Programming Applications
for Netscape Servers

Programming Applications for Netscape Servers

Kaveh Gh. Bassiri

ADDISON–WESLEY

An Imprint of Addison Wesley Longman, Inc.

Reading, Massachusetts • Harlow, England • Menlo Park, California
Berkeley, California • Don Mills, Ontario • Sydney
Bonn • Amsterdam • Tokyo • Mexico City

The publisher offers discounts of this book when ordered in quantity for special sales. For more information, please contact:

Corporate, Government, and Special Sales Department
Addison Wesley Longman, Inc.
One Jacob Way
Reading, Massachusetts 01867
(781) 944-3700

Library of Congress Cataloging-in-Publication Data

Bassiri, Kaveh Gh.
    Programming applications for Netscape servers / Kaveh Gh. Bassiri.
        p.   cm.
    Includes index.
    ISBN 0-201-41970-X
    1. Web servers.   2. Netscape Enterprise server.   I. Title.
    TK5105.888.B375   1998
    005.7'13769—DC21

                                                            98–23135
                                                            CIP

Text printed on recycled paper.

ISBN 0-201-41970-X
1 2 3 4 5 6 7 8 9—CRS—0302010099
First printing, September 1998

To my parents—the best of parents
and the best of friends

Contents

Preface

When I first began working as a consultant for Netscape, I had not planned on writing a book about the Netscape Server. At that time, the Netscape Server was only an enhanced version of the original NCSA HTTP Server written by Rob McCool. I was excited about the potential for developing Internet applications. Netscape was the first company to add an API to server programming options. The use of this API (NSAPI) opened a whole new realm of possibilities. I worked with Netscape to provide support, instruction, and examples for the Netscape Server. While working on NSAPI sample applications, I noticed the lack of essential information and resources. NSAPI was a new programming model, and its examples and documentation were sparse and rudimentary.

After my talk on NSAPI at the Netscape Developer Conference, I was asked to write a book on Netscape Server. I was hesitant. After all, I was busy developing and there was no time to write. Working as a Netscape server developer and training different Web administrators and programmers, however, I knew what other developers needed. What finally persuaded me to write such a book was the *need*.

So, I set out to write the book. I planned to write a book that discusses programming and technical issues not covered by other resources. I wanted to respond to some of the most frequently asked questions about the Netscape Server and how to extend it. I wanted the reader to gain not only a general review of server management and programming issues, but also an in-depth understanding of key programming options and different server configuration settings. My intended readers are experienced Webmasters who need to understand how the server works and how to customize its features, as well as developers who need to program for the Netscape Server.

In this book, server administrators will find information about the workings of the server—about how the server processes a request and the variety of server configuration settings. Programmers will find a review of different programming options for extending the server's processing of client requests. This book includes API reviews, examples, and walk-through tutorials for writing server applications. The programming options for Server 3.5.1 are so numerous that a single book cannot cover all the topics with meaningful study. This book focuses in on a review of CGI, NSAPI, CORBA, and WAI. CGI is the traditional server programming option and provides a good starting point. NSAPI is the least documented and most in need of a detailed discussion. CORBA opens the door for future methods of extending the server. WAI, itself a CORBA implementation, is the way of the future.

There still remains the problem of writing a book about a server that is updated so quickly. In this book, I try to address programming issues for anyone who runs a Netscape Server from Server 1.x to 3.5.1. Since many of you are using the latest version of the server or are planning to update to the latest version, I have focused on Enterprise Server 3.5.1. I kept in mind those who are still using earlier versions of the servers and made efforts to provide information about all the earlier servers. Much of the information covered in this book should remain the same for the future Netscape Server 4.x.

To supplement the materials in this book with more recent documents, you should always check Netscape DevEdge Online site (`http://developer.netscape.com`). You will find the latest revision of manuals, sample programs, articles, and other resources at this site. You should also check the Netscape Technical Support site (`http://help.netscape.com`) for the latest patches, FAQs, and Knowledge-base information. For the latest release notes, check Netscape's Web server directory (`http://home.netscape.com/eng/server/webserver/`). The release notes include important information about the latest updates, changes, and bugs. Netscape's online documentation provides the most current information about each version of the server. In an attempt to provide the most current information, much of this information may still be in revision. Online documents may be inaccurate or incomplete.

In this book, I have provided a tested review of the Netscape Server and its programming options. Although a printed book may not be as current as an online document, it has gone through a number of additional reviews and tests. Manuals or help files from a company usually provide the reference material and how-to instruction, but they do not provide an outsider's view. This book includes a number of warnings, bug reports, hints, and suggestions to assist you as a developer. The reason for the inclusion of this information is not to lessen the reputation of Netscape Server; instead, this information helps you find the source of a problem quickly and allows you to continue developing server solutions.

I hope you will find this book a source of learning and resources, because I really wrote it for my friends and colleagues.

What You Need to Know

To use the information in this book to greatest advantage, you should have a general understanding of the Internet, the Web, HTML, and Netscape Server. You should become familiar with Netscape Server and the Netscape client browser, both Navigator and Communicator.

You should also be familiar with the C programming language. You should have experience with the client/server environment. Knowledge of C++ is also helpful, especially when we discuss WAI and CORBA. In the CORBA and WAI section, we also discuss Java programming options, so an understanding of Java can be beneficial. Nevertheless, you do not need to know Java to develop CORBA or WAI applications. For CORBA, you can use C++ or Java. For WAI, you can use C, C++, or Java.

Conventions

The default server used for this book is Enterprise Server 3.5.1 for NT, but we will also refer to other platforms of Netscape Server. The main Netscape UNIX server used for testing and development for this book is Solaris. We will also refer to the Netscape FastTrack Server and previous versions of the Netscape Servers when needed. The name of the server is `foo`. The various examples of an IP address in this book use the fictitious IP address `1.2.3.4`. The default browser is the English version of Netscape Communicator 4.04 for NT. In general, references to Navigator 4.x also apply to Communicator 4.x, and vice versa. Navigator 4.x serves as the Navigator component of Communicator.

The default server path used for the Enterprise Server in this book is `c:/netscape/server/`. The forward slash (/) in the system path information is used to separate the components of the system path; however, at the Windows NT command prompt, you use a backslash (\) to specify a path.

Often, because of line-length limitation, the sample code may be split into multiple lines. In most cases, an attempt has been made to use the normal conventions of programming and server configuration. But this is not always possible, especially when information appears within a text paragraph. You should follow the standard convention of programming, the Internet, Netscape configuration files, and so on, when you encounter this type of information in the book. For example, when a URL is split into more than one line at a forward slash, you should input the URL without any space after the forward slash or before the rest of the URL.

The following conventions are used for formatting:

- `Courier font` is used for code, URL address, HTML tags, system paths, variables, data structures, file names, class names, syntax information, and information that may appear on your computer screen.

- **Bold** is used for functions, **obj.conf** and **magnus.conf** directives, and emphasis. For example, **Courier bold** is used to emphasize the main server configuration files: **obj.conf**, **magnus.conf**, and **mime.types**.

- *Courier Italic* is used for texts or descriptions of variables that you need to input or replace with actual data.

Acknowledgments

It would be impossible to name all the individuals who either directly or indirectly helped to make this book possible. I have been fortunate to work with so many accomplished and talented people.

I would like to thank the skilled staff of Addison Wesley Longman for supporting this book and working with me at each stage of its completion. I would especially like to thank the following people: Mary T. O'Brien, Elizabeth Spainhour, John Wait, Chanda Leary, Maureen Hurley, and former Addison Wesley Longman staff: Kim Fryer, Keith Wollman, and Ellen Wohl. They patiently supported and guided the project, as I went about writing, revising, and updating this book.

I would like to thank all the people at Netscape who have been so influential in the "information revolution." Without their work, the Internet revolution would not have formed in quite the same way. Netscape has been at the forefront, bringing us so many great Internet and Intranet applications. Where else would you get so many great people under one roof? In particular, I would like to thank Rob McCool (the person behind NSAPI), Robin Maxwell (the person behind WAI), and the rest of the great team of Netscape HTTP Server Engineers, including Ari Luotonen, Aruna Victor, Mike McCool, and Mike Belshe. I would also like to thank the following Netscape staff: Atri Chatterjee, John Dawes, Basil Hashem, John Ho, Ben Horowitz, Claire Hough, Clayton Lewis, Anh Nguyan, David Pann, Greg Sands, Ken Smith, and Bill Turpin. Working with the assiduous staff at Netscape has given me the necessary experience and insight to write this book.

The following people were responsible for the technical review and advice on the manuscript: Richard Careaga, Hitesh Bosamiya, Michael Blakeley, David Gulbransen, Guy Haas, and David Nelson. I would like to especially thank Richard Careaga for his many insightful suggestions. The following individuals are responsible for the additional programs available on the CD-ROM: Gregory Trubetskoy, Aaron Watters, Benjamin Sugars, Pedro Mendes, Mark Neal, Scott Alan Leerssen, Srividhya Gopala, Lincoln Stein, Steven E. Brenner, Thomas Boutell, Nick Kew, Daniel Doubrovkine, and Robert B. Denny. They have helped make this CD-ROM an asset for all Netscape programmers.

Finally, I would like to thank two people who have been the most instrumental in my work and this book: Emanuel Mashian for his continued inspiration, generosity, and encouragement, and JuLee Burdekin for her technical editing support and belief that I was the one who should write this book. I have known and worked with both Emanuel and JuLee for years, and continue to learn from them.

Part I

Introduction to Netscape Server

Part I comprises Chapters 1 and 2 and Appendixes A–D. Chapter 1 introduces the World Wide Web and the protocols employed to access it. It also reviews Netscape Server's evolution and compares the different server programming options. Chapter 2 is intended as an overview for server administrators and developers or those who want to have a better understanding of the workings of Netscape Server. In this chapter, we examine the steps that the server takes to process a client request and the way you can modify the server configuration. We also explore the major server configuration files, such as **magnus.conf**, **obj.conf**, and **mime.types**. (For built-in server functions, see Appendixes A and B.)

Chapter 1

Introduction

It was not until the advent of the World Wide Web (WWW or the Web) that the Internet became a hot topic for most businesses and consumers. Previously, the Internet had been primarily used by universities, the military, and select organizations. In the early 1990s, the addition of Hypertext Transfer Protocol (HTTP) and Hypertext Markup Language (HTML) catapulted the Internet to new heights. The Web, with its support of multimedia and hyperlinks, delivered an attractive interface to the previously unattractive world of the text-based Internet. By 1995, a slew of Web browsers and Web servers existed for almost any operating system. The Web singlehandedly revolutionized the use of the Internet. Today, use of the Internet and the Web has become part of the daily life of personal computer users and businesses.

The Internet is not limited to the Web. Consumers want to e-mail, download applications, chat with fellow users, share information using Internet conferencing, read information in newsgroups, and so on. New Web browsers from Netscape and Microsoft have already added many of these features. The browser is now the central client application for the network computer.

The Internet communication protocol, TCP/IP, has also become the standard for network communication—not just for the Internet, but also between different companies and inside organizations. In many organizations, proprietary architectures and protocols have been replaced by the standard network architecture and protocols of the Internet. Every day, new tools are being developed to take advantage of the existing infrastructure of the Internet and its various standard protocols.

The Internet, Intranet, and Extranet are changing the work environment. Businesses and organizations are using the Web and the Internet to enhance productivity, expand their consumer market, deliver updated information to clients, and provide customer support. The Internet has become not only a delivery mechanism for customers and clients, but also a means of commerce, customer support, delivery of products, and more. Electronic commerce is a key area of growth in the world of the Internet and the Web. The ease of use, flexibility, and low cost of browsers and Web servers, along with the common standards and the availability of new tools for developers, make the framework of the Web favorable to building internal client/server applications. Web tools, such as Web servers and clients (including browsers like Netscape Communicator), are now key components of the internal communication structures of many companies.

Intranet is a term coined for those who wish to use the capabilities of tools such as Web servers and browsers for internal use. It is currently the area of greatest growth. Companies like Netscape, Microsoft, and IBM are working on ways to make the tools you would need to develop your Intranet applications. The Extranet is another area of great interest. *Extranet* is a term used to denote the ability of securely connecting the Intranet, the internal company network of information, with a defined external network of business or corporate partners.

Netscape has been in the forefront of the Internet, Intranet, and Extranet revolution, and its various products are the mainstay of many users and organizations. Netscape browsers, such as the recently released Communicator, are still the most common browsers. They are the central client software for the Internet or Intranet. Netscape also provides a variety of servers, including Enterprise Server, Messaging Server, Compass Server, Collabra Server, Calendar Server, Proxy Server, Certificate Server, and Directory Server. These components are sold as part of a package called Netscape SuiteSpot. Each application provides a specific server component of the Internet or Intranet. The use of the Internet is not just limited to delivering information using a Web server such as the Netscape Enterprise Server. Different applications developed by Netscape provide additional functionality and features for networking. Even with all these additional components and programs, however, the Web client and server remain the central components of the network communication.

In this book, I focus on Netscape's Web servers. These Web servers deliver and manage various types of documents and information. Netscape's original Web servers were the Communication and Commerce Servers (that is, Netscape Server 1.x). The Commerce Server was Netscape's secured Web server. The FastTrack and Enterprise Servers 2.x and 3.x are the latest generations of the Netscape Web servers. FastTrack is a pared-down, less expensive version of Enterprise Server. Throughout this book, I use the term "Netscape Server" to refer to all of these Netscape *Web* servers. Although the Netscape Server can support different communication protocols, the primary protocol used by this Web server is HTTP. Web servers are, first and foremost, HTTP servers.

This introduction will first provide an overview of the general components of the Web and HTTP. Next, I will discuss programming options for different Netscape Web servers. If you are already familiar with HTTP and the Web, you can jump ahead to the section called Evolution of the Netscape Server.

Key Components of the Web

The model for the Web is a simple client/server architecture. Figure 1.1 illustrates the three essential components that make up the Web's client/server model: the Web client (user agent), normally a browser; the communication protocol (for example, TCP/IP and HTTP); and the Web server. The Web client can also be a spider (a robot that traverses the Web looking for various information) or any other type of end-user product that uses the Web model. The Web server may perform a number of tasks, but it is identified as a Web server because it serves the response to the client. The minimum communication protocols needed for client/server communication are TCP/IP and HTTP, but other protocols can also be used as part of the communication layer.

The browser makes a connection to the server using TCP/IP and HTTP protocols. It then sends a request to the server. The server listens on an established port and waits for a request. A connection is established when the server accepts the request for a connection from the browser. The server then receives a specific browser request, which it verifies and interprets. If the request is legitimate and the user is authorized to make it, the server processes the request. The server then returns a response to the client, again using standard communication protocols. The client interprets the request and presents the results to the user based on instructions in the document sent to the client.

The job of the Web client is twofold. First, the client connects to a server and passes the request. Second, after receiving the response, the client interprets and handles it. Normally, these two steps cause the Web browser to display the response according to the instructions set forth in the document's HTML code.

The job of the server is also twofold. First, the server waits for a connection from the client and receives the request, which it verifies and interprets. Second, the server returns to the client a response appropriate to the request. Figure 1-2 diagrams the communication between Web client and server.

The connection between the client and server can be broken by either the client or the server. The TCP/IP protocol provides the bottom layer of the communication. It actually transfers the messages (the request and response) between the client and the server. HTTP works on top of the TCP/IP layer. It delineates how the client makes the request and how the server returns the response.

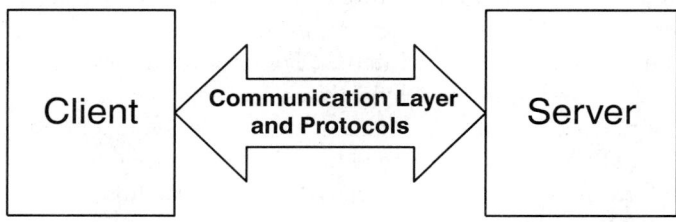

Figure 1-1   Web Client/Server Components

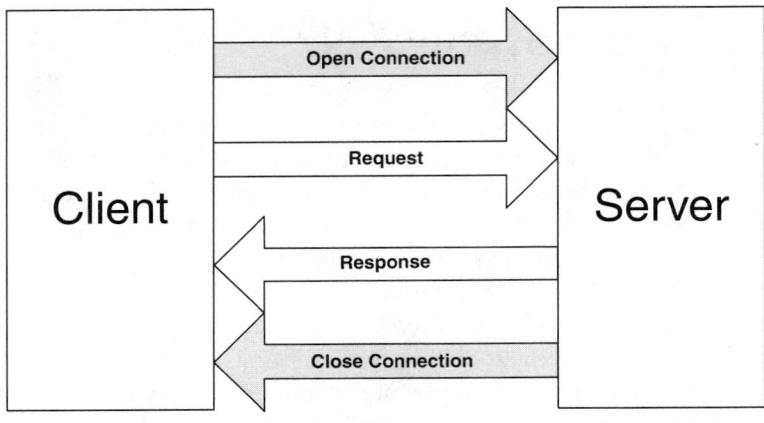

Figure 1-2   Web Client/Server Communication

URL and URI

The client uses a URL, or Uniform Resource Locator (a type of URI [Universal Resource Identifier]), to locate and retrieve resources on the server. A resource is the network data object or service identified by the URL. For example, the resource could be a file (such as `index.html`) or a program on the server that processes the client request (such as `guests.exe`).

A URL usually has the following format: `<scheme>://<server DNS or IP address>[:port]/[path][/resource]`. The first part, `scheme`, identifies the type of resource. It is usually a protocol name, which specifies the type of communication to be used. The protocol common to the Web server is HTTP. Thus, in the URL, `scheme` is `http` or `https` (a secured site). A secured site uses Secured Socket Layer (SSL). SSL protocol runs on top of TCP/IP, but below the HTTP protocol.

The `server DNS or IP address` identifies the machine in the network where resources are located; its value could be an Internet Protocol (IP) address or Domain Name System (DNS) address. An IP address is a series of numbers separated by dots that specify the exact location of a machine on the Internet. For example, the IP address `204.156.141.128` is a 32-bit number divided into four sets of eight-bit numbers (octets) converted into decimal numbers. You can also use the DNS address to locate the server machine. A DNS address, as defined here, is the fully qualified domain name (FQDN). In fact, the use of DNS is the recommended method of locating a server. The format of the DNS address is: `[machine name].[Domain Name].[type of organization].[country]`. An example of a DNS address is home.netscape.com. The information in the domain name starts with the most specific (home) and ends with the most general (com). In our DNS address example, home, the most specific description, refers to the name of the server machine. netscape refers to the specific registered domain name. com, referring to a commercial Web site, identifies the type of domain name or organization. Common domain classifications are com for commercial, edu for educational institution, mil for military, net for network organizations, and org for other miscellaneous organizations. Most countries also add an additional identifier at the end of the domain name. For example, uk identifies a site in the United Kingdom, as in the DNS address www.foo.com.uk.

The *port* information is the port address on which the server is listening. Usually, this port is defined as 80 for an unsecured server and 443 for a secured server. When using these two predefined ports, the client does not need to specify the port in the URL. If you use a different port for your server, however, the client must identify the port in the URL.

The *path* section identifies the directory where the resource is located. It is usually a directory path relative to the root directory of the documents, which your server intends to deliver to the client. The server maps this directory path to a physical path on your machine. The *path* does not need to match a physical path on your server machine. You can use a virtual path mapped to a physical location on your server machine.

The *resource* information names the item requested by the client. Normally it is a file (for example, news.html). Here, then, is an example of a complete URL: http://www.foo.com/news/news.html.

A URL may include additional information after the resource name or before the server address. For example, the user can include the user name and password before the server name (as in http://joe:password@www.foo.com/news/news.html). Additional information may also be added after the server name (as in http://www.foo.com/cgi/enter.cgi?name=joe). The information added after the requested resource is normally used by a program on the server. It may

---

Note ▶

When using HTML tags to identify a resource on your machine, you often use either a relative path or an absolute path, plus the resource name. You normally do not include a complete URL—that is, an absolute URL as described earlier. The absolute path always begins with a forward slash, as in /images/newsboy.gif. An absolute path is resolved based on the root document directory of your server. A relative path is resolved relative to the document from where the resource is being called, as in news/newsboy.gif. In other words, for an absolute path, the server always starts from the root directory and follows the path you specified to locate the file. For a relative path, the server starts at the current document directory and follows the path you specified.

include extra path information or data from a client HTML form input. We will discuss this additional information in later chapters.

For more information on URI, see the IETF (Internet Engineering Task Force) document "Uniform Resource Identifiers (URI): Generic Syntax and Semantics." You can find the latest draft of this document at the IETF–URI Working Group site (`http://www.ics.uci.edu/pub/ietf/uri/`).

TCP/IP

TCP/IP, or Transmission Control Protocol/Internet Protocol, is the network protocol used for the Internet. Every computer on the Internet (the network) supports TCP/IP. The data transferred across the network using TCP/IP are transmitted in packets. The protocols (including TCP/IP) used for the Internet are layered protocols. TCP/IP is actually two separate protocols. The IP protocol (the lowest layer) is a simple messaging protocol. IP is responsible for moving the packets from one location to another. It contains the addressing information that directs data from one place to another. The IP protocol does not guarantee the reliability of the data. Instead, TCP makes sure the data are transmitted without loss. The data delivered with TCP come in the form of IP packets, each of which contains the destination address. TCP guarantees the delivery of the data. It also serializes any data that exceed the size of an IP packet. TCP uses sequential numbers to order the packets of data. In addition to making sure that data arrive in the same order in which they were sent, TCP ensures that no packet is missing.

HTTP

HTTP is the underlying protocol of the Web. It runs on top of TCP/IP and determines the communication between the client and server. It specifies how a request is made and how the response is sent. To understand how the client request and the server response work, you need to understand how HTTP works. This section briefly reviews HTTP. For more information on HTTP, you should check W3C HTTP Overview (`http://www.w3.org/Protocols/`) or IETF HTTP Working Group site (`http://www.ics.uci.edu/pub/ietf/http/`).

History of HTTP

HTTP has changed in a number of ways since its first specification in 1990. The original version of HTTP supported by the first servers was HTTP/0.9. HTTP/1.0 added a number of new features, including support for different methods and MIME type headers. The headers provide specific information about the message requested by the client and sent by the server. HTTP/1.0 went through a number of revisions, and many of its features were implemented in most servers. Earlier Netscape Servers support HTTP/1.0. Because the HTTP proposed standard was not ratified and was constantly changing, not all servers provided support for HTTP/1.0 in the same way. A number of servers, such as Netscape Server 2.x, also attempted to include additional features to enhance the HTTP protocol. Some of these features were placed under consideration for the HTTP/1.1 standards. The current proposed HTTP standard is HTTP/1.1. Netscape Server 3.x is conditionally compliant with this protocol. In other words, it supports all "MUST" requirements of HTTP/1.1.

Brief Overview of HTTP

HTTP is a request/response protocol. Earlier in this chapter, in Components of the Web, I outlined the general model of how the client and server exchange information. This section explains in more detail the actual request sent by the client and the response returned by the server. But, before looking at the request and response, let's look at some special features of HTTP.

HTTP is stateless. In other words, unlike a typical client/server connection, which remains open, the HTTP connection is closed once the server finishes processing a client request. The server closes the HTTP (TCP/IP) connection after sending the response. The client can also easily close any connection. For example, by pressing the Stop (Back or Forward) button in the Navigator, a client closes the HTTP connection. The statelessness of HTTP allows your server to accommodate a greater number of clients. By closing the client connection, the server frees its resources for use during a new connection. The server can then handle a number of clients far exceeding the number of server threads. It can also take better advantage of various system resources, such as memory. There is no overhead for tracking client sessions between connections. On the other hand, the statelessness of the HTTP may be a problem when developing your applications. An application may need to track the client's navigation and maintain persistent data about the request. In this book, I discuss a number of options you can use to maintain state information. (See Chapter 10, Additional Programming Issues, for more information.)

As part of the statelessness of HTTP, each request from a client is handled in a separate connection. In the original specification of HTTP, each item requested by the client always took a separate connection. A separate TCP/IP connection was established for each URL. Thus, even for a Web page with a number of embedded multimedia items, a separate TCP/IP connection was opened and closed for each item. (The establishment of a new connection also occurs for each frame in a multiframe Web page.) The opening and closing of the connection is an unnecessary overhead for a request intended for multiple items. In other words, while it is beneficial for the connection to close before a client makes a request for a new page, it is actually more taxing to close and open a connection for a Web page with multiple items. To amend this weakness of the HTTP connection, HTTP/1.0 added the specification for a Keep-Alive connection. Keep-Alive keeps a connection open while the server delivers a number of files. In other words, the connection remains open while the server returns the HTML page with its embedded multimedia objects. Netscape Navigator 3.0 and later versions, and Netscape Server 2.x support Keep-Alive. To establish a Keep-Alive connection, the client must send a specific Keep-Alive request header.

HTTP/1.1, on the other hand, specifies persistent connection as the default type of connection between clients and servers that support HTTP/1.1. Persistent connection, an important new feature of HTTP/1.1, works similarly to Keep-Alive under Netscape Server 2.x, but enables even greater flexibility on the part of the client and server. The connection remains open until either the client or the server explicitly closes it. The server or client can send a connection header that signals the closing of the connection. This approach allows for better performance for the server and reduces the network traffic. Less memory and CPU time are used for handling the client request, and the number of TCP packets is reduced. An HTTP/1.1 client can also "pipeline" the request (that is, ask for multiple requests without waiting for the server to send each one). With Netscape Server 3.x, you can specify a timeout period for a persistent connection (which Netscape still calls a Keep-Alive connection at times) and a maximum number for the simultaneous persistent connections that the server will accept.

> **Note ▶**
>
> The connection between Netscape Navigator 4.x or Netscape Communicator 4.x and Netscape Server 3.x is still based on a Keep-Alive connection. Navigator 4.x uses an enhanced HTTP/1.0 protocol but does not explicitly support HTTP/1.1. So, although Netscape Server 3.x may support HTTP/1.1, the request is sent by Navigator 4.x and, therefore, the interaction between the server and the Navigator remains based on HTTP/1.0.

HTTP Request/Response Messages

The following discussion is based on the specifications of HTTP/1.1. An HTTP message is the basic unit of the HTTP communication used for a request or response.

Both request and response messages start with a specific request or response line. This line is followed by a number of message headers. The request message headers provide valuable information needed by the server to interpret a request. The response message headers provide information needed by the client to interpret the response. Message headers include general headers, request or response headers, and entity headers. The format of the message headers is [name]: [value] CRLF. Each header is specified in a separate line. The message headers are then followed by an empty line and the body of the message. The body of the message is also called the entity-body. Usually, when the server returns a document, the content of the page is the body of the response message. Not all messages, however, have a body. For example, the client request usually does not include a message body.

```
Request or Response Line
Message headers
CRLF
[Message Body]
```

An empty (blank) line separates the message headers and the body of the message. CRLF (carriage return line feed) refers to the end-of-line marker.

HTTP/0.9 did not support headers. HTTP/1.0, on the other hand, supports both request and response message headers. In fact, the core request and response message headers are generally the same for both HTTP/1.0 and HTTP/1.1. Here, we focus on the HTTP/1.1 headers that are actually applicable to both standards. Many of these headers are also supported by Netscape Server 2.x and 3.x, and Navigator 3.x and 4.x. All major browsers at least support HTTP/1.0. (Navigator 4.x supports HTTP/1.0.) Yet, significant differences remain between HTTP/1.1 and the various HTTP/1.0 proposed standards. Consequently, a number of headers discussed here are not included in the HTTP/1.0 specifications.

> **Note ▶**
>
> A final standard for HTTP/1.0 was never ratified. Any reference here to HTTP/1.0 is based on the various proposed drafts set forth by IETF. HTTP/1.1 is also not finalized. The information in this chapter is based on the current proposed standard Revision 03 (Rev-03), `draft-ietf-httpd-v11-spec-rev-03`. This draft, a major step toward the final HTTP/1.1 standard, addresses most of the significant issues regarding HTTP/1.1. (You can find a text version of this document under `http://www.ics.uci.edu/pub/ietf/http/draft-ietf-http-v11-spec-rev-03.txt`.) However, this draft expires on September 13, 1998. For the latest draft of the HTTP standard, you should visit the IETF HTTP Working Group site (`http://www.ics.uci.edu/pub/ietf/http/`).

Table 1-1 defines the general format and order of request and response messages. For the headers, it also includes the name of the headers as defined in the HTTP/1.1 specification. Although the order of the headers does not matter, common practice is to send the general headers first, followed by request or response headers and then the entity headers.

Table 1-1   Request/Response Messages

REQUEST	RESPONSE
Request-Line	*Status-Line*
(Method Request-URI HTTP-Version CRLF)	(HTTP-Version Status-Code Reason-Phrase CRLF)

General-Headers	
Cache-Control	
Connection	
Date	
Pragma	
Transfer-Encoding	
Upgrade	
Trailer	
Via	

Request-Headers	*Response-Headers*
Accept	Accept-Ranges
Accept-Charset	Age
Accept-Encoding	Etag
Accept-Language	Location
Authorization	Proxy-Authentication
Expect	Retry-After
From	Server
Host	Vary
If-Modified-Since	Warning
If-Match	WWW-Authenticate
If-None-Match	
If-Range	
If-Unmodified-Since	
Max-Forward	
Proxy-Authorization	
Range	
Referer	
TE (transfer coding)	
User-Agent	

Entity-Headers	
Allow	
Content-Encoding	
Content-Language	
Content-Length	
Content-Location	
Content-MD5	
Content-Range	
Content-Type	
Expires	
Last-Modified	

CRLF (an empty line)
Entity-Body

Request   After the client opens a connection to the server, it sends a request to the server. This request begins with a *Request-Line* followed by a number of message headers.

Request-Line   The *Request-Line* identifies the method of request, the URI, and the protocol version. The format of this line is as follows: *Method Request-URI HTTP-Version CRLF.* An example of such a line is

```
GET /index.html HTTP/1.0
```

Method specifies the method to be used on the resource specified in *Request-URI*. The most common method is GET. The client uses the GET method to get a file or resource—for example, an HTML file or a graphic file—from the server. Other common methods are HEAD, POST, and PUT. A HEAD method of request means that the client wants only the message headers. The body of the message is not sent. For example, a robot uses a HEAD request to verify a document's existence and its last modified date. A POST method is normally used with an HTML form. The client form input is appended to the body of the message for a POST request. A client may also use the POST method for annotating an existing resource or posting a message to a bulletin board or newsgroup. To take advantage of a POST method of request, a program is normally written. A PUT method is used to place the message body sent by the client on the server machine. Various HTML editors, such as Netscape Composer, use the PUT method to put a file (publish a file) on the server's Web site. For a PUT method, the *Request-URI* refers to the location on the server where the body of message should be stored. If the file does not exist, the server normally creates a new file for the message. If the file already exists, the content of the file on the server is replaced with the body of the message sent by the client. This book includes many examples that support client GET, POST, and HEAD methods of request. When writing a server program, most requests use the GET, POST, and HEAD methods. Other methods include OPTIONS, DELETE, TRACE, and CONNECT.

Request-URI specifies the location of the item requested by the client. Most browsers, including Netscape Navigator, use a partial URL (that is, the path and name of the resource) for the *Request-URI*. They do not include the complete (absolute) URL. The scheme (for example, http) and the server host name and port are already identified when the client uses the URL to connect to the server. Information about the server name (that is, the IP or DNS address and port of the server) is also specified in a separate HOST request header.

HTTP-Version specifies the version of the HTTP message supported and used by the client. The HTTP version should be HTTP/1.0 or HTTP/1.1.

Following the *Request-Line*, the client may send a number of additional message headers. The headers used for a request are general-headers, request-headers, and entity-headers.

> **Note ▶**
>
> Although the specific header names of the HTTP/1.1 specification use a capital letter for the first character in each word in the header name (for example, **C**ache-**C**ontrol), Netscape Server and its clients usually use lowercase letters for the header names (for example, **c**ache-**c**ontrol). The use of uppercase or lowercase naming conventions should not affect the actual workings of these headers.

General Headers   General headers accompany both requests and responses. They describe the message itself, not the body of the message (that is, the entity-body). They do not apply to the message body, but rather to the entire message.

The `Date` header specifies the date and time the message originated. The server usually includes a `Date` header with all responses. The `Date` message is an optional header for the request and is usually sent by the client when a message body (entity body) exists, such as during a `POST` or `PUT` request.

The `Connection` header identifies the type of connection. Netscape Navigator 3.x and 4.x use this header to specify a Keep-Alive connection: `Connection: Keep-Alive`. For HTTP/1.1, a `Connection: close` header is used by the client or the server to close a connection after the completion of the response.

`Pragma` is typically used by the client to specify that the server not employ caching. `Pragma` also applies to all other recipients along the request/response chain, such as the proxy or gateway programs. If you set the cache setting of the browser to zero (0) in the Preferences Dialog box for the Netscape Navigator (Communicator) 4.x, the Navigator sends the following header to the server: `Pragma: no-cache`. `Pragma` was previously identified as a request header under HTTP/1.0.

An HTTP/1.1-compliant client should use a `Cache-Control` header instead of `Pragma`—for example, `Cache-Control: no-cache`. Netscape Navigator (Communicator) 4.x, however, uses `Pragma`, not the `Cache-Control` header. `Pragma: no-cache` is equivalent to `Cache-Control: no-cache`. The `Cache-Control` header supported by Server 3.x allows for a great deal of control over the caching mechanism used by the server or any other program in the request/response chain. The directive is passed through all applications along the request/response chain. In other words, it affects the caching mechanism of an HTTP/1.1-compliant proxy server. A setting for a request does not necessarily apply to a response, or vice versa. With these directives, you can override the default caching algorithms. The `Cache-Control` directive includes a number of options, such as `no-cache`, `no-store`, and `max-age`. The directives for an HTTP request also differ from those for an HTTP response. Netscape allows you to set the `Cache-Control` directives using the Netscape Administration Server. (For more information on `Cache-Control`, see the HTTP/1.1 specification.)

Request Headers   Request headers include additional information about the request or the client for the server. Navigator (Communicator) 4.x sends the following headers by default: `Accept`, `Accept-language`, `Accept-Charset`, `User-Agent`, and `Host`. `Accept-language` and `Accept-Charset` are new to Navigator 4.x. Navigator 3.x does not send these headers automatically.

`Accept` specifies the type of media accepted by the client, such as `image/gif`, `image/x-xbitmap`, `image/jpeg`, `image/pjpeg`, `image/png`, or `*/*`. The acceptable media types are listed by their MIME (Multipurpose Internet Mail Extensions) type. (For information on MIME types, see the section mime.types in Chapter 2.) The use of the wildcard pattern (`*/*`) in the list of MIME types (content types) supported by Navigator means that Navigator also accepts any other MIME types not specified in this list.

`Accept-language` (for example, `en` for English) and `Accept-Charset` (for example, `iso-8859-1,*,utf-8`) specify the language and character set, respectively, that Navigator accepts.

`User-Agent` identifies the name of the client software (for example, `Mozilla/4.04 [en] (WinNT; I)` for the English Netscape browser 4.04 for Windows NT).

`Host` specifies the host name and port of the requested resource. The value of `Host` is determined by the HTTP URL used for the request. If no port is specified, a default port is assumed (usually `80`) for an unsecured server.

Other common request headers are `Authorization`, `If-Modified-Since`, and `Referer`. The `Authorization` header is used to authenticate a client with the server. The value of this header normally includes a base 64-encoded user name and password, plus the type of authentication, such as `authorization: Basic dG9tbXk6dG9t`. The `Referer` header names the absolute URL of the document where the current request originated, which is the URI of the resource from which the *Request-URI* was obtained. The `If-Modified-Since` header is used with a `GET` method to verify whether the requested document has changed since the time specified. If the requested resource has not changed since then, the server will not return the body of the message.

Tidbit ▶

`Referer` should really have four `r`'s. One is missing. It should have been named `referrer`.

Entity Headers   Entity headers include specific information about the body of the message (entity-body). They normally include specific meta-information about the entity body. If no body appears in the message, the request may use an entity header for the resource identified in the request. The client rarely uses an entity header if no entity-body is included in the request. Note that while an entity header in a response is used for the body of the response, the entity header for the client is normally intended for the entity-body that accompanies the request. An entity header sent as part of a request identifies the body of the request message, not the entity-body of the response. For example, the entity header content-type of a POST entity-body is application/x-www.form-urlencoded, while the content-type of the response could be text/html.

Most common entity headers are content-type and content-length. The content-type header specifies the media type, or MIME type, of the entity-body; for example, text/html. content-length specifies the length of the message. These two parameters should be always included with a response. content-type and other similar entity-headers, such as content-encoding and content-language, signal the client about how to interpret the response. The client normally sends an entity-header only when the request contains an actual entity-body—for example, with the POST or PUT method of request. In your programs, you can use this information to identify the type of input from the client or the length of the data stream sent by the client.

Other common entity-headers are Last-Modified and Expires. The Last-Modified header identifies the date when the entity-body (for example, the document being sent to the client), was last modified. Expires specifies the date when the entity-body will expire.

Example of a Request   The type of headers sent with a request may vary, depending on the request and the type of client. Different clients may send different headers. The following request information was sent by the Communicator 4.04. Navigator 3.x may not send the accept-language or accept-charset headers.

```
Get /index.html HTTP/1.0
connection: Keep-Alive
user-agent: Mozilla/4.04 [en] (WinNT; I)
host: www.foo.com
accept: image/gif, image/x-xbitmap, image/jpeg,
  image/pjpeg, image/png, */*
accept-language: en
accept-charset: iso-8859-1,*,utf-8
```

Response   Part of the job of the server and any program that you write for the server is to interpret and use the headers sent with the request. After the server processes a request, it prepares and returns a response. The server response starts with a *Status-Line* that is followed by a number of message headers.

Status-Line   The *Status-Line* includes the HTTP protocol version, status code, and reason string. The format of *Status-Line* is HTTP-Version Status-Code Reason-Phrase CRLF. An example of such a line is

```
HTTP/1.0 200 OK
```

The protocol version is similar to the HTTP protocol version specified in a request. The *HTTP-Version* in the *Status-Line,* however, specifies the HTTP version of the response message (not the request). *Status-Code* is a three-digit integer that indicates how the request was handled. The server returns a status code 200 when it successfully processes the client request. If the server was unable to process a request, it returns one of a number of error status codes. These codes explain the type of error that occurred. For example, the error could arise because a bad request was made (400) or because the client was not authorized to access the resource (401). *Reason-Phrase* is a plain-text explanation of the code. Although the status codes are standardized, *Reason-Phrase* may vary, depending on the server. You may also program a different reason string in your server application.

Status codes are grouped into five separate categories. 1xx status codes are used for informational purposes. 2xx status codes show a successful processing of a request by the server. 3xx status codes redirect the client to a different resource. 4xx status codes indicate client-specific errors. 5xx status codes indicate server errors that occur during the processing of a request. Table 1-2 lists common HTTP status codes and their Reason-Phrases. For more information on the various status codes and reason strings, see Chapter 6, HTTP Status Codes.

Table 1-2   Common Status Codes

STATUS CODE	REASON-PHRASE	DESCRIPTION
200	OK	Server successfully processed the request.
302	Found	Client is redirected to a new location.
304	Use local copy (Not Modified)	Client should use the local copy of the resource requested.
400	Bad Request	Server could not understand the request.
401	Unauthorized	Client was not authorized to access the resource.
403	Forbidden	Server understood the request, but access to the resource is forbidden.
404	Not Found	Server did not find the requested data.
500	Server Error (Internal Server Error)	A server error occurred while processing the request.

General, Response, and Entity Headers   The message headers for a response include the same general-headers and entity-headers described earlier for the request. This time, however, the headers apply to the response message or the entity-body of the response. Entity-headers, which are not necessarily an important part of a request, are especially crucial when the server returns a response. Most responses include an entity-body, and entity-headers are used to transmit important information about the body of the response to the client.

Specific (unique) response headers for a response also exist—response-headers. The most common response-headers are `Accept-Ranges`, `WWW-Authenticate`, and `Location`. The `Accept-Ranges` header specifies the acceptable range requests for a resource. Netscape Server usually uses `bytes` for the value of the `Accept-Ranges` header, meaning that the server can accept `byte-range`. In other words, the client can send a request of the content-type `multipart/byteranges`, which is self-delimiting. `Location` is used to route a client to a new location—that is, to redirect a client to a new URL. The `WWW-Authenticate` header is sent by the server to force authentication of the client. The user is then required to send a user name and password.

Normally, after the headers, the server returns the entity-body—that is, the body of the message. The body of the message is usually the content of the requested resource by the client. For example, if a client requests the file `index.html`, then the server returns the content of `index.html` after the headers. The response should include a blank (empty) line between the headers and the body of the response.

Example of a Response   The headers `Content-Type`, `Content-Length`, `Date`, and `Server` should always be part of the response. In the following example, the entity-body would be the specific HTML page that the client requested.

```
HTTP/1.0 200 OK
Date: Mon, 5 Jan 1998 20:36:04 GMT
Server: Netscape-Enterprise/3.5.1
Last-Modified: Mon, 24 Jun 1996 20:36:04 GMT
Content-Type: text/html
Content-Length: 200
Accept-Ranges: bytes
<empty line>
[Entity Body]
```

Additional Request and Response Headers   The client and server may also use other response or request headers. If the recipient of the header can recognize and handle the specific header, the client or server can use this extra header with the request or response. For example, a client can send a specific HTTP header that the server uses in interpreting the request. An example of such a header is the `cookie` header sent by the client and `set-cookie` sent by the server. Cookies are discussed in Chapter 10.

Evolution of the Netscape Server

Netscape as a company began as a collaboration between the developers of the most popular Web browser, MOSAIC, and the developers of the major free Web servers, NCSA and CERN. Starting with such a strong foothold, Netscape has continued to evolve and redefine the Web. In fact, the pace of Netscape's product evolution has been so rapid that keeping up is difficult.

The evolution of Netscape Server can be viewed from a number of different angles. Netscape has added new features to the server, enhanced the integration of the Web server with the Netscape client and other server products, and added new options and capabilities for application developers. In fact, the whole purpose of the Web server has shifted from delivering information to becoming a means of collaboration, integration with other legacy applications, and deployment of network-centric applications.

With each release of Netscape Server, Netscape has added more functionality and features to the server. Enterprise Server 3.x, Netscape's feature-rich Web server, includes new and enhanced features that were not available in previous versions. It now supports advanced features, such as Web publishing, content management, Netshare, intelligent agents, AutoCatalog, search, LDAP directory for user management, SNMP (Simple Network Management Protocol) version 1 and 2, centralized administration, and clustering of different Netscape Servers. You can enable and configure these options through Netscape's Administration Server.

Web publishing and content management allow for collaboration on the same document. They support access control as well as searching, editing, managing, and publishing documents on the server. The server also includes support for version control, document checkin and checkout, and link management. Users can publish, share, and manage various documents on the server.

> **Note ▶**
>
> With Enterprise Server 3.5.1, the clients can now download and install the Web Publisher Java applet on the local machine. Thus the applet does not need to be downloaded from the server each time it is launched. This method reduces the load time for the Web Publisher. Note also that the Web Publisher Java applet is not supported if SSL is used.

Netshare, which was introduced with Enterprise Server 3.01, permits users to set customizable, personal home pages. It provides a virtual workspace for users to manage their own server content. Users can work with this central workspace to maintain, share, and manage their own documents. They can also access the various server content management services, such as access control, revision management, agents, search, and link management.

Agents can be set up to perform a predefined task when a specific event occurs or a certain time is reached. For example, agents can notify an administrator when a specific URL has been updated. You can specify who has access to a specific agent, when and under what conditions an agent should be invoked, and what actions an agent should take when it runs.

AutoCatalog allows the cataloging (listing) of the documents on the Web server. It first gathers information about the URLs referenced in the files on the server and determines which URLs should be cataloged. Next, it generates a description of the

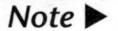

Note ▶

Although AutoCatalog appears as part of the Server Manager menus for the Enterprise Server for NT, this option is not supported under NT. Instead, you need to use Compass Server in conjunction with Enterprise Server.

result. The resulting information can be sorted by title, classification, author, and last-modified date.

Search allows users to search the content and attributes of the documents on the server. The server also converts a number of non-HTML files (for example, Microsoft Word and Adobe PDF files) to HTML for indexing. You can then customize the access to the search engine, the search query options, and the results of the search. For example, you can specify which words (for example, and or the) should not be indexed.

The LDAP (Lightweight Directory Access Protocol) directory allows for standardized, feature-rich users and groups management. By using Netscape Directory Server to manage the users directory of the Enterprise Server, you can take advantage of a powerful centralized users, groups, and resources management server that can support as many as 1 million users. Enterprise Server 3.5.1 is designed to be easily integrated with Netscape Directory Server 3.0. It also supports LDAP version 3, which includes many additional features, such as support for UTF-8 international character sets and real-time replication between multiple directory servers. (Communicator 4.04 has also been updated to support LDAP version 3.) To take advantage of LDAP version 3 for setting up users' and groups' preferred language, you need to use Directory Server 3.0 or later with Enterprise Server 3.5.1. Enterprise Server 3.5.1 can accommodate Asian and European languages that are represented natively in the Directory Server 3.0.

Support for SNMP allows you to integrate the server with other management systems, such as CA/Unicenter or IBM/Tivoli TME, for remote monitoring and managing of the server. Netscape Server 3.x also supports the centralized Administration Server with its capability to customize the functionality and access for different users. For instance, you can set up different administrators that can perform specific administrative tasks using the Administration Server. In addition, Administration Server allows you to cluster similar Netscape Servers that support clustering (for example, a group of different Enterprise 3.x Servers). You can then share one or more configuration files between the similar servers or administer the different servers from a central Administration Server.

Netscape has also improved the integration and supported features of its client and server products. Netscape Server shares a number of new features supported by Netscape clients. Netscape Server 3.x and the Netscape client (Communicator 4.x) both support programming options, such as Java, JavaScript, LiveConnect, and CORBA (Common Object Request Broker Architecture), as well as additional protocols, such as IIOP (Internet Inter-ORB Protocol), SSL 3.0, and LDAP. The next section outlines various programming options supported by the Netscape Server, including Java, JavaScript, LiveConnect, and CORBA.

The protocols SSL, IIOP, and LDAP run on top of TCP/IP and work in conjunction with HTTP to provide additional support. SSL provides a security layer between the client and server. IIOP provides a common protocol for communication between CORBA objects that can be implemented in different programming languages and run on different machines in the network. These programs can work in collaboration with Netscape clients and servers. IIOP also maintains state information, as it does not need to drop a client connection. LDAP provides the protocol for accessing the information kept in an LDAP directory server. Netscape Communicator and Netscape Server 3.x can work as clients for an LDAP directory server, such as the Netscape Directory Server. Although the use of programming features and protocols differs when it is intended for the client instead of the server, these options provide a uniform means of development, communication, and support for the client and server. Netscape itself uses these additional options for the integration and use of the client and server. For example, Netscape Administration Server uses the Navigator to administer the Netscape Servers with the help of JavaScript, Java, and LDAP.

You can also use these options when developing your own applications. For example, you can develop applications that perform specific tasks on the server (such as access to resources in a database), while other tasks can be performed by the client (such as verifying and validating the client HTML form input). In other words, applications can be created to take advantage of the specific features built into the server and client, distribute the work between the client and server, and communicate between the client and server using any of the supported protocols.

Netscape Web servers can also be used in conjunction with other Netscape Servers to provide optimal benefits. In fact, Netscape offers a group of its servers as part of the Netscape SuiteSpot package. For example, Netscape SuiteSpot 3.5 Standard Edition includes the following servers: Calendar, Collabra, Directory, Enterprise, and Messaging. It also includes LiveWire Pro. The different Netscape Servers can be combined with the Enterprise Server in many ways. As already mentioned, you can use Netscape Directory Server 3.0 to manage the users and groups of the Enterprise Server. You can have the Certificate Server assign and manage user SSL certificates. The users can then employ these certificates to access the Web site. Netscape Proxy Server can be used in conjunction with the Enterprise Server to provide caching and filtering of Web content. Proxy Server can filter content and control the access to information. Catalog Server, now called Compass Server, can be employed as a more feature-rich option (instead of the built-in AutoCatalog feature of the Enterprise Server) to provide a more powerful, centralized cataloging of the documents on your Web sites. LiveWire Pro adds a limited-deployment copy of the INFORMIX-Online Workgroup Server database software for use with the Enterprise Server. The agents of Enterprise Server 3.x can also take advantage of a mail or news server, such as Messaging Server 3.x and Collabra Server 3.x. The agent can post a message to a newsgroup or e-mail a specified user with the information it generates.

Programming Options for Netscape Server

The first generation of Web sites were predominately static, providing unchanging HTML pages for users to browse and search. But for users who wanted to do business on the Web or deliver a client/server application for internal use, static sites were not enough. To create a dynamic site, you need to program and use databases for maintaining the information. You also need to connect to existing applications and customize the site for each client. Users who wanted to take full advantage of Web technology soon realized that a glorified telephone book or library was not adequate. For the Web to become a truly powerful part of the desktop, it needed to provide features similar to the existing client/server architecture already in use in many organizations.

Figure 1-3 lists the various programming options to extend the capability of Netscape Servers. With each release of the server, the number of programming options has increased. This figure lists the key programming options for the different Netscape Servers, from Server 1.1x (Communication and Commerce Server) to Server 3.x (Enterprise Server 3.x and FastTrack Server 3.x). This list does not specify Netscape Server 3.x's programming options that allow you to customize a special feature of Netscape Server 3.x (such as writing an agent or a Web publishing client). Although you can write Servlets using JavaSoft or other third-party tools for earlier versions of Enterprise and FastTrack Servers, Netscape began supporting Servlets natively only with the release of Enterprise Server 3.5.1. Thus, this functionality is identified as a feature for Enterprise Server 3.5.1. In Figure 1-3, the programming options discussed in this book are highlighted with a background shadow.

CGI

As a means of developing applications, the original Web servers included support only for CGI (Common Gateway Interface). CGI is a standard interface supported by almost all Web servers. It allows you to write programs that can process a client request dynamically. A CGI program or script can be written in a number of different programming languages, such as C, C++, PERL, TCL, and Visual Basic. These programs are invoked by the client request. They run on the server, process the client request, and then return a response to the server. The server, in turn, returns the response to the client. CGI programs run in a different process than the server. Although CGI programs are easy to write, they do not provide optimal performance and cannot change the server's internal steps for handling a client request. As each request also invokes a separate CGI process, the CGI programs cannot easily support state maintenance.

All Netscape Servers provide full support for different methods of developing applications using CGI. Despite its shortcomings, CGI is a good choice for developing interactive and dynamic responses for the client. That is, if you wish to write a program in Visual Basic or a scripting language such as PERL, and if the performance and number of simultaneous connections to your server is not a significant factor, then CGI is an acceptable option. Since CGI is a standard interface for almost all major Web servers, it also allows you to write applications that can be deployed on other Web servers besides Netscape.

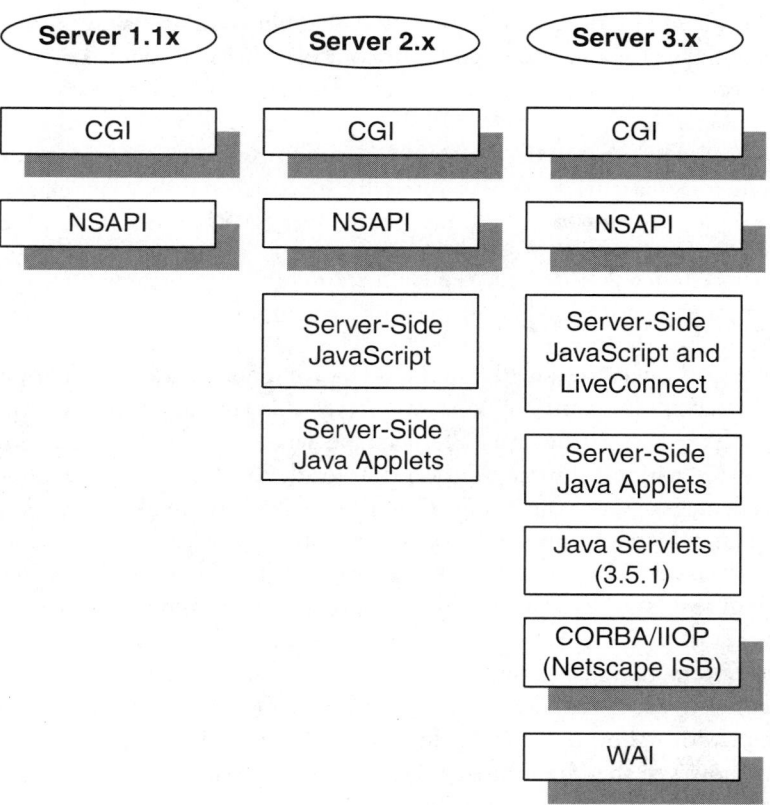

Figure 1-3   Main Programming Options for Extending Netscape Server

NSAPI

With later generations of its server, Netscape added a special Netscape-specific server API (NSAPI) for developing server applications. You can find NSAPI support in the Netscape Communication and Commerce servers. NSAPI is a subset of the server's own data structures and functions that directly exposes the working of the server. It allows you to write a program that directly interfaces with the server. NSAPI programs directly affect how the server processes a client request. Netscape has continued to enhance the NSAPI. Server 2.x included a number of major enhancements. For example, NSAPI in Server 2.x includes functions for thread locking and synchronization. Server 3.x includes even more functions and enhancements, although the changes in 3.x are relatively minor. Thus NSAPI remains primarily the same for Servers 2.x and 3.x. Binary applications developed under Server 2.x may run without any changes under Server 3.x, although not always. It is best to recompile the NSAPI application using the current NSAPI library and header files to ensure that it will work as intended.

NSAPI provides better performance and added functionality not available with CGI. NSAPI programs run inside the server process. They are loaded as dynamic libraries or shared libraries by the server. NSAPI applications can change the internal workings of the server and exert significant control over its behavior. These applications can also easily maintain persistent state information for client sessions. You can initialize a shared resource with NSAPI that can be accessed by your program when handling any client request. Because NSAPI applications run in the server process and directly interact with the server's internal data structures, they face a greater risk of crashing the server than CGI programs. Your NSAPI application must be thread-safe.

Server-Side Java Applet

With Server 2.x, Netscape added Server-side Java and Server-side JavaScript and Live-Wire to the server's programming options. Server-side Java allows you to write Java applets using the Server-side Java API. Netscape Servers 2.x and later include a JVM (Java Virtual Machine). Your application runs inside this JVM. Because the server starts and manages JVM, your application does not have to invoke a new JVM for each client request, which improves the Java application's response.

With Server-side Java, you can write Java applets that run on the server and can handle client requests. Netscape provides a number of server applet classes, `netscape.server.applet.*`, that you can use to write a server Java applet. These applets are intended to perform the same functionality as a CGI program. They provide access to the server and request specific variables. The applets also support persistent state information about the client session. Because they run as Java applets for Server 2.x, however, they are limited to certain security restrictions enforced in all Java applets. For example, you cannot execute an external application with your Java applet under Server 2.x. The applets also need to run under JVM 1.0.2, which is included with Server 2.x. You should use JDK (Java Developer Kit) 1.0.2 and Java 1.0.2 classes. Netscape removed the security restrictions for Java applets in Server 3.x. Enterprise Server 3.5.1 also includes an improved version of JVM that supports many of the features of JDK 1.1.[1] Nonetheless, Netscape does not recommend Server-side Java applets as a method of programming server applications. Instead, the company recommends that you use WAI for writing your server applications in Java (WAI is discussed later in this chapter). For a more standard Java interface programming for the server, you may also consider Servlets.

With Server 2.x, it is best to use CGI, NSAPI, or Server-side JavaScript for developing applications. Netscape does not intend to further develop the Server-side Java API. Support for server-side Java applets is included with Server 3.x for backward compatibility. It is also used to provide Servlet support in Enterprise Server 3.5.1. Future servers, however, may not support Server-side Java applets.

---

1. The JDK support included with Enterprise Server 3.5.1 still lacks a number of features, such as AWT 1.1, inner classes, internationalization, JNI (Java Native Interface), visible JavaBean, and a security model.

Java Servlet

The Java Servlet API includes a set of Java classes for writing applications to extend a Web server. Servlets are intended for Java-based Web servers, but can also be used by other Web servers, such as Netscape Enterprise and FastTrack Server. Support for Servlets has been available for Enterprise and FastTrack Servers by using JSDK (Java Servlet Developer Kit) from JavaSoft and through other third-party vendors. JSDK includes instructions for enabling and using Servlets with Netscape Servers. Other companies, such as IBM, New Atlanta Communication, LLC, and LiveSoftware, also provide Servlet classes that can be used with Netscape Servers. IBM provides Servlet-Express (`http://www.ibm.com/java/servexp/`), LiveSoftware offers JRun (`http://www.livesoftware.com/`), and New Atlantic Communications has developed ServletExec (`http://www.newatlanta.com/products.html`). You can use any of these packages with Enterprise and FastTrack Servers.

With Enterprise Server 3.5.1, Netscape includes native support for Servlets. Servlets provide a standard method of extending the server using Java. Unlike Server-side Java, Servlet is a Java-standard interface supported on a variety of Web servers. The support for Netscape Server Servlets is limited, however, and does not provide all the functionality offered by programming options such as NSAPI. You can use Servlets only to process client HTTP requests. Moreover, the Servlet support included with Enterprise Server 3.5.1 is based on JSDK 1.0.1. Netscape uses the Server-side Java API discussed earlier to support Servlets; it does not use the WAI interface for this purpose. A number of limitations in using various Servlet methods also exist. For example, the **getInitParameter**, **getServlet**, **ServletRequest.getAttribute**, and **destroy** methods do not work. (The third-party sources mentioned earlier may provide additional features not built into Enterprise Server 3.5.1's Servlet support.)

Netscape intends to support Servlets in future releases of the Netscape Server. Consequently, additional features and enhancements for Servlets are expected.

Server-Side JavaScript and LiveWire

Server-side JavaScript is an enhancement to JavaScript, Netscape's scripting language, that provides special support for server development. Unlike the client-side JavaScript, Server-side JavaScript is intended for use with the Netscape Server. With client-side JavaScript, you can control various components of HTML pages. With Server-side JavaScript, you can access various databases and support state management. Server-side JavaScript also addresses the limitation of the statelessness of HTTP. You can use this option to maintain persistent state information about the client and the client's Web session. In addition, you can deploy it to access databases.

LiveWire is the database connectivity component of Enterprise Server. It allows for native database connectivity to a number of major databases, such as Oracle, Informix, and Sybase databases. You can also access databases using ODBC. LiveWire was originally developed as an additional component that could be purchased with Enterprise Server 2.x. With Netscape Server 3.x, LiveWire is no longer a separate product. Instead, it is included with the server. Thus you no longer need to install LiveWire as a separate product. To obtain a development and limited deployment copy of the INFORMIX-OnLine Workgroup Server database or a development-only copy of Oracle7 Workgroup database, however, you should purchase LiveWire Pro 3.0.

Support for Server-side JavaScript and LiveWire in Server 3.x includes a number of added features. Server 3.x supports JavaScript 1.2, the current version of JavaScript. It allows you to access HTTP request and response headers. In addition, it supports native connectivity for the IBM DB2 database. With Server 3.x, you can have multiple, simultaneous database connections in a single JavaScript application and support for stored procedures. In contrast, Enterprise Server 2.x allowed only one database connection per application. UNIX versions of Enterprise Server 3.x now support ODBC as well. A new JavaScript SendMail class allows you to send e-mails using an SMTP (Simple Mail Transfer Protocol) mail server. For more information on the features of Server-side JavaScript and writing Server-side JavaScript programs for Netscape Server 3.x, see Netscape's document, "Writing Server-Side JavaScript Application" (http://developer.netscape.com/library/documentation/ enterprise/wrijsap/index.htm).

If the primary goal of your application is to access information in different databases and maintain client state information, then Server-side JavaScript delivers an effective and easy means of developing such an application. Server-side JavaScript, however, does not provide the same performance as NSAPI or WAI.

LiveConnect

LiveConnect allows for communication between JavaScript and Java. It is part of the Netscape Navigator versions 3.x and later. With Server 3.x, you can also use LiveConnect on the server. LiveConnect allows for two-way communication between Java and JavaScript. Thus you can write JavaScript programs that can interoperate with Java applications. Java classes can be used with JavaScript. JavaScript functions and Java methods can pass data between each other. You can use JavaScript to take advantage of functionality available in Java that is not directly available through JavaScript. JavaScript can be employed to control a Java application, access its public functions or variables, and set the values of a variable. This flexibility is highly desirable for developers who wish to take advantage of each programming tool. JavaScript is, after all, a script language and does not provide all the capabilities that may be needed to develop an application. On the other hand, you should not need to write extraneous code to accomplish tasks that a JavaScript script can do much more easily and quickly. LiveConnect extends the capability of your JavaScript application by allowing it to take advantage of Java classes and applications. If Server-side JavaScript is your intended programming tool, then consider using LiveConnect to extend the ability of your application.

CORBA/IIOP

Aside from Servlets support in Enterprise Server 3.5.1, Netscape Server 3.x adds two new programming options: CORBA/IIOP and WAI. CORBA is a standard specification for developing network-centric distributed client/server applications. It provides the framework for writing network-centric objects that can run as server or client objects. An object is a server when it provides a service for another object; an object is a client when it requests a service from another object. An object can also be a server to one object and a client to another.

ORB (Object Request Broker) is the core component of CORBA that allows the client and server objects to interact with one another. The ORB manages the interaction between the different CORBA objects. CORBA objects can communicate with one another independent of the operating system platform or the programming language of the object. The ORB locates the object, sends the request, and returns the result. Using the ORB, a client object can invoke a method on the server object. The client does not need to know the location of the object. When you write a server object, you define the services that the object provides and the type of data that the object can receive and send.

Enterprise Server 3.x and Communicator include Netscape's ORB (Internet Service Broker, or ISB). Communicator comes with a runtime version of ISB for Java. Enterprise Server 3.x comes with the Java and C++ ISBs for developing client and server objects. Enterprise Server 3.x also includes its own Web Naming Service for registering and locating CORBA objects. Server objects register themselves with the Netscape Naming Service. Client objects locate the server object (the object implementation) using this Naming Service.

IIOP is a platform-independent Internet protocol for communication between CORBA objects. The network protocol of choice for CORBA objects, it provides the necessary communication protocol for distributed objects. Unlike HTTP, IIOP preserves the state information. Both Enterprise Server 3.x and Communicator support IIOP. Using the Netscape ISB and IIOP, a CORBA client application using Communicator can access the services of other CORBA objects. With the Netscape ISB and IIOP support in the Netscape Server, you can develop CORBA client and server objects that can cooperate with the server when processing a client request.

Writing a CORBA application is not as easy as writing a server application using the other programming methods discussed here. You need to understand the working of the Netscape ISB and CORBA before you can write a CORBA application. If you plan to write a CORBA application to process a client request that uses HTTP, it is easier to take advantage of WAI. On the other hand, CORBA is the best means of extending the Netscape client and server tools in an existing network of CORBA objects. Applications can take advantage of IIOP instead of HTTP for exchanging information. You can write a CORBA interface for a legacy application enabling other CORBA objects to access the services of the legacy program. You can then integrate the CORBA object with the Netscape Server. You can also use JavaScript and LiveConnect to communicate with CORBA objects. Moreover, CORBA and IIOP are supported by a number of other third-party applications.

WAI

WAI (Web Application Interface) is a new programming interface developed to handle HTTP client requests. This unique extension of the Netscape CORBA offerings extends the server capabilities. WAI applications can be written in the server process, similar to an NSAPI application, or out of the server process, similar to a CGI application. They can also be deployed in a remote machine, although for security reasons you should not run a WAI application remotely. You can write a WAI application in C, C++, or Java. WAI is more closely integrated with the server than CGI is. It allows you to maintain state information and write to the server log files. A WAI application also provides better performance than CGI does. The server does not invoke a new process for each WAI request. With a WAI application that runs out-of-process, you have to manually start the application. Upon startup, the application registers itself with the Netscape Naming Service. Whenever a request is intended for your application, the server invokes a WAI method in your application to process the client request.

Unlike CGI, WAI is specific to Netscape Server and is not supported by other vendors' Web servers. Moreover, the current implementation of WAI does not provide all the features supported by NSAPI. It also does not give as good a performance as NSAPI does. On the other hand, WAI applications are easier to write than NSAPI applications are. The application interface for WAI is an abstract one. It does not directly expose the internal workings of the server. Netscape intends to continue to enhance WAI in the next release of the server. In fact, future versions of WAI may be better integrated than NSAPI may be with Enterprise Server 4.0. Thus using WAI may be the preferred way of developing server applications with Enterprise Server 4.0.

Note ▶

If you plan to use WAI with Enterprise Server 3.0 for Solaris and NT, you should run the WAI and Enterprise Server patches. You can find these patches under Netscape's "File Library" page (`http://help.netscape.com/filelib.html`). The Enterprise Server, after applying the server patch (for example, 3.0i for NT) and WAI patch `P85416`, will be comparable to Enterprise Server 3.01. You should first apply the latest Enterprise Server patch before applying the WAI patch. This book refers to Enterprise Server 3.0 with these upgrade patches as Enterprise Server 3.01; this version is the first release of Server 3.x for other supported platforms. The default version of the Netscape Server discussed in this book is Enterprise Server 3.5.1.

Additional Programming Options for Server 3.x

Besides the programming options that extend the server capability as an HTTP server that processes a client request, you can also customize a specific component of the Netscape Server 3.x with special server APIs. This book will not review these options. If you intend to customize a special feature of the Netscape Server that supports an API, however, you should review the documentation about these APIs found under

Netscape's developer site, DevEdge Online. (See the list of Enterprise Server 3.x documentation under `http://developer.netscape.com/library/documentation/index.html` for the latest server documentation, including documents on these specific APIs.) These additional APIs are new to Server 3.x and are not supported by previous versions of Netscape Server.

There are three main additional APIs that you can use with Netscape Enterprise Server 3.x: Agent API, Access Control API, and Web Publishing Client API.

Agent API is a C-language API that you can use to create and manipulate agents. This API can be seen as an extension of NSAPI. Agents allow you to set up an automatic action to be performed when a specific event occurs or a certain time is reached. With Agent API, you can create a new agent, manipulate an existing agent, or specify the event that should trigger an agent and the action that should be performed when the event occurs.

Access Control API is also a C-language API. Similar to Agent API, it can be viewed as an extension of NSAPI. Access Control API extends the access control capability of Netscape Server. With Access Control API, you define Loadable Authentication Services (LAS). You can read, evaluate, and manipulate the information in the Access Control List files, which include specific instructions for gaining access to the server resources. You can specify your own attributes for authentication or write your own authentication method. You can also use a different database for user information. For example, you can authenticate the user based on the client address. Access Control API is the preferred method of writing authentication functions for Netscape Server 3.x. With previous versions of the server, you had to write your own authentication method using NSAPI. With Server 3.x, however, you should use Access Control API. This API provides additional functionality and control and a more powerful, integrated means of writing authentication and authorization programs.

To supplement your authentication method, you may also consider the LDAP API, Directory Software Developer's Kit (SDK), and Certificate Mapping API. LDAP API allows you to build an LDAP client. You can write an application that connects to the LDAP Directory Server, make specific queries, retrieve specific information in the LDAP Directory Server, or update the entries in the directory. Directory SDK provides specific LDAP libraries. To take advantage of these APIs, you should use the Netscape Directory Server for managing user information. Certificate Mapping API allows you to manage and customize the certificate mapping process used during client authentication. With this API, you can customize how the server locates user information (entries) in the LDAP Directory Server for certificate authentication.

Unlike the previous two APIs, Web publishing API uses Java classes. These classes allow an application to manipulate the documents and directories on the server. The type of resource that you can manipulate using Web Publishing API are containers, which are typically file directories, and components, which are typically files. With this API, you can create, delete, move and copy a file or directory. You can also associate attributes to a specific resource on the server. You can then track and manage these attributes with your program. You can manipulate the attributes of files and directories. You can also lock or edit a resource.

Note on Installing Netscape Server

It is always best to *not* install a new version of the Netscape Server over a previous version. That is, always install to a new server root. This case is especially relevant with Enterprise Server 3.5.1. If you install Enterprise Server 3.5.1 over Enterprise Server 3.0, your server may not function properly. The installation program may not replace or add the necessary files needed to operate properly. For example, if you update the server with one of the server patches (for example, 3.0f for Enterprise Server 3.0 for NT), your file may have a later date than the version included in the 3.5.1 Server installation file. The installation program will not install the new files over the existing files of a later date. This situation can lead to problems, not only with Administration Server, but also with Enterprise Server 3.5.1. Furthermore, by maintaining an earlier version of the server, you can always resort to the previous version if the new version does not function properly.

For security reasons, Enterprise Server 3.5.1 for NT does not allow ~ (tilde) in the path used by a client. Thus you should not use ~ in the path names for your site documents and applications. This restriction holds true for the URL path used by the client and the physical path of a resource specified in the configuration file for use by the client. In other words, neither the URL for the resource nor the actual physical path location of the resource should include a tilde.

It is also recommended that you do not use a path with empty spaces for the location of your server or server resources. The use of spaces may complicate the specification of paths in the various configuration files. For instance, when you install Enterprise Server 3.5.1 for NT in a path that includes a space in the directory, the installation program may use a DOS-alternative directory name for the path. If you install Enterprise Server in `c:/program files/netscape/server`, the server may use `c:/PROGRA~1/netscape/server` as the path for the various resources in the different configuration files. Although this path may work with a number of internal resources of the server, it will not work for the path of a resource that is intended for use by the client. For example, the path for Servlet cannot accept the alternative DOS path—you cannot use `c:/PROGRA~1/netscape/server/plugins/java/servlets`. If you intend to use spaces in the path, make sure the full file name path is used in all the configuration files. Additional information on using paths in Netscape configuration files is provided in Chapter 2.

For Enterprise Server running under UNIX, make sure the operating system allows at least 1,024 open files within a single process and the system.

About This Book

The primary purpose of this book is to provide you with a strong foundation for using many of the programming options for extending Netscape Server. Additional topics covered in the book will also make it a valuable resource for server administrators or those who want to understand the workings of Netscape Server. On the other hand, some programming options are not covered in this book. For example, it does not discuss the special programming features of Netscape Server (such as Access Control API) that allow you to customize a specific feature of Netscape Server 3.x.

What Is Covered in This Book

The immediate Netscape Server covered in this book is Enterprise Server 3.5.1, but I have also attempted to discuss issues concerning previous Netscape Servers. Many readers may have not upgraded to the latest Netscape Server. You may not have seen any need to take advantage of the latest features of the Netscape Server, or you may have been asked to develop applications that must be deployed on different versions of Netscape Server. Much of the information in this book applies to all Netscape Servers. So, even if you are using Commerce Server 1.1x, you should still find the information in this book useful. I also discuss the differences between the many versions of the Netscape

Servers. This information is important if you plan to upgrade your server, or if you wish to develop applications to be deployed on different versions of Netscape Servers.

Even a developer needs to have a good understanding of how Netscape Server works and how it is configured. You need to know the existing features it supports. Netscape configuration files determine how the server handles a request. The global and general settings of the server, which determine how the server will perform, may also indirectly affect the working of your program. For example, the security and access control settings of the server may determine who will have access to your program. To use the different programming features of the server, you must enable and configure the programming feature. For example, to use a CGI program with the server, you must enable and configure the CGI setting of the server, either directly by manually editing the configuration file or indirectly by using Administration Server. For NSAPI applications, you manually update the Netscape configuration file, **obj.conf**, with instructions about your program.

The Netscape configuration file, **obj.conf**, also includes the instructions that the server uses when processing a client request. Some of these instructions are specific to your program; others are based on built-in server functions. These built-in functions may provide features that you may want or need. Instead of writing a program to accomplish a task, you may be able to use these functions to fulfill your requirement. The **obj.conf** file includes a list of the built-in functions that the server uses when processing a request. A number of built-in functions are included, by default, during installation; others may be added when you configure the server, using Administration Server. For some functions, you may need to manually edit and update the configuration file. (The various built-in server functions are described in Appendixes A and B.)

You can also configure specific settings for your program through the configuration file. These instructions affect the way in which the server recognizes and uses your program. For example, you can specify a parameter for CGI or WAI programs that the server then passes on to your program.

The rest of Part I of this book reviews how you can administer and configure Netscape Server. I discuss how to accomplish this goal by using Administration Server or by manually updating the Netscape configuration files. We outline how the Netscape Server processes a client request—in particular, how the **obj.conf** file determines the way in which the server responds to requests. This information can be useful for both administrators and developers. Understanding the **obj.conf** file is essential when you write an NSAPI application. Your NSAPI server application functions are registered with the server in a similar manner as other built-in server functions are. They can be assigned to perform a special task at a specific stage of the server's processing of a request. The discussion of Netscape Server configuration in Chapter 2 serves as background information for the rest of the book. I will expand and refer to this chapter throughout the rest of the book.

The remainder of this book discusses the different ways you can write server applications for Netscape Servers. The main programming options discussed are CGI, NSAPI, and WAI. To supplement these programming options, I will discuss some early ways of developing dynamic content for the client (that is, Server-side Include,

Imagemap, and ISINDEX). These simple-to-implement standards are supported by almost all Web servers. Server-side Include and ISINDEX are precursors to CGI, which provides a more powerful interface for developing server applications. To supplement our discussion of WAI, I will also consider CORBA/IIOP. Although CORBA/IIOP provides a powerful method of developing network-centric applications, the scope of such programs goes beyond HTTP, which is the main server protocol used for the programming methods discussed in this book.

As mentioned earlier, the developer's options for the Netscape Server 3.x include a number of different programming methods. No single book can cover all these topics thoroughly. If a book attempts to describe all the programming options supported by Netscape Server, it can make only a cursory review of the topics. Such a book may be useful for evaluating the available programming options, but it cannot provide the necessary programming discussions.

In this book, we have limited the range of programming topics so as to cover each topic more thoroughly. I will not discuss Server-side Java applets, Servlets, Server-side JavaScript, and LiveConnect. You should avoid writing Server-side Java applets, as Netscape does not recommend their use. Servlet support included with Enterprise Server 3.5.1 is also limited, although it provides a better solution than Server-side Java applets. Server-side JavaScript and LiveConnect, on the other hand, are viable programming options. You can develop powerful server applications using Server-side JavaScript, Java, and LiveConnect, although they do not provide the performance benefits of WAI and NSAPI. This book takes a different route for server programming. The dominant programming language here is C. C and C++ are still the most popular languages for developing mission-critical applications. To discuss Server-side JavaScript requires a review of the JavaScript language, which needs its own book. The topics of programming with JavaScript, Java, and LiveConnect also require extensive discussion, and should be covered in a separate book. Netscape provides different programming options for developers who plan to use Java. I will discuss the use of Java for developing CORBA client and server objects using Netscape ISB for Java and IIOP. I will also describe how you can develop a WAI application using Java. Even the discussion of CORBA and WAI will focus more closely on C++ and C as the main programming languages. Indeed, the examples included in this book are mostly written in C. To write an NSAPI application, you need to use C or C++. Netscape Server itself is written in C. By limiting the programming language to C, we can make a better comparison between CGI, NSAPI, and WAI for developing server applications.

Another purpose of this book is to supplement existing books and documents on Netscape Server programming. In this area, NSAPI and WAI have the greatest weaknesses. Because NSAPI is unique to Netscape Server and because many programmers have had difficulty in understanding its working, NSAPI is the least-documented programming feature of Netscape Server. Therefore, the largest portion of this book will be devoted to NSAPI. As WAI is a recently added development option to the Netscape Server, only limited documentation on this topic exists. WAI is also the recommended method of programming server applications for future Netscape Servers. Consequently, I will spend some time discussing WAI in detail.

The other major programming topics discussed in this book (that is, CGI and CORBA/IIOP) have been covered in a number of other books. Our focus on these topics is specific to Netscape Server. I discuss these topics not only as general programming tools, but also in terms of their specific relationship to Netscape. Since CGI and CORBA/IIOP are standards not limited to the Netscape Servers, much of the information available on these topics applies to Netscape as well. The implementation of these programming options, however, includes unique aspects relevant only to Netscape Server. This book first gives an overview of these programming topics. I then discuss these topics as they relate to Netscape Server. If you are familiar with these programming methods, you can use the information in this book to apply your programming knowledge for developing applications for Netscape Server. A review of CGI and CORBA also provides a good foundation for our discussion of NSAPI and WAI.

The organization of this book follows the evolution of Netscape Server itself. We begin our review of server programming with some early methods of providing dynamic content for the client, such as Server-side Include, Imagemap, ISINDEX, and CGI. These methods are supported by almost all Web servers. Server-side Include, Imagemap, and ISINDEX provide very rudimentary support for the server developer. Server-side Include is a method for including simple server commands directly into an HTML page. The server parses these HTML files and responds to the command tags defined in the file (hence the process is also referred to as Server-parsed HTML). Imagemap allows an image to be divided into predefined areas, with each area linking to a different URL. ISINDEX is a simple server programming method developed before forms were added to HTML standards. With ISINDEX, a program on the server can obtain client text input from an HTML page with an `ISINDEX` tag.

CGI, on the other hand, is a powerful way of writing server programs. In fact, most programmers today still use CGI as a way of extending the server's functionality. Many Web programs begin with programming CGI applications. You can write a CGI program using a script language (for example, PERL), Microsoft Windows programming language (for example, Visual Basic), or programming language that produces an executable program (for example, C or C++). To enable the shell scripts or Windows programs for the Windows version of Netscape Servers, you must enable WinCGI for Visual Basic programs and ShellCGI for the shell scripts. In this book, I will explain how you can configure the server to use your CGI program. I will review how the server uses a CGI program and how you write a CGI program. Although CGI programming is very powerful, it may not provide all the features that you need. It also cannot support the same scalability and performance that NSAPI and WAI applications do.

NSAPI is the next major programming method discussed. It was added as an option to address the weaknesses in CGI and to give programmers greater control over the server. NSAPI is a more difficult programming interface than CGI. Because NSAPI applications are directly linked with the server and run in the server process, you must write robust and thread-safe applications with this approach. On the other hand, NSAPI provides the greatest flexibility and performance. In fact, many of the Netscape Server features, such as Server-side JavaScript, were developed as NSAPI extensions for the server. You can also use NSAPI to program for the Proxy Server (Proxy Server programming is not covered in this book).

Little information is in print about NSAPI programming besides the documents provided by Netscape. Therefore, I will spend some time discussing different aspects of NSAPI. I will review the major data structures and functions used when writing an NSAPI application. I will also go through the steps involved in writing an NSAPI application, and the various types and purposes of NSAPI programs. I will discuss how these programs can affect the server's processing of the request. In addition, I will review how you can compile, register, and debug an NSAPI application. Finally, I will consider some advanced programming issues, such as threads.

Following the discussion of NSAPI, I will review CORBA and IIOP. Developing server applications using CORBA is a new option for Netscape Enterprise Server 3.x. This book will focus on the Netscape ORB offering (Netscape ISB) that you will use to develop CORBA applications. I will discuss its unique features as well as how you can write a CORBA client and server object. The examination of CORBA in this book is brief. You may choose to supplement it with the Netscape ISB for Java and C++ programming and reference guides. Other books on CORBA provide more detailed discussion on how to write CORBA applications in general.

The review of Netscape's CORBA offering is a good starting point for our discussion of WAI. WAI is a unique implementation of a CORBA server object for the Netscape Server. With WAI, you can process a client HTTP request. You do not need to understand CORBA to write a WAI application. Writing a WAI application is simple—you do not need to know the underlying CORBA implementation. You can write a WAI application in C, C++, or Java. You can also write a program in the server process or outside this process. I will discuss these various programming options for WAI. I will examine the various classes and functions that Netscape provides for WAI. I will also review the steps for writing a WAI application and go through some WAI examples. With the current Netscape Server 3.5.1, NSAPI is still the best way to realize additional functionality and superior performance. This situation might change with Server 4.0, however, as WAI is the recommended platform for the next generation of Netscape Servers.

The discussions of CGI, NSAPI, and WAI occur in parallel in this book. For each of these programming interfaces, I will discuss how you accept input from the client, process the request, and return a response. Common examples—a Hello Client and

---

Note ▶

The accompanying CD-ROM includes a number of very useful third-party programs and resources, in addition to the source code for the examples in the book. The materials on the CD-ROM supplement information in this book. For example, you will find CGI libraries for C, C++, and Perl, plus additional examples. These libraries will help you write CGI applications more quickly and efficiently. The CD-ROM also contains NSAPI extensions for Perl and Python. With these extensions, you can write NSAPI applications using Perl and Python instead of C.

Guest Book—are given for each of these interfaces. Throughout the book, I will frequently compare these programming interfaces. In later chapters, I will continue to build on topics discussed in earlier chapters. For example, the NSAPI section describes how you can get the equivalent values of the environment variables, which are used by CGI applications, using NSAPI.

Organization of the Book

This book contains four main parts, each of which is based on one of the major topics described above. Part I is an overview of the server. In addition to this chapter, Part I includes Chapter 2 and Appendixes A–D. Chapter 2 discusses the administration of Netscape Server and the major configuration files of the server. Appendix A includes the server directives used in the **magnus.conf** file for setting the global attributes of the server. Appendix B includes the server directive functions used in the **obj.conf** file. These directive functions are used to initialize a server setting and to direct the processing of a client request. Appendix C includes instructions for using the server's access control file. Appendix D includes instructions for the dynamic configuration of the server using special configuration files.

Parts II through IV cover the various programming interfaces. Part II, consisting of Chapter 3, covers Server-side Include, Imagemap, ISINDEX, and CGI. The CGI discussion is the main portion of this part. We also discuss WinCGI and ShellCGI. Part III (Chapters 4–11) covers the various aspects of NSAPI. Part IV (Chapters 12–15) covers CORBA, Netscape ISB, and WAI. Chapter 12 covers CORBA and Netscape ISB; Chapters 13–16 cover WAI. Depending on the programming interface that you want to study, you can skip to the appropriate part of the book. For example, if you are interested only in WAI, you can skip to Chapters 13–16.

The discussion of each programming interface begins with a general overview, followed by some reference material. You should briefly review the reference materials before you begin programming. This strategy will give you a better understanding of the interface components that you will use in programming your application. For NSAPI, the reference material includes descriptions of the various NSAPI data structures and functions. For WAI, the reference material includes the description of the WAI functions, classes, and methods. I will use the information in the reference sections for writing a server application, though it may be too detailed for general reading. You should use these sections for a general overview and for reference purposes. Once you begin programming, you can return to the reference materials when you need additional information. If you wish to start programming immediately, you may want to skip the reference sections. For example, to start programming with NSAPI, you may want to start with Chapter 6, Writing a Server Application Function.

Following the reference section, I will step through the method of processing a client HTTP request. I will discuss how to get information from the server and client, process this information, and return a response. I will also step through some examples. Because NSAPI is the programming interface most in need of further description, I have included additional information for NSAPI.

Chapter 2

Netscape Servers Configuration

Understanding how the Netscape HTTP server works is necessary if you intend to program applications for this server. The server goes through specific steps defined in the server configuration file, **obj.conf**, to process a request. If you plan to write a server application, you should understand these steps. This suggestion is especially true if you plan to write a server application function (SAF). NSAPI applications are normally written as SAFs. A group of SAFs can also be considered an NSAPI application. You need a good grasp of the server to understand how your SAF will interact with it. Moreover, the server's built-in functions provide specific features that work in concert with your program. These functions enable server applications, run CGI programs, provide the default instructions for the server, and so on. Your NSAPI applications should work similarly to the other built-in server functions. They should fulfill the necessary steps of processing a request as defined by the server. An understanding of the instructions in the configuration files, especially the **obj.conf** file, and the built-in server functions provides the needed groundwork for programming for Netscape Servers. You can also judge when the server already has a certain capability and how to take advantage of it. You may even find a built-in server function that already provides the feature you require.

In this chapter, first we will briefly describe how you can use Administration Server and the specific Server Manager. You can use Administration Server to modify or enhance your server. Next, we will review the major server configuration files. We will discuss the purpose and the workings of these configuration files. The discussion of the workings of the server in this chapter is based on the configuration files for the Netscape HTTP server, whether it is Enterprise, FastTrack, Commerce, or Communication Server. Some discussion of these configuration files may also apply to other Netscape Servers, although the focus in the book is on HTTP servers. For a more general description of the Netscape HTTP server, refer to Chapter 1.

As mentioned in Chapter 1, you can enhance the server's capability by using the different APIs that the server provides. These APIs can be used to extend a server (for example, NSAPI or WAI) or customize a specific feature of the server (for example, Access Control API or Web Publishing API). (Some of these features are supported only under Enterprise Server 3.x and not the FastTrack 3.x.) Besides writing a server program, you can also modify or enhance the server through Administration Server or through manual changes to the server configuration files.

Administration Server provides an easy-to-use graphic interface with which you can modify the server and enable various server features. The updates you make with Administration Server also modify the server configuration files. You can also modify these configuration files directly (manually). In fact, some of the options require you to make changes to the configuration files. These options, such as enabling your NSAPI function, cannot be done through Administration Server.

A Netscape Server includes a number of configuration files. The configuration files for the Netscape HTTP server (for example, Enterprise Server 3.5.1) can be located in the `<server path>/<server ID>/`config directory. Under this directory, you may find two different types of configuration files. There are general server configuration files (such as **magnus.conf** and **obj.conf**), which we will discuss in detail in this chapter. Other configuration files include the settings for a specific feature of Netscape Server. For example, `agent.conf` is the configuration file for the server agents. We will not discuss these specific configuration files here. In this book, we review only the APIs for extending the server and not the APIs for customizing a specific feature of the server. Therefore, we will review only the major server configuration files (that is, **magnus.conf**, **obj.conf**, and **mime.types**), which affect the server globally and are relevant to your programming of a CGI, NSAPI, or WAI application.

In the discussion of the server configuration files, we will refer to a number of server directives and built-in functions. The directives designate the server settings or the procedure the server takes to process a request. Directive functions determine the specific step that the server takes when it starts and when it processes a client request. The server built-in directives for **magnus.conf** and directive functions for **obj.conf** are listed and described in Appendixes A and B. You should use these appendixes in conjunction with this chapter to gain a better understanding of the server options and configuration files. If you are a developer and intend to use NSAPI, you should read this chapter in conjunction with Chapter 8. This chapter provides an overview of the server directives in **obj.conf**, while Chapter 8 provides more detailed information about server directives and their use for an NSAPI developer.

Although the primary audience for this book is the Netscape developer, the information in this chapter is broad enough to be useful for any administrator of Netscape Server. You can use this chapter to get a better understanding of how the server works and what capabilities it provides. The topics covered here encompass the necessary information you need to make modifications to your server. As an administrator, you should use this chapter in conjunction with Appendixes A and B.

Although versions of the Netscape Servers are very different from one another, much of the core functionality and concepts are the same for all versions of the Netscape HTTP server. The information in this chapter is first and foremost based on

Netscape Enterprise Server 3.5.1. Much of this information, however, can be applied to all Netscape HTTP servers, including earlier versions of FastTrack, Enterprise Server, or Commerce and Communication Servers. This situation is especially the case for the various versions of Enterprise Server 3.x, as most core components of Enterprise Server 3.0x and 3.5.1 are generally the same. We have attempted to note the changes between each version of the server throughout the book.

As this book covers only the HTTP server, we will refer to the Netscape HTTP server—for example, Enterprise Server or FastTrack Server—as the Netscape Server. This server is the one that you will be modifying and on which you will put your Web documents. The rest of this chapter covers the configuration options of this server.

This more general chapter does not cover all the details of the server's configuration and options. You may still need to refer to the Netscape Server manuals and help files or to your operating system manual so as to install and set up the server, enable some of the features of the Enterprise Server such as Web publishing, and so on. Subsequent chapters will expand on the constructs included here and provide additional detail, especially as needed for writing NSAPI applications.

The Administration Server

When you install the Netscape HTTP server, it installs two distinct servers: an Administration Server and your HTTP server (for example, Enterprise Server or FastTrack Server). Under NT, you can check in Control Panel under Services to find the Netscape Administration Server (for example, Netscape Administration Server 3.5), along with your installed Netscape Servers (for example, Enterprise, Messaging, or Certificate Servers). The HTTP server (for example, Enterprise Server) and the Administration Server are both HTTP servers, but they have different purposes. They also run on different ports. You can run them concurrently or separately. HTTP server is for general public use, while Administration Server is used to manage and configure other servers. Administration Server is a simple HTTP server (usually running as `root` under UNIX). It administers all servers installed under the main server path, such as Enterprise Server and Messaging Server. It uses Java, JavaScript, and CGI programs to manage and configure the Netscape Servers. It also performs a number of additional tasks, such as SNMP (Simple Network Management Protocol) duties, running `cron` utilities, and so on.

You can have many HTTP servers (secured or unsecured) or different versions of Netscape Server running on the same machine. Different Netscape Servers, however, may need to use a separate Administration Server. Each version of Administration Server includes different features and capabilities. It is also intended for a specific group of servers. Usually each version of Administration Server adheres to a separate version of SuiteSpot and its included servers. The different Administration Servers are not compatible with one another, although you can invoke an earlier version of Administration Server from a later version.

Administration Server 3.5 can be used to administer a number of appropriate 3.x Servers, such as Collabra Server 3.5, Enterprise Server 3.5.1, or Directory Server 3.0. For earlier servers (such as Directory Server 1.02 or Certificate Server 1.01), you need to use their appropriate Administration Servers. If you have multiple Administration Servers and different releases of Netscape Servers installed, Administration Server 3.5 can invoke the appropriate Administration Server if it is already running. It will not be able to administer those servers directly. For example, you can run the Administration Server 2.x for administering the Certificate Server 1.03.

It is not recommended that you run many servers on the same machine unless the server can handle the system resources and load requirements of all the servers. It is best to run different types of Netscape Servers on different machines. For example, run Directory Server on one machine and Enterprise Server on another.

To use Administration Server for Enterprise Server 3.5, you should run Netscape Navigator 3.x or later. Preferably you should use Netscape Communicator 4.04 or 4.05. You should also enable Java and JavaScript for the Navigator (Communicator) and allow cookies to be used. You use the URL for your server plus the specific port address of the Administration Server to access Administration Server. For example, if your server name is `www.foo.com` and the port for Administration Server is `8888`, then you invoke Administration Server by using `http://www.foo.com:8888/`. The server then redirects you to the central Administration Server page. The actual URL that will deliver the central Administration Server page is `http[s]://<server name>[:port]/bin/index`. The superuser that can access the Administration Server is defined when you install your server. It has full access to all features of Administration Server. (For the superuser to have access to the user list in a LDAP directory server database, you need to add the permissions in the directory server.) You can also use distributed administration options to give other users access to different parts of Administration Server.

As previously mentioned, Administration Server 1.x, 2.x, 3.0x, and 3.5 are different from one another, and you always need to use the appropriate Administration Server for your server. The differences between each point release of Administration Server are major in nature. In contrast, the overall differences between Administration Server 3.0x and 3.5 are minor in nature. Administration Server 3.5 includes additional features, such as tracking users licensed for different SuiteSpot servers. If you use Enterprise Server 3.5.1, you need to use Administration Server 3.5. The core features and the organization of the administration pages, however, are essentially the same for Administration Server 3.0x and 3.5. Therefore, much of the following discussion is relevant for, and refers to, both Administration Servers.

Servers managed by Administration Server 3.5 should be installed under the same server path (server root). 3.x servers not managed by Administration Server 3.5 should be installed in a separate directory. Enterprise Server 3.x cannot use Administration Server 2.x. The default directory for the 2.x servers is usually `c:\netscape\server` for NT and `/user/ns-home` for UNIX. For Enterprise Server 3.x, the default path is normally `c:\netscape\SuiteSpot` for NT and `/usr/netscape/SuiteSpot` for UNIX. Make sure that the path for the 2.x server uses a different server root

than the 3.x server. For example, under NT, you can install 2.x servers under
`c:\netscape2\server` and 3.x servers under `c:\netscape3\server`.

Administration Server 3.5 can include a link to Administration Server 2.x. You can find this link in the simple text file `sr2x` under the `<server path>/admin-serv/config/` directory. `sr2x` includes an absolute physical path to the Server 2.x root directory. For example, under NT, `sr2x` may contain `c:\netscape2\server`. If you installed a server that uses an earlier version of Administration Server after installing Enterprise Server 3.5.1, you can manually add the root directory of the server to the `sr2x` file. Make sure you run each Administration Server on a separate port. The two servers cannot share the same port if you want to use both concurrently.

Other differences exist between the Administration Server 3.x and 2.x. Under Administration Server 2.x, you had three distinct components: the Server Selector, the Administration Configuration, and the Server Manager. The Server Selector is the default (first) page delivered by the Administration Server. From this page, you can select to manage a specific server (for example, Enterprise Server) or configure the Administration Server. You can also install a new server or remove an existing server. (See Figure 2-1 for an example of the Server Selector page.) We will refer to the pages

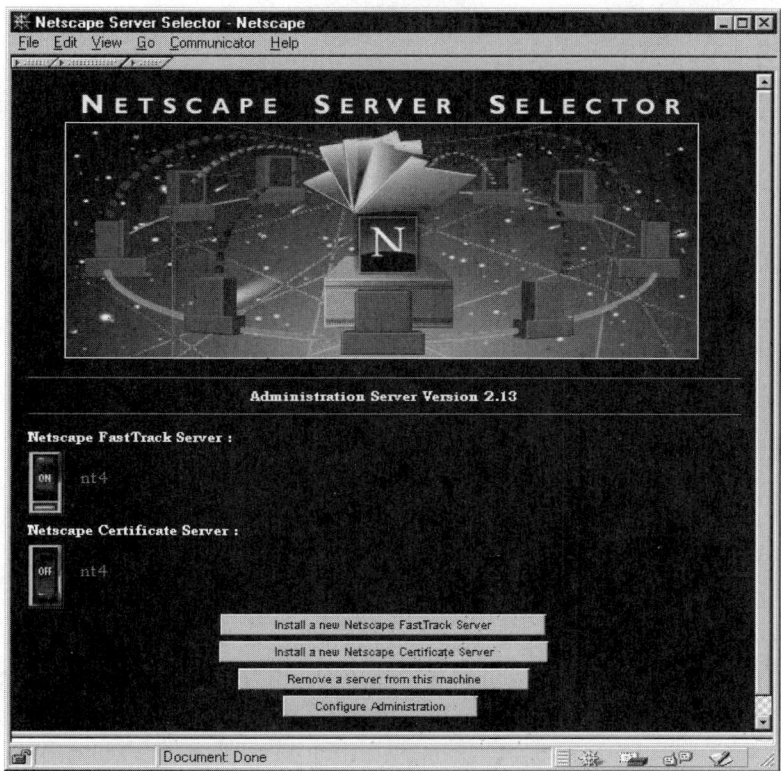

Figure 2-1   Netscape's Server Selector from Administration Server 2.x

for configuring the Administration Server as Administration Configuration and other specific servers' configuration pages as Server Manager. Server Manager is used to configure and manage a single server. Here, we use only the Server Manager for the HTTP server, such as Enterprise Server 3.5.1.

Under Administration Server 3.5, the Server Selector page is named Netscape Server Administration page (see Figure 2-2). The purpose of this page is roughly the same as the Administrative Server 2.x's Server Selector. From this page, you can go to the server's Server Manager pages. The Server Administration page of Server 3.x includes two main sections: a group of links to the General Administration pages, and a group of links to the Server Managers of different Netscape servers. The servers supported under the General Administration are listed under "Servers Supporting General Administration." These servers are part of SuiteSpot 3.5 and are installed under the

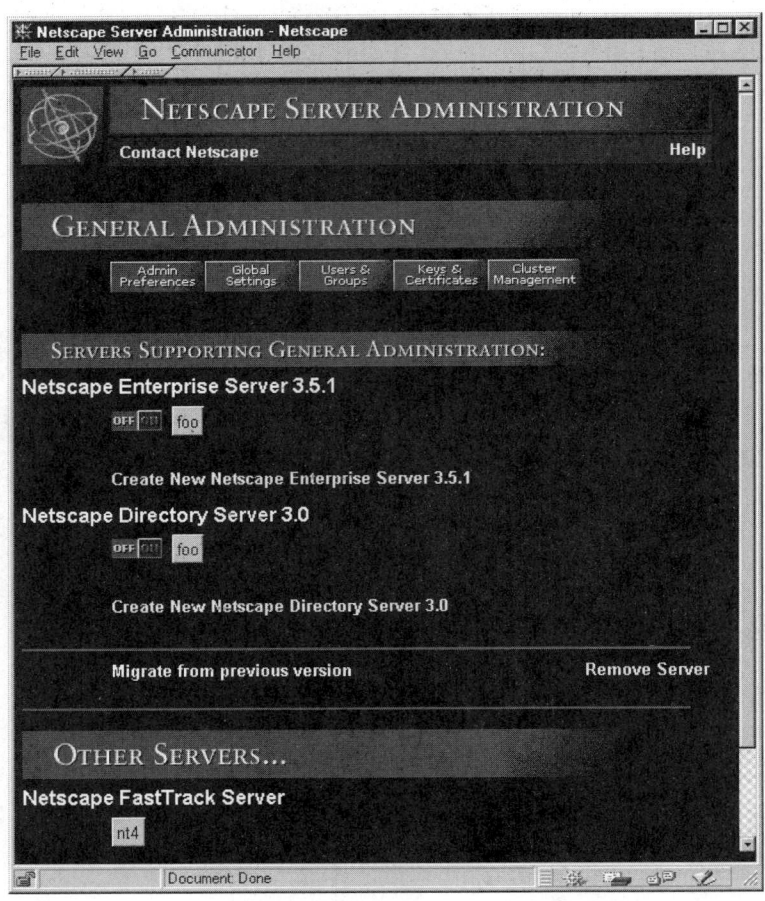

Figure 2-2   Netscape's Server Administration Page (Server Selector) from Administration
            Server 3.5

Server 3.5 root directory. For example, Enterprise Server 3.5.1 should be found under this heading. You can also invoke the Server Managers of earlier servers, which use a different Administration Server, from the Administration Server page. These earlier servers are listed under "Other Servers . . . ." These other servers should be found under a separate server path. You can also use the Server Administration page to add or remove a server or migrate the setting for a previous version of the server, such as Server 2.x.

In Administration Server 3.x, the Administration Configuration is part of General Administration (shown in Figure 2-3). Unlike the Administration Configuration for Administration Server 2.x, General Administration includes a number of additional features and options. Some of these options are specific to the Administration Server, such as the Admin Preferences pages. The Admin Preferences pages are very similar to the Administration Configuration for Administration Server 2.x. From Admin Preferences, you can start or shut down the Administration Server. You can also change the Administration Server port, set superuser access control options, set SSL security options for the Administration Server, view Administration Server's access and error log files, and so on. Other General Administration settings apply to all other 3.x servers directly managed by Administration Server. In other words, some settings for Enterprise Server 3.5.1, which the Server Manager handled for Server 2.x, are now set through General Administration. These General Administration settings relate to users

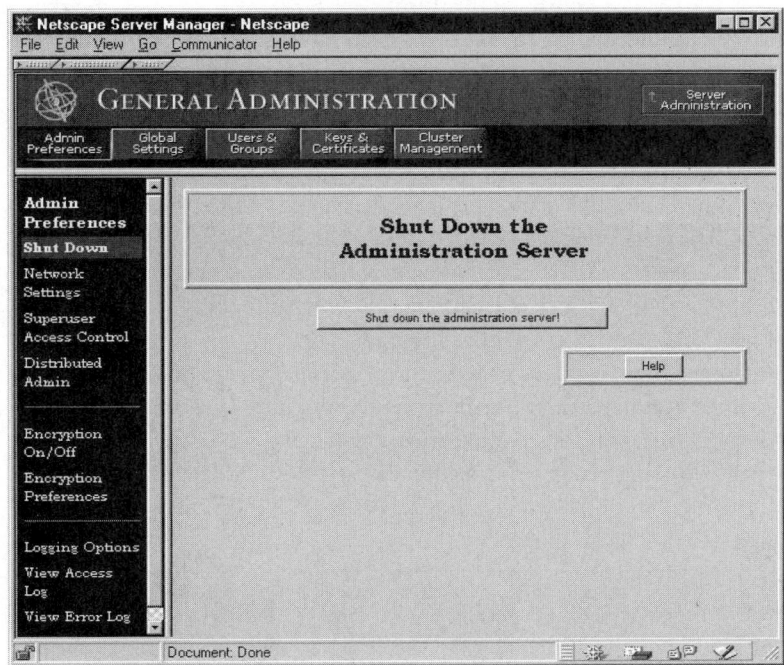

Figure 2-3   Administration Server 3.5 General Administration

and groups management and security. They allow the multiple servers to share keys and certificates and the user database. With 3.x servers, the users and groups are maintained from the General Administration pages. The users and groups database can be either a local database or an LDAP directory server, such as Netscape Directory Server 3.0. (The local database, unlike Netscape Directory Server, is limited to 1,000 entries.) With Administration Server 3.5, you can also customize the preferred language of the users and groups if you use Netscape Directory Server 3.0. This feature allows users to view their information in their preferred Asian or European characters. The Keys and Certificates are also installed, managed, and generated from the General Administration pages. For example, after installing the certificate and generating the key, you can specify an alias for the server's key-pair and certificate files under the General Administration Keys & Certificates menu. In the Server Manager of your server (for example, Enterprise Server), you can use this alias to enable security (Encryption) for your server (Server Preference|Encryption On/Off menu).

Note ▶

This book uses the convention of "[*top button name*]|[*left list name*]" in referring to the form pages of the Server Manager and General Administration.

Under Server 3.x, you may also administer multiple remote servers of the same type from a single Administration Server. For instance, multiple Enterprise 3.5.1 servers can use the same configuration. You can accomplish this goal by clustering, or grouping a number of servers, from the Cluster Management menu of General Administration.

You will make most of your modifications to a specific Netscape Server, such as Enterprise Server, in the Server Manager. We will discuss the Server Manager for the HTTP server in more detail shortly. To access the Server Manager for a specific server directly, you should use the following URL: `http[s]://<server name>[:port]/<server ID>/bin/index`. For example, you can access the Server Manager for the `foo` HTTP server using the following URL: `http://www.foo.com:8888/https-foo/bin/index`.

The use of different server management tools with very similar names might seem confusing. In fact, you might find documents that refer to one of these server management tools, but call it by a wrong or different name. In the real world, you will find that, although it may appear confusing on paper, it is actually easy to find out what each tool does and to navigate between them using Netscape Navigator (Communicator).

Note ▶

Unlike with Administration Server 2.x and 3.x, under 1.x Servers you could not configure a server while it was running.

Distributed Administration

With Server 3.x, you have the options of having multiple administrators, each of which has its own assigned capability. Server 3.x accommodates three types of users. The first type is the superuser, which has access to all features of the Administration Server. You use this user when installing the server. The second type is an administrator, which can have controlled access to the General Administration or the Server Manager of other servers. Finally, there is the end user. End users can modify only their own passwords or update their personal information.

To allow access for other administrators and end users, you first need to activate distributed administration from General Administration's, Admin Preferences|Distributed Admin menu. You must be a superuser before you can make any of the following changes for the first time. The options for the end users access are simple—you can allow or deny the end users access to the forms for modifying and changing their own passwords and personal information. The path to the user environment is http[s]:// <server name>:<admin port>/user-environment/bin/index. The end user can access this environment by typing http[s]:// <server name>:<admin port>/. You can also specify the groups that will constitute the administrator groups from the Admin Preferences|Distributed Admin menu, with the default group name being Administrators.

To demonstrate how you can set up different administrators, we will go through the additional steps for setting up an Administrators group. In our example, the Administrators group will have access to the HTTP server's Server Manager but not to the General Administration settings. To allow Administrators access to various portions of Administration Server, you need to create specific access control list (ACL) files. From General Administration, select Global Settings|Restrict Access, choose to create the ACL for Administration Server (admin-serv). The server will create the file and input the default access control rules. The admin-serv's ACL file can be found under <server path>/adminacl as admin-serv.acl. By default, the access control rules for the admin-serv state that no one and no group except Administrators can have access to the Administration Server's main page and the General Administration options. As we have not allowed the Administrators group to access the main Administration Server, no one will be allowed access to the main Administration Server page—that is, to http[s]:// <server name>:<admin port>/admin-serv/bin/index. For now, we can accept the default setting for the admin-serv. You can modify the Access Control settings for the admin-serv if you like. Press the submit button to continue. The server displays a warning, noting that you need to stop and restart the Administration Server for the changes to take effect. As we have not finished setting up the Administrators group, we go on making other modifications before shutting down and restarting the server.

In Global Settings|Restrict Access, choose your server from the list of the servers— for example, https-foo. Next, create the ACL file for your server. The ACL for the foo, https-foo.acl, can also be located under the adminacl directory. This time we will add the Administrators group to the list of access control rules. The default setting for the foo server is the same as the default setting for admin-serv. We now need to add the access control rules for our Administrators group. Use the New Line button to add a new line to the Access Control Rules table. You can then select anyone from the added line to choose a specific user or group for authentication. In the frame below the Access Control Rules table, choose "Only the following people" from the radio buttons and add the name of the Administrators to the Group text box. Next, press the Update button to update the access control rules. You can also click on all under the Programs column to select the specific program groups to which you intend to allow the administrator to access. Note that the list in the Program Groups reflects the top menu of the Server Manager. In our example, we will select Server Preferences. Thus the Administrator will have access only to the Server Preferences option of the foo Server Manager. After you have finished with the updates, you can submit the changes in the access control rules.

Listing 2-1 provides an example of an ACL file for the foo server. Note that the Administrators group is allowed access only to the Server Preferences program. (For more information on ACL files, refer to Appendix C.)

Listing 2-1   Example of an ACL File

```
Version 3.0;
acl "https-foo";

deny with file=
  "c:/netscape/server/adminacl/admin-denymsg.html";

authenticate (user,group) {
        prompt = "Enterprise Server Only";
};

deny (all)
  (user = "anyone");

deny absolute (all)
  group != "Administrators";

allow (all)
  (group = "Administrators") and
  (program = "Server Preferences");
```

Now you need to add a specific user to the Administrators group. First, add your user in General Administration from the Users & Groups|New User menu. If you wish to add an existing user to the Administrators group, you can skip this step. Next, use the menu User & Groups|Manage Groups to find the Administrators group. You can input the Administrators in the "Find group:" text box and press the Find button. This action should return the settings for Administrators. If the Administrators group was not found, you need to add the group, using the Users

& Groups|New Group menu options. Once you have the `Administrators` settings, you can add the user to the Group Members by using the Edit button. Find your user and add it to the Group Members of the `Administrators`.

You are now ready to shut down and restart the Administration Server. You can shut down the server from General Administration's Admin Preferences|Shut Down menu. To start Administration Server for NT, you can use the shortcut or the icon for Administration Server or select Administration Server from the Services in the Control Panel. Under UNIX, you can stop the server from the command line under the server root directory by typing `./stop-admin`. To start the server, you can type `./start-admin`.

Now we are ready to test our user. Open a new Navigator and try to access the Administrator Servers main page, such as `http://www.foo.com:8888/`. First, you are asked to enter your name and password. Even if the name and password are correct, the server should return the `admin-denymsg.html` page (Permission Denied). Next, try to access the Server Manager for the `foo` server directly, through `http://www.foo.com:8888/https-foo/bin/index`. The server should return the Server Manager with only the Server Preferences button available in the top frame.

In most cases, you may need to modify the ACL files manually. You cannot modify the default access control rules for Administration Server and Server Manager from the General Administration form. Because the default access control rules are hierarchical, they may conflict with a setting that you need to add. For example, to allow a single user who is not part of the `Administrators` group to access Server Manager, you need to remove the instructions for the `Administrators` from the file. For instance, you delete the following lines from the `https-foo.acl` file:

```
deny absolute (all)
 group != "Administrators";
```

In this case, the access control rule is identified as `absolute` and is the first instruction with the `absolute` attribute (see Listing 2-1). The `absolute` attribute means that, if the request matches the rule, then the server does not look at any other rules. Any user other than a member of the `Administrators` group satisfies this rule. Therefore, this rule is used and any additional rule will be ignored, unless the rule covers a user in the `Administrators` group. Appendix C provides additional information about ACL files.

Administration Server Files

As the Administration Server is itself an HTTP server, it has its own executable and program files. You can find the Administration Server 3.*x*'s program and documentation files under `<server path>/bin/admin`. The Administration Server also includes a number of configuration and log files. You can find these files under `<server path>/admin-serv`. Unlike with the Netscape HTTP server, you do not have access to a specific Administration Server API. Administration Server also does not include an **obj.conf** configuration file. The following list indicates the main Administration Server configuration files for Server 3.x found under the *<server path>*/admin-server/config directory.

- The ns-admin.conf file is very similar to a **magnus.conf** file (described in detail later in this chapter). ns-admin.conf is really a **magnus.conf** file for Administration Server. Administration Server does not have an **obj.conf** file (also described in detail later in this chapter). Unfortunately, this restriction means that you have limited control over how Administration Server works. For example, you cannot use NSAPI to customize Administration Server.

- ns-cron.conf and cron.conf are the cron configuration files for the server. cron (primarily used in the UNIX world) refers to a program that runs at pre-defined, regular intervals. For example, you can set up a backup routine for your log files to occur a certain time every week.

- The servers.lst file holds a list of the 3.x servers managed by Administration Server, including the HTTP servers. Each line includes *<product ID>*:*<product name>* (for example, https:Netscape Enterprise Server).

- admpw holds the username and password file for the Administration Server superuser. Administration Server has its own superuser username and password file, distinct from other servers' password files. This ASCII file holds the information needed to authenticate the superuser. The Administration Server superuser password must use eight or fewer characters.

- dsgw.conf, dsgwfilter.conf, dsgw-language.conf, dsgw-orgperson.conf, and dsgwsearchprefs.conf include specific programming instructions (JavaScript code), as well as LDAP- and Directory Server-related configuration information used by Administration Server when managing users and groups.

- sr2x (as described earlier) holds the absolute physical path to the Server 2.x root directory.

Under the *<server path>*/admin-serv/logs directory, you will find the main log files for Administration Server, access and errors. The access file logs

---

Note ▶

User and password information for the Netscape Administration Server superuser appears in a text file with a *<username>*:*<encrypted password>* format. If you forget your Administration Server password, shut down your server, open the user file (*<server path>*/admin-serv/config/admpw), and delete the password entry for your username. You can then access the server with a blank password and change this password from General Administration's Admin Preferences|Superuser Access Control menu. Make sure this file is in a safe location and is not accessible to other users.

the client access to Administration Server. `errors` logs any error that may occur while running Administration Server.

The Server Manager

The Server Manager is the part of Administration Server that manages a specific Netscape Server, such as an HTTP server. Netscape allows you to configure this server through its graphic and form-based Server Manager (see Figure 2-4). You can access the Server Manager for a specific Server 3.x directly, by using the following type of URL: `http[s]://<server name>[:port]/<server ID>/bin/index`. The server ID should be the ID of your server. For example, for the Enterprise Server `foo`, the server ID is `https-foo`.

If you have clustered a number of different servers, you can use the Server Manager to administer all servers in the cluster. You use the central (master) Administration Server's Server Manager to administer all the clustered servers. To use clusters, you must use Administration Server 3.x. The servers must also support clustering as, for example, Enterprise Server 3.5.1 does. FastTrack Servers and Netscape Servers earlier than the 3.0 version do not support cluster management. All servers in a cluster must be of the same type, using the same version and protocol. The central Administration Server must have access to the other server's Administration Server. The central Administration Server must also have the same administration user name and password as all the other clustered servers, as it employs this user name and password to access the other Administration Servers. To add, modify, and remove a server from the cluster, you use General Administration's Cluster Management menu in the central Administration Server.

The Server Manager, with its Web page interface, enables easy server administration. You can explore the Server Manager and use the Help option to review some of the server configurations.

> ### Note ▶
>
> There are three frames in Netscape's Server Manager, each of which has its own connection to the server. The frames use JavaScript, Java, CGI, and cookies to manage navigation and updating. Using Netscape Navigator 3.x, you might find some odd results when you navigate through these forms. For example, when you use the **Back** button or the **Back** menu option after pressing the right mouse button, different frames might go back at different rates. For instance, if you go from Server Preferences|View Server Settings to one of the previous URLs, you will not be able to return to View Server Settings by using the **Back** button.

Some other servers, such as O'Reilly's WebSite, provide more graphically enriched administration servers. WebSite uses the Windows operating system's GUI (graphical user interface) to provide an administration server that is more standard and intuitive to Windows users. Netscape opted for a browser-based Server Manager, because it provides the same interface across all platforms. Besides its Windows GUI-based administration server, Microsoft IIS (Internet Information Server) provides an HTML-based server manager. IIS version 3.0, however, does not provide the depth and capabilities of Netscape's Server Manager.

You can configure your server remotely—not just on different machines with the same operating system, but on all networked systems that allow you to run a browser with Netscape Navigator 3.x or later capabilities (supporting such advanced features as JavaScript, Java, cookies, and frames). As described in the previous section, with Administration Server 3.x, you can also name a specific administrator or a group of administrators that can manage a specific server using the Server Manager. You can also control what portion of the Server Manager that the administrator can use. Thus, unlike the previous versions of Netscape Server, you can separate the different tasks of managing Administration Server and managing the HTTP server.

Figure 2-4 shows a typical Server Manager page. To navigate through the Server Manager, first use the top-frame button menu as the top-level menu. Then use the list in the right frame to navigate between the pages of each section.

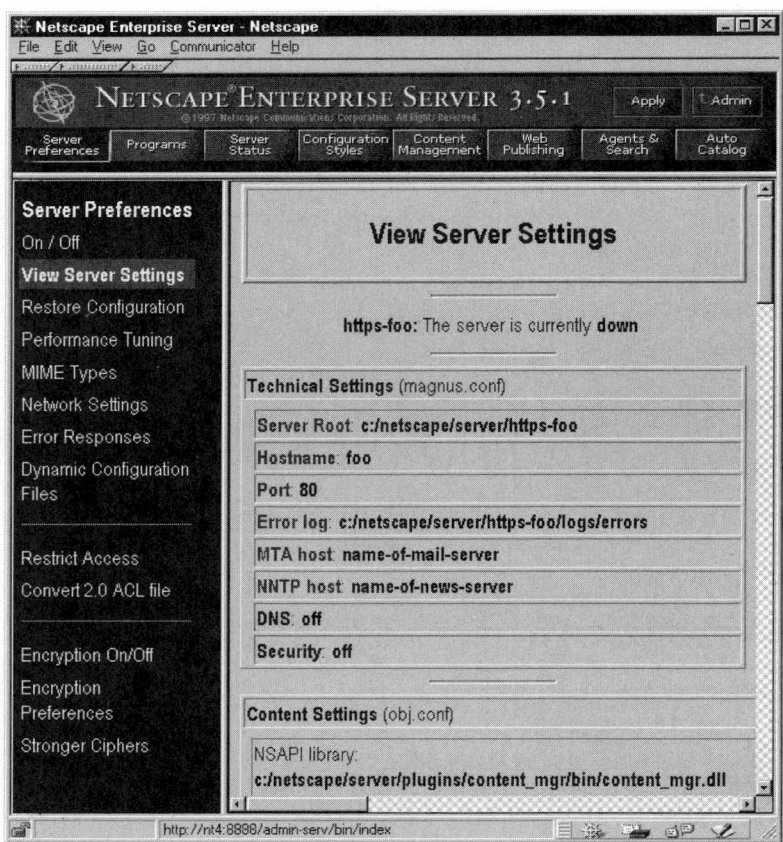

Figure 2-4   Netscape's Server Manager

You should spend some time reviewing the various Server Manager pages to examine the different server settings and the configuration options that the Server Manager provides. For example, you can check the View Server Settings page from the Server Preferences|View Server Settings menu of Netscape Server 3.5.1 to get an overview of the server's setting. From the Server Manager, you can enable various Enterprise Server features, such as Web Publishing, Agents, Search, and AutoCatalog. You should especially look under Programs for the specific settings of the CGI, WINCGI, ShellCGI, Query Handler, and WAI programming options. These programming options are discussed in this book. Throughout this book, we will refer to specific Server Manager pages whenever you can use the Server Manager to make modifications to the server for your programs.

You also can configure the server manually by directly modifying the configuration files. Your changes will take effect when you restart the server. If you make any manual changes to the configuration files, when you restart the Server Manager, you should update the Server Manager with your changes. Use the **Apply** button on the top right-hand corner of the Navigator/Communicator (see Figure 2-4).

Server Manager 2.x and 3.x recognize if a manual change has been made to the configuration files and ask if you want to apply those changes and update the Server Manager. They also allow you to update the Server Manager through the **Load Configuration Files** button. (Under Server 1.x, you needed to manually stop and restart the server for manual changes to be reflected in the Server Manager.) Server 2.x and 3.x then automatically restart, adding (rewriting) the changes that you made in the configuration files. (Unlike 1.x Servers, Netscape 2.x Servers cut off any active connection upon restart. Thus you should take all necessary precautions before you restart the server.)

The Server Manager keeps a backup copy of your configuration files. Under Server 2.x, you could find this backup under *<server path>*/admserv/*<server ID>*. Under Server 3.x, you can find these files under the *<server path>*/ *<server ID>*/conf_bk directory. The Server Manager uses these copies to find out if you have manually edited your configuration file. It also uses these files when you load a previously saved version of your configuration file through the Server Manager. When updating a configuration file, you should not make changes directly to these files, but rather change the files under the *<server path>*/*<server ID>*/conf

---

Warning ▶

Under Server Manager 2.x, when you make changes and save them using the Server Manager, the Server Manager overwrites the configuration files with your new configuration, but without any of your formatting or comment changes.

1. This process means that your formatting changes and commented lines will be erased! (So, make a backup of any manual configuration files.)
2. This is *not* the same as the **Save and Apply** or **Apply Changes** buttons, which overwrite your manual changes and apply the existing Server Manager's settings!

directory. Server Manager 3.x also includes an option for backing up the configuration files. You can set the number of backups and restore or view earlier versions of the configuration files through the Server Preferences|Restore Configuration menu.

Wildcard Options

Many server configuration options allow you to use wildcard patterns to specify a group of items. You are probably already familiar with this concept and are using wildcard patterns when you employ WWW search engines or when you attempt to specify a group of files under DOS, Windows NT's command prompt, or UNIX. You define a pattern that the specified items need to match. Thus you can define rules for a group of items even when you do not know what those items will be. For example, you define *.txt for all files that have a "txt" extension. Netscape's use of wildcards is similar to the pattern searching (matching) features available in many tools and operating systems. Although it is based on regular expression, it does not always conform to the regular expression syntax. The usage may also vary under certain circumstances. You should always test the usage of the wildcards to make sure the specific syntax is properly supported. For example, when using * in an IP address inside an ACL file, you can use the * only for an entire set of numbers in the IP address. In other words, you cannot use 204.156.128.2*, but you can use 204.156.128.*. The * wildcard character should also be the last character in the IP address. For example, you cannot use 204.*.128.200, but you can use 204.*. For more information on the use of wildcard characters in ACL files, see Appendix C.

Netscape Server 1.x provided a shexp.h header file for your NSAPI programs that included a few functions for supporting shell expressions. These functions, such as **shexp_casecmp**, can be used to readily compare a string with a shell expression. With Server 2.x and 3.x, there is also support for regular expressions. Under Server 2.x, you can find the definition of the regular expression functions in the regexp.h header file.

Wildcard Characters

The special wildcard characters you can use with your Netscape Server are described below. You can include multiple wildcards in one string.

---

* (asterisk, star)
*.txt
Use instead of any number of undefined characters in a string. The string can contain any number of characters, including zero. The asterisk should also be used in combination with a number of defined characters. For example, *.txt will define any file with the extension "txt".

? (question mark)

`l?ng`

Matches only one character in a string. The string can include any character in place of the question mark (?). For example, `l?ng` will match "long", "lang", and so on.

$ (dollar sign)

`continu$`

Matches the end of a string. The string can include any number of characters in place of the dollar sign ($). Unlike with `*`, you can use $ only at the end of a string. For example, `continu$` matches "continue", "continuing", "continues", "continuity", and so on.

\ (backward slash)

`*home\*`

Escape character. Any character after the escape character, backslash (\), will be recognized as a literal character instead of a special wildcard character. For example, `*home\*` will match any string that ends with "home*".

~ (tilde)

`*~home`

Logical NOT. All strings that include the characters defined after the tilde (~) are excluded. For example, `*~home` will match any string except the ones that end with "home".

| (pipe)

`(GET|POST)`

Logical OR. The pipe symbol (|) works as an "or" expression. The strings that you wish to include in your "or" expression need to be placed inside parentheses and separated by pipe symbols. The string can match any one of the strings in this group of strings. For example, `(GET|POST)` will match a string if it is either `GET` or `POST`. You can also include other wildcards in each substring.

[204]

`204.19[789]`

Matches at least one character in the brackets. The appropriate string will include one of the characters in the brackets. All characters except the bracket symbols, "[" and "]", can be included in the string. For example, `204.19[789]` will match 204.197, 204.198, or 204.199. (To use brackets in your string, add a backslash (\) in front of the bracket (for example, `\]`).)

[A–Z]

`20[A-Z]`

Matches at least one character in the brackets. The characters are members of the ASCII character set and match the range of ASCII characters. In this example, A–Z includes A and Z, but does not include the lowercase characters a–z. An ASCII table, commonly found in most introductory C programming books, lists the available characters. For example, `20[A-Z]` will match any string that begins with "20" and ends with a character between A and Z, inclusive.

---

[^12]

`20[^12]`

Matches any single character except the characters defined after the ^ (caret) symbol. For example, `20[^12]` matches any set of characters starting with 20, but not 201 or 202.

Main Server Configuration Files

Netscape Server includes configuration files that allow you to set global characteristics for your server and to tailor your server's response to particular scenarios. The principal Netscape configuration files are **magnus.conf**, **obj.conf**, and **mime.types**. For Enterprise Server 3.x, you can find these files under the *<server path>/ <server ID>*/config directory. You will normally modify these files to change a specific setting for the server or to enhance the server with a new feature. For NSAPI, you must modify the **obj.conf** file (and sometimes the **mime.types** file) with instructions about your program. All current and previous versions of the Netscape HTTP servers include these configuration files.

You will find additional configuration files under the config directory that are used for the different features of the Netscape Server. For example, for Enterprise Server 3.5.1, you may find the following configuration files.

jsa.conf is used for JavaScript server applications. This file contains the location and settings of each Server-side JavaScript application.

agent.conf includes the specific Netscape agent's configuration information. When you use the Server Manager forms from the Agent & Search menu to manage an agent, the changes you make are reflected in this file. Agents are used to manage automatically your Web server's files and folders. An agent can monitor your site for a predetermined event or a specified time. When the specific event occurs or the time of activation is reached, the agent will perform the tasks you have mandated—for example, sending an e-mail about the changes to an administrator.

filter.conf, rdm.conf, robot.conf, csid.conf, and process.conf are used for the AutoCatalog feature of Enterprise Server 3.x. You can use AutoCatalog to catalog the documents on your site and generate an HTML view of the content in your site based on title, classification, author, or last-modified date. AutoCatalog provides a subset of Netscape Catalog Server's (now called Compass Server) features and functionality. A catalog agent is used to handle the AutoCatalog. (Note that AutoCatalog is not supported under Enterprise Server 3.5.1 for NT.)

`Webpub.conf` is used by the Web Publisher, which clients deploy to access, edit, and manage files on the server.

You may also find a number of files with the extension `.clfilter`—for example, `magnus.conf.clfilter`. These files are used when a server is being administered as part of a cluster of servers. A group of Enterprise Servers, when clustered, can be managed from a central Administration Server. This book will not cover these specific features of the Netscape Server, so we will not review these configuration files in detail.

This chapter will examine the **magnus.conf**, **obj.conf**, and **mime.types** files. We will discuss these files in general and provide specific instructions for modifying them. Because **obj.conf** is critical for understanding the workings of the Netscape Server and for developing NSAPI applications, we will spend considerable time describing the different components of this file.

Within **magnus.conf** and **obj.conf** are sets of directives. **Directives** are specific instructions, or settings, that need to be defined for the server. They also define the type of function that will be applied to the server. In **magnus.conf**, the directives define the global settings for the server. In **obj.conf**, directives define the specific steps that the server will take to process requests. These directives identify a group of functions and their purpose, so any number of functions and function parameters can be defined for one directive. We will refer to the specific functions in **obj.conf** as directive functions.

After you install the server, these configuration files include a number of default settings. For example, **magnus.conf** includes a number of default directives and **obj.conf** includes several default directive functions. When you make a specific change through the Server Manager, these files will be updated with your changes. There are times, however, when you need to change these files manually. Not all options available through the built-in server directives and directive functions can be set through the Server Manager. You can modify these files by changing an existing directive or by adding or removing a directive or directive function.

Appendix A includes descriptions of the various server **magnus.conf** directives. Appendix B includes descriptions of the various server **obj.conf** directive functions. The default settings in **magnus.conf** and **obj.conf** do not include all built-in server directives for **magnus.conf** and directive functions for **obj.conf**. Appendixes A and B indicate whether a directive or a directive function is set as a default during installation.

Netscape's NT Server 1.1x does not work with **magnus.conf** and **obj.conf** files; instead it uses the NT registry. Microsoft recommends this method of configuring and registering applications because, as a database, the registry file provides more flexible security and cross referencing. (This reason is why Microsoft moved from using `win.ini` and `system.ini` for configuring Windows 3.1 to the registry database for Windows 95 and NT.) Updating the registry, however, is not only dangerous, but also cumbersome and slow. Ideally, programs should update the registry, with no further changes needed. That is, you should not need to hack regularly at the registry. "Hacking" is the norm for a program, such as Netscape Server 1.1x, that needs to modify the registry each time you add a new function. The many Netscape programmers who programmed for Netscape 1.1x under NT know the frustration of having to repeatedly change the registry. As a matter of fact, this requirement was annoying enough for the author that he wrote a program just to update and modify the registry with each function added or removed. This reason is also why Netscape began using the `*.conf` text files for configuring the later NT server. With Server 2.x, you can now easily write the configuration and transfer it between machines and operating systems. In other words, the configuration of **obj.conf** can be written for various platforms.

Many items for which you might consider writing a program can be accomplished through the existing functions of the Netscape Server directives. You might find a pre-defined function that does just what you want. For example, you might be thinking of writing a function that redirects a request for a certain directory to another location or path. The **NameTrans** directive used in the **obj.conf** file supports a built-in function that allows you to accomplish this goal. You invoke a function by adding it to your **obj.conf** file and setting its parameter and values. The function will then redirect the client request to a new location—just what you wanted. Review these already-available directives and think of what you intend to do before you start from scratch.

Warning ▶

Be careful not to modify configuration files manually unless you are sure about your actions. It is easy to render the server inoperative temporarily by incorrectly modifying these files. You should also make a backup copy of your configuration file, so you can always resort to a previously working configuration file. In addition, you can compare the different versions of the configuration files to identify changes made by the Server Manager. With Server Manager 3.x, you can automatically back up the server configuration files. The server can maintain a number of earlier versions of the configuration files. You can also restore a previously saved configuration file using the Server Manager. (See Server Preferences|Restore Configuration in the Server Manager.)

---

magnus.conf

magnus.conf holds the global server configuration. The origin of this file lies in the NCSA HTTPd's `httpd.conf` file. Under Netscape's UNIX Server 1.x, function initialization (**Init**) was placed in **magnus.conf**. With Server 2.x, there no longer exists a real need to include **Init** directives in the **magnus.conf** file. As **Init** functions were the main reason why you modified this file in Server 1.x, and this step is no longer necessary, you probably won't make manual changes to **magnus.conf**.

magnus.conf holds such global server information as the values of ServerName and Port. This information includes directives for the entire server—not specific information about how to handle directories, documents, and so on. For example, if your server is listening on port 86, you should specify Port 86 in the **magnus.conf** file. The server also uses **magnus.conf** information to configure its settings. See Appendix A for a description of the various **magnus.conf** directives.

Listing 2-2 provides an example of a **magnus.conf** file for Enterprise Server 3.5.1.

Listing 2-2 Sample **magnus.conf** file

```
#ServerRoot c:/netscape/server/https-foo
ServerID https-foo
ServerName foo
Port 80
LoadObjects obj.conf
RootObject default
ErrorLog c:/netscape/server/https-foo/logs/errors
MtaHost smtp.foo.com
NntpHost nntp.foo.com
DNS off
Security off
Ciphers +rc4,+rc4export,+rc2,+rc2export,+des,+desede3
SSL3Ciphers +rsa_rc4_128_md5,+rsa_3des_sha,+rsa_des_sha,\
+rsa_rc4_40_md5,+rsa_rc2_40_md5,-rsa_null_md5
ACLFile c:/netscape/server/httpacl/generated.https-foo.acl
ClientLanguage en
AdminLanguage en
DefaultLanguage en
AcceptLanguage off
RqThrottle 512
```

Conventions

Listing 2-2 demonstrates how the **magnus.conf** file includes a list of directives (specifications) that are defined for the server in the format shown in Table 2-1:

Table 2-1 Format of **magnus.conf** Directive

Format	Directive	Value
Example	ServerName	foo

Unlike the **obj.conf** directives, which identify a type of function, these directives identify a specific setting and its value. Although directives are case-insensitive, the convention is that the directive is initially capitalized. If it uses compound words, such as ServerName, each word begins with the initial letter capitalized (**S**erver**N**ame). The directives include the global variables for the server, such as ServerRoot and ServerName. Each new directive starts on a new line. In **magnus.conf**, directive order does not matter, as all of the instructions in the file load at the start and no information is reliant on previous instructions.

value, which follows the directive with a space, sets the directive's value (that is, defines the directive). Depending on the context of *value* and the type of directive, *value* may be case-sensitive. For example, the directory path for the **ErrorLog** file is case-sensitive under UNIX. In general, it is best to assume that values are case-sensitive.

Other Syntax

A **comment** line begins with a **pound sign** (#) and without any white spaces before the #.

Do not begin a directive line with any white **spaces**. If you use white spaces before the directive name, the Server Manager may not be able to read the information properly. Although your server will most likely function correctly, the Server Manager will report a blank for the value of the directive. Also, it is best to avoid trailing spaces after the value.

Use only **forward slashes** (/) in defining a path (for example, `c:/netscape/server`). They ensure that the server will find the correct files, even in operating systems like Windows where the path string usually utilizes a backslash (\). The path you specify could also include spaces.

Unlike with the **obj.conf** file, you should not include quotes around values in the **magnus.conf** file. If you add quotes around a value, even if the value is a directory path, the server will read the quote as part of the value.

> **Note ▶**
>
> A quote can be used for the value of parameters when a directive in the configuration file can include multiple and optional parameters (arguments), such as the **obj.conf** file. Do not use quotes around the value when directives, such as **magnus.conf** directives, include a single value.

The Server Manager writes each directive in its own line, independent of the length of the line. When you manually change a configuration file, however, each directive can be more than one line. As in C macro preprocessors (for example, in #define lines of code), you can use a **backslash** (\) to divide a line. You cannot split the directive into two lines unless you use a backslash. If you plan to use the Server Manager for configuring the server, however, you should avoid dividing the directive lines in the configuration files. The Server Manager will not be able to interpret a directive that is split into multiple lines. Moreover, when you change the **magnus.conf** file using the Server Manager, the Server Manager reformats the file, placing each directive on a single line. If, by any chance, you need to use a backslash that could be confused with a line break, you must include an escape character—that is, an extra backslash.

Table 2-2 shows examples of directives formatted properly and incorrectly.

Table 2-2   Use of Directives in `magnus.conf`

WRONG	WRONG	CORRECT	CORRECT
ErrorLog c:/my errorlog	ErrorLog "c:/my errorlog"	ErrorLog \\ c:/my errorlog	ErrorLog c:/\\ my errorlog

> **Warning ▶**
>
> A URL that points to a directory should always end with a forward slash. Netscape uses a call to redirect (status 302) to route a request for a directory that does not include a forward slash to a directory that contains the necessary forward slash (for example, it routes `http://www.foo.com` to `http://www.foo.com/`). This approach does not always work, however. If you have set up the Software Virtual Server (to respond to different URLs for the same IP address) and the browser that makes the request does not send the `Host` HTTP header, then the client might get a different server than the one requested. (See also the section Software Virtual Server later in this chapter.) For example, a request for `http://jackserver.com/news` might return `http://mainserver.com/news/`. The browser converts the server name in the URL to the IP address and will connect to the server using the IP address. If the host data is not sent by the browser, the server will have no way to identify which virtual server is requested. Therefore, it will look for the information in **magnus.conf** and return the directory based on the value of **ServerName** in the **magnus.conf** file. The client will receive the primary server name and not the one requested (for example, `http://jackserver.com` will send back `http://mainserver.com`).

obj.conf

Now that your server has its initial settings from **magnus.conf**, you need to direct it to respond to individual client requests. **obj.conf** contains directives that allow you to accomplish this goal. The directives define the type of functions to be applied to the server at a specific point in processing a client request. Once the server is running, it uses the settings of the **obj.conf** file to process the client request by loading specific functions and abilities. Whereas **magnus.conf** includes global server settings, **obj.conf** affects how the server processes specific directories, documents, and client requests. The word "directive" has a different meaning for the **magnus.conf** and **obj.conf** files. In **magnus.conf**, it refers to a specific global server setting. You can consider **magnus.conf** directives as global settings for the server. Under **obj.conf**, a directive refers to a specific step in the server's processing—a type of function. As we will see shortly, there can be any number of functions and function parameters for a given directive. You will find that most of the changes you make to the server settings are through **obj.conf**, so it is important to understand what is inside this file.

The server goes through **obj.conf** sequentially, starting from the top of the file. In the **magnus.conf** file, you have already defined where **obj.conf** is located (with the **LoadObjects** directive), and what the default Object is (with the **RootObject** directive). The server, after processing all **magnus.conf** directives, goes through the directives in your **obj.conf** file, starting with **Init** directives and then the default Object directives.

As its name implies, the **obj.conf** file is where you define Objects. Objects—sometimes called "resources" or "templates" (or "styles" in the Server Manager)—are not the same as the objects in object-oriented programming. In Netscape Servers, the term "Object-oriented" refers to a method of grouping server resources. These Objects are grouped and defined in the **obj.conf** file along with their functions. Such an Object directs the server to respond in a specific way to a client request.

The order of the information in this file is very important, especially inside each Object. Foremost, you need to know that a default Object should be defined before any other Objects, because many subsequent Objects are named and referenced by it. The default Object affects the entire server. Subsequent Objects do not need to appear in any specific order unless they refer to one another. The order of the directive functions *within* each Object, however, makes a difference in the way the server responds.

When you have a subsequent Object referenced from the default Object, the server processes this subsequent Object's directives next. The default Object's functions, however, are still processed as part of this new Object. In other words, if the directive in your subsequent Object does not include a needed function, the default Object's function will provide it. For example, if you do not write a **Service** function, such as **send-file**, files will be sent anyway. The server will use the default Object's **send-file** function to carry out that needed process. To inhibit the server from processing a certain default function, you can write your own function and provide an alternative procedure for the server.

> **Note ▶**
>
> It is rather confusing how Netscape has used different names in different circumstances to refer to Objects. The Server Manager refers to Objects as "styles." Some earlier documentation defines Objects as "templates" or "resources." This approach might have been taken because Netscape Objects needed to be distinguished from object-oriented structures, or because the term was not specific enough. Whatever the reason, it makes for a confusing work environment.

A Simple obj.conf

Listing 2-3 provides an example of a simple (plain) version of an **obj.conf** file. Your **obj.conf** file, especially if you enabled some of the features of the server, such as Server-side JavaScript, may look different from this listing. Listing 2-3 is similar to the default **obj.conf** file generated when you install Netscape's Enterprise Server 2.x or

FastTrack 3.01. The default **obj.conf** file for Enterprise Server 3.5.1 includes a number of additional lines, as the server enables search, agents, and Web publishing by default. If you disable these features, the **obj.conf** file should look similar to Listing 2-3. When you disable Web publishing using the Server Manager, however, the server may not remove a **NameTrans** directive line, similar to the line below, from the **obj.conf** file:

```
NameTrans fn="pfx2dir" from="/help"
  dir="c:/netscape/server/manual/https/ug"
```

The server uses this directive to locate the Web Publisher User's Guide help files that will be accessible to the various users.

Do not worry about what the code in Listing 2-3 actually does. The rest of the chapter and this book will explain its purpose. You can refer back to this code as you read about the general structure of the **obj.conf** file, each directive, and each directive's functions. For a discussion of a specific directive function, you should look in Appendix B.

Some of the lines in Listing 2-3 are also modified so that the function name—for example, fn="load-module"—will appear after the directive name (for example, **Init**).

Listing 2-3 Simple **obj.conf** File

```
Init fn=flex-init
  format.access="%Ses->client.ip% - \
%Req->vars.auth-user% [%SYSDATE%]\
  \"%Req->reqpb.clf-request%\" %Req->srvhdrs.clf-status%\
%Req->srvhdrs.content-length%"
access="c:/netscape/server/https-foo/logs/access"
Init fn=load-types mime-types=mime.types

<Object name=default>
NameTrans fn=pfx2dir from=/ns-icons
  dir="c:/netscape/server/ns-icons"
NameTrans fn=pfx2dir from=/mc-icons
  dir="c:/netscape/server/ns-icons"
NameTrans fn=document-root root="c:/netscape/server/docs"
PathCheck fn=nt-uri-clean
PathCheck fn=find-pathinfo
PathCheck fn=find-index index-names="index.html,home.html"
ObjectType fn=type-by-extension
ObjectType fn=force-type type=text/plain
Service fn=imagemap method=(GET|HEAD)
  type=magnus-internal/imagemap
Service fn=index-common method=(GET|HEAD)
```

Listing 2-3 Simple `obj.conf` File (*continued*)

```
type=magnus-internal/directory
Service fn=send-file method=(GET|HEAD)
 type=*~magnus-internal/*
AddLog fn=flex-log name="access"
</Object>

<Object name=cgi>
ObjectType fn=force-type type=magnus-internal/cgi
Service fn=send-cgi
</Object>
```

Syntax in the `obj.conf` *File*

A **comment** line begins with a **pound sign** (#) and without any white spaces before the #.

Do not begin a directive line with any white **spaces**. No spaces should appear before a new directive, at the end of a directive line, or between the name, equal sign, and value in [*name*]=[*value*] parameters. A space at the beginning of a new directive line or between [*name*]=[*value*] parameters can cause the server to misinterpret the directives or even crash. A white space divides each directive name, function specification, and parameters.

If a space in a value string of a parameter needs to be seen as a space, such as in a path that includes spaces, then put the value in **quotes** (for example, `"c:/Program Files/netscape one/server"`). This approach differs from the **magnus.conf** file, where you do not use quotes. Although, by convention, most value strings are placed in quotes, it is not necessary to do so unless they include spaces.

As mentioned in Chapter 1, Note on Installing Netscape Server, Netscape Enterprise Server 3.5.1 does not allow the use of the tilde (~) in a path that can be used either directly or indirectly by the clients. Therefore, you should not use ~ in a path defined in the **obj.conf** file. The server may itself use ~ to specify a directory name, if the directory includes spaces. For example, the server may convert the path `c:/program files/server/` to `c:/PROGRA~1/netscape/server`. This alternative DOS path was allowed by the previous version of the server, but may not work with Enterprise Server 3.5.1 for NT. Consequently, you should convert all paths in the **obj.conf** file to use the complete long directory and file path with the needed spaces. Make sure to include the path in quotes as well.

The Server Manager writes each directive in its own line, independent of the length of the line. When you manually change a configuration file, however, the directive line can be divided into separate lines. As with C preprocessors macros such as `#define`, you can use a **backslash** (\) to divide a line. Unlike with **magnus.conf**, in **obj.conf** code, when lines exceed your margin formatting (that is, you want to continue to the next line), you can use a white space at the beginning of the next line. You cannot break in the middle of a string this way, however, because the space will become part of the string. To break a line in the middle of a string, use a backslash but do not add any spaces before or after it or before the beginning of the next line. If you intend to use the Server Manager to change the configuration of the servers, avoid dividing the directive lines in the configuration files. When you apply new changes through the Server Manager, the Server Manager will reformat the file, allowing each directive only a single line. Moreover, although the server will most likely function properly, the Server Manager may not identify the information correctly if it is divided in multiple lines. If you are using a backslash that could be confused with a line break, you must use an escape character—that is, an extra backslash. Table 2-3 demonstrates the use of line breaks in **obj.conf**.

Table 2-3   Use of Line Break in **obj.conf**

WRONG	CORRECT	WRONG	CORRECT
`Init fn="myfunction" dir="c:/my directory"`	`Init fn="myfunction" dir="c:/my directory"`	`Init fn="my function"`	`Init fn="my\ function"`

In NSAPI C code, the program function cannot include dashes (–, which is the hyphen or minus character). Lexical convention in C does not allow for dashes. Normally, programmers use an **underscore** (_) to divide compound words. Netscape configuration files, however, can accept a dash instead of, or in place of, an underscore. Thus you can have an underscore in your function and use the same function in the **obj.conf** file with a dash instead of an underscore. With Server 2.x or later, you can also include underscores in the Netscape configuration files. Whichever option you choose, make sure to use the same convention to refer to the function throughout the configuration file.

Use only **forward slashes** (/) in defining a path (for example, `c:/netscape/server`). When you use a forward slash, the server will find the correct files, even in operating systems like Windows where the path string usually utilizes a backslash (\).

Unlike with **magnus.conf**, the order of the directive functions is important in the **obj.conf** file.

Order in the **obj.conf** File

Knowing how the server works and how to use the server's built-in functions requires an understanding of the server directives in the **obj.conf** file. We will discuss each directive and their built-in functions shortly, but will begin with some general information about the arrangement of directives within the file. (Later, we will discuss each directive in even greater detail, especially as it relates to writing your own NSAPI applications, in Chapter 8.) Each line in the **obj.conf** file begins with a tag (for example, `<Object ... >`) or a directive (for example, **Service**). A tag is used to group a number of directives. There are two types of tags: `Object` and `Client`. In the following sections, we go through a standard **obj.conf** file, such as the one shown in Listing 2-3.

Initialization   The first part of the **obj.conf** file includes initialization information about the features or functions that the server needs to load at the start of the server. It also includes information about the various modules (NSAPI programs) that the server should load. All of this information is conveyed through the **Init** directive functions. Since they are all initialized at the start of the server, their order does not matter—unless one **Init** function relies on information from an earlier **Init** function.

With Server 3.x, you can also use the optional `LateInit` parameter to have the **Init** function execute after the server process is forked. Thus the **Init** functions that have the value of `LateInit` set to `yes` (`LateInit="yes"`) are initialized after functions with the **LateInit** parameter set to `no`. The Init section later in this chapter provides more information on the **Init** function and the parameter `LateInit`.

Default Object and Order of the Functions   The second part of the file includes the settings of the default Object. This Object is called after the server has configured itself using **magnus.conf** and has loaded all the initialization functions of **obj.conf**. The default Object is unique, as it is always used by the server regardless of the request. Other Objects are called conditionally—that is, when a specific condition is met, such as when a specific directory is requested.

An example how an Object is defined follows.

```
<Object name="<name you provide>">
[Directive 1]
. . .
[Directive n]
</Object>
```

The Object tag should be reminiscent of HTML tags. The beginning tag includes `<Object name="<object name>">`. The end of the Object definition is identified with `</Object>`. All directives within these two tags are applied sequentially to the specific Object. An Object groups the directives.

Each directive has the following format:

```
<Directive> fn="<function name>" [first name=value
 parameters] . . . [last name=value]
```

`Directive` is the name of the type of function that will be applied to the server. Directives in an Object are processed in a specific order. They accomplish different steps in the processing of the client request. Each directive has a unique purpose, and the functions for that directive should accomplish that purpose. Each function can also include a number of parameters in the `[name]="[value]"` format.

In general, you should try to write a line of directive function in the most readable order, putting the functions (`fn`) before any other `[name]=[value]` parameters. With the Server Manager, however, the order is often switched around. As long as the directive name appears at the beginning, the order in which the individual functions' names and parameters are defined does not matter. You can, for example, define the function parameters first and name the function itself later in the line.

Figure 2-5 displays the progression of the server through the directives. (As mentioned previously, the order of the directives is important.)

The default Object can include any of six directives: **AuthTrans**, **NameTrans**, **PathCheck**, **ObjectType**, **Service**, and **AddLog**. In fact, it should always include all of these directives, except **AuthTrans**. The server builds a hash table of the functions listed in the **obj.conf** file when it is started. The functions are grouped based on their directive. The order of each function in that directive is important, because the server goes through each directive function in the order listed in the **obj.conf** file.

To make sure each function and each directive are processed properly, all directive functions should be grouped and placed in the order specified in Figure 2-5. For

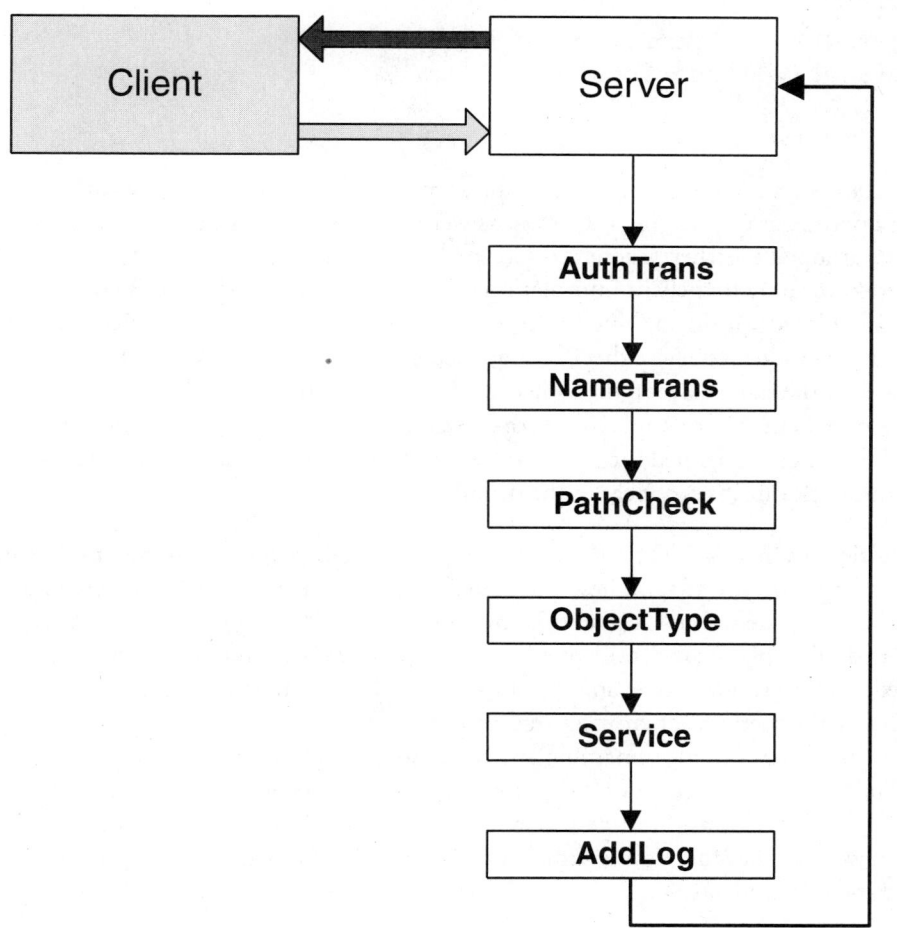

Figure 2-5   Directive Order

example, all **AuthTrans** functions should be placed first (before the **NameTrans** functions) in the list of directive functions in an Object. If **AuthTrans** is not included, but **NameTrans** is, then **NameTrans** must appear first and all other functions follow any **NameTrans** functions. The order then follows that shown in Figure 2-5. You may be able to place a specific directive function in a different location in an Object and have the server function properly, but this approach is not recommended. Proper ordering of the directives and their functions improves the readability of the information in the `obj.conf` file. It also ensures that the server functions properly. For some directives, if a function is placed after another function, the server may skip a needed function.

A Note Regarding Client Information   An Object identifies a set of instructions for the server. Another type of method for grouping a set of instructions is called Client. Client, in this context, is a special tag. It distinguishes a class criteria for a type of client and instructs the server to process requests from this special group of clients in a specific way:

```
<CLIENT1 [criteria]>
[Directive functions]
 . . .
</CLIENT>
```

Client tags can designate, for example, access restriction or secret key authorization for a particular type of client. Clients, as well as Objects, can have multiple instructions grouped together. Client is discussed later in this chapter. For now, however, you need know only that client information is included within an Object. A client tag is usually placed within an Object where a directive would go. The first directive in the Client tag indicates where the Client appears in the Object. The Client tag is positioned at the same place in the Object as this first directive would be if it were not inside a Client. For example, if a **PathCheck** directive is defined inside the Client tags, and the Client is defined for the default Object, then the Client tag is placed where **PathCheck** directives appear in the default Object.

Additional Objects   The default Object is followed by a number of other Objects, including ones you write. These additional Objects have one or more directives defined in them. You define an Object either by naming it or by using `ppath`. Objects are named using two **NameTrans** directive functions: **pfx2dir** or **assign-name**. `ppath` is used to identify a resource, an Object, based on the path to the resource. (I will describe the methods of creating an Object shortly.)

Below is an example of naming an Object (the CGI Object) subsequent to the default Object. Notice how CGI is first named in the default Object (name="cgi") with the **NameTrans** directive and later defined as an Object. (This approach is similar to how a member function is commonly declared in a C structure, or a C++ object, and then defined later.)

```
<Object name="default">
 . . .
```

```
NameTrans fn="pfx2dir" from="/cgi"
 dir="c:/netscape/server/cgi"
 name="cgi"
 . . .
</Object>

<Object name="cgi">
ObjectType fn="force-type" type="magnus-internal/cgi"
Service fn="send-cgi"
</Object>
```

In the cgi Object, there are two directive functions: **force-type** and **send-cgi**. **force-type** forces the MIME type of the cgi, `magnus-internal/cgi`, for any request that uses the `/cgi` path, `from="/cgi"`. **send-cgi** invokes the CGI applications. It sets the CGI environment variables and sends the request to the CGI program. It also returns the response from the CGI application to the client.

For `ppath`, however, you do not name an Object using **NameTrans** before defining it. The path information already includes instructions that delineate the scope to which the Object applies. In the next section, we will discuss how you can create and use a server Object.

After each Object's directive functions, the default Object's functions can be called. Therefore, whenever needed and missing, the default Object's functions complete the necessary steps in the processing of the request.

Creating an Object

Before we discuss the directives for an Object, let us first review how an Object is created.

Using the Server Manager to Create an Object   In the Server Manager, you create a style through the Configuration Styles|New Style menu of the Server Manager. This method, in effect, creates an Object. You then apply various predefined features to your Object from the Configuration Styles|Edit Style menu. The "Edit a Style" page contains a list of options you can define for the style. For example, you can choose from Log Preferences, Character Set, or Restrict Access. These options generate the directive functions for your Object. Under Configuration Styles|Edit Style, existing styles are listed in the Style List box, each of which is an Object defined in your **obj.conf** file (for example, CGI, Shell CGI). The style works just like a template. It is not actually applied until you associate it to some specific pattern or directory. You can use "Assign Style" to apply a style to a specific directory. From then on, a request for the directory will apply the specific style (that is, Object) features you assigned. Assigning a specific style in this way produces an **assign-name** function for the **NameTrans** directive. You can also "Apply Style" when you are adding "Additional Document Directories" through the Content Management|Additional Document Directories menu. (This method produces a **pfx2dir** function for the **NameTrans** directive.)

Creating an Object Manually   There are two ways to create an Object manually. First, you can associate an Object to a `ppath`. The server then recognizes the Object based on the path and carries out your Object's directives. Second, you can name an Object through the **NameTrans** directive, and then label it with the same name (as the one you specified in the **NameTrans** function). With this latter method, when the server encounters the **NameTrans** function you defined, it will know to go to the directives in your Object.

Table 2-4 shows the two types of Objects. The first uses `ppath` and associates an Object to a path. The second uses a `name` identified by a **NameTrans** function.

Table 2-4   Two Types of Objects

METHOD	EXAMPLE	PARAMETERS

Creating an Object by `ppath` association	`<Object ppath="c:/netscape/`
	`    server/docs/noaccess/*">`
	When you choose to set access control on a path in your server, the Server Manager will generate this type of Object.
		`ppath` (defines an Object by the path—the physical path; you can also use wildcards to specify the path)

Creating an Object by `name` association	`<Object name="cgi">` Server Manager produces this type of Object when you choose to define WinCGI, Shell CGI, CGI, Java, LiveWire, or any other type of style template.	`name` (defines an Object by the name defined in **NameTrans**)

Creating an Object with `ppath` *Association*   Creating an Object by association to a path evolved out of the NCSA HTTP Server's use of `.htaccess`. The `.htaccess` files can extend the server configuration settings and access control rules by allowing the instructions in these files to apply to specific resource directories of the server. By employing different `.htaccess` files in different directories, you can localize the configuration of the server to specific directories. `.htaccess` requires the server to make a linear search of all directories to locate the `.htaccess` files, a performance-intensive process. With Netscape Server, you can define an Object with `ppath`, for example, to extend control to a specific directory. Because these settings are specified in the main server configuration file, they do not have the performance drawback of the `.htaccess` files. (Netscape also provides support for `.htaccess` and `.nsconfig` files as part of dynamic configuration of the server. The `.nsconfig` files are a Netscape-specific alternative to `.htaccess` files. See Appendix D for more detail.)

You can define an Object by using the file system's path information. For example, you can define an Object by the path `c:/netscape/server/special/*`. All directives in this Object then take precedence in responding to a client request that referenced this path. You can also use a wildcard to define the type of files or directories that match with a specific Object. (For example, you can use `*.shtml` to define all the files that the server will parse and attach a certain document footer.) In addition, the Object can affect all the subdirectories of a path. You can, for example, define a subdirectory to be accessible to only a specific number of users (such as `/private/*`). You accomplish this goal by defining an Object, setting the directory information in the `ppath`, and defining the appropriate directive functions for the Object. When you define an Object using `ppath`, it is not placed in the default Object. Instead, it is defined as an Object after the default Object. The server will need to know only the path information to identify the Object.

While processing the **NameTrans** functions, the server checks other Objects to identify whether a specific Object applies to the path requested by the client. (We will discuss the **NameTrans** directive in more detail later in this chapter.) You must specify the physical path for the `ppath` parameter of the Object.[1] The `ppath` server variable refers to the partial (virtual) path before the **NameTrans** directive. By the time the server is ready to process your Object, it requires the physical path information. An existing **NameTrans** function in the default Object (usually **document-root**) has already set the path in the server variable `ppath` to the physical path before the server looks for other Objects. Your Object then has to match the physical path set by the **NameTrans** function—for example, **document-root**. As mentioned, you can use wildcards to specify the Object's `ppath` parameter. Therefore, `ppath (*/private/*)` identifies any path that will include the `private` directory in it.

Creating an Object by Name Association   Another, more powerful way to define a specific Object is by using **NameTrans**, or name translation, functions. First, you name an Object, as in the following example:

```
NameTrans fn="pfx2dir" from="/cgi"
 dir="c:/netscape/server/cgi" name="cgi"
```

In the **NameTrans** function, you also associate a directory with the named Object. Here, the `c:/netscape/server/cgi` directory is associated with the `cgi` Object. You then create an Object after the default Object in the **obj.conf** file and specify different settings, or directive functions, for this Object (for example, in the form of `<Object name="cgi">[directive functions] . . . </Object>`).

This method of naming an Object provides even greater flexibility than using `ppath` does. A named Object can be applied to any number of resources (directories) as specified by **NameTrans** functions. A named Object is like a template that can be applied to different resources. **NameTrans** functions can associate the template to a specific directory (resource). A **NameTrans** function can associate a named Object not only to a physical path, where the resources are kept, but also to a URI path (a virtual path), which a client can use. In the previous example, the Object will respond to the

---

1. This `ppath` is unlike the server variable `ppath` (found in server data structure *Request->vars*) that you may use with a **NameTrans** or **AuthTrans** function. The server variable `ppath` normally refers to the partial (virtual) path before the server finishes with the **NameTrans** directive.

URI path, /cgi, and look for the resources in the directory c:/netscape/server/cgi. A request for http://<server name>/cgi/<file name> will call your Object named cgi.

As with any Object, your new Object can control the server response when a request for your Object is made. An Object can include multiple functions or settings. Thus it can accomplish a number of unique tasks. What is special about an Object is that its functions take precedence over the default Object. With an Object, you can group together a number of instructions (directives' functions) that you wish to apply to a specific resource or directory. For example, the object can include a different authentication procedure, a unique way of processing a client request and responding, and a separate log file. (Note that the default object is named through the **magnus.conf** directive **RootObject**, not by a **NameTrans** function.)

Directives

Figure 2-5 listed the six major directives for each Object. In reality, there are eight directives, if you include **Error** and **Init**, in the **obj.conf** file. These two additional directives are a bit different—they do not define the server response to every request. Thus the server does not reevaluate these directives each time it responds. **Error** functions can be called after any directive, but only when an error occurs. Because of their functionality (that is, their ability to catch and process errors), they can also take precedence over any other functions. **Error** functions run only in case of an error, and can be called before any directive when an error occurs. **Init** functions are set once at the start of the server. As such, they more closely resemble a **magnus.conf** directive in that they are global.

The server proceeds through all **obj.conf** directives sequentially. The server first opens the log files and begins the logging process. It will also load any DLLs (Dynamic Link Libraries) or shared libraries, or initialization functions (**Init**). As a request comes in, if authorization data are sent, the server looks for authorization information and translates (authenticates) the client's authorization request (**AuthTrans**). It converts this information and compares it with the user or group database for authorization. (Users can be distinguished individually as a user or collectively in a group.) It does not allow or deny access to a specific directory at this point. Next, the server determines the path information and associates the requested URL to a specific system path and/or to a resource or object type (**NameTrans**). For example, the request <server name>/cgi-bin/test.cgi calls the CGI Object. **NameTrans** functions can also redirect a URL to another location. Then, the server verifies the path set by **NameTrans**. It also checks for the user (or group) information set by **AuthTrans** and allows or rejects the client request (**PathCheck**). ACL access control is also defined here. The server can perform a variety of useful path checking and conversions: converting the tilde (~) in the URL into the home directory of a specified user, or appending the forward slash (/) to a URL if needed. (The use of tilde to specify the user's home directory is supported under UNIX only. You should not use it in a path with Enterprise Server 3.5.1 for NT.) After **PathCheck**, the server determines the `content-type` (MIME type) of a requested document (**ObjectType**). It verifies the type of information that the client is requesting. **Service** is the next directive. The client input is interpreted (as in, for example, a form input) and a response is sent to the client. **Service** functions then return pages to the client. They also close the connection and socket after they finish sending the information. Finally, all access and error information is logged into the log files you have defined (**AddLog**).

Although we have emphasized the importance of maintaining the order of the directive, you should know that often a directive that may seem to be skipped actually does get processed. First, you need (**NameTrans**, **PathCheck**, and **ObjectType**) to process any request. The server processes the directives in the directives order, not necessarily the order in the `obj.conf` list. So although you may have placed a **Service** function between the **NameTrans** directives, the server will still process the directive with other **Service** functions. If you have declared an additional Object, the default Object's directive function can be called as part of your Object. In undefined or needed cases, the server responds with the default Object's directive functions. For example, you might not have defined an **AddLog** function in your Object, but errors do get logged through a "default" procedure defined in the default Object. The server also processes standard HTTP errors and returns an error page without your specification of an **Error** function. Moreover, a function can even be called by the server earlier than or before its appropriate time as outlined in the list of functions in the `obj.conf` file. For example, the **PathCheck** function **check-acl** is always called immediately after the **NameTrans** directive for Server 2.x, regardless of where it is placed in the `obj.conf` file. On the other hand, **check-acl** is called after all other **PathCheck** functions and before any **ObjectType** function for Server 3.x.

Based on what a directive function returns (for example, REQ_PROCEED or REQ_NOACTION), the server continues processing other functions in a directive or skips to the next directive. A function can force the server to skip other functions for that directive. For example, for the **NameTrans** directive, you should specify the **document-root** as the last function for the directive. **document-root** can force the server to skip other applicable **NameTrans** functions that come after it. (See Chapter 8, SAF Return Values and Order of the Directive Functions, for the specifics of what each function returns.)

Many other powerful features are available that go beyond what you can set using the Server Manager. You can consider these options as enhancements to your site. We will often imply that a directive does some *thing*. For example, **AuthTrans** authenticates. Of course, it is not the directive that does the action, but rather the server function and/or your code. Because Netscape Server goes through the steps of processing a request through these directives, one can nevertheless see each as a step (in the response of the server) that does some unique action. Let us look at each of these directives more closely.

Init   **Init** functions load at the start of the server. They initialize global server settings and variables (for example, enabling file caching and memory pool allocation). They also declare files (for example, access log and `mime.types` files) that are used by the server. All **Init** functions are initialized when the server starts and stay loaded as long as the server is active. For Server 2.x, they are called by the base server process and their data are inherited by any child process. You can use these types of functions to load shared resources or global settings that will apply to the server during its lifetime. These functions run before any request is processed. Therefore, unlike other functions written as a response to the client, **Init** functions always use persistent memory allocation. They also do not use the server data structures Session and Request, which are specific to a client or a client request and are used by other directive functions. We will review these data structures in detail when we will discuss NSAPI in the later chapters.

The function **load-modules** loads the functions that you write. Once you have written and compiled your shared library (so) or Dynamic Link Library (DLL), you load it with the function **load-modules**. You can also specify which functions should be added to the table of directive functions. These functions must be defined (for example, in the default Object) before they can be used by the server. You do not need to initialize all the functions inside your shared library.

If you wish to initialize a global resource or run a function before the server processes to client requests, then write it as an **Init** function. After you have loaded your shared library or DLL, you can initialize your function as "Init fn=your_function [*name1=value1*] . . . [*namex=valuex*]".

As all **Init** functions should be properly loaded at the start of the server, a REQ_NOACTION or REQ_PROCEED returned by an **Init** function is seen as success. The server goes to the next **Init** function and processes the rest of the **Init** functions. **Init** functions should return REQ_ABORTED upon error. If such a function fails, the server terminates during start-up. A failing **Init** function should insert an error string as the value of a variable named error in the server parameter block data structure (pblock) passed to an **Init** function by the server. The server then logs the error information before terminating. This procedure for logging errors is different from that followed by other directive functions.

Netscape Server 3.0 added support for an optional LateInit parameter for the **Init** functions. When LateInit with the value yes is added to the **Init** function (LateInit="yes"), the function is executed after the server process is forked. If the value of LateInit is no, the function is executed before the fork. When an **Init** function requires the creation of a thread (for example, with the **IIOPinit** function used for WAI), it should use the LateInit parameter with the value yes. Most NSAPI **Init** functions that you write will use the yes value for the LateInit parameter as well. If an **Init** function you are writing must perform an action before the server process is forked, you should use the LateInit="no" parameter for your **Init** function. For example, if you plan to write to a file that is owned by the user root, you should set the value of the LateInit parameter to no.

When you write an in-process WAI application, you write an **Init** function. You should also use the LateInit="yes" parameter with this type of **Init** function. For more information on the in-process WAI applications, see Chapters 13–16.

For descriptions of the built-in server **Init** functions, see Appendix B.

AuthTrans   The **AuthTrans**, or authorization translation, directive is used to authenticate the user. A better name for this directive is authentication translation. This directive is used to authenticate a user—that is, to verify the user authentication information. It is not used to allow authorization.

AuthTrans usually works in concert with the **PathCheck** directive. At the **AuthTrans** stage, the server translates and verifies the encrypted information sent by the client (such as `name:password`) to gain access to a specific directory or a file. For example, an **AuthTrans** function can verify the client information against a user database. This performance does not mean that an **AuthTrans** function cannot also deny access to a client. The normal and recommended procedure, however, is for an **AuthTrans** function to work in conjunction with the built-in **PathCheck** function **require-auth**. **AuthTrans** should verify the authentication of the user name and password. A **PathCheck** function (for example, **require-auth**) should then allow or deny access to the requested resource.

Supplying access control with **AuthTrans** occurs in two steps: authentication and authorization. Authentication verifies the user authentication information. Authorization forces the client to authenticate and allows or denies access. If you wish to write one function for both steps, then the preferred method is to use a **PathCheck** function. In fact, Netscape performs this procedure for the ACL. The **PathCheck** function **check-acl** performs both authentication and authorization and does not require an **AuthTrans** function. When you deny access to a directory through the Server Manager's Server Preferences|Restrict Access option, notice that the `obj.conf` file reflects a **PathCheck** directive (function **check-acl**) but no **AuthTrans** directive.

The built-in **AuthTrans** functions are **basic-ncsa** and **basic-auth**. You can write your own function as a user-defined **basic-auth** function. (The recommended method of writing an authentication function for Server 3.x, however, is to use the new Access Control API.)

Initially, **AuthTrans** translates the authentication information sent to it by the client. In this step, the function should decode and compare the authentication data sent by the client with a defined database (or one that you may provide). Next, the **AuthTrans** function sets the appropriate user information to be used by a later function or program—for example, a CGI application.

The **basic-ncsa** function obtains the necessary information (that is, the location of the user database and the authentication type `basic`) through its parameters defined in `obj.conf`. It will use this information to automatically authenticate the client against the user database. **basic-ncsa** does not use the local database of the Enterprise Server 3.x or an LDAP directory server. LDAP and the LDAP directory server are not supported by **basic-ncsa**. You can use only an NCSA-style user database or a DBM file. The NCSA-style user database (the default user database for Server 1.x) uses a flat file of users' names and passwords in a `<name>:<encrypted password>` format. A DBM file (default format of the Server 2.x user database) is a binary file that can hold the users' names and passwords. It provides better performance and gives faster access to the information than text files do. On the other hand, the DBM file used by

Server 2.x includes proprietary changes that make it difficult to modify programmatically. To use **basic-ncsa**, you not only need to add **basic-ncsa** to the **AuthTrans** directive list in the `obj.conf` file, but also add **require-auth** to the **PathCheck** directive list. By itself, the **AuthTrans** function does not deny or allow access for the client. It does not perform authorization. If **AuthTrans** fails to place the appropriate user information in the server data structure (`Request`), however, then the **PathCheck** function will deny access.[2]

In the second step (authorization), the server can insist (require) that the user information be present. Moreover, if it is missing, the server asks for the information again. This second step is performed by the **PathCheck** directive. The type of authentication you have requested and the data placed in the server variable `Request` (`Request->vars`) are checked by the **PathCheck** function **require-auth**. **PathCheck** will then allow or deny access. In other words, having an **AuthTrans** function by itself does not normally do anything unless the **PathCheck** function **require-auth** is also present. Once you add **require-auth**, then **AuthTrans** will proceed in the order described. In fact, the server must require authorization before going through this two-step process. The server goes through the directive once until **require-auth** sets the unauthorized status and requires authentication. The client then inputs a user name and password, and the server again goes through the directives to authenticate the client.

If you do not have the **AuthTrans** function, but only the **PathCheck** function **require-auth**, then the server will always deny access. There is no user database specified for the **require-auth** function, and the appropriate authentication data will not be available in the appropriate server data structure (`Request->vars`). **require-auth** needs **AuthTrans** to verify the user's data against the user database. It does not actually verify the accuracy of the client's information or authenticate the user.

On the other hand, **AuthTrans** requires the **PathCheck** function **require-auth** to actually get the client's user name and password. **require-auth** sets the `WWW-authenticate` response header, which causes the browser to invoke the authentication dialog box.

Netscape separated the steps of authentication and authorization to provide more flexibility and room for future support of other types of authentication, such as SHTTP. This separation provides for multiple translation methods and opens up a number of new possibilities. You can have multiple translation methods going through one required authorization step. For example, multiple **AuthTrans** functions can exist for one **PathCheck**. You can include **PathCheck**'s **require-auth** function, and write an **AuthTrans** function that records authentication information but does not refuse client access. Alternatively, the client's information can be verified and recorded through **AuthTrans**, with a **PathCheck** function requiring authentication and sending different responses to the client. You can also set specific server variables during the

---

2. The valid data are stored in the `Request->vars` data structure, which does not include any authentication information at the start of the **AuthTrans** step.

AuthTrans stage that can be used by a **PathCheck** function later. Moreover, you can use an **AuthTrans** function in conjunction with a CGI application. You can authenticate the user with an **AuthTrans** function and set the appropriate server variables for the user information. Your CGI program can access this authentication information through the specific CGI environment variables.

A return of REQ_PROCEED indicates that the user was successfully authenticated, and the server will skip subsequent **AuthTrans** functions. With REQ_NOACTION, the server continues processing other **AuthTrans** functions or the user is again prompted to authenticate. (See Chapter 8, **AuthTrans**, for more details.)

Netscape 2.01 and later Server have an additional **AuthTrans** function, **get-sslid**. **get-sslid** always returns REQ_NOACTION and places the SSL session ID in the appropriate server data structure (*Session*->client).

With Netscape Server 3.x, it is recommended that you use the Access Control API to manage and extend the access to your Web server. This API is an extension to NSAPI that provides greater control and functionality for authentication and authorization. You can define your own Loadable Authentication Service (LAS) with this API. Your LAS can use its own attributes, authentication methods, or databases to control access to a server resource.

This book will not discuss this Server 3.x API, as its description and use really require more extensive documentation. For more information on Access Control API, check the document called *Access Control Programmer's Guide* (http://developer.netscape.com/library/documentation/enterprise/accessapi/index.htm). For an example of a program using Netscape Access Control API, look in the directory *<server path>*/plugins/nsacl.

NameTrans **NameTrans**, or name translation, functions are used to redirect a client to a new location (**redirect** and **mozilla-redirect**), set the server's document root directory and/or the server's home page (**document-root** and **home-page**), and map a physical path to a virtual path (**assign-name** and **pfx2dir**). For descriptions of the built-in server **NameTrans** functions, see Appendix B.

The **NameTrans** directive translates a virtual path into a physical path. It turns the URI path sent by the client into a physical path address on the server. A **NameTrans** function reads the value of the partial path (the URI path) and uses the specific parameters set for it in the **obj.conf** file to produce the full physical path. It normally accomplishes this goal through the setting you have specified for the function in **obj.conf**. Thereafter, subsequent directives will have access to the physical path of the requested resource. To illustrate how **NameTrans** operates, consider a case in which a client requests http://www.foo.com/news/today.html. The ppath (partial path) variable in the **NameTrans** directive step would then be news/today.html. A **NameTrans** function will update ppath with the physical path of the resource—for example, c:/netscape/server/docs/news/today.html. The server then changes ppath (the virtual path) to path (the physical system path) after processing the **NameTrans** functions.

You can also use the **NameTrans** functions to name a new server Object, using the name parameter in the **assign-name** or **pfx2dir** functions. Once the server finds the Object defined in your **NameTrans**, it will call that Object's directive functions to process the request of the client. This feature can be very powerful. You can create your own Objects to take over from the default Object and process requests in the way you defined. Netscape calls these template Objects or styles. You can group your subsequent directives and have them respond only to your Object. For example, you can create an Object that will take over, initiate unique **Service** functions (such as processing forms), and then provide a log of its actions in its own log file (**AddLog**). Netscape uses this feature in creating Objects such as LiveWire and CGI. Consider the following example:

```
Init fn="load-modules"
 funcs="livewireInit,livewireNameTrans,livewireService"
 shlib="c:/netscape/server/bin/https/httpdlw.dll"
Init fn="livewireInit"
 objects="c:/netscape/server/https-foo/config/jsa.conf"

<Object name="default">
NameTrans fn="livewireNameTrans" name="LiveWire"
 . . .
</Object>

<Object name="LiveWire">
AuthTrans userfn="simple-userdb"
 userdb="c:/netscape/server/admserv/admpw" fn="basic-auth"
 auth-type="basic"
PathCheck realm="LiveWire Administration"
 fn="require-auth"
 path="(*appmgr*|*dbadmin*)" auth-type="basic"
Service fn="livewireService"
</Object>
```

For this LiveWire Object, LiveWire is loaded through the **Init** function **load-modules**. Multiple LiveWire functions are loaded here: **livewireInit**, **livewireNameTrans**, and **livewireService**. Next, the LiveWire function **livewireInit** is initialized as a user-defined **Init** function. In the default Object, the LiveWire Object is defined by **NameTrans**. Notice that this function does not use the predefined **pfx2dir** or **assign-name** functions to perform the **NameTrans** procedure. Instead it includes a user-defined function, **livewireNameTrans**, to handle the **NameTrans** procedure. After **livewireNameTrans** finishes, the LiveWire Object defined by name="LiveWire" is called. This Object has its own set of **AuthTrans**, **PathCheck**, and **Service** procedures. Once again, the server goes through all directives for a specific Object. Thus you can start with **AuthTrans**, even though there was no **AuthTrans** in the default Object (that is, you begin with any directive). After

AuthTrans, the **PathCheck** and **Service** directives are called. The server continues through the LiveWire Object directives. If LiveWire does not define and process a specific directive, then the server will use the default Object's directive functions.

The server performs some default actions based on the default Object's setting, even when no specific directive is defined for it. These actions will not stop unless you override them. For example, error logging occurs even if no specific **AddLog** function is defined for the Object. The new Object uses the default Object's **AddLog** functions to log errors or access information.

You can include multiple **NameTrans** functions, each naming a new Object. The server runs through each function until it finds the correct one. You can even have multiple **NameTrans** functions refer to the same Object.

To notify the server that name translation took place, the **NameTrans** function should return REQ_PROCEED. The server then goes on to the next directive. Once REQ_PROCEED is returned, the server updates the server variables with the physical path of the resource. Other directives can then access and use this path information. With a REQ_PROCEED, the server skips other **NameTrans** functions. Make sure your function is called in the proper order and is not superceded by an earlier **NameTrans** function. For example, **document-root** can set the physical path and return REQ_PROCEED before your function has a chance to do so. Thus you should always place **document-root** as the last function in the list of **NameTrans** functions. As a general rule, specify your own function as the first function in the list. A return of REQ_NOACTION means that the server should continue processing the rest of the **NameTrans** functions. Only one **NameTrans** function should set the physical path and return REQ_PROCEED.

PathCheck   The **PathCheck** directive accomplishes two tasks: It checks and verifies the path information, and it allows or denies access. In the first case, **PathCheck** checks and filters the path returned by **NameTrans** in the server data structure Request (*Request->vars*). It looks for the CGI path information and any errors or erroneous characters. It searches for characters such as / . / , / . . / , / / , \ . \ , \ . . \ , or \ \ . (Functions **nt-uri-clean** and **unix-uri-clean** perform this task.) It also appends a forward slash (/) when necessary (for example, when the request is for http://<*server name*>, a forward slash is added at the end of the path). In other words, **PathCheck** tries to resolve the path information. It also sets path-info, the path information for a CGI program, through the **find-pathinfo** function. Various other **PathCheck** functions help resolve possible path-related problems for the server. (For descriptions of the built-in server **PathCheck** functions, see Appendix B.) For example, you can define what your server will consider an index file by setting **find-index**. You define the type of index file that the server can look for in the **PathCheck** step. When a client requests a directory without a specific file, the server will look for the index file you defined through the **find-index** function. index.html, index.htm, home.html, and home.htm are the most common type of index files.

The **PathCheck** directive also performs a second task. It denies or allows access to a server, directory, or file. **PathCheck** accomplishes this goal in a number of ways. It permits access based on a client's authentication or through access control. It also denies access based on the client's host name or IP address.

We have already discussed one way that **PathCheck** verifies whether a client is allowed access—by requiring authentication through the **require-auth** function. Having been given the authorization information from **AuthTrans**, **require-auth** also allows or denies access. It works in conjunction with an **AuthTrans** function to accomplish this goal. (See the earlier discussion of **AuthTrans**.) The **AuthTrans** function sets the type of authentication (for example, `auth-type="basic"`) and the parameters for authentication (for example, `auth-password="xyz"`, `auth-db="c:/netscape/server/authdb/default"`, and `auth-user="john doe"`). This information will then become available during **PathCheck**'s directive step. Your program, or the default **PathCheck** procedures (**require-auth**), will then process that information and accept or deny the client request. With **require-auth**, **PathCheck** requires authentication. It returns an `Unauthorized` page, plus the HTTP response header `WWW-authenticate`. The server then seeks again to obtain authentication information before the client can receive the requested URL.

PathCheck verifies authentication in other ways as well. In fact, ACL access control is implemented under **PathCheck** through the **check-acl** function. **check-acl** uses the server's user database and ACL files to authenticate users. **check-acl** performs both authentication and authorization. You can enable access control through the Server Manager under the Server Preferences|Restrict Access menu. **get-client-cert** and **cert2user** are two new **PathCheck** functions that work in conjunction with SSL3 and client certificate to allow or deny client access. As mentioned earlier in the **AuthTrans** section, you can also use the Netscape Access Control API to control access to the various resources on your Web server.

The **PathCheck** function **check-acl** is unique. For Server 2.x, it is always called *before* any other **PathCheck** function, independent of the order in the **obj.conf** file. For Server 3.x, it is always called *after* all other **PathCheck** functions, independent of the order in the **obj.conf** file. If multiple **check-acl** functions are defined in the **obj.conf** file that apply to a request, the server invokes these functions using the order of the **check-acl** functions in the **obj.conf** file. **check-acl** also returns an `Unauthorized` page, plus the `WWW-authenticate` response header, to require the client to authenticate. An example of a `WWW-authenticate` header is `WWW-authenticate="basic realm=\"marketing department\""`. The server sends `WWW-authenticate` to inform the client of the type of authentication needed. The value of this parameter includes an authentication type, defined in **auth-type**, and realm information. (`realm` is a user-defined string that appears as part of the instructions for the client during the authentication process. It usually appears in the authentication dialog box and identifies the requested location or resource (for example, `Enter username for <realm> at <server name>`). If the client authentication fails, the status of the request will be set to `401 Unauthorized`.

Besides authenticating users through name and password and/or SSL client certificates, you can also deny or allow access by client IP or host name. This way you do not need to ask the client to input manually the authentication information. Instead, you can use the information that the browser sends you. **PathCheck** also provides a function that supports this option. The **PathCheck** function **deny-existence** can deny the existence of a directory or file from a specific client type. For example, you can deny all clients from hacker.com (*.hacker.com) access to your private directories (/private). (See the Client section later in this chapter for more information.)

You can also write your own **PathCheck** function to verify a client against your predefined list and deny access to those not in the list. As mentioned earlier, however, the recommended method for writing an authorization program for Netscape Server 3.x is to use the new Access Control API.

When the **PathCheck** function returns REQ_PROCEED and REQ_NOACTION, it usually signals success. The server continues to the next function to finish processing the client request. A return of REQ_NOACTION also means there is no need to ask the user to authenticate manually.

If the user does not have authorized access to the requested URL, then the function will typically return REQ_ABORTED with the protocol status set to PROTOCOL_UNAUTHORIZED or PROTOCOL_FORBIDDEN. The server will then return an Unauthorized or Forbidden page to the client. The status of the request will be either 401 Unauthorized or 403 Forbidden. (Note that 403 Forbidden should normally be reserved for server, rather than user, permission problems.) You can, of course, create other responses for your user. You can redirect the client to another page, send the page Not Found, and so on.

Unlike **NameTrans**, where one function does the work to process a client request, the server continues to process **PathCheck** functions, even after REQ_PROCEED or REQ_NOACTION has been returned. The server needs to verify all **PathCheck**-related functions. For **PathCheck**, **ObjectType**, and **AddLog**, the server continues processing all of the directives' functions. For the **PathCheck** function to require authorization, the function should return REQ_ABORTED, not REQ_PROCEED or REQ_NOACTION. With REQ_ABORTED, the server stops processing any other **PathCheck** functions. It then proceeds to **Error** and **AddLog** functions, and returns the appropriate page and headers set by the **PathCheck** function (that is, the Unauthorized page, WWW-authenticate response header, and so on).

ObjectType   If you guessed that this directive defines types of Objects, you guessed incorrectly. As the server receives a request, it needs to determine the nature (the MIME type) of the request: Is it a request for text, an image, or sound? **ObjectType** functions determine the MIME type of the file requested by the client. They look at the path information set by **NameTrans**, and possibly modified by **PathCheck** functions, and determine the MIME type for that file. Thus, if the request is for `*.html`, **ObjectType** assigns the MIME type HTML to it. **ObjectType** normally uses the **mime.types** file to determine the MIME type of a specific file extension, unless your function (or one of the predefined **ObjectType** functions) has defined an alternative. The most common way to determine a file type is by identifying its file extension. For example, a `*.html` or `*.htm` file is usually defined as `content-type text/html`. The function **type-by-extension** determines the MIME type by using the file extension and the **mime.types** file. The server then uses the MIME type information to process the request correctly.

ObjectType sets the MIME-related response headers (for example, `content-type` of the requested resource). This information will then be available for any future directive. It is used by the server to determine the **Service** function that pertains to the request. The client browser also uses the response headers (for example, `content-type`) to handle and display the returned data. The following is an example of `content-type` set by an **ObjectType** function:

```
content-type="magnus-internal/shellcgi"
```

Besides `content-type`, the MIME type can also include encoding and language information (that is, `content-encoding` and `content-language` headers). If no matching types exist, then the default type defined by the **ObjectType** function, **force-type**, is enforced. You can also use the **force-type** function to enforce a specific MIME type for a directory. For example, Netscape uses this function to enforce `magnus-internal/cgi` types for the CGI directory. If you wish to specify a MIME type using a unique expression in the path string, then use **type-by-exp**. With **type-by-exp**, you directly map a MIME type to a specific pattern in the request's path string, rather than using the **mime.types** file and the path's file extension.

All **ObjectType** functions are processed in the order that they appear in the **obj.conf** file. **ObjectType** functions set the MIME type information only once. No later **ObjectType** function should attempt to overwrite this MIME type. You should make sure to place the appropriate function first in the list of **ObjectType** functions. For example, you should place your **ObjectType** functions before the built-in **type-by-extensions** function. You should also place **force-type** last.

A response of REQ_PROCEED or REQ_NOACTION from an **ObjectType** function means success—that is, the server continues processing other **ObjectType** functions and goes to the next line in the **obj.conf** file. If the **ObjectType** function is defined already (that is, the `content-type` already exists), then the **ObjectType** function should return REQ_NOACTION. In other words, the function should take no action. The server continues on to the directive's next function. When the **ObjectType** function actually adds the `content-type` parameters, it returns REQ_PROCEED upon success. Whenever an **ObjectType** function sets these attributes, any later **ObjectType** function will not change the values. Instead, it will return `REQ_NOACTION`. Although not recommended, you can write your own function that will change a `content-type`.

For descriptions of the built-in server **ObjectType** functions, see Appendix B.

Service   The **Service** directive does most of the work in responding to the client request. The standard method of response is to return the content of the file (**send-file**) along with the appropriate header files to the client. If a file is not specified in a request, the server can return a directory listing (for example, **index-common**, **index-simple**). **Service** functions provide a number of other options for returning dynamically generated pages. The standard options (discussed in Chapter 3) include the use of imagemap (**imagemap**), server-parsed HTML (**parse-html**), ISINDEX (**query-handler**), and CGI (Common Gateway Interface) programs (**send-cgi**, **send-wincgi**, and **send-shellcgi**). Netscape also allows you to append trailers to an HTML file (**append-trailer**).

If you have been writing CGI programs, then you have been using a **Service** function. CGI programs are processed through **Service** functions. In fact, **send-cgi**, the main CGI-related **Service** function, runs the CGI program. It passes environment variables and standard input data to the program. The CGI program, in turn, returns the response that **send-cgi** processes and sends to the client.

Most of your NSAPI programs will also be **Service** functions. Some of the services this directive can perform are processing form requests, connecting to a database, and creating a dynamic page for the client. A typical **Service** function uses the specific information about a request (as determined by the server or other directive functions) to process a client request and return the response. The **Service** function can use other resources, such as a directory or a file, in addition to the request and client input. Chapters 6 and 9 will go into detail regarding how to write an NSAPI **Service** function.

> **Note ▶**
>
> There is also a specific **Service** function, **IIOPexec**, used for WAI applications. **IIOPexec** performs a function that is very similar to the function served by **send-cgi**. It prepares the necessary data for your WAI application and sends the data along with the client request to your program. **IIOPexec** also returns the response from your WAI application back to the client.
>
> A WAI application that runs in-process is not written as a **Service** function. Instead, you write an **Init** function for a WAI in-process application. (See Chapters 13–16 on WAI for more information.)

A **Service** function returns `REQ_PROCEED` when it successfully sends a response page to the client. Once it receives this return, the server skips other **Service** functions. Only one **Service** function should process a request and return a page. `REQ_NOACTION` is returned when you wish to send the HTTP response headers but not the entity-body. A **Service** function can also return REQ_NOACTION if another **Service** function should finish processing a client request. With REQ_NOACTION, the server will continue processing other **Service** functions.

Service class functions generally use two optional parameters: type and method. For the proper **Service** function to process a given request, a specific MIME type is declared and used. This case also holds true with the typical NSAPI **Service** function that you may write. (See also the **mime.types** section later in this chapter.) The server uses the MIME type of the requested resource (created by **ObjectType**) to determine whether a particular **Service** function should be applied. If the **ObjectType** directive was unable to specify the MIME type (for example, if no **ObjectType** function was used), the server always uses the first function in the list of **Service** functions to process all requests. As you might expect, this situation can lead to real problems if the first **Service** function is not the right one.

type defines the type of file that the **Service** class function processes. For example, **send-file** is applied to all MIME types that are not magnus-internal. If you look at **send-file** in your **obj.conf** file, you will notice that the type "*~magnus-internal/" is specified as a parameter for this function. type can be specified using a wildcard pattern. For example, "*~magnus-internal/" means that **send-file** should be used for all (*) types that do not (~) include magnus-internal. The MIME type magnus-internal is used to indicate a unique internal server MIME type, such as imagemap, parse-html, cgi, wincgi, shellcgi, directory, and any additional internal type you specify for your **Service** function. For instance, magnus-internal/directory is specified for the **Service** functions **index-common** and **index-simple**. This internal MIME type is used when no file is specified in a request, and the server should return a directory listing. For the server to return the directory listing, it needs to call either **index-common** or **index-simple**. The type parameter of these two functions identifies them as the correct function for the server.

To define an internal MIME type for your NSAPI **Service** function, you typically use magnus-internal/<your specified name>. The server uses this MIME type to recognize your **Service** function as the function that should process the request and return the data to the client. Typically, MIME types are associated with a specific file extension. The **ObjectType** function **type-by-extension**, for example, uses the information in the **mime.types** file to associate a file extension with a MIME type. Therefore, the specific file extensions of a MIME type must also be defined in the **mime.types** file. In other words, you must determine a file extension for the MIME types of your function in the **mime.types** file.

Unlike with NSAPI **Service** functions, you will not specify a specific MIME type for your WAI applications. The server recognizes a client request as a request for the WAI application based on the URI path of the request, normally /iiop/<WAI service name>. The WAI service registers itself with the server by using the specific functions or methods provided by Netscape.

The main purpose of a **Service** function is to interpret the client request and return a response. An HTTP method is used as a way to formulate a request. The common HTTP methods are POST, GET, HEAD, and PUT. A **Service** function processes the client request based on the method used. The function then processes the response appropriately and returns the correct response to the client. A **Service** function can specify a method that it expects through its method parameter. If the request does not use the specified method, then the function does not process the request. Instead, it sends an error.

method is the method of the request. If a method is not specified for a function, then all methods are acceptable. You can have a **Service** class function respond to one or more methods using wildcards. For example, a function can respond only to GET and HEAD methods by including the following parameter: method="(GET|HEAD)". The pipe symbol (|) works as a logical OR between the types of methods. For instance, **imagemap** uses the GET method to receive the regions of an image from a client. Therefore, in **obj.conf**, only the GET and HEAD methods are declared for the **imagemap** function. A HEAD method is commonly used by agents to verify the validity of a link, its accessibility, recent modifications, and so on. The server returns the meta-information about the file (response headers) without the actual content of the requested resource (entity-body).

Another optional parameter for a **Service** function is query. Although Netscape defines query as a standard option, it is mainly used with **query-handler** and ISINDEX. With query, you can define a pattern for the search query using wildcards. **query-handler** is used to pass on the client's query to the CGI program specified by its path parameter. It works with ISINDEX, which provides a defined instruction and a text field for client data input. An ISINDEX tag indicates that a document is a searchable index. Before HTML 2.0 defined the use of forms, ISINDEX allowed the client to send in a series of keywords separated with spaces. The server decodes the request string (for example, it replaces the spaces with a plus [+] character) and sends it to your CGI program as command-line arguments. The CGI program then processes the client's search request. The simple inclusion of ISINDEX or **query-handler** does not enable a search engine. You still need to write the actual search program. (See the ISINDEX section in Chapter 3 for more detail.)

Netscape Servers have continued to ease the process of publishing the Web documents to the server. Netscape Server 2.x included the option of Remote File Manipulation. Under Server 2.x, when you enable "Remote File Manipulation" (for instance, through the Server Manager's form in the Content Mgmt|Remote File Manipulation option), a series of **Service** functions are used: **delete-file**, **list-dir**, **make-dir**, **remove-dir**, **rename-file**, and **upload-file**. These functions allow you to update data on the server. The main function in this group is **upload-file**, which allows a PUT method of request from the client. With this method, a client can upload a file to the server. One advantage of Remote File Manipulation is its ability to enable Navigator Gold or Netscape Composer's one-button publish feature. (You must use the correct user name and password—for example, an authorized user's name and password—in your Navigator Gold or Netscape Composer settings to use this feature.) You still need to enable access control for Remote File Manipulation to implement this feature. When you install the server, write access is unavailable. You must first change the access control setting to permit any write access for Remote File Manipulation (that is, the same directories enabled for Remote File Manipulation). You can then limit who has access to Remote File Manipulation by defining who has write permission. The user account used by the server must also have write permission. (For more information on the server user account, see System User Account for the Server later in this chapter.)

Under Enterprise Server 3.x, Netscape provides a much more powerful Web publishing capability. You can still use Remote File Manipulation with Server 3.x, but the preferred method is to use Web Publishing. (You should not enable Remote File Manipulation and Web Publishing simultaneously.) You can enable Web Publishing and set its various settings from the Web Publishing menu in the Server Manager. When you enable Web Publishing, a slew of **Service** functions are added to the **obj.conf** file. They include **CM_StopRev**, **CM_StartRev**, **CM_GetPS**, **CM_GetAttrNames**, **CM_GetAttr**, **CM_SetAttr**, **CM_RevNum**, **CM_RevAdd**, **CM_RevLog**, **CM_RevLabel**, **CM_Unlock**, **CM_Lock**, **CM_Save**, **CM_Unedit**, **CM_Edit**, **CM_Copy**, **CM_Post**, **CM_MkDir**, **CM_Move**, **CM_Put**, **CM_Get**, **CM_Index**, and **CM_Delete**. All of these **Service** functions begin with CM_, which refers to Content Management, a name used earlier for Netscape Web Publishing. In addition to providing benefits similar to those that the Remote File Manipulation functions added to Server 2.x, these **Service** functions enable a large number of other features. They support version and revision control (**CM_StartRev**, **CM_RevLabel**, and so on), file locking (**CM_Lock**, **CM_Unlock**), and other options.

The actual interface for the Web Publisher that a client may use is a Java applet. You can also use a set of Java classes to write programs for Web Publishing (via the Web Publishing Client API). Underneath the Web Publisher, however, lies a Netscape Server application (NSAPI application) that interfaces between the Web Publisher and Netscape Server. The **Service** functions listed earlier are part of this NSAPI application. This NSAPI application (Content_mgr.dll for NT) handles the underlying protocol used by the Web Publisher. Web server publishing allows you to manage and update the Web server documents directly. The Web Publisher provides file management, version control, editing and publishing, search, agent services, controlled access, and link management. For more information on the Web Publisher, see *Netscape Web Publisher User's Guide* and *Administration Guide for Enterprise Server 3.x for Windows NT or UNIX.* For the Web Publishing Client API, see the document *Web Publishing*

Note ▶

You should place your **Service** functions before the built-in **Service** function **send-file** and the Web Publishing (content management) or Remote File Manipulation **Service** functions in the **obj.conf** file.

Client API Guide (`http://developer.netscape.com/library/documentation/enterprise/webpub/index.htm`).

For descriptions of the built-in server **Service** functions, see Appendix B.

AddLog   An **AddLog** directive logs information about the HTTP transaction into a log file. The server uses a number of log files. The default main log files are `access` and `errors`. There can also be additional log files depending on the server and its setting. For example, your server could also use the following: `agent.log`, `<secure>` (keysize), `<user-agent>`, and `pid`. The server, when started, generally opens a log file and keeps it open for the duration of the server. During this time, files are updated as needed. (Under UNIX, you can close and reopen the log files by sending a `-HUP` signal to the server process.) You normally define the name and path of the log file using the **Init** function **init-clf** or **flex-init**. The **AddLog** function then uses the name and any other information defined in these functions. For each Object the server is processing, all **AddLog** directives will be processed, including any **AddLog** functions in the default Object.

Before discussing the log files, we should note that you are not limited to these files for logging. You can create your own log file and log a variety of information into it. During the **AddLog** directive, you have access to most variables that became available to the server at the beginning of the request, plus any changes or additions made by the previous directive functions. You can log data from any server data structure available to an **AddLog** function, including the HTTP request or response header information. The server, client, or request specific information are usually available through the server's data structures: `pblock` (the parameter block set through the **obj.conf** file), `Session` (a **Session** data structure that applies to the entire session), and `Request` (a data structure that holds information about the request). We will review these data structures in detail when we will discuss NSAPI in later chapters. You also can use **AddLog** to store transactions in more than one log file.

Under UNIX, the server starts as `root`. If you are running the server as `nobody` or a specific Web user, you will need to change the owner or mode to enable the user (server) to write to the log file. The server does not make this change automatically. Use **chown** or **chmod** on the log file, after the log file is opened, to write to it.

A `REQ_PROCEED` result from an **AddLog** function indicates that the logging process was successful. The server will then go to the next **AddLog** function. A return of `REQ_NOACTION` means no logging occurred. The server will again go to the next **AddLog** function. A `REQ_PROCEED` and `REQ_NOACTION` returned by an **AddLog** function have the same effect—that is, the server will move on to the next **AddLog** function.

For descriptions of the built-in server **AddLog** functions, see Appendix B.

`access` *Log*   The `access` file records access information about a client request. Originally defined by NCSA and CERN, the Common Log Format (CLF) determined the format of the access file for the servers. It is still the most commonly accepted format, and many log analysis utilities assume data are recorded in this format. CLF includes the following fields: client host name or IP, authenticated user name, system date, full request, status, and content length.

Netscape also provides a more powerful (that is, containing more useful information) file format function called **flex-log**. When you install the server, the default format for the **flex-log** is the same as the CLF file format, but you can modify or add more variables to the list of data that will be recorded. (See also the discussion of the **Init** function **flex-init** in Appendix B for more detail.)

You can define the type of file format through **flex-init** or **init-clf**, both of which are **Init** directive functions (described in Appendix B), and **common-log** or **flex-log**, both of which are **AddLog** functions. The **Init** functions work with the **AddLog** functions to define the name, location, and format of the log file. Use **init-clf** and **common-log** for common log file settings, and use **flex-init** and **flex-log** for the flex log file. **init-clf** is a more generic function and does not provide formatting for the data that will be recorded. The Server Manager's form in the Server Status|Log Preferences section provides many settings for defining and formatting the access log file. (Refer to each function in Appendix B for more detail.)

The following example of a line from an access log file is wrapped for printing.

```
1.2.3.4 - - [27/Feb/1998:02:47:15 -0800] "GET / HTTP/1.0"
200 1064
```

errors *Log* errors will record information about specific server actions. In particular, any error that occurs during the server's lifetime, or from processing any client request, is recorded. This log also indicates the server's start and stop information. It records transaction data, starting with the time and date of the occurrence. Usually, a recorded occurrence is qualified with a type. The common types of "errors" are Info, Warning, Failure, Catastrophe, Config, and Security. Not all types of information logged in the error file are actually errors. The file can also include important server information. Info (information data) could include the start and stop of the server. Warning, Failure, and Catastrophe determine levels of error severity (similar to the error types Not found, Forbidden, and Server Error, respectively). When you set the severity of an error in your NSAPI program, the server will reflect your classification. This information may differ from the actual server error that can occur. Config refers to a configuration problem (such as an error in the **obj.conf** file directives, a missing parameter, and so on). Security records security errors (such as authorization errors).

Netscape Server 3.0 added a new type of "error" called verbose. If you set LogVerbose to on in the **magnus.conf** file, the server logs additional information that is labeled as verbose type.

The server uses its built-in error log functions and your **Error** functions to process errors as they occur. You can also write to the log file from inside your NSAPI functions. When you write your function, you can decide what will be recorded in the error log by using an NSAPI function, **log_error**. With WAI, you can use the function **WAILogError** for WAI applications written in C and **LogError** method for those written in C++ or Java. If you change the text and type of an error, the error information will not necessarily designate its original level of severity. Instead, the server records what you have specified as the error type. (Chapter 6 describes how you can log errors.)

The following example includes a few lines from an `errors` file, wrapped for printing purposes. Each line in the file begins with the time—for example, `[22/Nov/1997:06:44:59]`.

```
[22/Nov/1997:19:45:15] info: successful server startup

[22/Nov/1997:19:45:15] verbose: KeepAliveTimeout set to
 30s
[22/Nov/1997:20:45:15] security: for host 204.156.141.124
trying to GET /noaccess/, basic-ncsa reports: user suzy
password did not match database
c:/netscape/server/authdb/default

[23/Nov/1997:00:25:27] config: Agent Init : Mail server not
specified. Notifications will not work correctly.

[23/Nov/1997:00:05:27] failure: for host 204.156.141.124
trying to POST /newguest.frm, newguest reports: An I/O
error occurred before all form data could be read.

[23/Nov/1997:00:45:27] catastrophe: Cannot bind server to
specified IP home at address http://home.netscape.com;
cannot run.
```

Other Log Files   Other log files that your server may use are described below.

<secure> **keysize Log**   You can have a `secure` (keysize) file that keeps a record of the sizes of the security keys used by clients who attempted to access your secured server. You can use the **AddLog** function **record-keysize** to record the keysize information. This function works in conjunction with the **Init** function **init-clf**, which names the log file and its location. Client information, such as the IP address or DNS information, plus the date and time of the request and the size of the key used are all noted in this file.

The following is a line from a `secure` log file:

```
1.2.3.4: [22/Nov/1997:18:37:42 -0800] using keysize 128
```

<user-agent> **Log**   Using the **AddLog** function **record-useragent** and the **Init** function **init-clf**, you should be able to record the client-agent (browser) information from the HTTP request header. This information conveys the client's type of browser. For example, you can find out how many clients use a Netscape browser to determine whether you should depend upon the latest Navigator (Communicator) features when designing your site. This ability, of course, assumes that the browser actually sends user-agent information. You name the log file using the **init-clf** function. (See the discussion of the **AddLog** function **record-useragent** in Appendix B for more detail.)

The following is a line from a user-agent file:

```
204.156.141.124 Mozilla/4.04 [en] (WinNT; I)
```

This file will record the `user-agent` header from the HTTP request header after the IP address of each client. The data will be recorded for each request, including each request for images and other multimedia items embedded in an HTML page.

You do not need to use a specific user-agent file to record the client's user-agent. The server `access` log file can also include the user-agent header. For example, you can add the user-agent information in the log file by checking the HTTP header option, "user-agent," for the access log file in the Server Manager from the Server Status|Log Preferences menu.

`pid` **Log**   The `pid` file keeps a log of the process ID of the httpd daemon. Earlier versions of the Netscape Server used multiple processes under UNIX. Netscape Server 3.x, however, uses multiple threads with a single server process. `pid` is used in the UNIX environment to keep track of the processes that the server generates. A line in the `pid` file could be as follows:

```
1284
```

`agent.log`   `agent.log` is an example of a log file for a specific Netscape Server feature. If you enable the agent services for Enterprise Server 3.x, the server will create an `agent.log` to log the workings of the agents in the `<server path>/<server ID>/config` directory.

The following is a sample of the lines from an `agent.log` file, wrapped for printing purposes. Each line in the `agent.log` file begins with the time—for example, `[22/Nov/1997:06:44:59]`.

```
[22/Nov/1997:06:44:59]info: Agent controller initialized
successfully
[22/Nov/1997:06:44:59]info: EP:
_eventNumberToeventHandleStore=c:/netscape/server/
https-foo/agents-db/ns_event.num
[22/Nov/1997:06:44:59]info: EP:
_eventHandleStore=c:/netscape/server/https-foo/agent
s-db/ns_event.hdl
[22/Nov/1997:06:44:59]verbose: Done with AgentSystemInit
[22/Nov/1997:06:44:59]info: Agent System Initialization
 succeeded
```

Examining Log Files   You should not move or change the log file without shutting down the server. Otherwise, the data might not be recorded, and the server may stop functioning correctly. You can rename or move the log file manually (for example, to make it a backup file) when the server is not running; in that case, the server will re-create a log file with the original name and location defined in the configuration files upon restart. The server looks in the defined directories for the file it is appending with the log information. If the file is not there, it makes a new one. You can also use the Server Manager to archive a log file (see the Server Status|Archive Log option in the Server Manager).

You can even set a specific time when the server will rotate and archive your log files. You should rotate the log at regular intervals. Rotating the log file automatically may fail if the size of the log file exceeds 5 MB. The rotation time and date are kept in the `cron.conf` file under `<Server Path>/admserv/`. The following is an example of a `cron.conf` file for Server 3.x.

```
<Object name=https-foo_rotatelg0>
   Command
   "c:/netscape/server/bin/https/admin/bin/rotlog https-foo"
   User LocalSystem
   Time 0:30
   Days Sun Mon Tue Wed Thu Fri Sat
</Object>
```

You can open the log files with any text editor to view them. These files are in UNIX format, so, if you are using NT, you should select an editor that can open these files in a DOS format. If your editor is able to view the files without converting them, you do not need to convert the files. Another option is to use the Server Manager to view these file (see the View Access Log and View Error Log in the Server Status section of the Server Manager).

Log analysis utility programs are available from third-party developers. Netscape also provides tools for analyzing log files. You can generate a report from your `access` log file using the Server Manager's Server Status|Generate Report option. You can also use the programs that come in the directory `<server path>/extras/flexanlg` or `<server path>/extras/log_anly` (see the programs or server documentation for more detail).

Error   Netscape provides you with versatile error-handling options. The server may encounter an error in any number of places, from the initialization of **Init** functions to the processing of a client request and returning a response. An **Error** function is used to customize the server's error response and provide additional error handling when the server encounters an error during a request. These functions are used to customize the server page that is returned to the client when an error occurs.

Unlike the other server directives, an **Error** function can be called after any directive, but only when an error occurs. **Error** functions are defined as the last functions in an Object. Because of their functionality (that is, their ability to catch and process errors), however, they may take precedence over other functions. Actually, **Error** functions are called under most circumstances, unless a server function has set the status 200 (OK) and returned a requested document. In other words, **Error** functions are called even when a status 304 (Use local copy) is sent to the client.

Error functions are used by the server when a specified error occurs. The server then skips other directives and goes directly to these functions. Although you normally declare an **Error** directive as the last directive in an Object, it is actually called before the **AddLog** function. As the logging of information comes after a response is sent to the client, **AddLog** functions are called to log information after the **Error** directive. The server then logs the error in the errors log file.

Similar to a **Service** function, an **Error** function returns a page to the client. In other words, it takes on the responsibility of responding to a client. An **Error** function can be seen as a **Service** function that is applied only when an error occurs. In fact, the same **Service** function (such as **send-error**) can be deployed as an **Error** function. Netscape uses a number of similar functions as both **Error** and **Service** directive functions. Depending on the directive, these functions perform different tasks. The purpose of an **Error** function is to respond based on an error type, whereas a **Service** function responds to a specific type of request. These functions also expect different parameters. For example, **Service** functions expect method and type as parameters, while **Error** functions expect code or reason. Thus you should not confuse the use of a function for the **Service** directive with the use of the same function for an **Error** directive. The **PathCheck** function **deny-existence** also allows you to send a customized error page when a client requests a specific path.

You can use Netscape's built-in **Error** functions to replace the default error information (page) that the server sends to the client. The functions **query-handler** and **send-error** allow you to change the format of the default error messages. With **send-error**, a customized HTML page is sent when a specific error occurs. You can use this page to provide more details, nicer graphics, or a friendlier message. For example, you can add information about who should be notified when a server error occurs or an authorization is needed. The **send-error** function used as an **Error** directive function differs from the **send-error** used as a **Service** function. Although this function sends an error page to the client for both directives, its purpose for each directive varies. **send-error**, when used as a **Service** function, uses the type parameter to identify when to send the error page, whereas the same **send-error** function, when used as an **Error** function, uses the error status code or reason string. As a **Service** directive function, **send-error** sends the response page when a specific content-type is requested. As an **Error** directive function, it sends an error page when a specific error occurs.

query-handler allows you to run a CGI program when a specific error occurs. It gives you even more flexibility in not only sending back a specific page to the client, but also generating a tailored page based on the request. You can create your own customized error handling. For example, you can use the information sent by the client to customize the response. Again, the **query-handler** function as an **Error** directive function performs a different task than the **query-handler** function for the **Service** directive. As a **Service** directive function, **query-handler** is used to support ISINDEX.

In your server applications, you can use Netscape's NSAPI functions to log errors (for example, **log_error**) and to specify the type of error and customized error message to be sent to the client (for example, **protocol_status**). These NSAPI functions provide error-handling options for your program. They are specific to your program and are not applied to all types of errors. An **Error** directive function, on the other hand, provides an error-handling option for all errors of a specific type. Thus it provides customized server error-handling.

You can also write an NSAPI **Error** function that responds to a specific error. Similar to **query-handler**, such a function provides greater flexibility for error handling. In fact, because NSAPI functions have access to server variables, they are more versatile than **query-handler**, which can call only a CGI program. With an NSAPI **Error** function, you can also run additional clean-up procedures before sending the error page.

When an **Error** function returns REQ_PROCEED, the server skips any other **Error** function. Only one **Error** function is appropriate for a request that produced an error. A REQ_NOACTION returned by an **Error** function indicates that the server should skip to the next **Error** function.

The next section lists the common error types. Each error is defined by a three-digit number, or code, and a descriptive string, or reason. For example, 401 is the code and Unauthorized is the reason. Normally, you specify the error code or the reason string as a parameter for an **Error** function. In this way, the server identifies it as the correct function to use for an error type. (For a more detailed description of the various status codes and error types, see Chapter 6, Returning a Page Through an Error Function.)

For descriptions of the built-in server **Error** functions, see Appendix B.

Common Error Types

401—Unauthorized

PROTOCOL_UNAUTHORIZED

The client's authorization (for the request) is incorrect. The server was unable to authenticate the client. For example, the server may require HTTP user authorization to allow access, but the client's information is either missing, incorrect, or insufficient. As a result, client is not allowed access to the area requested.

403—Forbidden

PROTOCOL_FORBIDDEN

The server is forbidden from performing the requested task, perhaps because the server is running as a user that does not have adequate access to the area. For example, if this user does not have permission to run a program from the CGI directory, this error will arise. The server understands the request, but refuses to fulfill it.

In your programs, you will probably use this error type to handle many erroneous client requests, including errors caused by authorization problems, harmful requests, or, more generally, the server's failure to process a requested URL correctly. For example, this error is used to refuse access when the server does not wish to reveal the exact reason for the refusal.

404—Not Found

PROTOCOL_NOT_FOUND

The server could not find the requested data or page, perhaps because of a client error or a request for some item not present on the server. For example, this error occurs if the client sends extra path information as part of the URL when none was supposed to be there. You can also configure your server to respond with this error even when the requested data exist. This option can conceal the fact that authorization was sought or that the server actually can access the data. For an illustration of this error, see the discussion of **deny-existence**, a **PathCheck** function, in Appendix B.

500—Server Error

```
PROTOCOL_SERVER_ERROR
```
A critical error occurred on the server (that is, while the server was trying to process a client request). For example, your program might develop an I/O error, or the server might be configured incorrectly. This error occurs not in response to the client request, but as the result of the server's failure to process the request correctly.

Client

Objects group Netscape resources and provide specific features. Client is another method that groups Netscape resources, with the group being defined by the type of clients. For instance, an Object, as described earlier, can be defined through ppath association and can limit access to the directories defined in ppath by defining the **PathCheck** function **check-acl** for the Object. The following is an example of an Object for Server 3.x:

```
<Object ppath="c:/Netscape/server/docs/noaccess/*">
PathCheck fn="check-acl"
 acl=" c:/Netscape/server/docs/noaccess/*"
</Object>
```

With Client, you group resources by defining the client. You can also number the Client (for example, as Client1, Client2, Client3, and so on). You can specify the client type using wildcard options. (For example, *.netscape.com refers to any client from the netscape.com domain, while ~*.netscape.com refers to everyone who is not from netscape.com.) Consider the following example:

```
<Client1 *.hackers.com>
PathCheck fn=deny-existence
</Client>
```

Wildcards delineate the domain name of any clients (that is, *.hackers.com) affected by this grouping. Next, the **PathCheck** function **deny-existence** refuses access to any client by denying the existence of the file or directory that the client is requesting. This client is placed inside an Object where a **PathCheck** directive would be placed. The Object in which it resides will define the directories or files to which it applies. If you put the previously given code in the default Object, the server will deny existence of all documents to any client from *.hackers.com.

There are two main ways of defining a Client. The first distinguishes a client with a particular DNS, IP address, or keysize so as to attribute any number of functions to it.

The second distinguishes clients based on what they request. The Software Virtual Server section, which follows this section, describes the methods and drawbacks of this use of Client.

The following format defines a Client, which you can use to designate a number of functions within the Client tags.

```
<Client [wildcard parameter (criteria)]>
[Directive functions]
. . .
</Client>
```

The following example illustrates a Client type that can be added to an Object. It distinguishes specific clients that are not logged in the access log file.

```
<Client ip="*~1.2.3.4" dns="*~*.hackers.com">
AddLog fn="flex-log" name="log0"
</Client>
```

In the Server Manager's Server Status|Log Preferences section, if you choose "Do not log client accesses from:" in the Log Preferences Page option, it will produce a Client similar to the previous example. No client from the www.hacker.com domain or with an IP address of 1.2.3.4 will be logged. (The DNS and IP address in this example are fictitious.) Note that you do not need to use a number with the Client in the Client tag.

You can limit client access based on the type of secret keysize as well. When you "Require 128 bit secret key size for access" from the Server Preferences|Stronger Ciphers page, in fact, you are setting a Client type. (Do not use this function if you are running an unsecured server.) The server puts the following code inside the **obj.conf** file:

```
<Client secret-keysize="*~128">
Service fn="key-toosmall"
</Client>
```

The keysize, IP address, and DNS are the criterion categories used to define a Client. The Client is always placed within an Object. In most cases, the Client tag is placed in the Object where its first directive would be placed. For example, since the previously defined Client includes a **Service** directive function, it is placed in the Object where the Object's **Service** functions reside.

Besides using client certificates for security, Netscape provides other means of authorization, such as the following two easy ways to maintain security through denying access to your site. The first method is to deny access to a specific host name, IP address, or keysize. You accomplish this goal by creating a Client, then adding the appropriate directive functions to the Client (for example, **key-toosmall** or **deny-existence**). The second method is to exclude unauthenticated users from accessing an Object. Users' names (or groups' names) and passwords are added to a user database. This database, along with the ACL file, provides the necessary information on users' access privileges. The **PathCheck** function **check-acl** then checks the authenticity of the client's user information and either allows or denies access. The Object can specify the resource you are securing. For example, if **check-acl** is defined in the `default` Object, then you are authenticating the user for the full site.

Software Virtual Server

Netscape also uses Client as a part of its software-based virtual server feature. Whereas a hardware-based virtual server assigns the server more than one IP address (allowing it to respond to more than one IP), the software virtual server allows the server to assume several server names to *one* IP address. The use of Client as indicated here is somewhat different from the previously described usage. We are not assigning a group of functions to a specific client, but rather saying that any client who requests a certain URL will be processed through a particular set of functions. Here Client can be understood as anyone who uses Netscape Server. Client in the earlier case referred to some distinguishable group accessing the server. Client in this case refers to all those who are accessing the server, but with a distinguishable request (URL).

If you have multiple server names (DNS addresses) mapped to a single IP address, then you can create multiple clients that respond to each name. Usually, your first DNS is set when the server is installed. Consider the following example of an additional client:

```
<Client urlhost="oneeyed.jacks.com">
NameTrans fn="home-page"
 path="c:/Netscape/server/docs/oneeyedjacks/index.html"
</Client>
```

A request for this new URL routes the server to a new home page, which should be located in a subdirectory under the server's document root. You can use wildcards to define functions for a group of URLs that a client might request (for example, `*~www.(joe|jack|jill)`). You can also produce these clients by using the Server Manager's Software Virtual Servers option in the Content Management section. An ISP (Internet service provider) could use this feature to allow multiple customers to maintain their own home pages under the main server's home page (once the ISP has correctly set up the DNS information for the main server and its customers). The subdirectories for each customer are created with a virtual server for each subdirectory. With the proper browser (one that sends a `Host` variable—for example, Netscape 2.x and later) and the correct internal URL mapping for each server, anyone who is browsing the site should be able to access a specific customer page through the DNS. Note that the client must send the `Host` header for the software virtual server to work. If the client browser does not support `Host`, then the server will send back the primary server's home page. This method is not recommended, however, as a solution for any ISP. It is always best to provide a static IP for each server name. Moreover, Server 2.x uses serial handling for DNS look-ups. UNIX Server 2.x spawns a helper process for each server process to handle its DNS look-up duties. Thus, for a server using a single process for handling client requests, one process handles all DNS look-ups on a FIFO (First In, First Out) basis. This approach can have a severe impact on the performance, so you may want to disable DNS lookup for Server 2.x. (This DNS performance problem does not exist in Server 1.x and 3.x.) For more information on enabling DNS and the Server 2.x serialization bug, see the DNS directive in Appendix A.

Note ▶

When you use the Server Manager to set up a software virtual server, the server sets a home page for the virtual server, but not a document root. If you want to set up a document root for your virtual server, edit the **NameTrans** line for the client in your **obj.conf** file to reflect the function **document-root**.

```
<Client urlhost="oneeyed.jacks.com">
NameTrans fn="document-root"
 path="c:/netscape/server/docs/oneeyedjacks"
</Client>
```

Otherwise, use the HTML tag BASE to create a base root directory for your virtual server in your home page (for example,
`<BASE HREF="http://oneeyed.jacks.com/">`).

---

mime.types

The Official Definition Document (RFC 1521) defines MIME (Multipurpose Internet Mail Extensions), which was originally proposed as a mail extension. HTTP servers and browsers also support MIME. Your browser and the Netscape Server use this information to send multimedia, text, and binary files using the Internet (TCP/IP and HTTP protocol). Message parts are labeled, and the server or browser uses this defined information to interpret the data it receives. This information is essential if the server is to deal with the request correctly. The server will also send MIME type information back to the client for the client to interpret data it receives correctly.

The common method of identifying a MIME type is with file extensions. For example, the server recognizes the extension gif as a Graphic Interchange Format file, a popular format for graphic files on the WWW. The Netscape browser uses this MIME information to display the file as an image. Without this identification method, the browser would not be able distinguish between an HTML, text, or graphic file. Thus it would not interpret them correctly.

The **mime.types** file (usually located under your *<server path>*/config directory) holds the global MIME settings for your server. If you make any changes to this file, restart the server to make sure they take effect.

The file begins with the following text on the first line:

```
#--Netscape Communications Corporation MIME Information
```

Netscape uses this line to identify this file as **mime.types**. You can configure your server to point to different files; if a file contains this heading, then the server will recognize it as the global MIME type file. This line takes the form of a comment line, but is essential for the MIME type file. If you include other comment lines in this file, the server will ignore them. (A comment line always begins with a pound sign [#].)

The rest of the file includes the MIME type information. Every line holds one MIME type. You should have only one type/subtype per line and should not repeat any type or file extension. The format of each line is as follows:

```
type=<type/subtype> exts=<extension> icon=<name of icon>
```

The following is an example of a MIME type:

```
type=application/pdf exts=pdf icon=internal-gopher-binary
```

The `type/subtype` determines the MIME type; it is the same as the `content-type` entity-header information sent with an HTTP response. Types include `application`, `audio`, `image`, `text`, `video`, and `magnus-internal`. `application` refers to types that require an outside application to be interpreted fully. For example, `application/pdf` will require the use of Adobe Acrobat. The `audio`, `image`, `text`, and `video` types are what their names imply. You can, of course, have many subtypes for any given type. (For example, image can include `gif`, `jpeg`, `tiff`, `ief`, `x-portable-anymap`, `x-portable-bitmap`, `x-xwindowdump`, and so on.) A subtype starting with `x-` is an experimental type. HTML is a subtype of `text`. `magnus-internal` is an internal type specific to the server.

Note ▶

If you plan to add multiple extensions for a MIME type—for example, `exts=jpeg`, `jpg`, and `jpe`—do not add any spaces between each file extension. Thus `jpeg, jpg, jpe` is incorrect; `jpeg,jpg,jpe` is correct. Otherwise, the server will fail to start and will return an error.

When you write your NSAPI **Service** function, you use `magnus-internal/<your subtype>` to enable the server to recognize a request and run your program. You define a `magnus-internal` type for your program and set this information in the **obj.conf** file. You will then need to define a file extension for your program in **mime.types** that will be associated with the `magnus-internal` type you defined in the **obj.conf** file. When the client requests a file with the extension you defined, the server will recognize it as a request for your `magnus-internal` type and will run your program accordingly. CGI, imagemap, and parsed-html are all `magnus-internal` types. For your NSAPI functions, no actual file needs to be on the server machine that has the specified extension. Any call with the extension is a call for your function. The extensions are merely a way (a name or label) for the server to recognize the request as applicable to your function. You should also make sure the extensions you define for your NSAPI functions are not already assigned to another MIME type.

`exts` is the extension you associate with the MIME type. You can include more than one extension.

`icon` represents the name of the icon that the browser will display for the MIME types. Netscape Navigator (Communicator) uses a number of internal icons, including `internal-gopher-text`, `internal-gopher-unknown`, `internal-gopher-menu`, `internal-gopher-index`, `internal-gopher-image`, `internal-gopher-binary`, `internal-gopher-sound`, `internal-gopher-telnet`, and `internal-gopher-movie`. These icons are not found in a specific directory, but rather are built into Netscape Navigator. If the client browser does not include these icons, however, the server will provide them.

With Netscape Server 3.x, you can also use the Server Manager to edit, remove, or add a new MIME type for the server. See the Server Preferences|MIME types option in the Server Manager.

Let us look at a scenario where, even though the specified server directory includes icon files, Netscape Navigator uses its own internal icons. A client requests a directory listing (a directory without a file name). The server responds with a fancy index, as the directory included no index file. (See **index-common** in Appendix B for more details.) The server creates an HTML file that includes the names of the files or directories, their attributes, and so on, plus icons associated with those files or directories. Normally, the server will use the image files in the *<server root>*/ns-icons directory. If you look at the source for the HTML file, you will see links to images under the /mc-icons directory. This setup is allowed because, in the default installation, the **NameTrans** function **pfx2dir** redirects any request for /mc-icons to the /ns-icons directory. You can verify the use of these icons by using any of a number of browsers, including Microsoft Internet Explorer.

Netscape Navigator, as noted, uses its own internal icons. Consequently, although the HTML index list page indicates that the images are links to /mc-icons directory, they actually are not. You can verify this fact by comparing the images. For example, compare the GIF image on the HTML page with the `image.gif` file in /ns-icons directory: They are not the same. If you attempt to "view image" using the right mouse button, the server will return an error message: `Netscape is unable to find the file or directory named: /mc-icons/<file name>` . . . . These files are in the directory, however, so you can try accessing the file directly—for example, by using `http://<server name>/mc-icons/<file name>`.

The server takes care to deliver the icons, so you do not need to add them in the **mime.types** file, making the `icon` parameter unnecessary. In fact, during testing, this parameter was unable to specify any icons.

If you look in your **mime.types** file, you will notice special lines that do not conform to the `type=<type/subtype>` `exts=<extension>` format given earlier. These are encoded files, defined as follows:

```
enc=<type> exts=<extension>
```

Instead of type, you use enc. There are no subtypes with these types because enc is itself a type; its value is the subtype.

Listing 2-4 is an example of some of the MIME type information in a **mime.types** file.

Listing 2-4   Sample of MIME Types in **mime.types** File

```
type=application/octet-stream    exts=bin
type=application/oda             exts=oda
type=application/pdf             exts=pdf
. . .
type=audio/basic                 exts=au,snd
type=audio/x-aiff                exts=aif,aiff,aifc
type=audio/x-wav                 exts=wav
. . .
enc=x-gzip                       exts=gz
enc=x-compress                   exts=z
enc=x-uuencode                   exts=uu,uue
. . .
type=magnus-internal/imagemap    exts=map
type=magnus-internal/parsed-html exts=shtml
type=magnus-internal/cgi         exts=cgi,exe,bat
```

For more information on MIME support, see Netscape's "MIME (Multipurpose Internet Mail Extensions) Part One: Mechanisms for Specifying and Describing the Format of Internet Message Bodies" (http://home.netscape.com/assist/helper_apps/rfc.html).

User Database

This section will review the built-in user database support that comes with Netscape Servers. You can always write your own program to access a separate user database. For example, with Server 1.x and 2.x, you can write an NSAPI **AuthTrans** or **PathCheck** function that verifies the user information against a custom database. With Server 3.x, you can also use the Access Control API to write your own authentication methods and use a separate client database.

The default user database has changed with each major release of Netscape Server (1.x, 2.x, and 3x). Under 1.x, the user database was kept in a flat file with each user's <name>:<encrypted password> on a line of text. Under 2.x, Netscape used the

DBM files commonly found in the UNIX environment. These binary files hold `name-value` parameters. These new database files improved the performance of Netscape Server authentication. Instead of linearly searching through a text file, with DBM files the server can search using a more efficient **read** function call. With later versions of Netscape Server, if you wrote a program that looked up user information from a text file, your program will need to be revised. For example, Netscape Server 2.x provided programs under `/extras/database` that allow you to convert the 1.x user database to the 2.x version. You can also use the Server Manager to convert text files to DBM user database files.

Although Netscape supported the use of multiple user databases with Server 2.x, it discouraged their use, except when you have different kinds of servers. User databases are shared across different Netscape 2.x servers (HTTP, NNTP [news], and so on). In general, it is best to use groups to organize your users instead of employing multiple databases. Older servers, which did not support groups, supported multiple databases to cluster users. Under Netscape, you can create users and place them inside multiple groups. Each user will then have the same access privileges as the group. Thus, a single database can group users and also support groups within groups. All members of a group must reside within the same database. In Server Manager 2.x, look under Access Control to list, add, update, or delete databases, users, or groups. The default setting is to deny user access. A user gains access to an area of the server either by being added to a group that has that privilege or by receiving access on an individual basis (see Appendix C, ACL Files, for more information).

User Database for Server 3.x

With Netscape Server 3.x, you have the option of using the local database or an LDAP (Lightweight Directory Access Protocol) server, such as Netscape Directory Server. With Enterprise Server 3.5.1, you can use Netscape Directory Server 3.0 to take advantage of the LDAP version 3 support. (Communicator 4.04 has also been updated to support LDAP version 3.) The local database supported by Enterprise Server is a limited version of Directory Server. The user and group information is kept in a local LDAP-compliant directory. You can find the user database files under the `<server path>/userdb` directory (for example, in `c:/netscape/server/userdb/ldap/db`). You set the options for using the local database or an LDAP directory server in General Administration Global Settings. If your database does not include more than 1,000 records and you wish to use the same server machine for managing the user database, you can opt to use the local database. If you take this approach, you will not be able to take advantage of configuring some of the new LDAP version 3 features, such as support for international character sets for user and group information. If you wish to use the additional features of the Directory Server 3.0 and support a larger database of users remotely, you should consider using an LDAP directory server that supports LDAP version 3. For example, you can employ Netscape Directory Server 3.0 for managing the users for Enterprise Server 3.5.1. With the local database, you can access the database only through the Administration Server as the client.

Netscape also provides two other console utilities, `ldapmodify` and `ldapsearch`, found under `<server path>/userdb/ldap/tools` directory. You can use `ldapmodify` to add, delete, or modify entries; `ldapsearch` is used to search the database. With Netscape Directory Server, you can access the database using any LDAP-capable client. The client can use LDAP to comminute with Directory Server.

Netscape Administration Server 3.x allows the different Netscape Servers to use the same user database. In fact, unlike with previous versions of the server, you manage all users and groups with Administration Server instead of the Server Manager. With Administration Server 3.51, you can also track for which Netscape Server products users are licensed. Thus you can have a centralized user directory and can manage all users from the same interface. You add a new user or group or manage users or groups from General Administration Users & Group. (An earlier section in this chapter, Distributed Administration, explained how you set up different administrators and end-user options for Administration Server.) To set the permissions and access rights of the end users for Enterprise Server 3.x, you must first add the users to the user database via Administration Server (or the LDAP directory server). In the Server Manager of Enterprise Server, you can then set the access control rules for the end users or groups of Enterprise Server. These rules are kept in ACL files. ACL files for Server 3.x are different from those for the Server 2.x. (For more information on ACL files, see Appendix C.)

The Netscape Server 3.x user database provides greater functionality, better support, more features, and scalability. The local database of Enterprise Server supports the Internet standard, LDAP-compliant directory. Thus the database can be easily imported or used by other LDAP-capable directory servers. The local database, however, does not support all features of LDAP version 3 supported in Directory Server 3.0 and the LDAP protocol for network access. Consequently, you cannot access the data in the local database using an LDAP-capable client. When you use Administration Server to access the data in the local database, the server does not use LDAP. If you opt for a LDAP directory server for your user database, Administration Server uses LDAP to communicate with the directory server. You can also use other LDAP-capable clients to access the user database kept in the directory server. Thus the data in your database can be shared by other organizations, partners, and so on. Major vendors, such as IBM, Oracle, and Novell, have developed products that support LDAP. Netscape Directory Server can include not only text information about the users and groups, but also other types of data. For example, the client certificate information can be kept in Directory Server's user database. Directory Server can also handle a database of as many as 1 million users.

LDAP is a standard Internet directory protocol for accessing and managing directory services. A directory service, such as Netscape Directory Server, is a distributed database for managing the entries and attributes in a directory.[3] It manages your user and group database. LDAP is the protocol that defines the directory service and the possible ways

---

3. An LDAP directory is not the same as file system directory. The LDAP directory is a database of user and group information.

in which to access its service. An LDAP client, such as Netscape Administration Server, can access the entries and attributes kept in Directory Server by using LDAP.

LDAP directories maintain entries whose attributes contain descriptive information. The attributes describe specific information about each entry. Netscape Server 3.x uses an LDAP directory to manage users and groups. In this directory, you can specify information about the user contained in an entry, such as their name, e-mail address, and so on. The data maintained in the LDAP directory are organized hierarchically, and each entry is uniquely identified by a distinguished name (DN). The user information for Enterprise Server 3.5.1 should include a Common Name or full name (cn=John Doe), User ID (uid=jdoe), and SurName or last name (sn=Doe). The user DN will include the user ID and additional information, such as the user's organization name (o=companyname) and the particular branch of the organization in which he or she works (ou=Accounting). The order of the information in a DN starts with the narrowest attribute (for example, uid=jdoe) and ends with the broadest identifier (for example, o=companyname). The left-most value in the DN represents the entry's name, and each subsequent value represents a branch point above the entry. The hierarchical order of the information in the directory can be branched using a geographical location (for example, with a country location, c=US), a specific organization name, different organizational units, and so on. Each member of the organizational unit will be placed under its own associated branch.

To convert a Server 2.x database to a 3.x Server compatible local database, you can use Administration Server. From General Administration, under Users & Groups| Convert 2.0 Database, you can convert a 2.0 database to a 3.x database. You can also specify the DN branch (a specific location, such as an organization name, in the hierarchical directory entries) where you wish to add the users in the "Import at field" text box. Otherwise, the users will be added to the default Base DN specified in General Administration. A typical Base DN could be o=myCompany, c=US. A branch of the DN could be ou=marketing, o=myCompany, c=us. The use of a country designation is optional, and you can use other means of organizing the DN hierarchy. It is common practice to use the Internet domain name as the root DN in a Directory Server—for example, o=foo.com. For Netscape SuiteSpot Servers, the unique user ID (uid) is used to identify each user.

You can also convert all 2.x databases automatically from the General Administration main page by using the link "Migrate from previous version." Using this option, all entries in all the Server 2.x databases will be migrated to the default LDAP directory of Server 3.x. When using a local database for Server 3.x, the entries from the previous database will be added to the top of the tree in the local database. For an LDAP directory, the entries are added starting at the Base DN, which you specified in the General Administration Global Settings. You can change the Base DN temporarily before you migrate the 2.x user database to a different Base DN, enabling you to add the users to a different DN branch in Directory Server. When you migrate a 2.x database, the previous data is placed under the <server path>/authdb directory under Server 3.x.

For more information on user and group management under Netscape Server 3.x, see the help files for Administration Server or the administration documents for

Enterprise Server 3.x. For more information on the Netscape Directory Server, see the Netscape Directory Server documents. For help in writing client applications that communicate with an LDAP directory server using LDAP plug-in API, see *Netscape Directory Server Programmer's Guide.* You can find all of the recent developer and server specific documents at `http://developer.netscape.com/library/documentation/index.html`.

> **Note ▶**
>
> If you are using Netscape Directory Server to manage your user database for Enterprise Server 3.x, make sure Directory Server is running as well. Otherwise, Enterprise Server will not be able to verify the user information.

System User Account for the Server

To secure your server from outside tampering, you can limit the access of the server's user account (its system user account). If you have been working with Windows 3.1 or Windows 95, you may be unfamiliar with the concept of each server running as a user. Under NT and UNIX, all servers (services or daemons) run with the access privileges of a specific user, which you can specify. This user differs from the superuser employed with the Administration Server 3.x. The superuser for Administration Server is a user that has special administrative rights for administering the Netscape Servers. You can modify this user through General Administration's Superuser Access Control page. Administration Server's superuser is not necessarily the same as the user account of the Enterprise or Administration Server with the operating system. For example, in the NT Control Panel, under Service, look at any single service's "Start Up" option to review the "Log On As" settings. The user specified in this setting is the service's user account. The default user of Netscape Enterprise Server is the System Account (NT 4.0) or the LocalSystem (NT 3.51). Using a user account for the NT service allows you to control who can run a service and what a service program can do on your machine, based on the user account's system rights. You can limit the read and write access of the service—for example, by restricting Netscape Server to specific directories. The services can run even though no individual user is logged onto the machine, because services can log in on their own. Moreover, if you wish to map a network drive for use by the server, you must run the server with a user account other than System Account. For security reasons, System Account has a limited access to the local network.

Under NT, if you specify a user account (**User**) in **magnus.conf** or `ns-admin.conf`, this information will not have any effect on the NT Service's user account for Netscape Server (found in the Control Panel). You should change the user account of the server in the Control Panel, instead of using the **User** directive in the **magnus.conf** file.

Under UNIX, when the server is started by the superuser (root), the server will switch the user ID to the **User** defined in **magnus.conf**. (The login user account name must be eight or fewer characters.) Any child process created by this user will then have the same privileges. UNIX Servers that predate Server 3.0 use multiple processes. Netscape Server 2.x can use multiple processes with multiple threads. (See the **magnus.conf** directive **User** in Appendix A.)

To obtain the best results, you should create a dedicated account for the server. For example, under UNIX, do not use root, but rather create a special user account for the server (for example, http). Create a user account for your server that will have read-only access to the document files, execute (and write) access to the programs directories (for example, the CGI directory), and write access to the log files directory. Depending on the programs you are running, you might also provide other access privileges to this account. For example, if you run a database server, your server account will need to access the database. (Any major database, such as Oracle or Informix, also runs as a service, or daemon, and has its own user privileges.) As multiple Netscape SuiteSpot servers can share files, the user for the HTTP server may also need additional privileges. You can create a group of Netscape Server user accounts and add the Enterprise Server user account to this group. The group can then be defined to have specific privileges that are shared between the different servers.

Administration Server's user account needs to have write access for the configuration files. Under UNIX, when you run Administration Server as root, you will be able to add, start, and stop the other servers (or change their users) when the port is less than 1,024. (Usually, your unsecured HTTP server is set to port 80.) You can run the server as a different user, though this choice can limit what it can do. Thus, although it might be beneficial for security reasons to limit the server by limiting its user's capability, this approach is not recommended for Administration Server. On the other hand, because the Administration Manager has great powers to alter your server, take any precautions you deem necessary (including changing its user) to avoid a breach of security.

The following code gives an example of server user privileges under UNIX:

```
~server_root/http* directory rx
~server_root/http*/config directory rx
~server_root/http*/config/* files r
~server_root/http*/logs directory rwx and ownership
~server_root/http*/logs/* files rw and ownership
~doc_root directory rx
~doc_root/* files r subdirectories rx
~doc_root/*.cgi_filetype_exts files rx
~cgi-bin directory rx
~cgi-bin/* files rx
~mapped directories rx
~mapped/* files r
```

Under UNIX Server 2.x, if Administration Server and the Netscape HTTP server are running as different users, the certificate mapping through basic authorization will fail. The HTTP server needs to have permission to write to the `authdb` directory. You need to allow the appropriate permissions to the HTTP server or give the same user name to both servers.

> ### Note ▶
>
> For a secured NT or UNIX server, you can have the required SSL password read from a file, instead of manually inputting the password. Thus the server can start automatically without your typing in the password each time. If you save the password in a file, however, make sure to protect your password file from any unauthorized user. Keeping the password in a file increases the security risk.
>
> For UNIX, you have to modify the start script to read the password file. You need to redirect the server to look for the unencrypted (clear text) password from the password file. For example, you can add `</usr/netscape/SuiteSpot/https-foo/pass` after the path for the configuration files `/usr/netscape/SuiteSpot/https-foo/config $@` in the start script. For this example, the password is saved in the file `pass`.
>
> For NT, you can save the unencrypted password in a file named `password.txt` inside the configuration directory of the server—that is, `<server path>/<server ID>/config`. This option affects only the starting of the server through the Windows Services, not its start-up through the Server Manager. For manual input of the password for a server whose user account is System Account, you need to set the permission to allow the "Service to Interact with the Desktop" in the Service Startup dialog option. Otherwise, the required dialog box will not appear and the server will not start properly.

Summary

In this chapter, we reviewed the features of Netscape's HTTP configuration. Netscape Server is full of useful features. Its configuration files expose the server architecture. Studying these files makes evident how the server works, and how it processes and responds to a request.

The various functions of **magnus.conf** and **obj.conf** provide the general rules for configuring the server. **magnus.conf**, which must be set up correctly if the server is to run properly, includes the global server settings. **obj.conf** includes the necessary instructions for processing client requests. Its directives serve as the building blocks of Netscape Server. Directives direct the server to respond to client requests. The order of directives in **obj.conf** is important. The server steps through the directives sequentially when processing a request. At each step in the process, a directive has certain information available to it. A directive has its distinctive role in processing the client request and returns a specific value.

Multiple functions are available for a given directive. To program with NSAPI, you need to understand how your function fits into this sequential directive design. Thus you must know what the existing functions can do for you. When you write an NSAPI application, you need to write a directive function or a set of directive functions that work together. Consequently, you need to understand for which directives your functions will be written. For example, if you wish to write your own authentication procedure, you would write a function for the **AuthTrans** and **PathCheck** directives. To respond to a client request with data from a database, you would write a function for the **Service** directive. A custom log would be written for the **AddLog** directive.

The Server Manager is a convenient tool for prepping the server and enabling many server features, although many of the Server's built-in functions and features are not supported through the Server Manager. We showed how to modify the server manually, accessing features that otherwise are not available to you through the Server Manager. In fact, you must register your NSAPI application and its directive functions manually in **obj.conf**.

Use this chapter along with Appendixes A and B as a reference guide for configuring your server. Moreover, use the information in this chapter and the appendixes to understand the details of how the server works, what functions are available, and how you can implement your own directive functions for the server. In the following chapters, we will continue to examine these directives and their functions. We will also show how to write your own directive functions and provide a variety of examples.

Part II

Traditional Server Programming Options

Part II, which includes Chapter 3, covers SSI (Server-side Includes), imagemap, ISINDEX, CGI, ShellCGI, and WinCGI. CGI is the primary topic of this chapter. If you wish to review CGI and see how it is implemented in Netscape Server, you should go directly to the CGI section. We also refer to CGI in the NSAPI and WAI sections of this book, which provide NSAPI and WAI examples that parallel the CGI examples in this chapter.

Chapter 3

CGI Programming and More

This chapter reviews the HTTP programming features offered to a programmer before NSAPI emerged. Since the inception of HTTP servers, various methods for programming have been available. It was always the intention of server providers to include the capabilities of dynamic (interactive) HTML pages and greater client/server interactivity. The initial guidelines and features allowed for several options: imagemap, Server-side Include, ISINDEX, and CGI. Imagemap and Server-side Includes can be seen as enhancements to standard Web pages. ISINDEX is the first and simplest way for the server to obtain client text input. It was developed before forms were added to HTML standards. CGI is still the most popular programming method for the server. CGI programming is far more versatile than ISINDEX programming is. It still has limitations, however, which other programming options of the Netscape Server (for example, NSAPI, Server-side JavaScript (LiveWire), Server-side Java, CORBA, and WAI) attempt to address. These newer capabilities add speed, more control over the interaction of the client and the server, better integration with the server, and state maintenance. In this book, we will also cover NSAPI, CORBA, and WAI.

Server-side Include, imagemap, ISINDEX, and CGI are standards supported by almost all servers. You can consider them first-tier, first-generation, server-side programming options. They provide the basic support for developing interactive Web sites. This chapter will briefly review each of these first-generation options as they relate to Netscape Server. If you are especially interested in CGI, you should skip ahead to the CGI section.

The first generation of server programming, especially CGI, still dominates programming for the server. This chapter not only helps chart the evolution of server programming, but also can be used to compare these most frequently used methods to NSAPI and WAI programming methods. Many server programmers who intend to use NSAPI or WAI are already familiar with CGI.

Netscape's implementation of these first-generation features may also vary from other vendors' HTTP servers. In the rest of this chapter, we will describe what features Netscape provides, their unique enhancements or drawbacks, and their use with Netscape Server. For example, you may already know how to program a Shell script, but may need to know how Netscape supports shell programs and how they are enabled. Much of the general information about the use of these options is available in other books. If you want to pursue this line of programming, check each section for the recommended WWW sites or look in other books for more detailed descriptions.

Server-Side Include (Server-Parsed HTML)

Server-side Include (SSI) is a method for including simple server commands directly in an HTML page. The server parses an HTML file and responds to the command tags defined in the file—hence the term server-parsed HTML. SSIs are special tags that the server resolves into component commands. You include these simple commands in your HTML pages with tags. The tags are unique commands that the server reads and interprets. They do not appear on the client's document source. Instead, the result appears in the client browser in the place of the command. For example, the code `<!--#include file="address.html"-->` is added to an HTML file. The server parses the HTML file and processes the **include** command. The client receives the HTML page, including the contents of the file `address.html`. That is, the contents of `address.html` replace the SSI tag in the HTML file.

You can use a file extension to specify the type of file that should be parsed. For example, you normally set `.shtml` (a naming convention for HTML files containing SSI) as the extension for all files that are parsed. You are not limited to a specific type of file, however. You can also parse standard HTML files (`*.html`). (For UNIX servers, you can limit the parsing to HTML files whose execute bit is set to on.) SSI is a quick way to add dynamic features to your pages. Parsing files is obviously server-intensive. The server needs to parse the file, find and interpret your tags, process them, and send the result with the rest of the HTML file back to the client. If you define a specific type of file to be parsed, you limit the effects of parsing on the server response time. Another method of reducing performance drawbacks in SSI is by limiting the files to a specific directory. This isolation of SSI files can also increase security if you then take the appropriate measures in protecting the SSI directory.

You can also include **exec** tags, for executable programs, as a type of SSI. These "execute program" tags call CGI programs. Using **exec** as an option for your server-parsed HTML leads to even greater performance and security drawbacks. If you wish to use executables, write a CGI program instead.

Two functions in **obj.conf** determine how the server parses the files: **parse-html** and **shtml-hacktype**. **parse-html**, a **Service** function, parses a specific type of files. It reads the files and processes the SSI commands. It then returns the result as part of the content of the file to the client.

```
Service fn="parse-html" method=" (GET|HEAD)"
  type="magnus-internal/parsed-html"
```

The **parse-html** parameter `type` specifies the MIME type for server-parsed HTML files (`magnus-internal/parsed-html`). This MIME type is associated with the file extension `.shtml` in the **mime.types** file. You can activate server-parsed HTML using the Server Manager under the Content Management|Parse HTML menu or by adding this **Service** function manually to `obj.conf`. You can also modify the file extension for the `magnus-internal/parsed-html` MIME type by editing the **mime.types** file manually. Under Server 3.x, you can use the Server Manager to edit a MIME type under Server Preferences|MIME Types. The **parse-html** function in the previous example enables server-parsed HTML files for the GET and HEAD methods of requests. The file type is `magnus-internal` (a type internal to the server) and, more specifically, `parsed-html`. In the **mime.types** file, the `shtml` file extension is associated with the `magnus-internal/parse-html` types (`type=magnus-internal/parsed-html exts=shtml`). You can also limit the type of SSI that the server parses to exclude executables tags by using **parse-html**'s **opts** parameter or by selecting "Yes, without exec tag" in the Server Manager under Content Management|Parse HTML. (See the discussion of the **Service** function **parse-html** in Appendix B for more details.)

Once **parse-html** is added to your **obj.conf** file, the **ObjectType** function **shtml-hacktype** can be added to enable parsing for all HTML files. The line of code in the default Object would look something like the following:

```
ObjectType fn=shtml-hacktype
```

Additionally, for UNIX servers, you can check if the execute bit is enabled for the file with the **exec-hack** parameter. The server then parses only files whose execute bits are enabled. (See the discussion of the **ObjectType** function **shtml-hacktype** in Appendix B for more details.)

You can also limit server parsing to files in a specific directory by using the Server Manager or by directly modifying the **obj.conf** file. Creating a server Object and including the previously given code in that Object allows for targeted parsing. The following is an example of such an Object:

```
<Object ppath="c:/netscape/server/docs/parsed/*">
ObjectType fn="shtml-hacktype"
Service fn="parse-html" method=" (GET|HEAD)"
  type="magnus-internal/parsed-html"
</Object>
```

This code limits parsing to files only in the `/parsed` directory and subdirectories. Because the **shtml-hacktype** function is included, the server parses all HTML files in those directories.

The format of SSI commands in the HTML file is as follows:

```
<!--#[command] [name=value] [name=value] . . . -->
```

The command is lowercase and the attributes are in the usual `[name]="[value]"` pairs. `<!-- . . . -->` is how a comment line is defined in an HTML file. Adding a pound sign (#) to this comment line changes the nature of the comment line and enables SSI in the HTML file. No space should separate the first two dashes and the pound sign. The command line is ignored by a server that does not recognize an SSI command. It is seen simply as comment lines inside an HTML file.

The SSI commands initially supported by Netscape Servers were **echo**, **include**, **fsize**, **flastmod**, **exec**, and **config**. They are described later in this chapter. These specifications were defined by NCSA HTTPd (see "NCSA HTTPd Tutorial: Server Side Includes (SSI)" at `http://hoohoo.ncsa.uiuc.edu/docs/tutorials/includes.html`). Many servers support these specifications, including Microsoft Internet Information Server and Spy Web. A number of Web servers, such as Alibaba and WebQuest, also extend the original SSI with new options and features.

Netscape's Server-side JavaScript and Microsoft's VB Script both extend HTML with methods similar to SSI. They combine HTML with unique extended code (tags) that are interpreted in a predefined way by the server. The server replaces the tags with the result of the commands requested by those tags and then returns the result with the HTML page to the client. The Netscape and Microsoft methods each have their own unique features and tagging systems. Both are parsed by the server in a different way than server-parsed HTML files are.

SSI commands have access to all the CGI variables plus a few added variables. These added variables are listed in Table 3-1.

Table 3-1   SSI Specific Environment Variables

DOCUMENT_NAME	Name of the current file
DOCUMENT_URI	Virtual path to the current file
QUERY_STRING_UNESCAPED	Unescaped version of a search query, in which all shell characters are escaped with a backslash (\)
DATE_LOCAL	Current local time-zone data and time
DATE_GMT	Date based on Greenwich Mean Time
LAST_MODIFIED	Date that the current file was last modified

You can format date information in DATE_LOCAL, DATE_GMT, and LAST_MODIFIED using the **timefmt** function through the SSI command **config**.

Besides server-parsed HTML, you should also examine the **Service** function **append-trailer**. **append-trailer** allows you to globally append specific trailers to the end of an HTML page. You specify the trailer and the type of file to which you want the trailer to be added. The server adds the trailer dynamically to the file whenever a client requests the specified file's types. You can even specify **append-trailer** for a specific directory by creating an Object and declaring it for that Object. **append-trailer** removes the need for using server-parsed HTML to append specific custom signatures to each file. The server also does not need to parse each file before it can append the trailer. (See the discussion of the **Service** function **append-trailer** in Appendix B.)

SSI Commands Supported by Netscape

The SSI command **echo** replaces SSI variables with their values. It echoes these values at the position of the SSI command inside the HTML page and sends it to the client. Thus the result is sent back to the client. These variables are the same as the environment variables available to CGI programs, plus all the extended variables unique to SSI (defined earlier in this chapter). You can use the SSI command **config**, and the function **timefmt** to format any date that you want to echo. The parameter name for this command is *var.* Its value is the variable that is printed by the **echo** function. For example, `<!--#echo var="LAST_MODIFIED"-->` includes the last modified date of the file.

include tells the server to include another file you have specified within the HTML file. For example, `<!--#include file="address.html"-->` adds the content of the address file where this tag is located. You must, of course, provide the correct path, and the server must have access to that directory. You can access only other text files (including other parsed HTML files) when using the **include** command. There are two possible parameters (tags) for this command: *virtual* and *file. virtual* uses the virtual path to the document (that is, the path relative to the document root directory of server); *file* uses the current document's directory to reference the file. You can use a path relative to the current document's directory. You cannot use `../` in the path. You also cannot use an absolute path.

fsize includes the size of the file, which you can specify as being the current file or any other file. This command places the size of the file in the HTML page. **fsize** uses one of two parameters, *virtual* and *file,* to specify the file whose size should be included. *virtual,* as defined above, indicates the virtual path to the file relative to the server document root directory; *file* uses a path relative to the current directory for the file. For example, `<!--#fsize virtual="special/new.html"-->` places the size of the file `new.html` at the location of this SSI command. You can use this function to inform the client of the size of the file requested.

flastmod includes the date that the file was last modified. This function also uses the variables *virtual* and *file.* For example, `<!--#flastmod file="product.html"-->` includes the date that `product.html` was last modified. The client then knows whether the current html page is timely.

exec executes a shell command or CGI program (script) defined in the SSI command. It will then include the output from the shell or CGI program, instead of the SSI command, in the HTML file that is returned to the client. There are two possible parameter names for the **exec** command: *cmd* and *cgi.* *cmd* specifies the name and command-line parameters of a shell command. It is specific to the UNIX platform and works with `/bin/sh`. For example, `<!--#exec cmd=ls-->` adds a directory listing in the HTML document at the SSI command's location. In contrast, *cgi* can be used in both Windows and UNIX platform. The value of the *cgi* attribute is the virtual path to the CGI script. For example, `<!--#exec cgi=cgi-bin/answer.exe-->` executes the CGI script `answer.exe` and places the output in the HTML file. You need to make sure that you have enabled executables for your server as part of the SSI option. You must also make sure that the server has the necessary permissions to run the program. Finally, your program must deal with all necessary error checking (as the server will not be doing any error checking for you) and send the correct type of result. The CGI program returns data through standard output. This output should begin with `Content-type` and any other header needed, followed by a blank line and the body of the file.

> **Bug Report ▶**
>
> Under Server 2.x, the server-parsed HTML `exec cmd` tag does not work in the secured mode.

config controls the way that SSI tags are interpreted. It also specifies the error message that is sent to the client when an error occurs while parsing. There are three valid parameters for the **config** command: *errmsg, timefmt,* and *sizefmt. errmsg* defines the error message that is sent to the client when the server encounters a parsing error or when the required data are unavailable. This error is also logged in the error log file. *timefmt* defines the format of the date variables, such as the date information defined in **flastmod** or the `DATE_LOCAL` variable used with the **echo** command. The format of the date is based on a C runtime library function, **strftime**. For example,

`<!--#config timefmt="%A %d %B"-->` will display a day, date, and month format (for example, `Friday 13 September`). *sizefmt* defines the format of the file size as reported by the SSI command **fsize**. There are two values for *sizefmt*: *bytes* and *abbrev*. The value *bytes* reports the file size in complete formatted byte count—for example, `1,024`. *abbrev*, the default, provides the file size in kilobytes or megabytes. Unlike some programs such as Windows Explorer, the number is not rounded up; that is, `4.3 K` or `4.8 K` is seen as 4 K. For example, `<!--#config sizefmt="bytes" -->` lets the SSI command **fsize** report the size of the file in exact bytes. You can combine these **config** parameters together, as in `<!--#config timefmt="%A %d %B" sizefmt="bytes"-->`. Make sure you define the **config** commands before other SSI commands, as they define the settings that other SSI commands use.

Bug Report ▶

The `config` tag with the attribute `timefmt` does not work under Netscape Server 1.x.

Imagemap

You are probably already familiar with imagemap. Imagemap allows an image to be divided into predefined areas, with each linking to a different URL. Imagemap refers to an image that has a map definition (regions marked for a specific purpose—in this case, to respond to a client mouse click). Each region can be associated with a different URL and thus links to a different location.

There are two ways to define and use an imagemap: on the server and on the client. On the server, once you create your image, you can define the areas of the image that respond to client mouse clicks by using a `*.map` file. Some existing tools can also ease the demarcation of the areas of an image (such as the freeware Map This! by Todd C. Wilson). To define these areas, you first need to define the type of shapes that would hold these areas—that is, RECT (rectangle), CIRCLE (circle), and POLY (polygon). Then you can specify coordinates for each shape. RECT, the default shape, needs its four coordinates defined as left-x, top-y, right-x, and bottom-y. CIRCLE uses center-x,

---

Warning ▶

Although you can use as many as 100 coordinates with POLY, you should avoid using too many points. Under Netscape, the information about an area should be defined within one line of HTML code. If the line is too long, Netscape Server cannot process it.

---

center-y, and radius. POLY is used for irregular shapes; its coordinates are expressed in pairs (such as x1, y1, x2, y2, and so on). These pixel coordinates indicate the various points of the polygonal image's hotspots. Hotspots are the regions of the image associated to a specific HTML link. If no shape is specified, the server assumes the shape to be a default rectangle, RECT.

Once you have created your image and defined the type of shapes and the coordinates of the shapes' areas, you can write a *.map file and place the coordinates for each area in a separate line inside the file. The *.map file includes the instructional script that the server uses to process an imagemap. Use the following format:

[*Type of Shape*] [*URL (relative or absolute)*] [*Coordinates*]

The following is an example of a line of code in the *.map file:

```
rect   /new/news.html   0,0 85,25
```

Each line gives the shape, the associated URL, and the coordinates for the particular area you wish to link. Lines of code can be added for each new area of the image.

You also need to have the **Service** directive function **imagemap** defined in the **obj.conf** file. You need to include the following code in the **obj.conf** file (this line is normally included during installation by default):

```
Service fn="imagemap" method="(GET|HEAD)"
 type="magnus-internal/imagemap"
```

The type parameter defined in this **imagemap** function is a specific server-internal MIME type used for the imagemap file. It is associated with a file extension in your **mime.types** file. Usually, the extension map is used for an imagemap file. This function takes care of processing an imagemap.

For the client to use this image correctly and the server to recognize the imagemap, you need to correctly reference it in your HTML file. You can use an HREF attribute of the tag A to point to the *.map file. Next, include a reference to the image with the SRC attribute of the tag IMG. Include the IMG tag within the scope of the A tag. Also, include an ISMAP attribute for the IMG tag, as in the following example:

```
<A HREF="myimagemap.map"><IMG SRC="myimage.gif" ISMAP></A>
```

HREF refers to the imagemap script file on your machine, and SRC refers to the actual image. ISMAP identifies the image as an imagemap. You can also use any other image options with your IMG tag, such as ALIGN, BORDER, or ALT, to further delineate how the imagemap is displayed.

The server-side imagemap works with any browser that supports images. A more recent, and more frequently used, type of imagemap is the client-side imagemap. This method allows the processing of the imagemap script to occur through the client browser instead of the server. You, therefore, need to have a client browser that supports client-side imagemap. Netscape Navigator 2.0 and later support client-side imagemap.

You define the imagemap information using the MAP tag, a newly defined HTML tag. The regions and their associated URLs are delineated by AREA tags inside the scope of a MAP tag. A MAP tag begins with <MAP NAME=[*name to be referenced*]>, and its scope ends with </MAP>. Consider the following example:

```
<MAP NAME="myimagemap">
<AREA SHAPE="rect" COORDS="0,0,85,25" HREF="/new/new.html">
 . . .
</MAP>
```

NAME is a reference element that is used by an IMG tag to locate the imagemap information defined with the MAP tag. SHAPE, COORDS, and HREF are attributes that refer to the same types of information as described earlier for the *.map files. You can add NOHREF to the AREA tag if you want a blank region, which does not link to a URL. (Use this attribute instead of the HREF attribute.) You can also use the TARGET attribute with the AREA tag to handle the imagemap with frames. Thus you can link to and update a frame within a browser window instead of updating the entire browser window. (If two areas intersect, the one that appears first in the map definition takes precedence over the overlapping region.)

This information can be included in the HTML file or referenced from another file. For example, you can include the imagemap information from different images in one specific file. Each imagemap should have its own MAP tag and NAME attribute value. If an imagemap image is used in multiple places in your site, you can include the imagemap information under one file and reference it from the different HTML pages. In other words, by placing the imagemap's information in a separate file, you can have a single central source for the information that is easier to manage and alter.

You can reference the MAP tag information by using an IMG tag that includes a USEMAP attribute. Consider the following example:

```
<IMG SRC="myimage.gif" USEMAP="info.html#myimagemap">
```

SRC points to the location of the image. USEMAP points to the file that holds information about the imagemap regions (that is, the MAP file). It works similarly to an HREF attribute of the tag A. The #[*name value to reference*] is used to locate a tag with a NAME attribute in an HTML file. Thus it should have the same name value as the value of NAME defined in the MAP tag does. (In this example, myimagemap is used for the value of NAME.) If a file name is defined in the URL before the pound sign (#), then the server looks for the source of the MAP information in the specified file. In this example, the source for MAP should be inside the file info.html. You can then define the imagemap information inside a separate file, instead of in the same HTML file.

If a relative URL (a relative path) is included in the HREF attribute of the AREA tag, it will use the base path of the file that holds the imagemap information (that is, where the AREA tag is defined) and not the file from which it is referenced (that is, where the IMG tag is defined). In other words, if you include the imagemap information in a separate file in a different directory, you should reference files in the HREF attribute of the AREA tag relative to that file and not the file that includes the IMG tag.

You can use USEMAP in conjunction with ISMAP to provide both options and make sure that the imagemap is processed, independent of whether the client browser is capable of supporting client imagemap. The following code gives an example:

```
<A HREF="myimagemap.map">
 <IMG SRC="myimage.gif" USEMAP="info.html#myimagemap"
 ISMAP></A>
```

Using a client-side imagemap frees the server from processing the information and puts the load on the client browser and machine. On the other hand, not all browsers support client-side imagemap.

ISINDEX

ISINDEX was one of the earliest programming techniques for Web servers but has now been superceded by CGI and HTML forms. ISINDEX is used to pass a decoded value string to a CGI program as a command-line argument. Typically, this string includes various keywords that a CGI program uses as search terms. <ISINDEX> is an HTML tag that adds a brief instruction and a text input box inside an HTML page. The user reads the HTML page and types a string in the input box. The index terms (client input) can, for example, be used by a CGI program to search a site's documents. ISINDEX indicates that a document is a searchable page. By including this tag in your HTML page, you are not enabling a search engine, but rather providing a way for the client to input the searchable data. You still need to write the program that will perform the actual searching.

Once the Netscape Server locates the CGI program, it creates a CGI process for an ISINDEX request. The server can use the CGI-specific directive functions (such as **send-cgi**) to process the request or a specific ISINDEX function (such as **query-handler**). The directive function then produces the CGI process. The CGI program runs as a separate program in the CGI process. The server decodes the extended characters in the string and passes the data to your CGI program. This approach is different from how you normally receive and process data for CGI programs. For example, with the HTML form GET and POST methods of client request, the data are

---

Note ▶

With the official release of HTML 4.0, ISINDEX has depreciated. Although the current servers support ISINDEX, you should avoid using it. You should use HTML form tags (the INPUT tag) in place of the ISINDEX element tag. This section is intended to illustrate the use of this early programming technique for Web servers. See W3C's HTML home page (http://www.w3.org/Markup/) for more information on HTML 4.0.

URL-encoded. The CGI program first obtains these data through the environment variable QUERY_STRING or the standard input and then decodes it. With ISINDEX, the string is decoded (already converted) and passed to the CGI program as command-line arguments. You do not use an ISINDEX tag with an HTML form, as ISINDEX was developed before HTML was enhanced to include forms. It has its own prescribed method of sending information. Usually, the ISINDEX tag is placed inside a default page sent by a program you wrote to acquire specific information. When the client returns the query string, this string is sent to the same program. If you look at the URL address after a query is sent, you will see the originally requested document plus a question mark (?) and a number of keywords following the document's URL, as in the following example:

```
http://<server>/cgi/indexprog.exe?seasons+greetings%21.
```

The string sent by the client should not include a non-encoded equal sign (=) character. (This format differs from the client data usually returned from a form, which uses a [name]=[value] format after the question marks.) The server searches for the non-encoded equal sign in the query string to determine whether an ISINDEX query is being sent. If no such equal sign appears, the server sends the query after the question mark as a decoded command-line argument—which is what we want. The server accepts the encoded equal signs for ISINDEX. The server then decodes all the information (the query string). The decoding of the string is similar to the standard method of decoding of a URL-encoded string. The server replaces any plus symbol (+) with spaces. (The plus symbol is equivalent to the and in a Boolean search.) The server also replaces any extended (special) character that appears as a Hex value after a percent mark (%[Hex value]) with the equivalent ASCII character. The server adds a backslash (\) to the special character to distinguish it as a character (and to label it as not part of a command). This procedure is equivalent to how special characters are escaped under the UNIX shell or NT command prompt (DOS prompt). In the previous example, seasons+greetings%21 is passed to the program as seasons greetings\!

When the HTML page includes an ISINDEX tag (<ISINDEX>), the browser automatically displays an input box with an instructional phrase. For compatibility reasons, it is recommended that you place the ISINDEX tag within the HTML HEAD tag, although you can use the ISINDEX tag in other places in your document. Netscape Navigator processes the tag correctly, no matter where it is placed. For example, Netscape Navigator displays the default text shown in Figure 3-1 (other browsers may display the text differently).

Netscape also allows you to alter the descriptive text with a PROMPT attribute in the ISINDEX tag. The value of the PROMPT is placed as text before the text input box.

Listing 3-1 provides an example of a simple Perl program that returns client input back to the client in the form of an HTML list.

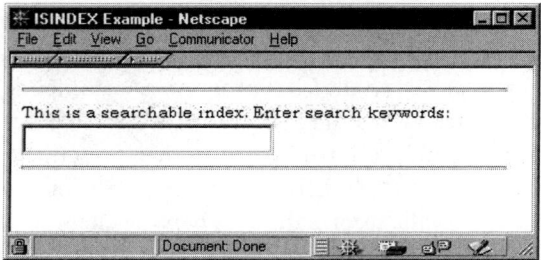

Figure 3-1   Default ISINDEX Text

Listing 3-1   Perl Version of an ISINDEX Example

```perl
#!/usr/local/bin/perl

# send the response header
print "Content-type: text/html\n\n";

$x = 0;
$input = $ARGV[$x];

print "<HTML>\n";
print "<HEAD>\n";
print "<TITLE>Simple ISINDEX Example</TITLE>\n";

# Print a list of words entered by the client. If the client
# has not sent any text, send the ISINDEX page and ask for
# input.
if ($input)
{
    print "</HEAD>\n";
    print "<BODY>\n";
    print "This is an ISINDEX test.";
    print "<P>";
    print "You entered the following words:\n";
    print "<STRONG>";
    print "<UL>";

    # read and print the command-line arguments
    while($input)
    {
        print "<LI>";
        print $input;
        $x = $x + 1;
```

Listing 3-1   Perl Version of an ISINDEX Example (*continued*)

```perl
        $input = $ARGV[$x];
    }

    print "</UL>";
    print "</STRONG>";
}
else
{
    print "<ISINDEX ";
    print "prompt=\"Please type in your text: \">\n";
    print "</HEAD>\n";
    print "<BODY>\n";
    print "This is an ISINDEX test.<P>This program prints ";
    print "out a list of the words you type into the";
    print "text box above";
}

print "</BODY>\n";
print "</HTML>\n";
```

The program in Listing 3-1 can be implemented as a Shell CGI program by placing it in your Shell scripts directory. (See the discussions of the Shell and Perl, in the CGI section later in this chapter for more details.) The program sends a standard HTML page with an ISINDEX tag when no input was sent by the client (that is, the first time the page is called and the client has not entered input). If there is an input string, the server returns a different page where each command-line argument is enumerated in an HTML list. $ARGV[] holds the command-line argument variables for the program. The first argument is argument 0, and so on. Because the server has already decoded each word in the string, the words appear as separate arguments. (The server, of course, must have appropriate permissions to run a program. Also, the program must be able to accept command-line arguments.)

You can combine your script or program with the power of other applications to deliver different information to the client. For example, you can run a **grep** program (a program commonly used to find files containing a specified string) to search in specific files. The command-line arguments are sent to **grep** as the search string. Another example of a program that takes command-line arguments is **finger**, an Internet (network) search application. For example, imagine that a client types in an Internet address. The server passes the address to your CGI program. The CGI program can use **finger** to obtain additional information about the user at that address. The CGI program then uses standard output to return that information to the client.

In Listing 3-1, the user calls up a program, which then generates an HTML page with an ISINDEX tag. Alternatively, you can create a separate HTML page that contains a link to your CGI program. The `ISINDEX` tag inside this HTML page calls the CGI program. When an `ACTION` attribute is added to the `ISINDEX` tag, the client input (query) is sent to the CGI program defined in the value of the `ACTION` attribute. This additional attribute is supported by Netscape. The following is an example:

```
<ISINDEX ACTION="shellcgi/myindex.pl"
  PROMPT="Please type in your text: ">
```

The client input is then sent as command-line arguments to the CGI program, `myindex.pl`.

Netscape also provides the **Service** function **query-handler** to direct a path request to a CGI program defined in the `path` parameter. **query-handler** was created to support the ISINDEX type of programming (that is, programs that take command-line arguments). This function is usually used in conjunction with an Object that has been defined for a specific directory. (Under Netscape Server 3.x, you can also enable **query-handler** using the Server Manager. See the Server Manager under the Programs|Query Handler menu.)

For example, the following **Service** directive routes any query (`query=*`) to the program specified by the path parameter:

```
Service fn="query-handler" query=*
 path="c:/netscape/server/cgi/myindex.exe"
```

You create an Object (for example, with `ppath`) and define the **query-handler** inside the scope of the Object. Any request for the path defined by `ppath` calls the CGI program defined in **query-handler**'s path parameter, as in the following example:

```
<Object ppath="c:/netscape/server/docs/index/*">
Service fn="query-handler" query=*
 path="c:/netscape/server/cgi/myindex.exe"
</Object>
```

Any ISINDEX request for the index directory calls the `myindex.exe` program. The important issue is that the parameters are sent as command-line arguments to your program. An example of a call to the previously given program from an HTML page could be tagged in the following manner:

```
<ISINDEX ACTION="/test/"
  PROMPT="Please type in your arguments: ">
```

You do not necessarily need to call the **query-handler** function using an `ISINDEX` tag. Nevertheless, your program should work the same way an ISINDEX program would work (that is, it must expect command-line arguments).

The program referred to by the `path` parameter of **query-handler** should be a CGI program, not a shell script. Listing 3-2 shows the C version of the Perl program in Listing 3-1.

Listing 3-2   C Version of an ISINDEX Example

```c
#include <stdio.h>
#include <stdlib.h>
#include <string.h>

int main(int argc, char *argv[])
{

    int x;
    char input[80];

    printf("Content-type: text/html\n\n");

    printf("<HTML>\n");
    printf("<HEAD>\n");
    printf("<TITLE>Simple ISINDEX Example</TITLE>\n");

    if(argv[1])
    {
        printf("</HEAD>\n");
        printf("<BODY>\n");
        printf("This is an ISINDEX test.");
        printf("<P>");
        printf("You entered the following words:\n");
        printf("<STRONG>");
        printf("<UL>");

        for(x = 1; x < argc; x++)
        {
            printf("<LI>");
            strcpy(input, argv[x]);
            printf("%s", input);
        }

        printf("</UL>");
        printf("</STRONG>");

    }
    else
    {
        printf("<ISINDEX ");
        printf("PROMPT=\"Please type in your text: \">\n");
        printf("</HEAD>\n");
        printf("<BODY>\n");
        printf("This is an ISINDEX test.<P>This program ");
        printf("print out a list of words you type into ");
```

Listing 3-2 C Version of an ISINDEX Example (*continued*)

```
        printf("the text box above.");
    }

    printf("</BODY>\n");
    printf("</HTML>\n");
    return 0;
}
```

With HTML forms, requests can be processed with the GET and POST methods. Although ISINDEX provides a simple way of getting information from the client, it lacks flexibility and features. You have a greater flexibility in getting client input with forms. Furthermore, Netscape Enterprise Server 2.x and 3.x both include a powerful search engine that you can use instead of ISINDEX.

CGI (Common Gateway Interface)

If you have been developing applications for the Internet, you probably have written CGI (Common Gateway Interface) programs. CGI quickly became the standard for developing applications for the WWW, with Perl being the most popular program language for developing CGI applications. A standard for interfacing external applications with the HTTP server, CGI was intended to provide a way for developers to create dynamic pages and Web sites. CGI's advantage is that it can be developed independently of the HTTP server type, and can be easily ported across different platforms. We will not cover CGI in great detail in this book, as there are already a number of good books available on the topic (for example, Thomas Boutell's *CGI Programming in C & Perl* and Shishir Gundavaram's *CGI Programming on the World Wide Web*). (For more information on CGI, you can also contact the following two Web sites: NCSA's "Common Gateway Interface" at http://hoohoo.ncsa.uiuc.edu/cgi/overview.html and Matt's Script Archive, Inc.'s "The CGI Resource Index" at http://www.cgi-resources.com/.) No significant difference exists between implementing a CGI program for Netscape and implementing such a program on any other server. Consequently, all the books on this topic are also relevant to programming for Netscape. Our intent, however, is to focus on application development tools

Bug Report ▶

Under Server 2.0 for Solaris and SGI, the server may hang during heavy CGI usage. You should upgrade to Server 2.01 to resolve this problem. You may also need to tune your server and system process table for heavy CGI use.

unique to Netscape. We will therefore provide a general understanding of how CGI works and include a few examples for comparison with later NSAPI and WAI examples. We will also try to provide valuable information for those who already know CGI and are interested in developing NSAPI or WAI applications.

Configuring the Server for CGI Programs

To use a CGI application, you need to enable CGI on your server. You have two options for setting up the CGI programs: You can enable CGI for a specific CGI directory, or you can enable it and associate CGI programs with a specific file type.

During installation, Netscape creates a default CGI Object (that is, `cgi`, but not a `ShellCGI` or `WinCGI` Object). You can use the Programs|CGI Directory menu in the Server Manager to specify the CGI directory for a specific URL prefix (a specific URI path). You specify the URL prefix that the client will use to invoke a CGI program (for example, `/cgi-bin`) and the absolute physical path of the CGI directory on your server machine. The CGI Object then is applied to the CGI directory. Any request for the specified URL invokes the CGI program in the associated directory. When you use this method, the server expects any file in that directory to be of the CGI type. When you set a CGI directory through the Server Manager, the server uses a **NameTrans** function (**pfx2dir**) in the default Object to specify your CGI directory for the `cgi` Object. Further down in the **obj.conf** file, inside the `cgi` Object, the server has defined the **ObjectType** function **force-type** to force the CGI MIME type (`magnus-internal/cgi`) for all files in that directory. It also has defined the **Service** function **send-cgi** to invoke the CGI programs.

You can also define the CGI programs as a file type, through the Programs|CGI File Type menu using the option "Activate CGI as a file type." In that case, the server will expect the CGI files to have a specific file extension. Under NT, the server defines the CGI file extensions as `exe`, `cgi`, and `bat`. You can change the file extensions by editing the **mime.types** file normally found under the *<server path>*/*<server ID>*/config directory. Under Server 3.x, you can also edit the MIME types using the Server Manager from the Server Preferences|MIME Types menu. Even when you have defined a CGI file type, you can still limit the directory where the CGI files are located. You are not required to define a directory, however. For example, you can set the file types for the entire server. In that case, any file with the specified extensions is seen as a CGI program. If you set the file types for the entire server, the server adds the **send-cgi** function to the `default` Object. If you limit the CGI file type to a specific directory, the server will create an Object using `ppath`. The value of `ppath` is the directory you specified. Inside this Object, the server includes a **send-cgi** function. As you do not want to force the CGI MIME type for the directory, the server will not add the **ObjectType** function **force-type** to the Object. (See Appendix B for more information on CGI-specific server functions.)

For security reasons, it is best to limit your program files to specific directories. You can then allow execution only for those directories and nowhere else. You can, of course, modify the **obj.conf** file manually, instead of by using the Server Manager. You can use the same built-in server functions and methods as described above to create a CGI Object, associate the Object with a CGI directory, or declare a CGI type file for a directory.

Note ▶

If you use `.exe` as a CGI file type extension, the client will not be able to download executable files (`*.exe`). The file extension .exe will be associated with the MIME type for CGI programs (`magnus-internal/cgi`) instead of with the MIME type for downloadable files (`application/octet-stream`). If you do not allow any file with the extension `.exe` to be downloaded, then you can keep the extension for the CGI programs.

If you do not use the extension `.exe` for the CGI programs, you can modify the **mime.types** file to associate the `.exe` extension with the MIME type of the downloadable files instead of with the MIME type of CGI programs. Remove `.exe` from the `magnus-internal/cgi` MIME type and add the extension to `application/octet-stream`.

A better alternative is to use a specific directory for the downloadable files. Add a **NameTrans** function **pfx2dir** to the `default` Object in the **obj.conf** file. The **pfx2dir** function should specify the location of the download directory, the URI path for the directory, and the name of the Object that forces the download. For example, the following **pfx2dir** associates the directory `c:/netscape/server/download` with the URI path `/download` and the Object `download`. When the client uses the URI path beginning with `/download` (for example, `http://www.foo.com/download/helpme.exe`), the server will look in the `c:/netscape/server/download` directory for the file.

```
NameTrans fn="pfx2dir" from="/download"
 dir="c:/netscape/server/download" name="Download"
```

Next, add the `download` Object, named with the **pfx2dir** function, after the `default` Object in the **obj.conf** file.

```
<Object name="download">
ObjectType fn="force-type" type="application/octet-stream"
</Object>
```

The **force-type** function in this `download` Object forces the MIME type of the downloadable files (application/octet-stream) for all files in `c:/netscape/server/download`. For example, when the URI path `/download/helpme.exe` is used, the file `helpme.exe` can be downloaded and saved by the client.

If you wish to allow fancy indexing of the directories and files under the download directory, you can add the following **type-by-exp** function before the **force-type** function in the `download` Object:

```
ObjectType fn="type-by-exp" exp="*/"
 type="magnus-internal/directory"
```

For more information, see Netscape's Tech Note, "Setting your server to let users download .EXE files," at `http://help.netscape.com/kb/server/960513-130.html`.

Configuring the Server for ShellCGI and WinCGI

Windows NT and 95 users should check the Server Manager's Programs section for ShellCGI and WinCGI settings. Shell CGI (ShellCGI) programs run with the operating system's existing file extensions. This ability is useful when you have associated a script with a program. In other words, when the script is called, it is passed to the executable program with which it is associated. ShellCGI scripts differ from executable CGI programs in that they are not compiled. They rely on another program, such as a Perl executable (Perl Interpreter), to run. For example, if you have associated `pl` extensions with Perl type files under NT, and you enable ShellCGI, Netscape Server should be able to run your ShellCGI script, with the file extension `pl`, as a Perl script. To use ShellCGI scripts, you need to have the script interpreter for your program—for example, the Perl Command Line Interpreter. Netscape Server comes with Perl Interpreter. You also need to associate the file extension of script files with the script interpreter using the Windows operating system's file type association.

You enable ShellCGI by defining a URL prefix and the ShellCGI directory in the Server Manager through the Programs|ShellCGI Directory menu. You specify the URL prefix that the client will use to invoke a ShellCGI program (for example, `/shellcgi`) and the absolute physical path of the ShellCGI directory on your server machine. (Make sure that Netscape Server has read and executed permission for the ShellCGI directory. Otherwise, you will not be able to run your ShellCGI programs.) The server then creates a `shellcgi` Object and associates the directory with the Object. In a process similar to the way that the server creates the `cgi` Object, it uses the **NameTrans** function **pfx2dir** to associate the directory with an Object—in this case, `shellcgi`. The server also designates the functions **force-type** and **send-shellcgi** for the `shellcgi` Object. Any request for a file under the ShellCGI directory is interpreted by the server as a request for a ShellCGI program. The server uses the MIME type of ShellCGI (`magnus-internal/shellcgi`) for all files in the ShellCGI directory. (See the discussion of the **Service** function **send-shellcgi** in Appendix B for more details.)

Windows programs are event-driven and normally use the graphic Windows interface (Graphic User Interface or GUI) to interact with the desktop or the user. Programming in Windows is different from programming in UNIX for which the original CGI specification was defined. Windows CGI (WinCGI) enables the use of Windows-based programs as CGI programs. It allows Windows-specific applications to work with the HTTP server. Netscape Server 1.x supports WinCGI version 1.1. With a few exceptions, Netscape Server 2.x and 3.x support WinCGI 1.3a specifications. (See the WinCGI section later in this chapter, for more details.) Robert B. Denny, the developer for WebSite (a different HTTP server), wrote the specifications for WinCGI and `Cgi32.bas` (the necessary file for Visual Basic applications). You can find more information on WinCGI at the O'Reilly & Associates, Inc. Web site, "Windows CGI 1.3a Interface" (`http://website.ora.com/wsdocs/32demo/windows-cgi.html`). WinCGI is an extension of CGI that allows Windows programs to run as CGI programs. It is intended for developers who would like to use

Windows programming tools like Visual Basic and Delphi. In this book, we will focus on Visual Basic 4.0 for developing WinCGI applications. Visual Basic 4.0 does not produce console applications that use that standard in (stdin) and standard out (stdout) libraries, and therefore, needs a special interface with an HTTP server. WinCGI includes the necessary files and headers needed for writing a Visual Basic program for the server.

When you enable WinCGI, your Windows CGI program runs like any other CGI program. You normally enable WinCGI by defining a URL prefix for the WinCGI directory. You specify the URL prefix that the client will use to invoke a WinCGI program (for example, /wincgi) and the absolute physical path of the WinCGI directory on your server. This task is easily done in the Server Manager through the Programs| WinCGI Directory menu. The server then creates a wincgi Object and associates the directory with this Object via the **NameTrans** function **pfx2dir**. This procedure is similar to how the CGI directory works. It also designates the functions **force-type** and **send-wincgi** for the wincgi Object. Any request for a file under the WinCGI directory is interpreted by the server as a request for a WinCGI program. The server uses the MIME type of WinCGI (`magnus-internal/wincgi`) for all files in the ShellCGI directory. (See the discussion of the **Service** function **send-wincgi** in Appendix B for more details.)

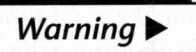

Warning ▶

WinCGI programs need to be placed on the same drive as the server root.

As with the standard CGI programs, you can also specify a file type for the WinCGI or ShellCGI applications. You can then associate this file type with a specific directory or the entire server. Unlike with CGI, however, you cannot set the ShellCGI and WinCGI file types using the Server Manager. No such option exists under the Server Manager's Programs menu.

To specify a file type for the WinCGI or ShellCGI programs, you need to add the specific file extensions to the MIME type of WinCGI or ShellCGI in the **mime.types** file. With Server 3.x, you can use the Server Manager to add or edit the MIME types under the Server Preferences|MIME Types menu. With earlier versions of Netscape Server, you manually must update the MIME type information in the **mime.types** file. For example, you can add the following MIME type to the **mime.types** file for ShellCGI: `type=magnus-internal/shellcgi exts=pl`. If the MIME type for ShellCGI is already in the **mime.types** file, you need to add only the file extension to the `exts` parameter. You should use a file extension that is not already associated with a different MIME type. For ShellCGI, make sure that the file extension you use is the same as the file extension you specified in the Windows operating system for the ShellCGI script files.

Setting the file type for ShellCGI or WinCGI programs does not do much unless you also enable ShellCGI or WinCGI for a specific directory or the entire server. In other words, you will need to add the **send-wincgi** function for WinCGI and the **send-shellcgi** function for ShellCGI to an Object in the `obj.conf` file. These two **Service** functions actually run the associated ShellCGI or WinCGI programs. When we enabled ShellCGI and WinCGI earlier, the server created the `shellcgi` and `wincgi` Objects and placed **send-wincgi** and **send-shellcgi** in the appropriate Object. The function **force-type** defined in these Objects, however, forces the specific MIME type for the ShellCGI or WinCGI directory. It does not matter which file types you associated with ShellCGI or WinCGI; **force-type** always sets the MIME type for all files in the associated directories. For example, `ObjectType fn=` `"force-type" type="magnus-internal/shellcgi"` forces the MIME type for ShellCGI for all files in the ShellCGI directory. By simply removing the **force-type** function from the `shellcgi` Object, you can allow the server to process all files in the ShellCGI directory using the file extension of the request file. If no **ObjectType** is specified in the `shellcgi` Object, the server uses the **ObjectType** functions in the `default` Object. The default procedure for processing files specified in the `default` Object uses the **ObjectType** function **type-by-extension** to set the MIME type based on the extension of the requested file. Now our file extensions come into play. If the file in the ShellCGI directory has the extension specified in the **mime.types** file (for example, `pl`), then the **Service** function **send-shellcgi** is used to invoke the ShellCGI program. Otherwise, the server uses the `default` Object's other **Service** functions to process the request. Thus the removal of **force-type** from the `shellcgi` Object causes the request for files in the ShellCGI directory to be processed by the server using the default procedure. The only difference is that, because **send-shellcgi** is declared for `shellcgi` but not the `default` Object, the server processes a request for a ShellCGI program only from the ShellCGI directory.

> ### Warning ▶
>
> Windows and NT 95 file systems preserve the case information about a file (that is, the uppercase and lowercase characters of a file name). The file system, however, does not make such a distinction when attempting to retrieve a file. You also cannot have two files that have the same name in different cases in the same directory. Thus requests for `/special/new.html` and `/Special/NEW.HTML` both retrieve the same file for the client. This process is, however, not the case with the directory extension you specify for your CGI, ShellCGI, or Windows CGI programs using the **NameTrans** functions **pfx2dir** and **assign-name**. The server, when it attempts to resolve the directory prefix in the client request URL, looks for the characters with the exact cases as specified in the `obj.conf` file. If you have specified the path for your ShellCGI program as `/shellcgi` in the **pfx2dir** function `from` parameter, the server recognizes only the same set of characters. In other words, a request for `/Shellcgi` is not recognized as a request for the ShellCGI program in the specified ShellCGI directory. The server more than likely returns a `Not Found` error page. The server looks for only `/shellcgi` in the URL of the client request.

To enable ShellCGI and WinCGI file types for the entire server, you can add **send-shellcgi** and **send-wincgi** to the default Object. As the server functions in the `default` Object apply to the entire server, including the ShellCGI and WinCGI directory, you can also remove the `shellcgi` and `wincgi` Objects and their applicable **NameTrans** function **pfx2dir** from the **obj.conf** file.

As with CGI, instead of using the Server Manager, you can make these modifications directly in the **obj.conf** file.

How CGI Works

CGI is used to develop dynamic documents by creating external programs. CERN and NCSA set the original CGI standards for communication between the server and an external program. CGI provides the gateway interface between the server and your CGI program. CGI programs are external programs that get their data from, and send appropriate information back to, the server. Usually, after the server has done some initial processing, it passes the request from the client, plus the environment variables, to the CGI program. The client request can also include data entered through a form. The environment variables are information that the CGI program needs to adequately process the request (for example, REQUEST_METHOD, CONTENT_TYPE). The server needs to be set up in such a way as to recognize the CGI program, execute it, and pass necessary information to it. The CGI program, in turn, processes information received by the server and, if necessary, calls other external resources (such as a database or a file). Once the CGI program executes its instructions, it returns the response through standard output to the Web server. The server then sends the appropriate data back to the client. The CGI program sends a Web page, a customized error page, or a redirection to another location.

Communication between the CGI program and the server takes place via the standard libraries, stdin and stdout. Thus you can use the standard I/O (input/output) defined by your chosen programming language. In C, you use functions such as **getc**, **fread**, **printf**, **scanf**, and so on. If you are developing in a graphical environment such as Windows, you may not be able to develop console applications that use stdin and stdout. WinCGI addresses this inadequacy of programming for the WWW.

CGI programs run as independent processes. They are initiated every time they are called. They run in their own process space, with each request creating one process. Their internal failure, therefore, will not normally crash or damage the server. Because you cannot easily crash the server, it remains protected from your program. This setup, on the other hand, has performance drawbacks, as the server must spawn a new process for each CGI program. Moreover, CGI program's failure, if it does not release the thread, can lead to a server crash. The client can close the connection from your server prematurely, and the program will be unable to detect this state. You may need to write the code for detecting a premature abort (for example, when a client presses the Stop button while the CGI program is in process). An example of CGI libraries that can identify a client premature abort can be found under Genome Database's (gdb) CGI Abort Libraries page, at

`http://wwwtest.gdb.org/browser/abort/cgiAbort.html`.

A Closer Look at CGI

Thus far, we have described CGI in general terms that apply to all servers. The following description of the CGI request is not only more detailed, but also applies more specifically to Netscape Server 3.x. Netscape UNIX Server 1.1x used multiple processes instead of threads. Netscape 2.x and 3.x for UNIX and NT work in a similar way when processing CGI application. Note, however, that Netscape 2.x UNIX Server can have multiple processes with multiple threads. Although most HTTP servers work in rather similar ways, there are still specific differences in their implementation of the CGI.

As Figure 3-2 shows, the server spawns a number of threads. Each thread waits for a request. If the server identifies the request as a request for a CGI program, the server invokes (forks) a CGI process in which the CGI program runs. This CGI process is like a mini-server process. It contains the communication information from the server. For the CGI process, the server produces the environment variables and, if needed, any standard input and command-line arguments. This information is then available to the CGI program. Once the CGI program does its work, it returns the response to the server by using the standard output. The server then returns the response (plus any other appropriate response headers) to the client.

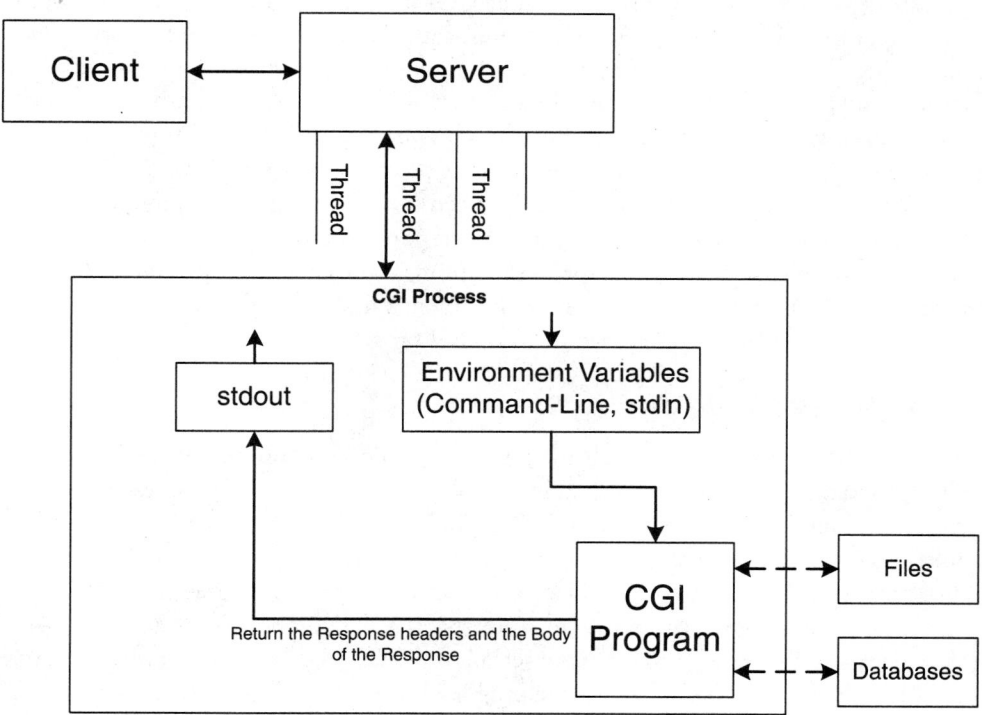

Figure 3-2   Processing a CGI Request

The Server Thread and the CGI Process

The following description pertains to standard CGI programs, although the same steps are also relevant to ShellCGI and WinCGI.

The server runs a pool of threads. These threads wait for a request from the client on a specified port. You define the port and the number of threads in the **magnus.conf** file (see the discussion of the **magnus.conf** functions in Appendix A for more details). Once a request comes in, one (and only one) of the threads takes the request and begins processing it. The server then goes through the directives specified in the **obj.conf** file. As we discussed earlier, specific functions are defined in **obj.conf** that identify a request as a CGI request. You can define what type of request or file the server accepts as a CGI program by using the Server Manager or by adding the appropriate directive functions or Objects to **obj.conf** and then making the appropriate changes to the **mime.types** file. After the server distinguishes the request as a CGI program, the server uses the built-in server function **send-cgi** to process the request. Note that, before the server reaches the **Service** function **send-cgi**, other server directive functions may prepare some of the information that will be sent to the CGI program. (See the Configuring the Server for CGI Programs section earlier in this chapter.)

For a CGI program, the server thread creates a new process, a CGI process. The CGI program runs in this CGI process. Each CGI request receives its own CGI process through the **send-cgi** function. The CGI process is like a miniature copy of the server that includes all the necessary communication information from the server. The server thread creates the right environment for your CGI program to process the request and return the response. **send-cgi** turns the client request and other server information into environment variables that can be accessed by your CGI program. It also creates a data pathway (a pipe) between the server and the CGI program. This pathway is used for the communication between the CGI program and the server. Your CGI program uses this pathway to return the response. The CGI process and the server communicate through interprocess communication (IPC). The server thread runs the CGI program and passes the environment variables, as well as any standard input or command-line arguments, to your CGI program.

Data Provided by the Server

As mentioned earlier, the server always sets a number of environment variables for the CGI program. It also passes standard input for the POST method of request as well as command-line arguments for ISINDEX. The actual value of the environment variables, however, can change based on the type of request.

Before the server reaches the **Service** function **send-cgi**, it may prepare some of the server variables for **send-cgi**. **send-cgi** converts these variables into environment variables, invokes your CGI program, and sets up the CGI process. For example, the server produces the physical path for the requested URI or extracts the extra path information from the client request. The **NameTrans** directive functions produce the physical path, and the **PathCheck** function **find-pathinfo** extracts the extra path information. (We will discuss extra path information shortly.) **send-cgi** then turns the information about the specific request into the environment variables for your CGI program. For instance, extra path information becomes available to the CGI program through the PATH_INFO environment variable.

Environment variables include server-, client-, and request-specific information. For example, they include the server host name, the client IP address, the content-type of the request, and so on. Environment variables are available in name-value pairs, where *name* is usually predefined and *value* is based on the Netscape Server, the client, the specific request, the user's input, and other factors. Some of the values are based on the server global information, such as the server name or server software. Others are based on client data, such as the user name, or the client IP address. Still others provide information about the request, such as the method of the request or the extra path information. (We will discuss environment variables in more detail shortly.)

Much of the information available through the environment variables is produced by the client browser without any direct input from the user (for example, the client IP address) or is predefined based on the requested resource (for example, the requested file's content type) or the server (for example, the name of the server). In other words, the actual user does not directly determine all the information produced by the server for your CGI program. To create a dynamic interaction between the user and your site, you need to have the user actively choose the data you desire or have the client input the data dynamically. The best and most frequently used method of obtaining dynamic input from the user is through HTML forms. With forms, the client enters information into a text field, selects an option from a check box or a radio button, or takes other actions.

When the client request uses a GET method, the HTML form input is appended to the end of the URL and sent to the server. The server then separates the input and places it as the value of the QUERY_STRING environment variable. With a POST method of request, standard input is used to send the client input to your program. Currently, the standard input type is defined as the form URL-encoded data (MIME type, application/x-www-form-urlencoded). If the client can send other types of data, you can also write a program that takes advantage of reading the specified type of data from stdin.

The URL for the CGI program can include additional information that your program can use. As already mentioned, with a GET method of request, the form input is appended to the URL of the CGI program. These data are appended to the end of the URL of the CGI program, as a query string after a question mark (?). For example, in the following URL, the query string is name=joe:

```
http://www.foo.com/cgi/myprogram.exe?name=joe
```

Besides using an HTML form, you can manually add the query string at the end of the hard-coded HTML hyperlink. Adding the query string manually does not provide the same flexibility as using an HTML form, however, because the information is usually predetermined. The client does not enter the data that are placed in the query string. (By using JavaScript in the HTML page, you may be able to produce the query string of an HTML link dynamically.)

Query strings, which appear after the question mark, can include any information. Normally, the information is defined in [*name*]=[*value*] pairs, with each pair being separated by an ampersand (&). The CGI program accesses this query string (QUERY_STRING) and decodes its value to get the variables that it needs to process the request. (The data in the query string are URL-encoded.)

In addition to the query string, the URL for a CGI program can also include extra path information. This information appears in the CGI URL after the name of the CGI program, but before the query string (before the question mark). It is separated from the CGI program name with a forward slash (/). You normally add this information manually to the HTML link. An HTML form does not automatically add extra path information to the URL. Extra path information can include any other data that your program may want. Normally, it is used to pass a path to a file that the CGI program can use to process the client request. The server goes through the server directive functions again so as to convert the extra path information into a physical path. The server sets this information as the value of the environment variable PATH_INFO, and delivers the translated extra path information to a physical path as the value of the environment variable PATH_TRANSLATED. You are not required to use extra path information for specifying a path, you can pass any information as part of the extra path information of the CGI URL. This information is available as the value of the environment variable PATH_INFO to the CGI program, independent of whether it is a file path. If it is a file path, the server does the necessary file conversion and provides the PATH_TRANSLATED environment variable.

You can also combine both the extra path information and the query string in a URL. The format for an extended CGI URL is usually as follows (see the URL and URI section in Chapter 1 for more detail):

```
http[s]://<server name>[:port]/<CGI path & program>/
[extra path info]?[query string]
```

Command-line arguments are intended for use with ISINDEX queries. The query string for an ISINDEX is processed differently than other types of query strings. If query does not include a non-encoded equal sign (=), the server processes the string as an ISINDEX query. The server then parses the input (query) and sends it as command-line arguments to your CGI program (see the ISINDEX section earlier in this chapter).

CGI Environment Variables

The following subsections include a list of CGI environment variables. Chapter 6 lists the NSAPI equivalent of these environment variables. For more information on CGI environment variables, you can read NCSA's documentation, "CGI Environment Variables," at http://hoohoo.ncsa.uiuc.edu/cgi/env.html.

The environment variables described below are divided into several categories. The first category includes the variables that exist for all types of CGI. That is, they are not request-specific. The second category lists the variables that apply to specific CGI requests. The third represents environment variable unique to Netscape Server. The fourth category includes the HTTP headers sent by the client, describing the client type and request. The fifth category lists variables for SSL secured HTTP. Under Server 2.x or later, you can also declare your own unique environment variables by adding the environment variables as `[name]="[value]"` parameters to the **init-cgi** function in the **obj.conf** file.

1. Global Variables

GATEWAY_INTERFACE
`CGI/1.1`
The version of CGI that the server supports. The format includes `CGI/` plus the numeric version (revision number) of the CGI.

SERVER_NAME (also known as SERVER_HOSTNAME)
`www.foo.com`
The fully qualified domain name, host name, or IP address of the server. It appears in the URL request of the client and is set by you in the Server Manager. When you need to reference the server URL (for example, to send back a complete URL path to the client), use this variable or `SERVER_URL` instead of hard-coding the server information. This way, your code can run on different servers without needing to change the value.

SERVER_SOFTWARE (also known as SERVER_VERSION)
`Netscape-Enterprise/3.5.1`
Name and version of your server software. It includes the server name, a forward slash, and the version number.

2. Variables Specific to a CGI Request

AUTH_TYPE
`Basic`
Defines the type of authentication used for the client request. If a server or CGI script needs authentication, this variable specifies the type required. It holds the type of

authentication method used to validate the client request. Netscape currently supports `Basic` (as part of the Basic user authentication supported under `HTTP/1.0` and `HTTP/1.1`). You can use `AUTH_TYPE` to find out if the CGI script requires authentication. The user must be authorized before accessing a CGI directory that is protected (see also `REMOTE_USER`, later in this section).

CONTENT_ENCODING

`x-gzip`

Determines the type of encoding used for the data sent by the client. It specifies the content type of the data as an encoded, usually compressed type. `x-compress` is for standard UNIX-type compression. `x-gzip` is for GNU-type zip compression. `x-uuencode` is for uuencoded format. The associated MIME types and their file extensions are defined in the **mime.types** file (for example, `enc=x-gzip exts=gz`). This variable differs from the response header `content-encoding` used to specify the encoding document returned by the CGI program to the client. Environment variable `CONTENT_ENCODING` is specific to the `POST` and `PUT` methods of client request. (See also `CONTENT_LENGTH` and `CONTENT_TYPE`, later in this section.)

CONTENT_LENGTH

`1024`

Number of bytes of form data being sent by the client. It provides a count of the data sent after the headers in a `POST` or `PUT` request. It should not be used for a `GET` request. The data is appended to the request after the request headers and can be accessed using stdin functions, such as **getc** and **fread**. `CONTENT_LENGTH` tells you how many bytes of data are being sent by the client. This variable can be used to determine if all the data from the client were received correctly. (It is also relevant for a `PUT` request.) (See also `CONTENT_TYPE`, below.)

CONTENT_TYPE

`application/x-www-form-urlencoded`

Determines the MIME type of the data sent by the client. It is limited to data being sent in the body after the headers, such as in the `POST` and `PUT` methods. This data is appended after the request headers and can be accessed using stdin functions, such as **getc** and **fread**. Currently, only form data can be sent from a client browser. `application/x-www-form-urlencoded` is defined as the type of data sent by a form (using the `POST` method). As the name implies, the content is form data, which are URL-encoded. This variable differs from the response header `content-type` that specifies the type of the data returned by the CGI program to the client. (See also `CONTENT_LENGTH`, above.)

PATH_INFO

`<http://www.foo.com/cgi/getx.exe>/data/info.txt`

Additional path information in the URL after the CGI program's path. Your program can use this information to access other relevant data. You can think of `PATH_INFO` as extra arguments for the CGI program. You can use the extra path information to return a path to data that the CGI program will use. You do not have to limit PATH_INFO to the actual file path—any type of data can be placed in this variable as long as they adhere to the guidelines for a URL. In the example, http://www.foo.com/cgi/getx.exe is the URL path to the CGI program. The rest of the URL /data/info.txt is the PATH_INFO, the extra path information that the client sent in the URL to the server. PATH_INFO is usually a virtual path. The program, getx.exe, can then use this information to get the data in info.txt that are needed to process the request. Thus you can provide different path information for the same CGI program, in order to use the CGI program in different ways. (See also PATH_TRANSLATED.)

PATH_TRANSLATED

c:/netscape/server/docs/data/info.txt

Additional path information (PATH_INFO) translated to a full physical path. As the additional path could be a partial (virtual or relative) path, this variable holds the translation of the partial path to a physical path. (Netscape Server translates a partial path to a physical path for both the original request and any additional path.) It is recommended that you use a virtual path for extra path information in the CGI URL and allow this function to provide the actual system path of the file, so that the file system information of your machine is not available to the client. In the example for PATH_INFO, the original PATH_INFO is /data/info.txt, and PATH_TRANSLATED is c:/netscape/server/docs/data/info.txt) (see also PATH_INFO).

QUERY_STRING

</cgi/getx.exe?>name=joe

Query information sent by the client to the server as a result of a GET request (passed through a form or as part of the URL) or an imagemap. This string is URL encoding, so you must decode the information to use it. For a GET request, this variable follows the URL, starting after a question mark (?). In the example, name=joe is the QUERY_STRING. If the request comes from a form, the form data are also attached to the URL after any QUERY_STRING you manually add to the URL. For example, if the example was part of a form request that included a password text input, then the rest of the query would be password=[client input].

For an imagemap, the coordinates of where the cursor clicked on the image are available through the QUERY_STRING.

REMOTE_ADDR

1.2.3.4

IP address of the browser (remote client) making the request. It differs from the client's actual IP address, as the IP address could be set dynamically by the client's ISP. Among other things, you can use this information to deny access to an IP address. Even when you do not have a REMOTE_HOST (host name) information, you still have this information. (If a proxy is used, the remote host information can be the same for many different users and, therefore, not an accurate confirmation of a specific user.)

REMOTE_HOST

`imagia.com`

Host name of the browser (remote client) after it is resolved through the DNS look-up. The server must resolve the domain name from the IP address. This fully qualified domain name includes all the necessary domain address information available (`[machine name].[server name].[type of server].[country code]`). If the remote host information is not available, REMOTE_ADDR should be used. If DNS is disabled, REMOTE_HOST may reflect the IP address of the client, which is the same as REMOTE_ADDR. (See also REMOTE_ADDR, above.)

REMOTE_IDENT

`johng`

User name sent by the user's machine. If the HTTP server supports RFC 931 identification and the remote user sent user information, then this variable holds the user name. The server must contact the remote machine to determine the user name. This information is available if the identification protocol is turned on by your server and an identification server is used by the client's machine. This information is voluntary, however, so many users may not send it. The accuracy of this information is also not verified. For example, identification daemons can be installed on an insecure system like Windows 3.1, which offsets the value and accuracy of the information being sent by the daemon. This variable is intended for logging purposes only. In general, you should not use this information.

REMOTE_USER

`joe`

Holds the authenticated user name, after the user has been authenticated. It is the name that the client (user) used for authentication. The accuracy of this information is based on the type of authentication that has taken place. It holds the local HTTP user name. Once the user has been authenticated, the client browser sends the authenticated user name and password every time a request is made. (See also AUTH_TYPE, earlier in this section.)

REQUEST_METHOD

`GET`

Method the client uses for his or her request, such as GET, POST, PUT, and HEAD. This variable is always set. Most requests that you make are of the GET type. Each time the user clicks on a link to get a new page, image, or sound, a GET request is made. You can also use the GET method for a form, but the preferred method of sending content of an HTML form is the POST method. You define the type of request for a form when you define the method of the form through a variable in the form tag (for example, `<FORM METHOD="GET" . . . >`). HEAD is used to request meta-information, such as the file size or file date. The server responds by sending the HTTP headers without the entity-body (that is, without the content of the file). HEAD can be used by the client to verify if a link is still valid and available. It can also verify whether a file was recently modified. In a CGI program, REQUEST_METHOD is used to verify the method of the client request and process the request accordingly. For example, with a GET request, QUERY_STRING contains the data sent by the client.

SCRIPT_NAME

`/cgi-bin/myprogram.cgi`

Virtual path to the CGI program. You can use this variable to obtain the path of the program. CGI scripts can use this information to reference themselves or to reintroduce the client to the program. You can use this variable instead of hard-coding a reference to the CGI program.

SERVER_PORT

`80`

Port address to which the request is sent. It is also the address of the port on which the HTTP server is listening. (Port 80 is normally used for an unsecured HTTP server.)

SERVER_PROTOCOL

`HTTP/1.0`

Version of HTTP protocol being used by the client and the server. The previous HTTP protocol version was HTTP/0.9, but almost all HTTP servers and browsers now support HTTP/1.0, with newer versions of HTTP protocol in the works. HTTP/1.1 is the version now being evaluated. Netscape Server 3.x is conditionally compliant with the version 1.1 proposed standards. It supports all the MUST requirements of HTTP/1.1. See the IETF Hypertext Transfer Protocol (HTTP) Working Group page (`http://www.ics.uci.edu/pub/ietf/http/`) for more information on HTTP/1.1. (See also the HTTP section in Chapter 1.)

3. Netscape-Specific Environment Variable

SERVER_URL

`http://www.foo.com:43`

Holds the URL that the client should use to access the server. This variable is available only with Netscape Servers and is not part of CGI revision 1.1. You can use this information to get the full server URL. (SERVER_NAME holds only the name of the server and not the full URL path.)

4. Additional HTTP Headers Besides the above environment variables, the client can send other information through the request headers, such as information about the request or the client. These data extend and enhance the request. These headers (for example, Accept, User-Agent, Referer) are based on the HTTP protocol specification. The CGI thread changes these HTTP headers to uppercase, replaces any hyphen (-) with an underscore (_), and adds the prefix HTTP_ to them. Thus Accept will become environment variable HTTP_ACCEPT. The CGI thread then makes these headers available to the CGI program as environment variables. The authorization request header is an exception. The value of the authorization header is available through the AUTH_TYPE and REMOTE_USER environment variables. Because it has already processed the authorization, the server excludes authorization as an HTTP header. Thus it is not part of the HTTP header environment variables defined here. The variables in this category can change or include additional variables based on the headers that a specific browser sends. For example, Netscape Communicator 4.x uses additional headers, such as HTTP_ACCEPT_CHARSET and HTTP_ACCEPT_LANGUAGE. HTTP_ACCEPT_CHARSET (iso-8859-1,*,utf-8) specifies the character set that the browser will support, and HTTP_ACCEPT_LANGUAGE (en for English) specifies the language that the browser will accept.

HTTP_ACCEPT

```
image/gif, image/x-xbitmap, image/jpeg, image/pjpeg,
image/png, */*
```

Lists the MIME types accepted by the client browser. This list includes the types of media supported by the client browser, separated by spaces. Not all browsers supply this information, and not all MIME types supported are included directly in the list. For instance, the example here lists the MIME type that Netscape Communicator 4.x accepts. As you can see, only a very few MIME types are actually listed. */* is added at the end to suggest that the browser supports everything else, which makes the information in this header rather useless. To use the value of HTTP_ACCEPT, you may want to verify the type of browser the client is using (HTTP_USER_AGENT). If the browser supports HTTP_ACCEPT, you can use this information to determine the type of file you can send. For example, the Netscape browser supports jpeg. If the request comes from a Netscape browser, then you can send a JPEG file instead of a GIF file.

HTTP_CONNECTION

```
Keep-Alive
```

Determines the type of connection between the client and server. Netscape Server 2.x supports a Keep-Alive connection. Netscape Server 3.x supports HTTP persistent connection. Persistent connection closely resembles the Keep-Alive connection under Server 2.x. With an HTTP/1.1-compliant client, the default connection with Netscape Server 3.x is a persistent connection. Persistent connection allows a client and the server to signal the closing of a TCP connection.

If the value of this environment variable is Keep-Alive, then Server 2.x and later will support a Keep-Alive connection with the client. The client sends the Keep-Alive request header, specifying that it can handle a Keep-Alive connection. Navigator 3.x and 4.x also support Keep-Alive connections. For these browsers, the server keeps the connection open until all the embedded items of the requested pages are delivered before disconnecting.

HTTP_COOKIE

`User=JoeBoxer`

Holds the cookie data returned by the client. You can use cookies to store specific state information on the client's machine. The server first sends a `Set-Cookie` header with specific information to be stored in the client's cookie file for later retrieval. When the proper type of request is made by the client, the client returns the cookie information that you can access through the `HTTP_COOKIE` environment variable.

HTTP_FROM

`joe@foo.com`

Holds the client's e-mail address. Netscape Navigator 0.9 was one of the first browsers that provided this feature. Its use, however, created privacy issues. Users did not want browsers to provide HTTP servers with their e-mail addresses. With version 1.0, Netscape removed this feature. It is no longer supported by Netscape browsers. (Note that other browsers may still provide this feature.)

HTTP_IF_MODIFIED_SINCE

`Monday, 1-Jan-96 12:00:00 GMT`

Contains the date in Greenwich Mean Time (GMT). The client can request that the data be sent only if the file date of the data is later than the date specified in this HTTP header. This variable can be used by the client to evaluate whether it should get the actual document or instead use a cached or saved file on the client's machine.

HTTP_REFERER (REFERER_URL)

`http://www.foo.com/index.html`

Holds the URL from whence the request came (that is, the URL that referred the client to the CGI program). It points to the last URL. To illustrate, imagine that the user's URL is `http://www.foo.com/index.html`. From this home page, the user goes to read the news on a subpage, `/new/news.html`. The referring page is then the original `http://www.foo.com/index.html`. If the news page includes images, then the `http://www.foo.com/new/news.html` is the referrer for the images. You can use this information, for example, to find out who points to your Web sites or from which locations your viewers are coming.

HTTP_USER_AGENT (also known as USER_AGENT)

`Mozilla/4.04 [en] (WinNT; I)`

Holds the name of the client browser. Not all browsers provide this information. You can use this variable to determine the type of HTML support that the client can receive so as to return the appropriate type of page. For example, if the client has Netscape Navigator 3.0 or later, you can send an HTML page that includes HTML 3.2 support plus features such as frames and JavaScript.

5. *Secured Server Environment Variables* This section includes a list of the standard default security environment variables for Netscape Servers. To include the client certificate and other certificate-related information in your CGI program, you need first to enable security from the Server Manager's Server Preferences|Encryption On/Off menu and require certificate through the Server Preferences|Encryption Preferences option. Once security is properly enabled, you will also need to declare the **PathCheck** function **get-client-cert** in the **obj.conf** file. This function generates the client certificate, which you can access through the environment variable CLIENT_CERT. The client certificate (CLIENT_CERT) is in MIME base-64 encoded, ASN.1 encoded X.509 format. Enterprise Server 3.5.1 also includes a number of additional certificate-related environment variables. The most important variables are CLIENT_CERT_ISSUER_DN and CLIENT_CERT_SUBJECT_DN. CLIENT_CERT_ISSUER_DN includes the distinguished name (DN) of the issuer of the certificate, and CLIENT_CERT_SUBJECT_DN includes the user's distinguished name. Enterprise Server 3.5.1 also parses the various DN fields and provides them separately for your use. For example, you could find the following environment variables: CLIENT_CERT_ISSUER_CN, CLIENT_CERT_ISSUER_O, CLIENT_CERT_SUBJECT_CN, and CLIENT_CERT_SUBJECT_O. (O is used for the organization name, and CN for the full name or common name.)

HTTPS
OFF
Holds information on whether the security is active. The value can be either OFF or ON.

HTTPS_KEYSIZE
128
Holds the number of bits in the session key used to encrypt it. Security must be active for this variable to be available.

HTTPS_SECRETSIZE
40
Holds the number of bits used to generate the private key of the server. Security must be active for this variable to be available.

HTTPS_SESSIONID
B+rZPf11DpxjCWGst6iFAmbUdgRKzLVRIJzPYW6PNWg
A new feature for Server 2.01 and later. If you include the **AuthTrans** function **get-sslid** in the **obj.conf** file, the server provides the base-64 encoding of the session ID as HTTPS_SESSIONID for your CGI programs.

Additional Variables

User-defined variables
GROUPS=buyers
You can also pass your own environment variables to your CGI programs by using the **Init** function **init-cgi**. You add **init-cgi** to the **obj.conf** file, and pass the environ-

ment variables as parameters to this **Init** function. The parameters are in `[name]=[value]` pairs. The CGI program can then access these parameters in the same way it accesses any other environment variables (for example, `getenv("GROUPS");`).

System-specific environment variables (for example, `PATH`)

`c:\Windows\system32;c:\Windows`

Your program can access other variables specific to your system through environment variables. To make sure you can access these variables, set the parameter `load-server-vars=true` for the **Init** function **init-cgi**.

`PATH` holds the system path information for the server machine. On NT, for example, this information is the same as the path information defined for the system. (See also "Path" in Windows NT Diagnosis by choosing the "System" button on the Environment tab.) This path is not the same as the path information for the local user.

Processing the Request

A CGI program makes use of the data provided by the server. For example, when writing a CGI program in ANSI C, environment variables are obtained through the function **getenv**. Reading and writing stdin data (the client input) work the same way as the normal standard I/O operations work. For example, reading stdin data can be accomplished through the **fread** function. To read the data from stdin, you should use the length of data available through the `CONTENT_LENGTH` environment variable to get the actual size of the data that need to be read. Command-line arguments can also be passed to your program. You can access them using the `argv` and `argc` parameters of your C programs.

The CGI program is responsible for verifying the data that are sent to it. You may need to parse the client input (for example, the query string from a `GET` form), verify that the input is of the correct type and size, or make sure the path does not include errors (such as `\ . \`). Once the CGI program does all the necessary error checking and parsing of the data, it then processes the request or calls any other program, database, or file needed. For instance, the CGI program can connect to a database and send an SQL query. The database sends the result to the CGI program. The CGI program manipulates the data and returns them through the server to the client (for example, as an HTML document).

The CGI Program Response

Because the CGI process includes server information, you do not need to include most of the specific HTTP protocol headers. The CGI process and the directive function **send-cgi** take care of this task. For example, **send-cgi** sets and sends the Status-Line. Normally, however, you will include the `content-type`. The headers should be followed by a blank line. The server parses all headers that you include before sending the data. It also verifies the headers for any error, and sends an error message if a header is incorrect. The body of document that comes after the header is sent in one package, without any parsing or evaluation by the server. It can include any type of data, such as HTML pages, images, sound, video, and so on. (Netscape, in general, takes care of many verifications of the information, such as the headers, before it sends it to your CGI program.)

As mentioned earlier, a CGI program returns one of three types of responses: redirection, a new document, or a custom error page.

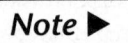

Note ▶

In the response, you need to put a single empty line after the last HTTP response header, but before the entity-body (the actual document). Otherwise, the server will return a server error. For example, in your code you can use newline characters to create an empty line. (For Windows, you can use two instances of \n.) The server then parses and evaluates all headers (everything above the empty line), but sends the entity-body unchanged directly to the client.

Returning a Redirect   The CGI program can redirect the client to another location by returning a new location. The status for a redirection is 302 Found. The program is not limited to redirecting a client to an HTTP URL; you can also redirect the client to an FTP, Gopher, and so on. The CGI program returns a new location using the following format, with the headers that you send being followed by a blank line.

```
Location: <new path>
<two newline characters(a blank line)>
```

The server will then recognize the request as a redirection and route the client to the location specified in the Location header.

If the new location points to a file that is on your server machine, you can use a partial (virtual or relative) path for it. A partial path includes only the URI path portion of the URL; it does not include the http[s]://<server name>[:port] portion. For example, the URI could be /new/newpage.html instead of http://www.foo.com/new/newpage.html. Two kinds of partial paths exist. One is relative to a specific document and its directory—that is, the path of the document from which the relative path is invoked. The other is relative to the base directory of the server documents (document root directory). To make sure that the partial path you specify in Location works, you need to use the document root as the starting directory. Thus your path needs to begin with the forward slash (for example, /new.html). When a path begins with a forward slash, the server reads it as a path relative to the document root. If a forward slash is not used, the path is relative to the document and the server does not process the program correctly. That is, the server will not be able to resolve such a path (in the **NameTrans** directive) and will return status 404 Not found.

When you use a partial path, the server retrieves the file by appending the partial path to the document root directory of the server. It then sends the new file specified with the Location to the client. The server goes through the directives twice before it can resolve the path and return the proper document. The first time, the server attempts to resolve the CGI request. Once the `Location` header is found, the server restarts the request by using the new URI (`LOCATION`) information. With the partial path location, the server does not restart the session. It also processes the **AddLog** directive functions after the second pass through the directives.

If the document contains other partial path hyperlinks (for example, links to images) which are relative to it, they are resolved as links from the CGI program's path and not from the document's directory. The server, not the client, resolves the URL request. The server resolves the links as if they were from the CGI directory, instead of the document's directory. Therefore, the document's internal links that are expected to be relative to the document can be broken. (This situation is especially relevant because CGI programs are usually kept in their own directory, not usually a subdirectory of the base document directory.) In other words, a link inside your document for `book.gif` is not resolved based on the document's directory. If the links in the document are relative to the document root (begin with a forward slash), however, then the server looks for the link based on the document root directory, instead of the document or the CGI programs directory. A link inside your document for `/image/book.gif` resolves relative to the subdirectory image from the root document directory, independent of the document or the CGI directory.

To avoid problems that may occur due to the use of partial paths, include the complete URL (the absolute path) for the `Location`. With the absolute URL, you include the `http[s]://<server name>`, as in `http://www.foo.com/new/newpage.html`. The `Location` header is then sent to the client, which resolves and requests the new URL. The client sees this new URL as the requested URL. The session is then restarted for the new request, and the server processes this request without reference to the CGI program. This situation also holds when the new URL references a file that is not on your machine (for example, `Location: http://www.newserver.com/`), except that the request is sent to a new server. The server sends the redirection header—`Location` header—to the client to be resolved. The client then processes this new URL and requests the pages specified in `Location` from the new server. All this activity occurs transparently, and the client receives the document as if it were the requested document.

Returning a New Document When the CGI program responds with a new document, it should inform the client of the type of document it is returning (`content-type`) before sending the entity-body (the document, such as an HTML page). If you do not specify `content-type`, no `content-type` is sent to the client. In some circumstances, this omission may not be a problem. For example, the Netscape browser can recognize and process a text or HTML file correctly, even if no `content-type` is sent. To guarantee that the document will be processed by the client properly, you should always include the `content-type`. The server usually takes care of any other necessary headers (for example, `content-length`). If you need to send any special response header (for example, `cookie`), you should send it after the `content-type` header. Normally, each header is placed on a separate line.

You also need to include a blank line after the response headers. If you do not include the blank line before sending the entity-body, the server will return a server error. (To bypass the CGI thread and send data directly to the client, you can use a nonparsed header file, discussed later in this chapter.) The format of the content-type information and the data you send is as follows:

```
content-type: <MIME type>
<two newline characters (a blank line)>
<Body of the document>
```

You can include any type of document as long as it matches the defined content-type and can be interpreted by the client. It is common practice to send the content-type at the beginning of the CGI program to avert a timeout by the server. Be careful to end your program by returning success, defined as zero (0) for C. As long as your program is alive, the thread will be busy and unavailable to any other request.

Returning a Custom Error Page   The server takes care of sending the status information to the client. Consequently, you do not need to return a Status-Line to the client. The server sets the status to 200 OK, if the request was successfully processed—that is, if the server was successful in returning your response to the client. The server also verifies the headers that your program returns and checks on the response you sent. If an error occurs during your CGI program, the server automatically sets the status and sends a server error page to the client. The server takes care of returning the predefined error page when an error occurs.

You may be able to set the status code and reason string of the response by using a status response header—for example, status: 403 Forbidden. But this approach may not always work. In fact, the server might even return a server error if you attempt to return a status header. For example, under FastTrack version 2.0 for NT, the server stops processing your response with a server error if you return a status header for a ShellCGI program. Server 2.0's process of setting the status information conflicts with the status that the ShellCGI program attempts to set. Even if you were able to set the status code and the reason string for the response, the server would not return the default error page associated with the status code. You would still need to send a custom error page. Nevertheless, the status code would appear as the status you set in the access log file.

You can always return your own customized error page. You would perform this feat the same way you return any other document to the client. You can catch an error and return an HTML page. These pages are not seen as errors by the server, but the client receives them as error pages (i.e., informing the client of an error that has occurred). The status for these error pages could also be 200 OK, even though they are sent in response to an error.

Nonparsed Headers

As noted, the server normally takes care of sending your response to the client. You send your response to the server, which parses and verifies your response headers. The server sets and sends the Status-Line and other necessary headers (general, response, and entity headers). It also sends the body of the response (for example, the HTML document) to the client.

If you wish to bypass the server and send your response directly to the client, you can use nonparsed headers. Nonparsed headers give you direct control over the connection between your program and the client. For example, you can use this method if you want to return a large amount of data or if you wish to send the data in a specific order.

Normally, data are buffered by the server and sent in one step. The server waits for the full response and then sends the complete response. If you wish the data to be sent at a certain interval, you can use nonparsed headers to control how the data are sent to the client socket.

To enable nonparsed headers, you need to name the CGI program as a nonparsed header file by using `nph-` as a prefix for the name of the program—for example, `nph-puzzler.exe`. The server processes any file with this prefix differently. It makes a copy of the socket connection between the server and client. Your program then writes directly to the client socket when it returns the response as standard output.

When you use nonparsed headers, the CGI program is responsible for all the necessary HTTP protocol headers of a response. (This task is normally carried out by the server.) Consequently, you must include the Status-Line and all the necessary HTTP headers (such as the date, time, and MIME type). All necessary headers must be sent before the body (entity-body) of the response. Otherwise, the client may not have the information necessary to recognize and interpret the response correctly. Any errors that can occur need to be handled by your program.

In Netscape Server, the standard output and standard error file streams are both returned to the server. In other words, the error and the output are processed in the same way. Normally, with a standard CGI program, the server sets the Status-Line. Thus your output does not conflict with the server's error handling. With nonparsed header files, you must set the Status-Line. If the status is set to OK and an error occurs later, the error status will conflict with the original status you set. The server will then send a server error. In other words, when using nonparsed headers, you can run the risk of a conflict between the standard error and the standard output or your program and the server's handling of the error.

Hello Client Examples

CGI programs can be written in a number of languages, including C, Perl, tcl, Bourne Shell, REXX, and so on. We will provide a very simple example, Hello Client, in ANSI C, Perl, and Visual Basic to show how each language approaches CGI. Because NSAPI is written in ANSI C, our other example, Guest Book, is also in C. Later on, we will write a Guest Book example using NSAPI and WAI.

A number of third-party libraries can also be used for writing your CGI applications. Consider using these libraries to reduce your development time. CGI libraries provide a great starting point and include support for form handling, data parsing, string manipulation, and so on. Two of the most popular C libraries are W3C's Sample Code Library, **libwww** (http://www.w3.org/Library) and Thomas Boutell's **cgic** (http://www.boutell.com/cgic/). For C++, you can use WebThing Ltd's **CGI++** Library (http://www3.pair.com/webthing/cgiplusplus/) or Daniel Doubrovkine's **MV4** CGI C++ Class Library (http://www.infomaniak.ch/~dblock/mozilla/index.html). All these libraries are also included with the CD-ROM that accompanies this book. (The CD-ROM also includes Perl Libraries. For more information see section ShellCGI [Perl].)

ANSI C

Listing 3-3   C Hello Client

```
/* Hello Client Program */

/* include files */
#include <stdio.h>
#include <stdlib.h> /* getenv */

int main(int argc, char *argv[])
{
    /* get the client IP address */
    char *client = getenv("REMOTE_ADDR");

    /* print out necessary header and empty line */
    printf("Content-type: text/html\n\n");

    /* print the body of the HTML file */
    printf("<HTML>\n");
    printf("<HEAD>\n");
    printf("<TITLE>Hello</TITLE>\n");
    printf("<BODY>\n");
    printf("<H1>Hello %s</H1>", client);
    printf("</BODY>\n");
    printf("<HTML>\n");

    return 0;
}
```

The code in Listing 3-3 is all you need to return an HTML page to the client. The program represents a small twist on the infamous "Hello World" example. Instead of saying hello to the world, we are saying hello, by way of the IP address, to the client. Compile this code for your operating system using the compiler of your choice before running it. Also, make sure you enable CGI for your server. (See the Configuring the Server for CGI Programs section earlier in this chapter for more details.)

Let's review the code. First, we include the standard I/O library `stdio.h` and `stdlib.h`, which includes the **getenv()** function. The **main** function is the entry point for your C or C++ code. The parameters for your **main** function include parameters for the standard I/O command-line arguments. They are declared, but not used.[1] For CGI programs, the programs mainly use environment variables and standard input to gain access to information.

Variables, such as the address of the client browser, are obtained through the function **getenv**. Here, the value we want is REMOTE_ADDR.

The rest of the code consists of simple **printf** functions that print out the strings defined in their parameters. We send back Content-type first. In this case, HTML. The two instances of \n in the parameter for the first **printf** line produce the necessary blank line after the header and before the content of the HTML page.

The code of the document (the page that is sent to the client) looks something like Listing 3-4.

Listing 3-4   HTML File for CGI Hello Client

```
<HTML>
<HEAD>
<TITLE>Hello</TITLE>
</HEAD>
<BODY>
<H1>Hello [1.2.3.4]</H1>
</BODY>
</HTML>
```

The user sees only the word "Hello" plus "[1.2.3.4]" (the client IP address) on the page that is returned.

A 0 return indicates success. This simple function does not include any error checking.

ShellCGI (Perl)

Perl (Practical Extraction and Report Language) was originally written to facilitate UNIX programming. It has since been ported to most platforms, including Windows. Perl is in the public domain and is easily available for almost all varieties of UNIX,

---

1. argc is an integer containing the number of arguments to be given in argv. argv is an array of null-terminated strings from the command-line arguments that are received from the server. argv[0] is the program; argv[1] is the first argument, argv[2] is the second argument, and so on. The last argv is always NULL. These arguments are usually used for an ISINDEX program, which uses command-line arguments.

Windows, DOS, and Macintosh. It is very similar to C, but includes features that make programming easier. These features resemble those provided by other scripting language (such as awk and sed). For example, it includes built-in functions for sorting, searching, and string manipulation. Perl variables can contain a variety of data types, including strings, integers, and floating-point numbers.

Perl is an interpretive language that does not compile into byte code or machine-readable code. Instead, it runs as script that the main Perl program (`perl.exe`) interprets and executes. The executable Perl file is also called Perl Interpreter. To run successfully, Perl must be installed correctly, and your script needs to locate the Perl Interpreter. Because Perl Interpreter deals with platform-specific issues, and because it is developed under a central umbrella, the language has far fewer compatibility problems across platforms. On the other hand, because the Perl Interpreter must always run when you run your script, and because it does not compile to byte code, it is slower than a programming language like C is. It also does not include many of the advanced features of C. For more information on the Perl language, check Tom Christiansen's "Perl Language Home Page" (`http://www.perl.com/perl/index.html`) or Earl Hood's "PerlWWW" (`http://www.oac.uci.edu/indiv/ehood/perlWWW/`).

Under Netscape Server 1.x, Perl Interpreter must reside in your CGI directory and be added to your URL path. You need to include both Perl and the script in the URL. This tactic, of course, is extremely dangerous, as it opens your server to hackers who can use the interpreter to wreak havoc on your server. The way to avoid vulnerability is to write a `.bat` (batch) file that calls Perl Interpreter and the script in the `.bat` file. Note, however, that `.bat` files have their own security risks.

Under Netscape Server 2.x and later, you can install Shell CGI using the Server Manager, which makes it easy to run any shell type of application, such as Perl. The specifics of the ShellCGI installation, as described in this chapter, are unique to the Windows platform. On the other hand, running Shell programs is not specific to Windows. You can write Perl programs for both Windows and UNIX versions of the server.

Listing 3-5 is the Hello Client example written in Perl.

Note ▶

Before implementing this or any other Perl program correctly, install Perl on your machine and enable Netscape Server for shell programs. Your Perl script needs to locate the executable Perl. Under NT 4.0, you can associate a Perl (`*.pl`) program with Perl Interpreter (`perl.exe`) by using file association in the File Manager or with "File Types" from the Explorer's View|Options menu. Then, enable ShellCGI for Netscape Server through the Server Manager's Programs|ShellCGI Directory option. If you have defined a directory for the ShellCGI, put all your Perl programs in that directory.

Listing 3-5 Perl Hello Client

```perl
#!/bin/perl
#Hello Client Example

#get client IP address
$client=$ENV{'REMOTE_ADDR'};

# Print out necessary header and empty line
print "Content-type: text/html\n\n";

# Print out the html text
print "<HTML>\n";
print "<BODY>\n";
print "<HEAD><TITLE>Hello</TITLE></HEAD>\n";
print "<H1>Hello ", $client, "</H1></CENTER>\n";
print "</BODY>\n";
print "</HTML>\n";
```

In the first line of the code, before any other statement, designate your code as Perl code and point to the location of your Perl program. Although a pound sign (#) normally defines a comment line, the combination of #! indicates the type of program—in this case, Perl. The text after #! is the path to the Perl executable, Perl Interpreter. If ShellCGI has been defined for Netscape Server and files with pl extensions have been associated with perl.exe, then this line of code can consist simply of #!perl and the script will run correctly. The server locates Perl Interpreter through file association, instead of via the path.

You can add the following line to the beginning of your script to ensure that the output is flushed immediately, instead of being buffered:

```perl
$|=1;
```

$| (dollar sign, pipe symbol), when set to a nonzero value, forces the output to be flushed. Thus the CGI output is sent immediately to the client. Additionally, in case of a busy server, CGI programs will not reach timeout. To make sure the output is properly flushed under Windows platform, you should always add the line of code given previously to your Perl script. Note, however, that keeping a CGI program from timing out is not always advantageous, as a hanging CGI program will not be terminated. Netscape also allows you to set a timeout period for CGI programs with the **Init** function **init-cgi**. (See the discussion of **init-cgi** in Appendix B for more information.)

After the comment lines, which begin with a pound sign, $ENV gets the environment variables' values for REMOTE_ADDR. The dollar sign defines a scalar variable, a variable that can store various types of data (such as strings, integers, characters, and so on).

Next, the `Content-type` of the message is printed out, with the necessary double newline characters that produce the blank line between the headers and the body of the HTML. Finally, the body of the message is printed as an HTML file. Perl uses the **print** function to write out each line of code. It is similar to **printf**. A series of strings (or variables) are sent through a single print function, with each item being separated by a comma. As you can see, although Perl is similar to C, it has its own unique features and functions.

The page returned is the same for all the Hello Client functions. (See the output in the ANSI C section earlier in this chapter.)

Many useful examples are available on the Web, or in books on Perl, that can help you program Netscape applications using this language. Some helpful sites containing examples, hints, and suggestions are Selena Sol's Public Domain CGI Script Archive (including guest book and mail-to examples) (`http://www.extropia.com/Scripts/`), The Webmasters Handbook (`http://www.informatik.th-darmstadt.de/~neuss/Handbook/book/`), and Matt's Script Archive (`http://worldwidemart.com/scripts/`). There are also some useful Perl libraries that help you with many tasks, including reading data from forms and connecting to a database. Two of the best known of these libraries are Steven Brenner's `cgi-lib.pl` (`http://cgi-lib.stanford.edu/cgi-lib/`) and Lincoln D. Stein's (Whitehead Institute/MIT Center for Genome Research) `CGI.pm` (`http://www-genome.wi.mit.edu/ftp/pub/software/WWW/cgi_docs.html`). Both of these libraries are included on the CD-ROM that accompanies this book.

WinCGI (Visual Basic)

As noted earlier, WinCGI enables Windows-based applications to work with the HTTP server. It is unique to Windows and does not apply to UNIX. The information in this section is for Visual Basic 4.0.

WinCGI uses INI files (profile files) and temporary files to process standard input and output. It uses spooled I/O for exchange of data between the server and the CGI program. To process the data, an INI file and any necessary temporary files are created for each request. The INI file processes the environment variables and handles the requirements for running a WINCGI application for the HTTP server. The data are processed by the server according to the WinCGI interface defined in the INI file. This information added to the INI file is passed to your CGI application. The main function for the Visual Basic application is defined in `Cgi32.bas`. You write your function as **CGI_Main**, which, in turn, is called by the **Main** function in `Cgi32.bas`. `Cgi32.bas` expects **CGI_Main** and works in conjunction with it, passing the necessary data back and forth. The temporary file holds the raw request content, such as in a `POST` or `GET` request. It uses a predesignated temporary file, such as `Output`, to process the standard out.

Note ▶

Before you use this example (Listing 3-6) or write your own Visual Basic 4.0 program, add `Cgi32.bas` to your Visual Basic project. (`Cgi32.bas` version 1.8 is included with the CD-ROM that accompanies this book.) Also, remove any files (such as Form1) from your project so that the project includes only your programs and `Cgi32.bas`. (In the Project Tab of the Options dialog box under Tools|Options, the Startup Form should be set to Sub Main.) Enable WinCGI for Netscape Server in the Server Manager through the Programs| WinCGI Directory option. If you have defined a specific directory for your WinCGI files, then you should put the executable file in that directory. Finally, compile your Visual Basic code for an executable (`*.exe`) program.

If you plan to run the compiled version of a WinCGI program on a machine that does not have the appropriate Visual Basic Dynamic Link Library (DLL), make sure to add the DLL to a directory on the system path. For example, for Visual Basic 4.0, you can place `vb40032.dll` in the [*windows*]`/system32` directory.

Netscape Server 3.x supports WinCGI 1.3a specifications with a few minor differences. Netscape has added support for the Netscape security environment variables `HTTPS`, `HTTPS Keysize`, and `HTTPS Secret Keysize` to WinCGI. In addition, `Document Root` in WinCGI may not refer to the actual document root under Netscape Server, as Netscape Server does not have a single document root. For example, you can set up a virtual server and have multiple document roots. Netscape then returns the root directory for the WinCGI program. Also, `Server Admin` and `Authentication Realm` are not supported under Netscape Server. Likewise, forms sent with `multipart/form-data` encoding are not supported.

`Cgi32.bas` is the main program needed to write a Visual Basic program for Netscape Servers. It takes care of creating the INI, output, and input files. It also deals with environment variables, parses the data sent by the client, sets procedures for handling error, and so on. The INI (profile) file passes data to your program and to the server (the CGI thread). This file has eight sections: `[CGI]`, `[Accept]`, `[System]`, `[Extra Headers]`, `[Form Literal]`, `[Form External]`, `[Form Huge]`, and `[Form File]`. The `[CGI]` section includes most of the environment variables (such as `Request Protocol`, `Request Method`, `Server Software`, `CGI Version`, and `Content-type`). `[Accept]` includes the `HTTP_Accept` environment variable. The `[System]` section includes information about the system and WinCGI (for example, Debug Mode, Output, and Content File). The `[Extra Headers]` section includes other HTTP headers (for example, User Agent information). `[Form Literal]` includes form input variables. `[Form External]` and `[Form Huge]` also support the decoding of form input. `[Form External]` is used for decoding value strings that are more than 254 characters long, while `[Form Huge]` is used for raw value strings that are more than 65,535 bytes long. Values in these sections point to the external temporary file where content is kept. `[Form File]` supports the MIME type `multipart/form-data` for uploading files. Each of these sections holds important information received from the client request, used by your program, and returned to the client.[2]

The **Main()** function in `Cgi32.bas` calls your function, which starts at **CGI_Main()**. The output file is open at this point. You can use the **send** function to write into it. **Inter_Main** is usually called before the **CGI_Main** function and intercedes when your program is run by itself and not as a CGI program. When the program is run without any command-line argument, or when the program is run by itself (for example, when you run the program by double-clicking on it in the Explorer), the program presumes that you want to run it interactively—that is, that you want to set up a screen, get input, and so on. For CGI programs, you normally do not want to take this action. Using **Inter_Main**, you can display a message box (MsgBox) instead. The message box informs the user that the program is not intended to be run by itself, but as a CGI program by your HTTP server.

Listing 3-6 gives the Hello Client code written for Visual Basic.

Listing 3-6 WinCGI Hello Client

```
` name of the module (this is optional)
Attribute VB_Name = "HelloWorld"

` Open a Message box if the program is run without HTTP server
Sub Inter_Main()

MsgBox "WinCGI program. Must be opened by the Web server", _
           16, "WinCGI error"
End Sub

`Send back the page to the client.
Sub CGI_Main()
    Dim client As String
    client = CGI_RemoteAddr

    Send ("Content-type: text/html")
    Send ("")
    Send ("<HTML>")
    Send ("<HEAD><TITLE>Hello</TITLE></HEAD>")
    Send ("<BODY>")
```

---

2. INI files, such as `win.ini` and `system.ini`, are often used in Windows 3.1. These two files are the main system files. They are updated by various programs and read by Windows before loading as initialization settings. They also include initialization settings for other programs. Many programs also maintain their own INI files (initialization file) so as to save specific settings.

Listing 3-6   WinCGI Hello Client (*continued*)

```
      Send ("<H1>Hello " & client & "</H1>")
      Send ("</BODY>")
      Send ("</HTML>")
End Sub
```

Comment lines in Visual Basic start with an apostrophe (') or the keyword REM followed by a space. The first line of code after the comment line defines the name of the Visual Basic module. You do not need to define any names here. If you want to define a name, use conventions similar to those in Listing 3-6. You can also name the module through the View|Properties options of the Visual Basic program, once you have opened the module and it is the active window. Visual Basic then adds the attribute name for the module automatically.

Next, the **Inter_Main** function is defined. If the function runs outside of the WinCGI, Netscape Server context, a message box opens with the parameters we have set here. We have defined three parameters for the function **MsgBox**. The first one is the text that will appear in the message box: "This is a WinCGI program run by the Web server". The " _" (space, underscore) is used to split the MsgBox line. The number for vbCritical, the visual basic critical error message box, is 16. It determines the type of message box that will appear. "WinCGI error" will appear as the text in the title bar of the message box.

CGI_Main is the main function of your program. Here, the client IP address comes from the variable CGI_RemoteAddr. All environment variables are defined in Cgi32.bas and begin with CGI_. It is not necessary to define a variable named client and assign it the value of CGI_RemoteAddr, as is done in Listing 3-6. Because CGI_RemoteAddr is global, it can be accessed directly by the **Send** function—that is, via Send("<h1>Hello" & CGI_RemoteAddr & "</h1>").

The **Send()** function defined in Cgi32.bas is a shortcut for writing to the client. It writes to the output file and thus back to the client. Each such function automatically includes a newline (line feed) character at its end, so you do not need to include one explicitly. We do need an extra line after the Content-type code and before the rest of the HTML file. Send ("") sends the second newline (line feed) character required before the rest of the HTML document is sent.

The returned page is the same for all the Hello Client function. (See the output in the ANSI C section earlier in this chapter.)

For more information on WinCGI, you can look at the O'Reilly & Associates, Inc. Windows CGI 1.3a Interface at http://website.ora.com/32demo/windows-cgi.htm/.

Guest Book Example in ANSI C

The Guest Book example is a longer example that includes familiar processes, such as reading and writing to a file. Some of the information, however, is specific to writing a

CGI program. This example is provided not only to give a complete example of a CGI program for your review, but also to enable a comparison with NSAPI (Chapter 9) and WAI (Chapter 16) examples.

You may find a Guest Book example in a variety of books. This useful program illustrates a number of commonly practiced programming tasks. The following features are covered: getting environment variables, reading and verifying client data from a form, dealing with a POST method of request, decoding a URL-encoded string, updating a file with data sent by the client, reading from a file, and formatting the data before sending it to the client. Many of these techniques are used whenever you are programming for a server. For example, decoding the URL is done for all client requests originating from a form.

The purpose of the following program is twofold: (1) It obtains client input and adds it to a Guest Book, and (2) it reads the updated Guest Book file, formats it in a table, and returns it to the client. Figure 3-3 shows the input form.

The HTML code for creating the Guest Book form is given in Listing 3-7.

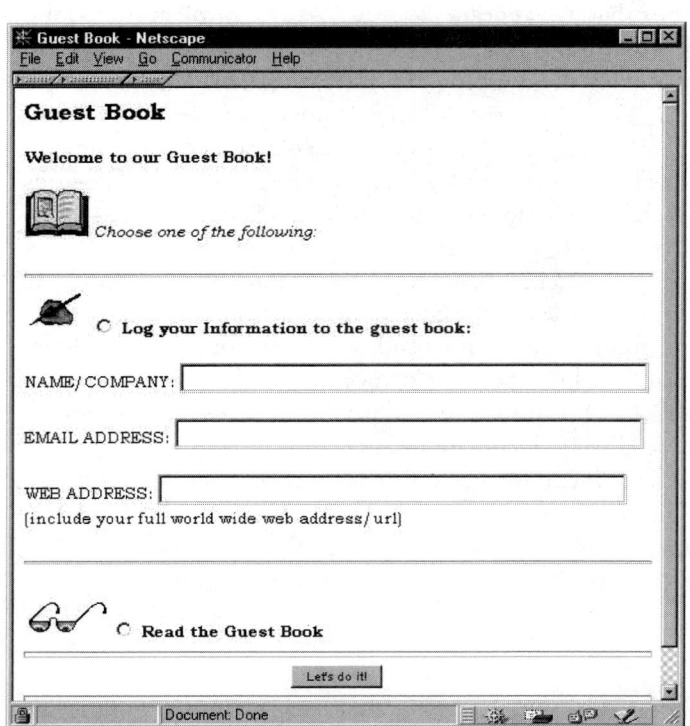

Figure 3-3   Guest Book Form

Listing 3-7   HTML File for the CGI Guest Book Form

```
<HTML>
<HEAD>
<TITLE>Guest Book</TITLE>
</HEAD>
<BODY>

<H1>Guest Book</H1>

<H4>Welcome to our Guest Book!</H4>

<IMG SRC="book.gif">

<I>Choose one of the following:</I>

<FORM method=POST action="cgi/guest.exe">

<HR>
<IMG SRC="hand.gif">
<INPUT TYPE="radio" NAME="action" VALUE="log">
<B>Log your information into the Guest Book:</B>
<P>
NAME/COMPANY:
  <INPUT TYPE="text" NAME="ename" SIZE=39 MAXLENGTH=39>
<P>
EMAIL ADDRESS:
  <INPUT TYPE="text" NAME="email" SIZE=39 MAXLENGTH=39>
<P>
WEB ADDRESS:
  <INPUT TYPE="text" NAME="web" SIZE=39 MAXLENGTH=39>
<BR>(<I>Include your full World Wide Web address/URL.</I>)

<P>
<HR>
<P><IMG SRC="glasses.gif">
<INPUT TYPE="radio" NAME="action" VALUE="read">
<B>View the Guest Book</B>

<HR SIZE=4>

<CENTER><INPUT TYPE="submit" VALUE=" Submit "></CENTER>
<HR SIZE=6>
</FORM>

</BODY>
</HTML>
```

Let's look first at the INPUT fields in Listing 3-7. The radio button INPUT is identified as INPUT TYPE="radio". There are two radio buttons, both named action but with different values. When the user chooses the radio button on the HTML page, the chosen value is returned (for example, action=log). In the case of radio buttons, if none is chosen, this variable is not returned. You can choose to turn one into the default checked button by adding the CHECKED attribute to its INPUT field. For this example, there is no default button selected. The other variables are received from the client input in the text box field. INPUT TYPE="text" defines the text box, with the size defining the size of the text box. It is important to keep this size to a reasonable input limit. Additionally, MAXLENGTH is used to limit the number of characters the client can directly input in each field. You define the name of the input types in the HTML page. The value is what the client inputs. For example, for NAME, the client can input kaveh@imagia.com. The browser returns ename=kaveh@foo.com. When the client submits a page, all text variables are sent back to the server, even when no data are typed in. Also, the order of the variables returned by the client is the same as the order of the INPUT fields as they appear on the HTML page. Therefore, if the first radio button in Listing 3-7 is chosen, the first variable sent to the server is action=log, and the fourth variable is web=[client input]. If the second radio button is chosen, when the user wants to read the Guest Book, the first variable is ename=[user input]. Thus action=read is the fourth variable.

The method of the request is defined in the FORM tag attribute, METHOD. The ACTION attribute points to the location of the CGI program. Because the result of this form is sent with the POST method, the client input is sent after the request header files as standard input (stdin). This method also safeguards you from any user returning data by adding it at the end of a URL instead of through a form. With a POST method of request, the client needs to use a form to send the data. As you can see, much information sent by the client is already predefined by the form's limitations. Therefore, these values conform to your definitions. This strategy avoids the need for extensive error checking of these predefined variables. For example, you will know that the name of the radio button will be action, in lowercase, and the value can be only log or read, again in lowercase. What is not predefined is the value of the text input fields.

Although value checking is provided in this CGI program, it is best to use JavaScript on the client side to provide verification of client input fields. This approach puts the load of error checking on the client's machine. It also provides a more effective and efficient error response. With a CGI program, errors are returned to the client only after the client has submitted the page (the form data). Moreover, a new HTML page must be returned to the client with the error information. The client must then return to the original page to resend the correct data. With JavaScript, an error message box pops up, informing the client of any error as it occurs, even before the client sends the HTML page. Figure 3-4 displays the page that a client receives when information has been sent correctly and adequately to the server.

Figure 3-5 shows an example of a guest book that may appear when the client requests to "View the Guest Book."

Listing 3-8 provides the code for the Guest Book example. There are many ways to

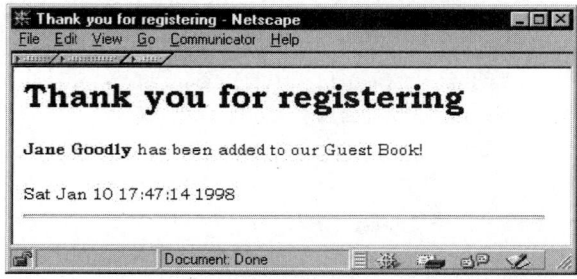

Figure 3-4   Thank You Page

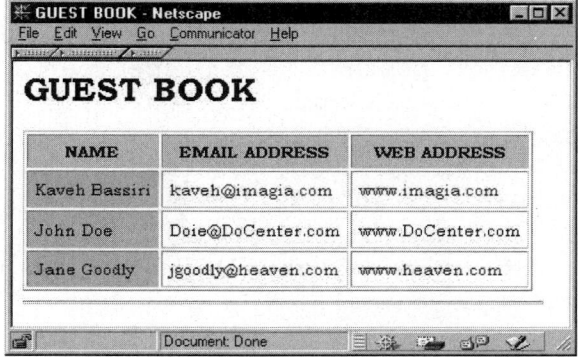

Figure 3-5   Guest Book Information

write a guest book—Listing 3-8 is merely one option. You may want to explore and write your own program. In our explanation of the code, we will indicate some alternatives in writing your guest book.

To implement this example, you must update the URL path of the Guest Book file in this program. Next, compile this file with your C compiler. Place the executable program in your CGI directory. (Make sure CGI is correctly enabled. See the ANSI C section earlier in this chapter for more details.) Next, place the Guest Book HTML pages in your document directory. Update the link on the HTML page to the location of the CGI program under your server. (Do not forget to copy the graphics as well.) You can find the program and the images in the accompanying CD-ROM. The complete program is separated, for ease of discussion, into Listings 3-8-1 through 3-8-4.

Listing 3-8-1   CGI Guest Book Main Function

```
/* Reading the client input, verifying the form data and
   returning an HTML page to the client.
 */
```

Listing 3-8-1 CGI Guest Book Main Function (*continued*)

```c
#include <stdio.h>      /* printf, fread, fwrite, etc. */
#include <stdlib.h>     /* malloc, getenv, free */
#include <string.h>     /* string functions */
#include <sys/timeb.h>  /* for adding the time to the
                           confirmation page returned to the
                           user */

#include <time.h>

/*----------------- DEFINES -----------------*/

/* In the following three constants, I define a specific
   set of numbers that I expect from the input.
   MAX_CONTENT_LENGTH is maximum content to be received
   from the POST.MAXLENGTH is the maximum length of each
   field input--that is, size of value of each name=value
   input. This is based on the value of the SIZE and
   MAXLENGTH attribute of INPUT (TYPE="TEXT") tags in the
   HTML page.  FIELDNUM is the maximum number of
   name=value input pairs expected. For this example,
   there are four pairs: action, ename, email, and eweb.
 */
#define MAX_CONTENT_LENGTH 300
#define MAXLENGTH 40
#define FIELDNUM 4

/* The path to the Guest Book file. You need to change
   this path to the path of the file on your machine. "\"
   is used to escape a backslash (\).
 */
#define GUESTBOOK_FILE \
   "c:/netscape/server/guests/gestlst.txt"

/* ----------------- DATA STRUCTURE -----------------*/

/* Structure to hold information from the form. I use
   pointers.You can use string arrays to avoid using
   malloc.
*/
typedef struct DATA
{
  char *name;
  char *mail;
  char *www_address;

}FORM_DATA;
```

Listing 3-8-1 CGI Guest Book Main Function (*continued*)

```c
/*----------------FUNCTION PROTOTYPES ----------------*/
int Append_Guest_File (struct DATA *user_form, char *path);
int Read_Guest_File (char **guestlist, char *path);
void error(char *error_string);
int parsing(char *string, char * name[], char *value[]);
void Remove_HTTP_Escapes(char *src, char *dest);
int HexToInt(int digit);

/*-------------------------------------------*/
/*---------------- main ----------------*/
int main(int argc, char *argv[])
{
    char *action = NULL;        /* holds the value of action,
                                   that is, log or read */
    char *query = NULL;         /* holds the client input */
    char *list = NULL;          /* the Guest Book information
                                   in the guest list file
                                   displayed in a table for
                                   the client to review */

    int  ichar = 1;             /* number of char in client input */
    struct _timeb timebuffer;   /* used to set time; time is
                                   added to Thank You page sent
                                   back to client */

    char *timeline;
    FORM_DATA *user_data;       /* holds the information from
                                   user */

    int clengthNumber;          /* size of the content sent by
                                   client in integer */
    char *clengthString=NULL;   /* length of the content sent
                                   by client in string format */
    int fields;                 /* number of fields in client input */

    char *name[FIELDNUM];       /* name of the fields in client's
                                   [name]=[value] input */

    char *value[FIELDNUM];      /* value of the fields in client's
                                   [name]=[value] input */

    /* Get the method type from the environment variable.
       We want only POST.
     */
    char *RequestMethod = getenv("REQUEST_METHOD");
```

Listing 3-8-1   CGI Guest Book Main Function (*continued*)

```
/* get the content type */
char *Content-Type = getenv("CONTENT_TYPE");

/* get the content length */
clengthString = getenv("CONTENT_LENGTH");

/* By sending the content-type in the beginning of the
   program we make sure that the CGI program will not
   be timed-out. Also, we send back an HTML page even
   in case of error, so the content-type does not
   change and can be set once.
 */
printf("content-type: text/html\n\n");

/* check on the method of the request */
if(strcmp(RequestMethod, "POST") != 0)
{
    /* Send error page if it is not POST. Error function
       deals with sending the page. You pass the string
       that describes the error to the client. Make sure
       there is no space after the "\".
     */
    error("<H1>Not a POST request</H1>\n \
          <STRONG>You need to submit the data using a \
          form.</STRONG>\n");
}

/* Check on the type of content requested. We expect only
   "application/x-www-form-urlencoded" for the POST
   method.
 */
if(strcmp(Content-Type, "application/x-www-form-urlencoded")
        != 0)
{
    /* Send error page if the type is incorrect--that
       is, if it is not data from a form. This rarely
       happens.
     */
    error("<H1>Content Type is Wrong</H1>\n \
          <STRONG>The Content Type your browser sent is \
          not correct.</STRONG>");
}

/* check on content length */
```

Listing 3-8-1   CGI Guest Book Main Function (*continued*)

```
if(!clengthString)
{
    /* send error page if content is missing */
    error("<H1>Content missing</H1>\n \
          <STRONG>There was no content sent.</STRONG>\n");
}

/* get the actual number for the content length in int.
   Content length is sent as string. */
clengthNumber = atoi(clengthString);

/* More content length checking. See if length is more
   than 0 and less than the maximum you set. This is use-
   ful if you want to limit the size of data you will
   receive.
 */
if((clengthNumber >= MAX_CONTENT_LENGTH) ||
   (clengthNumber < 1))
{
    /* send error page if content is not the right size */
    error("<H1>Content Length is not right.</H1>\n \
          <STRONG>The content of data your browser sent is \
          either empty or too long.</STRONG>\n");
}

/* query holds the content of the data sent by client */
query = (char *) malloc ((clengthNumber + 1) *
                          sizeof(char));

/* Read the data into the query. Read the data from
   standard input. Read number of bytes defined by
   clengthNumber.
 */
ichar = fread(query, sizeof(char), clengthNumber, stdin);

/* end the string of data we got with a NULL character */
query[ichar] = '\0';

/* Make sure all other data were received by verifying
   them against the expected length of the input. You
   can use ferror and feof to get the exact error, if
   you want to report it.
 */
if(ichar != clengthNumber)
{
```

Listing 3-8-1 CGI Guest Book Main Function (*continued*)

```
    /* free the malloced variables before exiting */
    free(query);

    /* send error page if the all data were not received */
    error("<H1>Content data read error</H1>\n \
        <STRONG>Was not able to correctly read all \
            the content.</STRONG>\n");
}

/* Parsing function parses the [name]=[value] input from
    the client. We send the query. The function updates
    the name and value array of string with the parsed
    variables.  It also returns the number of the
    variables. Even when the client requests to "read"
    the Guest Book, the variables email, ename, and eweb
    are sent. But the values of the variables are empty
    if the client has not input any data.
 */
fields = parsing(query, name, value);

/* make sure everything worked with the parsing
    function and we got the variables
 */
if(fields <= 0)
{
    free(query);

    /* If no pairs were sent, then something went wrong and
        we return an error page. We expect to get the
        variable pairs when a form is used, even if the
        client makes no input request.
     */
    error("<H1>An error occurred while verifying \
        the information</H1>\n \
        <STRONG>We were not able to process \
        your input correctly.</STRONG>\n");
}

/* Radio button field information (action=[value]) is not
    sent if the radio button is not chosen. Therefore, the
    number of fields will be less than 4. We check for
    this and require the client to choose a button. Today
    JavaScript does a better job of verifying field
    existence and value.
 */
```

Listing 3-8-1 CGI Guest Book Main Function (*continued*)

```
if(fields == 3)
{
    free(query);

   /* send an error requiring the client to choose a
      button */
   error("<H1>You did not select an action.</H1> \
        <STRONG>No radio button was picked.
        </STRONG>");
}

/* Action holds the type of action the client is
   requesting. Since this variable can be only "log" or
   "read", you can set the size to 5 characters.
 */
action = (char *) malloc (MAXLENGTH * sizeof(char));

/* Check for the value of "action". It is set in the
   first name (starting number is 0), if the client
   chooses to input information (update the Guest Book)
   and in the fourth name if the client requests to
   read the Guest Book. The order of the other
   variables does not change.
 */
/* if the first name is action */
if(strcmp(name[0], "action") == 0)
{
        /* This function replaces extended characters
           that appear in Hex with the equivalent ASCII
           characters and also replaces "+" with a
           space. What is returned is the value of the
           first variable. (This process is part of URL
           decoding.)
         */
        Remove_HTTP_Escapes(value[0], action);
}
/* if the first name is not action, check the third name */
else if(strcmp(name[3], "action") == 0)
{
        Remove_HTTP_Escapes(value[3], action);
}

/* if action is read, the guest file is read and
   formatted in an HTML table and sent to the client
```

Listing 3-8-1   CGI Guest Book Main Function (*continued*)

```
    */
if(strcmp(action, "read") == 0)
{
    /* malloc space for the guest list; make this large
       enough to hold the size of the information in
       the file and any extra HTML tags that are added
     */
    list = (char *) malloc(10000 * sizeof(char));

    /* set the list to blank */
    strcpy(list, "");

    /* call the Read_Guest_File function, which fills the
       list string with the information in the file
       formatted as HTML table
     */
    if(Read_Guest_File(&list, GUESTBOOK_FILE) == 0)
    {
        /* Document to be sent back to the client. List
           holds the dynamic data from the file.
         */
        printf("<HTML><HEAD><TITLE>GUEST \
                BOOK</TITLE></HEAD>\n");
        printf("<BODY BGCOLOR=FFFFFF>;
        printf("<H1>GUEST BOOK</H1>\n");
        printf("<TABLE BORDER CELLPADDING=5>\n");
        printf("<TR><TH BGCOLOR=C0C0C0>NAME<BR>");
        printf("</TH>\n");
        printf("<TH BGCOLOR=C0C0C0>EMAIL ADDRESS<BR>");
        printf("</TH>\n");
        printf("<TH BGCOLOR=C0C0C0>WEB ADDRESS<BR>");
        printf("</TH>\n");
        printf("</TR>\n");
        printf("%s", list);
        printf("</TABLE>\n");
        printf("<HR></BODY></HTML>");

        free(list);
    }
    else
    {
        /* Send an error in case Read_Guest_File failed.
           Normally, the errors in this function are
```

Listing 3-8-1 CGI Guest Book Main Function (*continued*)

```
                    handled inside it and the function exits the
                    program.
                */
                free(query);
                free(action);
                error("<H1>Sorry, an error occurred</H1>\n \
                       <STRONG>Could not read the guest \
                       file.</STRONG>");
            }
        }
        /* if the request is log, then read and parse the
           client's input, place it in the log file, and send
           back a Thank You letter
         */
        else if(strcmp(action, "log") == 0)
        {
                /* Malloc for the structure and all the fields.
                   Client data are placed in this data structure.
                 */
                user_data = (FORM_DATA *) malloc(sizeof(FORM_DATA));

                user_data->name = (char *) malloc(MAXLENGTH *
                                  sizeof(char));
                user_data->mail = (char *) malloc(MAXLENGTH *
                                  sizeof(char));
                user_data->www_address = (char *) malloc(MAXLENGTH
                                          * sizeof(char));

                /* This function parses the value and copies it
                   into the user_data structure. It replaces
                   extended characters that appear in Hex with
                   the equivalent ASCII character and replaces
                   "+" with a space.(This process is part of
                   URL decoding.)
                 */
                Remove_HTTP_Escapes(value[1], user_data->name);
                Remove_HTTP_Escapes(value[2], user_data->mail);
                Remove_HTTP_Escapes(value[3],
                                    user_data->www_address);

            /* Make sure that the input data from the client
               include at least the user name and email. You can
               also use JavaScript to do this.
             */
```

Listing 3-8-1 CGI Guest Book Main Function (*continued*)

```
if ((strcmp(user_data->name, "void") == 0) ||
    (strcmp(user_data->mail, "void") == 0) ||
    (*user_data->name == '\0') ||
    (*user_data->mail == '\0'))
{
    /* if the client missed the name or email field,
       ask the user to try again
     */
    free(query);
    free(action);
    free(user_data->name);
    free(user_data->mail);
    free(user_data->www_address);
    free(user_data);

    error("<H1>You did not fill out the form \
            completely.</H1> \
            <STRONG> You must at least include a name \
            and an e-mail address</STRONG>");
}
/* Update the Guest Book and send back a Thank You
   page. If updating of the file failed, return an
   error page. Append_Guest_File returns 0 upon
   success.
 */
if(Append_Guest_File(user_data, GUESTBOOK_FILE) == 0)
{
    /* time function for adding the time and date to
       the end of the HTML page
     */
    _ftime( &timebuffer );
    timeline = ctime( & ( timebuffer.time ) );

    /* thank you page to be sent to the client */
    printf("<HTML><HEAD><TITLE>Thank \
            you</TITLE></HEAD>\n");
    printf("<BODY><H1>Thank you!</H1>\n");
    printf("<B>%s</B> has been added to our Guest \
            Book!\n", user_data->name);
    printf("<P>%s\n", timeline);
    printf("<HR></BODY></HTML>");
}
else
```

Listing 3-8-1   CGI Guest Book Main Function (*continued*)

```
    {
        /* free variables before returning an error
           page
         */
        free(query);
        free(action);
        free(user_data->name);
        free(user_data->mail);
        free(user_data->www_address);
        free(user_data);

        error("<H1>Sorry, an error occurred</H1>\n \
                <STRONG>we weren't able to add you to the \
                Guest Book.</STRONG>");
    }

    /* free the structure and its data (specific to
       updating the Guest Book)
     */
    free(user_data->name);
    free(user_data->mail);
    free(user_data->www_address);
    free(user_data);
}
/* if action is neither log nor read, return an error
   page */
else
{
    free(query);
    free(action);

    error("<H1>Your form requested an invalid action.\
    </H1> <STRONG>Could not verify the data.</STRONG>");
}

/* free more variables */
free(query);
free(action);

/* return success */
return 0;
}
```

Listing 3-8-2 CGI Guest Book Utility Functions

```
/*----------- error -----------------------------------*/
/* This function returns an error page to the client. The
   error_string is customized by the calling function
   (where the error occurs). We use environment variable
   HTTP_REFERER to get the URL of the form. This
   environment variable holds the last URL.
 */
void error(char *error_string)
{
        char *formURL;

        formURL = getenv("HTTP_REFERER");

    printf("<HTML><HEAD><TITLE>Error</TITLE></HEAD>\n");
    printf("<BODY>%s", error_string);
    printf("<HR><P>Return to the <A HREF=\"%s\">", formURL);
    printf("Guest Book Form.</A>");
    printf("</BODY></HTML>");

    /* exit with error */
    exit(1);
}

/*----------- parsing -----------------------------------*/
/*  Parses the string sent to it, by separating pairs of
    variables (divided by "&") and by separating the
    [name] and [value](divided by a "=" sign). It then
    places the result in the name and value array of
    strings. The function also returns the number of
    variables it finds.
 */
int parsing(char *temp, char *name[], char *value[])
{
    int fieldnum = 0;

    while(*temp)
    {
        /* have the name point to the temp */
        name[fieldnum] = temp;

        /* go down the string until we find a "=" sign, at
           which time we put a NULL pointer in temp string--
           that is, NULL terminate the name string
         */
```

Listing 3-8-2   CGI Guest Book Utility Functions (*continued*)

```
while(*temp)
{
    if(*temp == '=')
    {
        *temp = '\0';
        temp++;

        /* get out of the loop */
        break;
    }
    else
    {
        temp++;
    }
}

/* set the temp to point to the value string */
value[fieldnum] = temp;

/* We look for "&", which divides the value from the
   next name. We put a NULL terminator at the end of
   the string, which also terminates the value
   string.
 */
while(*temp)
{
    if(*temp == '&')
    {
        *temp = '\0';
        temp++;
        break;
    }
    else
    {
        temp++;
    }
}

/* increase the number of variables */
fieldnum++;

/* We don't want more than four pairs of values. If
   there are more, return -1, which is interpreted
   as an error.
 */
```

Listing 3-8-2   CGI Guest Book Utility Functions (*continued*)

```
        if(fieldnum > FIELDNUM)
        {
            return -1;
        }
    }

    /* return the number of array of [name]=[value] */
    return fieldnum;
}

/*---------- Remove_HTTP_Escapes ---------------------*/
/* Removes the URL encoding of the name or value string.
   Replaces a "+" in the string (src) sent to the function.
   It also checks for Hex characters in the string and
   replaces them with equivalent ASCII characters. The
   result is placed in dest string.
 */
void Remove_HTTP_Escapes(char *src, char *dest)
{
    /* check for '+' and replace it with space */
    while(*src)
    {
        if(*src == '+')
        {
            *dest = ' ';
        }
        /* else check for '%' */
        else if(*src == '%')
        {
            int value;

            /* use HexToInt to transfer src to int */
            src++;
            value =  HexToInt(*src) * 16;
            src++;
            value += HexToInt(*src);
            *dest = value;
        }
        else
        {
            /* otherwise src and dest string are the same */
            *dest = *src;
        }
```

Listing 3-8-2   CGI Guest Book Utility Functions (*continued*)

```
        src++;
        dest++;
    }

    /* terminate the result string */
    *dest = '\0';
}

/*------------------- HexToInt -----------------------*/
/* This function turns Hex values into integers and is used
   by Remove_HTTP_Escapes to replace the Hex value with the
   ASCII character.
 */
int HexToInt(int digit)
{
    int value = 0;

    /* check for the Hex range and do the conversion */
    if(digit >= '0' && digit <= '9')
    {
        value = digit - '0';
    }
    else if(digit >= 'A' && digit <= 'F' )
    {
        value = digit - 'A' + 10;
    }

    /* return the integer in decimal */
    return value;
}
```

Listing 3-8-3   CGI Guest Book Read Function

```
/*-------------- Read_Guest_File ---------------------*/
/* This function reads the file gestlst.txt, formats the
   data in the file in an HTML table, and returns the result
   in a string by way of the parameter, guestlist. Pointer
   to a pointer string is used to update the calling string
   directly from this function. The function returns 0 if
   it was successful.
 */
int Read_Guest_File(char **guestlist, char *path)
{
    /* Table formatting HTML tags */
```

Listing 3-8-3 CGI Guest Book Read Function (*continued*)

```c
/* Beginning and end of a table field. <BR> allows for a
   better display of empty cells and for browsers that
   cannot display tables. Table cells for the name of
   the guests will be in color.
 */
#define BEGINITEM       "\n <TD>"
#define BEGINITEMCOLOR  "\n <TD BGCOLOR=#D2B48C>"
#define ENDITEM         "<BR></TD>"

/* beginning and end of a table row */
#define BEGINROW    "\n<TR>"
#define ENDROW      "\n</TR>"

/* enable e-mail and Web address link as hypertext */
#define BEGINMAIL  "<A HREF=\"mailto:"
#define BEGINLINK  "<A HREF=\"http://"
#define ENDLINK    "\">"
#define ENDREF     "</A>"

FILE *fd;                  /* file handle (descriptor) */
int  lnum = 1;            /* number of line in the file */
int  num;                 /* holds the switch/case value */
char line[MAXLENGTH + 1]; /* holds each line of info */

/* open and read the file pointed to by the path */
fd=fopen(path, "rt");

/* check for any system error in opening the file */
if(fd == NULL)
{
    /* send an error page if file was not opened */
    error("<H1>Could not open the file to read from \
           it.</H1>");
}

    /* Read each line of data until no more remain, one
       character at a time. We expect no more than
       MAXLENGTH + 1 (includes the line feed) for each
       line.
     */
    while(fgets(line, (MAXLENGTH + 1), fd) != NULL)
    {
        /* send an error message if an error occurs
           while reading the file
```

Listing 3-8-3   CGI Guest Book Read Function (*continued*)

```
    */
if(ferror(fd))
{
    /* close the file handle and send an
       error page
     */
    fclose(fd);

    error("<H1>Error reading the file.</H1>");
}

/* modulus operator is used to separate each
   line of the file into groups of three
 */
num = lnum % 3;

/* Read each line and place it in the guestlist
   string. Also format it with the correct tags.
 */
switch(num)
{
    /* first line includes the name of the user */
    case 1:
    {
        strcat(*guestlist, BEGINROW);
        strcat(*guestlist, BEGINITEMCOLOR);
        strncat(*guestlist, line,
                (strlen(line)) -1);
        strcat(*guestlist, ENDITEM);
        break;
    }
    /* second line include the e-mail address,
       which is also made into hypertext.
     */
    case 2:
    {
        strcat(*guestlist, BEGINITEM);
        strcat(*guestlist, BEGINMAIL);
        strncat(*guestlist, line,
                (strlen(line)) -1);
        strcat(*guestlist, ENDLINK);
        strncat(*guestlist, line,
                (strlen(line)) -1);
        strcat(*guestlist, ENDREF);
```

Listing 3-8-3   CGI Guest Book Read Function (*continued*)

```
                              strcat(*guestlist, ENDITEM);
                              break;
                    }
                    /* last line includes the Web address, which
                       is also made into hypertext
                     */
                    default:
                    {
                         strcat(*guestlist, BEGINITEM);
                         strcat(*guestlist, BEGINLINK);
                         strncat(*guestlist, line,
                                    (strlen(line)) -1);
                         strcat(*guestlist, ENDLINK);
                         strncat(*guestlist, line,
                                    (strlen(line)) -1);
                         strcat(*guestlist, ENDREF);
                         strcat(*guestlist, ENDITEM);
                         strcat(*guestlist, ENDROW);
                         break;
                    }
               }

               ++lnum;
          }

     /* guestlist gets freed through 'list' in the calling
        function
      */

     /* close the file */
     fclose(fd);

     /* 0 is returned when the function is successful */
     return 0;
}
```

Listing 3-8-4   CGI Guest Book Append Function

```
/*------- Update the guest file with client input -------*/
/*---------- APPEND_GUEST_FILE ------------------------*/
```

/* This function appends the guest file pointed to by the
   path parameter with the client input defined in user_form
   data structure. Each line of the structure is placed in
   a separate line in the file. As an enhancement, you can

Listing 3-8-4 CGI Guest Book Append Function (*continued*)

```
      update this function with a system lock of the file to
      make sure no other server thread will attempt to write
      to the file at the same time. This function returns 0
      upon success.
 */
int Append_Guest_File(struct DATA *user_form, char *path)
{
    FILE *fd;           /* file handle (descriptor) */
    int ret;            /* length of userinfo string */
    char *userinfo;     /* a string holding user information */

    /* open the file for appending the data */
    fd=fopen(path, "a+t");

    /* check for system error */
    if( fd == NULL)
    {
        /* Send back an error page if the file could not be
           opened for appending of the data. Then exit the
           program.
         */
        error("<H1>Could open the file to \
              write to it.</H1>");
    }

    /* Malloc userinfo to the max size of the user informa-
       tion fields combined. You can use strlen of each of
       the variables to get a more exact number for the size.
     */
    userinfo = (char *) malloc(((MAXLENGTH * 3) + 1) *
                                sizeof(char));

    /* Place all user data into one string. The \n puts each
       separate field into a separate line in the file.
     */
    sprintf(userinfo, "%s\n%s\n%s\n", user_form->name,
                  user_form->mail, user_form->www_address);

    /* put the string in the file */
    ret = fputs(userinfo, fd);

    /* check the return value of the fputs function to make
       sure the data were appended into the file
     */
    if(ret < 0)
```

Listing 3-8-4 CGI Guest Book Append Function (*continued*)

```
{
    /* send back an error page if an error occurred
       while writing to the file
     */
    error("<H1>Could not write to the file.</H1>");
}

/* close the file */
fclose(fd);

/* free userinfo data structure now that we are finished
   with it
 */
free(userinfo);

/* 0 means everything went OK */
return 0;
}
```

Stepping Through the Guest Book Example

There are five major sections to this program. We will begin with the first section of the Guest Book program, Listing 3-8-1. The **main** function reads the client input, verifies the type of request (in this program, a POST method), and receives the client input from the standard input stream. This procedure is broad enough to be applied to any program that attempts to respond to a POST request. The **main** function provides the general-purpose algorithm for getting the client input. Later, **main** calls other, more specific functions to accomplish the requested actions. These subsequent functions go through steps that vary depending upon the actual request.

The major section of this program (Listing 3-8-2) takes care of sending the error response, as well as the parsing of the data sent by the client. These general-purpose functions can also be used by any program you may write. By writing these utility functions and storing them in a specific file, you can then include them in any number of programs.

You can also write a general-purpose **main** function, based on the one in this program, that, with the utility functions, parses the client input for any type of form and passes the parsed variables to your specific function. Another function you can write can then access these variables to carry out the purpose of your program, using the particulars of the client request. Organizing tasks in this way allows you to share a **main** function, which verifies and parses client's data, to process various forms. Again, this approach reduces redundant code. Of course, the **main** function needs to identify which specific functions to call. You can pass the label or name of the function through the form, or you can have the function use the HTML page through which the server sent the request as the identifying token. If you wish to keep each form's response code separate, you can recompile your function with the generic **main** function and the utility functions to derive a different executable CGI program. In this example, however, the **main** function is designed to process one form, the Guest Book. It includes only the specifics of finishing such a request. In Chapter 9, we will write an NSAPI program that takes advantage of a shared main function to process two separate forms.

The third and fourth sections of our program (Listings 3-8-3 and 3-8-4) are not unique to HTTP server programming. These common C functions read from the Guest Book and append the client input to the Guest Book.

Back in the **main** function (Listing 3-8-1), the fifth and final section to our program finishes the processing of the request by verifying the client input. It calls the functions in Listings 3-8-3 and 3-8-4 and returns an HTML page to the client. This part of **main** is unique to the request (form). If the client chooses to add a name to the guest book, the **main** function calls the function in Listing 3-8-4 (**Append_Guest_File**) and adds the information to the Guest Book. The **main** function then returns a Thank You page. If the client chooses to see the Guest Book, **main** calls the function in Listing 3-8-3 (**Read_Guest_File**), which formats the data found in the file for an HTML table. The **main** function then returns an HTML page with the table of the guests' information to the client.

Let us look at the program in detail. Listing 3-8-1 begins with familiar information, such as the include files (standard libraries) and define preprocessor directives needed for the program. We use the define directives to define MAX_CONTENT_LENGTH, MAXLENGTH, FIELDNUM, and GUESTBOOK_FILE. MAX_CONTENT_LENGTH is the maximum length of the client input that is accepted, in case the data become too large. There is also a maximum length for the data from each input field (MAXLENGTH) and a maximum number of variable pairs expected from the client's form (FIELDNUM). You can change these numbers to suit your specific needs. (This program does not check the size of each client's input text against MAXLENGTH. We assume that the data will not be more than 39 characters because we used MAXLENGTH attribute in the INPUT tag to limit the client input.) GUESTBOOK_FILE points to the location of the Guest Book file.

In Listing 3-8-1, at the beginning of the **main** function, after declaring the appropriate variables, we get the various environment variables. The getenv([*environment variable name*]) function is used to get the environment variables. We make sure the request method is actually POST by using the **strcmp** function and comparing the

> **Note ▶**
>
> It is important to change the location of the Guest Book file in the code to match the location of the file on your machine. Otherwise, the program will not be able to find the file it needs. The location of this file can be anywhere that is accessible to your operating system. The server, however, needs to have the appropriate read and write permissions for the location.

request variable in REQUEST_METHOD with the string we expect, "POST". If it is 0, they are the same. The value of this variable is set by the METHOD attribute of the FORM tag sent by the client's form. We know, therefore, that it should be "POST" in uppercase. In fact, we know all the variable names sent by the client, plus the value of the action that the client can choose. These parameters are all defined internally in the form and are not dynamically altered by the client. A POST method of request is different from a GET method. With the POST method, the client's data are available through the standard input. (With the GET method, the data are sent in the QUERY_STRING environment variable.)

Before reading the information sent by the POST method, we make sure it was correctly sent and processed. We do the same for data sent by the client and the CONTENT_TYPE environment variable. The POST method returns the CONTENT_LENGTH environment variable, which is a string that holds the length of the body of the request. CONTENT_LENGTH is used to verify if anything actually was sent and that the data do not exceed the size we expect. (MAX_CONTENT_LENGTH limits the size of the content.) Since the variable is a string, we use **atoi** to convert the string into an integer. (The server also uses CONTENT_LENGTH to allocate the space needed for the client request before reading the data.) CONTENT_TYPE for a POST method should be application/x-www-form-urlencoded. The program does not handle anything else. (It is unlikely that a different content type is sent, because, generally, no other type of form input is supported.) If the content length is NULL (the server received no data) or if the content type is incorrect, an error message is sent.

After allocating memory for the client's data, we read it from the standard input. In this program, **fread** is used to read the complete length of the data from stdin in one step. There are other options for reading the data as well. The **fgetc** function, for example, reads the data one character at a time. With **fgetc**, you can parse the data as you read the characters from the standard input. **fread** suits our intended purpose. We will then verify and parse the data. Before parsing the string of data from standard input, the size of the data returned by the **fread** function is compared with the CONTENT_LENGTH to ensure that we received all of the data. Next, we terminate the string. These stages of reading and verifying data constitute the customary steps in responding to a POST request.

You might have noticed that in the beginning of the **main** function (after getting the environment variables), the content type was returned. By sending content-type early on, we make sure that the CGI program will not be timed-out. This program returns only HTML pages, even in case of error, so the content-type is always the same, text/html. We also no longer need to send the content-type each time we send back a page (for example, in case of error, or when we send the Thank You page). Another method of controlling the timeout of a CGI function is through the **Init** function **init-cgi**. With the parameter timeout, you can specify the number of seconds that the server waits for CGI output before terminating the program.

As seen in Listing 3-8-2, the **error** function prints out the text string (passed on as its parameter), which explains the specific nature of the error. If any errors occur, an

HTML page is returned through the **printf** function. The **error** function also uses the environment variable, HTTP_REFERER, to get the Guest Book input form's URL. A hyperlink to the Guest Book form is created. HTTP_REFERER holds the last URL— in this case, the URL of the Guest Book form page. This setup allows the user to re-attempt filling out the form and reinitiate the CGI program. Finally, we exit the program, using **exit(1)** when an error occurred.

The second utility function in Listing 3-8-2, the parsing function, is where the POST input string (query) is reformatted. There are four steps in URL decoding (parsing a URL-encoded string):

1. Separate all [name]=[value] pairs.

2. Separate [name] and [value] from one another.

3. Replace the + character with a space for all variables.

4. Replace Hex characters with the equivalent ASCII characters for all variables.

To separate the [name]=[value] pairs, the ampersand (&) character, which divides each pair, is identified and removed. Separation of [name] and [value] occurs by identifying the equal sign (=) in each pair. Steps 1 and 2 are accomplished through the **parsing** function. This function separates the string pointed to by the first parameter (temp) and places the result in the name and value arrays of strings (its second and third parameters). name and value are defined in the **main** function and passed on to this function as an address to the array of strings. Thus the **parsing** function can change the value of the name and value in the calling function (**main**). The **parsing** function goes through the temp string to get each variable's name and value. The main while loop (while(*temp)) is used to step through all the characters. The temp string is terminated with a null pointer when it reaches either an equal sign for name or an ampersand for value. This step also terminates the name or value variables, which point to the same temp string.

Once the main loop gets to the end of the string, the parsing function checks the number of variables. If the fieldnum is more than 4, then it sets the number to –1. The number should be either 3 or 4. Any other number is an error. The function returns the number of variables (fieldnum). The **main** function confirms that the number is not less than 0, otherwise it sends an error page to the client. If the return value is 3, the client has not chosen a radio button. Unlike the other (text) input fields sent by the client, a radio button is not sent to the server by the browser if it is not chosen. Instead, we return an error message to the client informing the user that a button must be selected.

Continuing through Listing 3-8-2, the last two parsing steps are completed by the **Remove_HTTP_Escapes** function. This function looks for any plus (+) character and replaces it with a space character. It also checks for Hex characters and replaces them with the equivalent ASCII characters. When the client sends text input, the browser encodes the value by replacing spaces with plus characters and most nondigit or alphabetical characters with the equivalent Hex values. For example, yes!#$%^ is replaced with yes%21%23%24%25%5E. The string is passed to **Remove_HTTP_Escapes** through its first parameter, src. It sends back the decoded string by updating its second parameter, dest. It calls the **HexToInt** function to change the Hex value to the equivalent ASCII character. It sends to the **HexToInt** function each integer or character of the Hex value after the % symbol. The result is then interpreted as an ASCII character and placed in the string. Once the function goes through the entire source (src) string, it terminates the destination (dest) string with a null pointer.

You can also use a structure to hold the pairs of variables sent by the client. In Listing 3-9, the **parsing** function has been altered to incorporate a structure. This modification is an easy task if you define the structure as a global structure that holds all name and variable pairs. The **parsing** function here alters the members of the global structure. The **main** function then accesses the variables through this same structure after the **parsing** function is called. We simply copy the first character of the temp string (which holds the client input) every time we go through the while loop in the appropriate name or value member of the structure.

Listing 3-9 CGI Alternative Parsing Function

```
/* Using Structure for Variables */
struct input
{
    char name[MAXLENGTH];
    char value[MAXLENGTH];

}VARIABLES[FIELDNUM];

int parsing(char *temp)
{
    int fieldnum = 0;

    while(*temp)
    {
        /* go down the string until we find a "=" sign, at
           which time we put a null pointer in temp string
         */
        while(*temp)
        {
            if(*temp == '=')
            {
                *temp = '\0';
                temp++;

                /* get out of the loop */
                break;
            }
            else
            {
```

Listing 3-9 CGI Alternative Parsing Function (*continued*)

```c
            /* copy the first temp character into the
               structure VARIABLES member name
             */
            strncat(VARIABLES[fieldnum].name, temp, 1);
            temp++;
        }
    }

    /* We look for "&", which divides the value from next
       name. We put a NULL terminator at the end of the
       string, which also terminates the value string.
     */
    while(*temp)
    {
        if(*temp == '&')
        {
            *temp = '\0';
            temp++;
            break;
        }
        else
        {
            /* copy the first temp character into the
               structure VARIABLES member value
             */
            strncat(VARIABLES[fieldnum].value, temp, 1);
            temp++;
        }
    }

    /* increase the number of variables */
    fieldnum++;

    /* We don't want more than four pairs of values. If
       there are more, return -1--that is, an error.
     */
    if(fieldnum > FIELDNUM)
    {
        return -1;
    }
}
/* return the number of array of [name]=[value] */
return fieldnum;
}
```

You can find many examples of how to parse URL-encoded strings on the Internet. For example, Listing 3-10 gives a cryptic method of converting Hex characters to ASCII characters. (This function comes from Rob McCool, the guru behind Netscape Server.)

Listing 3-10   Alternative Hex-to-Char Function

```
char x2c(char *what)
{
  char digit;

  digit = (what[0] >= 'A' ? ((what[0] & 0xdf) - 'A')+10
                : (what[0] - '0'));
  digit *= 16;
  digit += (what[1] >= 'A' ? ((what[1] & 0xdf) - 'A')+10
                : (what[1] - '0'));

  return(digit);
}
```

In Listing 3-10, the ternary conditional operator ([*expression 1*] ? [*expression 2*] : [*expression 3*]) evaluates the value of digit. If *expression 1* is true, the value is equal to *expression 2*; otherwise, it is equal to *expression 3*. The Hex constant 0xdf helps mask the high bits of the characters. It is used to invert the second digit of the high bits of the character—that is, 110 0011 (c) is turned into 100 0011 (C). The 0xdf binary equivalent is 1101 1111. When it is added to any other binary value by using the bit operator &, it turns the second digit of the high bits to 0. Any bit combined with 0 and using the & operator results in 0. Because the binary equivalent of a lowercase character has a 1 for the second digit of the high bit and the uppercase character has a 0, any lowercase letter is turned to uppercase.

Let us continue with Listing 3-8-1 of the program. In the **main** function, we checked the type of action. The client chooses the action through a radio button. If the client chose to add information to the Guest Book (by selecting the first [top] radio button), the value of action will be log. The value is the first pair of variables sent by the browser. If the client chose to read the Guest Book (by selecting the second radio button), the value will be read, the last pair of variables sent by the browser. The order of the variables is based on the order in which they appear in the HTML form. We check for the value to process each action accordingly.

If the client wants to read the Guest Book, the **Read_Guest_File** function (Listing 3-8-3) is called. We **malloc** a string to hold the guest book information and any HTML tagging we might add to the data from the file. We send the pointer address of this string to the **Read_Guest_File** function, along with the path, to the Guest Book file. This function can update the original string's value, because it accepts the address as a pointer to a pointer to the string.

In the **Read_Guest_File** function, we first define a set of HTML tags that is used to format the data from the file into a table. The HTML code also changes the e-mail and Web address to hypertext. We open the Guest Book file to read. The Guest Book file is a text file. Each line of the file includes one data field of a user's information. In other words, the first line includes the user's name, the second line includes the e-mail address, and so on. You may want to use a binary or a simple database file for quicker access and better support of advance features (for example, searching of the Guest Book). The **fgets** function reads each line of data in the file until no more lines remain. It returns NULL in case of an error or the end of file. It reads each line until it reaches the maximum line length (MAXLENGTH + 1) or until it encounters the first newline character. (The **fgets** function retains the newline character.) Every three lines are grouped together using a switch statement with the value of the modulus operator (lnum % 3). The data are then concatenated within the HTML tags. The complete data are then added to the guestlist string. Finally, the function frees any malloced variables, closes the file, and returns 0 for success.

In the **main** function, we first check for a number of possible errors. Finally, the guestlist (list in the **main** function) string is added to the rest of the HTML page and returned to the client.

If the client wants to add a name to the Guest Book, the function reads the input into the user_data structure. This structure includes pointers to the three client input strings: the name, e-mail, and Web address. The **Remove_HTTP_Escapes** function is used not only to decode the client's input string, but also to update the user_data structure with the decoded data. We also make sure that the client at least fills in a name and an e-mail address. You can do any additional error checking of the input value here. As mentioned earlier, however, if you expect the client browser to support JavaScript, you should implement the validation of the client input via JavaScript.

For this program, we know where each variable will be in the array of variables sent by the client. Thus we can access the values directly by pointing to the specific value— for example, value[1]. If you want a more general function, write a function to step through all the variables, looking for the correct variable name, to get the value for that variable.

In Listing 3-8-4, **Append_Guest_File** appends the Guest Book file with the client input, pointed to by the user_data structure. This structure is sent as the first parameter, and the path to the Guest Book file is transmitted as the second parameter. The function then opens the Guest Book file for appending the data. We **malloc** a string that holds all the member data in the user_form structure and copy the member data in to the string. Each variable is separated by \n, so each value is placed in a separate line in the file. The **fputs** function places the data at the end of the file stream. There is no system locking of the file in this function. If you want to create a multitasking program, you need to update this function to support multiple threads and to protect the file from being updated by different threads at the same time.

Upon successful updating of the Guest Book, the **main** function returns a

Thank You page to the client. We take the user name from the input, and the time from the **_ftime** and **ctime** functions, to dynamically customize the page. The date is returned unformatted. You can use functions, such as the runtime C library function **strftime**, to format a time string.

Finally, if everything went well, we free all the allocated memory and return 0 to indicate success.

A note on **malloc** and **free**: You may use arrays of characters instead of a pointer to a string to avoid using **malloc** and **free** to allocate memory for the string. You can also write a clean-up function instead of freeing all the allocated memory every time, before sending an error message. This program contains no error checking to make sure **malloc** actually allocated the space successfully. You may want to do so for greater safety.

Summary

This chapter has briefly reviewed the prevalent programming features for HTTP servers not specific to Netscape. SSI, imagemap, ISINDEX, and CGI were covered. Emphasis was placed on how each of these features is uniquely supported under Netscape Server. We reviewed how you can enable these features in the configuration file, how the CGI works under Netscape Server, and so on.

SSI and ISINDEX provide easier methods of developing a dynamic site. As a simple addition to HTML pages, you can implement SSI through SSI tags inside the HTML page. SSI also supports programming when executable tags are employed. ISINDEX acquires a simple variable string from the user. The server parses each word in the string and passes it as a command-line argument to your program.

Imagemap can be implemented both on the server and on the client. Instead of having to use multiple images, each linking to a unique URL, imagemap allows a single image to be used for site navigation purposes. It allows you to create an interactive image in which each section of the image routes the client to a different location on the Web. Imagemaps are best placed on the home page or at any central navigation page that links to other locations.

Much of this chapter reviewed CGI, the most common method of programming for an HTTP server. CGI is powerful enough to support many of your development needs. The three types of CGI programming reviewed were Standard CGI, ShellCGI, and WinCGI. ShellCGI supports CGI scripts such as Perl. WinCGI supports writing CGI programs via Windows programming tools such as Visual Basic. The Guest Book example, along with providing a review of CGI, permits a comparison with similar examples we will write using NSAPI and WAI.

You may opt for alternatives to CGI programming methods. For example, you may choose NSAPI programs to support features such as customized authentication and logging or to provide better performance. You may choose JavaScript on the server as an easier way of programming and integrating with the Web pages. You may also use

WAI to write an out-of-process application that, unlike CGI, does not fork a new process each time it is invoked. WAI applications provide better scalability and performance than CGI application. In Chapter 4, we will compare the benefits of using NSAPI versus those found with CGI. Nevertheless, you should not underestimate CGI as an easy and able method of programming. Most of the programs currently running on the Web are based on CGI programs. In fact, the Netscape Administrative Server is written as CGI programs.

Now that we have surveyed common programming methods, we will focus on Netscape and its API. You need to bring an understanding of the general topics covered in previous chapters. Even more than the methods covered in this chapter, writing NSAPI programs depends upon an understanding of how the Netscape Server is configured and how it works.

Part III

NSAPI

Part III (Chapters 4 through 11) covers NSAPI (Netscape Server API). We begin with an introduction to NSAPI in Chapter 4. In Chapter 5, we examine the major NSAPI data structures and functions. Chapter 6 introduces writing a Server Application Function (SAF) and NSAPI applications. Compiling, registering, and debugging an NSAPI application are covered in Chapter 7. Chapter 8 expands the discussion of server directives in Chapter 2. We review these directives as they pertain to writing an NSAPI application. In Chapter 9, we write a number of additional NSAPI programs. Chapter 10 includes some additional programming topics (such as cookies). Chapter 11 covers the topic of threads and processes for Netscape Servers. We also consider the steps you take to write a thread-safe NSAPI application.

Chapter 4

What Is NSAPI?

NSAPI (Netscape Server Application Programming Interface) is the name of Netscape's first server-specific framework and tool for creating custom functions (server application functions, or SAFs) and applications. Under Server 2.x, Netscape referred to NSAPI as the Server Plug-in Application Programming Interface. This name change did not affect the API architecture. Any changes to the API from Server 1.x to Server 2.0 and later have been evolutionary. In fact, you will notice that with Server 3.x, Netscape returned to the name NSAPI to refer to the built-in server API. The main purpose for the new name was to equate the client and the server programming options offered by Netscape. You are probably familiar with the API for the client's plug-ins (such as Macromedia's Shockwave). NSAPI is the equivalent server plug-in, however, "plug-in" is probably not the best description of NSAPI. Although the name "plug-in" provides an easier way for the user to compare Netscape's client and server offerings, it limits the understanding of what the Netscape Server API actually provides. NSAPI is more than just a plug-in. It not only provides a way to extend the server, but it also exposes and modifies the server architecture and resources. It allows the programmer to modify and change the various levels of the server's response to a request.

In this chapter, we will introduce the general concept of how your SAF fits into the server architecture and functionality. When you write a server application using NSAPI, you write one or more SAFs. We will compare NSAPI with different programming methods that you may recognize. If you are familiar with one or two other methods of programming for the Web, you can review these comparisons to gain a better sense of how NSAPI fits in relation to the available programming tools. In later chapters, we will discuss how you can write your own NSAPI programs and what the various server data structure and functions do; we will also provide some examples.

Generally Speaking . . .

Whenever the client makes a request, the server processes the request using the server directive functions defined in **obj.conf** file. Your SAF can be one of the directive functions that the server uses to process the request (see Figure 4-1). You place your SAF inside the directive function list of the server at the appropriate location in the relevant Object. The server then processes your SAF in the same way that it would process other built-in server functions. These directive functions define the various steps in the processing of a request, which include authenticating the client, verifying the request, sending a response, and logging access and error information. The server does not need to go through all the directives and their functions. Some directive functions can complete the processing of a request and make the server skip other directives or directive functions. Other directive functions may set variables that are used by later functions. When you write your SAF, you should be aware of the intended purpose of each directive and write your SAF accordingly. The server also returns the appropriate response to the client. This response could be based on the built-in server functions or

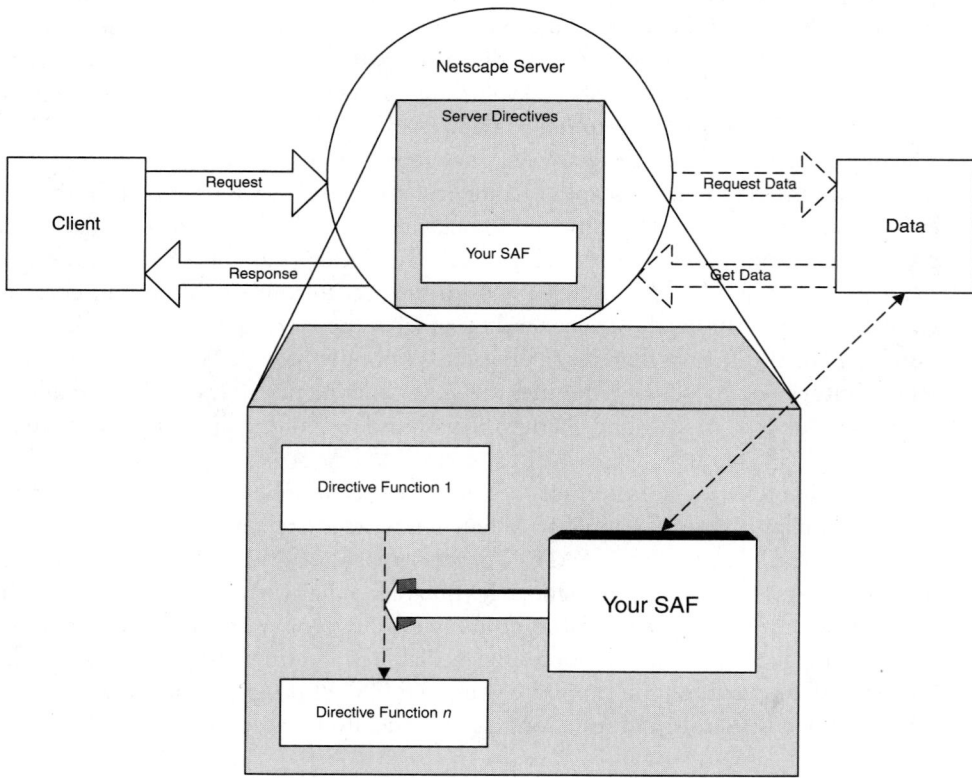

Figure 4-1   Your SAF in Relationship to the Rest of the Server

your SAF. For example, the built-in server function **send-cgi** runs your CGI program and returns the result to the client. Your SAF can also call other data (such as an HTML page, a graphics file, or a database) to process a request.

NSAPI includes a set of functions and data structures that are defined and made available in header files. In previous versions of the server, the various functions and data structures were defined in a number of different header files under the `<server path>/nsapi/include` directory. For Server 3.x, the functions and data structures are all defined in a single file, `nsapi.h`, under the `<server path>/include/nsapi` directory.

You use the NSAPI functions and structures to generate the features you need and to interface with Netscape Server. You can include these functions in your code and then write applications that extend the core functionality of the server. With NSAPI, you can write a variety of functions: plug-in applications, applications using databases, customized logging, version control, customized access control, customized user authentication, personalized Web sites for each client, and customized caching. You can also write an NSAPI application that uses more than one server directive function.

Other APIs, such as WINAPI, provide abstractions, a method of interfacing with a program. Insofar as it provides an interface and support for writing server applications, NSAPI is similar to other APIs. Unlike other APIs, however, Netscape's API directly exposes the server internals. Generally, an API is an abstraction layer separate from the server internals. NSAPI header files include a set of exportable server internal functions that your program can use. `NSAPI_PUBLIC` is a type definition added to all function prototypes that are meant for public use. These functions and data structures are a subset of the server's own functions and data structures. This NSAPI provides increased performance, as no layer separates your program and the server. It also gives more control to the programmer, because you are working directly with the server functions. The trick is that NSAPI also ties the API to the server structure. A change in the server's core function or architecture means a change in the NSAPI functions. Also, your program might have access to part of the internal server that was intended to be hidden.

Recognizing the above weaknesses, the 3.x version of Netscape Server provides an alternative API, Web Application Interface. (We will discuss WAI in detail in Chapters 13–16.) This new API allows you to write in-server process and out-of-server process applications in C, C++, or Java. WAI provides an abstraction layer, which is independent of the server's internal architecture. Consequently, the programs you write should have a better binary compatibility with each new release of the server. You cannot, however, write all the various type of server applications possible with NSAPI using WAI in Server 3.x. For example, WAI does not allow you to write authentication functions. Moreover, under Server 3.x, even if you run your WAI application in-process, the WAI application does not provide the same performance benefits as an NSAPI application does. Because the server uses the same server variables and similar server functions as your SAF when processing a client request, nothing is as close to the server's working or as efficient and fast as NSAPI. With future releases of the server, this advantage of NSAPI might disappear.

Netscape intends to support WAI in future releases of the server and provide better integration and features for it. Depending on the changes made to the server, WAI applications may be able to run as fast as NSAPI (or even faster) in the later versions of Netscape Server.

Server API

In response to the limitations of CGI, there has been a move toward using APIs as the preferred way of programming for WWW servers. Since Netscape introduced its API, other major server developers (such as Microsoft, Purveyor, and O'Reilly) have all added their own APIs. IBM Internet Connection Server even has an API, ICAPI, that is compatible with NSAPI. With a few exceptions, it allows many of the NSAPI programs to be easily ported to ICAPI.

Using the server API to program provides advantages not available with other methods of server programming. For example, there are performance and CPU overhead benefits. There are also advantages to writing customized programs not possible by other means, such as customized authentication and logging. We will cover some benefits when we compare CGI with NSAPI later in this chapter. There are also drawbacks in choosing NSAPI. Primarily, you must be more careful about how your program works, do more testing, and understand how the server works before actually writing your program.

Netscape Server comes in versions for many platforms, and there are distinct differences between each server. Some of these differences are due to the operating system and others are based on the choices Netscape has made.

Platform Differences

There are a number of platform differences between various versions of the Netscape Servers. Many of these differences are irreconcilable, because they are inherent in each operating system. You may already suspect differences, because you know your operating system works differently. If you review the NSAPI header files, you will notice that various functions and data structures are modified with #if and #ifdef processor macros so as to enable them to be supported under all platforms. Along with the API's multiplatform capabilities, your function can include similar macros to support platform-independent or separate versions of a function for different platforms. These differences are not limited to WIN32 and UNIX, but also exist between various UNIX platforms. For example, some UNIX platforms do not provide kernel (native) threading. All UNIX versions of Netscape Server 2.0 use user-level threads. For Enterprise Server 2.01, Netscape uses kernel threads for Solaris and IRIX and user-level threads for all other UNIX platforms. You may also notice that file locking (for example, **system_flock**) is done a bit differently on the BSD server than on other UNIX servers, or that semaphores are defined differently for IRIX. Netscape has tried to minimize these differences by providing platform-independent functions and data structures. You should, however, know that these functions and data structures may work differently on different platforms. A data structure may be defined differently and include a different member depending on the platform. For example, the `netbuf` function includes the member `address` only when used in conjunction with the WIN32 platform. These differences are especially noticeable between WIN32 and UNIX platforms. You can review the differences by looking at various header files, especially the `base/system.h` header file, which lists the general settings for each major platform. In Chapter 5, as we describe each data structure or function, we will point out some of these differences.

WIN32 and UNIX handle files differently. For example, WIN32 uses file handles, instead of integers, for file descriptors. It also uses the backward slash (\) instead of the forward slash (/) for file path information. Windows NT and 95 offer support for case-sensitive file and directory names, but it is only skin-deep. They display the case-sensitive files or directories but do not make any substantive distinctions between them. In other words, you cannot have both `nsapi.dll` and `Nsapi.dll` under the same directory, because they are both seen as the same file. You are probably familiar with these variations, but they are especially important when you are writing an NSAPI function that should work across different platforms.

C header files may vary based on the operating system. Thus you may need to include a different file or function for each platform. For example, under UNIX, the stat function is defined as **stat**. Under NT, it is defined as **_stat**. This difference is also reflected in Netscape's inclusion of various system header files. If you review the header files, you may see that, along with a `#include` reference in Netscape's own header files, Netscape may have a `#include` reference to a C system header file. So, for example, you may find `#include <sys/socket.h>` for UNIX and `#include <sys/winsock.h>` for WIN32. Again, Netscape has attempted to provide platform-independent support for some of these common functions, but there are still many functions unique to NT or UNIX. For example, Netscape header files define **system_winsockerr** and **util_delete_directory** for WIN32 only. On the other hand, there are a number of directives that are specific to UNIX, such as **Chroot** and **PidLog**.

There are also differences specific to Netscape Server as it runs on each platform. For instance, the UNIX version of Server 2.x supports multiple processes with multiple threads, while the NT version supports only multiple threads. (All versions of Server 3.x support only multiple threads.) Also, you can specify the maximum and minimum number of threads on UNIX Server 2.x, while the 2.x version of NT implements a predefined default setting for threads.

Between Server 1.x and 2.x, Netscape made major strides toward implementing a more unified cross-platform support. For example, earlier versions of the server include NT-specific header files. You also had to use the NT registry to register your function or alter the server configuration. The NSAPI server application function did not include a specific type cast, such as `NSAPI_PUBLIC`. To compile your function for NT, you had to define it as a DLL export type, `__declspec(dllexport)`. Some functions, such as **net_write**, were also defined differently under NT and UNIX. Under NT, **net_write** had four parameters; under UNIX, it had three. This variation meant that you had to modify each program before compiling the code or use specific preprocessor macros to support different platforms. With Server 2.x, all major functions of the server are defined in the same way for all platforms. This approach, however, does not mean that the actual way the function works or the members of a data structure are exactly the same for all platforms.

We should emphasize that, although you can often successfully write your NSAPI functions under one platform and then recompile them for use with another platform, this strategy will not always work. You should always test your programs on all platforms on which you plan to run your NSAPI applications and make sure you do not reference functions, data structures, or other features specific to one system. If you do use system-specific functions, make sure you select the appropriate preprocessor macros to specify which function should run under which platform. You should have some understanding of how your program will work under other platforms.

NSAPI 2.x versus NSAPI 1.x

Netscape version 1.x servers were divided into two types: Commerce and Communication Servers. Commerce Server, unlike Communication Server, included SSL security. With Netscape 2.x servers, the division was between Enterprise and FastTrack Servers. The cores of both these two servers are fundamentally the same. The default installation for Enterprise Server uses `https` (the standard for a secured server). FastTrack Server uses `httpd` (the standard for an unsecured server). Yet, they both support SSL. So, even though they appear to have different levels of security, they can both run as a secured server. In fact, both servers support SSL version 3.0 and you must enable security for both. FastTrack Servers, however, support 40-bit encryption only. To support 128-bit encryption, you should use Enterprise Server. Enterprise Server also includes features that are not part of FastTrack Server, such as search engine and version control. To find out more about each server, see the documentation that comes with it.

Note ▶

The use of a version associated with NSAPI in this book is based on the release number of the Netscape Server. In other words, NSAPI 1.1 refers to the version of NSAPI supported by Netscape Server 1.1.

As mentioned earlier, Netscape has attempted to provide a more integrated and easier environment with NSAPI 2.0. NSAPI 1.0 was a quick export of some of the major internal server headers and functions. It was also ported to NT without a major consideration of how it differed from UNIX. It has been a goal of Netscape to merge these platform differences and provide a powerful server API on all platforms. To this end, there have been many changes in both the servers and NSAPI. The header files and functions have been better organized and enhanced with new features. NSAPI_PUBLIC type cast is used to identify all exported functions, including your own functions. There are added features for memory pooling, which changes **MALLOC** to allocate space from the pooled memory instead of the heap. The memory block is allocated for a request and freed by the server when the request is finished. (You can use **PERM_MALLOC** to allocate persistent memory from the heap.) Netscape also enhanced the API with critical section and thread support functions and data structures. Under Server 1.x, NSAPI supported only semaphores, which are simply interprocess locks. There are many more small changes and updates to various functions or data structures, some of which are discussed in Appendix E.

There are also new updates for specific platforms. With Server 2.0, the UNIX server supports not only threads, but also processes with multiple threads. The NT version of the server now uses **magnus.conf** and **obj.conf** instead of the NT registry. The NT version is also better integrated with Event Viewer and Performance Monitor. There is even the addition of FastTrack for 95.

In Server 2.0, Netscape runs two server processes: ns-httpd and httpd. (Under NT 4.0, you can verify this fact by checking the running processes through the Task Manager|Processes tab.) ns-httpd manages the httpd servers that are running. If a server goes down, ns-httpd, which remains running, can restart the server. This enables the server to handle a variety of circumstances that could crash it. Thus a server can be automatically restarted even when it goes down.

Under Netscape 1.x, you could not invoke a server executable directly to debug your program. With Netscape 2.0, there is also an executable version of the servers. You can put the executable program httpd.exe found in *<server path>*/bin/http [s | d] and the server configuration files into the path of your debug session. This approach allows the programming environment, such as Visual C++, to call and run Netscape Server when you start a debug session. You can then set a break in your code and step through your code for debugging.

Netscape Server 2.01 includes a number of bug fixes for Server 2.0. For example, the NSAPI function **net_isalive**, which did not work properly under Server 2.0, works correctly under Server 2.01. Server 2.01 also added a few new functions, such as counting semaphores functions (**cs_***) and the **AuthTrans** function **get-sslid**. For information on counting semaphores, see Chapter 11. For a discussion of **get-sslid**, see Appendix B.

NSAPI 3.x

With each new release, Netscape HTTP servers continue to evolve and support additional features. Netscape continues to deliver FastTrack Server and Enterprise Server. As with previous versions of the server, FastTrack is a more limited version of Enterprise Server. It does not include all the features supported under Enterprise Server. For example, FastTrack Server does not support features such as search capability, SNMP-based monitoring, or the CORBA (Common Object Request Broker Architecture) distributed applications development tool.

With Server 3.0, Netscape added a number of new features to the server. For example, Enterprise Server now conditionally supports HTTP/1.1. The server also supports LDAP (Lightweight Directory Access Protocol), agents, advance Web publishing and content management, CORBA, and WAI. Many of these new features also support a programming interface, such as Access Control API, Web Publishing Interface, Agents API, Certificate Mapping API, and so on. These new features interface with the server by using their own built-in NSAPI functions. Some of these APIs can be seen as an extension of NSAPI. For example, Access Control API is a C-language API that allows you to write customized authentication methods and to assign your own permissions and access rights to server resources.

NSAPI functions and data structures that were defined in separate files under the `<server path>/nsapi` directory and under the subdirectories `base` and `frame` for Server 2.x are now placed inside a single file, `nsapi.h`. `nsapi.h` is located under the `<server path>/include/` directory. You can still find header files with the same name as the Server 2.x header files under the Netscape Server 3.x `include` directory. Except for `base/systems.h`, however, all other header files include only a reference to the `nsapi.h` file. Unlike with previous versions of the server, you no longer need to include different header files with your program. You need to include only the `nsapi.h` file.

NSAPI 3.x makes only minor changes to the NSAPI functions and data structures provided with Server 2.01. In fact, your binary NSAPI applications written for Netscape Server 2.x may run under Server 3.x without any modification. Note, how-

---

Bug Report ▶

Enterprise Server 3.5.1 for Solaris does not allow two NSAPI modules with conflicting symbols to coexist in the same process. You should update the server to the 3.5.1C version (patch `3.5.1C.solaris.export.tar.Z`) to resolve this problem. This patch includes updated versions of the `ns-httpd` and `ns-httpd.so` files. You can find this patch under Netscape Tech Support's File Library page (`http://help.netscape.com/filelib.html`).

---

ever, that this is not always the case. You may have to recompile your code using the NSAPI header and library files of your current Netscape Server. For information on running NSAPI applications compiled and linked with the Server 2.x or 3.0x library, see the next section, Running Earlier Versions of NSAPI Applications with Server 3.x.

If you are going to write NSAPI applications for Server 3.x, you may want to know of the changes in Server 3.x. In fact, NSAPI 3.5.1 makes a few more changes to NSAPI 3.0. In the next few chapters, whenever needed, we will note these changes. You should also check the `nsapi.h` header files to learn more about the NSAPI functions and to make sure the function you intend to use is supported by the server.

With a few exceptions, most functions that existed under Server 2.x are still supported as before under Server 3.x. A few NSAPI functions, such as **system_errmsg**, have changes. **system_errmsg** no longer takes a parameter. (The parameter for the previous version of **system_errmsg** was not used by the function anyway.) There are a few server variables and functions missing in Server 3.x. For example, `MAGNUS_VERSION_STRING` is not defined. On the other hand, a few functions have been added, such as functions for MD5 hash routines (**md5hash_create**, **md5hash_copy**, and so on), random number generation (**random_create**, **random_generate**, and so on), **func_replace**, **systhread_detach**, **systhread_set_default_stacksize**, and **getThreadMallocKey**. NSAPI 3.5.1 also includes a few more functions, such as **net_native_handle** and **netbuf_getbytes**.

Many of the changes to NSAPI have to do with the support for the new features of the server, such as ACL, agent, and HTTP/1.1. To support HTTP/1.1, new methods (for example, `METHOD_TRACE`, `METHOD_MAX`) and status codes (for example, `PROTOCOL_CONTINUE`, `PROTOCOL_SWITCH`, `PROTOCOL_URL_TOO_LARGE`) are added. To support these new features, many of the server data structures have also changed. For example, `FuncStruct`, `Session`, `Request`, and `conf_global_vars_s` all include new member variables. `conf_global_vars_s` for NSAPI 3.5.1 has also changed to support additional features such as FORTEZZA, a hardware-enhanced security services. These changes may also require you to recompile your code. FORTEZZA support is included with Enterprise Server 3.5 and 3.5.1. These servers support FORTEZZA Crypto Cards, which provide hardware-based cryptographic services for encryption, authentication, and data integrity. FORTEZZA is a National Security Agency (NSA) trademark for a family of hardware-based security products. Netscape has added FORTEZZA support to the SSL protocol. It provides support for a hardware-based cryptographic procedure instead of the software-based support existing in the previous version of the server. Other Netscape products also support FORTEZZA, including Communicator 4.04, Messaging Server 3.5, Collabra Server 3.5, and Directory Server 3.0. (An example of a Web site where you can find more information on FORTEZZA is FORTEZZA Developers Home Page, `http://www.armadillo.huntsville.al.us/`.)

Finally, there is a minor change in the settings for debugging NSAPI applications. Instead of specifying the location of the configuration file for the debug session, you use the name and port information of the Netscape Server. The NSAPI library file you should use to compile your NSAPI programs for Enterprise Server 3.5.1 is `ns-httpd35.lib`—not `ns-httpd30.lib`, which is used with Netscape Server 3.0x, or `libhttpd.lib`, which is used for Server 2.x. (See Debugging Your SAF in Chapter 7 for more information.)

> ### Warning ▶
>
> Because of the changes described here, your programs compiled under Server 2.x may not function properly under Server 3.x. Moreover, the function **net_write** may also fail to work properly under Enterprise Server 3.x, when SSL is enabled. To make sure your program runs properly under Server 3.0x or 3.5.1, you should make any modifications needed and recompile your code using the header and library files of the appropriate server.

Running Earlier Versions of NSAPI Applications with Server 3.x

Netscape Server 3.x allows you to run NSAPI applications that have been written for Server 2.x (for example, using the Server 2.x `libhttpd.lib` file). Server 3.5.1 also allows you to run NSAPI applications that have been linked and compiled with the Server 3.0x NSAPI library (for example, `ns-httpd30.lib`). To run these versions of NSAPI applications, the server must be able to locate a previous version of NSAPI shared or dynamic library files. For example, for the 2.x version, NT Server 3.x must find and use `ns-httpd20.dll`. For the 3.0x version, NT Server 3.5.1 must find and use `ns-http30.dll`. (The 3.5.1 version of the NSAPI dynamic library is `ns-httpd35.dll`.)

These files should have been installed by the more recent version of the server. The release version of Server 3.5.1 for NT may, in fact, lack the necessary library files. To obtain these missing files, you should download the NSAPI patch (`P106927`). Once you download the files, you can place them in a path that is accessible to the server, such as `c:/Winnt/system32` (`%systemRoot%\system32`).

To force the server to find and load the appropriate shared library (DLL file), you can use two special functions (`funcs`) with the **Init** function **load-module**. To load the 2.x version of the NSAPI dynamic or shared library (for example, `ns-httpd20.dll`), use the function **nsapi20_present**. For the 3.x version, use **__nsapi_table**.

The following code is an example of the line you can add to your **obj.conf** file for `ns-httpd20.dll`. You should change the path in the **shlib** parameter to point to the exact location of the file.

```
Init fn="load-modules" funcs="nsapi20_present"
  shlib="c:/netscape/server/https-foo/ns-httpd20.dll"
```

For the 3.0x version of the NSAPI library file, you can add the following line to the **obj.conf** file:

```
Init fn="load-module" funcs="__nsapi30_table"
  shlib="c:/netscape/server/https-foo/ns-httpd30.dll"
```

Writing NSAPI Applications Using Perl and Python

A number of third-party developers have extended the programming options for NSAPI by providing an interface for other programming languages. The most important of these extensions are for Perl and Python. Both Perl and Python are easier to use than C. With these extensions, you can take advantage of the speed and state maintenance capability of NSAPI while preserving the ease of use of Perl and Python. Your application will run in the server process. You can write NSAPI programs, using two of the most popular CGI programming languages. If you are familiar with Perl and Python, and would like to use them instead of C, you should definitely consider using these extensions.

Nsapy allows you to write NSAPI applications using Python. It embeds Python within the server using NSAPI. You can find more information at Gregory Trubetskoy's (the author of Nsapy, along with Aaron Watters) Nsapy Web page (`http://www.ispol.com/home/grisha/nsapy/nsapy.html`). **nsapi_perl** is an extension of NSAPI for Perl. It embeds the Perl Interpreter within the Netscape Server using NSAPI. It precompiles and caches CGI scripts allowing them to run inside the server process. For more information or the latest release, you can check Ben Sugars' nsapi_perl page (`http://interact.canoe.ca/~bsugars/nsapi_perl.html`). **Nsapy** and **nsapi_perl** are included in the CD-ROM that accompanies this book.

Comparison with Other Server APIs

There has been much discussion about the use of API instead of CGI for writing customized applications or faster server add-ons. In this section, we will review the major differences between programming with an API and programming with CGI. Obviously, there are also differences between the different server APIs. We will briefly compare NSAPI with IBM's ICAPI and Microsoft's ISAPI. ICAPI is based on the NSAPI architecture; it even provides support for NSAPI. ISAPI is a competitive alternative with which you may be familiar. We provide this comparison as a means to evaluate each API. Many Web developers need to program applications for a number of different servers. You can also use this information to make a transition from ISAPI to NSAPI—that is, if you are familiar already with ISAPI.

NSAPI versus ICAPI

ICAPI (Internet Connection Application Programming Interface) is a programming interface for the IBM Internet Connection Server (ICS). Its architecture is based on NSAPI, and it provides many of the same features as NSAPI. Much of the same code written for NSAPI also works on ICS. ICAPI comes with a compatibility module that allows NSAPI programs to run on ICS. ICAPI directives include many similar directives as NSAPI. Table 4-1 provides a quick review of ICAPI and NSAPI directives.

Table 4-1   NSAPI and ICAPI Directive Comparisons

NSAPI DIRECTIVE	ICAPI DIRECTIVES (PROCESS STEPS)
Init	Server Initialization (ServerInit) (required)
	PreExit (For compatibility with GoServe. This directive can be called after a request is read but before anything else has occurred.)
AuthTrans	Authentication
NameTrans	Name Translation (NameTrans)
PathCheck	Authorization
ObjectType	ObjectType
Service	Service
	Data Filter (Filters data as a "stream class," providing write access to the outgoing data stream.)
AddLog	Log
Error	Error
	PostExit (required) (For freeing memory and other clean-up, regardless of the return code from previous steps.)
	Server Termination (ServerTerm) (required) (For freeing memory and other clean-up after a standard shutdown or restart.)

As you can see, the ICAPI directives are very similar to the eight Netscape directives. The compatibility module for ICAPI was based on Netscape Server 1.x's design. Thus it does not support some of Server 2.0's features, such as critical section (`crit.h`). To use your NSAPI function with ICS servers, you must make a small modification of the configuration file for the correct module to be called. ICAPI needs to call `nsapi.dll` for the OS/2 and Windows NT systems, `nsapi.o` for the AIX system, `libnsapi.so` for the Solaris system, and `libnsapi.sl` for the HP-UX system. You must also recompile the code to include the ICAPI header files. For more information, see IBM's Internet Connection (Secure) Server's "Web Programming Guide" (`http://www.ics.raleigh.ibm.com/pub/icswpg.htm`).

NSAPI versus ISAPI

ISAPI and NSAPI are the two most popular HTTP server APIs. We will provide a brief comparison of ISAPI and NSAPI here. Other APIs, such as WSAPI for Website, also provide features similar to NSAPI. ISAPI, however, is backed by Microsoft. It is the other major API usually supported or mentioned by other server API developers. To learn more about ISAPI or any other server API, you should look at the relevant servers' Web sites for documentation and additional comparisons.

ISAPI was first developed by Purveyor. In its first installment, it was rather limited and provided only CGI-style plug-in support. There was limited support for writing customized add-on applications—mainly customized authentication. To write authentication, you had to use a separate module. Since then, and with the support of Microsoft, this API has become more formidable. (ISAPI is a subset of the INetAPI part of INetSDK.) With ISAPI, you can write a function in two ways: as an ISAPI application DLL or as an ISAPI filter function.

ISAPI application DLLs are similar to CGI programs except that they use DLL binding. These DLL applications use runtime dynamic linking and execute in the server process/address space. You write and compile the DLL to enable the server to link dynamically with it. The application uses the **GetExtensionVersion** and **HttpExtensionProc** functions to provide the entry points for the HTTP server. The server uses **Loadlibrary** and **GetProcAddress** to retrieve the starting address of the DLL function. It then uses the information provided by the DLL to link with it. Your program can use the ISAPI functions **GetServerVariable**, **ReadClient**, and **WriteClient** to read client input and the server variables, and to write back to the client. All the resources available to the HTTP server process are also available to the ISAPI DLL application.

The DLL application can be requested by the client in the same way that a CGI program is requested. For example, you can place the following URL in your HTML document where a CGI program would have resided: `http://www.foo.com/specialprogram.dll?name=joe`. When the client requests the DLL, the server loads your DLL and passes it the parameter `name=joe`.

ISAPI DLL applications resemble an NSAPI **Service** function. There is no additional overhead for each request. The server, unlike a CGI program, does not need to create a new process each time your program is invoked. This approach reduces the time it takes to process a request. ISAPI applications use less server RAM, since they do not need to support the overhead associated with a CGI process. Built-in caching also helps improve the performance. The server loads these functions on demand and unloads them as needed. The DLLs stay loaded until a set time, when they are unloaded if they have not been used.

Filter functions provide more flexibility and resemble Netscape NSAPI customized applications. You can write customized authentication, encryption, and logging, similar to programming with NSAPI. Filter functions are loaded through the server registry and allow modification of server workings. These filters stay loaded until the server is stopped. When the proper requests are sent by the client, the filter functions take over from the server. Filter functions use the **GetFilterVersion** and **HttpFilterProc** functions to specify the DLL entry point. They communicate with the server through the server notification, which starts with `SF_NOTIFY_`. Filters are registered for a specific notification. The server calls the filter's **HttpFilterProc** entry point for the specified notification. Filter functions tell the server what type of notification it needs. The server then calls the filter function whenever that particular event occurs. ISAPI also provides a set of data structures that contain data and function pointers (beginning with HTTP_) available to a filter function. Filter functions can read raw data, process headers, enable security, and return responses. Every filter is defined in a separate DLL. Filter functions, much like the DLL applications, include **GetServerVariable**, **ServerSupportFunction**, **ReadClient**, and **WriteClient**.

Table 4-2 compares Netscape directives with similar server notification and data structures for ISAPI. Unlike in Table 4-1 for ICAPI, this comparison is only a relative one. The notification and data structures are only loosely similar to how Netscape processes a request. In general, the order of the notification for ISAPI is SF_NOTIFY_RAW_DATA, SF_NOTIFY_PREPROC_HEADERS, SF_NOTIFY_AUTHENTICATION, SF_NOTIFY_URL_MAP, SF_NOTIFY_SEND_RAW_DATA, and SF_NOTIFY_LOG. The final notification is SF_NOTIFY_END_OF_NET_SESSION.

Table 4-2 NSAPI and ISAPI Directive Comparisons

NSAPI	ISAPI	
	NOTIFICATION DATA STRUCTURE	NOTIFICATION TYPE
Init		
AuthTrans	HTTP_FILTER_AUTHENT	SF_NOTIFY_AUTHENTICATION
NameTrans PathCheck	HTTP_FILTER_URL_MAP	SF_NOTIFY_URL_MAP
PathCheck	HTTP_FILTER_ACCESS_DENIED	SF_NOTIFY_ACCESS_DENIED
ObjectType	HTTP_FILTER_PREPROC_HEADERS (for preprocessed server headers)	SF_NOTIFY_PREPROC_HEADERS (for preprocessed server headers)
Service	HTTP_FILTER_RAW_DATA HTTP_FILTER_RAW_DATA	SF_NOTIFY_SEND_RAW_DATA SF_NOTIFY_READ_RAW_DATA
AddLog	HTTP_FILTER_LOG	SF_NOTIFY_LOG
Error		

ISAPI is similar to other APIs developed by Microsoft. It is an abstraction insulated from the server's internal structure. NSAPI, on the other hand, directly exposes the server internals and so provides the fastest response. NSAPI does not provide the same layer of abstraction that ISAPI does. NSAPI headers and functions are a subset of the server's headers and functions. As already mentioned, NSAPI exposes the server's structure. One negative effect of this close contact with the server is the threat of incompatibility with each upgrade of the server.

This section has presented a very brief description of how ISAPI works. One place to find more detailed information on ISAPI is Microsoft's Internet Server API Documentation (http://www.microsoft.com/win32dev/apiext/isalegal.htm).

NSAPI versus CGI

The most frequently sought-after benefit of using NSAPI is better performance than CGI. NSAPI provides such additional functionality as persistent data, and customized logging or authentication. You write a function that is loaded with the server, runs in the server context, and is directly linked to the server. Therefore, you should get better performance for your application. The server does not need to fork a new process and launch a new program, as it must for each CGI program. The API's improved performance has been repeatedly proven in benchmark tests. For example, representatives of both Illustra (a major database vendor that is now part of Informix) and Spider (a database connectivity tools provider) have attested to significant performance enhancement once these companies updated their programs from CGI to NSAPI. Depending on the type of application you wish to write, you can expect a range of improvement. This enhancement is especially great when you write an application that uses database features extensively.

When you write an SAF, you can use the server's built-in resources. Your functions can share data and communication resources with one another or with the server. For example, you can call an internal server function, such as the ones used in the **obj.conf** file. Because NSAPI functions are loaded once and can share data, you can easily have persistent data. Thus you can access the information for the server's entire lifetime (from when it starts to when it shuts down). You can control and customize the movement of a client through the pages of your site. You can also open a connection to a database once and use this same connection for queries from different clients. The use of persistent data, by itself, makes writing code easier and more powerful.

Moreover, NSAPI is designed to provide server functionality not possible with CGI, such as customized error handling and authentication. This ability is one of the main reasons for writing an NSAPI function. CGI programs provide the functionality of an NSAPI **Service** function, but they do not provide access to other directives of the server.

As your SAF function is not a program that is called by the user, you are less prone to security breaches. With NSAPI, your code is loaded with the server. The possibility of access to programs from anyone who does not have administrative access to your server is small. This improbability does not mean that you do not need to protect your code from any client sending wrong data. The difference is that NSAPI functions are loaded at the start of the server and are not called like a CGI program. Although not likely, with a CGI program the client might breach the security and gain access to unintended privileges, such as running programs for which the user does not have access rights. Therefore, with CGI you must take extra precautions to make sure CGI programs are in a secured directory and that the proper access privileges are set for clients and server resources.

Finally, although you can write your own set of utility functions (such as functions for parsing the URL), NSAPI provides some very useful built-in functions. They reduce the need for writing code. Moreover, these functions are already part of the shared resources. Therefore, unlike with CGI programs, they are not reloaded every time they are used.

Even with all the benefits mentioned so far, NSAPI programming is not suitable or desirable for every circumstance. It has certain drawbacks and limitations that a CGI program does not have. CGI programs are easy to write. You have more options in choosing what language you can use to write your program (for example, Perl, Visual Basic, C, and so on). Because CGI programs are not loaded with the server and are not in the server process, they are less likely to crash the server and easier to test. You do not need to have extensive knowledge of the server's workings. You do not need to understand advanced programming features, such as multithreading, before you can write a CGI program. CGI programs also work on most HTTP servers and are not limited to a specific vendor's API. APIs, on the other hand, are limited to specific servers.

As an alternative for CGI and NSAPI, you may consider writing a WAI application. WAI provides some of the benefits of NSAPI, such as better performance. You can also write a WAI application in-process, similar to NSAPI, or out-of-process, similar to CGI. For more information on WAI, see Chapters 13–16.

Table 4-3 lists the pros and cons of using an API versus CGI for programming.

Table 4-3   Benefits and Drawbacks of Using NSAPI versus CGI

ADVANTAGES OF USING NSAPI	DRAWBACKS OF USING NSAPI
Faster response and better performance. (An executable is not loaded each time it is called.)	Limited to specific operating systems and servers. (Less cross-platform support; vendor-specific.)
Support for built-in integration with the server. (Programs run in the server's address space. Also, they access and share server resources.)	More prone to crashing the server. (NSAPI programs are not separated from the server process. They do not run outside of the server process. They should be more closely tested, as they can easily break the system—for example, by corrupting the server's internal data.)
Better protection and security against outside tampering. (No specific program is called. None of the workings of the program is exposed.)	More difficult to write. Programs must be thread-safe. It takes extra steps to guarantee the program is working properly. (Programmers must deal with multiple thread handling, thread synchronization, clean-up, sharing states between multiple server processes, and so on. They also need to understand the server's working and learn the API.)
Less CPU-intensive. (Programs use less CPU overhead. No new process is forked or launched for each request.)	Limited to C and C++ language (although third-party utilities may allow you to use other languages, such as Perl and Python).
Better understanding of the server's workings. Can best take advantage of existing server capabilities and features.	More closely tied with server changes and, therefore, may need changing and updating to support a server upgrade.
Smaller programs and smaller footprints in memory use. (As the program uses existing functionality provided by the server and shared code and resources, you can write a smaller program. It also does not require the added resource of loading each new CGI process.)	More difficult to test, configure, and update code. (Every time you make a change in your program, you must stop and restart the server to reload the shared library. You must also configure each SAF in the **obj.conf** file.)

(continued)

Table 4-3 Benefits and Drawbacks of Using NSAPI versus CGI (*continued*)

ADVANTAGES OF USING NSAPI	DRAWBACKS OF USING NSAPI
Built-in functions and calling of a number of server's existing configuration functions.	
Advanced features and functionality that are particularly useful for writing server programs as the server improves with each version.	
Support of persistent data, state maintenance, and shared resources.	
Additional functionality not available through CGI (for example, customized logging and authentication).	

This section has outlined the general differences between programming for CGI and NSAPI. We have also kept CGI programmers in mind in other chapters. In particular, if you come from a CGI background, take special note of the CGI Environment Variables and NSAPI Variables section in Chapter 6.

Summary

This chapter provided an overview of NSAPI, its mode of operation, and its relationship to other APIs or CGI. You can use this information to evaluate whether NSAPI is the best tool for your needs. You can also use the comparisons as a guide for the cross-development of Internet applications. We also compared the various versions of the Netscape API, including a review of the changes in Server 3.01 and 3.5.1.

There are many options of programming for Netscape Server—NSAPI is only one, but it provides the best performance. Moreover, to really understand how Netscape Server works, you need to understand how Netscape's API works. Programmers have complained that documentation on NSAPI is sparse and confusing. In the rest of the book, I intend to clear up some of the confusion.

In the next chapters, we will cover the NSAPI data structures and functions that you need to know and use. We will write and install programs. We will also cover more advanced topics, such as threads. With this book and the existing server documentation, you should be able to write your own program applications easily. Often, the difficulty with programming with NSAPI comes from not knowing how the API works. To understand it is to take advantage of what it provides. Once you understand how the NSAPI works, you can use your existing programming knowledge to write your server programs. Much of your previous experience (such as database programming) can be easily incorporated into your NSAPI programs to provide the best performance and result.

Chapter 5

NSAPI Fundamentals

This chapter outlines the fundamentals of the Netscape Server API (NSAPI) programming components. NSAPI header files include external variables, data structures, and functions that allow your NSAPI program access to the server and to information about the server and client request. In this chapter, we will review the major server data structures and functions. Data structures contain core information that your program can access and manipulate. We will also review the major NSAPI functions, which usually match up with specific data structures. You use these functions to access the server variables, process the client request, and return a response. You can also use the functions to accomplish tasks not specific to HTTP, such as file I/O. Threads add a new programming consideration and require a more extensive discussion. We will discuss threads and processes and their related functions in Chapter 11, Threads and Processes.

The data structures and functions described in this chapter are intended first and foremost for Server 3.5.1. The discussion is also relevant for earlier versions of Netscape Server. The core component of NSAPI—that is, the main data structures and functions that you use for programming an NSAPI application—are basically the same for all releases of Netscape Server. Most functions covered in this chapter can be used with the earlier releases. Although many of the important server data structures have changed with each release of the server, the member variables of these data structures, which you normally use in your program, remain the same. The differences between the releases of the server have been noted in Chapter 4 and in Appendix E. In this chapter, we will continue to point out any specific data structure or function that is unique to Server 3.x or 3.5.1.

The information in this chapter is intended to complement Netscape's own programmer's guide and NSAPI header files. Additional information is also included where it is lacking in the existing documentation. The intention is to provide a starting point for you to gain an understanding of the most important server data structures and functions. The functions included in this chapter are neither a complete nor an exhaustive listing of all NSAPI functions. If you plan to read about NSAPI functions for Server 3.x, make sure you use the revised NSAPI Programmer's Guide (http://developer.netscape.com/docs/manuals/enterprise/nsapi/index.htm). This document includes a number of corrections and updates.

Header Files

Server 1.x and Server 2.x include a number of different headers. Therefore, you need to choose and add the appropriate header file before you write and compile your code. These header files are a subset of the server's own header files and, as such, they give you access to, and great power over, the server's internal workings. Appendix E briefly describes the content of each header file included with Server 2.x. You can use this appendix when you program for Server 2.x as a quick reference to decide which files to include with your program. With each new release of Netscape Server, the NSAPI header files and their content have also changed. Appendix E also includes a comparison of the header files for Server 1.x and Server 2.x.

Although Netscape Server 3.x includes header files similar to (header files with the same names) those found in Server 2.x under the <server path>/include/ directory, these header files do not include any definitions or declarations. With the exception of the system.h file found under the include/base directory, all other header files simply include a reference to the nsapi.h file. These additional files are included for backward compatibility with earlier NSAPI programs. If you look inside these Server 3.x additional files found under the include directory and frame or base subdirectories, you notice that all files basically include the following lines of code:

```
#ifndef PUBLIC_NSAPI_H
#include "../nsapi.h"
#endif /* !PUBLIC_NSAPI_H */
```

Consequently, with Server 3.x, you need to include only the nsapi.h file when compiling your NSAPI program.

Because of the changes to Server 3.x, reviewing the nsapi.h file for information about NSAPI functions is not as straightforward as reviewing the header files with the previous servers. NSAPI functions are now defined inside a dispatch vector table within the data structure nsapi_dispatch_s. You need to check in the nsapi_dispatch_s data structure for the function's parameter and return value. You then read the note about each function further down in the file, where each function is defined.

There are many functions defined in the nsapi.h file that you can use. Nevertheless, you do not need to understand all the functions to program for Netscape Server. Although the functions included in the nsapi.h file provide valuable features, most of the functions have very specific or limited usage. You mainly use a subset of these functions, which we will describe in this chapter.

Data Structures

There are a number of data structures in the Netscape Server headers. In the following sections, we will discuss the major data structures. As you might guess, some are more important to learn immediately. We will begin with the most commonly used and most important data structures: `pblock`, `Session`, and `Request`.

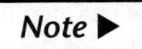

Note ▶

The data structure definitions included in this chapter are for Server 3.5.1. Servers 3.0x, 2.x, and 1.x may have different data structure definitions. The data structure variables may be different for various versions of the server. Throughout this chapter data structure's member variables that are unique to 3.0x and 3.5.1 Servers are noted.

Func, FuncPtr, and FuncStruct

Func is the prototype for a server application function (SAF), which is what you write when you write an NSAPI application. The declaration of Func is the same as the declaration of an NSAPI function (that is, it would include `pblock`, `Session`, and `Request` as parameters and return an integer). The definition of Func is as follows:

```
#ifdef XP_UNIX
typedef int Func(pblock *, Session *, Request *);
#else /* XP_WIN32 */
typedef int _cdecl Func(pblock *, Session *, Request *);
#endif
```

Your SAF may look something like `NSAPI_PUBLIC myfunction(pblock* param, Session *sn, Request *rq);`. XP_UNIX and XP_WIN32 are internal preprocessor flags for cross-platform support of Netscape Server.

FuncPtr points to a specific function. It is defined as follows:

```
typedef Func *FuncPtr;
```

FuncStruct is used for the static declaration of the functions. It creates a linked list of the functions. The server parses this list into a hash table during start-up. This list includes the functions declared in the **obj.conf** file. Func points to each function. The last entry in the list should be NULL. The FuncStruct definition is as follows:

```
struct FuncStruct {
    char *name;
    FuncPtr func;
```

```
        struct FuncStruct *next;

        /* added with Server 3.0 */
        int flags;

};
```

Sometimes you might like to wrap a new function around an existing function. For example, you might need to debug or log what happens in a function. In these circumstances, you can use `FuncPtr` and `FuncStruct` in addition to the **func_*** functions. The **func_*** functions include **func_find**, **func_insert**, and **func_exec**. With these functions, you can find an existing function, replace it with a new one, and execute the new function in place of the old one.

Three structures are also defined as part of the three parameters for a `Func` or your SAF: `pblock`, `Session`, and `Request`. These structures provide the core of information that you use to process a client request.

pblock

The heart of the HTTP variables (headers) consists of the *name-value* pairs of data sent by the client to the server and by the server to the client. Under Netscape Server, these variables are kept in the parameter block data structure (`pblock`). Each *name-value* pair is referenced by a single data structure, called `pb_param`. Each `pb_param` is one entry in the `pb_entry` linked list. `pblock`, in turn, is the hash table, which stores the *name-value* pairs.

Each `pb_param` data structure holds one *name-value* pair. `name` and `value` point to a string large enough to hold any size of parameters. They do not allow arbitrary types, however. They store text characters.

```
typedef struct {
    char *name,*value;
} pb_param;
```

The server also provides functions that enable you to create and free these parameters (**param_create** and **param_free**).

`pb_entry` is used to generate a linked list of the `pb_param` data structures.

```
struct pb_entry {
    pb_param *param;
    struct pb_entry *next;
};
```

`pblock` is a hash table of the linked list entries (that is, `pb_entry` structures) of single *name-value* pairs (`pb_param` structures). The hash table keeps a link to the first character of the name in the *name-value* pairs. `hsize` holds the number of parameter block entries. The default `pblock` holds a list of parameter block entries large enough to handle all sizes of entries. The actual entries are dynamically allocated per request.

For example, for a none-SSL secured server, no entry is allocated in the `client` pblock for `client->keysize`, `client->cypher`, and `client->secret-keysize`.

```
typedef struct {
    int hsize;
    struct pb_entry **ht;
} pblock;
```

The `pblock` data structure allows you to manipulate the group of *name-value* pairs as one variable and access each member, as you need it. Netscape provides a number of functions for managing parameter blocks. (We will discuss most of these functions in the `pblock` and `param` Functions section later in this chapter.) For example, there are functions that enable you to free, copy, remove, or create a `pblock` (**pblock_free**, **pblock_copy**, **pblock_remove**, and **pblock_create**). The hash table provides expeditious accessing of a parameter block. You can also use these functions to create a local copy of the parameters (that is, via **pblock_copy** and **pblock_dup**). There are functions to find or insert a value into a `pb_param` (**pblock_findval**, **pblock_nvinsert**, and **pblock_nninsert**). There are also functions that turn a string into `pblock` entries, or vice versa (**pblock_pblock2str**, and **pblock_str2pblock**).

A number of `pblock` elements in both `Session` and `Request` data structures are passed to your program. You can use these functions to access and manipulate these `pblock` members and their values. Also, settings (parameters) for your function (as defined in the **obj.conf** file) are passed to your program as `pblock` parameters. (A pointer to a `pblock` that accesses these settings from the **obj.conf** file is the first parameter of your SAF.)

Listing 5-1 gives all of the *name-value* pairs in a `pblock` data structure.

Listing 5-1   Reading Through `pb_entry`

```
/* pb_entry structure to hold the parameters */
struct pb_entry *EntryList;
int i;

/* walk through the pb_entry and get all the
   name-value pairs
 */
for (i = 0; i < pb->hsize; i++)
{
    for( entry = pb->ht[i]; EntryList;
         EntryList = EntryList->next )
    {

     /* Each EntryList's param->name includes the name.
        Each param->value includes the parameter value of
        the name-value pair.
```

Listing 5-1   Reading Through `pb_entry` (*continued*)

```
    */
    }
}
```

You can also access a specific `pb_param` by using **pblock_find** to find the *parameter* by its name or by using **pblock_findval** to get the value of the specific parameter. **pblock_pblock2str** can also turn a list of the `pb_param` entries into a string. It returns a string, which includes the `pb_param` entries in [*name*]="[*value*]" format, with the pairs separated by a space character.

Session

The `Session` data structure holds variables applicable throughout the entire session, from when the client connects to when it disconnects. `Session` provides information regarding a client's connection as well as a network buffer or socket link to that client. The following code details the `Session` data structure for Server 3.x.

```c
typedef struct Session {

    pblock *client;

    SYS_NETFD csd;
    netbuf *inbuf;
    int csd_open;

    struct in_addr iaddr;

#ifdef MCC_PROXY
    int req_cnt;
#endif

#ifdef MALLOC_POOLS
    pool_handle_t *pool;
#endif

    void *clauth;

    /* following variables are unique to Server 3.x */
    struct Session *next;
    int fill;
    struct sockaddr_in local_addr;

    struct PListStruct_s *subject;

} Session;
```

The parameter block `client` holds the client-specific information (for example, `dns`, `ip`, `cipher`, `keysize`, and `secret-keysize`). The following list gives the common `client` parameter block variables.

Session->client

- ip (always available)

  (for example, 1.2.3.4)

- dns

  (for example, imagia.com)

- cipher

  (for example, RC4-40)

- keysize

  (for example, 128)

- secret-keysize

  (for example, 40)

- issuer_dn (Enterprise Server 3.5.1 only)

  (for example, CN=Foo Certificate Server o=Foo)

- user_dn (Enterprise Server 3.5.1 only)

  (for example, UID=jdoe, o=Foo)

Although ip (the IP address) is always available, the other variables are available contingent upon your server setup and the request. For example, with a secured SSL server, cipher, keysize, and secret-keysize will be available. The server adds these parameters to the client parameter block. These variables are dynamically allocated. In other words, unless they are needed or specified, the variables will not be present in the client pblock. You can access the client information using the **pblock_findval** function. For example, you can get the IP address with the line pblock_findval("ip", sn->client);. To access the DNS information of the client, you should use the **session_dns** function (char *session_dns(Session *sn)). This function returns the DNS host name of the client, if available, and inserts dns into the client pblock.

csd is the platform-independent socket descriptor for the remote client. You can use it to return data to a client. For example, with **net_write**, you can write a specified number of bytes (len) of buffer (buf) to this socket (through net_write(sn->csd, buf, len)). csd_open is set to 1 when the socket is opened, which means the client is connected. inbuf is the input buffer for the socket descriptor. You can use this buffer to read the client's POST input (*Session*->inbuf).

iaddr holds the data structure for the raw socket information about the remote client. This information is used by the server for internal purposes. req_cnt is specific to proxy servers and is a new variable for this structure, as are the pool and clauth member variables. They were not available in Netscape Server 1.x. pool points to a memory pool that is used to allocate memory (using MALLOC, REALLOC, or another function). (The data in the Request parameter block are allocated using the new memory allocation macros and memory pool.) clauth points to the ACL client authentication information.

next, fill, local_addr, and subject are new variables added with Server 3.x. For example, next points to another Session data structure, and local_addr is the local address for the session. You normally do not reference these variables.

client, csd, and inbuf are the variables you will most likely use in your functions.

Request Data Structure

The Request data structure holds variables that are relevant only to specific requests. For the standard HTTP/1.0 protocol, each session has only one request. Thus Request, like Session, is also applicable for the whole session. With the Keep-Alive capabilities of Server 2.x, a session can be kept open for a request that includes embedded link items. The Keep-Alive connection header is sent by Netscape Navigator (Communicator). The server interprets a request as keeping the connection open until all embedded items are delivered. You can also write your own function for keeping a socket connection open while you accept more than one request.

With Server 3.x, Netscape supports persistent connection as specified in HTTP/1.1. Persistent connection works similar to Keep-Alive. With persistent connection, a session can be kept open until the server or client closes the connection. For a persistent connection to work, the browser needs to support HTTP/1.1. Netscape Communicator 4.x does not use persistent connection as defined in HTTP/1.1. Instead, it supports Keep-Alive. Server 3.x can also handle Keep-Alive connection. The Request data structure defined for Server 3.x includes a number of additional member variables that support HTTP/1.1 features.

```
typedef struct {

    pblock *vars;

    pblock *reqpb;

    int loadhdrs;
    pblock *headers;

    int senthdrs;
    pblock *srvhdrs;

    httpd_objset *os;
    httpd_objset *tmpos;

    char *statpath;
    char *staterr;
    struct stat *finfo;

    int aclstate;
    int acldirno;
    char *aclname;
    pblock *aclpb;
```

```c
        /* Server 3.x ACL list pointer */
        struct ACLListHandle *acllist;
#ifdef MCC_PROXY
        struct hostent *hp;
        char *host;
        int    port;
        void *socks_rq;
#endif

        int request_is_cacheable;
        int directive_is_cacheable;

        char *cached_headers;
        int cached_headers_len;
        char *unused;

/* no longer part of 3.x

        char *cached_date_header;
 */

/* Following variables are unique to Server 3.x.
   They support HTTP/1.1
 */
        time_t req_start;

#define REQ_TIME(x)        (x)->req_start
        short protv_num;
        short method_num;

        struct rq_attr
        {
#ifdef AIX
                unsigned abs_uri:1;
                unsigned chunked:1;
                unsigned keep_alive:1;
                unsigned pipelined:1;
                unsigned reserved:28;
#else
                unsigned long abs_uri:1;
                unsigned long chunked:1;
                unsigned long keep_alive:1;
                unsigned pipelined:1;
                unsigned long reserved:28;
#endif
        }rq_attr;
```

```
    char * hostname;
    int allowed;
    int byterange;
    short status_num;

    int staterrno;

} Request;
```

Four parameter blocks in the `Request` structure hold the HTTP request and response headers: `vars`, `reqpb`, `headers`, and `srvhdrs`. The actual parameters in these structures vary based on the server setup, the type of request, and the type of NSAPI function. The server allocates these variables as needed. In other words, unless they are needed, the variables will not be present in the parameter blocks. The parameter block entries are dynamically generated for each request. For example, authentication information is available if you have required it for your site. The `query` member variable for the `reqpb` structure is available only for a `GET` method of request.

You get the value of the parameters in the parameter blocks using **pblock_findval**—as in, for example, `pblock_findval("method", rq->reqpb)`. The `Request->headers` variables are an exception. Netscape provides a specific function **request_header** to access these variables—as in `request_header("user-agent", &ua, sn, rq)`. This function accesses the headers indirectly from your copy of the `Request` structure. You should use **request_header** to access `header` parameter block entries.

The type of server directive that is processing the request affects what information is available in these parameter blocks. (You can also write your own programs for a specific type of directive.) Each directive has specific information available to it. Although most of these variables are available for all directives, they are not *all* available for all directives. Less or different information may be given from one directive to another. As you might expect, there is usually more information available as you go down the list of directives. For example, there are more variables available for a **Service** function than for an **AuthTrans** function. Moreover, some directives are intended to work with specific information—that is, use a specific variable or alter a specific variable. Often, one directive is responsible for changing a variable, even when that variable is available to other directives. For example, `content-type` is not available before an **ObjectType** directive function. It is set by the **ObjectType** directive and is then available to a **Service** directive. (See Chapter 8, SAF and Server Directives, for more details.)

pblock (`vars`) for the Server Variables

The following list gives the important server's working variables (`vars`).

`Request->vars`

- ppath (always available)
  (for example, `/news`)

- `ntrans-base`

  (for example, `c:/netscape/server/docs`)
- `path`

  (for example, `c:/netscape/server/docs/news.html`)
- `path-info`

  (for example, `special/license.txt`)
- `url`

  (for example, `http://newserver/new.html`)
- `auth-type`

  (for example, `basic`)
- `auth-user`

  (for example, `john`)
- `auth-group`

  (for example, `engineers`)
- `auth-db`

  (for example, `c:/netscape/server/authdb/default`)
- `userdn`

  (for example, `uid=jdoe`)
- `auth-password`

  (for example, `awarded`)
- `started-keep-alive`

  (for example, `1`)
- `shellcgi-path`

  (for example, `c:/netscape/server/shellcgi/myprogram.pl`)
- `boundary`

  (for example, `--5682115017812`)
- `auth-cert`

  (in MIME base-64 encoded, ASN.1 encoded X.509 format)

`ppath` is always available for the request, regardless of the type of request. Other variables, however, are not always available. For example, if the server and client (such as Netscape Navigator 3.x and Server 2.x) use a `Keep-Alive` connection, then the `started-keep-alive` variable is set to 1. If the request is a Shell CGI program, the `shellcgi-path` variable is set. (You will obviously not use the information from `shellcgi-path`, as you are writing an NSAPI program and not a Shell CGI program!) Also, if you have required authentication, then the values for `auth-type`, `auth-user`, and so on, will be available. These variables are available for an

AuthTrans function to check values and verify authenticity. Normally, the `auth-db` variable indicates the location of the user database, which is in the NCSA and DBM format for Servers 1.x and 2.x, respectively. When using an LDAP directory server or the local database, which is also an LDAP directory, the Server 3.0x does not use or specify `auth-db`. On the other hand, Server 3.5.1 does add the `auth-db` entry in the `vars` parameter block with the value `default`. The variable `default` indicates that the default user database (LDAP directory specified for the server) is used for authentication. The **NameTrans** function sets the `path` information using the `ppath` and name translation base directory (`ntrans-base`). The **NameTrans** function actually changes the `ppath` information to reflect the system path. The server then converts (renames) the `ppath` to `path` once it is finished with the **NameTrans** directive. Thus, `ppath` is no longer available after the **NameTrans** directive. `path-info` is available if the request has extended path information. This information is relevant only for a CGI program. When the response status is set to redirect the client, the server looks to the `url` entry for the new location. (See Redirecting the Client in Chapter 6 for more details.) `boundary` is set by the server to support multipart MIME type messages. To have the client certificate (`auth-cert`) placed inside the `vars` pblock, you need to declare the **PathCheck** function **get-client-cert** in the **obj.conf** file. Security must also be set to `on` and the client must be required to send the certificate.

Unlike with `Request->headers`, the pblock entries that you might add to a `Request->vars` pblock are not checked by the server. The server does not verify the values of the `vars` pblock entries not produced by the server. Therefore, if you wish to add an arbitrary type of data to a `Request` pblock data structure, you can include it in this pblock. Later directive functions can also access this information. The server function **FREE** should also be able to free the memory of the value you add.

Request pblock (`reqpb`)

The pblock `reqpb` holds the main `Request` parameter blocks. `Request` parameter blocks include information in the standard Request-Line, *Method Request-URI HTTP-Version*. The following list contains the important `reqpb` variables.

`Request->reqpb`

- `method` (always available)
  (for example, `GET`)
- `protocol` (always available)
  (for example, `HTTP/1.0`)
- `uri` (always available)
  (for example, /news)
- `query`
  (for example, `name=john&phone=555-5555`)

- `clf-request` (always available)

  (for example, `GET / HTTP/1.0`)

`method`, `protocol`, and `uri` are all specific information about the request. `clf-request` is the full Request-Line and the first line of the client request. `clf` (common log file) refers to the fact that this information is also logged in the access log file. This information is always included with every client request. `query`, although part of `reqpb`, is not part of Request-Line. `query` is an exception that is available only for a `GET` method of request. For a `GET` request, the `query` is available for all directives. Typically, you use the information from `reqpb`—for example, `method`—with a **Service** function to process a client's `GET` or `POST` request. Most of these variables are available not only for any type of request, but also for any directive function you may write.

Headers pblock (`headers`)

pblock `headers` holds the request headers. Typically, they are the same as the CGI environment variables that start with `HTTP_`—that is, HTTP headers (with the exception of `authorization`, `host`, and `pragma`). They are the additional variables that specify the type of request or client. The `Request` data structure variable `loadhdrs` holds the number of headers that are loaded for the request (that is, the number of `entries` for the pblock `headers`). If more than one header value exists for a specific request header name, the values are separated by a comma. (For example, the `accept` header for Communicator 4.04 includes `image/gif`, `image/x-xbitmap`, `image/jpeg`, `image/pjpeg`, `image/png`, and `*/*`. Unlike CGI environment variables, these values are all in lowercase for NSAPI and do not begin with `HTTP_`. Also, they use a dash (-) instead of an underscore. The following list contains some of the important `header` variables.

Request->headers

- `host` (usually available)

  (for example, `www.traveller.com`)
- `authorization`

  (for example, `Basic a2F2ZWg6Z3JhdmU=`)
- `accept` (usually available)

  (for example, `image/gif`, `image/x-xbitmap`, `image/jpeg`, `image/pjpeg`, `image/png`, `*/*`)
- `user-agent` (usually available)

  (for example, `Mozilla/4.04 [en] (WinNT; I)`)
- `connection` (available with Navigator 3.x and 4.x)

  (for example, `Keep-Alive`)

- referer

  (for example, `http://home.netscape.com`)
- if-modified-since

  (for example, `Monday, 24-Jun-96 21:36:04 GMT; length=44263`)
- cookie

  (for example, `NETSCAPE_LIVEWIRE.name=cipher`)
- pragma

  (for example, `no-cache`)
- content-length

  (for example, `2096`)
- content-type

  (for example, `application/x-www-form-urlencoded`)
- content-encoding

  (for example, `x-gzip`)
- accept-language

  (for example, `en`)
- accept-charset

  (for example, `iso-8859-1,*,utf-8`)

Again, not all of these variables are available for every request. `host`, `accept`, and `user-agent` are usually sent by the client browser and are usually available. By default, Communicator 4.x also sends `accept-language` and `accept-charset`. The `authorization` variable is available for a request when you have required authorization. `connection` is usually set to `Keep-Alive`, when this type of connection is in use. `referer` is sent by the client when it is possible to specify the URI from which the current request was made. In other words, the client was referred to this location by clicking on a hyperlink in another document. `if-modified-since`, used with a `GET` method, lets the server know to send the data if the file has been changed since the specified date. Otherwise, the server sends back status 304 (`Local Copy`). `cookie` is available if there is a cookie set by `Request->srvhdrs`. The `pragma` variable is mainly used to tell whether caching is expected. `pragma: no-cache` is similar to the HTTP/1.1 header `Cache-Control: no-cache` and is used to provide backward compatibility with HTTP/1.0 clients and servers. If `pragma` is set to `no-cache`, the server must not use a cached copy for its response. `content-length` and `content-type` are specified for a `POST` request. NSAPI functions use this information to determine the size and type of data sent through a `POST` method of request. These `content-length` and `content-type` variables differ from the variables by the same name in the server response header pblock, `Request->srvhdrs`.

(content-length and content-type for *Request*->srvhdrs specify the length and size of the data being sent to the client.)

There can be any number of HTTP headers specified for a request. These headers are request-specific and can be different for different browsers. For example, Microsoft Internet Explorer 3.x also includes ua-cpu, ua-os, ua-color, and ua-pixels. If you wish to provide additional environment variables for a CGI program, you can add the headers to the *Request*->headers. These headers are then available as HTTP_* to your CGI program.

Server Header pblock (**srvhdrs**)

The pblock srvhdrs holds the server response headers—that is, the specific headers that are to be sent before the requested data (entity-body). This information is usually set by a **Service** directive and is also available for an **AddLog** function. But they can also be set by other directives. For example, status 401 Unauthorized is sent by an **AuthTrans** function. The following list contains the some of the important srvhdrs parameters.

Request->srvhdrs

- status (always returned to the client)
  (for example, 401 Unauthorized)
- WWW-authenticate (for example, basic realm=\"personal site\")
  —auth-type
  (for example, basic)
  —realm
  (for example, personal site)
- content-type (always returned to the client)
  (for example, text\html)
- content-length
  (for example, 223)
- content-encoding
  (for example, x-gzip)
- content-language
  (for example, en_US)
- magnus-charset
  (for example, ISO-8859-1)
- Expires
  (for example, Thu, 01 Jan 1998 16:00:00 GMT)

- `Date`

  (for example, `Sun, 15 Sep 1996 12:00:00 GMT`)
- `last-modified`

  (for example, `Sun, 15 Sep 1996 17:52:50 GMT`)
- `set-cookie`

  (for example, `NETSCAPE_LIVEWIRE.name=cipher; path=/appmgr`)
- `accept-ranges`

  (`bytes`)
- `Location`

  (for example, `http://www.newserver.com/`)

`status` includes the status information used in the Status-Line, the first line of response message. It includes Status-Code and Reason-Phrase. If authentication is required, `WWW-authenticate` is returned to the client, indicating the type of authentication required. `content-type` and `content-length` are usually returned as well. The client needs to know at least the type of data, so as to process the information and display the data correctly. With `status` "`304 Use local copy`", however, no `content-type` is sent and `content-length` is set to 0. These `content-type` and `content-length` variables differ from the variables of the same name sent by the client in `Request->headers`. In this context, the headers `content-length` and `content-type` specify the length and size of the data being sent to the client. You have to set `content-type` with your function. You can also set `content-length`. Your program, however, normally functions properly without it. Note that `content-length` must be present for the `Keep-Alive` connection to work. Unlike CGI programs, you need to set `content-length` with your function. The server does not handle this task automatically for you. If appropriate, `content-encoding`, `content-language`, and `magnus-charset` are also sent. This information lets the browser know the type of data it is receiving. For example, Netscape Communicator can then use the character set defined by `magnus-charset`. `Expires` is the date when the document expires. `Date` is the current date. The `last-modified` value can be used as a cache validator (for example, to let the client know to use cached data, if the data have not been modified since the `last-modified` value). To get the last-modified date of a file, you can use the **stat** function. (See the `finfo` (`stat`) section later in this chapter for more information.) You can also create a cookie using `set-cookie`. A `cookie` is a trigger text saved on the client machine and accessible to you through `Request->header`. `accept-ranges` indicates that the server accepts byte-range requests. `Location` is used to redirect a client to a new location.

Other Request *Data Structure Variables*

Other variables in the Request structure include os and tmpos. They hold the server Object sets constructed for processing the request. os (Object set) is created from the **obj.conf** file data, and tmpos (temporary Object set) is created from the .nsconfig file. (.nsconfig files are used for dynamic configuration of the server, as discussed in Appendix D).

statpath, staterr, and finfo contain stat-related information about the specific request last returned by **request_stat_path**. They give information about the file requested. statpath is the physical path to the file. staterr holds the error string when an error occurs while reading the stat structure. finfo holds the stat structure of the requested file. (See also the discussion of finfo in the File-Related Data Structures section later in this chapter.)

aclstate, acldirno, aclname, and aclpb hold the ACL (Access Control List) information. These variables are new to the Request data structure (they are not part of Netscape Server 1.x). They make ACL information available to your program. aclstate identifies the ACL state. acldirno holds the number of ACL directives. aclname holds the name of the ACL. aclpb holds the parameter block for the **PathCheck** functions that define the ACL (**check-acl**). Netscape Server 3.x Request also includes another ACL variable, acllist, which points to the ACL list. (See the discussion of ACL files in Appendix C and **PathCheck** function **check-acl** in Appendix B for more information.)

hp (DNS resolution result), host (host to connect to), port (port to connect to), and sock_rq (SOCKS request data) are specific for the proxy servers. host, hp, and port are new variables for Server 2.0 and later.

request_is_cacheable, directive_is_cacheable, cached_headers, cached_headers_len, and cached_date_header include settings and information about the cached headers, and whether the request and the directives are actually cached. Server caching of request variables is a new feature and was not part of Netscape 1.x servers. Netscape has improved the processing of client requests, largely through the use of cache. As a default, the server caches a response and sends the same response to different clients (when the requested file has not changed—that is, when the request generates the same response). The server can also cache the directive functions (for example, your NSAPI function). The default setting is TRUE for request_is_cacheable and FALSE for directive_is_cacheable. The caching of requests and directives improves the server's performance. You should cache your function only if the response is not dependent on the specifics of the request. In other words, if your function uses the client input, ip, or other request-specific information to process the request and generate the data it delivers, then you should not cache the directive. This suggestion is especially true for custom logging and authentication functions. In your program, you can change the value of these variables in the Request structure, thereby changing the way the server responds to the request. To illustrate, if you set directive_is_cacheable to TRUE (1), then your function is cached (that is, it is not called every time a client makes a request). If you find discrepancies in the server response even when directive caching is disabled, then make sure to disable request caching. If the server's caching of the request interferes with your function's dynamic generation of the correct information each time, then set the value for both of these Request variables to FALSE. For your NSAPI function to work properly, it is important that the cache settings for the request and directive be correct. Otherwise, the same information is sent to the various clients, even when the results should be different. Also, a new call to a database might not be made. Instead, the cached result of the previous call will be sent to the client. (Caching between a client and the server for performance improvement is also part of the HTTP/1.1 specification.)

req_start, protv_num, method_num, rq_attr, hostname, allowed, byterange, status_num, and staterrno are new variables for Netscape Server 3.x. They are added to provide HTTP/1.1 support. req_start and macro REQ_TIME(rq) are for the requested time and are used for verifying weak or strong cache validation. REQ_TIME(rq) is defined as (rq)->req_start (rq is for the request data structure). protv_num and method_num are used for the protocol version and method number, respectively. For Server 3.x, the current protocol version is 101 (CURRENT_PROTOCOL_VERSION 101). METHODS and their numbers are defined as follows in nsapi.h:

```
---METHODS for HTTP/1.1
#define METHOD_HEAD            0
#define METHOD_GET             1
#define METHOD_PUT             2
#define METHOD_POST            3
#define METHOD_DELETE          4
#define METHOD_TRACE           5
#define METHOD_OPTIONS         6

/* The following methods are Netscape method extensions */
#define METHOD_MOVE            7
#define METHOD_INDEX           8
#define METHOD_MKDIR           9
#define METHOD_RMDIR           10
#define METHOD_COPY            11

#define METHOD_MAX             12
```

METHOD_MAX is the maximum number of methods that the server supports. Macros for verifying method_num are defined as follows in the nsapi.h file (r is for the request data structure):

```
#define  ISMGET(r)       ((r)->method_num == METHOD_GET)
#define  ISMHEAD(r)      ((r)->method_num == METHOD_HEAD)
#define  ISMPUT(r)       ((r)->method_num == METHOD_PUT)
#define  ISMPOST(r)      ((r)->method_num == METHOD_POST)
```

```
#define ISMDELETE(r)    ((r)->method_num == METHOD_DELETE)
#define ISMMOVE(r)      ((r)->method_num == METHOD_MOVE)
#define ISMINDEX(r)     ((r)->method_num == METHOD_INDEX)
#define ISMMKDIR(r)     ((r)->method_num == METHOD_MKDIR)
#define ISMRMDIR(r)     ((r)->method_num == METHOD_RMDIR)
#define ISMCOPY(r)      ((r)->method_num == METHOD_COPY)
#define ISMTRACE(r)     ((r)->method_num == METHOD_TRACE)
#define ISMOPTIONS(r)   ((r)->method_num == METHOD_OPTIONS)
```

The `rq_attr` data structure is for the request-specific attributes. It includes the following variables: `abs_uri:1`, `chuncked:1`, `keep_alive:1`, `pipelined:1`, and `reserved:28`. The variable `abs_uri` is set to 1 when the absolute URI is used. `chunked` is set to 1 when the chunked transfer-coding is used. `keep_alive` is set to 1 when a `keep_alive` connection is used. `pipelined` is set to 1 when the requested packet is pipelined. Macros for these variables are defined as follows in `nsapi.h` (x is for the request data structure):

```
#define ABS_URI(x)      (x)->rq_attr.abs_uri
#define CHUNKED(x)      (x)->rq_attr.chunked
#define KEEP_ALIVE(x)   (x)->rq_attr.keep_alive
#define PIPELINED(x)    (x)->rq_attr.pipelined
```

`reserved` is set to a default of 28. You should reduce this number by 1 if a bit flag is added. `hostname` is for the host name used for the request and should not be NULL if the absolute URI is used (`abs_uri:1`). `allowed` specifies the number of allowed request METHODs for your server. `byterange` specifies the byte range as an integer. `status_num` is the status code for the request. `staterrno` is for private use by `rqstat`.

File-Related Data Structures

Specific file-related data structures are defined in the NSAPI header files. You can use these structures to take advantage of platform-independent file I/O support (such as reading and writing to a file or performing buffered I/O on a file). `stat` holds the system-related information about a file. `cinfo` holds content information about a file, which is typically unique to the HTTP use of the file (such as the MIME type of the file). The actual definition or member of the data structure may vary based on the operating system, but the entire data structure is a variable that works independent of the platform.

SYS_FILE

`SYS_FILE` specifies a file descriptor. It is defined as an integer for UNIX. You use a file descriptor to access a file. The specifics of the file descriptor are based on your operating system and the C system header files (such as `sys/file.h` and `sys/types.h`). You do not need to know what precisely a file descriptor is to use it.

For WIN32, SYS_FILE is defined as follows in the Server 2.x header file:

```
typedef struct {
    HANDLE fh;
    char *fname;
    SEMAPHORE flsem;
} file_s;

typedef file_s* SYS_FILE;
```

fh is the file handle. fname is the file name. flsem is the SEMAPHORE associated with the file. flsem is used later by **system_flock** and **system_ulock** for WIN32 (NT and 95). **system_flock** locks the current file against use by other processes. This data structure is hidden and is not defined in nsapi.h for Netscape Server 3.x.

SYS_FILE is used by a number of **system_***, **filebuf_***, and **pipebuf_*** functions. For example, SYS_FILE is the return value of system_fopenRO(char *path), which you can use to open a file. You can use the returned SYS_FILE variable to read from the file via system_fread(SYS_FILE fd, char *buf, int sz).

filebuffer (and filbuf or filbuf_t)

filebuffer is the other abstraction that you can use to perform file I/O. You can use filebuffer on the file to take advantage of buffered file I/O. (You must also declare a SYS_FILE to use with **filebuf** functions.) The default filebuffer data structure does not support mmap (memory mapping).

```
typedef struct {
    SYS_FILE fd;
    int pos, cursize, maxsize;

    /* for Server 3.x, inbuf is assigned
       to an unsigned char * instead of char *
     */
    unsigned char *inbuf;
    char *errmsg;
} filebuffer;
```

filebuffer includes SYS_FILE as a member. pos, cursize, and maxsize define the position of the cursor in a file, the size of the current file, and the maximum size. inbuf is the pointer to the buffer string. errmsg points to the error string that can occur with the buffer. It is obtained from the specific operating system, which allows for a platform-independent error messages. You can use this errmsg string instead of seeking the specific operating system error that occurred with the buffer.

```
#ifdef FILE_MMAP

typedef struct {
```

```
        SYS_FILE fd;
#ifdef FILE_UNIX_MMAP
        caddr_t fp;
#else /* FILE_WIN32_MMAP */
        HANDLE fdmap;
        char *fp;
#endif

        int len;

        /* for Server 3.x, inbuf is assigned
           to an unsigned char * instead of char *
         */
        unsigned char *inbuf;
        int cursize;
        int pos;
        char *errmsg;

} filebuffer;
```

If memory mapping (FILE_MMAP) is enabled, then the filebuffer given above is used. Memory mapping allows the file's contents to be mapped to the specified process's virtual address space. You can set file caching and the maximum amount of mmap files through the **Init** directive function **cache-init**. The parameters for **cache-init** are different for Server 2.x and 3.x. The mmap-max parameter is used for the **cache-init** function under Server 2.x to define the size of memory set aside for memory-mapped files. For Server 3.x, you use the parameter MaxTotalCacheFileSize. (See the discussion of **cache-init** in Appendix B for more details.) Memory mapping allows functions like **filebuf_getc** to use the elements len and fp for reading through the length of the file, one character at a time. Otherwise, **filebuf_getc** reads through the file using cursize, inbuf, and the function **filebuf_next**. (**filebuf_next** is used to load additional bytes of data into the buffer or return BUFFER_EOF or BUFFER_ERROR in case of error. See the filbuf Functions section later in this chapter for more details.)

For the UNIX filebuffer data structure, the fp member variable is a caddr_t type defined through the C system header file sys/types.h. For WIN32, fp is defined as char *. fdmap is used as a mapped file HANDLE. The variable len is used for the length of the file data. For filebuffer using mmap, there is no maxsize. The other elements of the filebuffer are the same for both the mmap version and the default version.

Netscape Server 3.x also includes a definition for filebuf_t, an alias for filebuffer defined in the nsapi.h file. filebuf_t is used in place of the filebuf alias used with the original Netscape Server 1.x and 2.x. filebuf_t replaces filebuf to resolve the conflict between the Netscape filebuf and the C++ class filebuf. If you want to write a program that is compatible with all versions of Netscape Server, use filebuffer instead of the alias filebuf or filebuf_t. In addition, note that the inbuf variable for filebuffer is defined as unsigned char * instead of char * for Netscape Server 3.x.

The filebuffer functions include **filebuf_getc**, **filebuf_create**, **filbuf_open_nostat**, **filebuf_buf2sd**, and so on. You normally create a filebuffer using **filebuf_open** or **filebuf_open_nostat** and then destroy the buffer using **filebuf_close**. With **filebuf_create**, **filebuf_open**, and **filebuf_open_nostat**, SYS_FILE is used as a parameter to create the file buffer. **filebuf_close_buffer** uses filebuffer as a parameter to close a file buffer. For samples of NSAPI programs that use the SYS_FILE and filebuffer data structures, look at Netscape's NSAPI addlog.c and service.c server examples. We will also use filebuffer in the Guest Book example in Chapter 9.

It is best not to access the members of the filebuffer data structure directly. Instead, you should use the **filebuf_*** functions that Netscape provides.

finfo (stat)

The stat (_stat for Windows NT) data structure holds the information about a file or directory. It serves as the operating system's data structure for a file or directory. The stat data structure includes different information for different platforms. You can obtain this data structure by using the system functions **stat** or **_stat** for Windows NT (for example, stat(<path of the file>, &<stat data structure>)). Netscape defines and uses finfo (file information) as a pointer to struct stat. For example, the **system_stat** function (equivalent to the system function **stat**) is defined as system_stat(char *name, struct stat *finfo).

util_can_exec, **protocol_stat_finfo**, **protocol_set_finfo**, **filebuf_open_nostat**, and **pipebuf_open** are other examples of functions that use finfo as a parameter. You can get the file information (finfo) by using the **stat** system function on a file or by using the NSAPI function **request_stat_path** or **system_stat**.

finfo can then be used by one of the functions (for example, **filebuf_open_nostat** includes the address of finfo as its third parameter). Once you have finfo, you can access the specific file information (for example, finfo.st_size obtains the size of the file whose stat you have). (See also the Netscape NSAPI example, service.c under <server path>/nsapi/examples, and the filebuf Functions section later in this chapter.)

The following code illustrates a typical stat structure (_stat) taken from the NT sys/stat.h file.

```
struct _stat {

    _dev_t st_dev; /* drive number of the disk containing
                      the file (NT) */
    _ino_t st_ino; /* number of information nodes (inode)
                      (UNIX) */
```

```
    unsigned short st_mode; /* Bit masks for file-mode
                               information. They include
                               information about the path
                               (file or directory), the
                               read/write permissions, and
                               the user execution bits. */
    short st_nlink; /* Number of links to a file. For NT, this
                       is always 1 on non-NTFS file systems. */
    short st_uid;   /* numeric identifier of the user who owns
                       the file (UNIX-specific) */
    short st_gid;   /* owner's group ID, numeric ID of the
                       group that owns the file (UNIX) */
    _dev_t st_rdev;  /* drive number of disk containing the
                        file (same as st_dev) */
    _off_t st_size;  /* size of the file in bytes */
    time_t st_atime; /* time of last access to file */
    time_t st_mtime; /* time of last modification to file */
    time_t st_ctime; /* time of creation of the file */
    };
```

st_ino, st_uid, and st_gid are specific for UNIX and have no purpose under NT. Under UNIX, inode (st_ino) describes the file data, time stamps, permissions, and content. It is used, for instance, when you create a soft link between two files. Those files then share the same inode. Look in the C system header file's stat.h file for more details.

The variables you will most frequently use are st_size, st_ctime, and st_mtime. Using **system_stat**, you are guaranteed only of retrieving the following elements: st_mode, st_size, st_ctime, and st_mtime.

cinfo

cinfo is the content information data structure of a file. It includes content-type, content-encoding, and content-language—that is, the standard MIME type information about the file. The cinfo data structure and functions can be used by an **ObjectType** directive function to map a file to a MIME type. Similar MIME type information is also specified for the body of the request in the HTTP entity-header and in the CGI environment variables. The cinfo definition is as follows:

```
typedef struct {
    char *type;
    char *encoding;
    char *language;
} cinfo;
```

type defines the type of data in the file. encoding determines whether any form of encoding (uuencode) or compression (x-gzip) is used on the file. language determines the language of the text and thereby the type of character set to be used for the text. If multiple types of attributes are used, they are listed in a string, separated with a comma. For example, encoding could include "-uuencode, x-gzip".

Curiously, if you look in the cinfo.h file for Server 2.x, you will see that other types of attributes have been specified for the cinfo data structure in the comment lines above the cinfo. description and viewer are explained as part of the cinfo data structure, but they are not part of the data structure. description is defined as the text string describing the file; viewer is the program used to view the file. These comments point to the expected additional file content information that Netscape intended for the 3.0 version of the server. Server 3.x, however, does not add any additional member variables for the cinfo data structure.

The **cinfo_find** function can be used to find the content information of a file by working with the file's URI or name (cinfo *cinfo_find(char *uri)). Other **cinfo_*** functions include **cinfo_init**, **cinfo_lookup**, **cinfo_terminate**, and so on.

Socket-Related Data Structures

Netscape provides abstract, platform-independent data structures—similar to file I/O—to support socket I/O and network buffering. These data structures, and their associated functions, allow the server to open and close a socket channel to a client. Sockets represent the end point of a communication between processes. They are bound to a network address (for example, an IP address). Two applications can exchange data across a network by sending and receiving packets of data to and from a socket, respectively. The server can also read and write from a socket by using network buffers for more efficient communication. SYS_NETFD is the socket descriptor. sockaddr_in specifies a socket address. netbuf is the data structure for the network buffer.

SYS_NETFD

SYS_NETFD is a platform-independent data structure for the socket descriptor. A socket descriptor is similar to a file descriptor. In fact, many of the same functions for reading and writing a file also work on sockets. It is best, however, to keep files and sockets separate and to use the appropriate functions defined for each. Under UNIX, a socket descriptor is an unsigned integer. Under NT, a socket descriptor is a HANDLE. You should review your specific operating system's resources for more information on socket descriptors. Socket information is available through sys/socket.h for UNIX and through winsock.h for WIN32. As with a file descriptor (HANDLE), however, you do not need to know what precisely a socket is to use it.

Netscape Enterprise Server 3.5.1 includes a new NSAPI function, **net_native_handle** (net_native_handle(SYSNETFD s)), that returns the native operating system's handle associated with a `SYS_NETFD`. The function returns an integer on UNIX and a `HANDLE` on NT.

`SYS_NETFD` is used in many **net_*** functions (for example, **net_read**, **net_write**, **net_connect**, **net_close**, and so on). **net_socket** returns the socket descriptor (`net_socket(int domain, int type, int protocol)`). During an HTTP request, a socket descriptor for the remote client is created in the `Session` data structure for each session. You use **net_write** to write a number of bytes from a defined buffer to the socket descriptor (`net_write(SYS_NETFD sd, char *buf, int sz)`). `SYS_NETFD` is also part of the `netbuf` data structure.

sockaddr_in *(and* sockaddr*)*

`sockaddr_in` is used to specify a socket address—that is, the local or remote address to which the socket will be connected. The data structure is defined in `winsock.h` for WIN32 and in `netinet/in.h` for UNIX platforms. The structure is defined for NT as follows:

```
struct sockaddr_in{
    short              sin_family;
    unsigned short     sin_port;
    struct in_addr     sin_addr;
    char               sin_zero[8];
};
```

`sin_family` is the address family, describing the format of the address. `sin_port` is the IP port. `sin_addr` is the IP address. Its structure is of type `in_addr`, the type of the IP address, which is a union that lets the address be seen as one long, two shorts, or four bytes. `sin_zero` is padding to keep the structure the same size as `SOCKADDR`. `SOCKADDR` is used for different types of socket connection (for example, `sockaddr_ipx` for an IPX address). `sockaddr_in` is for TCP/IP. We are interested in `sockaddr_in`, which is used to create a session in **session_create** (that is, `session_create(SYS_NETFD csd, struct sockaddr_in *sac)`). It is also used in **net_accept**, **net_bind**, **net_connect**, and **net_getpeername**. You will rarely use `sockaddr_in` or these **net_*** functions in your function.

netbuf

`netbuf` is a platform-independent network buffer data structure. You typically use this data structure to read from the client socket and to write to the client socket. The `netbuf` definition from `nsapi.h` header file for Server 3.x is as follows:

```
typedef struct {

    SYS_NETFD sd;

    int pos, cursize, maxsize, rdtimeout;
```

```
        /* for Server 3.x, inbuf is assigned
           to an unsigned char * instead of char *
         */
        unsigned char *inbuf;
        char *errmsg;
#ifndef XP_WIN32
        char address[64];
#endif

} netbuf;
```

As you might have expected, the `netbuf` data structure is similar to `filebuffer`.
The data structure `netbuf` includes comparable elements (like `pos`, `cursize`,
`maxsize`, `inbuf`, and `errmsg`). Although the structure is the same, these elements
apply to network socket and buffer information—not the file buffer. There is also no
memory-mapped (mmap) option available for `netbuf`. The data structure `netbuf`
includes an additional member `address` for Win32. Most likely, you will not refer
directly to any of the data structure's members. As with `inbuf` for `filebuffer`, the
`inbuf` member variable of `netbuf` is also assigned to an `unsigned char *` under
Server 3.x.

Functions for `netbuf` include **netbuf_buf2sd**, **netbuf_grab**, **netbuf_getc**,
netbuf_next, **netbuf_open**, **protocol_scan_headers**, and so on. **netbuf_open**
creates a new `netbuf` structure for processing buffered data input and output
from a socket. `netbuf` is also part of the `Session` data structure
(`Session->inbuf`) that is created for the session between the client and server.
You can use **netbuf_grab** and **netbuf_getc** to read the network buffer data (for
example, `Session->inbuf`). **netbuf_buf2sd** sends a specified number of bytes
of data from a predefined network buffer to a specified socket
(`netbuf_buf2sd(netbuf *buf, SYS_NETFD sd, int len)`).

Directory-Related Data Structures

`SYS_DIR` and `SYS_DIRENT` are two platform-independent data structures for directory manipulation. `SYS_DIR` points to a directory structure. `SYS_DIRENT` holds the
entries. The specific definitions of these data structures vary according to the operating
system. For UNIX, they are referenced from the C header file, `dirent.h`, and
defined as follows:

```
typedef DIR* SYS_DIR;
typedef struct dirent SYS_DIRENT;
```

For NT (Win32), they are defined as follows:

```
typedef struct {
    char *d_name;
```

```
} dirent_s;

typedef struct {
    HANDLE dp;
    WIN32_FIND_DATA fdata;
    dirent_s de;
} dir_s;

typedef dir_s* SYS_DIR;
typedef dirent_s SYS_DIRENT;
```

The directory function **dir_open** returns SYS_DIR for the specified path. **dir_read** then uses SYS_DIR as a parameter to read a directory and return SYS_DIRENT. Other functions include **dir_close**, **dir_create**, and **dir_remove**. (The last two functions are redefinitions of **mkdir** or **rmdir** for UNIX or **_mkdir** and **_rmdir** for WIN32.)

Memory-Related Data Structures

Two data structures are defined for sharing memory between different processes and different threads. The shared memory data structure is used across processes. The memory pool data structure gives each thread its own memory space from a pool of memory.

shmem_s

The shmem_s data structure provides platform-independent shared memory support. It is used to support data sharing and protection across multiple server processes. Shared memory is inherited by the child processes. It should be allocated in an **Init** function before any daemon process is spawned. Netscape uses files internally to manage shared regions. You can first allocate a shared memory space by using **shmem_alloc**, and then free the same region by using **shmem_free**. Shared memory regions should be protected from other regions of memory within the program. The designated memory can also be shared by the processes and the child processes, which should have unique names defined by the first parameter of **shmem_alloc**. You can use shared memory and semaphores (SEMAPHORE or COUNTING_SEMAPHORE) to take advantage of multiple server processes under UNIX.

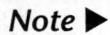

Note ▶

shmem_s and its related functions are no longer needed if you are using Server 3.x. No version of Server 3.x uses multiple processes.

shmem_s is defined as follows:

```
typedef struct {

    void *data;
#ifdef SHMEM_WIN32_MMAP
    HANDLE fdmap;
#endif

    int size;
    char *name;
    SYS_FILE fd;

} shmem_s;
```

data points to the shared memory region. fdmap, defined for WIN32 with mmap support only, is the mapped file descriptor handle. A similar type of HANDLE is defined for the WIN32 mmap filebuffer (also named fdmap). size holds the maximum length of the data. name is the file name that will be visible to other processes on your system if expose, the third parameter of the **shmem_alloc** function, is set to nonzero and your system supports shared memory space. name must be unique to the program that calls **shmem_alloc**. fd is the file descriptor for the shared memory region. name and fd are intended for internal use.

Bug Report ▶

The **shmem_realloc** function is mentioned in the comment section of the shmem.h file (for Server 2.x) and the nsapi.h file (for Server 3.x) as a way of reallocating a new size for the shared memory that does not automatically grow. No function prototype is defined, and no API function definition exists for this function in the Netscape's programmer's guide.

---

pool_handle_t

pool_handle_t provides for platform-independent handling of memory pool threads. This data structure is not supported under Server 1.x. Each thread creates its own pool for allocating data. These memory pools, which are defined to keep each thread safe and independent, are used in conjunction with platform-independent macros, such as MALLOC, REALLOC, STRDUP, and FREE. MALLOC, for example, uses the memory pool created for each session and is automatically freed by the server when the request is processed. (See the Memory Management Functions section later in this chapter for more details.) pool_handle_t is also defined as a member of the Session data structure if MALLOC_POOLS is allowed. In other words, memory pooling must be enabled (that is, it should not be disabled in the **Init** directive function **pool-init**). The data structure definition is as follows:

```
typedef void *pool_handle_t;
```

A number of **pool_*** functions manage memory allocation (such as **pool_create**, **pool_destroy**, and **pool_malloc**). **pool_create** creates a new memory pool (that is, it returns `pool_handle_t`). You usually do not call these functions directly. Instead, you use the memory functions (such as `MALLOC`) and let the server handle memory pooling. The specifics of the data structure, as well as its operation, may vary based on the operating system and Netscape settings. Also, as just noted, if the **Init** function **pool-init**'s parameter `disable` is set to true (in the **obj.conf** file), then the server will not use memory pooling.

Configuration File Data Structures

The following sets of structures are unique, in that they can be used to manage the data in, or derived from, the configuration files. These data structures begin with the smallest data structure member that holds one **obj.conf** file's function information. The largest data structure holds the information of all the configuration files. A number of data structures also reference other data structures. Let us begin with the smallest data structure and work our way to the largest one.

directive

```
typedef struct {
    pblock *param;
    pblock *client;
} directive;
```

The data structure for a directive holds only one instance of the directive—really, a single directive function. (As mentioned earlier, Netscape uses the term "directive" to refer to both a directive and a specific directive's function. In this book we distinguish between a directive type as *directive,* and a directive function as *function.* Alas, in this instance, we are stuck with the name `directive` for the directive function data structure.) `directive` includes `client` and `param` as members. `param` includes the parameters of the directive function. `client` includes client-specific, access-related data; it protects the directive. `client` includes the Client settings (as defined in the **obj.conf** file) that directly apply to `directive`. (See the Client section in Chapter 2.)

Warning ▶

We have made an effort to separate a directive function from a directive when using the two terms. Netscape, however, often uses a directive to refer to both a directive function (for example, **pfx2dir**) and the general directive (for example, **NameTrans**).

dtable

```
typedef struct {
    int ni;
    directive *inst;
} dtable;
```

Each dtable holds all the directive functions (directive structure) for each directive. This data structure stores the directive table for a specific directive. Each directive (for example, **AuthTrans** or **NameTrans**) can hold a number of directive functions. These functions are placed in an array referenced by dtable. Each directive has one dtable. inst refers to the array of functions (instances) of the directive (for example, **AuthTrans**). ni refers to the number of instances.

httpd_object

```
typedef struct {

    pblock *name;

    int nd;
    dtable *dt;

} httpd_object;
```

The data dtable structures are kept in httpd_object, which holds all the directives of a specific Object (for example, the Default or cgi Object). The name parameter block holds the name of the Object as well as other parameters associated with that Object, including the location associated with it. For example, an Object could be <Object ppath="c:/netscape/server/docs/special/*">, and therefore specify a specific physical path for the Object. An Object can also be defined by the **NameTrans pfx2dir** function (NameTrans fn="pfx2dir" from= "/cgi" dir="c:/netscape/server/cgi" name="cgi") and include references to a name, a virtual path, and a physical path. nd holds the number of dtable data structures. dt holds the dtable's array of directives. There are eight possible directives for the HTTP server (**AuthTrans**, **NameTrans**, and so on). (See Chapter 2 for a description of the directives.) Your function is responsible for defining the number of dtable structures that will be allocated. It also must keep track of which directive is associated with which nd number.

httpd_objset

```
typedef struct {

    int pos;
    httpd_object **obj;

    pblock **initfns;

} httpd_objset;
```

`http_objset`, the Object set, includes all Objects defined in the **obj.conf** file (obj), plus a `pblock` list of all **Init** functions (`initfns`). obj is a null-terminated array of Objects. `initfns` is a null-terminated array of **Init** functions. Each `initfns` parameter block holds the name and parameters of each **Init** function. `pos` points to the entry after the last entry in the `httpd_object` array. It is intended for use in finding the last entry. Netscape warns you not to change or modify this integer.

Let us review the order of these data structures. `dtable` holds the directive functions (`directive` structures); `httpd_object` holds the `dtable` data structures; and they are all held in the `httpd_objset` data structure.

For Servers 2.x and 1.x, you can include the `objset.h` header file in your program and get access to all of these data structures and functions. You might have noticed that all of the data structures are held in the `object.h` file, except `httpd_objset`. You need to include only the `objset.h` file, however, because it references the `object.h` file. For Server 3.x, you need to include only `nsapi.h`. All data structures and functions are defined in `nsapi.h`.

conf_global_vars_s

The `conf_global_vars_s` data structure has member variables that are the configuration settings for the server, which are usually defined in the **magnus.conf** and **obj.conf** files. This structure includes a list of the global variables (from the **magnus.conf** file) and the Object set data structure (`httpd_objset`, which consists of information from the **obj.conf** file). `conf_global_vars_s` is new to Server 2.0 and is also used with Server 3.x. Previously, most of these variables were not part of a data structure. They were declared as `extern` definitions (for example, `extern char *server_hostname`). `conf_global_vars_s` includes global variables such as `Vport` for server port or `Vuserpw` for the HTTP server user password. It also includes other information about the server settings, such as the SSL security settings (`Vsecure_keyfn`, `Vssl3_active`, and so on) or the root of the ACL data structure (`Vacl_root`).

Because the server features and setting has changed from Server 2.x to 3.0x and from Server 3.0x to Server 3.5.x, the actual member variables of `conf_global_vars_s` have changed as well. A number of variables used for multiple-process UNIX servers—for example, `Vpool_max`, `Vpool_maxthreads`, and so on—are now obsolete. Netscape UNIX Server 3.x does not use multiple processes. There are also added variables for Server 3.x, such as `log_verbose` (for logging additional information in the log file). Some of the variables are also dependent on the type of server. For example, `mtahost`, `nntphost`, and `agentFilePath` are used for support of agents in Enterprise Server 3.x.

Enterprise Server 3.5.1 does not use two member variables defined for Server 3.0x that have been renamed from `mp_optimization` and `concurrency` to `unused1` and `unused2`, respectively. Server 3.5.x also adds a number of members— `fortezza_card_mask`, `fortezza_personality`, and `krlname` for FORTEZZA hardware-based security support. An example of a Web site where you can find more information on FORTEZZA is the Department of Defense's Web site, FORTEZZA Developers Home Page (http://www.armadillo.huntsville.al.us/).

The conf_global_vars_s data structure definition contains a series of redefined variables for the data structure members that allow easy access to information. The **conf_getglobals** function is used to get the data structure (conf_global_vars_s) variables of the server and reassign them to a simpler variable. For example, the httpd_objset variable Vstd_os (which holds the Object set in the **obj.conf** file) is redefined as std_os (that is, #define std_os conf_getglobals()->Vstd_os). The value can be accessed, then, simply through std_os.

The following code gives the conf_global_var_s data structure for Enterprise Server 3.5.1 defined in the nsapi.h file. The redefinitions have been removed from the following listing to facilitate reading the structure.

```
typedef struct {

    int Vport;
    char *Vaddr;
    struct passwd *Vuserpw;
    char *Vchr;
    char *Vpidfn;

/* OBSOLETE variables, no longer used for Server 3.x.
   Used with multiprocess UNIX Server 2.x. */
    int Vpool_max;
    int Vpool_min;
    int Vpool_life;
    int Vpool_maxthreads;
    int Vpool_minthreads;
/* end of OBSOLETE variables */

    char *Vsecure_keyfn;
    char *Vsecure_certfn;

    int Vsecurity_active;
    int Vssl3_active;
    int Vssl2_active;
    int Vsecure_auth;
    int Vsecurity_session_timeout;
    long Vssl3_session_timeout;

    char *Vserver_hostname;
    char *Vroot_object;

    httpd_objset *Vstd_os;

    void *Vacl_root;

    char *Vmaster_error_log;
```

```
    char *Vserver_root;
    char *Vserver_id;
/* new for Server 3.x */

    int single_accept;
    int num_keep_alives;
    int log_verbose;
    int mmap_flags;
    int mmap_prots;

/* Server 3.0x includes the following members,
   which have been redefined as unused for Server 3.5.1

    int mp_optimization;
    int concurrency;
*/
    int unused1;
    int unused2;

/* Enterprise 3.x fields */
    int accept_language;

    char *mtahost;
    char *nntphost;

    void *Vacl_root_30;

    char* agentFilePath;

    int Allowed;

    pblock *genericGlobals;

    char* agentsACLFile;
    int wait_for_cgi;
    int cgiwatch_timeout;

/* additional member added for Enterprise Server 3.5.1 */
#ifdef FORTEZZA
    unsigned int fortezza_card_mask;
    char *fortezza_personality;
    char *krlname;
#endif

} conf_global_vars_s;
```

Let's look at the data structure pointer path to a parameter block of a function in the **obj.conf** file.

```
conf_getglobals()->Vstd_os->obj[0].dt[1].inst[0].param
```

As mentioned earlier, the **conf_getglobals** function gets the structure for the global variables of the server. Vstd_os is the httpd_objset for the server. obj[0] is the first Object (http_object) found in the **obj.conf** file. It is usually the default Object, but does not have to be. dt is the dtable that holds the table of directives. dt[1] looks for the second directive type in the Object. The numbers of directives in the array begin with 0. inst[0] points to the first instance of a function in that directive. param holds the parameter block for that function. In other words, we have reached the function and its parameters. Assuming everything works correctly, you should be able to use **pblock_*** functions to access the *name-value* pairs of the pblock entry held by the previously given code.

There is also a set of functions associated with these configuration data structures. The **objset_*** functions (for example, **objset_create**, **objset_add_object**, and **objset_findbyname**) are specific functions for manipulating the httpd_objset data structure. The **object_*** functions (for example, **object_add_directive** and **object_execute**) manage the httpd_object data structure. There are even a few **conf_*** functions that you can use, such as **conf_init**, **conf_getglobals**, and **conf_terminate**. You can use these functions to read a configuration file, get the global variables for a server, and perform other such tasks. When managing these data structures, you need to determine the actual index number of each structure and its members, and then allocate the appropriate space for them. For example, you need to allocate the right number of dtable data structures, keep track of the directive types, know which directive types maps to which dtable number, and so on.

Normally, you do not use these data structures and functions. Instead, you allow the server to deal with managing the information in the **obj.conf** file. These functions are useful mainly when writing an "administrative" plug-in that dynamically changes the server's configuration—not a common need. You can, however, use this discussion to get a better understanding of how server maintains the global settings and how the directive functions are maintained by the server.

Warning ▶

To access the members of the data structure conf_global_vars_s for Server 2.x, you have to set the NET_SSL compiler switch before you compile your program. Otherwise, the structure is offset and you may retrieve NULL or an incorrect value when attempting to retrieve the value of its member variables.

---

nsapi_dispatch_s *(Server 3.x only)*

The nsapi_dispatch_s data structure holds all the NSAPI functions. It is a dispatch vector table, holding the pointers to the NSAPI functions. This data structure provides a wrapper around the NSAPI functions that you can use.

Functions are defined in the following format in the data structure:

```
[function return] (*[function name])([parameters]);
```

Consider the following example:

```
SYS_FILE (*f_system_fopenRO)(char *path);
```

The names of the functions in this data structure begin with f_. The actual name of the NSAPI functions that you can use comes after the f_. In the above example, the NSAPI function's name is **system_fopenRO**.

Further down in the nsapi.h file, each NSAPI function is defined through a macro definition. For example, **system_fopenRO** is defined as follows:

```
#define system_fopenRO (*__nsapi30_table->f_system_fopenRO)
```

To review the comments about an NSAPI function in the nsapi.h file, you need to go to the location where the actual NSAPI function is defined in this file. To find out the function's return value or parameters, you need to look in the nsapi_dispatch_s data structure. The macro that defines the function only points to the function in this data structure.

Depending on the type of server you are running and its setting, number of different functions are defined in the data structure. For example, **f_pipebuf_next** (the NSAPI function **pipebuf_next**) is defined as int (*f_pipebuf_next)(filebuf_t *buf, int advance) for WIN32 (Windows NT) and as int (*f_pipebuf_next)(void) for other servers (UNIX servers).

```
#ifdef XP_WIN32
    int (*f_pipebuf_next)(filebuf_t *buf, int advance);
#else
    int (*f_pipebuf_next)(void);
#endif /* XP_WIN32 */
```

Thread-Related Data Structures

There are five data structures you can use to manage the server processes and threads in Server 2.01 or 3.x: SEMAPHORE, COUNTING_SEMAPHORE, SYS_THREAD, CRITICAL, and CONDVAR. The structures SYSTHREAD, CRITICAL, and CONDVAR were added to Netscape Server 2.0. COUNTING_SEMAPHORE was added to Server 2.01. Each data structure provides its own feature and support. These data structures and the related NSAPI functions are discussed in Chapter 11, Threads and Processes. These data structures and their uses are often platform-dependent. Refer to your operating system and your Netscape Server features and settings for details.

Important NSAPI Functions

You can use many functions to gain access to the variables in the data structures described earlier. We have already mentioned some of them when describing each data structure. Make sure to peruse the relevant data structures as well as read about the functions. We will not provide detailed API function definitions here. You should also review the header files and the NSAPI Programmer's Guide for more information about the NSAPI functions. In this book, we will focus on a specific subset of notable functions and their use in accomplishing common programming goals.

The server functions are usually grouped together by the kind of tasks they perform or the data they use. For easy identification, the first part of their names is the same. The word before the first underscore is the name of each group. This grouping normally reflects the data structure with which the group members are associated and the name of the header file where you can find them. (Before Server 3.0, the various NSAPI functions were defined in separate header files.) The main sets of functions described here are **pblock_***, **request_***, **protocol_***, **network_***, **filebuf_***, **system_***, **func_***, and **util_***. There are also a few important functions that are not part of a group, such as **log_error** and **daemon_atrestart**, as well as memory management functions, such as **MALLOC**.

Each version of the server may include a different or additional set of NSAPI functions. You should always review the header files or Netscape documentation for the different NSAPI functions supported by your version of the server. For example, with Server 3.x, Netscape included a set of random number generation functions (for example, **random_create**, **random_generate**, and **random_destroy**) and MD5 (Message Digest 5) message authentication hash routines (for example, **md5has_create**, **md5hash_begin**, and **md5hash_end**).

pblock and param Functions

The **pblock_*** and **param_*** functions are used to manage parameter blocks. These functions are most frequently used to get the headers and server variables available from the Request and Session data structures. They are also used to access the value of the NSAPI function's parameters defined in the **obj.conf** file. Netscape keeps most of the important variables that you need to use in parameter blocks (pblocks). Therefore, understanding **pblock_*** functions is essential for programming. You will use these key functions regularly in your programs. (See the pblock data structure discussion earlier in this chapter as well.) pblock is the hash table that contains the list (pb_entry) of *name-value* pairs (pb_param).

Creating and Freeing Parameter Block Entries

```
pb_param *param_create (char *name, char *value);
int param_free(pb_param *pp);
```

param_create and **param_free** are used to create and free, single parameter block entries' pb_param. The name and value parameter of the **param_create** function become a *name-value* entry pair (pb_param) returned by the function. You can use **param_create** to create a parameter block entry that you can later insert into the server's pblock data structures (for example, using **pblock_pinsert**, you can insert a pb_param into a pblock). This action, in effect, does the same thing as **pblock_nvinsert** (see the discussion of **pblock_nvinsert** later in this chapter).

param_free can free a pb_param that has been removed. For example, if you removed a parameter block entry via **pblock_remove**, **param_free** can deallocate the memory for the pb_param. The following function removes a pblock and then frees the memory:

```
param_free(pblock_remove("content-type", rq->srvhrdr));
```

Once it has removed content-type (a pb_param), **pblock_remove** (in the previous example) returns the pointer to the pb_param data structure that **param_free** will free. **pblock_remove** returns NULL if the pb_param was not found. **param_free** will then free the memory if its parameter (pp) is not NULL. **param_free** returns 1 if the pb_param was freed and 0 if the pp was NULL. Thus a 0 return indicates the parameter was not freed (removed).

Creating, Copying, and Freeing Parameter Blocks

```
pblock *pblock_create(int n);
void pblock_copy(pblock *src, pblock *dst);
pblock *pblock_dup(pblock *src);
void pblock_free(pblock *pb);
```

pblock_* functions allow you to create a list of pb_param entries and then copy, duplicate, or free it. You can create a pblock, for example, to hold a number of *name-value* pairs that you can later access using other **pblock_*** functions. Later, we will write an example where we create a pblock and insert the decoded query string sent by the client. Parameter *n* of the **pblock_create** function is the number of parameter block entries you want the server to create (that is, the number of pb_param entries to be created). Entries are kept in a hash table created by the server. (Actually, the hash table is the pblock data structure itself.) You determine the number of the list entries.

You can also make a copy or duplicate the pblock. For example, you can duplicate or copy a pblock from the Request data structure. This action gives you a local copy of the variables for quick access or so as to modify the copy but not the original. **pblock_dup** creates a new pblock and copies the src pblock into the pblock that is returned. If you create a parameter block (for example, through **pblock_create**), make sure that you free the parameter block using **pblock_free**, once you have finished with it.

Finding and Removing Parameter Block Entries

```
pb_param *pblock_find(char *name, pblock *pb);
pb_param *pblock_remove(char *name, pblock *pb);
```

Both **pblock_find** and **pblock_remove** are redefinition macros of the NSAPI **_pblock_fr** function (pb_param *_pblock_fr(char *name, pblock *pb, int remove)). (For **pblock_remove**, the remove parameter of **_pblock_fr** is set to 1. For **pblock_find**, the remove parameter is set to 0.) **pblock_find** finds and returns a pblock entry. **pblock_remove** removes a pb_param from the pblock. You are responsible for freeing the memory of the pblock parameters you removed. You can accomplish this goal by using **param_free**. name is the name of a *name-value* pair in the pblock (pb).

Finding the Value of a Parameter Block Entry

```
char *pblock_findval(char *name, pblock *pb);
```

Normally, you use **pblock_findval** (instead of **pblock_find**) to get an entry's value (in pb_param) from the pblock. The function returns either the value string for the entry specified by the name parameter or NULL if no value was found. You should not free the return value; instead use STRDUP and modify a copy of the return value. **pblock_findval** look for the *name-value* pair in the pblock specified by the pb parameter. You will use this function frequently. For example, you can obtain the value string of the entries from the pblock structures of the Request data structures (for example, pblock_findval("method", rq->reqpb)). You can also use this function to obtain the value of the NSAPI function's parameters defined in the **obj.conf** file (for example, pblock_findval("myparam", param)).

Inserting Parameters into a pblock

```
void pblock_pinsert(pb_param *pp, pblock *pb);
pb_param *pblock_nvinsert(char *name, char *value,
                          pblock *pb);
pb_param *pblock_nninsert(char *name, int value,
                          pblock *pb);
```

The **pblock_pinsert** function inserts an existing pb_param (pp) into the designated pblock, pb. **pblock_pinsert** inserts a pb_param that is already created and filled; it does not return a value. On the other hand, with **pblock_nvinsert** and **pblock_nninsert**, you can specify the pb_param directly through the name and value parameters. These two functions return a pointer to the pb_param that was inserted in the pblock (pb).

pblock_nvinsert inserts a string value for the *name-value* pair, whereas **pblock_nninsert** inserts an integer value. You can use these functions to insert a pb_param into the server response header (Request->srvhdrs). Each function allocates a new space for the added entry. For example, pblock_nvinsert ("content-type", "text/html", rq->srvhdrs) can be used to specify the type of content that the program is sending back to the client. To set the content-length value as an integer, you can use **pblock_nninsert**. (With NSAPI programs, you do not need to worry about placing the blank line after the last header; the server takes care of that task.)

Although the values are stored in a Last In, First Out (LIFO) method, only the name of the pb_param is used as the hash table key to access the value. Moreover, if the pblock contains multiple entries with the same name, only the first of these entries is returned by **pblock_findval**. If you insert a new pblock entry with the same name but a different value, **pblock_findval** returns the first pblock entry of the same name. The hash table also uses only the first ten characters of the name. If you use a unique name that is different from another only after the first ten characters, the **pblock_findval** interprets the two names as being the same. Thus you should first remove any pblock entry that you wish to replace before entering a new one with the same first ten characters in the name. You can also insert a new entry, but make sure the first ten characters are different from any other entry in the pblock.

You can also use **pblock_nvinsert** to report an error in an **Init** function (for example, pblock_nvinsert("error", "Invalid information submitted.", pb)). This function is used in lieu of the **log_error** function. (With all other directive functions except **Init** functions, you normally use **log_error** to report an error.)

Converting pblock Entries into Environment Variables

```
char **pblock_pb2env(pblock *pb, char **env);
```

pblock_pb2env converts the pblock (pb) table entries into environment variables (env). This function creates a new environment variable for each pb_param (*name-value* pair). You can use this function to pass a number of parameters or settings, as environment variables, from your NSAPI program to a shell program. Of course, you need to spawn the program directly. This function does not work with CGI programs that run outside of your server function (that is, programs that run by the built-in **Service** function **send-cgi** function). (See also the Manipulating Environment Variables section later in this chapter.)

Converting pblock Entries into Strings, and Vice Versa

```
char *pblock_pblock2str(pblock *pb, char *str);
int pblock_str2pblock(char *str, pblock *pb);
```

You can convert a pblock into a string with **pblock_pblock2str**, or a string into a pblock, by using **pblock_str2pblock**. **pblock_pblock2str** copies the parameter block entries specified in the pblock (pb) into the string (str). If the str is NULL, it will create a new string. Otherwise, it will allocate additional space for the string and append the existing string with the pblock entries. It will also return the new string. The server allocates the space for the string from the pool of memory created for the request and not from the heap. In other words, the string, str, is allocated using **MALLOC** or **REALLOC**—not **PERM_ALLOC** or **PERM_REALLOC**. The new string will include the *name-value* pair entries of the pblock as `[name]="[value]"`. The pairs are separated by a space. The function returns NULL upon failure.

The **pblock_pblock2str** function can provide the list of all `pb_param` entries from a pblock. To illustrate, the following code creates a string of pblock entries contained in the `Request` data structure's `reqpb` (`rq->reqpb`). Because the `str` parameter is set to NULL, it will create a new string. The resulting string includes the method, URI, protocol, and so on.

```
req_params = pblock_pblock2str(rq->reqpb, NULL);
```

pblock_str2pblock reads a string (`str`) of *name-value* pairs and adds them to a specified pblock (`pb`). For this function to work properly, the format of the string should be correct (see the Warning below). **pblock_str2pblock** returns the number of the pblock entries (`pb_params`) added to the pblock from the string. Upon failure or error, it returns −1.

In Chapter 9, we will write functions that use **pblock_str2pblock** when parsing a query string of *name-value* pairs sent by the client. To take advantage of the **pblock_str2pblock** function, we must first parse the query string. For example, we must replace all ampersands (&) with spaces. We will also need to deal with empty values. We have included a simple function (**remove_separator_plus**) that removes the ampersand and places default text into the string when there is no value for a *name-value* pair. The following code takes advantage of this function and **pblock_str2pblock** to copy

> ## Warning ▶
>
> There are some details that you should know about the **pblock_st2pblock** function. You need to have a list of *name-value* pairs in a string each separated by a space. These pairs can be in either of the following formats: [*name*]=[*value*] or [*name*]="[*value*]". If the *name* is missing, the pblock entries will end up with numbers in place of the *name*. In other words, the string "joe jack john" will result in the following `pb_param` entries: `1="joe" 2="jack" 3="john"`. The value must include quotes around it if it has any spaces—that is, `name="joe turner"` results in `joe turner` as the value of `name` in the `pb_param`. Also, all backslashes (\) should be followed by a literal character. Use a backslash to include a literal character that has a special meaning for the **pblock_str2pblock** function, such as an equal sign (=), a quotation mark ("), or another backslash. For example, you can use a backslash to escape the equal sign for its inclusion in a pblock entry.
>
> Finally, if there is an empty value, this function reads on until it finds the next pair and places everything in between as the value of `pb_param`. In other words, the string "name=lastname=email=myname@myplace.com" will become first `pb_param`, `name="lastname="`; second `pb_param`, `email="myname@myplace.com"`. For this reason, if you read an indeterminate string into parameter pairs, make sure to place default text where any parameters are missing. In other words, "name=&lastname=&email=myname@myplace.com" should be parsed into a string, such as "name=void lastname=void email=myname@myplace.com", before you use the **pblock_st2pblock** function.

the client's query string into a newly created pblock (`variables`). (The actual code for the function **remove_separator_plus** is not included here.)

```
/* get the query string */
query=pblock_findval("query", rq->reqpb);

newquery=(char *) MALLOC(MAXSIZE * sizeof(char));

/* Remove the "&" and place the default text if needed
   in the string. This function returns the number of
   pblock entries in the string. The new string will
   be newquery.
 */
varnum=remove_separator_plus(query, newquery,
                             DEFAULT_TEXT);

/* create a new pblock with the right number of entries */
variables=pblock_create(varnum);

/* insert the decoded string from remove_separator_plus
   into the new pblock
 */
pblock_str2pblock(newquery, variables);
```

After the string has been converted, you can walk through the pblock's `pb_param` entry table and remove the escape characters (`% [Hex]`) and the plus (+) characters from the query string. Alternatively, you can remove these characters from the query string before you place the *name-value* pairs in the pblock. (If you plan to replace the plus sign with a space in the string before using **pblock_str2pblock**, make sure the *value* string has quotes around it. Otherwise, **pblock_str2pblock** will interpret each separate word as an independent *name-value* pair with the *name* missing.)

Request Functions

There are a number of request functions that you can use to create, free, or manage a `Request` data structure. In this section, we will describe the two most frequently used **request_*** functions. **request_header** is used to read the client's HTTP request headers. **request_stat_path** gets the specified file's `stat` information.

Finding the Value of a Request Header

```
int request_header(char *name, char **value,
                   Session *sn, Request *rq);
```

When the pblock entry you are seeking is an HTTP header (that is, a header in the `Request->headers` pblock), Netscape prescribes the use of the **request_header** function instead of using **pblock_findval**. **request_header** can access the parameters indirectly, avoiding multiple calls. It can access the header values in your function's copy of the request data structure. If possible, **request_header** will not load headers until the first one is requested. The name parameter is the lowercase HTTP header name found in the `Request->headers` pblock (for example, `accept`, instead of CGI environment variable `HTTP_ACCEPT`). You specify the name of the header, and the function returns its value through the `value` parameter. You include the pointer to the address where you want the value placed. If no header was found, the `value` is set to NULL. You also can use your copy of the `Session` (sn) and `Request` (rq) data structures to verify a request in an asynchronous procedure. REQ_ABORTED is returned in case of an error; REQ_PROCEED is returned upon success. Consequently, you should make sure the function processed correctly by checking its return value. The following code checks for the `user-agent` header value (uagent). If an error occurred, we abort the function.

```
if(request_header("user-agent", &uagent, sn, rq) ==
                    REQ_ABORTED)
  return REQ_ABORTED;
```

Getting `stat` Information on the Requested File

```
struct stat *request_stat_path(char *path, Request *rq);
```

request_stat_path gets `stat` information about a requested file. Using the `path` parameter, it gives you information such as the size and last-modified date of the file. As with **request_header**, the use of this function eliminates multiple calls. You can use this function instead of using the **stat** function directly. **request_stat_path** keeps track of other calls. For example, a repeated call to this function, which references the same path, returns the previously found `stat`. The server also caches the `stat` of the current path. Thus **request_stat_path** gets the files' cached stat information. If no path is specified, the function uses the path variable in the `Request->vars` pblock. Consequently, `request_stat_path (NULL, rq);` checks for the path in `rq->vars`. You may want to use this code if you have changed the value of the `path` in `rq->vars` and want the server to update the cached `stat` of the current path with the new path information. If the function was unable to access the file (for example, if the file did not exist), it places an error message in the `Request->staterr` specified by the `rq` parameter and returns NULL. If the file can be read, the function returns the `stat` data structure of the file. Do not free the structure returned by this function. (See also the discussion of `stat` in the File-Related Data Structures section earlier in this chapter.)

Protocol Functions

A number of HTTP protocol-related functions are available in the server header files. The most important of these functions are **protocol_status**, **protocol_start_response**, and **protocol_set_finfo**. The **protocol_*** functions are actually redefinitions (macros) of **http_*** functions. In other words, these protocol functions currently support only the HTTP protocol. You use **protocol_status** to set the status of the response and **protocol_start_response** to send the response header to the client.

Setting the HTTP Protocol Status

```
void protocol_status(Session *sn, Request *rq, int n,
                     char *r);
```

protocol_status (**http_status**) sets the status code to the n parameter and returns the string pointed to by the r parameter as the description (reason) text for the status. The `status` entry, which includes both the status code and the reason string, is placed in the `Request->srvhdrs` pblock data structure. You can use this function to return an error status to the client. The descriptive text (`status`) is then sent back to the client with the rest of the error page. You can also set the status to PROTOCOL_OK and the descriptive string to NULL so as to return a response page from a **Service** directive function to the client (for example, `protocol_status(sn, rq, PROTOCOL_OK, NULL)`). This action is equivalent of sending the status 200 OK. This function does not return a value. (See Returning an Error Page in Chapter 6 for more details.)

Sending Headers to the Client

```
int protocol_start_response(Session *sn, Request *rq);
```

You should call **protocol_start_response** after defining all appropriate server headers and after calling **protocol_status**. Consider the following simple example. **pblock_nvinsert** inserts the content-type and **protocol_status** sets the status to OK. **protocol_start_response** then sends all the headers to the client.

```
pb_param *pblock_nvinsert("content-type", "text/html",
                          rq->srvhdrs);
void protocol_status(sn, rq, PROTOCOL_OK, NULL);
int protocol_start_response(sn, rq);
```

After **protocol_start_response**, you can begin writing to the client socket with the **net_write** function. In this case, you can send back a dynamically generated HTML page.

protocol_start_response sends all the appropriate response headers to the client. In other words, all headers (including the Status-Line, general-headers, and response-headers) are generated and returned using this function. The actual headers sent are usually found in `Request->srvhdrs`. Because HTTP/0.9 does not handle headers (for example, response-headers), both **protocol_status** and this function are ignored for an HTTP/0.9 request. For an HTTP/1.0 and later request, however, the headers will be sent.

Note what this function returns: REQ_NOACTION returned by this function means that the client does not want the contents of a page. Therefore, your function should not return the entity-body (the message body). This case typically occurs with a HEAD request, where the client requests the headers but does not want the actual entity-body. It is also the case when the client has the actual page cached. REQ_PROCEED is returned when the function sends the headers without any problem and the server stands ready to send the entity-body. REQ_ABORTED is returned in case of an error. Make sure you verify what is returned from this function before you proceed with the rest of your code. (See Returning a Dynamic Page in Chapter 6 for more details.) After **protocol_start_response** finishes, you can send the body of the response (entity-body).

Updating File stat

```
int protocol_set_finfo(Session *sn, Request *rq,
                       struct stat *finfo);
```

protocol_set_finfo sets the content-length and last-modified (date) headers for the specific session (sn) and request (rq) from the file information specified by finfo (the file information stat data structure). You should use this function when you are ready to return a document—for example, before a call to **protocol_start_response**. This function handles conditional GET requests in case of caching. In other words, it updates content-length and last-modified for the cached documents. After obtaining stat for the specific file, call this function. Similar to **request_stat_path**, this function can update the stat of a file that is cached. While **request_stat_path** is used for a requested file, **protocol_set_finfo** is used to update and verify the stat of a file being sent to the client. Because dynamic pages normally are not cached, however, you do not use this function when returning a document dynamically generated by your program. **protocol_set_finfo** returns REQ_ABORTED when the entity-body (the document) is not sent to the client. REQ_PROCEED is returned when the request is processed normally and a document is sent.

net and netbuf Functions

net_* functions are similar to standard socket functions available for your operating system. For example, **net_socket**, **net_connect**, and **net_close** are the same as the **socket**, **connect**, and **socket_close** socket functions used by Microsoft Windows Sockets or BSD's (Berkeley Software Distribution) socket API. There are two main **net_*** functions. **net_read** reads bytes directly from a specific socket. **net_write** writes bytes directly to a socket. These two functions are a bit different from the standard **recv** and **sent** socket functions. For example, **net_write** guarantees that the data are delivered. If you wish to convert an existing program that uses sockets to an NSAPI server application, replace your socket function with the equivalent NSAPI function. Also, include your operating system's specific socket header file in your program (for example, include winsock.h for Windows). Netscape's socket functions support SSL encoding and decoding. You may need to use other, specific system socket functions (for example, **gethostbyname**) in conjunction with Netscape's socket function.

The **netbuf_*** functions, such as **netbuf_getc** and **netbuf_buf2sd**, can also be used to read from and write to a socket through a network buffer. The function you use to read client input from a form sent via the POST method is **netbuf_getc**.

Reading Data from the Network Socket

```
int net_read(SYS_NETFD sd, char *buf, int sz,
             int timeout);
```

net_read reads from the socket (sd) into a buffer designated by the parameter buf. The function waits for data from the client until the timeout second is reached or until the actual number of bytes of data is read. You specify the socket descriptor (sd) used to communicate with the client. The maximum number of bytes to be read is specified in the third parameter, sz. The maximum seconds to wait for a read is designated in the fourth parameter, timeout. Set the timeout number large enough to ensure that all data are read and small enough to stop waiting when nothing is happening. You can also set the timeout to NET_ZERO_TIMEOUT or NET_INFINITE_TIMEOUT. The function returns the number of bytes read if all goes well; it returns a negative number, IO_ERROR (-1), if an error occurred. It should return zero if the remote client closes the socket. errno is set to EDTIMEDOUT if the function timed-out.

You do not use **net_read** to read data from a POST input. The data from a POST method, sent through a form, are usually placed inside the network buffer (Session->inbuf). You can read this information using **netbuf_getc**. Instead of reading from the socket, you access the data through the network input buffer's input string. The data for the POST request have already been read by the server. Thus nothing remains to be read from the socket. **net_read** can be used when your program has made a direct socket connection and wants to read data from the socket. In other words, you can use this function to read from the socket after you have created a socket and opened the connection (**net_socket**), established a connection to the client (**net_connect**), and begun listening at the specified port (**net_accept**).

When reading directly from the socket, data from other function calls can be in the network buffer. If you intend to use **net_read**, you must make sure that all the bytes are cleared (flushed) out of the buffer before you use it. You need to ensure that you read data starting from the pos position in the buffer.

Putting Bytes into the Network Buffer's inbuf

```
int netbuf_grab(netbuf *buf, int sz);
```

netbuf_grab takes data from the socket descriptor (sd) and places it into the network buffer's (buf) inbuf string. It puts the data from the underlying socket descriptor specified through buf into the buf->inbuf string. inbuf then points to the string of data. (Note that the inbuf variable of netbuf is cast to an unsigned char * instead of char * for Server 3.x.) **netbuf_grab** also sets netbuf's inbuf string to the size specified in sz. If the buffer is not large enough, it is resized. **netbuf_grab** takes care of allocating and deallocating of the buffer. In other words, netbuf's pos (current cursor position) and cursize (size of the inbuf) now reflect the new size. **netbuf_grab** returns the number of bytes read. This number must be less than the maximum number of bytes (sz) and more than 0. sz is the maximum number of bytes the server should try to read from the buffer. When the end of the file is reached or an error occurs, the function returns IO_EOF (0) or IO_ERROR (-1), respectively. If you need to know and use the size of the data read and are directly reading from a socket, use **netbuf_grab**. As with **net_read**, you do not use this function to read the client input from a standard POST request. This information is already read into the inbuf string by the server.

Reading Data from the Network Buffer into Your Buffer

```
/* Enterprise Server 3.5.1 only */
int netbuf_getbytes(netbuf *buf, char *buffer, int size);
```

netbuf_getbytes is a new NSAPI function for Enterprise Server 3.5.1 that can be used to read bytes of data from the network buffer (netbuf) into a specified buffer (buffer). You also specify the size of bytes that will be read (size). Upon success, **netbuf_getbytes** returns the number of bytes read. It returns NETBUF_EOF if no more data arrive on the socket and returns NETBUF_ERROR if an error occurs.

Reading Data from the Network Buffer One Character at a Time

```
int netbuf_getc(netbuf *b);
```

netbuf_getc reads one character at a time from the network buffer. The data are found in the input string (inbuf) inside Session's network buffer (inbuf) data structure (for example, netbuf_getc(sn->inbuf), where sn is a pointer to Session). Note that the inbuf member of the Session data structure is a netbuf data structure, whereas the inbuf member of the *Session*->inbuf (the inbuf member of inbuf) data structure is a character pointer. The following definition of **netbuf_getc** is found in the NSAPI header file. If you plan to read from the network buffer using your own function, you should take similar steps.

```
#define netbuf_getc(b) \
  ((b)->pos != (b)->cursize ? \
  (int)((b)->inbuf[(b)->pos++]) : netbuf_next(b,1))
```

netbuf_getc is a macro for a function that uses a ternary conditional operator. It reads one character at a time from the buffer. (b)->pos != (b)->cursize, the first expression, evaluates as true when the position of the cursor is not the same as the maximum size of the current buffer—that is, when pos is less than cursize and the end of the buffer has not been reached. When this expression is true, the function evaluates `(int) (b) ->inbuf[(b) ->pos++]. inbuf` is the actual char string buffer member of the `netbuf` data structure b. After it casts it to an integer, the function returns the character read. It also moves the position of the cursor one character. If the cursor reaches the end of the buffer (that is, `b->pos = b->cursize`), then the value of **netbuf_getc** will be equal to the result of `netbuf_next(b, 1)`. The **netbuf_next** function is defined as `int netbuf_next(netbuf *buf, int advance)`. Since we have advanced to the end of the buffer (that is, we have reached `cursize`), **netbuf_next** should return BUFFER_EOF (0) on reaching the end of the buffer or BUFFER_ERROR (–1) on encountering an error. In the **netbuf_next** function, `advance` is a number from the initial cursor position—in this case, the end of the buffer.

For the end of file, the **netbuf_getc** function returns 0 on EOF. In other words, it does not specify the number of bytes read. A way to get this bit of information is to use the **netbuf_grab** function.

Writing the Entity-Body to the Client's Socket

```
int net_write(SYS_NETFD sd, char *buf, int sz);
```

net_write writes a specified number of bytes (sz) from your buffer (buf) to the socket (sd). It returns IO_ERROR (–1) if an error occurred and IO_OKAY (1) upon success. You use this function to send a dynamically generated response to the client. It also guarantees that the response data are sent. With NSAPI, you do not use stdout. Instead, you use **net_write** to write to the client. With CGI, you use stdout to return data to the server. The server then takes the responsibility of sending the data to the client. With NSAPI, your function itself must send the data to the client. Typically, you create a buffer for the data you wish to send back and then use **net_write** to write to the client socket. Normally, sd is the socket descriptor from the Session data structure's csd (client sd). (See Returning a Dynamic Page in Chapter 6 for more details.)

Listing 5-2 is a program that returns a Thank You page to the client. Once you have sent all the headers (**protocol_start_response**), you are ready to send the page. buf is the string that will hold the HTML page code. **net_write** writes buf (of the size cl) to the client socket (sn->csd). If an error occurs, we free the malloced buffer and exit; otherwise we send back REQ_PROCEED.

Listing 5-2   Return a Thank You Page to the Client

```
protocol_start_response(sn, rq);

/* allocate a size for the buffer */
buf = (char *) MALLOC(300 * sizeof(char));

/* cl is the length of the buf to be used by net_write */
cl = util_sprintf(buf, "<HTML><HEAD>\n"
```

Listing 5-2   Return a Thank You Page to the Client (*continued*)

```
                        "<TITLE>Thank you</TITLE></HEAD>\n"
                        "<BODY><H1>Thank you!</H1>\n"
                        "Thanks for your comment."
                        "We appreciate your feedback."
                        "</BODY></HTML>");

/* send the confirmation */
if(net_write(sn->csd, buf, cl) == IO_ERROR)
{
    return REQ_EXIT;
}

return REQ_PROCEED;
```

Warning ▶

Contrary to what the Server 2.0's "Netscape Enterprise Server Programmer's Guide" states, **net_write** does not return the number of bytes written.
Moreover, **net_write** under NT version 1.x includes a fourth parameter, slot. In Server 1.x, you normally referenced slot from the Session inbuf for this parameter—that is, *Session*->inbuf->slot. This parameter is unnecessary and no longer exists. Make sure you revise any code written under NT Server 1.x, by removing the fourth parameter before recompiling the function for a later server.

Sending Bytes to the Socket

```
int netbuf_buf2sd(netbuf *buf, SYS_NETFD sd, int len);
```

netbuf_buf2sd can also be used to send a buffer to a socket. It sends a specified number of bytes (len) from the buffer (buf) to the socket (sd). If the socket descriptor's value (sd) is −1, the data are not to be sent. If the length is −1, **netbuf_buf2sd** writes until EOF is reached. If successful, it returns the number of bytes sent. If an error occurs, it returns IO_ERROR. You can use this function for interprocess communication (IPC) pipes to the client. Usually, the buffer has been read before using this function. **netbuf_buf2sd** calls **netbuf_grab** internally to grab the inbuf string before sending it to the socket.

Verifying the Domain Name

```
char *net_ip2host(char *ip, int verify);
```

The **net_ip2host** function takes the IP address as a parameter and returns the fully qualified domain name. verify, the second parameter, tells the server to take an extra step: Query to verify the domain name it receives. (It looks in the host name in the h_name and h_aliases entries of the data structure (hostent) returned by **gethostbyaddr** (a standard socket function) for a fully qualified domain name. This process is similar to calling **gethostbyname** of **gethostbyaddr**. For Servers 2.x and 3.x, it also attempts to guess the local domain name. If a host name is not found, the request is unverified. Setting this parameter to a number other than zero—for example, 1—verifies the domain name. This extra precaution confirms the domain name accuracy, especially in cases where you want to verify a domain name for security reasons. If DNS caching is enabled, it may take as long as 20 minutes before **net_ip2host** does another DNS look-up.

> ### Bug Report ▶
>
> Under Netscape Server 2.0, the **net_isalive** function does not work. This problem has been fixed in Server 2.01. **net_isalive** (net_isalive(SYS_NETFD sd)) should confirm whether the server is still connected to a specific remote host. You can use this function to verify whether a client is still connected or whether the request is canceled. **net_isalive** returns 0 if the socket is no longer connected to the remote host or 1 if it is connected.

File I/O Functions

Two significant function groups process file I/O. The **system_*** functions are platform-independent macros for system-specific functions that read from and write to files. For platform independence, use these functions instead of the operating system's "system" functions. For example, use Netscape's **system_fopen<xx>** function instead of C's **fopen**. The second type of I/O function encompasses the **filebuf_*** functions. They use file buffers to process file I/O, mainly to read the file data. These functions provide file buffer support even when the operating system does not provide such support. A few **file_*** functions are discussed below as well.

file_ * Functions

```
void file_unix2local(char *path, char *p2);
int file_setinherit(SYS_FILE fd, int value);
int file_notfound(void);
```

file_unix2local changes the path format specified in the path parameter, from a UNIX format to a local system format. It returns the new path in the p2 parameter. The function does nothing if the server is a UNIX system. It is useful only under Win32. **file_unix2local** can be used when you are running a Win32 version of the server but have a path in UNIX format. You can convert the format of the path to a Win32 format using this function.

file_setinherit designates whether the file descriptor (fd) can be inherited by the child process. If value is set to 0, fd cannot be inherited; otherwise it can. The function returns −1 if an error occurred.

Finally, **file_notfound** verifies whether a file error (errno) of the type ENOENT (not found) occurred. For example, if an error type ENOENT was returned while attempting to open a file using **system_fopenWA** (that is, no such file or directory), then a call to **file_notfound** returns TRUE.

System Functions

Opening a File

```
SYS_FILE system_fopenRO(char *path);
SYS_FILE system_fopenWA(char *path);
SYS_FILE system_fopenRW(char *path);
SYS_FILE system_fopenWT(char *path);
```

You open a file using one of the four **system_fopen<xx>** functions. The last two characters in each function define the actual way in which the file will be opened. After a file is opened through such a function, a separate function for the actual reading and writing is used (see the Reading from and Writing to a File section later in this chapter).

system_fopenRO opens an existing file in read-only mode. The file is specified by the path parameter. If successful, it returns the file descriptor (SYS_FILE). If the file does not exist, it fails and returns SYS_ERROR_FD. You can safely read from the file without the danger of modifying the content using this function.

system_fopenWA creates a file if the file does not exist. Otherwise, it opens the file for writing and appending. The new data are added to the end of the file.

system_fopenRW also creates a file if one does not exist. Otherwise, it opens the file for updating—that is, for both reading and writing. It does not, however, truncate the file to 0 length—that is, it does not destroy the existing data.

Use **system_fopenWT** to create a new file to write into it. If the file already exists, this function truncates the file to 0 length (writing over the data).

All of these functions open the file specified in the path parameter. They all return the file descriptor data structure (a handle to a file) if successful. They return SYS_ERROR_FD if an error occurs (for example, if the function was unable to open a file). As the value returned by these functions upon error can vary based on the operating system, verify the value by comparing it with SYS_ERROR_FD instead of directly looking for 0, −1, or NULL. Check for errors each time you use one of these functions.

> **Warning ▶**
>
> These **system_fopen** functions are not the same as **fopen** in UNIX. You should also not assume that the return values of the above functions are native file handles. Use the return value with other Netscape specific **system_*** functions.

Locking and Unlocking a File

```
int system_flock(SYS_FILE fd);
int system_ulock(SYS_FILE fd);
int system_tlock(SYS_FILE fd);
```

Once you have opened the file, you can use **system_flock** to lock it against any other processes. Notice that file locking locks a file only against other processes. Different threads in the same process can still access the file at the same time. Thus you still need to protect the file from other threads trying to write to the file at the same time. As Server 3.x does not use multiple processes, you no longer need to use this locking mechanism to lock a file against other processes. A better alternative for locking a file before writing to it is **system_fwrite_atomic**, which also automatically unlocks the file after updating the file.

system_flock takes the file descriptor returned from a **system_fopen<xx>** function. It returns IO_OK if the lock was successful and IO_ERROR if it failed. Make sure you unlock the file with **system_ulock** as soon as updating is finished. Use locking only when it is necessary (for example, when you are updating an existing file) because it can reduce server performance. With **system_tlock**, you can check whether a file lock is available. **system_tlock** returns zero (0) if it was able to hold the lock and a number less than zero if another process holds the lock.

Reading from and Writing to a File

```
int system_fread(SYS_FILE fd, char *buf, int sz);
int system_fwrite(SYS_FILE fd, char *buf, int sz);
int system_fwrite_atomic(SYS_FILE fd, char *buf, int sz);
```

system_fread, **system_fwrite**, and **system_fwrite_atomic** are for reading from and writing to a file. You must open the file (using a **system_fopen<xx>** function) before using these functions to actually read or write (see Opening a File earlier in this chapter). A file descriptor (fd) is returned (upon the successful opening of a file) by the **system_fopen<xx>** function. **system_fread** reads a specified number of bytes (sz) from this file into the buffer (buf). It also returns the number of bytes read. It returns IO_ERROR if an error occurred and IO_EOF if EOF was reached prematurely. **system_fwrite** writes a specified number of bytes (sz) from the buffer (buf) into the file specified by file descriptor (fd). Again, it returns IO_OK if successful and IO_ERROR in case of error. You cannot write to a file opened with **system_fopenRO**.

> **Note ▶**
>
> **system_fwrite** and **system_fread** do not work on pipes under NT. You should use **system_pwrite** and **system_pread** instead. For NT, **system_pwrite** is defined as `int system_pwrite(SYS_FILE fd, char *buf, int sz)` and **system_pread** is defined as `int system_pread(SYSFILE fd, char *buf, int sz)`.

As mentioned earlier, **system_fwrite_atomic** writes to a file as well. This function also provides file locking for the file to which you are writing.

Positioning the File Pointer

```
int system_lseek(SYS_FILE fd, int offset, int whence);
```

You can use **system_lseek** to set the position of (reposition) the file pointer in the file. The file pointer points to either the next character byte to be read from the file or to the location where writing will commence. offset defines the number of extra bytes from which the pointer should be offset (that is, the new location of the pointer). whence determines the origin where the offset should start. When whence is set to SEEK_SET, the file pointer points to the number of offset bytes in the file from the beginning of the file. When whence is set to SEEK_CUR, the pointer points to the number of offset bytes from the current position of the pointer in the file. When whence is set to SEEK_END, the pointer points to the number of offset bytes from the end of the file. If an error occurs, the function returns −1.

Closing the File

```
int system_fclose(SYS_FILE fd);
```

Once you have done the appropriate read and write procedures for the file, you must close the file descriptor with **system_fclose**. This function returns IO_ERROR in case of an error. Otherwise, it closes the file and returns 0.

The code in Listing 5-3 opens a file for appending some data. We then verify that the file was opened correctly. The path is specified for a Win32 system. **system_fwrite_atomic** is used to lock and write to the file the silly text "Add this to the file."

Listing 5-3   Writing to a File

```
SYS_FILE fd; /* file descriptor */
char *log;   /* data to be added to the file */
int len;     /* length of the data */

/* open the file for appending the data */
fd = system_fopenWA("c:/tmp/xfiles.html");

/* SYS_ERROR_FD is -1 for UNIX and NULL for Win32 */
if ( fd == SYS_ERROR_FD )
{
  /* add any error handling function here */

  return REQ_ABORTED;
}

log = (char *) MALLOC(80 * sizeof(char));
```

Listing 5-3   Writing to a File (*continued*)

```
/* data to be input */
len = util_sprintf(log, "Add this to the file");

/* this function locks the file while an update is being
   made */
system_fwrite_atomic(fd, log, len);

/* close the file */
system_fclose(fd);
```

filebuf Functions

You can use the **filebuf_*** (file buffer) functions in place of the system functions (for example, **system_fread**) to read from a file using buffers. For example, once you have opened a file, you can use a **filebuf_getc** function to read the data one character at a time. The file must be opened first, so you must call a **system_fopen<*xx*>** function before you attempt to use file buffering. You can then open a file buffer to read from the file. Using buffered I/O is a more efficient way of doing file I/O. Netscape provides platform-independent file buffering that also supports memory mapping (mmap). Memory mapping allows the file's contents to be mapped to the specified process's virtual address space. Even if the operating system does not support system-specific file buffering, these functions allow you to use buffers.

filebuf_* functions are very similar to the **netbuf_*** functions. (Under Server 2.x, both function types are defined in the base/buffer.h file.) Unlike **netbuf_***, however, **filebuf_*** functions can support memory mapping (mmap). **filebuf_open_nostat**, **filebuf_create**, and **filebuf_close_buffer** all have provisions for mmap.

Opening a File Buffer

```
filebuffer *filebuf_open(SYS_FILE fd, int sz);
filebuffer *filebuf_open_nostat(SYS_FILE fd,
                                int sz, struct stat *finfo);
```

filebuf_open opens a new file buffer for the file specified in the file descriptor fd. You can use one of the **system_fopen<*xx*>** functions to get the file descriptor before calling **filebuf_open**. The sz parameter is the size of the buffer in bytes. The function returns a pointer to the filebuffer data structure. It returns NULL if no buffer was opened. You can use this function to take advantage of the more efficient use of buffered file I/O. **filebuf_open** allows you to use buffered files even when it is not supported by the operating system. **filebuf_open_nostat** allows you to open a file buffer without a call to a **stat** function. Thus you should be sure to call a **stat** function (for example, **request_stat_path**) before calling this function. Repeated calls to this function do not need to make additional **stat** calls. Likewise, no additional

request_stat_path is called. Thus this function provides a more efficient way of opening a file buffer than **filebuf_open**. The finfo parameter points to the stat structure for the current open file (specified by fd). For **filebuf_open_nostat**, you can get the stat data structure finfo by calling **request_stat_path** or **system_stat** (system_stat(<*file name*>, &finfo)). This function takes advantage of memory-mapped files (FILE_MMAP). In fact, if memory mapping is not available or is disabled, a call to **filebuf_open_nostat** is interpreted as a call to **filebuf_open**. finfo is specifically defined for use with mmap. **filebuf_open** may return NULL if mmap is used under the UNIX operating system. You can always make a call to **system_errmsg** to check for a specific error message.

Reading from the File Buffer One Character at a Time
The function **filebuf_getc**,

```
int filebuf_getc(filebuffer *b);
```

is defined in Netscape's nsapi.h header file as follows:

```
#ifdef FILE_MMAP
#define filebuf_getc(b) \
  ((b)->pos == (b)->len ? IO_EOF : \
  (int)(unsigned char *) (b)->fp[(b)->pos++])
#else
#define filebuf_getc(b) \
  ((b)->pos != (b)->cursize ? \
  (int)((b)->inbuf[(b)->pos++]) : filebuf_next(b,1))
#endif
```

In earlier versions of the server, the value of (b)->fp[(b)->pos++] was not first cast to (unsigned char *).

Once the file buffer is open, you can read from the buffer using **filebuf_getc**. (You can also use **util_getline** to read from a file buffer. See the discussion of **util_*** functions later in this chapter for more details.) **filebuf_getc** reads a character from the current cursor position in the file. It works differently depending on whether mmap (memory mapping) is enabled. The function works similarly to **netbuf_getc** (see the net and netbuf Functions section earlier in this chapter for more details) if mmap is not defined. When mmap is defined, the function uses len and fp, which are filebuffer data structure members available to filebuffer only with mmap. The function then reads through the buffer, one character at a time, until the position of the file pointer reaches the size of the length of the buffer (that is, (b)->pos == (b)->len is true).

filebuf_getc reads through the file pointer, returning the current character and moving up the position of the file pointer by one character. It normally returns a char cast to an int. For Server 3.x, it returns an unsigned char cast to an int. Upon failure or reaching end of file, it returns IO_EOF.

Note that **filebuf_getc** cannot distinguish between an end of file (EOF) and a zero byte. For Server 3.x, if you want to make sure the actual end of file is reached and not an error or zero byte, you can use the new function **filebuf_iseof**.

Reaching the End of the File (Server 3.x)

```
int filebuf_iseof(filebuffer *b);
```

filebuf_iseof can be used to verify if the end of file (EOF) is reached. This function returns 0 if the end of file is not reached and 1 if the end of file is reached. You can use it in conjunction with **filebuf_getc** to make sure that the end of file has been reached rather than an error or zero byte.

Putting Bytes into the File Buffer's inbuf

```
int filebuf_grab(filebuffer *buf, int sz);
```

The **filebuf_grab** function takes data from the current file and puts them into the file buffer's (buf) inbuf string. (Note that the inbuf variable of filebuffer is cast to an unsigned char * instead of a char * for Server 3.x.) You can then use inbuf (buf->inbuf) instead of buf->fp to access the data in the file. inbuf points to the data in the file. **filebuf_grab** also sets the filebuffer structure's pos (current cursor position) and cursize (current size of buffer) to the size specified in sz. It returns the number of bytes read, which must be less than the maximum number of bytes (sz) and more than 0. The parameter sz sets the maximum number of bytes that the server should try to read from the file. In case of error, **filebuf_grab** returns IO_ERROR (-1). When the end of file is reached, it returns IO_EOF (0). This function works similarly to **netbuf_grab**.

Sending the File Buffer to the Socket

```
int filebuf_buf2sd(filebuffer *buf, SYS_NETFD sd);
```

You can send the contents of the file buffer to a specified socket by using **filebuf_buf2sd**. Once you have opened the file, and assuming you have not read from it, you can use this function to send the file's contents directly to the socket. Under Server 2.0, if you have read from the file previously, this function will not work. This method is the quickest way to send a file to a client. You can use **file_open_nostat** to open the file buffer and then employ this function to send the file's content to the client. If successful, the function returns the number of bytes sent to the client socket. If it fails, it returns IO_ERROR. In your function, you should check for an IO_ERROR return by this function. You can get the socket descriptor from the csd parameter of the Session structure.

Closing the File Buffer

```
void filebuf_close_buffer(filebuffer *buf, int clean_mmap);
void filebuf_close(filebuffer *buf);
```

You must close the buffer you have opened. Once you have read the data from the buffer, use **filebuf_close** to deallocate the buffer and close its associated file. **filebuf_close_buffer**, on the other hand, provides the file buffer clean-up without closing the underlying file (for example, this function deallocates the buffer while keeping the file open). If clean_mmap is set to 1, the file that was mapped in memory is unmapped. If clean_mmap is set to 0, the file is not unmapped.

Listing 5-4 uses a file buffer to read from a file and write to the client. The path for **system_fopenRO** is specified for a Win32 system. We get the file stat (finfo) for the file, and then use **filebuf_open_nostat** to open the buffer. **filebuf_buf2sd** then writes the buffer to the client socket specified with sn->csd. Closing the file buffer with **filebuf_close** also closes the file, so a **system_fclose** call is not needed.

Listing 5-4   Read from a File and Write to the Client

```
#define path "c:/tmp/xfile.txt"

filebuf *buf; /* file buffer */
SYS_FILE fd; /* file descriptor */
struct stat finfo; /* file stat */

/* open the file for reading the data */
fd = system_fopenRO(path);

/* SYS_ERROR_FD is -1 for UNIX and NULL for Win32 */
if(fd == SYS_ERROR_FD)
{
    /* Add any error handling function here. Also change
       return value to what you wish to happen upon failure.
     */

    return REQ_ABORTED;
}

/* get finfo */
if(stat(path, &finfo) == -1)
{
    /* Add any error handling function here. Also change
       return value to what you wish to happen upon failure.
     */
    system_fclose(fd);
    return REQ_ABORTED;
}

/* Get file buffer without a call to stat. FILE_BUFFERSIZE
   is defined as 4096.
 */
```

Listing 5-4   Read from a File and Write to the Client (*continued*)

```
buf = filebuf_open_nostat(fd, FILE_BUFFERSIZE, &finfo);

if(!buf)
{
    /* Add any error handling function here. Also change
       return value to what you wish to happen upon failure.
     */

    system_fclose(fd);
    return REQ_ABORTED;
}
/* send the buffer to client socket (csd) */
if(filebuf_buf2sd(buf, sn->csd) == IO_ERROR)
{
    /* Add any error handling function here. Also change
       return value to what you wish to happen upon failure.
     */

    filebuf_close(buf);
    return REQ_EXIT;
}
/* close buffer and exit */
filebuf_close(buf);

return REQ_PROCEED;
```

Func Functions

There are times when you may want to run a built-in server function and modify its actions. You may also want to redirect an existing SAF through a new function that will report the server processing of the original function. For example, you can call an existing server function (such as one of the functions defined in Appendix B) from within your program and use its result to extend the predefined features of the server. You can put a wrapper around a built-in server function. In such cases, **func_*** functions are used to handle server functions. At the start-up of the server, the server creates a table of these functions hashed by their names. This list includes the Netscape built-in server functions and any function you specify in the **obj.conf** file. The **func_*** functions find the built-in server functions, insert new functions into the hash table, or execute SAFs.

As noted in the Request Data Structure section earlier in this chapter, Netscape can cache directives. If the directive_is_cacheable is set to TRUE, the server directive is cached. This approach can pose a problem if the function is cached and therefore not called again to execute dynamically as you had planned. Thus you may need to disable directive caching.

Finding a Predefined Server Function

```
FuncPtr func_find(char *name);
```

You can verify whether a function is in the server function table and get a pointer to it. **func_find** finds the function named in its parameter and returns a pointer to that function. If no function is found, then **func_find** returns NULL. The function table is the list of built-in server functions and functions you defined in the **obj.conf** file. name is the name given to the server function in the **obj.conf** file and not necessarily the actual function's name. (When you name your function in the **obj.conf** file, you can use dashes instead of underscores.) Thus, if the actual function name is **get_stuff**, but you referenced it in **obj.conf** as get-stuff, in **func_find** you must use **get-stuff** as the name of the function. Function **check** found in the accompanying CD-ROM shows how you can use **func-find** to identify if a function is part of the Netscape's function table. This list includes all the server's built-in functions, even if they may not be defined in the **obj.conf** file.

Executing a Server Function

```
int func_exec(pblock *pb, Session *sn, Request *rq);
```

func_exec executes a function whose name is in the fn entry of the pblock (pb, **func_exec**'s first parameter). The server function is executed for the specific request determined by the Session and Request data structures. If the function was not found, then **func_exec** returns REQ_ABORTED.

If the pblock in the **func_exec** function is the same pblock that was passed to your server function, then **func_exec** executes your server function again. In other words, if you call **func_exec** using the pblock argument passed to your calling function (your function's first parameter), the pblock argument's fn entry of the **func_exec** function will be the same as the fn entry for your function in the **obj.conf** file.

If you want to use the same pblock as the one passed to your function, you must remove the name of the function and insert a new name for the fn parameter. One way to accomplish this goal is with the function **param_remove** or **pblock_remove**. They remove the existing function (fn) name from the pblock—for example, pblock_remove("fn",pb). Next, you must insert the new name into the pblock. **pblock_nvinsert** inserts the function into a pblock—for example, pblock_nvinsert("fn", <function name>, pb).

An alternative to renaming the fn entry of the pblock is to not use the same pblock that called your function in the first place. The pblock you are passing to **func_exec** does not need to be the same pblock that was passed to your function. You can create a new pblock and insert the function (fn) and any other parameter needed for the function. The new pblock can then be passed to **func_exec**.

The next two parameters of **func_exec**, Session and Request, are generally passed, as is, from your function. The information associated with the client request is typically utilized by the new function you are executing. **func_exec** works like any other server function you may write. In fact, the Func (server function) to which the FuncPtr points is defined as Func(pblock *, Session *, Request *). Your function is also written the same way, with pblock, Session, and Request as the three parameters.

A server function can be executed without **func_exec** by directly calling it in your function. For example, you can create a pblock for the function name and its parameters, calling the function directly by its name and passing it the pblock along with the Request and Session data structures. This method, in effect, works the same as calling **func_exec**. (See Chapter 6 for more details.)

If **func_exec** does not find the function, it returns REQ_ABORTED and logs the error. For example, if it does not find the name, it logs a LOG_MISCONFIG for the missing function name. Otherwise, it returns the return value of the function. You can use this return value to discover how the function processed the request.

Listing 5-5 provides an example in which an existing function is redirected to a new one. In this code, we execute a different SAF from inside an existing SAF.

Listing 5-5 Executing a Different SAF Using **func_exec**

```
int result;    /* return of calling the function */
pblock *newpb; /* new pblock to be used with the function */

/* create the new pblock */
newpb = pblock_create(2);

/* insert the pb_params into the pblock */
pblock_nvinsert("fn", "new_function", newpb);

pblock_nvinsert("xparam", "doit", newpb);

/* execute the new function */
result = func_exec(newpb, sn, rq);

/* free the new pblock */
pblock_free(newpb);

/* return the result of executing the new function */
return result;
```

Inserting or Renaming a Function into the Function Table

```
struct FuncStruct *func_insert(char *funcname, FuncPtr fn);

/* Server 3.x only */
FuncPtr func_replace(char *funcname, FuncPtr fn);
```

func_insert dynamically inserts a named function into the table of functions. It returns the function structure `FuncStruct`. `FuncStruct` is the hash table of the server's functions at the start of the server. This returned value could be put to use when freeing the `FuncStruct` for your function as the server restarts. `funcname` is the name of the function you wish to insert. `fn` is the address of the function. You can use `&<function name>` for the address of the function. Because this function does not specify a directive for the function or insert any of the parameters of the function, it is of little use for inserting a server application function.

func_replace is a new function added to Server 3.x. You can use it to replace a function in the server's table of functions with one that you have specified in the `fn` parameter. You specify the name of the function you want to replace in the `funcname` parameter and the address of the new function in `fn`. If **func_replace** is successful in replacing the function, it returns a pointer (`FuncPtr`) to the function you want to replace. Otherwise, it returns 0. Note that you can replace only the function, not the parameters set for the function in the **obj.conf** file.

Utility Functions

util_* functions are a series of utility functions not easily categorized in a specific group. Several of these **util_*** functions manage strings.

Formatting and Placing a String into a String Buffer

```
int util_sprintf(char *s, char *fmt, [arguments]);
int util_snprintf(char *s, int n, char *fmt, [arguments]);

int util_vsprintf(char *s, register char *fmt, va_list args);
int util_vsnprintf(char *s, int n, register char *fmt,
                   va_list args);
```

util_sprintf and **util_snprintf** are based on **sprintf** functions that use **printf**-type syntax to format a string and place it in a buffer. **util_snprintf** includes an added parameter, n, that holds the maximum number of bytes to be copied. You should use this function if you want bounds checking. The function returns the number of characters placed in the string, excluding the `NULL` terminator. s is the buffer that holds the formatted string. `fmt` is the formatted string. `[arguments]` can hold a number of arguments to be replaced by their values inside the formatted string. The following is an example of this kind of function call: `util_sprintf(ctbuf,` `"Content-type: %s\nContent-length: %d\n\n", content_type,` `finfo.st_size)`. The value of `content_type` will be placed where `%s` is located and the value of `finfo-st_size` will be placed where `%d` is located in the string. `fmt` handles only `%d` and `%s` (integer and string, respectively). It does not handle width and precision strings.

util_vsprintf and **util_vsnprintf** are based on **vsprintf** functions. They also format a string and place it in a buffer. Like **util_snprintf**, **util_vsnprintf** provides bounds checking. `fmt` is the register character pointer to a formatted string. It also supports only %d and %s (integer and string, respectively). va_list is the list of arguments you can obtain with a call to **va_start**, a macro that provides access to a function's arguments when that function takes a number of arguments. Typically, both are defined in stdarg.h for ANSI C and in varargs.h for UNIX System V. Both return the number of characters, excluding the NULL terminator, written into the buffer located by s. Usually, these two functions are not included, because the functionality typically needed is only formatting a string into a buffer. Your best choice, in such a case, would be either **util_sprintf** or **util_snprintf**.

Comparing Strings

```
int util_strcasecmp(const char *s1, const char *s2);
int util_strncasecmp(const char *s1, const char *s2, int n);
```

Other string manipulation functions include **util_strcasecmp** and **util_strncasecmp**. These functions compare two alphanumeric strings. They return 1 if the first string (s1) is greater than the second string (s2), 0 if s1 is equal to s2, and −1 if s1 is less than s2. With **util_strncasecmp**, you have the added advantage of defining the number of characters to compare. For example, to compare only the first three characters, n is set to 3. These two functions are not case-sensitive. (Under Server 2.x, they are defined in systems.h and not in util.h, where the other **util_*** functions are defined.)

These functions are simple macros for the system functions **strcasecmp** and **strncasecmp**. You will find greater flexibility in using the standard C string comparison functions instead of these functions.

Using Wildcards to Check a String

```
int shexp_cmp(char *str, char *exp);
int shexp_casecmp(char *str, char *exp);
int shexp_match(char *str, char *exp);
```

You can also take advantage of **shexp_*** functions to provide wildcard matching. (Under Server 2.x, **shexp_*** functions are defined in the base/shexp.h file.) Netscape's shell expression use is loosely based on zsh (the Z shell). **shexp_cmp** and **shexp_casecmp** first validate a string as an appropriate shell expression (exp) by using the appropriate wildcard expressions. They then compare the expression (exp) with the string (str). They return 0 if a match was found, 1 if no match was found, and −1 if the expression was invalid. **shexp_cmp** is case-sensitive. **shexp_casecmp** is the case-insensitive version of the function. **shexp_match** works in the same way, except that it does not validate the shell expression before comparing the expression with the string. As no validation of the expression takes place, **shexp_match** also does not return −1. Use these functions if you want wildcard matching of strings. (See Wildcard Options in Chapter 2 for more details.)

```
char *path = pblock_findval("path", pb);

if(shexp_casecmp(path, "c:\\tmp\\special.txt"))
```

```
{
    return REQ_ABORTED;
}
```

This code exemplifies the use of the **shexp_casecmp** function for comparing a path received from the server configuration with the expected path. If the paths are not the same, we exit the program.

Reading a Line from a File Buffer

```
int util_getline(filebuffer *buf, int lineno,
                 int maxlen, char *l);
```

Another useful **util_*** function is **util_getline**. This function reads one line of text at a time from a text file. It reads from the file buffer (buf) until it finds LF (line-feed) or CRLF (carriage return, line-feed). It terminates the line with a NULL terminator and removes the carriage-return and line-feed characters. Then, it places the data into the string pointed to by its fourth parameter (l). maxlen is the maximum length of the line (l) string in characters. This number limits the number of characters read into the l string. lineno is the line number. You must update lineno as you read the buffer. You can use lineno to indicate in an error message where an error occurred. You need to allocate the space for the l string. The function does not allocate or de-allocate space for the string automatically. The function returns 0 upon success, 1 if the function reaches the end of the file, and −1 if an error occurred. You should check the return value for the end of the file or if an error occurred. This function is an alternative to **filebuf_getc**.

Converting an Integer to a String

```
int util_itoa(int i, char *a);
```

util_itoa is a simplified version of the **itoa** function from the stdlib.h C header file. It converts an integer (i) to a string (a). a is the ASCII character string for the integer i. **util_itoa** returns the length of the string. You must allocate the space for the string. Make sure it is at least 32 bytes long.

Manipulating Environment Variables

```
char **util_env_create(char **env, int n, int *pos);
char *util_env_str(char *name, char *value);
void util_env_replace(char **env, char *name, char *value);
void util_env_free(char **env);
char *util_env_find(char **env, char *name);
```

The preceding code outlines functions for environment variable-related support. For example, if you want to set environment variables to be passed to a shell program run by your NSAPI function, use these functions to create, copy, find, and perform other operations on the environment variable strings. For more details, check the `util.h` header file for Server 2.x or the `nsapi.h` header file for Server 3.x, and the "NSAPI Programmer's Guide."

If you plan to use these functions to pass environment variables to a CGI program executed through **send-cgi**, you may be disappointed. The server does not pass the variables you define through these functions to the CGI program. Instead, you can use these functions to set the environment variables for a program that your SAF invokes.

To make sure your variables are passed to your CGI program, use the **pblock_nvinsert** function and insert your variables into the `Request->headers` pblock. These variables will then appear to the CGI program as the equivalent HTTP header variables (that is, `HTTP_*`). You do not add `HTTP_` to the name of the environment variable, as the server performs this task automatically. Your function needs to set these variables before **send-cgi** is invoked. For example, you can write a simple **NameTrans** function and add the variables in your function.

Another method of sending user-defined environment variables to a CGI program is to specify the variables as parameters for the built-in function **init-cgi**. These *name-value* pairs are then available to a CGI program in the same way as any other environment variables. The drawback in using **init-cgi** is that these variables are not dynamically generated. Instead, they are defined and loaded at the start of the server and are available to all CGI programs.

Getting the Server Host Name

```
char *util_hostname(void);
```

util_hostname is used to get the local host name of the server. The value is the same as the CGI environment variable `SERVER_NAME` and the global server variable `server_hostname`. **util_hostname** returns the name of the system running the server. This name must be a fully qualified domain name; otherwise, the function will return `NULL`.

Checking and Updating the URI

```
int util_uri_is_evil(char *uri);
void util_uri_parse(char *uri);
char *util_uri_escape(char *d, char *s);
void util_uri_unescape(char *uri);
```

uri_is_evil verifies if a URI includes unexpected characters—that is, if it is insecure. A URI is insecure if it includes the following path: `//`, `/./`, `/.`, `/..`, and `/../`. For NT, it should also not include `.` or `./`. **util_uri_is_evil** returns 1 if the URI is insecure (evil) and 0 if it is safe. You can then use **util_uri_parse** to remove the dangerous characters from the URI. **util_uri_parse** replaces each dangerous character with a single forward slash. It converts the dangerous characters in the URI, such as `/../`, `/./`, and `//`, to `/`. For example, once you find out that the URI `/./news.html` is insecure, you can convert it to `/news.html` by using **util_uri_parse**.

util_uri_escape can be used to escape any special character in the string s. The escaped string is then copied into the string specified in the d parameter. The process of escaping a special character converts the ASCII character to its Hexadecimal equivalent and places the Hex integer after a percent sign in place of the character in the string in d. The special characters include %, ?, #, :, +, &, ", ", <, >, or a space, carriage return (CR), and line-feed (LF). If d is NULL, **util_uri_unescape** allocates a string of an appropriate size, but does not do bounds checking on the d string. **util_uri_unescape** does the reverse of **util_uri_escape.** It unescapes the escaped characters in the URI. It replaces the % [*Hex*] characters with their equivalent ASCII characters. We will use **util_uri_unescape** in Chapter 9 to parse the URL-encoded input sent by the client using an HTML form. The URL-encoded input includes escaped Hexadecimal characters.

Verifying the Client Browser Version

```
int util_is_mozilla(char *ua, char *major, char *minor);
```

You can use **util_is_mozilla** to verify whether the client is using a Netscape browser of at least the specified version. ua is the user-agent string from the request header. You specify the major and minor parameters based on the version number. major is the release number before the decimal point. minor is the release number after the decimal point. For example, if the expected version number of the Netscape browser should be at least 1.2, you can use the major number 1 and the minor number 2. **util_is_mozilla** returns 1 if the user-agent matches the requirement. It returns 0 if the user-agent is not a Netscape browser or the version is less than the specified version. Note that **util_is_mozilla** verifies the client browser based on the user-agent header sent by the client. Other browsers, such as Microsoft Internet Explorer, may also return a user-agent header that includes the Mozilla version string.

Time Functions

```
int util_strftime(char *s, const char *format,
                  const struct tm *t);

struct tm *system_localtime(const time_t *clock, struct tm
                                   *res);
struct tm *system_gmtime(const time_t *clock, struct tm
                                   *res);
```

Finally, a few **util_*** functions provide the time. **util_strftime** is a thread-safe version of **strftime**. **strftime**, as defined in the time.h C header file, formats a time string and places it in a string buffer. **util_strftime** takes the data structure tm pointed to by parameter t and formats it based on the format arguments in the string pointed to by the parameter format. (This formatting is similar to how **printf** works, but the actual types of arguments enumerated in the format string are specific to the tm structure only.) **util_strftime** then puts the result in the string buffer s. Because there is no bounds checking, you must make sure that the size of the buffer is large enough. **util_strftime** returns the number of characters placed in the string buffer s and does not include the NULL terminator. To create the string in the HTTP expected format, use the constant HTTP_DATE_FMT. HTTP_DATE_FMT is defined as follows:

```
#ifdef XP_UNIX
#define HTTP_DATE_FMT "%A, %d-%b-%y %T GMT"
#else /* XP_WIN32 */
#define HTTP_DATE_FMT "%A, %d-%b-%y %H:%M:%S GMT"
#endif
```

To get the tm structure today, you can use the Netscape **system_*** functions: **system_localtime** or **system_gmtime**. (Under Server 3.x, **system_localtime** and **system_gmtime** are actually redefinitions of **util_localtime** and **util_gmtime**, respectively. With Server 3.x, you can also use **util_localtime** and **util_gmtime** if you like.) These functions are thread-safe versions of the standard C functions, **localtime** and **gmtime**. Both the **system_localtime** and **system_gmtime** functions return a pointer to the tm time data structure. **system_gmtime** returns the time based on Greenwich Mean Time. The first parameter of these two functions is a pointer to time_t, the time stored as a numerical value (the number of seconds since January 1, 1970). You get time_t from functions such as **time**, which is defined in the time.h C header file. **time** returns time_t. The second argument for both **system_localtime** and **system_gmtime** is the same value as the one returned by the functions and is added to provide compatibility with systems like OSF. Depending upon your operating system, the tm structure could be obtained from either the second parameter or the function's return value. (See your system's documentation or C programming documentation for more information.)

Listing 5-6 provides a simple example for producing a time string using **system_localtime**.

Listing 5-6   Creating a New Time String

```
time_t now;                 /* pointer to stored time */
struct tm *today;           /* time structure */
char *timestring;

/* Get the stored time (number of seconds since 1/1/70).
   You can use the time function's parameter or the
   returned value to save the stored time. Here, we use
   the return value and set the time parameter to NULL.
   Alternatively, we could have used time(&now);
 */
now = time(NULL);

/* get the time data structure for today */
today = system_localtime(&now, &today);
```

Listing 5-6   Creating a New Time String (*continued*)

```
/* malloc a space large enough for the string */
timestring = (char *) MALLOC(50 * sizeof(char));

/* put the time from the time data structure (today) in
   the string timestring
 */
util_strftime(timestring, "Today is %A, %B %d, %Y.", today);
```

This code uses the **time**, **system_localtime**, and **util_strftime** functions to include in a string today's day, month, date, and year (for example, Today is Friday, May 29, 1998).

Comparing Times

```
int util_later_than(struct tm *lms, char *ims);
int util_time_equal(struct tm *lms, char *ims);
```

The functions **util_later_than** and **util_time_equal** compare a time data structure (tm) specified in lms with the date string specified in ims. They handle RFC 822, RFC 850, and ctime formats. The functions return 1 if the relation is evaluated as true. For example, **util_later_than** returns 1 if the time in ims is the same as, or later than, the time in lms. The functions return 0 upon failure (for example, **util_later_than** returns 0 when the time in ims is earlier than the time in lms).

Memory Management Functions

Under Server 1.x, Netscape provided platform-independent memory macros, such as **MALLOC, REALLOC, STRDUP,** and **FREE.** They were simple substitute routines for the equivalent C library functions (for example, **MALLOC** substituted for **malloc**). Under Server 2.x, you can find these macros defined in the netsite.h file. For Server 1.x, these functions got their memory from the system heap and your code had to free any memory it allocated. With Server 2.0, Netscape provides memory pooling. (See the discussion of **pool_handle_t** earlier in this chapter for more information.) This new feature (also supported under Server 3.x) changes the way these macros work. It also improves the performance of the server. For each request, the server creates a memory pool and then uses this pool to allocate the Request data structure's parameter block elements. When you use these macros in your code for allocating memory, they use this memory pool. The server also frees the memory pool automatically after the request is processed, so you don't need to call **FREE** to free the memory. Of course, to use memory pooling, you must have memory pooling enabled (that is, you must not have disabled memory pooling through the **Init** function **pool-init** in the **obj.conf** file). Memory allocation works only for processing a request. In other words, the global server data, or data initialized with **Init** functions, do not use the memory pool. These data are allocated as permanent storage, because they need to last for the entire server's lifespan. (Even if you use **MALLOC**, the server uses persistent memory.) **MALLOC** allocates memory from the memory pool, while **PERM_MALLOC** allocates memory from the system's heap.

Allocating and Freeing Memory Blocks from the Memory Pool

```
#define MALLOC(size) system_malloc(size)
NSAPI_PUBLIC void *system_malloc(int size);

#define REALLOC(ptr, size) system_realloc(ptr, size)
NSAPI_PUBLIC void *system_realloc(void *ptr, int size);

#define STRDUP(ptr) system_strdup(ptr)
NSAPI_PUBLIC char *system_strdup(char *ptr);

#define FREE(ptr) system_free((void *) ptr)
NSAPI_PUBLIC void system_free(void *ptr);
```

MALLOC is used to allocate memory blocks. You pass the `size` of the space you want allocated to this function, and it will return a pointer to the allocated block. You can use a type cast on the returned value to specify the type of pointer (for example, `(char *) MALLOC (50 * sizeof(char))`. The function returns `NULL` if there is not enough memory available. **REALLOC** reallocates a new memory block. `ptr` points to the beginning of the existing (previous) memory block. `size` is the new size to be allocated. You use this function to change the size of a memory block you have already allocated with **MALLOC** or **STRDUP**. The contents of the block are unchanged up to the smaller of either the new or the old size. Any new space is not initialized. The pointer returned by **REALLOC** points to the new location of the memory block and could be different from the old location.

STRDUP is a macro for **strdup** in UNIX or **_strdup** in Win32. It duplicates a string. **STRDUP** calls **MALLOC** to allocate a new space for copying (duplicating) a string passed to it through the parameter `ptr`. It returns the pointer to the new string.

FREE frees (deallocates) the memory block allocated by any of the previously discussed functions (that is, **MALLOC**, **REALLOC**, and **STRDUP**). Make sure you **REALLOC** and **FREE** memory using the same type of function. If you use **PERM_MALLOC** to allocate memory, then use **PERM_REALLOC** and **PERM_FREE**. With **MALLOC**, **REALLOC**, and **STRDUP**, the server frees the memory when a request is finished. You can, however, still free the memory using **FREE**. On the other hand, you are responsible for freeing any memory that is allocated using **PERM_MALLOC**, **PERM_REALLOC**, and **PERM_STRDUP**.

Allocating and Freeing Memory Blocks from the Heap

```
#define PERM_MALLOC(size) system_malloc_perm(size)
NSAPI_PUBLIC void *system_malloc_perm(int size);
```

```
#define PERM_REALLOC(ptr, size) \
        system_realloc_perm(ptr, size)
NSAPI_PUBLIC void *system_realloc_perm(void *ptr, int
                                        size);

#define PERM_STRDUP(ptr) system_strdup_perm(ptr)
NSAPI_PUBLIC char *system_strdup_perm(char *ptr);

#define PERM_FREE(ptr) system_free_perm((void *) ptr)
NSAPI_PUBLIC void system_free_perm(void *ptr);
```

PERM_MALLOC, **PERM_CALLOC**, **PERM_REALLOC**, **PERM_STRDUP**, and **PERM_FREE** are new macros defined by Netscape. They perform the same roles as **MALLOC**, **CALLOC**, and so on under Server 1.x. They allocate persistent memory. You can use **PERM_MALLOC** to provide permanent storage for use with global variables or to control the freeing of memory. For example, if you want certain data to be available across multiple requests, make sure you allocate the memory by using **PERM_MALLOC**. Also, make sure you use **PERM_FREE** when freeing all of your permanently allocated memory. If you have disabled memory pooling, then **PERM_MALLOC** and **MALLOC** work the same way—that is, as persistent memory allocaters.

In general, you must be careful with memory allocation in your code. If the memory allocation has failed, the server does not tell you that the failure was due to memory allocation problem. The **PERM_*** macros are checked at runtime.

Warning ▶

Make sure you understand how **MALLOC** and **PERM_MALLOC** work. If your code written for Server 1.x was recompiled using the Server 2.x or 3.x header files, then the macros (**MALLOC, CALLOC,** and so on), will now use memory pooling, which could break your code. To have persistent memory for your allocated data, make sure to update your code with the **PERM_*** versions of these macros.

Other Functions

Besides the functions described so far, there are a few additional functions that are important to note, but do not fit into any group discussed so far. These functions are **log_error**, **daemon_atrestart**, **system_errmsg**, **cinfo_find**, **session_dns**, and **session_maxdns**.

Logging an Error

```
int log_error(int degree, char *func, Session *sn,
              Request *rq, char *fmt, [arguments]);
```

log_error logs an error of a given degree of severity for a function (func) into the errors log file. The fmt parameter works like the **printf** function. It uses arguments that you define for formatting the string to be placed in the errors log file. The function records the date and the degree you specify (for example, LOG_WARN for warning), plus the formatted string fmt. The degrees are LOG_WARN, LOG_MISCONFIG, LOG_SECURITY, LOG_FAILURE, LOG_CATASTROPHE, and LOG_INFORM. The following is an example of such a function call: log_error(LOG_WARN, "send-images", sn, rq, "%s%s not found", path, path-info). The Session *sn and Request *rq parameters refer to the appropriate Session and Request data structures that were passed to your function. The function returns 0 if the log entry was created and −1 if it failed. You will use this function frequently in your code to log any error that might occur in your program.

This function, along with **protocol_status**, provides the necessary error handling for your function. **protocol_status** sets the error status with the reason string to be sent to the client. **log_error** logs the error in the errors log file. (See Logging Errors in Chapter 6 for more information.)

Listing 5-7   Logging an Error

```
/* get the method used */
char *method = pblock_findval("method", rq->reqpb);

/* check if it is really POST being used */
if (strcmp(method, "POST") != 0)
{
    protocol_status(sn, rq, PROTOCOL_FORBIDDEN,
            "You must submit a form to access this URL.");
    log_error(LOG_WARN, "myfunction", sn, rq,
            "No form with POST method was submitted.");
    return REQ_ABORTED;
}
```

Listing 5-7 demonstrates the use of the three common steps (**protocol_status**, **log_error**, and **return**) taken in case of an error. In this code, we expected the client request method to be POST. The code returns an error and exits if it is not a POST method of request.

Running a Clean-up Function at Restart or Shutdown

```
void daemon_atrestart(void (*fn)(void *), void *data);
```

daemon_atrestart is used to register a function defined by the fn parameter that will run when the server restarts. Under Server 3.x and some releases of Server 2.x (see the Bug Report below), it is also invoked when the server stops. This updated function is used in place of **magnus_atrestart**, which, although still supported for backward compatibility, is now obsolete. **daemon_atrestart** is used to perform any necessary clean-up needed when the server stops or restarts. For example, the function can deallocate any resources allocated by an **Init** function. **daemon_atrestart** does the necessary clean-up before the server starts processing any new requests. The call-back function defined in fn parameter has a void pointer as its argument. You can use the second parameter data to pass on any necessary arguments to the function defined through fn. The parameter data is also a void pointer. Normally, you write **daemon_atrestart** as part of an **Init** function that runs when the server stops or restarts. **daemon_atrestart** calls your defined function at shutdown or restart. You can then free any variable, close a system lock, and perform similar operations in the function called by **daemon_atrestart**. **daemon_atrestart** is called by the base server process only. (For Server 2.x, it is called by the base server process before the server forks any child processes.)

Bug Report ▶

daemon_atrestart does not function properly under Server 2.0 for NT or IRIX.

Listing 5-8 calls the **finish** function by way of **daemon_atrestart** when the server stops or restarts. We set a global file descriptor that can be shared across different threads. The **finish** function closes the log file during shutdown or restart. The **my_init** function opens the log file. An additional function (not shown here) can then log what is needed into the log file.

Listing 5-8   Closing a File During Server Shutdown or Restart

```
/* file descriptor to be shared between threads */
static SYS_FILE log = SYS_ERROR_FD;

/* function called by daemon_atrestart */
NSAPI_PUBLIC void finish(void *parameter)
{
    /* close the log file */
    system_fclose(log);
    log = SYS_ERROR_FD;
}

/* an Init function that opens the log file
   shared between threads
 */
NSAPI_PUBLIC int my_init(pblock *pb, Session *sn,
                         Request *rq)
{
```

Listing 5-8   Closing a File During Server Shutdown or Restart (*continued*)

```
/* open the log file */
log = system_fopenWA("c:/tmp/log.txt");

/* check for errors in opening the file and return an
   Init type of error message
*/
if(log == SYS_ERROR_FD) {

    pblock_nvinsert("error",
      "my-init: failed to open the log file", pb);
    return REQ_ABORTED;
}

/* call finish to close the log file during server
   restart */
daemon_atrestart(finish, NULL);

return REQ_PROCEED;
}
```

Warning ▶

Under Server 2.0, when the server is restarted, a client will be cut off even in the middle of a request.

Returning the Last Error

```
char *system_errmsg(0); /* Server 1.x and 2.x */
char *system_errmsg();  /* Server 3.x */
```

system_errmsg returns the last error message that occurred while processing a system call. It is a macro for the **system_errmsg_fn** function. This function looks in the global array (`sys_errlist`) for the latest entry and returns the text string. It returns the last error for the most recent system call. Use this function for error handling. You can also include this function as an argument for your **log_error** function to get the actual error string reported with the rest of the error string, as in the following code:

```
log_error(LOG_WARN, "send-file", sn, rq,
         "error opening buffer from %s (%s)",
         path, system_errmsg());
```

Note ▶

You may find a reference to a specific parameter, such as a file descriptor (fd), for this function in earlier NSAPI examples. (See the example file service.c for Server 2.x.) Originally, Netscape had foreseen a use for this parameter. Because the function takes its cue from the global array of system error messages, however, the actual parameter is not used. For Server 1.x and 2.x, you have to use a parameter, although the actual parameter is not used by the server. Use 0 (zero) as a parameter. Under Server 3.x, **system_errmsg** does not take any parameter. Thus, if you are compiling a Server 2.x program that includes a **system_errmsg** function with 3.x header files, you must remove the parameter from the function.

Getting the Content Information Data Structure

```
cinfo *cinfo_find(char *uri);
```

The **cinfo_find** function finds the cinfo (content information) data structure of the file specified by the uri parameter. Content information includes the file's MIME type (for example, encoding information). (See the section on cinfo earlier in this chapter for more details.) uri can be a URI or a file name. The file name should be specified after the last forward slash (/) in the URI. If no slash is found in the uri parameter, **cinfo_find** expects only the file name as the parameter. File extensions should be separated by CINFO_SEPARATOR, which is defined as a period (.). For example, when a file has the extension *<file name>*.html.zip, the file type (text/html) and encoding (zip) are specified. File extensions, which are not case-sensitive, can include file type, encoding, and language. The function returns a pointer to a newly allocated cinfo data structure; otherwise, it returns NULL. The members of the cinfo data structure are pointers that point to the static data in the types database. You should not directly change any of these variables. If you want to change the data, make a copy of the elements (for example, with **STRDUP**) to create a new copy for your use. You must deallocate the cinfo data structure returned by this function when you have finished with it. Use this function to get the MIME type information for a file. For example, you can use cinfo to set the specific Request response headers of the file that are to be returned to the client.

Getting the Client DNS Address

```
char *session_dns(Session *sn);
char *session_maxdns(Session *sn);
```

session_dns and **session_maxdns** are used to get the DNS host name of a client. The client IP address and DNS are in the *Session*->client pblock. You can access the IP address, which is always available in *Session*->client, with **pblock_findval**. To get the DNS host name, however, you should use these functions. **session_dns** and **session_maxdns** insert the client host name into the client pblock and also return the client host name. You should use these functions to access the client DNS name instead of directly accessing the dns value in the *Session*->client pblock.

session_dns and **session_maxdns** are both macro definitions for session_dns_lookup(Session *sn, int verify). When verify is set to 1, as in **session_maxdns**, the function verifies that the DNS host name of the client is actually true. When verify is set to 0 (zero), as in **session_dns**, no verification is made after the DNS look-up. If you want to make sure the client is who it claims to be, use **session_maxdns**.

Summary

Netscape header files provide the necessary functions and data structures you need to program your NSAPI program. They are a subset of server's own API and, as such, represent a major resource for developing extremely efficient and speedy applications. Wherever possible in your code, you should take advantage of Netscape's NSAPI functions. These functions often provide the necessary platform independence or thread safety your program needs.

This chapter reviewed the major data structures and functions of NSAPI. It also provided an overview of the API. You do not need to understand every function or data structure to continue with the rest of the book, but a general understanding of what the API provides is important.

In Chapter 6, we will use some of these functions and data structures to write a number of examples. We will also review the steps you need to take to program an NSAPI application. Refer to these API chapters whenever you have a question about a function or a data structure.

Now that we have covered the main data structure and functions of NSAPI, it is time to write some code.

Writing a Server Application Function

The function you write for NSAPI is called a server application function (SAF). SAFs are directive functions. Your program can have many functions, some of which are SAFs. You can have any number of SAFs plus other C functions in your program. The function that interfaces with the server must be an SAF. Because the SAF is the function that is invoked by the server, you should begin writing your program by writing an SAF. Although an SAF should be the starting point of your program, your program can include a number of different SAFs. You can write a program that includes multiple server directive functions. These directive functions can work together to provide the specific feature that you need. The server passes information (for example, server variables and the client's input) to the SAF. These functions can also return appropriate responses to the server. An SAF can be an **AuthTrans**, **NameTrans**, or other directive's function. For example, you can write a **Service** function that processes a client's request. This function may call other C functions to read from and write to a file to process the request. The SAF can then return the appropriate response to the server.

To write an SAF, you first must decide which functionality you need and match it to a directive. You provide the added functionality by plugging your directive function (your SAF) into the server. Similar to how you add the built-in (predefined) server functions (previously described in Chapter 2), you also add your SAF to the `obj.conf` file, where a directive function like yours belongs (Figure 7-1, in the next chapter). The SAF can accomplish more than what a CGI function does (that is, reading input from a client, processing the client's request, and sending dynamic pages to the client). For example, you may want to write a customized authentication or logging function. You may even want to add features to the server, which a CGI program can later use. In Chapter 8, we will review all server directives (already discussed in Chapter 2), focusing on the directives as they are relevant for writing SAFs. We will discuss how to choose one directive over another, how the directives work, how you can take advantage of each directive step, and how to write a function for a specific directive.

In this chapter, we concentrate on **Service** functions. A **Service** function provides similar capabilities as a CGI program. It allows you to create a dynamic site. We have already reviewed the basic steps of a CGI program and you may already know how to write one. This chapter provides an overview of how you might transfer your existing CGI programs or skills to write an NSAPI program. **Service** is the directive for which you will write most of your functions. A few simple examples will provide you with a quick view of how NSAPI works, illustrating some of the frequently used features of NSAPI. In Chapter 9, we will expand on these examples and write more practical **Service** applications.

This chapter provides an outline of the common steps taken when writing an NSAPI program. It provides a basic understanding of how NSAPI works. We will return data to a client by sending an HTML page, redirecting a client, or sending an error status page. We will also read data from the server, including client input, global variables, and so on. You can check Figure 6-1 for an overview of how data are sent back and forth between the server and your server application function.

SAF Prototype

The declaration of your SAF is based on how server functions are defined by Netscape. If you look in the server header file (for example, the `nsapi.h` file for Server 3.x or the `func.h` file for Server 2.x), you will find the following code:

```
#ifdef XP_UNIX
typedef int Func(pblock *, Session *, Request *);
#else /* XP_WIN32 */
typedef int _cdecl Func(pblock *, Session *, Request *);
#endif
```

An SAF should have the following format:

```
NSAPI_PUBLIC int <function name>(pblock *<param>,
                                 Session *<sn>, Request *<rq>);
```

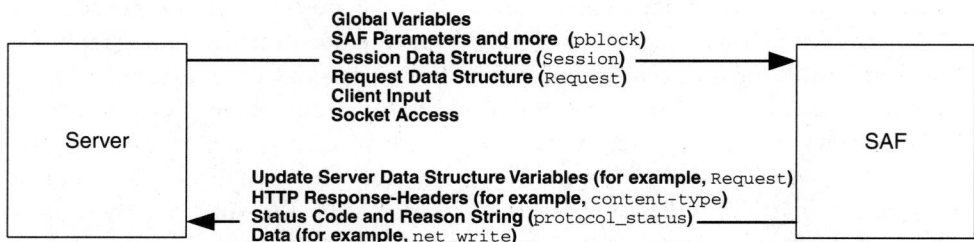

Figure 6-1   SAF's Relationship to the Server

As you can see, we defined the SAF declaration by following the same format as the **Func** definition does. You declare your function as type NSAPI_PUBLIC, with three predefined parameters and an integer as the return value. The server uses the functions defined in the **obj.conf** file to create a hash table of function declarations at the start of the server. The server looks for your SAF function in the **obj.conf** file to link to it.

Netscape NSAPI functions are declared as type NSAPI_PUBLIC so that your functions can use them. You also declare your function as type NSAPI_PUBLIC to allow the server to recognize it and link to it. These functions are then compiled into shared libraries for UNIX or DLLs for NT. For example, for NT NSAPI_PUBLIC is defined as __declspec(dllexport). This declaration is an extension to the C language for Windows programs. __declspec is a Microsoft-specific keyword that is used to qualify an extended attribute as a Microsoft-specific storage-class attribute. dllexport explicitly declares your function as exportable, enabling it to be exported from your DLL. Thus your function will become accessible to Netscape Server.

The parameters of an SAF are pointers to the three data structure types found in the server's header files. The first parameter of an SAF function stores the variables (parameters) defined for your function in the **obj.conf** file. When the server invokes your SAF (which you have placed in the **obj.conf** file), it passes the parameters defined there to your SAF through the first parameter (pblock *<*param*>). For an **AuthTrans** user-defined **basic-auth** function, an SAF's first parameter can also include other useful variables, such as the user name and password. The second parameter, *Session,* holds the session-specific data. This data structure includes data that are applicable session-wide (that is, from the opening to the closing of the connection between the client and the server). The third parameter, the *Request* data structure, holds request-specific information. With the exception of global server variables, you get all other relevant data from the server through these three data structures.

Your function should return an integer, the value of which is defined by the server. The server uses this return value to determine which action it should take. You should return REQ_PROCEED upon success. REQ_NOACTION is returned when, although no error has occurred, the function does not perform the expected action for the directive. REQ_ABORTED or REQ_EXIT is returned upon error. REQ_ABORTED does not abort the session, but rather aborts the request and begins returning the error page. REQ_EXIT is used for more severe cases when you wish your function to close the

---

Note ▶

In this book, we use *Session* and *Request* to refer to the data structures you will use in your program. In other words, we use *Session*->client to refer to the client pblock in the *Session* data structure. Because *Session* and *Request* are the reserved names for the internal server data structure, however, you must replace *Session* and *Request* with your own specified SAF parameter names. For example, in your code you might use sn->client but not *Session*->client. We will use param, sn, and rq for the three parameters of our SAF. These parameters are pointers to the internal server data structures.

session and exit immediately. (See SAF Return Values and Order of the Directive Functions in Chapter 8 for more details.)

Although your function's name can include only underscores (_) in its name, the name you use in the **obj.conf** file can include either underscores or dashes (–). (Under Server 1.x, you needed to replace underscores with dashes in the name of the function in the configuration file.) No matter which convention you use to refer to your function in the configuration file (**obj.conf**), make sure that it is the same for all references to your function in the configuration file. Also, make sure that the name of your function is unique and does not conflict with any built-in server function.

C++ and NSAPI

You normally write your NSAPI program in ANSI C. Although Netscape expects a C function for the SAF, you may be able to write your code using C++. To use C++, you should use C linkage (extern "C"). This option allows your C++ module to communicate with the C interface of Netscape's SAF. It allows you to compile your code using a C++ compiler. The compiler will then use the C naming convention and C linkage instead of the C++ type-safe naming (naming decoration) and C++ calling convention. This choice allows the server to use the right convention and symbols at load time. Declare your SAF and the include files inside extern "C" brackets.

```
extern "C"
{
   #include "nsapi.h"

   NSAPI_PUBLIC yourSAF(pblock *param, Session *sn,
                        Request *rq)
   {
       /* Your code */
   }
}
```

You cannot use exception handling when writing your NSAPI in C++. You must disable default exceptions generated by the compiler.

Include Files

To use the server data structures and functions, you should include the pblock.h, session.h, and req.h header files when compiling your SAF function for Servers 1.x and 2.x. These files are the standard header files needed for an SAF. session.h and req.h include the appropriate Session and Request data structures plus a number of other relevant functions. `pblock.h` includes the pblock functions and data structure.

For Server 3.x, you need to include only the `nsapi.h` file. All NSAPI functions and data structures are defined in this file. Because Server 3.x includes header files with the same name as the earlier header files, you can still use the earlier `include` directives (for example, `#include "base/pblock.h"`) when compiling your program for Server 3.x. For Server 3.x, these header files indirectly include the `nsapi.h` file. (As already mentioned, for backward-compatibility reasons, Server 3.x includes header files with the same name as the 2.x header files. These files simply include the `nsapi.h` file [`#include "nsapi.h"`].) You may opt to use the same `include` directives as Server 2.x for Server 3.x if you plan to write a program that can be compiled for both servers.

> **Note ▶**
>
> Under Servers 1.x and 2.x, there are a number of interdependencies between the various Netscape header files. Therefore, you may find that including one file may include a number of other header files. For example, `pblock.h` includes `netsite.h`, which, in turn, includes `systems.h` and `version.h`. So, by including `pblock.h` you also include another important file: `netsite.h`. In fact, by just including `req.h`, you already include `netsite.h`, `pblock.h`, and `session.h`. Nevertheless, for general compatibility, you should follow the suggestion of Netscape and include all three files for Servers 1.x and 2.x.

Sending Data to the Client

As with CGI, there are three types of information you can return to the client. You can return a dynamically generated page, redirect the client to an already existing page, or return an error page containing the default error status and an explanation. Unlike with CGI, you cannot simply use the **printf** function to write to the client. To write to the client, you must use functions such as **net_write**, **netbuf_buf2sd**, and **filebuf_buf2sd**. With NSAPI, you are not simply using stdin and stdout to communicate with the client. Instead, you use the access to the client's socket and to the network buffer to return data.

Returning a Dynamic Page

To write a page to the client, you usually take a series of steps. These steps send an HTML or text page to the client. It is not always necessary to take all these steps, as your function may use features that do not require every step. You can also reorder the following steps to suit your needs. For example, you can generate the response (Step 6), before sending the Status-Line and other response headers (Step 5). Nevertheless, it is important to review these steps and understand them before you make any changes. Some of these steps must precede others. For instance, you should not insert a response header (Step 3) after you have already sent the headers (Step 5). You should also look at Listing 6-1 to see these steps in action. We will refer to this example as we go through each step.

1. Remove the existing `content-type` (using **param_free** and **pblock_remove**).
2. Insert the new `content-type` (using **pblock_nvinsert**).
3. Insert any other appropriate headers—for example, `content-length` (using **pblock_nvinsert** or **pblock_nninsert**).
4. Set status to `OK` (using **protocol_status**).
5. Send the Status-Line plus other response headers (using **protocol_start_response**).
6. Create the data (response) to be sent to the client (for example, using the string buffer produced by **util_sprintf**).
7. Send the data to the client (using **net_write**, **netbuf_buf2sd**, or **filebuf_buf2sd**).
8. Verify whether the data were sent correctly (check for `IO_ERROR`).
9. Exit the SAF (send `REQ_PROCEED`).

As with any HTTP response, the server must return the Status-Line (that is, HTTP-Version Status-Code Reason-Phrase CRLF) as the first line of the response message. For NSAPI, you use **protocol_status** to set the Status-Line of the response. The server must also return any necessary HTTP response-headers (for example, `WWW-Authenticate`, `Location`, and so on), plus HTTP entity-headers (such as `content-type`, `content-length`, and `last-modified`). Response-headers provide additional information about the response that the server sends. They usually include information about access and the server. Entity-headers give additional information about the entity-body or message-body (the data) being sent or the resources requested by the client. They are intended to help the client recognize and process the data correctly. You normally do not have to set most of these headers. You do, however, need to take care of the `content-type` of the data being sent and the right status code. Netscape keeps the response-header and entity-headers in one pblock, `srvhdrs`, in the `Request` data structure. Thus all the headers you may want to send to the client should be inserted into `Request->srvhdrs`. In this book, we will usually refer to all of the headers (found in `Request->srvhdrs`) that your server may return to the client as response-headers.

Step 1. Remove `content-type`

When responding to a client as part of a CGI program, you return the `content-type`. Normally, you do the same with an NSAPI function. Before your **Service** function is invoked, however, a `content-type` is already set by the **ObjectType** directive. The `magnus-internal` MIME type defined for your function is already set as a content-type. Because a content-type is already specified, you must first remove the existing content-type before setting the one to be returned to the client. You do not have to take this step for CGI programs, as the **Service** function **send-cgi** takes care of setting the content-type for these programs.

If you do not remove the existing content-type, and simply attempt to insert a new content-type, the server will successfully place the new content-type in the pblock for a response header. When the server returns the content-type, however, it returns the first content-type in the Request->srvhdrs pblock— your function's content-type. Because the client's browser will not recognize a magnus-internal content type, it will not correctly process and display the file you are sending. The browser will either display an error message, saying it could not open the Internet site (as with Internet Explorer 3.x), or ask the client to specify the unknown file type (as with Netscape Navigator). (You can test for this condition by removing the line param_free(pblock_remove("content-type", rq->srvhdrs)); from the Hello Client example given later in this chapter.)

The MIME type (the request entity-header content-type) that the client uses to invoke your application (magnus-internal MIME type) is different from the MIME types that the client can accept as a response entity-header. As with CGI programs, the client requests a MIME type that your server recognizes and processes correctly (for example, magnus-internal/cgi for CGI applications). The CGI program or your SAF then returns a type of document (content-type) that the client can accept and process correctly.

To remove the content-type, use the **pblock_remove** function and pass it the name of the pblock entry (content-type) and the pblock for response headers (Request->srvhdrs). Removing a pblock entry does not free (deallocate) the memory used by the entry. **param_free** frees the pblock entry you have removed.

Steps 2 and 3. Insert New Headers

Once you have removed the pblock entry content-type, you can use **pblock_nvinsert** to insert the new content-type (that is, the type of data you are sending). For **pblock_nvinsert**, you specify the name and value of the pblock entry and the actual pblock into which they should be inserted. In the Hello Client example, we will insert the content type text/html, as we are sending an HTML file. You may also want to send other headers to the client. In that case, you can insert them in the same way we inserted the content-type header after you inserted the response's content-type. If the header you are returning is not already defined, then you do not need to worry about removing it from the Request->srvhdrs pblock. If it does exist, however, then you must take the same steps as we took with content-type. An example of another type of header you may want to insert is a cookie. Cookies are special tokens that can be saved on the client's machine. The client returns the value of these cookies to your server when it makes a request. To send a cookie response header, you insert the header set-cookie with the appropriate parameters. In Chapter 10, we will write an NSAPI application that uses cookies.

You may also want to set the content-length header. This information is used by the client and the server to establish a Keep-Alive or persistent connection. With Keep-Alive, a session connection can be kept open while a multipart request is processed. For example, a page with embedded images can be delivered in one connection. Without content-length, the server does not keep the connection alive. If you wish to use this feature, then you must send content-length with the rest of the response headers. If the value of content-length that you want to set is an integer, you should use **pblock_nninsert** instead of **pblock_nvinsert**. **pblock_nninsert** expects an integer for its value parameter.

Step 4. Set Status to OK

Once you have inserted the appropriate headers, you are ready to set the status to OK. You should send this status when everything has gone well and you are ready to return a page. The **protocol_status** function sets the status to be returned to the client. The server then creates the Status-Line to send to the client. You also use this function to return an error status. The status type is defined in the third parameter of the **protocol_status** (for example, PROTOCOL_OK). The fourth parameter is reserved for a descriptive reason string that should be returned with the page. This parameter can be used when you are sending an error status and you want to send added information about the error to the client. If you specify NULL for the fourth parameter, the server sends the default description for the status code. In the case of PROTOCOL_OK (status code 200), you should set the parameter to NULL and have the server send the default description, OK. After all, you will send the actual data through your program, not a predefined server error page. The Status-Line 200 OK means that the request was successfully processed. We will discuss the various server status codes and how to send an error page shortly.

Step 5. Send Status-Line and Headers

Now you are ready to send the headers to the client with **protocol_start_response**. These headers include the Status-Line and any other appropriate response-headers or entity-headers. Besides content-type and status, you normally do not need to worry about any other header, unless you are interested in changing or sending a specific header, such as content-length. content-length is used by the client and server to keep a connection alive with a Keep-Alive or persistent connection. If the server does not send content-length and you want the server to use the Keep-Alive feature or support persistent connection, you must insert content-length yourself. After **protocol_start_response**, you are ready to send the entity-body. The client is now also waiting to receive the actual content. In the Hello Client example, we will send the HTML page with the word "Hello" plus the client's IP address.

protocol_start_response also returns REQ_NOACTION if the request is a HEAD method of request. You should check for this value so as not to return data to the client. A HEAD request means that the client wants the headers but not the entity-body (for example, the actual Hello Client page). If the **protocol_start_response** returns

REQ_NOACTION, your SAF should send a return of REQ_PROCEED. The server then stops and will not continue with the rest of the code. The following code gives an example of this process:

```
if(protocol_start_response(sn, rq) == REQ_NOACTION)
{
    /* you should first free any allocated memory, close any
        file, and so on, before exiting */
    return REQ_PROCEED;
}
```

Step 6. Create the Response

In Hello Client, we will use **util_sprintf** to create the buf string that is sent to the client. The **util_sprintf** function also formats the string. Hence, we can use the %s format to include the IP address (which is a string) in the HTML page we are returning to the client. This process is similar to the way in which **printf** works. We also use the **util_sprintf** function's return variable length to specify the size of the data we are returning. You could also use the C function **strlen** to get the length of this buffer string.

In your program, you may use the length of the dynamically generated response to specify the content-length response-header that is sent to the client. You must set the response-headers before you use **protocol_start_response**. If you want to use the value of length returned by the **util_sprintf** function, for example, you need to set content-length before Step 5. For example, you can create the response (Step 6) and set content-length before setting the status to OK (Step 4) and sending the Status-Line and response-headers to the client (Step 5). You should also use **pblock_nninsert** instead of **pblock_nvinsert**. **pblock_nvinsert** expects a string for its value parameter. For the Hello Client example (Listing 6-1), we do not set content-length, as this step is not necessary for this example.

Step 7. Send Data

net_write writes the buffer we received from **util_sprintf** to the client's socket. You do not use a stdout function as you would with a CGI program. An NSAPI function does not use stdin and stdout to read from and write to the server. Your function is built into the server and has access to the same data as the server can access. Thus you actually write to the client's socket. This approach has the added benefit of allowing you to write a function that takes advantage of the socket connection between the client and the server. The client's socket is available through the Session->csd variable (sn->csd in the Hello Client example in Listing 6-1). For **net_write**, you also specify information about the buffer's string (buf) and its length.

Step 8. Error Checking

You should check for any errors while writing to the client's socket. **net_write** returns IO_ERROR if an error occurs. In case of error, your function should return REQ_EXIT, which stops the processing of the request.

Other functions that can be used to send a buffer to the client are **netbuf_buf2sd** (`netbuf_buf2sd(netbuf *buf, SYS_NETFD sd, int len)`) and **filebuf_buf2sd** (`filebuf_buf2sd(filebuffer *buf, SYS_NETFD sd)`). **netbuf_buf2sd** sends a buffer, usually previously read, to the socket. **filebuf_buf2sd** sends the contents of the specified file to the socket, as long as nothing was read from the `filebuffer`.

Step 9. Exit Your SAF

If everything went as planned, we return REQ_PROCEED. For a **Service** function, this return usually means the server has finished processing the request. If your **Service** function processes a request, no other **Service** function is called by the server.

Hello Client Example

For a quick comparison between a CGI and NSAPI program, see also CGI Hello Client examples in Chapter 3.

If you are using a version of Netscape Server earlier than Server 3.x, use the following code instead of the `include` directive in Listing 6-1.

```
/* The following three files are the standard header files
   needed for the SAF.
 */
#include "base/pblock.h"
#include "base/session.h"
#include "frame/req.h"

#include "base/util.h"          /* util_sprintf */
#include "frame/protocol.h"     /* protocol_start_response
                                   protocol_status */
```

Listing 6-1   Hello Client

```
/* include this file if you are using Server 3.x */
#include "nsapi.h"

/* This function sends an HTML page to the client */
NSAPI_PUBLIC int hello_client(pblock *param, Session *sn,
                              Request *rq)
{
   char *client; /* holds the client IP address */
   char *buf;    /* a buffer to be sent to the client */
   int length;       /* size of buf */

   /* get client's IP address from Session's client pblock */
   client = pblock_findval("ip", sn->client);
```

Listing 6-1   Hello Client (*continued*)

```
/* begin returning the HTML page */

/* Get rid of internal content type--usually the
   SAF's magnus-internal content type.
 */
param_free(pblock_remove("content-type", rq->srvhdrs));

/* set content type to html */
pblock_nvinsert("content-type", "text/html",
                rq->srvhdrs);

/* set status to OK */
protocol_status(sn, rq, PROTOCOL_OK, NULL);

/* send the headers and get ready for sending the page */
protocol_start_response(sn, rq);

/* malloc a rough size for buf */
buf = (char *) MALLOC(100 * sizeof(char));

/* put all the variables and the rest of the HTML page
   information into one buffer (buf)
 */
length = util_sprintf(buf,
                  "<HTML><HEAD>"
                  "<TITLE>Hello</TITLE>"
                  "</HEAD>\n"
                  "<BODY><H1>"
                  "Hello %s</H1>\n"
                  "</BODY></HTML>", client);

/* Send the information to the client. Also check
   for any error while sending the page to the client.
   If an error occurred, exit.
 */
if(net_write(sn->csd, buf, length) == IO_ERROR)
{
    return REQ_EXIT;
}

/* return success to the server */
return REQ_PROCEED;
}
```

Listing 6-1 includes some actions that were not discussed in the nine steps given earlier. For example, we use **pblock_findval** to get the IP address of the client from the server's `Session` data structure's `client` pblock (`sn->client`). We will shortly go through all the various data available from the server and how you can access them using NSAPI functions. Also, with **util_sprintf**, you must make sure the size of the string (`buf`) is large enough to hold the formatted string. Listing 6-1 does not do any bounds checking. Use **util_snprintf** if you need to perform this step.

Redirecting the Client

Sometimes you simply want to redirect a client to another location or document. You can accomplish this task in a number of ways. Netscape provides two built-in **NameTrans** functions, **redirect** and **mozilla-redirect**. These functions redirect a request for one location (defined by the `from` parameter) to a new location (defined by the `url` or `url-prefix` parameters). You can use these functions if you wish to always redirect a request for one path to another location. **mozilla-redirect** can be used only to redirect requests from Navigator Browser 0.96 or later. Both **redirect** and **mozilla-redirect** are best used when you know the path that will be requested, and you want to always redirect the client from that path. Another alternative is to write your own **NameTrans** function that routes the client to a new path. You can then specify some conditions that must be met before redirection occurs. For example, you may wish to redirect the client based on a cookie criterion you defined earlier.

You may also wish to redirect a client based on certain input. For example, there might be times inside a **Service** function when you want to redirect the client to an existing page instead of creating a dynamic page. In such cases, you can use `PROTOCOL_REDIRECT`, and the header `Location` or the pblock entry `url`.

In this section, we will discuss the use of redirection as part of a **Service** function. The use of the `Location` header is similar to how the header is used in a CGI program. The `Location` header points to the new location where the client is redirected. On the other hand, the server's error handling looks to the `url` entry in `Request->vars` for the new location. Thus you can also redirect the client by setting the value of `url` and returning an error. Listings 6-2 and 6-3, at the end of this section, are examples of redirecting a client using `Location` or `url`.

Redirecting the Client with a `Location` *Header*

You should take the following steps to set the `Location` header and redirect the client:

1. Remove any existing `Location` header (using **param_free** and **pblock_remove**).
2. Insert the `Location` response-header (using **pblock_nvinsert**).
3. Set the status to redirect (using **protocol_status** and `PROTOCOL_REDIRECT`).
4. Return the response-headers (using **protocol_start_response**).
5. Exit your function (using `REQ_PROCEED`).

These steps are simpler than sending a page to the client, as you do not have to create the page and write it to the client socket. You also do not need to set the `content-type`. The server returns a new location specified in the `Location` header to the client. The client then repeats the request, this time using the new location. Thus the server goes through the directives twice. It processes the request once with the current SAF path, and then again with the new path defined by `Location`. The physical path of the file is set by **NameTrans** functions. The `content-type` is identified through **ObjectType** functions, usually by the file extension. Thus the `content-type`, which originally reflected the `magnus-internal` `content-type` of your SAF, is finally determined through the file specified by the `Location` header.

You must insert the `Location` header into the `Request->srvhdrs` pblock. Again, we use **pblock_nvinsert** to insert the `Location` header. You may not need to remove the header first, as it probably is not already set. To make sure, we first attempt to remove any existing `Location` header using **pblock_remove** and free the pblock entry using **param_free**. After inserting `Location` in the server response-headers' pblock (`srvhdrs`), we set the status using **protocol_status**. This time, the status is set to `302 Found`—that is, `PROTOCOL_REDIRECT`. This status tells the client to seek the data in the new location specified in the `Location` header. Finally, **protocol_start_response** sends the headers to the client. As we have no data to return, but rather only the `Location` header, the response ends with this function. We should then exit, returning `REQ_PROCEED`, even though the function will work no matter what type of return value you return. The server response-header (`Request->srvhdrs`), however, could be different based on your function's return value. For example, the `Location` entry in the `srvhdrs` pblock might say `URL UNKNOWN` instead of the location you inserted if you return `REQ_ABORTED`.

The actual URL you set for the location (that is, `Location`'s value) is subject to some of the same restrictions as the value of the response-header `Location` set through CGI programs. The value of this header could include a partial (virtual or relative) path (`/<new location>` or `<new location>`) or a complete URL (`http://<server name>/<new location path>`). You can use a partial path if the file is located on your machine. On the other hand, with the complete URL, you can send a client to another machine or a different server. You are also not limited to HTTP URLs. For example, you can specify an FTP URL (for example, `ftp://ftp.foobar.com`). You need to bear in mind a number of considerations when choosing the type of path to specify, as discussed below. Also, a few differences exist in how the server processes the SAF method and a redirection for a CGI program.

Using a Partial URL for `Location`   For the `Location` value, the server processes the request a bit differently if `Location` includes a partial path and not a complete (absolute) URL. The server must resolve the path so as to redirect the client to the new file. The server resolves the path by appending `ppath` (the partial path sent by the client) to the server base directory (for example, the document root). The `path` variable in `Request->vars` will be the actual physical path of the file on your machine (for example, `c:/netscape/server/docs/new.html`). The first time the server processes the request, `ppath` is the partial path of the SAF function. After the server goes through all the directives, it returns the redirect status code `302`. The `Request->srvhdrs` (that is, Status-Line and other response-headers) could reflect something like the following:

```
status="302 Found" location="/new/newfile.html"
 content-type="magnus-internal/redirect"
```

In this code, the status is `302` (`PROTOCOL_REDIRECT`) and the location points to the new URI. With status `302`, the request is then re-sent, but this time the new URI path (location) is reflected in `ppath`. The server then attempts to resolve this new `ppath` and return the correct file. In its second attempt at processing the request, the server goes through the directives again. If everything went as planned and the file was found, `Request->srvhdrs` will include something like the following:

```
status="200 OK" accept-ranges="bytes"
 last-modified="Sun, 15 Sep 1996 16:52:50 GMT"
 content-length="369" content-type="text/html"
```

This code is different from how redirection for a partial path is processed for a CGI program. For CGI programs, the server stops after the **Service** directive the first time through and before it finishes processing the directives. It then goes through the directives again, this time using the new `ppath` (defined in `Request->vars`) and the new `uri` (the same value as `ppath` but defined in `Request->reqpb`). The value of URI in `clf-request` (also part of `Request->reqpb`), which is written in the common log file, will nevertheless reflect the CGI function path. The **AddLog** directive is not called until the second time around. For an SAF, the **AddLog** functions are called for each processing of the request: once when the server gets the redirection status, and a second time when the new location is processed. For CGI programs, **AddLog** functions are called after the second time and the session is not restarted. For the SAF, the session is restarted, and the value of `clf-request` is changed to reflect the new URI. In other words, with CGI, the server attempts to resolve the request itself instead of sending a redirection status and having the client resend the request using the URL specified in the `Location` header.

To get the server to respond to a CGI program in the same way as an SAF function, you can use the full (absolute) URL (`http://<server name>/<new location>`). When you use the complete URL, the client returns the request a second time with the new URL. The location entry in `Request->srvhdrs` will also reflect the complete URL. The following code is an example of the information in the `srvhdrs` pblock after the first attempt to process the CGI request:

```
status="302 Found"
 location="http://www.foo.com/newsite.html"
 content-length="0"
```

Notice the difference between these `srvhdrs` pblock entry values and the ones set the first time that the server went through the directives for an SAF request. There is a content-length zero, and there is no content-type. content-type is set by the server when it attempts to resolve the request the second time.

Another consideration when including a partial path for your new Location is whether it is relative to the site's document root or to the current directory or document. When you specify a forward slash (/) at the beginning of the partial path, the path is resolved from the root directory (document root). If you do not specify a forward slash as the first character of the URI path, the server resolves the path using the path of the original request or document. In other words, the path is appended to the path of the SAF. For example, when the client requests a redirection function with http://www.foo.com/old/get.new, get.new is used by the server to identify your SAF and run the function. (The server uses the magnus-internal MIME type you have defined for the file extension *.new to run your program.) Now, if the Location header specifies a newfile.html file, the server will append this file to the old directory. In other words, the server looks for the newfile.html file in <document root>/old/newfile.html. If the file is in that directory, the server returns the file. Otherwise, it returns 404 Not found. To make sure the file is specified based on the document and not the SAF path, use the forward slash and specify the path based on the document root directory. For example, if the value of the Location header is /newfile.html, the server looks for newfile.html in <document root>/newfile.html.

For the SAF, the server adds the forward slash before ppath, even if it is not specified in the Location header. This situation is not the case with a CGI program. With CGI, a URI that does not begin with a forward slash will also have none in the ppath and uri values. Thus the path is not resolved by the **NameTrans** functions and the server returns Not found (that is, status 404). For CGI programs, this problem is exacerbated by the fact that you normally specify a directory for each CGI program and keep the program files in that directory. This directory is usually not under the server document root.

Another problem may arise when the file to which the client is redirected includes links (other virtual [partial] paths) within it that are relative to the document path (that is, paths that do not include the forward slash). In these cases, the server resolves the links inside the document based on the SAF or CGI path, not the document's path. For example, you will redirect the client who is requesting http://<server name>/old/so.new to /newfile.html, and newfile.html includes a link to book.gif. The server looks for book.gif in <document root>/old/book.gif rather than in the root directory where it should be. If the link inside the document was specified as /book.gif, then everything would work as long as book.gif was in the root directory. If book.gif is in another directory, however, the path should reflect that directory relative to the root. To illustrate, if you keep all images in the image directory under the root directory, the path should be /image/book.gif.

Using an Absolute URL for Location   A simple way to safeguard against possible path problems is to use a complete (absolute) URL. When you use a complete URL, the client resolves the URL and reconnects to the server requesting the new URL.

The server responds to this new URL as if it was a new request and no longer references the SAF or CGI path. With a complete URL, you can also route the client to another machine or server, or to other services (such as gopher, FTP, news, and so on).

Redirecting the Client with a `url` pblock Entry

Instead of redirecting the client by using a `Location` header, you can use a `url` pblock entry. The following steps outline how this alternative method of redirecting the client works:

1. Insert the status for redirection, `PROTOCOL_REDIRECT` (using **protocol_status**).

2. Insert `url` (the new partial path or URL) into the pblock *Request->vars*.

3. Return `REQ_ABORTED`.

In this method, you use the `url` entry of the *Request->vars* pblock and the server's error-handling mechanisms to redirect the client. The server looks to `url` for the `Location` information when an error occurs. First, you set the status to `302` (`PROTOCOL_REDIRECT`) using **protocol_status**. Next, with **pblock_nvinsert**, you insert the new URL or partial path as the value of the `url` entry in the *Request->vars* pblock. Finally, you return an error, such as `REQ_ABORTED`. The server then obtains the new location from the `url`. The request is reprocessed with the new URL. This process also allows you to write other directive functions, such as **NameTrans**, to redirect the client.

Do not return `REQ_PROCEED`, as the directive will then attempt to process the request instead of redirecting the client. For example, if you return `REQ_PROCEED` in a **Service** function, the server will attempt to return a page with status `302`. As no such page exists, the client receives an error in the form of "`document contains no data.`" Also, do not use **protocol_start_response** to send the headers. If you do so, the server will return the `magnus-internal content-type` specified for your SAF along with the status `302`. Because this MIME type is not recognized by the client, the client will not be able to process it correctly. You could remove this `content-type` and insert a new `content-type` (for example, `text/html`), but this approach can lead to unpredictable results. Internet Explorer 3.x, for example, cannot process the response properly. It pops up an error dialog box, stating that it was unable to open the site and that the request header was not found. Netscape Navigator, on the other hand, will display an HTML page, stating that the document was removed. The text following will appear:

`Found`

`This document has moved to a new` <u>`location`</u>`. Please update your documents and hotlists accordingly.`

The text "location" is a hypertext link to the new location.

Remember not to call your function "redirect," which is the name of the server's built-in **NameTrans** function. If you do, the server will then look for this **NameTrans** function and will not run your function. You can test this case by renaming your function **redirect**. The server returns a server error page. Notice in the error log that the error states `redirect reports: missing parameter (need from, url)`. These parameters are needed for the **redirect** function and are not relevant to your function.

Redirection Examples

Listings 6-2 and 6-3 provide examples of redirecting the client. Listing 6-2 redirects the client using the `Location` header. Listing 6-3 redirects the client using the `url` pblock entry.

Listing 6-2   Redirect Client Using `Location`

```
/* include the following files if you are using a version
   of Netscape Server earlier than 3.x.

   #include "base/pblock.h"
   #include "base/session.h"
   #include "frame/req.h"

   #include "frame/protocol.h"
*/

/* include this file if you are using Server 3.x */
#include "nsapi.h"

/* this function redirects the client to a new location */
NSAPI_PUBLIC int my_redirect(pblock *param, Session *sn,
                                      Request *rq)
{
   char *address; /* holds the new URL */

   /* get the URL address defined as a parameter of this
      function in the obj.conf file
    */
   address = pblock_findval("address", param);

   /* insert the location header in the server header */
   pblock_nvinsert("Location", address, rq->srvhdrs);

   /* set status to redirect */
   protocol_status(sn, rq, PROTOCOL_REDIRECT, NULL);

   /* send out the headers */
   protocol_start_response(sn, rq);

   return REQ_PROCEED;
}
```

Listing 6-2 contains one additional step that was not covered earlier. In this function, `address` is defined as a parameter for the SAF function in the **obj.conf** file.

address should reflect the new location to which you want to route the client. You get the address using the **pblock_findval** function. The value of address is passed through the first pblock param to your function. This tactic allows you to easily change the value of the location in the **obj.conf** file. You will not need to hard-code the location in the file and recompile the code each time a change to the location is made.

Listing 6-3 Redirect Client Using url

```
/* include the following files if your are using a version
   of Netscape Server earlier than 3.x.

  #include "base/pblock.h"
  #include "base/session.h"
  #include "frame/req.h"

  #include "frame/protocol.h"
*/

/* include this file if you are using Server 3.x */
#include "nsapi.h"

/* this function redirects the client to a new location */
NSAPI_PUBLIC int my_redirect(pblock *param, Session *sn,
                                   Request *rq)
{
   char *address; /* holds the URL address */

   /* get the URL address defined as a parameter to this
      function in the obj.conf file
    */
   address = pblock_findval("address", param);

   /* set status to redirect */
   protocol_status(sn, rq, PROTOCOL_REDIRECT, NULL);

   /* insert the new URL in the Request vars pblock */
   pblock_nvinsert("url", address, rq->vars);

   /* exit with error (abort) */
   return REQ_ABORTED;
}
```

Returning an Error Page

Besides returning a document or redirecting a client, you may wish to return an error page. You can specify the type of error code and provide a reasoning for the error by using **protocol_status**. Just as we returned status OK (or 302 Found) with **protocol_status**, you can return other HTTP status codes as well. After your program inserts the status code using **protocol_status** and exits, the server finishes processing the request and returns an appropriate page to the client. The server usually does this task automatically without you having to define an **Error** directive function. The following demonstrates the **protocol_status**:

```
protocol_status(sn, rq, PROTOCOL_ UNAUTHORIZED,
 "You do not have the adequate access privileges");
```

The following is the definition of **protocol_status**. (For Server 2.x, you can find the definition in the `httpd.h` file under the `nsapi/include/frames` directory):

```
#define protocol_status http_status
NSAPI_PUBLIC void http_status(Session *sn, Request *rq,
                                int n, char *r);
```

As you can see, **protocol_status** is a redefinition of **http_status**. The function **protocol_status** sets the status code through the n parameter. It also returns the string pointed to by the r parameter as the description (reasoning) of the status. Normally, the description is returned with the rest of the error page to the client. Your error message—that is, the reasoning—will appear as HTML Heading 1. The standard error description defined for the status by the server follows. You can set the value for the fourth parameter, r, to NULL if you want the server to return only the predefined (default) reasoning. If no reason string is found for an error status code, the server returns Unknown reason as Heading 1 and An error has occurred as a further description. If the status code (n) is not defined, the server returns the default status code, PROTOCOL_SERVER_ERROR.

protocol_status sets the status entry in the *Request*->srvhdrs. The status string includes both the status code and the reasoning. If no reason is specified, the string will include the default string for the status code. For example, the status string for the previously given **protocol_status** function will be

```
"401 You do not have the adequate access privileges"
```

You should use this function frequently—whenever you include error-checking code and wish to inform the client of the type of error that occurred. This function typically works in concert with the **log_error** function, which logs error information in the errors log file.

HTTP Status Codes

Header lines (such as request-headers, response-headers, and Status-Line) are not supported under HTTP/0.9. Therefore, the status code, which is part of the server response (Status-Line), is ignored by an HTTP/0.9 protocol version. With HTTP/0.9, you simply send the response without any headers.

HTTP/1.0 supported HTTP status codes. Servers 2.x and 3.x support a number of these status codes as well. Table 6-1 lists the status codes supported by both Servers 2.x and 3.x. The most common status codes that your program returns are also defined in this table. The most frequently used status codes are indicated with an asterisk (*). (For

Server 2.x, you can find these status codes defined in the `httpd.h` file under the `nsapi/include/frames` directory.)

Netscape uses its own specific string definitions for each status code. Each string is defined as a macro for the status code number—for example, `#define PROTOCOL_UNAUTHORIZED 401`. In your program, you can use either the status code number (for example, `401`) or the status code string (for example, `PROTOCOL_UNAUTHORIZED`). Using the equivalent status code string makes your code more readable. In the Request for Comments (RFC) draft for HTTP protocol standards, all the words in the reason string are usually capitalized. In most cases, however, Netscape does not capitalize any words after the first one.

Table 6-1 Netscape Main Status Codes Supporting HTTP/1.0

HTTP STATUS CODE	DEFAULT REASON STRING—DEFINITION
SUCCESS (2XX) **Client request was successfully processed.**	
*`PROTOCOL_OK (200)`	`OK`—everything has gone well (successfully). You are now ready to send the headers and/or the data to the client. You should use this status code only with your **Service** function before returning the requested data to the client. Do not include a reason string with this status code.
`PROTOCOL_CREATED (201)`	`Created`—informs the client that a new resource was created. This new resource is accessible through the URI returned in the entity of the response. The URL can be specified in the `Location` header.
`PROTOCOL_NO_RESPONSE` `(204)`	`No response` (defined as `No Content` by the HTTP/1.1 proposal)—Informs the client that the request was fulfilled and no content was created. Your program should send this protocol if the request did not generate new output to return. A specific action is requested that will not change the user-agent's active document view (that is, the actual body of the response). For example, new entity-headers can be returned that apply to the existing document in the user-agent's active view.
`PROTOCOL_PARTIAL_CONTENT` `(206)`	`Partial content`—Informs the client that the partial content requested was sent. This code appears in response to a `GET` request asking for a range of data with the `Range` header. The response should include the Content-Range (`Range`) header for the data being returned. This new code is not part of HTTP/1.0 but is part of the HTTP/1.1 draft.
REDIRECTION (3XX) **The user-agent must take further actions to fulfill the request.** **Usually, this action is carried out without further user action.**	
*`PROTOCOL_REDIRECT` `(302)`	`Found` (previously defined as `Moved Temporarily` by earlier HTTP/1.1 drafts)—Sets the status for redirecting the client to a new URL. Use this function to send the client to a new location or another existing document. The server can also return a default page, which specifies the new location with a description and a hyperlink. (See the Redirection section for more details.) This status code was intended as a response to `GET` and `HEAD` requests. (See also the `ntrans.c` example included with Netscape Server.)

Table 6-1 Netscape Main Status Codes Supporting HTTP/1.0 (*continued*)

HTTP STATUS CODE	DEFAULT REASON STRING—DEFINITION

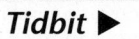

> **Tidbit ▶**
>
> Automatically redirecting a POST request by using a redirect status code can change the request to GET for some existing user-agents.

*PROTOCOL_NOT_MODIFIED (304)	Use local copy (defined as Not Modified by HTTP/1.1)—Used with a conditional GET request. For example, the client makes a GET request with the HTTP header, If-Modified-Since, asking for a modified file. This status code is sent if the requested file has not changed. Normally, the client can use the local copy of the file instead of getting the file from the HTTP server. No actual entity-body (message-body) should be returned.

CLIENT ERROR (4XX)
There is a client-side error in the request. The server, except in the
case of a HEAD request, returns an error page.

*PROTOCOL_BAD_REQUEST (400)	Bad request—Server could not understand and process the client's request. This syntax error is due to a faulty, unintelligible request made by the client. The client can then check for an error in the request and resend it.
*PROTOCOL_UNAUTHORIZED (401)	Unauthorized—Client was not authenticated. This code can be used with an **AuthTrans** or **PathCheck** directive. It informs the client that the authorization information was incorrect or incomplete (for example, if the client did not include the correct password). The response must include the WWW-Authenticate header field. The client may retry with the supposedly accurate authorization. Unlike PROTOCOL_FORBIDDEN, this function lets the client know that the error is specifically an authorization error.
*PROTOCOL_FORBIDDEN (403)	Forbidden—Client is forbidden access to the resources. Even if the client is authenticated, you can still forbid access to the specific files or resource by returning this code. It informs the client that the server understood the request, but that the client is explicitly forbidden access to the resource. Thus the server refuses to fulfill the request. This status code could also be an appropriate response to an erroneous or harmful request. You can forbid a faulty request.
*PROTOCOL_NOT_FOUND (404)	Not found—The requested data are not found. Return this code if the client requests data not on the server. Return this code if you wish the client not to have access to the specific files. You can use this code to deny access without letting the client know of the existence of the file. You can also use this code to inform the client of an inapplicable request.
PROTOCOL_PROXY_UNAUTHORIZED (407)	Proxy authorization required—Similar to PROTOCOL_ UNAUTHORIZED, except that this status code is normally used when programming for the proxy server. PROTOCOL_PROXY_ UNAUTHORIZED is used when the client's authentication did not occur at the proxy server. The server returns information about the authentication method. The client can use this information to reauthenticate itself. Use this feature if you are also running a proxy server (for example,

Table 6-1 Netscape Main Status Codes Supporting HTTP/1.0 (*continued*)

HTTP STATUS CODE	DEFAULT REASON STRING—DEFINITION
	Netscape Proxy Server) and you want the client to use the proxy server to be authenticated. The proxy server must return a `Proxy-Authenticate` header, requiring authentication.
SERVER ERROR (5XX) **A server error occurred. The server was unable to process a valid request.**	
*`PROTOCOL_SERVER_ERROR` (500)	`Server Error` (defined as `Internal Server Error` by HTTP/1.1)—A server error occurred. This error is specific to the server and not the client's request. Some of these errors are an error in the **`obj.conf`** file configuration, a read or write file error, and memory- or thread-related errors. This code is also used as a default status response if no status code is defined.
*`PROTOCOL_NOT_IMPLEMENTED` (501)	`Not Implemented`—The server does not know how to, or cannot, process the response. It lets the client know that the site has not implemented, or does not intend to support, the specific feature or type of request being made. You can return this status if a request method is `PUT` and your server does not support a `PUT`.

The current draft of the HTTP/1.1 proposed standard for HTTP from Internet Engineering Task Force (IETF) includes a number of additional status codes that support the newer features included with HTTP/1.1, such as persistent connection. Some of these status codes were also part of the HTTP/1.0 proposal at some point. Netscape Server 3.x supports several of these status codes.

Table 6-2 lists the status codes defined in the current proposed HTTP/1.1 standard by IETF. These status codes are based on the Revision 3 (Rev-03) version of the HTTP/1.1 proposed standard (`<draft-ietf-http-v11-spec-rev-03>`). You can find a text version of this draft at `http://www.ics.uci.edu/pub/ietf/http/draft-ietf-http-v11-spec-rev-03.txt`. This draft was issued on March 12, 1998, and will expire on September 13, 1998. For the latest on HTTP/1.1, you should check W3c's (World Wide Web Consortium) "HTTP Overview" page at `http://www.w3.org/pub/WWW/Protocols/`.

If the status code listed in Table 6-2 is supported by Netscape Server 3.x, the equivalent Netscape status code string (for example, `PROTOCOL_CONTINUE`) is included in the third column. As you can see, Netscape does not support a number of these status codes. For more information on the HTTP/1.1 status codes, especially the ones supported by Netscape Server 3.x and not included in Table 6-1, see the IETF's HTTP/1.1 Internet draft.

Table 6-2 HTTP/1.1 Proposal Status Codes

CODE	REASON	NETSCAPE-SUPPORTED STATUS CODE NAME
INFORMATIONAL (1XX)		
100	Continue	`PROTOCOL_CONTINUE`
101	Switching Protocols	`PROTOCOL_SWITCHING`

Table 6-2   HTTP/1.1 Proposal Status Codes (*continued*)

CODE	REASON	NETSCAPE-SUPPORTED STATUS CODE NAME
	SUCCESS (2XX)	
200	OK	PROTOCOL_OK (see Table 6-1)
201	Created	PROTOCOL_CREATED (see Table 6-1)
202	Accepted	(Not supported)
203	Non-authoritative Information (previously named Provisional Information)	(Not supported)
204	No Content	PROTOCOL_NO_RESPONSE (see Table 6-1)
205	Reset Content	
206	Partial Content	PROTOCOL_PARTIAL_CONTENT (see Table 6-1)
	REDIRECTION (3XX)	
300	Multiple Choices	(Not supported)
301	Moved Permanently	(Not supported)
302	Found (previously named Moved Temporarily)	PROTOCOL_REDIRECT (see Table 6-1)
303	See Other (previously named Method)	(Not supported)
304	Not Modified	PROTOCOL_NOT_MODIFIED (see Table 6-1)
305	Use Proxy	(Not supported)
307	Temporary Redirect	(Not supported)
	CLIENT ERROR (4XX)	
400	Bad Request	PROTOCOL_BAD_REQUEST (see Table 6-1)
401	Unauthorized	PROTOCOL_UNAUTHORIZED (see Table 6-1)
402	Payment Required	(Not supported)
403	Forbidden	PROTOCOL_FORBIDDEN (see Table 6-1)
404	Not Found	PROTOCOL_NOT_FOUND (see Table 6-1)
405	Method Not Allowed	PROTOCOL_METHOD_NOT_ALLOWED
406	Not Acceptable	(Not supported)
407	Proxy Authentication Required	PROTOCOL_PROXY_UNAUTHORIZED (see Table 6-1)
408	Request Timeout	(Not supported)
409	Conflict	PROTOCOL_CONFLICT
410	Gone	(Not supported)
411	Length Required	PROTOCOL_LENGTH_REQUIRED
412	Precondition Failed	PROTOCOL_PRECONDITION_FAIL
413	Request-Entity Too Large	PROTOCOL_ENTITY_TOO_LARGE
414	Request-URI Too Large	PROTOCOL_URI_TOO_LARGE
415	Unsupported Media Type	(Not supported)

Table 6-2 HTTP/1.1 Proposal Status Codes (*continued*)

CODE	REASON	NETSCAPE-SUPPORTED STATUS CODE NAME
CLIENT ERROR (4XX)		
416	Requested Range Not Satisfiable	(Not supported)
417	Expectation Failed	(Not supported)
SERVER ERROR (5XX)		
500	Internal Server Error	PROTOCOL_SERVER_ERROR (see Table 6-1)
501	Not Implemented	PROTOCOL_NOT_IMPLEMENTED (see Table 6-1)
502	Bad Gateway	(Not supported)
503	Service Unavailable	(Not supported)
504	Gateway Timeout	(Not supported)
505	HTTP Version Not Supported	PROTOCOL_VERSION_NOT_SUPPORTED

Returning a Page Through an Error Function

Netscape provides built-in **Error** functions, **send-error** and **query-handler**, for customizing the server's error response. **send-error** returns a designated error page when a specific error type occurs. **query-handler** runs a designated CGI program when a specific type of error occurs. The type of error is determined by the status code and reason string. The server calls these functions if the status string set by an earlier server function matches the information in the **Error** function's code or reason parameters. For instance, a **Service** function sets the status to PROTOCOL_FORBIDDEN (that is, 403). If an **Error** function was defined to handle type 403, it is used by the server to respond to the error. The following **Error** function, **send-error**, can be defined in the **obj.conf** file to deal with any 403-type errors:

```
Error fn=send-error code="403"
 path="c:/errors/forbidden.html"
```

send-error returns the file forbidden.html (specified in the path parameter) instead of the default error page. You can use an **Error** function to customize the error page, tailor the response to specific clients, or provide additional server clean-up. In Chapter 8, we will explain how you can write your own **Error** directive function.

Logging Errors

You should now have a general idea of how to return an error page to a client. Additionally, an SAF commonly includes error logging. As mentioned in the previous section, **protocol_status** sets the status of the request. If a problem arises, it returns an error page to the client. To log the error, an error-logging function (**log_error**) should be included at this stage as well. You first set the status for the error using **protocol_status** and then define the text to be returned with the error page to the client. Next, you use **log_error** to log the error in the errors log file. The prototype of **log_error** is defined in /nsapi/include/frame/log.h as follows:

```
NSAPI_PUBLIC int log_error(int degree, char *func,
                Session *sn, Request *rq, char *fmt, ...);
```

You specify the degree and the specific function (func—that is, your SAF) where the error occurs, plus any information you may wish to include (fmt). The fmt parameter is the formatted string you want to appear with the error message. It works like the **printf** function and can use arguments that you define so as to include dynamic information within the string you are adding. The server usually includes default error information based on the function and the Session and Request data structures, which you also specify. Your string is added to this default string. The Session *sn and Request *rq parameters refer to the appropriate Session and Request data structures that were passed to your function. For example, you may add a warning to specify that a client did not choose a button ("User did not choose a button") for your SAF function adduser. The error string can then include a string such as "warning: for host 204.156.141.124 trying to POST /register.run, adduser reports: User did not choose a button." The client invokes your program using the path /register.run. The following code gives a sample error string found in the errors log file:

```
[04/Sep/1996:02:56:38] warning: for host 204.156.141.124
trying to POST /register.run, adduser reports: User did
not choose a button.
```

This function records the date and time, plus the error string. The logged string includes the degree, the server-determined error string, and your specific error string. The function returns 0 if the log entry was created and −1 if it failed.

The following function can produce the error log described above:

```
log_error(LOG_WARN, "adduser", sn, rq,
        "User did not choose a button.");
```

You can also use the **system_errmsg** function (defined in base/file.h) to return the last error message that occurred after a system call. This function looks in the global array sys_errlist for the latest entry and returns the text string. It returns the last error for the most recent system call. The following code is an example of this function:

```
log_error(LOG_FAILURE, "write", sn, rq,
        "error opening file (%s)", system_errmsg(0));
```

The function adds the string "error opening file ...", which includes the message returned by **system_errmsg** in the parentheses. For Servers 1.x and 2.x, you need to specify a parameter for **system_errmsg** (for example, `system_errmsg (0);`), even though this parameter is not used by the function.

Table 6-3 lists the degrees (error message types) supported by Netscape Server. The string below each degree is the text that will be included in the log file for that degree. Server 3.x includes a new error degree called `LOG_VERBOSE`, which you can use to specify additional internal messages. (See `LOG_VERBOSE` in Table 6-3 for more information.)

Table 6-3   Error Message Types (Degrees)

DEGREE AND STRING IN LOG FILE	VALUE	DESCRIPTION
`LOG_WARN` `warning:`	0	Warning message—Usually a minor error caused by an incomplete or incorrect client request. This degree is typically based on client's error, which leads to the server being unable to process the request. You usually warn the client of the error and ask it to retry. Use this degree with the status codes `PROTOCOL_BAD_REQUEST` and `PROTOCOL_NOT_FOUND`. Errors can be due to the requested data not being found, a syntax error in client's request, or incomplete form input. Example Log File Output: `[31/Dec/1997:15:13:42] warning: for host 1.0.0.1 trying to GET /hack.hml, send-file reports: can't find c:/netscape/server/docs/hack.hml (File Not Found Error)`

`LOG_MISCONFIG` `config:`	1	Server configuration error—The server logs an error of this degree when it is unable to read and accurately process the system configuration files. The error could be due to syntax, missing parameters, or permission violations, perhaps reflecting an incorrect configuration of your SAF or a built-in server function in the **obj.conf** file. If your server failed to restart after you made specific changes to a configuration file, look for these error types in the error log file to find out more information about the failure.
		
		Example Log File Output:
		
		`[31/Dec/1997:17:13:42] config: for host 1.0.0.1 trying to GET /, func_exec reports: cannot find function named pblock_log`
		
		The error could also be due to an ACL configuration problem.
		
		Example Log File Output:
		
		`[06/Jan/1998:18:43:43] config: for host 1.0.0.1 trying to GET /, check-acl reports: ACL name special not defined`

`LOG_SECURITY` `security:`	2	Authentication error—This security message records the client's failure to authenticate, denies the existence of a resource, or forbids access to a resource. Normally, the server handles access control unless you write an **AuthTrans** or **PathCheck** SAF that specifically deals with client authentication. Log this error type when the HTTP status is `PROTOCOL_UNAUTHORIZED`, `PROTOCOL_FORBIDDEN`, or `PROTOCOL_PROXY_UNAUTHORIZED`.

Table 6-3   Error Message Types (Degrees) (*continued*)

DEGREE AND STRING IN LOG FILE	VALUE	DESCRIPTION
		If you deny the existence of a resource by using status `PROTOCOL_NOT_FOUND`, the error message should still be a security-type error and not a warning. Example Log File Output: `[06/Jan/1998:18:48:58] security: for host 1.0.0.1 trying to GET /private/, acl-state reports: access of c:/netscape/server/docs/private/ denied by ACL private directive 1`
LOG_FAILURE failure:	3	Server internal error—This more serious type of error stops the server from processing a request. This error should be based on the server (your program) being unable to process a complete and valid request. Use this degree of error in your program as a part of error handling when a failure occurs while processing the client's request. You should also inform the client that a server error occurred. The errors can include a file I/O error, socket read and write error, failure to access important data, and so on (for example, `[23/Jan/1997:16:31:56] failure: Unable to close socket for writing.`). For instance, if your program could not find a file needed to process a request, then use `LOG_FAILURE` instead of `LOG_WARN`. The server also logs this type of error for CGI programs or parse-html failures, such as when a CGI script exits prematurely or sends invalid headers. Example Log File Output: `[10/Jan/1998:16:14:30] failure: for host 1.0.0.1 trying to GET /shellcgi/Display, shellcgi-send reports: can't find file association of c:/netscape/server/shellcgi/ Display for execution`
LOG_CATASTROPHE catastrophe:	4	Catastrophic error—This fatal error causes the server to crash. The server can log the error as a catastrophe when it is unable to recover from it. The error can include running out of memory, threads, or processes, or system call failures, data corruption, and so on. Your SAF should protect itself from these types of errors. Thus you should not need to log them directly. Example Log File Output: `[11/Dec/1997:05:51:47] catastrophe: Cannot bind server to specified IP home at address http://home.netscape.com; cannot run`

Note ▶

These errors are rarely logged in the errors log file. Server errors are generally logged as degree failures in the errors log file.

Table 6-3   Error Message Types (Degrees) (*continued*)

DEGREE AND STRING IN LOG FILE	VALUE	DESCRIPTION

LOG_INFORM
info:
	5	Informative messages—Not really error messages, these messages do not reflect a failure of the server to process a request. Instead, they record useful messages, such as when the server starts and stops. You can also log informational messages useful for debugging or later analysis.
		
		Example Log File Output:
		
		`[10/Jan/1998:16:07:10] info: successful server startup`
		
		or
		
		`[09/Jan/1998:00:36:56] info: Suspend Httpd Service`

LOG_VERBOSE
verbose:
(Server 3.x only)
	6	Additional internal messages—This new message type is used with Server 3.x. You can use it to log additional internal messages. The server also sends a number of other messages about the workings of various components of the server (for example, IIOP and Agent) when you allow verbose logging. For these messages to be logged in the error log file, you must add the directive LogVerbose On to the **magnus.conf** file. This type of message is very useful for debugging purposes. The server provides additional information that you can use to determine whether the server is functioning properly. You can also write your own debugging message using LOG_VERBOSE. For example, you can set the directive LogVerbose to On, during debugging and log error messages using LOG_VERBOSE. When everything is working properly, you can remove the directive so that no verbose messages are logged.
		
		Example Log File Output:
		
		`[09/Jan/1998:00:37:00] verbose: Agent system built:`
		`Jun 8 1997 23:11:03`

Netscape Server provides additional error-log-related functions that you can use, including **ereport**, **ereport_init**, **ereport_terminate**, and **ereport_getfd**. You can use **ereport** to log an error much in the same way as **log_error**. **ereport** logs an error without a reference to the function, or the Session or Request data structure. The definition of **ereport** is as follows:

```
int ereport(int degree, char *fmt, ...);
```

You need to define only the degree and the error string for the **ereport** function.

Logging Errors for an Init Directive

Logging errors for an **Init** directive function is different from logging errors for any other directive. You use **pblock_nvinsert** to insert an error pblock entry into the pblock passed to the **Init** function through its first parameter (for example,

```
pblock_nvinsert("error", "An invalid information submitted.",
param)). You may also use **ereport** function to log an error from an **Init** function.
```

Obtaining Data

To write your program, you first need to obtain information from the server. These data could be general server information, information regarding a specific request, or client input data. In this section, we discuss how you can obtain data from the server. You can use methods similar to the ones discussed here to access variables that may not specifically be covered in this chapter. We will also look at several SAF examples that return NSAPI (server) variables.

We begin this section by comparing NSAPI variables with CGI environment variables. If you have been writing CGI programs, you are already familiar with environment variables. When writing SAFs, you often look for the same information. We will use the words "NSAPI variables" to refer to server variables available to your function. Just as CGI environment variables are used by the CGI programs, NSAPI variables are used by your SAF (or NSAPI program). With CGI, data are available through environment variables and standard input. Unlike CGI variables, NSAPI variables are located in different data structures and are available by different means. We also review the major types of NSAPI variables. Because most HTTP server programmers are familiar with CGI, we focus on NSAPI variables that provide the same values as the CGI environment variables. These variables constitute the majority of the variables you will access for your SAF. We show how to access these variables using NSAPI, and we also write an SAF that prints out the equivalent of CGI variables.

Your SAF needs data of different types, available through different methods, to process a client request. Global server variables are available globally or through the configuration data structure (`conf_global_vars_s`). You can also place parameters for your function in the configuration file that your SAF accesses through its first parameter (`pblock *param`). Other variables, which are available through the `Session` and `Request` data structures passed to your function, are specific to a client or a request. You usually get client input through the GET and POST methods. Typically, you use a form to get the client's input. These variables are available through the `query` string found in *Request*->reqpb for the GET method, and in the network buffer for the POST method. Finally, in addition to the data received from the server, you may need data from other sources, such as a database or file. For example, you may need to access a database to get the response for a client request.

Table 6-4 lists the common types of data provided by the server and available for use by your program. The table is organized by the type of information sought, not necessarily by the location of the data.

Table 6-4   Sample of Data Provided by the Server

SERVER-SPECIFIC INFORMATION
Global server information, some of which is set in the **magnus.conf** file (for example, server name or port)
Information in the **obj.conf** file, especially your user-defined SAF parameters

CLIENT- OR REQUEST-SPECIFIC INFORMATION
Client information (for example, client IP or DNS address, user name and password, or browser name)
Information about the requested resource (for example, content type or path information)
Additional request headers (for example, type of connection or cookie information)

CLIENT INPUT
Input from a GET method (query string sent with the request)
Input from a POST method (data provided through the network buffer)

CGI Environment Variables and NSAPI Variables

With CGI programs, it is easy to access the environment variables as they are all accessed via the same function. (For example, the **getenv** function is used for CGI programs written in C.) With NSAPI, these same variables are located mostly in different pblock data structures available through the Session and Request data structures. The pblock data structure holds a hash table of *name-value* pairs that resembles an environment-variable linked list. The requirement that you access variables through different data structures or functions may seem complicated and confusing to CGI programmers. We will try to make this transition easier by providing an overview of how you obtain data from the server.

With a typical CGI program, you get most of the data through the environment variables or through stdin. In this case, the environment variables are processed by the server and then passed to your application. Because a CGI program is a separate application spawned by the server, the relevant information must be passed to the CGI program through specific channels. Environment variables furnish an easy way to accomplish this task. NSAPI programs, however, access these variables as they appear to the server. An SAF, which works in the server process, has access to and can change the actual server variables. Moreover, information available to an NSAPI function may not be available to a CGI program. The value of a variable can also change before it becomes available to an SAF or a CGI program. A variable can be available for one directive and not another. A variable can also be changed in earlier directives for use by a later directive. For example, the physical path information (path) is derived from the ppath variables of *Request*->vars and a base directory of a **NameTrans** function. After the **NameTrans** directive is carried out, ppath is no longer available, whereas path becomes available for the later directives. In contrast, a CGI program is processed through the **Service** function **send-cgi**. Such a program cannot directly access or change the server variables that are available to **send-cgi**. Based on the directive function you write, your SAF, however, can access a specific subset of server variables. It can also change these variables and thereby affect how the rest of the server directives process a request.

NSAPI variables are available as they were intended for the server. In other words, they are organized based on the categorization appropriate for the server's processing of a request. Although variables passed to a CGI program are of different types (some include global server information, while others include specific request data), they are all environment variables, and are accessed through the same function. Netscape could have placed all of the NSAPI variables in a special parameter block and made it accessible to your program. Because the SAF uses the same information available to the server, however, these variables are not separated and parsed into one pblock for your function. For the server, the actual variables are of different types and are, therefore, processed in different data structures. For instance, a global server variable for the server port should be available through the server global variables and not through a specific request's variable. This strategy permits the tailored sharing of data and removes redundancy.

Other factors distinguish environment variables from NSAPI variables. For example, some environment variables (such as GATEWAY_INTERFACE) are not relevant to an NSAPI program. Moreover, NSAPI variables, unlike environment variables, appear as they are defined by HTTP protocol or Netscape Server. These variables are not converted to uppercase and do not use underscores. In place of underscores (_), dashes (-) are used to separate compound names. Also, the HTTP request header variables do not include the prefix HTTP_.

Note ▶

Whenever we use variables in CAPS (with the exception of MAGNUS_VERSION_STRING), we are referring to CGI environment variables and not NSAPI variables. As mentioned earlier, our intent is to show how you can access variables similar to CGI environment variables in an SAF function.

NSAPI Equivalents for CGI Environment Variables

Table 6-5 provides a quick overview of the CGI environment variables and their equivalent NSAPI variables. param, rq, and sn represent the names of the parameters of the SAF, as in NSAPI_PUBLIC int hello_client(pblock *param, Session *sn, Request *rq). The NSAPI information is also based on Servers 2.x and 3.x.

Table 6-5 NSAPI Equivalents for CGI Environment Variables

CGI ENVIRONMENT VARIABLE	NSAPI VARIABLES	LOCATION OF NSAPI VARIABLES
WHAT IT GIVES YOU	HOW TO ACCESS NSAPI VARIABLES—AN EXAMPLE	
	NOTES	

Global Request Variables

`GATEWAY_INTERFACE`	None	
CGI version information (for example, `CGI/1.1`)		
	Specific to CGI and not relevant to NSAPI.	
`SERVER_NAME`	`server_hostname` (global)	Global variable (also through `conf_global_vars_s`)
Server host name or IP address (for example, `www.foo.com`)	`conf_getglobals()->Vserver_hostname`	
	You can get the server name in a number of ways. For example, you can get the value through the `conf_global_vars_s` data structures or as a global variable, `server_hostname`. You can also use the **util_hostname** function to get the host name. (Make sure to compile your program with the `NET_SSL` compiler switch for Server 2.x. Otherwise, the structure is offset and you may retrieve `NULL` when attempting to retrieve the host name.)	
`SERVER_SOFTWARE`	`MAGNUS_VERSION_STRING` (for Server 2.x)	Global variable for Server 2.x
	`<version>` (for Server 3.x)	Use **system_version** for Server 3.x.
Server software name and version (for example, `Netscape-Enterprise/3.51`)	`char *version = system_version();` (Server 3.x)	
	Under Server 2.x, server software information is obtained through the global variable `MAGNUS_VERSION_STRING`. This variable is no longer available under Server 3.x. Under Server 3.x, however, you can use the new function **system_version** to get the server software information.	

Request-Specific Variables

`AUTH_TYPE`	`auth-type`	`Request->vars`
Authentication Type (for example, `Basic`)	`char *type = pblock_findval("auth-type", rq->vars);`	
`CONTENT_ENCODING`	`content-encoding`	`Request->headers`
Content encoding type sent by the client (for example, `x-gzip`)	`request_header("content-encoding", &hvalue, sn, rq);` (`hvalue` holds the `content-encoding` value.)	
	The desired method of accessing pblock `headers` entries is through the **request_header** function, but you can also access the value with the **pblock_findval** function. The variables `content-encoding`, `content-length`, and `content-type` defined in `Request->headers` are different from the variables of the same names defined for `Request->srvhdrs`. These HTTP variables (`headers`) are sent by the client to the server. The server headers (`srvhdrs`) are sent by the server to the client.	

Table 6-5 NSAPI Equivalents for CGI Environment Variables (*continued*)

CGI ENVIRONMENT VARIABLE	NSAPI VARIABLES	LOCATION OF NSAPI VARIABLES
WHAT IT GIVES YOU	**HOW TO ACCESS NSAPI VARIABLES—AN EXAMPLE**	
	NOTES	
	Request-Specific Variables	
CONTENT_LENGTH	content-length	*Request*->headers
Content length information sent by the client (for example, 1020)	request_header ("content-length", &hvalue, sn, rq); (hvalue holds the content-length value.)	
	See CONTENT_ENCODING.	
CONTENT_TYPE	content-type	*Request*->headers
Content type sent by the client (for example, application/x-www-form-urlencoded)	request_header ("content-type", &hvalue, sn, rq); (hvalue holds the content-type value.)	
	See CONTENT_ENCODING.	
PATH_INFO	path-info	*Request*->vars (available after the **PathCheck** function **find-pathinfo** is run)
Extended path information (for example, <*http://www.foo.com/cgi/getx.exe*>/data/info.txt)	char *extra_path = pblock_findval ("path-info", rq->vars);	
	Although this value is available in the Request pblock vars, you cannot actually use the extended path as part of the URL of an NSAPI **Service** program. Any extended path is seen as being part of the actual requested path. Consequently, the server looks for the extended path instead of your program. To pass values such as extra path information, use additional parameters for the NSAPI function found in the **obj.conf** file. These variables can then be accessed through the pblock parameter (param) that is passed onto your program.	
PATH_TRANSLATED	None	
Extended path information translated into a full physical path (for example, c:/netscape/server/data/info.txt)		
	See PATH_INFO for more information. The server goes through the directives a second time to translate the path found in path-info into a physical path—that is, PATH_TRANSLATED. This information is then passed to the CGI program as an environment variable.	
	For NSAPI, if you wish to convert a partial path (for example, PATH_INFO) into a complete physical path, you can use the NSAPI function **servact_translate_uri** (also defined as **request_translate_uri**). This function was removed from the main NSAPI functions under Server 3.0x. The NSAPI library file (ns-httpd30.lib), however, may still	

Table 6-5   NSAPI Equivalents for CGI Environment Variables (*continued*)

CGI ENVIRONMENT VARIABLE	NSAPI VARIABLES	LOCATION OF NSAPI VARIABLES
WHAT IT GIVES YOU	**HOW TO ACCESS NSAPI VARIABLES—AN EXAMPLE**	
	NOTES	

<table>
<tr><th colspan="3" align="center">Request-Specific Variables</th></tr>
<tr><td></td><td colspan="2">include it. Otherwise, for Server 3.0x, you need to write your own function to translate a URI path into a physical path. Server 3.5.1 does include this function.</td></tr>
<tr><td><code>QUERY_STRING</code></td><td><code>query</code></td><td align="center">Request->reqpb</td></tr>
<tr><td>Query string sent by the client (for example, <<em>NSAPI program path</em>>?name=joe)</td><td colspan="2"><code>char *query = pblock_findval("query", rq->reqpb);</code></td></tr>
<tr><td><code>REMOTE_ADDR</code></td><td><code>ip</code></td><td align="center">Session->client</td></tr>
<tr><td>Remote client's IP address (for example, <code>1.2.3.4</code>)</td><td colspan="2"><code>char *ip = pblock_findval("ip", sn->client);</code></td></tr>
<tr><td><code>REMOTE_HOST</code></td><td><code>dns</code></td><td align="center">Session->client</td></tr>
<tr><td>Remote client's DNS address (for example, <code>www.foo.com</code>)</td><td colspan="2"><code>char *client_dns = session_dns(sn);</code>
<code>char *client_dns = session_maxdns(sn);</code>
(sn is the current <code>Session</code> data structure.)</td></tr>
<tr><td></td><td colspan="2">You should use the session_dns or session_maxdns function to access the DNS information of the client instead of using the pblock_findval function. If these functions are not called, the <code>dns</code> variable is not inserted in the Request-><code>client</code>. You also need to have DNS enabled for this value to be available.</td></tr>
<tr><td><code>REMOTE_USER</code> (<code>AUTH_USER</code>)</td><td><code>auth-user</code></td><td align="center">Request->vars</td></tr>
<tr><td>Name of the authenticated user (for example, <code>joe</code>)</td><td colspan="2"><code>char *type = pblock_findval("auth-user", rq->vars);</code></td></tr>
<tr><td></td><td colspan="2">This variable is actually the environment variable <code>AUTH_USER</code>, which is equivalent to <code>REMOTE_USER</code>. For Enterprise Server 3.5.1, the value of <code>auth-user</code> and <code>REMOTE_USER</code> should be the same as the <code>UID</code> (user ID) defined in the directory server.</td></tr>
<tr><td><code>REQUEST_METHOD</code></td><td><code>method</code></td><td align="center">Request->reqpb</td></tr>
<tr><td>Client's request method (for example, <code>GET</code>)</td><td colspan="2"><code>char *method = pblock_findval("method", rq->reqpb);</code></td></tr>
<tr><td><code>SCRIPT_NAME</code></td><td><code>uri</code></td><td align="center">Request->reqpb</td></tr>
<tr><td>Virtual (relative) path to the requested program (for example, <code>/get.env</code>)</td><td colspan="2"><code>char *program_path = pblock_findval("uri", rq->reqpb);</code></td></tr>
<tr><td></td><td colspan="2">This path is used by the client to call your program—that is, it is the virtual (partial) path to your NSAPI program.</td></tr>
</table>

Table 6-5 NSAPI Equivalents for CGI Environment Variables (*continued*)

CGI ENVIRONMENT VARIABLE	NSAPI VARIABLES	LOCATION OF NSAPI VARIABLES
WHAT IT GIVES YOU	**HOW TO ACCESS NSAPI VARIABLES—AN EXAMPLE**	
	NOTES	

	Request-Specific Variables	
`SERVER_PORT`	`Vport`	`conf_global_vars_s`
Port address where the request is sent (for example, `80`)	`int port_num = conf_getglobals()->Vport;`	
	There is also a global variable for the server port that you can use. Under Server 2.x, `port` is defined as an `extern int` in the `conf.h` header file. You can directly access the value of the server port using the global variable `port`. Under Server 3.x, you can use the global variable `server_portnum`.	
`SERVER_PROTOCOL`	`protocol`	`Request->reqpb`
Version of protocol being used by the client (for example, `HTTP/1.0`)	`char *protocol = pblock_findval("protocol", rq->reqpb);`	

	HTTP Header Variables	
`HTTP_ACCEPT`	`accept`	`Request->headers`
Mime types accepted by the client's browser (for example, `image/gif`, `image/x-xbitmap`, `image/jpeg`, `image/pjpeg`, `*/*`)	`request_header("accept", &hvalue, sn, rq);` (`hvalue` holds the `accept` value.)	
	The correct method of accessing a pblock `headers` entry is through **request_header.** You can also access the variable with **pblock_findval.**	
`HTTP_CONNECTION`	`connection`	`Request->headers`
Verifies whether the connection is kept open—that is, whether `Keep-Alive` or persistent connection is used (for example, `Keep-Alive`).	`request_header("connection", &hvalue, sn, rq);` (`hvalue` holds the `connection` value.)	
	See `HTTP_ACCEPT`.	
`HTTP_COOKIE`	`cookie`	`Request->headers`
Cookie data sent by the client. The data must originally be set by your server (for example, `User=JoeBoxer`).	`request_header("cookie", &hvalue, sn, rq);` (`hvalue` holds the `cookie` value.)	
	See `HTTP_ACCEPT`.	

Table 6-5 NSAPI Equivalents for CGI Environment Variables (*continued*)

CGI ENVIRONMENT VARIABLE	NSAPI VARIABLES	LOCATION OF NSAPI VARIABLES
WHAT IT GIVES YOU	**HOW TO ACCESS NSAPI VARIABLES—AN EXAMPLE**	
	NOTES	
HTTP Header Variables		
`HTTP_FROM`	No longer supported	
`HTTP_IF_MODIFIED_SINCE`	`if-modified-since`	*Request*->headers
Date sent by the client. It is used to verify whether data should be sent (for example, `Monday, 1-Jan-98 12:00:00 GMT`).	`request_header("if-modified-since", &hvalue, sn, rq);` (`hvalue` holds the `if-modified-since` value.)	
	See `HTTP_ACCEPT`.	
`HTTP_REFERER`	`referer`	*Request*->headers
URL from which the request came (for example, `http://www.yahoo.com`)	`request_header("referer", &hvalue, sn, rq);` (`hvalue` holds the `referer` value.)	
	See `HTTP_ACCEPT`.	
`HTTP_USER_AGENT`	`user-agent`	*Request*->headers
Name of the client's browser (for example, `Mozilla/ 4.04 [en] (WinNT; I)`)	`request_header("user-agent", &hvalue, sn, rq);` (`hvalue` holds the `user-agent` value.)	
	See `HTTP_ACCEPT`.	
Security Variables		
`HTTPS`	`security_active`	Global variable (`conf_global_vars_s`)
Determines whether SSL security is enabled	`conf_getglobals()->Vsecurity_active;`	
	The variable `security_active` is not defined if the `NET_SSL` compiler switch is not specified for Servers 1.x and 2.x. You should compile with `NET_SSL` options to make sure all SSL variables are available. Otherwise, for Server 2.x, the data structure `conf_global_vars_s` is offset. The default makefile that comes with Netscape Servers 1.x and 2.x does not include this switch. For Enterprise Server 3.x, you no longer need to use the `NET_SSL` compiler switch.	
`HTTPS_KEYSIZE`	`keysize`	*Session*->client
Bit size of session key used for encryption (for example, `128`)	`char *k = pblock_findval("keysize", sn->client);`	
	SSL must be enabled.	

Table 6-5   NSAPI Equivalents for CGI Environment Variables (*continued*)

CGI ENVIRONMENT VARIABLE	NSAPI VARIABLES	LOCATION OF NSAPI VARIABLES
WHAT IT GIVES YOU	HOW TO ACCESS NSAPI VARIABLES—AN EXAMPLE	
	NOTES	
Security Variables		
`HTTPS_SECRETSIZE`	`secret-keysize`	*Session*->client
Bit size used to generate the server private key (for example, `128`)	`char *sk = pblock_findval("secret-keysize", sn->client);`	
	SSL must be enabled.	
`HTTPS_SESSIONID`	`ssl-id`	*Session*->client
Base-64 encoding of the SSL session value (for example, `B+rZPf11Dpx` `jCWGst6iFAmbUdgRKzL` `VRIJzPYW6PNWg`)	`char *sid = pblock_findval("ssl-id", sn->client);`	
	To have access to `ssl-id`, you must add the **AuthTrans** function **get-sslid** to the **obj.conf** file. SSL must also be enabled.	
Other Parameters	`[your parameter name]`	*param* (first parameter of your SAF)
Extra parameters sent through the **obj.conf** file	`char *extra = pblock_findval("extras", param);`	
	When you install your SAF, you can define a number of parameters in `[name]="[value]"` pairs in the **obj.conf** file. You then access these parameters from the pblock structure using **pblock_findval.** The parameters are passed to your function through the first parameter of your function.	

Data Received from the Server

The categories of the CGI environment variables used in Chapter 3 and in Table 6-5 were based on the original groupings of the CGI environment variables as defined by NCSA. With NSAPI, we must consider variables a bit differently. The following categories are based on how you obtain the NSAPI variables from the server. The four types of NSAPI variables are available as global variables, and through the data structures `Session`, `Request`, and *param*. `Session`, `Request`, and *param* are parameters passed to your function. As well as the four types of variables, you also have access to the socket and network buffer. The input from a POST method of request is usually accessed through the network buffer. You read the data from the network buffer using NSAPI functions (for example, **netbuf_getc**).

The following are the types of NSAPI variables.

1. Global variables pertain to the entire server, such as server name or server port. They are usually based on the server configuration and can be accessed directly.

2. The Session data structure is applicable to an entire client session. A session comprises the time between when a client connects and when it disconnects from the server. The information in this data structure persists until the server sends a response to the client. It includes general information about the client (for example, the client IP address) and the socket descriptor to the remote client.

3. Request contains the typical variables that NSAPI uses. These variables are appropriate only for a single request. The Request data structure includes a number of pblock structures, each with its own set of appropriate NSAPI variables. These variables determine the specifics of a client's request.

4. The first parameter of your SAF function (*param*) holds the parameters of your function as defined in the **obj.conf** file. Moreover, unlike other request-specific information, the information for authentication (for example, the user name and password) is also passed on through the *param* data structure, because the authentication programs are written as user-defined functions for the **AuthTrans** function **basic-auth**. You write your authentication (**AuthTrans**) function and define it through the userfn parameter of the built-in **basic-auth** function. **basic-auth** then passes the user information to your function through the *param* data structure.

NSAPI Variables

In this section, we will discuss how you can access the different types of NSAPI variables. We will maintain our focus on the NSAPI variables that are equivalent to the CGI environment variables. You can, however, use a similar method to access any NSAPI variable. In other words, you can use the methods discussed here to access any variable, even if it is not available to a CGI program. We will follow up this discussion about how to access the various NSAPI variables with examples of programs that obtain the NSAPI variables.

Global Variables   Global variables include information specific to the server's configuration and apply to the entire server. Global server information is usually found in your **magnus.conf** file. If you look in this file, you will notice that ServerName, Port, Security, and similar variables are defined for the server. You rarely reference these variables just to get your server configuration information. After all, you should know how your system is set up. On the other hand, you may want to use these variables to write a function for different systems, independent of the server configuration. You may use these global variables, for example, if you are writing a program that uses a global variable and will be implemented under a variety of different server configurations. The variables themselves are normally available through the server's global configuration variables data structure, conf_global_vars_s.

The conf_global_vars_s data structure holds information about the server port, the server host name, the address to which the server will bind, and so on. This data structure may include different variables depending on the type of server or the version of server you are running. Moreover, conf_global_vars_s is not supported under Server 1.x. (For more information on conf_global_vars_s, see Chapter 5 or the NSAPI header files.)

Under Server 2.x, Netscape provides some global variables that are not part of the conf_global_vars_s data structure—for example, MAGNUS_VERSION_STRING. You access these variables directly. With Server 3.x, you can access the global variables either through the conf_global_vars_s data structure or through a specific NSAPI function. Server 3.x does not include independent global variables, such as MAGNUS_VERSION_STRING.

Netscape also provides a number of simple macro redefinitions of the conf_global_vars_s member variables. You can use the variables defined by these macro definitions instead of directly accessing the variables in conf_global_vars_s. For example, the server name is available through the Vserver_hostname variable of the conf_global_vars_s data structure. You can access this variable by using the **conf_getglobals** function via conf_getglobals()->Vserver_hostname or directly through server_hostname. The variable server_hostname is defined as follows in the NSAPI header file:

```
#define server_hostname conf_getglobals()->Vserver_hostname
```

As already mentioned, most NSAPI variables that provide the commensurate CGI environment variables are passed to your function through the two data structures: Session and Request. A few general variables, however, affect the server as a whole and are not part of these data structures, which are sent to your SAF. These variables can be considered global variables. In CGI, you know these global variables as the environment variables SERVER_SOFTWARE, SERVER_PORT, SERVER_NAME, HTTPS, and SERVER_URL. This information is also available to your SAF, albeit through different means. Let us go through these options to see how you would obtain them for your SAF.

Under Server 2.x, you get the server software version (equivalent to the value of SERVER_SOFTWARE) by using the global variable MAGNUS_VERSION_STRING, defined in the <server path>/nsapi/include/netsite.h file. The value of this variable is automatically defined by the server in the <server path>/nsapi/include/version.h file when the server is installed. You can access this global variable directly. Under Server 3.x, you must use a new NSAPI function, **system_version**. This function does not take any parameters and returns the relevant version of Netscape Server.

The server port address, host name, and security information are found inside the conf_global_vars_s data structure. In conf_global_vars_s, Vport holds the port information, Vserver_hostname holds the host name information, and Vsecurity_active identifies whether SSL security is active. These NSAPI global variables include information commensurate to the CGI environment variables SERVER_PORT, SERVER_NAME, and HTTPS, respectively. You can access these conf_global_vars_s variables using the NSAPI function **conf_getglobals**.

The server port can be accessed through `conf_getglobals->Vport`. For Server 2.x, it can also be accessed through the global variable `port`. For Server 3.x, it can also be accessed through the global variable `server_portnum`.

The server name can be accessed through `conf_getglobals->Vserver_hostname` or through the global variable `server_hostname`. Netscape also provides an NSAPI function for accessing the host name, **util_hostname**. This function returns a fully qualified host name.

To find out if SSL security is enabled on the server, you can verify the value of the global variable `security_active`. If `security_active` is set to TRUE (1), then SSL is enabled. You can also verify this information by using `conf_getglobals->Vsecurity_active`.

Note that under Server 1.x and 2.x, you need to compile your code using the NET_SSL switch, otherwise the variables `Vsecurity_active` and `security_active` are not defined and will not be available to your program. The data structure `conf_global_vars_s` will also be offset, and you may retrieve NULL or an incorrect value when attempting to obtain the value of its member variables. (The default makefile for the NSAPI examples that comes with these servers does not include this needed compiler switch.)

The value of SERVER_URL is a bit more difficult to access, as no global variable is directly defined for it. To access the server's URL, you can use the API function **protocol_uri2url**. In fact, the server's name, port, and URL can all be accessed indirectly through this function.

protocol_uri2url takes a URI prefix and suffix, defined as its first and second parameter, and returns a full URL path to the server. The URL returned will be in the following format: `http[s]://<server hostname>[:port]/[prefix][suffix]`. If you set a null string for the prefix and suffix—that is, `protocol_uri2url("","")`— you should get the server root, as in `http://<server hostname>[:port]`. The port is ignored if it is the default port 80. You should then get `http://<server hostname>`. The result is, therefore, the server URL.

If you have problems accessing the server name, port, or URL, you can always use the function **protocol_uri2url**. For example, Listing 6-4 obtains the server name by using **protocol_uri2url**.

Listing 6-4   Getting the Server Name with the **protocol_uri2url** Function

```
char *getserver(void)
{
    char *url;      /* the full server url */
    char *tmp;      /* temporary string for getting server name */
    char *server;   /* holds the server name */
    int num;        /* number of string characters */

    /* allocate memory for string operation */
    server = (char *) MALLOC(80 * sizeof(char));
```

```
    /* get the server url, http://<server_hostname>[:port]. */
    url = protocol_uri2url("", "");

    /* look for the first ":" and remove the :// from the
       string until we get to the server name
     */
    tmp = strchr(url, ':');
    tmp = tmp + 3;

    /* look for the second ":" and use its location to
       copy the string into the server string without the
       port number
     */
    num = strcspn(tmp, ":");
    strncpy(server, tmp, num);

    FREE(tmp);

    /* return the name of the server as a string */
    return server;
}
```

In ensuring that we always get only the server's name, we must be careful about two factors. First, we cannot assume that the URL includes http://; it could be https://. Second, no port may be specified after the server name in the URL if it is the default port 80, but we also cannot assume that the port is always 80.

Listing 6-4 first gets the url, a string that holds the full server URL. You do not need to allocate the memory for the url string, because the function creates a newly allocated URL string. We then use **strchr** to look for the first occurrence of the colon character (:) in the URL. The function returns a pointer to the string beginning with :. We move up the string until we get to the server name, skipping ://. **strcspn** finds the first occurrence of the colon in this new temporary string. There should be only two unencoded colon characters in a server URL—one after the http[s] and one before the port number. **strcspn** returns the number of characters in the tmp string up to the colon character. The return value, num, is then used to specify the number of characters we want to copy into the new server string. The function returns the new string, which holds only the server name. You can use a similar function to get the port number from url.

Session **Variables** The Session data structure holds variables that apply to the entire session. It includes session information about the client (that is, information about the IP and DNS of the client), plus the SSL security information (for example, keysize). These variables are kept in the client pblock. The information available through the `Session` data structure is meant to apply to the entire session with the client, not just a single request.

`Session->client`

- `ip (REMOTE_ADDR)`
- `dns (REMOTE_HOST)`
- `keysize (HTTPS_KEYSIZE)`
- `secret-keysize (HTTPS_SECRETSIZE)`
- `ssl-id (HTTPS_SESSIONID)`
- `cipher`
- `issuer_dn (CLIENT_CERT_ISSUER_DN)`
- `user_dn (CLIENT_CERT_SUBJECT_DN)`

You get the IP address by using `pblock_findval("ip", sn->client)`. The **pblock_findval** function finds the value of a specified *name-value* pair in a pblock. You specify the name as the first parameter and the `client` pblock as the second parameter; the function then returns the value. **pblock_findval** is used to get most of the values of the *name-value* pairs in a pblock. Although we will continue to use this function to obtain other values, we use the **session_dns** or **session_maxdns** function (`char *session_dns(Session *sn)`) to get the value of the client's DNS. **session_dns** gets the DNS host name from the client's IP for the session specified in its parameter and inserts the value in the pblock `client`. This function does the actual look-up of the client's DNS. You also must have the DNS enabled for the server. **session_dns** returns the client's DNS number. You can also use **session_maxdns** to have the server look up and verify the client host name, providing for additional validation of the DNS.

The values for `keysize`, `secret-keysize`, `cipher`, `ssl-id`, `issuer_dn`, and `user_dn` can be obtained through the **pblock_findval** function. You must have SSL enabled for these variables to be present. Otherwise, the function returns NULL. For `ssl-id`, you must also add the **AuthTrans** function **get-sslid** to the `obj.conf` file. The distinguished name (DN) of the issuer of the client certificate (`issuer_dn`) and the client's distinguished name (`user_dn`) are available only with Enterprise Server 3.5.1. For example, if you had issued a certificate using Netscape Certificate Server, the `issuer_dn` could be `CN=my Certificate Server, o=my company` and the `user_dn` could be `UID=jdoe CN=john doe o=my company`. If no certificate is used, the values of these two entries will reflect `no certificate`. To have the `client` pblock include the issuer and user DN, you should require client certificate for all requests through the Server Manager's Server Preferences|Encryption Preferences menu.

Request Variables   The `Request` data structure holds variables that apply to a specific request. It includes three pblock data structures (`vars`, `reqpb`, and `headers`) that hold the NSAPI variables related to a client's request. These variables are request-specific headers. In this section, we will review each of these pblocks. The fourth pblock data structure (`srvhdrs`) holds the server response-headers. Each pblock holds a number of NSAPI variables.

Sample of *Request->*vars entries

- `path-info` (`PATH_INFO`)
- `ppath` (`SCRIPT_NAME`—virtual path)
- `ntrans-base` (translated root document directory)
- `path` (translated request path, physical path on the system)
- `url`
- `shellcgi-path`
- `auth-type` (`AUTH_TYPE`)
- `auth-user` (`REMOTE_USER`)
- `auth-group`
- `auth-db`
- `auth-password`
- `userdn`
- `auth-cert` (`CLIENT_CERT`)

This list gives some of the server's working variables contained in the *Request->*vars data structure. `vars` includes mostly authentication and path information. `path-info` (equivalent to the CGI environment variable `PATH_INFO`) is available through the `vars` pblock after the **PathCheck** directive's built-in server function, **find-pathinfo**, runs. You normally cannot use the extended path with your NSAPI **Service** function. If the extended path information is included after your function as part of a request (for example, `http://<server name>/<SAF name.SAF extension>/[extra path information]`), the server looks for the request in the extended path. It cannot distinguish between the SAF path and the extra path information. Thus your program will not be called, and a server error or a file not found error arises. You can, however, write an **ObjectType** function that uses `path-info`. The `PATH_TRANSLATED` environment variable is also nonconsequential, as it is the value of the extended path translated into a full physical path. The server goes through the directives a second time to correctly translate the path found in `path-info` into a physical path—that is, `PATH_TRANSLATED`. This information is then passed onto the CGI program as an environment variable.

`auth-type` and `auth-user` (equivalent to the CGI environment variables `AUTH_TYPE` and `REMOTE_USER`, respectively) are also defined in *Request->*vars. You get the value of these variables with the **pblock_findval** function. `auth_user` is not the name used for authentication, but rather the name of the user after authentication. To first get the user's name so as to authenticate a user in an **AuthTrans** directive function, you should get the name from the *param* parameter of your SAF function.

In other words, when writing a user-defined **AuthTrans** function for **basic-auth**, the user's name is obtained from your SAF's first parameter (*param*). Once you authenticate the user, **basic-auth** then places auth-user and auth-type in the Request->vars pblock. Your function should simply return REQ_PROCEED. This procedure also applies to auth-group, auth-db, and auth-password. The variable userdn holds the DN of the user in the local database or a directory server used by Server 3.x. To have the client certificate (auth-cert) placed inside the vars pblock, you need to declare the **PathCheck** function **get-client-cert** in the obj.conf file. You also need to require client certificates. The value of auth-cert will be in MIME base-64 encoded, ASN.1 encoded X.509 format. On the CD-ROM that accompanies this book, you will find an ASN.1 Certificate Decoder example, for decoding auth-cert, by Scott Leerssen.

Sample of Request->reqpb entries

- method (REQUEST_METHOD)
- protocol (SERVER_PROTOCOL)
- query (QUERY_STRING)
- uri (SCRIPT_NAME)

The reqpb pblock holds the Request-Line information (that is, "*Method Request-URI HTTP-Version*"). This line is sent by the client to inform the server of the method token, the URI, and the HTTP version of the request. reqpb also holds the query string. To access the CGI values gained from REQUEST_METHOD,

SERVER_PROTOCOL, or QUERY_STRING, look for the NSAPI values method, protocol, or query, respectively, in the pblock reqpb by using the **pblock_findval** function. uri (also accessed through **pblock_findval**) is the path to the NSAPI function sent by the client. As such, it gives the same value as SCRIPT_NAME.

Sample of *Request*->headers entries

- host (HTTP_HOST, usually the same as SERVER_NAME)
- authorization
- content-type (CONTENT_TYPE)
- content-length (CONTENT_LENGTH)
- content-encoding (CONTENT_ENCODING)
- accept (HTTP_ACCEPT)
- connection (HTTP_CONNECTION)
- cookie (HTTP_COOKIE)
- if-modified-since (HTTP_IF_MODIFIED_SINCE)
- referer (HTTP_REFERER)
- user-agent (HTTP_USER_AGENT)
- accept-charset (HTTP_ACCEPT_CHARSET)
- accept-language (HTTP_ACCEPT_LANGUAGE)

Note ▶

If you have declared your NSAPI application as a **Service** function in the default Object, the client can access your program independent of what directory path is used in the URI. The server uses the file extension associated with the NSAPI application's MIME type to recognize a request as being intended for your NSAPI application. To enforce your NSAPI application to work only under a specific directory, you should create a new Object in the **obj.conf** file and declare your function inside the Object. You also need to specify the path for your NSAPI application by using the ppath parameter of the Object or a **NameTrans** function (**pfx2dir** or **assign-name**) declared in the default Object. If you use **pfx2dir** or **assign-name,** the value of the name parameter of your Object should match the value of the name parameter you specify in the **NameTrans** function. You can then use the **ObjectType** function **force-type** to enforce the NSAPI application's MIME type for the directory. Place the **force-type** function before your NSAPI **Service** function. Normally, your server uses the same method to limit CGI programs to a specific directory. (See the section Configuring the Server for CGI Programs in Chapter 3 for more information.)

```
NameTrans fn="pfx2dir" from="/nsapi"
 dir="c:/netscape/server/https-foo/nsapi" name="nsapi"
...

<Object name="nsapi">
ObjectType fn="force-type" type="magnus-internal/nsapi"
Service fn="mynsapi" method="GET"
</Object>
```

The `headers` pblock holds the HTTP request-headers, which are additional protocol-specific headers. They comprise the NSAPI variables equivalent to the CGI environment variables that start with `HTTP_`. They are not limited to the HTTP response-headers, however. You will also find the equivalents of the CGI environment variables `CONTENT_TYPE`, `CONTENT_LENGTH`, and `CONTENT_ENCODING` environment variables here (`content-type`, `content-length`, and `content-encoding`, respectively). These variables are equivalent to HTTP entity-headers. They specify the type of data sent by the client (for example, the `POST` data type). `accept`, `connection`, `cookie`, `if-modified-since`, `referer`, and `user-agent` are equivalent to the environment variables `HTTP_ACCEPT`, `HTTP_CONNECTION`, `HTTP_COOKIE`, `HTTP_IF_MODIFIED_SINCE`, `HTTP_REFERER`, and `HTTP_USER_AGENT`, respectively. `host` is an additional variable. Its value is usually the same as the value of `server_hostname`, but `host` is the host name of your server as identified by the client. In other words, the value of `host` is obtained from the client's request, not from your server's setting. This variable is available if a browser, such as Netscape Navigator, actually sends the `host` header. Depending on the HTTP request-headers sent by the client, there may be additional entries in the headers pblock, such as `accept-charset` and `accept-language`.

You can look for the variables inside the `headers` pblock data structure by using **pblock_findval**. Netscape, however, recommends the use of the **request_header** function (`request_header(char *name, char **value, Session *sn, Request *rq)`). With this function, the server will not load the headers until the first one is requested. This function accesses the values indirectly, avoiding multiple calls. You can use a copy of the `Session` and `Request` data structures of the current request, plus the `name` of the variable (for example, `content-type`), as parameters. The function then places the value where the `value` parameter points. You must indicate the address of `value` for the **request_header** function to place the value where you specify. This function also returns a standard NSAPI function return code (for example, `REQ_ABORTED`) if an error occurred. You can use this return value for error checking.

Another pblock data structure (`srvhdrs`) is defined for `Request`. It holds the server response-headers. You send various header files to the client by inserting them into this pblock. You do not read these headers from a client request; rather, they are the headers you will send to the client. Do not mistake headers, such as `content-type`, that are specified by the client's request—and available in `Request->headers`—with the headers you specify in `Request->srvhdrs`. Although these headers may have the same name (such as `content-type`), they have different purposes. For the pblock `headers`, `content-type` is the header sent by the client as part of a `POST` method of request. For `srvhdrs`, `content-type` is the header determining the type of content sent to the client. You can use the NSAPI function **pblock_nvinsert** (`pblock_nvinsert(char *name, char *value, pblock *pb)`) to insert a *name-value* pair into a pblock hash table, for example, `rq->srvhdrs`.

param **Variables**   *param* refers to the name of the pblock data structure specified as the first parameter of your SAF. You can pass various [*name*]="[*value*]" parameters to your function by naming them in the **obj.conf** file. An example of such a function in the **obj.conf** file could be

```
NameTrans fn="my_redirect" address="/test/register.html"
```

These [*name*]="[*value*]" pairs can then be accessed via the **pblock_findval** function. If you have defined the parameter address="/test/register.html" (as in the above line in the **obj.conf** file), you can access this value with the following code in your SAF:

```
pblock_findval("address", param);
```

As mentioned earlier, for your user-defined **AuthTrans** function, the value of the user name and password are passed on through the *param* pblock. Again, you can use **pblock_findval** to access the user name and password. These values are passed to your function in the same way as other variables you may have defined for the **AuthTrans** function. The following code gives an example of an **AuthTrans** function defined in the **obj.conf** file:

```
AuthTrans fn=basic-auth userfn=my-auth
 auth-type=basic userdb=mydatabase
```

basic-auth is the server's built-in function for user-defined authentication. **my-auth** is the user-defined SAF function you need to write. **basic-auth**, then, sends the user name and password to your **my-auth** function through param. As you may expect, you can access the value of userdb through pblock_findval("userdb", param). You access the user name (user) through pblock_findval("user", param) and the password (pw) through pblock_findval("pw", param). The client inputs these values in the default authentication dialog box that appears during the basic authentication.

Examples of Obtaining NSAPI Variables

The following two sections provide different views of NSAPI variables. In the first section, we write out the CGI environment variables and their values using NSAPI functions (Listings 6-5 and 6-6). These functions reflect the information we have discussed so far, especially as shown in Table 6-5. In the second section, we write out the entries in the server's principal pblocks, *Session*->client, *Request*->vars, *Request*->reqpb, and *Request*->headers (Listing 6-7).

The information in both of these sections is similar, as the variables for the CGI-equivalent NSAPI variables are also primarily in the pblock data structure's entries. Because all of these examples are **Service** functions, only information available to a **Service** directive is available to them. Listings 6-5 and 6-6 show how to get many of the common NSAPI variables. Listing 6-7 allows you a peek at the variables inside the server.

NSAPI Variables Equivalent to Environment Variables Listing 6-5 writes the common NSAPI variables into an HTML page and then sends that page to the client. These variables are the NSAPI equivalents of CGI environment variables. As with other functions in this chapter, you must compile and install this function by using the instructions described in Chapter 7. We write this function as a **Service** function so as to return an HTML page containing the list of variables to the client. These variables are grouped based on the sections described above (that is, the global variables; the Session's pblock, client; and the Request's pblocks, vars, reqpb, and headers). This example is written for use with Server 3.x. You must include the Server 2.x header files and replace the **system_version** function with MAGNUS_VERSION_STRING to use this code with Server 2.x. You should include the following header files for Server 2.x:

```
#include "base/pblock.h"
#include "base/session.h"
#include "frame/req.h"

#include "base/util.h"          /* util_sprintf */
#include "frame/protocol.h"     /* protocol_start_response
                                   protocol_status */
#include "frame/conf.h"         /* conf_getglobals */
```

Listing 6-5 Writing CGI Environment Variables and Their NSAPI Values (Version 1)

```
/* header file for Server 3.x */
#include "nsapi.h"

/* this program sends the NSAPI values for the
   CGI environment variables as they are found in
   Netscape Server data structures to a client
 */
NSAPI_PUBLIC int print_env_var(pblock *param, Session *sn,
                                Request *rq)
{
    char *buf;    /* a buffer to be sent to the client */
    int cl;       /* size of buf */

    char env_var[2000]; /* string holds the NSAPI values and
                           their equivalent CGI environment
                           variable names */

    /* This function creates a string of name = value pairs
       for all appropriate NSAPI variables. It is divided
       into sections based on the type of variable (that is,
       Global, Session client, Request vars, and so on).
       Here, we use pblock_findval instead of the recommended
```

```
            request_header to get the headers' values.
         */
   util_sprintf(env_var, "<H3>Global variables</H3>\n"
                         "SERVER SOFTWARE = %s<P>\n"
                         "SERVER NAME = %s<P>\n"
                         "SERVER PORT = %i<P>\n"
                         "SERVER URL = %s<P>\n"
                         "HTTPS = %i<P>\n"

                         "<H3>Session client variables</H3>\n"
                         "REMOTE ADDRESS = %s<P>\n"
                         "REMOTE HOST = %s<P>\n"
                         "HTTPS KEYSIZE = %s<P>\n"
                         "HTTPS SECRETSIZE = %s<P>\n"

                         "<H3>Request vars variables</H3>\n"
                         "PATH INFO = %s<P>\n"
                         "AUTH TYPE = %s<P>\n"
                         "REMOTE USER = %s<P>\n"

                         "<H3>Request reqpb variables</H3>\n"
                         "REQUEST METHOD = %s<P>\n"
                         "SERVER PROTOCOL = %s<P>\n"
                         "QUERY STRING = %s<P>\n"

                         "<H3>Request headers variables</H3>\n"
                         "CONTENT LENGTH = %s<P>\n"
                         "CONTENT TYPE = %s<P>\n"
                         "CONTENT ENCODING = %s<P>\n"
                         "HTTP ACCEPT = %s<P>\n"
                         "HTTP CONNECTION = %s<P>\n"
                         "HTTP COOKIE = %s<P>\n"
                         "HTTP IF MODIFIED_SINCE = %s<P>\n"
                         "HTTP REFERER = %s<P>\n"
                         "HTTP USER AGENT = %s<P>\n",

                         system_version(),
                         server_hostname,
                         conf_getglobals()>Vport,
                         http_uri2url("",""),
                         security_active,

                         pblock_findval("ip", sn->client),
                         session_dns(sn),
```

```
                              pblock_findval("keysize", sn->client),
                              pblock_findval("secret-keysize",
                                             sn->client),

                              pblock_findval("path-info", rq->vars),
                              pblock_findval("auth-type", rq->vars),
                              pblock_findval("auth-user", rq->vars),

                              pblock_findval("method", rq->reqpb),
                              pblock_findval("protocol", rq->reqpb),
                              pblock_findval("query", rq->reqpb),

                              pblock_findval("content-length",
                                             rq->headers),
                              pblock_findval("content-type",
                                             rq->headers),
                              pblock_findval("content-encoding",
                                             rq->headers),
                              pblock_findval("accept", rq->headers),
                              pblock_findval("connection",
                                             rq->headers),
                              pblock_findval("cookie", rq->headers),
                              pblock_findval("if-modified-since",
                                             rq->headers),
                              pblock_findval("referer",
                                             rq->headers),
                              pblock_findval("user-agent",
                                             rq->headers));

    /* the rest of this code takes the standard steps
       for sending an HTML page to the client
     */

    /* get rid of internal content, which is usually the
       SAF's magnus-internal content type
     */
    param_free(pblock_remove("content-type", rq->srvhdrs));

    /* set content to html */
    pblock_nvinsert("content-type", "text/html",
                    rq->srvhdrs);

    /* set status to OK */
    protocol_status(sn, rq, PROTOCOL_OK, NULL);
```

```
    /* send the headers and get ready for sending the page */
    protocol_start_response(sn, rq);

    /* malloc a rough size for buf */
    buf = (char *) MALLOC(5000 * sizeof(char));

    /* put all the variables and the rest of the HTML page
       information into one buffer (buf)
     */
    cl = util_sprintf(buf,
                        "<HTML><HEAD><TITLE>"
                        "Environment Variables</TITLE>"
                        "</HEAD>\n"
                        "<BODY><H1>"
                        "Environment Variables</H1>\n"
                        "%s"
                        "<HR></BODY></HTML>", env_var);

    /* Send the information to the client. Also check
       for any error while sending the page to the client.
       If an error occurred, exit. No extra error
       information is processed here.
     */
    if(net_write(sn->csd, buf, cl) == IO_ERROR)
    {
        return REQ_EXIT;
    }

    /* return success to the server */
    return REQ_PROCEED;
}
```

print_env_var prints the value of the variables, independent of whether they are actually available. If they are not available, the function usually returns a NULL value. Normally, the server will not include a variable in the pblock if it is unspecified or not needed. In other words, the server dynamically generates the pblock *name-value* pairs based on the request and the server configuration.

We get each variable and include it in a string (env_var) by using **util_sprintf**. **util_sprintf** is an NSAPI function that formats a string based on the specifications defined in the second parameter of the function and its arguments. (The second—long—parameter ends with "HTTP_USER_AGENT = %s<P>\n".) The list of the arguments follows the second parameter. **util_sprintf** then places the formatted string in its first parameter (env_var). This approach is similar to how the **printf** function formats a string. **util_sprintf** is a long function that includes a string of variable names with specifications for the values (%s or %i). The functions that return the values are also defined as part of the **util_sprintf** arguments. Alternatively, you could create the final env_var string in separate stages by appending the string each time with the new variables. Also, **util_sprintf** does not do any bounds checking, so you should make sure that the size of env_var is large enough.

A few more points are relevant about how we get these variables. First, the values of the variables are placed directly inside the string. In other words, the **pblock_findval** functions are defined inside the **util_sprintf** function. **pblock_findval** returns the value to be placed inside the env_var string. If there is no value, it returns NULL. Also, we do not use **request_header** as suggested to get the variables from the Request->headers pblock. For now, this function uses **pblock_findval**. We will rewrite this same function in Listing 6-6 and take advantage of **request_header**.

REMOTE_HOST is NULL if DNS is not enabled for the server. HTTPS_KEYSIZE and HTTPS_SECRETSIZE are also NULL if SSL is not used. Listing 6-5 included PATH_INFO as a Request->vars variable, but as mentioned earlier, you cannot pass extra path information after your NSAPI function. (The server will not recognize your function if extra path information is present.) All other variables are derived based on the method described earlier. (See also Table 6-5 for more detail.)

Once we have all the variables in a string, we need to return them in an HTML page. The instructions conform to the standard practice we discussed earlier (see Returning a Dynamic Page earlier in this chapter). We first remove the current content-type. Next, we insert the new content-type, text/html, via the NSAPI function **pblock_nvinsert**. The function **protocol_status** then sets the appropriate status for the data being returned to the client (that is, Status: 200 OK). **protocol_start_response** sends the header files to the client. We then place the env_var string, along with the HTML tags, inside a new string before sending the buffer (buf) to the client. Finally, we send the buffer to the client's socket by using **net_write**, and exit the function with REQ_PROCEED upon successful delivery.

Listing 6-6 shows the same **print_env_var** function modified to use the **request_header** function. Notice that we declare the values and use **request_header** to get the values before placing them inside the env_var string. We also do not take advantage of the return value of **request_header** to verify whether an error occurred. If you believe that an error can occur while getting the headers, then check for the return value REQ_ABORTED.

Listing 6-6 Writing CGI Environment Variables and Their NSAPI Values (Version 2)

```
NSAPI_PUBLIC int print_env_var(pblock *param, Session *sn,
                               Request *rq)
{
    char *buf;    /* buffer to be sent to the client */
    int length;     /* size of buf */
```

```
char env_var[2000]; /* string holds the NSAPI values and
                       their equivalent CGI environment
                       variable names */

/* strings to hold the rq->headers variables */
char *http_content_type;
char *http_content_length;
char *http_content_encoding;
char *http_accept;
char *http_connection;
char *http_cookie;
char *http_if_modified_since;
char *http_referer;
char *http_user_agent;

/* Get all appropriate rq->headers. They are specified in
   the second parameter.
 */
request_header("content-length", &http_content_length,
               sn, rq);
request_header("content-type", &http_content_type,
               sn, rq);
request_header("content-encoding",
               &http_content_encoding, sn, rq);
request_header("accept", &http_accept,
               sn, rq);
request_header("connection", &http_connection,
               sn, rq);
request_header("cookie", &http_cookie,
               sn, rq);
request_header("if-modified-since",
               &http_if_modified_since, sn, rq);
request_header("referer", &http_referer,
               sn, rq);
request_header("user-agent", &http_user_agent,
               sn, rq);

/* This function creates a string of name = value pairs
   for all appropriate NSAPI variables. It is divided to
   sections based on the type of variable (that is,
   Global, Session client, Request vars, and so on). This
   time, we use the appropriate request_header function.
 */
```

```
util_sprintf(env_var, "<H3>Global variables</H3>\n"
                      "SERVER SOFTWARE = %s<P>\n"
                      "SERVER NAME = %s<P>\n"
                      "SERVER PORT = %i<P>\n"
                      "SERVER URL = %s<P>\n"
                      "HTTPS = %i<P>\n"

                      "<H3>Session client variables</H3>\n"
                      "REMOTE ADDRESS = %s<P>\n"
                      "REMOTE HOST = %s<P>\n"
                      "HTTPS KEYSIZE = %s<P>\n"
                      "HTTPS SECRETSIZE = %s<P>\n"

                      "<H3>Request vars variables</H3>\n"
                      "PATH INFO = %s<P>\n"
                      "AUTH TYPE = %s<P>\n"
                      "REMOTE USER = %s<P>\n"

                      "<H3>Request reqpb variables</H3>\n"
                      "REQUEST METHOD = %s<P>\n"
                      "SERVER PROTOCOL = %s<P>\n"
                      "QUERY STRING = %s<P>\n"

                      "<H3>Request headers variables</H3>\n"
                      "CONTENT LENGTH = %s<P>\n"
                      "CONTENT TYPE = %s<P>\n"
                      "CONTENT ENCODING = %s<P>\n"
                      "HTTP ACCEPT = %s<P>\n"
                      "HTTP CONNECTION = %s<P>\n"
                      "HTTP COOKIE = %s<P>\n"
                      "HTTP IF_MODIFIED_SINCE = %s<P>\n"
                      "HTTP REFERER = %s<P>\n"
                      "HTTP USER AGENT = %s<P>\n",

                      system_version(),
                      server_hostname,
                      conf_getglobals()->Vport,
                      http_uri2url("",""),
                      security_active,

                      pblock_findval("ip", sn->client),
                      session_dns(sn),
                      pblock_findval("keysize", sn->client),
                      pblock_findval("secret-keysize",
                                     sn->client),
```

```
                        pblock_findval("path-info", rq->vars),
                        pblock_findval("auth-type", rq->vars),
                        pblock_findval("auth-user", rq->vars),

                        pblock_findval("method", rq->reqpb),
                        pblock_findval("protocol", rq->reqpb),
                        pblock_findval("query", rq->reqpb),

                        http_content_length,
                        http_content_type,
                        http_content_encoding,
                        http_accept,
                        http_connection,
                        http_cookie,
                        http_if_modified_since,
                        http_referer,
                        http_user_agent);
/* the rest of this code is same as the version 1,
   Listing 6-5
 */

/* get rid of any existing content type */
param_free(pblock_remove("content-type", rq->srvhdrs));

/* set content to html */
pblock_nvinsert("content-type", "text/html",
                rq->srvhdrs);

/* set status to OK */
protocol_status(sn, rq, PROTOCOL_OK, NULL);

/* send the headers and get ready for sending the page */
protocol_start_response(sn, rq);

/* malloc a rough size for buf */
buf = (char *) MALLOC(5000 * sizeof(char));

/* put all variables and the rest of the HTML page
   information into one buffer (buf)
 */
length = util_sprintf(buf,
                "<HTML><HEAD><TITLE>"
                "Environment Variables</TITLE>"
                "</HEAD>\n"
```

```
                              "<BODY><H1>"
                              "Environment Variables</H1>\n"
                              "%s"
                              "<HR></BODY></HTML>", env_var);

    /* send the information to the client */
    if(net_write(sn->csd, buf, length) == IO_ERROR)
    {
        return REQ_EXIT;
    }


    /* return success to the server */
    return REQ_PROCEED;
}
```

Figure 6-2 shows an example of an HTML page returned to the client. In this example, the server name is foo. The server software used is Enterprise Server 3.5.1 for NT, and security is set to on. The client browser is Netscape Communicator 4.04 for Windows NT.

Writing Variables from the Server pblock Data Structures   In Listings 6-5 and 6-6, we returned the common NSAPI variables that are equivalent to CGI environment variables. Mostly, we searched for the NSAPI variables in the NSAPI data structures. Instead, you may want to write just the entries in the server's pblock data structures. **print_NSAPI_var** (Listing 6-7) writes the entries in the pblocks: *Session*->client, *Request*->vars, *Request*->reqpb, and *Request*->headers. (You can use a similar method to print out the *Request*->srvhdrs pblock as well.) It writes an HTML page that contains the NSAPI variables found in these pblock data structures. You can use this function to review the entries in each pblock. In Chapter 8, we will write a function that logs these variables for each server directive. **print_NSAPI_var**, however, is a **Service** function and returns the variables as they are available only to a **Service** directive. As mentioned earlier, the values of some of the variables change and are not necessarily available for a specific directive. Thus, the information in Listing 6-7 would be different if it were recorded for a different directive.

Listing 6-7   Writing NSAPI pblock Variables

```
/* include the following files if you are using a version
   of Netscape Server earlier than 3.x

  #include "base/pblock.h"
  #include "base/session.h"
  #include "frame/req.h"
```

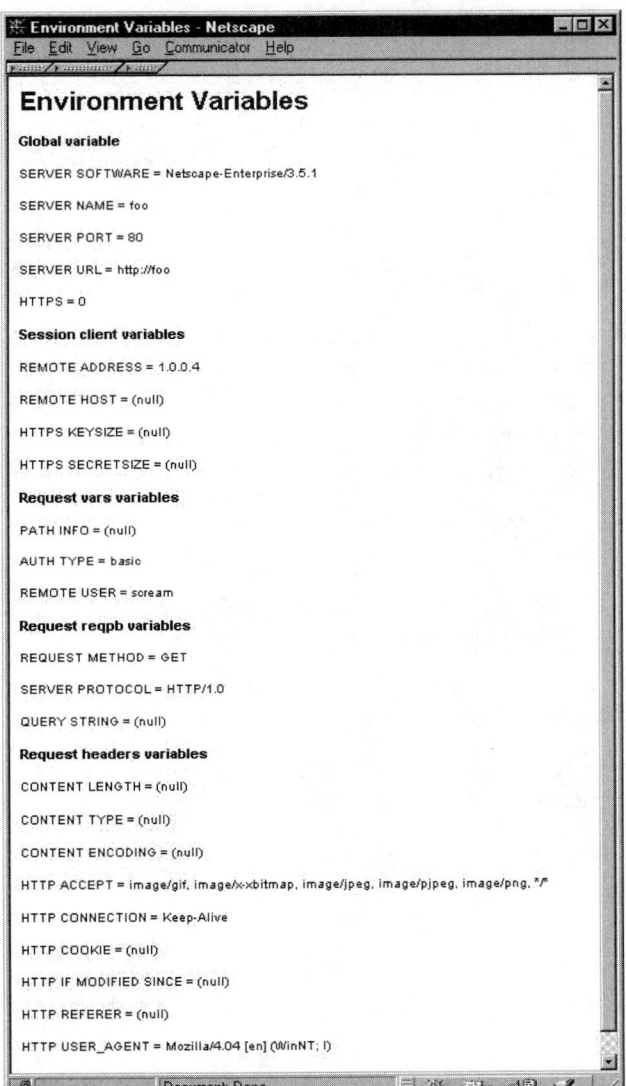

Figure 6-2 **Example of an HTML Page Returned by** print_env_var

---

Listing 6-7 Writing NSAPI pblock Variables (*continued*)

```
   #include "base/util.h"
   #include "frame/protocol.h"
*/

/* include this file if you are using Server 3.x */
#include "nsapi.h"
```

Listing 6-7   Writing NSAPI pblock Variables (*continued*)

```c
/* this function sends the server's pblock data structures
   to the client */
NSAPI_PUBLIC int print_NSAPI_var(pblock *param, Session *sn,
                                              Request *rq)
{
    char *buf;    /* a buffer to be sent to the client */
    int length;        /* size of buf */

    /* strings to hold pblock name-value pairs */
    char *client;    /* for sn->client */
    char *vars;        /* for rq->vars */
    char *reqpb;      /* for rq>reqpb */
    char *headers;    /* for rq->headers */

    /* get the Session's client pblock name-value pair */
    client = pblock_pblock2str(sn->client, NULL);

    /* get the Request's vars pblock name-value pair */
    vars = pblock_pblock2str(rq->vars, NULL);

    /* get the Request's reqpb pblock name-value pair */
    reqpb = pblock_pblock2str(rq->reqpb, NULL);

    /* get the Request's headers pblock name-value pair */
    headers = pblock_pblock2str(rq->headers, NULL);

    /* the rest of this code takes standard steps for
       sending an HTML page to the client
     */

    /* get rid of any existing content-type */
    param_free(pblock_remove("content-type", rq->srvhdrs));

    /* set content to html */
    pblock_nvinsert("content-type", "text/html",
                    rq->srvhdrs);

    /* set status to OK */
    protocol_status(sn, rq, PROTOCOL_OK, NULL);

    /* send the headers and get ready for sending the page */
    protocol_start_response(sn, rq);

    /* malloc a rough size for buf */
    buf = (char *) MALLOC(5000 * sizeof(char));

    /* put all the variables and the rest of the HTML page
       information into one buffer (buf)
```

Listing 6-7   Writing NSAPI pblock Variables (*continued*)

```
    */
    length = util_sprintf(buf,
                        "<HTML><HEAD><TITLE>"
                        "Environment Variables</TITLE>"
                        "</HEAD>\n"
                        "<BODY><H1>"
                        "Environment Variables</H1>\n"
                        "<H3>Session Client</H3>%s"
                        "<H3>Request vars</H3>\n%s"
                        "<H3>Request reqpb</H3>\n%s"
                        "<H3>Request headers</H3>\n%s"
                        "<HR></BODY></HTML>",
                        client, vars, reqpb, headers);

    /* send the buffer to the client */
    if(net_write(sn->csd, buf, length) == IO_ERROR)
    {
        return REQ_EXIT;
    }

    /* return success to the server */
    return REQ_PROCEED;
}
```

The function in Listing 6-7 is similar to the earlier functions (Listings 6-5 and 6-6) in the method it uses for returning the variables to the client. The main difference is in the way we get the data to be returned. We use the NSAPI function **pblock_pblock2str** to convert the entries in the pblock data structures to a string. **pblock_pblock2str** takes as its parameter a pblock data structure and returns the entries in the pblock hash table in the form of [*name*]=" [*value*] " pairs. These [*name*]=" [*value*] " pairs are each separated by a space. The second parameter of **pblock_pblock2str** is set to NULL to enable a new string to be allocated. Otherwise, you can specify a string to which the pblock *name-value* pairs are appended. Here, we use a separate string for each pblock. The function takes care of allocating memory using the memory pool.

Once we have all the strings for each pblock, we add the string to the HTML page by using **util_sprintf**. The HTML page is returned to the client in the same way as the functions in Listings 6-5 and 6-6 returned an HTML page. Figure 6-3 shows an example of an HTML page returned to the client by **print_NSAPI_var**.

Reading Data from a Socket or Network Buffer

So far, we have discussed information that is available through global variables or through the server's pblock data structures. This information is usually passed through

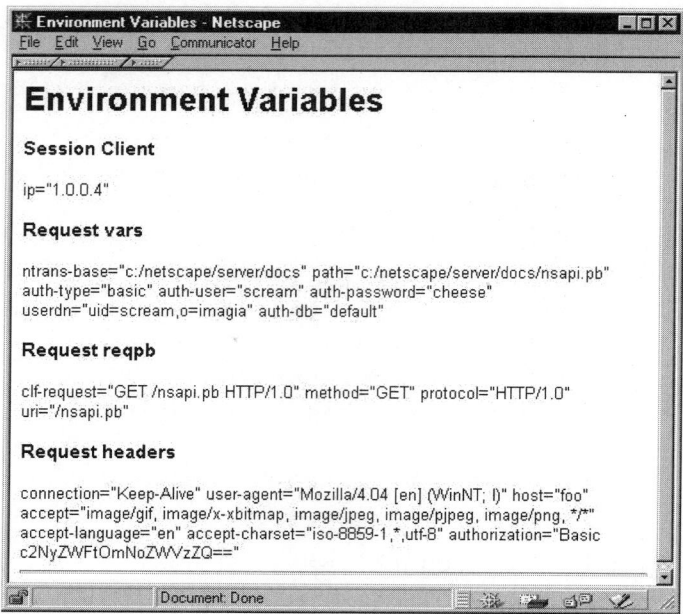

Figure 6-3   Example of an HTML Page Returned by print_NSAPI_var

various HTTP headers. Even the client input from a form that is sent through a GET method is available in a query header.

Let us discuss how data are received from a POST request. The server accepts the entity enclosed in the request (and sent by the client) as a new subordinate of the resource identified in the requested URI. For CGI programs, POST data are available through standard input after the other HTTP headers. Thus we read the data using the standard input functions (for example, **fread**). For your SAF, you have access to the client's socket and the network buffer. The network buffer is where POST data are found. You can access the buffer through the Session's network buffer string (*Session*->inbuf). You use NSAPI functions, such as **netbuf_getc**, to read the data from the network buffer. Note that with both the query string sent by a GET method and the network buffer data sent through the POST method (or the standard input data for the CGI program), you still must decode the data. The data are URL-encoded and need to be decoded before their use. The decoding functions can be the same for both the query string and the network buffer data. You can even use your existing CGI parsing functions to parse the data. Later we will write a parsing example that takes advantage of NSAPI functions.

A client inputs data into a form and then sends the data. If these data were sent through a POST method, the server places them into a network buffer string (*Session*->inbuf). Notice that both the Session's netbuf data structure and the string of input (a member of the `netbuf` data structure) are called `inbuf`. You can read the data sent through a POST method from the network buffer through *Session*->`inbuf` by using the **netbuf_getc** function. **netbuf_getc** reads from the network buffer's `inbuf` string one character at a time. The actual `inbuf` string includes the headers sent by the client and the client input data. **netbuf_getc**, however, starts reading at the position specified by `pos`, a member of the `netbuf` data structure. `pos` points to the client's input data. It is set to the position of the data sent, after the headers in the `inbuf` string. **netbuf_getc** returns each character that it reads as an integer. We can then place each character inside a newly allocated string for later use. You, of course, can directly read the data from the input buffer by using steps similar to those taken by **netbuf_getc**, but it is easiest just to use **netbuf_getc**. (See the discussion of `netbuf` in Chapter 5 for details on how this function works.) Listing 6-8 describes the typical steps taken to read a client's input from a POST request.

Listing 6-8 Reading POST Data

```
char *clstr;        /* content length as a string */
int clen =0;        /* length of content as an integer */
int ichar=IO_OKAY;  /* a character from the client's input,
                       IO_OKAY = 1 */
int curPos =0;      /* current position in client's input
                       string (post_data) */
char *post_data=NULL;   /* client's input */

/* get the length of the data sent by the client */
request_header("content-length", &clstr, sn, rq);

/* because the size defined for content-length is in a
   string format, we convert it to an integer
 */
clen = atoi(clstr);

/* malloc an appropriate size for the string to hold the
   POST data
 */
post_data = (char *)MALLOC(sizeof(char) *(clen+1));

/* read information into post_data, one character at a time,
   until the content length or the end of data (file) is
   reached.
 */
while (clen && ichar != IO_EOF)
{
   /* get a character from the network buffer */
   ichar = netbuf_getc(sn->inbuf);
```

Listing 6-8 Reading POST Data (*continued*)

```
    /* Check for any error while reading. If an error
       occurred, return error information, log the error, free
       post_data, and abort.
     */
    if(ichar == IO_ERROR)
    {
        protocol_status(sn, rq, PROTOCOL_SERVER_ERROR,
          "An I/O error occurred while reading POST data.");
        log_error(LOG_FAILURE, "myfunction", sn, rq,
          "An I/O error occurred while reading POST data.");
        FREE(post_data);
        return REQ_ABORTED;
    }

    /* place the character in the post_data string */
    post_data[curPos++] = ichar;

    /* reduce the size of content length until it is 0 */
    clen--;
}

/* terminate the string */
post_data[curPos] = '\0';
```

In Listing 6-8, we first declare a number of variables for reading the client's input. After these declarations, we get the length of the content sent by the client. As you probably know, a POST method of request returns both content-length and content-type. The content-type header should be application/x-www-form-urlencoded. The content-length header should include the length of the data sent. In Listing 6-8, we do not verify whether content-length, or any content at all, was actually sent. Normally, you should check for a return of REQ_ABORTED from **request_header** to ensure that content-length was sent. If content-length was not sent, **request_header** returns REQ_ABORTED. (We also do not verify whether the content-type is correct. You should also verify this information in your own function.) content-length, like other header variables, is sent as a string, so we need to convert the string to an integer. We use the standard C function **atoi** to do so. Once you get the actual content-length as an integer, you normally verify that the string is a number greater than zero. Otherwise, no content was sent. For simplicity, we have excluded a few of these error-checking steps. (We will write a full example of a function that processes a client input from a POST request in Chapter 9.)

We use content-length to allocate a string size large enough to hold the data we intend to read from the network buffer string. Next, we read through the client input until we reach content-length or the end of file, whichever comes first. We also verify that **netbuf_getc** was able to read the data correctly. If an error occurred, **netbuf_getc** returns IO_ERROR. In that case, we return an error page with a reason string to the client and log the error. As we read each character, we also place it in the post_data string. Finally, once we finish reading the data, we must terminate post_data. For safety, you may also want to verify that the number of characters read (curPos) is the same as the content length (clen). We are now ready to decode the data we read from the buffer.

Besides reading the client POST input, Netscape provides you with functions to make a socket connection and read data directly from the client's socket. You can use **net_socket** to create a socket descriptor and open a connection. **net_connect** then connects to a client. **net_accept** begins listening at a specified port. You can use **net_read** or **netbuf_grab** to read data from the client. **net_read** reads the data directly from the socket and places them in a buffer. **netbuf_grab**, on the other hand, puts the data from the network socket into the network buffer's inbuf string. These advanced functions provide added capabilities not available through a CGI program. Unless you have a special reason to do so, however, you will probably not read directly from the client socket.

Additional Information

Thus far, all of our examples have sought values that can be obtained through the server. You are not limited to this information alone. You can also use other resources, such as a database or other files, when processing a client's request. Moreover, stat information about a file, including a requested file, is also available. For example, to find out whether a file has been modified since a particular date (if-modified-since), you run the **stat** function and get the stat data structure for the file. The member data structure st_mtime usually holds the date that the file was last modified. You can use stat to get the length of the file (content-length) as well. You can use this file information along with the headers sent by the client. For instance, you can match the client's HTTP request header if-modified-since against the last-modified date of a file (st_mtime) to compare dates.

Summary

In this chapter, we examined some of the basic concepts of programming for NSAPI. NSAPI programs are not like CGI programs. They can work directly with the server variables and alter the server's response procedure. The two important concepts discussed in this chapter deal with how to send data to, and how to read data from, the server. In Chapter 7, we will review the steps you need to take to compile, register, and debug your function.

Specific procedures are followed to send a dynamic HTML page to the client. In this process, you use NSAPI functions like **pblock_nvinsert**, **protocol_status**,

protocol_start_response, and **net_write**. To send the response status code to the client, you must use **protocol_status**. To send response-headers, you use **pblock_nvinsert** and insert the header in pblock `Request->srvhdrs`. The response-header and Status-Line are then sent to the client via **protocol_start_response**. We also discussed how you could redirect a client or send an error page.

The data available to your program can consist of global variables, pblock entry variables found in a number of server data structures, or input from the socket or network buffer. You typically use **pblock_findval** to find a value in a server pblock entry. The important pblock structures are the `client` pblock in the `Session` data structure; `vars`, `reqpb`, and `headers` in the `Request` data structure; and the pblock `param` passed as the first parameter of your SAF. For a `POST` method of request, you can read the client input from the server's network buffer by using **netbuf_getc**.

The directive functions we wrote and discussed in this chapter are **Service** functions. Although a **Service** function is the most common and frequently written NSAPI program, it is not the only directive function you may write. More importantly, the type of directive function that you choose to write is directly related to the purpose of your function. You still need to know how to choose a certain directive and how to proceed once you choose the correct directive function. In Chapter 8, we will review each directive and its bearings on an SAF. For each directive function, we will also review the server data structure variables that you should change and the value you should return.

Chapter 7

Compile, Install, and Debug NSAPI Applications

In this chapter, we will discuss the methods for compiling, installing, and debugging NSAPI applications. We will first discuss the steps you need to take to compile your code. Compiling the code differs depending upon which platform you use. Netscape provides a sample makefile for compiling the examples that come with the server. You can use this sample as a starting point for your own makefile. Next, we will go through the process of registering an SAF with the server. To register your SAF, you must take at least two specific steps. First, you register the shared object (so) or dynamic linked library (DLL) that you have compiled, and declare the name of the function that the server should use. Second, you declare the actual SAF as a directive function. To illustrate, we will register some of the examples written in Chapter 6. These steps might seem more complicated than normal. Once you become familiar with them, however, you will see that they fit into the overall scheme of things and are not so difficult.

We will also discuss some of the debugging options you have with an SAF. Debugging a shared library is different from debugging a CGI program. Many ways of debugging your code exist, some of which should already be familiar.

This chapter is a general guide for these topics. We will not discuss the details of how each compiler works or how you actually debug C code. You should already be familiar with these concepts. Instead, we will focus on the specifics of these steps as they relate to NSAPI programming.

Compiling Your Code

SAF functions are compiled into a so for UNIX or a DLL for Windows. These modules are compiled for use by another application (that is, Netscape Server). They do not include a main function. They are not used as stand-alone applications. Instead, the files are loaded by the server at the start of the server. The server then calls the SAFs, whenever needed, at runtime. In other words, your code is part of the server's code (process). As such, it interacts with the server in a similar fashion as other internal server functions. You can load any number of so or DLL files.

You write your code, as we have done so far, in ANSI C and include any appropriate header files. (You may also be able to combine C++ code with your NSAPI application. For instructions on using C++ with NSAPI, see the C++ and NSAPI section in Chapter 6.) You may need to include not only the Netscape-specific header files, but also the C header files. Netscape header files already include directives for some of the standard header files, such as stdlib.h. You can compile the SAF functions using any standard ANSI C compiler. If you use any special C functions not already included, you need to include those header files as well.

All of the makefiles have a few steps in common. For example, they all compile the code by including the appropriate files and specific Netscape preprocessor definitions (such as MCC_HTTPD). Nevertheless, there are also specific settings unique to each platform and compiler. Netscape provides a default makefile unique to each platform. You can use this makefile to compile the examples provided by the server. The makefile and the examples can be found under <server path>/nsapi/examples. If any of the standard switches is missing from the makefile, you should add it. For example, with Netscape Servers 1.x and 2.x, NET_SSL is missing from the makefile included with the examples installed with the server. You should add this switch to the other standard switches—that is, MCC_HTTPD and XP_WIN32 for Windows or XP_UNIX for UNIX.

The simplest way to compile your code is to modify the existing makefile provided by Netscape to include your program. You can either use the makefile as a template to create your own or you can add your function to the existing file and then compile a new so or DLL file. Make sure you understand how a makefile works before you make any modification.

For any recompiled shared library to work, you must stop and start the server to have the changes reflected. It is not enough to use RESTART to restart the server. Rather, you should STOP and START the server in a two-step process. You can perform this task either through the Server Manager or directly. Under UNIX, you can also send the appropriate command-line instructions to stop or start the server process. For example, you can use the stop and start script provided by the server and located under the <server path>/<server ID>/ directory. From this directory, you can stop the server by entering ./stop. To start the server, you can use the following command: ./start. You can also use the command **kill** with the specific server process ID to stop the server: kill-9 <server pid>. Under NT, you can stop and start the server through the Control Panel|Services option.

Make sure you always recompile your code with the latest version of the server. The changes in each version of the server can break your program. Although you can run many binary NSAPI applications compiled under Server 2.x with Server 3.x, it is always based to recompile the code with the latest header and library files. For example, NSAPI programs that use **net_write** may not work properly if the code is compiled with Server 2.x header and library files and then run on the secured Enterprise Server 3.x (when SSL is enabled). It is also recommended that you recompile programs that were written for Server 3.0x when running them on Enterprise Server 3.5.1. You need to make any necessary changes and recompile the program for a new server. Also, if you attempt to compile your program and overwrite the shared library being used by the server, the compiler will generate an error. The server should be stopped first before you can delete or write over the existing shared library.

Compiling for UNIX

The makefile that Netscape provides assumes the use of the GNU make (**gmake**) program. You simply run the makefile through the command line to compile the examples. You can update the sample makefile to include your own functions. For example, your function can be added to the list of objects (`OBJS`) in the makefile. You can specify the object file using the name of your program file plus the extension `.o`. For example, if your file is `hello.c`, then add `hello.o` to the list.

To write your own makefile, you must include the necessary two-step command lines for compiling a source file: **gcc** for an object file and **ld** for linking the files into a shared library. Each command line includes different options (switches) based on the operating system. The order of the switches may also matter for the version of UNIX that you are using. The first line specifies the switches for the GNU compiler for compiling the source file without linking it. The output should be a `*.o` file. For example, for the Solaris platform, the first line would be

```
gcc -DXP_UNIX -DMCC_HTTPD -DNET_SSL -DSOLARIS -D_REENTRANT
 -Wall -c <file name>.c
```

Each preprocessor definition is defined with the `-D` switch. `-DSOLARIS` specifies a definition for the Solaris platform. `-D_REENTRANT` defines a multithreaded application option. `-DMCC_HTTPD`, `-DXP_UNIX`, and `-DNET_SSL` are specific definitions for Netscape Server. For instance, `NET_SSL` should be declared to support SSL and its applicable server variables. It is important to add this switch for Servers 1.x and 2.x. You should add the `-DNET_SSL` switch if it is missing. For Server 2.x, if `NET_SSL` is not used, the data structure `conf_global_vars_s` is offset, and you may retrieve `NULL` or an incorrect value when attempting to retrieve the value of its member variables. You do not need to include this switch with Enterprise Server 3.x, but including it should not cause any harm. `-Wall` options add all the warning options. `-c` specifies files to be compiled to an object file without linking. The second command line specifies the options for the GNU dynamic linker. For example, for Solaris, the line would be `ld -G <object file>.o -o <output file>.so`. `-G` produces a shared object and `-o` generates the output file.

Depending on the location of the source file or the header files, you might also need to specify the directories where these files are located. For example, you can use the `-I` switch with the appropriate directory path to specify where the compiler should search for the header files to be included (for example, `-Insapi/include/base`).

The following list gives selected system compiler and linking options for each platform. It assumes that the source files are in the current directory. You should also check the makefiles provided by Netscape for more information.

- Solaris 2.x (Sun Solaris on SPARC)
    - `gcc -DXP_UNIX -DMCC_HTTPD -DNET_SSL -DSOLARIS -D_REENTRANT -Wall -c` *`<file name>`*`.c`
    - `ld -G` *`<object file>`*`.o -o` *`<output file>`*`.so`
- SunOS 4x (Sun OS)
    - `gcc -DXP_UNIX -DMCC_HTTPD -DNET_SSL -DSUNOS4 -fpic -c` *`<file name>`*`.c`
    - `ld -assert pure-text` *`<object file>`*`.o -o` *`<output file>`*`.so`
- IRIX (Silicon Graphics IRIX)
    - `cc -DXP_UNIX -DMCC_HTTPD -DNET_SSL -DIRIX -D_SGI_MP_SOURCE -fullwarn -c` *`<file name>`*`.c`
    - `ld -32 -shared` *`<object file>`*`.o -o` *`<output file>`*`.so`
- HP-UX (Hewlett-Packard UNIX)
    - `cc -DXP_UNIX -DMCC_HTTPD -DNET_SSL -DHPUX -D_HPUX_SOURCE -Aa +DA1.0 +z -c` *`<file name>`*`.c`
    - `ld -b` *`<object file>`*`.o -o` *`<output file>`*`.so`
- OSF/1 (Digital UNIX)
    - `cc -threads -DXP_UNIX -DMCC_HTTPD -DNET_SSL -DOSF1 -c` *`<file name>`*`.c`
    - `ld -shared -all -expect_unresolved "*"` *`<object file>`*`.o -o` *`<output file>`*`.so`
- AIX
    - `cc -bM:SRE -berok` *`<object file>`*`.o -o` *`<output file>`*`.so -bE:`*`<text file>`*`.exp -lc`
    (`*.exp` is a text file that lists, one per line, the name of each function to be accessed by Netscape Server.)

The AIX version of the server is different from all other versions of the UNIX servers. For example, the AIX version of Server 2.0 does not support threads, because the server was built on AIX 3.x, which itself does not support threads. To compile your NSAPI functions under AIX, you must include a text file that lists all the functions to be exported for Netscape Server. Moreover, you also need to include the Netscape library file that lists all the functions of the server that will be imported into your shared object.

Compiling for Windows

The makefile that comes with the Netscape Server 3.x examples is intended for command-line compiling. You can use `nmake.exe`, the Microsoft Program Maintenance Utility that comes with Microsoft Visual C++, to compile the examples. You can build the examples by running the following command: `namke /f example.mak`. For `nmake.exe` to work properly, it must access all appropriate files. In other words, `nmake.exe` must be able to locate the source files, the NSAPI header and library files, and any other necessary C libraries and include files. You can also modify the makefile that comes with Netscape Server to add your code file to the list of example files. Notice that Netscape's makefile compiles two separate DLLs: `example.dll` and `cgiwatch.dll`. You can use the command-line instructions for these DLLs as a starting point for adding or writing your own makefile.

For Server 3.x, to use Microsoft Developer Studio 4.2's Windows-based interface, you must create a new project and specify its settings. You cannot use the makefile that comes with the examples under Developer Studio. (Microsoft Developer Studio 4.2 uses a different type of a makefile and supports `*.mdp` project files. `*.mdp` files are binary project workspace files.) We will go through the steps of configuring Developer Studio for compiling an NSAPI application shortly.

The makefile that comes with Netscape Server 2.x examples is in the Microsoft Visual C++ 2.0 format. You can also compile this makefile using `nmake.exe`, similar to the process with Server 3.x. Unlike with Server 3.x, however, you can convert the makefile of Server 2.x to the 4.2 format by using Developer Studio. Simply select Open Workshop from the File menu and choose Makefiles (`*.mak`) from the drop-down list box, List Files of Types: Developer Studio then allows you to convert the makefile and save it as a new project file. When you save the new file, it creates a make-file in the new format.

To create your own project and compile a new DLL using Microsoft Developer Studio 4.2, first choose to create a new Project Workshop from New . . . under the File menu. You need to create a DLL(not a Microsoft Foundation Class [MFC] version of DLL). Next, you need to make a few changes in the Project Setting, via the

---

Note ▶

Although the current version of Microsoft Visual C++ is version 5.0, the version of Microsoft Visual C++ discussed in this chapter is based on Visual C++ 4.2, also known as Microsoft Developer Studio 4.2. You should also be able to use Visual C++ 5.0 to compile your NSAPI applications. In fact, the instructions for Visual C++ 5.0 are very similar to the instructions for C++ 4.2 discussed here. Netscape, however, recommends the use of Visual C++ 4.2 for compiling NSAPI and WAI applications for Server 3.x. The server has been tested with Visual C++ 4.2.

Build|Settings . . . option. Under the C/C++ tab, add XP_WIN32, MCC_HTTPD, NET_SSL to the Preprocessor definitions. Make sure that the NET_SSL switch is added for Servers 1.x and 2.x. For Enterprise Server 3.x, you no longer need to specify NET_SSL, but specifying this switch should not cause any problem. Under the Link tab, remove most of the Object/library modules that do not pertain to the code you are writing. For example, you can remove references to ole*.lib if your code does not use OLE, or to odbc*.lib if you do not use ODBC. You also need to add the NSAPI library file to the Object/library list. Add ns-httpd35.lib for Server 3.5.1, ns-httpd30.lib for Server 3.x, libhttpd.lib for Server 2.x, and httpd.lib for Server 1.x. You add this file, because the project needs to have a list of functions and variables that are to be imported. You can find the library file under the <server path>/lib directory for Server 3.x. For servers that predate Server 3.x, you can find the library file in the same directory as the NSAPI examples—that is, <server path>/nsapi/examples. Specify where the file is located if it is not in a path already accessible to the project. Finally, add the appropriate path for the Netscape header files. You can add this path permanently to the Developer Studio by placing it in the list of included file directories under the Tools|Options menu. Choose the Directories tab to insert the new paths.

This procedure addresses the necessary steps for compiling a new DLL for Netscape Server. You may want to review a number of other settings that may optimize your project.

You are now ready to insert the new NSAPI program files into the project (through the Insert|Files menu) and build the DLL. Developer Studio can create two versions of DLL: Win32 Debug for debugging and Win32 Release as a final version that is both smaller and more efficient.

The settings described previously are specific to Microsoft Visual C++. The library file included with the server is intended for Microsoft Visual C++.

The following list provides a quick overview of the steps you have to take to compile your code.

Note ▶

Under Server 3.x, there may be additional library files for NSAPI. For example, the libhttpd.lib file included with Server 3.0 is the same as the release version of ns-httpd30.lib. (This file is different from the libhttpd.lib file that came with Server 2.x.) If you have upgraded the server using the Enterprise Server patch (e.g., 3.0i), however, then the ns-httpd30.lib file is updated but not libhttpd.lib. To make sure that you have the latest updated file, use ns-httpd30.lib when compiling your NSAPI application. With Enterprise Server 3.5.1, you should use ns-httpd35.lib.

1. Set the paths for the Netscape header files to enable the compiler to find them.

2. Include the preprocessor definitions (for example, `XP_WIN32`, `MCC_HTTPD`, and `NET_SSL`).

3. Add the Netscape library module (for example, `ns-httpd35.lib`) to the project.

4. Remove any unnecessary libraries from the project.

5. Compile for a DLL without support for object-oriented C++ libraries (such as MFC).

Registering SAFs

After compiling the program, we register its SAFs with Netscape Server. We must first load the module—that is, write instructions for the server to find and load the program. We also specify which functions, from the shared library or DLL, we want the server actually to use. Next, we specify what the functions need to do and how they should be used by the server. To do so, we declare the SAFs as server directive functions. Loading the module and declaring the SAFs are both accomplished by modifying the **obj.conf** file. We also might have to make other changes based on the type of directive function defined. For example, for a **Service** function, we should specify a content type (`type`) and modify the **mime.types** file to reflect this new content type.

The server can have more than one shared library, and a shared library can include more than one SAF. Each SAF inside a shared library is intended to accomplish a specific server action (that is, work as a unique directive function). For example, your DLL might contain both the **client_hello** and **my_redirect** SAFs (examples written in Chapter 6). The SAFs that you declare are then loaded at the start of the server and placed inside the table of available functions. The server maps the function pointers to a unique character string (defined by the `fn` parameter) that identifies it. The function is then accessible to Netscape Server (that is, the server calls your function at the appropriate time). The directives place the SAF within the server's steps for processing a request. When the server goes through the directives to process a request, it comes upon your directive function. If the request is handled by your function, it passes the appropriate data structures and parameters to your function. It waits for a response (a return value) from your function before continuing to process the request. Your function can be placed anywhere in the list of the directive functions. Normally, you place your function at the top of the list of the functions for its particular directive. Depending on your function's return value and the type of directive, the server continues processing other functions in the directive or skips to the next directive. Figure 7-1 illustrates how your SAF changes the way that the server processes a request.

Your directive function should take the necessary steps to accomplish what you intended. It should also take the appropriate steps expected from a server directive function. For example, if you write an **ObjectType** function, then you should check

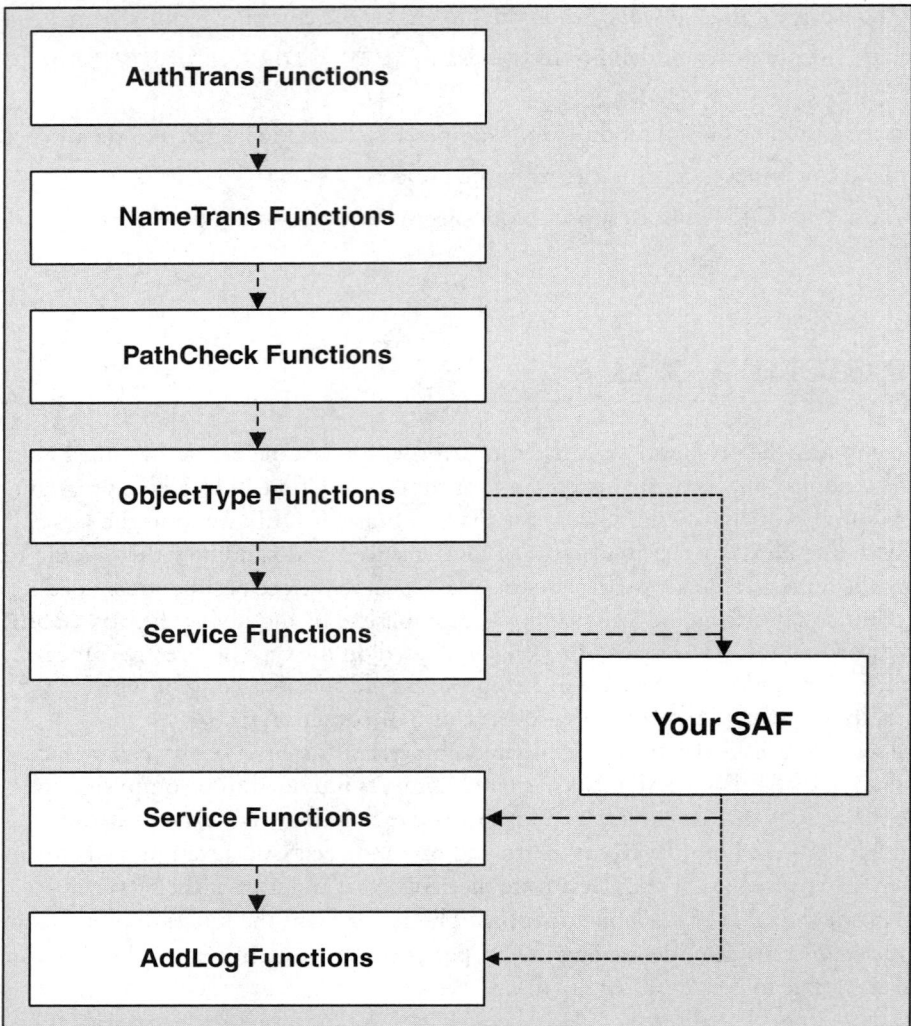

Figure 7-1   Example of Adding Your Service SAF to the List of Directive Functions

for and update `content-type` as needed. If `content-type` does not already exist and your SAF intends to add it, then your function should add `content-type` to `Request->srvrhdrs` and return `REQ_PROCEED`. In Chapter 8, we go through each directive, its purpose, and what your function should accomplish as a particular directive function.

You need to load the modules (the shared library) into the **obj.conf** file by using the built-in **Init** function **load-modules**. (See Appendix B for more details on **load-modules**.) What you actually load is your shared object or DLL file. You also specify the SAFs (modules) in the shared library that you want the server to load.

These modules are the functions you intend the server to use—functions you wish to declare as directive functions in the **obj.conf** file. Your shared library could include more than the SAF modules you intend to declare. These other functions are loaded with the shared library. They are not used until you have listed them in the funcs parameter of the **load-modules** directive function and then declared them as the specific directive functions in the **obj.conf** file. For the Hello Client example (Listing 6-1), if the DLL created was hello.dll, then the following directive function line can be added to the **Init** section of the **obj.conf** file:

```
Init fn="load-modules" funcs="hello_client"
 shlib="c:/netscape/server/nsapi/hello/hello.dll"
```

The order of the **Init** functions does not matter, unless one **Init** function relies on information from another. You manually must update the **obj.conf** file with the previously given line. This function tells the server to link to hello.dll at the start of the server. It also informs the server to look inside the DLL for the **hello_client** function to load the function. The location of the shared library can be anywhere on your machine.

Next, you declare the SAF as a particular directive function in the **obj.conf** file. You must specify the SAF as a directive type for one of the server Objects—most likely the default Object. This specification is done similarly to the way you specify the built-in server functions. The following code is an example of such a declaration for the **hello_client** SAF:

```
Service fn="hello_client" method="GET"
 type="magnus-internal/hello"
```

This function should be placed with the other **Service** functions in the default Object's directive list. **Service** functions should come after **ObjectType** functions and before **AddLog** functions. Only one **Service** function should process a client's request. The server chooses the appropriate function from the list, so the order of the functions within a **Service** directive does not matter. As a rule, unless your SAF relies on another server function from the same directive, you should always place it at the start of the list of each directive's functions.

You may also have to include specific parameters for your SAF. For example, for a **Service** function (such as **hello_client**), you should declare the function's MIME type and method. The type you declare is then used by the server to recognize a request as a request for your function. This declaration is not the MIME type of the document you send to the client, but rather the internal MIME type of your function that is used by the server. magnus-internal is used to specify the MIME type of a function as an internal server type. You also specify a subtype unique to your function. For the **hello_client** function, we declared the type magnus-internal/hello. The server looks to the **mime.types** file to find the extension associated with each type. Thus, in the **mime.types** file, you should declare your server internal type and specify an extension for it. (Under Server 3.x, you can also use the Server Manager to add the MIME type and its extension to the **mime.types** file. See the Server

Preferences|MIME Types option under Server Manager.) For the Hello Client example, we add the following line to the **mime.types** file:

```
type=magnus-internal/hello ext=hi
```

From that point forward, any request to the server for a file of type `*.hi` (for example, `http://<server name>/say.hi`) calls your Hello Client function. As an NSAPI function does not actually exist as a file, the path to this function is not relevant. The URI could include any path—even nonexistent directories. The server always calls your function as long as the file requested includes the correct extension.

For a **Service** function, like the Hello Client example in Chapter 6, we also declare a method comprising the method of the request that your function allows. For **hello_client**, we accept only a GET method. Any request other than a GET method will cause an error. You use wildcards to combine a number of methods. For example, if your function can accept both GET and POST, use `method="(GET|POST)"`.

The SAF function can also include any number of other parameters that you may add for your use. These parameters should also be in the form of `[name]="[value]"`. (Quotes are unnecessary if no space appears in the value.) As already discussed, you can then access these parameters in your SAF through the SAF's first parameter. This approach gives you flexibility in changing variables in the **obj.conf** file instead of hard-coding them in the program. It also allows for easier portability of the code. In other words, you need not change the program and recompile the shared library every time a change is made. For example, in the **my_redirect** functions (Listings 6-2 and 6-3), we pass the new location through the parameter `address`.

Assuming that we have compiled both SAFs, **my_redirect** and **hello_client**, into one shared library, we can load both modules as follows:

```
Init fn="load-modules" funcs="hello_client,my_redirect"
  shlib="c:/netscape/server/nsapi/hello/hello.dll"
```

The only change between this **Init** directive and the earlier one for **hello_client** is the addition of **my_redirect** in the `funcs` parameter.

Next, just as with the **hello_client** function, we declare **my_redirect** as a **Service** function. The following code is an example of this function directive:

```
Service fn="my_redirect" method="(GET|POST|HEAD)"
  type="magnus-internal/redirect"
  address="/test/register.html"
```

> **Warning ▶**
>
> Do not add parentheses around the method type if you have only one method type. `method="(GET)"` can lead to an error. Under Netscape 2.0 FastTrack Server, the server is unable to recognize GET as the method when contained in parentheses. This problem is resolved under Server 3.x.

my_redirect accepts the GET, POST, and HEAD methods. In other words, it responds to all standard methods of request. The MIME type for **my_redirect** is `magnus-internal/redirect`. We must also add the MIME type to the **mime.types** file, as in the following example:

```
type=magnus-internal/redirect exts=new
```

Any request that includes the extension `.new` will now be redirected to the address defined by the address parameter of **my_redirect**. As mentioned earlier, the address parameter is available to **my_redirect** through the SAF's first parameter. If you look back at the **my_redirect** function, you will notice that we used `pblock_findval("address", param)` to get the address we defined here in the **obj.conf** file.

Now you can compile **my_redirect** and **hello_client**, and make the above changes to the **obj.conf** and **mime.types** files so as to test these functions. As with compiling a new shared library, when you make any manual changes to the **obj.conf** file, you should also stop and start the server.

In addition, you should make sure that the name of your function and the MIME type you specify do not already exist. You should verify that your function's name does not conflict with any other existing NSAPI or built-in server function. For **Service** functions, you should make sure that the MIME type and file extension that you specify are not already assigned. Check the **mime.types** file to verify the existing MIME type definitions for your server.

> ### Note ▶
>
> With Server 3.x, you have the options of having your application employ user-level or kernel-level threads. When you load your module using the **load-modules** function, you can use the parameter `NativeThread` to specify that the server should use only user-level threads for your application. By default, the server uses kernel-level threads, whenever possible, for your SAF. By setting the value of `NativeThreads` to `no`, you can tell the server to use user-level threads instead. (For more information on threads, see Chapter 11.
>
> ```
> Init fn="load-modules" funcs="hello_client"
>   shlib="c:/netscape/server/nsapi/hello/hello.dll"
>   NativeThreads="no"
> ```

Alternative to Using the `mime.types` File for Service Functions

For the **Service** function examples in this book, we require the client to invoke our function by using the specified file extension associated with the MIME type. We specify the file extension in the **mime.types** file. Alternatively, you can force the MIME type of the **Service** SAF for a predefined path by using the server's built-in function **force-type**. Instead of requiring the client to invoke your function using the file extension, you can have the client invoke your SAF by requesting the prescribed path. We have already discussed this alternative for CGI applications in Chapter 3. The same method can be applied to your SAF.

Make sure you do not specify a file extension for the MIME type of your function in the **mime.types** file. If you do specify such a file extension, the server may return a server error. When attempting to process the client request, the server expects to find your **Service** function for the file extension. If the request is not for the specified path, the server cannot invoke your program and will therefore return a server error.

The following Hello Client function is invoked whenever the client uses the /hello path.

```
<Object default>
. . .
NameTrans fn=assign-name from="/hello*" name="hello"
. . .
</Object>

<Object name="hello">
ObjectType fn="force-type" type=magnus-internal/hello
Service fn="hello_client" method="GET"
  type="magnus-internal/hello"
</Object>
```

We use the built-in **NameTrans** function **assign-name** to associate the path /hello with the Object hello. In hello, we force the Hello Client MIME type (magnus-internal/hello) for all requests that use the path /hello. The Service function **hello_client** is then invoked to handle all requests for this path. Thus the requested URL http://www.foo.com/hello/, http://www.foo.com/hello/test, and even http://www.foo.com/hello/today/joe, will invoke the **hello_client** function.

Registering for Netscape NT Server 1.x

Under Netscape NT Server 1.x, you register your function in the NT registry—a cumbersome and dangerous process. The registry is a good place to register configuration information about a program that does not need to be updated on a regular basis. (The registry files provide more flexible security and cross referencing.) With Netscape Server, however, the configuration information of the server changes regularly. In fact, you must manually update the configuration information to register your functions. For that reason, Netscape Server 2.x was revised to support NT with the same text-based configuration files (**magnus.conf** and **obj.conf**) that were always used for UNIX. These text files allow one to transfer configuration information easily between different servers and operating systems without having to change the NT registry. **mime.types** was always a text file, so the instructions for updating this file are the same for all versions of the server.

As you no longer use the registry to register your function, we will not discuss this topic in depth here. We will simply provide the following instructions as an example of the procedures for updating the NT registry with your DLL. These instructions are similar to the changes you make to the **obj.conf** file for Server 2.x and later. They do not include any additional changes you must make to the **mime.types** file. The following instructions apply only to Netscape Server 1.1x on NT.

To register the Hello Client example, you need to add `hello.dll` and the **hello_client** SAF to the NT registry. Run `regedt32.exe` to edit the NT registry:

1. Add the key "InitFunction01" to HKEY_LOCAL_MACHINE\\Software\\ Netscape\\<*server name*>\\CurrentVersion\\StartUp. If InitFunction01 already exists, add the string "InitFunction" with a different number as the suffix (for example, as InitFunction02). Select the StartUp folder from the subtree. Then add the new key through the Edit|Add Key menu. Enter the key in the "Key Name" field and leave the "Class" field empty.

2. Add the parameters below as values to the key just added. You add the values through the Edit|Add Value menu. Enter each value, shown on the left side of the list below, in the "Value Name" field (for example, fn). "Data Types" should be left at the default REG_SZ. After pressing OK, enter the corresponding string shown on the right side of the list below (for example, load-modules). If you are adding more than one function to funcs, separate the functions with commas. Note that you first add the information on the left side of the colon (value name) and then, once the OK button is pressed, add the data on the right side (string). You actually do not type in the ":". It is added by the registry editor.

```
fn : load-modules
shlib : c:\netscape\ns-home\nsapi\examples\hello.dll
funcs : hello_client
```

3. Now you are ready to add the **hello_client** function to the **Service** directive in the default Object. Go to the following location (or to where the default Object— the "name: default" value—is located):

```
HKEY_LOCAL_MACHINE\\Software\\Netscape\\<servername>\\
CurrentVersion\\Objects\\Object1
```

4. Check for the Service Directive key under the Directive keys. A Service Directive key should already exist as "DirectiveName: Service." If you do not have a Service Directive key (which is unlikely), add one below the default Object (for example, Object1) key; add the key "Directive04" or whatever consecutive value is suitable for a key coming after the ObjectType key; and also add the value "DirectiveName: Service" to the Directive key.

5. For the Service Directive key, add the **hello_client** function to the Function key. Add a Function key below the Service Directive key as "Function01" (number it so that the function will be at the top of the list of Directive keys for Service).

6. Add the following values to the key you just added:

```
fn : hello_client
method : GET
type : magnus-internal/hello
```

Debugging Your SAF

An NSAPI program does not work alone, but rather in concert with the server. Therefore, two separate debugging concerns arise. The obvious debugging concern has to do with testing, revising, and making sure your code runs properly. You may also want to know how your function works in relation with other server directives. You may want to know how it actually integrates with the server's processing of a request. As you cannot trace through the actual server code, the best way to test how your SAF works with the server is by verifying the changes in the server data structure variables before and after your function. In Chapter 8, we will expand on the program **print_NSAPI_var** (Listing 6-7) to log the server's internal pblock information into a file. By registering this new function before and after your function, you can record changes to the server as the server steps through it. You can even wrap your SAF, using **func_exec**, inside another SAF that records the effect of your function on the server. In the rest of this chapter, however, we will discuss other debugging options available for an NSAPI application.

A simple method of debugging would be to write the appropriate data you are evaluating into a log file. You can print any information you wish at any given time to the error log file by using the **log_error** function. You do not even need to specify the information as errors. You can use the degree LOG_INFORM for instructive log information. For example, you can log a marker to make sure a specific section of code is being used, or place the value of the variable in the file to verify whether it is correct.

Another debugging method is to use the **protocol_status** function to send an error page to the client. You can send a reason string with **protocol_status**, which can include a variable you wish to evaluate. In your code, you need to return the Status-Line information using **protocol_start_response**. (See the redirection example, Listing 6-2, for more detail.) Although this method is the easiest to review (because the result appears in the browser), it does have some drawbacks. The obvious disadvantage is that the client connection is closed and the server has finished responding to a request once the error page is sent. Thus, you cannot continue tracing the request.

Most programmers would not be satisfied with the above methods. They would want to actually set break points and step through code as is normally done. You would want to stop the server before an error occurs and step through code dynamically. Every programmer has also a favorite debugger. To debug a shared library or DLL, the debugger needs to have access to the server's binary files and symbol table as well as to the shared library. Moreover, because the server runs as a process under UNIX and a service under NT, additional debugging steps are needed.

Before we review the options for debugging a UNIX or Windows NSAPI program, you should be aware of some general settings in the **magnus.conf** and **obj.conf** files that may help you in debugging your application. Unless you are specifically testing the use of threads in your program, you should set the number of simultaneous connections—that is, the number of threads—to 1. Under UNIX Server 2.x, you should also set the number of processes to 1. To accomplish this task, you can use the Server Manager or set the specific **magnus.conf** directive manually (for example, via **MaxThreads**, **MaxProcs**, and **RqThrottle**). **MaxThreads** and **MaxProcs** can be used to set the maximum number of threads and processes for UNIX Server 2.x. **RqThrottle** can be used for Server 3.x to set the maximum number of simultaneous transactions (active threads) for the server. Under Server 3.x, you can also reduce the number of **ListenQ**—that is, the number of connection requests to be queued when the server does not have any available threads. (For more information on the **magnus.conf** directives, see Appendix A.) If server caching conflicts with the result you are debugging, you should disable it. For example, you can disable file caching through the **Init** function **cache-init**. (For more information on **cache-init**, see Appendix B.) Finally, to make sure the data are not available to the browser from cache, set the memory and disk cache value of the browser you are using for testing to 0. Under Netscape Navigator 3.x, you can set these values in the Options|Preferences menu under the Cache tab. Under Netscape Communicator 4.x, you can set these values in the Edit|Preferences menu under the Advanced|Cache category.

For Server 3.x, you can set the **KernelThread** directive to on to make the server use only kernel-level threads. Netscape Server 3.x employs a combination of kernel-level and user-level threads whenever possible. Some operating systems may support scheduling of both types of threads natively. In most of these cases, Netscape allows the operating system to schedule these threads natively—for example, for the NT and Solaris versions of the server. In other cases, Netscape may use its own user-level thread model in combination with kernel-level threads—for example, in the IRIX version of Netscape Server 3.x. The standard compilers (and debuggers) cannot recognize these user-level threads; these compilers support kernel or native threads. To enable the kernel-threads-only mode for debugging, add the following line to the **magnus.conf** file: KernelThreads on. (For more information on threads, see Chapter 11.)

You should also make sure that your compiler compiles the debugging information. For instance, for Solaris, you should add the flag -g to the **gcc** command line. For Visual C++, you compile your code for Win32 Debug. There are a number of debugging options under the Build|Settings . . . menu. For example, you can generate browser information through the Browser Info and C/C++ tabs. You can also set the type of debugging information generated by the compiler under the C/C++ tab.

Debugging for UNIX

To debug the server process, first get the process ID of the server. One way to obtain it is to use the **ps** utility (for example, ps -ef | grep ns-httpd). **ps** returns the server's process IDs. If you had set the number of processes and threads to 1, there should be two IDs: one for the parent and another for the child. The higher-numbered process is the child process. For debugging, you can choose from several debuggers on the market. For example, the author uses GDB (the GNU project Debugger). The debugger must attach itself to the running child process, as this process started outside GDB. Run the debugger and use the command **attach** to attach the debugger to the server's process ID (`attach <process ID>`). The debugger also needs to access the symbol table of the server program and your shared libraries debug information. To make the server's binary accessible to the debugger, for example, you can change the current directory to the server's program directory, `<server path>/bin/http[d | s]/`. You are now ready to debug the program. Set the appropriate break points in your code, and instruct the debugger to continue. The debugger should stop when the server accesses the code where you have set the break point.

Debugging for Windows

Netscape Server 1.x does not include a stand-alone executable version of the program that can run from the command line. Consequently, debugging the service application is not straightforward. One way to avoid this problem is to hard-code the line `_asm int 3;` in your program at the point where you wish the server to stop. This assembly-code instruction forces the server to stop with an exception break point. A dialog box should pop up when the server encounters this line of code, stating that an application error has occurred in the server's executable and that a break point has been reached. If you press "Cancel," your debugger (Microsoft Developer Studio) should start. Developer Studio should load the server symbol library and your code and set the break point at the line `_asm int 3;`. A dialog should also pop up, stating that a user break point called from code at [*Hex value*]. You should now be able to step through the rest of the code. Remember to generate a browser information file so as to trace through your source code.

With Server 2.0 and later, Netscape provides an executable version of the server for debugging purposes. The file `httpd.exe` can be found under `<server path>/bin/http[d | s]/`. For Microsoft Developer Studio, under Build|Project Settings, choose the Debug tab and add the path for `httpd.exe` under "Executable for debug session:" (for example, `c:\netscape\server\bin\https\httpd.exe`). For Server 2.x, you also need to include the path for the configuration files (**magnus.conf**, **obj.conf**, and **mime.types**) in the "Program arguments:" (for example, `c:\netscape\server\https-foo\config`). For Server 3.x, you need to include the server ID in the "Program arguments:" (for example, `https-foo`). This step is the only one that you need to take. Now, if you choose Build|Debug, Developer Studio will run `httpd.exe` (not the service application). If you have set any break points, the server stops as soon as the code is reached and returns you to Developer Studio.

Remote Debugging for Windows

You can even use Developer Studio for remote debugging using the standard remote debugging procedure. The following instructions explain how to set up remote debugging with Visual C++ 4.x. Once you set up the local and remote machine, you can start debugging on the local machine.

Instructions for the Local Machine

1. Copy the NSAPI code to the local machine and open the project. When you compile this program, make sure to copy the same DLL to the remote machine. The two DLLs should match.

2. Set the Remote Connection setting from the Tools menu of Developer Studio to "Network (TCP/IP)." Choose the Settings and set the remote machine's name (IP address or DNS name). You can also specify a Debug monitor password here. This password should match the password set in the Debug Monitor that will run on the remote machine.

3. In the Project Settings from the Build menu of Developer Studio under the Debug tab, specify the path to the program you want to run in "Executable for debug session." This path leads to the program on the remote machine. If you connected to the remote machine and mapped the remote directory to a directory on your machine, then use the mapped directory path (for example, `n:\netscape\server\bin\httpd\httpd.exe`). For Server 2.x, also specify the path for the configuration files (**obj.conf** and so on) on the remote machine (for example, `c:\netscape\server\bin\https-foo\config`). This path is based on the path information on the remote machine, not the local machine (for example, `c:\` and not `n:\`). For Server 3.x, specify the server ID of the server on the remote machine. Finally, you need to specify the "Remote executable path and file name" of the file again based on the remote machine (for example, `c:\netscape\server\bin\httpd\httpd.exe`).

4. From the same debug tab, choose "Additional DLL" from the Category drop-down box. Make sure the check box "Try to locate other DLLs" is checked. When you run the debugger, the debugger asks for the local name of matching DLLs that the program will use. If you have a DLL on your machine that you wish to debug, then specify the local file. For example, specify a local file for the remote NSAPI DLL file. It represents the file you compiled on the local machine and copied to the remote machine. Otherwise, just press "Cancel" and let the process continue. Once the debugger asks you for all local machine names for the DLLs, you are ready to debug. If you missed any data during the debugging, you can come to this tab location to change the information.

Instructions for the Remote Machine

1. To run the program on the remote machine, the program must be installed, but not running, on the remote machine. You also need to have the following files on the remote machine: MSVCMON.EXE, SVCRT40.DLL, TLN0COM.DLL, TLN0T.DLL, and DMN0.DLL. If you already have Visual C++ installed on the remote machine, then just look in the bin directory and run MSVCMON.EXE. The important file for the remote machine is MSVCMON.EXE (Visual C++ Debug Monitor). You can find this program under the Visual C++ bin directory.

2. In the Visual C++ Debug Monitor, choose "Network (TCP/IP)," then choose "Settings," and specify the "local" machine's name or IP (where you will be debugging) as the remote machine. You should also specify the same password you used in the "local" machine's Visual C++ "Remote Connection" setup here.

3. Choose "Connect" from the Visual C++ Debug Monitor to connect to the local machine. You should see a dialog box, stating "Connecting . . ." with the button "Disconnect." This action is the only one that you need to take on the remote machine. The remote machine is now waiting for the call from the "local" machine.

Summary

In this chapter, we discussed the methods for compiling, registering, and debugging an NSAPI application. As the options for Windows and UNIX platforms are different, we reviewed the methods for each platform. We also reviewed any option that applies to a specific UNIX platform. Examples from Chapter 6 were expanded to demonstrate the method of registering an SAF.

To implement an NSAPI application, you first have to write and compile your code. You must compile your application into a shared library for UNIX or a DLL for Windows. Next, you must manually update the **obj.conf** file to reflect the shared library or DLL. You also have to register the specific SAFs that you have written in the appropriate location in the **obj.conf** file. Your SAF will operate as a server directive function.

You must make sure that your program runs properly. Therefore, it is important that you thoroughly debug your code before it is activated on the production server.

Chapter 8

SAF and Server Directives

We are now ready to cover the server directives as they relate to writing an SAF. We will examine each directive's intended purpose, and why and how you may write a function for it. This chapter should bring together some of the topics we have discussed in earlier chapters. In Chapter 2, we reviewed the server directives and the built-in server functions. That information will prove very useful here. Understanding how the server works through the existing directive functions is a necessary step in understanding what type of directive function you may write and what the SAF must accomplish for that directive. Each directive has a specific purpose. Your SAF, similar to other server directive functions, should accomplish the tasks set forth by the directive. You also register your functions in much the same way that the server built-in functions are registered in the `obj.conf` file (Chapter 7). In this chapter, the focus is on how and why you may choose to write an SAF for a specific directive.

In conjunction with this chapter, you can also use the information in Chapters 5–7 to gain a complete picture of how to write an SAF. Chapter 5 provided an overview of the essential NSAPI data structures and functions. You will use this information throughout this chapter and whenever you write SAFs. In Chapter 6, we reviewed the types of responses you can send to the client and the types of data you might read from the server. Although we focused on a **Service** function there, much of the information covered is relevant in this discussion as well. For any directive function you might write, you would use some of the steps covered in Chapter 6. Chapter 7 provided instruction for compiling, registering, and debugging your applications. You should use this information to register your SAF.

In this chapter, we will also review the return value of each function. What your function returns has a major bearing on how the server proceeds in stepping through each directive. The server may skip other directives, or other functions in a directive, based on what your function returns.

Server Directives

To write an SAF function, you must first decide what type of functionality you need. The functionality you may want from an SAF function can include more than standard CGI capabilities (that is, reading input from the client, processing the client request, and returning dynamic pages). For example, you may want to write a customized authentication or a logging function. You may even want to provide added features to the server that your CGI programs can use later. As mentioned earlier, you write a function for a specific directive. You provide this added functionality by plugging your directive function into the list of the server directive functions. Similar to how you add the built-in server functions in **obj.conf**, you then add your function. We discussed how you register an SAF in Chapter 7.

The server processes each directive sequentially. A directive defines the type of function to be applied by the server at a specific point in processing a client's request. Netscape specifies eight types of directives. When the server starts, it first runs the **Init** directive functions. It then goes through the default Object's directives (specified in **obj.conf**), usually beginning with **AuthTrans** and ending with **AddLog**. The server processes a request by going through the directive functions specified in the **obj.conf** file. The order of the directives and functions in each directive is important. The directive functions determine how the server processes a request. The server also processes additional Objects defined in the **obj.conf** file. An Object is used to group a set of directives that directs the server to respond in a specific way to a client's request. You can specify an Object by using path information or by naming it. To name an Object, you first specify the name with a **NameTrans** function.

Each directive has a specific purpose and usually works with a specific set of server variables. A server variable may be available for one specific directive, but not for another. Once a directive function changes or adds a server variable, the later functions have access to, and can use, these new data. For some directives, all functions are processed. For others, after a function processes a request, the server skips the rest of that directive's functions and goes to the next directive. In the following sections, we discuss these issues in more detail.

The eight directives are **Init**, **AuthTrans**, **NameTrans**, **PathCheck**, **ObjectType**, **Service**, **AddLog**, and **Error**. With the exception of the **Init** and **Error** functions, all other directive functions listed in the **obj.conf** file are processed for each request in the order specified in this file. The order of the directive functions in the **obj.conf** file should be based on the directive order shown above. **Init** functions are initialized once, at the start of the server. **Error** functions are called only in case of an error and can be called before any other directive—whenever an error occurs.

You write your function for a specific directive based on the information your function needs and the functionality you wish to provide. If you intend to write an authentication program, you can write a **PathCheck** or **AuthTrans** function. When you write an **AuthTrans** function, you normally also specify a **PathCheck** function to allow or deny access to a specific resource. If you plan to write a server Object that requires more than one server directive to accomplish its task (such as CGI or LiveWire Object), you should first name your Object in a **NameTrans** function. You can then write and define your functions for the Object. If you wish to write a function that accesses a specific database and returns a specific page based on the client input, you write a **Service** function. You can also write your own customized logging procedure with an **AddLog** function.

Netscape provides an example of server application functions written for all directives except **Error** under the `<server path>`/nsapi/examples directory. Review these functions to find out how you can take advantage of a function for each directive. The examples we will cover in this book are intended to complement the Netscape examples. Examples that come with the server are mostly intended to illustrate the use of SAF functions for each directive. Here, we intend to provide more practical examples (that is, the kinds of functions you will most likely want to write). We have already written a few **Service** functions (Chapter 6). In this chapter, we will write an **AuthTrans** function and a customized log function. To complement these functions, we will also write a **PathCheck** function for the **AuthTrans** example and an **Init** function for the customized log example.

You should also review the server built-in functions covered in Appendix B. You may find a functionality that you need is already provided in a built-in server function. Moreover, you may also use a built-in function in your program.

Init (Initializing Global Static Variables)

Init functions are initialized and processed at the start of the server. The initialized variables and settings are available as long as the server remains active. **Init** functions always use persistent memory allocation, so the memory is not automatically freed by the server. These functions are called before any request is processed. They are called by the base server (parent), and their resources are inherited by any child process. **Init** functions execute once in the base-parent process.

If you are using a Netscape Server that uses multiple processes, such as UNIX 1.x and 2.x servers, the values of the resources that the **Init** functions initialize are inherited by each child process. If you modify the value of a global variable in a child process, the other child processes still keep the original value (although the value changes for any thread that the child process forks). To modify a global variable in a multiprocess environment, you must use shared memory.

With Netscape Server 3.x, you can use a newly added parameter with all of your **Init** functions, LateInit. When LateInit with the value yes is added to the **Init** function (LateInit="yes"), the function is executed after the server process is forked. If the value of LateInit is no, the function is executed before the fork. When an **Init** function requires the creation of a thread, it should use the LateInit parameter with the value yes. Most NSAPI **Init** functions that you write will use the yes value for this parameter. If your **Init** function must perform an action before the server process is forked, you should use the LateInit="no" parameter for it. For example, if you plan to write to a file owned by the user root, you should set the value of the LateInit parameter to no. This parameter is especially important under the UNIX platform.

You use the server's predefined **Init** function **load-modules** to load your shared library (that is, your SAFs). You can also write your own **Init** function to initialize and load global resources or static variables that can be shared across threads or processes. You can then access these global resources from other directive functions. For example, you can open a connection to a database or open a log file with an **Init** function. The file or database will then stay open waiting for input. You read from the database or log information into the log files (using the global handle for the file or database) from another directive function. You should also initialize a critical section (CRITICAL), a conditional variable (CONDVAR), a semaphore (SEMAPHORE), or a counting semaphore (COUNTING_SEMAPHORE) in an **Init** function. You use the NSAPI function **daemon_atrestart** to free global variables you have initialized in the **Init** function during a server shutdown or restart. For example, in **daemon_atrestart**, you can close a file that was opened in the **Init** function.

A number of differences exist between an **Init** SAF and other SAFs. For example, all of the information available to an **Init** function comes from its first parameter, *param,* and the global variables. Session and Request are NULL. In other words, the only variables available to an **Init** function are the parameters you have declared for the function in the **obj.conf** file and the global variables. **Init** functions also log errors differently than other directives do. When writing an SAF, you normally use the **log_error** function to log errors in the errors log file. For **Init** functions, however, you use **pblock_nvinsert** to insert an error string for the predefined error parameter block entry (for example, pblock_nvinsert ("error", "could not open the file", param) ;). You can also use **ereport** function.

The static variable or global resources that you define with an **Init** function must be safe. For example, you can use a locking mechanism to lock multiple threads from changing the data simultaneously. It is not important to protect a value globally initialized in an **Init** function if you wish only to read the value. If the value needs to be modified, however, a locking mechanism is necessary. Netscape provides a number of functions for protecting the global or shared resources. You can use thread-safe functions (for example, **system_fwrite_atomic** locks a file before writing into it), or any NSAPI function affiliated with threads and semaphores (for example, **crit_init**, **crit_enter**, and **crit_exit**), to lock and manage threads and processes. Under Server 3.x, you are concerned only about threads. Server 3.x does not spawn multiple processes.

When writing an application for UNIX Server 2.x, which uses multiple processes with multiple threads, you are concerned not only with threads, but also with processes that might interfere with one another. Thus the processes also need to be safe. Netscape semaphores are simply interprocess locking mechanisms that use files. The function **sem_init** is used (in an **Init** function) to create a semaphore. Semaphores protect different processes from updating the same resource by providing a locking mechanism applicable to the shared resources in a multiprocess environment. To allocate a shared memory space across all processes, you can use the NSAPI function **shmem_alloc** in the **Init** function. You also free a shared memory region using **shmem_free**.

A semaphore locks a resource for processes, but not for the threads in the same process. Threads in a process or a child process can grab the semaphore ID (with **sem_grab** or **sem_tgrab**) and use it to gain access to the shared resource. To lock a resource from multiple threads in the same process, you need to use a thread-locking mechanism. Your function can then take the necessary action (for example, modify the value of the shared data). After your function is finished, it should release the lock on the thread and semaphore (**sem_release**). Netscape Server 2.01 also supports counting semaphores, which can be incremented and decreased. They more closely resemble the semaphores with which you might be familiar. (See Chapter 11 for more details.)

Netscape Security Model and Client Authentication

Much has been written about authentication, authorization, and the various models of security. Authentication can be seen as the step that verifies the user authentication information by comparing it against a specified source—for example, a user database. Authorization can be seen as the step that enforces the client authentication and allows or denies access. Authorization sets the permissions for a server resource. "Security" is a general term that specifies the mechanism for safety used during authentication and authorization. A detailed discussion of this complex topic is beyond the scope of this book.

Netscape provides a number of methods and means for authentication and authorization for Netscape Server. Each method includes its own pluses and minuses. When providing security for your site, several factors need to be considered. A good model of security requires support for a diverse number of users and groups, flexibility and diversity in the levels of security and the types of resources you can secure, and a guaranteed method of security. You need flexibility and advanced capability regarding for whom the service is provided, which resources need security, and how the security is implemented. Each of the following methods addresses these concerns. To provide the best means of security, you may need to combine these methods and options. For example, an LDAP (Lightweight Directory Access Protocol) directory server can be combined with client certificates supported under SSL 3.0 (Secured Socket Layer) and ACL (Access Control List). An LDAP directory server, such as Netscape Directory Server 3.0, provides the best features for user and group management. Client certificates and SSL provide the strongest method of client authentication. ACL provides a powerful means of authorization. You can use all of these features with Server 3.x. Enterprise Server 3.5.1 supports LDAP version 3. You can also use the new Netscape Directory Server 3.0 with Server 3.5.1. Moreover, with Server 3.x, you can write programs that take advantage of and extend the various security options provided by Netscape. For instance, you can manage users and groups in an LDAP directory by using LDAP SDK (Software Developer Kit). (To take this step, you need to use

Netscape Directory Server supported by Enterprise Server 3.x.) To manage client certificates, you can use the Certificate Mapping API. You can also write your own customized authentication and authorization procedure via the Access Control API.

In this chapter, we will discuss **AuthTrans** as a method of writing customized authentication functions. Netscape Server 3.x provides a much more powerful means of writing authentication or authorization functions, using the Access Control API. As the discussion of this API rightly requires its own document, we have not included it in this book. For more information, you should check the Netscape developer site (DevEdge Online). The document for Access Control API is called Access Control Programmer's Guide, `http://developer.netscape.com/library/documentation/enterprise/accessapi/index.htm`.

Before we write an authentication function for the **AuthTrans** directive, let us briefly review Netscape Server's security methods. The first security method, and one that we will cover in more detail here, is to use an **AuthTrans** function in conjunction with **PathCheck** function. For example, the built-in **AuthTrans** function **basic-ncsa** supports HTTP basic authentication. In other words, the client is required to input a name and password for authorization. Unless other means of security are used, this information is passed through the HTTP protocol specification using base-64 encoding. The user database supported by **basic-ncsa** is the NCSA-style user database or DBM-format user database. Server 3.x uses a local LDAP user database or an LDAP directory server, which is even more powerful and flexible than DBM. **basic-ncsa**, however, does not support LDAP or LDAP directory servers. By including **basic-ncsa** in a specific Object in the **obj.conf** file, you can limit the scope of authentication. You can also write your own **AuthTrans** function as a user-defined **basic-auth** function. We will write an example of such a function shortly. To enforce authentication for the **AuthTrans** function and to deny or allow access to the resource, you should combine the **AuthTrans** function with a **PathCheck** function, such as the built-in server function **require-auth**. Writing an **AuthTrans** function is the easiest way to create customized authentication.

A second method of security is to limit access to resources (files and directories) based on the client's IP or DNS address. Instead of verifying the client through name and password, you can use the client's IP, DNS, or secret-keysize. This way you do not need to ask the client to input authentication information manually. Instead, you can use the information that the browser sends. For example, you can specify a group of clients in the **obj.conf** file for whom you wish to deny access, as in the following code:

```
<Client *.hackers.com>
PathCheck fn=deny-existence
</Client>
```

Client, like an Object, can group specific directives. These instructions deny the existence of resources to clients from `*.hackers.com`. **deny-existence** performs the authorization. (See the Client section in Chapter 2 for more details.)

The third method of providing security is to allow dynamic authentication and authorization as an alternative to centralized authentication and authorization. This approach allows other qualified users to set up their own security settings for their specific directories. For example, as part of the dynamic configuration of the server using .nsconfig files, you can provide dynamic authentication and authorization using the functions **RestrictAccess** and **RequireAuth**. With dynamic configuration, some of the server's configuration settings (such as authorization) can be localized to specific directories. The server looks for these configuration files and uses the information inside the files to append the primary server configuration with these additional instructions. **RestrictAccess** restricts access to directories based on the user's IP or DNS address (much like the second method of authentication described earlier). **RequireAuth** requires client authentication and verifies the client's input against the user database. It is similar to the first authentication method described earlier (that is, the combined efforts of the **AuthTrans basic-ncsa** and **PathCheck require-auth** functions). With Enterprise Server 2.01 and 3.x, you can also use .htaccess files. You must manually enable .htaccess for the server by editing the **obj.conf** file. The .htaccess files support the following directives: **AuthName**, **AuthType**, **AuthUserFile**, **AuthGroupFile**, and **Limit**. (For more information on dynamic configuration, see Appendix D.)

The fourth method of delivering security is through use of ACL. ACL is supported through ACL files and the **PathCheck** function **check-acl**. You can set access control through the Server Manager without manually modifying the **obj.conf** file or writing your own authentication function. For Server 3.x, you set the access control rules under the Server Preferences|Restrict Access menu. You first specify the directory or resource for which you want to set the access rules. Under Server 3.x, you can set a number of different rights (for example, read, write, execute, or delete) for any number of users and groups. You can also limit access based on the host name or IP address of the client. You can specify the authentication method (for example, Basic or SSL) and the authentication database (normally the local database of your server). If you understand the syntax of ACL files, you can extend the access control rules by manually updating the ACL file. For example, you can specify a time when the resource can be accessed. You can also specify access control rules under Server 2.x, which uses **check-acl** and ACL files. The syntax and the options for Server 3.x, however, are different from Server 2.x. Compared with **basic-ncsa**, ACL provides greater built-in flexibility and ease. If you intend to use the built-in **basic-ncsa** function, we recommend using

Warning ▶

You cannot use an LDAP database or Enterprise Server 3.x's local database with .nsconfig or .htaccess files. With .htaccess files, you can use only a NCSA-style user database, similar to the user database supported under Server 1.x. With .nsconfig, you can use either a NCSA-style user database or the DBM files supported under Server 2.x.

check-acl and ACL files instead. The **PathCheck** function **check-acl** does not require an **AuthTrans** function. The authorization and authentication rules are set in the ACL file. **check-acl** is used to enforce these rules for a specific directory or resource. (See Appendix C for more details.)

The fifth, and more advanced, method of providing security is writing your own authorization and authentication scheme using the Access Control API. As already mentioned, Server 3.x provides a new Access Control API that can be seen as an extension of NSAPI. With this API, you can write your own authentication program in C. You can use the API to write your own access control rules for a directory or resource. You can specify your own user database, method of authentication, and rules of authorization. Previous versions of Netscape Server did not include an Access Control API. If you are planning to write an **AuthTrans** function similar to the one we will discuss shortly, consider using the Access Control API for Server 3.x instead. It provides greater functionality and support.

Two other important factors for security are the type of user database and the method of authentication. Server 3.x supports the use of LDAP and an LDAP directory server—for example, Netscape Directory Server. The user or group information for Enterprise Server 3.x is kept inside a local database or any LDAP-based directory server. The local database supported by Enterprise Server is a limited version of Directory Server. LDAP provides even greater functionality and flexibility, as well as additional features. It delivers a centralized directory service for managing users, groups, and access right information. The LDAP protocol works alongside of HTTP protocol. If you are using Netscape Directory Server, you can also take advantage of LDAP SDK. With the LDAP API provided with LDAP SDK, you can write your own LDAP clients that can search and retrieve an entry in the LDAP directory or add, update, delete, or rename an entry in the directory. Enterprise Server 3.5.1 supports LDAP version 3; to take advantage of these newer features, however, you may have to use Netscape Directory Server 3.0 with Enterprise Server.

Two main methods of authentication exist: basic and client certificate authentication (also known as strong authentication). Basic authentication uses the user name and password for authentication. Certificate authentication uses an authorized client certificate (a digital ID) issued by a trusted certificate authority (CA) for authentication. SSL, which is required for certificate authentication, can also be used with the basic method of authentication to ensure secured communication and privacy. SSL is a protocol that runs below the HTTP layer and above the TCP/IP layer. Netscape Server provides support for SSL through its HTTPS protocol. SSL includes procedures for encryption as well as support for certificate authentication. It provides the greatest level of security for your client–server transaction. For example, by enabling SSL on the server, you can have an SSL-enabled client (Navigator 3.0 and above) send the user name and password using SSL encryption. This strategy protects the information sent by the client from any security risk.

A client certificate is the most secured means of authentication. By itself, however, a client certificate does not provide for user and group management or access control rules. You need to combine the client certificate support with other means of user management and access control. For example, you can combine it with access control to limit access to a specific resource. Client certificates can be mapped to a user and employed as a means of authentication. In Server 2.x, the user must send a user name and password along with a certificate to the server. In Server 3.x, the server can use the certificate and digitally signed data sent by the client to allow access to a resource for a user. The digitally signed data are randomly generated for validating the client's security key. Netscape describes this method as single sign-on solution. Under this approach, the client can access different Netscape Servers by using a single certificate. Your server must first require a client certificate for the resource. The server verifies that the client certificate is valid and from a trusted CA. The server then uses the `certmap.conf` file to map the certificate to a user entry in the LDAP directory. The `certmap.conf` file is located under the `<server path>/userdb/` directory. If a certificate is correctly mapped to a user, the client is automatically authenticated. When the client sends the certificate, the server verifies the client's certificate by checking it against the mapped user information. The server then uses the appropriate ACL rule intended for the user to allow or deny access. For the server to verify the client certificate, the certificate must be published in the LDAP directory. For optimal use of the client certificate, you can use Enterprise Server in conjunction with Netscape Directory and Certificate Servers. Netscape Server 3.x also supports the Certificate Mapping API. To find out more about the single sign-on solution, see the Netscape documentation, Single Sign-On Deployment Guide (`http://developer.netscape.com/library/documentation/security/SSO/contents.htm`).

> **Bug Report ▶**
>
> Under Server 2.0, the user must exit and restart the browser after submitting the wrong certificate. With Server 2.01, this problem has been resolved. The SSL session is correctly invalidated when an ACL error occurs.

AuthTrans (Authenticating Clients)

Using **AuthTrans**, you can write a customized authentication application. The easiest method of writing a user-defined authentication function is to use the **AuthTrans** function **basic-auth** with the **PathCheck** function **require-auth**. This method uses the HTTP basic authentication, a simple scheme that is supported by most browsers.

> **Note ▶**
>
> The recommended method of writing an authentication or authorization function with Server 3.x is to use the Access Control API, which provides greater functionality and more features.

With basic authentication, the client is required to input a user name and password for authentication. Once authentication has been established, your manipulation of user information is limited only to your SAF. There are limitations and risks (such as security risks) involved in using the HTTP basic authentication as the sole method of getting the client's name and password. If this issue is a concern, you may want to enhance this option with other security features such as SSL. Here, we will provide a simple example of a user-defined **basic-auth** function that authenticates the client against Windows NT Server (versions 3.51 and 4.0).

If you use your own basic authentication function in conjunction with Netscape's built-in access control (**check-acl**), both functions need to work in concert. The client that you authenticate also needs to authenticate with the server through **check-acl**. In other words, the user or group you authenticated needs to exist in the server database used by **check-acl** and have the appropriate permissions before it can access the resource.

How the Client Gets Authenticated

The actual steps the server goes through to authenticate a user, through the **AuthTrans** and **PathCheck** functions, include multiple runs through the directives. The server goes through the directives the first time the client requests a page. Assuming the client was not authenticated (that is, did not send authentication data), the server reaches the **PathCheck** step and recognizes that authorization is required (that is, **require-auth** is declared). Because the authentication data (`auth-type`, `auth-user`, and so on) are not found, **PathCheck** sets the response status to "401 Unauthorized" and returns the `WWW-Authenticate` header. The server now skips other directives (**ObjectType** and **Service**) and goes straight to **AddLog**. The request needs to be repeated, this time including the authentication (user name and password) information. The following values are an example of the data that **PathCheck** function **require-auth** places inside the `Request->srvhdrs` (server response-header).

```
status="401 Unauthorized"
WWW-authenticate="basic realm=\"my personal server\""
content-type="text/html"
content-length="223"
```

Once the client browser receives this `Unauthorized` page with the `WWW-Authenticate` header, it will ask the user to authenticate. Instead of getting an `Unauthorized` page in the browser, an authentication dialog box appears, asking the user to input a name and password. After the user inputs this information and returns it to the server (by choosing the OK button), the server goes through the directive a second time. The user information is then translated and verified by the **AuthTrans** function. The **AuthTrans** function verifies the value of `user` and `pw` against the user database. This time, the client also sends an authorization header (an HTTP request-header found in `Request->headers`). Here is an example of such a header: authorization=`"Basic am9lOmJveGVy"`. The string after `Basic` is the encrypted [*user name*] : [*password*]. Unless this header is present, the **AuthTrans** functions, **basic-ncsa** and **basic-auth**, are not used for authentication by the server. **basic-auth** does not call your user-defined function (`userfn`) for authentication. If the client was authenticated, whenever the client makes another request to your host server, the client's browser sends the authorization header plus the user name and password. Thus **AuthTrans** continues to verify the client on any future request, unless the client's browser is closed and restarted. (Another instance of the browser program will also require its own authentication.) From now on, however, the authentication occurs behind the scenes. In other words, although the same process is repeated by the server, the user is not aware of the authentication process reoccurring. The authentication information—the name and password—are already available, and the client need not reinput the data. The information is sent by the browser without the client's direct input.

If the user information is correct, the **AuthTrans** function places the `auth-type`, `auth-password`, `auth-db`, and `auth-user` or `auth-group` values in *Request*->vars. If it is incorrect, **AuthTrans** should add nothing. The following is an example of the list of authentication data that an **AuthTrans** function inserts in the *Request*->vars pblock:

```
auth-type="basic"
auth-user="mouse"
auth-db="c:/netscape/server/authdb/default"
auth-password="cheese"
```

This information is set when **AuthTrans** returns `REQ_PROCEED`, which means the user was successfully authenticated. You can write your own **AuthTrans** function as a user-defined **basic-auth** function. If your function returns `REQ_PROCEED`, **basic-auth** automatically updates *Request*->vars with the appropriate user information. With a return of `REQ_PROCEED`, the server skips subsequent **AuthTrans** functions. A `REQ_NOACTION` return does not automatically place the user information in *Request*->vars, so another **AuthTrans** function should authenticate the user or the user should again be prompted to authenticate (in other words, authentication failed). With `REQ_NOACTION`, the server continues processing other **AuthTrans** functions. Remember that **require-auth** denies access and forces the authentication process to recur.

The **PathCheck** function **require-auth** looks for the user information in *Request*->vars. If the user is already authenticated, this information should already be present. If no information is found, then the function again sets the `status` to `Unauthorized`. In other words, the client is required to authenticate again. As its name implies, **require-auth** requires authorization from the client. **PathCheck** sets the status to `Unauthorized` and the server skips from the **PathCheck** directive to the **AddLog** function sending the `Unauthorized` page to the client. With Netscape Navigator 3.x and 4.x, the client sees the dialog box "Authorization failed. Retry?", plus the OK and Cancel buttons. The client can choose to cancel the authentication process or reenter a name and password. If the client opts to cancel, the Unauthorized page specified by the status code set by **PathCheck** will display in the browser. Choosing Cancel here is the same as choosing Cancel in the original authorization dialog box. On the other hand, if the client presses OK, the original authorization dialog box will reappear. With Microsoft Internet Explorer 3.x, if authorization failed, the authentication dialog box will reappear; there is no "Retry" dialog box. As you can see, each browser processes the basic WWW-Authenticate a bit differently.

The **require-auth** function does not actually check for all the specific auth-* variables in Request->vars. It expects auth-type="basic". In your user-defined **basic-auth** function, you do not need to directly insert the auth-* variables in the Request->vars pblock. **basic-auth** takes this step automatically when REQ_PROCEED is returned. If you do insert these variables, however, you will notice that inserting auth-type basic causes **require-auth** to stop requiring authentication. It assumes that everything was verified. If auth-type is available in Request->vars, then **require-auth** lets the request through. Thus the rest of the directive functions are processed by the server and the requested page is sent to the client.

During authentication, a dialog box (similar to the one in Figure 8-1) pops up, prompting the user for a name and password. The text unspecified in the string Enter user name for unspecified at foo: can be customized by defining a value for the realm parameter in **PathCheck**'s **require-auth** function (for example, "mysite"). In this case, server name is foo.

The default Unauthorized page sent by the server includes the following text:

```
Unauthorized

Proper authorization is required for this area. Either
your browser does not perform authorization, or your
authorization has failed.
```

If during authentication the client puts in a name and password that exists in the database, but does not have the specific access privileges being sought, the server returns the appropriate access-denied page (such as Forbidden or Not Found).

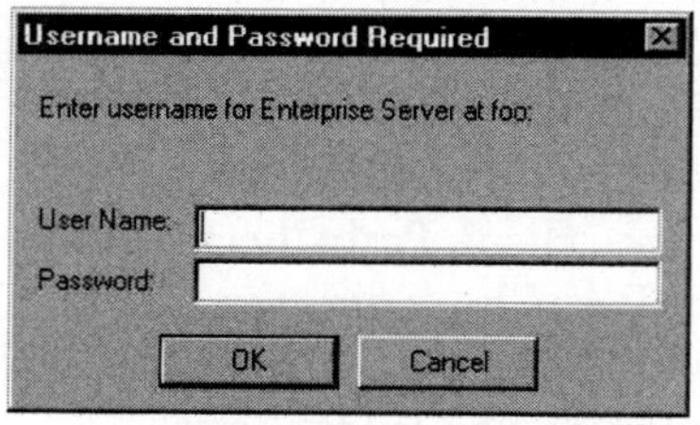

Figure 8-1   Authentication Dialog Box on NT

Writing a User-Defined basic-auth Function

Let us now go through the specifics of writing a user-defined **basic-auth** function. You name your function in the userfn parameter of **basic-auth**. The basic authentication data you need to validate the client are passed to your function by **basic-auth** through the first parameter of your function, param. In other words, client information from the authorization dialog box can be accessed through the param pblock. You can use the standard **pblock_findval** function to access the value of the user's name and password. The user name is found as the value of the pblock entry user. The password is found as the value of pw. For example, pblock_findval("user", param) returns the value of the user name. Once you have this information, you can verify it against your user database. If you return REQ_PROCEED, **basic-auth** places the appropriate auth-* header in the *Request*->vars pblock. The **require-auth** function takes care of the rest.

If you have enabled security, you will have access to a number of additional security-related variables during the **AuthTrans** directive step—for example, cipher, keysize, and secret-keysize. These variables are available through the *Session*->client pblock. For Server 2.01 and later, if you add the **AuthTrans** function **get-sslid** before your **AuthTrans** function, you will also have access to the SSL session ID, ssl-id. Finally, if you are using Netscape Server 3.5.1, you will have access to the distinguished name of the issuer of the client certificate (issuer_dn) and the distinguished name of the user certificate (user_dn). For our examples in this chapter, we will not use any of this information. (See also Chapter 6, NSAPI Variables, for more information on the various NSAPI variables.)

Writing Your Own AuthTrans Function

You can write your own customized authentication and authorization using **AuthTrans** and **PathCheck** functions. In the following scenario, the authentication and authorization steps are split between **AuthTrans** and **PathCheck**, but you can also combine these two steps in one server function (for example, a **PathCheck** function). To force the client to use the HTTP basic user authentication (that is, display the authorization dialog box), you first set the WWW-Authenticate header in *Request*->srvhdrs. Next, you return PROTOCOL_UNAUTHORIZED to the client. You should also return REQ_ABORTED to stop the server from processing any more **PathCheck** functions. The server then sends the header file and the Unauthorized page to the client. This step should normally be performed by a **PathCheck** function.

Next, your **AuthTrans** function (not the user-defined **basic-auth** function) needs to read the authorization header returning in *Request*->headers by using **pblock_findval**. Unlike with **basic-auth**, the server will not skip your function if it fails to find the authorization header in the *Request*->headers pblock. authorization should include the type of authentication (basic) and the encrypted user name and password. You must decrypt the data. The user name and password are encoded in base-64. The format is [user name]:[password]. Once you decrypt the user name and password, you are ready to check the user information against your user database. If the information was correct, you can set the appropriate `auth-*` entries in the pblock `Request->vars`—that is, `auth-type`, `auth-password`, `auth-db`, `auth-user`, or `auth-group`. Use **pblock_nvinsert** to insert the pblock entries into the `vars` pblock. You can include any of these data that you intend to use in your **PathCheck** function. You can also include other data to be passed to your **PathCheck** function.

Your **PathCheck** function can use the information it finds in the `Request->vars` pblock to allow or deny access. For example, it could check to see whether the `auth-user` or `auth-group` pblock entries exist in `Request->vars` and allow access if they do. A **PathCheck** function should return `REQ_PROCEED` or `REQ_NOACTION` to allow the server to continue. Your **PathCheck** function can again use the earlier method of sending the `Unauthorized` page and `WWW-Authenticate` header to force the client to retry.

This discussion has indicated how you can write your own **AuthTrans** and **PathCheck** functions. If your only purpose is to accomplish these steps, then user-defined **basic-auth** and **require-auth** functions may provide a much easier way of reaching your goal. Use the **AuthTrans** and **PathCheck** steps just described in combination with any unique features missing from **basic-auth** and **require-auth** to provide added functionality.

AuthTrans Example

Listing 8-1 uses the HTTP basic user authentication to get the user's name and password. It then checks the user information against the NT user database. We log the user on to the NT machine; if the logging process was successful, then the user name was found. This example is a user-defined **basic-auth** function called **ntauth**. For authorization to work, we must also use the built-in **require-auth** to force authorization, and deny or allow access to the resource. Although this example applies to Windows NT 3.51 and later, you can easily modify it to support other types of authentication.

Below are the lines of code you should insert in the **obj.conf** file to register the NT authentication example in Listing 8-1. According to the following instructions, the example should be compiled into `new.dll` and placed under the `c:/netscape/server/nsapi/examples/new/` directory. Modify the `shlib` parameter of **load-modules** to reflect the name and location of the compiled version of your program. If you added this function to an existing shared library (DLL), then simply add the functions to the list of the functions in the `funcs` parameter. The `userdb` parameter for **basic-auth** is a dummy, as we do not employ a user database in this function. `userdb` is not used by the **ntauth** function, so you can include any value you wish. You can also change `realm` (the parameter for **require-auth**) to display the desired instructions in the authentication dialog box.

```
Init fn=load-modules funcs="ntauth"
  shlib="c:/netscape/server/nsapi/examples/new/new.dll"
```

```
AuthTrans fn=basic-auth userfn=ntauth auth-type=basic
 userdb=none

PathCheck fn=require-auth auth-type=basic
 realm="my personal server"
```

Listing 8-1   NT Authentication Example

```c
/* include the following files if you are using a version
   of Netscape Server earlier than 3.x

   #include "base/pblock.h"
   #include "base/session.h"
   #include "frame/req.h"

   #include "frame/log.h"
*/

/* include this file if you are using Server 3.x */

#include "nsapi.h"

#include <winbase.h>     /* LogonUser */

/* function prototype */
int NTLogin(char *user, char *pw);

/* linked list holds the user name and password */
typedef struct user{
    char name[20];
    char pw[15];
    struct user *next;
} USERLIST;

/* global initialization of the user lists to be used
   for the server lifetime
 */
USERLIST *firstuser = (USERLIST *) NULL;
USERLIST *userx;

/* This function gets the user name and password from the
   user and checks it against a linked list of users. If
   the user name was found, it returns REQ_PROCEED;
   otherwise it checks with the NT user database. If the
   user was still not found, the server continues to ask
   for authentication. You can combine this function with
   the existing Netscape auth.c example included with the
   server package to search in a list of users/passwords.
```

Listing 8-1   NT Authorization Example (*continued*)

```
*/
NSAPI_PUBLIC int ntauth(pblock *param, Session *sn,
                                Request *rq)
{
   USERLIST newuser; /* hold the client name and password */

   /* get the user name and password, which are provided by
      the server
    */
   char *user = pblock_findval("user", param);
   char *pw = pblock_findval("pw", param);

   /* malloc space for new user */
   newuser = (USERLIST *) PERM_MALLOC(sizeof(USERLIST));

   /* initialize the new user */
   strcpy(newuser->name, "");
   strcpy(newuser->pw, "");
   newuser->next = NULL;

   /* initialize the list if it hasn't happened yet */
   if(firstuser == (USERLIST *) NULL)
   {
       firstuser = userx = newuser;
   }
   else
   {
       /* check if user is in the linked list */
       for(userx = firstuser; userx->next != NULL;
           userx = userx->next)
       {
           if((strcmp(user, userx->name) == 0) &&
                       (strcmp(pw, userx->pw) == 0))
           {
               return REQ_PROCEED;
           }
       }

       /* repeat the "if" statement, since the last
          userx data do not go through the above for loop
        */
       if((strcmp(user, userx->name) == 0) &&
                   (strcmp(pw, userx->pw) == 0))
       {
```

Listing 8-1   NT Authorization Example (*continued*)

```
            return REQ_PROCEED;
        }
    }

    /* Call the NTlogin function. If user was verified, then
       add the user to the linked list.
     */
    if(NTLogin(user, pw) == REQ_PROCEED)
    {
        /* point to the new malloced user and then go to it */
        userx->next = newuser;
        userx = newuser;

        strcpy(userx->name, user);
        strcpy(userx->pw, pw);
        userx->next = (USERLIST *) NULL;

        return REQ_PROCEED;
    }
    else
    {
        log_error(LOG_SECURITY, "ntauth", sn, rq,
        "User %s information was not registered under NT",
        user);

        return REQ_NOACTION;
    }

    /* free malloced space */
    PERM_FREE(newuser);
}
/* -------------------- NTLogin -------------------- */
/* this function logs the user to NT, and as a result veri-
   fies the user name and password
 */
int NTLogin(char *user, char *pw)
{
    HANDLE usertoken = NULL;

    /* This function logs the user and returns FALSE upon
       failure. If successful, you receive a handle to a
       token for the logged-on user. You can use
       GetLastError to get error information. LogonUser's
       calling process must have SeTcbPrivilege privilege.
```

Listing 8-1   NT Authorization Example (*continued*)

```
          Here is a brief description of the parameters: first,
          username; second, specifies the domain, ".." means use
          local accounts domain if this machine is not part of
          a domain; third, user password; fourth, type of
          logon: LOGON32_LOGON_BATCH (a batch-type logon),
          LOGON32_LOGON_INTERACTIVE (user must have an active
          connection), LOGON32_LOGON_SERVICE (service-type
          logon); fifth, LOGON32_PROVIDER_DEFAULT, for standard
          logon and recommended; sixth, pointer to variable
          that receives the token handle.
     */
    if (!LogonUserA(user, ".", pw,
               LOGON32_LOGON_INTERACTIVE,
               LOGON32_PROVIDER_DEFAULT, &usertoken))
    {
        return REQ_NOACTION;
    }

    /* close an open object handle; log off the user */
    CloseHandle(usertoken);

    return REQ_PROCEED;
}
```

In Listing 8-1, besides the standard NSAPI include files, we must include `winbase.h` to use the **LogonUserA** function to log the user on to the NT machine. USERLIST is an extra step in this function. Once the user name and password are confirmed through our **NTlogin** function, we add the users to the USERLIST linked list. This way we do not have to call **NTlogin** every time. If the user name is in the list, the user is not repeatedly authenticated by being logged on and off from NT with each request. This function uses a global linked list that holds the authenticated user list; it verifies the user against this list before checking the user against NT. Note that the user's name and password are passed on by the client each time a request is made (thus, a page with four images is requested five times). As this list is maintained in memory on the server, it should be safe from any tampering. However, it is not thread-safe. You should add thread safety by updating this function with the appropriate critical section (CRIT) functions to make sure multiple threads cannot corrupt the user list. (See Chapter 11 for more information on using critical section functions.)

You also have a number of other options. You can input this information in a file and verify the user against the file. This approach is not as efficient but does provide a user file as a secondary list of users that will be always available. For example, you can add the NT user's name and password to an existing user database after authentication. You can then check for the user against this database first before verifying the user information by logging the user into the NT machine. With USERLIST, the information disappears once the server stops.

In the **ntauth** function, we first get the user name and password through the param pblock. We then allocate a new user for USERLIST and initialize it. (Normally, we initialize global variables in an **Init** function.) We use this structure to add the user to the linked list. The next few lines provide standard linked list support. We make sure that a first user appears on the list. If it does not, we add the current user as the first user. Next, we go through the linked list looking for the user. If the user was found, we return REQ_PROCEED. We are then finished, and the server proceeds with the rest of the directives.

If the user was not in the list, we call the **NTlogin** function. This function uses NT's logging API function **LogonUserA** to log the user on to the NT machine. **LogonUserA** returns FALSE if the user information is incorrect and the client fails to log on. In **ntauth**, we verify whether **NTLogin** was successful. If it failed, we log an error string and return REQ_NOACTION. Otherwise, we add the user information to the linked list and return REQ_PROCEED.

Notes on NT User Logon API   With NT 3.51 and later, Microsoft provided a few new Logon API functions (**LogonUser**, **ImpersonateLoggedOnUser**, and **CreateProcessAsUser**). Here, we use **LogonUser**. (For more information on Logon API functions, look in Microsoft's NT API documentation.)

If you are using an earlier version of NT, or you intend to deploy this example on an earlier version, you can use the LAN Manager API to accomplish the same thing. The LAN manager API, found in NETAPI32.DLL, is not part of the core Windows NT networking API. It is included to support LAN Manager 2.x. The LAN Manager API is not network-independent, and some of its functions may not be supported in future releases of NT. (In Windows NT 3.1 and 3.5, there is no nonprivileged service that takes a user name and password and returns an indication of whether the user account password is valid.)

Currently, no NT API is available for checking user's password against SAM (the Secured Database of Users in NT). In our example, we log the user on to NT and authenticate the user based on the success of the LogonUserA function. You can keep the user logged on, but our example logs off the user as soon as authentication is complete.

In general, NT user authentication is not the best way to provide authorization for your server. Although this method provides the advantage of not replicating users, the current NT (version 4.0) user database is not well suited for a complex user database and the Internet. It is limited to the Windows platform and does not scale easily. The NT user database does not provide the features you may need to provide multiple domains with access to various directories for some users depending on their membership in a group, name, password, and other characteristics. This level of complexity can provide interdependencies, can duplicate user names with different accesses, and, in general, requires an intricate level of control. You may also need support for IP and domain name authentication and mixing of locations and user names. NT user authentication is a one-pass-through, flat database that does not distinguish between users and user groups (once a person is authenticated based on the user name or group affiliation, the process of authentication is finished). It also employs a user name and password for authentication and does not support client certificate authentication. Instead, an advanced directory server based on LDAP, the Internet standard (such as Netscape Directory Server), is best suited for complex user and group database management for your Netscape Server. Netscape Directory Server also supports synchronizing your NT directory with the entries in Directory Server. NT 5.0 will also include Active Directory, which is rooted in the LDAP, version 3, standard.

For the user to be logged on, the user must have the right to access the service. Moreover, **LogonUser** requires that the calling process have adequate privileges. A service running in the local system account will include these privileges. Otherwise, you need to add these privileges to the account by using the User Manager (MUSRMGR.EXE). Locate the User Rights Policy dialog box, through User Rights under the Policies menu. Check "Show Advanced User Rights" and select "Act as part of the operating system" from the Rights. You can then grant the needed privilege (SeTcbPrivilege) to the desired account.

NameTrans

A **NameTrans** function should accomplish one or two steps. Primarily, it should translate the requested URI path to a physical path on your system. It can also name a new server Object. As only one **NameTrans** function should set the physical path and return REQ_PROCEED, the order of the **NameTrans** functions is important. Always place your **NameTrans** functions first in the list of the **NameTrans** directive functions.

NameTrans (Determining the System Path)

The **NameTrans** directive is intended for translating a virtual path (the requested URI path) to a physical path. For a **NameTrans** function, the virtual (logical) path is available as ppath (the partial path) in *Request*->vars. The function updates ppath with the appropriate system path. Normally, one **NameTrans** function changes the value of the ppath entry to a physical path and returns REQ_PROCEED. The server then stops processing other **NameTrans** directives and renames ppath as path. In other words, only after the **NameTrans** functions are processed does the server translate (rename) the ppath pblock entry in *Request*->vars as path. The **NameTrans** function should not do this operation directly. The same **NameTrans** function that changes the value of ppath can also specify a base directory for name translation (ntrans-base). For example, the built-in **NameTrans** function **document-root** specifies the ntrans-base directory through its root parameter. **document-root** requires the root parameter, which it uses to determine the actual physical path. For **document-root**, the requested URL does not need to contain a reference to a file.

path is usually the combination of the requested URI path (uri) and the base directory (ntrans-base). For example, in the URL request http://

www.foo.com/new/new.html, the URI path is /new/new.html.
`Request->`vars will include the following pblock entry `ppath: /new/new.html`.
The **NameTrans** function changes the `ppath` entry to reflect the physical path:
`c:/netscape/server/docs/new/new.html`. It also inserts the `ntrans-base` entry, which is `c:/netscape/server/docs`. After the **NameTrans** function returns `REQ_PROCEED`, the server renames the `ppath` entry as `path`.

`ntrans-base` is the name translation's base directory. For standard HTML documents, it is usually the root directory of the documents (`docs`) under your server's directory. You can, however, use Netscape's built-in **NameTrans** functions **assign-name** and **pfx2dir** to specify a different base directory. For example, the default root directory for your documents could be `c:/netscape/server/docs`, and you might want to create a separate base directory for CGI programs and call it `c:/netscape/server/cgi`. Thus the `ntrans-base` entry for a CGI request that is `/cgi/*` will be `c:/netscape/server/cgi` and not `c:/netscape/server/docs/cgi`.

Because `path` gives the full path to the request directory or file, you will use `path` information frequently in your own programs. `path` does not need to include a specific file; it could identify only a directory. The directory path should include a forward slash (`/`) after the name of the last directory, otherwise the server will be unable to process the information correctly. If a file is missing, the server can use other functions to look for a default file in the directory. You can include a reference to the server's home page via the **NameTrans** function **home-page**. The server can also use the **PathCheck** function **find-index** to determine whether an index file should be sent. **find-index** updates the `path` entry to include a reference to an index file. If no index file is found, the server can generate a directory listing using the **Service** functions **index-common** or **index-simple**.

Your **NameTrans** function should not insert a `path` entry into the `Request->`vars pblock. If it attempts to do so, two `path` entries will appear at the end of the **NameTrans** directive. The first one is the entry you inserted, and the second one is the `ppath` entry the server renamed as `path`. The server needs to have a `ppath` directive in `Request->`vars. Otherwise, it returns the following configuration error:

```
process-uri-objects reports: no partial path after object
processing
```

Thus you cannot simply remove the pblock entry for `ppath` and insert a `path` entry into the `Request->`vars pblock. To set the physical path with a **NameTrans** function, you should get the pb_param ppath using **pblock_find**. You can then free the value of the existing `ppath` and insert a new value. Listing 8-2 provides an example of such a code.

Listing 8-2   **NameTrans** Redirect Example

```
/* include the following files if you are using a version of
   Netscape Server earlier than 3.x

   #include "base/pblock.h"
   #include "base/session.h"
   #include "frame/req.h"
*/

/* include this file if you are using Server 3.x */
#include "nsapi.h"

/* route any request for the server to the directory new */
NSAPI_PUBLIC my_ntrans(pblock *param, Session *sn,
                       Request *rq)
{
    char *new_path;  /* holds the new path */
    pb_param *virtual_path; /* holds the ppath */

    /* allocate space for the new path information */
    new_path = (char *) MALLOC(256 * sizeof(char));

    /* copy the new path string into the new_path */
    strcpy(new_path, "c:/netscape/server/docs/new/");

    /* get the pb_param for ppath */
    virtual_path = pblock_find("ppath", rq->vars);

    /* free the value of the ppath */
    FREE(virtual_path->value);

    /* set the value to new path */
    virtual_path->value = new_path;

    /* return success so the server will not
       process any more NameTrans functions
     */
    return REQ_PROCEED;
}
```

If you place the function in Listing 8-2 at the beginning of the **NameTrans** directive functions, the server routes any request to your server to the directory new. Make sure you include the last forward slash in the new_path string. Otherwise, the server will not be able to process the request correctly. The **PathCheck** function **find-index** will try to have the server reprocess the request using a new response location header that includes the forward slash. Because the URI of the request does not match new_path, things can go wrong. For example, if the request was for http:// <server name>, the uri will include only a forward slash. The **find-index** function then sets the location to //, which is incorrect. In this example, we do not include the ntrans-base entry. Or **NameTrans** function works properly without it.

A **NameTrans** function should return REQ_PROCEED when it actually updates ppath with the physical path of the requested resource, so that the server will skip other **NameTrans** functions. Otherwise, a **NameTrans** function should return REQ_NOACTION, which means that the physical path was not set. The server then continues through the **NameTrans** directive functions. You can also change the value of ppath and return REQ_NOACTION. In such a case, the server continues with the rest of the **NameTrans** directive. Another **NameTrans** function can then use this new ppath information. You can use this approach when you would like to change the value of ppath from one virtual path to another.

Built-in **NameTrans** functions are available that provide most of the functionality you need from such a directive. In general, there is no need to write a specific **NameTrans** function. **redirect** and **mozilla-redirect** redirect a client to a new location. **document-root** specifies the server's document root directory and **home-page** the server's home page. (You should always have **document-root** specified in your **obj.conf** file.) **assign-name** and **pfx2dir** map a physical path to a virtual path. Notably, you will use **pfx2dir** to map a physical path on your machine to a specific virtual path. For example, you can associate a request for /additional to a directory on another disk in your machine—for example, d:/moresites/docs/additional/. **assign-name** and **pfx2dir** also allow you to name a new Object and then associate a specific directory to it.

NameTrans (Creating Additional Objects)

The ability to create a server Object represents a powerful tool. There are times when you may want to apply a number of directives to a specific directory or combine different directives for a specific kind of request. In those cases, you can create your own Object to take over from the default Object and process requests in ways that you have declared. These directives will then respond only to the Object you defined. That is, they are not processed as part of the default Object. For example, you may want to provide your own **AuthTrans** or **PathCheck** function for authentication, process the request through a unique **Service** function, and log the information (**AddLog**) in a different file than the default log files. You can create a new Object and declare these directives inside your Object. You name that Object in a **NameTrans** directive inside the default Object. Netscape Server itself declares a number of Objects, including cgi, wincgi, shellcgi, server-applets, and LiveWire. The cgi Object is defined as follows:

```
<Object name="cgi">
ObjectType fn="force-type" type="magnus-internal/cgi"
Service fn="send-cgi"
</Object>
```

In your Object, the server can begin processing the directives with **AuthTrans**. You may also write your own **NameTrans** function instead of using **pfx2dir** and

assign-name, if you wish to pass additional variables to your Object. Remember that the default Object's directive are still called. Therefore, though you may not have specified a certain directive, the server uses the default Object's directive functions to complete the processing of a client request.

The default Object is unique because it is always used by the server, regardless of the request. Unlike other Objects, you identify the default Object with the directive **RootObject** in the **magnus.conf** file. During installation, Netscape names the default Object, `default`. It is recommended that you do not change the name of the default Object. Other Objects are called conditionally (that is, when a specific condition, such as a specific directory request, is met). In other words, a specific Object's directive functions are not called unless that Object is called. When it is called, its directive functions are processed first, before any default Object's directive function.

You could also declare an Object using `ppath` (partial path) information. This type of Object does not use an Object name and does not require a **NameTrans** function. The server processes this Object at the same time that it processes other **NameTrans** directive functions. In other words, when the server finishes processing the **NameTrans** directive functions in the `default` Object, it checks other Objects. If an Object's `ppath` matches the `ppath` information in the *Request*->vars pblock (the requested resource), then the server processes the directive in that Object. `ppath` should have already been modified by the **NameTrans** functions to reflect the physical system path of the resource. An Object's `ppath` should also reflect the physical system path. (See Creating an Object in Chapter 2 for more details.)

The following code is an example of such an Object declared with `ppath`:

```
<Object ppath="c:/netscape/server/docs/special/*">
PathCheck fn="check-acl"
 acl="c:/netscape/server/docs/special/*"
</Object>
```

PathCheck

The **PathCheck** directive has two separate responsibilities. **PathCheck** functions can be used to authenticate the client (for example, **check-acl** or **require-auth**). **PathCheck** functions also verify and update the system path of the request (for example, **nt-uri-clean**, **find-pathinfo**, or **find-index**).

PathCheck (Requiring Authorization)

As mentioned earlier, you could have a **PathCheck** function that handles both authentication and authorization (such as **check-acl**) or that works with an **AuthTrans** function (such as **require-auth**) to enforce authentication and permit access. Unlike other **PathCheck** functions, for Server 2.x, **check-acl** is called before any other **PathCheck** function, regardless of its location in the list of directive functions. For Server 3.x, **check-acl** is called after all other **PathCheck** functions. Because **check-acl** does both authentication and authorization, the value of the `auth-*` pblock entries in `Request->vars` are unavailable until after **check-acl** is called.

The **PathCheck** directive is also instrumental in three other methods of authorization. The **PathCheck** function **deny-existence** is used in combination with a specific client to deny the existence of a requested resource for the client. `Client` is specified using wildcards and IP addresses, DNS addresses, or secret keysizes. (See the Client section in Chapter 2 for more details.) The **PathCheck** function **load-config** enables dynamic configuration using `.nsconfig` files and specifies some of the options of the dynamic configuration (for example, the configuration file's name, base directory, and so on). The actual authorization requires two dynamic configuration functions: **RestrictAccess** and **RequireAuth**. You specify these functions in the `.nsconfig` file. Dynamic configuration using `.htaccess` is implemented as an add-on NSAPI application that you need to manually enable by editing the **obj.conf** file. The shared library or DLL for this application is found under `<server path>/plugins/htaccess`—for example, `htaccess.dll`. The functions you need to include are the **Init** function **htaccess-init** and the **PathCheck** function **htaccess-find**. (See Appendixes B and D for more information.) Netscape also provides **cert2user** and **get-client-cert** functions that support SSL3. **cert2user**, used with Server 2.x, maps the client certificate to a user in a user database. **get-client-cert** gets the client certificate from the SSL3 session and can require the presence of such a certification.

To have a **PathCheck** function require basic authentication and force the client to input a name and password in an authorization dialog box, you need to return an `Unauthorized` page and `WWW-Authenticate header`.

Listing 8-3 is an example of a **PathCheck** function that can replace the **require-auth** function.

Listing 8-3 PathCheck Require Authentication Example

```
NSAPI_PUBLIC my_require(pblock *param, Session *sn,
                        Request *rq)
{
    /* Check for auth-user and auth-password. If found,
       allow access. Otherwise, return WWW-Authenticate
       and status Unauthorized.
     */
    if(pblock_find("auth-user", rq->vars) &&
       pblock_find("auth-password", rq->vars))
    {
        return REQ_PROCEED;
    }
    else
    {
```

Listing 8-3   **PathCheck** Require Authentication Example (*continued*)

```
        pblock_nvinsert("WWW-Authenticate",
                        "basic realm=\"special site\"",
                        rq->srvhdrs);
        protocol_status(sn, rq, PROTOCOL_UNAUTHORIZED, NULL);

        protocol_start_response(sn, rq);

        return REQ_ABORTED;
    }
}
```

Listing 8-3 makes sure `auth-user` and `auth-password` are set in the *Request*->vars pblock. If they are not set, it sets the `WWW-Authenticate` header in the response-header (*Request*->srvhdrs) and returns an `Unauthorized` status. The pblock entries `auth-user` and `auth-password` must have been already inserted by an **AuthTrans** function. As you can see, this function does not verify the authenticity of the user information. You need to write an **AuthTrans** function to perform that task. You can use this function instead of **require-auth** with the **AuthTrans** example in Listing 8-1. Unlike **require-auth**, **my_require** checks for `auth-user` and `auth-password` and not `auth-type` in the *Request*->vars pblock. It does not look for and accept `auth-group`.

PathCheck (Verifying the System Path)

The path information of the requested resource is used and altered by a number of directives. As we have already shown, the path is derived from the client's requested URI path (ppath) and placed in *Request*->vars by a **NameTrans** function. A **PathCheck** function can then verify this system path information and update it when appropriate. **PathCheck** functions make sure the path does not include bad or dangerous characters or lack needed characters. For example, the **PathCheck** functions **nt-uri-clean** and **unix-uri-clean** are used to remove any dangerous or erroneous characters, such as / . /, / . . /, / /, \ . \, \ . . \, or \ \, from the path. Moreover, the **PathCheck** functions can update `path` with additional information necessary for processing a request. For example, the **PathCheck** function **find-index** is used to specify the name of index files. If a requested URL is for a directory but does not include a file name, **find-index** (based on the index names you have specified) looks for the index files in the directory. If such a file is found, it appends the `path` pblock entry with the index name. If **find-index** encounters a directory path without a forward slash at the end of the URL, the function adds it. It returns `REQ_ABORTED` and sets the response-header location to `http://<server name>/[URI path]/` (note the forward slash). The server then reprocesses the request, this time using the new URL.

The **ObjectType** function uses `path` to verify `content-type` (the MIME type of the requested data). **ObjectType** normally uses the file extension of the requested file as specified in `path` and the information in the **mime.types** file, thereby creating the response-header `content-type`. The **Service** functions, in turn, use this MIME type information to identify whether a specific **Service** function should be used. A **Service** function usually includes a `type` parameter that specifies the MIME types to which the function should be applied. Normally, if a file is not of the type `magnus-internal`, then the server uses the **Service** built-in function **send-file** to send the contents of the file to the client. Files of type `magnus-internal` (such as CGI, ShellCGI, and your SAF) are processed differently.

If you need to verify the path of the requested resource before it is processed by the **Service** or **ObjectType** functions, you should write a **PathCheck** function. For example, you might write a **PathCheck** function that provides extra path information for a **Service** SAF. The **PathCheck** function **find-pathinfo** produces the extra path information (the CGI environment variable `PATH_INFO`) for the CGI program, but does not support your user-defined **Service** SAF. As mentioned previously, you cannot use extra path information with an NSAPI **Service** function. If a request for your SAF function includes extra path information, the information is seen as part of the actual path. The server searches the extra path information for the appropriate file or directory. No built-in function removes the extra path information from an NSAPI application path. Normally, the server uses the file extension you specified in the **mime.types** file and the MIME type you specified in the `type` parameter of your function to recognize the request as one for your function. If extra path information is present, the server will not identify the correct file extension and your function will not be called.

You can write a function, such as **find_saf_pathinfo**, that reads the value of `path` from `Request->vars` and extracts the appropriate extra path information from the path string. The extra path information should appear after the file extension you have specified for the SAF function. For example, the extra path information in "`http://<server name>/safprogram.run/extra/path`" is "`/extra/path`" and the file extension for the SAF is "`run`." The server automatically removes the query string if one appears in the URL string.

An easy way to let **find_saf_pathinfo** know of SAF file extensions is to include the extension as a parameter to the **find_saf_pathinfo** function in the **obj.conf** file. Your program can then get this extension and look for it in the `path` string. Next, the extra path information should be removed from the string and inserted as a new pblock entry (for example, `saf-pathinfo`) in the `Request->vars` pblock. In this way, **ObjectType** functions can correctly identify the `content-type` of the request. The server will rightly call your **Service** function. Your SAF, in turn, can use the extra path information in `Request->vars` as it deems fit. The server caches the `stat` information of the current path. If you use **stat** and modify the path information, you should make sure to update `stat` for the file with the NSAPI function **request_stat_path**.

When a **PathCheck** function returns `REQ_PROCEED` or `REQ_NOACTION`, the server continues to process other **PathCheck** functions. As **PathCheck** functions accomplish multiple tasks, it is important for the server to process all of them. Return `REQ_PROCEED` when your **PathCheck** function is instrumental in processing the request—for example, when your function actually changes the `path` pblock entry. Return `REQ_NOACTION` when you simply want the server to skip your function, because it is not appropriate for the request. In either case, the server continues with other **PathCheck** functions. To require authorization, however, you should return `REQ_ABORTED`. With `REQ_ABORTED`, the server stops processing other **PathCheck** functions and proceeds to **AddLog**. It should return the appropriate page and headers set by your **PathCheck** function (that is, the `Unauthorized` page, `WWW-Authenticate` response-header, and so on).

ObjectType (Specifying MIME Types)

To this point, **NameTrans** has added the `path` entry to the `Request->vars` pblock. **PathCheck** verified and updated `path`. Now the **ObjectType** functions will use this path information to ascertain the MIME type of the request file. One **ObjectType** function then places the appropriate MIME type information in `Request->srvhdrs`. In other words, the **ObjectType** function determines the MIME type of the file to be returned to the client. These types of functions set the response-header `content-type`. MIME type information always includes `content-type` information, but it can also include `content-encoding`, `content-language`, and `magnus-charset`. The **ObjectType** function normally uses the file extension of the requested file, specified in `path`, and the MIME type specified for that file extension (in the **mime.types** file), to identify the resource's MIME information. The **ObjectType** built-in function **type-by-extension** performs this task for all file extensions specified in **mime.types**. If no type is found, the built-in function **force-type** enforces the default MIME types you specified.

For **ObjectType** to identify the correct MIME type, the **mime.types** file must include the MIME information for the file extension and the path must include the proper file extension. If you do not want to use this method to set `content-type`, you can use the built-in server function **type-by-exp** to map a MIME type (such as `content-type`) to a unique expression in the path. For example, with `ObjectType fn=type-by-exp exp=*.other type=text/html`, you can associate to HTML `content-type` (`text/html`) all files with the `.other` extension.

Only one **ObjectType** function should set the MIME type information. If a function finds that `content-type` is already defined in `Request->srvhdrs`, it should do nothing and return `REQ_NOACTION`. On the other hand, if your **ObjectType** function sets `content-type`, then you should return `REQ_PROCEED`. In either case, the server continues to process other **ObjectType** functions. Once `content-type` is set, however, other functions return `REQ_NOACTION` and do not reset the `content-type`. The order of **ObjectType** functions is important. Set your function as the first **ObjectType** function to ensure that your function always sets the `content-type` first, when appropriate. You can view **ObjectType** functions as a list of MIME types that the server goes through in order to find the right one for the requested path.

You may sometimes need to reset the MIME type that was already set by the **ObjectType** function—for example, when you write your own **Service** function and plan to return dynamic HTML pages. In Chapter 6, we mentioned that, to return an HTML page to a client, you had to remove the existing `content-type` and insert the `content-type` of the file to be returned. This situation occurs because the MIME type was already set by the **ObjectType** function. The **ObjectType** function **type-by-extension** used the extension of your SAF function and the MIME type you specified in the **mime.types** file to set the server response-header `content-type` to the `magnus-internal` MIME type of your SAF. This information is important for the server. The server uses `content-type` to identify your SAF and call your function for the request. It compares the `content-type` of your SAF with the `type` parameter you specified for your function in the **obj.conf** file. If they match, then your function is used as the **Service** function that processes the request.

Service (Processing Requests and Returning Pages)

Service functions lie at the heart of a server's response procedure. They determine how the server sends the requested response to the client. **Service** functions process and send data to the client. In Chapter 6, we wrote a few examples of **Service** functions and illustrated some of their main features. In Chapter 7, we went through the steps of installing some of the examples. In this chapter, we will expand our previous discussion. Chapter 9 will include a number of more advanced examples.

For a **Service** function, you can write programs that read the client's input or other request-specific data. We reviewed the types of data (such as the server variables) available to your function in Chapter 6. Your SAF can use this information to produce the appropriate response, such as a dynamically generated HTML page. For example, you can use the `accept` entry in the *Request*->`headers` pblock to identify the MIME types that the client's browser can accept. The following code is an accept header from Netscape Communicator 4.04:

```
"image/gif, image/x-xbitmap, image/jpeg, image/pjpeg,
image/png, */*"
```

Unfortunately, this information is not very useful, as it states that Communicator can accept any MIME type—that is, `*/*`. What you can use from this list is Communicator's ability to accept a number of image types, for example, `image/jpeg` and `image/pjpeg`. Thus you can send a JPEG file instead of a GIF file to the client.

Once you have ascertained the appropriate request information and have verified and decoded the client input, you can use the procedure described in Chapter 6 to return an HTML page. For both `POST` and `GET` methods, the client's input is URL-encoded. You must decode this information before you can use it. In Chapter 9, we will go through additional examples that process input from the `GET` and `POST` methods.

A client's request can require extra steps from your function. For example, the client could request a search of a database. Your function connects to the database and makes the appropriate search. It then uses the information returned by the database to generate the response page for the client. You can use the result of an SQL query to generate a dynamic HTML table that lists the results of the request. A **Service** function can take advantage of a number of other resources, such as existing files, databases, or other programs.

Netscape provides built-in **Service** functions that support standard HTTP processing of a request. For example, **send-file** sends the content of a request file directly to the client. Most of your site's static files (for example, HTML, text, graphic, multimedia, and so on) are sent to the client via **send-file**. Files are usually mapped in memory and sent to the client. A number of other **Service** functions support other programming options so as to dynamically generate pages (for example, **imagemap**, **parse-html**, **query-handler**, **send-cgi**, **send-wincgi**, and **send-shellcgi**). There are also specific files for remote file manipulation under Server 2.x or 3.x (**make-dir**, **list-dir**, **delete-file**, and so on) and Web publishing (content management) under Server 3.x (**CM_Edit, CM_Copy, CM_Put, CM_Get,** and so on). These built-in functions provide support for additional HTTP methods, such as PUT, and DELETE.

Unique to all **Service** functions are the two specific optional parameters: type and method. This information is especially important when you are writing your own **Service** functions.

type is a MIME type that you specify for your program in the **obj.conf** file. You can also use wildcards to specify a pattern of MIME types that your function supports. The server uses the MIME type set by the **ObjectType** function to identify which **Service** function should process the request. The MIME type of the **Service** function should match the MIME type that was set by the **ObjectType** directive. If the **ObjectType** directive was unable to specify the MIME type (for example, if no **ObjectType** function was used), the server always uses the first function in the list of **Service** functions to process all requests. For instance, if you had specified the **Service** function Hello Client (Listing 6-1) as the first **Service** function, and the MIME type was not set by an **ObjectType** function, then the server would always run this function, regardless of the request. Without the correct MIME type, your function is not called. No single **Service** function will process all requests. Therefore, no single MIME type is appropriate for all **Service** functions.

You identify a **Service** function that you write with a magnus-internal MIME type. The server uses magnus-internal to specify the MIME types that require unique processing (for example, magnus-internal/cgi for CGI programs). For example, we specified the MIME type magnus-internal/hello for the Hello Client example (Listing 6-1). Because you normally use file extensions to identify a MIME type, you also need to specify a unique extension for your function in the **mime.types** file. The built-in **ObjectType** function **type-by-extension** uses the file extension in the path entry found in *Request*->vars to identify the MIME types. **type-by-extension** uses the information in **mime.types** to make the correct file type association.

The MIME type associated with your function, however, is normally not the MIME type of the data you will return. Therefore, your function must remove `content-type` before returning the data (for example, an HTML page). **ObjectType** determines the `content-type` for the response-header by using the file extension intended for your program and the MIME type you specified for the file extension. Thus, the response-header's `content-type` will reflect your function's `content-type`. When you wish to return an HTML page, you must specify an HTML `content-type`. Although the MIME type specified by the **ObjectType** function is essential for the server to be able to call your function, it is not appropriate for the response-header. Therefore, in your function, you must remove this MIME type and insert the MIME type of the data you are returning in `Request->srvhdrs`.

method specifies the request methods that the function will accept. As with `type`, you can use wildcards to specify more than one method. For example, if your function accepts only `GET` and `HEAD` methods, you can add the parameter `method="(GET|HEAD)"` to your function. If no `method` is specified, then the function accepts all methods. If the request does not use the specified `method`, then the function will not process the request and sends an error.

The common HTTP methods are `POST`, `GET`, `HEAD`, and `PUT`, each of which delivers the client input differently. If your function accepts more than one method, you need to take separate steps in processing each method. You first need to identify the type of method used by the client by checking for the `method` entry in the `Request->reqpb` pblock. Next, for a `GET` method, you can look for client's input in the `query` entry in `Request->reqpb`. For a `POST` method, you can read the data from the network buffer found in `Session->inbuf`. These data are both URL-encoded, so you also need to decode them.

The server looks for the appropriate **Service** function in the list of the functions, inside the **obj.conf** file. Once the appropriate function is found, that function attempts to finish the request and return the response to the client. If the function was able to process the request successfully, it should return `REQ_PROCEED`. The server then stops processing other **Service** functions and goes to the **AddLog** directive. If a **Service** function returns `REQ_NOACTION`, the server continues through the other **Service** functions.

Normally, only one function is called by the server, and that function alone processes the request. You may return `REQ_NOACTION`, if two different SAFs respond to a particular MIME type. If you do not return the correct value, the client will receive mixed messages. We will look at two scenarios where `REQ_NOACTION` is returned by an SAF. This information should be instructional in your understanding of how the server processes a request. In these scenarios, your function returns `REQ_NOACTION`, with none of your other SAFs intervening. In most circumstances, this action leads to an error or a wrong response. No built-in server function is available to finish your SAF properly. You can, however, write another SAF that will finish your request. If your function intends to rely on a built-in server function to finish the request properly, then it must make all appropriate changes to the server variables and expect this follow-up function to send a response. For example, as your function no longer finishes the response, it must change the `path` variables in `Request->vars` and the `type` variable in `Request->srvhdrs` to reflect the information needed by the later function. For the follow-up function to be called, its `type` must match the MIME type set in `Request->srvhdrs`. As the URL path to your function is appropriate only for your SAF, no other built-in server can use this information to return a page, unless your functions change it. In the first scenario, we assume that your SAF comes before other **Service** functions. The second scenario assumes that your function is the last function in the list of **Service** functions.

The first scenario: If you return `REQ_NOACTION` before setting a new `content-type`, the server returns a server error. No other function is usually specified to process the client's requested MIME type (that is, your function's MIME type). If you change the response-header `content-type` to an acceptable type for a later function, the follow-up function finishes the request. For example, if you change `content-type` to `text/html`, the built-in **Service** function **send-file** is called. A problem arises, however. **send-file** is unable to find a file for the client's request of your SAF, so it returns a `Not Found` page. Your SAF is an internal server type, and is therefore processed differently from other documents in your site. When a client requests your SAF using the extension associated with your program, it is not actually asking for a specific physical document on your site. If your SAF actually sends a page to the client and also returns `REQ_NOACTION` afterward, the server first sends the data you returned. **send-file** then processes the request and returns the `Not Found` page. Thus the client will receive a page with two parts. The first half of the page includes the data you sent; the second half includes the body of the **send-file**'s `Not Found` page.

The second scenario: Your function—the last **Service** function in the list—processes a request and returns `REQ_NOACTION`. Unless the request is a `HEAD` request, the server automatically sees this return as an error. In other words, if the client requests a page using a `GET` method and your function does not send a page and return `REQ_PROCEED`, the server assumes that the request was not processed properly. One of the **Service** functions must send a page and return `REQ_PROCEED`, even if you return a page to the client before you return `REQ_NOACTION`. What you return is sent to the client but, because your function has returned `REQ_NOACTION`, the server still sees an error and sends an error page. If you set the status to `OK`, independent of whether you send the header or other data to the client, the server returns the reason string `OK` plus an error message: "`An error has occurred.`" In other words, if you return a dynamic page while also returning `REQ_NOACTION`, the client receives your page in the first half of the page and the body of the error page as the second half.

> ### Note ▶
>
> For NSAPI **Service** functions that respond to client form input, you may want to add a simple algorithm for handling requests that invoke your program directly instead of using the form. For example, you can redirect the client to an HTML form, if the client invoked the program directly.

You can also return REQ_ABORTED, REQ_EXIT, and REQ_RESTART. Use REQ_ABORTED if an error occurred and you want the server to return an error page to the client. With REQ_EXIT, the server does not return any more data to the client. Unless you have already sent the data, the client will receive nothing. You should be careful when you return REQ_RESTART. With REQ_RESTART, the server goes through the directives again, with the data from the previous request remaining in the server data structures. If your function repeatedly returns REQ_RESTART, the server can become stuck in an endless loop.

AddLog (Producing Customized Log Files)

AddLog functions allow you to create customized log files. Because most NSAPI variables remain available in an **AddLog** directive, you can write your own customized function and log any of these variables. The most common and useful log files produced by the server are the access and errors log files. access contains customizable information about the client's access (such as who accessed your site, when, from where, and what they requested). errors holds information about the server actions. In particular, it records any error that occurs during server's lifetime. (See AddLog in Chapter 2 for more details.)

For the access file, Netscape provides a number of alternatives for customizing the logged information. You can use the **Init** function **flex-init** to customize these data (see the flex-init and Formatting Log Files section in Appendix B). You can specify a number of options through **flex-init**. For example, you can require the server to log the name of the client's browser.

You can also use the Server Manager to view, customize, or generate log reports. Under Server Status, you can choose to view access or errors log files, monitor server activity, archive the log file, set log preferences, and generate a log report. Netscape also provides some rudimentary programs, under the <server path>/extras/log-anly directory, for analyzing the access file. In addition other third-party programs, such as WebTrends by Software, Inc., deliver advanced log analysis reports.

In case of an error, you have the option of logging a specific error message in the errors log file. You can use the **log_error** function, described in Chapter 6, to log an error degree with a reason string. This option does not change the actual processing of the client's request or set the response status. **protocol_status** sets the response status. In other words, logging information in the errors log file does not interfere with the server's processing of the request; it simply provides logging support. You can also log information that is not an error, such as specific information that you may later review for debugging or testing purposes.

Even with the options that Netscape Server provides, you may still want to write your own customized log function. For example, you may want to log an NSAPI variable that is not available through a **flex-init** option. You may also want to filter logged information. For example, you can specify that no information from a predefined group of clients should be logged. You can filter the data before they are logged, using a customized log function, or afterward, using a program that supports filtering options as part of log analysis.

An example of an **AddLog** function that logs information otherwise unavailable through the server's log file is the program `nosy.c`. The information delivered with this program was not available with Netscape Server 1.x's default `access` log file. You can find this program on the Netscape Web site. This program includes two functions: **nosy_init** and **nosy_log**. **nosy_init** is an **Init** function that opens the file for logging. **nosy_log** is an **AddLog** function that logs the appropriate information. For Windows NT, you can find this example under "Sample NSAPI to create a referrer log in NT" (`http://help.netscape.com/kb/server/960513-64.html`). For UNIX, you can find this example under "Sample NSAPI to create a referrer log in Unix" (`http://help.netscape.com/kb/server/960513-87.html`).

`nosy.c` logs the location from which a client came. In other words, it records the location of the previous site (page) that referred the client to your site (page). Netscape Server 1.x did not allow automatic logging of the `referer` header sent by the client. If you wanted to write the `referer` information into a file, you had to write your own **AddLog** function. `nosy.c` is such a program. With Netscape Server 2.0 and later, this program is no longer necessary, because you can customize the server to log the `referer` information. (For Netscape 3.x, you can initiate this setting through the Server Manager's Server Status|Log Preferences menu or through **flex-init** options.)

`referer` is an entry in *Request*->headers. It is sent by the client and specifies the URL from which the current request is made. It can be used to record the place from which each client of your site was referred. If you notice a link frequently listed as a `referer` link, then that page probably has a link to your site. `nosy.c` also logs information about the current requested URI, the client's DNS, and the client's user-agent (browser).

Steps for Writing a Customized Log Program

If you look at `nosy.c` or the `addlog.c` function that comes with Netscape Server, you will notice that they take certain steps. You normally take the following actions to write a customized log function:

1. Declare a global file descriptor that can be shared between processes (`static SYS_FILE`).
2. Open the log file in an **Init** function (**system_fopenWA**).
3. Close the file in case of restart or shutdown (**daemon_atrestart**).
4. Write another directive function (usually an **AddLog** function) to log the data.
5. Collect the desired data.
6. Write the information into the log file (**system_fwrite_atomic**).

To write the most efficient log file, you should write two separate SAFs. First, you need to declare a file descriptor as a global static variable. This variable can then be accessed by any SAF. You should open the file for writing and appending in an **Init** SAF. Thus the file is opened once at the start of the server and remains open until the server is shut down or restarted. You can also use the same procedure to open a connection to a database. In case of a restart or shutdown, you can use **daemon_atrestart** to call another function that will close the file.

Under UNIX, the server normally starts as root. If you are running the server as nobody or as a specific Web user, you need to change the owner or mode to enable the user (server) to write to the log file. The server does not carry out this step automatically. Use **chown** or **chmod** on the log file, after it is opened, to enable the server to write to it.

In the second SAF, you collect the appropriate information and log it. Although the second SAF can be declared as any directive function, the typical directive for logging is **AddLog**. Unlike the **Init** function, this SAF is called for every request. Remember that the server attempts to go through all the directives except **Init** and **Error** each time a request is made. This SAF uses the already-declared file descriptor to write to a file immediately. To make sure that your program is thread-safe, you should use **system_fwrite_atomic** to lock the file while you are writing into it. You can also protect your program using the NSAPI critical section, thread, or semaphore data structures and functions.

Customized Log Example

Listing 8-4 is similar to a program written by Basil Hashim (currently Product Manager for Netscape Enterprise Server 3.x). You can find Hashim's example, "sdump, an NSAPI Function to Write Session Data to a File," under http://help.netscape.com/kb/server/960513-90.html.

Our program is an extension of a previous example, **print_NSAPI_var** (Listing 6-7). **print_NSAPI_var** is a **Service** function and, as such, can access only the pblock entries available to a **Service** directive. It writes the entry information into an HTML page that is then sent to the client. Similar to **print_NSAPI_var**, Listing 8-4 uses **pblock_pblock2str** to turn the server's pblock data structure entries into strings. Because it writes the result into a file, however, the new program is more flexible. You can register a customized log function as any type of directive function. You can also log data while the server is processing the client's request. Unlike with **print_NSAPI_var**, which actually takes over the processing of the request to return a page to the client, the process of logging can work in the background. It does not need to interfere with the server response. Consequently, you can log information about any number of server responses. Listing 8-4 logs the various server variables for the specified directive stage during the server's normal response. You can then review the information at your convenience.

Following the instructions given earlier, we write two functions. **log_init** opens the log file. **pblock_log** writes the server pblocks' entries into the file. When you register these two SAF functions, you register the **Init** function once in the obj.conf file where other **Init** functions are registered; in contrast, you can register the **pblock_log** function as any directive function. You can also have many **pblock_log** functions registered for the same or different directives at the same time.

Listing 8-4 logs NSAPI variables found in the standard server's pblock data structures: *Session*->client, *Request*->vars, *Request*->reqpb, *Request*->headers, and *Request*->srvhdrs. This function could be used for debugging purposes or to review how the server processes each request.

The benefit of logging the server information at the **AddLog** directive is that the server has already gone through the other directives. Therefore, the pblock entries now reflect their final values. As **AddLog** functions come after the **Service** function, the NSAPI variables also include the information about the server's response-headers. **AddLog** functions log the result of the server's response after the request is processed (that is, after the data are sent to the client). They are called after the server stops communicating with the client. Because not all NSAPI variables are available during the **AddLog** step, and because directive functions can change the value of a variable, it is instructional to find out the values of these variables during each directive.

As already mentioned, you can declare a customized log function as any directive function. By selecting which directive function you declare the **pblock_log** for, you can access the particular NSAPI variables available during that directive stage. The declaration of an SAF as a specific directive type does not mean that it is required to act in the same way as that directive type function. Normally, we write an SAF for a specific directive, and our function should accomplish the directive's intended purpose. In this example, however, we write a directive function that can be used for all directives. As the purpose of this function is to record the changes in the server (NSAPI) variables during each directive stage, we need to declare this function at each stage (that is, as different directive functions). The logging of the server variables occurs alongside of the server's response. This process is, of course, the intention of any **AddLog** or logging function. The server steps through the functions in the **obj.conf** file mostly in the order they are listed. When you specify **pblock_log** as a specific directive function, the server calls the function during that directive's step.

For **pblock_log**, you should specify the name parameter. The value of name is then written into the log file. You use this information to label where in the list of the directive functions you have declared the **pblock_log** function. For example, by declaring the **pblock_log** function as a **NameTrans** function and declaring the name variable as NameTrans, you can identify the logged variables as variables during a **NameTrans** directive. Typically, you should register **pblock_log** as the first or last function in the list of the directive's functions.

Listing 8-4 also allows you to find out what changes are made by a specific directive function. By declaring the **pblock_log** function before and after a function, you can record the changes that the function makes. For example, by declaring **pblock_log** before a **NameTrans** function as NameTrans1 and after the function as NameTrans2, you can log the NSAPI variables before and after the function. You can then examine this information to evaluate any changes that the specific **NameTrans** function made.

Because the use of the name parameter is essential for identifying correctly the information in the log file, **pblock_log** requires you to specify a name parameter. You should also specify a different name for this mandatory parameter each time you register **pblock_log** in the **obj.conf** file.

By default, **pblock_log** returns REQ_NOACTION. For all directives, REQ_NOACTION allows the server to continue with other functions in that directive. The function logs the designated information without interfering with the server's stepping through the rest of the functions. **pblock_log** simply writes the pblock entries into the log file.

As an added feature, you can declare a return value for **pblock_log** through the parameter return. You can specify what **pblock_log** returns to find out how the server responds when a different type of value is returned. For example, by returning REQ_ABORTED or REQ_PROCEED, you can find out what happens when a directive function returns such a value. This parameter is optional. If you do not define it, the function returns REQ_NOACTION by default.

You should add the following lines of code to the **obj.conf** file to register this example. Modify the shlib parameter of **load-modules** to reflect the location of the compiled version of this program. If you added this function to an existing shared library, then simply add it to the list of the functions in funcs parameter. Also, update the file parameter of **log_init** to reflect where you would like the server to create the log file.

```
Init fn="load-modules"
 funcs="pblock_log,log_init"
 shlib="c:/netscape/server/nsapi/log/log.dll"
Init fn="log_init" file="c:/log/newlog.txt"
```

As mentioned, you can register the **pblock_log** function at any location in the directive list. For example, you can add the following line to the top of the list of **Service** functions:

```
Service fn="pblock_log" name="Service"
```

Listing 8-4   Logging Server pblock Entries for a Given Directive

```
/* include the following files if you are using a version of
   Netscape Server earlier than 3.x

   #include "base/pblock.h"
   #include "base/session.h"
   #include "frame/req.h"

   #include "base/util.h"
   #include "frame/protocol.h"
   #include "base/daemon.h"
   #include "frame/log.h"
*/
```

```
/* include this file if you are using Server 3.x */
#include "nsapi.h"

/* formatting string for separating the data in the file */
#define SESSION_BREAK \
"Session started\n\
*****************************************************\n\n"

#define REQUEST_BREAK \
"Request started\n\
*****************************************************\n\n"

#define PBLOCK_BREAK \
 "-----------------------------------"

#define DIRECTIVE_BREAK \
 "+++++++++++++++++++++++++++++++++++++++++++++++++++"

/*
 * file descriptor to be shared between the threads and
   processes
 */
static SYS_FILE logfd = SYS_ERROR_FD;

/*
 * this function is called by daemon_atrestart to close the
 * file on shutdown or restart
 */
NSAPI_PUBLIC void close_logfile(void *parameter)
{
    system_fclose(logfd);
    logfd = SYS_ERROR_FD;
}

/*
 * Init function log_init
 * opens the log file
 */
NSAPI_PUBLIC int log_init(pblock *param, Session *sn,
                          Request *rq)
{
    /* get the file name from the Init function as defined in
       the obj.conf file
     */
    char *fn = pblock_findval("file", param);
```

```
    /* Perform error checking */
    if(!fn) {
        pblock_nvinsert("error",
                        "log_init: log file's name is missing",
                        param);
        return REQ_ABORTED;
    }

    /* open the log file to write and append data */
    logfd = system_fopenWA(fn);

    /* send an error message if file was not correctly
       opened
     */
    if(logfd == SYS_ERROR_FD)
    {
        pblock_nvinsert("error",
                "log_init: error while opening the log file",
                param);
        return REQ_ABORTED;
    }

    /* close the file when server is restarted; call the
       function close_logfile on server restart
     */
    daemon_atrestart(close_logfile, NULL);

    /* return success */
    return REQ_PROCEED;
}


/*
    main function for writing the pblock entries into the
    log file
 */
NSAPI_PUBLIC int pblock_log(pblock *param, Session *sn,
                              Request *rq)
{
    char *directive;        /* normally name of the direc-
                                tive */
    char *return_string;    /* string value of return value */
    int   return_value;     /* return value in integer */

    char *directive_name;   /* string for name parameter */
```

```
char *pblock_client;    /* string for sn>client */

char *pblock_vars;      /* string for rq->vars */

char *pblock_reqpb;     /* string for rq->reqpb */

char *pblock_headers;   /* string for rq->headers */

char *pblock_srvhdrs;   /* string for rq->srvhdrs */

char *loginfo;          /* data to be placed in the file */
int   length;           /* length of loginfo */

/* Get the function's name parameter from obj.conf.
   Used to distinguish the NSAPI variables logged each
   time this function is called. Usually the name of
   the directive where pblock_log is declared.
 */
directive = pblock_findval("name", param);

/* the name parameter should be declared */
if (!directive)
{
    log_error(LOG_MISCONFIG, "pblock_log", sn, rq,
            "name is missing from the function.");
    return REQ_ABORTED;
}

/* Set a Session flag. The file then reflects each time
 * the session starts.
 */
if(pblock_findval("sflag", sn->client) == NULL)
{
    /* write the line that states session started */
    system_fwrite_atomic(logfd, SESSION_BREAK,
                        sizeof(SESSION_BREAK));

    /* insert the flag in the Session data structure */
    pblock_nvinsert("sflag", "true", sn->client);
}

/* Set a Request flag. The file will then reflect each
   time the Request is started. This code also groups
   the list of pblock entries of all registered
   pblock_log functions for a given request.
 */
if(pblock_findval("rflag", rq->reqpb) == NULL)
```

```
{
        system_fwrite_atomic(logfd, REQUEST_BREAK,
                                sizeof(REQUEST_BREAK));

    /* Insert the flag in the Request data structure.
       You can insert this variable in other pblock
       data structures, such as vars.
     */
    pblock_nvinsert("rflag", "true", rq->reqpb);
}
/* check if there is a return string for the pblock_log
   function defined in the obj.conf file
 */
return_string = pblock_findval("return", param);

/* You can define a return string to test what will hap-
   pen when the function returns a different variable.
   If none is set in the obj.conf file, this function
   returns REQ_NOACTION, which in effect lets the
   server continue processing the rest of the functions
   and directives.
 */
if(return_string)
{
    if (util_strcasecmp(return_string,
                        "REQ_PROCEED") == 0)
        return_value = REQ_PROCEED;
    else if (util_strcasecmp(return_string,
                        "REQ_NOACTION") == 0)
        return_value = REQ_NOACTION;
    else if (util_strcasecmp(return_string,
                        "REQ_ABORTED") == 0)
        return_value = REQ_ABORTED;
    else if (util_strcasecmp(return_string,
                        "REQ_EXIT") == 0)
        return_value = REQ_EXIT;
    else if (util_strcasecmp(return_string,
                        "REQ_RESTART") == 0);
        return_value = REQ_RESTART;
}
else
{
    return_value = REQ_NOACTION;
```

```
}

/* malloc space for the directive name */
directive_name = (char *) MALLOC(30 * sizeof(char));

/* Produce the directive_name string. We use "DIREC-
   TIVE" as the default label since you normally use a
   directive name for the name parameter of pblock_log.
 */
util_sprintf(directive_name, "DIRECTIVE: %s",
             directive);

/* insert the domain name in the client pblock */
session_dns(sn);

/* get the client pblock in string format */
pblock_client = pblock_pblock2str(sn->client, NULL);

/* get the vars pblock in string format */
pblock_vars = pblock_pblock2str(rq->vars, NULL);

/* get the reqpb pblock in string format */
pblock_reqpb = pblock_pblock2str(rq->reqpb, NULL);

/* get the headers pblock in string format */
pblock_headers = pblock_pblock2str(rq->headers, NULL);

/* get the srvhdrs pblock in string format */
pblock_srvhdrs = pblock_pblock2str(rq->srvhdrs, NULL);

/* determine a size for all the pblocks and various
   formatting texts
 */
loginfo = (char *) MALLOC(1024 * sizeof(char));

/* place all formatting data and pblock strings in the
   loginfo string and return the size of the loginfo
 */
length=util_sprintf(loginfo,
     "%s\n\n"
     ">>Session's Client pblock (sn->client)"
     "\n\n%s\n\n%s\n"
     ">>Server Variables pblock (rq->vars)"
     "\n\n%s\n\n%s\n"
     ">>Main Request pblock (rq->reqpb)"
     "\n\n%s\n\n%s\n"
```

```
                    ">>Request Headers pblock (rq->headers)"
                    "\n\n%s\n\n%s\n"
                    ">>Server Response Headers pblock (rq->srvhdrs)"
                    "\n\n%s\n\n\n%s\n\n",

                        directive_name,
                        pblock_client, PBLOCK_BREAK,
                        pblock_vars, PBLOCK_BREAK,
                        pblock_reqpb, PBLOCK_BREAK,
                        pblock_headers, PBLOCK_BREAK,
                        pblock_srvhdrs,
                        DIRECTIVE_BREAK);

    /* Write the data into the log file. This function locks
       the file as it writes into it.
     */
    system_fwrite_atomic(logfd, loginfo, length);

    /* free the malloced strings */
    FREE(directive_name);
    FREE(loginfo);

    /* return the value determined through return_string */
    return return_value;
}
```

We declare the file descriptor as a global static variable and set its value to error (SYS_ERROR_FD). SYS_ERROR_FD is –1 for UNIX and NULL for Windows. If function **system_fopenWA** was able to open the file, it sets the value to the actual file descriptor. The location where we would like **system_fopenWA** to create the log file is passed through **log_init**'s file parameter. If the log file already exists, **system_fopenWA** opens the file for appending. Notice that (as we mentioned in the **Init** section earlier) instead of **log_error**, we use **pblock_nvinsert** to insert an error in the function's pblock parameter. Finally, in the **log_init** function, we also call **close_logfile** through **daemon_atrestart**. When the server is stopped or restarted, **close_logfile** closes the log file and resets the file descriptor to SYS_ERROR_FD.

When we register the **pblock_log** function in the **obj.conf** file, we use the name parameter to specify where in the list of directives **pblock_log** was declared. This information is especially important when you register **pblock_log** multiple times in the **obj.conf** file. Therefore, we require that the name parameter be declared in the **obj.conf** file; otherwise, we log a server misconfiguration error. Listing 8-4 identifies the information as DIRECTIVE, as the best way to identify the location in the directive lists where we declared the **pblock_log** function is by the name of the directive for which the function was registered.

Next, we set two flags, sflag and rflag, to identify when a request or session is started. We set sflag in the *Session*->client pblock entries and rflag in the *Request*->reqpb entries. You can set the request flag in any other *Request* pblock. For Listing 8-4, we chose reqpb. We then look for the flag to discern whether it was already set. When a request flag is set, the flag remains there for the request's lifetime. In other words, if we set the request flag with a **pblock_log** function that is declared as an **AuthTrans** function, this request flag applies to all other **pblock_log** functions we declare thereafter. Thus, a **pblock_log** function declared as a **PathCheck** function will find this flag. These two flags group the **pblock_log** function's entries in the log file. If a flag is not there, **pblock_log** sets the flag and writes a heading for the start of the session or request in the log file. All the variables recorded from a given request are placed after a request heading in the log file. We can then use this information to evaluate the changes that occur to the NSAPI variables during a request. By including both a session and request heading in the log file, we also identify when a request restarts without a session restarting. For example, this situation can happen during a function that redirects a client (see Redirecting the Client in Chapter 6).

pblock_log also allows you to specify the function's return value through the optional parameter return specified in the **obj.conf** file. If the return parameter was used, **pblock_log** uses its value. Notice that the return parameter needs to be declared as REQ_PROCEED, REQ_NOACTION, REQ_ABORTED, REQ_EXIT, or REQ_RESTART. The case of the characters does not matter, but any value other than these is not accepted. If no return parameter is declared, or if the string is other than these five strings, the server uses the default REQ_NOACTION. Be careful if you plan to return REQ_RESTART. If a **Service** function returns REQ_RESTART, the server attempts to go through the directives again. This action could put the server in an endless loop and crash the server. The function forces the server to restart every time it reaches the **Service** function. Moreover, the directive functions continue to add server variables in the various pblock data structures.

Next, we must get all the data we intend to write to the log file. We use **pblock_pblock2str** to convert the pblock entries in *Session*->client, *Request*->vars, *Request*->reqpb, *Request*->headers, and *Request*->srvhdrs into strings. **pblock_pblock2str** allocates the space for the new string using the memory pool. We then place all the strings returned by **pblock_pblock2str** in a new string to be written into the log file. To facilitate reading of the data in the file, we also include the appropriate header texts and dividing line characters. Each group of data is divided by an appropriate header.

In the **pblock_log** function, we put the data in one string and write the data once with **system_fwrite_atomic**. You can also write the data immediately after they are returned by **pblock_pblock2str**. For example, you can write the string from *Session*->client before you write the *Request*->vars string.

The data placed inside the file by **system_fwrite_*** functions are in UNIX format (using the UNIX line breaks, CRLF). To open the file under NT, you must convert the file to a DOS format—that is, replace CRLF (carriage return and line-feed) with line-feed (LF) only. No lines of a string from a pblock entry are wrapped, a line could be rather long. Make sure you wrap the lines if you intend to print the results.

Example of Variables Logged by the pblock_log Function   Listing 8-5 shows the information placed in the log file after a request for the server (that is, `http://foo/`). The client requests the server's home page and the server returns the default `index.html` page. `index.html` also includes an embedded image, `title.gif`. The Netscape Server used for this example is Enterprise Server 3.5.1 for NT. Security is not enabled. Our server uses ACL for authorization (that is, a **PathCheck** function **check-acl** is defined in the **obj.conf** file).

For this example, we have declared the **pblock_log** function in the **obj.conf** file as the first function for each directive. In other words, we declare **pblock_log** for **AuthTrans**, **NameTrans**, **PathCheck**, **ObjectType**, **Service**, and **AddLog**. For the `name` parameter of **pblock_log**, we use the name of the directive **pblock_log**. The following code gives the declaration of **pblock_log** for the **AuthTrans** function in **obj.conf**:

```
AuthTrans fn=pblock_log name="AuthTrans"
```

We do not use the `return` parameter for **pblock_log**. Hence, **pblock_log** uses the default `REQ_NOACTION`.

When the client is prompted for a user name and password, we use the name "`mouse`" and password "`cheese`". For this situation, this information identifies a real user and the information is accurate! In other words, the client is authenticated when this user name and password are returned. The server returns the appropriate home page, which includes the `index.html` and `title.gif` files.

Listing 8-5 includes information only for a single client request, `http://foo/`. You can continue to log other actions of the server and review them in the log file. Depending on the request, the list of the variables and their values may differ. Listing 8-5 is formatted for easy reading, but with **pblock_log** the entries for each pblock are placed in a single line.

For this program, we have used Netscape Communicator 4.04, which sends different headers than Navigator 3.x does. For example, Communicator sends two additional request headers: `accept-language` and `accept-charset`. We have also set the cache setting in Communicator to zero (0). Thus the client will not send the `if-modified-since` header—for example, `if-modified-since="Thursday, 12-Sep-96 08:50:38 GMT; length=2927"`. Web publishing is also disabled, so its related server variables, such as the `reqpb` pblock variable `luri` and the response-header `Link`, are not created or logged. Although the server supports HTTP/1.1, the client supports HTTP/1.0 and sends HTTP/1.0 as part of the Request-Line (`clf-request`). The `connection` header sent by the client is also `Keep-Alive`.

The order of the information in Listing 8-5 and in the server's pblock data structures varies depending on the version of the server you use. For example, FastTrack 2.0a returns the following client pblocks:

```
dns="none" sflag="true" ip="1.2.3.4"
```

The actual information in these variables will also vary based on your server setting. For this example, security and DNS are set to off, so there is no DNS value and the security information is missing from the `client` pblock data structure.

Listing 8-5-1   Sample Data Logged by **pblock_log** (First Request's Server Variable List)

```
Session started
* * * * * * * * * * * * * * * * * * * * * * * * * * * * * * * * * * * * * * * * * * * * * * * * * * * * * *

Request started
* * * * * * * * * * * * * * * * * * * * * * * * * * * * * * * * * * * * * * * * * * * * * * * * * * * * * *

 DIRECTIVE: AuthTrans

>>Session's Client pblock (sn->client)

ip="1.2.3.4" sflag="true" dns="-none"

------------------------------------
>>Server Variables pblock (rq->vars)

ppath="/"

------------------------------------
>>Main Request pblock (rq->reqpb)

clf-request="GET / HTTP/1.0" method="GET"
protocol="HTTP/1.0" uri="/" rflag="true"


------------------------------------
>>Request Headers pblock (rq->headers)

connection="Keep-Alive" user-agent="Mozilla/4.04 [en]
(WinNT; I)" host="foo" accept="image/gif, image/x-xbitmap,
image/jpeg, image/pjpeg, image/png, */*"
accept-language="en" accept-charset="iso-8859-1,*,utf-8"

------------------------------------
>>Server Response Headers pblock (rq->srvhdrs)


++++++++++++++++++++++++++++++++++++++++++++++++++++++++

DIRECTIVE: NameTrans

>>Session's Client pblock (sn->client)

ip="1.2.3.4" sflag="true" dns="-none"
```

Listing 8-5-1 Sample Data Logged by **pblock_log** (First Request's Server Variable List) (*continued*)

```
-----------------------------------
>>Server Variables pblock (rq->vars)

ppath="/"

-----------------------------------
>>Main Request pblock (rq->reqpb)

clf-request="GET / HTTP/1.0" method="GET"
protocol="HTTP/1.0" uri="/" rflag="true"


-----------------------------------
>>Request Headers pblock (rq->headers)

connection="Keep-Alive" user-agent="Mozilla/4.04 [en]
(WinNT; I)" host="foo" accept="image/gif, image/x-xbitmap,
image/jpeg, image/pjpeg, image/png, */*"
accept-language="en" accept-charset="iso-8859-1,*,utf-8"

-----------------------------------
>>Server Response Headers pblock (rq->srvhdrs)

+++++++++++++++++++++++++++++++++++++++++++++++++++++
DIRECTIVE: PathCheck

>>Session's Client pblock (sn->client)

ip="1.2.3.4" sflag="true" dns="-none"

-----------------------------------
>>Server Variables pblock (rq->vars)

ntrans-base="c:/netscape/server/docs"
path="c:/netscape/server/docs/"

-----------------------------------
>>Main Request pblock (rq->reqpb)

clf-request="GET / HTTP/1.0" method="GET"
protocol="HTTP/1.0" uri="/" rflag="true"

-----------------------------------
>>Request Headers pblock (rq->headers)

connection="Keep-Alive" user-agent="Mozilla/4.04 [en]
(WinNT; I)" host="foo" accept="image/gif, image/x-xbitmap,
```

```
image/jpeg, image/pjpeg, image/png, */*"
accept-language="en" accept-charset="iso-8859-1,*,utf-8"

--------------------------------------
>>Server Response Headers Pblock (rq->srvhdrs)

++++++++++++++++++++++++++++++++++++++++++++++++++++
DIRECTIVE: AddLog

>>Session's Client pblock (sn->client)

ip="1.2.3.4" sflag="true" dns="-none"

--------------------------------------
>>Server Variables pblock (rq->vars)

ntransbase="c:/netscape/server/docs"
path="c:/netscape/server/docs/index.html"

--------------------------------------
>>Main Request pblock (rq->reqpb)

clf-request="GET / HTTP/1.0" method="GET"
protocol="HTTP/1.0" uri="/index.html" rflag="true"

--------------------------------------
>>Request Headers pblock (rq->headers)

connection="Keep-Alive" user-agent="Mozilla/4.04 [en]
(WinNT; I)" host="foo" accept="image/gif, image/x-xbitmap,
image/jpeg, image/pjpeg, image/png, */*"
accept-language="en"
accept-charset="iso-8859-1,*,utf-8"

--------------------------------------
>>Server Response Headers pblock (rq->srvhdrs)

status="401 Unauthorized"
WWW-authenticate="basic realm=\"private\""
content-length="223" content-type="text/html"

++++++++++++++++++++++++++++++++++++++++++++++++++++
```

Listing 8-5-2 Sample Data Logged by **pblock_log** (Second Request's Server Variable List)

```
Session started
***************************************************

Request started
***************************************************

 DIRECTIVE: AuthTrans

>>Session's Client pblock (sn->client)

ip="1.2.3.4" sflag="true" dns="-none"

------------------------------------
>>Server Variables pblock (rq->vars)

ppath="/"

------------------------------------
>>Main Request pblock (rq->reqpb)

clf-request="GET / HTTP/1.0" method="GET"
protocol="HTTP/1.0" uri="/" rflag="true"

------------------------------------
>>Request Headers pblock (rq->headers)

connection="Keep-Alive" user-agent="Mozilla/4.04 [en]
(WinNT; I)" host="foo" accept="image/gif, image/x-xbitmap,
image/jpeg, image/pjpeg, image/png, */*"
accept-language="en"
accept-charset="iso-8859-1,*,utf-8"
authorization="Basic dG9tbXk6dG9t"

------------------------------------
>>Server Response Headers pblock (rq->srvhdrs)

++++++++++++++++++++++++++++++++++++++++++++++++++++

DIRECTIVE: NameTrans

>>Session's Client pblock (sn->client)

ip="1.2.3.4" sflag="true" dns="-none"

------------------------------------
>>Server Variables pblock (rq->vars)

ppath="/"
```

```
------------------------------------
>>Main Request pblock (rq->reqpb)

clf-request="GET / HTTP/1.0" method="GET"
protocol="HTTP/1.0" uri="/" rflag="true"

------------------------------------
>>Request Headers pblock (rq->headers)

connection="Keep-Alive" user-agent="Mozilla/4.04 [en]
(WinNT; I)" host="foo" accept="image/gif, image/x-xbitmap,
image/jpeg,
image/pjpeg, image/png, */*" accept-language="en"
accept-charset="iso-8859-1,*,utf-8"
authorization="Basic dG9tbXk6dG9t"

------------------------------------
>>Server Response Headers pblock (rq->srvhdrs)

++++++++++++++++++++++++++++++++++++++++++++++++++++++

DIRECTIVE: PathCheck

>>Session's Client pblock (sn->client)

ip="1.2.3.4" sflag="true" dns="-none"

------------------------------------
>>Server Variables pblock (rq->vars)

ntrans-base="c:/netscape/server/docs"
path="c:/netscape/server/docs/"

------------------------------------
>>Main Request pblock (rq->reqpb)

clf-request="GET / HTTP/1.0" method="GET"
protocol="HTTP/1.0"
uri="/" rflag="true"

------------------------------------
>>Request Headers pblock (rq->headers)

connection="Keep-Alive" user-agent="Mozilla/4.04 [en]
(WinNT; I)" host="foo" accept="image/gif, image/x-xbitmap,
image/jpeg, image/pjpeg, image/png, */*"
```

```
accept-language="en"
accept-charset="iso-8859-1,*,utf-8"
authorization="Basic dG9tbXk6dG9t"

-----------------------------------
>>Server Response Headers pblock (rq->srvhdrs)

+++++++++++++++++++++++++++++++++++++++++++++++++++

DIRECTIVE: ObjectType

>>Session's Client pblock (sn->client)

ip="1.2.3.4" sflag="true" dns="-none"

-----------------------------------
>>Server Variables pblock (rq->vars)

ntrans-base="c:/netscape/server/docs"
path="c:/netscape/server/docs/index.html"
auth-type="basic" auth-user="mouse"
auth-password="cheese"
userdn="uid=mouse,0=factory, c=US" auth-db="default"

-----------------------------------
>>Main Request pblock (rq->reqpb)

clf-request="GET / HTTP/1.0" method="GET"
protocol="HTTP/1.0" uri="/" rflag="true"

-----------------------------------
>>Request Headers pblock (rq->headers)

connection="Keep-Alive" user-agent="Mozilla/4.04 [en]
(WinNT; I)" host="foo" accept="image/gif, image/x-xbitmap,
image/jpeg, image/pjpeg, image/png, */*"
accept-language="en"
accept-charset="iso-8859-1,*,utf-8"
authorization="Basic dG9tbXk6dG9t"

-----------------------------------
>>Server Response Headers pblock (rq->srvhdrs)

+++++++++++++++++++++++++++++++++++++++++++++++++++

DIRECTIVE: Service
```

```
>>Session's Client pblock (sn->client)

ip="1.2.3.4" sflag="true" dns="-none"

----------------------------------
>>Server Variables pblock (rq->vars)

ntrans-base="c:/netscape/server/docs"
path="c:/netscape/server/docs/index.html"
auth-type="basic" auth-user="mouse"
auth-password="cheese"
userdn="uid=mouse,0=factory, c=US" auth-db="default"

----------------------------------
>>Main Request pblock (rq->reqpb)

clf-request="GET / HTTP/1.0" method="GET"
protocol="HTTP/1.0" uri="/" rflag="true"

----------------------------------
>>Request Headers pblock (rq->headers)

connection="Keep-Alive" user-agent="Mozilla/4.04 [en]
(WinNT; I)" host="foo" accept="image/gif, image/x-xbitmap,
image/jpeg, image/pjpeg, image/png, */*"
accept-language="en"
accept-charset="iso-8859-1,*,utf-8"
authorization="Basic dG9tbXk6dG9t"

----------------------------------
>>Server Response Headers pblock (rq->srvhdrs)

content-type="text/html"

++++++++++++++++++++++++++++++++++++++++++++++++++++++

DIRECTIVE: AddLog

>>Session's Client pblock (sn->client)

ip="1.2.3.4" sflag="true" dns="-none"

----------------------------------
>>Server Variables pblock (rq->vars)

ntrans-base="c:/netscape/server/docs"
```

```
path="c:/netscape/server/docs/index.html"
auth-type="basic" auth-user="mouse"
auth-password="cheese" userdn="uid=mouse,0=factory, c=US"
auth-db="default"

-----------------------------------
>>Main Request pblock (rq->reqpb)

clf-request="GET / HTTP/1.0" method="GET"
protocol="HTTP/1.0" uri="/" rflag="true"

-----------------------------------
>>Request Headers pblock (rq->headers)

connection="Keep-Alive" user-agent="Mozilla/4.04 [en]
(WinNT; I)" host="foo" accept="image/gif, image/x-xbitmap,
image/jpeg, image/pjpeg, image/png, */*"
accept-language="en"
accept-charset="iso-8859-1,*,utf-8"
authorization="Basic dG9tbXk6dG9t"

-----------------------------------
>>Server Response Headers pblock (rq=->srvhdrs)

content-type="text/html"
last-modified="Thu, 12 Sep 1996 08:50:38 GMT"
content-length="2927" accept-ranges="bytes" status="200 OK"

++++++++++++++++++++++++++++++++++++++++++++++++++++
```

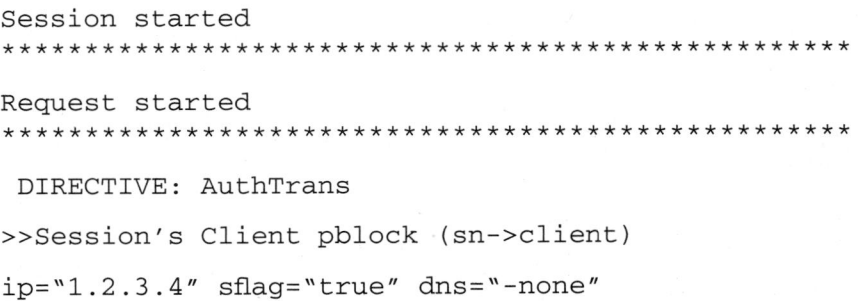

```
Session started
****************************************************

Request started
****************************************************

 DIRECTIVE: AuthTrans

>>Session's Client pblock (sn->client)

ip="1.2.3.4" sflag="true" dns="-none"
```

```
--------------------------------------
>>Server Variables pblock (rq->vars)

ppath="/title.gif"

--------------------------------------
>>Main Request pblock (rq->reqpb)

clf-request="GET /title.gif HTTP/1.0" method="GET"
protocol="HTTP/1.0" uri="/title.gif" rflag="true"

--------------------------------------
>>Request Headers pblock (rq->headers)

referer="http://foo/" connection="Keep-Alive"
user-agent="Mozilla/4.04 [en] (WinNT; I)" host="foo"
accept="image/gif, image/x-xbitmap, image/jpeg,
image/pjpeg, image/png, */*" accept-language="en"
accept-charset="iso-8859-1,*,utf-8"
authorization="Basic dG9tbXk6dG9t"

--------------------------------------
>>Server Response Headers pblock (rq->srvhdrs)

++++++++++++++++++++++++++++++++++++++++++++++++++++
DIRECTIVE: NameTrans

>>Session's Client pblock (sn->client)

ip="1.2.3.4" sflag="true" dns="-none"

--------------------------------------
>>Server Variables pblock (rq->vars)

ppath="/title.gif"

--------------------------------------
>>Main Request pblock (rq->reqpb)

clf-request="GET /title.gif HTTP/1.0" method="GET"
protocol="HTTP/1.0" uri="/title.gif" rflag="true"

--------------------------------------
>>Request Headers pblock (rq->headers)
```

```
referer="http://foo/" connection="Keep-Alive"
user-agent="Mozilla/4.04 [en] (WinNT; I)" host="foo"
accept="image/gif, image/x-xbitmap, image/jpeg,
image/pjpeg, image/png, */*" accept-language="en"
accept-charset="iso-8859-1,*,utf-8"
authorization="Basic dG9tbXk6dG9t"

-------------------------------------
>>Server Response Headers pblock (rq->srvhdrs)


+++++++++++++++++++++++++++++++++++++++++++++++++++++

DIRECTIVE: PathCheck

>>Session's Client pblock (sn->client)

ip="1.2.3.4" sflag="true" dns="-none"

-------------------------------------
>>Server Variables pblock (rq->vars)

ntrans-base="c:/netscape/server/docs"
path="c:/netscape/server/docs/title.gif"

-------------------------------------
>>Main Request pblock (rq->reqpb)

clf-request="GET /title.gif HTTP/1.0" method="GET"
protocol="HTTP/1.0" uri="/title.gif" rflag="true"

-------------------------------------
>>Request Headers pblock (rq->headers)

referer="http://foo/" connection="Keep-Alive"
user-agent="Mozilla/4.04 [en] (WinNT; I)" host="foo"
accept="image/gif, image/x-xbitmap, image/jpeg,
image/pjpeg, image/png, */*" accept-language="en"
accept-charset="iso-8859-1,*,utf-8"
authorization="Basic dG9tbXk6dG9t"

-------------------------------------
>>Server Response Headers pblock (rq->srvhdrs)

Vary="Accept-language"


+++++++++++++++++++++++++++++++++++++++++++++++++++++
```

```
DIRECTIVE: ObjectType

>>Session's Client pblock (sn->client)

ip="1.2.3.4" sflag="true" dns="-none"

-------------------------------------
>>Server Variables pblock (rq->vars)

ntrans-base="c:/netscape/server/docs"
path="c:/netscape/server/docs/title.gif"
auth-type="basic" auth-user="mouse"
auth-password="cheese" userdn="uid=mouse,0=factory, c=US"
auth-db="default"

-------------------------------------
>>Main Request pblock (rq->reqpb)

clf-request="GET /title.gif HTTP/1.0" method="GET"
protocol="HTTP/1.0" uri="/title.gif" rflag="true"

-------------------------------------
>>Request Headers pblock (rq->headers)

referer="http://foo/" connection="Keep-Alive"
user-agent="Mozilla/4.04 [en] (WinNT; I)" host="foo"
accept="image/gif, image/x-xbitmap, image/jpeg,
image/pjpeg, image/png, */*" accept-language="en"
accept-charset="iso-8859-1,*,utf-8"
authorization="Basic dG9tbXk6dG9t"

-------------------------------------

>>Server Response Headers pblock (rq->srvhdrs)

Vary="Accept-language"

+++++++++++++++++++++++++++++++++++++++++++++++++++++
DIRECTIVE: Service

>>Session's Client pblock (sn->client)

ip="1.2.3.4" sflag="true" dns="-none"

-------------------------------------
>>Server Variables pblock (rq->vars)
```

```
ntrans-base="c:/netscape/server/docs"
path="c:/netscape/server/docs/title.gif"
auth-type="basic" auth-user="mouse"
auth-password="cheese" userdn="uid=mouse,0=factory, c=US"
auth-db="default"

------------------------------------
>>Main Request pblock (rq->reqpb)

clf-request="GET /title.gif HTTP/1.0" method="GET"
protocol="HTTP/1.0" uri="/title.gif" rflag="true"

------------------------------------
>>Request Headers pblock (rq->headers)

referer="http://foo/" connection="Keep-Alive"
user-agent="Mozilla/4.04 [en] (WinNT; I)" host="foo"
accept="image/gif, image/x-xbitmap, image/jpeg,
image/pjpeg, image/png, */*" accept-language="en"
accept-charset="iso-8859-1,*,utf-8"
authorization="Basic dG9tbXk6dG9t"

------------------------------------
>>Server Response Headers pblock (rq->srvhdrs)

Vary="Accept-language" content-type="image/gif"

++++++++++++++++++++++++++++++++++++++++++++++++++++++
DIRECTIVE: AddLog

>>Session's Client pblock (sn->client)

ip="1.2.3.4" sflag="true" dns="-none"

------------------------------------
>>Server Variables pblock (rq->vars)

ntrans-base="c:/netscape/server/docs"
path="c:/netscape/server/docs/title.gif"
auth-type="basic" auth-user="mouse"
auth-password="cheese" userdn="uid=mouse,0=factory, c=US"
auth-db="default"

------------------------------------
```

Listing 8-5-3   Sample Data Logged by **pblock_log** (Third Request's Server
Variable List) (*continued*)

```
>>Main Request pblock (rq->reqpb)

clf-request="GET /title.gif HTTP/1.0" method="GET"
protocol="HTTP/1.0" uri="/title.gif" rflag="true"

------------------------------------
>>Request Headers pblock (rq->headers)

referer="http://foo/" connection="Keep-Alive"
user-agent="Mozilla/4.04 [en] (WinNT; I)" host="foo"
accept="image/gif, image/x-xbitmap, image/jpeg,
image/pjpeg, image/png, */*" accept-language="en"
accept-charset="iso-8859-1,*,utf-8"
authorization="Basic dG9tbXk6dG9t"

------------------------------------
>>Server Response Headers pblock (rq->srvhdrs)

Vary="Accept-language" content-type="image/gif"
last-modified="Mon, 24 Jun 1996 20:36:04 GMT"
content-length="44263" accept-ranges="bytes"
status="200 OK"


+++++++++++++++++++++++++++++++++++++++++++++++++++++++++++
```

As you can see, the server goes through the directives three times in Listing 8-5. The
first time (Listing 8-5-1), the server requires authentication and forces the client to
input the user name and password. The second time (Listing 8-5-2), the server evaluates the user name and password and sends the index.html page. The third time
(Listing 8-5-3), the server returns the image (title.gif).

At the outset of each session and request list, the **pblock_log** function has inserted
rflag and sflag in the Session pblock client and the Request pblock reqpb,
and has set their values to "true". These flags are used to identify when a new session
or request is started.

The browser used by the client is the English ([en]) version of Netscape Navigator
(Communicator) 4.04 for NT (user-agent in Request pblock headers is
Mozilla/4.04 [en] (WinNT; I)). The variables in the headers pblock can
differ depending on the browser. Try this request with Microsoft Internet Explorer, for
example, and you will see different entries.

During the first request (the first time the server goes through the directives; Listing
8-5-1), the **PathCheck** function **check-acl** sets the status to 401 Unauthorized
and inserts the header WWW-authenticate in the Request pblock srvhdrs. If
you use this program with Server 2.x, the **PathCheck** information will not be recorded

in the first pass. Under Server 2.x, **check-acl** is called before all other **PathCheck** functions and returns REQ_ABORTED. As a result, the other directive functions are skipped. Under Server 3.x, **check-acl** is called after other **PathCheck** functions, so our **pblock_log** is called first.

The first time the client needs to be authenticated, the **check-acl** function returns REQ_ABORTED to force the client to authenticate. This action, in turn, has the server skip other directive functions, except the **AddLog** functions. Although the client does not see the default Unauthorized page, it is sent by the server. Note that content-length and content-type of the Unauthorized page are specified in the srvhdrs pblock.

During the second request (Listing 8-5-2), the client sends back the authorization header ("Basic dG9tbXk6dG9t"). This header, found in the Request pblock headers, includes the type of authentication and the encoded user name and password. This time **check-acl** verifies the user name and password. As they are correct, **check-acl** inserts the user name (auth-user), user password (auth-password), the user's distinguished name (userdn), and the type of authentication (auth-type) in the Request pblock vars. For Server 2.x, there is no userdn. Enterprise Server 3.5.1 also inserts auth-db with the value default, for the default user database. In this case, the default user database is the local database of Enterprise Server 3.5.1. Server 3.0x, on the other hand, does not add the auth-db variable in the vars pblock, unless you have specified a special database when you set the access control rule for the user. For the second request, **check-acl** was able to accomplish its task and return REQ_PROCEED. Unless REQ_ABORTED is returned by a **PathCheck** function, the server goes through all **PathCheck** functions. Because our **PathCheck** function (**pblock_log**) was called first, these added server variables are not available to our function. You can verify that they are added by checking the Object-Type section of Listing 8-5-2.

After each **NameTrans** function, the ppath entry in the Request pblock vars is no longer available. Instead, there are path and ntrans-base entries. Note also that, during the second request, the path after **NameTrans** is c:/netscape/server/docs. In other words, no file is specified. The **PathCheck** function **find-index** then adds the index.html file to the path. After the **PathCheck** directive, the path is c:/netscape/server/docs/index.html.

Next, during the second request, an **ObjectType** function (**type-by-extension**) sets the value of content-type in the srvhdrs pblock, making it available for the **Service** functions. The **Service** function **send-file** then sets the value of the status to 200 OK and sends the index.html page to the client. This function also sets the last-modified, content-length and accept-ranges headers in the srvhdrs pblock. These headers, in turn, are sent with the content of the index.html page to the client.

During the third request (Listing 8-5-2), ppath is no longer the server root (/). The client is requesting the image ("/title.gif"). Note also, because title.gif is referenced from the index.html page, the client sends a referer header. You can find the `referer` header in the `Request` pblock `headers`. For the third request, `content-type` is set to "`image/gif`" and the image is sent to the client by the **Service** function **send-file**.

Error (Customized Server Error Response)

We have discussed how to send an error page or log an error message when an error occurs during the server's processing of your program. In Chapter 6, for example, we reviewed the use of the NSAPI functions **protocol_status** and **log_error** for error handling. **Error** directive functions, however, provide error-handling options that apply to all errors of a specific type. They allow customization of the server's error response and additional error handling for when a server encounters a particular type of error during a request.

    Error functions are unique in that they can be called after any function. Nevertheless, they can be called only when an error occurs. In other words, if the status information is set to OK (that is, the server processed the request without any error), then no **Error** function is called. On the other hand, **Error** functions are called for most other statuses, including a status such as 304 (PROTOCOL_NOT_MODIFIED). You normally declare an **Error** function as the last directive in a server Object. Because of their role (that is, processing errors), however, they take precedence over other functions. Once an error occurs, the server skips other functions and goes directly to the **Error** function (that is, if one exists). Although you declare an **Error** function as the last directive function in the Object, **AddLog** functions are still called after the **Error** function. Because the logging of information comes after a response is sent to the client, **AddLog** functions are called to log after the **Error** directive sends the error page.

    Similar to a **Service** function, **Error** functions should return a page to the client. In fact, an **Error** function can be seen as a **Service** function that is applied only when an error occurs. There are, however, distinct differences between an **Error** function and a **Service** function.

    Error handling is built into the server. The server returns the appropriate error page when a standard HTTP error occurs. Sometimes you may want to customize the response or send a different error message. Netscape provides the built-in **Error** functions **send-error** and **query-handler** for customizing the error pages returned to the client. With **send-error**, you can specify a default error page to be sent to the client when a specific error type occurs. With **query-handler**, the server runs the specified CGI program when a specific error type occurs. The CGI program can then review the request and return a tailored error response to the client. **send-error** and **query-handler** have different roles when called as **Error** directive function than the role they play as **Service** directive function. Do not confuse these different roles. An **Error** function is called when a specific error type occurs. A **Service** function, on the other hand, is called for a specific MIME type. For a **Service** function, the server looks for the `content-type` information specified in `Request->srvhdrs`, whereas for the **Error** functions, the server looks for the `status` in `Request->srvhdrs`.

You can also use **Service** function **send-error** and the **PathCheck** function **deny-existence** to customize the error response. The **Service** function **send-error** returns a customized error page when a client requests a specific MIME type. The **PathCheck** function **deny-existence** sends a customized error page when the client requests a specific path.

For the server to determine which **Error** function to use, it looks for the matching `status` information in the **Error** function's parameter. If the value of `status` in `Request->srvhdrs` matches the value of the **Error** function's parameter, then the **Error** function is used. You need to specify the error type through the **Error** function's parameters: `code` and `reason`. The `code` parameter is for the type of status code and `reason` is the specific textual description of the error code. Table 8-1 lists common error status codes and their respective reason strings. (For more information on status codes, see Returning an Error Page in Chapter 6.)

Table 8-1 Common Error Status Codes

STATUS CODE	REASON STRING
400	Bad request
401	Unauthorized
403	Forbidden
404	Not found
500	Server error

You can use either `code` or `reason`, or both, as the function's parameter. If you specify both parameters, then they should refer to the same error type. The `status` entry in `Request->srvhdrs` reflects both the status code and the reason string—for example, "`401 Unauthorized`". This `status` string is normally sent as the HTML heading and title of the error page to the client.

Writing an Error Function

You can also write your own SAF to handle an error type. It would be similar to the CGI programs called by **query-handler** to handle an error type. As SAFs have access to server variables and are part of the server process, they are actually more powerful. Consider writing your own SAF to customize the error response, tailor the response for different clients, or to provide additional clean-up. If you merely want to send a customized page for all errors of a specific type, then use **send-error**. On the other hand, if you need greater functionality, then write your own **Error** SAF. For example, you may use client name or `user-agent` (browser) to tailor your error response.

When you write your **Error** function, remember that the information for the Status-Line (`status`), which is sent to the client, has already been set by an earlier function. Thus, when you return your customized page to the client, you do not need to use

protocol_status to set `status`. To change the value of the Status-Line, you can remove the existing `status` entry and add a new `status` entry in the pblock `Request->srvhdrs`. The Status-Line set by the earlier function should not include the status code `200`. Status code `200` implies that the request is processed correctly and a page is sent to the client; therefore no error has occurred. For an **Error** function to be called, the status needs to be something other than `status` "200 OK". The earlier function should normally return `REQ_ABORTED` for the server to skip to the **Error** function. If the earlier function returns a value other than `REQ_ABORTED`, the server might not call your **Error** function. For example, if a **Service** function returns `REQ_PROCEED`, it indicates that the request was processed correctly and the page should have already been sent to the client. Therefore, the **Error** function should not be called. If the function returns `REQ_EXIT`, then the server should close the connection and exit without sending an error page.

As an **Error** function can be called after any directive function and is applicable to only one type of error, the NSAPI variables available to the **Error** function may vary. For example, if the error is of type `401 Unauthorized`, then `WWW-authenticate` would be available in `Request->srvhdrs`. On the other hand, if a server error (`500 Server Error`) occurs in an **AuthTrans** function, then a server variable, such as the request's `content-type`, can be unavailable to the **Error** function.

As mentioned earlier, **Error** functions are identified by the server through the `status` information. `status` is normally the common HTTP status `code` plus the default `reason` string. Typically, the server sends the default error messages for the standard errors without declaring an **Error** function. You write an **Error** function to provide a customized server response. If your **Error** function or the built-in **Error** functions **send-error** and **query-handler** are to work, you must specify a `reason` or `code` parameter. You also need to return an error page. If you specify an **Error** function and do not send an error page, there is no response for the client. It is the job of the **Error** function to return the error page to the client.

Because **Error** functions take responsibility for handling an error type, the specific type of error does not need to include the standard `code` or `reason` string. In other words, you can write an **Error** function that can handle a customized status `code` or `reason` string. For example, in an earlier function, you can use **protocol_status** and set the reason string to `special` (for example, `protocol_status(sn, rq, PROTOCOL_SERVER_ERROR, "special")`). This earlier function can return `REQ_ABORTED` to exit with an error. An **Error** function can then be declared to respond only when the reason string is "special", as in the following example:

```
Error fn="send-error" reason="special"
 path="c:/special/special.html"
```

The **send-error** function sends the `special.html` file when `status` includes the `reason` string "special". You can even specify a special error code that the **Error** function handles (for example, `PROTOCOL_PERSONAL` as code `999`). You can also specify a unique error code or reason string for your **Error** SAF (such as, `Error fn="my_error_function" reason="special"`).

SAF Return Values and Order of the Directive Functions

Earlier in this chapter, we mentioned that the order of the functions in **obj.conf** is important. In most cases, the server goes through the directives based on the predefined order of the directives (that is, **AuthTrans**, **NameTrans**, and so on) and the order of the functions in the **obj.conf** file. The server groups the functions of each Object based on the directive. Even if you have a function listed under another directive in the **obj.conf** file, the server calls the function during that function's directive stage (and not during the directive where it is placed in the **obj.conf** file). In most cases, the order of the functions of each directive is important. The server usually goes through each directive's functions in the order found in the **obj.conf** file. For safety and to make sure all the functions work properly, group the directives in the **obj.conf** file based on how the server processes them. Also, make sure you place the functions of each directive in the order you wish the server to process them.

As we have shown, each directive has a different purpose and different server variables can be available to each directive function. The functions for a directive carry out the directive's mission. They are all used by the server to respond properly to different clients' requests. Nothing stops you from writing a directive function that performs differently than expected. We did just that with our **pblock_log** function (Listing 8-4). However, with this approach, you run the risk of a server error or even a server crash if your directive function processes an action that varies from the order expected by the server.

Not all functions are called for every request. Some directives, such as **PathCheck**, accomplish different tasks, so more than one function may be needed to process a single request. On the other hand, only one **Service** function should respond to a specific request. Moreover, there are times when an error occurs, and the server should stop processing a request and respond with an error page. The server determines the next step it should take based on the value returned by a server function.

An SAF returns a code that instructs the server to proceed in a certain order. For example, the server can skip other functions or directives if a function encounters an error and returns REQ_ABORTED. Moreover, the server can skip other functions in a directive if a function accomplishes the necessary step of a request and returns REQ_PROCEED. In other words, the return code can stop the server from processing other directives or can force it to skip the rest of functions in a directive. Therefore, if your function followed another directive function that returns REQ_PROCEED, the server can skip your function. For example, if the **NameTrans** function **document-root** is placed before your **NameTrans** function, **document-root** can set the value of path to the root directory defined by its parameter. Your function can be disregarded by the server. To guarantee that your function is always processed, you should declare it as the first function in a directive.

There are a few exceptions to this rule. For example, under Server 3.x, the **PathCheck** function **check-acl** is always called after other **PathCheck** functions, no matter where in the list of **PathCheck** functions it is placed. Also, although all **ObjectType** functions are proceeded by the server, the first **ObjectType** function that sets `content-type` determines its value. The server ignores any additional `content-type` that is inserted by a later **ObjectType** function. The server processes only the request based on the first `content-type`. Therefore, your function should either be the first **ObjectType** function that attempts to insert the `content-type`, or it should remove the earlier `content-type` from the `Request->srvhdrs` pblock before inserting a new one. Finally, as we discussed, **Error** functions are unique. They are processed immediately after an error, but only when a specific error occurs.

Similar to other built-in server functions, your SAF should return one of the server's standard return codes. By returning a specific code, you instruct the server to take a specific step after your SAF is finished. You should review Tables 8-2 and 8-3 to decide when and what value your function should return. Generally, your function should return `REQ_PROCEED` when it actually accomplishes the step expected from its directive. It should return `REQ_NOACTION` when no content data should be sent to the client, or when your function did not finish the anticipated steps of a directive. This setup allows another server function to take the responsibility of fulfilling the directive's mission. Finally, your function should return `REQ_ABORTED` (or `REQ_EXIT`) in case of error.

There are five predefined return codes, each of which is determined by a specific number and a name beginning with `REQ_` (REQUEST). These codes direct the server response. Table 8-2 lists the common return codes.

Table 8-2　SAF Return Code

RETURN CODE	DEFINITION
`REQ_PROCEED` (0)	The function performed its intended directive purpose successfully. Proceed with finishing the response to the request (see Table 8–3 for more detail).
`REQ_NOACTION` (-2)	Proceed without performing the requested action. The function should be ignored by the server or did not perform its intended directive purpose. The function could have accomplished any number of tasks, but did not accomplish the steps expected from its directive (see Table 8–3 for more detail).
`REQ_ABORTED` (-1)	Abort the request. This action is not always the same as aborting the session. The connection can still be alive. It calls the error-handling functions, which set the status and return the HTML error response page. This value should not be returned in the middle of sending a response to a client. Typically, this return code means that an error occurred during the SAF. The server usually skips to the **Error** and/or **AddLog** functions to finish processing the request and return an error page. You should log an error (**log_error**) and return an error page to the client before returning `REQ_ABORTED`. You can return an error page to the client with **protocol_status** and/or an **Error** function. **protocol_finish_request** is called by the server to finish the request.
`REQ_EXIT` (-3)	Stops everything, immediately close the session and the connection to the client, and exit. Tear down the entire session. This code could be sent due to a response to a server error, such as file read and write. The server does not return an error page, but **protocol_finish_request** is still called by the server.

Table 8-2 SAF Return Code (*continued*)

Warning ▶

Although this function implies that the server stops processing other directives, in a test on FastTrack Server 2.x for NT and Windows 95, the server continued to process the directives. It even responded with the correct page when this code was returned by a directive function. In other words, this function exits your program, but does not stop the server from processing any other action. It does stop the server from returning an error page. Therefore, if you wish to stop the server from processing other directives so as to return an error page, use REQ_ABORTED.

REQ_RESTART (-4)   Restart the response procedure. The entire request–response process is restarted. The server goes through the entire request again, this time including the information from the earlier response. This action is not the same as restarting the request from scratch. When a **Service** function returns REQ_RESTART, the server goes through the directives again, but the server variables already include the values from the previous run. In other words, although the server begins with the first directive (that is, **AuthTrans** or **NameTrans**), the information in the server variables could include path from the earlier request as well as ppath from the new request. In a test, I was able to use this return value only for a **Service** directive function. Make sure you would like the server to take the action described here before you return REQ_RESTART. This return value creates a number of duplicate server variables and could even lead to an endless loop that causes a server crash.

Normally, the server responds the same way, independent of which function returns the value. For example, the server stops processing the request when REQ_ABORTED is returned. However, REQ_PROCEED produces a different result based on the type of directive. Table 8-3 delineates the different responses of the server when REQ_PROCEED is returned. To compare the server's response, we should also review how the server responds when a directive returns REQ_NOACTION. Although REQ_NOACTION always means that the server goes to the next function, this situation may also arise with REQ_PROCEED, as in **PathCheck** directive. Table 8-3 helps you decide when you should return REQ_NOACTION instead of REQ_PROCEED.

Table 8-3 Server Response Depending on the Directive and Return Value

DIRECTIVE	REQ_PROCEED	REQ_NOACTION
Init	Go to next **function** (All functions are processed once at the start [restart] of the server.)	Go to next **function** (Same as REQ_PROCEED. Because these functions are global, you should not return REQ_NOACTION. The function should either proceed or abort.)

Table 8-3 Server Response Depending on the Directive and Return Value
(continued)

AuthTrans	Go to next **directive** (**NameTrans**) (User was authenticated.)	Go to next **function** (Client was not authenticated. Another **AuthTrans** function can try to authenticate the client. If **AuthTrans** was returned in conjunction with **PathCheck**, then **PathCheck** can ask the client to authenticate again.)
NameTrans	Go to next **directive** (The server can go to the next directive in the current Object or to an Object identified by the `name` parameter of the function. Only one **NameTrans** function should translate the partial path to the physical path and return `REQ_PROCEED`.)	Go to next **function** (The function did not set the physical path information. Final name translation was not performed.)
PathCheck	Go to next **function** (The function is responsible for not only authorization, but also verification of the path information. Therefore, all functions are processed.)	Go to next **function** (The function did not perform its intended purpose. For example, the files are not loaded [**load-config**]; extra path information was not found [**find-path-info**]; authentication is not forced, and so on.)
ObjectType	Go to next **function** (More than one function can determine the type of file to return. For example, you can have **type-by-extension** and **image-switch**. The first function that sets an attribute determines its value. Later functions that attempt to set the same attribute are ignored. The order of the functions is important.)	Go to next **function** (The MIME type is already determined. `content-type` was already added. Skip to the next function.)
Service	Go to next **directive** (Only one function should process the client's request and return a response. If a document is sent, use `REQ_PROCEED`.)	Go to next **function** (The function was not used or did not return any data. A later function can finish processing the request.)
AddLog	Go to next **function** (The data were logged successfully. You can log information in different files using different functions. Therefore, all functions are processed. There is no other directive after this directive.)	Go to next **function** (No logging occurred. The function did not log any information.)
Error	Go to **AddLog** and **exit** (Only one function should handle a specific error type. Functions should return an error page. Otherwise, no data are sent to the client.)	Go to next **function** (Skip to the next error function. The function is not used. It did not return an error page.)

Summary

In this chapter, we expanded on our discussion of each server directive to look more closely at the purpose of each directive. We also considered how to write an SAF for each directive. Each directive has a unique purpose. You must decide which directive provides the functionality you need.

In addition, we wrote several examples of the type of functions you may write. We reviewed how you could take advantage of various authorization methods provided by the server. We also wrote a customized log file that can be very beneficial in examining how the server processes each request.

Your SAF can accomplish a variety of tasks. The various server directives provide needed flexibility. You can change the server variables, require authentication, redirect a client, set the response-headers, return a dynamic generated page, process a client's form input, return a customized response, log various server information, specify an error page, and provide error handling, among other actions.

We have not yet discussed in detail how you read data from a client's input. In Chapter 9, we will go through a few **Service** functions that read data from a form. We will write an example in which the client uses a GET method of request to return a mail response. We will also write an SAF that reads a client's input from a POST method. These two methods (POST and GET) are the standard HTTP methods for client input.

Processing Form Input

Thus far, we have covered the basics of programming an SAF. We have discussed how you choose a directive for your function, how you read data from the server or client, and how you return data to the client. We have also discussed how you install and register your program. In this chapter, we will focus on processing a client request entered through a form. We will go through the steps of reading and verifying the client input and generating a response based on that input. The examples in this chapter are **Service** functions.

The first two examples in this chapter read data and respond to specific client requests. Both examples are similar to CGI programs you may find on the Web. The first example uses a GET method of request and sends the client input as a mail message to a designated address. The second example is a POST example, similar to the Guest Book example we wrote in Chapter 3. We will also write a WAI version of this example in Chapter 16. Both examples in this chapter are complete programs that can be deployed and tested with little modification. Finally, we will go through a general-purpose function that can be used to process any form. You can include this last program with code you have written to process a specific form request. This program checks for the method of the request, parses the client input, and sends the input to your program in a pblock data structure.

Warning ▶

When you use the HTML files that are intended for the programs in this book, make sure you place these files in the document directory and open them using the server's URL. If you open these files using the File|Open File option in the browser, the programs will not run. This point may seem obvious, but in a number of cases the user took these steps and did not know why the programs were not working properly.

mailto Program—A GET Example

The first example (Listing 9-2) discussed in this chapter is **mailto**. The purpose of this SAF is to process the client input and mail the result to a designated recipient. You can find similar CGI examples on the Web or in different CGI books. This program asks the client to input some feedback about the Web site and sends the comment as part of a mail message to a designated recipient.

There are many ways of processing and mailing client input. One method is to use the new Server-side JavaScript SendMail Object, which is added to Netscape 3.x Server. You can also have the client input sent to a mail gateway as an attachment using the HTML `mailto` URL. In the HTML form, you specify the method of delivery as `POST` and the location where you would like the information sent. The following code is an example of such an HTML form tag:

```
<FORM ACTION="mailto:joe@foo.com" METHOD="POST">
```

You can even specify a subject after the `mailto:` address such as "`mailto: joe@foo.com?subject=comments`". Assuming that the client browser can handle the `mailto` URL and that the user has filled in the mail server information, the browser can automatically send the input to the `mailto` address. To send this information as an attachment, the client must use Netscape Navigator 2.0 or later. Moreover, the settings for the mail preferences for Navigator must include the correct information for the outgoing mail. (To set these preferences, check under the Options|Mail and News Preferences menu for Navigator 2.x or 3.x or under the category "Mail & Groups" from the Edit|Preferences menu for Navigator [Communicator] 4.x.) Some browsers, such as Navigator 1.2, can also send the input as the contents of the mail message instead of an attached document.

The attached file includes the contents of `POST`, which is a string of `[name]=` "`[value]`" data from the form. These data are URL-encoded. You must decode (parse) the information before using it. For instance, you can write your own parsing program based on the decoding functions we have already written for the Guest Book example in Chapter 3. On the other hand, you may use a freeware program, such as mailto: Formatter, to decode the e-mail message. You can find this freeware program under Robert Fries' Digital Playground site (`http://homepage.interaccess.com/~rpfries/`).

Here, we will write an SAF that parses the client input and then mails the result. With a mail program, you can have greater control over the client input. You can also combine the code for mailing a request with an NSAPI program that accomplishes additional tasks. For example, while processing a client request, you can send a mail message to a manager who needs to verify or review the request. An employee can request to buy supplies for his or her department. The order is then mailed to the manager for review and approval.

We have written this example as a `GET` method to illustrate how a `GET` request is processed by an SAF. Normally, you should use a `POST` method with a form. `POST` provides better security, as the client must use the form to send the request. With GET, the client can modify the query string in the URL instead of using a form. POST also allows for other MIME types. Moreover, there are limitations to the size of the environment variables and the data that can be passed on through a URL. The maximum size of a URL is 4K. Thus the input from a GET method can be truncated. The next two examples in this chapter (Listings 9-5 and 9-6) include instructions for processing a POST request. As a simple exercise, use the information in these later listings to add support for POST to the example in Listing 9-2.

Listing 9-2 is written for the NT platform, but can easily be modified to support UNIX. For instance, the functions **_spawnl** and **_tempname** are Windows-specific, but similar functions exist for UNIX. To write operating system-specific code and incorporate it with the code for other operating systems, use the conditional compiler preprocessor #ifdef with the identifiers XP_WIN32 and XP_UNIX. For example, use the following:

```
#ifdef XP_WIN32
    /* code specific for Windows */
#else
    /* code specific for UNIX
        (XP_UNIX) */
 #endif
```

Normally, one uses a mail user-agent, such as Netscape Mail or Eudora, to generate and send e-mail to the Simple Mail Transfer Protocol (SMTP) mail server. SMTP, a standard Internet mail protocol, is used to move messages between servers. This is different from other proprietary protocols used with cc:Mail and Microsoft Mail. The mail user-agent receives the e-mail through a POP3 (Post Office Protocol version 3) server that collects and processes the messages.

Our program needs to generate the message automatically and send it to the mail transport-agent (SMTP mail server). To mail the client input programmatically, we use a console utility and pass it the relevant mailing information (for example, the sender's and recipient's e-mail addresses) and the contents of the message. The client input is processed and used to create the arguments and the comment file that the console mail utility program needs. We then spawn a new process and pass this information to the program. You can also use this method to spawn other console applications. This console program needs to access an SMTP mail server (such as Netscape Mail Server) and pass our mail message.

Writing a **mailto** program under UNIX is, in fact, simpler than writing one under NT. The *sendmail* mail program, which routes and delivers mail using SMTP, should already be part of most UNIX systems. With NT, you normally need to obtain such a program. There are commercial ports of the UNIX sendmail program for NT, most notably MetaInfo's Sendmail 2.0 (http://www.metainfo.com/products/sendmail/index.htm). MetaInfo's Sendmail provides more than just routing a mail message to a mail server. For our example, we assume that you already have a SMTP mail server and that we need to pass only the mail message to the server using a simple utility program. Thus we use a freeware utility that is readily obtainable through Internet. For this example, we use Blat, a public domain Windows NT console utility that sends the contents of a file in an e-mail message using SMTP. You can find the program plus the source code in a number of different locations, including Blat! a WinNT SMPT mail client page (`http://gepasi.dbs.aber.ac.uk/ softw/blat.html`). The current version of Blat is 1.5. Blat is also included on the CD-ROM that accompanies this book. Other programs you might use include Jgaa's wSendMail (under Jgaa's Cgi-Bin page, `http://home.sol.no/~jarlaase/ cgi-bin.htm#wsendmail`) and Software.com's Postmail for NT (under Software. com's Postmail page, `http://www.software.com/Products/Postmail/ Postmail.html`). These programs are not complicated. You can even write your own "sendmail" utility and incorporate it with Listing 9-2 for a more efficient means of processing the client request. (The purpose of this function is not to advocate the use of Blat or any other SMTP gateway program, but rather to show how you can take advantage of such a program.)

mailto HTML Page

Listing 9-1 includes the HTML page that can be used for the **mailto** program. Figure 9-1 is the screen capture of the HTML page. Through the form, the client inputs his or her name and e-mail address. In the **mailto** example, the name of the client is used only for the Thank You page that is returned to the client upon success. You may want to change the program to include the name in the content of the e-mail message. The e-mail address is used as the sender's address. Next, the client chooses a specific topic on which to comment, rates the site based on predefined categories, and adds any other comments. By means of the **mailto** SAF, we require the client to specify all of the categories, except for the additional comments. As mentioned earlier, JavaScript is a good tool for field validation, so you may want to consider using it to make sure not only that the fields are filled, but also that they are properly entered.

Listing 9-1 takes advantage of the different form fields to categorize and organize the comments that are sent by different clients. The topic of the comment is used to specify a different recipient. When the client chooses a topic by selecting a radio button, a specific recipient is declared for the value of the button. Thus the sale representative (`salesguy@imagia.com`) will get only the comments regarding the sales department. As with the Guest Book example discussed in Chapter 3, when a client does not choose a radio button, the `[name]=[value]` information is not passed to the **mailto** program. If you like, you can add the parameter CHECKED to the INPUT TYPE="radio" tag to make the specified radio button be the default checked button. Listing 9-1 does not use CHECKED, because we want to make sure the client manually chooses the radio button.

The rating scale is used for the subject of the e-mail, and the detailed comment is used for the actual body of the e-mail. Thus the client's response can be organized in the specific recipient's mail program by subject (that is, the rating scale).

You can modify these form options or write your own HTML page. If you plan to use this form, make sure you change the radio buttons' descriptions to reflect the section (category) of the site for which you wish the user to comment and their values to reflect the e-mail address of the appropriate recipient.

The use of forms for mailing information is flexible enough to work with a variety of different topics, not just a feedback page. With a few minor changes, you can update the **mailto** example to work with a different form.

Remember that we are using predefined values for different fields, such as the radio buttons. Thus the program expects a specific value. With a GET method, however, the client can simply change the value in the query string and send a wrong value with the request URL. This tactic can lead to errors. Although the **mailto** function includes some error checking, it does not attempt to catch all of the different types of errors that are possible.

Listing 9-1   mailto Example's HTML Page

```
<HTML>
<HEAD>
<TITLE>Give us your feedback!</TITLE>
</HEAD>

<BODY>

<H1>Feedback Page</H1>

<H2>Help us make this site better<BR>
 give us some feedback to help us grow</H2>

<HR>
<FORM ACTION="mailto.send" METHOD="GET">

<B>Please enter your name:</B>
    <INPUT TYPE="text" NAME="name" SIZE="39" MAXLENGTH=39>
<P>
<B>Enter your email address:</B>
    <INPUT TYPE="text" NAME="address" SIZE="39" MAXLENGTH=39>
<P>
<H3>Choose the topic you wish to comment on:</H3>

<!--following values are imaginary and need to be replaced-->
<INPUT TYPE="radio" NAME="recipient"
  VALUE="prodinfo@imagia.com">Product Information<BR>
<INPUT TYPE="radio" NAME="recipient"
  VALUE="salesguy@imagia.com">Sales Department<BR>
<INPUT TYPE="radio" NAME="recipient"
```

Listing 9-1   **mailto** Example's HTML Page (*continued*)

```
    VALUE="webmaster@imagia.com">Web related<BR>

<H3>Select how well you think we are doing:</H3>

<SELECT NAME="subject">
    <OPTION>Excellent
    <OPTION>Above Average
    <OPTION>Average
    <OPTION>Below Average
</SELECT><BR>

<H2><I>Your detailed comment:</I></H2>

<TEXTAREA NAME="comment" ROWS=4 COLS=50></TEXTAREA><BR>

<HR SIZE=4>

<INPUT TYPE="submit" VALUE="SEND FEEDBACK">
<INPUT TYPE="reset" VALUE="START OVER">
</FORM>

<HR>

</BODY>
</HTML>
```

Instructions for Blat

The following code gives the description of Blat's (version 1.5) command-line arguments:

```
blat <file name> -t <recipient>
                [-s <subject>
                 -f <sender>
                 -i <address>
                 -c <recipient>
                 -b <recipient>
                 -mime
                 -server <address>]
```

- `<file name>` holds the message body.
- `-t <recipient>` is the recipient's address (use with `-c` for a carbon-copy recipient list and with `-b` for a blind carbon-copy list). Use a comma to separate addresses.
- `-s <subject>` is the subject line.
- `-f <sender>` is the sender's address. Use it to override the default sender. *This address must be known to the SMTP server.*

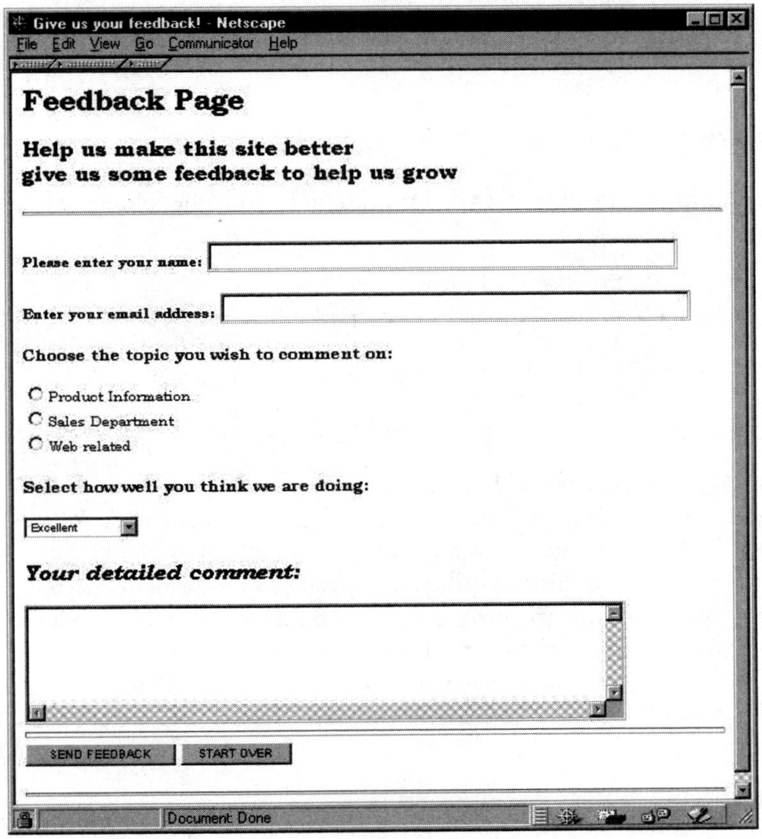

Figure 9-1 Screen Capture of the `mailto.html` **Page**

- `-i <address>` holds the `From:` header address (which does not need to be known by the SMTP server). (The actual `<sender>` address is stamped in `Reply-to:` and `Sender:` lines.)
- `-mime` gives the MIME Quoted-Printable Content-Transfer-Encoding information. It specifies the MIME type.
- `-server <address>` overrides the default SMTP server.

To run Blat, you need first to install it by running

```
blat -install <server address> <sender address>
```

This line puts the information for the default SMTP server and the sender's address in the NT registry for later use. You can override these values through Blat's command-line arguments. You must also make sure that the files `blat.exe` and `gensock.dll` are placed in a directory accessible by this code or in the proper path.

(See the readme file that comes with Blat on the accompanying CD-ROM for detailed instructions.)

Registration Instructions

To install the SAF in Listing 9-2, you need to compile it and include the following line in the **obj.conf** file:

```
Init fn=load-modules funcs=mailto
 shlib="c:/netscape/server/nsapi/examples/mailto.dll"

Service fn=mailto method="(GET|HEAD)"
 type="magnus-internal/mail"
 mail-program="c:\\netscape\\server\\blat.exe"
```

If you added this SAF to an existing DLL, then modify the existing **load-modules** line in the **obj.conf** file by adding the function to the funcs parameter list. You should also update the shlib parameter to reflect the correct location of the DLL. mail-program is the location of the Blat utility. We specify this information here instead of hard-coding the location in the program. You should change the information to reflect the location of the mail program on your machine.

To enable the server to recognize this **Service** SAF, you should also update the **mime.types** file. In **mime.types**, add the following line (or any other extension [exts] you may wish to use with the SAF):

```
type=magnus-internal/mail exts=send
```

As mentioned earlier, this function is specific to NT. You must modify **load-modules** and the mail-program information to use the modified version of this program with UNIX.

The temporary directory where the comment file can be created is hard-coded (TEMPDIR). You should change the path for this directory (c:\\temp) to the path of the temporary directory on your machine. This directory must also be accessible to the server, and the server must have permission to read and write from the directory.

Listing 9-2 was written for Server 3.x. You need to include the following NSAPI header files for Server 2.x, instead of including nsapi.h. You also need to add a dummy parameter (for example, zero [0]) for the NSAPI function **system_errmsg**. The version of this function supported by earlier Netscape Servers expects a parameter for this function.

```
/* Include files for Server 2.x */
#include "base/pblock.h"
#include "base/session.h"
#include "frame/req.h"

#include "frame/protocol.h" /* protocol_start_response */
```

```
#include "frame/log.h"          /* log_error */
#include "base/util.h"          /* util_sprintf */
```

Listing 9-2-1   mailto Example (mailto Function)

```c
/* include this file if you are using Server 3.x */
#include "nsapi.h"

/* _tempnam, _spawnl, strcmp etc. */
#include <stdio.h>
#include <process.h>
#include <string.h>

/* header file for the general-purpose functions we will
   write, including parse_query
 */
#include "forms.h"

/* temp directory for comment file */
#define TEMPDIR "c:\\temp"

/* default value for parse_query */
#define DEFAULT_VALUE "void"

NSAPI_PUBLIC int send_simple_response(char *title,
                 char *content, Session *sn, Request *rq);

/* main Service function mailto */
NSAPI_PUBLIC int mailto(pblock *param, Session *sn,
                        Request *rq)
{
   char *mail_program;      /* path to the mail program */
   char *query;             /* form's information */
   pblock *variables;       /* holds the form information in
                               pblock */
   char *name;              /* name of the client */
   char *address;           /* e-mail address of client */
   char *recipient;         /* recipient's address */
   char *subject;           /* subject of mail */
   char *comment;           /* body of mail */
   SYS_FILE fd;             /* file handle for the comments */
   char *filename = NULL;   /* holds the temporary file name
                               that is passed to the console
                               program; contains the client's
                               comment */
```

Listing 9-2-1   mailto Example (**mailto** Function) (*continued*)

```
char arguments[1024];        /* arguments to be passed to
                                mail_program */
char response_content[256]; /* content of Thank You page */
int ret;                     /* send_simple_response return
                                value */
int return_value = -1;       /* mailto return value; -1
                                equals REQ_ABORTED */

/* get the name of the mail program */
mail_program = pblock_findval("mail-program", param);

/* make sure the mail program was specified */
if(!mail_program)
{
    protocol_status(sn, rq, PROTOCOL_SERVER_ERROR,
            "A server configuration error occurred.");
    log_error(LOG_MISCONFIG, "mailto", sn, rq,
      "No mail program was specified in obj.conf file.");
    return REQ_ABORTED;
}

/* get the query string */
query = pblock_findval("query", rq->reqpb);

/* Check for query. It should be there. With the GET
   method of request, the input is sent through
   the query string.
 */
if (!query)
{
    protocol_status(sn, rq, PROTOCOL_BAD_REQUEST,
        "Your browser didn't send any information.");
    log_error(LOG_WARN, "mailto", sn, rq,
        "The browser didn't send any information.");
    return REQ_ABORTED;
}

/* parse_query does all the parsing of the query and
   returns a pblock structure with the client input
 */
variables = parse_query(query, 5, DEFAULT_VALUE);

/* get the value of name, address, recipient, subject, and
   comment from the pblock returned by parse_query
```

Listing 9-2-1   mailto Example (**mailto** Function) (*continued*)

```
*/
name = pblock_findval("name", variables);
address = pblock_findval("address", variables);
recipient = pblock_findval("recipient", variables);
subject = pblock_findval("subject", variables);
comment = pblock_findval("comment", variables);

/* Check if the fields are filled. "comment" can be empty. */

/* check for name */
if (!name || (strcmp(name, DEFAULT_VALUE) == 0))
{
    protocol_status(sn, rq, PROTOCOL_FORBIDDEN,
                    "You did not fill in your name.");
    log_error(LOG_WARN, "mailto", sn, rq,
              "Form was not filled out completely.");

    goto done;
}

/* check for address */
if (!address || (strcmp(address, DEFAULT_VALUE) == 0))
{
    protocol_status(sn, rq, PROTOCOL_FORBIDDEN,
              "You did not fill in your e-mail address.");
    log_error(LOG_WARN, "mailto", sn, rq,
              "Form was not filled out completely.");
              goto done;
}

/* Check recipient's value (address is defined in the
   form itself). We don't verify if the value is actu-
   ally changed in the URL's query string.
 */
if (!recipient || (strcmp(recipient, DEFAULT_VALUE) == 0))
{
    protocol_status(sn, rq, PROTOCOL_FORBIDDEN,
                    "You did not choose a topic.");
    log_error(LOG_WARN, "mailto", sn, rq,
              "Form was not filled out completely.");

    goto done;
}

/* create a random file name using TEMPDIR path
   and the prefix "mail"
```

Listing 9-2-1   mailto Example (**mailto** Function) (*continued*)

```
    */
    filename = _tempnam(TEMPDIR, "mail");

    /* if successful, write the comment into the file
       to be passed to the mail program
     */
    if(filename)
    {
        fd = system_fopenWA(filename);

        /* make sure file was properly opened */
        if(fd == SYS_ERROR_FD)
        {
            protocol_status(sn, rq, PROTOCOL_SERVER_ERROR,
                        "Sorry, server was unable to process \
                        your comment.");
            log_error(LOG_FAILURE, "mailto", sn, rq,
                        "error opening %s (%s)",
                        filename, system_errmsg());

            goto done;
        }

        /* write into the file and check for errors */
        if (system_fwrite_atomic(fd, comment,
                                strlen(comment)) !=IO_OKAY)
        {
            protocol_status(sn, rq, PROTOCOL_SERVER_ERROR,
                        "Sorry, server was unable to process \
                        your comment.");
            log_error(LOG_FAILURE, "mailto", sn, rq,
                        "could not write to the file.");

            goto done;
        }

        /* close the file */
        system_fclose(fd);
    }
    else
    {
        /* if filename was not properly created */
        protocol_status(sn, rq, PROTOCOL_SERVER_ERROR,
                    "Sorry, server was unable to process \
                    your comment.");
```

Listing 9-2-1   **mailto** Example (**mailto** Function) (*continued*)

```
        log_error(LOG_FAILURE, "mailto", sn, rq,
                "Error while creating the temp mail file.");

      goto done;
    }

  /* set the parameter for mail_program using the program's
     settings and the information we got from the form
   */
  util_sprintf(arguments,
                "\"%s\" -s \"%s\" -t \"%s\" -f \"%s\"",
                filename, subject, recipient, address);

  /* Load mail_program and send it the arguments. _P_WAIT
     suspends calling the process until execution of the
     new process is complete (synchronous _spawnl). The
     exit status is 0 if the process terminated normally.
   */
  if(_spawnl(_P_WAIT, mail_program, mail_program,
            arguments, NULL) == REQ_PROCEED)
  {
      /* generate the content of the page to be returned
         to the client, if everything has gone as planned.
       */
      util_sprintf(response_content,
                  "%s, thanks for your comment. "
                  "We appreciate your feedback.", name);

      /* send the HTML Thank You page to the client */
      ret = send_simple_response("Thank You",
                                  response_content,
                                  sn, rq);

      /* check if the sending of the page was successful */
      if(ret != REQ_PROCEED)
      {
          return_value = ret;
          goto done;
      }
  }
  /* send an error message if an error occurred while
     spawning the mail program
```

Listing 9-2-1   mailto Example (**mailto** Function) (*continued*)

```
    */
    else
    {
        protocol_status(sn, rq, PROTOCOL_SERVER_ERROR,
                        "Sorry, server was unable to process \
                        your comment.");
        log_error(LOG_FAILURE, "mailto", sn, rq,
                    "Error occurred while sending information \
                    to the mail_program.");

         return REQ_ABORTED;
    }

    /* set the status to success, clean up, and exit */
    return_value = REQ_PROCEED;
    goto done;

    done:

    /* free memory and remove the comment file */
    if(filename)
    {
        if (remove(filename) == -1)
        {
            /* log an error if we were unable to
               remove the comment file
             */
            log_error(LOG_FAILURE, "mailto", sn, rq,
                        "Could not delete the temp file \
                        created for mailto.");
        }

        free(filename);
    }

    /* free pblock variables */
    if(variables) pblock_free(variables);

    return return_value;
}
```

Listing 9-2-2   mailto Example (**send_simple_response** Function)

```
/* This function is a generic function that generates
   a standard HTML page and sends it to the client.
   The dynamic information of the page, -- that is, title
```

Listing 9-2-2   mailto Example (**send_simple_response** Function) (*continued*)

```
       and content, -- are passed on to this function.
   */
NSAPI_PUBLIC int send_simple_response(char *title,
                   char *content, Session *sn, Request *rq)
{
      long int cl;                  /* length of buffer */
      char *buf = NULL;             /* holds the information to be
                                       passed to user */

      /* remove the existing content-type */
      param_free(pblock_remove("content-type", rq->srvhdrs));

      /* set the content-type to HTML */
      pblock_nvinsert("content-type", "text/html",
                      rq->srvhdrs);

      /* set status to OK */
      protocol_status(sn, rq, PROTOCOL_OK, NULL);

      /* if NOACTION (request was HEAD) then do not send the
         HTML page */
      if(protocol_start_response(sn, rq) == REQ_NOACTION)
      {
          return REQ_PROCEED;
      }

      /* allocate a rough size for buf */
      buf = (char *) MALLOC((52 * sizeof(char)) +
                        ((strlen(title) * 2) * sizeof(char)) +
                        ((strlen(content)) * sizeof(char)));

      /* cl is the length of the buf to be used by net_write */
      cl = util_sprintf(buf,
                  "<HTML><HEAD><TITLE>%s</TITLE></HEAD>\n"
                  "<BODY><H1>%s</H1>\n"
                  "%s</BODY></HTML>",
                  title, title, content);

      /* send the HTML page */
      if(net_write(sn->csd, buf, cl) == IO_ERROR)
      {
          FREE(buf);
          return REQ_EXIT;
      }

      FREE(buf);
      return REQ_PROCEED;
}
```

Stepping Through the mailto Program

The **mailto** program includes two separate functions; **mailto** and **send_simple_response**. **mailto** does the bulk of the work. It checks the client input and spawns the process for the mail program (Blat). **send_simple_response** is a generic function that is used to return an HTML page to the client. You pass the title and the content of the HTML page, and the function generates and sends the page. In this example, we use this function to send a Thank You page. The **mailto** function also uses a parsing function, **parse_query**. In the section Parsing Functions, we will step through **parse_query**.

Let us now walk through the **mailto** program. In Listing 9-2-1, we first declare the include files. Along with the NSAPI header file, we also include the process.h file, where the **_spawnl** function is declared. Although we included stdio.h (for **_tempnam** and **remove**) and string.h (for **strcmp**), it is not necessary to add these files here, as they are already indirectly included through the NSAPI header files forms.h. is the header file where we declare the general-purpose functions that are used by other SAFs. In forms.h, we declare these external functions as external NSAPI functions (extern NSAPI_PUBLIC). For now, this file contains the **parse_query** function declaration. Later, we will add the declaration for **send_simple_response** and other functions.

As mentioned earlier in the instructions for installing this function, you can change the temporary directory for the comment file. Instead of hard-coding this directory, you can pass this information through a parameter of the **mailto** function in the **obj.conf** file. The value of DEFAULT_VALUE is used by the **parse_query** function. (We will discuss **parse_query** and parsing of a URL-encoded string in detail in the section Parsing Functions.)

In the **mailto** function, we first get the path to the mail program (mail_program). This information is essential to mailing the client's feedback. We make sure the parameter is declared in the **obj.conf** file. Otherwise, we return a server error page and log a misconfiguration error in the log file. We could also verify that the request is GET, but this step is really unnecessary. We set the methods for this function as GET and HEAD in the **obj.conf** file. Any other method causes a server error before our function is even called. Try changing the METHOD in the HTML form to POST and then use the form to send in a comment. The server should return a server error page before the **mailto** function is called.

Next, we check for the query string, which includes the client input. With the GET method, the client input is found in the query entry in *Request->reqpb*. We make sure the client sent a query string, as we cannot process anything without it. To parse the query string, we call the function **parse_query**. We pass **parse_query** the query string to be parsed, along with the number of fields in the form and the DEFAULT_VALUE ("void"). DEFAULT_VALUE is used when value of the [*name*]=[*value*] pair of data is empty (NULL). **parse_query**, in turn, returns the parsed variables in a pblock data structure. We look in the returned pblock for the value of each field by using **pblock_findval**. The **parse_query** function does not truncate any spaces in the client input. In other words, if the client entered "   John Smith   ", the value of the name will be "   John Smith   " and not "John Smith". Moreover, if the client entered a space for any of the values, **mailto** assumes that there is a valid value for the fields and does not report an error. Because none of the information in this form is critical and spaces do not cause a critical error, we do not provide extra error checking here. For example, even if there are spaces before or after the client's address, the spaces are ignored when they are used as part of the arguments for the mail program. If you want to make sure all the values are accurate, however, you may choose to update this program for additional error checking.

Next, we verify that the client entered a name and e-mail address and chose a topic for comment. We require that this information be sent by the client. The name is used only to customize the Thank You page, but you may also add it to the body of the mail message. The e-mail address overrides the default e-mail address of the sender we specified during Blat's installation. The topic of the comment is essential, as it specifies to whom (recipient) the comment is sent. The recipient is NULL if the client does not choose a radio button. As already mentioned, the error-checking code in Listing 9-2-1 is rudimentary. It simply verifies whether the client sends information for each field. If you want to make sure the client's e-mail message is actually in e-mail format or inform the client when multiple fields are empty, you should update the code with additional error checking. Moreover, since the method is GET, the values of these variables could be modified directly in the URL sent by the client. Our code does not check for such changes to the query string. You may also want to check for these errors in the query string, especially for changes in the recipient's e-mail address. Except for the direct changes to the query string, you should consider JavaScript for error checking. JavaScript is the best and easiest way of providing these types of form validation.

We also generate a random file name in the TMP directory with the prefix mail. We have used **_tempnam** to generate the file name, but there are other functions you can use to generate a unique temporary file name. (Also, make sure to use a thread-safe function or provide for thread safety in your program.) The **_tempnam** function first looks for the TMP directory specified by the TMP environment variable of your system. If such directory is not found, it uses the directory specified as part of its argument (that is, the TEMPDIR). If the directory in TEMPDIR is not found, **_tempnam** uses the P_tmpdir specified in STDIO.H or the current working directory, in that order. If **_tempnam** was successful, we open and write the client's detailed comment into it. **system_fopenWT** seems like a logical choice, as the comment is never appended to an existing file. **system_fopenWT** does not always function properly, however. To make sure the SAF is able to open the file and write into it, use **system_fopenWA**. (**system_fopenWT** does work properly under some earlier versions of Netscape Server.) We write into the file using **system_fwrite_atomic**. It guarantees that the file is locked while we write into it. For this program, we do not need to worry about locking a file before writing into it, because every comment should have its own file. After writing into the file, we close the file (**system_fclose**).

As noted earlier, the parsing function (**parse_query**) uses the DEFAULT_VALUE in place of any empty input field. Therefore, the comment fields will reflect the

DEFAULT_VALUE ("void")—that is, the mail message will include the text void—if the client did not input any comment.

We are now ready to create an argument string that can be passed to mail_program (Blat). With **_spawnl**, we can specify each command-line argument directly through **_spawnl** parameters. Here, we put the command-line arguments in one string and then use this string as the arguments for mail_program. **_spawnl** creates and executes a new process. It executes mail_program as a new process and passes the arguments to it. **_spawnl**'s first parameter, _P_WAIT, causes the calling function to wait until the spawned process returns (synchronous) before it continues executing. We use this option to remove the file after we have finished sending it. It guarantees that the message is already mailed before the server continues through our code. With _P_WAIT, **_spawnl** has access to the console and opens a command-prompt window for the output of mail_program. Once the mail is sent, the console window is closed. You must explicitly flush or close any stream before calling **_spawnl**. Enough memory must be available for loading and executing the new process. **_spawnl** returns 0 if the process terminated normally and –1 in case of an error when the process is not started. You can then check errno for different types of errors. For example, the value is ENOENT if the file or path for the mail program is not found or ENOMEM if not enough memory is available to execute the process. **_spawnl**, however, does not verify if Blat was actually able to connect to the mail server. You should make sure the mail server is running and is accessible to Blat before using this function. As with **_tempnam**, you may consider other functions for running a process that mails the comment message. For example, you can create a pipe and then execute the program.

After the message is sent, we call **send_simple_response** (Listing 9-2-2) to send a Thank You page to the client. We also use the name of the client to customize the response_text (body) of this page. **send_simple_response** is a straightforward function, using the same steps we discussed in the section Returning a Dynamic Page in Chapter 6. The unique aspect of this function is that we allow another function to call it and pass the title and content of the page. The title you pass to this function (first parameter) is also used as the HTML heading for the page. In Listing 9-2-1, the size of the message content (response_content) is set to 256. To enable the function to use the Session and Request data structures of the calling function, we also pass these two data structures. **send_simple_response** returns the standard SAF return value (for example, REQ_PROCEED for success). Later, we will add **send_simple_response** to the general-purpose functions file and to the forms.h header file. Different SAFs will then be free to use the same function.

If the HTML page was properly sent to the client, we begin the clean-up process and exit. We first remove the file (filename) that was created for the comment. To remove this file, we use the ANSI C function **remove**. We also free the string (filename) that **_tempnam** created. Next, we free the pblock data structure (variables) that holds the client's input. You do not have to use FREE to free the memory block you allocated using MALLOC. For compatibility with earlier versions of the server and for general clarity, however, it is recommended that you free any memory block you malloc.

We use **protocol_status** and **log_error** throughout this program to send back an error page and log an error. Sometimes it may be difficult to decide which status code (used with **protocol_status**) or degree of error (used with **log_error**) is best suited for the specific error. You should consider the status code and degree of error as general guidelines for clarity and organizational purpose; they normally do not change the fundamentals of how the server responds. The server responds in the same way by sending the error page to the client and logging the error in the log file. You specify the type of error. As a rule, for the status code, decide which error message gives the right information to the client and describes the error that occurred. The server returns a separate default text (along with your description, if specified) for different status codes. For the degree of error, you should decide the degree based on how you would want the information to appear in the errors file. For instance, make your choice based on how you would like the function's errors to be categorized in a report. You should also review the sections Returning an Error Page and Logging Errors in Chapter 6 for more detailed information. In this example, we use the following status codes: `PROTOCOL_SERVER_ERROR`, `PROTOCOL_FORBIDDEN`, `PROTOCOL_BAD_REQUEST`, and `PROTOCOL_OK`. We use the following error degrees: `LOG_MISCONFIG`, `LOG_WARN`, and `LOG_FAILURE`.

Sending HTML Mail

The **mailto** example uses the standard text-based mail message. After all, the client input is from a `TEXTAREA` field that can accept only text. There are times, however, when you may wish to take advantage of a richer type of e-mail. For example, you may want to e-mail an HTML page that includes graphic links. In such cases, you can take advantage of the new HTML mail feature of Netscape Navigator 3.0 and later. For example, Netscape Navigator 3.x's mail program (Netscape Mail) allows you to accept an HTML page as a mail message. In other words, instead of receiving mail in the standard text, you can receive Web pages that include graphics, tables, forms, and so on. These pages can include reference and links to other locations. A good example of the use of HTML mail is when you wish to e-mail a form to a recipient. For instance, suppose you have set up an internal ordering system for your office using Netscape Server, but you require that all orders be approved by a supervisor before they are processed. Your program can mail an HTML approval form to the supervisor after an employee orders some items. The supervisor then accepts or denies the order using the form you sent through e-mail. The form can invoke another program that marks the order in the database for processing or mails a Not Approved page to the employee who placed the order.

Normally, a mail program such as Eudora or Netscape Mail does not allow you to type in an HTML page (a message with HTML tags) and mail it as HTML mail. If you write an HTML page, tags and all, in the mail program's input window, the mail program sends the message as text. The mail program makes certain assumptions about the type of message you are sending, as does Blat. To send an HTML page without the utility program or the mail user-agent predetermining the `MIME-Version`,

Content-type, and other headers, you must use a program that allows you to directly send the headers and content of the message. You need to override the MIME types of the content.

For the mail user-agent, you can send an HTML page as an attachment using Netscape Navigator or Communicator. For instance, compose an HTML page using Netscape Gold's Editor, or the Netscape Composer included with Communicator 4.x, and send the document, after you have saved it, as an attachment. For example, choose Send Page from the File menu of Netscape Composer to transmit the file using Netscape Mail. (You can also delete the URL of the file that is automatically placed in the input windows.)

To send an HTML page directly or through your SAF, you can use sendmail under UNIX or a port of such a program under NT. For instance, you can use the freeware program postmail, mentioned earlier. With postmail you can directly send the message file with the appropriate headers. To illustrate, the following command line e-mails the HTML page news.html to the recipient defined in the To: header line in the message file. The -H argument specifies the SMTP server, and -t specifies that postmail should parse the message for the To: header.

```
postmail -Hsmtp.foo.com -t < d:\news.html
```

In your message file, you must specify all necessary headers. Next, you need to include a blank line after the headers and before the content of the e-mail. This setup is similar to how you send a regular HTML page through the server. The following is a list of typical headers you can include:

```
MIME-Version: 1.0
Content-Type: text/html
Subject: Test Subject
From: joe@foo.com
To: someone@foo.com

[Content of the HTML page
  <HTML>. . .</HTML>]
```

Depending on the mail utility program used, some of the headers can be specified through command-line arguments or procured from the system's settings. You should, however, specify the MIME-Version and Content-type in the file you are routing to the mail utility program.

To make sure the links in the HTML page work properly, include a BASE tag in the page you are sending. For example, if you wish the links to be from a subdirectory, /new/, in your site, specify a BASE tag like the following inside the <HEAD> tag of the HTML page:

```
<HEAD>
<BASE HREF="http://www.foo.com/new/">
<HEAD>
```

The links in this page are resolved based on the BASE URL.

Parsing Functions

An essential part of processing client input from a form is parsing the data that are received. Independent of whether the input is obtained through a GET or POST method, the data are received in URL-encoded format. This setup does not mean that for both methods the data are part of the URL, but rather that the same encoding method is used for the data independent of the method of delivery. In other words, [*name*]=[*value*] pairs of information that are delivered are in an encoded string. (In Listing 9-2-1, the string is query.) Each pair of data is separated by a separator character, &. In the string, spaces are replaced by +, and special characters are replaced by their equivalent Hex characters. For example, # is replaced by %23. To use the client input, we need to decode and separate each [*name*]=[*value*] pair. You can parse the URL-encoded query string with the same functions that we used for the Guest Book example in Chapter 3. In this section, we will use NSAPI functions as much as possible to parse the query string. The steps we take to parse the string are roughly the same, independent of whether we use standard ANSI C or NSAPI functions. We took the following steps for the Guest Book example in Chapter 3:

1. Separate all the [*name*]=[*value*] pairs.
2. Separate [*name*] and [*value*] from one another.
3. Replace the + character with a space for all variables.
4. Replace Hex characters with the equivalent ASCII characters for all variables.

In this chapter, we will do things a bit differently. There is no single function in NSAPI that allows you to parse a URL-encoded string quickly. There are, however, two useful functions we can use to help write our parsing function: **pblock_str2pblock** and **util_uri_unescape**. In Listing 9-3, the main function that parses the encoded string is **parse_query**. The calling function passes the encoded string, the number of fields in the form, and a default value to this function. **parse_query**, in turn, calls other functions (including the NSAPI functions) to decode the string. It returns the data in the string as entries in a pblock data structure.

pblock_str2pblock reads through a string and puts the [*name*]=[*value*] data into entries in a pblock data structure. To use this function, we must first prepare the string. At first glance, it may seem that if we just remove the separator, &, we can use **pblock_str2pblock** to convert the string's [*name*]=[*value*] pairs into pblock entries. **pblock_str2pblock** looks for a space separating each pair of data. After some testing, however, you will find that **pblock_str2pblock** does not work properly for our purpose if there is no [*value*] for a [*name*]. Normally, we do not need to worry about a missing (empty) [*name*], as this information is specified in the HTML. On the other hand, the [*value*] is usually entered by the client and can be empty. If there is no [*value*] for a [*name*], **pblock_str2pblock** reads the next [*name*]=[*value*] pair as the value of the current [*name*]. For example, if the string is "firstname= lastname=smith", **pblock_str2pblock** inserts only one pblock entry with the name firstname and the value lastname=smith. This scenario is a problem, because we want two entries—one for firstname with no value, and another for lastname. To resolve this problem, we must place some default value for each empty [value] via the DEFAULT_VALUE we defined in Listing 9-2-1. Once we remove the separator, &, we look for an empty value and replace it with DEFAULT_VALUE. With this small modification, we can now use **pblock_str2pblock**.

pblock_str2pblock returns a pblock with each [name]=[value] pair in a separate entry. We still need to remove the escaped characters. We can use **util_uri_unescape** to remove these characters. Although **util_uri_unescape** was written to unescape a URI, we can also use it to unescape our encoded strings. We step through the data structure and remove the escaped characters. **util_uri_unescape** replaces only the Hex escaped characters. It looks for the %[Hex value] and replaces it with the equivalent ASCII character. We still need to replace the + character with a space in the entries. To do so, we have written **insert_space** (found in Listing 9-3).

The following is the order of the steps we will take to parse the client input in Listing 9-3:

- Replace the separator character (&) between the [name]=[value] pairs with a space. If there is no [value], insert a default value in place of it (**remove_separator_plus**).

- Create a pblock into which to insert the pairs (**pblock_create**).

- Insert the updated [name]=[value] pairs into the pblock entries (**pblock_str2pblock**).

- Remove the escape characters from the pblock entries (**pblock_remove_escapes**):

  Replace + with a space (**insert_spaces**);

  Replace %[Hex value] with the equivalent ASCII character (**util_uri_unescape**).

The order of these steps is important. For example, if you replace the + characters first, before calling **pblock_str2pblock**, the result will be faulty. **pblock_st2pblock** sees the spaces as the separator between the [name]=[value] pairs. Therefore, "name=joe smith" will be seen as name=joe 2=smith. In other words, two separate entries will be inserted by **pblock_str2pblock**. When **pblock_str2pblock** finds a value without a [name], it uses a default numeric string for the name. It also expects a non-encoded equal sign (=) to separate [name] and [value].

If you plan to replace the + characters before calling **pblock_str2pblock**, you should place the value string in quotes (name="joe smith"). (Listing 9-4 includes an alternative method of accomplishing these steps by using a revised **remove_separator_plus**. Besides accomplishing what the **remove_separator_plus** function in Listing 9-3 does, the **remove_separator_plus** function in Listing 9-4 also replaces the + characters with spaces and puts quotation marks around each value string. This function eliminates the need for the **insert_spaces** function.)

You should not use **util_uri_unescape** before calling **pblock_str2pblock**, because **util_uri_unescape** replaces each encoded character with the actual ASCII character.

This substitution can cause **pblock_str2pblock** to return an error (−1). For example, **util_uri_unescape** can turn encoded quotation marks into actual quotes, leading to an improper number of quotes in the string. As already mentioned, **pblock_str2pblock** expects quotes around [*value*]. An extra quotation mark can cause this function to return −1. Moreover, **pblock_str2pblock** sees a backslash character (\) as an escape character that is followed by a literal character. Thus, if you convert the Hex encoded backslash into the equivalent ASCII character, **pblock_str2pblock** will ignore the backslash, because it recognizes it as an escape character. Finally, a non-encoded equal sign (=) is used to separate [*name*] and [*value*] pairs. If **util_uri_unescape** replaces an encoded equal sign with an actual ASCII character, **pblock_str2pblock** will then see this character as a separator of the [*name*] and [*value*] pairs.

Our parsing functions here do not make provisions for when a client uses spaces for a value or when spaces are placed before or after a value. These spaces are seen as part of the value. In other words, the value " `Joe Smith` " is not interpreted as "`Joe Smith`". If such a use of spaces in the client input is inappropriate for your function, you can modify the parsing functions or verify the values in the pblock returned by **parse_query** to make sure the values are correct. You may also use JavaScript in the HTML pages to validate or update the client input before it is passed to your function.

Listing 9-3 Parsing Functions Using NSAPI Functions

```
/* include the following files if you are using a version
of
   Netscape Server earlier than 3.x.

   #include "base/pblock.h"
   #include "base/session.h"
   #include "frame/req.h"

   #include "frame/log.h"
   #include "base/util.h"

/* include this file if you are using Server 3.x */
#include "nsapi.h"

/* Produces a string (dest) that is the same as src but
   has a space instead of the separator &. Also, if there
   is no value after [name]=, insert the default_value
   in place of the empty value.
 */
NSAPI_PUBLIC int remove_separator_plus(char *src,
                      char *dest, char *default_value)
{
   int i, x;          /* used to navigate through
default_value */
```

Listing 9-3   Parsing Functions Using NSAPI Functions (*continued*)

```
int sepnum = 1;        /* number of separators, --that is,
                          [name]=[value] pairs found */

/* while there is the source string step through it */
while(*src)
{
    /* If the character is '&' then make sure the
       character before it is not '='. If it
       is, insert the default value. Otherwise, add
       a space instead of &.
     */
    if(*src == '&')
    {
        src--;
        if(*src == '=')
        {
            x = strlen(default_value);

            /* place the default_value in the dest string */
            for(i = 0; i < x; i++)
            {
                *dest = default_value[i];
                dest++;
            }
        }

        /* insert the space */
        *dest = ' ';

    /* increase the value of the name=value pairs by 1 */
        sepnum++;

        src++;
    }
    /* the rest of destination string should
       be the same as the source
     */
    else
    {
        *dest = *src;
    }

    src++;
    dest++;
}
```

Listing 9-3   Parsing Functions Using NSAPI Functions (*continued*)

```
    dest--;

    /* Check to see if the last name does not have a value.
       If there is no value, place the default text.   */
    if(*dest == '=')
    {
        dest++;

        x = strlen(default_value);

        /* place the default text in place of the empty
           value */
        for(i = 0; i < x; i++)
        {
            *dest = default_value[i];
            dest++;
        }
    }
    else
    {
        /* if there is a value, step to the end of the string */
        dest++;
    }

    /* terminate the destination string */
    *dest = '\0';

    /* return the number of [name]=[value] pairs */
    return sepnum;
}

/* This function is similar to remove_separator_plus
   except that there is no need to add a default value. It
   replaces the plus character (+) with spaces.
 */
NSAPI_PUBLIC void insert_spaces(char *src, char *dest)
{
    while(*src)
    {
        if(*src == '+')
        {
            *dest = ' ';
        }
        else
        {
```

Listing 9-3 Parsing Functions Using NSAPI Functions (*continued*)

```
                   *dest = *src;
           }

           src++;
           dest++;
       }
     *dest = '\0';
}

/* Remove the Hex characters and replace them with the
   equivalent ASCII characters. Also call insert_spaces to
   replace the plus character (+) with spaces.
 */
NSAPI_PUBLIC void pblock_remove_escapes(pblock *pb)
{
   int i;

   /* Go through the pblock and remove the special
      characters. hsize is the size of the hash table, -- that
      is, the number of entries in the pblock pb.
    */
   for(i=0; i < pb->hsize; i++)
   {
       /* an entry includes a pb_param (param) and a
          pointer to the next pb_param
        */
       struct pb_entry *entry = pb->ht[i];

       /* as long as there is a pblock entry, do the update */
       while(entry)
       {
           insert_spaces(entry->param->name,
                         entry->param->name);
           util_uri_unescape(entry->param->name);

           insert_spaces(entry->param->value,
                         entry->param->value);
           util_uri_unescape(entry->param->value);

           entry = entry->next;
       }
   }
}

/* the main parsing function calls the appropriate
   functions to parse the query string
```

Listing 9-3   Parsing Functions Using NSAPI Functions (*continued*)

```
*/
NSAPI_PUBLIC pblock *parse_query(char *query,
int max_fields, char *default_value)
{
    char *newquery;  /* new query string after separator is
                        removed*/
    int  num;      /* number of pblock entries to be created */
    pblock *vars; /* pblock that will hold client input */

    /* malloc the newquery for the size of query plus the
       size of default_value times the maximum number of
       pblock entries that will be created
    */
    newquery=(char *)MALLOC((((strlen(query)) +
            (max_fields * (strlen(default_value))) + 1) *
            sizeof(char));


    /* remove the separator and insert the default_value */
    num = remove_separator_plus(query, newquery,
                                default_value);

    /* Create a pblock that will hold the client input.
       Number of entries (num) is based on the number of
       [name]=[value] pairs of data that was found in the
       query string.
    */
    vars = pblock_create(num);

    /* put query string [name]=[value] data into pblock vars
    */
    pblock_str2pblock(newquery, vars);

    /* remove special characters from vars pblock entries */
    pblock_remove_escapes(vars);

    /* free the newquery because we are done with it */
    FREE(newquery);

    /* return the parsed pblock */
    return vars;
}
```

Let us go through the functions in Listing 9-3. We start with the last function, which is the main parsing function **parse_query**. In **parse_query**, max_fields is used to allocate the size of the new query string (`newquery`) that will hold the client input after **remove_separator_plus** has updated the string. The exact size may vary, but make sure it is big enough to hold the new string. As we do not know which value in the [`name`]=[`value`] pairs sent by the client is empty, we malloc a large-enough size to allow all of the original values to be empty and thus replaced by `default_value`.

> ### Note ▶
>
> The parameter `max_fields` is not essential to the workings of **parse_query**. You can remove this parameter as long as you MALLOC a large-enough string to hold `newquery`.

Next, we call **remove_separator_plus** to parse the `src` string (`query`) and place the new string in `dest` (`newquery`). In the new string (`dest`), the separators (&) are replaced with spaces and, if [`value`] is empty, `default_value` is put in its place. **remove_separator_plus** steps through the source string (`src`) and updates `dest` with data from the `src` string. We step through the string looking for the separator &. To identify whether the value is empty, we step back in the `src` string to look for the equal sign, character =. If = is found, then the value was empty (as in, `firstname=&lastname=boxer`). We therefore insert the default value (`default_value`) in the destination string. If the value was not empty, we replace & with a space in the `dest` string. To make sure a space still separates each [`name`]=[`value`] pair, we add a space at the end of `default_value` to the `dest` string.

Under Netscape Servers predating Server 3.x, you did not need to add `default_value` for the last [`value`] in the string if the value was empty. **pblock_str2pblock** processed the last [`name`]=[`value`] pair correctly, even when the last value was empty. It created a pblock entry for the last [`name`]=[`value`] entry with an empty (NULL) entry for the value. This situation has changed with Server 3.x, so we must also ensure the last value in the [`name`]=[`value`] pairs is not empty. If it is, we insert `default_value`.

Once we have finished copying the information into the new string, we terminate the destination string and exit. The function returns the number of [`name`]=[`value`] pairs it finds.

Back in **query_string**, the return value from **remove_separator_plus** (`num`) is used to specify the number of pblock entries (*name-value* pairs) for the new pblock, `vars`. **pblock_create** creates the `vars` pblock. `num` is the size of the hash table (`vars->hsize`). We could have used the number of fields (`max_fields`) that is passed to **query_string** to designate the number of pblock entries. To be more exacting and so as not to create extra entries in the pblock, we will use the return value from **remove_separator_plus**. As mentioned earlier, sometimes the number of [*name*]=[*value*] pairs in the string may be less than the number of fields in the form. For example, if the client does not choose a radio button, then the [*name*]=[*value*] information for the radio button is not sent. You may also use the same SAF to process a number of forms. The value of the max_fields then should be the number of fields in the form with the greatest number of fields. With the return value of **remove_separator_plus**, **query_string** creates a pblock specific to each form and/or client input. This number can be less than the number of fields in the form having the greatest number of fields. A nonexisting *name-value* entry in the pblock returned by **query_string** is easily handled in the calling function. You can use **pblock_findval** to look for the value of a *name-value* pair. If **pblock_findval** returns NULL, then the *name-value* pair was either missing or the client did not input any value for the specific field.

pblock_str2pblock is used to populate the pblock vars with the [*name*]=[*value*] data from newquery. We still must decode the entries (*name-value* pairs) in the hash table. **pblock_remove_escapes** steps through vars to decode the *name-value* pairs. To move through the hash table, we must step through pblock's pb_entry hash table (pb->ht[i]). Each pb_entry holds a pointer to a pb_param (name and value) and a pointer to the next pb_entry. We work through the hash table until we reach the size of the pblock entries (pb->hsize). The size of the hash table (pb->hsize) should be greater than i. The *name-value* pairs are in the pb_param data structure, param, found in the pb_entry hash table. pb->ht[i]->param->[*name* or *value*] holds one of the [*name*] or [*value*] entries from client input. The actual variables can be found in pb->ht[i]->next or in pb->ht[i]. Thus we will loop through pb->ht[i] looking for param->name and param->value in pb->ht[i] or pb->ht[i]->next. As we step through the hash table entries, we replace any + character with a space via the **insert_space** function. **insert_space** is a simpler version of **remove_separator_plus**, used because we do not need to worry about inserting a default_value in the destination string (dest). The source (src) and destination string (dest) are the same pblock entry for **insert_space**. **insert_space** simply updates the entry. Finally, we will remove any Hex character using the NSAPI function **util_uri_unescape**. With **util_uri_unescape**, we send it the string (pblock entry) and the function updates the string.

Back in **parse_query**, once the pblock vars is parsed, we free the newquery string's memory block we malloced and return the pblock vars. The calling function can then use **pblock_findval** to find the value of each entry.

Alternative remove_separator_plus

The **remove_separator_plus** function in Listing 9-4 is an alternative for the function with the same name in Listing 9-3. To use this function, you should also modify **pblock_remove_escapes** by removing references to **insert_space**. In addition to what the function in Listing 9-3 does, the function in Listing 9-4 does the task accomplished by the **insert_space** function. It looks for the + character in the src string and places a space in place of it in the dest string. Listing 9-4 also places quotation marks (") before and after each value. A quote is placed immediately after the = character and before the separator & is replaced by the space character in the dest string. Notice that the process of checking for the last value in the string is a bit different from that in Listing 9-3. As the code inside the while loop places a quotation mark after any equal character (=), the last value in the destination string (dest) will be a quotation mark (") if there is no value in the source string (str). Consequently, we must step back twice (dest--), to check for the equal sign, as in [name= "value" ... name]=".

Listing 9-4   Revised **remove_separator_plus**

```
/* This function is a revised version of the function with
   the same name in Listing 9-3. Here we also replace the
   + character with a space and put quotes around the value.
 */
NSAPI_PUBLIC int remove_separator_plus(char *src,
                          char *dest, char *default_value)
{
    int i, x;          /* used to navigate through
                          default_value */
    int sepnum = 1;      /* number of separators */
/* while there is the source string, step through it */
while(*src)
{
    /* if the character is a +, replace it with a space */
    if(*src == '+')
    {
        *dest = ' ';
    }
    /* if it is a =, add " to the dest string */
    else if(*src == '=')
    {
        *dest = *src;
         dest++;
        *dest = '"';
    }
    /* If it is &, add the default_value if the value is
       void or a space if it is not. Also put a quote
       before the space.
     */
    else if(*src == '&')
    {
        src--;
```

Listing 9-4 Revised **remove_separator_plus** (*continued*)

```
            if(*src == `=')
            {
                x = strlen(default_value);

                for(i = 0; i < x; i++)
                {
                    *dest = default_value[i];
                    dest++;
                }
            }

            *dest = `"';
             dest++;
            *dest = ` ';

            sepnum++;

            src++;
        }
        else
        {
            *dest = *src;
        }

        src++;
        dest++;
}

/* we must step back twice to check for = character,
   since the above code has already added " character
   to the string */
dest--;
dest--;

/* Check to see if the last name does not have a value.
   If it does, we add the default value.
 */
if(*dest == `=')
{
    dest++;
    dest++;

    x = strlen(default_value);

    /* place the default value in place of the empty value */
    for(i = 0; i < x; i++)
    {
```

Listing 9-4   Revised remove_separator_plus (*continued*)

```
                    *dest = default_value[i];
                    dest++;
            }
        }
        else
        {
            /* if there is a value, step back to the end of the
               string
             */
            dest++;
            dest++;
        }

        /* place the final quote character around the last value */
        *dest = '"';

         dest++;
        *dest = '\0';

        return sepnum;
}
```

guestbook Program—A POST Example

The example in Listing 9-5 is an NSAPI version of the CGI Guest Book example reviewed in Chapter 3. With this program (**guestbook**), the client can choose to add a name, e-mail address, and Web address to the guest file or to view the guest list. Many of the relevant details of this NSAPI program are the same as the CGI program in Listing 3-8. This version uses the same HTML file (Listing 3-7). In other words, it decodes the same type of form data. It also reads and writes to the same type of guest book file and returns a similar response page to the client. Moreover, the general algorithm—the steps we take to process the client request—is similar. The program in Listing 9-5 is an SAF, however, and uses NSAPI functions to accomplish several tasks: to read and parse the client input, read from and write to the guest file, and respond to the client. As we have already discussed the guest book program in detail in Chapter 3, we will not repeat the same discussion here. Instead, we will focus on the aspects of this program that are different from the previous CGI example. We will step through the example focusing on the NSAPI functions and the different methods of accomplishing the same tasks. You should refer to Chapter 3 for additional information about the accompanying HTML page and the general information and algorithm of this program. You should also compare this example with the WAI Guest Book example in Chapter 16.

Registration Instructions

Below we provide instructions for registering the SAF **guestbook** (Listing 9-5). You should have already compiled the program to a DLL or shared library. This program was originally written for NT, but it should work without any specific modification under UNIX.

Add the following line in the **obj.conf** file:

```
Init fn=load-modules funcs=guestbook
 shlib=c:/netscape/server/nsapi/examples/guestbk.dll

Service fn=guestbook method="(POST|HEAD)"
 type=magnus-internal/guest
 guestfile="c:/netscape/server/guestlst/guestlst.txt"
```

If you added this SAF to an existing DLL or shared library, then modify the **load-modules** line in the **obj.conf** file by adding the function's name (guestbook) to the funcs parameter list. You should also update the shlib parameter to reflect the correct location of the DLL (or the shared library file for UNIX). The guestfile parameter of the **Service** function **guestbook** points to the location of the guest book file. We specify this information here instead of hard-coding the location in the program. You should change the path to reflect the location of the guest book on your machine.

To enable the server to recognize this **Service** SAF, you should also update the **mime.types** file. In **mime.types**, add the following line (or any other extension [exts] you may wish to use with the SAF):

```
type=magnus-internal/guest exts=gst
```

As with the **mailto** example in Listing 9-2, you must make several small modifications to this code to use it with Netscape Server 2.x. You need to include the following NSAPI header files instead of including nsapi.h. You also need to add a dummy parameter (for example, zero [0]), for the NSAPI function **system_errmsg**.

```
/* Standard headers for Server Application Functions */
#include "base/pblock.h"
#include "base/session.h"
#include "frame/req.h"

#include "base/file.h"     /*system_fopenWA, system_fopenRA,
                             system_fclose */
#include "frame/protocol.h"  /* protocol_start_response,
                             protocol_status */
#include "frame/log.h"       /* log_error */
#include "base/util.h"       /* util_sprintf, util_getline
*/
#include "base/buffer.h"     /* filebuffer, etc */
```

Listing 9-5-1   Guest Book Example (guestbook Function)

```
/* include this file if you are using Server 3.x */
#include "nsapi.h"

/* header file for the general-purpose functions we will
   write, including parse_query and send_simple_response
 */
#include "forms.h"

/* for adding the time in the confirmation page returned to
   the user */
#include >time.h>
#include <sys/timeb.h>

#include <string.h> /* string function */

/* maximum size of each line in the file (based on the maximum
   length attribute [also MAXLENGTH] of each input field)
 */
#define MAXLENGTH 40

/* maximum content to be received from POST */
#define MAX_CONTENT_LENGTH 300

/* default text for parsing function */
#define DEFAULT_VALUE   "void"

/* function prototypes */
NSAPI_PUBLIC int Append_Guest_File(pblock *user_form,
                       char *path, Session *sn, Request *rq);
NSAPI_PUBLIC int Read_Guest_File(char **guestlist,
                       char *path, Session *sn, Request *rq);

/* global file descriptor (handle) to be shared between
   threads and processes
 */
SYS_FILE fd;

/* main guest book function */
NSAPI_PUBLIC int guestbook(pblock *param, Session *sn,
                            Request *rq)
{
   char *path;               /* path of the guest list file */
   char *type;               /* content type of the request */
   char *clengthString=NULL; /* length of the content sent
                                by client in string format
                              */
```

```
int clengthNumber;          /* size of the content sent by
                               client in integer */
int tmpclength;             /* clengthNumber used to go
                               through the Session inbuf */
char *query;                /* client input */
int curPos = 0;             /* current position for
                               navigating through user info */
int ichar = IO_OKAY;        /* number of char to go
                               through to read user info,
                               IO_OKAY = 1 */
pblock *variables;          /* will hold client input */
char *value = NULL;         /* value of method type */
char *email = NULL;         /* user e-mail address */
char *ename = NULL;         /* user name */
char *response_content;     /* content of the message returned */
struct _timeb timebuffer;   /* needed to set time */
char *timeline;
char *list = NULL;          /* list includes the file data for
                               dynamic generation of the HTML */
int ret;                    /* return value from
                               send_simple_response */
int return_value=REQ_PROCEED; /* guestbook's return
                               value */

/* get the path of the guest file from obj.conf */
path = pblock_findval("guestfile", param);

/* if not found, return configuration error */
if(!path)
{
    protocol_status(sn, rq, PROTOCOL_SERVER_ERROR,
            "A server configuration error occurred.");
    log_error(LOG_MISCONFIG, "guestbook", sn, rq,
        "No guestfile was specified in obj.conf file.");
    return REQ_ABORTED;
}

/* Get the content-type. Use request_header
   instead of pblock_findval to access rq->headers.
 */
request_header("content-type", &type, sn, rq);

/* make sure the content-type is right */
```

```
    if(util_strcasecmp(type,
                "application/x-www-form-urlencoded") != 0)
    {
        protocol_status(sn, rq, PROTOCOL_FORBIDDEN,
                "Your browser sent the wrong content type.");
        log_error(LOG_WARN, "guestbook", sn, rq,
                    "Browser sent the wrong content type.");
        return REQ_ABORTED;
    }

    /* check whether content-length was sent */
    if (request_header("content-length", &clengthString,
                    sn, rq) == REQ_ABORTED)
    {
        protocol_status(sn, rq, PROTOCOL_FORBIDDEN,
                "Your browser didn't send any content.");
        log_error(LOG_WARN, "guestbook", sn, rq,
                    "Error in getting content length.");
        return REQ_ABORTED;
    }

    /* Get the actual number for the content-length in int.
       Content length is sent as a string.
     */
    clengthNumber = atoi(clengthString);

    /* Check if the content-type is right. It should be
       less than the maximum size we specified and greater
       than zero.
     */
    if(clengthNumber >= MAX_CONTENT_LENGTH ||
        clengthNumber < 1)
    {
        protocol_status(sn, rq, PROTOCOL_FORBIDDEN,
                    "The right amount of data was not sent.");
        log_error(LOG_WARN, "guestbook", sn, rq,
            "Content length is less than 1 or too long.");
        return REQ_ABORTED;
    }

    /* we want to keep clengthNumber unchanged to verify
       if the right amount of the data was read
     */
    tmpclength = clengthNumber;
```

```
/* now reading information sent by the form */

/* will hold the POST data */
query = (char *) MALLOC((clengthNumber + 1) *
  sizeof(char));

/* You should set this value for Servers 2.x. Otherwise,
   the server can hang while sending an error status you
   set. The name must be "data-removed" but the actual
   value does not matter. Here, value is set to "done".
 */
pblock_nvinsert("data-removed", "done", rq->vars);

/* read information into query string */
while (tmpclength && ichar != IO_EOF)
{
    ichar = netbuf_getc(sn->inbuf);

    /* check for any error while reading */
    if(ichar == IO_ERROR)
    {
        protocol_status(sn, rq, PROTOCOL_SERVER_ERROR,
                        "Error reading form data.");
        log_error(LOG_FAILURE, "guestbook", sn, rq,
                  "Error reading form data from buffer.");
        FREE(query);
        return REQ_ABORTED;
    }

    query[curPos++] = ichar;
    tmpclength--;
}

/* terminate the query string */
query[curPos] = '\0';

/* make sure the size of data we read from buffer is the
   same as the content-length sent by the client
 */
if(curPos != clengthNumber)
{
    protocol_status(sn, rq, PROTOCOL_SERVER_ERROR,
                    "Error reading the input.");
    log_error(LOG_FAILURE, "guestbook", sn, rq,
              "Did not read all data from buffer.");
```

Listing 9-5-1   Guest Book Example (**guestbook** Function) (*continued*)

```
        FREE(query);
        return REQ_ABORTED;
    }

    /* parse_query does all of the parsing of the query and
       returns a pblock structure with the client input
     */
    variables = parse_query(query, 4, DEFAULT_VALUE);

    /* get the POST action input type */
    value = pblock_findval("action", variables);

    /* check to make sure one of the buttons is checked */
    if(!value)
    {
        protocol_status(sn, rq, PROTOCOL_BAD_REQUEST,
                        "You did not select an action.");
        log_error(LOG_WARN, "guestbook", sn, rq,
                  "Form results had an invalid action.");

        return_value = REQ_ABORTED;
        goto done;
    }

    /* if user chooses to look at the guest list, get the file,
     * generate a table with the data, and send it to the user
     */
    if(util_strcasecmp(value, "read") == 0)
    {
        /* malloc space for the guest list, making it large
           enough to hold the size of the information in the
           file and any extra HTML tags that will be added
         */
        list = (char *)MALLOC(10000 * sizeof(char));

        /* set the list to blank */
        strcpy(list, "");

        /* Read_Guest_File fills the list with the
           information in the file, formatted as an HTML table
         */
    if (Read_Guest_File(&list, path, sn, rq) == REQ_PROCEED)
```

Listing 9-5-1   Guest Book Example (**guestbook** Function) (*continued*)

```c
    {
        /* size of the content of the response page */
        response_content = (char *)MALLOC
        ((strlen(list)+300) * sizeof(char));

        /* add TABLE tags and the content of the table
           from the list
         */
        util_sprintf(response_content,
            "<TABLE BORDER CELLPADDING=5>\n"
            "<TR><TH BGCOLOR=C0C0C0>NAME<BR></TH>\n"
            "<TH BGCOLOR=C0C0C0>EMAIL ADDRESS <BR></TH>\n"
            "<TH BGCOLOR=C0C0C0>WEB ADDRESS<BR>/</TH>\n"
            "</TR>\n"
            "%s</TABLE>\n<HR>", list);

        /* send the table of the guest list to the client */
        ret = send_simple_response("GUEST BOOK",
                                   response_content,
                                   sn, rq);

       /* check if the sending of the page was successful */
        if(ret != REQ_PROCEED)
        {
            return_value = ret;
            goto done;
        }
        goto done;
    }
    /* if we were unable to read the guest book */
    else
    {
        return_value = REQ_ABORTED;
        goto done;
    }
}
/* if the action is log, write the user information into
   the file and return a Thank You page
 */
else if(strcmp(value, "log") == 0)
{
    /* get the value of ename and email */
```

Listing 9-5-1   Guest Book Example (guestbook Function) (*continued*)

```
ename = pblock_findval("ename", variables);
email = pblock_findval("email", variables);

/* Make sure that both email and ename are filled.
   We use our default text, 'void', for checking.
 */
if ((util_strcasecmp(ename, DEFAULT_VALUE) == 0) ||
    (util_strcasecmp(email, DEFAULT_VALUE) == 0)
    || (*ename == '\0') || (*email == '\0'))
{
    protocol_status(sn, rq, PROTOCOL_BAD_REQUEST,
        "You did not fill out the form completely.");
    log_error(LOG_WARN, "guestbook", sn, rq,
        "Form was not filled out completely.");

    return_value = REQ_ABORTED;
    goto done;
}

/* write the client input into the guest file and
   return a Thank You page
 */
if(Append_Guest_File(variables, path, sn, rq) ==
                    REQ_PROCEED)
{
 /* time function to add the time and date to the end
    of the response page
  */
    _ftime( &timebuffer );
    timeline = ctime( & ( timebuffer.time ) );

    /* will hold the content of the page to be sent
       to the client
    */
    response_content = MALLOC(256 * sizeof(char));

    util_sprintf(response_content,
                "<B>%s</B> "
                "has been added to our Guest Book!\n"
                "<P>%s\n<HR>", ename, timeline);

    /* send the HTML Thank You page to the client
       function reference from forms.h
     */
    ret=send_simple_response(
```

```
                                    "Thank you for registering",
                                    response_content, sn, rq);

        /* check if the sending of the page was successful */
        if(ret != REQ_PROCEED)
            {
                return_value = ret;
                goto done;
            }

            goto done;
        }
        /* if we were unable to write to the file */
        else
        {
            return_value = REQ_ABORTED;
            goto done;
        }
    }
    /* make sure the action is log or read */
    else
    {
        protocol_status(sn, rq, PROTOCOL_FORBIDDEN,
                        "Your form made an invalid request.");
        log_error(LOG_WARN, "guestbook", sn, rq,
                        "Form results had an invalid action.");

        return_value = REQ_ABORTED;
        goto done;
    }

    goto done;

    done:

    FREE(query);
    pblock_free(variables);

    if(response_content) FREE(response_content);

    if(list) FREE(list);

    return return_value;
}
```

Listing 9-5-2   Guest Book Example (Read_Guest_File Function)

```
/* This function reads the guest list file, formats the
   data in the file for an HTML table, and returns the
   result through guestlist. session *sn and request *rq
   are used with protocol_status, log_error, and so on.
 */
NSAPI_PUBLIC int Read_Guest_File(char **guestlist,
                    char *path, Session *sn, Request *rq)
{
   /* table formatting HTML tags */

   /* Beginning and end of a table field data. <BR> allows
      for better display of empty cells and for browsers
      that cannot display tables. Table cells for the name
      of the guests will be in color.
    */
   #define BEGINITEM    "\n <TD>"
   #define BEGINITEMCOLOR "\n <TD BGCOLOR=#D2B48C>"
   #define ENDITEM   "<BR></TD>"

   /* beginning and end of a table row */
   #define BEGINROW   "\n<TR>"
   #define ENDROW     "\n</TR>"

   /* e-mail and Web address link as hypertext */
   #define BEGINMAIL "<A HREF=\"mailto:"
   #define BEGINLINK "<A HREF=\"http://"
   #define ENDLINK    "\">"
   #define ENDREF     "</A>"

   filebuffer *guestbuf;    /* file buffer */
   int endcheck;            /* lets us know when the end of
                               file is reached */
   int  lnum;               /* number of lines in the file */
   int  num;                /* holds the switch/case value */
   char line[MAXLENGTH +1]; /* holds each line of info */
   int return_value = REQ_PROCEED; /* function's return
                                      value */

   /* open and read the file pointed to by the path */
   fd=system_fopenRO(path);

   /* Check for any system error in opening the file. If file
      was not found, then set the status to not found.
      Otherwise set the status to forbidden.
```

Listing 9-5-2   Guest Book Example (**Read_Guest_File** Function) (*continued*)

```
    */
    if( fd == SYS_ERROR_FD)
    {
        protocol_status(sn, rq, (file_notfound() ?
                    PROTOCOL_NOT_FOUND : PROTOCOL_FORBIDDEN),
                        "Could not write to the guest file.");
        log_error(LOG_FAILURE, "guestbook", sn, rq,
                    "error opening %s (%s)", path,
                    system_errmsg());
        return REQ_ABORTED;
    }

    /* open a buffer reading the specified file */
    guestbuf = filebuf_open(fd, FILE_BUFFERSIZE);

    if(!guestbuf)
    {
        system_fclose(fd);
        protocol_status(sn, rq, PROTOCOL_SERVER_ERROR,
                        NULL);
        log_error(LOG_FAILURE, "guestbook", sn, rq,
            "error opening buffer for guest file, (%s)",
            system_errmsg());
        return REQ_ABORTED;
    }

    /* this function reads each line of the file and places
       the appropriate tags around them
     */
    for(endcheck = 0, lnum = 1; endcheck == 0; ++lnum)
    {
        endcheck = util_getline(guestbuf, lnum,
                                (MAXLENGTH + 1), line);

        /* -1 means an error occurred. The logged error
           information includes the system error message and the
           error returned by the function found in the line.
         */
        if(endcheck == -1)
        {
            protocol_status(sn, rq, PROTOCOL_SERVER_ERROR, NULL);
            log_error(LOG_FAILURE, "guestbook", sn, rq,
                    "error reading %s (%s). %s",
```

Listing 9-5-2   Guest Book Example (**Read_Guest_File** Function) (*continued*)

```
                        path, system_errmsg(), line);
        return_value = REQ_ABORTED;
        goto done;
    }

    /* util_getline returns 1 upon EOF */
    if(endcheck != 1)
    {
        num = lnum % 3;

        switch(num)
        {
            /* first line includes the name of the user */
            case 1:
            {
                strcat(*guestlist, BEGINROW);
                strcat(*guestlist, BEGINITEMCOLOR);
                strcat(*guestlist, line);
                strcat(*guestlist, ENDITEM);
                break;
            }
            /* second line includes the e-mail address,
               which is also made into a hypertext
             */
            case 2:
            {
                strcat(*guestlist, BEGINITEM);
                strcat(*guestlist, BEGINMAIL);
                strcat(*guestlist, line);
                strcat(*guestlist, ENDLINK);
                strcat(*guestlist, line);
                strcat(*guestlist, ENDREF);
                strcat(*guestlist, ENDITEM);
                break;
            }
            /* last line includes the Web address, which
               is also made into a hypertext
             */
            default:
            {
                strcat(*guestlist, BEGINITEM);
                strcat(*guestlist, BEGINLINK);
                strcat(*guestlist, line);
```

Listing 9-5-2   Guest Book Example (**Read_Guest_File** Function) (*continued*)

```
                    strcat(*guestlist, ENDLINK);
                    strcat(*guestlist, line);
                    strcat(*guestlist, ENDREF);
                    strcat(*guestlist, ENDITEM);
                    strcat(*guestlist, ENDROW);
                    break;
                }
            }
        }
    }

    done:

    /* guest list is freed through 'list' in the calling
       function
     */

    /* close the buffer, which also closes the file */
    filebuf_close(guestbuf);

    return return_value;
}
```

Listing 9-5-3   Guest Book Example (**Append_Guest_File** Function)

```
/* This function appends the guest file pointed to by the
   path parameter with the client input defined in the
   user_form data structure. Each line of the structure is
   placed in a separate line in the file. We need session
   and request to make the calls to protocol_status,
   log_error, and so on.
 */
NSAPI_PUBLIC int Append_Guest_File(pblock *user_form,
                      char *path, Session *sn, Request *rq)
{
    int len;                 /* length of userinfo string */
    char *userinfo;          /* a string of user information */
    int return_value = REQ_PROCEED; /* function's return
                                       value */
    char *webaddress;  /* holds the Web address of client */

    /* open the file for appending the data */
    fd=system_fopenWA(path);
```

Listing 9-5-3   Guest Book Example (**Append_Guest_File** Function) (*continued*)

```
/* Check for system error. If file was not found, then
   set the status to not found. Otherwise set the status
   to forbidden.
 */
if( fd == SYS_ERROR_FD)
{
    protocol_status(sn, rq,
            (file_notfound() ? PROTOCOL_NOT_FOUND :
             PROTOCOL_FORBIDDEN),
                "Sorry, could not write to the guest file");
    log_error(LOG_FAILURE, "Append_Guest_File", sn, rq,
            "error opening %s (%s)", path, system_errmsg());
    return REQ_ABORTED;
}

/* get the Web address of the client */
webaddress = pblock_findval("web", user_form);

/* If the Web address was not specified, the value
   would be set to DEFAULT_VALUE ("void") by the parsing
   function. Here, we replace DEFAULT_VALUE with an
   empty string.
 */
if(util_strcasecmp(webaddress, DEFAULT_VALUE) == 0)
{
    strcpy(webaddress, "");
}

/* Malloc userinfo to the max size of the user
   information fields combined. You can use strlen of each of
   the variables to get a more exact number for the size.
*/
userinfo = (char *) MALLOC(((MAXLENGTH * 3) + 1) *
                        sizeof(char));

/* Place all user data into one string. The \n puts each
   separate field into a separate line in the file.
 */
len = util_sprintf(userinfo, "%s\n%s\n%s\n",
                    pblock_findval("ename", user_form),
                    pblock_findval("email", user_form),
                    webaddress);
```

Listing 9-5-3   Guest Book Example (**Append_Guest_File** Function) (*continued*)

```
    /* Write the user information into the file. This
       function locks the file while writing into it.
       Check for any errors.
     */
    if (system_fwrite_atomic(fd, userinfo, len) != IO_OKAY)
    {
        protocol_status(sn, rq, PROTOCOL_SERVER_ERROR,
                    "Sorry, could not write to the guest file");
        log_error(LOG_FAILURE, "Append_Guest_File", sn, rq,
                    "could not write to the guest file.");
        return_value = REQ_ABORTED;
    }

    /* close the file */
    system_fclose(fd);

    /* free the userinfo data structure now that we are
       finished with it
     */
    FREE(userinfo);
    return return_value;
}
```

Stepping Through the guestbook Program

Unlike in the CGI example (Listing 3-8), with our new **guestbook** function, the path of the guest book file is not hard-coded. Instead, it is specified in the **obj.conf** file as a parameter for the **guestbook** function. **pblock_findval** is used to get the guest book file's path from the entry guestfile. We use the **request_header** function to get content-type and content-length, as these two variables are in the Request->headers pblock. As discussed earlier, you should use **request_header** instead of **pblock_findval** to access the entries in the headers pblock. We make sure content-type is application/x-www-form-urlencoded. To compare the two strings, we use the NSAPI function **util_strcasecmp**, which compares two alpha-numeric strings not using case sensitivity. Next, we check if content-length is greater than 0 and less than the maximum length (MAX_CONTENT_LENGTH). To use the content-length information, we convert content-length, available through **request_header**, from a string into an integer. These steps are the standard verification procedure for a POST request. As with the **mailto** example, we do not verify if the request is using the POST method, as we specify that a POST method of request is required when registering the **Service** function **guestbook**.

To get the client input from a POST request, we must read the data from the network buffer (*Session*->inbuf). Unlike in the CGI program, the data are not available from the standard input but rather from the network buffer. We use the NSAPI function **netbuf_getc** (instead of **fread** used in the CGI program) to read the data. **netbuf_getc** reads the POST data one character at time. We step through the buffer until we reach the end of the buffer (IO_EOF) or until we read the length of the content (content-length). Because we decrement the value of content-length as we step through the buffer, a temporary integer (tmpclength) is used. The character (ichar) returned by **netbuf_getc** is then placed in the query string. If successful, **netbuf_getc** returns the value of the character as an integer. Otherwise, it returns IO_EOF when end of buffer is reached or IO_ERROR when an error occurs. After the characters are placed in the query string, we terminate the string. We then use the value of the original content-length (clengthNumber) to make sure the right number of characters were read from the buffer. If this value is different, then something went wrong in our reading of the data.

Once we make sure the content is correct, we are ready to parse the information. This query string is in the same format as the query string from a GET request (as in Listing 9-2-1). In other words, it is URL-encoded and we must decode it. As with the previous **mailto** example, we use the **parse_query** function to parse the string and get a pblock data structure (variables). variables should now hold the client input.

Once the client input is parsed, we look for the value of each input in the variables pblock using **pblock_findval**. The first value we seek is action. action is sent when the client chooses a radio button requesting to view the guest list or to add the user information to the guest book. If there is no value for action, then the client did not choose a radio button. This method of verifying if a button was selected is different from that in the CGI program. In the CGI program, we used the number of [name] = [value] pairs of data in the query string to verify if a button was selected.

Warning ▶

To make sure the server will not hang trying to read data from the socket when there are no such data to be read, you should insert the entry data-removed into the *Request*->vars pblock data structure. The value of the entry does not matter. In Listing 9-5-1, the following line is used to insert data-removed with the value done in the vars pblock:

```
pblock_nvinsert("data-removed", "done", rq->vars);
```

This problem, which is related to how the two internal server programs **ns-httpd** and **httpd** work, is new to Netscape Servers 2.0. It occurs during a POST or PUT method and can cause the server to hang for a long time, up to a minute or two, before a response is sent. In Listing 9-5-1, the problem occurs when you use **protocol_status** to set the status to an error message and return REQ_ABORTED. Instead of responding with an error page immediately, the server waits and sends the response after some time. By inserting data-removed, you make sure the server has flushed all the data and is no longer waiting to read data from the socket.

Moreover, with the CGI program, the parsing of the data in the **main** function occured in separate steps. Thus, the data were not fully parsed until we verified that `action` was `read`. With the NSAPI function **guestbook**, the input is parsed in a single step (**parse_query**).

Listing 9-5 continues to use **protocol_status** to set the return status and specify a description for the error. You may opt to return an HTML page that informs the client of the type of error instead. This alternative method is a better solution if you wish to send back a customized error page to the client. For example, you can return an HTML page that includes specific steps that the client should take to fix the problem. Use **send_simple_response** to write this type of HTML page to the client.

If the client chose a button, `action` should be either `log` or `read`. If the value of `action` is `read`, we `MALLOC` a large-enough size to hold the guest book list (`list`) and set its initial value to empty (`NULL`). Make sure you increase the size of memory for `list` to match the size of the guest book file plus the additional HTML tags. We then use **Read_Guest_File** to read from the guest book. **Read_Guest_File** updates `list` with the data in the guest book file. As with a similar function in Chapter 3, **Read_Guest_File** wraps the data from the file with HTML formatting tags. The result is an HTML table with e-mail and Web addresses of the guests as hyperlinks. We use **system_fopenRO** to open the file for read-only access. Unlike with the CGI example, we then open a file buffer to read the content of the file. **filebuf_open** returns a pointer to the `filebuffer` `guestbuf`. `FILE_BUFFERSIZE`, defined in the NSAPI header file as `4096`, is the I/O size for the buffer. You may choose to use **filebuf_open_nostat** instead, so as to read the data without a call to the function **stat**. Once the file and a new file buffer were successfully opened, we use **util_getline** to read each line of data from the file buffer. Each line of data in the file holds one specific piece of information about the guests (that is, name, e-mail or Web address). **util_getline** reads from the buffer (`guestbuf`) until it finds the end of the line (`LF` or `CRLF`) or maximum number of characters (`MAXLENGTH`). It then places the data in the string `line`. **util_getline** returns 0 if successful, 1 if the end of file (`EOF`) is reached, and −1 if an error occurs. If an error occurred, **util_getline** places an error description instead of the line of data from the file in the string `line`. We step through each line of the file (`lnum`) until **util_getline** returns a value other than 0. With **util_getline** (unlike with the **fgets** function used in the CGI program), `CRLF` or `LF` is removed from the string before it is placed in the string `line`. We place the data from the file, plus all the other formatting tags for the table, in the `guestlist` string. Once finished with the file, we close the file buffer (**filebuf_close**), which also closes the file, and return `REQ_PROCEED`.

Back in the **guestbook** function, if **Read_Guest_File** finished successfully, we use the updated `list` string, which now holds the HTML-formatted data from the file, to produce the `response_content` string. `response_content` holds the content of the page that is returned to the client. To return the table of the guest list, we also add the HTML beginning and end tags for a table (`<TABLE . . . > . . . </TABLE>`) to the `list` string. Finally, as with the **mailto** function, **send_simple_response** is called to return the HTML page to the client. Unlike the

mailto function, however, **send_simple_response** is declared outside of Listing 9-5. As with the parsing function, we use the header file `forms.h` to include **send_simple_response**, which is defined in another file with other frequently used functions.

If the value of `action` is `log`, we use **Append_Guest_File** to write to the guest file. First, we get the value of the user name (`ename`) and e-mail address (`email`). **guestbook** makes sure that the client inputs at least `ename` and `email`. Otherwise, the status is set to `PROTOCOL_BAD_REQUEST`, an error is logged, and `REQ_ABORTED` is returned. As with the **mailto** example, we do only a limited amount of error checking here. If you wish to include additional error checking, you should update this program or use JavaScript.

We are now ready to write the data into the guest book file. This example reads and writes from a text file, which has the added advantage of being easily modifiable by any text editor. You can also use binary files and linked lists. With a binary file, you can take advantage of more efficient functions for updating, deleting, sorting, and other operations on the data. Unlike with the CGI program, we pass the client's input through the pblock `variables` to **Append_Guest_File**. With the CGI program, we place the client's input first in a data structure and then send the data structure to **Append_Guest_File**. In Listing 9-5, the client's input is already in the `variables` data structure. The easiest way to pass the client's user information is to pass `variables`. We pass `variables`, `path` of the guest book file, and the `Request` (`rq`) and `Session` (`sn`) data structures. The `Request` and `Session` data structures are used by **Append_Guest_File**, **Read_Guest_File**, and **send_simple_response** to call NSAPI functions (for example, **protocol_status**) that require `Request` and `Session`.

Append_Guest_File writes the client's user information into the guest file. It uses the NSAPI functions **system_fopenWA**, **system_fwrite_atomic**, and **system_fclose** to write the data to the file. The data from the client are available through the `user_form` pblock (`variables` from the **guestbook**). **Append_Guest_File** makes a string buffer of the data before writing the information into the file. We get the user input from the `user_form` pblock by using **pblock_findval**. (Alternatively, you can create the string in the **guestbook** function and pass it to **Append_Guest_File**. To do this, you must change the first parameter of **Append_Guest_File** to accept a string instead of pblock.) As we allow the client to not input a Web address, the parsing function may place the `DEFAULT_VALUE` (`"void"`) for the Web address (`web`) in the pblock data structure `user_form`. In **Append_Guest_File**, we check for the value of the web entry in the `user_form` pblock. If it is `DEFAULT_VALUE`, we replace the value of the Web address with an empty string (`""`). (We do not want to use the string `"void"` for the Web address in the guest book file.) We then open the file for appending the new information (**system_fopenWA**) and use **system_fwrite_atomic** to write the data. The input string is then passed to **system_fwrite_atomic** to write the data into the file. **system_fwrite_atomic** locks the file while it writes the data. Once the file is properly updated, we close it with **system_fclose**. **Append_Guest_File** returns `REQ_PROCEED` if successful.

Back in the **guestbook** function, if **Append_Guest_File** returned REQ_PROCEED, we return a simple Thank You page with a time stamp to the client. We create the content of the page (response_content) and pass the content and title of the page to **send_simple_response**. **send_simple_response**, in turn, returns the HTML page to the client.

Finally, we free any memory block or pblock that was created or allocated before exiting. (As mentioned earlier, with an NSAPI function written for Server 2.0 and later, you do not need to FREE the memory block if MALLOC and memory pooling were used.)

A General-Purpose formresponse Function

Listing 9-6 is a general-purpose function (**formresponse**) that can process a number of different forms. It can also be seen as a template for writing any function that needs to parse client input from a form using the GET or POST method. **formresponse**'s main purpose is to verify the client input and parse the data so as to pass that information to an appropriate function that can finish processing the client request. As the steps of verifying and parsing a request are the same for different **Service** functions, **formresponse** eliminates the need to repeat these steps for each function.

formresponse can be used as a switchboard for a number of different **Service** functions. These functions can be developed in separate files and then called by **formresponse**. You can access these functions as external functions (extern). On the other hand, you can use a special header file (for example, forms.h) to include the declarations for functions that are used by **formresponse** but kept in separate files. **formresponse** uses the name of the file requested by the client without the extension to identify which function should be called. In other words, if the client requests mail.frm, **formresponse** uses the name mail to identify the function mail that should be called. Thus, you need to identify only one file extension (for example, frm) and register only **formresponse** to process different forms.

In Listing 9-6, we use **formresponse** to call a modified version of **mailto** (Listing 9-2) called **mail** and a version of **guestbook** (Listing 9-5) called **guest**. **formresponse** passes the parsed client input (variables) to the designated function (for example, **mail**), which then finishes processing the request. To use **formresponse** with other **Service** functions, such as **mailto**, you need to modify these functions to accept the parsed input (variables) as a parameter. For example, the function prototype for the **mail** function is NSAPI_PUBLIC int mail(pblock *variables, pblock *param, Session *sn, Request *rq);. **formresponse** also passes its own parameters (param, Session, and Request). Thus the called function, such as **mail**, has access to the same Session and Request data structures. **formresponse** passes any parameters that are declared in **obj.conf** to the function through the `param` parameter. For example, for the **mailto** function, we passed the parameter `mail-program` through **obj.conf**. Here, we specify this same parameter for **formresponse**. When the `param` pblock is passed to the function (**mail**), the parameters of **formresponse**, which now include `mail-program`, are also passed to the function.

As you might expect, **formresponse** includes some of the same code as the **mailto** and **guestbook** functions. To modify these functions for use with **formresponse**, you should remove any section of the code that is already part of **formresponse** from Listings 9-2 and 9-5. You should remove the steps involved in verifying or parsing the client input, and any declaration or freeing of the memory blocks that are part of this process, such as `query`.

Registration Instructions

The instructions below are specific to Listing 9-6. They are intended to work with the modified version of the **mailto** (**mail**) and **guestbook** (**guest**) functions. You need to compile these functions along with the other functions (**mail**, **guest**, parsing function, and so on) into the shared library or DLL before registering **formresponse**. As with the previous examples, you should modify the `shlib` parameter of **load-modules** to point to the appropriate shared library or DLL. With the **formresponse Service** function, you also need to include the parameters that were passed to **mailto** and **guestbook**. Change these parameters, `guestfile` and `mail-program`, to point to the correct location of the mail program and the guest book file. You should add the following lines to **obj.conf** (this information is specific to NT or Windows 95):

```
Init fn=load-modules funcs=formresponse
 shlib=c:/netscape/server/nsapi/examples/formresponse.dll

Service fn="formresponse" method="(GET|POST)"
 type="magnus-internal/formresponse"
 guestfile="c:/netscape/server/guestlst/guestlst.txt"
 mail-program="c:\\netscape\\server\\blat.exe"
```

This information is all you need to add to the **obj.conf** file. You no longer need to register the **mailto** or **guestbook** function.

To enable the server to recognize your new **Service** function, you should update the **mime.types** file. In **mime.types**, add the following line (or any other extension [exts] you may wish to use with the SAF):

```
type=magnus-internal/formresponse exts=frm
```

The forms that you intend to use to invoke the **formresponse** function should include the appropriate file name in the ACTION parameter of the FORM tag. The name of the file must be the same as the name expected in **formresponse**, with the extension specified here (.frm). For this example, `mail.frm` should be used for the **mail** function and `guest.frm` for the **guest** function.

Listing 9-6 **formresponse**—A Form-Processing Switchboard

```
/* include the following files if you are using a version of
   Netscape Server earlier than 3.x.

   #include "base/pblock.h"
   #include "base/session.h"
   #include "frame/req.h"

   #include "frame/protocol.h"
   #include "frame/log.h"
*/

/* include this file if you are using Server 3.x */
#include "nsapi.h"

/* header file for the general-purpose functions we will
   write, such as parse_query
 */
#include "forms.h"

/* this is the default value for function parse_query */
#define DEFAULT_VALUE "void"

/* maximum content to be received from the forms */
#define MAX_CONTENT_LENGTH 300

/* maximum fields we expect from the forms */
#define MAX_FIELDS 5

/* This function is a "switchboard" for a number of other
   Service functions that are written to respond to
   a client request. It handles the POST and GET methods of
   request and calls the appropriate functions to finish the
   request.
 */
NSAPI_PUBLIC int formresponse(pblock *param, Session *sn,
                                Request *rq)
{
    char *method;              /* method of request */
    char *query;               /* client input */
    char *type;                /* content type of the request */
    char *clengthString=NULL;  /* length of the content sent
                                  by client in string format
                                */
    int clengthNumber;         /* size of the content sent by
                                  client in integer */
```

Listing 9-6   formresponse—A Form-Processing Switchboard (*continued*)

```
int tmpclength;                  /* clengthNumber used to go
                                    through the Session inbuf */
int curPos = 0;                  /* current position for
                                    navigating through user info */
int ichar = IO_OKAY;             /* number of char to go through to
                                    read user info, IO_OKAY = 1 */
pblock *variables;               /* will hold client input */

char *path;                      /* forms path information */
char *name;                      /* name of the file */
int return_value=REQ_PROCEED;    /* formresponse's return
                                        value */

/* get the method used */
method = pblock_findval("method", rq->reqpb);

/* process the data if the method is GET or POST */
if(util_strcasecmp(method, "GET") == 0)
{
    /* get the query string */
    query = pblock_findval("query", rq->reqpb);

    /* check if query string exists (With the GET
       method, there are no content-type and
       content-length. Instead, the form information
       is an encoded query string appended to the URL.)
     */
    if (!query)
    {
        protocol_status(sn, rq, PROTOCOL_NOT_FOUND,
            "Your browser didn't send any information.");
        log_error(LOG_WARN, "formresponse", sn, rq,
            "The browser didn't send information.");
        return REQ_ABORTED;
    }
}
/* check if it is POST */
else if(util_strcasecmp(method, "POST") == 0)
{
    /* Get the content-type. Use request_header
       to access rq->headers.
     */
    request_header("content-type", &type, sn, rq);
```

Listing 9-6 **formresponse**—A Form-Processing Switchboard (*continued*)

```
/* make sure the content-type is right */
if(util_strcasecmp(type,
            "application/x-www-form-urlencoded") != 0)
{
    protocol_status(sn, rq, PROTOCOL_FORBIDDEN,
          "Your browser sent the wrong content type.");
    log_error(LOG_WARN, "formresponse", sn, rq,
            "Browser sent the wrong content type.");
    return REQ_ABORTED;
}

/* check if content-length was sent */
if(request_header("content-length", &clengthString,
                  sn, rq) == REQ_ABORTED)
{
    protocol_status(sn, rq, PROTOCOL_FORBIDDEN,
              "Your browser didn't send any content.");
    log_error(LOG_WARN, "formresponse", sn, rq,
                "Error in getting content length.");
    return REQ_ABORTED;
}

/* Get the actual number for content-length in int.
   content-length is sent as a string.
 */
clengthNumber = atoi(clengthString);

/* Check if the content-type is right. It should be
   less than the maximum size we specified and
   greater than zero.
 */
if(clengthNumber >= MAX_CONTENT_LENGTH ||
   clengthNumber < 1)
{
    protocol_status(sn, rq, PROTOCOL_FORBIDDEN,
            "The right amount of data was not sent.");
    log_error(LOG_WARN, "formresponse", sn, rq,
        "content-length is less than 1 or too long.");
    return REQ_ABORTED;
}

/* we want to keep clengthNumber unchanged to
   verify if the right amount of the data was read
 */
```

Listing 9-6 formresponse—A Form-Processing Switchboard (*continued*)

```
tmpclength = clengthNumber;

/* will hold the POST data */
query = (char *)MALLOC(clengthNumber+1) * (sizeof(char));

/* You should set this value to make sure the server
   will not hang while sending an error status you
   set. The name must be "data-removed" but the
   actual value does not matter. Here, value is set
   to "done".
 */
pblock_nvinsert("data-removed", "done", rq->vars);

/* read information into query string */
while (tmpclength && ichar != IO_EOF)
{
    ichar = netbuf_getc(sn->inbuf);

    /* check for any error while reading */
    if(ichar == IO_ERROR)
    {
        protocol_status(sn, rq, PROTOCOL_SERVER_ERROR,
                    "Error reading form data.");
        log_error(LOG_FAILURE, "formresponse", sn, rq,
                "Error reading form data from buffer.");
        FREE(query);
        return REQ_ABORTED;
    }

    query[curPos++] = ichar;
    tmpclength--;
}

/* terminate the query string */
query[curPos] = '\0';

/* make sure the size of data we read from buffer is the
   same as the content-length sent by the client
*/
if(curPos != clengthNumber)
{
    protocol_status(sn, rq, PROTOCOL_SERVER_ERROR,
                    "Error reading the input.");
    log_error(LOG_FAILURE, "formresponse", sn, rq,
                "Did not read all data from buffer.");
```

Listing 9-6 **formresponse**—A Form-Processing Switchboard (*continued*)

```
                FREE(query);
                return REQ_ABORTED;
        }
}
/* We accept only POST and GET.
   If the value is not POST or GET, return an error.
 */
else
{
    /* in case of error */
    protocol_status(sn, rq, PROTOCOL_BAD_REQUEST,
            "Your browser sent the wrong type of request.");
    log_error(LOG_WARN, "formresponse", sn, rq,
        "No form with POST or GET method was submitted.");
    return REQ_ABORTED;
}

/* parse_query does all the parsing of the query and
   returns a pblock structure with the client input
 */
variables = parse_query(query, MAX_FIELDS,
                        DEFAULT_VALUE);

/* Get the path of the client request. We use the
   request's file name to identify the function that
   should be called. The name of the function is same as
   the name of the requested file without the extension.
 */
path = pblock_findval("path", rq->vars);

/* look for .frm in the path string */
name = strstr(path, ".frm");

/* set everything after '.frm' including '.frm' to NULL */
*name = '\0';

/* go back up the string and get the full name of the
   file without the extension
 */
while (*name != FILE_PATHSEP)
{
    name--;
}

/* remove the FILE_PATHSEP from the name */
```

Listing 9-6 **formresponse**—A Form-Processing Switchboard (*continued*)

```
    name++;

/*--------------- Your code goes here --------------- */

    /* You can use this space to call your functions. Here,
        we call a modified version of the mailto and guestbook
        examples. You need to update the examples to reflect
        the new name and parameters and remove  the extra
        codes that are duplicated in this program.
    */
    if(util_strcasecmp(name, "mail") == 0)
    {
        return_value = mail(variables, param, sn, rq);

        goto done;
    }
    else if(util_strcasecmp(name, "guest") == 0)
    {
        return_value = guest(variables, param, sn, rq);

        goto done;
    }
    else
    {
        /* if there is no matching function */
        protocol_status(sn, rq, PROTOCOL_NOT_FOUND,
            "Server was not able to process the request.");
        log_error(LOG_WARN, "formresponse", sn, rq,
            "No function is declared for the request.");

        return_value = REQ_ABORTED;
        goto done;
    }

/*---------------------------------------------------*/

    done:

        if(query) FREE(query);
        pblock_free(variables);

        return return_value;
}
```

Stepping Through the formresponse Program

Let us quickly step through the function in Listing 9-6. Much of the code in this function was discussed during our review of Listings 9-2 and 9-5. First, we should note that the values of MAX_FIELDS and MAX_CONTENT_LENGTH apply to all forms that this function calls. Therefore, you should set these values to a size appropriate for the form with the greatest number of fields (MAX_FIELDS) and the greatest amount of input (MAX_CONTENT_LENGTH). In Listing 9-6, we verify the method of the request. This function expects only GET or POST as a method. If the method is different, **formresponse** sets the status to PROTOCOL_BAD_REQUEST and the server returns an error message. The query string holds the URL-encoded client input before it is parsed. If the request is GET, the value of query is found in the pblock rq->reqpb. For the POST method, we first verify content-type and content-length. We make sure the length is greater than 0 and less than the maximum number specified (MAX_CONTENT_LENGTH). We then read the data from the Session's network buffer (sn->inbuf) into the query string. We also verify if the entire client input was read from the buffer. The **parse_query** function is used for both POST and GET requests to parse the URL-encoded client input (query). Although the value of MAX_FIELDS may be greater than the specific number of [name]=[value] pairs in the input, this greater value will not cause any harm. MAX_FIELDS is used to MALLOC a large-enough string to hold the new query string once the separator character has been removed and DEFAULT_VALUE is added.

Finally, we get the path of the client request from rq->vars. We step through the path and get the name of the requested file. The extension for the requested file must be frm. The name of the file can be found after the last forward slash and before the string .frm. After we have the name, we need to call the appropriate function based on this information. In Listing 9-6, we have specified two functions: the modified version of **mailto** (**mail**) is called when name is mail, and the modified version of **guestbook** (**guest**) is called when name is guest. The return value of the **mail** or **guest** function is used as the return value of **formresponse**. If no function is specified, the status is set to PROTOCOL_NOT_FOUND. You can also add your form-processing functions to the list of the functions that **formresponse** can call.

Summary

In this chapter, we expanded on some topics from previous chapters and put information from Chapter 6 to practical use. This chapter included **Service** SAFs that process client input from a form. It provided examples that process POST or GET methods of requests using NSAPI. The first example, **mailto**, was written to handle a GET request and call a console SMTP mail utility that sends the client input from a form as a mail message to a designated administrator. The second example, **guestbook**, allowed a user to add user information to a guest book file and to view the guest book file in an HTML table. These examples are the typical type of functionality you may wish to add to the server.

Much of the information in this chapter can be utilized by other **Service** functions you may write. For example, the parsing function **parse_query**, which uses NSAPI functions, can be used to decode the client input from any form. **send_simple_response** can be used to return an HTML page to the client. You can use **send_simple_response** to return a response to the client or to return a specific error page. For instance, instead of deploying **protocol_status** to send the default server error page, use **send_simple_response** to send a customized error page. Finally, **formresponse** can be used as a switchboard for any additional SAF form-handling function you may write. You can update **formresponse** to call your function. **formresponse** not only reduces some redundant code, but also simplifies the amount of updating you need to make to the **obj.conf** file. With **formresponse**, you update the **obj.conf** once with its information. From then on, you need to add only the additional parameter that should be passed to your function by the **Service** function **formresponse**.

In Chapter 10, we will discuss a number of additional options or advance considerations. We will discuss how you can maintain state information, write status update while the client is waiting, use templates, and so on.

Chapter 10

Additional Programming Issues

By now, you should be familiar with how SAFs work and how you can write your own SAF. In previous chapters, we wrote a number of SAFs and discussed some of the common concerns you may have in writing your functions. As you begin programming for Netscape Server, a number of additional issues arise. In this chapter, we will review some of these issues and delineate ways you can deal with them.

The first topic that we will discuss is how you can overcome the limitation of the HTTP connection and the server's physical disconnection after sending a response to the client request. HTTP protocol is a lightweight protocol and by itself does not support many additional features you may need for an interactive application.[1] On the other hand, HTTP is flexible enough that, with the options provided with Netscape Server and the client, you could easily compensate for some of these limitations. HTTP communication between server and client is stateless. Every request for a document is a new connection. Once the server returns the requested data to the client, the connection is closed. The server, besides logging each connection, does not keep track of the clients and their requests. Every request is a new request. A feature of developing an interactive site, however, is to keep an extended session with the client. In other words, you want to keep track of the user's requests and collect specific data about the user's interaction with the site, including how the client moves through each page of your site. You may also want to maintain detailed information about each client to keep track of each visit or to customize the site based on the client's specification. In the first section of this chapter, we will discuss how you can use URL encoding, client's default response-headers (for example, IP address), cookies, and/or the server (using

---

1. HTTP/1.1 addresses a number of these issues. For example, HTTP/1.1 supports persistent connection as a means of keeping a connection open between the client and the server. Netscape Server 3.x takes advantage of HTTP/1.1. Server 2.x supports Keep-Alive as a method of maintaining a connection while the server returns a page along with its embedded resources, such as an image.

shared memory, a file, or a database on the server) to maintain additional or more accurate information about the clients and their requests.

Next, we will consider client pull and server push as methods of "keeping the connection alive" and delivering information at determined intervals. With these methods, you can send a response sequence to a client. For example, you can use this method to develop a slideshow. Moreover, with server push, you can update a response page in a specific, predetermined order. You can use this method to send status information to the client while the client is waiting for an operation on the server to finish.

Finally, we will briefly review templates as a means of separating content production from programming and discuss how you can incorporate a database with your program. Just as Server-side Includes and Server-side JavaScript use specific tags in an HTML page to tell the server that a specific action should take place, you can define specific tags for your program. Your program can then read the content page and update the information by replacing the tag with dynamic information that your program has produced. The result can be sent to the client. Most advanced Web sites use a database for maintaining a variety of different information, such as client data, product data, Web site content, interactive data, purchase orders, and so on. NSAPI provides the fastest and most effective way of communicating with a database. If you intend to use a database, and speed of access and control of your communication with the database are important issues, you should definitely consider writing an NSAPI application and incorporating your database with it. It is easy to add database connectivity to your NSAPI program. You can easily add existing database code to your NSAPI program.

Maintaining State (Persistent Data)

The need for persistent data or maintaining state is simple to demonstrate. Suppose you have a client fill a form with some information that you may need later. To access the information again, you need to save it first. Once you have processed the client request and returned the response, data from the client input are no longer available unless you take specific action to save them. Even if you have saved the client input, you still need to associate these data to a uniquely identifiable client. Because each request from a client is a separate connection, any such request is seen as a separate, unique request by the server. A future request by the same client is seen as a new request, and the server will go through the steps of processing this request all over again. The server is aware of the user only when a transaction is in process. Except for cases specified in your server setting, such as authentication, the server does not distinguish between one client and another. To associate the client input with a particular client, you must take additional action. You need to identify and keep track of the client as well as associate the client input to the unique client identifier that you have specified. In this section, we will discuss how you can keep data persistent and maintain state information about a client.

You can categorize the use of persistent data based on the scope and lifetime of that use. The lifetime of the information can be very short (such as between HTML pages) or permanent (such as between different client sessions in different months).[2] The scope of the data can also vary between two HTML pages and between various clients.

The simplest type of persistent data is information that can be transferred (maintained) between two requests or HTML pages. With this type of data, you can customize the following page based on the information from the previous request. That is, you can associate a previous transaction with a current transaction from the same client. We have already written such an example in previous chapters. Each time we send a dynamic response based on the client request, we have used this type of persistent information. Moreover, by continuing to pass the data between pages, you can keep the data persistent for as long as you wish.

The second type of persistent data lasts for the entire client session. By client session, we mean the time the client spends navigating through the group of pages on your site that provides a unified Web application. (This use of the word *session* is different from the use of the data structure Session used in NSAPI programming.) This definition does not imply that there is a persistent network connection. You can maintain information about the client's selections as he or she goes through your Web site. In other words, you want to track clients' movements and selections as they navigate through the site. Thus the persistent data bring together a group of multiple pages as an application. The client can then dynamically interact with your Web application. This type of data does not need to be permanent; rather, it needs to last only while the client actively moves through your site. The server and/or client can keep this information in memory.

The third type of data is more permanent and is intended to last between each client session. It needs to be saved in a file or database. Your program can then specify how many days the data should be kept. The data are used to identify a client each time the client returns to the site.

Finally, you can have data that can be shared or used between clients. You can have information or selections from one client made available to another client. An example of this last type of persistent data is information about the guests in the Guest Book example that each client can view (see Chapter 9 for this example). You can also use this type of information to keep track of the number of users who visit your site or allow two clients to play a game together using your Web application.

In this chapter, we will focus more closely on the second and third types of persistent data. Unlike the first type of data, which is specific to requests and HTML pages, and the fourth type of data, which comprises global data saved on the server and shared between clients, the second and third types of data are more specific to a client. You can consider these types as short-term or long-term client data.

The kind of client data that you may wish to save can be simple, such a single tag

---

2. By permanent, we mean information that you can keep beyond the short time of the client's session. Your program can usually specify how long the information should be saved.

that identifies a client uniquely, or more complex, such as a list of client information or client selections and choices. You can use this information for processing the client's request, online ordering, tracking the user's navigation through your site, and so on.

Examples of Persistent Client Data

Before we examine ways to produce and maintain persistent data for your program, let us review some examples of the use of such client data. Each of the following examples has a different goal, and you can use different methods to accomplish these goals.

The shopping-cart scenario for online ordering can be an example of the second type of persistent data (short-term client data). The site can use a shopping-cart metaphor to collect different selections of the client and then use this information for the final processing of the client's order. Thus the site can distribute the client input across a number of pages. The client can order multiple items and select specific features by going through various order forms. In the final order page, you can use the client's various selections and input data from the previous pages to process the order. Sites like amazon.com use this type of persistent information to process a client's order. Although online ordering is the main use of this type of persistent data, similar methods can be used to track the client's navigation for other purposes.

Another example of an application for persistent information is the use of specific information from the client to customize the Web site. You can use the information gathered from or entered by the client to target different information for each user. Many commercial sites use this type of data to target advertisements. For example, they use the client information or a unique client tag to make sure a different advertisement banner appears each time the user visits the site or while the user is browsing a specific page. Some advertisers even require that their advertisements be displayed a minimum number of times or in a specific rotation. For example, Focalink uses persistent data to keep track of which ad banner has been shown and the number of times it was clicked on in its product SmartBanner. (See "meet SmartBanner" at `http://www.focalink.com/home/sb/sb2.html`.)

You can also use client selection or input to allow the user to customize (personalize) your site. Instead of using the client information to determine how you display information, you can allow users to select how *they* wish the information to be presented. Each client can use the specific criteria or selections you have defined to choose what type of information should be presented and how the information is to be organized or displayed. Unlike with the previous online ordering example, for this type of information to work, the information about the user and the user's preferences needs to be persistent beyond a single session. Therefore, this type of information should be of the third type of persistent data (long-term client data). Netscape, for example, provides such a customization of its site. (See Netscape PowerStart Setup at `http://personal.netscape.com/custom/index.html`.)

Finally, persistent client data can also be used to reduce repetitive or redundant input for the client. For example, the user's name and password can be saved and passed on automatically without the client having to re-input a name, password, or any other additional information each time he or she visits the site. The New York Times Web site, for example, uses such a technique to maintain a persistent identity of the registered users.

It is easy to come up with ways of taking advantage of persistent client data. This topic is popular in discussions found in various newsgroup or Internet programming books and journals. In fact, one key feature of JavaScript on Netscape Server (Server-side JavaScript) is its ability to provide various ways of maintaining state. You probably have already come up with additional examples of how you may want to use persistent client data. Once you gain access to client's information, it is tempting to use this information for your commercial or research purposes. You should, however, be cautious about using the information in ways that infringe on the user's privacy rights.

> ### Note ▶
>
> There has been a great deal of concern regarding privacy and misuse of the client information by various Web sites. You should be aware that many users are reticent and will refuse to give any personal information. To entice the users to provide such information, you should consider these options:
>
> - Make the input of additional information that is not essential for the processing of the client request voluntary.
> - Make sure the data will safely be delivered, processed, and maintained by your site. Provide the necessary security (for example, SSL) to make sure the client information will not be vulnerable to outside intruders or hackers.
> - Provide rewards and bonuses for anyone who actually fills the input forms.
> - Specifically identify why you are asking for the information.
> - State how you intend to use the information and why the client should provide such information.

Producing and Maintaining State Information

Let us now look at ways in which you can create and maintain persistent data. As the simple diagram in Figure 10-1 shows, the communication between the client (for example, Netscape Navigator) and the server (for example, Enterprise Server) includes three major components, just as with any client/server architecture. During an HTTP communication, the client requests a specific resource using a URL. The server receives the request and returns a response to the client. For any data to be persistent, the information needs to be kept by the client, delivered in the request, or saved and present on the server.

URL Encoding

A simple way of creating and maintaining persistent data is to take advantage of the URL used by the client. You can encode the state information that needs to be passed

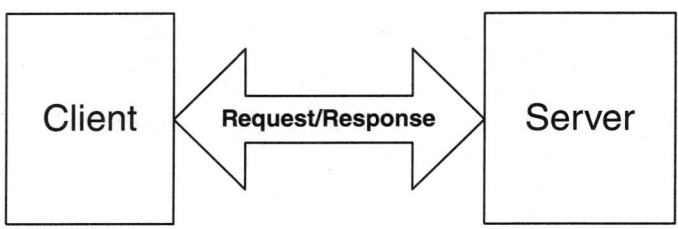

Figure 10-1   A Simple HTTP Client/Server Model

between the clients in the URL string. For this method, if the data are created dynamically, then you also need to produce the URLs dynamically. You need to pass the encoded information between all links that need to know the state information. The information can be placed at the end of the URL in the same way that extra path information or a query string is placed after the URL. (See URL and URI in Chapter 2.) You can place a specific string in the extra path information or standard [*name*]=[*value*] pair information in the query string. (For a **Service** function, you cannot use extra path information, unless you also write another directive function that can parse the extra path information, similar to the **PathCheck** function **find-pathinfo**.) Your program then reads these data from the URL string to get the client's information and to produce the next set of dynamic URLs embedded in the response page. In addition, for a POST request, you can use hidden fields to pass the information. The data from the hidden fields are then available to your program and should be again processed and added to any future link that requires the persistent data to be present. The advantage of using URL encoding is that it works with all browsers. URL encoding also has limitations. The size of the URL is limited depending on the browser and server. You can generally assume that the total size of the URL string should be less than 4K. Any further information in the string will be truncated. Moreover, because much of the data are dynamically generated based on the client's information or input, all URLs that need to maintain the persistent data must be dynamically generated. The dynamically generated data are also available only for the specific client session. Your program must take extra steps to maintain and manage the URLs. For a large Web application that includes many links and pages, this requirement could be rather complex and cumbersome. Changes to the site can also lead to a number of additional revisions. You need to keep track of the URL and make sure the right URL is used by the client. The complex URL string can also be confusing and distracting to the user. In general, you should use this method whenever the number of pages for which you wish to keep the data persistent and the amount of the data being saved are both small.

Client IP Address

Under HTTP/1.0 and higher, the data passed between the client and server include various headers (request and response headers). In Chapter 6, we discussed how you can obtain and use these headers to identify specific information about the client—for example, client IP or DNS address (the fully qualified domain name), the client browser type, and so on. Some of these headers are sent automatically by the client for each request, such as the IP address of the client (the `ip` entry in the `Session->client` pblock) or the client user-agent's (browser's) name (the `user-agent` entry in the `Request->headers` pblock). Because all major clients send these headers for each request, you can use these default headers as persistent data. For example, you may use the IP address of the client to identify the user during each visit to your site. Although these headers include essential and useful information, they do not include the necessary or assured information you may need to identify the client correctly each time. For example, the client IP address can be dynamically assigned by the user's Internet service provider (ISP). Thus, it could change each time the client visits your site. If each user has a different static IP address in the Intranet network of your company, you can assume that this information is always the same. You cannot assume that in the world of Internet, where many ISPs use dynamic IP addresses, that the client IP address will always be the same. This problem also exists if the client visits your site through a proxy server. With the proxy server as the middleman between your server and the client, you may have access to only the proxy's IP address. Moreover, the type of data sent by default from the client is predefined and limited. You cannot specify which data should be sent by the client each time. The client cannot dynamically specify the data. The only data that are dynamically entered by the client and repeatedly sent by the client for each request comprises the authentication information. For example, once the client inputs a name and password during the basic authentication, this same name and password are continuously sent by the client, each time the client requests a page from your site. The authentication information is lost as soon as the user closes the browser (client). Thus the user needs to re-input the name and password each time he or she starts the browser and attempts to visit your secured site.

Cookies

To overcome the limitations of the default headers that the client sends, Netscape provides the HTTP cookies protocol. Cookies are special tokens that your server can send to the client to be saved in a cookie file on the client's machine or in the memory of the browser. The client will return the value of these cookies to your server each time it makes a request. The cookies are sent by the server as part of the response-headers and are returned by the client as part of the HTTP request-headers. The values of these cookies are available only to the domain that sends the cookie to the client. While your site has access to the cookies it sets, it cannot have access to cookies set by another site that does not have the same domain. A cookie is a unique type of header (found in the pblock `Request->headers`) that the client repeatedly sends to your server for a URL that your server has specified. You can also specify whether the cookie should be saved, instead of being kept in the client's memory pool, and when it should expire.

As with all the options discussed here, there are advantages and disadvantages to using cookies. The advantage is that cookies are easy to implement and the maintenance of the data is done by the client. The data do not take extra memory or disk space from the server. You need only to set the cookie and expect it to be returned by the client. You are also guaranteed that the cookie is correctly associated with the client, because only the same client can return the cookie. On the other hand, a weakness of using cookies is that the cookie file is unique for each client/browser. In other words, if a user uses different browsers, the cookie saved when using one browser is not available through another browser. This setup applies independent of whether the user has multiple browsers on different machines or the same machine. Moreover, not all browsers support cookies, and the client can disable cookies for the browser. Another limitation is the number and size of the cookies you can set. The total number of cookies that a client can have is 300. If the number exceeds 300, the client (for example, Netscape Navigator) deletes the oldest cookie. The full size of a cookie cannot be more than 4K. When a cookie is larger than 4K, the cookie is truncated to 4K. For any given specified domain, there can be no more than 20 cookies. If the number of cookies for a specific domain exceeds 20, the client deletes the oldest cookie for the domain. The transferring of the cookies between client and the server also adds to the network traffic, especially if the size and number of cookies is large.

You should use cookies whenever you want to make sure of the identity of the client. With the Internet you cannot be certain that a client will always send a cookie, so you should use a cookie as a convenient and beneficial feature. It should supplement alternative options. For example, you can use cookies to save the user's login information. The user will not need to log in if the cookie sent by the client includes the correct information. If the cookie was not sent by the client, however, the user should be reauthenticated. Use cookies whenever the size and the number of the data that need to be sent by the client are both small. Cookies are especially useful as a client session key (session ID) or as an index token to data saved on the server. (To learn more about cookies, see the section More About Cookies later in this chapter.)

Server-Side Persistent Data

Another alternative is to save the client's information in the server's shared memory pool or in a file or database on the server. This option has the added benefit of working with all browsers, as it is limited only to the server's ability. The data are also not dependent on the client. For example, the client can delete the cookie file, but the data saved on the server remain in your hands. There is no predetermined limit (such as in client cookies) to the size and number of data you can save on the server. Server-side persistent data also reduces the network traffic between the client and server, as the data are not passed from the client to the server. Because the data are kept and maintained by the server, however, this option can have adverse effects on the server's performance. Saving data on the server requires additional disk space and/or memory for the server. It also demands more work, in the form of processing power, from the server. If the size of the data kept in the server memory pool gets too large, you should write a mechanism for pruning the data. You should erase data no longer in use.

To decide the best way to save information on the server, you should consider the speed of access, the size and type of the information, and the expected lifespan of the data. If the information needs to be kept for only a short time, you can save it in a data structure in the server's shared memory space. On the other hand, if the information needs to be available for a long time, you should save the data in a file or database. If the size of the information is large and the speed of access is important, you should consider a commercial database, such as Microsoft Access or an even more powerful database such as Oracle Workgroup Server. Otherwise, a simple binary file or a DBM file may suffice. Your program can then access and use the information as needed.

Saving general information or client input and retrieving the same data are rather simple operations. For example, we have already performed these tasks when we created a guest book file that different users can browse. Yet, to associate the saved information with a client is not a given, if the information is saved only on the server. To identify the saved information on the server as unique for a client, you must identify the client uniquely as well.

There are a number of ways that you can associate information on the server with a client. If you wish to save the client information only for a session, then the use of the client IP address may be all that you need. Even when the IP address is dynamically generated by the ISP, it stays the same during the client's login session with the ISP. The user can hang up the connection or be disconnected from the server while in the middle of a session with your site, in which case the ISP may reassign the client to a new IP address. This problem of correctly identifying the user is also present when the client is using a proxy server. All clients using the proxy server use the proxy's IP address to access your site. If the loss of such a connection or the existence of a proxy server is considered a significant drawback to your program, you need to use other options. Moreover, if you wish to identify clients each time they visit your site (for example, after a specific number of days), then you need to combine the use of information saved in the server side with other options. Another alternative is to combine the associated saved data on the server with a client cookie. For example, you can use a client ID as a client cookie to identify the client, but maintain the actual client information on the server. You can also use a login procedure to identify the client and then associate the authenticated client with the data saved on the server. Because the authentication information (for example, the `auth-user` or `auth-password` entry in *Request*->`vars`) continues to be sent by the client (browser), you can use this information across a client session with the data saved on the server. Finally, you can use URL encoding in conjunction with the data saved on the server. You can add a specific unique identifier to the URL that can be associated to such information. As long as the unique identifier is in existence in the URL or through the hidden form fields, the association between the data on the server and the client can be maintained.

Additional Options

You have additional options for maintaining state information that primarily take advantage of features unique to Netscape Navigator 3.x or 4.x (with the exception of some other browsers, such as Microsoft's Internet Explorer, that also support these features). These options include the use of frames or layers (now available with Navigator

4.x and Communicator) in conjunction with JavaScript. These browsers allow you to dynamically generate layers, frames, or windows whose various objects and HTML tags can be shared and controlled from other layers, frames, or windows. You can then change and modify the values in this shared environment and provide dynamic updates that span the layers, frames, or windows. You can also use LiveConnect to allow JavaScript to share information with Java applets or plug-in applications.

In addition, you can use BeanConnect, now available with Communicator 4.x. BeanConnect allows Java or IFC components to be distributed across different pages or frames but share a single execution context in the Java virtual machine. With Bean-Connect, you can also control the program objects and their lifetimes. (See "Bean Connect: Using Java Objects to Implement Crossware Programs" at `http://developer.netscape.com/library/wpapers/beanconnect/index.html`.)

More About Cookies

Let us look at how cookies work. We should first warn you that cookies have not yet been standardized by the Internet Engineering Task Force (IETF). The RFC (Request for Comments) 2109 was the original *proposed* standard. The current Internet draft is named "HTTP State Management Mechanism." The preliminary specification written by Netscape differs from both RFC 2109 and "HTTP State Management Mechanism." You can find additional information about the preliminary specification written by Netscape, "Cookie Persistent Client State—HTTP Cookies," under `http://home.netscape.com/newsref/std/cookie_spec.html`. This specification is also included on the CD-ROM that accompanies this book. For the latest Internet draft from IETF, see "HTTP State Management Mechanism" under the IETF's HTTP Working Group site (`http://www.ics.uci.edu/pub/ietf/http/`). The IETF cookie specification ("HTTP State Management Mechanism") discussed in this book is based on the February 16, 1998, draft, which expires on August 16, 1998. You can find this document, `draft-ietf-http-state-man-mec-08.txt`, under `http://www.ics.uci.edu/pub/ietf/http/draft-ietf-http-state-man-mec-08.txt`. For more information on cookies, you can also check the Cookie Central site, `http://www.cookiecentral.com/`.

In this section, we will refer to both the Netscape and IETF proposed standards. Because the Netscape proposal is the standard currently supported by most browsers, we will focus most closely on the Netscape specifications. The accompanying example (Listing 10-2) also uses the Netscape specifications' syntax.

Netscape Cookie File

As mentioned earlier, cookies are simple tokens or text strings that the server sends to the client (browser). They include state information passed from an origin server to a user-agent, such as a browser. The actual value of a cookie could be in clear or encoded text. The client (user-agent) saves this information in memory or in a cookie file.

Netscape cookie files are flat files. Under Windows, they can be found as `cookies. txt` under the root directory for Netscape Navigator 2.x and 3.x. For Netscape Communicator, you can find the cookie file under the Communicator subdirectory `Users`. For Netscape Communicator, there is a different cookie file for each user. Under Macintosh, the file name is `MagicCookie` and can be found under the System folder|Preferences folder. For UNIX, the file name is `cookies` and can be found under the Netscape Navigator directory for Navigator 2.x and 3.x or under the `Users` directory for Netscape Communicator. Other browsers may use different methods for saving cookies. For example, Microsoft Internet Explorer 3.x and 4.x for Windows keeps the cookies in the `<Windows path>\profiles\<user name>\cookies` directory. You can check the cookie file of your Netscape Navigator (Communicator) for examples of cookies set by different servers. Listing 10-1 provides one sample of cookies from a Netscape Communicator cookie file.

Listing 10-1   Sample Cookies from the Netscape Communicator's Cookie File

---

```
# Netscape HTTP Cookie File
# http://www.netscape.com/newsref/std/cookie_spec.html
# This is a generated file!  Do not edit.
.msn.com   TRUE  /  FALSE  921198891
    MC1       GUID=0238130629B9D1118D6F0000F84AAB52
www.zdnet.com      FALSE  /  FALSE  892620000
    ad-tracking-ziffd3  +
.excite.com  TRUE  /  FALSE  946641111
    registered  no
```

Listing 10-1   Sample Cookies from the Netscape Communicator's Cookie File
(continued)

```
.infoseek.com  TRUE  /  FALSE  921049878
   InfoseekUserId  AFF8001043D48FFD963FA8B8CD47AC2E

home.netscape.com  FALSE  /  FALSE  890266520
   menu_ret_state  0

.amazon.com  TRUE  /  FALSE  889947419
   session-id-time  889948800
```

In the Netscape Navigator (Communicator) cookie file, each cookie is placed on a single line starting with the host or domain name of the server that sent the cookie. In Listing 10-1, the lines are wrapped to fit on the printed page. In the actual cookie file, each cookie takes up a single line and there is no space between each line. There are seven columns of data, separated by tabs, saved for each cookie in the cookie file. The important columns you want to review are the first, third, sixth, and seventh columns. The following list, which breaks down these columns, includes the value of each column from the first cookie in parentheses after each description.

1. Domain or host name of the server sending the cookie. (.msn.com)
2. Code for whether the first field is a host or domain name. The value is either FALSE or TRUE. TRUE means that the first field is a domain name. (TRUE)
3. The virtual or partial path (a subset of the URL) for the domain or host name specified. It gives the path of the documents on the server for which the cookie is valid. The cookie is also valid for any subdirectory of the specified path. (/)
4. Specifies whether a secured socket connection is required for the client to send the cookie. The value is either FALSE or TRUE. If this value is TRUE, the cookie is sent only if the communication is secured—that is, if SSL is used. (FALSE)
5. Time of expiration. (921198891)
6. The name of the cookie (the name the server specified for the cookie). Your program can access the cookie's value using this name. (MC1)
7. The value of the cookie, which consists of the actual cookie data that you wished the client to save. (GUID=0238130629B9D1118D6F0000F84AAB52)

Set-Cookie *Response-Header*

You set a cookie by passing the HTTP response-header Set-Cookie to the client. The IETF specification uses Set-Cookie2. This specification allows the two methods to coexist. IETF specifies that a client, which receives both Set-Cookie and Set-Cookie2 response-headers, should discard the Set-Cookie information. A client that receives and supports Set-Cookie2 should use the IETF specification for returning a cookie.

For NSAPI, you can use pblock_nvinsert to send the header. For example, `pblock_nvinsert("set-cookie", "ID=123", rq->srvhdrs)` inserts a cookie named `ID` with the value `123` in the response-header. You can also specify a number of attributes for the cookie that determine how it functions. Not all of these attributes are required for the cookie to be accepted. For the Netscape specifications, only the name and value of the cookie ([*NAME*] = [*VALUE*]) are required. For IETF, you should also add the `Version` attribute.

The syntax for `Set-Cookie` based on the Netscape specification is as follows:

```
SetCookie: [NAME]=[VALUE]; expires=[DATE];
 path=[PATH]; domain=[DOMAIN_NAME]; secure
```

The [*NAME*] = [*VALUE*] pair is the first attribute of a cookie and is mandatory. It includes the name of the cookie, which your program uses to access the value. The client uses the name to find the value. You can use any string for the NAME or VALUE. You should not include semicolons (;), commas (,), quotes (" "), or spaces in the [*NAME*] = [*VALUE*] string. There should be no extra space before or after the equal sign. If you need to include any of these excluded characters, you can first use URL encoding for the characters. Your program can then decode the encoded string sent by the client. (For example, you can use the NSAPI function **util_uri_escape** to escape characters, such as the quote characters, in the string.)

The `expires` attribute specifies when the cookie should expire relative to GMT time. If you do not specify the `expires` attribute, the cookie expires when the user closes the browser. The format of the [DATE] is `Wdy, DD-MON-YY HH:MM:SS GMT`. It is based on RFCs 850, 1036, and 822. The only legal time zone is GMT, and the date variables must be separated by dashes. Make sure you include the `expires` attribute if you want the client to save the cookie in the cookie file.

The `path` attribute determines the path in the URL (the URI path) for which the cookie should apply. Any path under the specified path will also receive the cookie. Thus, if you specify the path `/custom`, the path `/custom/new` will also receive the cookie. The forward slash (/) is used to specify the root directory and all the subdirectories of a server. If you do not specify a path with `Set-Cookie`, `path` will be set to the path of the original request.

The domain name is the domain name of the server sending the cookie (that is, your server)—the domain for which the cookie is valid. You should use a domain name that includes at least two periods, as in, `.netscape.com`. Therefore, a domain such as `.org` or `.com` cannot be declared. All valid domains should begin with a period. If the domain does not include at least two periods or does not begin with a period, Navigator views the entry as the host name of the server sending the cookie (for example,

Bug Report ▶

For Netscape Navigator 1.1 and earlier, you had to specify the path as "/" for the value of the cookie to be saved on the client.

home.netscape.com). Domain names are more general and can refer to more than one host name. They allow multiple servers within the same domain. For example, .netscape.com matches both home.netscape.com and developer.netscape.com. If you check the Netscape's cookie file, you will notice that all domains that do not include at least two periods and do not begin with a period are classified as FALSE by the next column—that is, seen as the host name. The host name usually refers to an individual machine. You cannot specify a domain that does not match your server's domain or host name. An IP address is seen as the host name. It is recommended, however, that you use a domain name instead of an IP address. If you do not specify a domain name, the host name of the server that generated the cookie is used. The client verifies whether the domain you specified matches the origin server (your server) that sent the Set-Cookie header. The client also uses the domain information to verify whether the cookie header should be sent with the rest of the request-headers to the requested server. If your server does not match the domain, you will not receive the cookie.

secure is used to declare that the cookie should be transmitted only when a secured channel is available. With this attribute, you specify that the cookie should be sent over an SSL layer. If no secure attribute is declared, the cookie is sent over unsecured channels. For this attribute, there is no value. You specify only the string: secure.

IETF Set-Cookie2 *Response-Header*

IETF-based syntax for Set-Cookie2 is different from Set-Cookie defined earlier. IETF specification defines the Set-Cookie2 syntax as follows:

```
set-cookie     =       "Set-Cookie2:" cookies
cookies        =       1#cookie
cookie         =       NAME "=" VALUE *(";" set-cookie-av)
NAME           =       attr
VALUE          =       value
set-cookie-av  =       "Comment" "=" value
               |       "CommentURL" "=" <"> http_URL <">
               |       "Discard"
               |       "Domain" "=" value
               |       "MaxAge" "=" value
               |       "Path" "=" value
               |       "Port" [ "=" <"> portlist <"> ]
               |       "Secure"
               |       "Version" "=" 1*DIGIT
portlist       =       1#portnum
portnum        =       1*DIGIT
```

This describes a Set-Cookie2 that is similar to Netscape's Set-Cookie, but has a number of important differences. It specifies the use of Max-Age for the expiration (not expires). The Max-Age attribute specifies the lifetime of the cookie in seconds, not the time of expiration. The IETF specification also includes `Comment`, `CommentURL`, `Discard`, `Port`, and `Version` attributes. `Comment` can be used by the server to describe the use of the cookie for the user. `CommentURL` specifies a URL where the comment is kept by the server. Because the value of a cookie can be encrypted, the comment attributes allow the server to describe the use of the cookie for any user who inspects the information. `Discard` instructs the client to discard the cookie when the client is terminated. `Port` restricts the port where a cookie can be returned. Port numbers should be placed in a comma-separated list with quotes around them. Like `Path`, the `Port` attribute allows you to limit the scope of the cookie. If no `Port` is specified, the cookie can be returned to any port. Unlike the other attributes, the `Version` attribute is mandatory. `Version` is a decimal integer that specifies the version of the state management specification to which the cookie conforms. Currently, only `Version=1` should be used. Unlike the Netscape specification, the IETF specification allows more than one cookie, separated by a comma, to be sent using a single `Set-Cookie2` response-header. Under the Netscape version, you had to devise a unique scheme to include more than one cookie. Your program needs to combine the cookies in such a way that you can later decode and separate them. IETF also recommends using quotes around the values of each attribute. Older clients, however, may not accept quotes.

It is expected that older clients (ones that do not support the IETF standard) should ignore the `Set-Cookie2` response-header. If a client can respond to both `Set-Cookie` and `Set-Cookie2`, it should return the `Cookie2: $Version="1"` request-header to notify the server that it can accept `Set-Cookie2` headers. An older server (one that does not support the IETF standard) should send `Set-Cookie` and not `Set-Cookie2`. If the server can support both versions, it may send both `Set-Cookie` and `Set-Cookie2`. A client that supports `Set-Cookie2` should then discard the `Set-Cookie` information and return a request-header based on `Set-Cookie2` and the IETF specification. This IETF specification is different from the RFC 2109 specification, which also uses `Set-Cookie` and not `Set-Cookie2`.

Cookie HTTP Request-Header

Once a cookie is successfully sent to the client, the client verifies the accuracy of the cookie information by validating the domain information. Based on the existence and value of the `expires` or `Max-Age` attribute, the client either keeps the cookie alive in memory or saves it to the file. If the cookie has not expired, Netscape Navigator (the client) saves the cookie to the cookie file when it is closed. The client also loads the cookie information from the cookie file into memory when started. Whenever the user makes a request for a server, the client verifies whether the requested URL matches the specification of a cookie with the correct domain name and path information. For `Set-Cookie2`, the client should also verify the `Port` information. If such a cookie is found and has not expired, the client sends a `cookie` HTTP request-header with each request that matches. The value of this cookie will include all the cookies that match. The cookies are generally sent back separated with semicolons. IETF specifies that cookies can also be separated by commas. Under the IETF specification, the cookie information should also include `Version`. Depending on whether `Path`, `Domain`, or `Port` was sent by the `Set-Cookie2` response-header, `Path`, `Domain`, or `Port` will also be included in the cookie request-header. Under the IETF specification, the attributes of all cookies should begin with $, as in `$Path="/news"`. The `Version` attribute should always come before the actual cookie. Your program needs to separate the cookies before using them.

The following code gives two `Set-Cookie` examples based on Netscape:

```
Set-Cookie: USER=Joe; path=/
Set-Cookie: Order=1234; path=/orders
```

The same examples based on IETF follow:

```
Set-Cookie: USER="Joe"; Version="1"; Path="/"
Set-Cookie: Order="1234"; Version="1"; Path="/orders"
```

Netscape Navigator returns the following code as `cookie` in response to a request with the URL path `/orders`:

```
cookie: Order=1234; USER=Joe
```

A browser that supports IETF spec will return the following code:

```
cookie: $Version="1";
        Order=1234; $Path="/orders";
        User="Joe"; $Path="/"
```

Updating or Deleting a Cookie

To update a cookie with a new value, you should specify a new cookie that matches the main attributes of an existing cookie—that is, [*NAME*], `domain`, and `path` of the preexisting cookie. For the same `domain` and `path`, the client accepts only one cookie with the same name. To delete a cookie, just replace an old cookie with a cookie that has the same attributes but has already expired or has its `Max-Age` attribute set to zero. For `Set-Cookie`, change the expiration date to a date that has already passed. The client will delete such a cookie.

Cached Cookies

Sometimes the use of caching on the HTTP or proxy server and/or client can lead to problems with your use of cookies. The server could cache the `Set-Cookie` header along with the document, and the client could cache the documents.

The server should not cache a `Set-cookie` or `Set-Cookie2` header that is intended for a single user. To stop the caching of a document, you should return the header `cache-control: no-cache` for HTTP/1.1 or `pragma=no-cache` for HTTP/1.0. You can also use `cache-control` to disable caching for a specific header—for example, `Cache-control: no-cache="set-cookie2"`. Other options include `cache-control: private; cache-control: must-revalidate,max-age=0; cache-control: max-age=0;` and so on. For more information on `cache-control` and its use for cookies, see "HTTP State Management Mechanism." For general information on `cache-control`, see the HTTP/1.1 specification.

If a document is cached by the client, then your cookie may not be sent. The client asks the server to send a document only if it has changed since a specified date, by sending the `If-Modified-Since` request-header. If the document has not changed, then the server returns status `304` and no document is sent. Thus your cookie could also not be sent. To avoid this problem, you can force the document not to be cached by sending the `no-cache` header. You can also remove the `If-Modified-Since` header from *Request*->headers or modify its value before sending the `Set-Cookie` header. Moreover, you can send the `Expires` header with the document to force the document to expire immediately after it is read by the client. `Cache-control` directives should override the `Expires` header for HTTP/1.1 proxies.

Cookie Example—newuser

The example in Listing 10-2 uses the cookie information to redirect a client. It is implemented as a **Service** function, so the **newuser** SAF is called only when the appropriate file extension is used by the client. Normally, you use a cookie for your entire site or for a specific directory in your site. You indicate a specific path to which the cookie should apply. In this example, however, we limit the use of the cookie to our SAF. When the client makes a request with the file extension specified in the **mime.types** file, the server sends the cookie.

In Listing 10-2, we first check whether a cookie is sent by the client. If the client did not send a cookie, we send back a cookie and route the client to the location specified in **obj.conf**. We actually return two cookies: The first cookie records the day it was sent, and the second records the number of times the cookie was sent. For the first visit, we set the number of cookies, which reflects the number of the client's visits, to one (1). You can modify this program to return one cookie with both the date and number of visits. Here, we intend to show how easy it is to return multiple cookies. We also set the expiration date to a day far in the future, so this cookie is kept for a while.

The next time the client requests our SAF, it also returns the cookies we sent. Both cookies are returned together in the cookie header. We read the data in the cookie header and return a new set of cookies that updates the date and the number of visits. We also print out the date and number of cookies for the client.

This process allows you to quickly review the result of the cookie. In your programs, you will probably find a better use of the cookie than to return the cookie information to the client. For example, you can route the client to a different location each time the user returns. You can also modify this program to remember the client's password. The first time the client visits, you can route the client to a page for input of a user name and password. You then set this information in the cookie and send it to the client. The next time the client visits, you will read this information to authenticate the user.

If the name and password are correct, you can route the client to the requested location. Otherwise, you can return the client to another page, requiring the user to re-input a name and password.

Listing 10-2 shows how you can send cookies, read the content of cookies, update cookies, and use cookies to route the client to a different location.

Following are examples of cookies in the client's cookie file sent by our server:

```
www.foo.com FALSE / FALSE 930816001 DATE Monday+July+27+1998
www.foo.com FALSE / FALSE 930816002 NUM 4
```

Because we do not specify a domain name, the server host name is used. Some browsers require a domain name. This example is intended for Netscape Communicator/Navigator. Other browsers may expect different information in the cookie string.

Registration Instructions

The following instructions apply to registering the SAF **newuser** (Listing 10-2). You should have already compiled the program to a DLL or shared library. This program was originally written for NT, but it should work without any specific modification under UNIX. Add the following lines in the **obj.conf** file:

```
Init fn=load-modules funcs=newuser
  shlib=c:/netscape/server/nsapi/examples/newuser.dll

Service fn="newuser" method="GET"
  type="magnus-internal/newuser" address="/first.html"
```

If you added this SAF to an existing DLL or shared library, then modify the **load-modules** line in the **obj.conf** file by adding the function's name, **newuser**, to the funcs parameter list. You should also update the shlib parameter to reflect the correct location of the DLL (or the shared library file for UNIX). The address parameter of **newuser** points to the file that you should return the first time the client asks for your SAF. You should change the path to reflect the location of the file you wish the server to return.

To enable the server to recognize this **Service** SAF, you should also update the **mime.types** file. In **mime.types**, add the following line (or any other extension [exts] you may wish to use with the SAF):

```
type=magnus-internal/newuser exts=ask
```

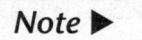

Note ▶

The Functions **pblock_remove_escape** (Listing 9-3) and **send_simple_response** (Listing 9-2-2) are referenced in Listing 10-2 through forms.h. You should look in Chapter 9 for the actual functions.

This **Service** function is called only when this extension is used as the extension of the file that the client is requesting.

Listing 10-2   Cookie Example—newuser

```
/* include the following files if you are using a version of
   Netscape Server earlier than 3.x

   #include "base/pblock.h"
   #include "base/session.h"
   #include "frame/req.h"

   #include "base/util.h"
   #include "frame/protocol.h"
*/

/* include this file if you are using Server 3.x */
#include "nsapi.h"

/* Header file for the general-purpose functions. We
   discussed the use of this file in Chapter 9.
   pblock_remove_escapes and send_simple_response are
   referenced from this file.
 */
#include "forms.h"

/* sets a cookie with the name=value in the response-header
 */
NSAPI_PUBLIC void insert_cookie(char *name, char *value,
                                        Request *rq);

/* redirects the client to a location specified
   in param->address
 */
NSAPI_PUBLIC int new_direction(pblock *param, Session *sn,
                                        Request *rq);

/* replaces the separator character with a space in the dest
   string
 */
NSAPI_PUBLIC int remove_separators(char *src, char *dest,
                                        char *separator);

/* returns the parsed cookies in a pblock */
NSAPI_PUBLIC pblock *parse_cookies(char *cookies_str);

/* This is the expiration date we set for the cookie.
```

Listing 10-2   Cookie Example—newuser (*continued*)

```
    Without the expires attribute the cookie expires
    after the session==that is, when the client shuts down
    the browser.
 */
#define EXPIRATION_DATE "Thursday, 01-July-99 08:00:00 GMT"

/* path attribute of the cookie */
#define COOKIE_PATH "/"

/* This function routes the client to a new location the
   first time it is called by the client. After that,
   it returns an HTML page with the last date
   of the client's visit and the number of visits
   to this new page.
*/
NSAPI_PUBLIC int newuser(pblock *param, Session *sn,
                            Request *rq)
{
    time_t now;                 /* pointer to stored time */
    struct tm *today;            /* time structure */
    struct tm tmpday;          /* local times data structure */
    char *timestring;          /* value of DATE cookie, date of
                                  last client visit */

    int i;                      /* holds the number of visits */

    char *cookie_string=NULL;  /* cookie string sent by
                                    client */
    pblock *cookie_jar;        /* parsed cookies in a pblock */

    char *day;                 /* date of client's last visit */
    char *times;               /* number of client's last visit */
    char *new_times;           /* new number of client's visit */

    char *response_content;   /* content of the page sent to
                                    client */
    int return_value = REQ_PROCEED; /* function's return
                                        value */

    /* get the stored time (number of seconds since 1/1/70) */
    now = time(NULL);

    /* get the current local time data structure */
    today = system_localtime(&now, &tmpday);

    /* malloc a large-enough space for the time string */
    timestring = (char *) MALLOC(50 * sizeof(char));
```

Listing 10-2   Cookie Example—newuser (*continued*)

```
/* put the time from the time data structure (today) in
   the string timestring
 */
util_strftime(timestring, "%A+%B+%d+%Y", today);

/* retrieve the cookie string from the client */
request_header("cookie", &cookie_string, sn, rq);

/* first time to the site */
if(!cookie_string)
{
    /* set new cookies for the current time and
       number of visits (1)
     */
    insert_cookie("DATE", timestring, rq);
    insert_cookie("NUM", "1", rq);

    /* since this is the first time we route the client
       to the special location specified in obj.conf
     */
    return_value = new_direction(param, sn, rq);

    goto done;
}
else
{
    /* parse the cookie string and place the
       data in the cookie_jar pblock
     */
    cookie_jar = parse_cookies(cookie_string);

    /* get the value of DATE and NUM cookies */
    day = pblock_findval("DATE", cookie_jar);
    times = pblock_findval("NUM", cookie_jar);

    /* If the values are not found then we haven't set
       them. We could have other cookies but not the
       ones we want.
     */
    if(!day || !times)
    {
        /* if the cookies we want are not there, then we
           process this request as if it is the first time
         */
        insert_cookie("DATE", timestring, rq);
```

Listing 10-2   Cookie Example—**newuser** (*continued*)

```
                    insert_cookie("NUM", "1", rq);

                    return_value = new_direction(param, sn, rq);

                    goto done;
          }
          /* we found the cookies */
          else
          {
                    /* update the cookie with current DATE value */
                    insert_cookie("DATE", timestring, rq);

                    /* we must convert the number of client visits
                        to integer before increasing the value by one
                     */
                    i = (atoi(times)) + 1;

                    /* We must convert the new number of client
                        visits to a string (new_times). When 1 is
                        added to 9 the result is 10 (two characters).
                        We therefore add an extra char to the size of
                        new_time.
                     */
                    new_times = (char *) MALLOC((strlen(times) + 2)
                                                * sizeof(char));

                    /* convert i (integer) to new_times (string) */
                    util_itoa(i, new_times);

                    /* update the number of visits by setting a new
                        cookie with the updated number
                     */
                    insert_cookie("NUM", new_times, rq);

                    /* will hold the content of the page to be sent
                        to the client
                     */
                    response_content =(char *)MALLOC(512 *
                                                    sizeof(char));

                    /* create a string for the content of the response,
                        which shows the number of visits the client has
                        made and the time of last visit
                     */
                    util_sprintf(response_content,
                            "You last visited this site on %s.<P>"
                            "Number of times your have visited this "
```

Listing 10-2   Cookie Example—newuser (*continued*)

```
                        "page = %s.",
                        day, times);

            /* Send the response page to the client.
               send_simple_response was written earlier and is
               referenced from forms.h.*/
                return_value = send_simple_response(
                        "Welcome Back", response_content, sn, rq);
            goto done;
        }
    }

    done:

    FREE(timestring);
    if(new_times)
        FREE(new_times);
    if(cookie_jar)
        pblock_free(cookie_jar);
    return return_value;
}
/* set the cookie header in the server response-header
   pblock (rq->srvhdrs)
 */
NSAPI_PUBLIC void insert_cookie(char *name, char *value,
                                Request *rq)
{
    char *cookie_value;  /* the value of set-cookie */

    cookie_value = MALLOC(256 * sizeof(char));

    /* create the value of the set-cookie by adding
       the cookie's name and value plus expires and
       path attributes
     */
    util_sprintf(cookie_value,
                "%s=%s; expires=%s; path=%s",
                name, value, EXPIRATION_DATE, COOKIE_PATH);

    /* insert the set-cookie in the response-header */
    pblock_nvinsert("set-cookie", cookie_value, rq->srvhdrs);

    FREE(cookie_value);
}
/* this function redirects the client to a new location */
```

Listing 10-2 Cookie Example—**newuser** (*continued*)

```
NSAPI_PUBLIC int new_direction(pblock *param, Session *sn,
                                      Request *rq)
{
    char *address; /* holds the new URL */

    /* get the URL address defined as a parameter of newuser
       in the obj.conf file
     */
    address = pblock_findval("address", param);

    /* insert the location header in the server header */
    pblock_nvinsert("Location", address, rq->srvhdrs);

    /* set status to redirect */
    protocol_status(sn, rq, PROTOCOL_REDIRECT, NULL);

    /* send out the headers */
    protocol_start_response(sn, rq);

    return REQ_PROCEED;
}

/* place the source character without the separator character
   in the dest string. Replace the separator character with
   a space character.
 */
NSAPI_PUBLIC int remove_separators(char *src, char *dest,
                                      char *separator)
{
    int x = 1;  /* holds the number of cookies */

    /* step through the source string */
    while(*src)
    {
        /* if the source character is the separator,
           then replace it with a space in the
           dest string
         */
        if(*src == *separator)
        {
            *dest = ' ';

            /* each cookie is separated by a separator,
               so the number of separators is one less
               than the number of cookie items
             */
```

Listing 10-2   Cookie Example—newuser (*continued*)

```
            x++;
        }
        /* otherwise src and dest should be the same */
        else
        {
            *dest = *src;
        }
        src++;
        dest++;
    }

    /* terminate the destination string */
    *dest = '\0';

    /* return the number of cookies */
    return x;
}

/* Separate each cookie (name=value) pair
   and place them in a pblock data structure. Also
   remove any spaces and Hex-encoded character from the
   data in the pblocks.
 */
NSAPI_PUBLIC pblock *parse_cookies(char *cookies_str)
{
    char *separate_cookies; /* holds the cookie string after
                               remove_separators */
    int num;                /* number of cookies */
    pblock *cookies_pb; /* pblock that will hold the cookies */

    /* malloc a string to hold the parsed cookies */
    separate_cookies = (char *)MALLOC((strlen(cookies_str)
                       + 1) * sizeof(char));

    /* separate the cookies by replacing ; with a space */
    num = remove_separators(cookies_str,
                            separate_cookies, ";");

    /* Create a pblock that will hold the cookie. The
       size of the pblock (number of entries) is
       determined by the number of cookies (returned
       by remove_separators).
     */
    cookies_pb = pblock_create(num);
```

Listing 10-2   Cookie Example—**newuser** (*continued*)

```
    /* put the data in the string separate_cookies into
       pblock cookies_pb
    */
    pblock_str2pblock(separate_cookies, cookies_pb);

    /* Replace the Hex characters in cookies_pb entries
       with equivalent ASCII characters and + with
       spaces. Here we want to replace the + in the
       DATE cookie.
     */
    pblock_remove_escapes(cookies_pb);

    FREE(separate_cookies);
    return cookies_pb;
}
```

Stepping Through the newuser Program

Listing 10-2 includes five functions: **new_direction**, **insert_cookie**, **remove_separators**, **parse_cookie**, and **newuser**. **new_direction** redirects the client to the location specified in the **obj.conf** file, similar to the redirect function we wrote in Listing 6-2. **insert_cookie** inserts the set-cookie response-headers. **remove_separators** and **parse_cookie** parse the cookies returned by the client in the cookie request-header. These two functions are very similar to the parsing functions we wrote to parse a query string (Listing 9-3). **parse_cookie** also uses the **pblock_remove_escapes** function that we wrote in Listing 9-3. **newuser** is our SAF, our main function. It calls the other functions.

We first define the expiration date (EXPIRATION_DATE) for the cookies as a date far in the future and specify the path (COOKIE_PATH) to /, root document directory. We do not declare a domain name, but you may want to modify this program to include a domain name parameter for the cookies.

In **newuser**, we first create a timestring that we will use as the value of the first cookie (DATE). We use the NSAPI function **system_localtime** to get the local time (today). **util_strftime** is used to create the timestring based on today's day, month, date, and year (for example, Monday+July+27+1998). We use a plus sign (+) for the space between each field. Next, we see if there is any cookie header sent by the client (request_header("cookie", &cookie_string, sn, rq);). **request_header** looks for the cookie header. If we were writing a CGI program, we would have looked for HTTP_COOKIE.

If no cookie was sent by the client, we use **insert_cookie** to insert the DATE and NUM cookies. We then redirect the client using **new_direction**.

We pass the name and value of the cookie to the function **insert_cookie**. **insert_cookie** uses EXPIRATION_DATE and COOKIE_PATH to specify the expires and path attributes of the cookie. If you intend to use a domain name, you should add the domain name (domain=[DOMAIN_NAME]) here. The cookie_value is then inserted in the response-headers by pblock_nvinsert (pblock_nvinsert("set-cookie", cookie_value, rq->srvhdrs);). The cookie_value is placed in the response-headers as the value of set-cookie (Set-Cookie) header. Although the header's name is given Set-Cookie in the cookie specification, it seems to be safer to use set-cookie (all lowercase) as the name of the header. Some browsers have a difficult time handling Set-Cookie. As we will not use the cookie_value string any longer, we also FREE it at the end of the **insert_cookie** function.

The param, sn (Session), and rq (Request) parameters of the **newuser** function are passed to the function **new_direction**. **new_direction** needs the param pblock to get the address of the new location. We get the value of the parameter address defined in the **obj.conf** file for the SAF **newuser** using **pblock_findval** (pblock_findval("address", param);). **new_direction** also needs the Session and Request parameters to set the status to redirect (protocol_status) and send the headers (**protocol_start_response**). We return REQ_PROCEED and set the return value of **newuser** to REQ_PROCEED.

Back in **newuser**, we free any string we had allocated and use the return value of **new_direction** to exit. If the client had returned a response cookie header (that is, cookie_string exists), we would continue with **newuser**. We first parse the cookies using **parse_cookies**.

We pass the cookie string from the client to the **parse_cookies** function. The cookie string is similar to a query string. It includes a number of cookies in the form of [NAME] = [VALUE] pairs separated by semicolons. **parse_cookies** calls **remove_separators**, which separates the cookies in the cookie string by placing a space between each cookie. Next, in **parse_cookies**, we create a cookie pblock (cookies_pb). We use **pblock_str2pblock** to place the parsed string (separate_cookies) from **remove_separators** into the pblock cookies_pb entries. We also use the **pblock_remove_escapes** function (from Listing 9-3) to remove any escaped characters from the cookie entries in cookies_pb. For our cookies, this function replaces only the + character in DATE with spaces. You can also use **pblock_remove_escapes** to remove any additional encoding. As already mentioned, it is best to URL-encode your string before sending it to the client. Because **pblock_remove_escapes** decodes an URL-encoding string, you do not need to write a separate decoding function. If there are additional cookies that your server has sent to the client, **parse_cookies** parses and decodes them. In the end, **parse_cookies** returns the updated pblock cookies_pb.

Back in the **newuser** function, we get the value of DATE and NUM cookies using pblock_findval from the cookie_jar returned by **parse_cookies**. For example, pblock_findval("DATE", cookie_jar); returns the value of DATE cookie. If the DATE and NUM cookies were not found in the cookie_jar, then we had not set them. We must therefore insert these cookies in the response-headers using **insert_cookie** and redirect the client just as we did earlier. We need to repeat this action because the server could have specified other cookies but not the ones we want and that our function has set. If your server had sent other cookies to the client, when we checked for client's cookie in the request-header, we would have found them. They are not the cookies in which we are interested, however.

If the DATE and NUM cookies were found, then we update their values. We need to update DATE and NUM to reflect the current time and the number of the client's visit. We use the timestring we created earlier to set the DATE information to the current date. By resending the same DATE and NUM cookies with a new value, we actually update the existing cookies. The client replaces the value of the cookies with the new value, instead of inserting additional cookies in the cookie list. To update the NUM value, we need to convert the value of NUM from the cookie_jar to an integer. The value of cookies and the pblock entries are in string format. We can then update the NUM integer by one. To return the cookie, we convert the value of NUM back to a string. This time we use the NSAPI function **util_itoa** to convert an integer to a string. We then use insert_cookie to insert the cookies in the response-header.

We are now ready to return the HTML page stating the last date the client visited the site and the number of times the client has visited the current page. Because the client did not get this dynamic page the first time around, we return the number of visits from the client's cookie request header instead of the updated response-header cookie. In other words, if it is the second time the client requested your SAF, then we return this dynamic page and state that it is the first time the client has visited this new page. **send_simple_response**, a function found in Listing 9-2-2, is used to return the page to the client.

Finally, we free timestring (value of the DATE cookie), times (value of the NUM cookie as a string), and the cookie_jar pblock that held the client cookies. If everything went as planned, we also return REQ_PROCEED.

Maintaining a Connection Using Push and Pull

In the previous section, we spoke of ways you can maintain state information; in this section, we will discuss how you can maintain the HTTP connection beyond a single request. Both of these techniques allow you to gain greater control over the interaction with the client. In this section, we will discuss two ways of updating the client page at specified intervals. The methods described here are different from the use of persistent connections supported by the server to maintain a connection while a page with its embedded resources is sent to the client.

Push technology is the subject of much debate and discussion lately. Push technology (also called Webcasting), which was delivered first with PointCast, allows information to be delivered automatically to the client without the user having to take any additional steps. The content is updated automatically at regular intervals. In other words, the server can push content to the client. Push content is the "TV" version of the Web, except that it allows for greater customization and interaction. The idea is to allow users to choose what information they wish to get and how the information should be displayed on their screens. The information then gets updated regularly using a number of different methods.

Originally, these tools were demonstrated by third-party providers using proprietary means. PointCast and Marimba Castanet are the two most famous early advocates of this new technique. Today, Netscape and Microsoft are getting into the act. Netscape provides Netcaster and works closely with Marimba, while Microsoft provides Channel Definition Format (CDF) and works with PointCast. These standards are recent technologies and require the latest versions of the browsers. You will need Netscape Communicator or Netscape Navigator 4.x with Netcaster or Microsoft Internet Explorer 4.x. Netcaster uses a combination of cascading style sheets, HTML, JavaScript, and Java. Microsoft, on the other hand, has proposed a new standard with CDF. It recommends the use of Visual Basic, Active X, and Dynamic HTML for its push support. To take the greatest benefit from these technologies, you may also need special servers. The use of push, as intended by these providers, is not limited to sending Web content; it also includes updating and serving of actual software application. For additional information on the use of push by these companies, check out the Web sites of each company.

In this chapter, we will discuss some earlier versions of this technique that provide limited support for pushing content to the client. Before the new generation of push technology was delineated and implemented by Netscape, Microsoft, and other third-party developers, Netscape proposed two simple standards that supported basic push: client pull and server push. Unlike the techniques discussed previously, these standards are supported by earlier browsers. For example, both client pull and server push are supported by Netscape Navigator 1.1 and later. Many other browsers, such as Microsoft Internet Explorer, support these features as well, although the implementation might be a bit different. Client pull and server push should be seen as features that enhance existing Web sites and the current use of Internet HTTP communication. They are not intended to be a new way of delivering Web content.

Client pull is simple. You include a META tag in the document that you wish to be updated at regular intervals. The client interprets this META tag (or the equivalent HTTP response-header) and continues requesting the same page or a new page based on a predefined time interval. The work of client pull is normally done by the browser (the client). The browser must understand and execute the tag (the specific HTTP header) properly. Server push, on the other hand, works as collaboration between the client and the server. The client recognizes the header sent by the server and keeps the connection open. The server can then send back data in any order it wishes. With server push, you can update data such as an image in a specific page instead of reloading a new page each time. You must write a program to take advantage of server push, however. In the program, you can dynamically control and modify the order and timing of the data sent to the client. Once the server has finished sending the data, it returns a new header that tells the browser to shut down the connection. Server push uses a special MIME type, `multipart/mixed` or `multipart/x-mixed-replace`, to accomplish this task. The client needs to recognize these MIME types and process the response properly for server push to work.

With client pull, you do not keep the connection open. With server push, the HTTP connection is held open until the server tells the client to end the connection. Of course, both these options cannot stop a client from interrupting the connection manually and going to a new page. Once the client moves to a new location (page) on the Web, the connection is closed and the data are no longer updated.

Client Pull

Client pull is a relatively simple technology. You do not need to write a program to take advantage of it. You simply add a META tag to the HEAD part of the HTML page that instructs the client to upload the data from your server on a regular basis. Of course, you are not limited to using the META tag in HTML pages; you can also specify the instruction as an HTTP response-header.

You can use client pull in two different ways. First, client pull allows you to refresh a page by having the client ask for the same page every few seconds. This method is commonly used to update statistical information on Web sites. Web sites use client pull to update stock information, sports results, and so on. For example, Yahoo uses client pull to have the statistics of current sport events periodically updated. If you visit Yahoo! Sports: Major League Baseball (http://baseball.yahoo.com/mlb/), you can watch the page update every 300 seconds with the latest game statistics. Second, client pull can tell the client to download a different page. After the specified number of seconds, the client requests a new page. For example, you can use this method to create a slideshow. Each time a new page is sent to the client, the URL in the META tag points to the next slide. Thus the client goes through each slide based on the refresh rate you specify.

The following code is an example of a META tag you can use to produce client pull:

```
<META HTTP-EQUIV="Refresh" CONTENT="300">
```

This tag states that the document should be refreshed every 300 seconds. Make sure to include the META tag in the HEAD section of your HTML document before the TITLE tag.

META tags are standard HTML 3.x tags that specify unique metainformation about the document. They are often used by search engines for indexing and cataloging documents. They are also used to generate HTTP response-headers from within an HTML document. META tags can be extracted and used by both the client and the server. The server can translate specific META tags to equivalent HTTP response-headers and return the headers and their values with the document to the client. The META tag can also be read and interpreted by a client. The above META tag, for example, is understood by Netscape Navigator as the equivalent HTTP response-header. If you open a file with this tag in the browser, you will notice that the client refreshes the file every 300 seconds. META tags normally include HTTP-EQUIV or NAME as the attribute to determine the name of the response-header. The CONTENT attribute is used to define the value of the response-header. Thus the example META tag is interpreted as HTTP header `refresh:300`. For the refresh HTTP tag to work, the browser needs to understand this HTTP tag and respond by refreshing the document. You can include any number of HTTP headers this way. For example, you can include the `Expires` header as a META tag, as in `<META HTTP-EQUIV="Expires" CONTENT= "Wednesday, 01-Jan-99 24:00:00 GMT">`.

In addition to reloading the same page, you can have the client request a different page or automatically redirect the client to a new location after the specified time. To accomplish this goal, you can add the URL attribute to the META tag. For example, the following tag tells the client to reload the page `doc2.html` after 300 seconds:

```
<META HTTP-EQUIV="refresh" CONTENT="300
 URL=http://www.foo.com/doc2.html">
```

The equivalent HTTP response-header for this META tag is

```
Refresh: 300, URL=http://www.foo.com/doc2.html
```

You should use an absolute URL for the document. Do not use relative paths or a partial path. In other words, include the complete URL of the document, including `http://`, the server information, and the path to the document. If the following page does not include the `Refresh` META tag, however, the client will not refresh the page. Each META tag tells the client to refresh the page once. If the new page also includes the `Refresh` META tag, the client refreshes the page again.

As mentioned earlier, you do not need to use the META tag to have the client refresh a document. You can also send the specific HTTP response-header directly via a CGI or NSAPI program you have written. By using the `Refresh` header in your program, you can have greater control over when the document should be refreshed.

Server Push

Server push allows you to keep the connection with the client alive while you update the information being sent to the client. Thus the server can decide when and how often the data should be sent. With client pull, the client continues to reconnect to the server and request the information based on intervals you defined. Unlike client pull, server push keeps the connection alive. As the connection is kept open, server push is a more efficient way of updating pages. Because of the same open connection, however, server push takes more resources away from the server. The server has to dedicate a TCP/IP port for the connection. Unlike client pull, you also must write a server program (for example, a CGI or NSAPI program) to take advantage of server push.

Server push uses special MIME types to let the client know that multiple-part data are being sent. The client then waits for all parts of the data to be sent before closing the connection. Normally, the MIME type identifies one type of data that is sent to the client—for example, `Content-type: text/html`. You can also use a MIME type, which identifies a message that includes many separate parts and/or different types of data. The MIME type normally used to identify a multiple-part message is

multipart/mixed. Netscape also uses another MIME type, multipart/
x-mixed-replace. Type multipart/x-mixed-replace is an experimental
MIME type, as identified by the x-. This MIME type implies not only that multipart
data are being sent, but also that the new block of data sent by the server should *replace*
the previous block of data.

To enable the client to recognize where the beginning of the new block of data is, a
boundary string is used. When this boundary string is used to introduce a new
block of data, it should begin with two dashes (--). In other words, you add two
dashes to the boundary string before sending it to the client. When the last block
of data is sent, the server returns the boundary string with dashes both in the beginning and at the end of the string. The client recognizes this string as the last data and
shuts down the connection. The format of the Content-type you should use for a
multiple-part response is as follows:

```
Content-type: multipart/x-mixed-replace; boundary=<string>
```

or

```
Content-type: multipart/mixed; boundary=<string>
```

The boundary string can be any string you choose, as long as you use the same string
to separate each block of data that the server sends. The following is an example of blocks
of data sent by the server after sending Content-type with MultipleData as
the boundary string:

```
--MultipleData
Content-type: text/html
[any additional header]

[First block of data.]

--MultipleData
Content-type: text/html
[any additional header]

[Additional data.]
---MultipleData--
```

While these data are being sent, the HTTP connection is kept alive. If you look at the
Netscape Navigator (Communicator) logo on the top right-hand corner of the Navigator
window, you can see that it is animated—that is, the connection is active. Your program
has control over when to send each block of data. For example, you can set a timer and
send each block after a few seconds. If you do not send the last boundary string that
tells the client to disconnect, the client stays connected until the user manually disconnects. The user can disconnect the connection by closing the browser, pressing the
Stop or Back button, and so on. Each block of data can have its own headers, so a different type of data can be sent each time. With multipart/x-mixed-replace,
the important thing to note is that each block of data is sent to replace the previous

block. You do not use this option to write the text of a page in increments, but rather to update the page with new data. When the client receives the new response-headers (for example, `Content-type: text/html`), it clears the previous document and waits for the new data. The client then usually displays the new data after it receives the boundary string, such as `--MultipleData`. This procedure can continue until you send the final boundary string, such as `--MultipleData--`.

A common example of server push is to write a program that produces an animation of an in-line image. Before animated GIFs became the standard for creating simple graphic animations, this use of server push was one of the ways of producing basic animations. You can find an example of such a program in the NSAPI example, `service.c`, that comes with your server. You can also find a CGI example of such a program as `doit.c` under `http://search.netscape.com/assist/net_sites/mozilla/doit.c`. What you get with server push is flexibility in choosing the interval in which the data are displayed and the type of data that you can send. For example, the images you send back could be a combination of GIF and JPEG. Animated GIF (GIF89a format), however, is now a better way of producing simple animation, as it is easier to create and distribute such an animation and does not take away resources from the server. With animated GIF, the HTTP connection is not kept alive. The image sent by the server includes all the frames and instructions for generating the animation.

Although it is not recommended that you use server push for the purpose of creating simple animations, it is still a useful feature. The best use of server push is when you want to send information to the client that needs to be updated regularly, while at the same time controlling when and what type of data should be sent. If you simply want the client to request a page that is updated regularly, or if you wish to create a slideshow, then client pull is probably the easier method. If you want greater control over the client connection, then server push is the better way. For example, with server push, your program can disconnect the connection whenever it sees fit.

Server Push Example—wait

The following example uses server push to update incrementally the information on a page sent to a client. Once the page is updated, the SAF **wait** (Listing 10-3) sends back a new page. The page begins with the following text:

```
Starting Wait
Please wait. System is processing.
```

Every three seconds, the server sends an additional "`Please wait. System is processing.`" string. This cycle continues six times. After the last string is sent, the server sends a new page with the following text:

```
Thank you. Server is finished.
```

Although by itself this example is not very useful, it does show how you can combine server push with a page that returns status information to the client. For example, suppose your program takes a long time processing a request. You can use an SAF program similar to the one in Listing 10-3 to return status information to the client while the user is waiting. You can also use a similar SAF to return the result of a multiple-source search. For example, if your program searches a number of different databases to get the response, you can send an update for each search as it becomes available.

With CGI, you can use nonparsed functions (nph-) to take control of sending the response to the client. (See the Nonparsed Headers section in Chapter 3.) You can then write each portion of the data to the client and flush the output. This process should allow you to send incremental data to the client. You cannot, however, use the same method with your SAF. The main NSAPI function that we use to write information to the client is **net_write**. This function usually writes the data to the client all at once. The server generally attempts to cache the response. Even if you use a number of different **net_write** functions in your program, all data are sent to the client in one batch. It is not your program, but rather the server, that decides when data should be sent to the client. By simply using multiple calls to **net_write**, you cannot control the timing of the data that are delivered to the client. You cannot return information in intervals.

Listing 10-3 uses a modified server push in conjunction with **net_write** to send incremental updates. As mentioned earlier, the use of the MIME type `multipart/x-mixed-replace` is intended for replacing an existing content with new data. In our example, we use the MIME type `multipart/mixed`. Unfortunately, Netscape browsers respond to these MIME types in the same way. In other words, Navigator does not interpret `multipart/mixed` as a MIME type for pages that are updated incrementally. Thus we must devise a way to make the browser display the data as they are piped down to the client.

As noted earlier, Navigator clears the existing page once the new `Content-type` header is sent. If we begin each block of data with a new `Content-type` header, Navigator clears the existing content. Sending the `boundary` string will not help. Without the new `Content-type` header, Navigator may display no additional data, so information can be received by the client but not displayed.

After some testing, we would notice that, whenever the content of the data sent to the client is followed by two line-feeds (a line break), the client displays the data. This line break is the same as the line break that is always sent after the response-headers. To update a page, we therefore send the `Content-type` of the page. As the `Content-type` of the page is always the same, we do not need to change it or send a new `Content-type` each time we return an update for the page. Most likely, it will be `text/html`. After the response-header, we return each block of data followed by two line-feeds, which causes the data to appear via Navigator. Each new set of line-feed characters forces the previous block of data to display. In general, the action of each **net_write** occurs after the following **net_write** is sent. We also do not return any `boundary` string until we are finished with the page.

For the new page, we return a new `boundary` string followed by the new `Content-type` and the body of the new page. We end the connection by sending the `boundary` string with two dashes, `--`, at the end of the string.

Note that while we use **pblock_nvinsert** to insert the `Content-type` `multipart/mixed`, we do not send the additional response-headers for each block of the data the same way. We write the response-headers and the body of the content more like a CGI program. In other words, we first send each header in a line followed by the two linefeed characters. Next, we write the content of each block. The difference is that we use **net_write** instead of a CGI function (for example, the C function **printf**).

> **Note ▶**
>
> With an SAF, another way of keeping the socket connection open is by setting the value of `Session>csd_open` to 0 and returning REQ_EXIT or REQ_PROCEED from the **Service** function. You are then also responsible for keeping and closing the socket. To close the socket, you can use the function **net_close.**

Registration Instructions   The following code gives the instructions for registering the SAF **wait** (Listing 10-3). You should have already compiled the program to a DLL or shared library. This program was originally written for NT, but it should work without any specific modification under UNIX. Add the following lines in the **obj.conf** file:

```
Init fn=load-modules funcs=wait
  shlib=c:/netscape/server/nsapi/examples/wait.dll

Service fn="wait" method="GET" type="magnus-internal/wait"
```

If you added this SAF to an existing DLL or shared library, then modify the **load-modules** line in the **obj.conf** file by adding the function's name, **wait**, to the funcs parameter list. You should also update the shlib parameter to reflect the correct location of the DLL (or the shared library file for UNIX).

To enable the server to recognize this **Service** SAF, you should also update the **mime.types** file. In **mime.types**, add the following line (or any other extension [exts] you may wish to use with the SAF):

```
type=magnus-internal/wait exts=wait
```

This **Service** function is called only when this extension is used as the extension of the file that the client is requesting.

Listing 10-3   Server Push—wait Example

```
/* include the following files if you are using a version of
   Netscape Server earlier than 3.x

   #include "base/pblock.h"
   #include "base/session.h"
   #include "frame/req.h"
```

Listing 10-3 Server Push—**wait** Example (*continued*)

```
    #include "base/util.h"
    #include "frame/protocol.h"
*/

/* include this file if you are using Server 3.x */
#include "nsapi.h"

/* error string if the browser is not supported */
#define WRONG_BROWSER "Browser is not compatible."

/* multipart content-type */
#define MULTIPART "multipart/mixed; boundary=Wait\n\n"

/* boundary strings */
#define FIRSTMSG "--Wait\n"
#define MIDDLEMSG "\n--Wait\n"
#define ENDMSG "\n--Wait--\n"

/* introductory content of the first page */
#define PAGE_INTRO "<HTML><HEAD>\n \
<TITLE>Please Wait</TITLE>\n \
</HEAD>\n<BODY>\n<H1>Starting Wait</H1>"

/* update string for the first page */
#define WAIT "<B>Please wait. System is processing.<B><P>"

/* content of the next page */
#define DONE\
"<HTML>\n<HEAD>\n<TITLE>Done</TITLE>\n</HEAD>\n \
<BODY>\n<H3>Thank You. Server is finished.</H3>\n \
</BODY></HTML>"

/* line-feed characters used to make Navigator display the
   content of the update string */
#define linebreak "\n\n"

/* This program writes out a first page and sends back
   continuous status information six times. After that, a
   new page is returned.
 */
NSAPI_PUBLIC wait(pblock *param, Session *sn,
                  Request *rq)
{
    char first_header[100]; /* holds the response-header
                               of the first page */
    char last_header[100]; /* holds the response-header
                              of the second page */
```

Listing 10-3   Server Push—wait Example (*continued*)

```
int first_len;          /* length of the response-header
                             for the first page */

int last_len;           /* length of the response-header
                             for the second page */

int x = 1;              /* used to count the number of
                             status strings (WAIT) sent */

char *ua;               /* user agent */

/* this function is intended to work only with Netscape
   Navigator 1.1 and higher.
 */
if(request_header("user-agent", &ua, sn, rq) ==
                   REQ_ABORTED)
    return REQ_ABORTED;

/* Check to make sure the client has the right browser.
   Navigator 1.0 is not supported, nor is any other
   browser that is not Netscape's. Microsoft's Internet
   Explorer returns Mozilla as part of the user-agent
   string, which we use to identify Navigator, so we
   also make sure the browser is not Microsoft Internet
   Explorer. We check for MSIE (Microsoft Internet
   Explorer String) to identify if the browser is
   Internet Explorer.
 */
if((strstr(ua, "Mozilla") == NULL) ||
   (strstr(ua, "Mozilla/1.0") != NULL) ||
   (strstr(ua, "MSIE") != NULL))
{
    /* return an error page and write an error status
       in the log file if the browser is not compatible
     */
    protocol_status(sn, rq, PROTOCOL_FORBIDDEN,
                    WRONG_BROWSER);
    log_error(LOG_FAILURE, "wait", sn, rq,
              WRONG_BROWSER);

    return REQ_ABORTED;
}

/* get rid of the internal content-type, which is
   typically the NSAPI magnus-internal content-type
 */
param_free(pblock_remove("content-type", rq->srvhdrs));
```

Listing 10-3   Server Push—**wait** Example (*continued*)

```
/* set status to OK */
protocol_status(sn, rq, PROTOCOL_OK, NULL);

/* set content-type for multipart/mixed */
pblock_nvinsert("content-type", MULTIPART, rq->srvhdrs);

/* send the response-headers */
protocol_start_response(sn, rq);

/* send the first boundary string */
if(net_write(sn->csd, FIRSTMSG, strlen(FIRSTMSG)) ==
                    IO_ERROR)
    return REQ_EXIT;

/* content-type of the first page */
first_len = util_sprintf(first_header,
                            "Content-type: text/html\n\n");

/* send the content-type */
if(net_write(sn->csd, first_header, first_len) == IO_ERROR)
    return REQ_EXIT;

/* send the first page's introductory text */
if(net_write(sn->csd, PAGE_INTRO, strlen(PAGE_INTRO)) ==
        IO_ERROR)
    return REQ_EXIT;

/* Send the wait string six times. After that, return a
    new page. */
while( x < 8)
{
    if( x == 7)
    {
        /* send the boundary string for the second page */
        if(net_write(sn->csd, MIDDLEMSG,
                    strlen(MIDDLEMSG)) == IO_ERROR)
            return REQ_EXIT;

        /* content-type of the second page */
        last_len = util_sprintf(last_header,
            "Content-type: text/html\n\n");

        /* send the content-type of the second page */
        if(net_write(sn->csd, last_header, last_len) ==
                    IO_ERROR)
            return REQ_EXIT;
```

Listing 10-3   Server Push—**wait** Example (*continued*)

```
            /* send the content of the second page */
            if(net_write(sn->csd, DONE, strlen(DONE)) ==
                        IO_ERROR)
                return REQ_EXIT;

        /* send the last boundary string for the client
           to disconnect
        */
            if(net_write(sn->csd, ENDMSG, strlen(ENDMSG)) ==
                        IO_ERROR)
                return REQ_EXIT;
    }
    else
    {
        /* send the wait (status) string */
        if(net_write(sn->csd, WAIT, strlen(WAIT)) ==
                    IO_ERROR)
            return REQ_EXIT;

        /* send the line-feed characters that make the
           browser display the wait string
        */
        if(net_write(sn->csd, linebreak,
                    strlen(linebreak)) == IO_ERROR)
            return REQ_EXIT;
    }

    /* wait for 3 seconds */
    Sleep(3 * 1000);

    x++;
    }

    return REQ_PROCEED;
}
```

Stepping Through the wait Program   In Listing 10-3, we first define the boundary string (Wait) and specify the contents of the pages that are sent to the client. We include the HTML tags—<HTML>, <HEAD>, <TITLE>, <BODY>, and so on—for each page that is sent to the client. The browser does not display any <TITLE> for a multipart/mixed content. You can send just the BODY of the HTML page if you like.

In the **wait** function, we first verify if the user's browser is Netscape Navigator 1.1 or higher. This function does not work with any other browsers. Microsoft Internet Explorer 3.x does support multipart documents and keep the connection alive, but it does not support a boundary string for separating blocks of text and sending a new page.

We remove the `magnus-internal` content-type of the NSAPI function and return the `multipart/mixed` content-type. We use the standard NSAPI functions for sending response-headers to the client—that is, **protocol_status**, **pblock_nvinsert**, and **protocol_start_response**. Next, we send the first `boundary` string followed by the `Content-type` of the first page and the introductory body of the page. From now on, we use **net_write** to write (send) the content to the client.

We use a `while` loop to send the status page to the client. For the first six times through the loop, the function writes the `WAIT` string followed by the line break (`\n\n`). The browser therefore displays each status string after it is sent. Alternatively, you can include the line breaks at the end of the `WAIT` string. The server waits three seconds before sending each `WAIT` string (status line) using the C function **Sleep**.

After the `WAIT` strings have been sent, we send the second page. We first send a new `boundary` string, followed by the `Content-type` of the second page and the body of the page. In Navigator, this new page replaces the previous data that were sent. To have the client disconnect, we also return the `ENDMSG` (`--WAIT--`).

Customized Server Tags and Template Files

The browser reads the HTML tags to process and display the content sent by the server. For example, it uses the `IMG` tag and its attributes to display an image. It did not take long for developers to realize that similar uses of tags (instructions) could be implemented by a program on the server side. A number of different companies now support optional tags for server files that their programs read and process on the server side. Such server tags can be interpreted and used by the server program alone. Therefore, the actual tag can be removed from the file before the result is sent to the client. For example, when a client requests a server file, the server application can read the file and its server tags to produce the response for the client. The file and its tags are processed by the server program before the response is sent to the client. These tags can include programming instructions or instructions for formatting the response. For instance, a tag may instruct the server to pass a query (sent to the server by the client) to a database and return the results in place of the tag. The server program then replaces the tag with the appropriate data from the database. These server tags can be placed inside an HTML document that includes additional information to be sent to the client. Thus, the server response can include the standard HTML document in addition to the result of the server's processing of the tag.

An example of the use of server tags is Server-side JavaScript. Server-side JavaScript is implemented as an NSAPI server application. The JavaScript program you may write is identified by the directory of the file that the client is requesting. Any file in the JavaScript directory is processed by the server JavaScript implementation. The Server-side JavaScript SAF (**livewireService**) reads the requested JavaScript/HTML file, looking for the special Server-side JavaScript tags you have included in the file. It interprets and processes these tags along with any additional information sent by the client. Unlike the JavaScript tags interpreted by the client, the server tags are kept hidden from the client. The result is sent with the rest of the HTML file to the client. When you write a Server-side JavaScript application, you do not need to worry about how the server (and the Server-side JavaScript SAF) is processing the tags. You simply use the tags as they were intended.

You may consider these special files, which a server program interprets, to be template files. They include the default data plus a number of tags that help generate dynamic information. For both content developers and server programmers, the use of template files and server tags allows greater control and flexibility. Using template files, the development of content can be separated from the development of server applications. Instead of the server program generating the entire content of the response, the program can use the already-developed content. Moreover, the content developer can take advantage of including tags in files to produce dynamic data. Individuals who develop the content of the site can develop a more interactive response, while the programmer can focus on developing the dynamic information.

Content providers can have a greater control over the site content, and its look and "feel," because they can produce responses that include dynamic information. They also control the content and format of the responses that are returned by server programs. Depending on the complexity of the tags that your program can support, many simple programming steps can be passed to the content developers as well. Thus, the business logic and the difficult aspects of the program can be separated from the implementation. For example, the core of the program, such as connecting to a database and passing a query, can be separated from the actual use of the query and the database response.

Template files allow a single program to produce dynamic data for different implementations. They give the developer greater flexibility and allow a program to work with any file that includes the appropriate tags. The programmer can program the application with only the specific tags in mind. An existing file does not need to be associated with the program. The programmer does not need to worry about the actual file that is sent to the client. It is the job of the content provider to use the tags in the documents. Moreover, the program does not need to be modified each time a change to the content of the Web document is made.

In general, whenever you have a complex site that requires a number of similar server programs with separate implementations, you should consider using a template file.

You can easily write a program that supports template files. Just as we read the Guest Book file in the Guest Book example (Listing 9-5), you can read the template file. Your program can look for the server tag and generate the requested result. With NSAPI, you have great control over the type of tags you can support. NSAPI is best suited for the use of template files. As with Server-side JavaScript, you can even develop complex tags that allow developers to produce their own programs using your server-specific tags. You can also specify a directory or a special file extension for all the template files, in order to restrict their use and their effect on the server.

A good use of server tags is to make calls to a database. You can use the server tags to encapsulate the database connectivity and calls. Your program can support tags that accept database queries and formatting specifications. Content developers can include such tags in the HTML files. For example, they can specify name of the database, produce a database query based on the expected client input from a POST data, and determine the format of the output of the response in an HTML table. Your program then uses the client POST data and the instructions in the HTML file to make a call to a database and return the result as specified. You should also protect your program against any misuse of these tags.

Using a Database with NSAPI

One of the best uses of NSAPI is to provide quick access to a database so as to make direct queries or updates. NSAPI code provides the best performance for a database call. It is easy to write an NSAPI application that uses a database, as many of the database programs that you may have already written can be directly ported to an NSAPI application. NSAPI does not limit how you make a database call or how the data are sent to the database. Of course, you need to know how to write a database program to write such a program using NSAPI. The only requirement is that the database should be accessible through the NSAPI code that you have written in C. You may use your database's proprietary API, ODBC (Microsoft's Open Database Connectivity), SQL, or any third-party tool. Another important limitation with which you should be concerned is that the application you write to update the database should be thread-safe.

Just as we wrote an application that read from and wrote to a file, you can write an application that reads and writes from a database. You can use any type of database, from a simple DBM file to an Oracle workgroup server. The type of database you intend to use and the type of API or library you will use to access the database are up to you. In general, if the data you access are critical and your server makes many database calls, you should use a robust database from a major database vendor (for example, Oracle, Sybase, Microsoft, IBM, or Informix). Also, you usually get the best performance if you use the database vendor's specified API to access the database, instead of a generic API (such as ODBC for Windows NT or a third-party API to access a database). Most vendors' specific APIs include optimization and feature enhanced capabilities that go beyond a generic standard API. On the other hand, your program will not be portable to other types of databases if it is written using proprietary functions.

You first open a connection to the database before sending your query, usually in the form of a SQL statement to the database. Your program can then use the result returned by the database. For example, a typical ODBC connection can use the following functions: **SQLAllocEnv**, **SQLAllocConnect**, **SQLConnect**, **SQLAllocStmt**, and **SQLExecDirect**. **SQLAllocEnv** allocates the SQL environment handle. **SQLAllocConnect** allocates the connection handle. **SQLConnect** makes the connection to the database. **SQLAllocStmt** allocates a statement handle used for sending SQL commands to the database server and for retrieving the response from the server. **SQLExecDirect** sends SQL strings to the ODBC driver, which in turn sends the strings to the DBMS (the database) or directly executes the SQL statement. You can retrieve the data using other ODBC functions. For instance, **SQLFetch** and **SQLGetData** can be used to retrieve a column of data. **SQLGetData** can get the data in a row, one column at a time. Alternatively, you may use **SQLNumResultCols** with **SQLDecribeCol** to get the data from an unknown number of columns before using **SQLFetch** and **SQLGetData**. Finally, you use **SQLFreeStmt**, **SQLDisconnect**, **SQLFreeConnect**, and **SQLFreeEnv** to free the environment handles and disconnect from the database.

To gain the best performance benefit from your SAF, you should open a connection to the database in an **Init** function. You can then use the handle to the already-open database in a later function, such as a **Service** SAF. This method removes the necessity of opening and closing a database each time. This simple procedure should improve the performance of your NSAPI application over a similar CGI program. A CGI program must establish a new connection to the database before sending each request to the database.

An important consideration when incorporating database connectivity into your NSAPI program is thread safety. You should make sure that calls to the database are thread-safe. You do not want to have two separate threads that are not safely synchronized update the database at the same time. Netscape provides a number of thread synchronization functions (for example, **crit_***) that you can use to make sure a query or update to a database is safe. In Chapter 11, we will review Netscape's thread and process model and discuss the thread and process data structures and functions included with NSAPI.

Warning ▶

When you write a NSAPI program to access a client/server database, make sure that Netscape Server has the proper access to the database. The server has to have permission to open the database and make queries or updates as needed. For instance, the user that the Netscape HTTP server is running as should have the permission to access the database.

Summary

In this chapter, we went through some advanced concepts of programming for Netscape Server. The features discussed here can greatly enhance your Web site. They relate to some of the most commonly asked Web programming questions.

The first topic we covered was how to maintain state in a stateless HTTP environment. We reviewed various ways you can maintain state, from URL encoding and server-side persistent data to cookies. Cookies are the most common means of maintaining state. They are easy to implement and leave the work of their maintenance to the client. Cookies are simple tokens or text strings that the server (your program) can save on the client machine. You can save different types of information on the client side using cookies. The client returns the cookie as part of its response-header, so you can obtain and use it. When you plan to save a greater amount of data associated with a client, you may want to combine cookies with a server-side database. To illustrate how cookies work, we discussed the different features and standards of cookies and wrote a simple example.

Next, we looked at push technology. We briefly discussed the advances in push technology in recent years. We focused closely on two specific features (client pull and server push) that the Netscape client and server provide to allow a "persistent" connection between client and the server. Client pull allows you to tell the client to refresh a page every few seconds. It is done by adding a special META tag to the HTML page. Server push allows you to keep a connection with the client alive while you update the data sent to the client. For server push, you must write a program, so we wrote a simple program to demonstrate this feature.

We ended this chapter with a brief discussion of the use of templates and databases. Templates allow you to separate content production from programming. You designate special tags for the content that your program can interpret and replace with the appropriate dynamic information. This option gives more flexibility and control to the content producer, while relieving the programmer from having to develop the different response pages. Databases are a standard part of Web site development, and NSAPI provides the fastest and most effective way of using a database. In most cases, you can easily incorporate your existing database program into an NSAPI program.

In Chapter 11, we will discuss threads and processes. Make sure you read this chapter, because it includes important information needed to write thread-safe NSAPI programs.

Chapter 11

Threads and Processes

Threads are a wellspring for many discussions in the programming world. Many questions arise about how threads work on the server and how you can write a thread-safe program. You need only pick up various magazines, like *Dr. Dobbs* or *Windows Developer's Journal,* to see a number of new articles on the subject of threads. Especially since the advent of NT and Win32, programmers have been moving to the new world of that multithreading operating system from the world of DOS and Windows, where threads were a nonissue.

In this chapter, we will discuss the use of threads and processes under Netscape Server. Different versions of Netscape Server may use different models of threads and processes. When you write your SAF, you need to understand the model of threads and processes supported by your Netscape Server. You also *must* make sure that your program is threadsafe. If your program updates a global variable or an external data, such as a field in a database, you need to use threadsafe functions. You can also use NSAPI thread-locking functions to lock a thread while the data are being updated. Otherwise, one thread can overwrite or corrupt the information that another thread is writing. We will review how threads and processes are used by the server and the specific NSAPI functions and data structures you can use to write a threadsafe SAF.

We will first discuss threads and processes in general. Our emphasis will be on how they are applicable to Netscape. This chapter is by no means a complete study of these subjects. You should look in your operating system's documentation for specifics of thread support for your system. Most systems provide specific documentation on how threads are actually implemented on those operating systems. There are also books dedicated to this topic, such as *Multithreaded Programming with Windows NT* by Thuan Q. Pham and Pankaj K. Garg and *Programming with UNIX Threads* by Charles J. Northrup. (See also the newsgroup comp.programming.threads for a more detailed discussion of threads.)

The focus of this chapter is on Netscape Server 2.x and 3.x. Most of the thread- and process-specific functions and data structures discussed in this chapter are not supported under Server 1.x. Moreover, the UNIX version of Netscape Server 1.x did not support processes with multiple threads. Instead, the server used multiple processes, each with a single thread. Under Server 2.x, the UNIX platforms support multiple processes, with each process supporting multiple threads. The Windows NT and 95 versions of Netscape Server support one process with multiple threads. Netscape Server 3.x no longer uses multiple processes, so all the information in this chapter that refers to managing multiple processes is not needed for Server 3.x.

How threads work is also affected by your server setting, especially the **magnus.conf** directives. For example, you can set the UNIX Server 2.x to support one process and one thread through the specific **magnus.conf** directives. We will also discuss the server settings that directly affect the use of threads and processes by the server.

Finally, we review the data structures and functions that you can use to write a thread-safe program. Netscape provides five data structures that are directly related to writing a thread (and process)-safe program. Each data structure is supported by a number of functions. As you will see shortly, Netscape attempts to provide a uniform set of data structures and functions for your use in an NSAPI function. Although the internal implementation of these data structures and functions may vary on different platforms and for different versions of the server, the Netscape data structures and functions provide a consistent method of writing thread (and process)-safe applications. So as long as you use NSAPI-specific thread functions and the platform on which you intend to use the program supports the thread model, your program should be portable to the other platforms. We will first review the thread and process data structures. Next, we will go through the various functions. We will also provide information on how you can write a thread-safe application using Netscape's NSAPI thread and process functions.

> **Note ▶**
>
> Enterprise Server 3.x no longer supports multiple processes. Multiple processes with multiple threads are supported under only the UNIX version of Server 2.x.

More on Threads and Processes

The key issue with threads and processes is how you can take advantage of running multiple simultaneous series of actions while making sure that they do not write over one another's memory space, corrupt the data, and so on. Because Server 3.x is a multi-threaded application but does not use multiple processes, the focus of this chapter is on threads.

Multithreading means better performance and simultaneous execution of multiple requests. The data and functions in your code can be processed by more than one thread at a given time. This situation could lead to two or more threads simultaneously accessing the same data or part of code and cause data corruption or undesirable changes to data. For example, one thread could be accessing data that are currently being changed by another thread, leading to an inaccurate result. You need to protect the threads from one another by supporting synchronization and locking or by using thread-safe functions to make sure that one thread cannot interfere with another or write in another's memory space.

Netscape Server 3.x takes advantage of multiple threads, which allows the server to provide increased performance and support for simultaneous client access. With a CGI program, you generally do not need to worry about threads, as each CGI program is run separately in its own process and does not share resources. With WAI, on the other hand, you do have to worry about threads. The WAI application must be thread-safe. Since an out-of-process WAI application runs in its own process, however, its thread is less likely to conflict with server threads and cause a server crash. We will discuss WAI in detail in Chapters 13–16.

NSAPI programs run in the server processes. They directly plug into your server and share context, memory, and other resources with the server. Thus you have to be sure your code uses threads properly; you must make sure your program is thread-safe. Even when you set the server to use a single process with a single thread, the thread for your program can still interfere with other server threads.

As mentioned earlier, different releases of Netscape Server may use different models of threads and processes. Operating systems may handle native processes and threads differently, which affects how they work under Netscape. The Netscape thread model may differ depending on the platform and version of the server. Consequently, you should verify which thread options are available with your server. For example, Netscape Server uses user-level threads for all UNIX versions of Server 2.0. With Server 2.01, Netscape began supporting native threads. The Solaris and IRIX versions of Netscape UNIX Server 2.01 support native threads. The NT version of the server has always supported native threads. Many 3.x servers (such as, NT, Solaris, and IRIX) support a combination of user-level and kernel-level threads.

Before Server 2.0, there was little in the way of NSAPI programming functions and data structures for writing thread-safe programs that could work across various platforms. Only interprocess locks (SEMAPHORE) were supported for Netscape Server 1.x. With Server 2.0 and later, Netscape has provided a number of data structures and functions that you can use to handle threads and provide thread and process safety. When programming for the UNIX version of Netscape Server 2.x, you need to be concerned about not only multiple threads, but also multiple processes. With Server 3.x, you need to be concerned only with thread safety. You can use the data structures and functions provided by the server to write a platform-independent, thread-safe application. You can also create and manage your own threads using NSAPI functions. Moreover, NSAPI provides several thread-safe versions of standard C functions that you can use. We will discuss the NSAPI thread- and process-specific functions shortly.

Processes

A process is an instance of the executable program. All major operating systems support processes as a way of running multiple programs or instances of a program. A process has its own virtual address space and resources. In general, UNIX platforms support multiple processes, but not all versions of UNIX support multiple threads. Recently, however, most UNIX vendors have provided some level of support for threads in their operating systems.

UNIX versions of Netscape Server that predate version 3.x supported multiple processes. Netscape 1.x UNIX servers supported multiple processes with single threads. Netscape 2.x UNIX servers also support multiple processes, but each process can spawn multiple threads. (Under UNIX Server 2.x, you can specify the number of processes and threads the server will create in the **magnus.conf** file.) Netscape Server 3.x uses one process with multiple threads.

For Server 2.x, each process then runs one or more threads, depending on the server and its setting. As a rule, you should run one process for each processor (CPU) on your machine. By running multiple processes, the server can support parallel execution of the program. Each process is a mini-server that has a private virtual address space and resource. At the start of the server, the process gets loaded into memory and waits for execution. A process includes the code, virtual global data, and other system resources, such as files and pipes. Netscape also allows for shared resources between processes. It uses shared memory (shmem_s) to support multiprocess sharing. This shared information is accessible from a thread. To share data across multiple server processes in your program, you must write the mechanism for sharing the resource across the processes via shared memory. You also have to protect the shared memory against other threads and processes. A thread, in turn, responds to a client request. The thread executes the part of the program that responds to the request. It can also fork another thread.

Threads

Each process can run one or more threads. Under Enterprise Server 3.x, the server first determines the number of processors (CPUs) that your system is running. It then creates the appropriate number of threads to take advantage of all processors.

A thread is like a lightweight "process." Each thread is allocated CPU time from the system. The threads maintain a set of structures for saving the context. The context can include machine registers, the kernel stack, environment variables, the user stack, and so on. All threads share the virtual address space of the process and can access the global variables and system resources of the process. They also share open files. On the other hand, the threads have their own separate stack and control registers. Except for the stack and registers, all data are shared between threads. Because threads share the same address space and resources, it is easier to switch between threads than between processes. Threads are mapped into the address space of the process at the outset, whereas process code has to be loaded. Therefore, threads provide better performance.

POSIX-style thread is the common type of thread on UNIX systems. Microsoft Win32 has its own thread system.

There are two common types of thread implementation (model): kernel-level (native) or user-level (user-space or user-mode).

Kernel-Level Threads

A kernel-level thread is scheduled by the native operating system. The order in which the thread is awakened or processed is dependent on the operating system. The thread competes with other kernel-level threads, including the core system threads, for scheduling. Because of this scheduling, kernel-level threads can be expensive.

The system processes each kernel-level thread based on its priority and its process's priority. In a preemptive multitasking operating system, a thread can be suspended when its time slice elapses. The server can then restore and save the context of the suspended thread. Scheduling is the process in which the operating system decides which thread should be executed in what order.

On a multiprocessor (multiple-CPU) system, processes and threads can run simultaneously when they have been written in such a way that they can support it, such as on Netscape Server. Processes are distributed among the available processors. Because the operating system schedules the kernel-level threads, it can also specify the threads to take advantage of multiprocessors (CPUs) on the system. It can distribute the threads across multiple processes. Context switching, switching CPUs, or switching control between multiple processes and threads, especially on a single-processor machine, can actually slow down a system. For Server 2.x, you should not run more than one server process if your system has only one CPU. Context switching between threads in a process is more economical than between two processes. Context switching between user-level threads is also more efficient than kernel-level threads.

Not all UNIX servers support kernel threads. For example, the AIX version of Enterprise and FastTrack Server 2.0 was compiled on AIX 3.x, which does not support threads. (Version 4.x of AIX now supports threads.) AIX 4.x, IRIX 6.2, HPUX 10.20, Solaris 2.6, and Windows NT are some examples of operating systems that support kernel-level threads.

User-Level Threads

User-level threads maintain their state in the user space. A user-level thread is usually implemented by a program (the process); the operating system is not involved. Netscape Server 2.0 provides user-level threads across all UNIX servers. It is usually the user (the program) that schedules the thread. Because the mechanism and scheduling logic of a user-level thread are implemented by the software vendor, a user-level thread can exist for any operating system. It is not easy to debug a user-level thread using the standard debugger or the compiler that comes with the operating system. The implementation of the thread is not exposed (known) to the debugger. Most debuggers are developed to take advantage of kernel-level or native threads. Also, when the thread is not scheduled by the operating system, it cannot take advantage of the multiple processors on the system.

Some operating systems, however, support user-level threads and can schedule a user-level thread along with kernel-level threads (for example, Solaris). If the operating system does not manage the user-level threads, you need to use the API provided by the software vendor to take advantage of a user-level thread. In other words, for Netscape Server 2.0, you should use only Netscape's thread API. On the other hand, for the Solaris version of Enterprise Server 3.x, you can use Solaris's native thread in conjunction with Netscape's NSAPI thread model. Enterprise 3.x uses Solaris's native thread and supports both kernel- and user-level thread models. As a rule, when a user-level thread is involved, you should not combine it with third-party programs or libraries that use a separate threading mechanism. This setup could lead to a lock up or a server crash.

User threads are more efficient because they do not have to compete with kernel threads for scheduling. In fact, you can gain as much as ten times faster performance from a user-level thread during context switching. Netscape states that the server performs 25% to 50% faster using user-level threads.

Combination of User-Level and Kernel-Level Threads

As mentioned earlier, some operating systems can support and schedule both user-level and kernel-level threads. In such cases, when a process creates a thread, the operating system decides whether it is best to create a kernel-level or a user-level thread. The operating system decides which of the two types of thread models provides the best result and performance.

As a rule, it is always best for context switching to happen in the current context. In other words, it is best not to switch between kernel-level and user-level threads. Some thread functions are best suited for kernel-level threads and others for user-level threads. For example, I/O-bound threads are best handled by kernel-level models. On the other hand, process signal models, such as threads called by the **sigwait** or **sigsuspend** functions, can be handled in user-level models (as is done by Solaris).

Netscape Server 3.x attempts to use a combination of kernel-level and user-level threads whenever possible. If the operating system supports scheduling of both user- and kernel-level threads, Netscape usually allows the operating system to do the scheduling.

Netscape Thread Models

All NT versions of Netscape Servers use kernel-level threads. The UNIX version of Netscape 1.x Server does not use multiple threads for a process. All UNIX versions of Netscape Server 2.0 use user-level threads only.

The Solaris and IRIX versions of Netscape Server 2.01 use kernel-level threads. Thus you can safely use the native thread library of these operating systems. This model can, however, lead to incompatibility between the 2.0 and 2.01 versions of Netscape Server under Solaris and IRIX. If a 2.0 version of a program you have written was not native thread-safe, it probably will not work under version 2.01. Under Server 2.01, all programs should be native thread-safe.

Under NT, when a thread is created by an **Init** function, it persists for the server process. For the 2.x version of IRIX, the thread will exist only in the base process. It will not be distributed to the child processes. For all other version 2.x UNIX servers, the thread created in the **Init** function will exist both in the base process and in all of the child (worker) processes.

Netscape Server 3.x attempts to use a combination of user-level and kernel-level threads. If the operating system supports both types of threads, Netscape Server will support the operating system's implementation of the thread. In other words, Netscape allows the operating system to schedule the threads, as is the case with Solaris and NT. When the operating system supports kernel-level threads but does not support scheduling of user-level threads, Netscape Server will attempt to combine the use of the server kernel-level threads with Netscape's user-level threads. Netscape uses kernel-level threads to take advantage of multiple processors and programming flexibility. For performance reasons, however, it also supports user-level threads. Typically, the server runs enough kernel-level threads to support all processes. It then uses user-level threads that run inside the kernel-level threads. Each client request is processed by a user-level thread. If the server does not provide kernel-level thread, Netscape uses user-level threads. For example, Netscape Server for HPUX supports only user-level threads. HPUX 10.10 and 10.20 do not support native threading.

With Server 3.x, you also have the option of running the server threads as kernel-level only, if the operating system supports kernel-level threads. You can specify that the server not use user-level threads via the **magnus.conf** directive **KernelThreads**. In the **magnus.conf** file, you should use the value on for the **KernelThreads** directive, as in KernelThreads on. You can also specify that your NSAPI application use a kernel- or user-level thread by using the parameter NativeThread when you load your NSAPI application via the **Init** function **load-modules**. By default, your application uses kernel-level threads when possible. If you use the parameter NativeThreads and set its value to no, the server uses user-level threads for your application.

Note ▶

Although IRIX version 6.2 of the operating system provides a pthreads package, which supports both user-level and kernel-level thread scheduling, Netscape Server 3.x does not use pthreads for thread implementation. Instead, Netscape uses its own combination of user-level and kernel-level mechanisms.

Process and Thread-Related Server Settings

For debugging purposes, you may want to set the value of process and threads to 1. Later on, you can change these values to provide the best performance for your program. This approach makes it easier to debug your code. It also prevents multiple requests from entering your NSAPI application at the same time. Setting the thread and process numbers to 1, however, does not guarantee that your code will be thread-safe. Beside its performance drawbacks, a server with one process and one thread can still end up with thread conflicts. **magnus.conf** directives such as **MaxThreads**, **MinThreads**, **RqThrottle**, and **RqThrottleMinPerSocket** apply only to the request-handling threads. Other threads created by the server for maintenance purposes may still conflict with your NSAPI threads. Thus you should always make sure your code is thread-safe.

For Server 2.x, if you set up your server to support one process with multiple threads, the threads can share context without sharing memory. This flexibility makes the programming of your code easier, as you need to worry only about the shared context in relationship to the threads. You can then increase the number of threads to provide multithreading without the added complexity of multiple processes. The system can usually create a thread more quickly than a process because the code for a thread has already been mapped into the address space of the process. This default scenario applies to the NT version of all the servers and all Enterprise 3.x servers. Multithreaded programs can take the best advantage of running concurrent (and identical) tasks and connections, such as reading from and writing to a file request by multiple clients.

For Netscape UNIX Server 2.x to gain the optimal results for a site that is heavily used (that is, carries high traffic), you may want to balance the number of processes and threads. You may choose to run more than one process, each with its own set of threads. As the number of threads for each process will be smaller than if all threads were running from the same process, the virtual address space for each process will be less and therefore increase the performance of threads. A good rule of thumb is to have a separate process for each additional processor (CPU) on your machine. The added overhead of context switching and various locking of threads has, of course, the drawback of reducing performance. Consequently, you should balance the needs of your server, the number of requests you expect, and the benefit of creating the most fitting number of thread or process. In all cases, increasing the memory (and processors) on a busy server leads to better performance.

There are a number of articles written on how to optimize your server. You should test your server to find out the optimal setting. There are a number of server benchmark programs, such as, WebBench 1.1 from ZiffDavis (`http://www.zdnet.com/zdbop/webbench/webbench.html`), Webstone 2.0.1 (`http://www.sgi.com/Products/WebFORCE/WebStone/`), and SPECweb97 (`http://www.specbench.org/osg/web97/`).

Netscape provides a number of specific server settings that you can use to control the operation of the server's process and threads. With these parameters, you can also prepare your server for optimal performance. Before you begin programming your NSAPI function, you should check and determine these settings for your server. Most of these settings are declared in the **magnus.conf** file, as **magnus.conf** determines the server's global settings. Netscape also added new options for Enterprise Server 3.x, which we will also discuss later in this chapter.

magnus.conf Directives

There are a number of **magnus.conf** directives that affect the server's thread and process settings. Some of these directives may apply only to a specific version of the server. This section lists important **magnus.conf** directives that affect the use of threads and processes on your server. For more information on these directives or other **magnus.conf** directives, see Appendix A.

MaxProcs

MaxProcs is a specific directive for the 1.x and 2.x versions of UNIX Servers. It allows you to limit the number of processes that the server uses to handle client requests. **MaxProcs** specifies the maximum number of active processes for the server. You should use a number no greater than the number of CPUs on your machine. The number should also be below the size of your operating system's process table. Because Netscape Server 3.x no longer uses multiple processes, this directive is not needed for Server 3.x. If this directive is used, you should set its value to one (1).

MaxThreads and MinThreads

MaxThreads and **MinThreads** can be used to limit the number of threads used by UNIX Server 2.x for processing client requests. **MaxThreads** specifies the maximum number of concurrent threads used by the server to handle client requests. **MinThreads** specifies the minimum number of concurrent threads spawned by the server. For Server 2.x for NT, the server determines the appropriate number of threads. You do not specify the maximum or minimum number of threads in the **magnus.conf** file. The number of threads you specify using these directives is not the same as the actual

---

Warning ▶

Netscape Servers use data structures to hold statistics about child threads that are created to handle client requests. These data structures are called *statistics slots*. If you have gotten the error message `unable to find empty statistic slot`, you may need to increase the maximum number of threads. The error could occur when threads have terminated without freeing the slot or the server has run out of empty slots.

---

number of maximum or minimum threads that the server spawns. By default, the NT server spawns as many as 40 threads.

For Server 3.x, Netscape uses **RqThrottle** and **RqThrottleMinPerSocket**. These **magnus.conf** directives are similar to **MaxThreads** and **MinThreads**. (See the section on **RqThrottle** and **RqThrottleMinPerSocket** below for more information.)

magnus.conf Directives for Server 3.x

The following directives are specific to Server 3.x. For Server 3.x, you should use these directives instead of the directives described earlier.

RqThrottle and RqThrottleMinPerSocket

RqThrottle determines the maximum number of simultaneous HTTP connections for your server. It specifies the number of active requests allowed at one time. If the maximum number is reached by the server, the server waits until one of the requests is finished before allowing another connection. The value of **RqThrottle** determines the maximum number of simultaneous requests across the multiple virtual servers. The default number of maximum simultaneous requests has been increased from 128 for Server 3.0 to 512 for Server 3.01 and 3.5.x.

RqThrottleMinPerSocket specifies a suggested minimum number of threads that wait for the HTTP connection to the server socket. This actual number of waiting threads used by the server may be slightly higher or lower than the number you specify.

KernelThreads

To allow even greater control over the type of threads the server makes, Netscape provides the **magnus.conf** directive KernelThreads. As mentioned earlier, a number of Netscape Server 3.x versions (for example, Solaris, NT, and IRIX) support both kernel-level and user-level threads. This combination provides the optimal performance and flexibility. For debugging purposes, however, you may want to limit the server to only kernel-level threads. By adding the directive KernelThreads on to the **magnus.conf** file, you tell the server to use only kernel-level threads.

StackSize

The default stack size for a process has been changed to 64KB under Enterprise 3.x Server. Stack size for Server 2.x was 256KB. The process and each thread use some of the space on the stack, so it is possible for the server to run out of stack space. For example, if you use a recursive SSI include command, you will get a stack overflow. A stack overflow can lead to a general protection fault (GPF) or a segmentation fault, both of which should be avoided at all costs. If you notice any problem with the stack size, you should increase this number. Add the directive **StackSize** with a new stack size to the **magnus.conf** file. A smaller stack size uses less memory, which is good, but not if it is too small. Increase this number incrementally until the stack size is large enough. **StackSize** affects all server threads, not just your program.

> **Warning ▶**
>
> Sun recommends a default stack size of 2 Meg for threads on Solaris. Netscape Server also has a predefined stack size. When you write your NSAPI application, make sure the stack size does not exceed this size. For example, instead of using an array on the stack that is larger than the expected stack size, you should allocate memory using `MALLOC` or `PERM_MALLOC`.

NativeThreads Parameter of load-modules

In Enterprise 3.x, an additional parameter has been added to the **Init** function **load-modules** called **NativeThreads**. You can use this parameter with the value no to have the server run user-level threads instead of kernel-level threads. This setup can improve the performance of your code. Before making this change, make sure your code does not rely on any native threading functions. In other words, you should not be using native functions for thread locking, local storage, or socket I/O in your code. The default setting for your NSAPI application is to use kernel-level threads. In other words, if you do not use the parameter **NativeThreads** and set its value to no, the server uses kernel-level threads for your program.

NSAPI Data Structures and Functions

It is paramount that the SAF you write be thread-safe. NSAPI programs that are not thread-safe run the risk of system crash and data corruption. They can lead to undesirable or unpredictable results. Netscape provides two options for writing a thread-safe application. First, you can use NSAPI functions that are process- and/or thread-safe, such as **system_fwrite_atomic**, **system_gmtime**, and **system_localtime**. We discussed a number of these functions in Chapter 5. Second, you can use specific data structures and functions that Netscape has provided to create and manage threads or to protect the processes and threads. You can use these functions to lock a section of code from other threads or processes. Whenever possible, you should use these two options to make sure your code is thread-safe.

By using NSAPI functions, you also provide support for all the Netscape platforms. Your program can be easily ported to other platforms of Netscape Server. This idea, however, does not mean that different versions of the server are fully compatible. There are significant differences between version 1.x, 2.x, and 3.x of Netscape Server. There are also important differences between 2.0 and 2.01 versions or 3.0x and 3.5.1 versions of Netscape Server. Netscape has taken many steps to make these versions compatible, but a number of differences remain. We have already discussed the main differences between the different versions of the server. You should be familiar with these differences when you port your program to a different version of the server.

Moreover, Netscape's thread and process functions do not work the same way under each platform. Netscape has provided general functions that you can use, but each function may work differently for each platform. For example, using **sem_*** functions under NT will work similar to **crit_*** functions; under UNIX Server 2.x, they provide protection for shared resources between processes.

Using Other Libraries with Your NSAPI Application

Although Netscape provides a number of options to protect and deliver a thread-safe application, it cannot provide a function for all of your potential uses. You may need to resort to other C libraries, and even to a third-party library or API, to write your program. Whenever you attempt to combine other library functions with your code, make sure they are compatible and thread-safe. Make sure you understand how your server works and what type of processing and threading model it supports. You may use the information in an earlier section, Netscape's Threads Model, to assess your server's thread support. You should also understand how your operating system handles threads and processes and what type of functions and threads model it supports. If possible, use standard multithreaded versions of libraries that are supported across different platforms, POSIX, for example, is a standard interface for UNIX platforms. If you are using a third-party library, then you need to understand how this library is implemented. You need to know if the functions are multithreaded and thread-safe. Avoid using any third-party, user-level thread libraries with Netscape Server. Also, avoid mixing kernel-level libraries with Netscape Server's libraries that use user-level threads.

The best solution for integrating other libraries with NSAPI is to replace specific C functions with the equivalent NSAPI function. Sometimes, however, you may not have access to the original functions or the function you may need does not have an NSAPI equivalent. In such cases, you need to evaluate whether the function or code that you are using can lead to a thread conflict. Functions that support other threads and processing models; accept thread or process locking; use semaphores or mutex; support local storage calls, socket calls, or pipe I/O calls; or enable database updates should be reentrant or thread-safe. Also, global resources or data shared between processes or threads should be thread-safe. You should protect the code (algorithm) or data, which can be used by more than one thread, by placing it in a safe block of code. For example, you can execute the function in a block of code that is locked by using Netscape thread synchronization functions that begin with **condvar_*** and **crit_***. Also, use these thread synchronization functions to protect global data and socket and file I/Os. Lock global data structures, variables, files, and other resources while they are being updated. This solution, however, may not help a function that uses a different type of thread model than Netscape Server. In general, a third-party thread model or a model not compatible with Netscape should not be used in conjunction with your program. Running two different thread models with the same process will more than likely not work.

Most operating systems include a set of multithreaded functions (libraries) that are thread-safe or reentrant. These functions are usually variations of the standard C library, libc. Microsoft, for example, provides `libcmt.lib` as a reentrant library for creating multithread programs. (The `libc.lib` library for Windows provides single-thread static support.) Compile your code using this library, if you want to write a thread-safe multithreaded program. Under UNIX, POSIX functions that are thread-safe usually end with `_r`. Check the POSIX version supported by your operating system for the list of reentrant functions.

Reentrant code can be shared by different processes and threaded at the same time. The program can safely use a reentrant function without failing. Multiple processes or threads can execute the same reentrant code. In fact, other programs and processes can interrupt and restart execution of reentrant code. Because variables inside a reentrant procedure are not altered (shared) by different threads that reenter the procedure, they are thread-safe. The function will not use a static global variable, so a reentrant function is thread-safe. Not all thread-safe functions are reentrant, however. A function or code can become thread-safe if you produce a thread synchronization scheme, which protects the code. In other words, you can use NSAPI thread-locking functions (**crit_*** and **condvar_***) to protect threads from entering a nonentrant code section.

For Netscape Servers that do not support kernel-level threads, you should use NSAPI functions instead of system function calls or the native thread library. Netscape's user-level threading implementation does not support concurrent system calls. Netscape Servers do not perform threading preemptively. When a system call blocks, it blocks all threads in that process. Instead of system calls, it is best to use NSAPI functions that do not block the entire process. If you want to use the system's libraries (`libc`), you can use standard C functions as long as they are reentrant. Avoid using an operating system's kernel-level thread libraries with Netscape Server's libraries that use user-level threads.

In most cases, Netscape Servers that support kernel-level threads can be safely combined with your operating system's native multithreaded library functions. They can safely work with native socket I/O, system calls, or native local storage functions. You may still need to use a reentrant version of a function such as **localtime_r** and **gmtime_r** or an NSAPI version of the functions **system_localtime**, or **system_gmtime**. Always check to see if the function is reentrant. For Solaris and IRIX platforms, make sure you compile your program using `-D_REENTRANT` and `D_SGI_MP_SOURCE`, respectively.

For Enterprise Server 3.x, if the program you are writing uses functions that are threadsafe and do not conflict with Netscape's threads model, you can tell the server to use user-level threads for your module. By adding `NativeThreads=no` to the **Init** function **load-modules**, which specifies your shared library or DLL, you tell the server to not use kernel-level threads. This setup can provide even better performance for your NSAPI program. (See the earlier section, NativeThreads Parameter of load-modules, for more details.)

Process and Thread Data Structures

The following sections give a brief description of the process- and thread-related NSAPI data structures—that is, `SEMAPHORE`, `COUNTING_SEMAPHORE`, `SYS_THREAD`, `CRITICAL`, and `CONDVAR`.

SEMAPHORE *and* COUNTING_SEMAPHORE

Netscape's SEMAPHORE provides platform-independent, interprocess locking support. These interprocess locks are not the same as the traditional semaphores used by programmers. Netscape's SEMAPHORE and its supporting functions, with names beginning with **sem_**, provide simple interprocess locking mechanisms that use files. SEMAPHORE uses a file created in the temporary directory (/tmp) for locking. These **sem_*** functions process binary semaphores.

Netscape Server 2.01 added COUNTING_SEMAPHORE and **cs_*** functions for counting semaphores. A counting semaphore can be incremented and decreased. It more closely resembles the semaphores with which you might be familiar.

Both SEMAPHORE and COUNTING_SEMAPHORE are used to provide mutual exclusion across processes. Use them to exclude and allow access to shared memory available across server processes. Netscape semaphores do not protect a shared resource from different threads in the same process. Instead, they are intended for protection of the shared resources from different processes.

Unlike the thread-related data structures and functions, SEMAPHORE is also supported by Netscape Server 1.x. You do not need to use Netscape semaphores for the NT version of Netscape Server, as these servers do not support multiple processes. You also no longer need to use SEMAPHORE and COUNTING_SEMAPHORE with Server 3.x, as it does not use multiple processes.

For WIN32, the definition for a SEMAPHORE found in the base/sem.h file of Server 2.x is as follows:

```
typedef HANDLE SEMAPHORE;
```

For IRIX, the definition is

```
typedef struct {
    usptr_t *arena;
    usema_t *sem;
} semirix_s;
typedef semirix_s* SEMAPHORE;
```

For the rest of the platforms, the definition is

```
typedef int SEMAPHORE;
```

COUNTING_SEMAPHORE is defined as follows:

```
typedef void *COUNTING_SEMAPHORE;
```

SYS_THREAD

The SYS_THREAD data structure is a platform-independent system thread variable. There is also a set of supporting functions that begin with **systhread_**. For example, you can use these functions to start a thread, yield the processor to another thread, or terminate a thread. SYS_THREAD (and its supporting functions) is different from

CRITICAL and CONDVAR. **sys_thread_*** functions provide support for managing threads, but not a means for thread locking and synchronization. SYS_THREAD is defined as follows:

```
typedef void* SYS_THREAD;
```

CRITICAL

The CRITICAL data structure is a platform-independent critical-section variable. You use this data structure to lock (protect) part of your code (that is, a set of data and functions). A critical section is executed by one thread at a time and protects the data from being overwritten or affected by another thread. The CRITICAL data structure and its supporting functions, which begin with **crit_***, are new features of Netscape Server 2.x and later. You can use them to isolate a thread. Unlike SYS_THREAD functions, however, they do not support features for starting, stopping, and managing threads. Also, unlike SEMAPHORE and COUNTING_SEMAPHORE functions, they apply to threads and not to processes. CRITICAL is defined as follows:

```
typedef void* CRITICAL;
```

CONDVAR

CONDVAR provides platform-independent support for conditional variables. It offers conditional control over a thread and is used for thread synchronization. The CONDVAR data structure and its supporting functions, which begin with **condvar_***, are new features of Netscape Server 2.x and later. You can use this data structure in combination with the critical-section data structure, CRITICAL, and its functions to have a thread wait for another thread to notify it about a condition that has been met before processing. Unlike the SEMAPHORE and COUNTING_SEMAPHORE functions, CONDVAR applies only to threads and not to processes. CONDVAR is defined as follows:

```
typedef void* CONDVAR;
```

Process and Thread Functions

Once you have set up your server with the optimal settings, you can use the group of NSAPI functions, each associated with a specific data structure to program your code. To protect shared memory across processes, as in UNIX Server 2.x, you should use semaphore functions (**sem_***, **cs_***). Semaphore functions are intended for control of processes. You can initialize a semaphore, gain exclusive access to a semaphore, release a semaphore, and so on.

With threads, there are three sets of functions: **systhread_***, **crit_*** and **condvar_***. All of these functions work in the current process. You start, initialize, terminate, and perform other operations on a thread using the **systhread_*** functions. These functions actually create and manage a new thread. Use these functions for general thread management aside from thread locking. **crit_*** functions are used to lock or protect a thread. These locks are set for a specific thread. **crit_*** functions provide mutual exclusion without any conditional support. You can use them to lock the current thread that is processing a request or a thread that was created by a **systhread_*** function. **condvar_*** functions, on the other hand, provide conditional synchronization of threads. When just locking a thread is not enough, you can use **condvar_*** functions to have a thread wait to be notified about a condition by another thread.

SEMAPHORE *and* COUNTING_SEMAPHORE *Functions*

Netscape's semaphores, SEMAPHORE and COUNTING_SEMAPHORE, provide a more global locking mechanism. They allow for serverwide mutual exclusion (locks) between processes, but do not protect (lock) the resource from different threads in the same process. Netscape semaphores are used to control shared resources between processes. They are intended for a multiprocess server. Each process is like a mini-server program that has a private virtual address space. It usually includes various global data and other system resources, such as files and pipes. These resources are then accessed by each thread that the process spawns. The threads are run in the context of the process.

Netscape allows processes to share memory between processes. You can use the shared-memory data structure (shmem_s) and shared-memory functions (**shmem_*** functions, such as **shmem_alloc**) to create a shared memory space. As a rule, you create your shared object, shared memory, and so on in an **Init** function. You can then use Netscape semaphores to synchronize (protect) the shared memory. Without shared memory, the values set by the **Init** function are passed to all child processes. When a child process changes one of these global variables, it changes only the variable of the specific process; the variables of all other processes stay the same. You should therefore use shared memory to share specific data across processes.

There are two types of semaphore functions, each with its own semaphore data structure: **sem_*** functions for SEMAPHORE and **cs_*** for COUNTING_SEMAPHORE. Netscape's SEMAPHORE is a binary semaphore. It can be true or false. **sem_*** functions are used for mutual exclusion. A COUNTING_SEMAPHORE function can take any value between 0 and a larger integer value. Two processes can access the same critical section using COUNTING_SEMAPHORE. You can also use a wait condition (**cs_wait** and **cs_trywait**) with a COUNTING_SEMAPHORE.

A SEMAPHORE should be used only with Netscape UNIX Server 1.x and 2.x and a COUNTING_SEMAPHORE with Netscape UNIX Server 2.01. Other Netscape Servers support one process with multiple threads. Therefore, there is no need to support shared memory across multiple processes.

Note ▶

As mentioned earlier, Netscape's semaphore functions should be used only for UNIX Server 1.x and 2.x, where the server supports multiple processes. Under NT and Server 3.x, you need to use only the thread functions.

SEMAPHORE **Functions**   Use SEMAPHORE and **sem_*** functions to protect resources that are shared across processes. For example, these functions are useful for shared memory, global variables, or shared files. SEMAPHORE works as file lock. It supports mutual exclusion. A SEMAPHORE should be initialized in an **Init** function.

```
SEMAPHORE sem_init(char *name, int number);
int sem_grab(SEMAPHORE id);
int sem_tgrab(SEMAPHORE id);
int sem_release(SEMAPHORE id);
int sem_terminate(SEMAPHORE id);
```

You can use the **sem_*** functions to access the shared memory safely to read and alter the variables. You initialize a SEMAPHORE with **sem_init** in an **Init** function. This information is then inherited by the child process. You get a SEMAPHORE by using **sem_init** function. The function takes a file name (name) and an ID number (number) as parameters and returns a SEMAPHORE. Netscape uses a file for inter-processes locking. The file name defined by name should be a file name that a server can access. Because **sem_*** functions work with files, the name should be an appropriate file name (for example, not com1, which is reserved for devices). The name is just a file name, not a path with a file name. Netscape uses your system's temporary directory for the location of the file. The number, which will be a unique identification number for the SEMAPHORE, will become part of the file name like a file extension. For example, sem_init("sushi", 13) can create a file named sushi.13 in your temporary directory tmp—that is, /tmp/sushi.13. The server must be able to write to the temporary directory. In fact, the server already uses similar semaphore files to handle global and other interprocess data. **sem_init** returns a SEMAPHORE that you can use to lock a shared process or SEM_ERROR (−1) if it was not able to initialize a SEMAPHORE.

The child process can then use **sem_grab** or **sem_tgrab** to grab the semaphore. Your specific code performs all the necessary actions between the **sem_grab** and **sem_release** functions. **sem_release** releases the semaphore you grabbed. To deallocate the semaphore, you use **sem_terminate**. In your **Init** function, you can deallocate any semaphore that might have been left. For example, your **daemon_atrestart** function can call a function that uses **sem_terminate** to terminate (deallocate) any semaphore that was initialized by **sem_init** and is still around. These **sem_*** functions take a semaphore identification number as their parameter. **sem_grab**, **sem_tgrab**, and **sem_release** return 0 upon success and −1 in case of error. **sem_terminate** returns void (that is, nothing).

sem_tgrab and **sem_grab**, which are used to gain exclusive access to a given semaphore, work a bit differently. **sem_tgrab** tests whether exclusive access is available, but does not actually block the caller. If it is not available, **sem_tgrab** returns −1. With **sem_grab**, the caller is blocked if exclusive access is not available. You should use **sem_grab** when you actually want to lock a shared resource and make the caller wait until access is available. Use **sem_tgrab** to test whether the access is available; you may then use the result of the test to take other actions.

COUNTING_SEMAPHORE **Functions**   A counting semaphore allows two or more processes into a secured section of code—that is, a shared memory area. You can use a counting semaphore when more than one process can run the code. It gives you greater control over when a process can access a shared memory area. You can also specify a condition before entry. You can queue the processes to manage access to a shared memory area. For example, you can set the count for a counting semaphore to 2, when two different write operations can occur on separate disks. The server will then allow two processes to write before stopping the operation. When a third write operation is requested by a new process, that process must wait until one of the processes is finished before writing.

A counting semaphore takes an initial value you set (`initial_count`). It can be any number greater than zero, usually a number greater than 1. Two separate actions are taken on the counting semaphore: wait and release, often known as WAIT and SIGNAL, respectively. When a wait operation is performed on the counting semaphore (**cs_wait**), the value of the count is decreased by 1. When release is performed, the value of the count is increased by 1 (**cs_release**). Another thread that may be waiting to access the shared memory area can now enter the code. Another Netscape function, **cs_trywait**, tells the process to enter the shared memory area, if the value of count is greater than zero.

```
COUNTING_SEMAPHORE cs_init(int initial_count);
int cs_wait(COUNTING_SEMAPHORE csp);
int cs_trywait(COUNTING_SEMAPHORE csp);
int cs_release(COUNTING_SEMAPHORE csp);
void cs_terminate(COUNTING_SEMAPHORE csp);
```

cs_* functions are similar to **sem_*** functions. They initialize a semaphore that can be used to safely access shared-memory data. As with **sem_init**, you initialize the semaphore in an **Init** function. Unlike **sem_*** functions, however, **cs_*** functions produce counting semaphores, COUNTING_SEMAPHORE. A COUNTING_SEMAPHORE can take any initial integer you specify. You do not need to specify a file or an ID for COUNTING_SEMAPHORE. It is also not limited to mutual exclusion. More than one process can access the shared memory area. **cs_init** initializes a COUNTING_SEMAPHORE with the initial count you specify as its parameter (`initial_count`).

cs_init returns a `COUNTING_SEMAPHORE` or zero upon failure. You can use **cs_wait** to wait before entering the secured block of code. This function returns 0 if successful or −1 upon failure. **cs_trywait** enters the block of code only when the semaphore count is greater than zero. If the count was zero, or in case of an error, **s_trywait** returns −1. When a process is waiting, you allow its thread to enter the block of code by releasing the `COUNTING_SEMAPHORE` via **cs_release**. **cs_release** returns 0 upon release of the lock or −1 upon failure. To delete a `COUNTING_SEMAPHORE`, you can use **cs_terminate**. The function **cs_terminate** returns 0 if successful and −1 upon failure. As with **sem_terminate**, you can use **cs_terminate** in **daemon_atrestart** to deallocate any semaphore that might have been left.

System Thread (systhread_*) Functions

Let us now look at Netscape's thread functions. As mentioned earlier, **systhread_*** functions provide support for creating and managing threads. Thread support and the data structures and functions associated with **systhread_***, **crit_***, and **condvar_*** are unique to Netscape Server 2.0 and later; they were not part of Server 1.x. As we discussed earlier, there are a number of different thread models (for example, kernel-level and user-level threads). Netscape uses a different model for different operating systems. When you use Netscape's NSAPI functions, however, you do not need to worry about which thread model the server is using. Netscape takes care of how the threads are actually implemented.

Threads are spawned by a process. They share the processes' virtual address space, global variables, and other resources. Usually, a separate thread is spawned by the server to process each client request. A thread executes a portion of a program. Thus, there is a specific starting address for the code, which is executed. Under Netscape, this address is a pointer to a function. Threads also keep a set of data structures that hold their context as they wait for their scheduled time of execution. The context includes various thread-related information such as machine registers, kernel stack, environment variables, and so on. The order in which threads are awakened or executed is determined by Netscape Server and/or the operating system. The process's and thread's priorities affect the order in which the thread is executed. Under a multiprocessor system, multiple threads can be executed at the same time (parallel processing).

Start a Thread

```
SYS_THREAD systhread_start(int prio, int stksz,
                void (*fn)(void *), void *arg);
```

We begin with **systhread_start**, which creates a thread. You set the priority with the `prio` parameter. This number is system-dependent. Look into your operating system settings for thread priority. The default `SYSTHREAD_DEFAULT_PRIORITY` is 16. An example of a thread priority under NT is `HIGH_PRIORITY_CLASS`, with the normal base priority level of 13. Base priority level is measured by the priority value of the thread and its process class. The system usually executes each thread based on its level of priority and when it was placed in the schedule of threads to be executed. The size of the stack allocated for the thread is defined with stksz. If stksz is set to zero, then the default stack size (usually the initial size of the thread) is allocated. For Enterprise Server 3.x, it is 64KB. For Server 2.x, it is 256KB. The fn parameter is the function that is called, and its arguments are defined in the parameter arg. As mentioned earlier, a thread can execute a part of your code. The function specified here (fn) is that code that is called once the time to execute is reached. **systhread_start** returns a new SYS_THREAD structure if successful and SYS_THREAD_ERROR (NULL) upon failure.

Under NT and Server 3.x, when a thread is created by an **Init** function, it persists for the server process. For the 2.x version of IRIX, the thread will exist only in the base process; it will not be distributed to the child processes. For all other version 2.x UNIX servers, the thread created in the **Init** function will exist both in the base process and in all of the child (worker) processes.

Get the Current Thread and Make a Thread a Netscape Thread

```
SYS_THREAD systhread_current();
SYS_THREAD systhread_attach();
```

You can get the current thread using **systhread_current**. This function returns a pointer to the current thread. **systhread_attach** makes an existing thread to a Netscape thread, a platform independent thread. The function returns a pointer to the platform-independent thread.

Create, Set, and Get Thread-Private Data

```
int systhread_newkey(void);
void systhread_setdata(int key, void *data);
void *systhread_getdata(int key);
```

systhread_newkey, **systhread_setdata**, and **systhread_getdata** are functions you can use to identify a variable (data) that you want to use in the current thread only. For instance, you can use these functions to set the variable differently between threads. Use **systhread_newkey** to get an integer key to identify a localized thread data, the thread-private data. This function allocates an integer ID (key) for the thread-private data. You can then use **systhread_setdata** to associate a value with the key for the thread. You can use the integer (key) returned by **systhread_newkey** and a pointer to the specific thread-private data to associate the data with the specific key. data points to the string of thread-private data. You can then get the data using the **systhread_getdata** function. You pass the key, and **systhread_getdata** returns the pointer to the data. **systhread_getdata** returns NULL if it failed—for example, if you had not set the data using **systhread_setdata**.

Change a Thread's Timing

```
void systhread_sleep(int milliseconds);
void systhread_yield(void);
void systhread_timerset(int usec);
```

There are also functions for delaying a thread from responding or yielding to another thread. **systhread_sleep** puts a thread to sleep—that is, makes a thread inactive. It sets the current thread to sleep for the given milliseconds defined in the function's parameter. **systhread_yield** yields the processor to another thread. In other words, the thread is not processed. You can use this function in conjunction with a conditional setting you may have instituted to have the processor yield when the condition is met. If your system allows the timer interval for the threads to be changed, **systhread_timerset** can reset or start the interrupt timer.

Terminate a Thread

```
void systhread_terminate(SYS_THREAD thr);
```

After you have finished with the thread, you can terminate it using **systhread_terminate**. This function takes the thread (thr) that it will terminate as a parameter. You can have the SYS_THREAD value through **systhread_start** or **systhread_current**. If you had started a thread, you can close it using this function.

Bug Report ▶

systhread_terminate does not function properly. You may want to use a native thread termination or a conditional variable with a thread that checks for the condition.

New System Thread Functions For Server 3.x

```
/* NEW to Server 3.x */
void systhread_set_default_stacksize(int size);
void systhread_detach(SYS_THREAD thr);
```

For the UNIX version of Server 3.x, you can use a new NSAPI function, **systhread_set_default_stacksize**, to change the default stack size. This process is similar to setting the StackSize in the **magnus.conf** file. Using this function, you can dynamically change the stack size without having each administrator manually update the **magnus.conf** file. This function should be called in an **Init** SAF. You can use it to increase the stack size, if your program needs more space for its stack. The new stack size is specified in the parameter size. This function sets the stack size for all threads created by the server.

systhread_detach detaches a thread that was previously attached using the **systhread_attach** function.

CRITICAL *and* CONDVAR *Functions*

crit_* functions are used for critical section support. A *critical section* is a standard concept in the multithreaded systems, referring to a specific section of the code that is owned by one thread at a time. It includes code that will not work properly (is unsafe) if more than one thread is accessing it simultaneously. The critical section prevents multiple threads from using a thread-unsafe function or from updating a static global variable, a file, or database at the same time.

Consider the following scenario where a critical section is needed. You have a global variable that you want to update whenever a specific client request is made (for example, the number of connections to a database). This variable, because it is global, can be accessed by your specific code, which can then update its value. If you are running a multithreaded environment, thread A can access the variable and read it; before it attempts to do the update, however, thread B, which has also read the variable, makes an update. The problem is that when thread A actually updates the same variable, it will not read the revised (new) variable. Instead, it will update the original variable. Thus the changes of thread B will be ignored, and you will get an erroneous response.

condvar_* functions are used for conditional variable support. A *conditional variable* allows you to provide a condition for blocking a thread. The condition of entering the critical section of one thread can be based on another thread. One thread is made to wait until it is notified by another thread about a certain condition having been met before proceeding.

crit_* functions are used in mutual exclusion of threads. **condvar_*** functions are used in synchronization of threads based on a conditional variable. Unlike **systhread_*** functions, both **crit_*** and **condvar_*** functions are used only for thread isolation and synchronization—not for creating and manipulating a thread directly. Also unlike **sem_*** functions, they are used only for threads—not for processes. You should use **crit_*** and **condvar_*** functions whenever you need thread safety for your code.

CRITICAL **Functions**
```
CRITICAL crit_init(void);
crit_enter(CRITICAL id);
crit_exit(CRITICAL id);
crit_terminate(CRITICAL id);
```

To use the critical section, you first need to create a new critical-section variable (data structure). You use **crit_init** to initialize and return a critical-section variable, an instance of type CRITICAL. At the time of the creation of the CRITICAL variable, no thread owns the critical-section. The place to initialize a critical section variable is in an **Init** function. In fact, the CRITICAL variable should be a static global variable that is initialized in an **Init** function. Thus the CRITICAL variables will be available to all threads.

To take ownership of the critical section, you need to enter it using **crit_enter**. This function uses the CRITICAL variable returned by **crit_init**. If another thread has taken ownership of the critical section, the thread waits (is blocked) until the other thread exits. When the thread enters the critical section, it has exclusive access to the code and variables inside the section. To enter the critical section use **crit_enter** before the part of the code you want to protect inside your standard directive function (for example, a **Service** function). The code you may want to protect could include functions that are not thread-safe, functions for accessing a database or a file, functions for updating of a global variable, and so on. The size of code that you declare in a critical section should be as small as possible, preferably only a few functions. You do not want the threads waiting to gain access, as it can slow the performance of the server.

Once the thread has stepped through the code in the critical section, it should exit the critical section with **crit_exit**. The critical section is then available to other threads. The next thread waiting to enter the critical section is allowed access. Your code should not call **crit_enter** again, before exiting the critical section by calling **crit_exit**.

To terminate (eliminate) a critical-section variable, use **crit_terminate**. It is not the same as **crit_exit**, as **crit_terminate** actually removes (releases) the CRITICAL variable that you created with the **crit_init** function. The critical variable will no longer be available for **crit_enter**, so you should not called **crit_terminate** unless necessary. A good place to call this function is from the **Init** function where the CRITICAL variable was initialized. For example, you can use **crit_terminate** inside a function that is called by **daemon_atrestart**. **daemon_atrestart** is used to do clean up upon shutdown or restart of the server (for example, deallocating resources initialized by an **Init** function). Thus, if a CRITICAL variable is still in memory, it is freed. When you call **crit_terminate**, all threads should have exited the critical section, and no thread should be waiting to enter the critical section.

Critical Section Example   Listing 11-1 is a mock example of how to use **crit_*** functions. It is not complete, but rather covers the necessary part of the critical section that you will need to add to your code. You should be able to incorporate this code easily within your program. For example, you can use the critical section to update a ticker that records the number of requests for your NSAPI program. Declare the ticker as a global static integer variable and increase the value of the ticker by 1 in the critical section. A complete example of the use of the critical section is included on the accompanying CD-ROM.

Listing 11-1   Example Using crit_* Functions

```
/* static global variable for critical section */
static CRITICAL ThreadLock;

/* cleanUp function called by daemon_atrestart */
NSAPI_PUBLIC void cleanUp(void *parameter)
{
   /* check if the critical section variable is still
      around and remove it
    */
   if(ThreadLock)
   {
        crit_terminate(ThreadLock);
   }

   /* the rest of your cleanUp function to be called at
      server restart or shutdown
```

Listing 11-1   Example Using crit_* Functions (*continued*)

```
      */
}

/* Init function to initialize global variables, critical
   section, and so on
 */
NSAPI_PUBLIC int yourInitFunction(pblock *pb, Session *sn,
                                    Request *rq)
{
   /* allocate the critical-section variable */
   ThreadLock = crit_init();

   /* check if the critical section variable was allocated */
      if(ThreadLock == 0)
   {
       /* do appropriate action upon failure, e.g. exit */

       return REQ_ABORTED;
   }

   /* the rest of your Init function */
   /* call the cleanUp function at shutdown or restart */
   daemon_atrestart(cleanUp, NULL);

   return REQ_PROCEED;
}

/* your main function */
NSAPI_PUBLIC int yourServiceFunction (pblock *param, Session
                                       *sn, Request *rq)
{

   /* first part of your code */

   /* Enter critical-section code. Thread will take
      ownership.
    */

   crit_enter(ThreadLock);

   /* your code that requires locking, such as connecting
      to a database and updating a record, updating a
      global variable, and so on

    */

   /* Exit the critical section. Allow other threads access. */
      crit_exit(ThreadLock);
```

Listing 11-1   Example Using **crit_*** Functions (*continued*)

```
    /* the rest of your code */

    /* return the appropriate return value for your function */
    return REQ_PROCEED;
}
```

As you can see in Listing 11-1, you write three separate functions to use the **crit_*** functions: **yourInitFunction**, **cleanUp**, and **yourServiceFunction**. After you declare a global static variable for the critical-section variable, you initialize the CRITICAL variable in an **Init** function (**yourInitFunction**) using **crit_init**. To deallocate any global variable at the server restart or shutdown, you call **crit_terminate** inside another function, **cleanUp**. **cleanUp** is called by **daemon_atrestart**, which is declared inside **yourInitFunction**. The actual critical-section code, which you enter and exit using **crit_enter** and **crit_exit**, is called in yet another function, **yourServiceFunction**.

CONDVAR **Functions**   There are times when using critical functions, **crit_***, by themselves is not enough. You not only want to lock a section of code from other threads, but you also may want to include special conditions on when such lock should occur. The condition of entering the critical section of one thread can be based on another thread. In other words, you want a thread to wait until it is notified by another thread about a certain condition having been met before proceeding. For such a circumstance, you use **condvar_*** functions. This method of locking is more complicated and requires greater care when programming. If you want only simple mutual exclusion with a condition that can be based on a global variable, you should use **crit_*** functions instead.

condvar_* functions include a wait and notify procedure to coordinate the execution of the critical-section code between dependent threads. **condvar** stands for "condition variable" for a critical section. **condvar_*** functions work in conjunction with CRITICAL variables and **crit_*** functions to provide the ability for your program to set a condition on when a certain critical section of code should be blocked. You use **crit_*** functions to define the critical section. After a thread enters the critical section, you can use two **condvar_*** functions, **condvar_wait** and **condvar_notify**. **condvar_wait** has the thread wait until a condition is met, while **condvar_notify** has the thread notify another thread (the thread with **condvar_wait**) that the condition is actually met.

```
CONDVAR condvar_init(CRITICAL id);
void condvar_wait(CONDVAR cv);
void condvar_notify(CONDVAR cv);
void condvar_terminate(CONDVAR cv);

/* NEW for Server 3.x */
void condvar_notifyAll (CONDVAR cv);
```

condvar_init is used to initialize and allocate a conditional variable. You pass it the CRITICAL variable initialized by **crit_init**, and it returns the CONDVAR variable (data structure). You must call **crit_init** before calling **condvar_init**. Both functions should be initialized in an **Init** function, because the variables they return are to be accessed by all threads. The CONDVAR variable returned by **condvar_init** should be declared first as a global static variable. You can then initialize this variable in the **Init** function. In the previous example, you can simply have the **condvar_init** function appear immediately after the **crit_init** function, as in ThreadVariable = condvar_init (ThreadLock);. ThreadVariable can be defined similar to ThreadLock as static CONDVAR.

Once you have initialized the conditional variable, you need to run the appropriate condvar_* functions (for example, **condvar_wait** and **condvar_notify**). The **condvar_wait** thread waits for a condition to be met before executing the rest of the critical section. In other words, the rest of the code after **condvar_wait** is blocked until the condition referenced from the **condvar_wait** parameter is met. This requirement does not mean that another thread cannot enter the critical section. **condvar_wait** locks only its own thread and critical section.

The condition variable parameter, cv, of **condvar_wait** should be the variable originally initialized by **condvar_init**. Another thread using the **condvar_notify** function can then notify this thread, which is waiting, that the condition is met. Both functions, **condvar_wait** and **condvar_notify**, share the same CONDVAR variable as the parameter. **condvar_notify** notifies **condvar_wait** based on the shared CONDVAR parameter.

Each of these functions, **condvar_wait** and **condvar_notify**, needs to be placed inside a separate critical section that was begun by a separate **crit_enter**. **condvar_wait** is called in a separate thread from **condvar_notify**. **condvar_notify** is not declared after the same **crit_enter** that **condvar_wait** follows. It is declared after a **crit_enter** that uses the same CRITICAL variable. The **crit_enter** functions for **condvar_wait** and **condvar_notify** use the same CRITICAL variable as the parameter, but they are called by different threads.

A single thread is normally used to process a client request. If that thread finds a critical section with **condvar_wait**, the thread is placed on hold. The server will not finish sending the response until another thread, by another request, notifies it that the condition has been met. Another request can enter a thread with a critical section having the same CRITICAL variable and find **condvar_notify** with the same CONDVAR variable as **condvar_wait**. This new thread then notifies the waiting thread (via **condvar_wait**) to proceed. Thus both the original thread and the new thread will finish processing their requests.

If you intend to use **condvar_wait** and **condvar_notify** in the same NSAPI program that responds to a single client request, your program must spawn the appropriate threads. It must spawn a thread that waits (**condvar_wait**) and another thread that notifies the waiting thread (**condvar_notify**). Otherwise, the program waits each time it encounters **condvar_wait** and will not finish processing the client request. In other words, if you simply follow the code for the critical section with **condvar_wait** by inserting the code for the critical section with **condvar_notify**, **condvar_notify** will not execute. The thread that is responding to the client request will stop processing and begin waiting when it encounters **condvar_wait**.

When a **condvar_wait** function is found inside a critical section that a thread has entered, the **condvar_wait** function releases the critical section and its variable (CRITICAL) and waits to be notified. In other words, the CRITICAL variable defined as the **crit_enter** parameter is available for another thread (**crit_enter** function) to use. The **condvar_wait** function will not hold the critical section. **condvar_wait** holds only its own thread and critical section. Another thread can now enter a critical section with the same CRITICAL variable. This thread can even enter the same **condvar_wait** code. Thus more than one thread can be waiting for **condvar_notify**.

When a new thread finds a thread with the same CRITICAL variable and a **condvar_notify** with the same CONDVAR variable, it calls **condvar_wait**. **condvar_wait**, in turn, regains control of its critical section, and the rest of the critical section is executed. **condvar_notify** can notify (awaken) only one thread with **condvar_wait**, even when multiple threads have called the same **condvar_wait** code. **condvar_notify** notifies the first thread waiting with **condvar_wait**. If the thread with **condvar_wait** surrenders ownership to the critical section (that is, exits the critical section with **crit_exit**), a second thread with **condvar_notify** can notify the next thread waiting with **condvar_wait**. Thus multiple threads could be waiting for notification from **condvar_notify**.

With Server 3.x, you can use a new function, **condvar_notifyAll**, to notify (awaken) all threads waiting with **condvar_wait**. In other words, unlike **condvar_notify**, **condvar_notifyAll** awakens all threads blocked for the given conditional variable.

As we are dealing with a multithreaded environment, both threads with **condvar_wait** and **condvar_notify** will finish their processes concurrently. If you are using **condvar_notifyAll**, all threads with the appropriate **condvar_wait** and **condvar_notifyAll** threads finish their processes concurrently. Critical sections for both the thread with **condvar_wait** and the thread with **condvar_notify** (or **condvar_notifyAll**) should be exited with **crit_exit**.

You can also terminate (release) a condition variable with **condvar_terminate**. Again, as with **crit_terminate**, you should use **condvar_terminate** only when necessary—for example, before the server restart. You can use **condvar_terminate** inside a function called by **daemon_atrestart**. Thus, if a CONDVAR variable is still in memory, it is freed. The CONDVAR variable is a global variable that should be available while the server is running, so that various threads can access it. **condvar_terminate** frees the allocated CONDVAR variable defined by its parameter.

The following code is an example of using **condvar_***. We first declare the CRITICAL and CONDVAR variables as global static variables:

```
/* static global variable for critical section */
static CRITICAL ThreadLock;
static CONDVAR ThreadVariable;
```

Next, we initialize both variables in an **Init** function:

```
ThreadLock = crit_init();
ThreadVariable = condvar_init(ThreadLock);
```

We can also use **crit_terminate** and **condvar_terminate** in a function called by **daemon_atrestart**, just as we did in Listing 11-1. This action will deallocate (free) the CONDVAR and CRITICAL variables, if they are still in memory, at the restart of the server.

To use **condvar_wait** and **condvar_notify**, we need to create two separate threads. The server must be able to enter both these threads. When the server is stopped during the processing of one thread, **condvar_wait**, another thread must be able to enter the critical section, which includes **condvar_notify** (or **condvar_notifyAll**).

In thread A, you can use **condvar_wait**:

```
/* enter the thread with condvar_wait */
crit_enter(ThreadLock);

/* take any action before calling condvar_wait */

/* thread will wait until the condition is met */
condvar_wait(ThreadVariable);

/* finish the critical section */

/* Exit the critical section. Allow other threads access
*/
crit_exit(ThreadLock);
```

In thread B, you use **condvar_notify**:

```
/* enter the thread with condvar_notify */
crit_enter(ThreadLock);

/* Take any action before calling condvar_notify. For
   example, you can verify if a condition is met before
   calling condvar_notify. If the condition is not met,
   you can exit the critical section.
 */

/* notify the waiting thread (condvar_wait) if condition
   was met */
condvar_notify(ThreadVariable);

/* the rest of the critical-section code */

/* Exit the critical section. Allow other threads access.
*/
crit_exit(ThreadLock);
```

An example of the use of conditional variables is included on the accompanying CD-ROM.

Summary

Chapter 11 is the final chapter on NSAPI. By now, you should be ready to write your own NSAPI programs. This chapter covers a difficult subject, threads and processes. It is difficult to cover all the important aspects of programming of threads and processes in one chapter. If you are not already familiar with these topics, you may need to use supplemental reading to learn more about them. The difficulty of this topic is also augmented by the fact that various operating systems and Netscape Server versions and platforms use different thread and process models. Thus, you not only need to understand the thread and process model of your operating system, but you also need to understand how your version of Netscape Server implements its own model.

Many programmers may ignore this chapter because, when they created CGI programs, they did not have to worry about threads. With NSAPI, however, you should be concerned that your code is thread-safe. Otherwise, you run the danger of data corruption, server crashes, or server lock-up.

To write a thread-safe application, you should first study your operating system's thread and process model. You can then use the information in this chapter to get a better understanding of how your Netscape Server implements threads and/or processes. If you are using Netscape Server 1.x or 2.x on UNIX, you should also review the sections on processes, such as SEMAPHORE and COUNTING_SEMAPHORE. UNIX versions of Netscape 1.x and 2.x use multiple processes. The UNIX version of Netscape 2.x uses multiple processes with multiple threads. Thus you should also review the section on threads.

If you are using Enterprise Server 3.x or any version of the server on NT (Win32), you can safely ignore the sections on processes and focus more closely on thread implementation and functions. The easiest way to make sure your code is thread-safe using NSAPI is to take advantage of CRITICAL variables and **crit_*** functions. This approach allows you to lock a section of the code (critical section) for use by a single thread. Other threads must wait for the current thread to finish stepping through the critical section before entering it. If you need more control over thread locking and require conditional variables that can specify access for one thread based on another thread, then you should consider adding **condvar_*** functions to your program. In this chapter, we reviewed the appropriate thread functions and stepped through a couple of mock examples to show how you can use these functions.

Part IV

CORBA/IIOP and WAI

Part IV (Chapters 12 through 16, plus Appendix F) covers the new Common Object Request Broker Architecture (CORBA)-based programming features of Netscape Server 3.x. In Chapter 12, we review CORBA in general and the Netscape Internet Service Broker (ISB) in particular. Chapters 13–16 cover the Web Application Interface (WAI). WAI is an extension of Netscape CORBA support that allows you to process HTTP client requests. Chapter 13 covers the general topics of WAI. Chapter 14 is a reference chapter, where we will discuss the details of this new API. In Chapter 15, we step through the process of writing a WAI application. Chapter 16 includes a number of WAI programming examples. Appendix F includes a discussion of osagent and osfind, two utilities that are used only with Enterprise Server 3.0.

Chapter 12

CORBA and Netscape ISB

Common Object Request Broker Architecture (CORBA) is an object-oriented model that defines a framework for distributed objects. Enterprise Server 3.x includes a CORBA Object Request Broker (ORB) runtime and development license that Netscape has named the Internet Service Broker (ISB). An ORB is the core component that enables communication between CORBA objects. You can use the Netscape CORBA development tools to write CORBA applications for the Enterprise Server so as to expand the use of the server and integrate other distributed objects with your programs. You can also develop CORBA applets for Netscape Communicator. Netscape Communicator includes a runtime ORB. Thus, with Communicator at every desktop, you have access to a CORBA ORB on every machine.

The scope of programming using CORBA and IIOP is far greater than the scope of Netscape's earlier server programming tools. CORBA programming goes beyond HTTP and HTML-based programming models supported by Netscape Server (such as CGI, NSAPI, or even WAI). CORBA is very extensible. Netscape Enterprise Server and Communicator, when using the built-in CORBA ORB, become part of a larger network of distributed applications. By supporting CORBA and IIOP, Enterprise Server and Netscape Communicator become two nodes in a much greater programming plan that can include CORBA client and server applications developed by other vendors or programmers. CORBA is supported by many of the major software providers (including IBM, Oracle, SUN, Borland, and Novell). Consequently, you can develop applications to take advantage of these CORBA-enabled services from other vendors.

CORBA is a general-purpose client/server application model. With CORBA, you can distribute the application logic among different objects over the network. You can encapsulate a legacy application, allowing it to interoperate with other CORBA objects. If your organization uses CORBA, then you should definitely consider taking advantage of the CORBA support in Netscape Server and Communicator. If you want to integrate an existing client/server application or a legacy system, you can also use

CORBA to leverage your existing architecture. CORBA application development separates the interface and implementation of objects. It allows you to write applications that can communicate with one another regardless of the programming language, operating system, or network location of the CORBA objects. If you are interested only in using CORBA to extend the server's processing of HTTP requests, then you should use Web Application Interface (WAI). We will discuss WAI in detail in Chapters 13 through 16.

In this chapter, we will briefly review CORBA, IIOP, and other CORBA-related terms and concepts. Much of the information in this section is based on the CORBA standard. However, there is also specific information that is unique to Netscape and its ISB, such as Netscape Naming Service (also known as Web Naming Service). We will spend more time discussing these special features. We will also review the development tools that Netscape provides. Finally, we will walk through the steps of writing a CORBA client/server application. Throughout this chapter, the focus is on what Netscape provides, instead of CORBA specifications in general.

Netscape provides CORBA development tools for both Java and C++. With these tools, you can write CORBA client and server applications that can talk to one another. These applications use the Netscape ORB and Naming Service to locate and then communicate with one another. You can deploy these applications for use by Netscape Enterprise Server or Netscape Communicator. We will focus more closely on C++ (as opposed to Java) as C has been the main programming language throughout the book. There also will be notes and comments unique to Java. In fact, the Java CORBA offerings of Netscape provide more options and features than the C++ offerings.

The Netscape CORBA development environment is intended for applications dependent on Enterprise Server. Enterprise Server includes a Java and C++ ORB licensed from Visigenic. The ISB, the CORBA ORB included with Enterprise Server 3.x, is a modified version of Visigenic's ORB. The actual licensing from Visigenic Software (`http://www.visigenic.com`) requires applications to be built for the server. The tools themselves, however, are not limited to Netscape Server. You can get similar tools from Visigenic (for example, VisiBroker for C++ or Java, and VisiBroker Naming Service) or other vendors to develop distributed objects or CORBA client/server applications. In other words, much of the discussion in this chapter can be used to develop any type of CORBA application. You should use the Netscape ISB for applications intended for use with Netscape Enterprise Server.

Some of the features discussed here are unique to the version of Visigenic ORB included with the Netscape Server. Other features are modifications or enhancements

---

Note ▶

Visigenic was recently acquired by Borland (recently renamed as Inprise Corporation), and its products will be incorporated into the existing Borland product line.

of the ORB unique to Netscape ISB. For example, with Server 3.01, Netscape removed an essential component of Visigenic ORB, osagent. Netscape uses its own Naming Service. Using the built-in Naming Service, your program will be dependent on the Netscape Server. In this chapter, we discuss Enterprise Server 3.0, as well as Enterprise Servers 3.01 and 3.5.1. We will discuss the use of osagent that comes with Enterprise Server 3.0 as well as Netscape Web Naming Service. (For more information on osagent, see Appendix F.)

Unlike the CGI and NSAPI chapters, this chapter has a broader scope. It is intended for writing distributed CORBA applications in general. You can use this information to write your own CORBA client or server applications that work with Enterprise Server. As noted earlier, if you intend to extend Netscape Server's processing of client HTTP requests (as you would with CGI or NSAPI), you should consider writing a WAI application. WAI is an extension of the Netscape CORBA support intended for handling HTTP requests. It is built using Netscape ISB. Writing a WAI application is also easier than writing a CORBA application. To write a CORBA application, you need to understand the CORBA architecture, ORB, IIOP, and more. WAI, on the other hand, shields you from these complexities. Unlike Netscape ISB, WAI is provided with both FastTrack 3.x and Enterprise Server 3.x. FastTrack 3.x does not include the ISB for developing CORBA distributed applications.

To use Netscape Naming Service for registering and locating CORBA objects, you need to enable WAI. In the Server Manager, you can enable WAI from the Programs| WAI Management menu. Depending on the kind of WAI application you want to write and whether you wish to use Communicator ORB, you may also need to enable Web Publishing and set the appropriate access privileges. See the Important Settings for Java ISB and Naming Service section later in this chapter for more information.

Note ▶

To upgrade your Solaris or NT version of Enterprise Server 3.0 to Enterprise Server 3.01, you should use the latest server patch (for example, 3.0i for NT) and the WAI patch (P85416). You should first update the server with the server patch and then apply the WAI patch. You can find these patches in the File Library page under Netscape's Tech Support site (http://help.netscape.com/filelib.html). These patches include a variety of server- and WAI-specific updated files that will replace your existing 3.0 files. Read the instructions that come with these patches for the specific steps you should take to update your server. You should also regularly check the File Library page for additional updates or recent patches for your server.

CORBA

This section on CORBA is very basic. It is intended only to provide you with a simple overview of how CORBA works. You can also use this information for a better understanding of how WAI works.

CORBA is an established standard that is supported by many vendors (such as Netscape, IBM, and Oracle). These vendors provide applications that support CORBA or programming tools for CORBA. There are also a number of good books on CORBA including *The Essential Distributed Objects Survival Guide* by Orfali, Harkey, and Edwards. Because CORBA has gathered a great deal of attention recently, you should expect many more articles and books on CORBA in the future. You can also find additional information in the Netscape developer site, DevEdge Online (`http://developer.netscape.com`), and Object Management Group (OMG) site (`http://www.omg.org`). CORBA specification version 2.0, supported by Netscape Server 3.x, and the current version 2.2 are included on the CD-ROM that accompanies this book.

Netscape also provides a number of CORBA-related documents for Netscape Enterprise Server (*Netscape Internet Service Broker Programmer's Guide for C++, Netscape Internet Service Broker Programmer's Guide for Java, Netscape Internet Service Broker Reference Guide for C++,* and *Netscape Internet Service Broker Reference for Java*). You can find the latest version of these documents on the Netscape developer Web site, DevEdge Online (`http://developer.netscape.com`). These documents cover the necessary information you need to program a CORBA application for Netscape Enterprise Server using C++ or Java. There are many differences between the C++ and Java implementations of ISB. You should look in the appropriate book for more detailed information. Here, an attempt was made to give an overview that is applicable to both; a number of more specific references, however, are applicable to either C++ or Java, but not to both.

CORBA, CORBA Objects, and Object Implementation

CORBA is an object-oriented specification set forth by Object Management Group (OMG) that provides the framework for network-centric distributed objects. These objects can work together, independent of the client or the server operating system, the location of the objects, and the programming language. Netscape Server 3.x supports OMG's CORBA 2.0 standard. CORBA delineates the specifications for writing distributed objects. It is based on the Core Object Model (COM), which describes the objects and Object Management Architecture's (OMA) Reference Architecture for distributed objects. CORBA is an architecture standard, not an implementation standard. A CORBA object is a software component that can provide a specific service. An object is a server when it provides a service for another object; it is a client when it requests a service from another object. Another way to refer to a server object is as an object implementation. Sometimes it is also called a service. Object implementation is the actual service that the server object provides. In many cases, a server object is another object's client. An object can be both a client and a server. A server application can include multiple object implementations. It can also include client objects.

The CORBA module includes the interface and methods for such operations as creating, duplicating, and releasing a CORBA object. It also includes the definition of how these objects should communicate with one another.

ORB and Netscape ISB

The components that CORBA defines include objects and ORBs. An ORB is the glue that connects various client/server objects. It helps a client find and communicate with other CORBA objects transparently. It is the objects' request broker. All CORBA objects must include an ORB for locating and communicating with other CORBA objects. A CORBA client object needs to know only what the name of the server object is and how to use its interface to interact with it. The ORB takes care of locating the object, passing the request of the client object, and returning the response of the server object. It handles the details of the communication layer. The ORB does not have to know how the server object actually processes the request. It simply passes the request (parameters) and accepts the response (return value). The client does not need to know the location or the language of the server object. The ORB provides interoperability between objects, independent of the type of system and the location of the object.

An ORB is not an executable program. It is a set of libraries, interfaces, and resources. It includes a number of interfaces: client stub, server skeleton, Dynamic Invocation Interface, Dynamic Skeleton Interface, Object Adapters, and ORB interface (each of which will be discussed later in this chapter). The CORBA specification for the ORB includes a general architecture. It is up to the ORB provider to deliver the implementation. Here, we will focus on the Netscape ORB implementation.

As already mentioned, the Netscape ORB (ISB) is a modified version of Visigenic ORB (VisiBroker for C++ and VisiBroker for Java). Netscape ISB and Visigenic VisiBroker have some differences. VisiBroker includes a program called Gatekeeper to support HTTP tunneling for locating objects and wrapping IIOP in HTTP. Thus the client can use HTTP to locate and invoke a method on the server object through the gateway program, Gatekeeper. Netscape, on the other hand, uses its own Netscape Web Naming Service. Visigenic also uses the osagent that is no longer included with Servers 3.01 and 3.5.1. We will discuss Netscape Web Naming Service and IIOP shortly. (For more information on osagent, see Appendix F.)

Figure 12-1 illustrates the three core components of the CORBA model: the client or requester, the server and its object implementation, and the ORB.

IIOP

Internet Inter-ORB Protocol (IIOP) is the open-standard network protocol for communication between different ORBs (see Figure 12-2). It is based on the General Inter-ORB Protocol (GIOP) specification. IIOP, similar to HTTP, runs on top of TCP/IP. It governs how the objects will communicate over the Internet. The ORBs can come from any number of vendors. As long as they use IIOP, objects should be able to communicate with one another. IIOP adds the necessary communication protocol for CORBA to delineate a truly distributed object standard. IIOP specifies the protocol for operating and transporting messages on top of the TCP/IP layer. It defines the standard for identifying an object, its reference (Interoperable Object Reference),

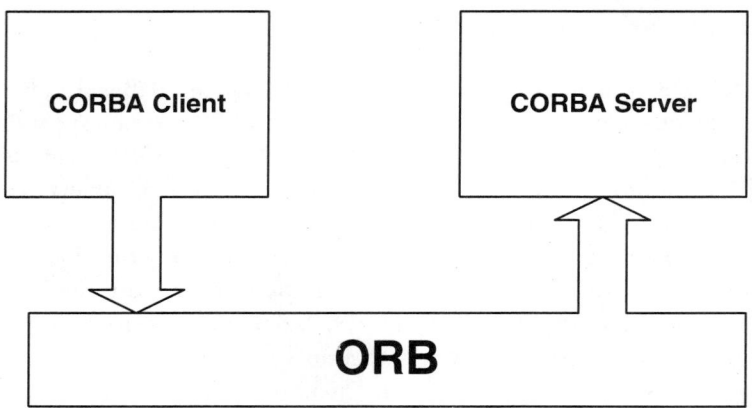

Figure 12-1   CORBA Client and Server Using the ORB

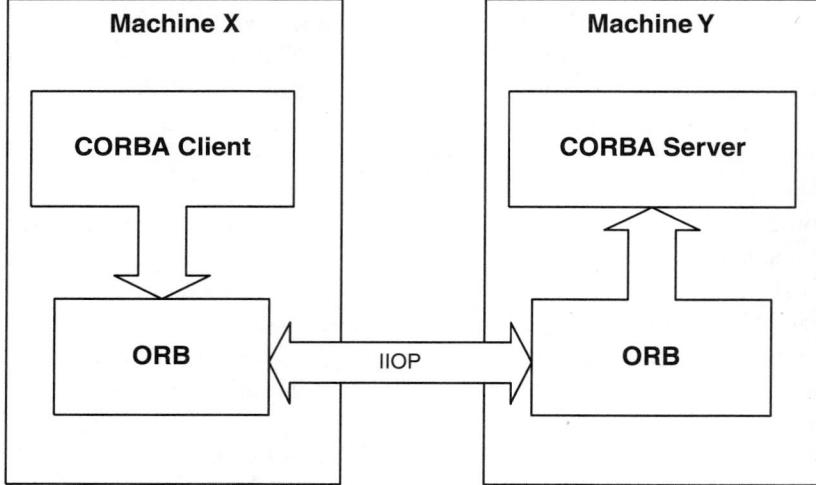

Figure 12-2   CORBA Client and Server Using IIOP

acceptable communication messages between ORBs (Inter-ORB message formats), and the standard data transfer syntax (Common Data Representation).

Netscape's support of IIOP means that the Communicator 4.x, besides using HTTP and FTP, can communicate with other CORBA-compliant servers via IIOP. Unlike TCP/IP, IIOP preserves the state information across multiple connections and various object invocations.

There is no standard port address associated with IIOP. Therefore, you must know the IIOP port address in advance before you can use IIOP. Different ORBs must agree upon a port address.

Object Reference and Interoperable Object Reference

Each instance of your object has an object reference that identifies it. This object reference is used to reference an object and invoke the methods of the object. In other words, a client object needs an object reference to the server object to invoke one of its methods. Object references are opaque. There are no standards for the format and implementation of object reference, although all object references include information about the name, location, and interface type of the object. The scope of the object reference is limited to the local ORB. An object reference is transient. It lasts only for the duration of the client's session with the ORB. An object reference can be made persistent through the process of stringification, the process of converting an object reference to a string. (We will discuss stringification shortly.) Other objects can use the stringified object reference to get the actual object reference.

Normally, you do not need to know how the object reference is implemented. The object reference is intended for use by your ORB. You reference the object by its interface name and an object name that may be given to the object implementation. Netscape ISB also provides specific methods for using and producing persistent and transient object references.

For your program, you normally use a Naming Service to locate an object reference for an object implementation. You use a Naming Service for a persistent object. A persistent object has a global scope and a persistent object reference. Persistent objects normally register themselves with the Naming Service and are available through that service. Transient objects, on the other hand, are not registered with the Naming Service. For transient objects, you need a direct access to the object reference. Transient object references last for the duration of the process that creates them.

Because the Naming Services can vary based on the CORBA vendor, the methods for registering and locating an object can be different. For example, for Netscape Server 3.0, your server object registers itself with the osagent (a directory service—a simplified Naming Service included with Server 3.0) and/or the built-in Netscape Web Naming Service. (We will discuss osagent in Appendix F, and Naming Service later in this chapter. The important thing to note is that osagent is part of Enterprise Server 3.0 but not Enterprise Server 3.01 and 3.5.x. For Enterprise Server 3.01 and 3.5.x, you should use the Netscape built-in Naming Service and its designated methods.)

For the C++ version of ISB for Server 3.0, the client uses osagent to locate the object implementation. The name given to the object implementation and the object's interface name are used by the client to find and invoke the services of the server object. Using osagent, the client can locate the server object through the **bind** method (for example, _**bind**). The client uses the name of the object implementation class (the interface name and any specified object name for the object implementation) assigned during instantiation of the server object and the object implementation class bind method. The client invokes the bind method to get the object reference of the server object. The bind method returns a reference to the server object. The client uses osagent via the ORB. The ORB contacts osagent to locate the server. It then establishes the connection between the server and the client. Depending on where the server resides, the ORB will produce a TCP/IP connection and a proxy object for the client's use. For instance, if the host is on a remote machine, the ORB will use TCP/IP for the connection between the client and the server object. It then creates a proxy object that the client uses to invoke the methods. All methods (server object invocations) are, in turn, packaged and sent to the remote server. The client uses the methods of the proxy object as if the object were local.

With Server 3.01 and 3.5.x, you no longer use the bind method or osagent. The ORB procedure for getting an object reference and establishing a connection with the server object, however, is very similar. For C++, you can use **resolveURI** to get an object reference for an object implementation. (For Java, you can use the method `netscape.WAI.Naming.resolve`.) You use the host name and port number of the Netscape Server, the URI path of the Naming Service, and the interface name and object name of the object implementation. (You also use the C++ method **_narrow** to narrow the object to the exact object reference. Narrowing turns an object reference of type CORBA Object into the specific type of object you need.) The ORB then contacts Netscape Naming Service to locate the server object using the interface name and/or object name. The use of the object name is optional. If the server object is transient, then there will be no object name. The ORB establishes the connection between the server object (object implementation) and the client. For a local server object, the ORB can use shared memory for sending the client object's request when both the client and server are multithreaded. If the server object is on a remote machine, a TCP/IP connection is used for the client request. The ORB again creates a proxy object for the client use. If the server object is in the same process as the client, then the ORB uses a pointer to the object implementation. The client then directly invokes the methods on the object implementation.

IOR

Interoperable Object References (IOR) is used to invoke methods on an object in another ORB. An IOR is also used by a client object to invoke a method on a remote server object. It is an essential component, along with IIOP, for providing location-independent, standardized communication between different ORBs. Unlike object references that are specific to an ORB, IOR is intended to provide interoperability between different vendors and ORBs and, therefore, has a standardized format. Netscape uses IOR for the objects that are registered with its Naming Service.

For your programming purposes, there is no difference between an object reference and IOR. You get an IOR in the same way that you get an object reference.

An ORB uses the IOR to locate the remote object and create a local proxy for the object. It then uses IIOP to access the remote object and make any method calls on that object. An IOR contains a type ID, the protocol ID (which should be IIOP, ID zero), and other specific information about the object. The IOR includes a profile that lets other ORBs know how to use it. An IIOP profile is used to enable an ORB to tell another ORB how to use the IOR properly. You can think of IOR as a resource locator, as it points to the location of the object. IOR has the necessary information to route your object's request to the appropriate object.

If the object implementation that your object needs to reference is implemented in the same way (by the same vendor) as your client, then you can use a simple ORB method to obtain the object reference, for example, **resolve_initial_references**. **resolve_initial_references** is vendor-specific. If you want to obtain an object reference for an object by another vendor, however, you must take a different approach. A Naming Service from your vendor may be able to obtain the IOR of the object you need. Otherwise, you must obtain the stringified object reference of the server object and convert it to an IOR by calling the ORB method **string_to_object**. The **string_to_object** method should be supported by all vendors that support IIOP. To access a stringified object reference, the server object's constructor must implement the procedure. ISB provides an ORB class that supports **object_to_string**.

It is common to have the stringified IOR saved in a file that a client can access. Thus the client can find an object implementation without a Naming Service. Once the client gets the stringified IOR, it can call **string_to_object** and **narrow** to get the object implementation's object reference. Narrowing converts a general supertype object reference to a more specific subtype. **narrow** turns an object reference of type CORBA Object to the specific type of object you need. It is called when multiple CORBA interfaces are implemented and results in a valid object reference. An example of an IOR file can be found in your system under /wai/NameService/—for example, https-<*server name*>.IOR. This file includes the IOR of your server. The following string is an example of the IOR found in such a file. (Here, the IOR line, normally a single line in the file, is wrapped for typesetting purposes.) The data following the text, IOR:, is the Hexadecimal stringified IOR that can be converted to an object reference.

```
IOR:01202020280000049444c3a6f6d672e6f72672f436f734e616d69
6e672f4e616d696e67436f6e746578743a312e300001000000000000
61000000010100200a0000003132372e302e302e31003a0f4900000001
504d43000000001900000000436f734e616d696e673a3a4e616d696e6743
6f6e746578740020202010000068747470732d6e74343030303030
303030068747470732d6e743400
```

CORBA Services and the Naming Service

CORBA also includes a number of standard specifications for additionally needed services. These services are beyond the services provided by a typical CORBA object that you may write—that is, your server object's object implementation. These low-level services are intended for all kinds of object communication. Some of these services include Event Service, Trading Service, Naming Service, and so on. Various vendors that provide CORBA ORBs and tools, such as Visigenic, also provide several of these service packages based on CORBA standards. These services are implemented as CORBA interfaces. (The actual implementation may also include proprietary features.)

These low-level services are an essential part of a CORBA implementation. Let us look at one of the critical CORBA services, Naming Service. CORBA Naming Service allows CORBA clients to locate another CORBA object by its name. It identifies an object and its service to other objects. It maps the CORBA object reference to a simple, unique name. This procedure is termed "binding an object." Getting an object reference that is bound to a name is known as "resolving the name." The server object and Naming Service determine what the name of the object will be. Naming Service is the mechanism that allows a client object to locate another object without knowing the specific location of the server object.

Normally, when a service starts, a new object reference is created. Moreover, although you can access the information in an object reference, the object reference itself is opaque and concealed. To provide a persistent and more readable object identifier, Naming Service is used.

The CORBA standard Naming Service (CosNaming module) includes two CORBA interfaces, one for the name context (NamingContext) and another for the binding iterator (BindingIterator). For an example of such a module, see cosnaming.idl under <server path>/wai/idl directory. NamingContext provides the interface for creating Name and binding Name with an object reference. NamingContext is used to resolve Name and returns an object reference. With NamingContext you can have full access to CosNaming module. Name is a sequence of NameComponent values. With the Netscape ORB, a forward slash (/), is used to separate components (similar to the use of the forward slash by UNIX file systems). (Some parts of the CosNaming specifications are left to the vendors.) Contexts organize the names in a hierarchical structure, like a file directory, with subcontexts. If a name has more than one component (which they usually do), the first component is resolved first to a subcontext and the rest of the name is sent to the subcontext to be resolved. Once there are no remaining components, the object reference is returned. You can also use NamingContext to bind to another NamingContext or to create a new NamingContext. Interface BindingIterator is used to iterate across the object references contained in a NamingContext. It allows you to go through the list of named object references. You can also retrieve the named object references. Similar to the process with other CORBA server objects, you can access a NamingContext or BindingIterator through its object reference.

There are specific NamingContext methods for obtaining an object reference and adding or removing a Name. For instance, after you get an object reference to a NamingContext, your object implementation can call the method **bind** of NamingContext to pass on an object reference and a Name for an object to be placed in the NamingContext. The client can call the method **resolve** (another NamingContext method) of a NamingContext with a named object implementation to get the object reference. You can also use the method **unbind** to unbind an existing service. With **unbind**, you can unregister an object that is registered with the Naming Service.

Different vendors also provide specific Naming Services and methods that support easy binding and resolving of an object. They provide specific mechanisms for naming and binding an object, managing the object reference and their object identifier, and locating an object. For example, the **_bind** method used with the Netscape 3.0 C++ ISB is specific to Visigenic. It is different from the **bind** method of `NamingContext`.

Netscape Naming Service

Netscape Server 3.x includes a built-in Web Naming Service for Java. Servers 3.01 and 3.5.x also include a Naming Service for C++. The Web Naming Service is unique to Netscape Server. (We will also refer to this Web Naming Service as Netscape Naming Service.) Netscape provides this Naming Service in place of the Visigenic Gatekeeper as osagent. Enterprise Server 3.0, however, does use the Visigenic osagent to resolve and locate a server object. (osagent is a program included with Server 3.0 that provides Naming Service support. See Appendix F for more details.) Enterprise Server versions 3.01 and later no longer include osagent. Instead, you should use the Netscape Naming Services for C++ and Java.

Web Naming Service allows an HTTP URL to be associated with an object. Thus a client can locate a CORBA object and get its object reference using a specified URL. The client object uses the URL path of an object implementation, which is registered with Naming Service, to get its object reference. The server object, in turn, uses the URL of Netscape Naming Service to register the object implementation with Naming Service. The use of URL integrates Netscape Server and your server or client objects. Your objects need Netscape Server to register and locate objects. As you might expect from a Web server, Netscape Server uses the HTTP URL of the client request to locate the requested resource. The use of the URL with server or client objects provides a similar kind of support for CORBA objects. HTTP and URL can be used for registering, identifying, and locating objects. A Web browser may also be used to locate and invoke a server object using the URL. For an example of using a URL to locate a CORBA server, see the WAI implementation discussed in Chapters 13–16. Web Naming Service uses a one-to-one association between the URL and the object reference.

If SSL is enabled, you do not use the URL. Instead, you need to use the file indicator (protocol) and the name or path of the Netscape Server IOR file. You can find the server IOR file in the `NameService` directory under the `wai` directory, `<server path>/wai/NameService/`. The file name begins with the server ID and includes the extension `IOR`—for example, `https-foo.IOR`. The server object uses the IOR file location that you provide, plus the environment variable that you may need to set, to locate the IOR file of Netscape Server. It then uses the IOR information in the file to get the object reference for Naming Service and register its object implementation with Naming Service. For more information on the use of file indicator for SSL enabled servers, see Tables 12-1 and 12-2 later in this chapter.

In the following two sections, we will discuss the various C++ and Java methods you can use to register a CORBA service with Netscape Naming Service and get the service's object reference from Naming Service. (In Chapter 13, we will also discuss the settings for IIOP and the Naming Service in the **obj.conf** file under the section Enabling WAI on the Server.)

C++ Naming Service

To use the C++ Naming Service, you should include the `NameUtil.hpp` header file in your server or client application code. C++ Naming Service functions are used for both WAI and the general CORBA servers and client objects. `NameUtil.hpp` includes functions useful for your CORBA application, such as **registerObject** and **resolveURI**. The method **registerObject** registers your object implementation. You use the **resolveURI** function to get the object reference for an object implementation. There are also specific functions for WAI applications, such as **registerWAS** and **resolveWAS**. Methods that include **WAS** as part of their name are defined specifically for WAI applications, which are called Web Application Services (WAS). **putObject** and **putContext** are for internal use. Do not call these functions directly.

As with the **register** and **resolve** methods for Java, **registerObject** and **resolveURI** use a URL to locate and register the object implementation. Netscape's predefined path for Naming Service is `/NameService`. This path is also declared in the `obj.conf` file for the purpose of locating and getting the object reference of Netscape Naming Service and other CORBA objects. For example, for the client to get the object reference for `guest`, it uses a path similar to the following: `http://<server name>[:port]/NameService/guest`. In this path, `guest` is the name of the object implementation as defined by **registerObject**. The WAS path also comes under the `/NameService` path. `/NameService/WAS` is used for WAS (WAI applications).

registerWAS and **resolveWAS** enable CORBA applications to take advantage of WAI. For example, a CORBA client object can use **resolveWAS** to get the object reference for a WAI application. Although you can use these Naming Service functions when writing a WAI application (WAS), you normally do not use these functions directly in your WAI program. Instead, you use **registerService** to register your WAI application. Because your WAS is a server application, you normally do not have a use for **resolveWAS**. Instead, the client typically invokes your WAI application with a browser using the URL for your WAI application.

The Naming Service functions are of type DLLEXPORT. DLLEXPORT defines the Naming Service functions as type _declspec(dllexport) for Windows. The return value type for **registerObject** and **resolveURI** is WAIReturnType_t. The return value is WAISPISuccess when **registerObject** or **resolveURI** is successful in accomplishing its task, and WAISPIFailure upon failure. It is especially important to check whether the object implementation was able to register properly with the Naming Service. If a server object failed to register, no client can access its methods. The return value for the **registerWAS** function is of type WAIBool. **registerWAS** returns WAI_TRUE when successful and WAI_FALSE upon failure to register successfully.

Table 12-1 lists the appropriate Naming Service methods for C++. When you read these methods, make a special note of the unique steps for registering an object implementation when registering with an SSL-enabled server. For example, if SSL is enabled, you should specify file:<*server IOR file*> instead of <*server name*>[:*port*] for the host parameter of **registerObject** or **registerWAS**.

Table 12-1　C++ Naming Service Functions

FUNCTION PROTOTYPE	DESCRIPTION
	FOR NETSCAPE ISB APPLICATIONS

`WAIReturnType_t DLLEXPORT`
`registerObject(const char *host, const char *object_name,`
`CORBA::Object_ptr obj);`
	Registers the object implementation (obj) with Netscape Naming Service. You should use this function when you write a server application (object implementation) using Netscape ISB. The host parameter should be used for the host name and the port address of Netscape Server when SSL is not used. If SSL is enabled, you should use the file indicator and the location of the server IOR file—for example, file:<*server IOR file*>. If the server root and server ID are different from the default setting, you should specify the environment variables NS_SERVER_ROOT and NS_SERVER_ID. These variables should be accessible to your application. Note that once you specify these environment variables, the object may register using this information independent of what you specify in the host parameter. Netscape documentation uses the name url for the second parameter of the **registerObject** function. url is actually an incorrect name for the second parameter of the **registerObject** function; what you need to specify is a unique object name for your object implementation. This name does not have to be the same as the name of your object implementation (obj). You can specify any name you wish as long as no other object implementation uses the same name. Your object implementation will use this instance name when registering with Naming Service. Naming Service registers your object with the name you specify here. The client uses this name in the URI path for your object implementation. obj should be used for your object implementation. It is the actual object you wish to register. **registerObject** generates the appropriate URL for registering the object implementation. The URL will be http://<*host (server name:port)*>/NameService. /NameService is the path for Netscape Naming Service. **registerObject** gets the object reference for Naming

Table 12-1 C++ Naming Service Functions (*continued*)

FUNCTION PROTOTYPE	DESCRIPTION

Service and registers your object implementation with it. The URL associated with your object will be `http://<host (server name:port)>/NameService/<object_name>`.

registerObject returns `WAISPISuccess` if the registration was successful, and `WAISPIFailure` upon failure. You can verify the return value to make sure the object implementation was properly registered. If the registration failed, the client object will be unable to get the object reference of your object implementation.

(See also **registerWAS** below.)

Warning ▶

Do not use a URI path for the second parameter of **registerObject**. Specify a name for your object implementation instead.

```
WAIReturnType_t DLLEXPORT
resolveURI(const char *host, int port, const char *uri,
CORBA::Object_ptr& obj);
```

Gets the object reference for the object implementation identified in `uri`. You should use this function with your client application (client object) to obtain the object reference of an object implementation. `host` and `port` are for the Netscape Server host name and port address. `uri` should point to the Naming Service path for the object implementation.

If SSL is enabled and file protocol is used, you can set `host` to an empty string, `" "`, and `port` to 0. If the server root and server ID are different from the default setting, you should specify the environment variables `NS_SERVER_ROOT` and `NS_SERVER_ID`.

`uri` should include both the partial path for Naming Service, `/NameService`, and the instance name of the object implementation as identified by the **registerObject** function. **resolveURI** creates a URL from the `host`, `port`, and `uri` information—for example, `http://<host (server name:port)>/NameService/<object_name>`. It then locates Naming Service and requests the object reference.

resolveURI returns the object reference through the `obj` parameter. You should have already declared a variable of `CORBA:Object_ptr` for this parameter based on the interface implementation class you wrote.

resolveURI returns `WAISPISuccess` if the object reference was retrieved, and `WAISPIFailure` upon failure. You can verify the return value to make sure the object reference was successfully obtained.

You normally follow **resolveURI** with a narrow method (**_narrow**) to narrow the object reference returned by **resolveURI** to the exact object reference you need.

(See also **resolveWAS** below.)

```
WAIBool DLLEXPORT
registerWAS(const char *host, const char *object_name, CORBA::Object_ptr obj);
```

Registers the `obj` (object implementation) with the Naming Service. You can use this function to register a WAS (WAI application) with Netscape

Table 12-1 C++ Naming Service Functions (*continued*)

FUNCTION PROTOTYPE   DESCRIPTION

Naming Service. (Normally, to register a WAI application, you use **registerService**, not **registerWAS.** We will discuss **registerService** in Chapter 14.)

`host` should include the host name and port number of Netscape Server. `object_name` registers the name of the object implementation. You can specify any name you like for the object implementation as long as no other object implementation uses the same name. This name does not have to be the same as `obj` (the object implementation). **registerWAS** registers the object implementation using the path of WAS for Netscape Naming Service— that is, `http://<host (server name:port)>/NameService/WAS`. The URL associated with the WAS will be `http://<host (server name:port)>/NameService/WAS/<object_name>`. The function returns `WAI_TRUE` upon successful registration and `WAI_FAILURE` upon failure.

If SSL is used for Netscape Server, **registerWAS** needs to access the IOR file of Netscape Server instead of using HTTP URL. Instead of using the Netscape Server host name and port address, specify a file indicator with the location of the IOR file name of your server, `file:<server IOR file>`. **registerWAS** also uses the default server root and server ID of Netscape Server to locate the file. If this information is other than the default value, you should set an environment variable for the server root, `NS_SERVER_ROOT`, and/or server ID, `NS_SERVER_ID`. The environment variables should be accessible to your application. Note that once you specify these environment variables, the application may register using this information independent of what you specify in the `host` parameter.

(See also **registerObject** above.)

```
CORBA::Object_ptr DLLEXPORT resolveWAS (const char
*object_name);
```
Once a WAS is registered with the server, **resolveWAS** gets the object reference for the WAS object implementation. With **resolveWAS**, you specify only the name of the object implementation, `object_name`. The server should already have adequate information to create the appropriate URL for the object implementation—that is, `http://<host (server name:port)>/NameService/WAS/<object_name>`. **resolveWAS** returns the object reference for the object implementation.

(See also **resolveURI** above.)

FOR INTERNAL USE BY THE SERVER

```
WAIBool DLLEXPORT putObject (const char *url, CORBA::Object_ptr obj, WAIBool
create_intermediate_nodes=WAI_FALSE);
```
This method is for the internal use of the server. Do not call this method.

```
WAIBool DLLEXPORT putContext (const char *url, WAIBool
create_intermediate_nodes=WAI_FALSE);
```
This method is for the internal use of the server. Do not call this method.

Java Naming Service   Netscape provides two separate Java Naming Service classes: `netscape.WAI.Naming` and `netscape.WAI.NameUtil`. Both classes provide specific functions for registering an object with Netscape Naming Service and retrieving the object's object reference.

netscape.WAI.Naming include two public static methods: **register** and **resolve**. netscape.WAI.Naming is included with both Netscape Server (`<server path>/WAI/java/nisb.zip`) and Netscape Communicator (`<communicator path>/Program/Java/Classes/iiop10.jar`). **register** registers an object implementation with the server. **resolve** obtains the object implementation's object reference. When you register an object, you specify a URL for the object implementation. The URL must include the host name of Netscape Server, as well as a port number if the port is different from the standard HTTP port. You also need to specify the name of the object implementation. For Server 3.0 and the Communicator ORB, you must include a path for the location of IOR file as well. For Server 3.01 and later, you include only the name of the object implementation. The client, in turn, uses the method **resolve** and the URL of the object implementation. The URL should be the same URL used with the **register** method. **resolve** connects to Netscape Naming Service. Netscape Naming Service resolves the client's requested URL and returns the object reference. This procedure does not require osagent, even under Server 3.0.

As mentioned earlier, under Server 3.0 and with the Communicator ORB, you need to specify a specific path for the URL location of the object reference when using the **register** method. Server 3.0 and Communicator use the HTTP PUT method to place the object reference (IOR) of the object implementation at the specified location. You also need to set the appropriate access privileges with the server for the directory where the IOR is saved. The server object needs to be able to save the file in the specified location. For Server 3.0, this path is usually `/iiop_objects`. For example, for the object implementation `guest`, you may use the following URL: `http://foo/iiop_objects/guest`. With Communicator ORB, you use `/NameService`, that is, `http://foo/NameService/guest`. The directory `NameService` is the default location of Netscape Naming Service files. It is also where you find the IOR of the services that register with Netscape Naming Service for Server 3.01 and later. The actual location of the server object can be anywhere, as long as it can reach the Netscape Server and the Netscape Server can also access it.

Under Server 3.01 and later, the server uses the default `/NameService` path for the location of the IOR. When you use **register** or **resolve** functions, however, you should not include `/NameService` as part of the URL path. The server automatically adds this string to the path immediately after the host name (and port) information. In other words, if you specify the URL `http://foo/hello` when registering your object, the **register** function registers your object implementation using the following path: `http://foo/NameService/hello`. This case also arises with **resolve**. Note that you still need to use `/NameService` in the URL when using these methods with the Communicator ORB.

netscape.WAI.NameUtil is included only with Netscape Server (`<server path>/WAI/java/WAI.zip`). The netscape.WAI.NameUtil class includes an alternative method for registering and resolving object implementations. Instead of using **register** and **resolve**, you can use **registerObject** and **resolveURI**. As with the **register** method for Server 3.01 and later, **registerObject** uses the Naming Service path for the object (that is, `/NameService`). You specify the server host name and port information, plus a specific name for the object implementation. **registerObject** generates the appropriate URL to register your service with Naming Service. The object is then associated with the URL path for Naming Service (that is, `http://<server name>[:port]/NameService/<object_name>`).

resolveURI returns the object reference for the server object implementation. Unique to **resolveURI** is the parameter `protocol`. As with C++ Naming Service functions, when SSL is enabled, use the `file` protocol instead of the `http` protocol. During registration, use the `file` indicator and the location of the server IOR file. Specify `file:<location of IOR file>` instead of `<host name>[:port]` for the `host` parameter of **registerWAS**. Note that with Java you use the location of the IOR file, not the name of the file and environment variables.

There is also a specific function for registering a WAS in the `NameUtil` class. **registerWAS** functions closely resemble **registerURI**, except for the fact that the default path generated includes `/NameService/WAS` instead of `/NameService`. The object is also associated with the path for WAS—that is, `/NameService/WAS`.

Although you can use **registerWAS** to register WAI applications (WAS objects), you normally do not employ this method. Instead, you use the WAI method **registerService**. The **registerWAS** and **resolveURI** methods can be used by other CORBA implementations to take advantage of WAI applications. We will discuss **registerService** and the procedure for registering a WAI application in Chapters 14 and 15.

Finally, `NameUtil` includes two additional methods for direct access to CosNaming's `NamingContext`: **getRootNaming** and **NameFromString**. If you plan to use `NamingContext` and its methods, you can use **getRootNaming** to get the `NamingContext` object of the server.

Table 12-2 lists and describes the different Naming Service methods of Java.

Table 12-2   Java Naming Service Methods

METHOD PROTOTYPE	DESCRIPTION
NETSCAPE.WAI.NAMING	
`public static void register(String url, org.omg.CORBA.object obj);`	Registers the object implementation (`obj`) with Netscape Naming Service. The URL you associate with the object implementation in `url` is used by the **resolve** method to get the object reference for the object implementation. `url` should include the host name (and port number if it is different from the default HTTP port address) of Netscape Server and a unique name for the object implementation—that is, `http://<server name>[:port]/[path]/<object_name>`. For Server 3.0, `path` can be an arbitrary path. If the server object has more than one object implementation, then you can use `path` to organize the objects under the same umbrella directory. For Server 3.01 and 3.5.x, you should not include a directory path in the URL. **register** automatically adds the path `/NameService` to the URL after the host name (and port). You can choose any name you wish for `object_name` as long as no other object implementation uses the same name. This method throws a `SystemException` exception. (See also **registerObject** below.)

Table 12-2   Java Naming Service Methods (*continued*)

METHOD PROTOTYPE	DESCRIPTION

NETSCAPE.WAI.NAMING

`public static org.omg.CORBA.Object resolve(String url);`

Gets the object reference for the object specified in `url`. `url` should be the same URL used with the **register** method. As with the **register** method, you should not include `/NameService` in the URL path for Server 3.01 or 3.5.x. **resolve** automatically adds this string to the path in the URL. This method also throws a `SystemException` exception.

You normally follow **resolve** with a narrow method (**narrow**) to narrow the object reference returned by **resolve** to the exact object reference you need. (See also **resolveURI** below.)

NETSCAPE.WAI.NAMEUTIL

`public static CosNaming.NamingContext getRootNaming(String host, int port);`

Gets the object reference for the `NamingContext` object of Netscape Server. `host` is for the host name of the Netscape Server machine. `port` is for the port address of Netscape Server. Use this function if you want to use `NamingContext` to access the object references that are registered with the server. This method throws a `SystemException` exception.

`public static CosNaming.NameHolder NameFromString(String s, String sepchar);`

Converts the string specified in `s` to a `NameComponent` list. **NameFromString** returns a list of name components. `sepchar` specifies the character that separates the components. Normally, this character is a forward slash (`/`). This method throws a `SystemException` exception.

`public static boolean registerObject(String host, String object_name, org.omg.CORBA.Object obj);`

You can use this function instead of **register** to register a server object (object implementation) with Naming Service. The `host` parameter should be used for the host name (server name) and the port address of Netscape Server when SSL is not used. If SSL is enabled, you should use the `file` indicator and the location of the server IOR file—for example, `file:<location of IOR file>`.

`object_name` is a unique name for your object implementation. It does not have to be the same as the name of your object implementation (`obj`). You can specify any name you wish as long as no other object implementation uses the same name. Your object implementation uses this instance name when registering with Naming Service. Naming Service registers your object with the name you specify here. The client uses this name in the URI path for your object implementation.

`obj` should be used for your object implementation. It is the actual object you wish to register.

registerObject generates the appropriate URL for registering the object implementation. The URL for Naming Service will be `http://<host (server name:port)>/NameService`. **registerObject** gets the object reference for Naming Service and registers your object implementation with it. The URL associated with your object will be `http://<host (server name:port)>/NameService/<object_name>`.

The function returns `true` if the method was successful in registering the object, or `false` upon failure. Check the return value to make sure the function was properly registered. **registerObject** throws the following exception:

```
CosNaming.NamingContextPackage.NotFound
CosNaming.NamingContextPackage.CannotProceed
CosNaming.NamingContextPackage.InvalidName
org.omg.CORBA.SystemException
java.lang.Exception
```

Table 12-2   Java Naming Service Methods (*continued*)

METHOD PROTOTYPE	DESCRIPTION
	NETSCAPE.WAI.NAMEUTIL

```
public static org.omg.CORBA.Object resolveURI(String protocol,
String host, int port, String uri);
```

You can use this function instead of **resolve** to get the object reference for an object implementation. `host` and `port` are for the Netscape Server host name and port address. `uri` should point to the Naming Service path for the object implementation. If SSL is enabled and file protocol is used, you can set `host` to an empty string, `" "`, and `port` to 0. **resolveURI** returns the object reference.

uri should include both the partial path for Naming Service, `/NameService`, and the instance name of the object implementation as identified by the **registerObject** function. **resolveURI** creates a URL from the `host`, `port`, and `uri` information—for example, `http://<host (server name:port)>/NameService/<object_name>`. It then locates Naming Service and requests the object reference.

This function throws a `SystemException` exception.

(See also **resolve** above.)

```
public static boolean registerWAS(String host,
String object_name, org.omg.CORBA.Object obj);
```

Registers a WAS with Netscape Server. `host` should include the host name and port number of Netscape Server. If SSL is used for Netscape Server, **registerWAS** needs to access the IOR file of Netscape Server instead of using the HTTP URL. Instead of using Netscape Server's host name and port address, you should specify a `file` indicator with the location of the IOR file of your server, `file:<location of IOR file>`. Use `object_name` to specify a specific instance name for the WAS object. The name can be any name that you wish as long as no other WAS object implementation uses the same name. The `obj` parameter is used for the actual object implementation that should be registered.

This function generates the appropriate URL of WAS for Netscape Naming Service based on the parameters you set—that is, `http://<host (server name:port)>/NameService/WAS`. The URL associated with the WAS will be `http://<host (server name:port)>/NameService/WAS/<object_name>`. The function returns `true` if the method was successful in registering the object, or `false` upon failure. Check the return value to make sure the function was properly registered. This function throws the following exceptions:

```
CosNaming.NamingContextPackage.NotFound
CosNaming.NamingContextPackage.CannotProceed
CosNaming.NamingContextPackage.InvalidName
org.omg.CORBA.SystemException
```

(See also **registerObject** above.)

Object Adapter and BOA

The Object Adapter allows your server object to interact with the ORB. It serves as the adapter between the server object and the ORB. The server object uses the Object Adapter to access the ORB. The ORB uses the Object Adapter to manage the runtime environment of the object implementation. There can be different Object Adapters for different implementations. Currently, CORBA includes only one standard interface for an Object Adapter, Basic Object Adapter (BOA). BOA is used by the server object to initialize the object, generate an object reference, activate and deactivate the server object, and wait for incoming requests. BOA generates and interprets the object reference. It also activates and deactivates the object implementations and individual objects. The interface between BOA and ORB is a proprietary interface. The support for BOA is built into the Netscape ISB.

The object implementation uses BOA to tell the ORB that it is ready to be used. After an object implementation (ORB object) is instantiated in the server process, BOA is notified (**BOA_init**). BOA is also notified when the object is activated and ready to receive request from client objects (through the BOA methods **object_is_ready** and **imp_is_ready**). **imp_is_ready** readies the implementation of the request dispatch loop. This dispatch loop is similar to an event loop. It keeps the application alive, waiting for client requests and method invocations.

There are four BOA activation policies for a CORBA server: shared server, unshared server, persistent server, and per-method server. These activation policies define how objects are created in the server process. BOA makes sure these activation policies are enforced. BOA activation policies are used only during the creation of the object. They do not specify anything about the actual connection between the client and the server.

As mentioned earlier, there are two types of server objects: transient and persistent. A transient object lasts only for the duration of the server's process. It does not register itself with the osagent, Naming Service, or OAD (ORBeline Activation Daemon or Object Activation Daemon). Therefore, only objects that have access to its transient object reference can call its method. A persistent object stays alive even after the server process that created it terminates. It has a global scope and its object reference stays available beyond the server life. Persistent objects are used for long-term services.

OAD

Object Activation Daemon (OAD) can also be used (with the ISB for C++) to register a persistent server object. OAD provides the automatic activation of an object implementation. You can use OAD to have a server object automatically start instead of starting it manually.

OAD is implemented as a CORBA object. You can find an Interface Definition Language (IDL) interface for object activation under the `<server path>/wai/idl` directory, `oad.idl`. The `oad.idl` file includes the definition for the `Activation` module and the `OAD` interface. You can write your program in such a way that it uses the `OAD` interface. The `OAD` interface is used by BOA to register the object reference of a server object upon activation. It is also used by the ORB to locate a server object.

The Netscape ISB also includes an OAD program (ORBeline Activation Daemon) that you can use, `oad.exe`. `oad.exe`, a Visigenic product, can be found under `<server path>/wai/bin`. You can register an object with OAD through command-line arguments (for UNIX systems) or through the menu register (for Windows systems) of `regobj.exe`. OAD automatically starts the server objects that are registered with it. `regobj.exe` registers the objects with OAD. You can find `regobj.exe` under the `/wai/bin` directory. `oad.exe` should already be running before you use `regobj.exe` to register a server object. To register an object implementation, you must specify all necessary information for the object implementation—that is, the interface name (the object's IDL interface name), object name (a name for the object implementation), path to the file (the location of the server object), and activation policy. The default activation policy is a shared server, which means that multiple objects of the same object implementation share the same server. For WAI applications, use an asterisk (*) for the interface name of the server object. You can also specify additional arguments, environment variables, and reference data. `regobj.exe` is a console application under UNIX and a Windows application under the Windows system. For more information on `regobj.exe` and its argument or menu options, see *Netscape Internet Service Broker for C++ Reference Guide.*

Another way of registering and unregistering an object with OAD is through programming, using methods such as `BOA::create`. Objects registered by OAD are automatically activated when a client requests to bind with them. A client object can also directly bind with OAD and verify the status of the registered objects using the OAD object's interface. You also must use the `CreationImplDef` class, derived from the `ImplementationDef` class, when setting the necessary information for OAD. You set the properties `_path_name`, `_policy`, `_args`, and `_env`, which are similar to the information that you must specify when using `regobj.exe`. OAD uses this information to activate the ORB object. You use `BOA::deactivate_impl` to deactivate an object implementation that was started by OAD.

Objects registered with OAD are stored in an implementation repository that OAD maintains (Figure 12-3). The information from the implementation repository is kept in a file named `impl_rep`. This file can be found under the `orb` directory—for example, under `/user/local/isb/adm/impl_dir/` or `c:/orb20/admin/impl_dir`.

With Server 3.0, you use OAD in conjunction with osagent. Usually, a client request is first made to the osagent by the ORB. If an ORB requests an object that is registered with OAD, osagent returns OAD's address. The ORB then connects to

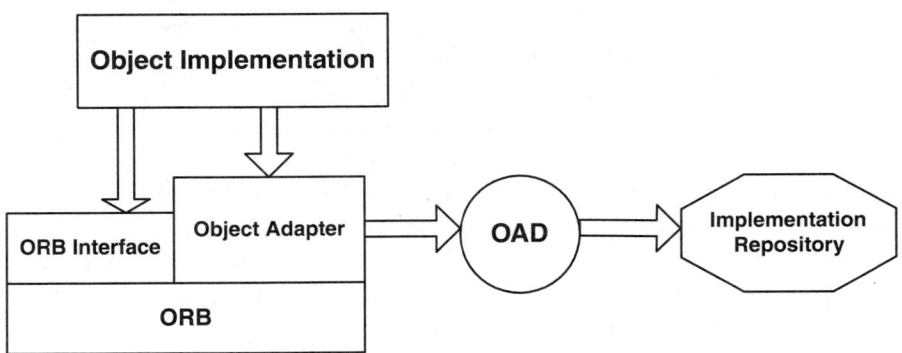

Figure 12-3   Registering an Object with OAD

OAD to obtain the object reference. Beside objects registered with osagent, osagent also keeps a list of objects registered with OAD.

You can also use OAD with Enterprise Server 3.01 and later. Netscape Naming Service, which comes with Server 3.01 and 3.5.x, also supports OAD. To use OAD, you must specify a number of environment variables, including NS_SERVER_ROOT, NS_SERVER_ID, ORBELINE_IMPL_NAME, ORBELINE_IMPL_PATH, and LD_LIBRARY_PATH. These variables should be available to Netscape Server and the OAD application:

- NS_SERVER_ROOT—Location of the root directory of the Netscape Servers (for example, c:/netscape/server).

- NS_SERVER_ID—Server ID (for example, https-foo).

- ORBELINE_IMPL_NAME—Name of the OAD utility file (for example, oadfiles). OAD creates a file to track object implementations.

- ORBELINE_IMPL_PATH—The path where OAD will create the OAD utility file for tracking the object implementations (for example, /tmp). This directory needs to exist and be accessible to the OAD. (See also ORBELINE_IMPL_NAME.)

- LD_LIBRARY_PATH (or SHLIB_PATH for HP-UX and LIBPATH for AIX)— Location of the shared library or DLL files that the server object needs (for example, c:\netscape\server\wai\lib;c:\netscape\server\bin\https; c:\netscape\server\lib;c:\netscape\server\wai\java).

Before registering your server object with OAD, first have the object implementation register itself with Naming Service.

IDL

Interface Definition Language (IDL) is the CORBA definition language used to define the interface for the CORBA client and server objects. This interface describes the specifications of the object and its implementation methods. It describes the services that the server object provides and the client object requests. The IDL interface of each object informs other objects of which services it provides, how to use these services, and what results the services will produce. An interface describes the methods of an object implementation and its calling conventions, without asserting how those methods are actually implemented. IDL resembles C or C++, but is its own separate language. An interface defined in IDL looks very similar to a C++ class definition. IDL is used to define (describe) the object's interface, not to program an application. None of the actual programming algorithm is included in the IDL file. A definition language, IDL describes an interface, not an implementation. If you are familiar with Java, you should know what an interface is. Although the IDL interface is different from a Java interface, it provides the same functionality. It describes which services (methods) an object (class) should provide (implement). It does not specify how an object (class) should implement the service. An interface, similar to an API, hides the implementation from the objects that use it. Therefore, different implementations can be developed, or the internal working of the implementation can change, without the need to redefine the object and its services. The IDL interface is independent of the actual programming language of the CORBA object. There are a number of different implementations of IDL for different programming languages.

Enterprise Server includes a number of CORBA IDL modules for its CORBA services and implementation. A module contains one or more interfaces. (An IDL module is similar to Java package.) A module groups interfaces together. You can also have one module inside another. For example, `Employees::Managers` identifies the module `Managers` inside the module `Employees`. You can find the Server's IDL modules in IDL files under the IDL directory, `<server path>/wai/idl`. An IDL file has the extension `.idl`. These files include IDLs for the Naming Service, OAD, Interface Repository, and WAI. Netscape WAI, for instance, is defined as a set of IDL interfaces. The WAI interface defines the methods for getting HTTP request-headers, client input, and server information, as well as methods for returning a response. WAI IDL and its Netscape implementation make the writing of CORBA applications easy for processing client HTTP request. They shield you from having to write the CORBA component (the IDL files and its implementation) from scratch. You can use the WAI-specific interface, and its classes and methods for Java and C++ or functions for C, to write your WAS without having to worry about how the actual CORBA component is defined and working.

In IDL, you declare the interface for your object and its name and methods. The methods include parameters that should be included when the interface is invoked. IDL exposes the object and its methods and services to other CORBA objects. By writing an IDL interface for an existing program, you can expose its services to other CORBA objects. An interface can also be inherited from another interface. The following `HttpServerContext` interface is defined in `server.idl` (you find `server.idl` under the IDL directory):

```
interface HttpServerContext {
        HttpServerReturnType getInfo(in string name,
                                     out string value);
        long getPort();
        string getName();
        string getHost();
        string getServerSoftware();
        boolean isSecure();
};
```

In IDL, as with C++, all variables must be declared before they are used. The interface definition specifies the name of the object and all its methods—for example, the `getName` method for the interface `HttpServerContext`. Types `long`, `string`, and `boolean` are examples of the generic IDL data types. For example, `name` is of the generic type `string`. `in`, `out`, and `inout` define the purpose of parameters (the type of the parameter). `in` is used for the input parameter. `out` is used for the output result. `inout` is used for a parameter that both is an input and holds the output. In the previous example, `name` is an input parameter and `value` holds the output.

`return` is used for the return value of an operation on an interface. `oneway` methods, on the other hand, have no return value.

An interface can also include an attribute, `attribute`. An attribute is, by default, read-write. The following is an example of an attribute:

`attribute string product.`

Beside interfaces and their methods, you can include data type definitions (`typedef`), data structures (`struct`), enumeration (`enum`), and constants. IDL includes the constructed types `enum`, `struct`, `union`, `sequence`, and `array`. The following example of an enum (`state`), struct (`ObjectStatus`), and `typedef sequence` (`ObjectStatusList`) from the `oad.idl` file is also found under the IDL directory:

```
enum State {
    ACTIVE,
    INACTIVE,
    WAITING_FOR_ACTIVATION
};

struct ObjectStatus {
    long      process_id;
    State     activation_state;
    Object    objRef;
};

typedef sequence<ObjectStatus> ObjectStatusList;
```

As with C, you can include other IDL files in your IDL file by adding an `include` directive—for example, `#include "trader.idl"`.

IDL Compiler

In order to use an IDL module or interface, you have to compile it. Netscape Enterprise Server 3.x includes IDL compilers for Java and C++. An IDL compiler provides two essential features. First, it generates the necessary CORBA component needed for your object to work with the CORBA ORB, BOA, and other CORBA objects. The IDL compiler generates much of the CORBA-specific part of the code. Second, an IDL compiler uses a predefined standard for language mapping to map a generic CORBA IDL into a specified programming language. Each IDL compiler can handle a specific programming language. So not only is much of the necessary code generated, but the code is also in the language of your preference. The generated files (CORBA objects and methods) can then be integrated with an existing program or used to write and integrate a new program with the generated CORBA components. The result will be a CORBA-compliant client and/or server object.

The IDL compiler helps you write both the client and the server CORBA objects. For example, you can write an IDL interface for an existing program and then compile it using the IDL compiler. You then integrate the components generated by the IDL compiler with your client and server programs, write a few additional lines of code, and recompile with your programming language compiler. The newly compiled programs will be the CORBA client and server applications. As mentioned earlier, Enterprise Server includes an IDL compiler for C++ and Java (`Orbeline` for C++ and `idl2java` for Java, both found in the `<server path>/wai/bin` directory). These compilers generate Java or C++ classes from the CORBA interfaces. They also convert the parameters and other generic IDL data types to the language-specific data types.

Besides the two IDL compilers mentioned previously, Netscape provides two additional unique IDL compilers for Java. `java2iiop`, the Caffeine compiler, allows Java-to-Java compiling. This compiler lets you work completely in Java. The compiler generates the IIOP-compliant CORBA client stub and server skeleton from the interfaces you defined in Java. (The client stub and server skeleton are essential components of IDL compilers that we will discuss shortly.)

Netscape also includes a Java-to-IDL compiler called `java2idl`. You can find `java2iiop` and `java2idl` in the `/wai/bin` directory.

To compile an IDL program, run the program as an argument for the IDL compiler. IDL compilers are console applications and can run from the command line. You can also include optional flags for an IDL compiler. Check the documentation for the appropriate flags you can use with the IDL compiler. The following line compiles the `hello.idl` file using the C++ IDL compiler:

```
[prompt]>Orbeline hello.idl
```

IDL and the IDL compiler are the key components of CORBA that allow objects written in different languages to communicate with one another. Using IDL for the objects, the CORBA objects can use each other's services through the ORBs. (You, of course, must take additional steps to generate the CORBA object.) You need to write the IDL interface only once. Different IDL compilers can compile IDL into different languages. If there is an IDL compiler for your preferred programming language, you can generate the CORBA components for that language. The IDL compiler allows you to write your program in the programming language of your choice. Thus you can write one IDL and provide different implementations. With Netscape Server, you use C++ and Java. You can compile your IDL program with the Netscape C++ or Java IDL compiler and write your implementation and CORBA client in C++ or Java. With WAI, you can also use C.

IDL and the IDL compiler allow you to integrate legacy code with your CORBA objects. You simply write an IDL interface for your program and compile your IDL file with the IDL compiler of your choice. The compiler writes the necessary code for the CORBA interface. It takes care of converting the generic language-neutral IDL code to your preferred programming language. It also generates the object reference for the classes (objects). You need to add only your specific implementation of the server object and then integrate it with the existing legacy application. You can also incorporate the generated IDL code for the client with your client application. The interface you define in IDL is the essential component that must be shared between the client and the server. It defines the object and methods that the client object wants to invoke and the server object needs to respond to the client. You write the implementation of the server object's services (methods) and the client-specific code in the designated programming language. You then recompile the code with the programming language compiler to generate the client and server application.

> **Warning ▶**
>
> With Enterprise Server 3.0, 3.01, and 3.5.x, you cannot use any preprocessor code in the Java IDL file. `idl2java` does not perform any preprocessing on the IDL file.

Language Mapping

Language mapping is the mechanism by which the IDL names, data types, and so on are mapped to the equivalent classes, data types, and declarations in the appropriate programming language. It is also the mechanism used by the IDL compiler to generate the language-specific code. The specifics of the standard language mapping for a number of popular programming languages, such as C++ and Java, are defined by OMG. The compilers use these specifications to support a standardized conversion of IDL to the programming language. For example, the IDL `octet` type (an 8-bit quantity) is converted to the ISB C++ type `CORBA::Octet`, which is equivalent to the C++ `unsigned char`. Under Java, `octet` is converted to the Java type `byte`.

Note, however, that language mapping is not an exact science. A data type may be platform-dependent or a specific IDL data type may not be supported by the programming language. The mapping might need additional steps to ensure that data are properly converted. You may also need to take special steps in your CORBA application to make sure that your data types are compatible with the standard set by the compiler and the Netscape ISB. For example, you should use the CORBA functions **string_alloc** and **string_free** to dynamically allocate a string. In general, when easy mapping is not available, the IDL compiler's language mapping attempts to provide alternative means or methods for achieving the appropriate mapping.

Language mapping is also important when a client makes a call to a server object that is written in a different language. The underlying ORB handles these transfers using the appropriate language mapping. When a language does not support a specific IDL data type, an alternative type or procedure is used by the generated IDL compiler files to handle the appropriate conversion and transfer. You also must use these methods when you write your CORBA application. For example, a Holder class is defined in Java to support the passing of parameters by reference and call-by-value methods. It supports the passing of `out` and `inout` parameters that cannot be directly mapped into Java.

To become more familiar with the language mapping of IDL to Java or to C++, you can review the relevant chapters, "IDL to Java Mapping" and "IDL to C++ Language Mapping," in the Netscape ISB programming books for Java and C++, respectively.

Steps of Writing a CORBA Client/Server Application

There are three main steps in writing a CORBA application. First, you write a CORBA IDL interface for the client and server applications. Next, you compile the IDL code using the IDL compiler. Finally, you write the client and server application using the files and data generated by the IDL compiler. The client and server applications do not need to be compiled by the same programming language compiler. For example, the server application can be developed using the C++ IDL compiler, while the client application can be developed using the Java compiler.

You can find a number of examples of CORBA applications with Netscape Enterprise Server under the `<server path>/wai/examples` directory. These examples include any necessary IDL files, plus the additional CORBA client and server implementation files, which you normally must write. In this section, the steps of writing a CORBA application are accompanied by a sample C++ Hello World example for Server 3.01 and later versions. A Java version of this example is included on the accompanying CD-ROM.

You can find the header files used for developing C++ CORBA applications under `<server path>/wai/library`. The Java classes can be found under the Java directory `<server path>/wai/java`.

Overview of Steps for Writing a CORBA Client/Server Application

Let us quickly outline the steps of writing a CORBA client/server application. This outline is a generalization of the procedure. The actual steps may vary based on your chosen language and the IDL compiler used. After this section, we will go through the steps in writing a C++ CORBA client/server application. Once the IDL compiler has generated the appropriate files, you may take two separate paths to generate the client and server applications. It is not necessary to generate a separate application for each client and server object. Client and server objects can be implemented inside the same application.

1. You must identify the object, methods, and method parameters of the server object that is also used by the CORBA-compliant client applications. You then write the interface for the server (client) object in the IDL language and save it, along with any additional IDL declaration, in an IDL file.

2. Choose a programming language to write your CORBA applications, and use the appropriate IDL compiler to compile the IDL file. This step will generate the server skeleton and client stub files, plus any number of additional important CORBA definition and implementation files. The result will be in the specific programming language of the IDL compiler. You will write the client and server applications in this programming language.

3. Write an implementation class (interface) to be used by your server application. This step provides the necessary abstraction—that is, the separation between implementation and interface. The implementation interface you define can be used by different applications. You must extend the skeleton class to write the server class.

4. Write a client application using the classes, methods, and other data types generated by the IDL compiler. Fill in the standard necessary steps needed to initiate the ORB, locate the server object, and so on. The client application uses the result returned by the server object to produce whatever response is expected from the client. You may also incorporate previously written applications with the client application. Thus, the result of the client CORBA application can be used by another application, or the CORBA application can use the result of another application.

5. Compile the client application using your programming language compiler. The compiler should be based on the IDL compiler and the programming language of your client.

6. Write a server application that takes advantage of the skeleton class and other files generated by the IDL compiler. You also use the implementation class that you wrote earlier. The server object needs to process the client request and return the results. Write the main server application function, register the server object, and take other necessary steps. By combining the server application with a legacy application, you can access the legacy data and make them available to any number of CORBA-compliant client applications.

7. Compile the server application using your programming language compiler.

8. Integrate the client and server applications with Enterprise Server 3.x or Netscape Communicator 4.x. For example, you can run a client CORBA-compliant Java applet in Communicator that talks to a CORBA server object on the Enterprise Server machine or to a server object on another remote machine. Alternatively, a CORBA application on the server side can run as a client to a CORBA server object on a remote machine. You can use IIOP as the communication protocol between the various server and client objects. Alternatively, you can complement an existing HTTP communication between Communicator and Enterprise Server with other CORBA client and server objects that use IIOP. There are a variety of options that you can explore. For instance, you can use JavaScript and LiveConnect to communicate with Java server or client objects on Enterprise Server or on a separate remote machine. Make sure you check for any security risks when implementing your CORBA client/server applications. In Chapter 13, we will briefly review some of the security issues of CORBA and WAI.

Figure 12-4 shows the great flexibility that CORBA and IIOP provide. Not only can you use HTTP and IIOP to provide communication between Enterprise Server and Netscape Communicator, you can also use IIOP between CORBA objects and Netscape Communicator. Enterprise Server can also use IIOP to communicate with CORBA objects that reside on a local or remote machine.

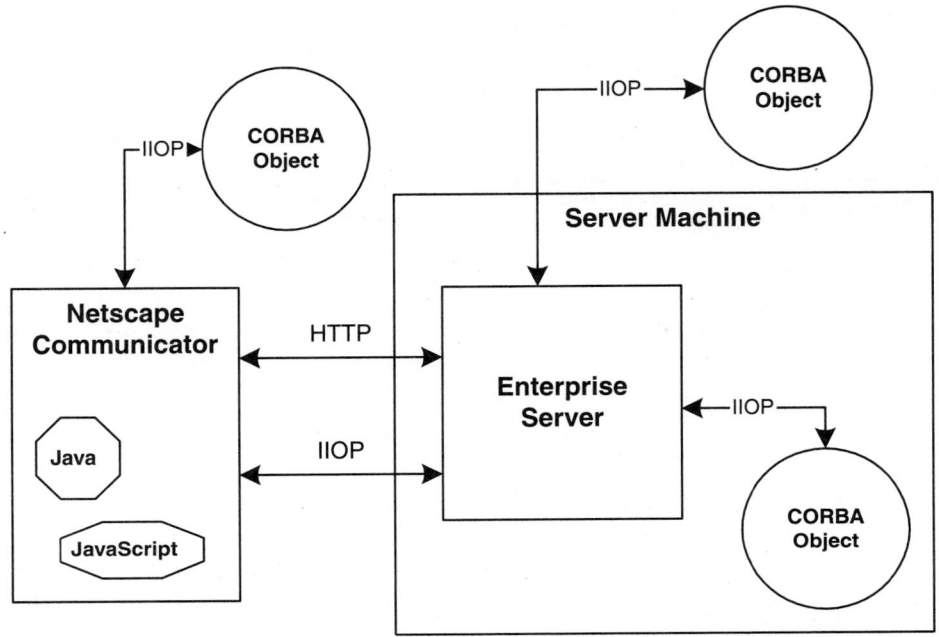

Figure 12-4   Uses of CORBA Objects with Enterprise Server and Communicator

Write a CORBA IDL Interface (Step 1)

Before you can write a CORBA client/server application, you must identify the object and methods that will be shared by (distributed or used by) the CORBA-compliant clients and the server application. In other words, you must delineate the interface and methods that any CORBA-compliant client application will use to access and obtain the correct response from the server. The interface and methods should also reflect the server object and its public methods needed by the client. In other words, the core of the server object should be defined as an interface in the CORBA IDL file. Each object must have an IDL interface. You write this IDL interface in the IDL language. (With Java, you may also write the interface in Java and use the `java2idl` program to generate the IDL file.) The IDL file should also include a definition of all necessary data to be passed between the client and the server application. These data should be defined in the IDL language as well.

The interface can include an interface to a previously existing application (legacy application). It can include the methods needed by the client for passing on the appropriate information to the server object. The server object, in turn, can get the necessary results from the legacy application by making a request based on the client request to the legacy application.

Once you have the IDL file, you can use the IDL compiler to generate language-specific code that you use to write the CORBA applications.

Listing 12-1 is an example of an IDL module for client and server Hello World applications.

Listing 12-1   IDL for the Hello World Example

```
module HelloWorld
{
   interface Hello
   {
      string Hi();
   };
};
```

Compile the IDL File with the Netscape IDL Compiler (Step 2)

A language-specific IDL compiler generates a native-language client stub (client proxy) and a server skeleton (server proxy) for your server and client CORBA objects from the IDL file. The client stub and server skeleton are the unique proxies that manage the communication between the client and server (Figure 12-5).

A client stub is like a placeholder (a stub) for the method called by the client. It stands in for the class and methods that the client needs. When a client invokes the method found in its stub, because the actual implementation is not defined in its program, the client, using the ORB, sends the request and its arguments as a message to the object

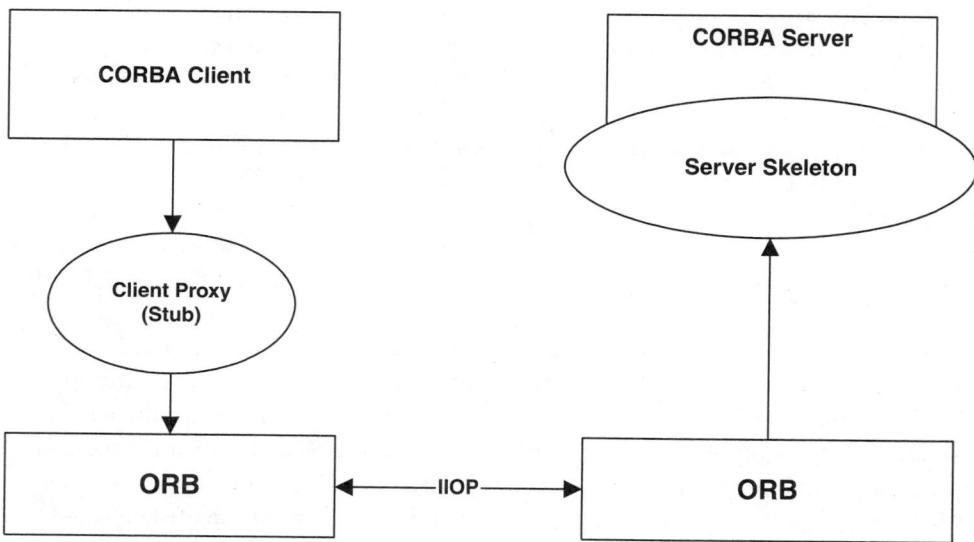

Figure 12-5   Client and Server Communication through the Skeleton and Stub

implementation (the server object). The client then waits for the response. The ORB, in turn, packages this message for the server object, and sends the request and its parameters to the object implementation (server object). The ORB also returns the response to the client. The client application can then decode the response and process it. You still need to write a client program that takes advantage of this information and produces the needed response.

The server skeleton holds the skeleton (framework) of the implementation class and skeleton methods. The skeleton class is the frame upon which you build your class. It is derived from the client's stub class; you then derive your implementation class from the skeleton class. The skeleton class also includes a reference for the methods you must write for the server object. The skeleton methods are used by the ORB to open (unwrap) the client request and parameters. The ORB then invokes the implementation that you have written for the server object. The ORB also waits for the response from your method implementation, wraps the response for the client application, and returns the response to the client. You still need to write a server program that initializes the ORB and BOA, creates and implements the server object and methods, and finally processes the server services. The server object normally waits for the client requests to arrive.

Do not modify the files generated by the IDL compiler. Instead, write your own server and client files that include (import) the generated files.

To compile the Hello World IDL (Listing 12-1) with the Netscape C++ IDL compiler (`Orbeline`), you can run the following command from the command prompt. The name of the IDL file is `hello.idl`.

```
[prompt]>Orbeline hello.idl
```

C++-Generated Files

Let us look more closely at what the IDL compiler produces and how you use this information. Here, we will examine the C++ compiler and the procedure for producing client and server CORBA applications in C++. The C++ IDL compiler generates client and server files with the extensions `.hh` and `.cc`. You can distinguish these files from your program files based on these extensions. A typical set of files generated by IDL compiler are `<name>_c.hh`, `<name>_c.cc`, `<name>_s.hh`, and `<name>_s.cc`. `<name>` should be based on the interface name or the `<name>.idl` file name. In the author's experience, they are generated based on the file name. `_c` and `_s` specify whether the file is for a client or a server object, respectively. `*.hh` files include the type and class definitions, like typical C header files. `*.cc` files include the implementation of the different functions and methods.

By looking in the client stub header file `*_c.hh`, you should be able to identify the specific class definitions and methods for your interface in C++. This class will be inherited from a public virtual class, `public virtual CORBA_Object`. The methods you specified in the IDL are generated as part of a stub class for the client. When the client object invokes this class's methods and passes it the parameters, the ORB will create a request object for the method invocation. It packages the request and its parameters for the server object. This process is called marshalling. Marshalling takes the method the client is invoking, and the types and values of its argument, from the specific programming language of the client and places them into a format suitable for sending across the network. The client stub header file should also include the type definition and other data types you defined in the IDL file. Besides the methods and other data you defined in the IDL file, the class definition should include a number of other methods, including some of the CORBA methods, such as **_bind** and **_narrow**. Some of these functions you will never use, as they are intended for the internal workings of the CORBA implementation. Others can be used by your client program; for example, with Netscape Enterprise Server 3.0, you can use **_bind** and **_narrow** to locate and invoke a service on the server object.

The client stub header file also includes other CORBA header files by including `corba.h`. These files provide the underlying support for much of the code and the internal CORBA implementation. Again, you will not have to make any direct use of these classes and functions. If you wish to review what these CORBA header files contain, however, look for the files under the *<server path>*`/wai/include` directory. Some of the major header files you may want to review are `corba.h`, `boa.h`, `impldef.h`, `orb.h`, and `request.h`.

The `*_c.cc` file, which includes the client-side implementation, also includes the client stub header file (`*.c.hh`). It contains a number of implementations, including the **_bind** and **_narrow** implementations. These implementations can be used by the client application to communicate with the ORB, locate the server object, and request the response from the server object. The **_bind** method, for example, can be used to ask the ORB to locate and connect to the server object. The ORB then creates a proxy object for the server object that your program can reference. (The **_bind** method is specific to Server 3.0. With Enterprise Server 3.01 and 3.5.x, do not use the **_bind** method to locate the object reference of an object implementation. Instead, you use the **resolveURI** method of Netscape Naming Service.)

The client files handle the object reference for the server object with two types of object references, *<class_name>*`_var` and *<class_name>*`_ptr`. The `*_var` object reference provides automatic memory management. It is allocated from the stack. When the object is deleted or reinitialized, the object reference is also deleted. Memory is returned when the object reference goes out of scope. The `*_ptr` object reference needs to be freed and allocated manually. You must support the memory management. It is best to use the `*_var` object reference, as it is easier to manage. Memory management is then taken care of by the system. If you seek greater control, or for better performance, consider using the `*_ptr` object reference.

Looking in the server skeleton header file `*_s.hh`, you should find the definition for the skeleton class, `_sk_<class_name>`. This class is derived from the client's stub class. The skeleton header file `*_s.hh` includes the client stub header file (`#include <name>_c.hh`). You derive your server implementation class from this class. You must write the constructor for the object that calls the skeleton classes' constructor to initialize and register your object with the ORB. Server methods invoked by a CORBA client should be extended from the skeleton class.

The skeleton class is an abstract class. It includes a number of methods, such as the skeleton methods for the methods defined in the IDL interface. The skeleton methods are used internally by the ORB. They are invoked by the BOA for a client request. For example, the ORB uses the skeleton method of your IDL interface method to open (unwrap) the parameters from the client application's request. It then invokes the actual method implementation you have defined. Skeleton methods start with an underscore (_), `_<method>`. The actual implementation method that you write is not a skeleton method. It does not begin with an underscore. The server object should not directly invoke the skeleton method. The skeleton method calls your implementation method. You derive your implementation method from another method (function) defined in the skeleton class. This predefined method is a pure virtual function, `virtual CORBA::<type function(parameters)>=0;`. Your derived server object class must override a pure virtual function.

The skeleton methods also receive your response and package (marshal) the return value to be sent to the client.

The skeleton header file also contains a class template, `_tie_<class name>`. You can use this template class instead of deriving your own class from `_sk_<class name>`. You can use the template class to create wrapper classes that cannot be inherited. These classes are not inherited from any IDL-generated server or client classes.

`*_s.cc` includes the implementation for the skeleton methods. This file also includes the server skeleton header file, `#include <name>_s.hh`.

These IDL-generated files may seem complicated at first, especially the client files. As mentioned earlier, however, you do not use most of the functions directly. Much of the code in these files is for internal CORBA implementation. In fact, you can safely ignore most of the code and focus on writing your own client and server programs. To write your programs, you will use specific functions and classes derived from these generated files.

Review these generated files to get a better understanding of how the CORBA client/server implementation works. Do not alter the content of these files, however. Instead, you will write your own server and client application files. Your files will include these generated files, use the functions generated by the IDL compiler, and inherit the classes and methods.

Java-Generated Files

The Java IDL compiler generates a different set of files and works differently from the C++ compiler. You can read about both the C++ and Java implementations of the server in the Netscape ISB documents.

Besides generating the skeleton (`_sk_<interface name>.java`) and stub (`_st_<interface name>.java`) files, the Java IDL compiler generates an interface declaration file, `<interface name>.java`, and an "example" file that holds the core of the implementation of the interface, `_example_<interface name>.java`. It also generates the following files: a helper file, *<interface name>*Helper.java; a holder file, *<interface name>*Holder.java; an operations file, *<interface name>*Operations.java; and a tie file, _tie_*<interface name>*.java.

The class in the interface declaration file is based on the defined IDL interface. You need to complete the object implementation for the "example" file. This file is like a template that needs to be completed. You should fill in the implementation operation for the class _example_*<interface name>*. Use a different name for the file and the class when you write your own object implementation. This new name will help you distinguish between the interface definition and the implementation. You then need to compile your file with a Java compiler. You will use this object implementation when you develop your client and server applications.

The holder and helper files include the Holder and Helper classes. These classes provide the *_var IDL functionality. The Holder class is used to pass parameters during the client request. It is the holder of the passing parameters. It supports passing of parameters by reference. The Java language supports passing of parameters by value. To support passing of the IDL out and inout parameters, therefore, the Holder class is generated by Java IDL compiler for all the basic IDL data types and the interfaces defined in the IDL file. The Helper class includes utility methods for your interface class and other user-defined IDL data types. It helps by not loading unnecessary methods. It also provides various methods for getting the typecode or the repository ID, and for reading and writing the IDL type from and to a stream.

The Java IDL compiler can also generate a tie class (_tie_*<class name>* in _tie_*<class name>*.java) and interface operations class (*<interface name>*Operations in *<interface name>*Operations.java). These classes allow the server object to support CORBA objects but inherit from a class other than the skeleton class. The tie class includes a delegate implementation that inherits from org.omg.CORBA.Object. This implementation delegates any request (method invocation) to a specified implementation class, which itself can be inherited from another class. You need to initialize the tie class with an instance of your implementation class. The tie class then delegates the responsibility of implementation to this other implementation class, called *<interface name>*Operations.

Write an Interface Implementation (Step 3)

The first step you should take in writing your CORBA client and server applications is to write a simple implementation for the CORBA interface defined in the IDL file. Derive an implementation class (your server class) from the skeleton class generated by the IDL compiler. The skeleton class is an abstract class. It does much of the work that your server application needs to accomplish. The skeleton class gets and converts the client request and its parameters, and it invokes your object implementation. You must write the code for the specific methods—the object implementation—of your server class. These methods should provide the server's service for the client. You declared these same methods in the IDL file.

For C++, you must write the code for the interface implementation yourself. For Java, the IDL compiler generates an example file, _example_<*interface name*> that you can use as the framework for your implementation. Instead of updating the example file with your implementation class, it is best to write your own implementation file based on the example file. Use the information in the example file as a framework. Write an implementation class with a different name and save the file with a different name.

In your interface implementation file, write the implementation class, its constructor, and its specific implementation methods. Save the interface implementation in a separate file and include the file with the server application that you write. This approach allows you to include the implementation file with a number of different server applications. The methods you write should provide the services of the server object. The client then invokes these methods of the server object. The constructor should call the skeleton class constructor or should be derived from the skeleton class constructor. It calls the skeleton class constructor to provide the necessary internal initializations. In your implementation class constructor, you can also initialize any additional variables you may need. For Java, you can then compile the interface implementation file.

Listing 12-2 is an example of a C++ interface implementation class based on the Hello World IDL module we wrote earlier.

Listing 12-2   Interface Implementation for the Hello World Example

```
#include "hello_s.hh"

class HelloWorldImpl: public _sk_HelloWorld::
                                   _sk_Hello
{
   public:
       HelloWorldImpl(const char* object_name=NULL) :
               _sk_HelloWorld::_sk_Hello(object_name)
       {
       };

   char* Hi()
   {
       return "Hello World!";
   };
};
```

Write the Client and Server CORBA Applications (Steps 4 and 6)

You still must write client and server CORBA applications. In other words, you need to write programs that can be compiled into a server and/or client executable program. In the case of Java, these programs may be applets. You must write the main function and include the necessary files generated by the IDL compiler. Also, include (import) any necessary files generated by the IDL compiler in your program. For example, for the C++ client applications, include the client stub header file, *<name>*_c.hh. With the server application, include the interface implementation file. Because you will be using Netscape Naming Service, include the NameUtil.hpp file with both the client and server applications. Figure 12-6 traces the path of the Hello World client application's request as it uses the ORB and Netscape Naming Service to reach the Hello World server application's object implementation. In the rest of this section, we will write the relevant Hello World client and server applications.

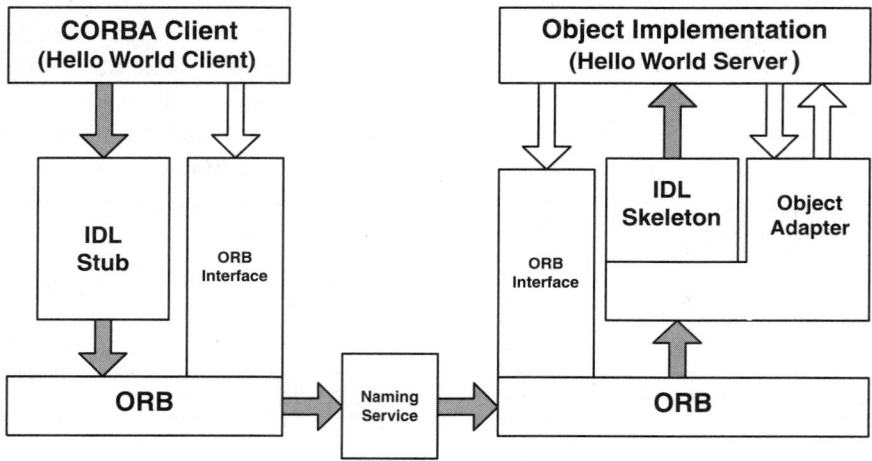

Figure 12-6 **Overview of the Hello World Implementation with the Path of the Client Request Highlighted**

The Client Application (Step 4)

The client application needs to initialize the ORB, locate the server object, invoke the method on the server object, and process the result returned by the ORB. It can then generate any response that you would expect from the client application. The client application needs to know only the registered name of the server object and the specific method it intends to invoke. You first call the CORBA ORB initialization function. In C++, this function call is CORBA::ORB_init(argc, argv). If there is a specific setting (for example, the ORB or BOA location) that the ORB may need to know about, then pass it through the **ORB_init** argument, argv. Next, you locate and invoke the methods of the server object. You must get the object reference for the server object. For Enterprise Server 3.0 using C++, use the **_bind** method of the client object generated by the IDL compiler to locate and establish a connection with the server object. Also, use exception handling (try and catch statements) to detect any exception. The actual implementation of **_bind** is produced by the IDL compiler. The **_bind** method returns the object reference that your client application uses to invoke the method. You can then invoke the specific methods defined in the IDL file for the returned object.

You do not need to worry about how this invocation actually works. The files generated by the IDL compiler, CORBA ORB, and server object handle the process. In the client application, you simply invoke the method and pass the appropriate parameters. Again, use exception handling for this invocation. The ORB does the background work of marshalling your request and its parameter, passing it to the server object and returning the response. You can then use the response to finish your program and generate the result for the client application. If the client application takes any parameters, such as command-line parameters, then your program should also verify this information. The command-line arguments can be used to pass arguments for use with **ORB_init** or the name and port of Netscape Server. It may also include other arguments that your client application can use.

With Server 3.01 and 3.5.x, you will use the **resolveURI** function instead of the **_bind** method. **resolveURI** gets the object reference for the CORBA object you specify. It is the supertype of the object implementation's object reference. You pass the host name and port number of Netscape Server plus the URI path for the object implementation that the client needs. The URI should include the name of the object implementation as specified by the server object and Netscape's Naming Service path, `/NameService`. For the Hello World example, the URI will be `/NameService/Hello`. Also, verify the **resolveURI** return value to make sure you got the object reference. **resolveURI** returns `WAISPIFailure` if it failed. You then must use the **_narrow** method of the client class specified in the client file—for example, `HelloWorld::Hello` in `hello_c.hh`. **_narrow** gets the exact object reference you need. It returns a new object reference for the server object implementation. The parameter of the **_narrow** method should be the object reference that was returned by **resolveURI**. Make sure you have the object reference for the object implementation before you invoke its method. Also, include exception handling for `CORBA::SystemException`. Besides the client-generated header file (for example, `hello_c.hh`) include the `NameUtil.hpp` header file where **resolveURI** is declared.

Listing 12-3 is an example of the source code for the C++ version of the Hello World client application. For this example, the Netscape Server host name is `foo` and the port address is `80`. The object implementation's name is `Hello`. This application is written for an unsecured Server 3.01 and later. It uses Netscape Naming Service. If SSL is enabled, you must make the appropriate modifications. If basic authentication is required, this application will not work. The authentication information is not provided by the client application.

Listing 12-3 CORBA Client Code for the Hello World Example

```
#include "hello_c.hh"
#include <iostream.h>
#include <NameUtil.hpp>

int main(int argc, char* const* argv)
{
```

Listing 12-3   CORBA Client Code for the Hello World Example (*continued*)

```
try
{        CORBA::ORB_ptr orb = CORBA::ORB_init(argc, argv);

    HelloWorld::Hello_var SimpleHello;

    CORBA::Object_ptr HelloObject;

    if(resolveURI("foo", 80, "/NameService/Hello",
                HelloObject) == WAISPIFailure)
    {
      cout << "Failed to get the object implementation."
            << endl;

      return 1;
    }

    SimpleHello = HelloWorld::Hello::_narrow(HelloObject);

    if(SimpleHello == NULL)
    {
        cout << "Failed to narrow the Object Reference."
            << endl;

        return 1;
    }

    cout << SimpleHello->Hi() << endl;
}
catch (CORBA::SystemException& e)
{
    cerr << e << endl;
    return 1;
}

return 0;
}
```

The Server Application (Step 6)

For the server application, your program needs to accomplish the following tasks: initialize the ORB and BOA; create and activate the server object; register the object implementation with Naming Service (if Netscape Naming Service is used); notify the BOA that the object is ready; and wait for the client request. The server application may also take any number of additional steps you wish. For example, it may log information about the start of the server object into a log file. As with the client application, you can pass important settings or valuable information as arguments to your server application. The server application should verify this information and use it as needed.

For example, information about the name and port of Netscape Server or specific settings for the ORB and BOA can be passed dynamically as arguments to the server application. The server application also initializes a server object using the interface implementation class. Thus you need to include the interface implementation file with your server application code.

As with the client application, for C++, you use **ORB_init** to initialize the ORB (`CORBA::ORB_init(argc, argv);`). Next, you must initialize the BOA. For C++, invoke the **BOA_init** (`BOA_init(argc, argv);`) method of the ORB that was returned by **ORB_init**. If you have implemented the server object and its methods, you now activate the server object. (See the section Write an Interface Implementation earlier in this chapter for information on implementing the server object.) Although recommended, you do not need to write a separate interface implementation file. You may include the server class implementation with your server application file. You must write the server class before you initialize the server object in the main function of your server application. If you have finished implementing the server object, you can instantiate and activate it in the main function after initializing the BOA.

You are now ready to register your object with the BOA. With Enterprise Server 3.0, you use the **obj_is_ready** method. Call the BOA method **obj_is_ready** and pass it the instance of the server object you created. **obj_is_ready** notifies the BOA that the server object is now ready. In C++, the code will be something like `boa->obj_is_ready(&<server object>)`. For Enterprise Server 3.01 and 3.5.x, register your object implementation with Netscape Naming Service first. To do so, you use Netscape Naming Service functions. For C++, you use the **registerObject** function. **registerObject** is found in the `NameUtil.hpp` file. Make sure to include this file in your server application file. For **registerObject**, you specify the host name and port of Netscape Server. You must specify a port if it is different from the default HTTP port, `80`. Also, declare a name for the object implementation. The name you give to the object implementation can be any name as long as no other object implementation uses the same one. Finally, you pass the server object that you created as a parameter for **registerObject**. Check the return value of **registerObject** to make sure the registration was successful. **registerObject** returns `WAISPIFailure` if it failed to register your object implementation. Once you have finished registering the object implementation with Netscape Naming Service, you call **obj_is_ready**. If you have more than one object implementation that you want to start, you must register and invoke **obj_is_ready** for each object.

Finally, you call the function **impl_is_ready**, which starts the event loop that waits for the client request. As with **obj_is_ready**, this method is a method of BOA. You may use the following code to invoke such a method in C++: `boa->impl_is_ready()`. The server application is kept alive with **impl_is_ready** waiting for a request from the client application. **impl_is_ready** puts the server application in an endless loop waiting for a client request. Any code that you write after **impl_is_ready** will not be executed.

Listing 12-4 is the source code for the server Hello World application written in C++. For this example, the Netscape Server host name is `foo` and the port address is `80`.

This application is written for an unsecured Server 3.01 and later. It uses Netscape Naming Service. If SSL is enabled, you must make the appropriate modifications. This client/server application will not work if basic authentication is required.

Listing 12-4   CORBA Server Code for the Hello World Example

```cpp
#include "HelloWorld.cpp"
#include <NameUtil.hpp>

int main(int argc, char* const* argv)
{
    CORBA::ORB_var orb = CORBA::ORB_init(argc, argv);
    CORBA::BOA_var boa = orb->BOA_init(argc, argv);

    HelloWorldImpl* HelloObject = new HelloWorldImpl();

    if(registerObject("foo:80", "Hello", HelloObject) ==
                        WAISPIFailure)
    {
        cerr << "Object registration failed." << endl;
        return 1;
    }

    boa->obj_is_ready(HelloObject);

    cout << "Server object is ready." << endl;

    boa->impl_is_ready();

    return 0;
}
```

Additional Notes

As mentioned earlier, a server application can implement both the client and server object. You can implement an application that includes both the client and server implementations. Thus the same executable code can handle both the client and server procedures.

Java Applications

As with the files generated by the IDL compiler, the steps of writing Java client and server applications may include additional and different steps than the ones undertaken for C++ applications. With Java, you first implement the interface class based on the "example" file. The client and server applications then use the compiled interface implementation. The Java client application can use the `Naming` (`netscape.WAI.Naming`) method **resolve** and the helper class method **narrow** to locate and get the object reference for the server object. On the server side, the server object can use the `Naming` method **register** to register itself with Netscape Naming

Service. These two methods are both part of Netscape Web Naming Service. You can also use **registerObject** and **resolveURI** with Java applications for Server 3.01 and 3.5.x. (For additional information on Netscape Java Naming Service, see the Java Naming Service section earlier in this chapter.)

Compiling and Running the Client and Server Applications (Steps 5 and 7)

Netscape 3.0x includes makefiles for the CORBA and WAI C++ examples that come with the server. You can find the makefile, `Makefile`, for each example under the example directory, `<server path>/wai/examples/<example name>`. Netscape also provides a general makefile for all C++ CORBA examples, `stdmk`, found in the example's root directory. The makefiles found in the example directories include the specific instructions for each example. They also have instructions for including `stdmk`, the standard makefile.

The release version of Enterprise Server 3.5.1 does not include the C++ CORBA examples that came with Server 3.0x. You can, however, use the information in this section to write your own makefile.

The following makefile instructions can be used with the Hello World example. As with other Netscape examples that came with Server 3.0x, `Makefile` for Hello World uses the `stdmk` file. It also assumes that the `stdmk` file is placed in the example's root directory and that the Hello World example files are placed under the examples directory—for example, `<server path>/wai/examples/<hello>`. The `stdmk` file needs to include both `orb_r.lib` and `ONEiiop10.lib` in its library path. If `ONEiiop10.lib` is missing from the file, add it. Also, include the path for the NSAPI include directory. If this path is missing, then add it to the `CCINCLUDES` line of the `stdmk` file. For example, in Listing 12-5-1 (the `stdmk` file), we have added the line `NSAPI_INC=..\..\..;` to the `CCINCLUDES` line, we have added `-I$(NSAPI_INC)\include`.

The `stdmk` file (Listing 12-5-1) and the specific `Makefile` (Listing 12-5-2) generate the client and server Hello World applications for Windows NT. You need to use Visual C++ for these makefiles. The name of the implementation file (Listing 12-2) is `helloworld.cpp`. The name of the client application's source file is `hellocl.cpp` (Listing 12-3) and the name of the server application's source file (Listing 12-4) is `hellosrv.cpp`.

Listing 12-5-1   Makefiles for the Hello World Example—Part I `stdmk` File

```
# stdmk (standard makefile)
# This file is based on the stdmk file provided by Netscape
# for Server 3.0x. It is used with the Hello World
# example's Makefile.

CC = CL -DWIN32 -DXP_WIN32 /GX   /MT
```

```
DEBUG = /Z7

ORBELINEDIR = ..\..

NSAPI_INC = ..\..\..

ORBCC = $(ORBELINEDIR)\bin\orbeline  -v _c -m _s -c cpp

CCINCLUDES = -I. -I$(ORBELINEDIR)\include \
             -I$(NSAPI_INC)\include

CCFLAGS = $(CCINCLUDES) $(DEBUG)

LIBDIR = $(ORBELINEDIR)\lib

STDCC_LIBS = wsock32.lib kernel32.lib

LIBORB = $(LIBDIR)\orb_r.lib $(LIBDIR)\ONEiiop10.lib

.SUFFIXES: .CPP .obj .h .hh

.CPP.obj:
  $(CC) $(CCFLAGS) -c $<
```

Listing 12-5-2 provides the content of `Makefile` for the Hello World example.

Listing 12-5-2   Makefiles for the Hello World Example—Part II `Makefile` File

```
# Makefile for Hello World example
# This file uses the stdmk file.

include ../stdmk

EXE =  hellocl.exe hellosrv.exe

all: $(EXE)

clean:
  del *.obj *.hh *_c.cpp *_s.cpp $(EXE) *.log

hello_c.cpp: hello.idl
  $(ORBCC) hello.idl

hello_s.cpp: hello.idl
  $(ORBCC) hello.idl

hellocl.exe: hello_c.obj hellocl.obj
  $(CC) -o hellocl.exe hellocl.obj hello_c.obj \
        $(LIBORB) $(STDCC_LIBS)
```

```
hellosrv.exe: hello_s.obj hello_c.obj helloworld.obj \
              hellosrv.obj
   $(CC) -o hellosrv.exe hellosrv.obj helloworld.obj \
              hello_s.obj hello_c.obj   $(LIBORB)
$(STDCC_LIBS)
```

To compile the client and server applications using these makefiles, you should use the console make program. You can run the Microsoft Visual C++ utility `nmake` to compile the client and server Hello World applications. Run the `nmake` program with the parameter `all`—for example, `nmake all` or `namke -f Makefile`.

You do not need to run the osagent for Netscape Server 3.01 and 3.5.x, but you do have to enable WAI. You can enable WAI through the Programs|WAI Management menu of Netscape Server's Server Manager. We will discuss WAI settings in Chapter 13.

Before you run the CORBA programs, Netscape Server must be started. Additional environment variables may need to be set as well. The client and server programs need to be able to access Netscape Server and the additional necessary shared library or DLL files. For example, under NT, the CORBA applications need to access `ONEiiop10.dll` and `orb_r.dll` or `orb.dll`, which can be found under the `<netscape server>/wai/bin` directory. For more information on Java settings, see the section Important Settings for Java ISB and Web Naming Service later in this chapter.

Once everything is ready for running the CORBA applications, you can run the server application (`hellosrv`) followed by the client application (`hellocl`). For the Hello World example, once you run the client application, the following line is printed to the console: `Hello World!`

Alternatives to the Server Skeleton and Client Stub

The use of client stubs and server skeletons is also known as static interface, because the interface is known at the time of compilation. In a static invocation, the actual code is generated specifically for a predetermined interface. An alternative to the client object's use of the client stub and the server object's use of the server skeleton is to use a dynamic interface. Dynamic Invocation Interface (DII) is an alternative for the client object, and Dynamic Skeleton Interface (DSI) is an alternative for the server object. Both of these methods can be used to generate your client and server applications (Figure 12-7). Dynamic interface does not know the interface prior to compilation. The interface type is discovered or declared at runtime.

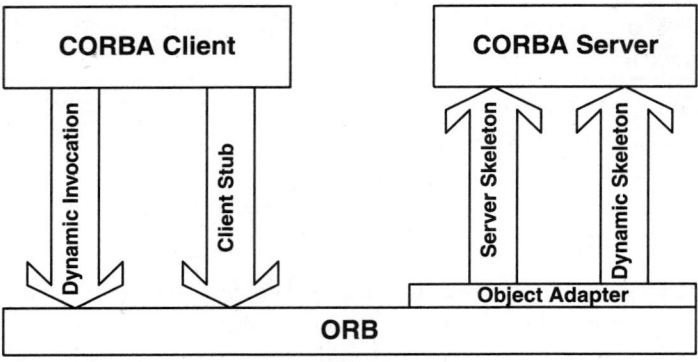

Figure 12-7   Use of Dynamic and Static Invocations

Dynamic Invocation Interface (DII)

DII allows the client to invoke dynamically a method on a server object using the interface repository. The client application will not use the client stub generated by the IDL compiler. Instead, the client application uses the interface repository to obtain the server object, its object reference. It then creates a `Request` object (dynamic invocation request) and invokes the request for the server object using DII. The client application must produce and send the request to the server object found in the interface repository. With the client stub, the server object is identified during the client compilation. It is not dynamically identified. The client stub is generated from the same IDL interface just as the server object uses a predefined server object.

The interface repository (IR) keeps various data about the ORB objects, including information about the interface, modules, type definitions, attributes, exceptions, and so on. There is an IDL interface that your client program can use to locate a registered object (interface) with IR. The client can also obtain specific language binding information.

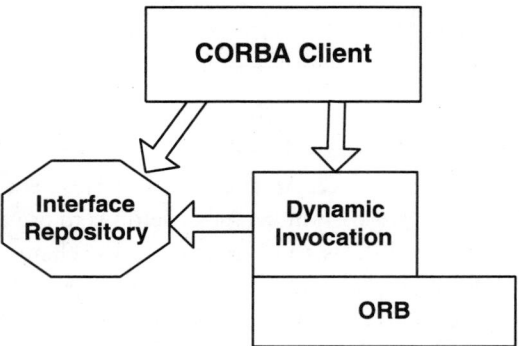

Figure 12-8   Relationship Between CORBA Client, DII, and Interface Repository

When using DII, your program first gets a reference to an IR object (Figure 12-8). It then must traverse the IR to acquire the object reference and interface type of the server object. Next, it must create a `Request` object (class) for the method it intends to invoke on the object implementation. The client constructs the `Request` object (class) dynamically. It also initializes the `Request` object, its arguments, the return value, and so on. A `Request` object includes an object reference, an operation name, and value and type information for the arguments. The `Request` object is then written to a buffer and sent to the object implementation. The client invokes the `Request` object and retrieves or waits for the results. The server object responds to a client request using DII in the same way as a client request that uses a client stub.

With a client application that uses the client stub, you call the methods generated by the IDL compiler to bind with the server object and invoke the method. The actual process happens via the generated code and the ORB, which makes using the client stub easier. With DII, you must generate the `Request` object. DII, on the other hand, provides the flexibility in that the client application does not need to know the server object at the time of compilation. Moreover, you do not need to recompile the client application each time the server object is changed or modified.

Dynamic Skeleton Interface (DSI)

Just as DII provides dynamic support for the client application, DSI provides dynamic support for the server application. DSI allows the server application to write a server object that is not derived from the server skeleton class. The server application can write an object implementation and register it with the BOA dynamically. As far as the client application is concerned, server objects generated through the skeleton class and through DSI are the same.

When you write an object implementation using DSI, you must write your own object implementation. You need to create and activate the server object and its methods. You will derive your class from the CORBA `DynamicImplementation` class. Under C++, you derive your class from `CORBA_DynamicImplementation`. Under Java, you extend the `org.omg.CORBA.DynamicImplementation` abstract class. You must implement the **invoke** method that the ORB uses to invoke your object implementation methods. You pass the `ServerRequest` object (for example, C++, `ServerRequest_ptr`) to the **invoke** method. You also must register your object implementation with the BOA. Unlike when you derive the server object from the skeleton class, you must implement the steps generated by the IDL compiler for your server object. You must determine the client request passed by the ORB, interpret the parameters and arguments of the request, and process the request. Finally, you must return the appropriate return value.

DSI provides greater flexibility. For example, it supports a server object that has multiple implementations and interfaces. Netscape Enterprise Server 3.0x includes an example that uses DSI under the `<server path>/wai/examples/dsi` directory.

Threads

Similar to NSAPI programming, an important aspect of programming CORBA applications using Netscape ISB is the use of threads and thread safety. The ISB provides thread support for the ORB and your program. The ISB for Java is multithreaded, using threads for its internal processing. A separate thread is used for each client and server session. The ISB for C++ supports both multithreaded and single-threaded operations. Netscape provides two separate libraries for C++: one for single-thread use, and another that supports multithreads and that is reentrant and thread-safe. When you use the multithreaded library, ISB for C++ also uses multithreading for its internal processing. The interface for both libraries is the same. The single-threaded libraries for UNIX are orb, orb.sl, liborb.so, and liborb.a. For Windows, the library is ORB.DLL. Multithreaded reentrant libraries for UNIX libraries are orb_r, orb_r.sl, iborb_r.so, and liborb_r.a. The counterpart Windows library is ORB_R.DLL. You can use the single-thread library to get better performance if your application does not use threads.

If you use the multithread library for C++ or Java, make sure your client or server objects are thread-safe. When using your programming language libraries, make sure the functions and methods you use are thread-safe. If you use methods or functions that are not thread-safe, be sure to use a locking mechanism to protect the critical section of the code from other threads.

Multiple Threads in ISB for C++

With the ISB for C++, both the client and the server objects can use multiple threads if the platform supports threads. The server thread can use threads to handle different clients. A client can use multiple threads to create multiple connections with the server object or to make multiple thread requests for the same connection.

The main thread of the server object can use worker threads to handle different clients. It spawns a new worker thread for each client. This working thread then handles all of the client's requests. When the client is disconnected, the thread will be released. There will be a new worker thread for each client.

The client can use threads for connections to or requests from the server object. The client can use multiple threads to make multiple connections to the server object or for a single connection so as to make simultaneous requests to the server object. The client can use the object reference that is returned from a single bind with the server object for multiple-thread requests. It can spawn new threads and pass the object reference to each thread. The server object then uses a single connection (worker thread) to process the multiple-thread requests from the client. On the other hand, the client can make a different bind (connection) request for each thread, using a separate object reference for each thread. The server then uses a separate connection (worker thread) to handle each client thread request. In other words, you can use threads either before binding or after binding.

You can also use the **_clone** method to make multiple connection threads to a server object. The client can **_clone** (copy) an object reference, making a new connection to the server object.

Netscape provides a method for integrating the ISB for the C++ events loop started by **impl_is_ready** with your operating system or another event-handling procedure. For a multithreaded system, you can use one thread for the ISB and another for the other event-driven procedure.

If you cannot use multiple threads to support a Netscape event loop and your system-driven event loop, you may be able to use the `Dispatcher` and `IOHandler` classes to integrate all event-driven procedures. `Dispatcher` detects the events and dispatches them to the `IOHandler` class using file descriptors. `IOHandler` handles events for a particular file descriptor. You can use `Dispatcher` and `IOHandler` if your platform does not support threads. For XWindows, the ISB provides the `XDispatcher` class. You can use `XDispatcher` to integrate your program events with XWindows events, with both being handled by the `Xt` event loop. For Windows NT, Netscape provides the `WDispatcher` class. You can use `WDispatcher` to integrate your program events with Windows message events. With both `XDispatcher` and `WDispatcher`, you must instantiate the dispatcher class before you initialize the ORB and BOA. All of these options should be used for single-threaded servers only. For more information on threads and the various options that Netscape ISB provides, read the chapter, "Advanced Programming Topics," of *Netscape ISB for C++ Programmer's Guide*.

If possible, use a multithreaded CORBA server instead of integrating your CORBA program event loop with the operating system event loop. For example, multithreaded CORBA servers for Windows NT can process multiple requests simultaneously. The requests can be distributed across different CPU processors. Moreover, if a thread hangs or fails, other worker threads can still process requests.

Multiple Threads in ISB for Java

The ISB for Java supports thread-per-session. With thread-per-session, a new thread is created for each session—that is, for each client connection to the server object (object implementation). The threads are created and destroyed based on the sessions.

> **Warning ▶**
>
> Contrary to what the original Netscape ISB for Java Programmer's Guide for Enterprise Server 3.0 states, Netscape ISB does not support thread pooling. Netscape includes a modified version of Visigenic 2.5 for Java, which does not support thread pooling. Thread pooling is supported under Visigenic 3.0. With thread pooling, a single connection is used for each client. All client requests are then supported by this connection, which assigns a thread for each of the requests.

When the server uses thread-per-session, the server creates a new worker thread for each client connection. The worker thread handles all client requests. The requests are processed based on the order in which they are received. A different connection will exist for every client. Different worker threads are used for each client.

To use multiple threads to process a single client's requests, you can take advantage of the **_clone** operation. **_clone** clones a new connection for the client application using the server's object reference. The new request is processed in a new worker thread.

Important Settings for Java ISB and Naming Service

If you plan to write a program using the ISB for Java, you must take a few additional preliminary steps. First, make sure that you have JDK 1.1.x and that the PATH environment variables for the JDK and the ISB binary directories are properly set. The ISB binary directory is in `<server path>/wai/bin`. You will also need to set the CLASSPATH environment variables for JDK and Enterprise Server's ISB. Enterprise Server's ISB and WAI classes are in the `<server path>/wai/java` directory (`nisb.zip` and `wai.zip`). Finally, the server needs to write to the specific directory where the IOR information of your service will be saved. In other words, for Netscape Server 3.01 and 3.5.x, the server should be able to write to the `<server path>/wai/NameService` directory.

When running your Java application under Enterprise Server 3.0, include the parameter –DDISABLE_ORB_LOCATOR—for example, `java –DISABLE_ORB_LOCATOR <client or server application>`. DISABLE_ORB_LOCATOR means that the program will locate Netscape Server directly, instead of using osagent to locate the Netscape Server ORB. The program will not register with the osagent. Moreover, when you use –DDISABLE_ORB_LOCATOR, you should specify OAport (BOA port) in the **obj.conf** file as a parameter to **IIOPinit**. (See the section IIOPinit Parameters in Chapter 13 for more details on **IIOPinit** parameters.) You may also need to delete the files under `/wai/NameService` before running your Java application. The information in these files may include IOR information that conflicts with your Java application directly registered with the server. In your program, also specify the appropriate location and port information for the BOA as arguments for the **ORB.init** and **BOA_init** functions.

For Server 3.0 and Communicator ORB, you also need to make sure that Web Publishing is enabled and that the CORBA server and client have the appropriate access to the directory where the IOR of the object implementation resides. Both of these steps are needed for Web Naming Service to work properly when using Server 3.0 or the Communicator ORB. You must enable Web Publishing and allow HTTP PUT for the IOR directory. When you use the **register** method to register your server object, Web

Naming Service places the IOR for the service in a file under the specified directory using the HTTP PUT method. For the server to perform this task, Web Publishing must first be enabled. Next, you specify the location of the IOR directory and set the permission for the directory. The directory where the server will place the IOR (for example, `iiop_objects`) should be found under the document root directory or be mapped as a directory under the server. You can also use the `/NameService` directory, the default directory for Naming Service. For Communicator with Server 3.01 and later, you should use this directory. The server objects need to create (execute) and write the IOR files in the assigned directory to register themselves. The client objects need to read the IOR files to get the IOR of the named server objects. As Web Naming Service does not employ user authentication, you need to allow the appropriate read, execute, and write access for `anyone` (everyone). You can identify the server and client object based on the IP or DNS address of the machine where they are running. By allowing anyone from the specified IP address access to write to the IOR directory, Web Naming Service can write the IOR of the service in the IOR directory. Look in the Server Manager under the Web Publishing|Web Publishing State menu to enable Web Publishing and under the Server Preferences|Restrict Access menu to specify the access control for the IOR directory. You need to know the path of the IOR directory (for example, `c:/netscape/server/docs/iiop_objects`) before setting the access control rules for the directory. To use `/NameService` directory, you need to specify the access control rules for the `iiopnameservice` style. Choose `iiopnameservice` from the Style list in the Configuration Styles|Edit Style menu. Then press the "Edit this style" button and select Restrict Access from the list of Edit options. Allow write and delete access for any machine running a CORBA server and read access for any machine running a client.

For Server 3.01 and 3.5.1, the server writes the IOR information for your service in a file (for example, `https-foo.sav`) under the `NameService` directory, `<server path>/wai/NameService`. It does not use a separate file for each service's IOR. The files under the `NameService` directory maintain the IOR information for all CORBA services, including C++ objects. Thus you do not need to specify a specific directory for the IOR under the document directory. You also do not need to enable Web Publishing and set the access controls for the IOR directory, if you are using the ORB from Server 3.01 and 3.5.x for your client and server objects. The **register** and **resolve** methods that you use with Server 3.01 and 3.5.x work differently from the same methods used with Server 3.0 and the Communicator ORB. For more information, see the earlier section Java Naming Service.

Netscape CORBA Offerings

Netscape Communicator and Enterprise Server 3.x both provide runtime licenses for the Java ORB. Enterprise Server also includes the runtime license for the C++ ORB. Netscape ORBs (ISBs) are modified versions of Visigenic ORBs. These ORBs are based on the Visigenic ORB release 2.5 for Java and 2.1 for C++, respectively. (The Visigenic ORB is called VisiBroker.) Visigenic Software is one of the first and major developers of CORBA technology. The CORBA components of Netscape Communicator and Enterprise Server support IIOP, DSI, DII, and Netscape Naming Service. They are based on the CORBA 2.0 standard. Between Communicator and Enterprise Server 3.x, you can communicate using HTTP or IIOP protocols. You may also use IIOP to communicate with other CORBA applications. (Note that the Java ORB included with Enterprise Server 3.01 and 3.5.x includes different and additional functionality from the ORB included with Communicator.)

Enterprise Server also includes a single-user development license for the Java and C++ ORBs, plus additional development tools. These tools include IDL compilers for Java and C++, ORBeline Activation Daemon, Naming Service, osagent, osfind, and so on. Netscape Server 3.01 and 3.5.x no longer include osagent and osfind. One of the most exciting development tools included with Enterprise Server is Caffeine, which includes a Java-to-Java compiler. You can use this compiler (`java2iiop.exe`) to generate the client stub and server skeleton from a Java interface. With Caffeine, you no longer need to use IDL. Caffeine allows a Java object to be passed by value. It also includes the `java2idl` program that generates IDL files from the Java interface.

The development license can be used to write CORBA applications. It is applicable to the same machine where Enterprise Server resides. The runtime license allows the CORBA object to run and communicate with Enterprise Server or Communicator. You can execute a CORBA Java applet in Communicator. You can also execute C++ or Java applications that are dependent on Enterprise Server. The license does not allow for execution of applications that are not dependent on Enterprise Server or Communicator.

FastTrack Server 3.x does not include the Netscape ISB. You need Enterprise Server to develop CORBA client and server applications. FastTrack does, however, include a WAI programming interface.

Summary

This chapter provided a general overview of CORBA. We covered various CORBA-related terms and concepts, such as IIOP, ORB, BOA, IDL, and so on. We reviewed a few of the important CORBA development tools that Netscape Server provides, such as IDL compilers and Netscape Naming Service. We also described the steps you must take to write CORBA client/server applications.

The topics covered in this chapter are specifically related to Netscape Enterprise Server. Although FastTrack Server 3.x includes WAI, it does not include the ISB. There are also some differences between Netscape Enterprise Server versions 3.0, 3.01, and 3.5.x. Server 3.01 and 3.5.x no longer support osagent. Instead, you should use Netscape Naming Service with these releases. Netscape's built-in Naming Service is unique to Netscape.

Writing a CORBA application is not a simple process. You have to understand not only the various CORBA specifications, but also the implementation of these specifications in Netscape Server. The CORBA specifications as defined by OMG are general specifications and standards. They are intended as the framework for any CORBA vendor that provides various CORBA tools and applications. The review of these specifications will give you a better understanding of CORBA and IIOP and their purposes, benefits, and goals. When you write a CORBA application, however, you will use a specific vendor's implementation of CORBA. In our case, we used Netscape's CORBA offering, which is licensed from Visigenic. The documents from vendors such as Netscape provide more specific descriptions of the actual implementation of CORBA. They are intended to help you write your CORBA applications. They also cover the various features and tools that the CORBA vendor provides. If you intend to understand the general CORBA specification, refer to the OMG Web site (`http://www.omg.org`) and publications for details of the standards. Once you are ready to program your CORBA application, read the documentation provided by Netscape or look in the Netscape developer Web site (`http://developer.netscape.com`) for more detailed information. In this chapter, we tried to combine both approaches. We included a general overview of CORBA. As the topics became more specific and implementation-oriented, we added various Netscape-specific implementation issues. Nevertheless, you must resort to the OMG specifications and Netscape documents to get a better understanding of the topics covered in this book.

Netscape CORBA ORBs and development tools support C++ and Java. These different ORBs and development tools do not always work the same way, however. There are clear distinctions between how you develop a CORBA application using Java or using C++. If you know the programming language in which you plan to develop your CORBA applications, focus on the ISB books provided by Netscape for that language. Netscape provides a set of ISB programming and reference books for both Java and C++.

## Chapter 13

Web Application Interface (WAI)

Web Application Interface (WAI; pronounced "way") is the latest programming interface included with Enterprise Server 3.x. WAI is a unique addition to Netscape's CORBA-based offerings for writing applications that extend the server. The current release of WAI in Enterprise Server 3.x allows you to write applications that process a client HTTP request. A WAI application is invoked via a client HTTP request. A WAI application works like an NSAPI **Service** function or a CGI application. It processes the client request and returns a response to the client. Netscape still supports earlier programming options such as CGI and NSAPI, which we have also discussed in this book. In an attempt to provide the better performance and the state maintenance ability of NSAPI while maintaining the flexibility and ease of programming with CGI, Netscape has added WAI to its list of programming options. WAI is the recommended programming interface for future versions of Netscape Server. WAI also fits into Netscape's plan of supporting CORBA as the main framework of integrating the server with other distributed objects. Netscape Enterprise Server 3.x and Netscape Communicator 4.x have added CORBA/IIOP support to their cores.

In Chapter 12, we discussed CORBA in general and Netscape tools (Netscape ISB) for developing CORBA client/server applications. We also wrote a simple CORBA client and server application. This information can be very useful when reviewing WAI. Although you should be using the Netscape ISB to develop applications only for Netscape Server, the actual tools and our discussion are not limited to Netscape. Because of Netscape's licensing agreement with Visigenic, you are supposed to write applications specific to Netscape Server. Unlike with WAI, however, the CORBA development tools are not limited to Netscape. You could get similar tools directly from Visigenic and develop your own distributed objects or CORBA client/server applications. Netscape's CORBA development tools, on the other hand, are customized for use with Netscape Server. With Netscape Server 3.01 and 3.5.x, you use Netscape Naming Service, which requires your CORBA programs to register with Netscape Server. CORBA, IIOP, and Visigenic ORB and development tools are general-purpose standards and tools for distributed application development. The Visigenic ORB (VisiBroker) is also included with a number of other companies' offerings (for example, Oracle, Novell).

In the remaining chapters of this book, we will discuss WAI. We will review how WAI works, how you can write WAI application, and the WAI functions or methods you will use. We will also write a few WAI examples. WAI is a Netscape-specific implementation of a CORBA-based programming interface for processing HTTP requests. WAI is supported only by Netscape Server 3.x and later. You do not need to understand CORBA to program WAI applications. WAI shields you from much of the difficulty and complexity of directly developing a CORBA-compliant application.

WAI hides the complexity of CORBA and provides an easy way of processing client input. Beside C++ and Java, you can also use C to program your WAI application. Many of the details of the CORBA implementation, such as how your application links with the ORB, how the name registration works, and so on, are accomplished behind the scenes by Netscape's internal implementation of WAI. You do not need to write an IDL file, compile IDL files, or deal with server skeleton, for example. You need to write only an application based on the programming interface that Netscape provides. Unlike other CORBA applications you may write, WAI applications can also run in the server process space.

A program written with WAI is called a Web Application Service (WAS). A WAS can run in-process, out-of-process, or remotely. In other words, your program can run outside of the Netscape Server process, just as CGI applications do, or in the server process, like NSAPI applications. Figure 13-1 shows the various ways you can write and use a WAS.

As an out-of-process application, a WAI program runs in parallel with your server process on a local or remote machine. It uses the Netscape ISB to communicate with the server. Unlike a CGI program, the server does not need to spawn a new process (for example, run a CGI program) each time it executes your application. This difference allows a WAI application to run faster than a CGI program and use less of the server's processing power. Running a program outside of the server process (outside of the server memory space and execution context) also removes much of the risk of interfering with the server threads and crashing the server. A crash of a program that runs outside of the server process usually does not lead to a server crash. Your WAI application, however, must still be thread-safe. A WAI server object can handle multiple requests simultaneously and support shared resources. Thus your code should provide the nec-

---

Note ▶

There are significant differences between the ISB and WAI implementations in Netscape Server 3.0, 3.01, and 3.5.1. Throughout these CORBA and WAI chapters, we will include references for the different versions of the server. Whenever needed, information specific to Netscape Server 3.0, or to Server 3.01 or 3.5.1, is noted.

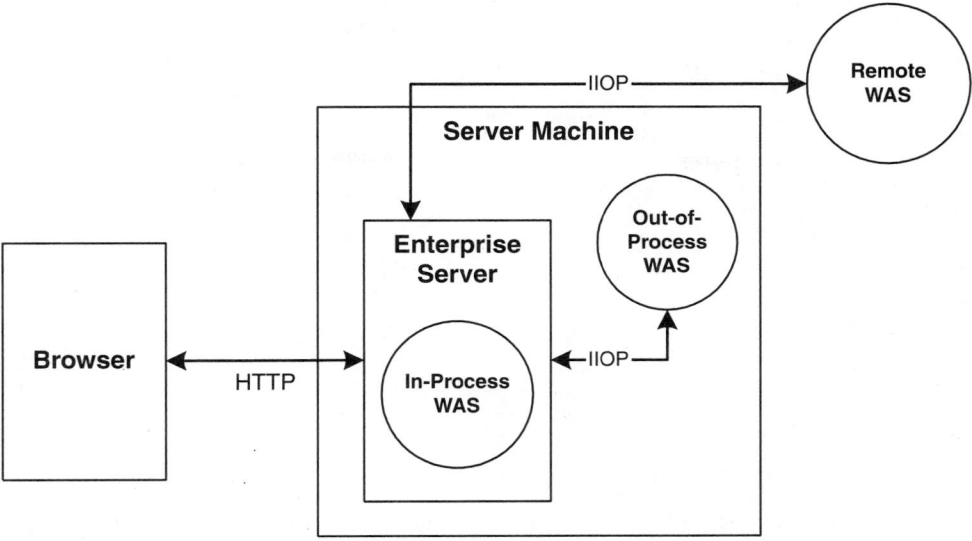

Figure 13-1   WAS Running In-Process, Out-of-Process, and as a Remote Application

essary thread safety for the shared (global) resources. In fact, this shared resource ability is one of the key benefits of WAI. Because the application does not exit after each request, you can easily use persistent data or maintain state information, similar to NSAPI.

You can also deploy an out-of-process application remotely. By distributing applications that can tax your system to a remote machine, you can indirectly increase the resources and processing power of your server. Because of the possible security risks, however, you should not use a WAI application remotely.

Running a program in-process usually provides additional performance benefits. On the other hand, a WAI that runs in-process sustains the same risks and requires the same thread safety as an SAF (NSAPI program). You can write only a C or C++ in-process WAI application. An in-process WAI application may also benefit from using some of the NSAPI functions.

As we have focused on programming using ANSI C throughout this book, we will continue to focus on the C version of WAI. For example, in Chapter 16 we will write a guest book example similar to the NSAPI guest book example (Chapter 9) and CGI example (Chapter 3). You can then compare the examples and functions of CGI, NSAPI, and WAI with ease. Note, however, that WAI is best suited for those who intend to write C++ or Java applications. As mentioned earlier, CORBA itself is an object-oriented framework. For more information on WAI, you should read Netscape's document *Writing Web Applications with WAI* and check Netscape's DevEdge Online Web site (http://developer.netscape.com).

WAI versus NSAPI and CGI

You can think of the current release of WAI as an API that is a trade-off between NSAPI and CGI. As mentioned earlier, programming with NSAPI requires a greater understanding of the workings of Netscape Server, as well as knowledge of its thread and process models. NSAPI applications must be thread-safe. These functions use built-in server functions and can easily cause a server to crash. NSAPI programs run in the server process. They are not insulated from the internal workings of the server. This issue makes writing an NSAPI program more difficult than writing a CGI or WAI program. Moreover, with each version of the server, the NSAPI must change to conform to the new features. This changing environment makes it more difficult to maintain a standard that works on all versions and platforms.

WAI is simpler to write and debug than NSAPI. You do not need to stop and restart the server when you make changes to a WAS that is running out-of-process. An out-of-process WAI application does not easily crash the server. You do not have to use a Netscape-specific threading model and functions in your out-of-process application. Unlike with NSAPI, you can also write a WAS in Java, as well as in C and C++. WAI is best suited for object-oriented programming. It provides a number of specific functions or classes and methods that make reading server variables and request headers or CGI/1.1 environment variables easy. These functions or methods are not part of the server in the same way as an NSAPI function is. Instead, they are implemented as wrapper functions or as part of wrapper classes. WAI programming is a higher level of programming than NSAPI. Thus WAI applications are distinct from the internal server's workings and do not need to be revised or modified with each server version. (This benefit, however, does not mean that Netscape will not change the specification of WAI to include new and improved features.)

On the other hand, WAI functions and methods provide only limited functionality and support for your program. WAI does not expose the server and its internal request processing to your program. Similar to CGI programs and NSAPI **Service** functions, WAI programs provide only HTTP request/response support. They do not allow modification of the steps that the server takes to respond to a request. They do not provide the same fine-grain control over the server as NSAPI functions. You can write a WAI application only for Server 3.x and later. Previous versions of the server do not support WAI, whereas NSAPI is supported under even Netscape Server 1.x.

If you want higher performance, you can also write a WAI application in-process. However, an in-process WAI will have the same limitations as an NSAPI application. If you write an in-process WAI, you must declare it as a server function in your **obj.conf** file, just as with NSAPI functions. Unlike with an NSAPI **Service** function, however, you declare an in-process WAS as an **Init** function.

Unlike with CGI, the WAI application does not invoke a new process for each client request. WAI also provides functionality unavailable with CGI. For example, the Netscape agent API is built using WAI. Moreover, you can even use NSAPI functions with a WAI application. WAI applications can maintain state information and support multithreaded server operations. They can also run remotely. Similar to NSAPI, you can also write error information into the server errors file using WAI. On the other hand, writing a WAI application is not as easy as writing a CGI program. You do not simply read and write from the standard input and output. Your program has to take additional steps to return data to the client. WAI is also supported only by Netscape, unlike CGI, a standard supported by all major Web servers.

WAI versus Other Java Programming Options

You can only write an out-of-process WAI application in Java. For writing a WAI application, you should not use the Java server applet package (`netscape.server.applet`) that was introduced in Server 2.0. Server-side Java API (`HTTPApplet`) is not compatible with writing a WAI application. With WAI, you write a Java application, not an applet. Server-side Java applet programming is a separate method of writing a server application. Netscape no longer recommends the use of this package. Server 3.x provides this package for backward compatibility. Netscape no longer intends to provide further functionality or development for this package. Instead, you should write an out-of-process WAI application.

Enterprise Server 3.5.1 also supports writing Java Servlets. This version of Java Servlets, however, uses Server-side Java applet interface and not the WAI interface.

If you are developing programs for Enterprise Server 3.x, you can use LiveConnect, Server-Side JavaScript and Java CORBA applications to process a client request. This method, however, is different from writing a WAI Java application. For more information on writing Server-side applications using JavaScript, LiveConnect, Java and CORBA objects, see the document "Writing Server-Side JavaScript Applications" under Netscape developer Web site, DevEdge Online (`http://developer.netscape.com/library/documentation/enterprise/wrijsap/index.htm`).

Benefits and Drawbacks of WAI

Table 13-1 presents a basic review of the benefits and drawbacks of using WAI as it is currently implemented.

Table 13-1 Benefits and Drawbacks of WAI

BENEFITS OF WAI	DRAWBACKS OF WAI
Can be written in C, C++, and Java. Supports object-oriented programming with C++ and Java.	Does not provide all the features of NSAPI. You can write only a server **Service** function with WAI. You cannot write a function for other directives, such as **AddLog**, **AuthTrans**, and so on.
Can run in-process, out-of-process, and remotely. You can even write a single WAI application that can serve multiple servers.	Unlike with NSAPI, your WAI application works only on Enterprise Server 3.x. Unlike with CGI, there is little in the way of third-party or existing tools and resources available for WAI. Moreover, a CGI program works on almost all Web servers, not just Netscape.
Easier to write and debug than NSAPI. The interface more closely resembles CGI than NSAPI. There is a set of functions and classes used to gain access to server variables, request and response headers, and so on. You can also access actual CGI-type variables with WAI. You do not need to stop and restart the server when you make changes to a WAS, as long as the WAS is running out-of-process.	There are a number of security issues regarding WAI and CORBA. There is no current standard for IIOP over SSL. IIOP does not use a standard port for communication, so direct IIOP communication across a firewall may not work. (Netscape Server 3.01 and 3.5.x provide special procedures for supporting and writing WAI applications when SSL is enabled on the server.)
Provides better performance than CGI. The server does not need to fork a new process (run a CGI program) each time to process the client request.	An out-of-process WAI application is slower than an NSAPI application, as it requires additional steps for communication between your object, which is outside of the server space, and the server. When you invoke a WAI method in an out-of-process application, you actually make a

Table 13-1   Benefits and Drawbacks of WAI (*continued*)

BENEFITS OF WAI	DRAWBACKS OF WAI
	remote procedure call to the server. The server then processes your request and returns the response to your program.
Supports CORBA objects and can communicate with other CORBA objects. Can be integrated with other ORBs written by you or other vendors.	When running an application out-of-process or remotely, you must make sure the right WAI application is invoked by the client. Your Web application has to register itself with Enterprise Server Naming Service. You must know that the correct application is being registered and called.
Running a WAI application remotely can improve the server performance by transferring the load of a computationally heavy transaction to a remote machine.	Running WAI outside of the Netscape Server process, especially remotely, can open your server to security risks. Another program can register itself with Netscape Server and wreak havoc. Another program can replace your Web service and provide a different service than the one you expect.
Reduces the risk of server crashes, as a WAS can run outside of the server's shared memory space. This benefit does not exist if you run the application in-process.	WAI does not expose the server and its internal processing of a request to your program. WAI does not teach you about the working of the server.
WAI is shielded from internals of the server. It does not provide direct access to the server functions. Therefore, changes to the server do not need to affect WAI.	You still have many of the same issues, such as thread safety and server vulnerability to your code, especially when you run a WAI application in server process. You also must register an in-process WAS in the same way as you register an NSAPI application.
Can save state information and supports multithreaded server operations.	WAS can have a larger footprint in memory use, as it requires running the ORB. With Netscape Server 3.0, osagent must also be running.
Unlike NSAPI, CORBA is a standard supported by many vendors. The specific implementation of WAI, however, is unique to Netscape.	You must understand how CORBA and IIOP work to take full advantage of WAI. (One benefit of using WAI is its support for CORBA and IIOP.)
Provides greater functionality than CGI. Because it is closely integrated with the server, you can do things with WAI not possible with CGI, such as writing to the server error log file when an error occurs.	There are still aspects of writing a WAS that resemble writing an NSAPI program. Writing a WAS is not always as easy as writing a CGI program. For example, in a WAS written in C, you must use WAI functions like **WAIStartResponse** and **WAIWriteClient** to send a page to the client.

When to Use WAI

If you plan to write in C++ or Java, you should definitely consider writing your application using WAI. If you want to extend the server with CORBA, WAI provides an easy starting point. You can then explore the specific C++ and Java ORBs and services that Netscape provides to write a CORBA object on your own. If you or your company have already invested in CORBA, then you should definitely consider WAI. In fact, you should consider writing your own CORBA objects. CORBA, unlike NSAPI, is a standard that many third-party vendors support. Also, if you have not explored writing an NSAPI application, but wish to take advantage of its better performance, you should consider writing a WAS. WAI provides the opportunity for you to easily move a program from being in-process to out-of-process, or vice versa. For example, you can write and test your program as an out-of-process WAI application and then convert it to an in-process WAI application to take advantage of the better performance of an in-process application. WAI also allows you to transfer your application to a remote machine.

On the other hand, if you are already familiar with NSAPI, then currently you have no real reason to write a WAI application. NSAPI provides the best performance and functionality. It also allows you to tweak and modify the workings of the server. You can write an NSAPI function for any server directive, not just **Service**. If you intend to write an in-process WAI to take advantage of the best performance, you lose much of the protection that an out-of-process WAI provides. Your applications can easily crash the server if they do not function properly. You must also make sure that the program functions properly in the server space and is thread-safe in the server environment. For example, you may use NSAPI thread-locking functions with your WAI application written in C to protect a critical section in your code. Furthermore, if you are developing applications that need to run on earlier versions of Netscape Server, you must use NSAPI or CGI.

Before you write a WAI application, you should first review the security concerns surrounding WAI. Some of these concerns may affect your decision-making process. For example, you may consider writing your server application using WAI, because of the remote deployment possibility it provides. Running a WAI application remotely may expose your server to potential security risks. In the following section, we discuss some of the security issues with WAI.

Security Issues with Netscape ISB and WAI

The current version of Netscape's ISB and WAI may produce a number of security risks. First, there currently is no standard implementation of IIOP over SSL, although different vendors provide specific solutions to this problem. Visigenic 3.0, for example, supports IIOP via SSL. (The version of the Visigenic ORB included with Netscape Server is 2.5 for Java and 2.1 for C++.) Netscape also intends to provide better IIOP/SSL support with the next release of Enterprise Server.

Although not based on a standard IIOP/SSL support, Netscape Server 3.01 and 3.5.x do support the use of WAI with a secured server. Netscape supports registering and locating WAI or CORBA server objects using Netscape Naming Service when SSL is enabled for Netscape Server. This approach allows you to use your CORBA objects or WAI applications with a secured Netscape Server. To register a CORBA server object or locate an object reference for a server object, you can use Netscape Naming Service methods (for example, **registerWAS**, **resolveURI**) or the WAI method **registerService**. When registering your WAI application or server object, instead of passing the host name and port of Netscape Server, you should specify a file indicator with the name or path of the server's Interoperable Object Reference (IOR) file. To enable the registration to work, you should point the registration method to the IOR file of the server. The IOR file holds the object reference information for Netscape Naming Service. For example, with **registerWAS** in C++, you specify `file:<server IOR file>` for the `host` parameter. With **registerService** in Java, you specify the full path to the IOR file—for example, `file:c:/netscape/ server/wai/NameService/https-foo.IOR`. For more information on Netscape Naming Service, see the C++ Naming Service section and the Java Naming Service section in Chapter 12. For more information on registering a WAI application, including registering for a secured server, see Chapter 15 (for example, the section Registering Your Service with an SSL-Enabled Server).

If SSL is a significant part of your server communication strategy, you must make sure that what Netscape Server 3.01 and 3.5.x provide with Netscape Naming Service fits properly and securely with your system. The use of the Naming Service methods to register server objects may provide the necessary security for a server object that you wish to implement. On the other hand, it might not fit into a client/server model that intends to use certificates and trust-based delegation for the CORBA ORBs, IIOP, LiveConnect, JavaScript, Netscape Communicator 4.x ORB, or client-based Java applet. You may need to wait for the support of IIOP/SSL in the next versions of Netscape Server and Communicator. The IIOP/SSL in the next release of the server should include point-to-point authentication and certification support. Moreover, because IIOP does not use a standard port for communication, a firewall or proxy server might not be able to handle communication with the CORBA objects properly. There is no current standard for IIOP communication that handles proxy and firewall issues. To resolve this problem, HTTP tunneling can be used to convert IIOP packets into HTTP packets so that firewalls can recognize them. HTTP tunneling places IIOP calls in an HTTP envelope sent to an HTTP daemon on the server host machine. Netscape Proxy Server supports access from CORBA remote objects. You need to make sure your firewall or proxy server handles CORBA objects communication properly.

To provide added security, you can enable ACL security for the WAI directory. Any request for a WAI application will then require authentication.

One of the benefits of using CORBA and WAI is that applications can reside anywhere in the network. Unfortunately, this same feature can produce a security hole. Running a WAS outside of the server process (out-of-process or remotely) allows other CORBA applications to register with the server. Another Web service can register itself with Netscape Naming Service (or osagent for Netscape Server 3.0) using the same name as your Web service. If your WAS did not register itself first or if your service crashes, then this other service is called to respond to the client request. This setup can be very dangerous. You must make sure the right WAI application is called when running an application out-of-process or remotely.

You also do not want any WAI application, other than the ones you have prescribed, to register with the server. It would mean that a client could invoke an application that you have not authorized. The potential harm that such an application can cause can be grave, especially when remote applications are allowed. Just because your machine is secure does not mean that a remote application is unable to register with the server's Naming Service. If you allow remote use of WAS, any service in your network can register itself with your server's Naming Service or the osagent of Netscape Server 3.0.

To reduce the danger of a security hole, you should run your WAS only on the local machine. You should make sure that all your WAI applications start automatically with your system. You should not change the configuration of Naming Service to accept remote services. The default setting of Naming Service and its BOA is set to listen to localhost only—that is, 127.0.0.1. If you change the setting of the **IIOPinit** directive in the **obj.conf** file so that the BOA listens on a specific IP address, then other services on different machines can register with Naming Service. For Netscape Server 3.0, you should limit osagent to accept only services on the local machine. Run osagent with the command option -a 127.0.0.1. (For more information on osagent, see Appendix F.)

Because WAI applications that run outside of the server process run as executables outside of the server process, they run the same risk as CGI programs. These files can be removed or replaced. You should take the same precautions that you take with CGI with your WAI application. Run your applications as read-only—that is, write-protect your program. Make sure your machine is secure. Make sure no unauthorized user has access to Enterprise Server. Set the appropriate read, write, and execute privileges for your server directories. Also, make sure that users do not have write access to directories where your program resides.

WAI applications are even more susceptible to security risks than CGI programs are. Unlike CGI programs, any Web service application that runs on the local machine can register itself with your server. This ease holds even when you have limited osagent and Naming Service to register service only on the local machine. You cannot limit the Web service to a specific directory. Therefore, a program may run from a separate directory, where you have allowed other users executable or write access, and register itself with your server's Naming Service. To safeguard against such security risks, you should allow only authorized user write or execution access to your machine. You should avoid guest login on your local machine.

Note ▶

localhost is a special IP address, 127.0.0.1. It is used as a loopback interface. Only the local machine has access to this interface. This IP address is reserved for the local machine to point to itself. 127.0.0.1 always refers to the local machine, no matter which network IP address your system is using. For example, your system can talk to itself using localhost and a different port address. TCP stack recognizes that 127.0.0.1 refers to the local machine and directs the connection to the specific port without sending any data across the network.

Although running your WAS in-process removes many of the potential risks that we have discussed, it does not safeguard against out-of-process services.

Communicator includes additional security features for Java and JavaScript of which you should be aware if you plan to use JavaScript code and Java applets that work on the client side. The new security model safeguards the client from receiving applets or JavaScript code that can produce dangerous or undesired effects. Netscape provides a security class used to enable applet call-back security privileges (for example, `netscape.security.PrivilegeManager.enablePrivilege`). The client needs to give your applet these privileges before the applet can take advantage of the CORBA features.

Enabling WAI on the Server

Before you can use WAI and write a WAS, you must enable WAI on the server. Unlike NSAPI, WAI is not a straight extension of the server. Netscape has written the server's interface for IIOP and WAI for you. This NSAPI interface is similar to LiveWire, WinCGI, and other server extension program interfaces used with the server. In the Server Manager, you can enable WAI through the Programs|WAI Management menu. (For Netscape Server 3.0, make sure osagent is running before you enable WAI services. Moreover, for security reasons discussed in the previous section, you should start osagent with the `-a 127.0.01` parameter.)

When you enable WAI, the server writes the IOR of Netscape Server in a file under `<server path>/wai/NameService`—for example, `https-<server name>.IOR`. This file is updated each time the server is restarted. With Server 3.0, osagent must be running before the server will update the IOR file.

The `NameService` directory includes a binary "save" and a "backup" file— `https-<server name>.sav` and `https-<server name>.bak`, respectively. These two files hold the latest saved and backup settings and IOR information of the registered CORBA services with Netscape Naming Service—for example, Netscape WAS Naming Service for use with WAI applications, and your Web services. With Netscape Server 3.0, the Netscape ISB and WAI require osagent. Every time you run osagent, Netscape Server, and any WAI service, these files are updated as needed. You should start osagent first, then the server, followed by the WAI service. With Netscape Server versions 3.01 and later, you should start Netscape Server before running your

Warning ▶

If you are running more than one server on the same machine, you should enable WAI on only one of the servers. Do not enable WAI on more than one server running on the same machine.

WAI application. You do not need to start osagent. If you start a WAI service before starting the server, the service will not be able to register with the server's Naming Service, because the server is not running. The "save" file in the `NameService` directory is also not updated with your service.

The information in the `NameService` directory files is essential for proper operation of WAI and Netscape Naming Service, and for proper registration of your CORBA and WAI services. If you made a specific change to your system and the server was not able to handle the WAI applications properly, stop the server and delete the files in the `NameService` directory. The server recreates these files upon restart. Deleting the files in the `NameService` directory ensures that you start with a clean slate and that no previously existing information in the `NameService` directory files cause an error or conflict.

For example, for Server 3.0, if you failed to run osagent before enabling WAI, incorrect information may be placed in the files under the `NameService` IOR directory. Even if you disable WAI, start osagent, and reenable WAI, the information in these files may remain incorrect. Also, if you change the IIOP settings of the server, the change may affect the information in the IOR files. For example, if you add `OAport` or `OAipaddr` parameters to the **IIOPinit** directive function in the **obj.conf** file to specify the BOA address and port, these new settings may cause a problem when you try to run Netscape Server or a WAI application. The solution is to stop the server and delete the existing files in the `NameService` directory.

Warning ▶

For Enterprise Server 3.0, it is essential that osagent is running before you enable WAI. To upgrade your Enterprise Server from version 3.0 to 3.01, use the most current server patch (for example, 3.0i for NT) and the WAI patch (P85416) found under the File Library page, `http://help.netscape.com/filelib.html`.

Checking with osagent and osfind

Let us now look at what registers with osagent, when the server has started and WAI is enabled. osagent is available only with Netscape Server 3.0, so the information regarding osagent and osfind are not directly relevant to Server 3.01 and 3.5.x. The concepts behind how a server object registers with a Naming Service can nevertheless be helpful in the general understanding of a CORBA Naming Service and Netscape's WAI implementation.

Table 13-2 lists the interfaces and objects that have been manually started. As you can see, the interface `NamingContext`, which identifies Netscape Naming Service, has started on the local machine (`127.0.0.1`). The server ID is `https-foo`. The `WAS` string stands for Web Application Services. `netscape::WAI::HttpServerContext`, which holds the server context (server global information), has also started.

Table 13-2 Netscape Server Registered with osagent

MANUALLY STARTED INTERFACES	MANUALLY STARTED OBJECTS

`CosNaming::NamingContext`	`\127.0.0.1\`
	`\127.0.0.1\https-foo00000000000https-foo`
	`\127.0.0.1\WAS0000000001https-foo`

`netscape::WAI::HttpServerContext`	`\127.0.0.1\` `\127.0.0.1\https-foo`

As soon as you run a WAI application, the additional interfaces and objects shown in Table 13-3 also register with osagent. For Table 13-3, the WAI hello example is running out-of-process. As you can see, two additional WAI interfaces, `netscape:WAI::WebApplicationBasicService` and `netscape::WAI::WebApplicationService`, are now manually started. We will discuss these two interfaces in Chapter 14.

Table 13-3 WAI Application Registered with osagent

MANUALLY STARTED INTERFACES	MANUALLY STARTED OBJECTS
`netscape::WAI::WebApplicationBasicService`	`\127.0.0.1\` `\127.0.0.1\hello`
`netscape::WAI::WebApplicationService`	`\127.0.0.1\` `\127.0.0.1\hello`

To find the information in Tables 13-2 and 13-3, run the osfind application found under Netscape 3.0's WAI bin directory, *<server path>*`/wai/bin`. ORBeline Smart Finder (osfind) finds the various agents, OAD, interfaces, and objects that are registered and running. For more information on osfind and osagent, see Appendix F.

Changes to the `obj.conf` File

Let us review what happens to the server settings when you enable WAI. These settings are also required for any CORBA application that you may want to write for the server using Netscape ISB. A number of server functions (SAFs) are automatically added to the `obj.conf` file. Netscape has written the appropriate NSAPI components for invoking and executing WAI services. Your WAI application uses these SAFs, along with Netscape's ISB and the built-in support for CORBA and IIOP, to process a client request. The rest of this section relies on your understanding of the server directive functions and `obj.conf` file. If you are not familiar with the server directives, you may want to read about them in Chapter 2.

The following code is an example of the code added by the server to the `obj.conf` file when WAI is enabled on a system:

```
Init fn="load-modules"
  funcs="IIOPinit,IIOPexec,IIOPNameService"
```

```
shlib="c:/netscape/server/wai/bin/ONEiiop10.dll"

Init fn="IIOPinit" LateInit="yes"

NameTrans fn="assign-name" from="/NameService*"
 name="iiopnameservice" stop=""

NameTrans fn="pfx2dir" from="/iiop" dir="/iiop"
 name="iiopexec"

<Object name="iiopnameservice">
Service fn="IIOPNameService"
</Object>

<Object name="iiopexec">
Service fn="IIOPexec"
</Object>
```

Three main SAFs are used for WAI: **IIOPinit**, **IIOPexec**, and **IIOPNameService**.
Similar to how we registered our NSAPI functions, these functions are first loaded as
part of a shared library for UNIX (so) or a dynamic linked library (DLL) for the NT
version of the server. The Windows DLL file that contains these SAFs is
ONEiiop10.dll. For UNIX, you load the shared library libONEiiop.so.10.
The server **Init** function **load-modules** loads the library. The parameter shlib points
to the location of the shared library on the system. The parameter funcs lists the
server directive functions that also need to be declared in the **obj.conf** file.

IIOPinit is an **Init** function that initializes the ORB, BOA, and Naming Service. A
number of parameters can be used with this function (these parameters are listed in the
next section).

IIOPNameService is a **Service** function that provides a service for the server's built-
in Naming Service and any application that wants to register with Naming Service.
It is also used by CORBA clients to locate the object reference (IOR) for an object
implementation. The **NameTrans** built-in function **assign-name** is used to associate any request with a URL that matches /NameService* with the Object
iiopnameservice defined in the **obj.conf** file. **IIOPNameService**, which is

---

Note ▶

To guarantee the proper functioning of IIOP and WAI, make sure the **load-modules**
directive function for the IIOP shared library or DLL and the **IIOPinit** function are at the
top of the list of **Init** functions in your **obj.conf** file. When you enable the server, these
two **Init** functions are added to the **obj.conf** file, but they are not necessarily placed
at the top of the **Init** functions. You can edit the **obj.conf** file and move these two
Init directive functions to the top of the list. As you expect, the **load-modules** directive
function should come before the **IIOPinit** function, because the module should be
loaded before declaring a specific function inside the module.

defined inside the Object `iiopnameservice`, is a **Service** function that processes the requests for this Object. For example, for the request `/NameService`, **IIOPNameService** delivers the object reference (IOR) of the server's Naming Service. This request is made to register a CORBA service or a WAS with Naming Service.

The following lines are added to the **obj.conf** file and relate to **IIOPNameService**:

```
NameTrans fn="assign-name" from="/NameService*"
  name="iiopnameservice" stop=""

<Object name="iiopnameservice">
Service fn="IIOPNameService"
</Object>
```

You find the **NameTrans** function with other **NameTrans** directive functions in the default Object `<Object name="default">` and the Object `iiopnameservice` at the end of the list of Objects in the **obj.conf** file, along with the `iiopexec` Object.

Here is how **IIOPNameService** works. When WAI is enabled, Netscape Naming Service is started with Netscape Server. Naming Service waits for a server object wanting to register with it or a client object wanting to get an object reference for a server object (CORBA object implementation). For Netscape Server 3.0, Enterprise Server registers itself and its Naming Service upon start with osagent. osagent then notifies the server when a new service wants to register with its Naming Service. As soon as you run an out-of-process WAI application, the WAS attempts to register itself with osagent. The WAS also uses the **RegisterService** method (or the **WAIregisterService** function for C) to register its service with Netscape Server. (For Netscape Server 3.0, if you use `-DDISABLE_ORB_LOCATOR` with a Java WAI application, the application attempts to register with Naming Service without going through and registering with osagent.) For Server 3.01 and 3.5.x, the WAI application directly registers with Naming Service without osagent. The CORBA server and WAI application locates Netscape Server's Naming Service through the host name and port information that you specify in the parameter of the **RegisterService** method or **WAIregisterService** function. If the Web application failed to locate Naming Service so as to get its object reference, your service will not be registered.

The server receives a request from a CORBA server object or the WAI application wanting to register with its Naming Service (Figure 13-2). Netscape Server runs through the standard server directives defined in the **obj.conf** file by using the URL provided by the application. For example, the application can use `http://<server name>[:port]/NameService/WAS` or `http://<server name>[:port]/NameService`. For Server 3.5.1, the WAI applications written in C and C++ use `/NameService`, while Java applications use `/NameService/WAS`. This process happens automatically without your being aware of it. The `user-agent` or `accept` request-header of this registration request may also be different from the header for a request from your browser. For example, for a Java WAI application, the `user-agent`

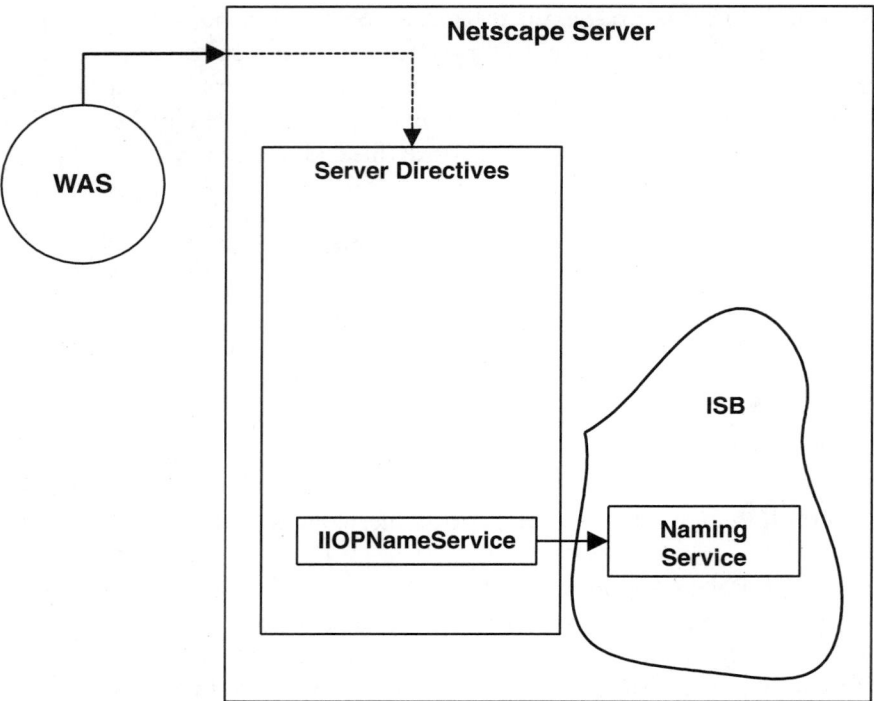

Figure 13-2   WAS Registering with Netscape Naming Service

is Java11 and the accept header is
text/html, image/gif, image/jpeg, *; q=.2, */*; q=.2. (If you are
running a program for logging the server variables based on the example described in
the section Example of Variables Logged by the **pblock_log** Function in Chapter 8,
you can see that the server has gone through the directives by looking at the log file
that the example generates.)

Once the server reaches the **NameTrans** directive function **assign-name** for the
iiopnameservice object, it stops processing other **NameTrans** functions. To
make the server stop processing other **NameTrans** directives, the server has added the
stop="" parameter to the **assign-name** directive function for iiopnameservice.
The stop="" parameter tells the server to skip over other **NameTrans** functions.
When it comes time for the server to step through the **Service** directive functions, the
server goes to iiopnameservice and runs **IIOPNameService**. **IIOPNameService**
returns the object reference of Netscape Naming Service or the server's WAS implementation. Your CORBA object implementation or WAI application then uses this
information to register its service or object implementation with Naming Service. You
can verify the IOR for Netscape Naming Service by invoking the URL
http://<server name>[:port]/NameService or by looking in the server
IOR file <server name>.IOR in the <server path>/wai/NameService

directory. For the WAS implementation's IOR, you can invoke the URL `http://<server name>[:port]/NameService/WAS` or look in the binary "save" IOR file in the `NameService` directory, `<server name>.sav`.

There will also be an IOR for your WAI application. You can verify the IOR of your WAI application by requesting a URL for your service via the `NameService` path. You specify the name of a Web service when you create a Web service object in your program. To verify whether your service is properly registered with the built-in Naming Service, run the following URL: `http://<server name>[:port]/NameService/WAS/<service name>`. For example, the URL for a hello example could be `http://www.foo.com/NameService/WAS/hello`. The server then returns the IOR for your service. The response should look something like the following code:

```
IOR:0120202030000000049444c3a6e657473636170652f5741492f5765
624170706c69636174696f6e426173696963536572766963653a312e3000
010000000000000059000000010100200a0000003132372e302e302e31
0099074100000001504d43000000002a0000006e657473636170653a3a
5741493a3a5765624170706c69636174696f6e426173696963536572769
63650020200050000005741535000
```

What the server actually returns is displayed in one line; the above example is formatted for printing purposes. This information is also reflected in the "save" IOR file. If your service has not been registered or was unable to register with Naming Service, the server returns a `Not Found` page.

The final WAI SAF is **IIOPexec**. The following instructions from the **obj.conf** file are used for **IIOPexec**:

```
NameTrans fn="pfx2dir" from="/iiop" dir="/iiop"
 name="iiopexec"

<Object name="iiopexec">
Service fn="IIOPexec"
</Object>
```

As with **IIOPNameService**, a **NameTrans** function is used to route a specific client request to an Object in the **obj.conf** file. This time, however, the **NameTrans** built-in function **pfx2dir** is used. **pfx2dir** associates the Object `iiopexec` to the URI identified in the `from` parameter. The `from` parameter identifies the URI path to which **pfx2dir** responds. If the path of the client request includes the `/iiop` directory, **pfx2dir** routes the request to the specified Object—that is, `iiopexec`. The `dir` parameter is normally intended for the actual directory where the application resides, so it points to a complete system path. Here, however, `dir` does not point to the exact location of the WAI application. The location of the application can be anywhere on your system. As long as the request is for the `/iiop` path, the server responds properly. Alternatively, Netscape could have used **assign-name**, as was done with

IIOPNameService. The following **NameTrans** function **assign-name** works similar to the **pfx2dir** function that the default WAI setting uses:

```
NameTrans fn="assign-name" from="/iiop*" name="iiopexec"
```

Similar to the use of /NameService*, using the address /iiop* with **assign-name** means that any URL that includes /iiop in its path is serviced by the iiopexec Object. In other words, the server responds to the path, http://www.foo.com/iiop_long/hello, in the same way it responds to the plain /iiop/ path, http://www.foo.com/iiop/hello. The server also responds to the URI /iiop/long/hello in the same way. The **pfx2dir** function, on the other hand, responds only to a path based on /iiop/—that is, http://www.foo.com/iiop/hello.

Once a client makes a request for your WAI application (your WAS) using the URI path specified in the from parameter of **pfx2dir**, the **NameTrans** function takes over and assigns the Object iiopexec for handling the client request (Figure 13-3). When the server gets to the **Service** directive, it uses the **Service** directive function in the Object iiopexec instead of the default Object's **Service** directive functions. **IIOPexec** is the **Service** directive function that calls your WAI application. It invokes the "run" method of your Web service object. For C++ and Java, this method is the **Run** function of your WAI service object. Once you have finished processing the request, you return the response to the **IIOPexec** function, which in turn returns the response to the client. Insofar as it calls your application that processes the response and expects the response from your application, **IIOPexec** is similar to the CGI built-in server functions, **send-cgi**.

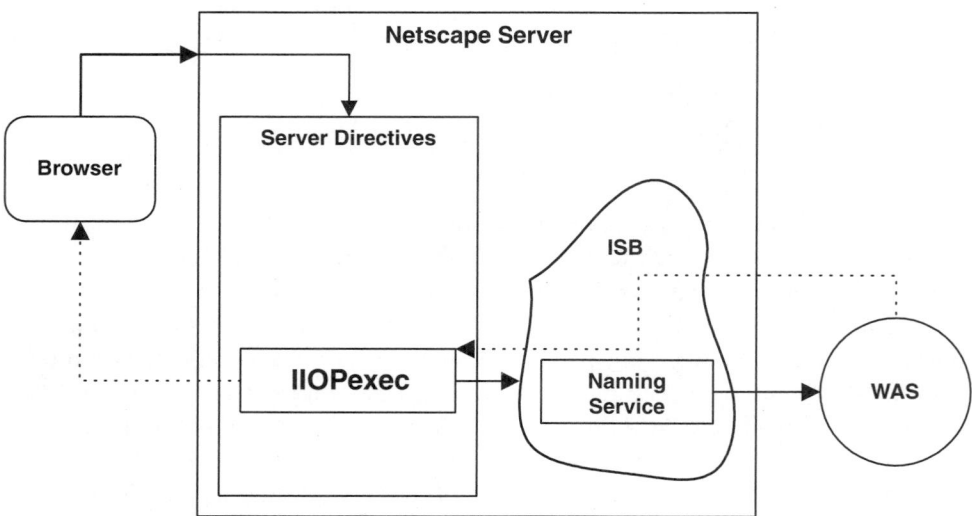

Figure 13-3   Client Request for a WAI Application, a WAS

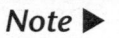
IIOPinit Parameters

You can set the parameters given in Table 13-4 for the **Init** server function **IIOPinit**.
These parameters determine various important settings regarding osagent, ORB, BOA,
and so on. Whenever you wish the server to use a different setting than the default for
the ORB and BOA, you should specify these parameters in the **obj.conf** file.

The parameters for the **Init** directive function **IIOPinit** determine the settings for
the ORB, osagent, and BOA for Netscape Server. You can also specify these settings for
your application through the parameters of **ORB_init** and **BOA_init**. With the
IIOPinit function, these parameters are set for Netscape Server, not your application.

When you program a CORBA application using the Netscape ISB for C++, you can
specify the ORB and osagent parameters for your application using `ORBagentaddr`,
`ORBagentport`, `ORBsendbufsize`, `ORBrcvbufsize`, `ORBmbufsize`, and
`ORBshmsize`. You can specify the BOA settings using `OAipaddr`, `OAport`,
`OAsendbufsize`, `OArcvbufsize`, `OAnoshm`, and `OAshm`. You use these parameters with the methods **ORB_init** and **BOA_init**. **ORB_init** initializes the ORB and
BOA_init initializes the BOA. You define the ORB and BOA settings through the
`argv` parameter—for example, `ORB_init(argc, argv)` or
`BOA_init(argc, argv)`. `argc` is an integer that determines the number of arguments in `argv`. The arguments are set through the `argv` parameter as `-[name]`
`[value]` pairs—for example, `-ORBagentaddr 1.0.0.2`. For WAI applications
written in C++, you can specify these parameters using the appropriate Web service
class constructor that supports passing of the arguments. In other words, the constructor includes the `argc` and `argv` parameters. For WAI applications in C, you can
specify the ORB or BOA parameters in the `argv` parameter of
WAIcreateWebAppService. Normally, you pass these parameters as command-line
arguments to your application, which in turn passes the arguments to the **ORB_init**
and **BOA_init** methods by way of the `argc` and `argv` variables of your application's
main function, `main(int argc, char** argv)`. For Java, **BOA.init** and
ORB.init do not expect any arguments.

The information in the parameters of **IIOPinit** should match the information that
you specify in your application, and vice versa. Your application needs to know the settings of Netscape Server. In other words, if you specified a specific IP address for the
BOA using the `OAipaddr` parameter of **IIOPinit**, you should also specify the same
information for your Web application. Pass `OAipaddr` as a parameter (`-OAipaddr`)

to the methods or functions that initialize the ORB or BOA or create your Web service object.

The most common settings that you may use are `ORBagentaddr`, `ORBagentport`, `OAipaddr`, and `OAport`. For Netscape Server 3.0, use `ORBagentaddr` and `ORBagentport` when the osagent is on a different machine, IP address, or port. By default, Netscape Server 3.0 expects osagent to run on `127.0.0.1`, the localhost IP address. Use `OAipaddr` when you have multiple IP addresses on the server machine and the BOA should be associated to a specific port. You also need to set the BOA to a specific IP address, your server's IP address, to use a remote WAI application. By default, the BOA is set to `127.0.0.1`. Thus the server accepts requests only from objects on the same local machine as Netscape Server. To allow the server to register a remote WAI application, you must set the BOA to the specific network IP address where the server is running. Use `OAport` to specify a port where BOA is listening.

Table 13-4   IIOPinit Parameters

PARAMETER	DESCRIPTION
ORB AGENT (OSAGENT)-RELATED SETTINGS	
ORBagentaddr (for Server 3.0 only)	Designates osagent's IP address, the IP address of the host where the osagent is running. If osagent has a different IP address than the IP address of the localhost machine (`127.0.0.1`), you should specify osagent's IP address with `ORBagentaddr`. (osagent is included with only Netscape Server 3.0.)
ORBagentport (for Server 3.0 only)	As with `ORBagentaddr`, if osagent is using a different port than the default port, `14000`, you should specify osagent's port number with `ORBagentport`. This option can be used for multiple ORB domains.

Table 13-4   IIOPinit Parameters (*continued*)

PARAMETER	DESCRIPTION
	OTHER ORB-RELATED SETTINGS
ORBsendbufsize	Sets the size of the buffer that is used to send the client requests. Use this parameter to specify a specific size for the buffer. Otherwise, the server determines the appropriate size. The size should be in bytes.
ORBrcvbufsize	Sets the size of the buffer that is used to receive the response. Use this parameter to specify a specific size for the buffer. Otherwise, the server determines the appropriate size. The size should be in bytes.
ORBmbufsize	Sets the size of the intermediate buffer used by the ORB. When this parameter is not set, the ORB uses a pointer to the argument instead of producing an intermediate copy of the argument. The size should be in bytes.
ORBshmsize	Sets the size of the shared memory buffer used by the ORB for sending and receiving data between your application and the server. Use this parameter to specify a specific size for the shared buffer. Otherwise, the server determines the appropriate size. The size should be in bytes. (See also OAshm and OAnoshm.)
	BOA-RELATED SETTINGS
OAipaddr	Names the IP address for Netscape Server's BOA. If the IP address for the BOA is anything other than the localhost IP address of the machine (127.0.0.1), you should specify the IP address with OAipaddr. For example, if your machine has multiple IP addresses, you can use this parameter to associate the BOA to a specific IP address. Otherwise, the server uses the localhost's default IP address, 127.0.0.1. You should also set the BOA IP address to the network IP address where Netscape is running to allow remote WAI applications to locate and register with Netscape's Naming Service.
OAport	Names the port number where Enterprise Server's BOA is listening. Use this parameter to specify a specific port for the BOA. Otherwise, the server uses an existing, unused port.
OAsendbufsize	Sets the size of the "sent" buffer for sending messages. Use this parameter to specify a specific size for the buffer. Otherwise, the server determines the appropriate size. The size should be in bytes.
OArcvbufsize	Sets the size of the "receive" buffer for receiving messages. Use this parameter to specify a specific size for the buffer. Otherwise, the server determines the appropriate size. The size should be in bytes.
	GENERAL SHARED MEMORY SETTINGS AND LATEINIT
OAshm	Allows shared memory to be used for transmitting messages. This parameter has no value. (See also OAnoshm.)
OAnoshm	Does not allow shared memory to be used for transmitting messages when the server and your application are located on the same machine. This parameter has no value.
LateInit	A default parameter set to yes by the server when WAI is enabled. This parameter can be used by any **Init** function when using Server 3.x. A yes value means that the **Init** function is executed after the server process is forked.

Log Verbose

You can have Netscape Server log additional information about your WAI application by adding the line `LogVerbose on` to the **magnus.conf** file. Messages will be logged as type `verbose` in the error log file. These errors are of type `LOG_VERBOSE`, which is defined as 6. The information logged is not an error, but rather additional data about the initialization of the server modules and termination of the server. Other types of errors include `LOG_WARN`, `LOG_MISCONFIG`, `LOG_INFORM`, and so on. The following code is a sample of `verbose` information from one server's error log file:

```
[17/Mar/1998:18:17:39] verbose: IIOPinit - starting
                initialization.
[17/Mar/1998:18:17:39] verbose: IIOPinit - initialization
                complete.
[17/Mar/1998:18:17:41]] verbose: livewireInit reports:
        Starting Server-Side JavaScript build: 98.027.1852
```

As you see in this sample code, there is specific information about the initialization of IIOP added to the error log file. Set `LogVerbose` to on for debugging purposes. The disadvantage of using `LogVerbose` is that the size of your error log file increases.

Summary

This chapter provided an overview of WAI. We covered such general topics as what is WAI, when should you write a WAS, and what are the security risks involved. If you want to write a faster CGI application that can maintain state information, WAI is a good alternative. WAI does not provide all of the functionality and features of NSAPI. Unlike NSAPI applications that can be written for any server directive, WAI applications are of the **Service** directive type. On the other hand, WAI is easier to write. You can also write your application out of the server process and even as a remote application. Unlike NSAPI, which is normally written in C, you can write a WAS (a WAI Service Application) in C, C++, or Java.

By using WAI as a way of extending your server, you may run a number of risks. There is currently no standard for IIOP running on top of SSL. Moreover, any application that runs on the local machine can register itself with Netscape Naming Service. Running a WAI remotely can be even more dangerous. You should protect your server and WAI applications against any security risk.

Finally, we went through the steps of enabling WAI. We also discussed the changes that enabling WAI makes to the **obj.conf** file. The information in this section requires a general understanding of the server directives. You need to be familiar with how the server processes a request as it steps through the directives. If you are not familiar with the server directives, read Chapter 2, where we discussed the **obj.conf** file and the server directives.

Chapter 14

WAI Fundamentals

This chapter is a general reference chapter for WAI. It focuses on the details of what Netscape provides with WAI. If you want to start writing WAI applications and examine this reference material later, you may want to skip this chapter and go straight to Chapters 15 and 16. Chapter 15 covers how you write WAI applications. Chapter 16 includes a number of WAI examples that you can use as a starting point for your own applications.

In this chapter, we begin with an overview of the CORBA interface of WAI. To fully appreciate this section, you may need to have some general understanding of CORBA. You should read Chapter 12 (if you have not yet done so) to get a better understanding of some of the issues discussed. The information we will discuss in the CORBA and WAI section is based on the IDL specification of WAI, which is CORBA-specific. This specification is the central interface for all of the different programming language implementations of WAI—that is, for C, C++, and Java. CORBA allows you to write one CORBA interface and then have different implementations for that interface. By reviewing the CORBA IDL interface, you will gain a general overview of the WAI interface. We will use the information in this section to supplement the later language-specific discussions of WAI for C, C++, and Java.

Next, we will compare the WAI interface with NSAPI. If you are currently using NSAPI and are planning to move to WAI, you should review this section. We will also discuss how you can use NSAPI functions with your WAI programs. Although not recommended, you can use a number of NSAPI functions with your in-process WAI applications written in C and C++.

The rest of this chapter is dedicated to the specific programming languages that you will use to write your WAI applications. We will discuss the files, classes, methods, and functions that you will use. The main classes are based on the WAI CORBA interface discussed in the CORBA and WAI section. The core WAI classes are `WAIWebApplicationService` and `HttpServerRequest`. You use `WAIWebApplicationService` to write your Web service class, create your Web service object, and register the object with Naming Service. For C++ and Java, you derive (extend) `WAIWebApplicationService` to write your own Web Application Service (WAS). This class is provided by Netscape to facilitate the development of your WAS programs. It is based on the CORBA interface, `WebApplicationService`, and `WebApplicationBasicService`. `HttpServerRequest` is actually the WAI CORBA interface for processing client HTTP requests. You use this interface to get client request-specific information and to return a response to the client. A reference to the `HttpServerRequest` object is passed to your program. You use this reference to invoke the `HttpServerRequest` methods and get the request-specific information you need. You also use the `HttpServerRequest` to write your response to the client. For C++ and Java, `HttpServerRequest` provides indirect access to the `HttpServerContext` object, which includes the methods for accessing the server-specific information—for example, the server name.

The final WAI class is the `FormHandler` class. This class was added to WAI with Server 3.01 for C++ and Java and allows you to easily process the client input from an HTML form. Unfortunately, the necessary library file and the function definitions that you need to use the `FormHandler` class for C++ were inadvertently missing in the release version of Server 3.5.1. Thus you cannot use the C++ `FormHandler` with the release version of Server 3.5.1. Netscape should provide a patch to resolve this problem.

Writing a WAI application for C is a bit different from writing applications for C++ and Java. Because C is not an object-oriented language and does not support classes, Netscape has provided wrapper functions that allow you to create the Web service object and register it with the server. These functions also allow you to invoke the methods of `HttpServerRequest` and `HttpServerContext` objects. You cannot, however, use `FormHandler` with C.

CORBA and WAI

WAI is a CORBA-based programming interface. It defines a set of CORBA-specific interfaces written in Interface Definition Language (IDL), the language of CORBA. (For information on IDL, see the IDL section in Chapter 12.) These interfaces determine how a CORBA object can get information about an HTTP request or additional data about the server, and return a response to the client. They also define the kind of object that you will write—that is, a WAS. You use WAI to extend Netscape Server's ability to process client HTTP requests. It is not intended for writing stand-alone or other types of CORBA-compliant applications.

As mentioned earlier, WAI hides the complexity of CORBA. Much of the detail of the CORBA implementation, such as how your application links with the ORB, is accomplished behind the scenes by Netscape's internal implementation of WAI. You do not need to write an IDL file, compile IDL files, or deal with the server skeleton, for example. You merely write an application based on the programming interface that

Netscape provides. An understanding of CORBA, however, can help you better understand how WAI is actually implemented.

In the first part of this chapter, we will review the WAI IDL files, which include the IDL specification of WAI. You do not use these IDL files directly. They include only the CORBA specification. Netscape has already included the appropriate programming interface (and wrapper classes) for C, C++, and Java to enable you to program WAI applications easily. Because the WAI programming interface for all supported languages is based on the WAI IDL, we will review the IDL interface first. It provides the core definition of WAI that is shared by all the supported programming languages. Although the actual implementations for these languages differ, the IDL definition remains the same. In CORBA terminology, we will review the signature of the WAI IDL methods (that is, the names, parameters, and result types).

WAI IDL Files

The WAI IDL files can be found under the `<server path>/wai/idl` directory. These IDL files determine how you should write your program and which functions or methods you should use. If you are familiar with CORBA, you may be able to use the IDL files. You normally do not use these IDL files, however. Instead, when writing your program, you use the programming language-specific functions or methods that Netscape provides for C, C++, or Java.

There are two specific IDL files: `server.idl` and `WebAppService.idl`. Both these files are part of the module `netscape::WAI`. They determine the interface of WAI and the methods used by your WAS. `server.idl` includes the interfaces for accessing HTTP request-specific and global server data. `WebAppService.idl` includes the interfaces that your WAS uses to write and register its service. It also incorporates the file `server.idl` (`#include "server.idl"`).

As discussed in Chapter 12, IDL uses `module` to group different interfaces. `interface` determines the specification of an object and its implementation methods. Netscape IDL interfaces for WAI are part of the `netscape::WAI` module. Each interface includes a number of methods. The data and parameter types used in the WAI IDL files are specific to IDL. For example, in IDL, `in` is used for the input parameter (what you should specify) and `out` for the output parameter (what the method delivers). These methods and data types are programming language-neutral, and different implementations can be generated from them. Netscape provides C, C++, and Java implementations for WAI.

In the following sections, we review the WAI IDL files and describe the interfaces and methods defined in them. As already mentioned, because the functions or methods you use are generated from these methods, the actual functionality of the methods remains the same. Although the functions and methods and their return values and parameters differ depending on the programming language you use, the purpose of the functions or methods flows from the IDL definition. A review of the methods defined in the IDL files therefore provides an overview of the specific methods and functions for each WAI language implementation.

server.idl

In the `server.idl` file, two interfaces are declared: `HttpServerContext` and `HttpServerRequest`.

`HttpServerContext` includes methods for accessing server-specific information—for example, the port, host name, server software, and so on. These static and global server data determine the context of the server. You use these methods to get information about Netscape Server. Much of the global server information comes from the server settings defined in the **magnus.conf** file. The global server data are not specific to any particular request.

`HttpServerRequest` includes methods for processing the HTTP requests—for example, getting request-header and client information, reading data from the client input or setting response-headers and writing data to the client. The variables you can get using the `HttpServerRequest` methods are specific to a session or request. They are valid only for that session. They are similar to the information you can get from the NSAPI data structures `Session` and `Request`.

In the `server.idl` file, an enum `HttpServerReturnType` is used as the return value for many of the methods. The value of `HttpServerReturnType` is either `Success` or `Failure`. This return value is used to verify whether a method was successful in accomplishing its task. Most methods of `HttpServerRequest` return an `HttpServerReturnType` value. `HttpServerBuffer` (`typedef sequence <octet> HttpServerBuffer;`) is a binary data buffer for the transfer of data between your WAI application and the server `Request` object. It is used to read data from, and write data to, the client.

The methods defined in the `server.idl` file are used by you to get various global or request-specific data so as to process the request. You do not extend or derive from the interfaces in this file. Instead, you use the reference to a request object to invoke these methods and get their values from the server.

`HttpServerContext`　　Table 14-1 describes the methods defined for `HttpServerContext`. With C++ and Java, you do not call these methods directly. Instead, you use the method **getContext** of `HttpServerRequest` to get `HttpServerContext` and invoke its methods. The C++ implementation of this

interface is the class `WAIServerContext`. The Java implementation is
`netscape.WAI.HttpServerContext`.

The method **getInfo** is unique because you can access all global and static server
variables directly from this method. Other methods of `HttpServerContext` provide a quicker means of accessing the most frequently used global server variables. The
main CGI environment variables supported by **getInfo** are `GATEWAY_INTERFACE`,
`SERVER_PORT`, `SERVER_NAME`, `SERVER_ID`, `SERVER_SOFTWARE`, and `HTTPS`.

getInfo does not support the CGI environment variable SERVER_URL, which is a unique variable for Netscape Web servers and is not part of the CGI/1.1 specification.

Table 14-1 HttpServerContext Methods

METHOD	DEFINITION
HttpServerReturnType **getInfo** (in string name, out string value);	Gets the global server information, including the global variables determined by the rest of the methods of this interface. name is the name of the variable you wish to retrieve—for example, GATEWAY_INTERFACE or SERVER_PORT. This name is same as the name of the CGI environment variable. The value of the variable is placed in the value string (for example, CGI/1.1). **getInfo** returns Success (HttpServerReturnType is Success) if the method was successful in obtaining the value string.
long **getPort** ();	Returns the port number of Netscape Server (for example, 80). It is similar to the value of the CGI environment variable SERVER_PORT.
string **getName** ();	Returns the internal name of Netscape Server, the server ID (for example, https-foo).
string **getHost** ();	Returns the host name of the server machine (for example, www.foo.com). It is similar to the value of the CGI environment variable SERVER_NAME.
string **getServerSoftware** ();	Returns Enterprise Server's name and version information as in the version information string NetscapeEnterprise/3.5.1. It is similar to the value of the CGI environment variable SERVER_SOFTWARE.
boolean **isSecure** ();	Returns TRUE if the server is using SSL security. It is similar to the CGI environment variable HTTPS.

HttpServerRequest   Table 14-2 includes the methods defined for HttpServerRequest. You use these methods to process a client request. We have grouped the methods into five categories (discussed later in this chapter).

Most HttpServerRequest methods retrieve the result as part of one of their parameters. The return value, HttpServerReturnType, on the other hand, is used to verify whether the method was able to retrieve the results. Other methods, such as the ones that set the response-header, also return HttpServerReturnType. This return value is Success if the method was able to fulfill its intended purpose and Failure if it failed. You should check the return values of all methods that return HttpServerReturnType to make sure the method was able to properly retrieve or set the value you intended.

1. Getting Request- and Client-Related Information   The first group of methods—**getRequestInfo**, **getRequestHeader**, and **getCookie**—is used to get request-headers and CGI environment variables. As a rule, a method that begins with **get** is used to get information about a request, while a method that starts with **set** sets the response-headers. Netscape provides two methods for getting the value of the request-headers: **getRequestInfo** and **getRequestHeader**. **getRequestInfo** uses the CGI environment variable naming convention for the name of the request-header to be retrieved—for example, HTTP_ACCEPT. **getRequestHeader** uses Netscape's internal naming convention for the request-headers—for example, accept. The internal names are based on the HTTP specification header names, except that you need to use all lowercase letters for the name. These names do not start with HTTP_.

You can use **getRequestInfo** to get the CGI/1.1 environment variables. Thus **getRequestInfo** allows you to access more than just request-headers. Beside all HTTP_* environment variables, **getRequestInfo** supports these environment variables:

- AUTH_TYPE
- CLIENT_CERT
- CONTENT_LENGTH
- CONTENT_TYPE
- HOST
- HTTP_* (for example, HTTP_COOKIE)
- HTTPS
- HTTPS_KEYSIZE
- HTTPS_SECRETKEYSIZE
- PATH_INFO
- PATH_TRANSLATED
- QUERY_STRING
- REMOTE_ADDR
- REMOTE_HOST
- REMOTE_USER
- REQUEST_METHOD
- SCRIPT_NAME
- SERVER_PROTOCOL
- URI
- URL

These variables are a superset of the CGI/1.1 environment variables. You can, for example, use **getRequestInfo** to get client-related information, such as the client IP address (REMOTE_ADDR). **getRequestInfo** is very useful when converting a CGI program to a WAI application. If you are already familiar with CGI environment variables, this method makes the conversion easy, because it uses the same naming convention. For more information on the CGI environment variables, see the section CGI Environment Variables in Chapter 3.

You can use **getRequestHeader** to get any variable that is inside the headers parameter block (pblock) of the server's Request data structure. We used the same names with NSAPI. If you are familiar with NSAPI, you may want to use **getRequestHeader** to get the request-headers. The headers pblock includes all major HTTP request-headers plus a number of additional headers that are actually general or entity-headers as delineated by the HTTP specification—for example, connection, content-length, and content-type. **getRequestHeader** retrieves only request-headers. To obtain additional client information or CGI environment variables that do not have an equivalent request-header, you must use **getRequestInfo**. For more information on the Request data structure and its parameter blocks, see the Request Variables section in Chapter 6.

getCookie provides a quicker means of accessing cookies. You can also get the cookies using the request-header CGI environment variable `HTTP_COOKIE` with **getRequestInfo** or the request-header `cookie` with **getRequestHeader**.

2. Getting Additional Information   The next group of methods—**getConfigParameter**, **getContext**, and **ReadClient**—gets the additional data that you need to process the client request. Just as in NSAPI, we can access the parameters set for your program in the **obj.conf** file with WAI. With NSAPI, you access your SAF's parameter from the `pblock` parameter of the SAF using **pblock_findval**. **IIOPexec** is the SAF that invokes your WAI applications, whether they are in-process or out-of-process. **IIOPexec** is defined as a **Service** function inside the `iiopexec` object in the **obj.conf** file.

```
<Object name="iiopexec">
Service fn="IIOPexec"
</Object>
```

You can set any parameter for **IIOPexec**. In your program, you can retrieve the value of the parameter using its name and **getConfigParameter**.

getContext returns the `HttpServerContext` object for the server. You use **getContext** when you program with C++ and Java to access `HttpServerContext`'s methods. **ReadClient** reads the additional data sent by the client after the request-headers (usually the HTTP `POST` data). It returns the number of bytes that were read. You may want to use this return value to make sure the entire buffer of data was read.

3. Setting, Getting, and Deleting Response-Headers   **addResponseHeader**, **setResponseContentType**, **setResponseContentLength**, **setCookie**, **setResponseStatus**, **setRequestInfo**, **getResponseHeader**, **getResponseContentLength**, and **delResponseHeader** are all used to handle response-headers. The response-headers are sent before the actual document to the client by the server. They describe the response. As with many of the other methods of WAI, you have access to a general-purpose method that supports an unspecified group of headers and a specific method intended for a single header. To set the response-headers, you can use **addResponseHeader** to add any number of response-headers, including `content-type`, `content-length`, and `set-cookie`, as well as `pragma`, `content-language`, and other types of response-headers. **setResponseContentType**, **setResponseContentLength**, and **setCookie** all provide a convenient (and recommended) way of setting a specific response-header—that is, `content-type`, `content-length`, and `set-cookie`, respectively. They also provide additional benefits. **setResponseContentType** and **setResponseContentLength**, for example, replace the default `content-type` or `content-length` set by the server. With **setResponseContentLength**, you do not need to convert the length of the content to a string before setting it. **addResponseHeader** expects the value to be a string. You can even use **addResponseHeader** to set the status. **setResponseStatus**, however, is the recommended way of setting status—for example, `404` (`PROTOCOL_NOT_FOUND`). **setResponseStatus** allows you to include a reason string for the status as well. The reason string provides a description for the status code. Note that just by setting the status, the server does not actually return the default response page for the status. In other words, by setting the status to `404`, the client does not automatically receive a `Not Found` HTML page. You must write the `Not Found` page and return it to the client. You generally need to set only `status`, `content-type`, and `content-length`. Therefore, the methods that WAI provides should satisfy most circumstances. The method **setRequestInfo**, which was probably intended for setting response-headers using CGI environment variables as the counterpart to **getRequestInfo**, is currently nonfunctional. You should not use **setRequestInfo**.

Additional methods—**getResponseHeader**, **getResponseContentLength**, and **delResponseHeader**—can be used to retrieve or delete an existing response-header. **getResponseContentLength** returns the content length of the response based on an existing `content-length` response-header. Although it is not very useful, you can use this method to verify whether your program has set the correct `content-length` before sending the response-header to the client. You can also use **getResponseHeader** to get any existing response-header, including `content-length`. **delResponseHeader** can be used when you need to remove an existing header from the response-headers. For example, you may want to remove the default `content-type text/html` before adding a new `content-type` using **addResponseHeader**.

4. Sending the Response and Headers   The fourth group of methods—**StartResponse** and **WriteClient**—is used to send the response-headers and the actual document to the client. Once you have set the response-headers, **StartResponse** can send them. If the client uses the HTTP 0.9 protocol, the server does not send any response-header. HTTP 0.9 does not support request- and response-headers. **StartResponse** works similarly to the NSAPI **protocol_start_response** method. You should verify the return value of **StartResponse** before sending the body of the response—that is, the actual document. If **StartResponse** returns `REQ_NOACTION` (the same as **protocol_start_response**), you should exit without sending the body. A return of `REQ_NOACTION` (`-2`) by **StartResponse** means that a `HEAD` method of request was used by the client. A `HEAD` request asks for the response-header but does not want the body of the response. If the response was `REQ_PROCEED` (`0`), then you are ready to send the actual document—the body of the response—to the client. **WriteClient** writes the data—for example, the HTML document—to the client. You may want to use the return value of **WriteClient** to make sure all of the data were sent properly. **WriteClient** returns `-1` if an error occurred.

5. Additional Methods   The last group—**BuildURL**, **LogError**, and **RespondRedirect**—includes additional useful methods. **BuildURL** is used to create a URL. It appends the prefix and suffix string that you specify in its parameter to the server URL to create a complete URL—that is, `http://<server name>[:port][prefix][suffix]`. **LogError** is used for error logging, and **RespondRedirect** is used to redirect a client to a new location.

Table 14-2   `HttpServerRequest` Methods

METHOD	DEFINITION
METHODS FOR GETTING REQUEST- AND CLIENT-RELATED INFORMATION	
`HttpServerReturnType` **getRequestInfo** `(in string name, out string value);`	Retrieves data about the client, session, and request. These variables are request-specific. You use the CGI environment variables (CGI/1.1) for the name parameter, as in `AUTH_TYPE`, `CONTENT_TYPE`, `QUERY_STRING`, and so on. **getRequestInfo** also supports all of the HTTP environment variables beginning with `HTTP_*`. The parameter `value` will hold the value of the variable. (See also **getRequestHeader** and the section, "Getting Request- and Client-Related Information," for the environment variables that **getRequestInfo** supports.)
`HttpServerReturnType` **getRequestHeader** `(in string header, out string value);`	Retrieves the request-headers from the client request. You can also use **getRequestInfo** to retrieve the request-headers using the CGI environment variables. With **getRequestHeader**, you use a request-header name for `header`. The header names are based on the parameters that Netscape Server expects for processing the request, which are in turn based on HTTP request-header names. These names are the same request-header names used in NSAPI applications, found in `Request->header` pblock. (See also **getRequestInfo**.)
`HttpServerReturnType` **getCookie** `(out string cookie);`	Provides quick access to the cookie request-header. Instead of using **getRequestHeader** or **getRequestInfo**, you can use this method to get the cookies sent by the client. It retrieves the cookie string and places it in the parameter `cookie`. (For information on cookies, see the Cookies section in Chapter 10.)
METHODS FOR GETTING ADDITIONAL INFORMATION	
`HttpServerReturnType` **getConfigParameter** `(in string name, out string value);`	Retrieves a parameter set for the Netscape **Service** function **IIOPexec** in the `obj.conf` file. You specify the `name` parameter and the `value` is placed in the `value` parameter. **IIOPexec** is the **Service** directive for the WAS. You can add any number of parameters to this **Service** directive, such as `Service fn="IIOPexec" database="oracle2"`. **getConfigParameter** then gets the value of the `database` parameter (that is, `oracle2`) and places it in `value`.
`HttpServerContext` **getContext** `();`	Instead of accessing the methods of `HttpServerContext` directly, with C++ and Java you gain access to `HttpServerContext` through **getContext**. This method returns `HttpServerContext`. You can then use the return value to get the server's global information using `HttpServerContext` methods. With Java and C++, the

Table 14-2   `HttpServerRequest` Methods (*continued*)

METHOD	DEFINITION
METHODS FOR GETTING ADDITIONAL INFORMATION	
	server passes only the `HttpServerRequest` and the object is passed to your implementation method (**Run**). (See the `HttpServerContext` section earlier in this chapter for more details on `HttpServerContext` methods.)
`long` **`ReadClient`** `(inout HttpServerBuffer buffer);`	Reads any additional client input after the request-headers. You use this function to read the `POST` data from an HTML form. The buffer holds the data read from the client. **ReadClient** returns the number of bytes read. You can check this number against the request-header `content-length` to make sure all of the data were read.
	Netscape Server 3.01 and 3.5.x include a new class called `FormHandler`. You can use `FormHandler` when you write a WAI application in C++ or Java to read and parse the input from an HTTP `POST` or `GET` method. For example, the constructor for the `FormHandler` class reads and parses the `POST` data. (For more information on `FormHandler` and its methods, see the `FormHandler` Class section later in this chapter.)
METHODS FOR SETTING (ADDING), GETTING, AND DELETING RESPONSE-HEADERS	
`HttpServerReturnType` **`setResponseContentType`** `(in string ContentType);`	Adds the response-header `content-type`. `content-type` specifies the type of the body of the response that you are sending to the client. The default `content-type` is `text/html`. You do not need to set a new `content-type` if the response document is of the type `text/html`. If you wish to specify a different content type, you can use **setResponseContentType**. It replaces the default `content-type` and sets a new `content-type` based on the information you give, `ContentType`. Although it is not recommended, you may also use **addResponseHeader** to add a `content-type`. (See **addResponseHeader** for more details.)
`HttpServerReturnType` **`setResponseContentLength`** `(in unsigned long Length);`	Adds the response-header `content-length`. `content-length` specifies the length (size) of the body of the document to be sent to the client. For proper handling of the request, you should always set this parameter. Unlike with **addResponseHeader**, you use an integer for the parameter (`Length`) of **setResponseContentLength**.
`HttpServerReturnType` **`setCookie`** `(in string name, in string value, in string expires, in string domain, in string path, in boolean secure);`	Sends the cookie you specify to the client. Adds a `set-cookie` header for the response-headers. `name` is the name of the cookie, and `value` is the cookie's content. `expires` sets the expiration date for the cookie. If no expiration date is specified, then the cookie expires when the client closes the browser and is not saved in the cookie file. `domain` and `path` are the server domain and URI path, respectively, for which the cookie is set. If no `domain` is specified, then the server uses the host name of the server setting the cookie. You cannot set a cookie for a domain other than your server's domain. `secure` specifies whether a secured channel (SSL) should be used during the sending and receiving of the cookie. All of the parameters are optional, except the `value`

Table 14-2 `HttpServerRequest` Methods (*continued*)

METHOD	DEFINITION
METHODS FOR SETTING (ADDING), GETTING, AND DELETING RESPONSE-HEADERS	
	parameter. For more information on cookies and its parameters, see the Cookies section in Chapter 10.
HttpServerReturnType **setResponseStatus** (in long status, in string reason);	Adds a status-header to the response-headers. You specify the status code—for example, `200` for `PROTOCOL_OK` or `404` for `PROTOCOL_NOT_FOUND`. The `reason` parameter can be used to declare a reason for the status. If you do not specify a `reason` string, the server uses the default built-in reason string for the status code. You should not add a reason string for the status code `200` (`PROTOCOL_OK`). Use `" "` instead for the reason string. This method is similar to the NSAPI function **protocol_status**. Unlike with the use of **protocol_status** for NSAPI applications, however, you must write the response page that is returned to the client for WAI. For information on the various status codes and default reason strings, see the section Returning an Error Page in Chapter 6. You should also review the section Setting the Response Status in Chapter 15 for more information on **setResponseStatus**.
HttpServerReturnType **setRequestInfo** (in string name, in string value);	Currently has no use. It was probably intended as an alternative to **addResponseHeader** that uses CGI environment variables similar to **getRequestInfo**, which is used as an alternative to **getRequestHeader**.
HttpServerReturnType **addResponseHeader** (in string header, in string value);	Used to add a header with the name (`header`) and value (`value`) to the response-headers. The value should be of the string type, not an integer. The actual data type varies based on the programming language you intend to use (that is, C, C++, or Java). This method does not set a response-header, but rather adds a response-header. Thus more than one header can be added for a given response-header type. (See also **setResponseContentType**, **setResponseCookie**, and **setResponseContentLength**.)
HttpServerReturnType **getResponseHeader** (in string header, out string value);	Retrieves a response-header from a list of existing headers. Use this method to evaluate the value of an existing header.
HttpServerReturnType **getResponseContentLength** (out unsigned long Length);	Gets the `content-length` header from the existing response-header lists. You can use this method to verify whether the correct `content-length` has been set by your program before sending the response-header to the client. This method is rarely used, as you should already know the `content-length` of the response-header you are sending.
HttpServerReturnType **delResponseHeader** (in string header);	Just as you can add a response-header, you can also delete a header from a list of the existing response-headers. If the header specified by the parameter `header` is found, then it is removed. You may use this method to remove any default response-header that the server sets, such as `status` or `content-type`. You can also use this method to delete a response-header that you added earlier.

Table 14-2 `HttpServerRequest` Methods (*continued*)

METHOD	DEFINITION
METHODS FOR WRITING THE RESPONSE	
`long` **StartResponse** `();`	Sends the response-headers to the client, if the HTTP protocol is version 1.0 or later. HTTP 0.9 does not support request- or response-headers. **StartResponse** returns REQ_NOACTION (-2) if the client used a HEAD method for the request. A HEAD request asks for the response-header but does not want the body of the response. If the response was REQ_PROCEED, then you are ready to send the actual documents, the body of the response, to the client using **WriteClient**. This function is similar to the NSAPI function **protocol_start_response**.
`long` **WriteClient** `(in HttpServerBuffer buffer);`	Writes the body of the response to the client. Use this method to send the actual content of the response to the client. `buffer` should include the data being sent. **WriteClient** returns 1 if it was successful in writing the data and -1 if an error occurred. You should verify the return value to make sure the data were properly sent. Use this function after setting and sending (**StartResponse**) the response-headers. This function is similar to the NSAPI function **net_write**.
ADDITIONAL METHODS	
`string` **BuildURL** `(in string prefix, in string suffix);`	Returns a full URL by adding the URI prefix string and the URI suffix string to the server URL—for example, `http://`<*server name*>`[`:*port*`][`*prefix*`][`*suffix*`]`. To get the server URL, set the prefix and suffix to empty strings, `""`. This function is similar to the NSAPI function **protocol_uri2url**.
`HttpServerReturnType` **LogError** `(in long degree, in string func, in string msg, in boolean clientinfo);`	Places an error message for the function specified by `func` in the error log file. This function is very similar to the NSAPI function **log_error**. You specify the degree of the error, ranging from 0 for a warning to 5 for an informational message. For the list of error degrees, see the section Logging Errors in Chapter 6. There is an additional error degree, 6, for internal messages, which is logged if the directive LogVerbose on is set in the **magnus.conf** file. LogVerbose lets the server know that you want to use the verbose mode while logging. The parameter `msg` is used for logging a customized message describing the error. By setting the `clientinfo` parameter to `true`, you can also include information about the session, such as the client IP address, and the request, such as the requested path and method used. `clientinfo` can also be set to `false`. The following is a warning error for the WAS named **guests** when the `clientinfo` is set to true: `[08/Jul/1997:00:05:29] warning: for host 1.2.3.4 trying to POST /iiop/guest, guests reports: Form was not filled out completely.`
`HttpServerReturnType` **RespondRedirect** `(in string url);`	Redirects the client to the URL specified in the `url` parameter. You can use this function to redirect the client to a new location. In Chapter 15, in the section Redirecting a Client, we will discuss how you can redirect a client to a new location.

WebAppService.idl *and* WAIWebApplicationService

The `WebAppService.idl` file includes two interfaces:
`WebApplicationService` and `WebApplicationBasicService`.
`WebApplicationService` includes the method **getServiceInfo**, which records
information about the author, version, and copyright of the WAS.
`WebApplicationBasicService` is derived from `WebApplicationService`
and includes the **Run** method. These interfaces provide the procedures for integrating
your WAI application, Netscape Server, and Netscape ORB. They also identify the service that your WAS provides. After all, WAS stands for Web Application Service. In
other words, it is a `WebApplicationService`.

When you program your WAS, you do not need to worry about actually invoking
classes directly generated from the interfaces in `WebAppService.idl`. Instead, you
use the base wrapper class `WAIWebApplicationService`, which implements
these interfaces for you. You derive (extend) your class from this base class. The derived
class is your Web application service class. In other words, you derive an implementation class for your application from `WAIWebApplicationService`. First, you
must write the constructor class for your service class. With C++, you have a number
of different base constructors that you can use. (In the next sections, which are
dedicated to each target language, we will discuss how you derive your service
class from `WAIWebApplicationService` for each programming language.)
You also must write the **Run** and **getServiceInfo** methods for your class. In
`WAIWebApplicationService`, these methods are declared as virtual functions
that your program must implement. The server invokes the **Run** function of your
service, which in turn processes the client request. Unlike a CORBA server object
that you may write, the method that the client object invokes is predefined. The
Run method is the method that the client object, Netscape Server, calls.
`WAIWebApplicationService` also includes a **RegisterService** method that
you use to register your WAI application with Netscape's Naming Service. Instead of
using Naming Service methods, which we discussed in Chapter 12, you can use
RegisterService. This method is simple to use. All you normally include as its parameter is the host name and port of the Netscape Server machine. The method returns
`true` if your service was successfully registered, or `false` upon failure.

There are also several other methods defined for `WAIWebApplicationService`:
ActiveWAS, **StringAlloc**, **StringDelete**, and **StringDup**. These methods are mainly
used for C++ WAI.

Unlike `HttpServerRequest` or `HttpServerContext` methods, when
you invoke the method of `WAIWebApplicationService` for your service
object, the method is executed in your application's process. When you invoke a
`HttpServerRequest` or `HttpServerContext` method, you make a request to
the server. For an out-of-process WAI, you make a remote procedure call to the server.
The server then processes your request and returns the response to your application.

C programming does not support classes and is not object-oriented. In other words,
you do not derive a class from `WAIWebApplicationService`. To derive a class

directly from `WAIWebApplicationService`, you must write your application in C++ or Java. For C applications, you must take a different set of steps to create and register your Web service. As mentioned earlier, CORBA is an object-oriented specification. Netscape's C version of WAI hides the object-oriented interface of CORBA. The C version of WAI is built as a layer on top of C++. Netscape provides wrapper C functions that create your `WAIWebApplicationService` object (**WAIcreateWebAppService**) and register your service with Netscape Server (**WAIregisterService**). **WAIcreateWebAppService** creates an instance of the Web application service—that is, **IIOPWebAppService**. **WAIregisterService** registers the Web service returned by **WAIcreateWebAppService**.

Because the methods for creating and registering your service differ depending on the target language used, we will discuss the `WAIWebApplicationService`-related functions for creating and registering your Web service in the following sections for specific programming languages.

NSAPI and WAI Methods

Writing an NSAPI application is obviously different from writing a WAI application. With NSAPI, you do not need to create a Web service object. Thus the information about `WAIWebApplicationService` and `WebAppService.idl` are not relevant to NSAPI. Other WAI methods used to process a client's HTTP request, however, perform similar tasks as a **Service** directive NSAPI function. Consequently, a comparison of the `HttpServerContext` and `HttpServerRequest` methods and their equivalent NSAPI functions can be useful.

Tables 14-3 and 14-4 list equivalent NSAPI functions for the IDL methods from the `server.idl` file. You can use these tables to convert an NSAPI **Service** application to a WAS or vice versa. Although WAI includes some of the functionality of NSAPI and some of its methods are similar to NSAPI functions, WAI is very different from NSAPI. In fact, it is easier to convert a CGI application to a WAI application than to an NSAPI application. NSAPI provides a great deal of additional functions, complexity, and options that are not part of WAI. If you have used NSAPI functions for much of your code, you might need to rewrite your application to convert the code to a WAS. For example, in the Parsing Functions section in Chapter 9, we use NSAPI pblock data structure and functions to parse the query string and client POST input. The pblock functions are not part of WAI. Instead, you should use a parsing procedure similar to the parsing functions for the CGI program Guest Book, discussed in Chapter 3. With Netscape Server 3.01 and later, the C++ and Java versions of WAI include a new `FormHandler` class for handling HTML form input. You can use the methods of `FormHandler` to read and parse the client input from an HTML form. You may also be able to use NSAPI functions with your WAI applications. For example, you can use a number of NSAPI functions with an in-process WAI application written in C (although Netscape does not recommend this approach).

For more information on the NSAPI functions, see Chapter 6, which covers the major NSAPI functions used to process client requests. Chapter 6 also shows how you can access the equivalents of CGI environment variables by using NSAPI. This discussion can be useful in comparing CGI, NSAPI, and WAI.

Unlike with WAI, where you can access all of the CGI environment variables using **getRequestInfo** and all additional server global settings from **HttpServerContext**, there are a number of different functions and ways of getting the same information using NSAPI. The actual request and client information that you wish to retrieve via NSAPI are kept in different server data structures, while a number of global server settings are available as global static variables. This setup makes writing WAI applications easier than writing NSAPI applications, as you do not need to know where to look before retrieving the data.

WAI provides two methods for accessing request-headers, **getRequestHeader** and **getRequestInfo**. **getRequestHeader** uses the same name for the request-headers as NSAPI, while **getRequestInfo** uses the CGI environment variable names. In other words, with WAI you can use the HTTP request-header names, as in NSAPI, or you can employ CGI environment variables, as in CGI. With NSAPI, you use the **request_header** function to get the request-headers. The name of the request-headers that you use with the NSAPI functions are based on the HTTP request-headers and are the same as the names you use with **getRequestHeader**. With **getRequestInfo**, you can get additional client-related information using CGI environment variables. The functionality of **getRequestInfo** is not available to NSAPI, because NSAPI does not use the CGI environment variables. There is no wrapper server function, such as **IIOPexec** for WAI and **sendcgi** for CGI, that can produce CGI environment variables for your NSAPI function. With NSAPI, to access the same information that **getRequestInfo** provides, you must use different NSAPI functions and look in a number of different server data structures. The CGI Environment Variables and NSAPI Variables section of Chapter 6 provides a parallel listing of the CGI environment variables and the equivalent NSAPI variables. It also lists the functions you can use with NSAPI to get the equivalent CGI environment variable. You can also use this information to determine which request-header names you can use with the **getRequestHeader** method.

NSAPI programs are mainly written in C, so the references to WAI and NSAPI are mainly relevant to developers who intend to use C to write a WAS. Although you can also use this information for C++ or Java, the actual procedure of programming in these object-oriented languages is different from C programming. Later in this chapter, Tables 14-6 and 14-7 list the language-specific C functions that you can use to write your WAI programs. For now, we will consider only the comparisons in Tables 14-3 and 14-4, which are based on WAI IDL methods and NSAPI functions. In Chapter 16, we also rewrite the guest book example, which we have already written in NSAPI (Chapter 9) and CGI (Chapter 3) using WAI and C. You can use this program to compare WAI with NSAPI and CGI. All of the guest book examples are written in C.

The procedures for writing, registering, and enabling WAI and NSAPI **Service** applications are different. We have already discussed how you can write an NSAPI function in Chapters 6 and 7. In the remaining chapters, we will discuss the steps of writing, compiling, and registering your WAI. The WAI method of registering and enabling the application also differs depending on whether you are writing an in-process or out-of-process application.

Some WAI methods have a parallel NSAPI function, as in the case of **LogError**. (Unlike CGI, both NSAPI and WAI allow you to log errors in the server's error log file.) For these cases in Table 14-4, we have included the function prototype of the NSAPI functions. Other WAI methods perform a function that can be reproduced by an NSAPI function or a set of NSAPI functions. There is no one-to-one parallel between NSAPI functions and WAI methods, however. For these WAI methods in Tables 14-3 and 14-4, we have included a possible example of the NSAPI function, plus a method of accomplishing the same task using NSAPI. The variable that the WAI function retrieves may be available as a global variable to the NSAPI function as well. This case applies to much of the global server data retrieved through the `HttpServerContext` methods.

WAI provides a number of convenient and recommended specific methods (for example, **setResponseContentType**), which can accomplish particular tasks that can also be fulfilled through general-purpose functions (for example, **addResponseHeader**). NSAPI does not provide such convenient functions, but it does provide functions that support the general-purpose WAI functions.

The process of handling of the response-headers and writing the response to the client in WAI is similar to the NSAPI process. With both NSAPI and WAI, you can retrieve, remove, and replace a server response-header. Once you have set the correct response-headers, you send these headers followed by the body of the response. With NSAPI, you use **protocol_start_response** and **net_write** to send the header and the body of the response. With WAI, you use **StartResponse** and **WriteClient**.

The NSAPI SAF functions include three parameters: `pblock`, `Session`, and `Request`. `pblock` holds the parameters of the SAF from **obj.conf**. `Session` includes the session-specific data, such as the client IP address. `Request` holds only request-specific information, including the request- and response-headers. Tables 14-3 and 14-4 assume that the default SAF function has three parameters: `param`, `sn`, and `rq`. The following code is an example of such a function:

```
myNSAPIfunction(pblock *param, Session *sn, Request *rq);
```

In other words, the NSAPI functions in Tables 14-3 and 14-4, which deliver the same results as their equivalent WAI functions, use `param`, `sn`, and `rq` as their source data structures. It is as if these NSAPI functions were written for **myNSAPIfunction**.

Table 14-3   `HttpServerContext` Methods

IDL METHOD	NSAPI EQUIVALENT

`HttpServerReturnType`
`getInfo` `(in string name,`
`out string value);`
	There are different methods for accessing the global server information. There is no single function that you can use. Usually you can find the global server information as global variables that your NSAPI can access directly. For more information, see the rest of the methods for `HttpServerContext`.

`long` **`getPort`**`();`	Global variable `port` (`conf_global_vars_s()->Vport`)
`string` **`getName`**`();`	Global variable `server_id` (`conf_getglobals()->Vserver_id`)
`string` **`getHost`**`();`	Global variable `server_hostname` (`conf_getglobals()->Vserver_hostname`) or the return value of the function `char *util_hostname();`
`string` **`getServerSoftware`**`();`	Global variable `MAGNUS_VERSION_STRING` for Server 2.x `system_version()` for Server 3.x
`boolean` **`isSecure`**`();`	Global variable `security_active` (`conf_getglobals()->Vsecurity_active`)

Table 14-4   `HttpServerRequest` Methods

IDL METHOD	NSAPI EQUIVALENT
METHODS FOR GETTING REQUEST- AND CLIENT-RELATED INFORMATION	

`HttpServerReturnType`
`getRequestInfo` `(in string`
`name, out string value);`
	In NSAPI, you do not have access to the CGI environment variables, but you can access the same information using a number of different NSAPI functions. The NSAPI variables equivalent to the CGI environment variables can be found in a number of different pblocks inside the data structures passed to your NSAPI function. The following is a list of the NSAPI functions that you can use to get the same information that **getRequestInfo** retrieves. You need to specify the name of the variable you wish to retrieve in *<name>*. `value` will hold the value of the header.
	
	`value = pblock_findval("<name>", sn->client);`
	(For client-specific variables, such as the client IP address.)
	
	`value = pblock_findval("<name>", rq->vars);`
	(For server working variables, such as `path-info` and `auth-type`.)
	
	`value = pblock_findval("<name>", rq->reqpb);`
	(For request-line–related data, such as `method` and `uri`. You also use this function for the `query` string.)

Table 14-4 `HttpServerRequest` Methods (*continued*)

IDL METHOD	NSAPI EQUIVALENT
METHODS FOR GETTING REQUEST- AND CLIENT-RELATED INFORMATION	
	`request_header("<name>", &value, sn, rq);` (For the HTTP request-header, such as `user-agent`, `content-type`, and `referer`.)
	(See Chapter 6 for more details on NSAPI functions.)
`HttpServerReturnType` **getRequestHeader** (in string header, out string value);	`request_header("<header>", &value, sn, rq);` (`rq->headers`)
	(You mainly use the **request_header** NSAPI function to access request-headers that are found in the `Request->headers` pblock (`rq->headers`). You must specify the request-header name in *<header>*. `value` will hold the value of the header. For other types of request- or client-related information, see **getRequestInfo**.)
`HttpServerReturnType` **getCookie** (out string cookie);	`request_header ("cookie", &cookie_string, sn, rq);` (`cookie_string` holds the cookie from the client.)
METHODS FOR GETTING ADDITIONAL INFORMATION	
`HttpServerReturnType` **getConfigParameter** (in string name, out string value);	`value = pblock_findval("<name>", *param);`
	(`param` is the pblock data structure passed to the SAF. *<name>* is for the name of the parameter. **pblock_findval** returns the value of the parameter. Unlike with WAI, each NSAPI SAF that you write can have its own set of parameters in the **obj.conf** file. With WAI, all WAI applications access the parameter of the same **IIOPexec** function.)
`HttpServerContext` **getContext**();	Not relevant to NSAPI. This division between global server variables and request-specific variables is unique to WAI.
`long` **ReadClient** (inout `HttpServerBuffer` buffer);	A number of different functions can be used. The most common function is as follows:
	`int netbuf_getc(netbuf buf);`
	(`buf` holds the client input. **netbuf_getc** reads one character at a time from the buffer.)
	Other functions include the following:
	`int net_read(SYS_NETFD sd, char *buf, int sz, int timeout);` `int netbuf_grab(netbuf *buf, int sz);`
METHODS FOR SETTING (ADDING), GETTING, AND DELETING RESPONSE-HEADERS	
`HttpServerReturnType` **setResponseContentType** (in string ContentType);	`pblock_nvinsert("content-type", "<value>", rq->srvhdrs);`
	(You specify the content type in *<value>*.)

Table 14-4 `HttpServerRequest` Methods (*continued*)

IDL METHOD	NSAPI EQUIVALENT
METHODS FOR SETTING (ADDING), GETTING, AND DELETING RESPONSE-HEADERS	

`HttpServerReturnType` **setResponseContentLength** `(in unsigned long Length);`	`pblock_nninsert("content-length", <value>,`
	`                 rq->srvhdrs);`
	
	(You specify the length of the content in `<value>`.
	`<value>` is an integer.)

`HttpServerReturnType` **setCookie** `(in string name, in string value, in string expires, in string domain, in string path, in boolean secure);`	`pblock_nvinsert("set-cookie", "<The Cookie>",`
	`                 rq->srvhdrs);`
	
	(`<The Cookie>` should be the full cookie string, including the name, value, expires, domain, path, and secure information.)

`HttpServerReturnType` **setResponseStatus**`(in long status, in string reason);`	`void protocol_status(Session *sn, Request *rq,`
	`                      int n, char *r);`
	
	(n is the status code, and `r` is the reason string. Unlike with the use of **protocol_status** for sending an error page, with WAI you cannot simply set the status and expect the server to respond with a default error page. Similar to CGI, with WAI you must write an error page and send it to the client.)

`HttpServerReturnType` **setRequestInfo**`(in string name, in string value);`	Currently has no use in WAI.

`HttpServerReturnType` **addResponseHeader**`(in string header, in string value);`	`int pblock_nvinsert("<header>", "<value>",`
	`                     rq->srvhdrs);`
	
	or
	
	`int pblock_nninsert("<header>", <value>,`
	`                     rq->srvhdrs);`
	
	(**pblock_nvinsert** adds a header with a string `value`. **pblock_nninsert** adds a header with an integer value. Unlike with **addResponseHeader**, with NSAPI you are not limited to response-headers. You can add and remove information to and from any of the pblock data structures passed to your function through the `Session` and `Request` data structures—for example, rq->headers, rq->vars, rq->reqpb, and sn->client.)

`HttpServerReturnType` **getResponseHeader**`(in string header, out string value);`	`value = pblock_findval("<header>",`
	`                        rq->srvhdrs);`
	
	(`value` is a string holding the value of `<header>`.)

`HttpServerReturnType` **getResponseContentLength** `(out unsigned long Length);`	`value = pblock_findval("content-length",`
	`                        rq->srvhdrs);`
	
	(`value` is the string [not an integer] holding the length of the content.)

Table 14-4 `HttpServerRequest` Methods (*continued*)

IDL METHOD	NSAPI EQUIVALENT
METHODS FOR SETTING (ADDING), GETTING, AND DELETING RESPONSE-HEADERS	

`HttpServerReturnType` **delResponseHeader** `(in string header);`	`param_free(pblock_remove("<header>",`
	`                          rq->srvhdrs);`
	
	(**pblock_remove** removes the header. **param_free** then frees the memory. Unlike with **delResponseHeader**, with NSAPI you are not limited to response-headers. You can add and remove information to and from any of the pblock data structures passed to your function through the `Session` and `Request` data structures—for example, `rq->headers`, `rq->vars`, `rq->reqpb`, and `sn->client`.)

METHODS FOR WRITING THE RESPONSE	
`long` **StartResponse** `();`	`int protocol_start_response(Session *sn,` `                             Request *rq);`
`long` **WriteClient** `(in HttpServerBuffer buffer);`	`int net_write(SYS_NETFD sd, char *buf, int sz);` (`sd` is the socket descriptor. `buf` is the buffer. `sz` is the size of the buffer.)
ADDITIONAL METHODS	
`string` **BuildURL** `(in string prefix, in string suffix);`	`char *protocol_uri2url(char *prefix,` `                        char *suffix);`

`HttpServerReturnType` **LogError** `(in long degree, in string func, in string msg, in boolean clientinfo);`	`int log_error(int degree, char *func,`
	`              Session *sn, Request *rq,`
	`              char *fmt, . . .);`
	
	(There is no `clientinfo` parameter with **log_error**.)

`HttpServerReturnType` **RespondRedirect** `(in string url);`	There are different ways of redirecting a client. One way is to use the following functions:
	
	`pblock_nvinsert("Location", <url>, rq->srvhdrs);`
	
	and
	
	`protocol_status(sn, rq, PROTOCOL_REDIRECT,`
	`                NULL);`

Using NSAPI Functions with WAI Applications

Beside using the CORBA ORB (Netscape ISB), WAI is also implemented as an NSAPI extension. It interacts with the server through an NSAPI interface. Moreover, the WAI applications may be able to access and use NSAPI functions. The header file ONEiiop.h, which you include with your WAI C applications, includes the NSAPI header file netsite.h (#include "netsite.h"), which in turn includes the main NSAPI header file nsapi.h.

You may be able to use some NSAPI functions with your C or C++ WAI applications. Nevertheless, the use of NSAPI is limited. If you plan to use NSAPI functions, you should write an in-process application. Most NSAPI functions are not available with out-of-process applications. It is also best to use C for your WAI applications. Although many of the NSAPI functions may work when used in in-process applications and some may even work in out-of-process WAI C applications, it is recommended that you do not mix NSAPI code with WAI applications. In general, you should use WAI functions with WAI applications and NSAPI functions for your NSAPI applications. Because NSAPI is a C API, you cannot use NSAPI function with Java. An SAF written with NSAPI cannot be directly implemented in Java.

Likewise it is best not to use NSAPI with WAI applications written in C++. NSAPI is not object-oriented and does not use C++'s methods and functionality. It does not support C++ exception handling. If you plan to use NSAPI functions with your C++ applications, write a C++ in-process application and avoid using C++ conventions or libraries. Use Netscape stream classes found in `<server path>/wai/include/reqstrm.hpp` and avoid C++ stream classes. You should place your entire code in `extern "C"` brackets, so as to allow the compiler to use the correct symbols and the appropriate naming convention.

```
extern "C"
{
#include . . .
/* Your code */
}
```

As mentioned earlier, if you wish to mix NSAPI functions with a WAI application, consider writing a WAI C application that runs in the server process. Although you may be able to use some NSAPI functions with an out-of-process WAI C application, you should avoid using NSAPI functions when running the application out-of-process. NSAPI relies on data structures that are in the server process. These data structures are not available to an out-of-process WAI application. Out-of-process applications use the data structures invoked through CORBA. They do not have direct access to the data structures of the server process. For example, you can use **util_sprintf** with C or C++ out-of-process applications, but you cannot use `system_*` or `crit_*` functions with such an application.

An in-process WAI application is written as an **Init** function that runs at the start of the server. A WAI **Init** function can use a number of NSAPI functions. But, it does not have access to the server's request-specific data structures. With an in-process WAI application, the request-specific information is passed by way of the built-in WAI **Service** function **IIOPexec** to the function in your WAI application that processes the client request.

NSAPI functions, which do not access or rely on the server `Request` or `Session` data structures, can be used with your WAI in-process C (or C++) applications. These NSAPI functions are mainly platform-independent functions based on standard system calls. In other words, file I/O, threads, and **util_*** functions can be used in your

WAI in-process applications. These NSAPI functions are not intended for handling the CORBA request object. You may want to use these functions for the thread safety and the cross-platform support that they provide. To demonstrate the use of NSAPI with WAI applications, in Chapter 16 we will modify the guest book example to use a number of NSAPI functions. If you plan to use NSAPI with your WAI applications, you also need to include the NSAPI library, `ns-httpd30.lib` for Server 3.0x and `nshttpd35.lib` for Server 3.5.1 (found under *<server path>*`/lib`), when you compile and link these programs.

You also should not use WAI functions with your NSAPI applications. NSAPI code does not have access to the CORBA methods and request objects.

Target Language Files, Classes, Methods, and Functions

WAI is built on top of NSAPI, CORBA, IIOP, and the Netscape ORB, but the complexity of these interfaces is hidden from you. The process of compiling the WAI IDL files and writing the appropriate CORBA classes and methods has already been completed by Netscape. Netscape has also written the core CORBA and NSAPI components of WAI. With WAI, Netscape even goes a step further and provides simple wrapper classes and functions for your programming. Netscape hides much of the complexity of CORBA and exposes only those classes, methods, and functions that you need to write your applications. The actual CORBA implementation of WAI remains hidden. What is exposed is the part of implementation that your code needs to use.

Netscape provides the specific programming language files that your program requires to interact with the server and to process the client request. You include (import) these files in your WAS source file. These language-specific files include the wrapper classes for C++ and Java and wrapper functions for C that your program uses to process client requests. The classes, methods, and functions are based on the WAI CORBA interface that we discussed in the previous section.

You write your WAI applications using the specific classes, methods, and functions identified for your chosen programming language—that is, C, C++, or Java. These wrapper classes and functions are similar to an API that you can use to write server programs. Your job is to finish writing the object implementation for the service the server needs to deliver. First, you write a program that declares a `WAIWebApplicationService` class, creates a service object, and registers its service with the server. The service's implementation function or method (that is, the **Run** method) should process the client request and return the response using the specific functions that Netscape provides. You use the `HttpServerRequest` interface's methods for your chosen programming language to process the client request and return the response to the client. The files and the actual classes, methods, or functions that you use will differ depending on the programming language you choose.

In Chapter 15, we will go through the steps of writing WAI applications for C, C++, and Java. In the rest of this chapter, we will examine all the major components that Netscape provides for C, C++, and Java. We will list the language-specific files, classes, methods, or functions that you need to include and use. There are three main interfaces (and classes) intended for all the WAI programming languages: `WAIWebApplicationService`, `HttpServerRequest`, and `HttpServerContext`. In the following sections, we will use these interfaces and classes to list and describe the programming language specific implementation provided by Netscape. Since `WAIWebApplicationService` is a wrapper class based on the `WebApplicationBasicService` IDL interface and its implementation varies depending on the programming language, we will list all of the methods of this class for each language and describe their uses. On the other hand, as `HttpServerContext` and `HttpServerRequest` methods are based on the CORBA IDL interface described in the CORBA and WAI section (Tables 14-1 and 14-2), we will list only the appropriate methods or functions of a specific language with their IDL equivalents. `HttpServerContext` and `HttpServerRequest` are actually interfaces, while `WebApplicationBasicService` is a class provided by Netscape for writing your WAI applications in C++ and Java. For more information on the specific use of these methods, see Tables 14-1 and 14-2.

We will also discuss the `FormHandler` class for C++ and Java. You can use this class to access the client POST or GET input.

WAI C and C++ Files

As with most programs that you may write, there are three main types of files needed for writing a C or C++ WAI application. The first group of files includes the header files you need to include with your source file. The second group contains the library files to which your program needs to link. These files need to be available during the linking and compiling of your program. The third type includes the shared library or DLL files that the WAI program needs to use (dynamically link to) when it is running. These files need to be accessible to your program. Besides any additional files that your program, system, or compiler may require, you must also use a number of Netscape-specific files.

In the following section, we will look closely at the two core header files for WAI: `ONEiiop.h` (for C) and `ONESrvPI.hpp` (for C++). We will also look at the `FormHandler.h` file included with Server 3.01 and later for C++. Unlike the shared object, library, or DLL files that you need for compiling and linking your application, header files can be reviewed and studied for the declaration of the functions or classes that you can use.

Other header files for CORBA and WAI programming are found in the `<server path>/wai/include` directory, such as `NameLib.hpp` or `NameUtil.hpp` for Naming Service. Another header file, `reqstrm.hpp`, includes stream and stream buffer classes for C++ WAI. You can use these classes to write directly to the client or to read the client input. The classes include `reqStreamBuf` for the stream buffer and `oreqstream`, `ireqstream`, and `ioreqstream` for the output, input, and input/output stream used by the IIOP request object. Normally, you do not use these classes, so you can also safely ignore other header files in the WAI include directory. When you program a WAS, you mainly need to be concerned with `ONESrvPI.hpp` for C++ and `ONEiiop.h` for C.

There are specific library files that you need to include when you program your C or C++ WAS, such as `ONEiiop10.lib` for Windows NT and `libONEiiop.so.10` for Solaris. The compiler needs to link with these files. These library files differ depending on the platform for which you are programming. We will list the library files you need to include in your project when we go through the steps of compiling a WAI C or C++ application in Chapter 16.

Your compiled C++ and C WAI applications also need to use a specific number of shared libraries or DLLs. In other words, for your program to run, it needs to be able to find and access methods or functions in the shared or dynamically linked libraries. For example, a simple NT version of a WAI application for Server 3.5.1 needs to have access to at least the following files: `ns-httpd35.dll`, `nslch32v30.dll`, `nsldap32v30.dll`, `ONEiiop10.dll`, `mtld.dll`, `msvcrt.dll`, `libesnspr20.dll`, `msvcirt.dll`, and `orb_r.dll`. These files include a number of essential core libraries, from Enterprise Server and LDAP libraries to IIOP, WAI, and ISB specific libraries. When you install the server, Netscape places these files in the Windows NT system32 directory or under the Netscape Server bin directory—for example, `<server path>/bin/https`. These directories should be already accessible to your program. If you were to place your program on a remote machine where Netscape Server is not installed, however, then your program would ask for these missing files.

ONEiiop.h—*C Header File*

The header file `ONEiiop.h`, found under the `<server path>/wai/include` directory, includes the declarations of the C functions that you can use to write your WAI applications. The C version of WAI is built as a layer on top of C++. `ONEiiop.h` includes the NSAPI header file `netsite.h`. It is dependent on the NSAPI header files for some of its definitions; for example, the `NSAPI_PUBLIC` type definition is defined in the NSAPI header files. The NSAPI header files are also used when writing in-process WAI C functions.

Unlike a file generated by an IDL compiler, `ONEiiop.h` does not include implementation code. `ONEiiop.h` is a header file that includes the declarations for the data types and functions you need to write your program. Only the interface that you need to program your application is exposed in this file. None of the underlying functions and methods that accomplish the CORBA implementation is included. You can safely forget about dealing with the details of the CORBA layer.

`ONEiiop.h` provides wrapper C functions and data types for developing a WAS. You do not use classes and methods, as you typically would for the object-oriented CORBA programming. The C++ classes or methods are not exposed in C. Unlike the header file for C++, there are no class equivalents to the `HttpServerContext` and `HttpServerRequest` interfaces. Instead, the C functions use a specific reference (handle) to the server session object. This object is accessed through the first parameter of the WAI C functions. The ORB passes a reference to the request's session object to your WAI callback function that handles the request. You also pass this reference to the specific WAI functions that you intend to use.

Functions in `ONEiiop.h` are programming language prototypes based on the `server.idl` methods. They include similar parameters to their parallel IDL methods, plus the additional parameter for the server session object (`ServerSession_t`). This parameter allows access to the HTTP request object (`HttpServerRequest`). For example, the IDL method **getRequestHeader** defined in `server.idl` is

```
HttpServerReturnType getRequestHeader(in string header,
 out string value);
```

The C function for the method **getRequestHeader** is

```
NSAPI_PUBLIC WAIReturnType_t WAIgetRequestHeader(
                                    ServerSession_t p,
                                    const char *header,
                                    const char *value);
```

The data structure for `ServerSession_t` is defined as

```
typedef struct{
      void *reserved;
} *ServerSession_t;
```

As in NSAPI, `NSAPI_PUBLIC` is mainly used to identify a function as type `_declspec(dllexport)` for Windows NT and as type `extern` for other operating systems. The names of all C WAI functions begin with `WAI`.

The return value, `WAIReturnType_t`, of most WAI C functions is used to verify whether the function performed its task properly. A return of `WAISPISuccess` indicates success, while a return of `WAISPIFailure` indicates failure. `WAIReturnType_t` is based on IDL enum `HttpServerReturnType`. `WAIReturnType_t` is defined as follows:

```
enum WAIReturnType {
    WAISPISuccess,
    WAISPIFailure
    WAISPIBadparam,
    WAISPINonameservice
};
typedef enum WAIReturnType WAIReturnType_t;
```

`WAISPIBadparam` and `WAISPINonameservice` are new constants added to enum `WAIReturnType` for Netscape Server 3.01 and later. They are intended for use with the C++ Naming Service methods.

Other important data structures defined in `ONEiiop.h` are `IIOPWebAppService_t` and `ServerContext_t`. You do not actually use `ServerContext_t` directly, but `IIOPWebAppService_t` is used for registering WAI applications. `IIOPWebAppService_t` is the handle to the IIOP Web application service structure. There are four specific functions for creating, registering, readying, and deleting your WAI application: **WAIcreateWebAppService**, **WAIregisterService**, **WAIimplIsReady**, and **WAIdeleteService**.

`WAIWebApplicationService`-**Related C Functions**   Table 14-5 describes the various `WAIWebApplicationService`-related functions for C.

Table 14-5   `WAIWebApplicationService`-Related C Functions

FUNCTION	DESCRIPTION
`typedef long (*WAIRunFunction) (ServerSession_t session);`	The prototype for the call-back function you write to process the client requests. The server calls this function, which you register with the server through **WAIcreateWebAppService** and **WAIregisterService**. This function should return 0 when it exits successfully.
`NSAPI_PUBLIC IIOPWebAppService_t` **WAIcreateWebAppService** `(const char *name, WAIRunFunction func, int argc, char **argv);`	Creates a Web service and identifies your C call-back function that processes the client requests. (See above for the prototype of the call-back function.) `name` is the name of the WAI service. You can choose any name you wish as long as it is not used by any other Web service. The client uses this name in the HTTP URL to invoke your WAS. `argc` and `argv` are used to pass additional ORB or BOA settings. You may need to specify a BOA address if it is different from the default loopback address, `127.0.0.1`. In other words, if you specified a unique BOA address with the **IIOPinit** directive function in the **obj.conf** file, you may need to send this address as an argument (`argv`) for **WAIcreateWebAppService**. If no additional argument is needed, you can set `argc` and `argv` to 0. `IIOPWebAppService_t`, which is returned by **WAIcreateWebAppService**, is the handle to the IIOP Web application service structure.
`NSAPI_PUBLIC WAIBool` **WAIregisterService** `(IIOPWebAppService_t p, const char *host);`	Registers the WAI service created by **WAIcreateWebAppService** (p) with Netscape Server's Naming Service. The `host` parameter should be used for the name of the Netscape Server host machine. If the port is different from the default HTTP port (`80`), you should also specify the port in the `host` parameter—that is, `<host name>[:port]`. The host name and port information can be passed to your program through command-line arguments. If SSL is enabled, you should use the `file` protocol and the name of the server IOR file—for example, `file:<server IOR file>`. (For more information, see Chapter 15, Registering Your Service with an SSL-Enabled Server.) The function returns 1 (`WAI_TRUE`) if successful and 0 (`WAI_FALSE`) if it failed to register your service.
`NSAPI_PUBLIC void` **WAIimplIsReady** `(void);`	Like the CORBA method **impl_is_ready**, **WAIimplIsReady** activates the implementation. It starts the event loop that waits for the client request. **WAIimplIsReady** puts the server application in an endless loop waiting for a request. Any code that

Table 14-5 `WAIWebApplicationService`-Related C Functions (*continued*)

FUNCTION	DESCRIPTION
	you write after **WAIimplIsReady** is not executed. Place this function at the end of your main function before exiting.
`NSAPI_PUBLIC void` **WAIdeleteService** `(IIOPWebAppService_t WebAppService);`	Used to delete a service you created using **WAIcreateWebAppService**.
`NSAPI_PUBLIC void` **WAIstringFree** `(char* s);`	Used to free a string that was previously allocated.
`getServiceInfo,` `StringDup` and `StringAlloc` are defined for C++ but not C.	

When you create a Web application service, **WAIcreateWebAppService** returns `IIOPWebAppService_t`, a pointer to an instance of a WAI Web service class (a Web service object). The parameters for **WAIcreateWebAppService** are the name of the instance of the service and the name of the function that the Netscape Server invokes to respond to a client request. The name you give to the Web service is the same name that the client uses to invoke your application. Unlike with C++ and Java, with the C version of WAI, you specify the name of the function that processes the client requests. The server does not assume that the name of the function of your Web service object is **Run**. The prototype of a function that processes the client request is `typedef long (*WAIRunFunction)(ServerSession_t session);`. The function returns a `long` and receives a reference to a server session object (`ServerSession_t`) as a parameter. This parameter represents the HTTP request object (`HttpServerRequest`). The following is an example of this function:

```
long MyFunction (ServerSession_t obj);
```

Next, you register the Web service object with Netscape Server by using **WAIregisterService** and the handle to the IIOP Web application service structure, `IIOPWebAppService_t`, returned by the **WAIcreateWebAppService** function. You also specify the name of the Netscape Server host machine and its port address, if it is different from the default HTTP port address (`80`), as a parameter of **WAIregisterService**. If SSL is enabled, you should use the `file` indicator and the name of the server IOR file—for example, `file:<server IOR file>`. If the server root and server ID are different from the default settings, you should specify the environment variables `NS_SERVER_ROOT` and `NS_SERVER_ID`. Note that once you specify these environment variables, the application may register using this information, independent of what you specify for the `host` parameter of **WAIregisterService**. (For more information, see Chapter 15, Registering Your Service with an SSL-Enabled Server.) Finally, you use **WAIimplIsReady** to start a loop that waits for the client request. Your application remains active while waiting for client requests. Any code that you write after **WAIimplIsReady** is not executed.

HttpServerContext- and HttpServerRequest-Related C Functions

Tables 14-6 and 14-7 list the WAI C functions that are used to process client requests. You use these functions in the WAI function that processes the client requests—that is, the same function that you declared with the **WAIcreateWebAppService** function. Unlike with C++ and Java, the distinction between HttpServerContext and HttpServerRequest is not relevant to C functions. You do not need to get HttpServerContext by using **getContext** before accessing the HttpServerContext methods. Instead, you get the global server data directly with specific **WAIget*** C functions. For example, you get the server port address via **WAIgetPort**.

Tables 14-6 and 14-7 list the IDL methods on which these WAI C functions are based. The use of these C functions is dependent on the purposes of the IDL methods. For more information on the use of these functions, see Tables 14-1 and 14-2. These C functions include parameters similar to those of their IDL methods. All of the following HttpServerContext- and HttpServerRequest-related C functions also include matching a parameter for the server session object (ServerSession_t). These functions need to identify the server session object (the HTTP request object) to invoke its specific method.

Table 14-6 HttpServerContext-Related C Functions

C PROTOTYPE	IDL METHOD
WAIBool **WAIgetInfo** (ServerSession_t p, const char *name, char **value);	HttpServerReturnType getInfo (in string name, out string value);
NSAPI_PUBLIC char* **WAIgetHost** (ServerSession_t p);	string getHost();
NSAPI_PUBLIC char* **WAIgetName** (ServerSession_t p);	string getName();
NSAPI_PUBLIC long **WAIgetPort** (ServerSession_t p);	long getPort();
NSAPI_PUBLIC char* **WAIgetServerSoftware** (ServerSession_t p);	string getServerSoftware();
NSAPI_PUBLIC WAIBool **WAIisSecure** (ServerSession_t p);	boolean isSecure();

Table 14-7 HttpServerRequest-Related C Functions

C PROTOTYPE	IDL METHOD
FUNCTIONS FOR GETTING REQUEST- AND CLIENT-RELATED INFORMATION	
NSAPI_PUBLIC WAIReturnType_t **WAIgetRequestInfo** (ServerSession_t p, const char *name, char **value);	HttpServerReturnType getRequestInfo(in string name, out string value);

Table 14-7 `HttpServerRequest`-Related C Functions (*continued*)

C PROTOTYPE	IDL METHOD
FUNCTIONS FOR GETTING REQUEST- AND CLIENT-RELATED INFORMATION	
NSAPI_PUBLIC WAIReturnType_t **WAIgetRequestHeader** (ServerSession_t p, const char *name, char **value);	HttpServerReturnType getRequestHeader (in string header, out string value);
NSAPI_PUBLIC WAIReturnType_t **WAIgetCookie** (ServerSession_t p, char **cookie);	HttpServerReturnType getCookie(out string cookie);
FUNCTIONS FOR GETTING ADDITIONAL INFORMATION	
NSAPI_PUBLIC WAIReturnType_t **WAIgetConfigParameter** (ServerSession_t p, const char *name, char **value);	HttpServerReturnType getConfigParameter(in string name, out string value);
Not used.	HttpServerContext getContext();
NSAPI_PUBLIC long **WAIReadClient** (ServerSession_t p, unsigned char *buffer, unsigned buffsize); (With **WAIReadClient**, you also must specify the size of the buffer [bufsize] that is read.)	long ReadClient(inout HttpServerBuffer buffer);
FUNCTIONS FOR SETTING (ADDING), GETTING, AND DELETING RESPONSE-HEADERS	
NSAPI_PUBLIC WAIReturnType_t **WAIsetResponseContentType** (ServerSession_t p, const char *ContentType);	HttpServerReturnType setResponseContentType (in string ContentType);
NSAPI_PUBLIC WAIReturnType_t **WAIsetResponseContentLength** (ServerSession_t p, unsigned long Length);	HttpServerReturnType setResponseContentLength (in unsigned long Length);
NSAPI_PUBLIC WAIReturnType_t **WAIsetCookie**(ServerSession_t p, const char *name, const char *value, const char *expires, const char *domain, const char *path, WAIBool secure);	HttpServerReturnType setCookie (in string name, in string value, in string expires, in string domain, in string path, in boolean secure);
NSAPI_PUBLIC WAIReturnType_t **WAIsetResponseStatus** (ServerSession_t p, long status, const char *reason);	HttpServerReturnType setResponseStatus(in long status, in string reason);
Not used.	HttpServerReturnType setRequestInfo (in string name, in string value);

Table 14-7 `HttpServerRequest`-Related C Functions (*continued*)

C PROTOTYPE	IDL METHOD
FUNCTIONS FOR SETTING (ADDING), GETTING, AND DELETING RESPONSE-HEADERS	
NSAPI_PUBLIC WAIReturnType_t **WAIaddResponseHeader** (ServerSession_t p, const char *header, const char *value);	HttpServerReturnType addResponseHeader (in string header, in string value);
NSAPI_PUBLIC WAIReturnType_t **WAIgetResponseHeader** (ServerSession_t p, const char *header, char **value);	HttpServerReturnType getResponseHeader (in string header, out string value);
NSAPI_PUBLIC WAIReturnType_t **WAIgetResponseContentLength** (ServerSession_t p, unsigned long *Length);	HttpServerReturnType getResponseContentLength (out unsigned long Length);
NSAPI_PUBLIC WAIReturnType_t **WAIdelResponseHeader** (ServerSession_t p, const char *header);	HttpServerReturnType delResponseHeader (in string header);
FUNCTIONS FOR WRITING THE RESPONSE	
NSAPI_PUBLIC long **WAIStartResponse** (ServerSession_t p);	long StartResponse();
NSAPI_PUBLIC long **WAIWriteClient** (ServerSession_t p, const unsigned char *buffer, unsigned buffsize); (With **WAIWriteClient**, you also must specify the size of the buffer [bufsize] that is read.)	long WriteClient (in HttpServerBuffer buffer);
ADDITIONAL FUNCTIONS	
NSAPI_PUBLIC char* **WAIBuildURL**(ServerSession_t p, const char *prefix, const char *suffix);	string BuildURL (in string prefix, in string suffix);
NSAPI_PUBLIC WAIReturnType_t **WAILogError**(ServerSession_t p, long degree, const char *func, const char *msg, WAIBool clientinfo);	HttpServerReturnType LogError (in long degree, in string func, in string msg, in boolean clientinfo);
NSAPI_PUBLIC WAIReturnType_t **WAIRespondRedirect** (ServerSession_t p, const char *url);	HttpServerReturnType RespondRedirect (in string url);

ONEsrvPI.hpp—*C++ Header File*

The main header file for C++ WAI is ONEsrvPI.hpp. ONEservPI.hpp also includes the WAI header file ONEiiop.h (#include "ONEiiop.h"). It uses ONEiiop.h for some of its type definitions.

Like ONEiiop.h, ONEservPI.hpp is not the same as the file generated by an IDL compiler. If you compile the WAI IDL files with the C++ IDL compiler, you get different files with different sets of classes and methods. ONEservPI.hpp exposes only the parts of the WAI interface that you need to write your programs. Your job is to finish writing the server object based on the classes that ONEservPI.hpp provides.

Unlike ONEiiop.h, ONEsrvPI.hpp closely resembles the WAI IDL interfaces and methods. It includes specific C++ classes, WAIServerContext and WAIServerRequest, for the IDL interfaces, HttpServerContext and HttpServerRequest. The WAIWebApplicationService class is used to create an instance of your WAI Web service and register it with the server. These three C++ classes, which are the basis of C++ WAI, are defined as type DLLEXPORT. DLLEXPORT is used to identify these classes as _declspec (dllexport) for building an in-process DLL application for Windows NT. For other circumstances, DLLEXPORT is set to blank (nothing).

The three internal classes—HttpServerRequest, HttpServerContext, and WebApplicationServiceSkeleton—are used by the WAI C++ classes you are supposed to write. You do not use these classes directly, however. They are for internal use by the ORB. There are also pointers to WAIServerContext, WAIServerContext_ptr, for use by the WAIServerRequest method **getContext**, and a pointer to WAIServerRequest, WAIServerRequest_ptr, for use by the WAIWebApplicationService method **Run**.

WAIWebApplicationService **Class**

Table 14-8 WAIWebApplicationService C++ Methods

METHOD	DESCRIPTION
For Server 3.x: **WAIWebApplicationService** (const char *service_name); or WAIWebApplicationService (const char *service_name, int argc, char **argv); Added to Server 3.01 and later: WAIWebApplicationService (const char *service_name, WAIBool activeObj);	Constructor for WAIWebApplicationService. You use the WAIWebApplicationService class constructor to write your WAS class constructor. You derive your Web application service class from WAIWebApplicationService. You then use the constructor in the main function of your application to instantiate your Web service object. You can also initialize any additional Web service variables in your constructor. The service_name variable is the name you give to your Web service. You can use any name you wish as long as no other Web service uses the same one. The client uses this name in the HTTP URL to invoke your WAS. There are four possible base constructors used, each of which was a different parameter. The first two constructors can be used for all versions of Netscape Server 3.x. The next two constructors are new constructors for Server 3.01 and later. All constructors use the service_name as a parameter. The new constructors also include a parameter activeObj. You

Table 14-8 `WAIWebApplicationService` C++ Methods (*continued*)

METHOD	DESCRIPTION
`WAIWebApplicationService` `(const char *service_name,` `int argc, char **argv,` `WAIBool activeObj);`	set `activeObj` to `WAI_TRUE` if you want the object to be immediately activated. If you set `activeObj` to `WAI_FALSE`, you must use the method **ActiveWAS** to activate the object. (See **ActiveWAS** for more information.) The parameters `argv` and `argc` can be used to pass additional ORB or BOA settings. You may need to specify a BOA address if it is different from the default loopback address, `127.0.0.1`. In other words, if you specified a unique BOA address with the **IIOPinit** directive function in the `obj.conf` file, you may need to pass this address as an argument (`argv`). If no additional argument is needed, you can set `argc` and `argv` to `0`.
`~WAIWebApplicationService();`	The `WAIWebApplicationService` destructor. A destructor is automatically called when your service object is destroyed. You do not need to call this method.
`virtual char*` **`getServiceInfo`**`();`	Used to return specific information about the author, version, and copyright information of the application. It is a pure virtual function that your class has to override.
`WAIBool` **`RegisterService`** `(const char *host);`	Registers the Web service with Netscape Server's Naming Service. The `host` parameter should be used for the name of the Netscape Server host machine. If the port is different from the default HTTP port (`80`), you should also specify the port in the `host` parameter—that is, `<host name>[:port]`. The host name and port information can be passed to your program through command-line arguments. If SSL is enabled, you should use the `file` indicator and the name of the server IOR file—for example, `file:<server IOR file>`. (For more information, see Chapter 15, Registering Your Service with an SSL-Enabled Server.) The method returns `WAI_TRUE` when the service was properly registered and `WAI_FALSE` if the registration failed.
`virtual long` **`Run`** `(WAIServerRequest_ptr` `session);`	Processes the client requests. The **Run** function is a pure virtual function that your class must override. When Netscape Server receives a client HTTP request that asks for your Web service, the server invokes the **Run** function of your Web service. A pointer to the server request object is passed to your **Run** method. This object provides access to the `HttpServerRequest` interface. You use this object to get the HTTP request information and to return a response. (See Table 14-10 for `HttpServerRequest` methods that you can use to process a client request.) The **Run** method should return `0` when it exits successfully.
`void` **`ActiveWAS`**`();`	Activates the Web service object. Instead of having the service object be activated when you invoke its constructor, you can set the parameter `activeObj` for the constructor of the service object to `WAI_FALSE` and use **ActiveWAS** to activate the service object. Thus you can activate your service object at a later point after the object is constructed. You can use **ActiveWAS** in conjunction with OAD to have your program automatically activated for the UNIX version of the server. (For more information on OAD, see the OAD section in Chapter 12. For

Table 14-8 `WAIWebApplicationService` C++ Methods (*continued*)

METHOD	DESCRIPTION
	information on registering your WAI application with OAD, see Registering an Out-of-Process WAI Application with OAD in Chapter 16.)
char* **StringAlloc** (size_t size);	Used to allocate memory for a string. `size` is the string that should be allocated. **StringAlloc** returns a pointer to a newly allocated buffer.
void **StringDelete**(char *s);	Used to free a string that was allocated.
char* **StringDup** (const char *s);	Used to duplicate (copy) a string. The function also allocates a buffer for the new string. `s` is the string that should be duplicated. The function returns a pointer to the newly allocated string.

Table 14-8 lists the methods (functions) defined for `WAIWebApplicationService`. You derive your WAI application service from the `WAIWebApplicationService` class. You must derive a constructor class from `WAIWebApplicationService` and write the **getServiceInfo** and **Run** methods. **getServiceInfo** should return the general application information—for example, the author name, version, copyright, and so on. The **Run** method is your service's actual implementation method. It processes the client request. You use the methods of `WAIServerContext` and `WAIServerRequest` in the **Run** method. The ORB passes a pointer to the request object (`WAIServerRequest_ptr`) to your **Run** method. You use the methods of this object (`WAIServerRequest`) to get information about the request and return a response. To get a pointer to the `WAIServerContext` (`WAIServer_ptr`) so as to invoke the `WAIServerContext` methods, you must use the **getContext** function of `WAIServerRequest`.

You must also register the Web service object you initialize in your WAI application's main function by using the method **RegisterService** of your Web service object. You specify the name of the Netscape Server host machine and a port address, if it is different from the default HTTP port address, as a parameter of **RegisterService**. If SSL is enabled, you should use the `file` indicator and the name of the server IOR file—for example, `file:<server IOR file>`. If the server root and server ID are different from the default settings, you should specify the environment variables `NS_SERVER_ROOT` and `NS_SERVER_ID`. For example, the default setting for `SERVER ID` is `https<host name>`. Note that once you specify these environment variables, the application may register using this information, independent of what you specify in the `host` parameter. (For more information, see Chapter 15, Registering Your Service with an SSL-Enabled Server.)

Netscape Server 3.01 has added a new parameter to the `WAIWebApplicationService` constructor, `activeObj`. You can set this parameter to `WAI_FALSE` if you want to activate your object at a later stage. You then use the new method **ActiveWAS** to activate the Web service object. Thus the object is activated when **ActiveWAS** is called, rather than when the constructor is invoked.

`WAIServerContext` and `WAIServerRequest` **Classes**   Table 14-9 lists the methods (functions) for the `WAIServerContext` class, and Table 14-10 lists the methods for the `WAIServerRequest` class. The methods listed in these tables are virtual functions of the two classes. These virtual functions are based on the IDL methods. The matching IDL methods for the C++ functions are also included. For more information on the use of these functions, see Tables 14-1 and 14-2, which describe the purpose of each IDL method. You do not need to worry about the other methods of the `WAIServerContext` and `WAIServerRequest` classes, as they are used for internal purposes.

Unlike the C functions, the C++ functions that process the client request are virtual functions of a class. The names of the C++ functions do not begin with `WAI`, and there is no need for the `ServerSession_t` parameter. Some of the parameters of the C++ functions are also of different types than the parameters of the C functions.

Except for **ReadClient** and **WriteClient**, the C++ methods do not include any parameters other than the ones identified by the IDL files. The return values of many of the C++ functions are `WAIReturnType`. The return value `WAIReturnType` is `WAISPISuccess` upon success of the function or `WAISPIFailure` upon the failure.

Table 14-9   `WAIServerContext` (`HttpServerContext`) C++ Methods

C++ FUNCTION	IDL METHOD
`WAIReturnType getInfo` `(const char *name,` `char *&value);`	`HttpServerReturnType getInfo` `(in string name, out string value);`
`char* getHost();`	`string getHost();`
`char* getName();`	`string getName();`
`long getPort();`	`long getPort();`
`char* getServerSoftware();`	`string getServerSoftware();`
`int isSecure();`	`boolean isSecure();`

Table 14-10   `WAIServerRequest` (`HttpServerRequest`) C++ Methods

C++ FUNCTION	IDL METHOD
FUNCTIONS FOR GETTING REQUEST- AND CLIENT-RELATED INFORMATION	
`WAIReturnType getRequestInfo` `(const char *name,` `char *&value);`	`HttpServerReturnType getRequestInfo` `(in string name, out string value);`
`WAIReturnType` `getRequestHeader` `(const char *header,` `char *&value);`	`HttpServerReturnType getRequestHeader` `(in string header, out string value);`
`WAIReturnType getCookie` `(char *&cookie);`	`HttpServerReturnType getCookie` `(out string cookie);`

C++ FUNCTION	IDL METHOD
FUNCTIONS FOR GETTING ADDITIONAL INFORMATION	

`WAIReturnType`
`getConfigParameter` `(const char`
`*name, char *&value);`
	`HttpServerReturnType getConfigParameter`
	`(in string name, out string value);`

`WAIServerContext_ptr` **`getContext`**`();`	`HttpServerContext getContext();`

`long` **`ReadClient`**
`(unsigned char *buffer,`
`unsigned buffsize);`
 	
(With **ReadClient**, you also must
specify the size of the buffer
[`bufsize`] that is read.)
	`long ReadClient`
	`(inout HttpServerBuffer buffer);`

FUNCTIONS FOR SETTING (ADDING), GETTING, AND DELETING RESPONSE-HEADERS	

`WAIReturnType`
`setResponseContentType`
`(const char *Content-Type);`
	`HttpServerReturnType`
	`setResponseContentType`
	`(in string ContentType);`

`WAIReturnType`
`setResponseContentLength`
`(unsigned long Length);`
	`HttpServerReturnType`
	`setResponseContentLength`
	`(in unsigned long Length);`

`WAIReturnType` **`setCookie`**
`(const char *name,`
`const char *value,`
`const char *expires,`
`const char *domain,`
`const char *path,`
`WAIBool secure);`
	`HttpServerReturnType setCookie(in string`
	`name, in string value, in string expires, in`
	`string domain, in string path, in boolean`
	`secure);`

`WAIReturnType`
`setResponseStatus`
`(long status,`
`const char *reason);`
	`HttpServerReturnType`
	`setResponseStatus`
	`(in long status, in string reason);`

Not used.	`HttpServerReturnType`
	`setRequestInfo`
	`(in string name, in string value);`

`WAIReturnType`
`addResponseHeader`
`(const char *header,`
`const char *value);`
	`HttpServerReturnType`
	`addResponseHeader`
	`(in string header, in string value);`

`WAIReturnType`
`getResponseHeader`
`(const char *header,`
`char *&value);`
	`HttpServerReturnType`
	`getResponseHeader`
	`(in string header, out string value);`

`WAIReturnType`
`getResponseContentLength`
`(unsigned long &Length);`
	`HttpServerReturnType getResponseContentLength`
	`(out unsigned long Length);`

Table 14-10 `WAIServerRequest` (`HttpServerRequest`) C++ Methods
(continued)

C++ FUNCTION	IDL METHOD
FUNCTIONS FOR SETTING (ADDING), GETTING, AND DELETING RESPONSE-HEADERS	
WAIReturnType **delResponseHeader** (const char *header);	HttpServerReturnType delResponseHeader(in string header);
FUNCTIONS FOR WRITING THE RESPONSE	
long **StartResponse**();	long StartResponse();
long **WriteClient** (const unsigned char *buffer, unsigned buffsize); (With **WriteClient**, you also must specify the size of the buffer [bufsize] that is read.)	long WriteClient(in HttpServerBuffer buffer);
ADDITIONAL FUNCTIONS	
char* **BuildURL** (const char *prefix, const char *suffix);	string BuildURL (in string prefix, in string suffix);
WAIReturnType **LogError** (long degree, const char *func, const char *msg, WAIBool clientinfo);	HttpServerReturnType LogError (in long degree, in string func, in string msg, in boolean clientinfo);
WAIReturnType **RespondRedirect** (const char *url);	HttpServerReturnType RespondRedirect (in string url);

`FormHandler.h`—`FormHandler` *Class for C++*

Netscape Server 3.01 added a new class, `FormHandler`, that handles the parsing and managing of the client input. `FormHandler` can be used when you write a WAI application in Java or C++. The methods you use and how you take advantage of the `FormHandler` class will differ depending on whether you use Java or C++.

The `FormHandler` class makes your life easier. With `FormHandler`, you can quickly access the data from the client input. If the data are sent using the POST method, `FormHandler`'s constructor (**FormHandler**) parses the data. You can retrieve the data using the **Get** method of `FormHandler`. If the data are sent using the HTTP GET method, you must first parse the data using **ParseQueryString**. The

---

Warning ▶

The correct function definitions for the C++ `FormHandler` class are not available in the library file included with the release version of Server 3.5.1. Thus you cannot use `FormHandler` with the release version of Server 3.5.1. Netscape should provide a patch to resolve this problem.

data from the HTTP GET method are found in the query string sent with the client's requested URL. Again, you can use the **Get** method of FormHandler to get the value of a named *name-value* pair. If you do not know the name in the *name-value* input from the client, or if there is more than one value associated with the same name, then you should use the **InitIterator** and **Next** methods of FormHandler. **InitIterator** returns a pointer to the first *name-value* pair in the list of parsed input data. You can then step through the list and read the name and value of each pair using the **Next** method. To use the FormHandler methods, you should first create an instance of the FormHandler class using the **FormHandler** constructor. Table 14-11 lists and describes the FormHandler methods that you can use.

You can find the FormHandler class in the formHandler.h header file under the *<server path>*/wai/include directory. To use FormHandler methods, you should include the FormHandler header file in your source file.

Bug Report ▶

The WAI patches (P85416) for upgrading the NT and Solaris versions of Enterprise Server 3.0 may include a FormHandler bug. With NT, when you use the FormHandler class to parse the query string from a GET method (that is, **ParseQueryString**), the parsed information is not available when you use the **InitIterator** or **Get** method. Using FormHandler for the POST method of requests works correctly. Check Netscape's File Library page, http://help.netscape.com/filelib.html, for updated WAI patches for your Netscape Server that may fix problems you may be having.

Table 14-11   FormHandler C++ Methods

METHOD	DESCRIPTION

`FormHandler`
`(WAIServerRequest_ptr`
`request);`
	Constructor for the FormHandler class. Before you can use its methods, you must instantiate an instance of the FormHandler class (create a FormHandler object). You pass the pointer to the request object (WAIServerRequest_ptr request) to the **FormHandler** constructor. This pointer is passed by the ORB to your **Run** method.
	
	If there is any input from an HTTP POST method of request, **FormHandler** reads and parses it. You can then use the **Get** or **InitIterator** and **Next** methods to obtain the value of the *name-value* pair of data submitted through the POST method. The POST data are normally submitted through an HTML form. To parse data in HTTP GET method of request, you must call the FormHandler method **ParseQueryString**.

`~FormHandler();`	FormHandler class destructor.
`WAIBool IsValid();`	Use this method to verify whether the data that the **FormHandler** constructor read from a POST method are valid. As with all FormHandler methods, you first must create an instance of the FormHandler class before calling its methods. If **FormHandler** was not able to read and parse the POST data, **IsValid** returns WAI_FALSE. Otherwise, it returns WAI_TRUE.

Table 14-11 `FormHandler` C++ Methods (*continued*)

METHOD	DESCRIPTION
`char* GetQueryString();`	You can use this method to get the query string from an HTTP `GET` method of request. **GetQueryString** returns the query string intact. You do not need to call this method before calling **ParseQueryString** to parse the query string. If you want to find out the value of the query string, however, use this method. You can also use **getRequestInfo** to get the query string with the `QUERY_STRING` environment variable. The query string is appended to the end of the client's requested URL after a question mark (for example, `http://www.foo.com/iiop/form?name=joe`).
`WAIBool ParseQueryString();`	Parses the query string of an HTTP `GET` method of request. The `FormHandler` object has access to the query string through the request object you pass to it. Use this method to parse the query string. **ParseQueryString** places the *name-value* pairs of data from the query string in a data structure that you can access. Unlike with the `POST` data, you must call an additional FormHandler method to parse the query string from a `GET` method (that is, **ParseQueryString**) before actually obtaining the value of a name-value pair of data in the `GET` query string. After the query string is parsed, you can use the **Get** or **InitIterator** and **Next** methods to access the values of the *name-value* pairs of query string data. If the method was able to parse the query string, it returns `WAI_TRUE`. Otherwise, it returns `WAI_FALSE`. Check this return value to make sure that the query string was valid and properly parsed.
`const char* Get (const char *name);`	Use this method for both the `POST` and `GET` methods of HTTP request. You can use **Get** to obtain the value of a named *name-value* pair found in the `POST` data or the query string. You specify the name of the *name-value* pair in the `name` parameter. **Get** returns the value. If there is more than one value for a name (that is, if there are multiple *name-value* pairs with the same name), you should use the **InitIterator** and **Next** methods to step through the pairs. For query strings, you should call **ParseQueryString** before using **Get**.
`WAIBool Add (const char *name, ; const char *value)`	You can add a *name-value* pair to the parsed query or HTTP `POST` data. This method returns `WAI_TRUE` if **Add** was able to add the *name-value* pair identified by the parameters `name` and `value`. **Add** returns `WAI_FALSE` if it failed to add the *name-value* pair. You rarely use the **Add** and **Delete** methods. You mainly use the **Get** or **InitIterator** and **Next** methods to get the value in the parsed data from a `GET` or `POST` method of request.
`WAIBool Delete (const char *name);`	You can delete a *name-value* pair in the parsed query or HTTP `POST` data. This method returns `WAI_TRUE` if **Delete** was able to delete the *name-value* pair identified by the parameter name. **Delete** returns `WAI_FALSE` if it failed to delete the *name-value* pair. You rarely use **Add** and **Delete** methods. You mainly use the **Get** or **InitIterator** and **Next** methods to get the value in the parsed data from a `GET` or `POST` method of request.
`WAIBool InitIterator();`	Used instead of the **Get** method to get the value of parsed *name-value* pairs, you can use the **InitIterator** and **Next**

Table 14-11 `FormHandler` C++ Methods (*continued*)

METHOD	DESCRIPTION
	methods together. **InitIterator** places a pointer to the beginning of the parsed *name-value* pairs. **Next** gets the value of each *name-value* pair iteratively. If you want to place the pointer to the beginning of the list again, then call **InitIterator** one more time. **InitIterator** returns `WAI_TRUE` if it was able to place a pointer at the beginning of the list of *name-value* pairs. It returns `WAI_FALSE` if an error occurred.
`WAIBool` **Next** `(const char *&name, const char *&value);`	Used to step through the list of parsed *name-value* data pairs. The `name` and `value` parameters hold the next *name* and *value* of the parsed *name-value* pair of data. First, call **InitIterator** to place yourself at the top of the *name-value* pairs of data. Then, you can iterate (enumerate) through the list using **Next**. If there are no more *name-value* pairs, **Next** returns `WAI_FALSE`. Make sure you check for the return value as you step through the *name-value* list. **Next** returns `WAI_TRUE` if a *name-value* pair was found and obtained.

WAI Java Classes and Method Files

You can find the Java WAI classes in `WAI.zip` under the `<server path>/wai/java` directory. `nisb.zip`, which holds Netscape's ISB classes is under the same directory. You need to add both of these zip files to your `CLASSPATH` environment if you plan to write `WAI` applications in Java. `WAI.zip` includes the `CosNaming.*` and `netscape.WAI.*` classes. `nisb.zip` includes `org.omg.CORBA.*`, among other classes. (It also includes the `netscape.WAI.Naming` class.) In addition to the standard Java classes, you use these three sets of Java classes (`CosNaming.*`, `netscape.WAI.*`, and `org.omg.CORBA.*`) in your project.

Unlike the C++ header files, the Java class files are in bytecode—that is, `*.class` files. Netscape does not provide the source code, so you must resort to the documentation to find out what the WAI Java interface provides, what methods exist for each class, which classes you need to use, and so on. If you look in the `WAI.zip` directory, you will find all of the relevant files that you would expect when you compile the IDL files with a Java compiler. There are many classes represented in these zip files.

If you look under `netscape.WAI`, you will find the CORBA implementation files for WAI. There are the server skeleton files (`_sk_*`), client stub files, (`_st_*`), tie class ("template" class) files, (`_tie_*`), and example (core of object implementation) files, (`_example_*`) for `HttpServerContext`, `HttpServerRequest`, `WebApplicationBasicService`, and `WebApplicationService`. There are also `*Helper.class`, `*Holder.class`, and `*Operations.class` class files for `HttpServerContext`, `HttpServerRequest`, `WebApplicationBasicService`, and `WebApplicationService`. For example, for `HttpServerRequest`, there are `HttpServerRequest.class`, `_sk_HttpServerRequest.class`, `_st_HttpServerRequest.class`, `_tie_HttpServerRequest.class`,

`_example_HttpServerRequest.class`,
`HttpServerRequestHelper.class`,
`HttpServerRequestHolder.class`, and
`HttpServerRequestOperations.class`. In other words, `WAI.zip` includes the CORBA implementations for the main four IDL interfaces `HttpServerContext`, `HttpServerRequest`, `WebApplicationBasicService`, and `WebApplicationService`). Do not worry about these CORBA implementation files; they are used for internal implementation of WAI. When you program a WAI application in Java, you use only a few classes and methods. We will discuss the relevant classes and methods shortly.

In addition to the previously mentioned files, `netscape.WAI` includes `NameUtil.class`, `FormHandler.class`, `WAIWebApplicationService.class`, and the relevant files for `HttpServerBuffer` and `HttpServerReturnType` (for example, `Helper` and `Holder` files).

`NameUtil.class` includes the interface for the `NameUtil` class used to register and locate CORBA object implementations using Netscape's Naming Service. `Naming.class` (`netscape.WAI.Naming`) includes the other Java class used for locating and registering CORBA object implementations. Unlike `NameUtil.class`, `Naming.class` is included with `nisb.zip`. This class is included with Netscape Communicator's ORB. Both of these classes use Netscape Naming Service. We discussed these classes and their methods in the section Java Naming Service in Chapter 12. Although you can use these classes in your Java WAI applications, you do not normally register your WAI application using the methods in `Naming` and `NameUtil` classes. Instead, the `WAIWebApplicationService` class provides the **RegisterService** method that you use to register your WAI application with Netscape Naming Service.

`FormHandler.class`, added to the `WAI.zip` file with Netscape Server 3.01, is used for the `FormHandler` class, which can be used to parse and manage input from a client `POST` or `GET` method of request. See the section FormHandler Class later in this chapter for more details.

`WAIWebApplicationService.class` is an important class, which you use to create the instance of your Web service and register your service. We will discuss the methods of this class in the next section.

You should also be familiar with the `Holder` classes, which are used to pass parameters during an operation request. With `Holder` classes, parameters can be passed by reference. `Holder` classes support the CORBA IDL types `out` and `inout`. (Unlike C and CORBA IDL data types, Java parameters are passed by value, not by reference.) You can use the `StringHolder` class (`org.omg.CORBA.StringHolder`) or the `IntHolder` class (`org.omg.CORBA.IntHolder`) with a number of Java methods. `HttpServerBufferHolder` is used for reading the client input (**ReadClient**). Before you can use the `netscape.WAI.HttpServerBufferHolder` class with the **ReadClient** method, you must create the buffer holder. You also must initialize the number of bytes to be read (a byte array) from the client. With Netscape Server 3.01

and later, you can use the `FormHandler` class and its methods to read and parse the input from a client `POST` input, instead of using the **ReadClient** method and writing your own parsing functions.

The `HttpServerReturnType` class is used for the return value of the majority of the `HttpServerRequest` methods. `HttpServerReturnType` is `Success` when the method is successful in accomplishing its intended task (`netscape.WAI.HttpServerReturnType.Success`) and `Failure` if the method failed to accomplish its task (`netscape.WAI.HttpServerReturnType.Failure`).

If you are familiar with CORBA or if you read Chapter 12 on CORBA, you may have a general understanding of the purposes of the Java class files included with the `WAI.zip` file. You do not need to understand how the actual CORBA implementation works to write your WAI application in Java. What you must know are the three main classes (plus `FormHandler` for Netscape 3.01 and later) and a few additional CORBA and WAI methods that you need to use. The three main classes with which you need to concern yourself are `WAIWebApplicationService`, `HttpServerContext`, and `HttpServerRequest`.

WAIWebApplicationService *Class*

Table 14-12   `WAIWebApplicationService` Java Methods

METHOD	DESCRIPTION
public **WAIWebApplicationService** (java.lang.String name);	Constructor for `WAIWebApplicationService`. You extend your Web application service class from `WAIWebApplicationService`. In your Web application service class constructor, you should first call the constructor for the superclass (`super(name);`). You can then initialize any additional server object variable that you like. You use the constructor to create an instance of your class (a Web service object). name is the name of the service. You can use any name you wish as long as no other Web service uses the same one. The client uses this name in the HTTP requested URL to invoke your WAS. The constructor can throw the following exceptions: `CosNaming.NamingContextPackage.CannotProceed`, `CosNaming.NamingContextPackage.InvalidName`, `CosNaming.NamingContextPackage.AlreadyBound`, and `org.omg.CORBA.SystemException`.
public abstract java.lang.String **getServiceInfo**();	Used to return specific information about the author, version, and copyright information of the application. It is a public abstract method that your class needs to override (define).
public boolean **RegisterService** (java.lang.String host);	Registers the Web service with the server. host is the host name of the Netscape Server machine. If the port is different from the default HTTP port (80), you should also specify the port in the host parameter—that is, <host name>[:port]. The host name and port information can be passed to your program through command-line arguments. If SSL is enabled, you should use the file indicator and the path of the server IOR file—for example, file:<path>/<server IOR file>. For

Table 14-12 `WAIWebApplicationService` Java Methods (*continued*)

METHOD	DESCRIPTION
	instance, for the server `foo` under NT, the path can be `file:c:/netscape/server/wai/NameService/httpsfoo.IOR`.

> **Bug Report ▶**
>
> This method should return `true` upon successful registration of your service and `false` upon failure. As tested under the NT version of Enterprise Server 3.0 using WAI patch and Server 3.5.1, however, it returned `false` even when the service was able to register with Naming Service. Make sure this method returns the proper response before you take advantage of its return value.

METHOD	DESCRIPTION
`public abstract int` **Run** `(netscape.WAI.HttpServerRequest session);`	Processes the client requests. The **Run** method is a public abstract method that your class must override. When the server calls your service, it invokes the **Run** method of your service. A reference to the server request object (session) is also passed to the **Run** method. This object represents `HttpServerRequest`. It allows you to get the HTTP request information and lets you return a response. The **Run** method should return 0 when it exits successfully.

Before you can create an instance of your WAI service, you should write an implementation for your service class. Similar to the process in C++, you derive (extend) your Web application service from `WAIWebApplicationService`. You must write a constructor and the **getServiceInfo** and **Run** methods. Table 14-12 describes the methods of the `WAIWebApplicationService` class.

When you write the constructor for your class, you should first call the constructor for the superclass in your constructor. You should also declare the naming context and system exceptions that the constructor can throw. The following is an example of such a code:

```
class SpecialWebApplicationService extends
                          WAIWebApplicationService
{
    String SpecialName;

    SpecialWebApplication(java.lang.String name) throws

    CosNaming.NamingContextPackage.CannotProceed,
    CosNaming.NamingContextPackage.InvalidName,
    CosNaming.NamingContextPackage.AlreadyBound,
    org.omg.CORBA.SystemException
    {
        super(name);
```

```
        SpecialName = name;
    }
}
```

As with WAI for C++, you must write the **getServiceInfo** and **Run** methods of your Web service class. The **Run** method is the service's actual implementation method. It processes the client request. In the **Run** method, you use the methods from `netscape.WAI.HttpServerContext` and `netscape.WAI.HttpServerRequest` to process the request. The ORB passes a reference to the `HttpServerRequest` object to your **Run** method. You must use the **getContext** function of `HttpServerRequest` to get the `HttpServerContext` object and use its methods.

You also must register your Web service object with Netscape Naming Service. Use the **RegisterService** method of the Web service object that you have created to register it with the server. (This step is part of writing your WAI application's main function.) You specify the name of Netscape Server's host machine and a port address, if it is different from the default HTTP port address, as parameters of **RegisterService**. If SSL is enabled, you should use the `file` indicator and the path of the server IOR file— for example, `file:<path>/<server IOR file>`. For instance, for server `foo` under NT, the path could be `file:c:/netscape/server/wai/ NameService/https-foo.IOR`. You should also put quotes around a path that includes spaces—for example, `file:"c:/program files/server/wai/ NameService/httpsfoo.IRO"`. Note that you use a path, not just the server IOR file name with Java.

`HttpServerContext` *and* `HttpServerRequest` *Classes*

Tables 14-13 and 14-14 list the methods for the `HttpServerContext` and `HttpServerRequest` classes, respectively. The methods listed in these tables are public methods of the classes and are based on the IDL methods. We have also included the matching IDL methods for these Java methods. The return value for many of these methods is `netscape.WAI.HttpServerReturnType`. The return value is `netscape.WAI.HttpServerReturnType.Success` upon success if the method accomplished its task or `netscape.WAI.HttpServerReturnType.Failure` upon failure. You should check for the return value when you use the appropriate `HttpServerRequest` methods to make sure the method functioned properly.

As mentioned earlier, some of the Java methods use a `Holder` class—for example, `StringHolder`, `HttpServerBufferHolder`, and `InitHolder`. `Holder` classes support the passing of CORBA IDL `out` and `inout`. (Unlike C and CORBA IDL data types, Java parameters are passed by value, not by reference.) All of the basic IDL data types (such as `String`) have a `Holder` class (`StringHolder`). The WAI-specific data types also have a `Holder` class, `HttpServerBufferHolder`.

The use of the methods in Tables 14-13 and 14-14 is based on the purpose of the IDL methods. For more information on the use of these methods, see Tables 14-1 and 14-2, where the purpose of each IDL method is described.

Table 14-13 `HttpServerContext` Java Method Prototypes

JAVA PROTOTYPE	IDL METHOD
public netscape.WAI.HttpServerReturnType **getInfo** (java.lang.String name, org.omg.CORBA.StringHolder value);	HttpServerReturnType getInfo(in string name, out string value);
public java.lang.String **getHost**();	string getHost();
public java.lang.String **getName**();	string getName();
public int **getPort**();	long getPort();
public java.lang.String **getServerSoftware**();	string getServerSoftware();
public boolean **isSecure**();	boolean isSecure();

Table 14-14 `HttpServerRequest` Java Method Prototypes

JAVA PROTOTYPE	IDL METHOD
METHODS FOR GETTING REQUEST- AND CLIENT-RELATED INFORMATION	
public netscape.WAI.HttpServerReturnType **getRequestInfo** (java.lang.String name, org.omg.CORBA.StringHolder value);	HttpServerReturnType getRequestInfo (in string name, out string value);
public netscape.WAI.HttpServerReturnType **getRequestHeader** (java.lang.String header, org.omg.CORBA.StringHolder value);	HttpServerReturnType getRequest Header(in string header, out stringvalue);
public netscape.WAI.HttpServerReturnType **getCookie** (org.omg.CORBA.StringHolder cookie);	HttpServerReturnType getCookie (out string cookie);
METHODS FOR GETTING ADDITIONAL INFORMATION	
public netscape.WAI.HttpServerReturnType **getConfigParameter** (java.lang.String name, org.omg.CORBA.StringHolder value);	HttpServerReturnType getConfigParameter (in string name, out string value);
public netscape.WAI.HttpServerContext **getContext**();	HttpServerContext getContext ();
public int **ReadClient** (netscape.WAI.HttpServerBufferHolder buffer);	long ReadClient (inout HttpServerBuffer buffer);

Table 14-14 `HttpServerRequest` Java Method Prototypes (*continued*)

JAVA PROTOTYPE	IDL METHOD
METHODS FOR SETTING (ADDING), GETTING, AND DELETING RESPONSE-HEADERS	

`public`
`netscape.WAI.HttpServerReturnType`
`setResponseContentType`
`(java.lang.String ContentType);`
	`HttpServerReturnType`
	`setResponseContentType`
	`(in string ContentType);`

`public`
`netscape.WAI.HttpServerReturnType`
`setResponseContentLength``(int Length);`
	`HttpServerReturnType`
	`setResponseContentLength`
	`(in unsigned long Length);`

`public`
`netscape.WAI.HttpServerReturnType`
`setCookie``(java.lang.String name,`
`java.lang.String value,`
`java.lang.String expires,`
`java.lang.String domain,`
`java.lang.String path,`
`boolean secure);`
	`HttpServerReturnType setCookie`
	`(in string name, in string value,`
	`in string expires, in string domain,`
	`in string path, in boolean secure);`

`public`
`netscape.WAI.HttpServerReturnType`
`setResponseStatus`
`(int status,`
`java.lang.String reason);`
	`HttpServerReturnType`
	`setResponseStatus`
	`(in long status, in string reason);`

Not used.	`HttpServerReturnType setRequestInfo` `(in string name, in string value);`

`public`
`netscape.WAI.HttpServerReturnType`
`addResponseHeader`
`(java.lang.String header,`
`java.lang.String value);`
	`HttpServerReturnType`
	`addResponseHeader(in string header,`
	`in string value);`

`public`
`netscape.WAI.HttpServerReturnType`
`getResponseHeader`
`(java.lang.String header,`
`org.omg.CORBA.StringHolder value);`
	`HttpServerReturnType`
	`getResponseHeader(in string header,`
	`out string value);`

`public`
`netscape.WAI.HttpServerReturnType`
`getResponseContentLength`
`(org.omg.CORBA.IntHolder Length);`
	`HttpServerReturnType`
	`getResponseContentLength`
	`(out unsigned long Length);`

`public`
`netscape.WAI.HttpServerReturnType`
`delResponseHeader`
`(java.lang.String header);`
	`HttpServerReturnType`
	`delResponseHeader`
	`(in string header);`

METHODS FOR WRITING THE RESPONSE	
`public int `**`StartResponse`**`();`	`long StartResponse();`
`public int `**`WriteClient`** `(byte [] buffer);`	`long WriteClient` `(in HttpServerBuffer buffer);`

Table 14-14   `HttpServerRequest` Java Method Prototypes (*continued*)

JAVA PROTOTYPE	IDL METHOD
ADDITIONAL METHODS	

`public java.lang.String`
`BuildURL``(java.lang.String prefix,`
`java.lang.String suffix);`
	`string BuildURL(in string prefix,`
	`in string suffix);`

`public`
`netscape.WAI.HttpServerReturnType`
`LogError` `(int degree,`
`java.lang.String func,`
`java.lang.String msg,`
`boolean clientinfo);`
	`HttpServerReturnType LogError`
	`(in long degree, in string func,`
	`in string msg,`
	`in boolean clientinfo);`

`public`
`netscape.WAI.HttpServerReturnType`
`RespondRedirect`
`(java.lang.String url);`
	`HttpServerReturnType`
	`RespondRedirect`
	`(in string url);`

`FormHandler` *Class*

As with C++ and Netscape Server 3.01 or later, you can use the `FormHandler` class to parse and manage the client input. You no longer have to write special functions to handle the data sent by a client. The methods you use with Java to access the client input after it is parsed, however, are different from the methods used with C++.

The `FormHandler` constructor or its method **ParseQueryString** parses the URL-encoded *name-value* pairs of data that are sent by the client via the HTTP GET or POST method. First, you must create an instance of the `FormHandler` class using the `FormHandler` constructor, **FormHandler**. The **FormHandler** constructor also reads and parses the input from an HTTP POST method. You no longer need to call the **ReadClient** method of `HttpServerRequest` to read the input. If the data are sent using the HTTP GET method, you must invoke `FormHandler`'s **ParseQueryString** method to parse the query string. The data from the HTTP GET method are found in the query string sent with the client's requested URL. Once the data are parsed, you can invoke the **GetHashTable** method of `FormHandler` to get a `Hashtable` that holds the parsed *name-value* pairs of data. You can use the `java.util.Hashtable` methods to access the value of a *name-value* pair. The `Hashtable` returned by **GetHashTable** uses the name from the *name-value* pairs of parsed data as the key. The values are stored as Java Vectors (`java.util.Vector`). Table 14-15 includes a description of the methods of the `FormHandler` class.

> **Note ▶**
>
> The accompanying CD-ROM includes an alternative form handling class written by Srividhya Gopala called `MyFormHandler`. You should check this Java class before using the `FormHandler` class. Unlike the `FormHandler` class, `MyFormHandler` is designed to handle forms with a large number of data. It also uses the same interface for accessing data submitted through both POST and GET methods of request.

Table 14-15   FormHandler Java Methods

METHOD	DESCRIPTION
public **FormHandler** (HttpServerRequest request);	Constructor for the FormHandler class. Before you can use its methods, you must first instantiate an instance of the FormHandler class (create a FormHandler object). You pass the request object (HttpServerRequest request) to the **FormHandler** constructor. The request object is passed by the ORB to your **Run** method.
public boolean **IsValid**();	You can use this function to verify whether the data that the **FormHandler** constructor read from a POST method are valid. As with all FormHandler methods, you first must create an instance of the FormHandler class before calling its methods. If **FormHandler** was not able to read and parse the POST data, **IsValid** returns false. Otherwise, it returns true.
public String **GetQueryString**();	You can use this method to get the query string from an HTTP GET method of request. **GetQueryString** returns the query string intact. You do not need to call this method before calling **ParseQueryString** to parse the query string. If you want to find out the value of the query string, however, use this method. You can also use the **getRequestInfo** method of HttpServerRequest to get the query string by using the QUERY_STRING environment variable. The query string is appended to the end of the client's requested URL after a question mark (?).
public boolean **ParseQueryString**();	Parses the query string of an HTTP GET method of request. The FormHandler object has access to the query string through the request object you passed to it. Use this method to parse the query string. **ParseQueryString** parses the URL-encoded *name-value* pairs of data from the query string. You can then call **GetHashTable** to get a Hashtable of the parsed data. Unlike with the POST data, you must call **ParseQueryString** to parse the query string from a GET method before actually using **GetHashTable** to get the Hashtable of *name-value* pairs. If the method was able to parse the query string, it returns true. Otherwise, it returns false. Check this return value to make sure that the query string was valid and properly parsed.
public Hashtable **GetHashTable**();	Returns a Hashtable that holds the parsed *name-value* pairs of data from a POST or GET method of request. To access the data in this Hashtable, you must use the methods of the Java utility Hashtable class, java.util.Hashtable. The Hashtable class implements a hash table data structure that associates a value with a specified key. **GetHashTable**'s Hashtable uses the name from the *name-value* pairs of data as the key. The values are stored as Java Vector objects. The java.util.Vector class implements an array of objects. Netscape uses the Vector class for the value so as to support an array of objects whose size is not known in advance. Thus multiple objects (values) can be associated with a single name (key). The Hashtable and Vector classes provide a number of public methods. For example, you can use the **get** method of Hashtable to retrieve the value of a *name-value* pair. Other

Table 14-15 `FormHandler` Java Methods (*continued*)

METHOD	DESCRIPTION
	`Hashtable` methods include **put**, **remove**, **keys**, and **elements**. `Vector` methods can be used to access a specific value from the array of values. `Vector` methods include **elements**, **lastElement**, and **firstElement**. To enumerate (iterate) through the list of values and retrieve a specific value, you can use `java.util.Enumeration` class and its methods **hasMoreElements** and **nextElement**. A number of `Hashtable` and `Vector` class methods return an `Enumeration`. For example, the `Vector` method **elements** returns an `Enumeration` of the objects stored in `Vector`.

Summary

In this chapter, we reviewed the core foundation of WAI and its components. We began with a review of the WAI IDL files. In particular, we looked at the two main IDL interfaces for processing client request: `HttpServerContext` and `HttpServerRequest`. `HttpServerContext` is used to get global and static server information, such as the server IP address. `HttpServerRequest` is used to get the request-header, CGI environment variables, and client input. For example, the **getRequestInfo** method is used to access the value of CGI/1.1 environment variables. You also use `HttpServerRequest` to send response-headers and the body of the response.

Next, we discuss the WAI methods and functions you need to use for the supported programming languages C, C++, and Java. You do not use the WAI CORBA IDL interface directly to write your application. Instead, you use the C, C++, or Java classes, methods, and functions that Netscape provides.

When you write your WAI application, you need to create a Web application service object and register this object with the server. For C, you use the WAI functions **WAIcreateWebAppService** and **WAIregisterObject**. For C++ and Java, you first need to extend the `WAIWebApplicationService` class and write a constructor, **getServiceInfo**, and **Run** method for your class. You can then initialize the class in your application's main function using the constructor and register the object you created using the **RegisterService** method of your object. The **Run** method is invoked by the server when a request is made for your WAI application. This method is then responsible for processing the client request.

The ORB passes a reference to the request object (`HttpServerRequest`) to your application that you use to get the client request and other relevant information and then write and send a response to the client. This object holds the appropriate methods that you need to call to process the request. With C++ and Java, to invoke the methods of `HttpServerContext`, you first need to get a reference to the

`HttpServerContext` object by using the `HttpServerRequest` method **getContext**. For an out-of-process application, when you use the request object's methods, your application makes a remote procedure call to the server to invoke the server request object method and get the response.

In Chapter 15, we will go through the steps of writing WAI applications in greater detail. We will expand on the information we discussed in this chapter and put the WAI functions and methods to use.

Chapter 15

Writing a WAI Application

This chapter goes through the steps of writing a WAI application, a WAS (Web Application Service). Here, we will review the steps of writing a WAS out-of-process or in-process. We will cover all of the target programming languages together under the general procedures of writing a WAI application. By reading the combined instructions for writing a WAI application in C, C++, or Java, you can compare the differences between the programming procedures. For example, if you are a C programmer, you can use this comparison to find out how you can write the same application in C++ or Java. Many steps for writing a WAI in C, C++, or Java are similar, although you may use a different function or method to accomplish the task. For example, the steps for processing a client request are very similar for all the programming languages. There are also important variations of which you should be aware. For example, how you create your Web service object is very different when you write a C program versus a C++ application.

Writing an out-of-process WAI is different from writing an NSAPI or CGI application. Unlike with NSAPI, a WAI application can run as a separate application and have its own console or Windows interface. You write a WAI out-of-process application as a separate console or a Windows application. You need to start such applications individually, after the server is started. Unlike with CGI, WAI applications start once and stay alive for as long as you want them. They run in parallel with the server on a separate process. When started, these applications locate Netscape's Naming Service and register themselves with the server. They then wait for the server to call them. If a client HTTP request is made for your specific WAI application, the server calls your application and invokes its run method. Your function or method processes the request and returns the response to the server. The server, in turn, sends the response to the client.

Throughout the chapter, there are descriptions and instructions for the specific programming language functions and methods that are covered in the WAI chapters. This information is mainly intended for individuals who are familiar with one of the supported WAI programming languages, enabling them to review the procedures for writing a WAI in another language. You should be familiar with at least one of the WAI programming languages—C, C++, or Java—to take advantage of WAI. For a Microsoft Windows version of a WAI application, you should also be familiar with the Windows API. It is not the intent of this chapter to teach programming in C, C++, Java, or the Windows environment. We cover only the basic aspects of programming in C, C++, and Java that are needed to write a WAI application.

Brief Overview of a WAS in Action

When you write a WAI, you are actually writing a CORBA object implementation. Netscape Server calls this implementation to process a specific client request. For out-of-process applications, the server calls your application using a CORBA remote procedure call (IIOP). The client invokes your WAS by requesting a specific URL, which includes the path for your WAI application. The URL should look like the following: `http://<server name>[:port]/iiop/<your service name>`. The string `iiop` is the predefined part of the path for all WAI applications. You do not need to place your application in such a directory. In fact, you do not even need to have an `iiop` directory. The server uses this information only to identify the request as a WAS request.

For your application to work as a WAS, it must write and create a Web service object and register this object with Netscape Naming Service. You name your WAI service when you write the code for registering your application with Netscape Server's Naming Service. You give a specific object name to your WAS. Your application registers with Netscape Naming Service using the name you specified. The client uses this name to invoke your specific application. The server also uses this name to recognize the client request as one for your application. Netscape Server then locates and calls your application. Make sure this name is unique and other services do not use the same name.

The server returns a `Not Found` page if it was unable to locate your WAI service with Naming Service—in other words, if it could not find the interoperable object ref-

---

Note ▶

There are two main objects (IDL interfaces) involved in the interaction between the server and your application. The first object is the Web service object you write to process the client request. You write the server implementation for this object. The Netscape server includes a client stub for it. Netscape uses the client stub to invoke your applications run method (**Run** for C++ and Java). This object is based on `WebApplicationBasicService` interface. The second object is implemented by the server. You invoke this object's method using the HTTP request object passed to your run method. For this object, your application is the client object (uses the client stub) and the server's implementation is the server object. This object is based on the `HttpServerRequest` interface.

---

erence (IOR) for your service. This situation can happen if your application was never registered with the server. The IOR is like an address that is used to locate CORBA implementations. Netscape Naming Service saves the IOR of all implementations that register with its service in a file under <*server path*>/wai/NameService. If your service was registered with Naming Service, but for some reason the server could not invoke it, the server returns a Server Error page to the client. In other words, if the server was able to find your application's object reference (IOR) with Naming Service, it expects that your service should be available. If your application was shut down or crashed, the server does not see it as an application not found, but rather as a server error, because it was unable to call it. (For more information on IOR and Netscape Naming Service, see Chapter 12.)

Under Server 3.0, the server requires osagent for registering and locating your service. You must run osagent before running your application. Your application registers with both osagent and Netscape Naming Service. Netscape Server and Netscape Naming Service also register with osagent. osagents from different machines on the local network also communicate with one another, sharing information about the registered server objects. Figure 15-1 shows the process of a WAS registration under Enterprise Server 3.0. (For more information on osagent, see Appendix F.)

Under Server 3.01 and 3.5.x, the server no longer uses osagent. Your program directly registers with the server's Naming Service, which then locates your object based on the

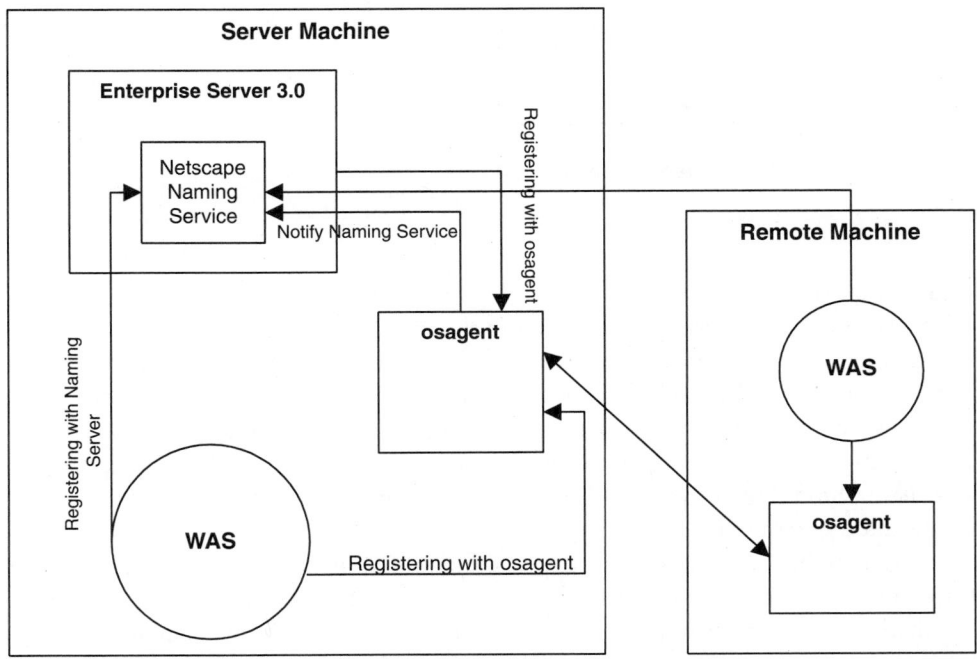

Figure 15-1   WAS Registration Process Under Enterprise Server 3.0

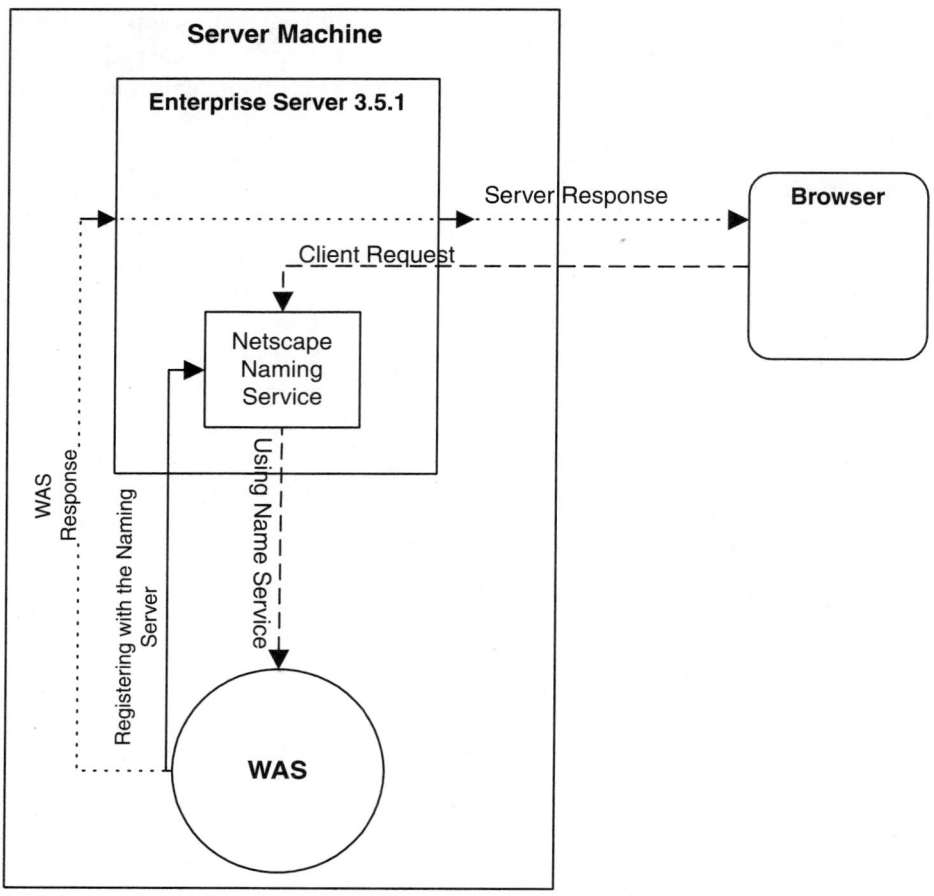

Figure 15-2   WAS Under Enterprise Server 3.5.1

information you have provided it. Figure 15-2 shows the process of registration of the WAS with Netscape Naming Service. It also shows the route that a client request takes before it receives the response. The request is sent by Netscape Server through Naming Service to the WAS. (We will discuss the details of this process shortly.) The WAS returns a response to the server, which then sends the response to the client. Figure 15-2 displays the working of WAS running on the local server machine. A remote WAS functions in a similar fashion if the server could accept remote registration and the WAS was able to locate and register with Naming Service.

In your application, you include a special function or method (for example, **Run** for C++ and Java) that processes the client HTTP request. Netscape invokes your method or function to process client requests. This function is the actual implementation method of your Web service application. The ORB passes an HTTP request object (also known as the session object) to your implementation function or method. This object provides the necessary means for getting specific data about the request and the server. When you ask for client request information, you actually invoke one of the methods of this HTTP request object. Netscape provides a number of functions or methods that you can use to get client, request, or server information. For C, which does not handle objects, Netscape has included wrapper functions that provide access to the methods of the HTTP request object. You use the information returned by these functions to process the request.

For an out-of-process application, when you invoke the request object's methods or functions, they actually call the server and ask the server to execute the comparable internal methods and return the response to your program. In other words, you make a remote procedure call (IIOP call) to the server, asking the server to process your request and return a response. This process differs from the workings of a CGI program, where all information is passed to your CGI application as environment variables.

Once you have processed the client request and taken any action for which your program is designed, you return the response using the functions or methods that Netscape provides—that is, the request object's methods. The server then passes your response to the client. The server also sets a default Status-Line (`200 OK`) and `content-type` (`text/html`) response-header for your response.

A WAI application can also be written as an in-process application. In that case, as with an NSAPI application, it is loaded as a shared library or dynamic linked library (DLL) when Netscape Server is started. When you write an out-of-process application, you actually start an application in parallel to Netscape Server. Unlike with CGI, you start the out-of-process WAI application after you start the server. The server does not start the application each time a request is made. An out-of-process application is an independent application running in its own process that can communicate with Netscape Server. If you set the server to accept remote WAI applications, you can place your WAI application on a remote machine. Your application must then locate the server to register with its Naming Service. Because of the security risks that running a remote WAI application may cause, it is recommended that you run a WAI application only on the same machine that your server is running.

Steps for Writing a WAS

There are three major parts to writing a WAS. If you are using C++ or Java, you first write a WAS class for your program. You derive your Web service class from `WAIWebApplicationService`. For C, you skip this step. Next, you write a C function or a **Run** method for your Web service class that processes the client HTTP request. Finally, you write a main function for your WAI application. In the WAS's main function, you also must create a Web service object and register it with Netscape Naming Service. As expected, for C++ and Java, you must first write the Web service class before you create an instance of your Web service class (a Web service object) in the application's main function.

The first part—deriving a Web service class from WAIWebApplicationService—is unique to Java and C++. This class can be the source of any number of Web service objects. In this book, however, we instantiate only one instance of the class for the WAS examples. (For C, you do not derive a Web service class. Netscape does that step internally.) In the first step, you write the constructor and **getServiceInfo** method of your Web service class. (You must also write a **Run** method for your Web service class, but we will discuss this method shortly as part of Step 2.) You should place the code for your service class outside of the main function of your WAI program. For Java, you must write at least two separate classes: one that implements the Web application service class and another that provides the main function of your application. You can also write the Web service class in a separate file.

In the second step of writing a WAS, you write a function (or a method) that processes the client request and returns a response. For C++ and Java, this function is the **Run** method of the WAI service class (your service object). We will consider the writing of the **Run** method to be the second step, as the **Run** method is the central method from which you process the client requests. This step can be much more complicated than writing a simple class constructor and **getServiceInfo** method for your Web service class (step 1). You also write a callback function similar to the **Run** method for C applications. For C, you name this function when you create the WAI service object. It does not have to be called **Run**, but it provides the same functionality as the **Run** function in C++ or Java. In our examples, we will call this function **RunFunction**. The server invokes this C function or the **Run** method of your Web service object when a client asks for your WAI application. The request object (or server session object) is also passed to your **Run** method (or C function). This part of the code is similar to a CGI application. WAI language-specific functions or methods based on the IDL methods for HttpServerRequest and HttpServerContext interface are used to process the client request. To process the client request, you can also invoke other methods or functions in **Run** or **RunFunction**.

In the third part of your program, you write the main function for your WAI application. First, determine what type of application you are planning to write, whether it is a stand-alone application—that is, an executable out-of-process WAS—or a DLL or shared library (so)—that is, an in-process WAS. For an out-of-process application, you must also decide whether you want to write a Windows application or a console application. The procedures for writing a Windows out-of-process WAS, a console out-of-process WAS, or a DLL or shared library in-process WAS are different. This decision determines how you will write the main function and the steps you must take in the function.

For all the different types of applications that you can write, the main function of the WAS must at least create the Web service object and register it with Netscape Server Naming Service. The rest of the steps of writing the main function differ depending on the type of application you write. For example, for Java, you must write a separate public class for your application and include a main function for that class. This main function will be the WAI application's main function, its starting point.

In the main function, you create a Web service object by using the constructor for your Web service class. For C, you use the WAI function **WAIcreateWebAppService**. This step creates the CORBA server object that will communicate with other CORBA objects. You then register your Web service object with Naming Service.

The three steps discussed in this chapter may seem complicated at first glance, especially as we will be discussing all the options for each step in this chapter. Actually, only a few lines of code can accomplish most of the required steps of writing a WAI application. What may take longer to write is the specifics of how your program will process the client request (step 2). Fortunately, this part of writing your code is very similar to writing any other type of server application, such as a CGI program or an NSAPI **Service** function. For WAI examples that you can use as starting points for writing your own WAI applications, you can look in the next chapter. Chapter 16 includes a simple Hello Client example for all major types of WAI applications that are discussed in this chapter and that you may decide to write on your own.

Files to Include with the Code

With C WAI applications, you should include the header file ONEiiop.h (#include "ONEiiop.h"). With C++ WAI applications, you should include ONESrvPI.hpp (#include "ONESrvPI.hpp"). With Java, you can use the following classes: netscape.WAI.*, org.omg.CORBA.*, and org.omg.CosNaming.*.

As you would expect, you still need to include other header files or other classes depending on the functionality that your program needs. You may need to include other general C or C++ header files or Java classes. For example, for Java, you may need to import java.io.*, java.lang.*, java.util.*, java.net.*, and so on.

Part I: Write a Web Service Class (for Java and C++ Only)

For C++ and Java, you must declare a WAS class that derives from or extends Netscape's base WAI Web Application Service class, as outlined in the steps in Table 15-1. You must derive (extend) a Web service class from WAIWebApplicationService. The WAIWebApplicationService class implements the WebApplicationService and WebApplicationBasicService CORBA IDL interface for you. You can name your class anything you want. For your Web service class, you should write a constructor, **getServiceInfo**, and a **Run** method. In the following sections, we will review the constructors for C++ and Java, and the **getServiceInfo** method. For the **Run** method, see Part II.

Table 15-1 Write a Web Service Class for C++ or Java

Derive (extend) a class from `WAIWebApplicationService`.
Write a constructor for your class.
Write a **getServiceInfo** method.
Write a **Run** method (see Part II for more information).
Declare any additional member variables.
Write any additional methods.

Constructors for C++

With C++, you can choose from a number of constructors.

```
WAIWebApplicationService(const char *service_name);
WAIWebApplicationService(const char *service_name,
                         int argc, char **argv);
WAIWebApplicationService(const char *service_name,
                         WAIBool activeObj);
WAIWebApplicationService(const char *service_name,
            int argc, char **argv, WAIBool activeObj);
```

The first two of these constructors can be used for all 3.x Servers. The second two constructors are new to Netscape Server 3.01. You can use all of these constructors with Server 3.0.1 and 3.5.x.

service_name is the name that you give to your Web service. You specify this name when you create an instance of your service class in the main function of your application. If you must pass a specific ORB or BOA setting during initialization of your Web service object, then use a constructor that includes the argc or argv parameters. For example, you can pass the IP address of the BOA, -OAipaddr, using the argv parameter. You can also set the argc and argv parameters to 0 if no argument is needed.

The new Server 3.01 and later constructors add an additional parameter, activeObj. If you want the service object to be activated at a later point using the **ActiveWAS** method of your service object, then use one of the two new constructors. You can also use this method when you want your application to be automatically started by the Object Activation Daemon (OAD). We will go through the steps of registering your service with the OAD in the section Registering an Out-of-Process WAI Application with OAD in Chapter 16. (The use of the OAD with WAI applications is limited to the UNIX versions of the server.)

You derive your constructor from WAIWebApplicationService. The following code is an example of a constructor for the MyWAIService class derived from the WAIWebApplicationService(service_name, argc, argv) constructor:

```
MyWAIService::MyWAIService
        (const char *service_name, int argc, char **argv):
```

```
               WAIWebApplicationService(service_name, argc, argv){
}
```

You may want to declare your constructor as the default constructor for your class. The default constructor should have a default value for all of its arguments. The default constructor for `WAIWebApplicationService` is `WAIWebApplicationService(const char* service_name = 0);`. The default constructor is called whenever you define an instance of the class without an explicit initial value. Moreover, it is used for initializing an array of objects. A separate default constructor is called for each object in the array. The following code includes the declaration of the `MyWAIService` constructor, defined previously, as the default constructor for the `MyWAIService` class.

```
MyWAIService:public WAIWebApplicationService
{
   public:
      MyWAIService(
               const char *service_name=(const char *)NULL,
               int argc=0, char **argv=0);

      char *getServiceInfo();
      long Run(WAIServerRequest_ptr session);
};
```

You can include additional parameters for your constructor as well. If you have declared a variable for your service object, you can initialize the variables in the constructor. Unlike with CGI, these variables are available for the lifetime of your WAI application, not the lifetime of the client session. Thus you can have persistent data across client sessions. The constructor is a good place to initialize any step that affects your application globally. For example, you can open a file or connect to a database with the constructor. You do not have to use the constructor to initialize a variable; you can use other methods of your service class for initializing and updating a Web service member variable. Netscape Server invokes your Web service object's **Run** method when it calls your WAI application (your Web service object). The constructor, on the other hand, is called once by your main WAI application function for instantiating your Web service object.

Constructor for Java

The constructor for `WAIApplicationService` in Java is

```
public WAIWebApplicationService (java.lang.String name);
```

As with C++, you extend your Web service class constructor from the `WAIWebApplicationService` class. `name` is the name of the Web service object. You specify this name when you create an instance of your service class in the main function of your application. You can also include additional parameters for your constructor.

In your class constructor, you should first invoke the superclass (WAIWebApplicationService) constructor by calling the **super** method with the name of the Web service as its parameter (that is, super (name) ;). The superclass constructor also expects the name of the Web service object as its parameter. You specify the **super** method because you want the superclass constructor invoked and the name of the Web service passed to the constructor. The Java compiler places an implicit call to the superclass without any parameters (that is, super ()). We, however, want to specify a parameter for the **super** method. You should call **super** *before* any statement in your constructor method. You can initialize an instance name for the name of the Web service by assigning the service name (name) to your instance name (for example, ServiceName). This step, however, is not required. You should also declare all of the exceptions that the constructor may throw by using throws. The following code is an example of a constructor for MyWAIService in Java:

```
MyWAIService(java.lang.String name) throws
    CosNaming.NamingContextPackage.CannotProceed,
    CosNaming.NamingContextPackage.InvalidName,
    CosNaming.NamingContextPackage.AlreadyBound,
    CORBA.SystemException{

        super(name);
}
```

You place the constructor inside your class declaration. In the following code, we also declare an instance name for the class:

```
class MyWAIService extends WAIWebApplicationService{
    String ServiceName;

    MyWAIService(java.lang.String name) throws
        CosNaming.NamingContextPackage.CannotProceed,
        CosNaming.NamingContextPackage.InvalidName,
        CosNaming.NamingContextPackage.AlreadyBound,
        CORBA.SystemException{

            super(name);
            ServiceName = name;
    }
. . .
```

As with C++, you can initialize any member variables that you have declared in the constructor.

getServiceInfo

For both C++ and Java, you must override the **getServiceInfo** method. You have to write the implementation of this method for your service class. The **getServiceInfo** method is declared as a pure virtual function for C++ and an abstract class in Java. You use **getServiceInfo** to return information about your Web service. You can return the name of the service, its author, its version, copyright information, and so on. There is no specific guideline to what information you must return with this method. You should return any important product information that another user of your WAI application may need. Other applications or classes can use this method to get information about your Web service. **getServiceInfo** is defined as `virtual char *getServiceInfo();` for C++, and `public abstract java.lang.String getServiceInfo();` for Java.

The following code is an example of a **getServiceInfo** method for the `MyWAIService` class in C++:

```
char* MyWAIService::getServiceInfo(void)
{
    return StringDup("Simple Apps\nCompany AppWriter\n\
                    Version 3.2\nCopyright AppWriter Inc.");
}
```

For C++, we use **StringDup** to allocate storage space for the string we are returning. **StringDup** allocates storage space for a copy of the string and places the copy into the newly allocated buffer in memory.

The following code is an example of a **getServiceInfo** method for the `MyWAIService` class in Java:

```
public java.lang.String getServiceInfo(){

    return "Simple Apps\nCompany AppWriter\n" +
           "Version 3.2\nCopyright AppWriter Inc.";
}
```

Additional Member Methods or Variables

You can add any number of member functions and variables to your Web service class. These member functions and variables can be private or public. Normally, they are private members of your class, as they are mainly used by your class. You can then write public methods that can read or change these variables.

Member variables can be used to maintain state information or to prepare your application for handling a client request. For example, you can have a ticker that measures the number of client requests or a handle to a file that the **Run** method will use to record the client HTML form input. You can then initialize the member variables in the constructor and use them with the **Run** method or any other method that you write for your Web service class. You can also declare a Web service class variable that a member method can update or use. For example, if the initialization information of a variable is passed through an argument to your WAI application, you can use a method of your service object to initialize this variable in the main function of your WAI application. The member variable can be an integer, a string, a stream, another class, a handle to a file, and so on. It can be available to all invocations of the **Run** method. These variables are available for the lifetime of the WAI application and during the processing of every client request. For more information on adding methods to the Web service class to support persistent data, see the section Persistent Data and WAI, later in this chapter.

The member functions or methods can perform any additional tasks that your program needs to accomplish. These additional methods can support your **Run** method. As with any object-oriented program, you divide the tasks that your class will accomplish and write different member functions for each task or procedure. One method can call another method to finish its task. With the Web service class, your core method is the **Run** method. This method is invoked by Netscape Server when a client asks for your WAI application. Thus other methods that you write for your Web service class are usually called either directly or indirectly from your **Run** method. You may also write a method that the main function of your WAI application can use to initialize a Web service class variable that your **Run** method can use. In the main function, you can invoke the method after you have created your Web service object—that is, created an instance of your Web service class.

Part II: Process the Client Request

The second step of writing your program for Java and C++ is to write a **Run** method that will process the client request. You write this method for your Web service class. You should also write a function in C that can handle client requests. For C, this step is the first step of writing a WAI application. With C, you can name this function anything you like. In the main function of your WAI application, when you create your Web service object, you also specify the name of the function that handles the client requests. This function will be the **Run** method of the Web service object that you create.

When the server calls your WAI application, it invokes the **Run** method or its equivalent C function. In CORBA terminology, Netscape Server makes a client request to your object implementation (your Web service object), invoking the **Run** method of your object. A reference to the HTTP request object is also passed to your function. This object enables you to invoke the WAI-specific functions or methods for processing the client request. You need this object to get information about the server and the client's HTTP requests. You also use this object to return a response to the client.

The request object you receive is based on the `HttpServerRequest` IDL interface. It is a reference (a stub) for the server HTTP request object. What is actually passed to your run function is different for C, C++, and Java. In C, you receive an "object" of type `ServerSession_t`, which is a pointer to an internal data structure that allows you access to the HTTP request interface. You then pass this value to all WAI functions that you call. In C++, it is of type `WAIServerRequest_ptr`, which is a pointer to an internal `WAIServerRequest` class. This class includes all the methods necessary to process the client request. In Java, an `HttpServerRequest` object of the `netscape.WAI.HttpServerRequest` class is received. You also use the method of this class to process the client request.

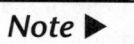
The following functions are examples of the **Run** methods and equivalent C functions. For these functions, the name of the session object is `session`.

C
```
long RunFunction(ServerSession_t session)
```

C++
```
long MyWAIService::Run(WAIServerRequest_ptr session)
```

Java
```
public int Run(HttpServerRequest session)
```

You use the methods or functions that Netscape has exposed for your programming purposes to get information about the server or request and to return a response. The processing of the client request occurs either directly or indirectly from inside the **Run** method or C equivalent function. This function is the core of your WAI application, where you process the client request. You can also write additional methods or functions that can support this core method or function.

The WAI methods you use are directly related to the session object (HTTP request object) passed to your program. With C++ and Java, the methods you use are the methods of the session object. For example, for Java, in the **Run** method given previously, you can use `session.getRequestInfo("REMOTE_ADDR", <value>);` to get the client IP address. For C++, the method is `session->getRequestInfo ("REMOTE_ADDR", <value>);`. For C, the function is `WAIgetRequestInfo (session, "REMOTE_ADDR", <value>);`. As you can see, the methods for C++ and Java are methods for the session object (`session`). For C, you must pass the session object as the first parameter of all WAI functions you invoke in your C "run" function—for example, **RunFunction**.

Table 15-2 lists three steps for processing a client request: getting information for processing the client request, processing the client request, and returning a response. In the first and third steps, you will use the appropriate methods or functions that Netscape provides. In the second step, you process the information that you get from the first step. This part of the code varies greatly, based on what you wish to do with the information from the request. The code in the second step can be very simple and short, or long and complex, depending on the purpose of your WAI application. It can also call other functions or methods to process the client request. Some of the steps in Table 15-2 are optional. You do not have to accomplish all steps to process a client request.

Table 15-2 Functions for Handling HTTP Requests

C (Function is specified with **WAIcreateWebAppService**)	C++ (**Run** method of your Web service class)	JAVA (**Run** method of your Web service class)
GET INFORMATION FOR PROCESSING THE CLIENT REQUEST		
Get information from the `obj.conf` file, **IIOPexec** parameters (**WAIgetConfigParameter**)	Get information from the `obj.conf` file, **IIOPexec** parameters (**getConfigParameter**)	Get information from the `obj.conf` file, **IIOPexec** parameters (**getConfigParameter**)
	Get a pointer to the server context `HttpServerContext` (`WAIServerContext_ptr`), using **getContext**	Get the server context object `HttpServerContext` (`netscape.WAI. HttpServerContext`), using **getContext**
Get server's global settings (for example, **WAIgetHost**, **WAIgetPort**)	Get server's global settings, using the server context object returned by **getContext** (for example, **getHost**, **getPort**)	Get server's global settings, using the server context object returned by **getContext** (for example, **getHost**, **getContext**)
Get request-headers or CGI environment variables (for example, **WAIgetRequestHeader** or **WAIgetRequestInfo**)	Get request-headers or CGI environment variables (for example, **getRequestHeader** or **getRequestInfo**)	Get request-headers or CGI environment variables (for example, **getRequestHeader** or **getRequestInfo**)
Get additional client input, such as HTTP POST data (**WAIReadClient**)	Get additional client input, such as HTTP POST data (**ReadClient**)	Get additional client input, such as HTTP POST data (**ReadClient**)
	With Server 3.01 and later, you can also use the `FormHandler` class and its methods (for example, **ParseQueryString**) to parse and get the POST or GET data	With Server 3.01 and later, you can also use the `FormHandler` class and its methods (for example, **ParseQueryString**) to parse and get the POST or GET data
PROCESS THE CLIENT REQUEST		
Process the response based on the data you received, contact a database, evaluate the client's response, write to a file, read data from a file, and so on	Process the response based on the data you received, contact a database, evaluate the client's response, write to a file, read data from a file, and so on	Process the response based on the data you received, contact a database, evaluate the client's response, write to a file, read data from a file, and so on
RETURN THE RESPONSE		
Get an existing response-header to evaluate its value. You may want to take this step to find out if you need to set a new response-header or delete an existing one (**WAIgetResponseHeader**).	Get an existing response-header to evaluate its value. You may want to take this step to find out if you need to set a new response-header or delete an existing one (**getResponseHeader**).	Get an existing response-header to evaluate its value. You may want to take this step to find out if you need to set a new response-header or delete an existing one (**getResponseHeader**).

Table 15-2   Functions for Handling HTTP Requests (*continued*)

C (Function is specified with **WAIcreateWebAppService**)	C++ (**Run** method of your Web service class)	JAVA (**Run** method of your Web service class)
RETURN THE RESPONSE		
Delete an existing response-header if it conflicts with one that you want to add (**WAIdelResponseHeader**)	Delete an existing response-header if it conflicts with one that you want to add (**delResponseHeader**)	Delete an existing response-header if it conflicts with one that you want to add (**delResponseHeader**)
Add the response-headers (for example, **WAIaddResponseHeader**)	Add the response headers (for example, **addResponseHeader**)	Add the response-headers (for example, **addResponseHeader**)
Set the response status (**WAIsetResponseStatus**)	Set the response status (**setResponseStatus**)	Set the response status (**setResponseStatus**)
Send the status and response-headers (**WAIStartResponse**)	Send the status and response-headers (**StartResponse**)	Send the status and response-headers (**StartResponse**)
Write the response to the client (send the body of the response) (**WAIWriteClient**)	Write the response to the client (send the body of the response) (**WriteClient**)	Write the response to the client (send the body of the response) (**WriteClient**)

There are also a few other important functions and methods that you use in your **Run** method or C equivalent function that we will discuss in the section Additional Steps, later in this chapter. These additional steps include a method for redirecting a client to a new location and the procedure for logging errors.

Get Information for Processing the Client Request

There are four types of data that you may need from the server to process the client request: specific global settings for your WAS; general server global variables or settings; request- or client-related information; and the client input.

Many of Netscape's WAI methods or functions return a success or failure value. You should always check the return value of these methods or functions to make sure the function accomplished its intended task. For C and C++, the return value is usually WAISPISuccess if the function was successful and WAISPIFailure if it failed. For Java, the return value is netscape.WAI.HttpServerReturnType.Success upon success and netscape.WAI.HttpServerReturnType.Failure upon failure. For example, in the following code, we check the return value of the WAI method or function after we get the cookie from the request-header.

C

```
char *storecookie = NULL;
if(WAIgetCookie(session, &storecookie) != WAISPISuccess)
    . . .
```

C++

```
char *storecookie = NULL;
if(session->getCookie(storecookie) != WAISPISuccess)
. . .
```

Java

```
org.omg.CORBA.StringHolder storecookie =
                new org.omg.CORBA.StringHolder();
if(session.getCookie(storecookie) !=
                HttpServerReturnType.Success)
. . .
```

With C and C++, set the initial value of the string that you get from the WAI "get" methods or functions (for example, **getCookie** or **WAIgetCookie**) to NULL at the outset. Also, after you use the string returned by the functions, you should delete it by using the **StringDelete** method for C++ and the **WAIstringFree** function with C. Your program is responsible for freeing the memory. Moreover, you should free the string buffer or stream that you prepare for sending the output of the body of response to the client. If you do not free the memory, future requests may receive incorrect information.

The StringHolder and IntHolder classes are used with a number of Java methods (for example, **getCookie**). The StringHolder class is used with **getInfo**, **getRequestInfo**, **getRequestHeader**, **getCookie**, **getConfigParameter**, and **getResponseHeader**. The IntHolder class is used with **getResponseContentLength**. The StringHolder class is used for string information and IntHolder for integers. For example, the parameters you specify for **getCookie** use an org.omg.CORBA.StringHolder object. To get the value of the data you need from StringHolder or IntHolder, you should use the **value** method of the StringHolder or IntHolder class. For example, to get the value of storecookie, use storecookie.value.

Global Data Passed to Your Program   The first type of data that you may need or want to use in your WAI application consists of global variables that can be specified outside your program. This information can be configuration information or specific variables that should be passed to your program when it starts. For example, you can pass the location of a file that your program needs to process the client requests. Unlike the client request information, this type variable is specified only once and is available at all times to your program.

Instead of hard-coding this information in your program, you have two common ways of passing such global data to your program. First, if you are running an out-of-process WAI, you can pass the information as arguments to your program. The variables passed as arguments to your program can change each time you restart the WAI application. If you want the flexibility of having the information dynamically entered each time the program is invoked, then use the command-line arguments of the WAI application to pass the information to your program. This method can be also used to pass information to your program that the Web service object may need. A common use of application arguments is to pass the host name and port or the BOA IP address of Netscape Server. We will discuss this use in Part III, when we write the WAI application's main function. You may also pass the arguments indirectly to your **Run** method. You can invoke a method of your service object in the main function that initializes a variable for your Web service object. This variable can then be used by your **Run** method. Alternatively, for C, you can initialize a global variable in your main function that the C equivalent **Run** method can use.

The second method of passing global variables to your application is to define the information in the Netscape configuration file, **obj.conf**. You can specify any number of parameters for the **IIOPexec** directive function in the **obj.conf** file. In your program, you can retrieve this information by using the **getConfigParameter** method for C++ and Java or the **WAIgetConfigParameter** function for C. The parameters are available to your **Run** method at all times. You simply invoke the **getConfigParameter** or **WAIgetConfigParameter** function. This information is set once by the administrator of the server and is available to all WAI applications, unlike a command-line argument for a WAI application. **IIOPexec** is used to process all WAI applications. You can also use this information with an in-process application. The parameter you specify in the **obj.conf** file is available only in the **Run** method of your Web service object or in the C function that processes the client request. You need to have access to the session object (HTTP request object) before you can invoke **getConfigParameter** or **WAIgetConfigParameter** to get the **IIOPexec** parameters. This information is not available in the WAI application's main function.

For example, you can specify the location of a database that you need to process a client request as a parameter to **IIOPexec**. You can find the **IIOPexec** directive function in the iiopexec Object in the **obj.conf** file.

```
<Object name="iiopexec">
Service fn=IIOPexec database="c:\mydatabase\users.dat"
</Object>
```

In your **Run** method, you can get the value of database using the following methods or functions.

C++
```
char *DatabaseLocation = NULL;
session->getConfigParameter("database", DatabaseLocation);
```

Java
(To get the value of database from DatabaseLocation, you must use the StringHolder class method **value**—for example, DatabaseLocation.value.

```
org.omg.CORBA.StringHolder DatabaseLocation =
                        org.omg.CORBA.StringHolder();
session.getConfigParameter("database", DatabaseLocation);
```

C

```
char *DatabaseLocation = NULL;
WAIgetConfigParameter(session, "database", &DatabaseLocation);
```

> **Note ▶**
>
> Unlike with C++ methods, you usually have to use the address of the string variable to
> retrieve the value from the WAI C function's parameter (that is, `WAIgetConfig`
> `Parameter(session, "database", &DatabaseLocation);`).

Server Information   There are several Web server settings or other information
that you may want to use in your program. These data are the server port (for
example, 80), server host name (for example, www.foo.com), server ID
(for example, https-foo), name of the server software (for example,
Netscape-Enterprise/3.5.1), and whether the server is using SSL security.

In C, you can access this information directly using **WAIgetPort**, **WAIgetHost**
(server host name), **WAIgetName** (server ID), **WAIgetServerSoftware**, and
WAIisSecure. For example, to get the host name of the server, you can use the following function:

```
char *host_name = NULL;
host_name = WAIgetHost(session);
```

You can also access the information about the server using **WAIgetInfo**. To use
WAIgetInfo, you must specify the CGI/1.1 environment variable name of the server
data that you want (that is, GATEWAY_INTERFACE, SERVER_PORT, SERVER_NAME,
SERVER_ID, SERVER_SOFTWARE, or HTTPS). Consider an example:

```
char *host_name = NULL;
WAIgetInfo(session, "SERVER_NAME", &host_name);
```

WAIgetInfo returns a string through its third parameter. For the server port
(SERVER_PORT), you must therefore convert the string to an integer.

With C++ and Java, you must first get the server context object
(HttpServerContext) before you can invoke any of its methods. For C++, you
must get a pointer to a server context object, WAIServerContext_ptr. Note that
the server context class in C++ is called WAIServerContext. For Java, you must get
an object of the netscape.WAI.HttpServerContext class. To get the server
context object, you can use the **getContext** method of the session object (HTTP server
request object). You can then use the **getPort**, **getHost**, **getName**, **getServerSoftware**,
isSecure, or **getInfo** methods of the server context object.

The following code gets the server name in C++. The session object passed to the
Run method is named session.

```
char *host_name = NULL;
WAIServerContext_ptr server = session->getContext();
host_name = server->getHost();
```

You can also use the **getInfo** method, similar to the C function **WAIgetInfo**, to get the server name.

```
char *host_name = NULL;
WAIServerContext_ptr server = session->getContext();
server->getInfo("SERVER_NAME", host_name);
```

The following code gets the server name in Java.

```
String host_name;
HttpServerContext server = session.getContext();
host_name = server.getHost();
```

You can also use the **getInfo** method. To get the value of the server name from host_name provided by the **getInfo** method, you should use the **value** method of the StringHolder class, host_name.value.

```
org.omg.CORBA.StringHolder host_name = new
                     org.omg.CORBA.StringHolder();
HttpServerContext server = session.getContext();
server.getInfo("SERVER_NAME", host_name);
```

Request- or Client-Related Information   With HTTP 1.0 and later, when the client sends a request to your Web server, it also sends a number of request-headers. You often use the information in these headers to process the client request. The request-headers provide information about the request. With C++ and Java, you can use the **getRequestInfo** and **getRequestHeader** methods to get the request-headers. With C, you use the functions **WAIgetRequestInfo** and **WAIgetRequestHeader**. You must use the CGI environment variable naming convention to access the headers when using **getRequestInfo** and **WAIgetRequestInfo**. With **getRequestHeader** and **WAIgetRequestHeader**, you use the HTTP header naming convention. The request-header names are the same names you use in NSAPI applications.

With **getRequestInfo** and **WAIgetRequestInfo**, you get the value of the CGI/1.1 environment variables. Some of these environment variables are based on HTTP request-headers; others provide additional useful information. Usually environment variables for the HTTP request-headers start with HTTP_ (for example, HTTP_USER_AGENT or HTTP_ACCEPT). Other environment variables hold important data about the client, such as the client IP address (REMOTE_ADDR), client host name (REMOTE_HOST), or authenticated user name (REMOTE_USER). The environment variables include additional information about the request as well, such as the method the client used for sending the request (REQUEST_METHOD), the type of authentication used for the request (AUTH_TYPE), and additional path information in the request URL (PATH_INFO). **getRequestInfo** and **WAIgetRequestInfo** are very powerful. They provide much more information than **getRequestHeader** and **WAIgetRequestHeader**. If you have written CGI applications, you should be familiar with the CGI environment variables. Otherwise, review Chapter 3 for information on the CGI environment variables. For a list of the CGI 1.1 environment variables that **getRequestInfo** and **WAIgetRequestInfo** support, see the section in Chapter 14, Getting Request- and Client-Related Information.

> ### Note ▶
>
> Unlike with NSAPI **Service** functions, you can use PATH_INFO to get additional path information from the client. The additional path information is placed after the path for your WAI application and before any query string in the client's requested URL—for example, http://<server name>[:port]/iiop/<WAI application>/ [additional path]?[query string].

The following examples use **getRequestInfo** or **WAIgetRequestInfo** to get the method of the client request (that is, REQUEST_METHOD).

C
```
char *method = NULL;
WAIgetRequestInfo(session, "REQUEST_METHOD", &method);
```

C++
```
char *method = NULL;
session->getRequestInfo("REQUEST_METHOD", method);
```

Java
```
org.omg.CORBA.StringHolder method = new
                    org.omg.CORBA.StringHolder();
session.getRequestInfo("REQUEST_METHOD", method);
```

You can also use **getRequestHeader** for Java and C++ and **WAIgetRequestHeader** for C to get a number of request-headers. These headers include all the HTTP request-headers as defined in the HTTP specification, plus a number of other headers, such as connection, content-type, and content-length. These headers are actually variables in the headers pblock of the server's Request data structure. (See the section Request Variables in Chapter 6 for more information.) The actual names of the request-headers are based on HTTP specifications, except that they should use all lowercase letters for the names. (See the section HTTP Request/Response Messages in Chapter 1 for more information.) Unlike CGI environment variables, request-header names do not use underscores (_); instead they use dashes (as in accept, if-modified-since, referer, user-agent, and so on). They also do not begin with HTTP_.

The following examples use **getRequestHeader** or **WAIgetRequestHeader** to get the URL of the location from which the request originated (that is, `referrer`). You can get the same information by using the `HTTP_REFERRER` environment variable with **getRequestInfo** or **WAIgetRequestInfo**.

C
```
char *source = NULL;
WAIgetRequestHeader(session, "referer", &source);
```

C++
```
char *source = NULL;
session->getRequestHeader("referer", source);
```

Java
```
org.omg.CORBA.StringHolder source = new
                    org.omg.CORBA.StringHolder();
session.getRequestHeader("referer", source);
```

For Java, to get the value of the resource you specified with **getRequestInfo**, **getRequestHeader**, or **getCookie**, you should use the **value** method of the `StringHolder` class (for example, `source.value`).

getCookie and **WAIgetCookie** can be used to retrieve a cookie that you sent to the client earlier. You can also use **getRequestHeader**, **WAIgetRequestHeader**, **getRequestInfo**, and **WAIgetRequestInfo** to get a cookie, though **getCookie** makes the retrieval easier. See the beginning of the section, Get Information for Processing the Client Request, earlier in this chapter, for examples of **getCookie** and **WAIgetCookie**.

Client Input   The client can also send additional data to your application after the request-headers. This method of sending data is commonly used to `POST` client input from an HTML form. To read the data from the `POST` method of request, you can use **ReadClient** for Java and C++ and **WAIReadClient** for C. You also need to specify a buffer where the data should be received.

The procedure for handling a `POST` method is fundamentally the same whether you write a WAI, CGI, or NSAPI application. First, you normally have to verify whether the client input is sent using the `POST` method. Use **getRequestInfo** for C++ and Java and **WAIgetRequestInfo** for C to get the method (`REQUEST_METHOD`) used by the client. You may also want to verify if the `content-type` that the client sent is correct (that is, `application/x-www-form-urlencoded`). You expect this type of content from a `POST` method. Next, you should get the `content-length` of the data sent by the client. You can use the functions or methods we discussed earlier to get the `content-type` and `content-length` of the data sent by the client (that is, **getRequestInfo** or **getRequestHeader** for C++ and Java and **WAIgetRequestInfo** or **WAIgetRequestHeader** for C). You then need to convert `content-length` to an integer and create a buffer for the data that **ReadClient** or **WAIReadClient** will read, using the `content-length` information. Finally, you read the data with **ReadClient** or **WAIReadClient**. Remember that even after you get the data from the client, you still need to decode this information. Just as with the query string sent with the GET method, the POST data from a form are URL-encoded.

For an example of a WAI application that uses **WAIReadClient** to read data from a form, see the guest book example in Chapter 16.

Netscape Server 3.01 and later include a new class, `FormHandler`, that you can use with C++ and Java WAI applications to handle a client's POST or GET input. Using these classes makes the job of writing an application to handle HTML forms much easier. Thus, you do not have to read the data using **ReadClient** and then write parsing function to parse the URL-encoded data that were sent by the client.

FormHandler *Class*

One of the first programs that you write for a Web server is usually a program that processes client input from an HTML form. In fact, we wrote a number of programs in this book that read and processed input from HTML forms. The data from the HTML form, independent of whether the POST or GET method is used, are delivered as a string of URL-encoded *name-value* pairs of information. We wrote specific functions for NSAPI and CGI that parsed these data to access the value of each of the *name-value* pairs.

`FormHandler`, a new class added to Netscape 3.01, makes the handling of the form input easy. With the `FormHandler` class, you can quickly get and parse the client input. You can then use the `FormHandler` methods or the appropriate Java `Hashtable` or `Vector` class methods to retrieve the parsed *name-value* pairs of data sent by the client. `FormHandler` supports both the GET and POST methods. The `FormHandler` constructor gets and parses the input from a POST method. **ParseQueryString** parses the query string from a GET method.

With C++, you can use `FormHandler`'s **Get** method to access any value from the *name-value* pairs, as long as you know the correct name. You can also repeatedly call the **Get** method of `FormHandler` to locate all the values of a given name. **Get** returns NULL if no other value is associated with the name. If you do not know the name, then you can iterate through the *name-value* pairs using the **InitIterator** and **Next** methods.

With Java, you first call `FormHandler`'s **GetHashTable** method to get a `Hashtable` of the parsed *name-value* pairs. In a hash table, keys are mapped to specific values. You can then use `java.util.Hashtable` methods to access the name or value from the *name-value* pairs in the hash table. The `Hashtable` returned by **GetHashTable** uses the name component of the *name-value* pairs as the key. For example, if you know the name of the *name-value* pair, you can use the **get** method of `Hashtable` to retrieve the value. You can also use the **keys** method to get an `Enumeration` of the keys in the hash table or the **elements** method to get an `Enumeration` of the values in the hash table. The `Enumeration` class includes a series of elements. You can use the `Enumeration` class methods, **hasMoreElements** and **nextElement**, to iterate (enumerate) through the list of the names or values in the hash table. **hasMoreElements** verifies whether the enumeration contains any more elements. It returns false if there are no more elements. **nextElement** returns the next element in the enumeration.

The values of the *name-value* pairs in the hash table are stored as Java `Vector` entries (`Java.util.Vector`). The `Vector` class is normally used for an array of objects that can grow or shrink as needed. Netscape uses the `Vector` class for the value so as to support an array of objects whose size is not known in advance. Thus multiple objects (values) can be associated to a single name (key). `Vector` methods can be used to access a specific value from the array of values. You normally use an integer index to access the components (data) in a vector. For example, the **elementAt** method returns the component at the index you specify. You can also use the method **elements** to get an enumeration of the components of the vector. You can then use `Enumeration` class methods, mentioned earlier, to iterate through the components and retrieve the value. The method **size** returns the number of components in the vector. For more information on the `Hashtable` and `Vector` class, see your Java API documentation.

(For information on the various methods of `FormHandler`, see the `FormHandler` class sections for C++ and Java in Chapter 14.)

`FormHandler` **for Java—An Example**   Listing 15-1 is a simple **Run** method written for Java WAI that parses the input from any HTML form input and returns the *name-value* pairs of data from the form in an HTML list. We use the `FormHandler` class constructor to parse the input from a `POST` method and **ParseQueryString** to parse the input from a `GET` method. This program supports both `GET` and `POST` methods. You can also use the method **IsValid** of `FormHandler` to verify whether the constructor was able to parse the client `POST` input, although Listing 15-1 does not use this method. To verify the method of the request, we invoke the method **getRequestInfo** with the environment variable `REQUEST_METHOD`. Note that if the method specified in an HTML form is anything other than `GET` or `POST`, **getRequestInfo** returns `GET`. What you specify in the HTML `FORM` tag for the `METHOD` does not change the fact that the default method is `GET`. If you specify anything other than `POST`, the `GET` method is used.

We use **GetHashTable** to get the `Hashtable` of the parsed *name-value* data pairs and the **keys** method of the `Hashtable` class to get an `Enumeration` of the keys in the hash table (`data`). We then step through the keys using the **hasMoreElements** method of the `Enumeration` class. When **hasMoreElements** returns false, there are no more keys. We get the name (the key) of the *name-value* pairs by using **nextElement**. If there is no key, we print `Name is missing!` Otherwise, we print the name from the *name-value* pair. Next, we get the values associated with each key by using the **get** method of `Hashtable`. We then use the `Vector` method **elements** to get an enumeration of the values. We step through the values in the same way that we step through the names (keys), by enumerating through the values in the `Vector`. We also print the values in a sublist for each name.

The rest of this code includes instructions for creating an output stream and sending the response to the client. We will cover these steps in the next section, Processing the Client Request. Generating the HTML page is rather straightforward; we simply print a list of names with the values in a sublist for each name. If there is no value, the list is empty.

Listing 15-1   Example of a Run Method Using `FormHandler` **in Java**

```java
/* Send a list of name-value pairs of data from a form */
public int Run(HttpServerRequest session){

    /* Create a new byte array of output stream. We write
       the output that will be sent to the client into this
       stream. The array automatically grows as data are
       written into it.
     */
    ByteArrayOutputStream streamBuffer = new
                                ByteArrayOutputStream();

    /* Used to output to the stream. We use the print or
       println method of PrintStream to print to the stream.
     */
    PrintStream page = new PrintStream(streamBuffer);

    /* StringHolder method to hold the method of request */
    org.omg.CORBA.StringHolder method = new
                            org.omg.CORBA.StringHolder();

    /* check for the method of request */
    if(session.getRequestInfo("REQUEST_METHOD", method) ==
                            HttpServerReturnType.Success){

        /* create the FormHandler object */
        netscape.WAI.FormHandler forms = new
                                FormHandler(session);

        /* if the method is get, then call ParseQueryString
         */
        if(method.value.equalsIgnoreCase("GET"))
            forms.ParseQueryString();

        /* get a hash table of the name-value pairs */
        Hashtable data = forms.GetHashTable();

        /* get the enumeration of the keys (names) */
        Enumeration e1 = data.keys();

        /* The beginning of the HTML page that will be
           returned to the client. Print the HTML code into
           the output stream. */
```

```
page.println("<HTML><HEAD>");
page.println("<TITLE>Form Data</TITLE>");
page.println("</HEAD><BODY>");
page.println("<H2>Form Data</H2>");
page.print("The following is a parsed list of ");
page.println("the name-value pairs of data from");
page.println("the form:");
page.println("<P><UL>");

/* Enumerate through the list of names; if there is
   a name, start making the list. */
while(e1.hasMoreElements()){

    /* get the name */
    String name = (String)e1.nextElement();

    /* If the name is empty, print that the name
       is missing. Otherwise list the name. */
    if(name.compareTo("") != 0)
        page.println("<LI><B>" + name + "</B> = ");
    else
        page.println(">LI><U>Name is missing!</U>");

    /* get all the values for a name */
    Vector AllValue = (Vector) data.get(name);

    /* get an enumeration of the values */
    Enumeration e2 = AllValue.elements();

    /* i is used to check if there is more than one
       value for a name. If there is more than one
       value, we send a different set of HTML tags.
     */
    int i = 1;

    /* enumerate through the list of the values */
    while(e2.hasMoreElements()){

        /* get each value */
        String value = (String)e2.nextElement();

        /* Write out each value. If there is no
           value, leave it blank.
         */
        if(i < 2)
            page.println("<UL>" + "<LI>" + value);
        else
```

```java
                            page.println("<LI>" + value);

                i = i + 1;
            }
            page.println("</UL>");
        }

        page.println("</UL>");
        page.println("</BODY></HTML>");
    }
    /* if the method is not GET or POST, then send an error */
    else{
        page.print("Couldn't get the method of request.");
    }

    try{
        /* set the content-length of the response using the
           current size of StreamBuffer
         */
        session.setResponseContentLength(streamBuffer.size());

        /* send the response-headers */
        session.StartResponse();
    }
    catch(org.omg.CORBA.SystemException e){
        System.out.println("CORBA system exception.");
        System.err.println(e);
    }
    catch(java.lang.Exception e){
        System.out.println("Failed to send the output.");
        System.err.println(e);
    }

    /* retrieve the data in the output stream and write
       them as the body of the response to the client */
    session.WriteClient(streamBuffer.toByteArray());

    return 0;
}
```

FormHandler for C++—An Example   Listing 15-2 is a simple **Run** method for C++. It returns the *name-value* pairs of data sent by the client through a form in an HTML list back to the client. Unlike the Java example in Listing 15-1, this example lists all of the *name-value* pairs without organizing the values of a specific name as a sublist of that name. (If you wish, you can easily modify this function to write a list similar to the Java program—that is, with values as a sublist of the same name.) In this example, we simply write out the *name-value* pairs after iterating through the parsed list that Formhandler provides. In the parsed list, *name-value* pairs with the same name are grouped together. When we iterate through the list, if there are multiple form inputs with the same name, they are listed consecutively. There is no specific order to the *name-value* pairs grouped by name.

In this **Run** method, as with the Java example, we first get the method of the request, in this case by invoking **getRequestInfo** with the environment variable REQUEST_METHOD. Note that what you specify in the HTML FORM tag for the METHOD does not change the fact that the default method is GET. If you specify anything other than POST, the GET method is used.

If the method is GET, we parse the query via **ParseQueryString**. We also check the return value of **ParseQueryString** to make sure the method was successful in parsing the query string. This step is important because, due to a bug in the WAI patch (P85416) released for the NT version of Enterprise Server 3.0, **ParseQueryString** may not parse the query string as expected. In other words, **ParseQueryString** may return WAI_FALSE. In that case, we return an error page. (Check Netscape's File Library page, http://help.netscape.com/filelib.html, for an updated WAI patch for your Netscape Server that may fix problems or bugs.) If the method is POST, the FormHandler constructor parses the form input. This method functions properly with the WAI patch (P85416). You may also want to verify whether the constructor successfully parsed the POST data (that is, that the data from the POST method were valid), by calling the FormHandler method **IsValid**.

We iterate through the parsed *name-value* pairs of data sent by the client using the FormHandler method **InitIterator**. The **InitIterator** method begins at the top of the list. We use the FormHandler method **Next** to get the name and value of each pair. If there are no more *name-value* pairs, **Next** returns WAI_FALSE. We then print the name and value to the output stream. If there is no name for a *name-value* pair, we print Name is missing!.

The rest of the code in Listing 15-2 includes instructions for creating an output stream and sending the response to the client. We will cover these steps in the next section. The following function is only the **Run** method of the WAI application. You must write the rest of the code, including the rest of your Web service class and the main function for your program. Also, make sure to include the formHandler.h header file with your source code.

Listing 15-2   Example of a **Run** Method Using `FormHandler` in C++

```
/* send a list of name-value pairs of data from a form */
long MyWebService::Run(WAIServerRequest_ptr session)
{
    char *method;        /* method used by the client */

    /* Class supporting output string stream, output to
       in-memory strings. The constructor internally
       allocates an expandable string.
     */
    ostrstream outstream;

    /* get the method of the client request */
    if(session->getRequestInfo("REQUEST_METHOD", method) ==
                                        WAISPISuccess)
    {
        const char *name;   /* name of the name-value pairs */
        const char *value;  /* value of the name-value pairs */

        /* create the FormHandler object */
        FormHandler forms(session);

        /* If the method is GET then parse the query
           string. strcmp does a case-sensitive string
           comparison. If you wish to make a case-
           insensitive comparison, use stricmp for Windows
           or strcasecmp for UNIX.
         */
        if(strcmp(method, "GET") == 0)
        {
            /* Parse the query string if the method is GET.
               If ParseQueryString failed to parse the query
               string, return an error string.
             */
            if(forms.ParseQueryString() == WAI_FALSE)
            {
                outstream <<
                "WOOPS! Couldn't parse your input." << endl;

                goto send;
            }
        }

        /* HTML data for the file we are returning, output
           to the output stream
         */
```

Listing 15-2   Example of a **Run** Method Using FormHandler in C++ (*continued*)

```
outstream << "<HTML><HEAD>" << endl;
outstream << "<TITLE>Form Data</TITLE>" << endl;
outstream << "</HEAD><BODY>" << endl;
outstream << "<H2>Form Data</H2>" << endl;
outstream << "The following is a parsed list of the ";
outstream << "name-value pairs of data from the form:";
outstream << "<P><UL>" << endl;

    /* step through the parsed name-value pairs and
       put them in the output stream
     */
    if(forms.InitIterator() == WAI_TRUE)
    {
        /* get all the name-value pairs */
        while(forms.Next(name, value) == WAI_TRUE)
        {
            /* check if there is a name. */
            if(strcmp(name, "") == 0)
            {
                outstream << "<LI>" <<
                            "<U>Name is missing!</U>"
                            << " = " << value;
            }
            else
            {
                outstream << "<LI>" << name << " = "
                            << value;
            }
        }
    }
    outstream << "<UL>\n</BODY></HTML>" << endl;
    goto send;
}
else
{
    outstream << "Couldn't get the method of request."
              << endl;
    goto send;
}

send:
```

```
/* Set the content-length of the HTML page to be
   returned. The size is based on the number of bytes
   stored in the stream buffer. */
session->setResponseContentLength(outstream.pcount());

/* send the response-headers */
session->StartResponse();

/* write the body of the response to the client */
session->WriteClient((const unsigned char *)
                outstream.str(), outstream.pcount());

/* Unfreeze the stream that was frozen by the call to
   str. Delete the current buffer. */
outstream.rdbuf()->freeze(0);

return 0;
}
```

Finishing the Client Request

Once you get all the data that you need, you should do any processing of the request that you deem necessary. This part of the code is left up to you to fill. You can take any actions you wish. You can log the client input into a file, return data from a database, evaluate whether the client response is correct, process a client order, and so on.

Note on Preparing Data to Be Sent to the Client   This section will quickly review some options that you can use to manage the data that are later sent to the client. Because you will often develop the output that you write to the client in different parts of the code, it would be nice to be able to create a stream in memory where you can input the output buffer. When you write the data to the client using **WriteClient**, you use a buffer. In C and C++, the buffer is a pointer to char (const unsigned char *). With Java, it is an array of bytes (byte [ ]). Before you get to **WriteClient**, you may want to build a buffer in memory that you can easily send to the client.

In C, you can initialize a buffer large enough to hold the response either by allocating the size of the buffer or by specifying the size of the array of characters. You can then use the string or stream manipulation functions, such as **strcat** or **sprintf**, to update the string where the data to be sent to the client are kept.

With C++ and Java, a number of classes support reading and writing to stream. Some of these classes can also dynamically allocate the size of the buffer—that is, the array can expand as needed without you having to keep track of the size. For C++ examples in this book, we use the class `ostrstream`. You can find this class in `strstrea.h` in Windows or `strstream.h` under UNIX. The `ostrstream` class is an output string stream class. You construct an object of class `ostrstream` by calling its constructor. If you do not specify a length for the character array, the constructor internally allocates an expandable array. You can then write to the buffer using the operator <<. This procedure is very similar to writing to a file or to the console. To get the array, you use the method **str**. The method **str** returns a pointer to the stream content. **str** also freezes the array, so make sure you call it immediately before **WriteClient**. After writing the data, you should also call `rdbuf->freeze(0)` to unfreeze the array.

With the Java examples in this book, we use the `ByteArrayOutputStream` class to create an output stream buffer that grows automatically as new data are written into it. To write into the output stream, we use the `PrintStream` class and its **println** and **print** methods. We specify the output stream, created using the **ByteArrayOutputStream** constructor, as the parameter for the **PrintStream** constructor. **print** and **println** are used to write the data into the output stream. **println** also places a newline character at the end of the string. `PrintWriter` is a new class in Java 1.1 that supercedes the `PrintStream` class. We use the `PrintStream` class primarily to overcome version compatibility issues. You may not be able to use Print-Writer in your WAI application.

Netscape Stream and Stream Buffer Classes for C++   Netscape also provides a set of input, output, and input/output stream classes (`oreqstream`, `ireqstream`, `reqstream`) and a stream buffer (`reqStreamBuf`) class for C++. You can find these classes declared in the header file `reqstrm.hpp` under the *<server path>*`/wai/include` directory. These classes can be used in an in-process WAI application.

You can create an `oreqstream` object to write output directly to the client or an `ireqstream` object to read the client input. For example, the following **Run** function writes the output directly to the client. Unlike with `ostrstream`, with `oreqstream` we do not first create the output stream buffer and then write the buffer to the client using **WriteClient**. Instead, the stream is directly sent to the client.

```
#include "reqstrm.hpp"
. . .
long MyWebService::Run(WAIServerRequest_ptr session)
{

    /* start sending the response */
    session->StartResponse();

    /* create an output stream using oreqstream class */
    oreqstream outstream(*session);

    /* write the Hello World page to the client */
    outstream << "<HTML><HEAD>" << endl;
    outstream << "<TITLE>Hello World</TITLE></HEAD><BODY>";
    outstream << "<H1>Hello World" << "</H1>";
    outstream <<  "</BODY></HTML>";

    return 0;
}
```

With `ireqstream`, you can use the **read** method of the `istream` class to read the client input. The constructors for the Netscape stream classes use the `WAIServerRequest` object passed to your **Run** method in their parameters. Use these classes in an in-process, not an out-of-process, WAS. You can find an example of `oreqstream` in the CD-ROM that accompanies this book.

Returning the Response

Once you have processed the client request, the next step is to return a response. Before you send the body of the response, you must send the response-header. You must make sure the correct response-headers are sent to the client. Once you set and send the response-headers, you can write the data to the client.

The following subsections discuss the basic steps that you might take to write a response to the client. You do not have to include all these steps, but you should go through at least the following three steps whenever you return a page to the client. Using **setResponseContentLength** for C++ and Java, and **WAIsetResponseContentLength** for C, set the `content-length` of the response body. Next, invoke **StartResponse** or **WAIStartResponse** to send the response-header. Finally, send the body of your response using **WriteClient** for Java and C++ and **WAIWriteClient** for C.

Listing 15-3 is a simple Hello World function written in C that sends the string `Hello World!` to the client. For more examples, see Hello Client examples in Chapter 16.

Listing 15-3   C Function That Returns Hello World to the Client

---

```
long RunFunction(ServerSession_t session)
{
    char buffer[13] = "Hello World!\n";

    /* set the content-length */
    WAIsetResponseContentLength(session, 13);

    /* send the response-headers */
    WAIStartResponse(session);

    /* write Hello World! to the client */
    WAIWriteClient(session, (const unsigned char *)buffer,
                   13);

    return 0;
}
```

Getting an Existing Response-Header   Although it is rare, there might be times when you want to verify an existing response-header. You may want to see whether the server has already placed a response-header. For example, the `status` response-header is set to `200 OK` by default. You may also want to verify whether a header that you added to the response-header using **addResponseHeader** for Java and C++ or **WAIaddResponseHeader** for C is actually there.

To find out if a header already exists in the response-header and to get its value, you can use **getResponseHeader** with Java and C++ and **WAIgetResponseHeader** with C. If there is more than one response-header associated with the same name, **getResponseHeader** or **WAIgetResponseHeader** retrieves the last header, which was set for the given name.

The procedure for getting a response-header is very similar to the procedure for getting a request-header. What you get, instead of the request-header, is the response-header. You must specify the response-header name as a parameter in the **getResponseHeader** or **WAIgetResponseHeader** function.

The following examples verify that a `status` already exists in the response-headers. `stype` will hold the value of the response-header `status`. `session` is passed by the ORB to the **Run** method or your C equivalent function. If you have not set or deleted the status response-header before calling this code, you should get `200 OK` (status OK) in `stype`. For Java, to get the value of `status`, you should use the **value** method of the `StringHolder` class, `stype.value`.

C
```
char *ctype = NULL;
WAIgetResponseHeader(session, "status", &stype);
```

C++
```
char *ctype = NULL;
session->getResponseHeader("status", stype);
```

Java
```
org.omg.CORBA.StringHolder ctype = new
                    org.omg.CORBA.StringHolder();
session.getResponseHeader("status", stype);
```

Deleting a Response-Header   Besides getting the response-header, you may also want to remove an existing response-header. For example, you can remove a header that was added by using **addResponseHeader** for C++ or Java and **WAIaddResponseHeader** for C.

To remove a response-header, you can use **delResponseHeader** for C++ and Java or **WAIdelResponseHeader** for C. You have to specify the response-header's name in the function parameter (for example, `session->delResponseHeader` `("content-type");`). If there is more than one response-header for a given name, then the function (or method) deletes the last response-header set for that name. To remove all response-headers for a given name, you can repeatedly invoke **delResponseHeader** or **WAIdelResponseHeader** (for C). For Java, **delResponseHeader** returns `netscape.WAI.HttpServerReturnType.Failure` if it could not delete a header (that is, a header was not found). Likewise, **delResponseHeader** for C++ and **WAIdelResponseHeader** for C return `WAISPIFailure` upon failure.

Normally, it is the job of the browser (the client) to handle the response-headers. For example, if multiple response-headers with the same name are sent to Netscape Navigator (Communicator), Navigator uses the last response-header associated with a given name (last in, first out). If there are two content-type headers—for example, text/html and text/plain, in that order—Netscape Navigator uses the content-type header text/plain to display the document. Thus even an HTML page will appear as text (that is, you can see the source without any HTML formatting). On the other hand, a browser like Microsoft Explorer 3.x may recognize the tags for HTML and display an HTML page even when the content-type explicitly states that the content is text/plain and not text/html. If you believe that a pre-existing response-header may conflict with the proper display of your document, you can remove the response-header by using **delResponseHeader** for C++ and Java or **WAIdelResponseHeader** for C.

Adding a Response-Header   Before you send a response to the client, you normally have to specify a response-header. The most common response-header, and one that you should normally set before sending the response to the client, is content-length. content-length lets the client know the size of the content that you are sending. To set content-length, use **setResponseContentLength** for C++ and Java or **WAIsetResponseContentLength** for C. For example, if the size of the data you are sending is 80, then you can use setResponseContentLength(80); for Java or WAIsetResponseContentLength(session, 80); for C. For WAI, the size (content-length) is of type unsigned long for the C function and C++ method, and int for Java. Normally, because you generate dynamic content, you use a function or method to get the size of the buffer that you plan to send to the client.

To send a content-type other than the default text/html (for example, text/plain), you should use **setResponseContentType** for C++ and Java or **WAIsetResponseContentType** for C to specify the type of content that will be sent. To send a cookie, use **setCookie** for C++ and Java or **WAIsetCookie** for C.

The methods or functions mentioned previously are used to add the most common response-headers. Netscape also provides a general-purpose function that you can use to add any type of response-header. You use **addResponseHeader** with C++ and Java or **WAIaddResponseHeader** with C to add any number of response-headers (such as pragma or content-language). You can also use **addResponseHeader** or **WAIaddResponseHeader** to set content-type, content-length, or cookie (set-cookie). You are better off, however, using the specific methods or functions that Netscape provides. For instance, **setResponseContentType** or **WAIsetResponseContentType** can replace the preexisting content-type specified by the server (text/html) with the content-type you specify. **addResponseHeader** and **WAIaddResponseHeader**, on the other hand, simply add your content-type to the response-headers. In other words, if you use **addResponseHeader** or **WAIaddResponseHeader** to add a content-type, two separate content-type headers will exist. In addition, it is always best to send one response-header for each response-header type. This approach ensures the most consistent results with different clients. Moreover, unlike **setResponseContentLength** and **WAIsetResponseContentLength**, **addResponseHeader** and **WAIaddResponseHeader** accept only a character array or a string as the value of the response-header. If you were planning to use **addResponseHeader** to add a content-length, then you may have to convert the size of the content from an integer to a string.

With **addResponseHeader** and **WAIaddResponseHeader**, you can add multiple headers with the same name. **setResponseContentType**, **setResponseContentLength**, **WAIsetResponseContentType**, and **WAIsetResponseContentLength** set content-length and content-type only once. If you invoke these methods multiple times in your program, only the last method or function that you invoke places the appropriate response-header. These methods will also remove any previously existing response-header with the same name.

Setting the Response Status   The default status set by the server is 200 OK. You can also specify a different status code using **setResponseStatus** with C++ and Java or **WAIsetResponseStatus** with C. When you set a new status code, the server returns this new status header with the rest of the response-headers to the client. The status code is also recorded in the access log file. For example, you can use **setResponseStatus** to set the status to 301, Moved Permanently. The status 301 along with the Location response-header that you can add using **addResponseHeader** can redirect the client to the path specified by the Location header. (See Redirecting a Client, later in this chapter, for more information.)

If you set the status to an error status code, such as 404 Not found (PROTOCOL_UNAUTHORIZED) or 401 Unauthorized (PROTOCOL_UNAUTHORIZED), you still need to return an error page to the client that describes the type of error that occurred. The client needs to get the content of the page that describes the error. Unlike with the procedure for returning a quick error page using **protocol_status** in NSAPI, you must write and send a response page to the client with WAI. The server does not send the default error page for an error status code you specify. If you do not write such a function, no document data will be sent to the client. Consequently, Netscape Navigator (Communicator) may pop up a warning, stating Document contains no data. Similar to the situation with CGI, therefore, you should write an error response function or method. You can then invoke this error method or function to return an error page to the client whenever you detect an error.

The WAI function in Listing 15-4 is a simple error-handling function written in C. You can invoke this function inside your C function intended for handling the HTTP client requests. **error** returns an error page to the client that includes the error_string you specify. This function is very similar to writing a regular response page to the client. We first try to remove any preexisting status code via **WAIdelResponseHeader**. Next, we set the status code and the reason string based on the information passed to **error** through its parameters. We also specify the content-length based on the size of the error page we are returning. Finally, we write the error page to the client.

Listing 15-4   A Default Error Function

```
/* Return an error page to the client. The description of the
   error is customized by the value of the error_string parameter.
 */
```

Listing 15-4   A Default Error Function (*continued*)

```
int error(ServerSession_t session, int status,
          char *error_string)
{
   char buffer[500]; /* error page to be sent to the client
 */int length;        /* size of the error page */

   /* error page */
   length =  sprintf(buffer,
              "<HTML><HEAD><TITLE>Error</TITLE></HEAD>\n"
              "<BODY><H2>%s</H2></BODY></HTML>",
              error_string, fromURL);

   /* remove any existing status header */
   WAIdelResponseHeader(session, "status");

   /* set the new status header */
   WAIsetResponseStatus(session, status, error_string);

   /* specify the content-length of the error page */
   WAIsetResponseContentLength(session, length);

   /* send the response-headers */
   WAIStartResponse(session);

   /* write the error page to the client */
   WAIWriteClient(session, (const unsigned char *)buffer,
                  length);

   return 0;
}
```

Sending the Response-Headers   Once you have set or added all the response-headers that you need, you should invoke **StartResponse** for C++ and Java or **WAIStartResponse** for C to send the response-headers to the client. You should invoke the function before writing the body of the document to the client and after you set the status and your response-headers. This function is very similar to the NSAPI function **protocol_start_response**.

StartResponse and **WAIStartResponse** can distinguish between whether the client should receive the response-header or not. If the HTTP 0.9 protocol is used by the client, the server does not send any response-header (HTTP 0.9 does not support request- and response-headers). Otherwise, **StartResponse** starts the response by sending the response-headers and the status.

You can also use the return value of **StartResponse** or **WAIStartResponse** to determine whether you should return the body of the document. If the function returns –2

(REQ_NOACTION, as defined in the nsapi.h file), you should exit without sending the body of the response. A return of –2 (REQ_NOACTION) means that a HEAD method of request was used by the client. A HEAD method of request asks for the response-headers but does not want the body of the response. A HEAD request is commonly performed by an automatic program (a robot) that searches the Web verifying the existence of any changes to documents. If **StartResponse** or **WAIStartResponse** returns 0 (REQ_PROCEED, as defined in the nsapi.h file), you should send the body of the document. Note that the REQ_NOACTION and REQ_PROCEED macros defined in nsapi.h (the header file for NSAPI applications) are available only to C and C++ WAI applications. You cannot use these macros in Java. Instead, you should use their equivalent integer values for Java.

The following are examples of **StartResponse** in C++ or Java.

C++

```
. . .
   if(session->StartResponse == REQ_PROCEED)
   {
       /* write the response using WriteClient */
   }

   return 0;
}
```

Java

```
. . .
   if(session.StartResponse == 0)
   {
       /* write the response using WriteClient */
   }

   return 0;
}
```

The following is an example of **WAIStartResponse**.

```
. . .
   if(WAIStartResponse(session) == REQ_PROCEED)
   {
       /* write the response using WAIWriteClient */
   }

   return 0;
}
```

Writing the Body of the Response   Once you have sent the response-header, you are ready to write the body of your document to the client. You should use **WriteClient** with Java and C++ and **WAIWriteClient** with C. To make sure no error occurred while writing the content of the document to the client, you should verify the return value. **WriteClient** and **WAIWriteClient** return 1 if they were successful in sending the data and –1 if an error occurred. With C and C++, you must specify the size of the data that you are sending in the last parameter of the function.

Additional Steps

There are two additional WAI functions that are very useful when you write your program. We will discuss these functions in the following subsections.

Logging Errors   Just as with NSAPI but unlike CGI, Netscape allows you to write an error information into the server's error log file. You can find the error log file, `errors`, in the `<server path>/<server ID>/logs/` directory. You use **LogError** with Java and C++ and **WAILogError** with C. These error-logging functions work similarly to the NSAPI function **log_error**.

When you use **LogError** or **WAILogError**, you should specify the name of the function where the error occurred or your WAI application's name, and write a specific customized message that will be logged. The messages that are logged in the error log file are categorized based on the error's degree of severity. Below is a list of the degrees you can use. For more information on the error degrees, see the section Logging Errors in Chapter 6. In the following list, the code in the parentheses is the name of the degree as it appears in the error log file.

- 0—Warning message (`warning:`)
- 1—Server configuration error (`config:`)
- 2—Authentication or security error (`security:`)
- 3—Server internal error or failure (`failure:`)
- 4—Catastrophic error (`catastrophe:`)
- 5—Informative message (`info:`)
- 6—Additional internal message (`verbose:`) (new with Server 3.x)

Bug Report ▶

LogError and **WAILogError** are supposed to return `WAISPISuccess` for C or C++ and `netscape.WAI.HttpServerReturnType.Success` for Java. You may notice, however, that the function will not return the appropriate value. For example, under Server 3.5.1, **WAILogError** returns `WAISPIFailure` after successfully logging the error instead of `WAISPISuccess`. Make sure the function returns the appropriate value before you use this value in your program.

You should select a degree that best suits the type of information or error that you want to log. When you produce a log report, the information will be organized according to the error degree. If you specify the proper degree, you can then easily locate or evaluate the degree by reviewing the log report. You can also use the new internal message degree (`verbose`) for debugging purposes. You can enable the logging of the `verbose` error types by adding the `LogVerbose` on directive to the **magnus.conf** file. You can set the directive to on during debugging, when you want to have additional information logged. If everything is working properly, you can remove the directive so that none of the verbose messages is logged.

`clientinfo` is the final parameter for **LogError** and **WAILogError**. If you set this parameter to `true`, additional information about the session and request is included with your message in the error log file. For example, the message in the error log file will include `for host 1.0.0.4 trying to POST /iiop/guest`. The following code is an example of a warning message from an error log file when the last parameter of **LogError** was set to `true`:

```
[19/Mar/1998:13:41:46] warning: for host 1.2.3.4 trying to
POST /iiop/guest, guests reports: Form was not filled out
completely.
```

The following is an example of **WAILogError** for C:

```
WAILogError(session, 1, "MyWAIService",
  "The parameter in the obj.conf file is incorrect.", false);
```

The following are examples of **LogError**:

C++
```
session->LogError(1, "MyWAIService",
  "The parameter in the obj.conf file is incorrect.", false);
```

Java
```
session.LogError(1, "MyWAIService",
  "The parameter in the obj.conf file is incorrect.", false);
```

Redirecting a Client   With WAI, you have two options for redirecting a client. The first option automatically redirects the client to a new location, without the client knowing that a redirect has occurred. To redirect the client automatically, you use the standard HTTP status `301 Moved Permanently` or `302 Found` and the `Location` response-header. This procedure is not unique to WAI. You can use a similar procedure with CGI and NSAPI. You should use this procedure if you are moving a document or a site permanently and if you want the redirect to happen automatically.

First, add a `Location` response-header with the path for the new location. (See the section Redirecting the Client in Chapter 6 for more information on redirecting the client.) Next, set the status to `301` or `302`. `301` is the status code for pages or sites that have been permanently removed. You can also use `302` for pages or sites that have been temporarily redirected. You may also want to delete any existing status header before setting the status to 301 or 302. Finally, send the response-headers and status by using **StartResponse** for C++ or Java and **WAIStartResponse** for C.

Listing 15-5 is an example of a C function that automatically routes a client to a new location.

Listing 15-5   C Function for Redirecting the Client Using the `Location` Header

```
long MyWAIService(ServerSession_t session)
{
    WAIaddResponseHeader(session, "Location",
              "http://home.netscape.com");

    WAIdelResponseHeader(session, "status");
    WAIsetResponseStatus(session,302, "Moved to Netscape!");

    WAIStartResponse(session);

    return 0;
}
```

Listing 15-6 is an example of a **Run** method in C++ for automatically routing a client to a new location.

Listing 15-6   C++ Method for Redirecting the Client Using the `Location` Header

```
long MyWAIService::Run(WAIServerRequest_ptr session)
{
    session->addResponseHeader("Location",
                               "http://home.netscape.com");

    session->delResponseHeader("status");
    session->setResponseStatus(302,
                               "Moved to Netscape!");

    session->StartResponse();

    return 0;
}
```

Listing 15-7 is an example of a **Run** method in Java for automatically routing a client to a new location.

Listing 15-7   Java Method for Redirecting the Client Using the `Location` Header

```java
public int Run(HttpServerRequest session){

    try {
        session.addResponseHeader("Location",
                        "http://home.netscape.com/");

        session.delResponseHeader("status");
        session.setResponseStatus(302,
                        "Moved to Netscape!");

        session.StartResponse();
    }
    catch(org.omg.CORBA.SystemException e){
        System.out.println("CORBA system exception.");
        System.err.println(e);
    }
    catch(java.lang.Exception e) {
        System.err.println(e);
    }

    return 0;
}
```

The second method of redirecting a client is unique to WAI and uses the WAI method **RespondRedirect** for Java and C++ and **WAIRespondRedirect** for C. You can write a program in CGI or NSAPI to accomplish the same task, but the Netscape WAI function does this duty for you automatically. With this option, you simply use the redirection method or function and start the response using **StartResponse** for C++ or Java or **WAIStartResponse** for C.

The server generates and sends a `Moved Temporarily` page with the new location as a hyperlink to the client. The page that the server returns includes the following text, with the word `location` being a hyperlink to the new location specified in the WAI function:

`Moved Temporarily`

`This document has moved to a new location. Please update your documents and hotlists accordingly.`

As this server-generated page implies a temporary move of a document, you should use this method for documents that have not been moved permanently. Notice that this method returns the `302 Moved Temporarily` status code. Also, consider using this option if you do not want clients automatically redirected. Clients are informed of the fact that there is a new location for the document, so they can update their bookmarks (hotlists).

Listing 15-8 is the C function that uses **WAIRespondRedirect**.

Listing 15-8 C Function for Redirecting the Client Using **WAIRespondRedirect**

```
long MyWAIService(ServerSession_t session)
{
    WAIRespondRedirect(session,
                        "http://www.imagia.com/new.html");

    WAIStartResponse(session);

    return 0;
}
```

Listing 15-9 is the code in C++ using **RespondRedirect**.

Listing 15-9 C++ Method for Redirecting the Client Using **RespondRedirect**

```
long MyWAIService::Run(WAIServerRequest_ptr session)
{
    session->RespondRedirect
                        ("http://www.imagia.com/new.html");

    session->StartResponse();
    return 0;
}
```

Listing 15-10 is the code in Java using **RespondRedirect**.

Listing 15-10 Java Method for Redirecting the Client Using **RespondRedirect**

```
public int Run(HttpServerRequest session){

    session.RespondRedirect
                        ("http://www.imagia.com/new.html");

    try {
        session.StartResponse();
    }
```

```
catch(org.omg.CORBA.SystemException e){
     System.out.println("CORBA system exception.");
     System.err.println(e);
}
catch(java.lang.Exception e){
     System.err.println(e);
}

return 0;
}
```

Part III: Write the Main Function for WAS

We are now ready to write the actual implementation of WAI as a separate application or a shared library or DLL. To use the **Run** method or C function that processes the client request, and to take advantage of the WAI service class, we first write a WAI application. We write a main function—an entry point—for our application. In the main function, we create a Web service object and register this object with the server. In this section, we will go through the steps of writing in-process and out-of-process applications. We will discuss the procedure for writing a main function for an out-of-process WAI console application in C, C++, and Java. We will also discuss writing a Windows application for Windows NT to show that your application does not have to be a console application. The main function you write for each of these approaches is different, so we will review the differences between the various approaches.

Before we go through the steps of writing the WAI main program function, let us briefly discuss the difference between writing a CGI or NSAPI application and an out-of-process WAI application. An out-of-process WAI application is unique, because it is not just a process running outside of the server process; it is also a separate application running parallel to your server. The processing of a client request and the return of a response to the server (client) is only one of the actions that your program can take. Besides performing the necessary communication with the server and processing an HTTP request, your application can handle its own input and output or maintain state information.

An Out-of-Process WAI Application

Writing an out-of-process WAI application is different from writing a CGI, NSAPI, or in-process WAI application. With CGI, the program is invoked by the server. The CGI program processes the client request and outputs the response to the server, which in turn returns the response to the client. The connection between the server and the CGI program lasts only for the specific request. A separate CGI process is run for each request. When you write an output using the standard out (for example, **printf**) in

CGI, you are actually sending data to the server. NSAPI applications work inside the server process. Therefore, they do not live outside of the server. An in-process WAS application is the same as an NSAPI application. An out-of-process WAI application, on the other hand, runs as an independent application on a separate process than the server. It runs in parallel to the server and communicates with it. Unlike a CGI program, the out-of-process WAS should be started only once after the server has started. Once your Web service application registers with the server, it is ready to process the client requests. During its lifetime, your application simply waits for a request from the server. Because the same running application responds to all client requests, it is easy to maintain state information even when the application is running out of the server process. We will discuss persistent data in a later section, Persistent Data and WAI.

The main purpose of the out-of-process WAI application is to process the client HTTP request. Using the ORB and IIOP, your WAI application receives the client request from the server and returns a response to the server. Your application can take other actions as well. An out-of-process application is a separate Windows or console application; it is also a separate CORBA distributed application. For example, you can have your application be a client to another CORBA server object or include another implementation of a server object. Your application does not have to receive a request and send a response only to Netscape Server. Besides performing the necessary communication with the server and processing an HTTP request, it can handle its own input and output. You can write output to the console, a Windows client area, other applications, a file, and so on, as well as to the client browser. These outputs are independent of the output to the server. Thus, while you can write output to the server, you can also write separate output or receive input from another application. For example, with C, you can write output to the console using **printf**. In other words, as well as writing a response to the client using a WAI function such as **WAIWriteClient**, you can write a response to the console using **printf**.

You can use this multiple functionality of the WAI application in a variety of ways—the real purpose of writing a multithreaded distributed CORBA application. Two very useful and easy ways of using a separate output from your application are described below.

In your main function, you should output to the console or your Windows client area, printing any error that occurs during the creation and registration of your service object. You can also write other status update or information about the success of the main function. For example, you can print out information about the Web service object, or the host name and the port of the server that your Web service used for registering with the server. You may also write an error message to the console if the creation of the Web service object failed or if the object was not able to connect to Netscape Server. Remember that, because you do not have access to the session object (HTTP request object) in your main function, you cannot write messages directly to the client. Only the **Run** method or its C equivalent function can directly or indirectly write to the client. Moreover, in the main function, you cannot use **LogError** or **WAILogError** to log specific information in the server's error log file. So, although the server writes specific error information regarding the success of your program in registering and communicating with the server, you cannot write an error message into the server error log file directly from the main function.

You can also write to the console or the Windows client area from other methods or functions in your WAI application. For example, you can write to the console from the **Run** method. Use this option for debugging during processing of a client request. At any point in your **Run** method, you can write output to the console using the appropriate functions or methods of your programming language. For example, you can use **printf** in C or **system.out.println** in Java.

Your WAI application must be thread-safe, especially when it supports multithreaded steps. To avoid any thread locks or performance degradation, you should not use this method of output to a different source unless there is a specific reason (for example, for debugging). Once the server has stepped through the main functions, your WAI application should process only the HTTP request and return a response to Netscape Server (that is, the clients).

WAI Out-of-Process Main Function—An Overview   The final step of writing an out-of-process WAS is to write an application that works as your WAI application. To write such a program, you must write a main function for your application. You also must take specific steps in this main function to create (instantiate) the Web service object that will work with the Netscape ORB and WAI interface. Next, you register this object with Netscape Naming Service.

Table 15-3 lists a typical set of steps that you may take in your application's main function. Table 15-3 is based on writing a console application for C, C++, or Java.

Table 15-3   Main WAS Console Application Function

C	C++	JAVA
		Write a public class that provides the main function of your application.
Write a main function (**main**).	Write a main function (**main**).	Write a main function (**main**).
Find the host name and port of Netscape Server (for example, through command-line argument `argv`).	Find the host name and port of Netscape Server (for example, through command-line argument `argv`).	Find the host name and port of Netscape Server (for example, through command-line argument `argv`).
Get additional application arguments that your program can use (`argv`).	Get additional application arguments that your program can use (`argv`).	Get additional application arguments that your program can use (`argv`).
		Initialize the ORB (**ORB.init**).
		Initialized the BOA (**BOA_init**).
Create (instantiate) the Web service object (**WAIcreateWebAppService**). Specify the name of your service.	Create (instantiate) the Web service object using your Web service class constructor. Specify the name of your service.	Create (instantiate) the Web service object using your Web service class constructor. Specify the name of your service.

Table 15-3 Main WAS Console Application Function (*continued*)

C	C++	JAVA
Register the Web service with Netscape Server (**WAIregisterService**) using the host name and port of Netscape Server.	Register the Web service with Netscape Server (**RegisterService**) using the host name and port of Netscape Server.	Register the Web service with Netscape Server (**RegisterService**) using the host name and port of Netscape Server.
If SSL is enabled, then use a file indicator with the name of the server IOR file found in the `NameService` directory for **WAIregisterService**, `file:<server IOR file>`.	If SSL is enabled, then use a file indicator with the name of the server IOR file found in the `NameService` directory for **RegisterService**, `file:<server IOR file>`.	If SSL is enabled, then use a file indicator with the path to the server IOR file found in the `NameService` directory for **RegisterService**, `file:<path to server IOR file>`.
Verify that the registration with the server was successful (`WAI_TRUE` was returned).	Verify that the registration with the server was successful (`WAI_TRUE` was returned).	Verify that the registration with the server was successful (`WAI_TRUE` was returned).
Print a confirmation about the Web server object and its registration with the server to the console.	Print a confirmation about the Web server object and its registration with the server to the console.	Print a confirmation about the Web server object and its registration with the server to the console.
Get ready to receive requests (**WAIimplIsReady**). Start the implementation loop of the Web service object.	Write a loop that keeps the program alive.	Get ready to receive requests (**impl_is_ready**). Start the implementation loop of the Web service object.
	May also include exception-handling code.	Include exception-handling code.

Table 15-4 describes the general steps you can take to write a Microsoft Windows WAI application. The steps covered in Table 15-4 include the minimum steps you must write to produce a window for your Windows application using the Windows API. These steps are relevant to **WinMain**, the Windows application's main function. Besides writing a **WinMain** function, you must also write the Windows procedure function that will handle the Windows messages. Table 15-4 is based on writing a C++ version of a Windows WAI application.

Table 15-4 Writing a Simple Windows WAI Application for C++

WRITE A WINDOWS APPLICATION MAIN FUNCTION (WINMAIN)
Find the host name and port of Netscape Server (for example, through the command-line argument `lpCmdLine`).
Get additional application arguments that your program can use (`lpCmdLine`).
Specify a Windows class and register it (**RegisterClass**).
Create the window (**CreateWindow**).
Show the window (**ShowWindow**). Have the window display.
Create (instantiate) the Web service object (**createWebAppService**).

Table 15-4 Writing a Simple Windows WAI Application for C++ (*continued*)

WRITE A WINDOWS APPLICATION MAIN FUNCTION (WINMAIN)
Register the Web service with Netscape Server (**RegisterService**) using the host name and port of Netscape Server. If SSL is enabled, then use the file protocol with the name of the server IOR file found in the `NameService` directory for **WAIregisterService**, `file:<server IOR file>`.
Verify that the registration with the server was successful (`WAI_TRUE` was returned).
Write a `while` loop that gets the Windows messages (**GetMessage**). This loop will keep the program alive.

WRITE A WINDOWS PROCEDURE FUNCTION
Handle the Windows messages, such as close window, `WM_DESTROY`.
Use the default Windows procedure for all messages that you do not want to handle directly (**DefWindowProc**). The default Windows procedure handler deals with the rest of the messages.

Writing a WAI Out-of-Process Main Function

In the following sections, we will describe how you write a main function for the various versions of WAS. We will describe the procedure for creating a Web service object and registering it with the server (Creating and Registering a Web Service Object). There are also other important steps that you will have to take in your main functions (Additional Steps for the Out-of-Process WAI Main Function). Other steps are not essential—for example, you do not have to read the Netscape Server host name and port from the command line. You may assume that the program is always running on the same machine as the server and that the port is the standard port (80). Thus you can use a function such as **gethostname** to get the host name of the machine or even hard-code the host name and port information.

To write a WAS, you need to write either an executable, stand-alone application for an out-of-process WAS or a UNIX shared library (`so`), or Windows DLL for an in-process WAS. If you are writing an out-of-process application, you must write a main function that can be used for a console application in UNIX or Microsoft Windows, or a Windows-specific main function for the Microsoft Windows NT operating system, X Windows, and so on. To write a console application, you will need to write a **main** function. For a Windows application in C and C++, we will use **WinMain**. **WinMain** is the entry point (main function) for an application that can run under Microsoft Windows. **WinMain** and **main** are the initial entry point functions for out-of-process applications. These programs start executing with **WinMain** or **main**. In Java, everything is implemented in classes, so you must write a class that supplies the **main** function of your application.

C, C++ Console Application Main Function (main)   The main function for a C, C++ console application is the same standard **main** function that you use for writing a standard C program with an `int` as the return value—that is, `int main(int argc, char **argv)`. `argv` holds the arguments that are passed through the command line of the application. You should check this variable for any arguments that your program may need. For example, Netscape Server `<host name>[:port]` information can be sent through the command-line argument. You may also send additional command-line arguments that your program can use. By using command-line arguments, you can input dynamic data at the start of your application.

C, C++ Windows Application Main Function (WinMain)   Microsoft Windows applications using the Windows API can be written in C or C++. The main function for the Windows application is **WinMain**. The **WinMain** function prototype is:

```
int WINAPI WinMain(HINSTANCE hInstance, HINSTANCE
        hPrevInstance, LPSTR lpCmdLine, nCmdShow nCmdShow);
```

`hInstance` is a handle to the current instance of the application. `hPrevInstance` is a handle to the previous instance of the application. This parameter is `NULL` for Win32 applications. `lpCmdLine` points to the command-line arguments, a null-terminated string. As with the **main** console function, you can check for the arguments sent through the command-line arguments. For example, the host name and port can be sent through the command-line argument. You may also send additional arguments. In your program, you must parse the `lpcmdLine` string to get the various parameters. Unlike the console command-line arguments (`argv`), `lpcmdLine` does not include the name of the program as the first parameter. `nCmdShow` is used to specify how the windows will show. The various values for this parameter are `SW_HIDE`, `SW_MINIMIZE`, `SW_RESTORE`, `SW_SHOW`, `W_SHOWMAXIMIZED`, `SW_SHOWMINIMIZED`, `SW_SHOWMINNOACTIVE`, `SW_SHOWNA`, `SW_SHOWNOACTIVATE`, and `SW_SHOWNORMAL`. You do not have to include any other Windows-specific code for the WAI application.

If you want a window to appear, you must register a Windows class (**RegisterClass**), create the window (**CreateWindow**), and show it (**ShowWindow**). You also must write a message loop and a function that will handle Windows procedures. When you write a Windows application, you should use the Windows message loop to ensure that your window functions properly. Do not invoke the CORBA or WAI event loop (for example, **WAIimplIsReady**) before or after the Windows message loop in the main function. You should also make sure any updating or procedure handling of the Window application does not conflict or interfere with your handling of the HTTP request. Your application must be thread-safe. (See also Table 15-4.)

Java Application Main Function (main)   Unlike Server-side Java applications, you cannot write a WAS as a Java applet. The Java WAS must be an application. For a Java application, there needs to be a class with a main function. Everything in Java is contained in classes. You therefore need to have a new class for your application, separate from the Web application class, and write a main function for that class. The name of this class should be the same as the name of the file (for example, if the class is `foobar`, the file should be `foobar.java`). Normally, each class has its own file, but you can also write both the Web service class and your WAI application class in the same file. The prototype of the main function is `public static void main(java.lang.String[] argv)`.

```
public class foobar {
    public void main(java.lang.String[] argv) {
        // your code
    }
}
```

As with C and C++, the main function of a Java application is called **main**. You can use command-line arguments to pass dynamic data, which your application can use later, at the start of the application. For example, if the host name and port are passed through command-line arguments, you can check for them in `argv`. The parameter `argv` is an array of strings. With C, you get the number of arguments through `argc`; with Java, the number of arguments can be determined by the method **length** for the String class, `argv.length`. Unlike in C and C++, the first argument in Java is not the name of the function.

If you use the `InetAddress` class methods **getLocalHost** and **getHostName** in your main method to get the host name of the machine where the server is running, you should declare the exceptions that these methods throw in a `throws` clause. In other words, add the `throws` clause to the main function and list the exception—for example, `UnknownHostException`.

```
public class foobar {
    public void main(java.lang.String[] argv) throws
                    UnknownHostException {

    // your code
    }
}
```

Writing a WAI In-Process "Main" Function

If you are writing an in-process application, you must write an NSAPI application, a Server Application Function (SAF). Running a WAI in-process is equivalent to running an NSAPI application. You can write an NSAPI function in C or C++. Therefore, your in-process WAI application should also be in C or C++. Netscape expects a C function for the SAF. To write a C++ WAI application, you must use C linkage (`extern "C"`).

You can write an in-process C function that calls a Java WAI application, but it defeats the purpose of writing an in-process application. There is no performance benefit, as you must still invoke an out-of-process application.

Normally, when you write an NSAPI function to process a client request, you write a **Service** function. Your SAF becomes another directive of the server. With an in-process WAI application, you need to create and register your WAI service object at the start of the server. Thus you write an **Init** directive function instead. **Init** functions are loaded once, at the start of the server. Unlike other directive functions, they are called only once. The data initialized in an **Init** function are global variables that remain available for the lifetime of the server. Using an **Init** function also allows your application to initialize and share state information between different client requests. With NSAPI, to initialize a global variable or to maintain state information, you usually write an **Init** function as well.

An SAF uses the following format:

```
int <function name>(pblock *param, Session *sn,
                    Request *rq)
```

Your **Init** function should be an external function that can link with the server. In other words, for Windows your function should be _declspec(dllexport), an exportable DLL function that links with the server. For UNIX, it should be an extern function—that is, an external function that links with the server. The way you implement your **Init** function is a bit different when you use C++ or C. The NSAPI application and your SAF are normally written in C, so your C++ SAF must use C linkage. We will discuss the procedure for writing an SAF for C and C++ shortly.

The server passes the value of the parameters param, sn, and rq to your application. With WAI, unlike NSAPI, you do not have to worry about these parameters. You write an SAF that is very similar to other WAI main functions. The code inside the SAF function is similar to what you write inside an out-of-process WAI main function. In other words, you create a service object and register the object with the server.

In your SAF function, you create a Web service object similarly to how you would create a service object for an out-of-process C or C++ WAI application. You normally declare your service object as a global variable outside of your SAF and instantiate a service object inside the SAF using the **WAIcreateWebAppService** function in C or the constructor for your Web service class in C++. You then register your Web service object using the **WAIregisterService** function in C or the **RegisterService** method of your Web service object. Unlike with an out-of-process WAI application, you do not have to use the host name or port number of the server when registering your Web service. Because the in-process application is directly linked to the server, the application does not need extra instructions to locate the server's Naming Service. You also do not have to worry about using the file protocol and the IOR file name if a secured server is used. With a shared library or DLL, you do not have any command-line arguments. You can specify a parameter for the **IIIOPexec** directive function in the **obj.conf** file and then retrieve the parameter in your **Run** method or the C equivalent function. Finally, you do not need to use the implementation loop (for example, **WAIimplIsReady**) or write a loop that keeps the program alive. When you write an **Init** function, the function is loaded at the start of the server and the service object you create is available for the lifetime of the server. You can also initialize any additional global variables that you may wish to use with your program in the **Init** function.

Unlike with an out-of-process WAI application, if your **Init** function fails or was not able to load properly, the server will fail to function correctly. When you write a shared library or DLL, similar to the case with NSAPI, your code must be thread-safe and function properly for the server to run. You also need to stop and restart the server if you make any changes to your WAI in-process application.

Once you have written your SAF function and the rest of your WAI application code, you compile your application into a DLL or shared library. Your DLL or shared library then links with the server. To accomplish this goal, you register your WAI application in the **obj.conf** file, similarly to how you register an NSAPI function. You use the built-in server **Init** directive function **load-modules** to specify the location of your DLL or shared library (shlib parameter) and to load your SAF (funcs parameter). You then declare your **Init** WAI function as an **Init** directive function inside the **obj.conf** file. Remember that you must stop and restart the server for any changes to **obj.conf** to take effect. We will discuss the process of registering your SAF in greater detail in Chapter 16 under the section, Registering an In-Process WAI Application.

In-Process WAI SAF Function in C   When you write an in-process application in C, you can define your function as NSAPI_PUBLIC. This definition basically means that the function is of type _declspec(dllexport) for Windows (WIN32), and extern for UNIX. You may also use the appropriate types directly, instead of using NSAPI_PUBLIC. Listing 15-11 is an example of an in-process WAI **Init** function, MyWAS.

Listing 15-11   In-Process WAI SAF Function in C

```
IIOPWebAppService_t obj;

  NSAPI_PUBLIC int MyWAS(pblock *param, Session *sn,
                            Request *rq)
{
  // Create a Web service
  obj = WAIcreateWebAppService("<Service Name>",
                                  <Run Function>, 0, 0);

  // Register the Web service
  WAIregisterService(obj, "");

  return 0;
}
```

We declare the service object (obj) that is returned by the **WAIcreateWebAppService** function outside of the main function. In the main function, we first create a WAS object and then register the object with Netscape Naming Service. Notice that the "main" function for an in-process WAI is very simple. You do not need to worry about the third and fourth parameters (argc and argv) of **WAIcreateWebAppService**, as these are specific to an out-of-process application. You can set the second parameter (host) of **WAIregisterService** to an empty string. We will discuss **WAIcreateWebAppService** and **WAIregisterService** object in a later section, Creating and Registering a Web Service Object.

Unlike with NSAPI applications, if you wish to specify a parameter for your WAI function, you should not set the parameters for the **Init** function in the **obj.conf** file. Instead, you can set parameters for **IIOPexec** in the **obj.conf** file. You can then retrieve the parameters using **WAIgetConfigParameter** in your WAI function that processes client requests. (To access the **Init** function parameters, you need to use NSAPI functions.)

In-Process WAI SAF Function in C++   With C++, you must declare your in-process application a bit differently. You should use extern "C" when initializing your **Init** function. This strategy allows your C++ module to communicate with the C interface of the server's SAF. You should also use _declspec(dllexport) for a Windows version of your **Init** function. Listing 15-12 is an example of an out-of-process **Init** function for WAI.

Listing 15-12   In-Process WAI SAF Function in C++

```
#if defined(WIN32)
#define DLLEXPORT __declspec(dllexport)
#else
#define DLLEXPORT
#endif

/* MyWAIService class declaration */
MyWAIService *obj;

extern "C" {
   DLLEXPORT int MyWAS(pblock *param, Session *sn,
                       Request *rq);
}

int MyWAS(pblock *param, Session *sn, Request *rq)
{
   obj = new MyWAIService("<Service Name>");
   obj->RegisterService();
   return 0;
}
```

In Listing 15-12, we first define DLLEXPORT, so that we can use _declspec (dllexport) for an exportable DLL function in Windows (Win32). We do not have to specify extern for UNIX, as the **Init** function is specified as extern "C". Next in your code, you should include the declaration for your WAI service class. For this example, the class is called MyWAIService. We then declare an object of the type MyWAIService—for example, obj. The combination of extern "C" and DLLEXPORT allows the C++ **Init** function to work with Netscape Server. The server can then link and use our SAF. Your C++ function can be accessed by the C interface of Netscape Server. Your compiler will use the C naming convention and C linkage instead of the C++ type-safe naming (naming decoration) and C++ calling convention. We do not use NSAPI_PUBLIC as we did in the C version of the in-process WAI application. In the **Init** function, MyWAS, we create an instance of the WAI service class (obj) using the class constructor, and then register the object with Netscape Naming Service (**RegisterService**).

Creating and Registering a Web Service Object

In your main WAI application function, you must create or instantiate a WAS object, so as to create an instance of a WAI service class. For C++ and Java, you use the constructor for your Web service class to create the WAI service object. We already discussed how you create your WAI service class in the previous section, Part I: Writing a Web Service Class. For C, you use the WAI function **WAIcreateWebAppService**. You then register the Web service object (WAS object) using the object's method **RegisterService** for C++ and Java or **WAIregisterService** for C.

These two steps of creating the WAS object and registering it with Netscape Server should be included for all WAI applications, whether they are in-process, out-of-process, a Windows application, and so on. Any additional code that you may write to support creation or registration of your service object may be unique to that type of WAI application.

Creating a Web Service Object in C   To create a WAS (a Web service object) in C, you will use the function **WAIcreateWebAppService**. Unlike in C++ and Java, you do not have to declare a WAS class derived from WAIWebApplicationService; Netscape does it for you. You simply declare an object as IIOPWebAppService_t type and use **WAIcreateWebAppService**. **WAIcreateWebAppService** returns an object of type IIOPWebAppService_t that you can use to register your service. The prototype for **WAIcreateWebAppService** is as follows:

```
WAIcreateWebAppService(const char *name, WAIRunFunction
                       func, int argc, int argv);
```

For example, you can use the following code to create a hello service object, obj:

```
IIOPWEbAppService_t obj;

obj = WAIcreateWebAppService("hello",
                 <Function to process request>, <argc>,
                 <argv>);
```

As with the Java and C++ constructor, the first parameter of **WAIcreateWebAppService** identifies the name of the service. The second parameter is unique to C. With C++ and Java, the server will invoke the **Run** method of your service object. With C, you must specify which function the server should invoke. func should be the name of the call-back function that the server invokes and to which the HTTP request object (the session object) is passed. You write this function to process the client request and return the response. We have already discussed how you can write such a function in Part II: Process the Client Request. `argc` and `argv` work the same way as the `argc` and `argv` parameters in the C++ class constructor. As with C++, you can pass ORB or BOA settings through the `argc` and `argv` parameters. (See the section Creating a Web Service Object in C++ and Java, below, for more details on the use of `argc` and `argv`.)

Creating a Web Service Object in C++ and Java   To instantiate your WAS object for C++ and Java, you must invoke the constructor for your Web service class derived from the `WAIWebApplicationService` class. The constructor creates an actual instance (a physical entity) of your WAI service class. As you might expect, the constructor for a class has the same name as the class. For more information on the C++ and Java constructors, review the sections on these functions found earlier in this chapter.

You also must assign a special name to the Web service. The name you specify for your Web service can be anything you like, as long as no other Web service uses the same name. It is different from the name of the WAS object you create. The name does not have to be the same as the name of the instance of the WAS object or the name of your WAI application. You specify the Web service name in the name parameter of your constructor. The name you specify in the Web service class constructor's parameter is an instance name for your Web service. Your service registers itself with Netscape Naming Service using this instance name. The clients also use this name to invoke your service.

C++   The following code lists several different C++ constructors that you can use to create a WAS object (`obj`). You should have specified the type of constructor that you want to use when you declared your service class constructor. In the main function, you can then invoke the constructor for your Web service class (WAS class). Decide on which constructor you want based on the type of options that you wish to have when you create your service object. For example, if you want to activate your object at a later point using the C++ method **ActiveWAS**, you should use the third or fourth constructor types. These two constructors are not supported by Server 3.0. The Web service class for the examples below is `MyWAIService`.

```
MyWAIService obj = MyWAIService("<service name>");
MyWAIService obj = MyWAIService("<service name>",
                                <argc>, <argv>);
MyWAIService obj = MyWAIService("<service name>",
                                <activeObj>);
MyWAIService obj = MyWAIService("<service name>",
                                <argc>, <argv>,
                                <activeObj>);
```

You may also use the short form of invoking the constructor:

```
MyWAIService obj("<service name>");
MyWAIService obj("<service name>", <argc>, <argv>);
```

```
MyWAIService obj("<service name>", <activeObj>);
MyWAIService obj("<service name>", <argc>, <argv>,
                 <activeObj>);
```

The instance of the WAS class (`MyWAIService`) created is `obj`. The *service name* can be any name you want (for example, `hello` for a Hello Client example).

`argc` and `argv` can pass the appropriate ORB or BOA settings to the ORB and BOA of your WAI application. For instance, if you specified a BOA address for the **IIOPinit** directive function in the **obj.conf** file, you can pass the IP address of the BOA, `-OAipaddr`, using the `argv` parameter. In the `argc` parameter, you can specify the number of parameters that you are passing with `argv`. You can also specify the various BOA- or ORB-related arguments through your application's command-line argument. For a console application, you can directly pass the application's command-line arguments to the constructor. You can use the same `argc` and `argv` variables from the **main** function with the constructor. The constructor (Netscape ORB) can parse and get the various parameters it needs. For a Windows application, you must first parse `lpCmdLine`, which holds the command-line arguments, before you can pass the arguments using the `argc` and `argv` parameters of the constructor. You need to identify the number of arguments in `lpCmdLine` to set the `argc` parameter. If no argument is needed, you can set both `argc` and `argv` to 0. There is no argument for an in-process WAS. For an in-process WAS, you should set the parameters to 0 if you use a constructor that includes `argc` and `argv` parameters.

`activeObj` is a new parameter added to the C++ constructor with Netscape Server 3.01. You set the `activeObj` parameter to `WAI_FALSE` if you want to activate your WAS object at a later point using the **ActiveWAS** method of your object. When you set the `activeObj` parameter to `WAI_FALSE`, your WAS object is not activated until you invoke **ActiveWAS**. You also use a constructor with the `activeObj` parameter and set its value to `WAI_FALSE` when you want your application to be started automatically by the OAD. We will go through the steps of registering your service with the OAD in the section Registering an Out-of-Process WAI Application with OAD, in Chapter 16. (The use of OAD with WAI applications is limited to UNIX versions of the server.) This parameter is not relevant for an in-process WAI application. You register only an out-of-process WAI application with OAD.

The following two examples illustrate how to create a Web service object in C++.

```
MyWAIService obj("hello", argc, argv);
MyWAIService obj("hello", 0, 0, WAI_FALSE);
```

Java   Creating your WAS object with Java is simple. There is only one constructor for the WAS class. When you invoke the constructor, you simply pass the name of the instance of your Web service. There is no additional argument for the constructor—no `argc`, `argv`, or `activeObj` parameter. We also use the `new` operator to create an instance of the Web service class (a task done implicitly by the C++ constructor), as in the following example:

```
MyWAIService obj = new MyWAIService("hello");
```

With Java, you should also put the code for creating and registering your Web service object inside a `try` block and catch and handle the exceptions that the code may produce using `catch`. You need to catch the CORBA exceptions, `CORBA.UserException`.

```
try {
   // create the Web service object
   MyWAIService obj = new MyWAIService("hello");

   // register the Web service object
   obj.RegisterService("foo:80");

   // additional code . . .
}
catch (org.omg.CORBA.UserException e){
   System.out.println("CORBA user exception.");
   System.err.println(e);
}
catch(java.lang.Exception e){
   System.out.println("Service failed to initialize.");
   System.err.println(e);
}
```

Note that writing the code for creating and registering a WAS object in Java is different from doing so in C++ and C. The code you write is similar to what you would write in any CORBA object implementation. You must initialize the ORB (**ORB.init**), initialize the BOA (**BOA_init**), and call **impl_is_ready** when you have finished registering your object. We will go through these steps in the section Additional Steps for the Out-of-Process WAI Main Function, later in this chapter.

Registering Your Service   Once you have created your service object, you are ready to register the service with Netscape Naming Service. It is theoretically possible to register your service with more than one Netscape Server. For now, however, you need to employ a Web service object for a single server. Netscape states that, on the same machine, you should not enable WAI on more than one server. Moreover, there are performance drawbacks and thread-locking and safety risks if a WAI service responds to multiple servers.

There are a number of ways to register CORBA services with Netscape Naming Service, including different methods for registering a WAS. We discussed several of these methods for Java and C++ in the section Netscape Naming Service in Chapter 12. In this section, we review the standard way of registering your WAI service with Netscape Server. Instead of using the methods discussed in Chapter 12, we use the **RegisterService** instance method of our Web service object or **WAIregisterService** for C.

Under C++ and Java, **RegisterService** is a method of a Web service class. You use the **RegisterService** instance method of the Web service object that you instantiated to register your service with Netscape Server's Naming Service. The name of the host where Netscape Server resides and the port where the server is listening are normally used as parameters for **RegisterService**. This information is needed to enable the WAS to locate Netscape Server and to get the object reference of Netscape Naming Service. The method generates a URL for Netscape Naming Service based on the predefined path for it and the host name and port you specify. For example, for server `foo`, the URL could be `http://foo/NameService/WAS`. **RegisterService** passes this request to Netscape Server. The server then returns the object reference (IOR) for the server's Naming Service or the built-in WAS implementation. If the request is `http://foo/NameService`, the server returns the Naming Service IOR. If the request is `http://foo/NameService/WAS`, the server returns the IOR of the WAS implementation. **RegisterService** uses this information to register your service with Naming Service. For SSL-enabled servers, your application does not use HTTP and the URL to get the object reference for Naming Service. Instead, you use the file indicator (protocol) and the name or path of the server IOR file to locate the object reference. We will discuss registering your service with an SSL-enabled server in the next section.

You may hard-code the host name and port information in your program. The typical means of getting the host name and port for Netscape Server, however, is through the command-line argument used with the WASI application. As another alternative, you can use a C or Java programming language function to get the host name of the server machine. For example, you can use the **getLocalHost** and **getHostName** methods of the `InetAddress` class in Java or **gethostname** in C or C++. **gethostname** and **getHostName** return the host name of the machine where the WAI application is running. You should use these functions only if Netscape Server is on the same machine as your WAI application. You also need to add the port for Netscape Server if it is different from default port (80). **getHostName** and **gethostname** will not return the port address of your Web server. If you do not specify a port when registering your application, the default port (80) is used for finding and registering your service with the server.

For example, to register a Hello WAS object (`obj`) in Java or C++, you can use the following function. Netscape Server is on the host machine `foo` and the port on which it is listening is `100`.

```
obj.RegisterService("foo:100");
```

Under C, you use the function **WAIregisterService**. The Web service object reference (type `IIOPWebAppService_t`) that the **WAIcreateWebAppService** function returns is used as the first parameter of **WAIregisterService**, and the host name and port information as the second parameter. To register the Hello WAS object (`obj`) in C, you can use the following function:

```
WAIregisterService(obj, "foo:100");
```

Because it is essential for Web service objects to properly register with Netscape Server, you should always check the return value of **WAIregisterService** or

RegisterService. These functions return WAI_TRUE (or true for Java) upon success and WAI_FALSE (or false for Java) upon failure to register. You can then exit the program and write out an error string. With Java, you should place this code, along with the constructor for creating the Web service object and **impl_is_ready**, inside a try block and catch and handle the exceptions that the code may produce using catch. (See the section Creating a Web Service Object in C++ and Java, earlier in this chapter, for an example of the use of try and catch.)

With in-process WAI applications, you do not need to specify any parameter for **RegisterService** or **WAIregisterService**. Because the WAS is directly linked with the server in a shared library or DLL, **RegisterService** and **WAIregisterService** do not need any additional information to register your service with the server.

Bug Report ▶

The **RegisterService** method for Java should return true upon successful registration of your service and false upon failure. As tested under Server 3.0 for NT using the WAI patch (P85416) and Server 3.5.1, however, it returns false even when your service was able to register with Naming Service. Make sure the WAI register method or function returns the proper value before you rely on its value in your program. You should also check Netscape's File Library page, http://help.netscape.com/filelib.html, for an updated WAI patch for your Netscape Server that may fix this problem.

Registering Your Service with an SSL-Enabled Server   To register your WAI application when SSL is enabled on your server, you use the WAI registration function (that is, **WAIregisterService** for C and **RegisterService** for C++ and Java). Instead of using the host name and port information of the server, however, you should use the file indicator (protocol), file:, along with the location or name of the Netscape Server IOR file. When host name and port information is used, your application generates a URL for the server based on the information you have input. When SSL is enabled, your application—instead of using the HTTP and URL to get Naming Service's object reference—needs to directly locate the IOR file of Netscape Naming Service. The IOR file for the server, <server ID>.IOR (for example, https-foo.IOR), is located under <server path>/wai/NameService. Inside this IOR file is the object reference for Netscape Server's Naming Service. Once the registration function gains the object reference, it can register your service with Naming Service.

For the host parameter of **WAIregisterService** in C, and **RegisterService** in C++, you should specify the file indicator and the name of the IOR file, file:<server IOR file>. You should also set the environment variables NS_SERVER_ROOT and NS_SERVER_ID if they are other than the default values. The registration function can use the environment variables and the value you specify in the host parameter to locate the IOR file of the server. Set NS_SERVER_ROOT to the root directory of your server (such as c:/netscape/server) and NS_SERVER_ID to the server ID. Do not set NS_SERVER_ROOT to the root of a specific Netscape Server, as in c:/netscape/server/https-nt4. The default server ID is https-<server name>. You should specify these environment variables so that your WAI application can access them. You can set these variables with **setenv** in UNIX or **set** in Windows NT. You can also add these variables in the Environments tab of the Systems Properties dialog box from the Control Panel of Windows NT 4.0.

For Java, you should use the full path to the IOR file in the host parameter of **RegisterService**. Note that the path you specify is different from the path that a browser may use to open the file. For instance, to open the `https-foo.IOR` file in Netscape Navigator, the following path is used: `file:///c|/netscape/server/wai/NameService/https-foo.IOR`. Do not use this file path format. Use the path format based on your operating system for the file instead. For example, under NT, you can use `file:c:\\netscape\\server\\wai\\NameService\\https-foo.IOR`. (You must use the backslash escape character to insert the backslash character in the path.) You can also use `file:c:/netscape/server/wai/NameService/https-foo.IOR`. The path under UNIX could be `file:/user/netscape/server/wai/NameService/https-foo.IOR`. If the path you specify includes a space, you should use quotes around the path—for example, `file:"c:/program files/netscape/server/wai/NameService/https-foo.IOR"`.

In the following example of **RegisterService** under NT, `obj` is the name of the Web service object.

```
obj.RegisterService(
    "file:c:/netscape/server/wai/NameService/https-foo.IOR");
```

Additional Steps for the Out-of-Process WAI Main Function

There are a number of additional methods or functions that you need to invoke in your main function for an out-of-process WAI application. Unlike a function that you may invoke for the unique purpose of your application, these methods or functions are essential to the working of a WAI application. You do not have to invoke any additional steps for an in-process main application.

All out-of-process applications need to produce a loop that keeps the WAI application alive while waiting for requests from Netscape Server. You need to invoke this loop at the end of your main application. In addition to this step, you must write specific steps for out-of-process Windows applications and for WAI applications in Java. As you might expect, a Windows application requires specific steps for creating and showing a window and for processing keyboard and mouse input from the client. In this book, we will write a simple Windows application for Windows NT that uses the Windows API. This WAI application simply displays a window. No specific input is painted in the client window. As for Java, similar to a CORBA server object that you may write, the Java WAI application needs to invoke specific CORBA methods for initializing the ORB and BOA.

WAI Implementation Loop   Once you have registered your Web service, you need to invoke a WAI implementation loop that will place your application in an endless loop waiting for requests from the server. This step should be the last one in your main function. You should perform this task only after you have registered your application and have finished all appropriate processing in your main function. The only statement that you should include after this implementation loop should be the return statement, `return 0`.

C   Netscape provides a specific function for this loop in C. **WAIimplIsReady** puts the application in an endless loop. Your application is now ready to receive client input. The WAI application stays alive until it is manually shut down. There is no parameter for **WAIimplIsReady**. You simply call the function, `WAIimplIsReady();`. As already mentioned, do not include any additional statements after **WAIimplIsReady**. Any code that you write after **WAIimplIsReady** will not be called.

C++   For C++, there is no specific WAI implementation that you can call. You must write your own loop that suspends the application thread. A simple `while` loop can be used to keep the program alive indefinitely. For example, you can use the following `while` loop.

```
. . .
  while(1)
    Sleep(1000)

  return 0;
}
```

Because this loop is always true, your application's thread will be suspended for an infinite time. The millisecond of time you specify for the **Sleep** function is an arbitrary number, as the program does not exit the loop. This code is only one example of an endless loop; you can write any type of loop you like. The important thing is that the loop should keep your application alive while waiting for requests.

Java   For Java, you can use the CORBA BOA method **imp_is_ready**. You should have first initialized the BOA with **BOA_init** before you invoke this method. You can place **imp_is_ready** along with the method for creating and registering your Web service object in the same `try` and `catch` block of code. The following code is an example of this approach:

```
. . .
ORB orb = org.omg.CORBA.ORB.init();
BOA boa = orb.BOA_int();
. . .

   try{
       // create the Service object (obj)
       MyWAIService obj = new MyWAIService("hello");

       // register the object with Naming Service
       obj.RegisterService("foo:80");

       // Wait for incoming requests
       boa.impl_is_ready();
   }
   catch (org.omg.CORBA.UserException e){
       System.out.println("CORBA user exception.");
       System.err.println(e);
   }
   catch(java.lang.Exception e)
   {
       System.out.println("Service failed to initialize.");
       System.err.println(e);
   }
. . .
```

Windows API   For Windows applications, you should use the Windows-specific message loop instead of writing your own or using the function provided by Netscape (for example, **WAIimplIsReady**). For example, for a Microsoft Windows application using the Windows API, you write a message loop—a `while` loop with the **GetMessage** function. Consider the following example:

```
MSG msg;
. . .
   while( GetMessage( &msg, NULL, 0, 0 ) )
   {
```

```
            TranslateMessage( &msg );
            DispatchMessage( &msg );
    }

    return 0;
}
```

This loop gets the message from the message queues for your WAI application. If the message is anything other than WM_QUIT, **GetMessage** returns TRUE, a nonzero value. **GetMessage** removes the message from the message queue. Parameters NULL, 0, and 0 are used with **GetMessage** to get all messages for all windows created by our program. **TranslateMessage** retrieves input from the keyboard. **DispatchMessage** returns msg back to Windows, which then sends the message to your window procedure function. Your window procedure function then handles the message, processing the messages for your window. For example, the simple window procedure in Listing 15-13 closes the application window if the user chooses Close from the system menu or presses Alt-F4.

Listing 15-13 Simple Windows Procedure Function

```
LRESULT CALLBACK MainWndProc( HWND hWnd, UINT msg,
                              WPARAM wParam, LPARAM lParam)
{

    switch(msg)
    {
        /*for closing the window */
        case WM_DESTROY:
            PostQuitMessage( 0 );
            break;

        /* use default window procedure for handling other
           messages
         */
        default:
            return(DefWindowProc(hWnd, msg, wParam, lParam));
    }

    return 0;
}
```

WM_DESTROY is the message for destroying a window. **DefWindowProc** sends any other message back to the system for default processing. This message loop and window procedure function are extremely basic. When you write a Windows application, you usually write much more code for handling a variety of inputs and outputs.

For a complete example of a basic Windows WAI example, see the section Out-of-Process WAI Windows Example in Chapter 16.

Special Steps for Java   For Java, you must also initialize the ORB and BOA. Before you create your service object, you should initialize the ORB by calling **ORB.init()**, as in `org.omg.CORBA.ORB.init()`. You then initialize the BOA for the ORB returned via **ORB.init**. The following example illustrates these two steps:

```
ORB orb = org.omg.CORBA.ORB.init();
BOA boa = orb.BOA_init();
```

boa is also used to call **impl_is_ready**. When you register the BOA and ORB, make sure to catch any `CORBA.SystemException`. Listing 15-14 is an example of a complete Java class (`Hello`) with the main function, for a WAI application.

Listing 15-14   Example of an Out-of-Process WAI Main Function for Java

```java
class Hello{

    // WAI application main function
    public static void main(java.lang.String[] args)
            throws UnknownHostException{

        try {
            // initialize the ORB
            ORB orb = org.omg.CORBA.ORB.init();

            // initialize the BOA
            BOA boa = orb.BOA_init();

            // get the host information from the command line
            if(args.length > 0){

                StringBuffer host;
                host = new StringBuffer(args[0]);

                try{
                    // create the Service object (obj)
                    MyWAIService obj = new
                                    MyWAIService("hello");

                    // register the object with Naming
                    // Service
                    obj.RegisterService(host.toString());

                    // wait for incoming requests
                    boa.impl_is_ready();
                }
                catch (org.omg.CORBA.UserException e){
                    System.out.println(
                                    "CORBA user exception.");
```

```
                        System.err.println(e);
                    }
                    catch(java.lang.Exception e){
                        System.out.println(
                                "Service failed to initialize.");
                        System.err.println(e);
                    }
                }
                else{
                    System.out.println("Missing host parameter.");
                }
            }
            catch(org.omg.CORBA.SystemException e){
                System.out.println("CORBA system exception.");
                System.err.println(e);
            }
        }
    }
```

Persistent Data and WAI

One powerful feature of a WAI application is that it can easily maintain and update state information. WAI applications can support persistent data. Because a single WAI application can handle all client requests for the application, you can maintain, update, and alter a state information that can be kept for the lifetime of the application. Any global variable or a Web service class variable that you declare persists for the application's lifetime. Multiple or different threads of your application can access the global variable or your Web service object's variables.

The only catch to using WAI for supporting persistent data is that your code must be thread-safe. If you are using a multithread version of WAI, and you update or change a global variable or a Web service object's variable, you must make sure that the update happens in a thread-safe manner. Multiple threads of a WAI application that are handling different client requests simultaneously can end up corrupting or writing incorrect information. You should use a thread synchronization method that protects critical data from simultaneous access. For example, you can use your programming language system-specific thread-handling functions to lock a thread before updating it. You can then release the thread once the update is made.

In Java, you can use the `synchronized` keyword to lock a class or an instance method. By locking a class or an instance of the class (object), you make sure that no other thread can modify the object or class. `synchronized` prevents simultaneous access by different threads to the critical data. You can also use the **wait**, and **notify**, or **notifyAll** methods of `java.lang.Object` to synchronize the access to a thread. **wait** has the thread wait until a specified condition is met. **notify** notifies a waiting thread about the condition. **notifyAll** notifies all waiting threads. The Java thread class can be found in `java.lang.Thread` (`Java.Lang.ThreadGroup` is for groups of threads). The `java.lang.Thread` methods can be used to create, run, stop, yield, resume, and perform other operations on a thread. Make sure the method you use is properly supported by Netscape for the type of application that you are writing. For instance, some Java methods are not supported for LiveConnect applications (for example, `java.lang.Thread`'s **suspend** and **resume**).

With C and C++, you can use your favorite thread synchronization mechanism (such as critical section, mutex, semaphores, and so on). For a C version of an in-process WAI application, you may also be able to use Netscape's NSAPI thread model. (See Chapter 11 for more information about the NSAPI thread model and the various NSAPI functions that support thread handling.)

Let us look at an example that uses persistent data. In Java or C++, you can declare a public or private member variable for your Web service class. The member variable can be an integer, a string, a stream, another class, a handle to a file, and so on. You can then write a method for your class that updates or uses this variable safely. You invoke this thread-safe method in the **Run** method of your Web service class to make the update and/or get the variable. Because the **Run** method is invoked every time a client makes a request, the variable can be retrieved and updated based on each request. With C++, you can also override the default destructor for the Web service class. In the destructor, you can perform any necessary clean-up. For example, you can free (delete) the memory for any member variable of your class in the destructor.

Listing 15-15 is written in Java and uses `synchronized` for thread safety. In this example, we keep track of the number of visitors to our site from a predefined location outside our site. To verify the point from which the client is coming, we use the `referer` HTTP request-header. This header is sent by the client when the client is directed to our WAI application from another page. If the client directly requests the program by inputting the URL in the browser (for example, in the `Location` text box of Navigator), there is no `referer` header. If the client uses a link in another page to invoke our program, the location of that page is sent as the value of the `referer` header. You can use `referer` to find out if the client used a listing or an ad placed in another site to get to your site. For this example, we expect the URL value of the `referer` header to be the fictitious `http://www.wizards.com/oz.html`. This expected URL, which we use to verify whether the client was referred from the desired location, is hard-coded in Listing 15-15. You can have this URL be declared as a parameter of **IIOPexec** in the **obj.conf** file. You then retrieve the URL using **getConfigParameter**.

If the client is referred from `oz.html`, we update the `OZService` variable `hits`. **addhits** is a thread-safe method that increments the value of `hits` by 1. If the number of `hits` is less than 100, **addhits** returns 0. Once we reach the 100 mark, the value of hits is set back to 0, the value of counts is set to counts + 100, and **addhits** returns counts. Thus we can identify every 100 hits to our site from the oz.html page. Both counts and hits are initialized to 0 in the constructor.

In the **Run** method, we invoke **addhits** to increment hits by 1 and watch for every hundredth visitor. If the client requesting our program comes from oz.html and hits the 100 mark, we return a congratulatory page. Otherwise, we return the Welcome to OZ page for clients referred by oz.html and the Welcome to Kansas City page for all other requests.

Note that this function does not identify whether the same user is making each request. In a real-world scenario, you would normally allow one hit for each client or at least one hit for each client for a given time period or number of hits. Consequently, you would not have the same user trying to access your site repeatedly to reach the 100 marks. To limit the clients to one hit, you must keep track of the clients. For example, you may use a linked list to keep track of the clients by their IP addresses. You then update the hits only when a new client invokes your program. Once the hundredth person is reached, you may clear the list of users and start from scratch. You can also use a cookie to keep track of the users.

In Listing 15-15, we have included only the class definition and methods of OZ Service. You still must write your WAI application class and its main method before you can use this example. Once you create and register your Web service object using the OZService class, your object will keep track of the persistent data and process the client request.

Listing 15-15   Example of a Web Service Class That Uses Persistent Data

```
/* OZService class extends WAIWebApplicationService class
 */
class OZService extends WAIWebApplicationService
{
    int hits;         /* number of hits from OZ */
    int counts;       /* counts for hundred hits */

    /* class constructor */
    OZService(java.lang.String name) throws
        CosNaming.NamingContextPackage.CannotProceed,
        CosNaming.NamingContextPackage.InvalidName,
        CosNaming.NamingContextPackage.AlreadyBound,
        org.omg.CORBA.SystemException
        {
            /* call the superclass constructor */
            super(name);

            /* initialize our variables in the constructor */
            hits = 0;
            counts = 0;
```

```
    }

   /* Thread-safe updating of the number of hits
      from oz.html. counts will mark every
      hundredth visitor. addhits returns 0 if
      the number of hits is not 100.
    */
   private synchronized int addhits(){
    if(hits == 99){
        hits = 0;
        counts = counts + 100;
        return counts;
    }
    else{
        hits++;
    }
    return 0;
}

/* Method for processing client request. If the client
   is from the external OZ link, we return the OZ page.
   If the client is the hundredth visitor from the OZ
   link, we return a congratulatory page. Otherwise
   we return the Kansas page.
 */
public int Run(HttpServerRequest session)
{
    /* Create a new byte array of output stream. We
       write the output that will be sent to the client
       into this stream. The array automatically grows
       as data are written into it.
     */
    ByteArrayOutputStream streamBuffer =
                        new ByteArrayOutputStream();

    /* Used to output to the stream. We use the println
       method of PrintStream to print to the stream.
     */
    PrintStream page = new PrintStream(streamBuffer);

    /* StringHolder class is used to hold the referring
       link--that is, the location from which the client
       comes
```

```
        */
        org.omg.CORBA.StringHolder referred = new
                            org.omg.CORBA.StringHolder();

    /* Check if a referer header is sent. If the client
        directly asks for our program by typing the URL
        in the browser, then there will be no referrer
        header. Return the Kansas page.
    */
    if(session.getRequestHeader("referer", referred) ==
                        HttpServerReturnType.Success)
    {
        /* Check if the referer header is OZ. If the
            visitor didn't come from the OZ link, return
            the default Kansas page.
        */
        if(referred.value.compareTo (
                    "http://www.wizards.com/oz.html")==0)
        {
            /* update the number hits and get the counts */
            int num = addhits();

            /* If counts isn't the hundredth increment, send
                back the OZ page. Otherwise send the
                congratulatory page.
            */
            if(num == 0)
            {
                /* write the OZ page */
                page.println("<HTML><HEAD>");
                page.println("<TITLE>OZ Site</TITLE>");
                page.println("</HEAD><BODY>");
                page.println("<H1>Welcome to OZ</H1>");
                page.println("</BODY></HTML>");
            }
            else
            {
                /* write the congratulatory page */
                page.println("<HTML><HEAD>");
```

```
                    page.println("<TITLE>Winner</TITLE>");
                    page.println("</HEAD><BODY>");
                    page.print("Congratulations. ");
                    page.print("You are the ");
                    page.print(num + " visitor to OZ.</B>");
                    page.println("</BODY></HTML>");
             }
         }
         else
         {
         /* write the default Kansas page */
         page.println("<HTML><HEAD>");
         page.println("<TITLE>Kansas Site</TITLE>");
         page.println("</HEAD><BODY>");
         page.println("<H1>Welcome to Kansas</H1>");
         page.println("</BODY></HTML>");
         }
    }
    else
    {
        page.println("<HTML><HEAD>");
        page.println("<TITLE>Kansas Site</TITLE>");
        page.println("</HEAD><BODY>");
        page.println("<H1>Welcome to Kansas</H1>");
        page.println("</BODY></HTML>");
    }

    try
    {
        /* set the content-length of the response using
           the current size of StreamBuffer
         */
         session.setResponseContentLength(
                              streamBuffer.size());

        /* send the response-headers */
        session.StartResponse();

        /* retrieve the data in the output stream and
           write them as the body of the response to
           the client
         */
```

```
            session.WriteClient(
                                streamBuffer.toByteArray());
        }
        catch(org.omg.CORBA.SystemException e){
            System.out.println("CORBA system exception.");
            System.err.println(e);
        }
        catch(java.lang.Exception e){
            System.out.println(
                            "Failed to send the output.");
            System.err.println(e);
        }

        return 0;
    }

    /* provide information about your service */
    public java.lang.String getServiceInfo()
    {
        return "OZ Example\nVersion 1.0\n";
    }
}
```

Summary

In this chapter, we went through the basic steps of writing a WAI application. The procedure for writing a WAI application varies depending on what programming language you use (C, C++, or Java), and whether you want to write an in-process or out-of-process application. We covered all the major steps you must take when you write a WAI application for these different options. Writing such an application always takes at least two major steps. You must write a method or function that is the nexus for processing the client request. This method or function is invoked by the server each time the client makes a request. In this chapter, we considered this step to be the second step. For your WAI application, you also must write a main function that is the entry point to your application. For in-process applications, you write a server **Init** function as the entry point. In the main function, you create and register your Web service. We consider this procedure to be the third step. For Java and C++, you also must write a Web service class. We regard this special procedure to be the first step.

The division of writing of a WAI application into the three steps is based on the common procedures that you must take to write your application. Each step delivers a specific predefined purpose. The code you write for each step, however, will be different for each type of WAI application.

In general, the first and third steps remain the same for different services you write for a specific type of WAI application. In other words, if you write an out-of-process application in C++, the process of writing the core of the service class and the main function of your WAI application remains essentially the same for all applications. You need to make only simple modifications to the code to support a different Web service. For the first step in Java and C++, you must derive (or extend) the `WAIWebApplicationService` class and write the constructor and the **getServiceInfo** method for your class. For the third step, you must write a simple main function for your application. Unlike the **Run** method of your service, the main function is executed (invoked) once when your application is started. For Java, you must write a separate class that should include the main method for your application. In the main function, you must create a Web service object and register it with Netscape's Naming Service. For C++ and Java, the Web service object, which is instantiated, is based on the Web service class you wrote in the first step. Depending on the programming language and whether you are writing an in-process or an out-of-process application, your program may have to take a few additional actions. For example, for an out-of-process application, you must invoke an implementation loop or write your own simple loop that keeps the program alive while waiting for the client request. Note that you cannot write an in-process Java application.

The second step, on the other hand, usually differs according to the service that your application provides. In this step, you write a **Run** method for your Web service class for Java and C++ or a call-back function for WAI applications written in C; this method or function processes the client request. For C, the function that processes the client request is declared when you create the Web service object in the main function. This step can be seen as part of the first step for Java and C++, as you write the **Run** method for your Web service class. Because of the unique purpose of this method and because most of your work is in writing the **Run** method, however, we consider the writing of the **Run** method as a separate step. Through its parameter, the **Run** method or the equivalent function in C gets a reference to the session object (HTTP request object). You use this object to process the client request. For example, you invoke the methods of the session object to get specific client, request, or server information. You process the requests as you see fit using the programming language-specific functions, methods, or classes. Once you have finished processing a request, you normally return a page to the client via the WAI functions or methods.

Writing a WAI application is easier than writing a CORBA application or an NSAPI application. The service you write is intended only to process the HTTP request of a client. As such, the scope of the programming is not as broad as a CORBA client/server application or an NSAPI service function.

In the next chapter, we have developed a version of the Hello Client example for a number of different types of WAI applications. You can use these examples as a framework for writing your own WAI applications. Because the examples in Chapter 16 are complete applications, you can also review them as simple implementations of the steps discussed in this chapter.

Chapter 16

WAI Examples

In this chapter, we will put what we discussed in the previous chapters into practice by writing a number of different versions of the Hello Client example. You may remember that we wrote a similar example for NSAPI, CGI, WinCGI, and ShellCGI. We will write the Hello Client example first as an out-of-process console application for C, C++, and Java. Next, we will write a Windows version of Hello Client in C++ for Windows NT. We will also write a C version of an in-process Hello Client example. You can use these examples as the basic foundation for writing your applications.

Regardless of the type of WAI application that you may write, the steps you must follow when writing the application's main function and your WAI service class remain mostly the same. Therefore, these Hello Client examples are a good starting point for writing your Web Application Service (WAS). More importantly, these two steps, for the main function and the WAI service class, include the most WAI and CORBA specific part of writing a server application. Although your particular application may include additional parts in the main function and as part of your WAI service class definition, the core components are the same. These steps include procedures unique to WAI, which is dependent on Netscape's ORB, the foundation of Netscape's CORBA support. What will differ with each WAI application you may write are the steps for processing the client request and returning a response. Unlike the steps for creating and registering the WAI service object, the steps for processing a client request are similar to the steps for writing an NSAPI or CGI application. Although the actual methods or functions that you will use for a WAS are different than for NSAPI or CGI functions, the general procedure for processing a client request remains the same. In general, all server applications accomplish similar tasks. You use the WAI classes, methods, or functions to get the client, request or server information, and client input. You then process the request as you see fit. Once you are finished, you return the response, again using WAI methods or functions. We have already used similar steps when writing the CGI and NSAPI examples, so you should already be familiar with how a server application processes an HTTP request. If you familiarize yourself with the unique steps of writing a WAI application and with the specific WAI methods or functions, the writing of your own applications will be straightforward.

After writing the Hello Client applications, we will go through the necessary steps of compiling and running a WAI application. As you would expect, compiling a C or C++ application is different from compiling a Java application. We will also discuss how you can use a remote WAI and register an in-process application with the server.

We finish the chapter by writing a more useful WAI example in C, Guest Book. Because the majority of the programs in this book are written in C, we also chose C for this example. You can compare this example with the similar C example written for CGI in Chapter 3 and for NSAPI in Chapter 9. Because writing a WAI application in C does not provide the support for the `FormHandler` class, we will be unable to use this class to handle `POST` and `GET` input data from the client. Instead, we will use the same functions we wrote for CGI to parse the query string or the input from the `POST` method. If you are writing a WAI application in C++ or Java, you should consider using the `FormHandler` class. For more information on the `FormHandler` class, and examples of a **Run** method using the `FormHandler` class, see Chapter 15.

> ### Note ▶
>
> For the following examples and for any program you may write for most UNIX platforms, you need to set the environment variable `LD_LIBRARY_PATH` to point at `<server path>/wai/lib;<server path>/lib;<server path>/bin/https`. On HPUX, you need to set the environment variable for `SHLIB_PATH`. On AIX, you need to set the environment variable for `LIBPATH`.

Hello Client Examples

The following Hello Client examples return a simple HTML page with the word `Hello` and the client IP address. To get the client's IP address we use the WAI function **WAIgetRequestInfo** for C and the **getRequestInfo** method for C++ and Java. To get other client, server, or request-specific data, you use this same function or method or other methods or functions that WAI provides, depending on the information you need. To find out more about how you can get various server, client, or session information from the server, see the section Get Information for Processing the Client Request in Chapter 15.

The Hello Client examples, Listings 16-1 through 16-5, do not require a detailed description, as they use the procedures that we have set forth in Chapter 15. Besides reading the comments included with each listing and the brief notes before the listings, you should refer to that chapter for additional information about the methods or functions used in the examples.

Out-of-Process WAI Console Examples

Listings 16-1 through 16-3 are console applications. You should invoke them from the command prompt. They also require that the host name and port be passed through the first command-line argument. If there is no argument for the WAI application, the console application returns an error message and exits. For the C and C++ examples, you may use additional ORB- or BOA-specific arguments for your program. These arguments are then passed to **WAIcreateWebAppService** for the C example or to the Hello client's Web service class constructor for C++ (**HelloService**). The first argument must be the host name (and port). The ORB and BOA arguments should begin with a dash (-) —for example, –OAipaddr 1.2.3.4.

These examples are intended for the Windows NT or Solaris platform. You may have to make some minor modifications to run them under other Netscape Server UNIX platforms.

The **Run** method of the C++ and Java examples and the C function **RunFunction**, which process the client requests, include only basic error checking. Most WAI methods or functions include a return value that you may use to verify whether the procedure was successful. For example, **WAIgetRequestInfo**, **getRequestInfo**, **WAIsetResponseContentLength**, **setResponseContentLength**, **WAIWriteClient**, and **WriteClient** all return a Boolean-type return value that can be checked to determine success or failure. If an error occurs, you can log the error in the error log file, using **WAILogError** for C or **LogError** for Java and C++.

As the return status for the following examples is the default 200 and the content type of the response is text/html, we do not need to set the Status-Line (status) and content-type. Unlike for NSAPI and CGI applications, the server (**IIOPexec**) sets a default content-type (text/html) for all WAI applications. We will set the content-length of the response. For CGI applications, the server (for example, **send-cgi**) sets the content-length automatically. As with the WAI examples, you may also want to set the content-length for the NSAPI **Service** applications, as the server does not perform this function automatically.

Hello Client in C

In Listing 16-1, **RunFunction** is the designated function that processes the client request. We specify this function when we use the **WAIcreateWebAppService** function to create the Web service object. The service uses the name helloc when registering with Naming Service. To invoke this application, the client must use the same name (that is, http://<server name>[:port]/iiop/helloc).

Listing 16-1   Out-of-Process Hello Client in C

```
/* make sure to include ONEiiop.h */
#include "ONEiiop.h"
```

Listing 16-1   Out-of-Process Hello Client in C (*continued*)

```c
/* function for processing client requests */
long RunFunction(ServerSession_t session)
{
    char *client = NULL;  /* client IP address */
    char buffer[256];   /* HTML page data for the client */
    unsigned int length;  /* length of buffer */

    /* get the client IP address */
    WAIgetRequestInfo(session, "REMOTE_ADDR", &client);

    /* create the HTML page that is returned to the client */
    sprintf(buffer,
                "<HTML><HEAD><TITLE>Hello</TITLE></HEAD>\n"
                                "<BODY><H1>Hello %s</H1>\n"
                                "</BODY></HTML>", client);

    WAIstringFree(client);

    length = strlen(buffer);

    /* set the content-length */
    WAIsetResponseContentLength(session, length);

    /* send the response headers if the request is not
        HEAD */
    if(WAIStartResponse(session) == REQ_PROCEED)
    {
        /* send the HTML document */
        WAIWriteClient(session,
                    (const unsigned char *)buffer,length);
    }

    return 0;
}

/* WAI application main function */
int main(int argc, char **argv)
{
    IIOPWebAppService_t obj;      /* Web service object */
    char host[80];                /* hostname of the machine */

    /* Get the host name from the command-line. We expect
        the host name as the first argument after the program
        name.
     */
    if((argc > 1)  && (*argv[1] != '-'))
```

Listing 16-1   Out-of-Process Hello Client in C (*continued*)

```c
{
    strcpy(host, argv[1]);

    /* create the Web service object and name the
       service and function that will process the
       client requests
     */
    obj = WAIcreateWebAppService("helloc", RunFunction,
                                 argc, argv);

    /* Register the service with the server's Naming
       Service. If registration failed, print an error
       message.
     */
    if(WAIregisterService(obj, host) == WAI_FALSE)
    {
        printf("Couldn't register with the %.", host);
        return 0;
    }
    else
    {
      /* print a message if registration was successful */
        printf("Object is ready. Server on host %s.\n",
               host);
    }

    /* Start the implementation loop. Application is
       now ready to receive client requests from the
       server.
     */
    WAIimplIsReady();
}
/* if host name (and port) is not sent through the
   command-line argument, return an error */
else
{
    printf(
    "Server host name should be the first argument.\n");
}

return 0;
}
```

Hello Client in C++

For the C++ example in Listing 16-2, we use a constructor for the Web service class that supports arguments from the command line (`argc` and `argv`) but does not use the `activateObj` parameter. If the application was able to register successfully with Naming Service, we use the **getServiceInfo** method to print out specific information about the Web service application.

The Web service in this example uses the name `hellocpp` when registering with Naming Service. To invoke this application, the client must use the same name (that is, `http://<server name>[:port]/iiop/hellocpp`).

Listing 16-2   Out-of-Process Hello Client in C++

```
/* make sure to include ONESrvPI.hpp */
#include "ONESrvPI.hpp"

/* for ostrstream class */
#ifdef WIN32
#include <strstrea.h>
#else
#include <strstream.h>
#endif

/* HelloService class derived from
   WAIWebApplicationService */
class HelloService: public WAIWebApplicationService
{
   public:
       HelloService(const char *object_name =
                 (const char *)NULL, int argc=0,
                 char **argv=0);
       long Run(WAIServerRequest_ptr session);
       char *getServiceInfo();
};

/* HelloService constructor used with
   argc and argv parameters and no activeObj
 */
HelloService::
   HelloService(const char *object_name,
             int argc, char **argv):
         WAIWebApplicationService(object_name, argc, argv)
{
}

/* this method will process the client requests */
```

Listing 16-2   Out-of-Process Hello Client in C++ (*continued*)

```
long HelloService::Run(WAIServerRequest_ptr session)
{
    char *client;              /* client IP address */

    /* Instantiate the output stream object. We
       use outstream to create the output string
       for the content of the HTML page. The constructor
       internally allocates an expandable string.
     */
    ostrstream outstream;

    /* get the client IP address */
    session->getRequestInfo("REMOTE_ADDR", client);

    /* create the HTML page that is returned to the client */
    outstream << "<HTML><HEAD>" << endl;
    outstream << "<TITLE>Hello</TITLE></HEAD><BODY>"
              << endl;
    outstream << "<H1>Hello " <<  client << "</H1>"
              << endl;
    outstream <<  "</BODY></HTML>" << endl;

    /* deallocate the memory block of the client IP */
    StringDelete(client);

    /* Set the content-length. The size is based on the
       number of bytes stored in the stream buffer.
     */
    session->setResponseContentLength(outstream.pcount());

    /* send the response-headers */
    if(session->StartResponse() == REQ_PROCEED)
    {
        /* send the HTML document. str gets the string
           stream's content. pcount returns the size of the
           stream buffer.
         */
        session->WriteClient((const unsigned char *)
                    outstream.str(), outstream.pcount());

        /* Unfreeze the stream that was frozen by the call to
           str. Delete the current buffer.

         */
        outstream.rdbuf()->freeze(0);
```

Listing 16-2 Out-of-Process Hello Client in C++ (*continued*)

```
   }

   return 0;
}

/* provide information about your service */
char *HelloService::getServiceInfo(void)
{
   return StringDup(
              "Hello Client\nTest App\nVersion 1.0\n");
}

/* WAI application main function */
int main(int argc, char **argv)
{
   char host[80];    /* hostname of the machine */

   /* Get the host name from the command-line. We expect
      the host name as the first argument after the program
      name.
    */
   if ((argc > 1) && (*argv[1] != ''))
   {
       strcpy(host, argv[1]);

       /* instantiate the Web service object and name your
          service
        */
       HelloService obj("hellocpp", argc, argv);

       /* Register the service with Naming Service.
          If registration failed, print an error message.
        */
       if(obj.RegisterService(host) == WAI_FALSE)
       {
           cout << "Couldn't register with the " << host
                << ".\n" << endl;
           return 0;
       }
       else
       {
           /* prints out the information about the service
              if registration was successful
            */
           cout << obj.getServiceInfo() << endl;
```

Listing 16-2   Out-of-Process Hello Client in C++ (*continued*)

```
            cout << "Object is ready. Server on host "
                << host << ".\n" << endl;

            /* set up a while loop that will keep the
               program alive waiting for the request from
               the server
             */
            while(1)
                Sleep(1000);
        }
    }
    /* if the host name (and port) is not sent through the
       command-line argument, return an error */
    else
    {
        cout <<
            "Server host name should be the first argument.\n"
            << endl;
    }

    return 0;
}
```

Hello Client in Java

Listing 16-3 is a console Java application. It does not include a graphic interface for the application. You can produce a graphic user interface (GUI) for the application if you like, but it is not necessary.

The **main** method for the Java Hello Client application is declared as part of the hello class, so the name of the file for the Hello Client example should also be hello. When you compile this application using the Java compiler, it will generate two class files: HelloService.class and hello.class.

With the C and C++ examples, we checked for REQ_PROCEED (0) to determine whether we should send the body of the Hello Client example. If a request is a HEAD request, **StartResponse** returns REQ_NOACTION (-2). For a HEAD request, you should send the response-headers without the body of the response page. With Java, you do not have access to these names—that is, REQ_PROCEED and REQ_NOACTION. These macros are defined in nsapi.h file and are available only to C and C++ applications. For Java, we use the equivalent number—for example, 0 for REQ_RROCEED.

The Web service in Listing 16-3 uses the name hellojava when registering with Naming Service. To invoke this application, the client must use the same name (that is, http://<*server name*>[:*port*]/iiop/hellojava).

Listing 16-3   Out-of-Process Hello Client in Java

```java
/* import the needed Java classes */
import java.io.*;
import java.net.*;
import java.lang.*;

/* import the CORBA-specific classes */
import org.omg.CORBA.*;
import CosNaming.*;
import netscape.WAI.*;

/* HelloService class extends WAIWebApplicationService
   class */
class HelloService extends WAIWebApplicationService
{
    /* an instance name for HelloService */
    String instanceName;

    /* class constructor */
    HelloService(java.lang.String name) throws
        CosNaming.NamingContextPackage.CannotProceed,
        CosNaming.NamingContextPackage.InvalidName,
        CosNaming.NamingContextPackage.AlreadyBound,
        org.omg.CORBA.SystemException
        {
            /* call the superclass constructor */
            super(name);

            instanceName = name;
        }

    public int Run(HttpServerRequest session)
    {
        /* Create a new byte array of output stream. We
           write the output that will be sent to the client
           into this stream. The array automatically grows
           as data are written into it.
         */
        ByteArrayOutputStream streamBuffer =
                            new ByteArrayOutputStream();

        /* Used to output to the stream. We use the println
           method of PrintStream to print to the stream.
         */
        PrintStream page = new PrintStream(streamBuffer);
```

Listing 16-3 Out-of-Process Hello Client in Java (*continued*)

```java
    /* StringHolder client to hold the client IP address */
    org.omg.CORBA.StringHolder client = new
                         org.omg.CORBA.StringHolder();

    /* get the client IP address */
    session.getRequestInfo("REMOTE_ADDR", client);

    /* write the HTML content to the stream */
    page.println("<HTML><HEAD><TITLE>Hello</TITLE>");
    page.println("</HEAD><BODY>");
    page.println("<H1>Hello "+ client.value + "</H1>");
    page.println("</BODY></HTML>");

    try
    {
        /* set the content-length of the response using
           the current size of StreamBuffer
         */
         session.setResponseContentLength
         (streamBuffer.size());

        /* send the response-headers */
        if(session.StartResponse() == 0)
        {
            /* retrieve the data in the output stream
               and write them as the body of the
               response to the client
             */
            session.WriteClient
                        (streamBuffer.toByteArray());
        }
    }
catch(org.omg.CORBA.SystemException e){
    System.out.println("CORBA system exception.");
    System.err.println(e);
}
catch(java.lang.Exception e){
    System.out.println("Failed to send the output.");
    System.err.println(e);
}

    return 0;
}
```

Listing 16-3   Out-of-Process Hello Client in Java (*continued*)

```java
    /* provide information about your service */
    public java.lang.String getServiceInfo()
    {
        return "Hello Client\nTest App\nVersion 1.0\n";
    }
}
/* the WAI application main class */
class hello{
    /* WAI application's main function */
    public static void main(java.lang.String[] args)
            throws UnknownHostException{

        try {
            /* initialize the ORB */
            ORB orb = org.omg.CORBA.ORB.init();

            /* initialize the BOA */
            BOA boa = orb.BOA_init();

            /* verify if host command-line argument was
               sent */
            if(args.length > 0){

                /* Get the host name (and port) from the
                   command line. We use a StringBuffer
                   object for the host string. host should
                   be the host name of the machine where
                   the server is running.
                 */
                StringBuffer host;
                host = new StringBuffer(args[0]);

                try{
                  /* create the Web service object and
                     name your service
                   */
                  HelloService obj = new
                            HelloService("hellojava");

                    /* Register the object with Naming
                       Service. host must be there and
                       correct for this function to work.
                     */
                    obj.RegisterService(host.toString());
```

Listing 16-3   Out-of-Process Hello Client in Java (*continued*)

```
                    /* print out the information about the
                       service if registration was
                       successful
                     */
                    System.out.println
                                    (obj.getServiceInfo());
                    System.out.print("Object is ready. ");
                    System.out.println("Server on host " +
                                      host + ".");

                    /* this will keep the program alive and
                       waiting for the request from the
                       server
                     */
                    boa.impl_is_ready();
                }
                catch (org.omg.CORBA.UserException e){
                    System.out.println(
                                    "CORBA user exception.");
                    System.err.println(e);
                }
                catch(java.lang.Exception e){
                    System.out.println(
                      "Service failed to initialize.");
                    System.err.println(e);
                }
            }
            /* if the host name (and port) is not sent
               through the command-line argument, return an
               error
             */
            else{
                System.out.println(
                            "Missing host name parameter.");
            }
        }
        catch(org.omg.CORBA.SystemException e) {
            System.out.println("CORBA system exception.");
            System.err.println(e);
        }
    }
}
```

Out-of-Process WAI Windows Example

Listing 16-4 is a bit more complex than the previous examples, including specific codes for running a Windows program under NT. We use the Microsoft Windows API to create and display a window for our application. You are not limited to the Windows API, however; you can use other libraries or classes, such as MFC (Microsoft Foundation Class), for your WAI application. The use of a graphic window interface for the WAI application is also not limited to Microsoft Windows platform. You can use X Windows or other APIs supported by your operating system to produce a window interface for your WAI application. Make sure these APIs are compatible with WAI and its thread model before you use them.

The HelloService class declaration and the **Run** method of HelloService are the same as in the console C++ application. The main function of the Windows example is different. If you are familiar with programming for Windows, then this code should be easy to follow. The example does only the minimum needed to generate and display a window.

In the main function, we first check to see if a previous instance of our application is running. If there is a previous instance of our window class registered with Windows, we will defer to the previous window and exit. Otherwise, we specify the needed information about our window class and register the class with the Windows operating system. The name of the class is HelloAppClass. Once we have registered the window class, we create a window using **CreateWindow**. The window caption is Hello Client. The additional settings for the window class use the standard default setting. We then show the window using **ShowWindow**.

Unlike with the C++ console application, if there is no host name (and port) argument specified for the application, we use the **gethostname** function to get the host name of the machine where the application is running. **gethostname** gets only the host name of the machine where the WAI application is running. Thus, unless Netscape Server is running on the same machine and the port is the default 80, you may still need to input the host name and port as part of the application's arguments.

To pass the arguments to the application under Windows NT 4.0, you can invoke the application from the command prompt with the argument or you can use a batch file that runs the application (for example, c:\netscape\server\wai\examples\hello\hellowin.exe [host name] [:port]). You can also create a shortcut for the application and specify the parameter in the Properties dialog box of the shortcut. Add the arguments after the program in the Target text box under the Shortcut tab. To retrieve the arguments, we look in the lpCmdLine parameter of **WinMain**. Unlike in a console application, lpCmdLine will not include the program name as the first argument. The only argument in the command line (lpCmdLine) should be the host name and port information. We do not expect any other command-line arguments for this application. Therefore, the parameters argc and argv of the constructor that creates the Web service object is set to 0. You may also use a constructor that does not include these two parameters.

For information about the registration of our service, we use the Windows default message dialog box, `MessageBox`. If an error occurred, a message box is displayed stating the error. Also, once the application successfully registered with Naming Service, we use a message box that informs us of the success.

Instead of using a `while` loop and **sleep** function as in the console application, we use the standard Windows message retrieval and dispatch loop in this application. This loop keeps the application alive and waiting for input. The application responds to both window-specific inputs and requests from Netscape Server.

MainWndProc is the name of the Windows procedure function for our example. The application does not handle any unique procedure; it simply uses the default Windows procedures.

The Web service in Listing 16-4 uses the name `hellowin` when registering with Naming Service. To invoke this application, the client must use the same name (that is, `http://<server name>[:port]/iiop/hellowin`).

Listing 16-4   Windows Version of Out-of-Process Hello Client

```
/* make sure to include ONESrvPI.hpp */
#include "ONESrvPI.hpp"

/* for Windows API functions */
#include <windows.h>

/* for ostrstream class */
#include <strstrea.h>

/* Windows Procedure function prototype */
LONG WINAPI MainWndProc(HWND, UINT, WPARAM, LPARAM);

/* HelloService class derived from
   WAIWebApplicationService */
class HelloService: public WAIWebApplicationService
{
   public:
       HelloService(const char *object_name =
           (const char *)NULL, int argc=0, char **argv=0);
       long Run(WAIServerRequest_ptr session);
        char *getServiceInfo();
};

/* HelloService constructor */
HelloService::
       HelloService(const char *object_name,
                    int argc, char **argv):
       WAIWebApplicationService(object_name, argc, argv)
{
```

Listing 16-4   Windows Version of Out-of-Process Hello Client (*continued*)

```
}

/* this method will process the client requests */
long HelloService::Run(WAIServerRequest_ptr session)
{
    char *client;      /* client IP address */

    /* Instantiate the output stream object. We
       use outstream to create the output string
       for the content of the HTML page. The constructor
       internally allocates an expandable string.
     */
    ostrstream outstream;

    /* get the client IP address */
    session->getRequestInfo("REMOTE_HOST", client);

    /* create the HTML page is returned to the client */
    outstream << "<HTML><HEAD><TITLE>Hello</TITLE></HEAD>";
    outstream << endl;
    outstream << "<BODY><H1>Hello " <<  client << "</H1>";
    outstream << endl;
    outstream <<   "</BODY></HTML>" << endl;
    /* deallocate the memory block of the client IP
       address
     */
    StringDelete(client);

    /* Set the content-length. The size is based on the
       number of bytes stored in the stream buffer.
     */
    session->setResponseContentLength(outstream.pcount());

    /* send the response-headers */
    if(session->StartResponse() == REQ_PROCEED)
    {
        /* Send the HTML document. str gets the string
           stream's content. pcount returns the size of the
           stream buffer.
         */
        session->WriteClient((const unsigned char *)
                    outstream.str(), outstream.pcount());

        /* Unfreeze the stream that was frozen by the call
           to str. Delete the current buffer. */
```

Listing 16-4   Windows Version of Out-of-Process Hello Client (*continued*)

```
            outstream.rdbuf()->freeze(0);
   }

   return 0;
}

/* provide information about your service */
char *HelloService::getServiceInfo(void)
{
  return StringDup(
                  "Hello Client\nTest App\nVersion 1.0\n");
}

/* WAI application main function */

/*
   hInstance          handle to current instance
   hPrevInstance      handle to previous instance
   lpCmdLine          command-line arguments
   nCmdShow           initial show state of the window
*/
int WINAPI WinMain(HINSTANCE hInstance, HINSTANCE
            hPrevInstance, LPSTR lpCmdLine, int nCmdShow)
{
   WNDCLASS wc;      /* Window class structure */
   MSG msg;          /* message structure */
   HWND hWnd;        /* handle to a window */

   char host[80];    /* host name of the machine */

   char buffer[256]; /* buffer for message box */

   /* Check for another instance of the application
      running. If we find another instance of the WAI
      application window, we close our window and defer to
      the previous instance.
    */
   hWnd = FindWindow ("HelloAppClass", NULL);

   if(hWnd)
   {
       /* If the previous window is minimized, restore it
          to its original size and position. (Open the
          window.)
        */
       if (IsIconic(hWnd)) {
```

Listing 16-4   Windows Version of Out-of-Process Hello Client (*continued*)

```
                    ShowWindow(hWnd, SW_RESTORE);
        }

        /* Active the window. Put it in foreground. */
        SetForegroundWindow (hWnd);

        /* exit our program, deferring to previous instance */
        return 0;
    }
    /* name of our window class */
    wc.lpszClassName = "HelloAppClass";
    /* name of our window procedure function */
    wc.lpfnWndProc = (WNDPROC) MainWndProc;
    /* no specific class style is used */
    wc.style = 0;
    /* instance handle */
    wc.hInstance = hInstance;
    /* use the predefined icon for the window */
    wc.hIcon = LoadIcon( NULL, IDI_APPLICATION );
    /* use the predefined cursor for the window */
    wc.hCursor = LoadCursor( NULL, IDC_ARROW );
    /* set background of the client area of the window */
    wc.hbrBackground = (HBRUSH)( COLOR_WINDOW+1 );
    /* there is no menu */
    wc.lpszMenuName = NULL;
    /* no extra space for class or windows structure is
       used */
    wc.cbClsExtra = 0;
    wc.cbWndExtra = 0;

    /* register the windows class */
    if(!RegisterClass( &wc ))
        return 0;

    /* Create a window based on our class. Caption is
       Hello Client. The window is an overlapped window.
       The initial position of the window is set to the
       default position for overlapped windows
       (CW_USERDEFAULT).
     */
    hWnd = CreateWindow(
        "HelloAppClass",      // class name
        "Hello Client",       // caption
```

Listing 16-4   Windows Version of Out-of-Process Hello Client (*continued*)

```
            WS_OVERLAPPEDWINDOW,  // style
            CW_USEDEFAULT,        // initial x position
            CW_USEDEFAULT,        // initial y position
            CW_USEDEFAULT,        // initial x size
            CW_USEDEFAULT,        // initial y size
            NULL,                 // handle for the parent
                                  // window
            NULL,                 // menu handle
            hInstance,            // instance handle
            NULL                  // creation parameter
    );

    /* if the window was not created, exit the program */
    if(!hWnd)
        return 0;

    /* show the window using the initial show state */
    ShowWindow(hWnd, nCmdShow);

    /* Check if there is a command line. lpCmdLine should
       include the host name (and port), if one was
       specified. Unlike the argv parameter of a console
       main, lpCmdLine does not include the name of the
       program. If the parameter is for an IIOP setting and
       includes a dash, then skip it.
     */
    if(*lpCmdLine)
    {
        if(*lpCmdLine != '-')
        {
            int i = 0;

            /* get the host name */
            while((*lpCmdLine) && (*lpCmdLine != ' '))
            {
                host[i] = *lpCmdLine;
                lpCmdLine++;
                i++;
            }

            host[i] = '\0';
        }
    }
```

Listing 16-4 Windows Version of Out-of-Process Hello Client (*continued*)

```
    /* If the host name was not specified, use gethostname
       to get the machine's host name. We will use the
       machine's host name instead.
     */
    else
    {
        gethostname(host, sizeof(host));
    }

    /* create a service object and name your service */
    HelloService obj("hellowin", 0, 0);

    /* Register your service with Naming Service. If an
       error occurred, display an error message box.
     */
    if(obj.RegisterService(host) == WAI_FALSE)
    {
        sprintf(buffer,
            "Failed to register with the server %s.", host);

        MessageBox(hWnd, buffer, "Error",
                MB_OK|MB_ICONERROR);

        return 0;
    }

    /* if registration was successful, display a success
       message box
     */
    sprintf(buffer, "Service is ready. Server on host %s.",
            host);
    MessageBox(hWnd, buffer, "Service Ready",
            MB_OK|MB_ICONINFORMATION);

    /* message retrieval-and-dispatch loop for our window */
    while( GetMessage( &msg, NULL, 0, 0 ) )
    {
        TranslateMessage( &msg );
        DispatchMessage( &msg );
    }

    return msg.wParam;
}
```

Listing 16-4   Windows Version of Out-of-Process Hello Client (*continued*)

```
/* Windows procedure function for our window. This
   function handles client input for the window. For our
   example, we handle only a destroy window message.
 */
LONG WINAPI MainWndProc(HWND hWnd, UINT msg,
                        WPARAM wParam, LPARAM lParam)
{
    /* Identify the message we received and process it. We
       handle only the WM_DESTROY message. For all other
       messages, we use the default Windows procedure.
     */
    switch(msg)
    {
        case WM_DESTROY:
            PostQuitMessage( 0 );
            break;

        default:
            return(DefWindowProc(hWnd, msg, wParam, lParam));
    }

    return 0;
}
```

In-Process WAI Example

Running an application in-process is even simpler than writing an out-of-process application. The "main" function that you write for the in-process application usually includes only three lines of code. The first line creates the Web service object. The next line registers the service with Naming Service. The last line returns the success value (that is, 0). Note that the "main" function is actually a standard server **Init** SAF similar to a NSAPI function. You can name this function anything you like as long as the name does not conflict with that of any already existing server function. Listing 16-5 is a C version of an in-process application. For a C++ example, you need to specify the function as `extern "C"`. See the section In-Process WAI SAF Function in C++, in Chapter 15, for more information. Because an in-process WAI application directly links with the server, we set the values of the `argc` and `argv` parameters of **WAIcreateWebAppService** to 0. We do not need to specify a host name and port information when registering the Web service object. The host parameter for **WAIregisterService** is set to an empty string, " ".

The Web service in Listing 16-5 uses the name `helloin` when registering with Naming Service. To invoke this application, the client must use the same name (that is, `http://<server name>[:port]/iiop/helloin`).

The procedure for compiling and registering an in-process WAI application is very different from that for an out-of-process WAI application. You need to compile the following application into a DLL or a shared library, similarly to an NSAPI application. You also need to modify the **obj.conf** file and add the appropriate lines for loading and initializing the example. See the Registering an In-Process WAI Application section later in this chapter for more information. You cannot write an in-process WAI application in Java.

Listing 16-5   In-Process Hello Client in C

```c
/* make sure to include ONEiiop.h */
#include "ONEiiop.h"

/* function for processing client requests */
long RunFunction(ServerSession_t session)
{
    char *client = NULL; /* client IP address */
    char buffer[256];    /* HTML page data for the client */
    unsigned int length; /* length of buffer */

    /* get the client IP address */
    WAIgetRequestInfo(session, "REMOTE_ADDR", &client);

    /* create HTML page to be returned to the client */
    sprintf(buffer,
            "<HTML><HEAD><TITLE>Hello</TITLE></HEAD>\n"
                "<BODY><H1>Hello %s</H1>\n"
                "</BODY></HTML>", client);

    length = strlen(buffer);

    /* set the content-length */
    WAIsetResponseContentLength(session, length);

    /* send the response-headers */
    if(WAIStartResponse(session) == REQ_PROCEED)
    {
        /* send the HTML document */
        WAIWriteClient(session,
                    (const unsigned char *)buffer, length);
    }
```

Listing 16-5 In-Process Hello Client in C (*continued*)

```c
    return 0;
}

/* global Web service object variable */
IIOPWebAppService_t obj;

NSAPI_PUBLIC int helloInit(pblock *pb, Session *sn,
                                 Request *rq)
{
    /* create a Web service object and name the service and
       the function that will process client requests
     */
    obj = WAIcreateWebAppService("helloin", RunFunction,
                                    0, 0);

    /* register the service with the server Naming Service */
    WAIregisterService(obj, "");

    return 0;
}
```

Compiling Your WAI Application

To compile the previously given examples or the examples that come with Netscape Server, you need to use an appropriate compiler, such as Microsoft Visual C++ version 4.2 or 5.0 for the C and C++ examples in Windows NT, or Symantec Café for the Java examples. You also need to set the path for the files that your program needs to include in its project. For C and C++, you must include the necessary include and library files.

> **Note ▶**
>
> The makefiles that come with Netscape Server's examples for NT are intended for compiling with the `nmake.exe` utility file of Microsoft Visual C++. These makefiles include the instructions for compiling your application in text. The Developer Studio uses a binary file with the file extension `*.MDP` as the workspace configuration file for your program. To compile your application using the Visual C++ 4.2 (or 5.0) Developer Studio interface, you need to create a new Project Workspace and make the appropriate modifications, as discussed later in this chapter, to the Project Settings dialog box found under the Build|Settings . . . menu. The "Preprocessor definitions:" under the C/C++ tab should include WIN32 and XP_WIN32. You need to add XP_WIN32. The "Object/library modules:" list of libraries under the Link tab should include `ONEiiop10.lib` and `Wsock32.lib`. Finally, you should specify that the code be generated using a multithreaded DLL runtime library. You can choose this option from the C/C++ tab, under the category "Code Generation," where you select multithreaded DLL for "Use run-time Library:".

For Java, you must include the path for `WAI.zip` and `nisb.zip`. In the following two subsections, we will describe the procedures for compiling for C or C++ and Java WAI applications.

Compiling a C or C++ WAI Application

To compile C or C++ WAI applications, you first need to have the appropriate compiler for your operating system. Next, you should add the include files and the library files to the search path for your compiler and linker. You also need to include the necessary library files in your project and specify a number of compiler flags (preprocessor flags), depending on the operating system that you are using.

You can use the makefiles for the examples that come with Netscape Server as a starting point for your own makefile. The makefiles are found under the examples directory for the WAI, `<server path>/wai/examples`. For example, the makefiles for the NT examples are named `Makefile.WINNT` and the Solaris makefiles are named `Makefile.SOLARIS`. The makefiles that come with the server are intended for command-line compiling of your application. In other words, for Windows NT, you can use `nmake.exe`, the Microsoft Program Maintenance Utility, to build the project. This utility program comes with Microsoft Visual C++. You can build the existing example by running `nmake /f Makefile.WINNT`.

To compile your own applications, you can modify the makefiles that come with Netscape Server's WAI examples to identify your source file and produce the programs you need. You can also write your own makefile or use programs such as Visual C++ to compile your application. The following instructions outline the steps you should take for writing your own makefile and compiling your application. We include only the steps unique to writing a WAI program. Other steps that you must take to compile your application are specific to your compiler and linker or are common to writing any C or C++ application. You should already be familiar with them.

Note ▶

Due to the specific use of Windows NT kernel, you cannot compile C or C++ WAI applications under Windows 95.

Step 1. Choosing a Compiler

The following list includes selected compilers that you can use to compile your WAI application.

Windows NT

- Microsoft Visual C++ 4.2 or 5.0

Solaris 2.5.x

- SparcWorks C++ Compiler version 3.0.1

IRIX 6.2
- IRIX C++ compiler version 7.1

AIX version 4.x
- AIX C/C++ compiler

HP-UX
- HPCPLUSPLUS version A.10.28

Digital UNIX (DEC)
- C compiler V5.2-036 and C++ compiler V5.5-004

Step 2. Include Files Directories

The include files that your WAI program needs to use can be found in the following directories. You should add the paths for these directories to enable the compiler to locate the necessary include files.

Windows NT
- `<server path>\include;<server path>\wai\include`

UNIX platforms
- `<server path>/include;<server path>/wai/include`

For example, for Microsoft Developer Studio 4.2, you can add paths for the include files in the Options dialog box under the Directories tab. From "Show directories for:" select the "Include files" and add the path for the include files to the "Directories:" list. You can find the Options dialog box under the Tools|Options menu.

Step 3. Necessary Libraries and Program Paths

The additional WAI-specific libraries that you need to include in your project for the linker can be found in the following directories. You should include these paths so that the compiler/linker can locate the necessary library files.

UNIX platforms
- `<server path>/lib`
- `<server path>/wai/lib`
- `<server path>/bin/https`

Windows NT
- `<server path>\lib`
- `<server path>\wai\lib`
- `<server path>\bin\https`

For example, for Microsoft Developer Studio 4.2, you can add the path for the library files in the Options dialog box under the Directories tab. From "Show directories for:" select the "Library files" and add the path for the library files to the "Directories:" list. You can find the Options dialog box under the Tools|Options menu.

On Solaris, for the linker to be able to search for the shared objects in the libraries during runtime, you should use the -R flag. For IRIX, use the -rpath flag.

The list at the end of this section indicates the libraries to which the linker needs to link. These libraries are found under the library paths we just added or under a path already accessible to your compiler/linker. For example, Wsock32.lib for Windows NT is found under the visual C++ lib directory. The linker may also need to link with other operating system-specific libraries. These system-specific libraries, such as, kernel32.lib for Windows NT applications, should already be in the path of your compiler/linker. Furthermore, there may be additional Netscape-specific libraries (DLL or shared objects) needed by your application. These libraries or shared objects should be accessible for your program. For example, the WAI application for Windows NT needs to access orb_r.dll, which is located under the <server path>\bin\https directory.

You should add the appropriate libraries based on the following list to the list of the libraries that the compiler/linker will use. For example, for Microsoft Developer Studio 4.2, you can add ONEiiop10.lib and Wsock32.lib to the libraries found for "Object/library modules:" under the Link tab of the Project Settings dialog box. You can find the Project Settings dialog box under the Build|Settings . . . menu.

> **Note ▶**
>
> The exact names of the files that you need to use for your program may be different from those in the following list. The files you need to use may include specific version designations. For example, the shared library libONEiiop for Solaris is libONEiiop.so.10. Another example is the libldap file. Server 3.01 includes libldap10.so. Server 3.01 supports the LDAP shared library files that are based on Netscape Directory Server 1.0. Netscape Enterprise Server 3.5.1, on the other hand, includes libldap30.so. Server 3.5.1 supports LDAP version 3 and Netscape Directory Server 3.0. You may need to verify the exact file name before including it in your project.

Windows NT
- wai\lib\ONEiiop10.lib
- Wsock32.lib
- Other standard Windows NT libraries (for example, kernel32.lib)

Solaris
- lib/libldap[xx].so (for example, libldap10.so)
- lib/liblcache[xx].so (for example, liblcache10.so)
- wai/lib/libONEiiop.so

- `wai/lib/liborb_r.so`
- `bin/https/ns-httpd.so`
- `libthreads.so`
- `libposix4.so`
- `libresolv.so`
- `libnsl.so`
- `lib/libnspr.so`
- `wai/lib/libIIOPsec.a`

IRIX

- `lib/libldap[xx].so` (for example, `libldap10.so`)
- `lib/liblcache[xx].so` (for example, `liblcache10.so`)
- `wai/lib/libONEiiop.so`
- `wai/lib/liborb_r.so`
- `bin/https/ns-httpd.so`
- `wai/lib/libIIOPsec.a`

HPUX

- `dce.sl`
- `wai/lib/orb_r.sl`
- `wai/lib/ONEiiop.sl`
- `bin/https/nshttpd.sl`
- `wai/lib/IIOPsec.sl`

AIX

- `wai/lib/libONEiiop_shr`
- `wai/lib/IIOPsec`
- `bin/https/nshttpd_shr`
- `lib/nspr_shr`
- `wai/lib/orb_r`

> **Note ▶**
>
> `ns-httpd30.lib` is the appropriate NSAPI library file for Server 3.0x and `ns-httpd35.lib` is the appropriate NSAPI library file for Server 3.5.1. You can find each file under `<server path>/lib`. If your application uses NSAPI, you need to add this library to the list of libraries to which your program needs to link. Even if your code does not rely on NSAPI, you can safely add this library to the list of libraries used by the linker.

- `dcepthreads`
- `C_r`

Digital UNIX
- `lib/ldap[xx].so` (for example, `ldap10.so`)
- `lib/lcache[xx].so` (for example, `lcache10.so`)
- `wai/lib/ONEiiop.so`
- `wai/lib/orb_r.so`
- `bin/https/ns-httpd.so`
- `wai/lib/IIOPsec.so`

Step 4. Compiler Flags

You should specify the following flags for the compiler. The compiler uses these pre-processor definitions while compiling your code. For example, by using `WIN32` and `XP_WIN32` for a Windows NT WAI application, you tell the compiler to use the appropriate Windows-specific functions or methods provided by Netscape libraries.

Solaris
- `-DXP_UNIX -D_REENTRANT KPIC`

Windows NT
- `-DXP_WIN32 (XP_WIN32) -DWIN32 (WIN32) /MD`

IRIX
- `-o32 -exceptions -DXP_UINX -KPIC`

HP-UX
- `-DXP_UNIX -D_REENTRANT -DHPUX`

AIX
- `-DXP_UNIX -D_REENTRANT -DAIX $(DEBUG)`

Digital UNIX
- `-DXP_UNIX KPIC`

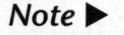

Note ▶

For UNIX platforms, if you use a relative path for the location of the libraries, you should specify a path relative to the Netscape Server executable program (`ns-httpd.exe`) (that is, `<server path>`/bin/https).

To set these flags in Microsoft Developer Studio 4.2, add XP_WIN32 and WIN32, if they are not already there, to the "Preprocessor definitions:" in the C/C++ tab of the Project Settings dialog box. The Project Settings dialog box can be located under the Build|Settings . . . menu.

Compiling an In-Process Application

The procedure for compiling an in-process application is basically the same as that for compiling an out-of-process application. The target application, however, should be a shared object (library) for UNIX or a DLL for Windows NT. Thus the compiler options you specify for building a shared object or DLL differ from the options for compiling a WAI executable application (out-of-process). For example, using Microsoft Developer Studio 4.2, when selecting a new Project Workspace you should choose dynamic link library. Developer Studio will then use the specific options for compiling a DLL.

Compiling an in-process application is also the same as compiling an NSAPI application. (Refer to Chapter 7 for more information.) The instructions for NSAPI are directly relevant to an in-process WAI application.

Compiling a Java Application

To compile a Java application, you need to use a Java compiler (such as Javasoft Java Development Kit 1.1.x or Symantec Café 1.8). Your compiler should be compatible with JDK 1.1.x. You should not use JDK 1.2. To access the Java compiler and interpreter from anywhere on your machine, you may want to add the path to these programs, usually under the bin directory of your Java development tool, to the PATH environment variable.

You should add the path for nisb.zip and WAI.zip to the class path. nisb.zip and WAI.zip can be found under the <*server path*>/wai/java/ directory. You can add the path for WAI.zip and nisb.zip either directly to the CLASSPATH environment variable or to the classpath flag option of the Java compiler. Also make sure that the standard Java classes (classes.zip) are included in the class path.

Starting a WAI Application

Starting an out-of-process application is different from starting an in-process application. An out-of-process application runs as a separate application with its own process in parallel to the server. An in-process application is started automatically when the server starts.

To run an out-of-process WAI application, you should start the application after the server has already started. For Netscape Server 3.0, osagent must also be running before you start your out-of-process application. If you run your application before starting the server, your application will not be able to register with the server's Naming Service.

To start an in-process WAI application, you must register the application with Netscape Server by adding the appropriate directive information to the server **obj.conf** file. Thereafter, the application automatically starts with the server; you do not manually start the application.

Starting an Out-of-Process WAI Application

Running an out-of-process application is easy. You can run the console applications from the command line. If the program requires the host name and port information to be passed as arguments, then make sure to include them as arguments. For example, if you compile the C or C++ example given earlier to an executable program (for example, `hello.exe`), you can run the program from the command prompt by typing the file name and the host name and port of the server (for example, `hello foo:80`).

You can invoke the Windows version of a WAI application, just as with the console applications, from the command prompt. Unlike with the console applications, you can also invoke the Windows applications through the File Manager or Explorer interface of Windows NT. If you invoke the application from the File Manager or Explorer by double-clicking on the program name, however, you will not be able to add the command-line argument. The Windows version has the added advantage that you can shut down the application by closing the window. With the console applications, you must kill the application process. For example, under NT 4.0, you can use the Task Manager to end the process for your application by selecting the application from the list of processes under the Processes tab and using the End Process button.

To invoke a Java application, you must run the Java interpreter and pass the compiled class file of your program as its parameter. For example, after the Java Hello Client example was compiled to `HelloService.class` and `hello.class`, you can run this program by passing `hello`, the main class of your application, to the Java interpreter, `java hello`. If you need to pass any additional arguments, such as the host name of the server machine, then add the argument after the class name—for example, `java hello foo:80`. Under Netscape Server 3.0, you should run the Java application with the `DISABLE_ORB_LOCATOR` flag (for example, `java DISABLE_ORB_LOCATOR hello`). The application can then register with the server and bypass osagent.

If your application was able to successfully register with Naming Service, you should be able to get the object reference (IOR) of your application by requesting the following URL: `http://<server name>[:port]/NameService/WAS/<service name>`. Otherwise, the server will return a `Not Found` page.

If a client request is for a Web service that does not exit and is not registered with Naming Service, the server returns a `Not Found` page to the client. If the service was registered with Naming Service, but the server was not able to locate the application so as to pass the request to it, the server returns a server error page to the client.

Once a service is registered with Naming Service, the server expects the service to be available for a client request. The IOR information of the service is available and saved in the `<server path>/NameService/<server ID>.sav` file. Therefore, if your application was not started, a request for your service that is already registered with the server will cause the server to return a server error page.

Registering an In-Process WAI Application

To start an in-process application, you must register your application with the server. You register your application by adding two specific directive functions to the **obj.conf** file. **obj.conf** is located under the `<server path>/<server ID>/`config directory. This file includes the instructions for loading specific DLLs for Windows NT or shared objects for UNIX and the steps for processing client requests. Both directive functions that you add are **Init** functions. **Init** functions are initialized at the start of the server. They are placed before the `default` Object's directive functions (before `<Object name="default">`) in the **obj.conf** file. You should also add the **Init** functions for the in-process WAI application after the **load-modules** and **IIOPinit** directive functions that initialize the WAI interface. The following is an example of the **Init** functions for the WAI interface of the server:

```
Init fn="load-modules"
 funcs="IIOPinit,IIOPexec,IIOPNameService"
 shlib="c:/netscape/server/wai/bin/ONEiiop10.dll"
Init LateInit="yes" fn="IIOPinit"
```

The procedure for registering an in-process WAI application is the same as that for registering an NSAPI server application function (SAF). (Review the section Registering SAFs in Chapter 7 for more information on registering an SAF.) Note that the SAFs you commonly write for processing a client request for NSAPI are **Service** directive functions. The WAI in-process functions are **Init** functions.

You first load your module (your shared object or DLL). To load the module, you use the built-in server function **load-modules**. You also specify the function that you wish the server to use and the location of the shared object or DLL as additional parameters for the **Init** function **load-modules**. The function you want the server to load is your in-process WAI **Init** function (for example, **helloInit**). The following code is an example of the **Init** function for loading the Hello Client example's DLL (`hello.dll`):

```
Init fn="load-modules" funcs="helloInit" LateInit="yes"
 shlib="c:/netscape/server/wai/examples/hello/hello.dll"
```

With Server 3.x, you should add the `LateInit` parameter to the **Init** functions that load your NSAPI or WAI in-process functions. `funcs` includes the list of the functions that you intend to declare and use (for example, **helloInit**). `shlib` should point to the physical location of the shared object or DLL. The actual location of the file could be anywhere that is accessible to the server.

After you load your shared object or DLL, you need to initialize the function you specified in the `funcs` parameter of **load-modules**. The following code is an example of the **Init** function for **helloInit**:

```
Init fn="helloInit" LateInit="yes"
```

As with **load-modules**, we add the `LateInit` parameter to the **helloInit** directive function.

Once you start the server, it locates and dynamically loads the shared object or DLL that you specified. It then initializes your WAI application (your **Init** SAF). If this process fails, the server will not be able to function properly. SAFs are part of the server process and as such can directly affect the operation of the server. If your application fails, the server will also fail. You may be able to look in the errors log file for an error that might have occurred during loading or initializing your WAI application. Make sure your application is working properly before you enable it as an in-process WAS. You also need to stop and restart the server to enable any changes to the `obj.conf` file to take effect. You can always test your program as an out-of-process WAI application and then modify it to work as an in-process WAI application.

Running a WAI Remotely

The following instructions for running an out-of-process WAI application remotely apply to Netscape Server 3.0.1 and 3.5.x. Server 3.0 included a number of limitations that made running an out-of-process application remotely inoperable. You should still consider running an out-of-process application locally due to security risks. Running a WAI application remotely exposes your server to a number of possible security risks. (For more information on the security issues related to running a WAI application remotely, see the section Security Issues with Netscape ISB and WAI in Chapter 13.)

To run a WAI application remotely, you must allow Netscape's Naming Service to accept registration from a remote application. The default setting of Netscape Server is set to accept requests only from the local machine. You must add the `OAipaddr` parameter to the **IIOPinit** directive function in the `obj.conf` file and specify the network IP address of the machine where the server is running as its value. For example, if the IP address of the server machine is `1.2.3.4`, you need to add the parameter `OAipaddr=1.2.3.4`. `OAipaddr` is used to specify the IP address for the BOA. The default IP address is set to the localhost machine IP address, `127.0.0.1`. If you do not change the IP address of the BOA to the network IP address, when attempting to register with Naming Service the server will return an error message and the registration of your application will fail.

Bug Report ▶

Although it is the intention of Netscape to provide the option of writing WAI applications remotely, you may discover that some of your WAI applications do not work from a remote machine. In a number of tests, the author was unable to run C or C++ applications on a remote NT machine. The program was able to register with Naming Service, but the server was not able to locate the program so as to invoke the **Run** method of the Web service object. WAI Java applications, however, functioned properly from remote Windows 95 and NT machines.

With C and C++ applications, you can also specify `OAipaddr` in the parameter `argv` for the **WAIcreateWebAppService** function for C and the constructor for the Web service object for C++.

To run an application remotely, the WAI application needs to be able to locate the necessary shared object or DLL for C or C++ applications and the Netscape ISB and WAI classes for Java. You cannot just place the C or C++ executable program (such as `hello.exe`) or the Java classes (such as `hello.class` and `HelloService.class`) on the remote machine and expect the program to run. If you have installed Netscape Server 3.x on the remote machine, the appropriate files or classes are available for your program. Otherwise, the application needs to locate the necessary files before you can run the remote application. For Java, besides the standard Java classes (`class.zip`), the Java interpreter needs to locate the `nisb.zip` and `WAI.zip` files. C++ and C WAI applications need to access the server and WAI-specific shared objects or DLL. For example, under Server 3.5.1 NT, the application needs access to at least the following files: `orb_r.dll`, `ONEiiop10.dll`, `ns-httpd35.dll`, `nslch32v30.dll`, `nsldap32v30.dll`, `libesnspr20.dll`, `mtld.dll`, `msvcrt.dll`, and `Msvcirt.dll`.

You may also be able to execute the WAI application on separate machines running different operating systems. For example, you can run the Java WAI applications on a Windows 95 machine. In contrast, you cannot run C or C++ WAI applications remotely on a Windows 95 machine.

Registering an Out-of-Process WAI Application with OAD

On UNIX machines using Netscape Server 3.01 or 3.5.x, you can have the OAD automatically start your C++ out-of-process application. If your application is not running, the OAD automatically starts your application, so you do not have to start each application manually.

To register a WAI application with the OAD, you need to use a constructor for your Web service class that takes *activeObj* as a parameter and sets this parameter to `WAI_FALSE`. You can then activate your WAS by invoking the **ActiveWAS** method of the Web service object.

Before you register your service with the OAD, you must register your service with Netscape Server's Naming Service. Run your application once before you register the service with the OAD to make sure it registers with the server. The OAD requires that your application be already registered with Netscape's Naming Service.

Note ▶

You can use the OAD to activate your WAI applications automatically only for WAI applications on UNIX platforms. This option is not supported on Windows NT. You also cannot use the OAD with applications written in Java.

If you have not already added the environment variables for `NS_SERVER_ROOT`, `NS_SERVER_ID`, `OBERLINE_IMPL_NAME`, `OBERLINE_IMPL_PATH`, and `LD_LIBRARY_PATH`, then you should add these environment variables before you start the OAD. You need to add these environment variables for the OAD, your application, and Netscape Server. `NS_SERVER_ROOT` should point to the location of the server root (for example, `/user/netscape/server`). `NS_SERVER_ID` is used for the server ID, `https-<your server>`. `ORBELINE_IMPL_NAME` specifies the name of the file that the OAD produces to keep track of the services (object implementation) registered with it. You can name the file anything you wish. `ORBELINE_IMPL_PATH` should point to an existing directory. The OAD will create the file specified with `ORBELINE_IMPL_NAME` in the directory you specify with `ORBELINE_IMPL_PATH`—for example, `/user/oad/`. `LD_LIBRARY_PATH` should have already been set for the path of the shared libraries, `<server path>/wai/lib;<server path>/lib;<server path>/bin/https`. For HP-UX, you should use `SHLIB_PATH`. For AIX, use `LIBPATH`. The environment variables for the library paths should be set for all UNIX platforms, regardless of whether you intend to use the OAD. You may use `setenv` to set the environment variables for the C shell (for example, `setenv NS_SERVER_ID httpsfoo`).

Once you start the OAD, it uses the information you specified in `ORBELINE_IMPL_PATH` and `ORBLINE_IMPL_NAME` to create a file in the specified directory for maintaining the CORBA object implementations, including your Web service object. You can find the OAD (`oad.exe`) under the `<server path>/wai/bin` directory.

To register your object, you can run the `regobj` program found under the `/wai/bin` directory. Under UNIX, `regobj` is a console application. The following code is an example of the command line you can use to register the C++ Hello Client example (Listing 16-2) with the OAD:

```
regobj o "*,hellocpp" -f /user/local/wai/examples/hello
-a httpServerName=foo:80
```

Specify the `-o` flag to name the CORBA interface name and the object name of your Web service object (the CORBA object implementation) (for example, `-o "*,hellocpp"`). For WAI applications, you do not specify an interface name, but use * instead. You must specify the object name, however. The object name is the name you give to your service when you create the Web service object (for example, `hellocpp`). Next, use the `-f` flag to specify the location and name of the WAI application (for example, `-f /user/local/wai/examples/hello`). Finally, add the flag for the additional arguments, `-a`, that are passed to your application (that is, host name and port information). You should add the host name and port as the value of `httpServerName` (for example, `-a httpServerName=foo:80`). If you wish to pass any specific environment variable, you can use the `-e` flag followed by the environment variable. The activation policy can be the default, which is shared. You can also specify the activation policy through the `-p` flag, `-p shared`. For more information on OAD, see the OAD section in Chapter 12.

Debugging a WAI Application

To debug your WAI application, you must use a compatible debugger. For example, you can debug a C or C++ application with Microsoft Visual C++ 4.2. Debugging an out-of-process application is simple. You can set break points in your application and run it in a debug session. If the break point was set during the function for processing client request, such as the **Run** method of your service class for C++, the program will stop when it reaches the break point while processing the client request. You can then step through the debugger. You do not have to use any special setting for an out-of-process application. The debugging procedure is the same as the debugging procedure for any other application.

For in-process applications, you should use the same method used for debugging an NSAPI application for Netscape Server 3.x. See the section Debugging Your SAF in Chapter 7 for more detail. For example, for Microsoft C++ Developer Studio 4.2, you should run the server as an executable program for the debug session. You should stop the server, if it is running, and have the Developer Studio start the server. Specify the path for the server, `httpd.exe`, in the Project Settings dialog box under the Debug tab. You can bring up the Project Settings dialog box through the Build|Settings . . . menu. You should include the path for the Netscape Server program (for example, `c:\Netscape\server\bin\https\httpd.exe`) under "Executable for debug session." You also need to specify the server ID as an argument for the server. Add the server ID, `https<server name>`, to "Program arguments:" in the Debug tab of the Project Settings dialog box.

Guest Book Example in C

The Guest Book example (Listing 16-6) is based on the ANSI C CGI Guest Book example, found in Chapter 3. We used C for the WAI Guest Book example to facilitate comparing this example with the NSAPI (Chapter 9) and CGI Guest Book examples previously discussed. Unlike with NSAPI, however, you can also write the Guest Book example in Java or C++. This example is an out-of-process WAI application. The client, using the guest book HTML form, can choose to view the guest list in an HTML table or input his or her own information in the guest book. The HTML form is the same form we used with the CGI and NSAPI examples, but you must modify the value of the ACTION attribute of the FORM tag to reflect the URI of the WAI application. Here is an example of the modified FORM tag:

```
<FORM METHOD="POST" ACTION="/iiop/guestbk">
```

In this section, we will briefly review the WAI example and discuss the specific differences between it and the NSAPI and CGI Guest Book examples. For more detailed information about the Guest Book example, you should review the CGI example in

Chapter 3. You may also review the NSAPI example in Chapter 9 for additional information and NSAPI-related issues.

A number of functions in this example are almost exactly the same as those in the CGI example. The WAI example uses the same **parsing**, **Remove_HTTP_Escapes**, and **HexToInt** (part of Listing 16-6-4) functions to parse the client's POST input. We use these CGI functions, because the pblock data structures and functions used with the NSAPI example are specific to NSAPI. For an out-of-process WAI C application, it is best to avoid using any NSAPI functions. As the example is written in C, we cannot use the FormHandler class, which is available for C++ and Java only. If you use C++ or Java and Server 3.01 or later, you should consider using the FormHandler class instead of writing your own parsing functions. The FormHandler class includes methods that can easily parse and retrieve the client POST and GET input from an HTML form.

Append_Guest_File and **Read_Guest_File** (Listing 16-6-3) are also the same as their counterparts in the CGI example. They are used to write the client input into the guest file and to read the guest list from the guest file. Note that these functions do not provide any thread-safety mechanism. You must update the program with an appropriate thread-locking mechanism to make sure multiple requests cannot update the guest file at the same time. In a later section, we will update **Append_Guest_File** to use the NSAPI **system_fwrite_atomic** function. This function locks the file while it is being updated. To use the NSAPI function, we need to rewrite the program as an in-process WAI C SAF. In other words, instead of the out-of-process **main** function, we use an NSAPI (in-process WAI) **Init** function. This update to the Guest Book example also demonstrates an example of a WAI application, which uses NSAPI functions.

The **main** (Listing 16-6-2), **RunFunction** (Listing 16-6-1), and **error** (part of Listing 16-6-4) functions of the WAI example are different from those functions in the CGI example. The **main** function for the WAI Guest Book example is the same as the function in the out-of-process Hello Client example (Listing 16-1) earlier in this chapter. The difference is that the service object registers with Naming Service using the name guestbk instead of helloc. You would have to pass the host name and port information of the server as the first argument of the Guest Book example when you invoke the program from the command prompt.

RunFunction is the core function for processing the client request. In **RunFunction**, we verify whether the client input is actually from a POST method of input and read the input from the client. This example works only with the POST method of request. After we have verified the data, we check for the client-requested action. If the client chose read, we call **Read_Guest_File** to read the data from the file. We then return the formatted response to the client. If the client request was log, we verify the client input and write the data to the guest file. We then return a Thank You page to the client.

The best way to compare the WAI application with the NSAPI or CGI program is to review **RunFunction**. In **RunFunction**, we use **WAIgetRequestInfo** to get the value of REQUEST_METHOD, CONTENT_TYPE, and CONTENT_LENGTH. We use the name of the variable (for example, REQUEST_METHOD) and the pointer to the server HTTP request object (`session`) passed to our **RunFunction**. These variables have the same names as the CGI environment variables. In the CGI example, we used the **getenv** function to get the value of the environment variables. We take a number of precautions to make sure that we received the correct information and that **WAIgetRequestInfo** was able to retrieve the variables from the client request. **WAIgetRequestInfo** returns `WAISPISuccess` if it was successful in getting these values.

If an error occurred, we invoke our own **error** function to return an error page to the client. We pass `session`, the error status, and the error reason string to the **error** function. For the error status, we use the HTTP status code name as defined in the `<server path>/include/nsapi.h` file (for example, `PROTOCOL_BAD_REQUEST`, `PROTOCOL_SERVER_ERROR`, and so on). We used these same status code names with NSAPI programs. If you wish, you can use the standard integer value of the status code (for example, `400` for `PROTOCOL_BAD_REQUEST`). You must use the integer value of the status code when programming in Java. We will discuss the **error** function shortly.

Unlike in the CGI example, when an error occurs, before exiting the function, we also log the error in the error log file using **WAILogError**. This function is similar to **log_error** in the NSAPI example. We specify the different error degrees based on the type of error—`LOG_WARN`, `LOG_FAILURE`, and so on. The names we use are defined in `nsapi.h`. As with the status code, you can also use the number associated to each error type (for example, `0` for `LOG_WARN`). (Because Java programs do not have access to `nsapi.h`, you should use the degree number for a Java WAI application.) For the name of the function, the third parameter of **WAILogError**, we use `guestbk`, the name of the WAI service. We also set the last parameter of `WAILogError` to `TRUE`, so that information about the session and request, such as the client IP address, is logged. In this example, we log all errors in the error log file. You may decide to log only critical errors. For example, you do not have to log an error when a client forgets to fill in the user information in the form. You may also want to check the return value of **WAILogError** to make sure the error was properly logged. **WAILogError**, however, may not return `WAISPISuccess` as intended. Testing this function under NT using original WAI patch and Server 3.5.1, **WAILogError** failed to return `WAISPISuccess` upon success. In Listing 16-6, therefore, we do not check for the return value of **WAILogError**. If this function returned the proper value upon failure, you may want to write an error message (for example, `printf("Was unable to log the error.\n");`) to the console. Thus you can verify whether the logging of the error failed by checking the console output. Once we have returned the error page and logged the error, we exit the program.

We use the WAI function **WAIstringFree** to free the memory for the values of the variables furnished by **WAIgetRequestInfo** after we have finished using them. In this example, we also use **WAIstringFree** to free the memory for the strings that were allocated in our program. **WAIstringFree** frees only the memory for a string. Thus, to free the data structure, `user_data`, we must use the C function **free**. You can also use the standard C function, **free**, to free the memory for a string (though it is best to use **WAIstringFree** for string functions).

To read the client's POST input, we use the **WAIReadClient** function. This function returns the number of bytes read. We use the return value to make sure we read all intended data. In other words, the number of bytes read should match the value of CONTENT_LENGTH.

We get the location of the guest file from the guestfile parameter of **IIOPexec**. You must add this parameter to the **IIOPexec** directive function in the **obj.conf** file. **WAIgetConfigParameter** retrieves the value of the guestfile parameter (that is, the location of the guest file).

To return the Thank You page or the guest list, we use the standard WAI functions—**WAIsetResponseContentLength**, **WAIStartResponse**, and **WAIWriteClient**. First, we set the response-header content-length based on the size of the response page. If we failed to set content-length, we log the error in the error log file. It is always best to set the content-length header before sending the body of response, although the client browser should be able to handle a response without this header. Because the response header content-type is the same as the default text/html, we do not have to set content-type (that is, use **WAIsetResponseContentType**). We also do not have to set the status (that is, use **WAIsetResponseStatus**, because the status for a correct response is the default 200 OK).

Next, we send the response-headers using **WAIStartResponse**. We check the return value of **WAIStartResponse** to find out if the request expects us to send the body of the response. If **WAIStartResponse** returns REQ_NOACTION, then we should not send the HTML page. Normally, **WAIStartResponse** returns REQ_NOACTION for a HEAD method of request that expects to receive the response-headers but not the body of the response. Because we accept only the POST method of request in this example, **WAIStartResponse** should always return REQ_PROCEED.

Finally, we return the body of the response—the HTML page—by using **WAIWriteClient**. If this function fails, it returns -1. We log the error and print out the error to the console.

The **error** function writes an error page to the client. Before we create this page, we get the referring HTML page (the URL of the guest book HTML form) by using **WAIgetRequestHeader** and the header referer. You can also use **WAIgetRequestInfo** with HTTP_REFERER to get the referring URL. We use this information to create a link back to the form. If there is no referring page, we return an error page without the link. For example, if the client directly invokes our program (that is, http://<server name>[:port]/iiop/guestbk), there is no referring page. As the error page is also of type text/html, we do not have to set the content-type response-header. On the other hand, the status code for the error page is not the default, 200 OK. Thus, we must set the error status for the response page. By default, the status 200 OK is included in the response-headers. We first remove this existing status header with **WAIdelResponseHeader**, via WAIdelResponseHeader(session, "status");. We then set the new status code using **WAIsetResponseStatus**. The program should function properly even if the original status header was not removed. To avoid having two status codes, however, it is best to remove the existing status header before setting a different type of status code.

The rest of the **error** function uses the same procedure as **RunFunction** to send the error page. We use **WAIsetResponseContentLength**, **WAIStartResponse**, and **WAIWriteClient** to write the error page to the client. In Listing 16-6-4, the **error** function always returns 0. You may want to set the return value to −1 upon failure, and use this information in **RunFunction** to verify that the **error** function was able to return the error page properly.

Listing 16-7 WAI Guest Book Example

```c
/* for adding the time to the confirmation
   page returned to the user
 */
#include <time.h>
#include <sys/timeb.h>

/* standard WAI header file for C */
#include "ONEiiop.h"

/* -------------------- DEFINES -------------------- */

/* In the following three constants, we define a specific
   set of numbers expected from the input.
   MAX_CONTENT_LENGTH is maximum content to be received
   from the POST. MAXLENGTH is the maximum length of each
   field input--that is, size of value of each name-value
   input. It is based on the value of the SIZE and
   MAXLENGTH attribute of INPUT (TYPE="TEXT") tags in the
   HTML page. FIELDNUM is the maximum number of name-value
   input pairs expected. For this example, there will be
   four pairs: action, ename, email, and eweb.
 */
#define MAX_CONTENT_LENGTH 300
```

Listing 16-6   WAI Guest Book Example (*continued*)

```
#define MAXLENGTH 40
#define FIELDNUM 4

/* ---------------- DATA STRUCTURE ---------------- */

/* Structure to hold information from the form. We use
   pointers. You can use string arrays to avoid using
   malloc.
*/
typedef struct DATA
{

   char *name;
   char *mail;
   char *www_address;

}FORM_DATA;

/* --------------- FUNCTION PROTOTYPES --------------- */

int Append_Guest_File (struct DATA *user_form, char *path);
int Read_Guest_File (char **guestlist, char *path);
int error(ServerSession_t session, int status,
           char *error_strings);
int parsing(char *string, char * name[], char *value[]);
void Remove_HTTP_Escapes(char *src, char *dest);
int HexToInt(int digit);
```

Listing 16-6-1   RunFunction

```
/* ----- Function for processing client requests ----- */
long RunFunction(ServerSession_t session)
{
   char *action = NULL;      /* holds the value of action--
                                that is, log or read */
   char *query = NULL;       /* holds the client input */
   char *list = NULL;        /* the guest book information
                                in the guest list file
                                displayed in a table for
                                the client to review */
   int  ichar = 1;    /* number of char in client input */
   struct _timeb timebuffer; /* Used to set time. time is
                                added to the Thank You
                                page sent back to client.
                              */
```

Listing 16-6-1 **RunFunction** (*continued*)

```
char *timeline;
FORM_DATA *user_data;    /* holds the information from
                               user */

int clengthNumber;          /* size of the content sent by
                               client in integer */
char *clengthString=NULL; /* length of the content sent
                               in string format */
int fields;           /* number of field in client input */
char *name[FIELDNUM];   /* name of the field in client's
                            [name]=[value] input */
char *value[FIELDNUM];    /* value of the field in
                             client's [name]=[value]
                             input */
char *RequestMethod=NULL; /* method of client request */
char *ContentType = NULL; /* content-type of request
                             input */
char *guestfile = NULL;   /* locates the guest book file */
char *data = NULL;        /* holds the content to be
                             returned */
int length;                 /* length of the data */

/* get the method used */
if(WAIgetRequestInfo(session, "REQUEST_METHOD",
                     &RequestMethod) != WAISPISuccess)
{
    error(session, PROTOCOL_NOT_FOUND,
          "Couldn't get the method of the request.");
    WAILogError(session, LOG_FAILURE, "guestbk",
       "Couldn't get the method of the request.", TRUE);
    return 0;
}

/* check if it is POST */
if(strcmpi(RequestMethod, "POST") != 0)
{
    error(session, PROTOCOL_NOT_FOUND,
          "Your need to submit the data using a form.");
    WAILogError(session, LOG_WARN, "guestbk",
          "Client did not use the POST method.", TRUE);
    return 0;
}

/* free the RequestMethod string */
```

Listing 16-6-1 RunFunction (*continued*)

```
WAIstringFree(RequestMethod);

/* get the content type */
if(WAIgetRequestInfo(session, "CONTENT_TYPE",
                        &ContentType) != WAISPISuccess)
{
    error(session, PROTOCOL_NOT_FOUND,
      "Could not get the content-type of the request.");
    WAILogError(session, LOG_FAILURE, "guestbk",
    "Could not get the content-type of request.", TRUE);
    return 0;
}

/* Check on the type of content requested. We expect
   only "application/x-www-form-urlencoded"
   for the POST method.
 */
if(strcmp(ContentType,
                "application/x-www-form-urlencoded") != 0)
{
    error(session, PROTOCOL_FORBIDDEN,
            "Your browser sent the wrong content type.");
    WAILogError(session, LOG_WARN, "formanswer",
            "Browser sent the wrong content type.",
            TRUE);
    return 0;
}

WAIstringFree(ContentType);

/* get the content length */
if(WAIgetRequestInfo(session, "CONTENT_LENGTH",
                        &clengthString) != WAISPISuccess)
{
    error(session, PROTOCOL_FORBIDDEN,
            "Your browser didn't send any content.");
    WAILogError(session, LOG_FAILURE, "guestbk",
            "Error in getting content length.", TRUE);
    return 0;
}
```

Listing 16-6-1   RunFunction (*continued*)

```
/* Get the actual number for the content length in int.
   Content length is sent as string. */
clengthNumber = atoi(clengthString);

WAIstringFree(clengthString);

/* More content length checking. See if length is more
   than 0 and less than the maximum we set. This
   information is useful if you want to limit the size
   of data you will receive.
 */
if((clengthNumber >= MAX_CONTENT_LENGTH) ||
    (clengthNumber < 1))
{
    error(session, PROTOCOL_FORBIDDEN,
          "The right amount of data was not sent.");
    WAILogError(session, LOG_WARN, "guestbk",
          "Content length is less than 1 or too long.",
            TRUE);
    return 0;
}

/* query will hold the content of the data sent by
   client */
query = (char *) malloc ((clengthNumber + 1) *
                          sizeof(char));

/* Read the data into the query. Read the number of
   bytes defined by clengthNumber.
 */
ichar = WAIReadClient(session, query, clengthNumber);

/* end the string of data we got with a NULL character */
query[ichar] = '\0';

/* Make sure all other data were received by verifying
   them against the expected length of the input. You
   can use ferror and feof to get the exact error, if
   you want to report it.
 */
if(ichar != clengthNumber)
{
    /* free the query string before exiting */
    WAIstringFree(query);
```

Listing 16-6-1   RunFunction (*continued*)

```
        error(session, PROTOCOL_SERVER_ERROR,
                "Error reading the input.");
        WAILogError(session, LOG_FAILURE, "guestbk",
                "Did not read all data from buffer.", TRUE);
        return 0;
    }

    /* Parsing function parses the [name]=[value] inputs
       from the client. We send the query. The function
       updates the name and value array of the string with
       the parsed variables. It also returns the number of
       variables. Even when the client requests to "read"
       the guest book, the variables email, ename, and eweb
       are sent. The values of the variables are empty if
       the client has not entered any data.
     */
    fields = parsing(query, name, value);

    /* make sure everything worked with the parsing
       function and we got the variables
     */
    if(fields <= 0)
    {
        WAIstringFree(query);

        error(session, PROTOCOL_BAD_REQUEST,
                "Error with the data received.");
        WAILogError(session, LOG_WARN, "guestbk",
                "Error getting the form data.", TRUE);
        return 0;
    }

    /* The radio-button field information (action=[value])
       will not be sent if the radio button is not chosen.
       Therefore, the number of fields will be less than 4.
       We check for this case and require the client to
       choose a button. Today JavaScript does a better job
       of verifying field existence and value.
     */
    if(fields == 3)
    {
        WAIstringFree(query);

        error(session, PROTOCOL_BAD_REQUEST,
                "You did not select an action.");
```

Listing 16-6-1   RunFunction (*continued*)

```
         WAILogError(session, LOG_WARN, "guestbk",
               "Form results had an invalid action.", TRUE);
      return 0;
}

/* action holds the type of action the client is
   requesting. As this variable can be only "log" or
   "read," you can set the size to 5 characters.
 */
action = (char *) malloc (MAXLENGTH * sizeof(char));

/* Check for the value of "action". It is set for the
   first name (starting number is 0) if the client
   chooses to input information (update the guest book)
   and for the fourth name if the client requests to
   "read" the guest book. The order of the other
   variables does not change.
 */

/* if the first name is action */
if(strcmp(name[0], "action") == 0)
{
         /* This function replaces extended characters
            that appear in Hex with the equivalent ASCII
            characters and also replaces "+" with a
            space. What is returned will be the value of
            the first variable. (This process is part of
            URL decoding.)
          */
         Remove_HTTP_Escapes(value[0], action);
}
/* if the first name is not action, check the third */
else if(strcmp(name[3], "action") == 0)
{
         Remove_HTTP_Escapes(value[3], action);
}

/* Get the guest file location from the IIOPexec
   parameter in obj.conf. Make sure the location is a
   directory accessible to this application.
 */
if(WAIgetConfigParameter(session, "guestfile", &guestfile)
                    != WAISPISuccess)
```

Listing 16-6-1   **RunFunction** (*continued*)

```
{
    WAIstringFree(query);
    WAIstringFree(action);

    error(session, PROTOCOL_SERVER_ERROR,
            "Server Error!");
    WAILogError(session, LOG_MISCONFIG, "guestbk",
      "Missing file parameter for IIOPexec in obj.conf.",
            FALSE);
    return 0;
}

/* if action is read, the guest file is read and
   formatted as an HTML table and sent to the client
 */
if(strcmp(action, "read") == 0)
{
    /* Malloc space for the guest list. Make this space
       large enough to hold the size of the information
       in the file and any extra HTML tags that will be
       added.
     */
    list = (char *) malloc(10000 * sizeof(char));

    /* set the list to blank */
    strcpy(list, "");

    /* call the Read_Guest_File function, which will
       fill the list string with the information in the
       file formatted as an HTML table
     */
    if(Read_Guest_File(&list, guestfile) == 0)
    {

        data = (char *) malloc((strlen(list) + 300)
                                    * sizeof(char));

        /* Document to be sent back to the client. List
           holds the dynamic data from the file.
         */
        length = sprintf(data,
                "<HTML><HEAD><TITLE>GUEST BOOK</TITLE>"
                "</HEAD>\n<BODY BGCOLOR=FFFFFF>"
                "<H1>GUEST BOOK</H1>\n"
                "<TABLE BORDER CELLPADDING=5>\n"
```

Listing 16-6-1   RunFunction (*continued*)

```
                        "<TR><TH BGCOLOR=C0C0C0>NAME<BR></TH>\n"
                        "<TH BGCOLOR=C0C0C0>EMAIL ADDRESS<BR>"
                        "</TH>\n<TH BGCOLOR=C0C0C0>WEB ADDRESS"
                        "<BR></TH>\n</TR>\n%s</TABLE>\n<HR>"
                        "</BODY></HTML>", list);

            WAIstringFree(guestfile);
            WAIstringFree(list);
        }
        else
        {
            /* send an error in case Read_Guest_File failed */
            WAIstringFree(query);
            WAIstringFree(action);
            WAIstringFree(guestfile);
            WAIstringFree(list);

            error(session, PROTOCOL_SERVER_ERROR,
                    "Error reading from the guest file.");
            WAILogError(session, LOG_CATASTROPHE, "guestbk",
                "Error reading from the guest file.", TRUE);
            return 0;
        }
    }
    /* if the request is log, then read and parse client's
       input, place it in the log file, and send back a
       Thank You page
     */
    else if(strcmp(action, "log") == 0)
    {
        /* Malloc space for the structure and all of the
           fields. Client data will be placed in this data
           structure.
         */
        user_data = (FORM_DATA *) malloc(sizeof(FORM_DATA));

        user_data->name = (char *) malloc(MAXLENGTH *
                            sizeof(char));
        user_data->mail = (char *) malloc(MAXLENGTH *
                            sizeof(char));
        user_data->www_address = (char *) malloc(MAXLENGTH *
                                    sizeof(char));
```

Listing 16-6-1   RunFunction (*continued*)

```
/* This function will parse the value and copy it
   into the user_data structure. It replaces
   extended characters that appear in Hex with the
   equivalent ASCII characters and replaces "+"
   with a space. (This process is part of URL
   decoding.)
 */
Remove_HTTP_Escapes(value[1], user_data->name);
Remove_HTTP_Escapes(value[2], user_data->mail);
Remove_HTTP_Escapes(value[3],
                       user_data->www_address);
/* Make sure that the input data from the client
   include at least the name and email. You should
   now use JavaScript to do this task.
 */
if ((strcmp(user_data->name, "void") == 0) ||
    (strcmp(user_data->mail, "void") == 0) ||
    (*user_data->name == '\0') ||
    (*user_data->mail == '\0'))
{
    /* if the user missed the name or email field,
       return an error page
     */
    WAIstringFree(query);
    WAIstringFree(action);
    WAIstringFree(guestfile);
    WAIstringFree(user_data->name);
    WAIstringFree(user_data->mail);
    WAIstringFree(user_data->www_address);
    free(user_data);

    error(session, PROTOCOL_BAD_REQUEST,
           "Form was not filled out completely.");
    WAILogError(session, LOG_WARN, "guestbk",
        "Form was not filled out completely.", TRUE);
    return 0;
}

/* Update the guest book and send back a Thank You
   page. If updating of the file failed, return an
   error page. Append_Guest_File returns 0 upon
   success.
 */
```

Listing 16-6-1   **RunFunction** (*continued*)

```
if(Append_Guest_File(user_data, guestfile) == 0)
{
    /* time function for adding the time and date to
       the end of the HTML page
     */
    _ftime( &timebuffer );
    timeline = ctime( & ( timebuffer.time ) );

    /* malloc enough space to hold the data for the
       return page
     */
    data = (char *) malloc(400 * sizeof(char));

    /* Thank You page to be sent to the client */
    length = sprintf(data,
            "<HTML><HEAD><TITLE>Thank "
            "you</TITLE></HEAD>\n"
            "<BODY><H1>Thank you!</H1>\n"
            "<B>%s</B> has been added to our Guest"
            " Book!\n<P>%s\n<HR></BODY></HTML>",
             user_data->name, timeline);
}
else
{
    /* free variables, and so on, before returning
       an error page
     */
    WAIstringFree(query);
    WAIstringFree(action);
    WAIstringFree(guestfile);
    WAIstringFree(user_data->name);
    WAIstringFree(user_data->mail);
    WAIstringFree(user_data->www_address);
    free(user_data);

    error(session, PROTOCOL_FORBIDDEN,
            "Error writing to the guest file.");
    WAILogError(session, LOG_CATASTROPHE,
            "guestbk",
            "Error writing to the guest file.", TRUE);
    return 0;
}

/* free the structure and its data (specific to
   updating the guest book)
```

Listing 16-6-1   RunFunction (*continued*)

```
            */
        WAIstringFree(user_data->name);
        WAIstringFree(user_data->mail);
        WAIstringFree(user_data->www_address);
        free(user_data);
    }
    /* if action is neither log nor read, return an error
       page */
    else
    {
        WAIstringFree(query);
        WAIstringFree(action);
        WAIstringFree(guestfile);

        error(session, PROTOCOL_FORBIDDEN,
                "Form results had an invalid action.");
        WAILogError(session, LOG_WARN, "guestbk",
                "Form results had an invalid action.", TRUE);
        return 0;
    }

    /* set the content length based on the length of the
       response page
     */
    if(WAIsetResponseContentLength(session, length) !=
                                    WAISPISuccess)
    {
        WAILogError(session, LOG_FAILURE, "guestbk",
        "Could not set the response contentlength.", TRUE);
    }

    /* Send the response-headers. The content-type
       response-header is the default text/html. status is
       the default 200.
     */
    if(WAIStartResponse(session) == REQ_PROCEED)
    {
        /* send the content of the response page to the
           client */
        if(WAIWriteClient(session,
                (const unsigned char *)data, length) != 1)
      {
          WAILogError(session, LOG_FAILURE, "guestbk",
```

Listing 16-6-1 **RunFunction** (*continued*)

```
                "Was not able to send the page to the client.",
                    TRUE);
                printf("Was unable to send the response.\n");
        }
    }

    /* free more variables */
    WAIstringFree(query);
    WAIstringFree(action);
    WAIstringFree(guestfile);

    /* return success */
    return 0;
}
```

Listing 16-6-2 **main** Function

```
/* WAI application's main function */
int main(int argc, char **argv)
{
    IIOPWebAppService_t obj;      /* Web service object */
    char host[80];               /* host name of the machine */

    /* Get the host name from the command line. We expect
       the host name as the first argument after the program
       name. You could also use a port address with the
       host name.
     */
    if(argc > 1)
    {
        strcpy(host, argv[1]);

        /* create the Web service object and name the
           service and function that will process client
           requests
         */
        obj = WAIcreateWebAppService("guestbk", RunFunction,
                                    argc, argv);

        /* Register the service with Netscape Naming
           Service. If registration failed, print an error
           message.
         */
        if(WAIregisterService(obj, host) == WAI_FALSE)
```

Listing 16-6-2   **main** Function (*continued*)

```
            {
                printf("Couldn't register with the %.", host);
                return 0;
            }
            else
            {
        /* print a message if registration was successful */
                printf("Object is ready. Server on host %s.\n",
                       host);
            }

            /* Start the implementation loop. Application is
               now ready to receive client requests from the
               server.
             */
            WAImplIsReady();
        }
        /* if the host name (and port) is not sent through the
           command-line argument, return an error */
        else
        {
            printf(
            "Server host name should be the first argument.\n");
        }

        return 0;
    }
```

Listing 16-6-3   **Read_Guest_File** and **Append_Guest_File**

```
/* --------------- Read_Guest_File --------------- */
/* This function reads the guest book information from the
   guest book file, formats the data for an HTML table, and
   returns the result in the string by way of the
   parameter guestlist. A pointer to a pointer string is
   used to update the calling string directly from this
   function. The function returns 0 if it was successful.
 */
int Read_Guest_File(char **guestlist, char *path)
{
    /* table formatting HTML tags */

    /* Beginning and end of a table field. <BR> allows for a
       better display for empty cells and for browsers that
```

Listing 16-6-3 Read_Guest_File and **Append_Guest_File** (*continued*)

```
         cannot display tables. Table cells for the name of
         the guests will be in color.
      */
     #define BEGINITEM "\n <TD>"
     #define BEGINITEMCOLOR "\n <TD BGCOLOR=#D2B48C>"
     #define ENDITEM "<BR></TD>"

     /* beginning and end of a table row */
     #define BEGINROW   "\n<TR>"
     #define ENDROW     "\n</TR>"

     /* enable email and Web address link as hypertext */
     #define BEGINMAIL "<A HREF=\"mailto:"
     #define BEGINLINK "<A HREF=\"http://"
     #define ENDLINK    "\">"
     #define ENDREF     "</A>"

     FILE *fd;                  /* file handle (descriptor) */
     int  lnum = 1;            /* number of lines in the file */
     int  num;                 /* holds the switch/case value */
     char line[MAXLENGTH + 1]; /* holds each line of info */

     /* open and read the file pointed to by the path */
     fd=fopen(path, "rt");

     /* check for any system error in opening the file */
     if(fd == NULL)
     {
         /* send an error page if file was not opened */
         return 1;
     }

         /* Read each line of data until no more remain, one
            character at a time. We expect no more than
            MAXLENGTH + 1 (includes the line feed) for each
            line.
          */
         while(fgets(line, (MAXLENGTH + 1), fd) != NULL)
         {
             /* send an error message if an error occurs
                while reading the file
              */
             if(ferror(fd))
             {
             /* close the file handle; return 1 for error */
```

Listing 16-6-3   **Read_Guest_File** and **Append_Guest_File** (*continued*)

```
        fclose(fd);

        return 1;
    }

    /* modulus operator is used to separate each
        line of the file into groups of three
     */
    num = lnum % 3;

    /* Read each line and place it in the guestlist
        string. Also format it with the correct tags.
     */
    switch(num)
    {
      /* first line includes the name of the user */
        case 1:
        {
            strcat(*guestlist, BEGINROW);
            strcat(*guestlist, BEGINITEMCOLOR);
            strncat(*guestlist, line,
                    (strlen(line)) 1);
            strcat(*guestlist, ENDITEM);
            break;
        }
        /* Second line includes email. The email
            address is also made into hypertext.
         */
        case 2:
        {
            strcat(*guestlist, BEGINITEM);
            strcat(*guestlist, BEGINMAIL);
            strncat(*guestlist, line,
                    (strlen(line)) -1);
            strcat(*guestlist, ENDLINK);
            strncat(*guestlist, line,
                    (strlen(line)) -1);
            strcat(*guestlist, ENDREF);
            strcat(*guestlist, ENDITEM);
            break;
        }
      /* The last line includes the Web address.
        The Web address is also made into
        hypertext.
```

Listing 16-6-3 **Read_Guest_File** and **Append_Guest_File** (*continued*)

```
                    */
            default:
            {
                strcat(*guestlist, BEGINITEM);
                strcat(*guestlist, BEGINLINK);
                strncat(*guestlist, line,
                        (strlen(line)) -1);
                strcat(*guestlist, ENDLINK);
                strncat(*guestlist, line,
                        (strlen(line)) -1);
                strcat(*guestlist, ENDREF);
                strcat(*guestlist, ENDITEM);
                strcat(*guestlist, ENDROW);
                break;
            }
        }

        ++lnum;
    }

    /* guestlist gets freed through 'list' in the calling
       function
     */

    /* close the file */
    fclose(fd);

    /* 0 is returned when the function is successful */
    return 0;
}

/* --------------- Append_Guest_File --------------- */
/* This function appends the guest file pointed to by the
   path parameter with the client input defined in the
   user_form data structure. Each line of the structure
   is placed in a separate line in the file. As an
   enhancement, you can update this function with a system
   lock of the file to make sure no other server thread
   will attempt to write to the file at the same time. This
   function returns 0 upon success. Note that with WAI,
   unlike CGI, you can have a global file handle.
 */
int Append_Guest_File(struct DATA *user_form, char *path)
{
```

Listing 16-6-3   **Read_Guest_File** and **Append_Guest_File** (*continued*)

```
FILE *fd;              /* file handle (descriptor) */
int ret;               /* length of userinfo string */
char *userinfo; /* a string holding user information */

/* open the file for appending the data */
fd=fopen(path, "a+t");

/* check for system error */
if( fd == NULL)
{
    /* send back an error page if the file could not be
       opened for appending of the data, then exit the
       program
     */
    return 1;
}
/* Malloc userinfo to the maximum size of the user
   information fields combined. You can use strlen of
   each of the variables to get a more exact number for
   the size.
 */
userinfo = (char *) malloc(((MAXLENGTH * 3) + 1) *
                           sizeof(char));

/* Place all user data into one string. The \n puts
   each separate field into a separate line in the file.
 */
sprintf(userinfo, "%s\n%s\n%s\n", user_form->name,
        user_form->mail, user_form->www_address);

/* put the string in the file */
ret = fputs(userinfo, fd);

/* check the return value of the fputs function to make
   sure we were able to append the data into the file
 */
if(ret < 0)
{
    /* send back an error page if an error occurred
       while writing to the file
     */
    return 1;
}
```

Listing 16-6-3   **Read_Guest_File** and **Append_Guest_File** (*continued*)

```
     /* close the file */
     fclose(fd);

     /* free the userinfo data structure now that we are
        finished with it
      */
     free(userinfo);

     /* 0 means everything went OK */
     return 0;
}
```

Listing 16-6-4   Utility Functions (**error, parsing, Remove_HTTP_Escapes,** and **HexToInt**)

```
/* -------------------- error -------------------- */
/* This function returns an error page to the client, with
   the error_string being customized by the calling
   function (where the error occurs). We use the
   environment variable HTTP_REFERER to get the URL of the
   form. This environment variable holds the last URL.
 */
int error(ServerSession_t session, int status,
          char *error_string)
{
   char *formURL = "";
   char buffer[2048];
   int length;

   /* Get the referring page's URL. If there is no
      referring page, send a different error page.
    */
   if(WAIgetRequestHeader(session, "referer", &formURL) ==
      WAISPISuccess)
   {
       /* content of the error page */
       length = sprintf(buffer,
               "<HTML><HEAD>"
               "<TITLE>Error"
               "</TITLE></HEAD>\n"
               "<BODY><H1>%s</H1><HR>Return to the "
               "<A HREF=\"%s\">Guest Book Form.</A>"
               "</BODY></HTML>",
```

```
                        error_string, formURL);
}
else
{
    /* content of the error page */
    length = sprintf(buffer,
                "<HTML><HEAD>"
                "<TITLE>Error"
                "</TITLE></HEAD>\n"
                "<BODY><H1>%s</H1></BODY></HTML>",
                error_string);
}

WAIstringFree(formURL);

/* delete the default status 200 */
WAIdelResponseHeader(session, "status");

/* set the status of the error page */
if(WAIsetResponseStatus(session, status, error_string)
                        != WAISPISuccess)
{
    WAILogError(session, LOG_FAILURE, "guestbk",
            "Could not set the status for the error page.",
            TRUE);
    return 0;
}

/* set the content-length of the response */
if(WAIsetResponseContent Length(session, length)
                            != WAISPISuccess)
{
    WAILogError(session, LOG_FAILURE, "guestbk",
      "Could not set the content-length for error page.",
      TRUE);
}

/* Send the response-headers. The content-type
   response-header is the default text/html.
 */
if(WAIStartResponse(session) == REQ_PROCEED)
{
    /* send the content of the response page to the
       client */
```

```c
        if(WAIWriteClient(session,
                (const unsigned char *)buffer, length) != 1)
        {
            WAILogError(session, LOG_FAILURE, "guestbk",
                "Could not send the error page.", TRUE);
            printf("Was unable to send the error page.\n");
        }
    }

    return 0;
}

/* -------------------- parsing -------------------- */
/*
  Parses the string sent to it, by separating pairs of
  variables (divided by "&") and by separating the [name]
  and [value] (divided by a "=" sign). It will then place
  the result in the name and value array of strings. The
  function also returns the number of variables it finds.
 */
int parsing(char *temp, char *name[], char *value[])
{
    int fieldnum = 0;

    while(*temp)
    {
        /* have the name point to temp */
        name[fieldnum] = temp;

        /* go down the string until we find a "=" sign, at
            which time we put a null pointer in temp
            string--that is, null-terminate the name string.
         */
        while(*temp)
        {
            if(*temp == '=')
            {
                *temp = '\0';
                temp++;

                /* get out of the loop */
                break;
            }
            else
```

```c
        {
            temp++;
        }
    }

    /* set temp to point to the value string */
    value[fieldnum] = temp;

    /* We look for "&", which divides the value from
        the next name. We put a NULL terminator at the
        end of the string, which will also terminate the
        value string.
     */
    while(*temp)
    {
        if(*temp == '&')
        {
            *temp = '\0';
            temp++;
            break;
        }
        else
        {
            temp++;
        }
    }

    /* increase the number of variables */
    fieldnum++;

    /* We don't want more than four pairs of values. If
        there are more, return -1, which will be
        interpreted as an error.
     */
    if(fieldnum > FIELDNUM)
    {
        return -1;
    }
}

/* return the number of array of [name]=[value] */
return fieldnum;
}

/* -------------- Remove_HTTP_Escapes -------------- */
```

```c
/* Removes the URL encoding of the name or value string.
   Replaces a "+" in the string (src) sent to the
   function. It also checks for Hex characters in the
   string and replaces them with equivalent ASCII
   characters. The result is placed in the dest string.
 */
void Remove_HTTP_Escapes(char *src, char *dest)
{
    /* check for '+' and replace it with space */
    while(*src)
    {
        if(*src == '+')
        {
            *dest = ' ';
        }
        /* else check for '%' */
        else if(*src == '%')
        {
            int value;

            /* use HexToInt to transfer src to int */
            src++;
            value =  HexToInt(*src) * 16;
            src++;
            value += HexToInt(*src);
            *dest = value;
        }
        else
        {
        /* otherwise src and the dest string are the same */
            *dest = *src;
        }

        src++;
        dest++;
    }

    /* terminate the result string */
    *dest = '\0';
}
```

```
/* ------------------ HexToInt ------------------ */
/* This function turns Hex values into integers and is
   used by Remove_HTTP_Escapes to replace a Hex value with
   the ASCII character.
 */
int HexToInt(int digit)
{
   int value = 0;

   /* check for the Hex range and do the conversion */
   if(digit >= '0' && digit <= '9')
   {
       value = digit  '0';
   }
   else if(digit >= 'A' && digit <= 'F' )
   {
       value = digit  'A' + 10;
   }

   /* return the integer in decimal */
   return value;
}
```

Adding NSAPI Functions to the Guest Book

Let use now make a few modifications to the **Append_Guest_File** function (Listing 16-6-3). We want to use **system_fwrite_atomic** to take advantage of its platform-independent file-locking support. **system_fwrite_atomic** locks the file while it is being updated and releases the lock after it is finished. To use this function, we also use the NSAPI file handle type, SYS_FILE, for the file and open the file using **system_fopenWA**. Because the file handle has to be set globally, we will specify SYS_FILE outside of the **Append_Guest_File** function as a global variable. If you plan to use NSAPI with **Append_Guest_File**, it is also best to modify **Read_Guest_File** to use the same SYS_FILE handle and NSAPI functions for reading the file.

   system_fopenWA opens the file for writing and appending data to the end of the file. We then update the guest file with the client input via **system_fwrite_atomic** and close the file via **system_fclose**. **system_fwrite_atomic** returns IO_OKAY upon success. When a function works in conjunction with an NSAPI function, such as **system_fwrite_atomic**, you should always use the appropriate NSAPI function instead of the standard ANSI C function or your system-specific function. **Append_Guest_File** (Listing 16-7) now resembles the NSAPI function

Append_Guest_File (Listing 9-5-3) more than the CGI function **Append_Guest_File** (Listing 5-8-4)!

You can also add other NSAPI functions to the WAI Guest Book program. For example, you can use **util_sprintf** instead of **sprintf**.

Listing 16-7   Modified Append_Guest_File Using NSAPI Functions

```
SYS_FILE fd;   /* place this global file handle with the
                  rest of the global variables for this
                  example
               */

int Append_Guest_File(struct DATA *user_form, char *path)
{
    int len;                 /* length of userinfo string */
    char *userinfo;          /* a string holding user
                                information */

    /* open the file for appending the data */
    fd=system_fopenWA(path);

    /* check for system error */
    if( fd == SYS_ERROR_FD)
    {
        return 1;
    }

    /* Malloc userinfo to the maximum size of the user
       information fields combined. You can use strlen of
       each of the variables to get a more exact number
       for the size.
     */
    userinfo = (char *) malloc(((MAXLENGTH * 3) + 1) *
                                    sizeof(char));

    /* Place all user data into one string. The \n puts
       each separate field into a separate line in the file.
     */
    len = sprintf(userinfo, "%s\n%s\n%s\n",
                    user_form->name, user_form->mail,
                    user_form->www_address);

    /* write the client input into the guest file */
    if(system_fwrite_atomic(fd, userinfo, len) != IO_OKAY)
    {
        return 1;
    }

    /* close the file */
```

Listing 16-7   Modified **Append_Guest_File** Using NSAPI Functions (*continued*)

```
    system_fclose(fd);

    /* free the userinfo data structure now that we are
       finished with it
     */
    WAIstringFree(userinfo);

    /* 0 means everything went OK */
    return 0;
}
```

To be able to use Listing 16-7, you must write the Guest Book example as an in-process application. You cannot use **system_fwrite_atomic** with an out-of-process application. You can use the **guestInit** function in Listing 16-8 instead of the **main** function of the out-of-process WAI application (Listing 16-6-2). This function registers the Guest Book Web service object using the name `guestin` with Naming Service.

Listing 16-8   In-Process **guestInit** Function for the Guest Book Example

```
/* global Web service object variable */
IIOPWebAppService_t obj;
NSAPI_PUBLIC int guestInit(pblock *pb, Session *sn,
                           Request *rq)
{

    /* create a Web service object and name the service and
       the function that will process client requests
     */
    obj = WAIcreateWebAppService("guestin", RunFunction,
                                 0, 0);

    /* register the service with the server's Naming Service
     */
    WAIregisterService(obj, "");

    return 0;
}
```

The following code is an example of the directive functions you can add to the **obj.conf** file to enable the **guestInit** function to run as an in-process application. These instructions apply to Windows NT. For UNIX, you should change the `shlib` parameter to point to your shared object. Also, compile this program as a shared object or DLL and include appropriate NSAPI library (for example, `nshttpd35.lib` for Server 3.5.1) in your project while compiling and linking your application.

```
Init LateInit="yes" fn="load-modules" funcs="guestInit"
  shlib="c:/netscape/server/wai/guest/guest.dll"
Init LateInit="yes" fn="guestInit"
```

Summary

In this chapter, we completed our discussion of WAI by writing a few examples. We also discussed the steps for compiling or debugging a WAI application and registering an in-process WAI application.

Writing a WAI application includes two components. This first component is more general and is shared between all WAI applications of the same type. In other words, part of your code remains mostly the same for all applications of C++ developed as out-of-process console WAI applications. When you write this part of your code, you do not define the specific HTTP request-handling service that your program provides. For example, the main function of your application usually remains the same. For this service-independent component of your WAI application, the Hello Client example included in this chapter can provide a foundation on which to build your own programs. For example, you can easily modify the main Hello Client function of the C++ example to support a separate service (for example, a different **Run** function).

The second component of your program depends on what you need to accomplish. Part of this code is the standard reading of the input from the client and writing of an output page. You can use the discussion in Chapter 15 to facilitate writing this portion of your code. The other service-dependent portion of your code can range from simple processing of the client request, such as the Guest Book example given in Listing 16-7, to complex database checking, validation, commerce transaction processing, and so on. This part of your program is always left to your discretion. You can include existing functions or classes in your code; write new methods, functions, or classes; or connect to an existing legacy application.

An example of a more powerful use of WAI can be found in the example directory containing Netscape's agents, `<server path>/plugins/agents/examples`. The Netscape agent example (`agentapi.cpp`) uses WAI to implement an agent server plug-in. Agent services can be used to monitor server files and directories. An agent can notify you when a specific event occurs related to a document or a directory. For example, a client can be notified in an e-mail when a URL or file is updated. The Netscape agent example is a C++ in-process WAI application. The WAI application demonstrates the use of the Agent API for developing customized agent applications. The Agent API functions run in the server process. This example was originally developed for Server 3.0, however, and does not take advantage of Server 3.01 or 3.5.x features such as the `FormHandler` class.

WAI can be a very easy, fast, and powerful means of developing Netscape Server applications. The current WAI implementation is still being enhanced and updated. Some problems remain to be addressed. Netscape has stated that it is committed to WAI and intends to support it in future versions of the server. Thus, you can be sure that the investment you make in writing WAI applications will be worthwhile.

Appendix A

`magnus.conf` Directives

This appendix covers the **magnus.conf** directives for Netscape HTTP servers. These specifications set the global attributes of the server. Other Netscape Servers that may use a similar file to **magnus.conf** may include additional directives. For example, nsadmin.conf, which is used by Administration Server 3.x, includes the directives **Backups** and **ONEACLDir**.

Whenever a directive applies to only a specific version of Netscape Server, we have made a note of the applicable servers in parentheses after the directive name (for example, Server 3.x). Also, we have noted the default directives that are declared by the server in the **magnus.conf** file during installation.

ACLFile

```
ACLFile c:/netscape/server/httpacl/\
generated.https-foo.acl
```
(Default value is set during installation.)

Defines the location of the Access Control List (ACL) files, usually under the *<server path>*/httpacl/ directory. ACL files hold the information on who has access to what part of your site. ACL files contain the access control rules for the users and groups in the user database. The acl directives in an ACL file work in conjunction with the **PathCheck** function **check-acl** to set access

Note ▶

While you can specify multiple ACL files in the **magnus.conf** file, Web Publisher uses only the first ACL file that you specify for the resources that do not have a specific ACL referenced in the **obj.conf** file. Therefore, you should use the **PathCheck** function **check-acl** to reference the ACLs in the ACL files in the **obj.conf** file. (See **check-acl** in Appendix B for more information on its use.)

control restrictions for your server. (See Appendix B for description of **check-acl**.) You can have more than one **ACLFile** directive in your **mangus.conf** file. The server reads all ACL files at start-up. The name of each ACL file must be unique. The format of the ACL files for Server 3.x is different from that for Server 2.x. You can convert a Server 2.0 ACL file to a Server 3.0 file using the Server Manager; see the Server Preferences|Convert 2.0 ACL file menu. (See Appendix C for more information on ACL files.)

ACLCacheLifetime (Server 3.5.1)

`ACLCacheLifetime 0`

Sets the cache for the ACL. The default value, `120` seconds, is also the default cache for Enterprise Server 3.0x. You can set this value to `0` to turn off ACL caching. When a number other than `0` is used, the ACL information about the user is cached. Thus the user information set in the LDAP directory may not take effect for the server for the duration of the cache. User cache stores mapping for user and password information and user Distinguished Name (DN) and certificate information about the user and user DN.

AcceptLanguage (Server 3.x)

`AcceptLanguage on`

(Default value is set to `off` during installation.)

(In the Server Manager, set "Parse Accept Language Headers:" to Yes from the Content Management|Document Preferences menu.)

By setting this directive to `on`, you allow `Accept-Language` request-header parsing by the server. If a client is using HTTP/1.1, it can send an `Accept-Language` request-header that specifies the languages that the client can accept. By setting this directive to `on`, the server parses this language information and sends the appropriate language version of the document based on what the client can accept. You should set this value to `on` only if your server supports multiple languages. (See also **AdminLanguage**, **DefaultLanguage**, and **ClientLanguage**.)

Address

`Address http://www.foo.com`

(In the Server Manager, set this directive with the "Bind to Address" option from the System Settings|Nework Settings menu for Server 2.x or with Server Preferences| Network Settings for Server 3.x .)

Instructs your machine to answer to an additional IP address. When you set your server to multiple IP addresses, you use this directive to tell the server to which additional IP address it belongs. You must configure your system to listen to an additional IP address before using the `Address` directive.

AdminLanguage (Server 3.x)

`AdminLanguage en`

(Default value is set during installation.)

> For an international version of the server, you can use this directive to specify the language used for the Server Manager and other administrative pages. You can set the value to en (English), fr (French), de (German), or ja (Japanese). (See also **AdminLanguage**, **DefaultLanguage**, and **AcceptLanguage**.)

AsyncDNS (Server 3.x)

`AsyncDNS off`

(In the Server Manager, set this directive with the "Enable Async DNS" option from the Server Preferences|Performance Tuning menu.)

> Specifies whether asynchronous DNS is allowed. The value is either on for enabled or off for disabled. When the server uses DNS, multiple threads are serialized. By setting **AsyncDNS** to off, you disable serialization and enable asynchronous DNS look-up. You should have **DNS** set to on before setting **AsynDNS** to on. Asynchronous DNS will improve your system's DNS look-up.
>
> For Enterprise Server 3.0, make sure to apply the Server 3.0 update patch (for example, the 3.0i patch for Windows NT version of the server). This patch solves the problem with asynchronous DNS intermittent failure. You can find the patch under Netscape's File Library page
> (`http://help.netscape.com/filelib.html`). (See also **DNS** directive.)

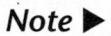

Note ▶

Although **AsyncDNS** is documented for NT and can be set in the Server Manager, it seems to work only under UNIX.

Certfile

`Certfile c:/netscape/server/alias/cert-foo.db`

(Netscape Server 2.x documents this directive as ServerCert Certfile.)

(For Server 2.x, security information is set in the Server Manager's Encryption menus [for example, Installing Certificate, Managing Certificates]. For Server 3.x, you set all the keys and certificates information in General Administration. Choose Keys & Certificates from the General Administration menu. You can then select the appropriate menu, such as Install Certificate, Manage Certificates, and so on. In the Server Manager, you can enable encryption from Server Preferences|Encryptions On/Off.)

> Points to where the certificate file database for the server is located. Part of installing the server certificate. You can use an absolute path or a relative path from the server path (root). The certificate file format for each version of Netscape Server is different. The Netscape Server 3.x certificate file format is different from the Netscape Server 1.x or 2.x format. For Server 3.x, the files are normally placed under the *<server path>*/alias directory. You can use

Administration Server to convert a 2.0 `Certfile` (and the `keyfile`) to 3.x format. See General Administration's Keys & Certificates|Convert 2.0 Certdb menu. (See also **keyfile**.)

Chroot (UNIX)

`Chroot /usr/ns-home/www`
(For UNIX Server 3.x, choose Server Preferences|UNIX Chroot in the Server Manager to enter the chroot directory.)

Changes the root directory that the server will use. Limits the server to specific directories under the **Chroot** directory. Use this directive to safeguard your server from hackers seeking access to other parts of your system. You can set your document root directory as the **Chroot** directory. Make sure **Chroot** refers to the documents' root directory and that server root and log and configuration files are stored outside of the **Chroot** directory. In other words, you want to bar others from accessing the important files but allow the server to log information. Also, the Server Manager must be able to change the configuration files. There are limitations to using **Chroot**. For example, the server must start as the superuser. You cannot use `-HUP` to soft-restart the server. The CGI programs must all be placed in the **Chroot** directory and statically linked. You also need to place the `pid` file under the **Chroot** directory. Modify the **PidLog** directive (discussed later in this appendix) to point to a file in a directory under the **Chroot** directory. For Solaris, you also need to create a directory for TCP and UDP devices. (See Netscape TechNote, "Chrooting a Netscape Web Server," at `http://help.netscape.com/kb/server/960804-9.html`, for more information.) Before using this option, read about it in the Netscape Server Administrator Guide or your operating system manual. Make sure it does what you want.

Ciphers and SSL3Ciphers

`Ciphers +rc4,+rc4export,+rc2,+rc2export,+des,+desede3`
(Default value is set during installation.)
(For Server 2.x, security information is set in the Server Manager's Encryption|Security Preferences. For Server 3.x, you can specify the ciphers from Server Preferences|Encryption Preferences.)

Enables and defines ciphers (encryption functions) for the server. The ciphers are listed with a plus sign (+) signifying that the cipher value is active, or a minus sign (–), signifying that the cipher value is inactive. Valid cipher options are `rc4`, `rc4export`, `rc2`, `rc2export`, `ides`, `des`, `desede3`, `rsa_rc4_128_md5`, `rsa3des_sha`, `rsa_des_sha`, `rsa_rc4_40_md5`, `rsa_rc2_40_md5`, and `rsa_null_md5`. There are different settings for Secure Sockets Layer (SSL) 2.0, the default ciphers, than for SSL 3.0 ciphers. SSL 2.0 has now been replaced by SSL 3.0. SSL 2.0 is mainly supported for compatibility with earlier browsers. (SSL3 is supported under Netscape Navigator 3.0 and later.)

Table A-1   SSL Ciphers for Server 2.x

SSL 2.0	SSL 3.0
RC4 with 128-bit encryption	RC4 with 128-bit encryption and MD5 message authentication
RC4 with 40-bit encryption	RC4 with 40-bit encryption and MD5 message authentication
RC2 with 40-bit encryption	RC2 with 40-bit encryption and MD5 message authentication
RC2 with 128-bit encryption	No encryption, but MD5 message authentication
DES with 56-bit encryption	DES with 56-bit encryption and SHA message authentication
Triple DES with 168-bit encryption	Triple DES with 168-bit encryption and SHA message authentication

Table A-2   SSL Ciphers for Server 3.x

SSL 2.0	SSL 3.0
RC4 with 128-bit encryption and MD5 message authentication	RC4 with 128-bit encryption and MD5 message authentication
RC4 with 40-bit encryption and MD5 message authentication	RC4 with 40-bit encryption and MD5 message authentication
RC2 with 40-bit encryption and MD5 message authentication	RC2 with 40-bit encryption and MD5 message authentication
RC2 with 128-bit encryption and MD5 message authentication	No encryption, but MD5 message authentication
DES with 56-bit encryption and MD5 message authentication	DES with 56-bit encryption and SHA message authentication
Triple DES with 168-bit encryption and MD5 message authentication	Triple DES with 168-bit encryption and SHA message authentication

For example, `rc4` stands for RC4 with 128-bit encryption. `rc4export` stands for RC4 with 40-bit encryption, as exporting encryption is limited to 40-bit encryption. Any cipher name that includes "40" refers to a cipher with 40-bit encryption, whereas "128" refers to 128-bit encryption.

ClientLanguage (Server 3.x)

`ClientLanguage en`
(Default value is set during installation.)

If you are using an internationalized version of Netscape Enterprise Server, you can specify the language for the client messages as `en` (English), `fr` (French), `de` (German), or `ja` (Japanese). The specific server messages (for example, `Not Found`) will then be displayed in the appropriate language. For more information on the internationalized server settings, see the Netscape Enterprise Server Administration Guide, Appendix B, "Using the Internationalized Server." (See also **AdminLanguage**, **DefaultLanguage**, and **AcceptLanguage**.)

DaemonStats (UNIX Server 3.x)

`DaemonStats off`

> By adding this directive to the **magnus.conf** file and setting its value to `off`, you disable the collection of some daemon statistics by the server. This directive may improve the performance of the server, but it also reduces the statistics that the server may gather.

DefaultLanguage (Server 3.x)

`DefaultLanguage en`

(Default value is set during installation.)

> If you are using an internationalized version of Netscape Enterprise Server, you can specify the default language for the server. The default language is used for both the client responses and administration, if a requested resource cannot be found. For more information on the international servers, see the Netscape Enterprise Server Administration Guide, Appendix B, "Using the Internationalized Server.") (See also **AdminLanguage**, **ClientLanguage**, and **AcceptLanguage**.)

DNS

`DNS on`

(Default value is set during installation.)

(You can set this directive in the Server Manager with the "Enable DNS?" option from the System Settings|Performance Tuning menu for Server 2.x or with the Server Preferences|Performance Tuning menu for Server 3.x.)

Bug Report ▶

Under Server 2.x, DNS look-up is serialized. Serial handling of DNS look-up can result in a severe performance drawback. Under UNIX for Server 2.x, each server process spawns a helper process to handle all of its DNS look-up. Therefore, when your system is using a single process (as is expected in a single-CPU machine), one server process attempts to do all DNS look-up. NT versions of the server always use a single process. If there is a lengthy delay in processing a DNS look-up, all requests are put on hold. The DNS look-up requests are handled in first in, first out (FIFO) fashion. For Server 2.x, you should disable DNS look-up to avert this problem. If you wish to keep DNS enabled, you can improve the response by disabling access log DNS look-up, by using the `iponly` parameter of the **flex-log** function. For more information, see the **Init** functions **common-log** and **flex-log** in Appendix B. To better the performance drawback of using DNS, you can also use DNS caching. See **dns-cache-init** in Appendix B.

Under UNIX Server 1.x, the server used a separate process for handling each request and the DNS look-up. Thus the performance drawback was far less than with Server 2.0. This problem has been resolved with Server 3.x. For Server 3.0, you should update the server with the latest patch from Netscape's File Library page (`http://help.netscape.com/filelib.html`). Server 3.x also supports asynchronous DNS look-up. (See the **AsyncDNS** directive.)

Enables DNS look-up. The server obtains the client `hostname` from the client IP address. This procedure can slow the process of your server, but it provides more detailed information for your programs, access control, and log files.

ErrorLog

`ErrorLog c:/netscape/server/https-foo/logs/errors`
(Default value is set during installation.)

Designates the full path for the server's error log file. For UNIX, you can replace the path with `SYSLOG` if you want to use `syslog` instead of the error file.

Init (Server 1.x)

(See **Init** functions in Appendix B.)

Unless you are using Netscape Server 1.x, you should not declare **Init** functions in the **magnus.conf** file. Although you can use **magnus.conf** to define the **Init** functions as was done in Server 1.x, you should not do so for later versions of the server. Declare your **Init** functions in the **obj.conf** file. Keep **Init** in **obj.conf** and leave **magnus.conf** as is, with minimal or no updating. This way you can limit almost all your changes to the **obj.conf** file.

KeepAliveTimeout

`KeepAliveTimeout 90`
(Default value is set during installation, but may not show up in **magnus.conf**. You can always add this directive if you want a different timeout than the default. For Server 3.x, in the Server Manager, you can set KeepAliveTimeout from HTTP Persistent Connection Timeout in Server Preferences|Performance Tuning.)

Determines the maximum time that the server holds open an HTTP Keep-Alive connection. Netscape Server 2.x added the feature Keep-Alive, which allows the client/server connection to continue while the server processes the client request (for example, processing a request for a page with embedded images). The Keep-Alive packet is sent through the TCP/IP connection. The client usually sends the Keep-Alive request-header, specifying that it can handle a Keep-Alive connection. The response should also include the `content-length` response-header for Keep-Alive to work.

As part of HTTP/1.1 support, Netscape Server 3.x supports HTTP persistent connection. Persistent connection is similar to Keep-Alive under Server 2.x. With an HTTP/1.1-compliant client, the default connection is a persistent connection. Persistent connection allows a client and the server to signal the closing of a TCP connection. You still need to set a timeout for the persistent connection. **KeepAliveTimeout** sets the timeout setting of the persistent connection to stop the connection from continuing and consuming additional system resources. (See also **MaxKeepAliveConnections**.)

KernelThreads (Server 3.x)

`KernelThreads on`

Netscape Server 3.x supports both kernel-level and user-level threads whenever the operating system supports kernel-level threads. If the operating system does not support context switching and scheduling of kernel-level and user-level threads, Netscape provides a model that can support it. This Netscape-specific model, however, can make it difficult to debug your NSAPI program using the debugger provided by your operating systems. Normally, the standard debugger and compiler of your system are intended for use with kernel-level threads. By setting the value of `KernelThreads` to on, you make the server use only kernel-level threads. This option can also help when you combine Netscape's thread model with third-party options that support kernel-level threads. (See also Chapter 11.)

Keyfile

`Keyfile c:/netscape/server/alias/key-foo.db`
(Netscape Server 2.x documents this directive as ServerKey Keyfile.)
(For Server 2.x, in the Server Manager, security information is set through Encryption menus—for example, On/Off, Generate Key, and Change Key Password. For Server 3.x, you set the keys and certificates information from the General Administration menu. Choose Keys & Certificates from General Administration. You can then select the appropriate menu, such as Generate Key or Change Key Password. In the Server Manager, you can enable encryption through Server Preferences|Encryptions On/Off.)

Points to the location of the server's encryption keys—that is, the `Keyfile` location. For Server 2.x, if the `Keyfile` is in the *<server path>/<server ID>/*config directory, then you simply specify the file name. For Server 3.x, you should specify the absolute path for the `keyfile` or the relative path from the server root. Normally, for Server 3.x, the `keyfile` is placed in the `alias` directory under the server path. The `Keyfile` format is different for each version of the server. Thus the Netscape Server 3.x `keyfile` format is different from that of Server 1.x or 2.x. You can use Administration Server to convert a 2.0 `keyfile` to 3.x format. See General Administration's Keys & Certificates|Convert 2.0 Certdb menu.

ListenQ (Server 3.x and UNIX Server 2.x)

`ListenQ 100`
(Under Server 3.x, you can set this value in the Server Manager under Server Preferences|Performance Tuning. See option "Listen Queue Size:".)

Defines the number of incoming connections for a server socket. **ListenQ** specifies the parameter for the socket call that the server will make. It lets the operating system know the number of connection requests to queue when the server does not have any available threads (or processes for Server 2.x). The queued connection request will then use a thread when it becomes available. The default number is set to 128. You rarely need to increase this number. If you change this number, make sure your system can support the new size. You should check to find out the maximum size of the listen queue supported by your system. For example, some earlier versions of Solaris force a limit of 5 for the listen queue size. If the number can be modified, then you should set it in such a way that it could support the size of the listen queue for Netscape Server. If the server requests a size larger than the maximum listen queue size for your system, the size is set to the system's maximum size. If the size of the listen queue is too large, it may actually diminish the performance of your server. The server will be overloaded with connections that it cannot handle. On the other hand, if the listen queue is too small and is filled up, the connections may be dropped.

LoadObjects

LoadObjects obj.conf
(Default value is set during installation.)

Defines which files are loaded with the server as the configuration files for your objects—that is, the **obj.conf** file.

> **Warning** ►
>
> The Server Manager assumes that there is only one file, **obj.conf**, and that it is placed in the *<server path>*/*<server ID>*/config/ directory. To use the Server Manager, you should keep the **obj.conf** file in the default directory and not change the default value of this directive in the **magnus.conf** file.

LogVerbose (Server 3.x)

LogVerbose on

Not all server messages are logged in the server's error log file. For example, initialization messages for Web Application Interface (WAI) are normally not logged. By setting LogVerbose to on, the server will log these additional messages. These messages appear in the log file with severity level LOG_VERBOSE (verbose:). Because this directive actually increases the size of the log file, you should use it only if you wish to review the additional logged message.

MaxKeepAliveConnection (Server 3.x)

MaxKeepAliveConnection 100
(Default value is set during installation, but may not show up in **magnus.conf**. You can always add this directive if you want a different timeout than the default.)

Maximum number of Keep-Alive connections (persistent connections) for the server. It is the maximum number of simultaneous Keep-Alive connections that the server will allow. The default value is 200. Persistent connection keeps the client/server connection alive while the server processes the client request (for example, processing a request for a page with embedded images). You should increase this number only if your system can support the additional connections. (See also **KeepAliveTime**.)

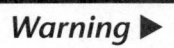

Warning ▶

You should be careful when increasing the number of Keep-Alive connections for UNIX servers. UNIX operating systems use a file descriptor for the socket connection. Normally the maximum number of open files is set to 1024. If the number of Keep-Alive connections is too high, the system may run out of open file descriptors.

MaxProcs (UNIX Server 1.x and 2.x)

MaxProcs 2
(Default value is set during installation.)

Maximum number of active processes for the server. Under Netscape Server 2.x for UNIX, you can have multiple processes, each with its own number of threads. Set this value to a number no greater than the number of CPUs on your machine. The number should also be smaller than the size of your operating system's process table. Make sure that the number of processes does not outrun the system's process tables. When you determine the optimal number of processes and threads for the server, consider the following issues: the number of CPUs on the server machine; the number of simultaneous connections you expect; the forking overhead; the system memory size; and any speed increase due to an increase in the number of processes or threads. Remember also that for Server 2.0, the server process spawns a child process to perform DNS look-up.

This directive is no longer needed for Server 3.x. Server 3.x does not use multiple processes. If this directive is used, you should set its value to 1. (See also **MaxThreads**, **MinThreads**, and **RqThrottle**.)

MaxThreads (UNIX Server 2.x)

MaxThreads 20
(Under Server Manager 2.x for UNIX, you can set the number of maximum threads through the option "Maximum Threads" from the Server Settings|Performance Tuning menu.)

Maximum number of concurrent threads spawned by the server for processing client requests. This number is not the same as the maximum number of threads that the server spawns. The server may spawn additional threads for maintenance purposes. With UNIX servers, you can specify the maximum and minimum number of threads for handling client requests in the **magnus.conf** file. Netscape UNIX Server 2.x can use multiple processes with multiple threads. The NT version of Server 2.x automatically determines the maximum and minimum number of threads. You do not specify the maximum number of threads in **magnus.conf**. When you determine the optimal number of processes and threads for the server, consider the following issues: the number of CPUs on the server machine; the number of simultaneous connections you expect; the forking overhead; the system memory size; and any speed increase due to an increase in the number of processes or threads.

Netscape UNIX Server 3.x also supports multiple threads. With Server 3.x, however, you use a new directive, **RqThrottle**, to specify the number of simultaneous requests that the server can accept. (See **RqThrottle** for more information. See also **MinThreads**, **MaxProcs**, and **RqThrottleMinPerSocket**.)

> ### Warning ▶
>
> Netscape Server 2.x and 3.x use data structures to hold statistics about child threads that are created to handle client requests. These data structures are called *statistics slots*. If you have gotten the error message `unable to find empty statistic slot`, you may need to increase the maximum number of threads. The error could occur when threads have terminated without freeing the slot or the server has run out of empty slots.

MinThreads (UNIX Server 2.x)

```
MinThreads 5
```

Minimum number of concurrent threads spawned by the server for processing client requests. This number is not the same as the minimum number of threads that the server spawns. The server may spawn additional threads for maintenance purposes. With UNIX servers, you can specify the maximum and minimum number of threads for handling client requests in the **magnus.conf** file. Netscape UNIX Server 2.x can use multiple processes with multiple threads. The NT version of Server 2.x automatically determines the maximum and minimum number of threads. You do not specify the maximum number of threads in **magnus.conf**. When you determine the optimal number of processes and threads for the server, consider the following issues: the number of CPUs on the server machine; the number of simultaneous connections you expect; the forking overhead; the system memory size; and any speed increase due to an increase in the number of processes or threads.

Under Server 3.x, Netscape allows you to set a rough number for the minimum number of threads waiting for a connection with **RqThrottleMinPerSocket**. (See **RqThrottleMinPerSocket** for more information. See also **MaxThreads**, **MaxProcs**, and **RqThrottle**.)

MtaHost (Server 3.x)

```
MtaHost proxymail
```

(In the Server Manager, set the MTA host from the Server Preferences|Network Settings menu.)

Specifies the name of the SMTP mail (messaging) server (Message Transfer Agent [MTA] host) used by the agents. For reports to be sent automatically to a mailing address, the mail server needs to be identified.

NntpHost (Server 3.x)

`NntpHost news2`

(In the Server Manager, set the NNTP host from the Server Preferences|Network Settings menu.)

> Specifies the name of the news (Collabra) server (Network News Transfer Protocol[NNTP] host) used by the agents. When you enable the server agents, the server checks to ensure **MtaHost** and **NntpHost** are set.

Personal (IRIX 2.x and 3.x)

`Personal on`

> This directive is set for some servers shipped by SGI. It is used to reduce the footprint of the server. When it is set to `on`, the server's footprint is roughly less than one megabyte of memory. If you are using the server for personal use or for testing, you may keep this directive. Remove this directive from the **magnus.conf** file for production servers that require more memory.

PidLog (UNIX)

`PidLog /usr/ns-home/https-foo/logs/pid`

(Default value is set during installation.)

> Location for the file where the base server pid (process identification) is recorded. The default location is under `/logs`. Every process has an ID logged, including your server. You can stop (`kill`) the server by using its `pid` number. The user account under which the server is running must have write permission for the `logs` directory. The server needs to be able to log the process ID to run.

Port

`Port 80`

(Default value is set during installation.)

(You can set this directive in the Server Manager with the "Server Port" option in the System Settings|Network Settings menu for Server 2.x and with the Server Settings| Network Settings menu for Server 3.x.)

> TCP port for the server. Can be a number between 0 and 65,535. If this number is anything other than `80` (unsecured server) or `443` (secured server), clients must specify a port to access your server. Under UNIX, if the port number is less than `1024`, the server must be started as a root. You can only have one **Port** directive in your **magnus.conf** file.

ProcessLife (UNIX 1.x)

`ProcessLife 128`

(Default value is set during installation.)

> Defines the number of child processes that the server will spawn during its life. Once the number is reached, the server stops the processes and restarts them. This behavior allows the server to free up memory and any resources or memory

leaks. Default is 64. This directive is applicable only for Netscape Server 1.x under UNIX.

RqThrottle (Server 3.x)

`RqThrottle 128`

(Default value is set during installation.)

(In the Server Manager, you can set this directive with the "Maximum Simultaneous Requests:" options from the Server Settings|Performance Tuning menu.)

Specifies the maximum simultaneous requests that the server accepts. It is the number of active requests allowed at one time. The default value for Server 3.0 is 128 requests. Netscape has increased the default value to 512 for Server 3.01 and later. If the maximum number is reached by the server, the server waits until one of the requests is finished. If a client stops a request midway, the server waits 30 seconds or more before timing out. The value you set with this directive specifies the maximum simultaneous requests across multiple virtual servers. The server does not do any load balancing. This directive replaces the **MaxThreads** directive used for Server 2.x. (See also **MaxThreads** and **RqThrottleMinPerSocket**.)

RqThrottleMinPerSocket (Server 3.x)

`RqThrottleMinPerSocket 90`

Specifies an approximate number for the minimum number of threads that wait for an HTTP connection for the server socket. This number is only a suggested number: the actual number of waiting threads may be slightly greater or lesser than the number you specify. The default number is 48. (See also **RqThrottle**.)

RootObject

`RootObject default`

(Default value is set during installation.)

Defines the default server Object in the **obj.conf** file. You can have multiple Objects in **obj.conf**, but you need to name a default Object in **magnus.conf**. This default Object is necessary, because the server must have a place to begin processing a client request. The directives specified in this Object affect the entire server and every request. The Server Manager assumes that `default` is the default Object's name, so try to keep the default Object's name as `default`.

Security

`Security on`

(Default value is set during installation.)

(In Server Manager 2.x, you can choose to have security by setting the "Encryption" option to on from the Encryption|On/Off menu. For Server 3.x, you will find the Encryption On/Off page under Server Preferences|Encryption On/Off. Of course, you need a certificate and key pair file and correct settings for the security to actually work. Otherwise, you will receive an error message.)

Defines whether SSL security is enabled. For Server 2.x, you specify the encryption-related settings for your server from the Server Manager of your server under the Encryption menu. You should not turn off security if the server is set to SSL3 and 128-bit encryption is enabled. Turn the secret key size to 40-bit access (in the Server Manager, through Encryption|Stronger Cipher) before turning off security.

For Server 3.x, you first need to create the certificate and key pair file and specify an alias for them under General Administration's Keys & Certificates Menu. You can then use the alias when enabling encryption.

ServerCert
(See **Certfile**.)

ServerID (Enterprise Server 3.5.1)
`ServerID https-foo`
(Default value is set during installation.)

This new directive allows you to specify the server ID in the **magnus.conf** file. The server ID for Enterprise Server comprises `https` and the name of the server—for example, `https-foo`.

ServerKey
(See **Keyfile**.)

ServerName
`www.foo.com`
(Default value is set during installation.)
(You can set this directive in the Server Manager with the "Server Name:" option from the System Settings|Network Settings menu for Server 2.x or with the Server Preferences|Network Settings menu for Server 3.x.)

Server host name. The domain name defined here is used by the server when it automatically generates a URL. It should be a fully qualified domain name. Clients also use this name to access the server. You should not have more than one `ServerName` in the **magnus.conf** file.

ServerRoot
`#ServerRoot c:/netscape/server/https-foo`
(Default value is set during installation.)

Defines the root directory of the server. This default directive set during installation is "commented out" in the **magnus.conf** file. The server uses **#ServerRoot** as the directive name. You should keep this directive name as is. Unlike other **magnus.conf** directives, the server expects this directive to start with #. If you remove # from the **ServerRoot** directive name, the Server Manager may not be able to function properly. It will report an incorrect usage error.

SSL2

```
SSL2 off
```

Enables Secure Sockets Layer (SSL) version 2 encryption for your server. If you are using the SSL version 2 encryption, then you should enable this directive. You can set this directive to either on or off. This directive works with the **Security** directive; the **Security** directive has precedence over this directive. If **Security** is set to off, then this function is ignored. SSL2 is now superceded by SSL3.

SSL3

```
SSL3 on
```

Enables Secure Sockets Layer (SSL) version 3 encryption for your server. If you are using SSL version 3 encryption, then you should enable this directive. You can set this directive to either on or off. This directive works with the **Security** directive; the **Security** directive has precedence over this directive. If **Security** is set to off, this function is ignored. (SSL3 is supported by Netscape Navigator 3.0 and later.)

SSL3Ciphers

```
SSL3Ciphers +rsa_rc4_128_md5, +rsa_3des_sha,\
+rsa_des_sha, +rsa_rc4_40_md5,\
+rsa_rc2_40_md5, -rsa_null_md5
```

Determines the SSL3 ciphers for the server. (See **Ciphers** for more detail.)

SSLClientAuth

```
SSL3ClientAuth on
```

(For Server 3.x, you can set this directive in the Server Manager under Server Preferences|Encryption Preferences, by selecting the option for "Require client certificates (regardless of access control):".)

Determines whether SSL3 (client certificate) will supersede any other ACL type you might have defined. The value can be either on or off. If set to on, it requires SSL3 client authentication for all requests. This directive is not necessary if you plan to use client authentication with access control. If it is set to on, only clients that have already been mapped to a certificate will have access to the site. (SSL3 is supported only under Netscape Navigator 3.0 and later.)

SSLSessionTimeout

```
SSLSessionTimeout 100
```

Sets the length of SSL2 session caching (in seconds). If it takes longer than the number defined for the cached SSL2 session to be validated, it becomes invalid. The default number is 100. If this directive is used, the value of seconds is silently constrained to between 5 and 100 seconds, inclusive.

SSL3SessionTimeout

`SSL3SessionTimeout 3600`

> Sets the length of SSL3 session caching (in seconds). If it takes longer than the number defined for the cached SSL3 session to be validated, it becomes invalid. Default number is `86400` (that is, 24 hours). If this directive is used, the value of seconds is silently constrained to between 5 and `86400` seconds, inclusive.

StackSize (Server 3.x)

`StackSize 256`

> Determines the stack size used by the server. For Server 3.x, Netscape has reduced the size of the default stack to 64 KB. Previously, stack size for Server 2.0 was `256` KB. A small stack size uses less memory, reducing the size of memory used by the server threads and your NSAPI program. If your NSAPI program requires a larger stack, you should increase the stack size. The increase of the stack size affects all server threads. To minimize the effect of the stack size on server memory, increase this number only when it is needed.

TerminateTimeout (Server 3.x)

`TerminateTimeout 10`

> Sets the time that the server waits before closing outstanding connections (timing out). The value is in seconds. Default is set to 3 seconds. During server shutdown, the server does not take any new connections and waits to close any existing connections based on the value you set for **TerminateTimeout**. The server terminates only after the time specified in TerminateTimeout is over.

User (UNIX)

`User http`

(Set during installation, but may not appear in that **magnus.conf** file.)
(For Server 2.x, you can set this directive in the Server Manager with the "Server User" option from the System Settings|Network Settings menu. Under Server 3.x, you can specify the user in the Server Manager under Server Preferences|Network Settings.)

> Operating system's user account that the server runs on. Under UNIX, the user name should be eight characters or less (login name of a user account). The user account (for example, `http`) must have read access to all server directories, read and write access to the log directory, and execute access for programs (for example, CGI programs). It may also require other privileges, such as access to the shared files between different Netscape Servers or to a specific program, such as a database that the server uses. To protect your server, you create a specific user account for the server.
>
> In UNIX, if the server is started by the operating system's `superuser` (`root`), the server binds to the specified server port and changes the user ID to this `User`. Otherwise, this directive is ignored. If there is no **User** directive, the server starts with the user account, which started the server. Under UNIX, if you

intend to use nobody as the user account, make sure that the user ID for nobody is greater than 0. If your operating system uses a number less than 0, Netscape will fail during installation.

The default user account on NT is the LocalSystem (NT 3.51) or the System Account (NT 4.0). You should set the user in the Control Panel under Services for your server (for example, Netscape Enterprise Server 3.5.1 [foo]). Choose Startup and select "This Account" under "Log On As:" to input the user account. Do not set a **User** directive in the **magnus.conf** file. Under NT, the **User** directive does not specify the specific user, which the server runs as. (See the section User Account for the System Server in Chapter 2 for more details.)

Note ▶

Under NT, the server works as a service that normally logs on with system account privileges. When you change the user information in the Server Manager for Server 2.x or through the **magnus.conf** file, it does not affect the user as defined under Services in NT. The user information in the NT Services and the information in **magnus.conf** are not directly related. A setting in one does not automatically change the setting in the other. You should modify the user account of your server in the Control Panel, not the **magnus.conf** file. The Server Manager for Server 3.x no longer allows you to set a user account for the NT server.

Appendix B

`obj.conf`
Directive Functions

Note ▶

A number of directive functions, such as **image-switch,** discussed in this appendix are not accessible through the Server Manager. If you add these functions manually to the `obj.conf` file, they may appear as Unknown Settings in the Server Manager under Server Preferences|View Server Settings. In other words, the Server Manager does not recognize these functions. This information under View Server settings does not mean that the functions will not operate properly.

This appendix describes the built-in server directive functions used in the `obj.conf` file. We have included all of the unique built-in server functions that provide general support for the server and ones relevant to the server features covered in this book—that is, CGI, WinCGI, ShellCGI, and WAI.

Other features of Netscape Server also use server directive functions. When you enable these features from the Server Manager, a number of server directive functions are added to the `obj.conf` file. For example, if you enable Server-side JavaScript (also called LiveWire in Server 2.x) from Programs|Server Side JavaScript with Server Manager 3.x, the server adds specific directive functions needed for Server-side Java-Script. These functions initialize and enable the use of the feature for the server. For Enterprise Server 3.5.1, these special server features include Server-side JavaScript (LiveWire), Server-side Java, Servlets, agents, search, Web Publishing, and AutoCatalog (catalog agent). Support for Servlets was first added with Enterprise Server 3.5.1.

The server directive functions for these features are loaded with the **Init** function **load-modules**. The server first loads the shared library or dynamic linked library (DLL) needed for these features. The functions are included in the library. For example, for NT, the DLLs are `httpdlw.dll` for Server-side JavaScript, `libsjava.dll` for Server-side Java applets and Servlets, `agents.dll` for agents, `nsir.dll` for search, `content_mgr.dll` for Web Publishing, and `rdm.dll` for AutoCatalog. An example of **load-modules** used for a server feature is the following directive for Server-side Java and Java Servlets from one NT Enterprise Server 3.5.1 `obj.conf` file:

```
Init fn="load-modules"
 funcs="java-init,java-run,java-find-applet,java-run-applet"
 shlib="c:/netscape/server/plugins/java/bin/libsjava.dll"
```

These Enterprise Server features also include their own initialization functions (**Init** functions): **livewireInit** for Server-side JavaScript, **java-init** for Server-side Java applets and Servlets, **ns-agentInit** for agents, **es-search-init** for search, **CM_Init** for Web Publishing (content management), and **rdm-init** for AutoCatalog. These **Init** functions should come after the appropriate **load-modules** function.

Enterprise Server 3.x also includes a special library (for example, `libsjboot.dll` for NT) and **Init** function, **SJavaBootInit**, for loading and initializing the various Java class libraries used by the server. The Java classes include classes for Server-side Java and Netscape Internet Service Broker (a CORBA ORB).

All of the server features include at least one **Service** function that enables the use of the specific feature. These **Service** functions often provide the plug between your application and the server. The main **Service** functions are **livewireService** for Server-side JavaScript, **java-run-applet** for Server-side Java applets, **java-run** for Servlets, **ns-agentCmdHandler** for agents, **es-search** for search, and **rdm-service** for AutoCatalog. Web Publishing includes a number of different **Service** functions based on the specific method of the request (for example, **CM_MkDir** for `MKDIR` and **CM_Put** for `PUT`).

Because AutoCatalog and Web Publishing apply to all documents of the server and should be enabled as part of the default processing of the client requests, their service functions are added to the `default` Object in the `obj.conf` files.

Other features are invoked through a specific URI path. They are identified through a **NameTrans** directive function by the server, which determines the specific URI path for the feature and its respective server Object. The server then looks in the specific Object for the server directive functions needed to process the request. The **Service** functions are declared inside the appropriate Object, similar to the workings of other server features covered in this book (for example, as in CGI and WinCGI). Unlike CGI, WinCGI, ShellCGI, and WAI, however, Netscape uses a special **NameTrans** function for these features: **livewireNameTrans** for Server-side JavaScript, **java-find-applet** for Server-side Java applet, **agent_name_trans** for agents, and **es-search-nametrans** for search. The Objects for each feature are `LiveWire` for Server-side JavaScript, `server-applets` for Server-side Java applets, `agents` for server agents, and `search` for search. You can find these Objects after the `default` Object in the `obj.conf` file.

Each of these Enterprise Server features may include additional, unique server functions. For example, agent uses **ns_agentType** as an **ObjectType** function. They may also use the standard built-in server functions. For example, Server-side JavaScript uses **basic-auth** and **require-auth** for authentication.

The following code gives examples of the directive functions added to the **obj.conf** file for two specific features, Web Publishing and Server-side JavaScript. This information is from the author's **obj.conf** file of Enterprise Server 3.5.1 for NT.

Server-Side JavaScript

```
Init fn="load-modules"
  funcs="livewireInit,livewireNameTrans,livewireService"
  shlib="c:/netscape/server/bin/https/httpdlw.dll"

Init fn="livewireInit"
  objects="c:/netscape/server/https-foo/config/jsa.conf"

<Object name="default">
. . .
NameTrans fn="livewireNameTrans" name="LiveWire"
. . .
</Object>

<Object name="LiveWire">
AuthTrans fn="basic-auth" userfn="simple-userdb"
  userdb="c:/netscape/server/admserv/admpw"
  auth-type="basic"
PathCheck fn="require-auth"
  realm="LiveWire Administration"
  path="(*appmgr*|*dbadmin*)" auth-type="basic"
Service fn="LivewireService"
</Object>
```

Web Publishing

```
Init fn="load-modules" NativeThread="no"
  funcs="CM_Init,CM_Delete,CM_Index,CM_Get,CM_Put,CM_Move,\
CM_MkDir,CM_Post,CM_Copy,CM_Edit,CM_Unedit,CM_Save,\
CM_Lock,CM_Unlock,CM_RevLabel,CM_RevLog,CM_RevAdd,\
CM_RevNum,CM_SetAttr,CM_GetAttr,CM_GetAttrNames,\
CM_GetPS,CM_StartRev,CM_StopRev"
  shlib="c:/netscape/server/plugins/content_mgr/\
bin/content_mgr.dll"

Init fn="CM_Init"
  webconfig="c:/netscape/server/https-foo/config/webpub.conf"

<Object name="default">
. . .
```

```
Service fn="CM_StopRev" method="STOPREV"
Service fn="CM_StartRev" method="STARTREV"
Service fn="CM_GetPS" method="GETPROPERTIES"
Service fn="CM_GetAttrNames" method="GETATTRIBUTENAMES"
Service fn="CM_GetAttr" method="GETATTRIBUTE"
Service fn="CM_SetAttr" method="SETATTRIBUTE"
Service fn="CM_RevNum" method="REVNUM"
Service fn="CM_RevAdd" method="REVADD"
Service fn="CM_RevLog" method="REVLOG"
Service fn="CM_RevLabel" method="REVLABEL"
Service fn="CM_Unlock" method="UNLOCK"
Service fn="CM_Lock" method="LOCK"
Service fn="CM_Save" method="SAVE"
Service fn="CM_Unedit" method="UNEDIT"
Service fn="CM_Edit" method="EDIT"
Service fn="CM_Copy" method="COPY"
Service fn="CM_Post" method="POST"
Service fn="CM_MkDir" method="MKDIR"
Service fn="CM_Move" method="MOVE"
Service fn="CM_Put" method="PUT"
Service fn="CM_Get" method="(GET|HEAD)"
Service fn="CM_Index" method="INDEX"
Service fn="CM_Delete" method="DELETE"
. . .
</Object>
```

> **Note ▶**
>
> Web Publishing, a new feature of Server 3.x, includes a different set of server directive functions than Remote File Manipulation. To allow clients to publish documents for Server 2.x, you use Remote File Manipulation. You can also enable Remote File Manipulation for Server 3.x. For example, for Server 3.5.1, you can enable Remote File Manipulation from Content Management|Remote File Manipulation in the Server Manager.
>
> You should not enable both Web Publishing and Remote File Manipulation for Server 3.x at the same time. The preferred method of enabling client manipulation of documents on Server 3.x is Web Publishing. Web Publishing includes a number of additional features not supported with Remote File Manipulation. These additional features require their own **Service** functions. The Web Publishing **Service** functions replace similar functions used for Remote File Manipulation. Functions **CM_Delete**, **CM_Index**, **CM_MkDir**, **CM_Move**, and **CM_Put** are used in place of **delete-file**, **list-dir**, **make-dir**, **remove-dir**, **rename-file**, and **upload-file**. There are also additional **Service** functions for Web Publishing, such as **CM_GetAttr** and **CM_GetAttrNames**. All Web Publishing **Service** functions begin with **CM_**.
>
> Also, note that the **remove-file** function listed in Netscape's documentation for Server 2.x should be **delete-file**.

It is unlikely that you will need to change the directive functions for these Enterprise Server features in the **obj.conf** file. Instead, you can use the Server Manager to make your specific modifications. The changes you may want to make should be limited to updating the different paths used by the feature—for example, the path for the shared library or DLL or the URI path in the **NameTrans** function.

A full discussion of these Enterprise Server features and their uses is beyond the scope of this book. You should refer to the Netscape Server manuals, the Server Manager's help feature, or the documents under Netscape's developer site, DevEdge Online (`http://developer.netscape.com/library/documentation/index.html`), for more information.

The Init Functions

For Server 3.x, all **Init** functions can include a `LateInit` parameter. Setting this parameter to `yes` (`LateInit="yes"`) means that the **Init** function will be executed after the server process is forked. A `no` value means that the **Init** function will be executed before the server process is forked.

acl-set-default-method (Server 3.x)

```
Init fn=acl-set-default-method method=SSL
```

Sets the default method for any ACL that does not specify a method. ACLs are access control lists that specify the access to a specific server resource. They are contained in the server ACL files, which are named in the **magnus.conf** file with the **ACLFile** directive. The default method is `Basic`. With basic authentication, the client is required to enter a user name and password before accessing a requested resource.

Parameter: <u>method</u> (Specifies a default method for any ACL that does not specify a method.)

cache-init (Server 2.x and 3.x)

For Server 2.x:

```
Init fn=cache-init cache-size=1024 mmap-max=20000
```

For Server 3.x:

```
Init fn=cache-init MaxNumberOfCachedFiles=1024
```

Enables file caching and designates its settings. File caching improves the server performance. You can fine-tune these numbers to get the best results. When considering the size, include all the static HTML, image, and sound files, but not the dynamically created pages or data. For best results, set the cache size to a number less than your RAM. The parameters for this directive have changed for Server 3.x.

Parameters for Server 2.x: <u>cache-size</u> (number of items—that is, URIs—in the cache. It can be a number between 32 and 32,768, inclusive. This number should be greater than the number of static HTML pages. It is the number of pages, not the size of the memory. The default is 512. Because CGI and NSAPI programs return dynamic information, you should not include them in the size of the cache.); **mmap-max** (Maximum amount of memory in kilobytes for mapping in memory of your document files. These files are kept open by the server. This parameter can be a number between 512 and 524,288 [512 * 1,024], inclusive. This number can be the number of your static HTML pages times their sizes. The default is 10,000 KB.); **disable** (Disables caching. Set this parameter to `true` to disable caching.)

Parameters for Server 3.x: **MaxNumberOfCachedFiles** (Similar to the `cache-size` parameter, it specifies the number of cache entries, or URIs. This directive maps a URI to a specific static file on your machine. With this parameter, you indirectly specify the number of files that are cached.); **MaxTotalCacheFileSize** (Maximum amount of memory in kilobytes used to cache the document files. It can be a number between 512 and 524,288, inclusive. This number can be the number of your static HTML pages times their sizes. If the maximum size of the cached files is reached, no additional file is cached. The default is 10,000 KB.); **MaxCacheFileSize** (Maximum size of a cached file. If the size of the file in your site is greater than the size specified here, the file is not cached. The default size is 537,600 bytes. With this parameter, you can limit the type of files, which are cached, based on their size.); **PollInterval** (Maximum amount of time that can pass before the server checks the disk again to make sure that the file has not changed. Default value is 5 seconds. You can set this value to zero seconds, to make sure the file is checked for every request.); **disable** (Disables caching. Set this parameter to `true` to disable caching.)

Bug Report ▶

Under Server 2.0, file caching did not function properly. You should set **cache-init** to `disable` if you are using Server 2.0. File caching should work properly under Server 2.01. You should upgrade the server to 2.01 to take advantage of file caching and so as to use this **Init** function.

---

cindex-init

```
Init fn=cindex-init widths=25,2,2,30 opts=i
  ignore=*.secret icon-uri=/myicon
```

Sets the global settings for fancy indexing (formatted presentation of directory and file listings with graphics). When the user requests a directory that does not have a default index file, this function sets how fancy indexing, once enabled, will work. File names starting with a period (.) are ignored. `/mc-icons` is the default location of the GIF images for the file types and directory. (Usually Netscape shares all icons under one directory. It links any reference to either the `/mc-icons` or `/ns-icons` directory to this shared directory, (`<server root>/ns-icons`, using the **NameTrans** function **pfx2dir**.) Binary files do not appear with the `binary.gif` icon. Instead, they appear as an `unknown.gif` icon. The settings in this function are used by the **Service** function **index-common**, which returns the HTML page with the fancy indexing to the client. (See also **index-common**.)

   Parameters: <u>widths</u> (Width for each column displayed—that is, Name, Last-modified, Size, and Description. The default is `widths=22,1,1,33`. Use a comma-separated list of numbers for the width of columns. A zero width should disable the column.); <u>**opts**</u> (Optional settings—that is, `i` links all icons, `s` adds the HTML title, `<TITLE>`, of the files to the description column.); <u>**ignore**</u> (Defines which files to ignore. The default setting ignores all file names starting with a period. You can also use wildcards.); <u>**icon-uri**</u> (Points to your alternative icon path. By default, the icons for the fancy indexing are found under the `/mc-icons` directory. You should also specify a **pfx2dir** function in the **obj.conf** file that sets the new physical path of the icons.)

Bug Report ▶

The optional parameter `opts` does not work correctly. When using the `s` option, if the file is larger than 255 bytes, it causes a server crash when the server attempts to read the title of the HTML page. The `i` parameter is the default setting, so having it does not matter. Moreover, although documented, the description information in the fancy indexing does not seem to work.

---

dns-cache-init (Server 2.x and 3.x)

```
Init fn=dns-cache-init cache-size=2048 expires=300
```

(You can set this directive in the Server Manager with the "Cache DNS Entries?" option from the System Settings|Performance Tuning menu for Server 2.x and with the Server Preferences|Performance Tuning menu for Server 3.x.)

   Enables DNS caching. The client `hostname` (DNS) and IP address are cached for quicker retrieval. You can define the maximum size of the cache and the time when the information will expire. You must have DNS enabled to use this function. (See **DNS** in Appendix A.)

   Parameters: <u>**cache-size**</u> (Defines the maximum number of DNS entries [IP address/DNS name look-up] that are cached. It can be a number from 32 to 32,768, inclusive. The default number is 1024); <u>**expires**</u> (Lifetime of the DNS information in seconds. It can be from 1 second to 1 year. The default is 1200 seconds.)

---

flex-init

```
Init fn="flex-init"
 access="c:/netscape/server/https-foo/logs/access"
 format.access="%Ses->client.ip% - \
%Req->vars.auth-user% [%SYSDATE%] \
\"%Req->reqpb.clf-request%\" \
```

```
%Req->srvhdrs.clf-status% \
%Req->srvhdrs.content-length%"
```
(Default value set at installation.)

(In the Server Manager, you can set most **flex-init** options in the "Log Preferences" option under the Server Status|Log Preferences menu.)

Defines the location of the flexible log file and the format of the data that will be placed in the file. The server then opens this file and keeps it open until the server is shut down. This function works with the **flex-log** function in the **AddLog** directive (see **flex-log**). **flex-log** does the actual logging of the request transaction, but you need an **Init** function to open a file once, at the start of the server. The flexible log format, unlike the common log format, allows flexibility in extending or removing information from the log file (see **init-clf**). You specify what is going to be logged. There already should be a **flex-init** function in your **obj.conf** file. Netscape uses this function to specify the access log file. You can also have multiple **flex-init** functions in the **obj.conf** file. The Flex-init and Formatting Log Files section, later in this Appendix, shows the various options for formatting the log file using the format.<*name*> parameter.

Parameters: <u>*<name>*</u> (Points to the name and location of the log file. The *name* you specify here, as part of <*name*>=<*file location*>, is also used in **AddLog** function **flex-log** as the value of its name parameter. *name* should be unique, but does not have to be the same as the file name. This method of naming allows multiple **AddLog** functions to work with one log file defined in the **Init** function. You specify the path for a log file once in this parameter. It also allows multiple files to use the same format.<*name*> parameter as long as *name* is the same. Use the complete system path to point to the actual location of the access log file. You can specify multiple *name* parameters with **flex-init**; <u>**format.*<name>***</u> defines the format of the data placed in the log file; <u>**no-format-str.access**</u> is used only with Server 3.x. This parameter can apply to multiple log files when the same *name* parameter is used for different files. See the Flex-init and Formatting Log Files section, for various formatting options. This parameter specifies whether the format string should be included in the log file. Normally, the log file begins with a format string, specifying the format of the information in the log file. The proxy server's log analyzer requires the format string in the log file. Other third-party log analyzers may not require this string at the top of the file, so you may use this parameter to exclude the format string from the file. Set this parameter to yes to exclude the format string or to no to include the format string.)

IIOPinit (Server 3.x)

```
Init fn=IIOPinit LateInit="yes"
```
(When you enable WAI services in the Server Manager from Programs|WAI Management, this function, along with other IIOP server functions [**IIOPexec** and **IIOPNameService**] are added to the **obj.conf** file.)

Initializes the ORB, BOA, and Naming Service for Server 3.x. **IIOPinit** also has a number of parameters: ORBagentaddr, ORBagentport, ORBsendbufsize, ORBrcvbufsize, ORBmbufsize, ORBshmsize, OAipaddr, OAport, OAsendbufsize, OArcvbufsize, OAshm, and OAnoshm. These parameters determine various important settings regarding osagent, ORB, BOA, and so on.

Similar to other specific add-on server applications (such as Server-side JavaScript), the specific WAI server functions—**IIOPinit**, **IIOPexec**, and **IIOPNameService**—are loaded as server functions through a shared library or DLL at the start of the server using the **Init** function **load-modules**. **IIOPinit** should come after the **load-modules** function that loads the shared library or DLL (for example, ONEiiop10.dll). (For more information on **IIOPinit** and other WAI-related server functions, see the section Changes to the **obj.conf** File in Chapter 13.) (See also **IIOPexec** and **IIOPNameService**.)

Parameters: (See the section IIOPinit Parameters in Chapter 13 for the specific parameters.)

init-cgi

```
Init fn=init-cgi timeout=120 SOURCE=/data/data.txt
```
Sets a time limit and additional environment variables for your CGI programs. This function also ensures that all environment variables are loaded for your CGI program. (See also **send-cgi**, **send-wincgi**, and **send-shellcgi**.)

Parameters: **timeout** (Number of seconds that the server waits for the CG output before terminating it. The default timeout is five minutes. This parameter is optional.); **load-server-vars** (Tells the server to load all environment variables. Under Server 2.x, the server does not export all system environment variables to the CGI process. Add this parameter if you have an environment variable that is not being exported. The value for this parameter is true or false. This parameter is optional.); **[environment variable name]="[value]"** (You can pass any additional name=value parameter as an environment variable to your CGI program. You can also have multiple name=value parameters.)

init-clf

```
Init fn=init-clf
 global="c:/netscape/server/https-foo/logs/access"
```
Uses the Common Log Format (CLF—the standard formatting of the access log file) to record access information. The server then opens this file and keeps it open until the server is shut down. This function works with the **common-log** function of the **AddLog** directive. You specify the location of the log file with this function. **common-log** does the actual logging of the request transaction. You also use this function with **AddLog** functions **record-keysize** and **record-useragent**. You can include multiple files with the same **init-clf** function.

Unlike with **flex-init**, you should call this function only once in the **obj.conf** file. If multiple **init-clf** functions are included, the last **init-clf** function is used. If you wish to have a more flexible log file, use the **flex-init** function. (See also **flex-init**.)

Parameters: **_<name>_** (Sets the location of the log file. Although _name_ should be unique, it does not need to be the same as the file name. `global` is the default _name_. `access` is the name of the server's default log file. The _name_ you specify here, as part of `<name>=<file location>`, should also be used in **AddLog** function **common-log** as the value of its `name` parameter. This method of naming allows multiple **AddLog** functions to work with one log file defined in the **Init** function. You also need to use an **Init** function to open a file once at the start of the server. Use the complete system path to point to the actual location of the log file. You can specify multiple _name_ parameters (log files) with the same **init-clf** function).

Note ▶

In referring to the formatting of the common log file (CLF), Netscape's documentation uses Common Log Format, Common Logfile Format, and Common Log File interchangeably.

---

init-uhome (UNIX)

```
Init fn=init-uhome pwfile=/etc/passwd
```

(In the Server Manager, you can choose Load Entire Database on Startup from Content Management|User Document Directories menu.)

Loads specifications of the user's home directories into internal hash tables for faster access. You can also point to a different password file, such as a password file you have created. Lines in the `passwd` file should have the following format:

```
username:<name>:<password>:groupid:<ID>:homedir:<dir>.
```

Parameter: _pwfile_ (Points to the location of the full system's file path. Default is `/etc/passwd`.)

Warning ▶

If you allow users to use their UNIX login to set up and maintain their own content under Server 2.x for UNIX (for example, under `http://www.foo.com/~userx`), you should load the entire user database on server start-up. Otherwise, this option may not work properly.

---

load-modules

```
Init fn="load-modules"
  funcs="livewireInit,livewireNameTrans,livewireService"
  shlib="C:/netscape/server/bin/https/httpdlw.dll"
```

(When you install Server-side JavaScript, Server-side Java applets, Java Servlets, or WAI programs from the Programs menu in the Server Manager, these programs' central functions are loaded with the **load-modules** function.)

Loads the shared library or the DLL. It also specifies which functions should be defined and used by the server. You use this function to load your NSAPI server applications. With Server 3.x, you can also specify whether the application will use user- or kernel-level threads.

Parameters: <u>**funcs**</u> (Name of the functions defined in the shared library that are called by the server. Separate each function with a comma and no space.); <u>**shlib**</u> (Location of the DLL or shared library.); <u>**NativeThread**</u> (A new parameter for Server 3.x. Netscape Server 3.x supports both kernel- and user-level thread models. You can specify the server to use user-level threads by setting this parameter to no. If this parameter is set to yes (the default setting), the application uses kernel-level threads. User-level threads provide the best performance. Your program must not use any native thread calls, if you set this parameter to no. For more information on threads, see Chapter 11.)

---

load-types

```
Init fn=load-types mime-types=mime.types
  local-types=/special/local.types
```

(Default value set at installation.)

Points to the **mime.types** file. The server uses the file mapping information in the **mime.types** file to associate a specific file extension with a MIME (Multipurpose Internet Mail Extensions) type. It maps a file's extension to the file's content-type, content-encoding, and content-language. It is how, for instance, the server recognizes a `*.gif` file as an image file. This function should be included in your **obj.conf** file. **load-types** must be declared before the server can use the function **type-by-extension**.

Parameters: <u>**mime-types**</u> (Points to the location of the MIME types file. The default location is the `<server path>/<server ID>/`config directory. Use a full path to the file or a relative path to the config directory for the location of the **mime.types** file. See also mime.types in Chapter 2 for more details.); <u>**local-type**</u> (Points to the location of an optional MIME types file for your local server only. If you want your server to share a global MIME types file with other servers and have its own local MIME types file, you can use this parameter.)

pool-init (Server 2.x and 3.x)

```
Init fn=pool-init disable=true
```

Supports memory allocation pooling. With pooled memory, the server automatically cleans up all memory allocated by **MALLOC**, **REALLOC**, and **STRDUP** when the request is completed. You can enable or disable this feature. Enabling this feature improves the performance of the server. **pool-init** cleans up only the memory that was allocated during the processing of a request. As **Init** functions are run before any request, they use persistent memory allocation. Even when **pool-init** is defined, and you use **MALLOC** or similar operations, the **Init** functions still use persistent memory allocation.

Parameters: <u>disable</u> (Allows you to disable memory pooling. Values include `true` and `false`. The default value is `false`.); <u>freesize</u> (Maximum size of the free block list in bytes. The value should not be greater than `1,048,576`.)

Warning ▶

pool-init affects any NSAPI code compiled with Server 2.0 or later header files. With **pool-init** enabled, the server will automatically clean up all memory allocations allocated by **MALLOC**, **REALLOC**, and **STRDUP** when the request is completed. Thus you do not need to free any memory. Freeing memory that is already freed, or attempting to use a memory space that is already deallocated (freed), can break your code. To use persistent memory allocation, use the **PERM_*** version of these functions: **PERM_MALLOC**, **PERM_REALLOC**, **PERM_STRDUP**, and **PERM_FREE**.

---

user-defined

```
Init fn=initialize-myfunction file=/code/mystuff.txt
```

Write your own **Init** function and pass it any `[name]="[value]"` parameter you wish. **java-init** and **livewireInit** are two examples of specialized **Init** functions written by Netscape.

Parameter: any `[name]="[value]"` parameter set by you and passed on to the function.

flex-init and Formatting Log Files

The **flex-init** function's format parameters allow you to customize the content and format of the access log file. Unlike the common log file (the older standard of log files) with its predefined format, you can change the flexible file. You can format, add, and remove the information in the flexible log file. Adding extended formatting characters improves the readability of the data. **flex-init** works in conjunction with the **AddLog** directive function **flex-log** to allow you to define and format the access log file. The **flex-init** file allows for a customized access log file, whereas **init-clf** uses the predefined CLF. For more information on log files, see the AddLog section in Chapter 2. This section describes the parameters of the flexible log file.

You specify the format of the data that will be logged with the `format.<name>` parameter. With the **flex-init** function, you create a template for the line of data that is logged in the access log file. This template includes the names of variables (as in `name-value`) whose values will be reflected in the log file. The names of the template variables are enclosed inside percent signs (`%`). You can also include other formatting characters (such as, `[`, `]`, and `-`) for readability purposes. The `name-value` pairs are usually typical server variables, such as client `IP=1.2.3.4` or `hostname=www.foo.com`. Netscape does not use the CGI environment variable naming conventions. Instead, these template variable names are the Netscape Server variables based on HTTP standards. (You use these same variables in your NSAPI programs.) For example, in the format string, `Ses->client.ip` holds the client IP name. Its value is the actual IP address that is, in turn, logged in the log file. `Ses` refers to the server data structure `Session`, and `req` refers to the `Request` data structure.[1] (See Chapter 5 for more information on the `Session` and `Request` data structures.)

The complete string of the **flex-init** `format.<name>` parameter needs to be inside quotes. Some variables inside this parameter may also require quotes around them, because the values could include spaces, as in user-agent. You need to use the escape character backslash (`\`) with these quotes, because you are adding quotes within the format string quotes (for example, `\"Req->reqb.clf-request%\"`).

When the server is installed, it usually installs a flex log file as your default access log file. The format of this flex log file is the same as the CLF. The following is an example of the server's default flex log file's format definition:

```
format.access="%Ses->client.ip% - \
%Req->vars.auth-user% [%SYSDATE%] \
"%Req->reqpb.clf-request%\" \
%Req->srvhdrs.clf-status% %Req->srvhdrs.content-length%"
```

This code uses CLF, which is used by many Web servers and various log analysis utilities. (See the World Wide Web Consortium's "Logging Control In W3C httpd," `http://www.w3.org/hypertext/WWW/Daemon/User/Config/Logging.html`, for more details.) You can use the Server Manager to customize the flexible log file and define it as your default log file. When you take this step, you modify the information, which will appear in the access log file. Not all the parameters you can add, however, are listed in the options found under the Server Manager's Server Status|Log Preferences menu. For example, the extensions `%Req->headers.accept%`, `%Req->headers.if-modified-since%`, and `%Req->headers.authorization%` are not included. You can add these options to the **obj.conf** file manually. Be careful when you make changes to data that are logged into the log file. Some third-party log

---

1. `name-value` pairing as defined by Hypertext Transfer Protocol (HTTP) is the cornerstone of many procedures for HTTP and for your programming. The `name-value` pairs are accessible through parameter blocks in pblock, `Request`, or `Session` server data structures (except for `%SYSDATE%`, which is the system date and is not defined in the server's parameter blocks).

analysis utilities expect CLF. They will not work properly if the information is changed. This situation is particularly the case if you modify the first six default template variables that are specified by the server.

Table B-1 lists all the variables you can use to customize your flexible log file.

Table B-1 Variables for Customizing Flexible Log File

NAME OF THE VALUE IN **FLEX-INIT**	WHAT IT REFERENCES	EXAMPLE OUTPUT
DEFAULT COMMON LOG FORMAT		
`%Ses->client.ip%`	Client IP address (host name)	`1.2.3.4`
`%Req->vars.auth-user%`	Authenticated user name	`Joe`
`%SYSDATE%`	System date, time of request	`03/Sep/1996:12:50:55 -0700`
`\"%Req->reqpb.clf-request%\"`	Client's full request	`GET /appmgr/images/Banner.gif HTTP/1.0`
`%Req->srvhdrs.clf-status%`	Status code server returned	`200`
`%Req->srvhdrs.content-length%`	Content length in bytes of the data sent to the client	`21661`
ADDED EXTENSIONS		
`\"%Req->headers.referer%\"`	HTTP header, referrer (page where the request came from, previous page of client)	`http://<server name>/appmgr/banner.html`
`\"%Req->headers.user-agent%\"`	HTTP header, user-agent (browser type of the client)	`Mozilla/4.04 [en] (WinNT; I)`
`%Req->reqpb.method%`	Request method used by the client (such as GET, POST, or HEAD)	`GET`
`%Req->reqpb.uri%`	URI path (the virtual path of the requested resource)	`/appmgr/images/banner.gif`
`%Req->reqpb.query%`	Query string sent by the client (what comes after "?" in the URI path used in the GET method)	`stuff=supplies&sql=1`
`\"%Req->reqpb.protocol%\"`	Protocol used by the client	`HTTP/1.0`
EXTENSIONS NOT INCLUDED IN SERVER MANAGER'S OPTIONS		
`%Req->headers.accept%`	HTTP header, accept (MIME type accepted by the browser)	`image/gif, image/x-xbitmap, image/jpeg, image/pjpeg`
`%Req->headers.if-modified-since%`	HTTP header, if-modified-since (specifies that the request should be sent only if it has been modified since the given date) (Magically, the character length appears as well.)	`Tuesday, 03-Sep-96 20:55:20 GMT; length=382`

Table B-1 Variables for Customizing Flexible Log File (*continued*)

NAME OF THE VALUE IN **FLEX-INIT**	WHAT IT REFERENCES	EXAMPLE OUTPUT
EXTENSIONS NOT INCLUDED IN SERVER MANAGER'S OPTIONS		
`%Req->headers.date%` (rather uncommon)	HTTP header, `date` (date and time when the message originated)	`Tuesday, 03/Sep/1996 20:55:00 GMT`
`%Req->headers.authorization%`	HTTP header, `authorization` (type of authentication and encoded user name password)	`Basic YWRtaW46Z3JhdmU=`

Below are a few examples of the formatted information taken from one access file. All of the options in Table B-1 were included in the **flex-init** format parameter. When the output is NULL, a dash replaces the data. These lines will not be wrapped in the log file.

```
1.2.3.4 - suzy [11/Sep/1996:19:40:40 -0700] "GET
/appmgr/images/banner.gif HTTP/1.0" 200 21661
"http://www.foo.com/appmgr/banner.html" "Mozilla/3.0Gold
(WinNT; I)" GET /appmgr/images/banner.gif - "HTTP/1.0"
image/gif, image/x-xbitmap, image/jpeg, image/pjpeg  - "-"
Basic c3V6eTpjaGV1c2U=

1.2.3.4 - - [11/Sep/1996:19:51:37 -0700] "GET
/database.frm?stuff=supplies&sql=1 HTTP/1.0" 200 -
"http://www.foo.com/odbctest.html" "Mozilla/3.0Gold
(WinNT; I)" GET /database.frm stuff=supplies&sql=1
"HTTP/1.0" image/gif, image/x-xbitmap, image/jpeg,
image/pjpeg, */* - "-" -

1.2.3.4 - - [12/Sep/1996:02:53:09 -0700] "GET /title.gif
HTTP/1.0" 304 0 "http://www.foo.com/" "Mozilla/3.0Gold
(WinNT; I)" GET /title.gif - "HTTP/1.0" image/gif,
image/x-xbitmap, image/jpeg, image/pjpeg  Monday,
24-Jun-96 21:36:04 GMT; length=44263 "-" -
```

The AuthTrans Functions

basic-auth

```
AuthTrans fn=basic-auth userfn=ntauth userdb=NT
  auth-type=basic
```

> Allows you to write your own authentication function. Netscape documentation for Server 2.0 states that this function is obsolete and has been superseded by **basic-ncsa**. Actually, **basic-auth** is the way you can write your own user-defined

function to process basic authentication. You cannot write your own function using **basic-ncsa**. In fact, Netscape Server-side JavaScript (LiveWire) uses **basic-auth**. With **basic-auth**, you can call a user-defined function to authenticate the client. You normally use this function in conjunction with a **PathCheck** function, such as **require-auth**. Under Server 3.x, you should use the Access Control API to write your authentication program instead of using **basic-auth**. (See also **require-auth**.)

Parameters: <u>userfn</u> (User-defined function name—the name of your function that will authenticate the user. Your function must already be loaded with the **Init** function **load-modules**.); <u>auth-type</u> (Type of authentication to be used. Currently only `basic` is used.); <u>userdb</u> (If you want to use the default user files, such as a DBM file, this function can point to the database's location. It is not required to reference such a file. In the **AuthTrans** example listed above, `userdb` is used only as a marker to identify the type of authentication file. In this case, NT's internal user database is used and `userdb` does not actually point to a user database. `usrdb` works in conjunction with the `userfn` parameter.); <u>groupdb</u> (Path to the group database file. You use this parameter in conjunction with the `groupfn` parameter. For example, the NCSA-style group file is a text file with each line as `group:user1 user2 . . . usern`. Each user is separated by a space. This parameter is optional.); <u>groupfn</u> (Similarly to `userdb`, you can also write your own group management function. This function can then reference the file pointed to by the `groupdb` parameter. This parameter is optional); **_[user-defined parameters]_** (any number of `[name]="[value]"` parameters passed to your function. `userdb` in this example works as one such parameter.)

---

basic-ncsa

```
AuthTrans fn=basic-ncsa auth-type=basic
  dbm="c:/netscape/server/authdb/new/"
```

Translates using the basic predefined server authorization method. This method is similar to the HTTP basic authentication scheme. It uses either the DBM or NCSA-style user database type. You cannot use this function with the local database of Enterprise Server 3.x or Directory Server. LDAP and LDAP directories are not supported by **basic-ncsa**.

Parameters: <u>auth-type</u> (Type of authentication to be used. Currently only `basic` is allowed.); <u>dbm</u> (Full system path for the DBM user database file—do not include the file name! Server 2.x uses DBM file format for the user database. The DBM file, based on Berkeley hashed DBM file and commonly used in the UNIX world, is a hashed file format of `name-value` pairs of data. You should use either the `dbm` parameter or the `userfile` parameter.); <u>userfile</u> (Full path of the NCSA-style user database. For this parameter, include the name of the file in the path. Netscape 1.x used an NCSA-style user database file. This type of file is a text file with each line including a null-terminated `username:encrypted password`. You should use either the `dbm` parameter or the `userfile` parameter.); **grpfile** (NCSA-style group file. In this text file, each line is written as `group:user1 user2 . . . usern`. Each user is separated by a space. This parameter is used in conjunction with the `userfile` parameter to define the groups of users specified in `userfile`. This parameter is optional).

get-sslid

```
AuthTrans fn=get-sslid
```

This function is for Netscape Server 2.01 and later. **get-sslid** always returns `REQ_NOACTION`. If security is enabled, it creates a variable named `ssl-id` in the `Session` data structure's `client` pblock, which is the base-64 encoding of the SSL session value. Your server application function can then use this information. This value is also accessible to a CGI program as `HTTPS_SESSIONID` (for example, `HTTPS_SESSIONID=B+rZPf11DpxjCWGst6iFAmbUdgRKzLVRIJzPYW6PNWg`).

Parameter: None.

The NameTrans Functions

assign-name

```
NameTrans fn="assign-name" from="/private/*.exe"
 name="shellcgi"
```

(In the Server Manager, you assign a name by first creating a style through Configuration Styles|New Style. This action creates the Object. "Assign a Style" from the Configuration Styles|Assign Style menu by assigning a URL prefix to the style. The style is applied to the URL prefix you defined. You can view the list of assigned names through Configuration Styles|List Assignments. You can also add directives to the style/Object using Configuration Styles|Edit Style.)

This function applies a named Object to a specific URL prefix. Apply the Object to a directory under the document path by using the prefix (for the URL) after the document root. You can also use a wildcard to define a specific set of files to which the Object is applied. In the accompanying example, the Shell CGI Object applies only to `*.exe` files. The server uses the directives in the defined Object when a request originates from that specific URL prefix. This function tells the server that once the request comes from the specified URL, it should go to the Object you have defined and continue the response using that Object's directive functions. This function always returns `REQ_NOACTION`, unless you use the new Server 3.x parameter `stop`. Unlike with **pfx2dir**, you do not map a system path to a prefix. (See also **pfx2dir**.)

Parameters: **from** (Directory to which you want to apply the defined Object. Include the prefix of the directory. You can also use wildcards to narrow the type of files to which this Object applies.); **name** (Name of the Object that you want to use for the defined URL.); **stop** (A new parameter for Server 3.x. It tells the server to stop processing other **NameTrans** directive functions. The value of this parameter does not matter. You can set the value to a blank string, `stop=""`. When you use this parameter, **assign-name** returns REQ_PROCEED instead of the typical REQ_NOACTION.)

> ### Note ▶
>
> In the Server Manager, when you "Create a New Style," you are creating a new Object. Then, when you "Edit a Style," you are attributing directives to that style (Object). If you "Assign a Style" to a directory, you actually create a **NameTrans** function **assign-name** in the default Object (assign a directory to that style). Now, if you remove that style (with the "Remove a Style" option), you remove only the Object you created (and its directives), but not the **NameTrans** function. You still need to delete the **NameTrans** function. To do so, search for and delete it from the **obj.conf** file, or reassign the directory to a blank style (by choosing "NONE").

document-root

```
NameTrans fn=document-root
 root="c:/netscape/server/docs" address="1.2.3.4"
```
(Default value set at installation.)
(In the Server Manager, you can change your document root by changing the directory in the "Primary Directory" option from the Content Management|Primary Document Directory menu. This function is also defined when you define "Hardware Virtual Servers" from the Content Management|Hardware Virtual Servers menu.)

Defines the actual location (physical path) of the root documents. It is where the server looks for documents when the user requests your server (for example, `http://www.foo.com/`). This function usually should be set in your **obj.conf** file. Place this function after other **NameTrans** functions. **document-root** should be seen as the default **NameTrans** function called if other **NameTrans** functions did not set the physical path. If no other function has set the path, this function sets the path based on the `root` directory. **document-root** always returns REQ_PROCEED. Other **NameTrans** functions placed after **document-root** will not be used by the server.

Parameters: root (Points to the location—the physical path—of the document root on your machine. Don't use a forward slash after the last directory.); **address** (IP address of a hardware-based virtual server. It allows your server to respond to multiple IP addresses. All hardware- or software-based virtual servers share the server configuration file. You cannot have one virtual server be secure and another not be secure. If you wish to have separate configurations for each IP address, then install separate instances of the server for each IP address. This parameter is optional).

home-page

`NameTrans fn=home-page path=home.html`

(In the Server Manager, you can set the home page through the "Document Preferences" options from the Content Management|Document Preferences menu. This function is also defined when you set the "Software Virtual Servers" from the Content Management menu.)

Besides defining the location of the root directory (**document-root**), you might want to define the default home page that the server will use. Here, you define a specific page (file) that is sent when the client requests your server home page (for example, `http://www.foo.com/`). This function is different from the **PathCheck** function **find-index**. With **find-index**, you are defining the type of file that the index file is (for example, `home.html`, `home.htm`, `index.htm`, and so on). As a rule, the file identified by **find-index** is sent to the client when a directory is requested without specifically requesting a file in that directory. With the **home-page** function, you actually define the home page of your site, not a default index file for the server directories. You should use an HTML or text file as the home page.

If you specify a file name in the `path` parameter (`home.htm`), **home-page** adds the name of the file to the requested URI path—for example, / turns `/home.htm`, and returns `REQ_NOACTION`. The server then continues to the next **NameTrans** directive. Normally, the server identifies the root directory through **document-root** and processes other links, even links in the home page, based on it. **document-root** uses the new URI set by **home-page** to identify the physical path of the client's requested resource. **home-page** should come before **document-root** in the `obj.conf` file.

Under UNIX, you can also specify the path of the home page—for example, `netscape/server/docs/joe/home.htm`. When the path starts with the forward slash, **home-page** identifies the path as a physical path. It then sets the server variable `path` based on the value of **home-page**'s `path` parameter and returns `REQ_PROCEED`. The server now skips other **NameTrans** directives.

You cannot use a physical path as the value of the `path` parameter under NT, because the physical path under NT begins with the directory information (for example, `c:\`) and not a forward slash. You can use only the file name of the home page for the `path` parameter under NT—for example, `home.htm`. In other words, you can define a home page only for a file in the document root directory. Also, do not add a forward slash before the file name.

Parameter: **path** (The path and file name or the file name of the home page. See the discussion above for details on the use of this parameter.)

mozilla-redirect

`NameTrans fn=mozilla-redirect from=/ url=http://newplace/`

You can redirect a request from Navigator 0.96 or later to a new URL. This function works with requests that send a `user-agent` of Mozilla 0.96 or later (that is, Netscape Navigator 0.96 or later). This function works in the same way as **redirect**, except that it responds only to Netscape Navigator 0.96 and later. It could be used by site designers who want to have a basic HTML version (or text version) of the site for clients without Netscape Navigator capabilities. Clients who have Netscape Navigator can be routed to a fancier graphic and form-based site.

Parameters: **from** (The directory from where you want the server redirected. In the example, it is the root directory.); **url** (The new URL that you want to send to the client.)

> **Tidbit ▶**
>
> If you try to test **mozilla-redirect** with NCSA Mosaic, you will notice no redirection takes place and a default index file is sent back. If you try this operation with the Microsoft Explorer, you will be redirected. Microsoft has decided to define its user-agent as Mozilla and, therefore, returns a Mozilla string as the type of `user-agent`. Clever—you are not Mozilla, but you think you are.

pfx2dir

```
NameTrans fn="pfx2dir" from="/shellcgi"
  dir="c:/netscape/server/shellcgi" name="shellcgi"
```

(This function is set for `ns-icons` and `mc-icons` when you install the server. It is a reference to the icons library that the server uses. The server uses these icons, for example, to display a fancy directory listing when the client requests a directory that does not have an index file.)

(In the Server Manager, this function is set in various ways. You can define a URL prefix to map to a directory [the **pfx2dir** function] for an existing style [an Object] through Content Management|Additional Document Directories. Also, when you define one of the "Programs" menu options [such as WinCGI], the Server Manager asks you to define a "URL prefix" [such as a WinCGI directory] for the program [the Object] and adds a **pfx2dir** function for the Object [the program].)

This function is frequently used to replace a long directory path or a location outside of the server path with an easy-to-use or alternative prefix. It maps a directory prefix—a virtual path (what the client uses in its URL)—to a physical path on your machine. The client then requests a short URL path, and the server looks for the data in the defined physical path. The server sees the links relative to this new prefix, URL path. You can also include an Object name here. By including a name parameter, you can associate the directory with an Object that you have defined. This function will then work similarly to the **assign-name** function. (You do not use wildcards in this function, however.) You can evaluate both functions, **pfx2dir** and **assign-name**, to decide which is best suited for the Object you are defining. **pfx2dir** does not require an Object, but if you define one, any request for the defined URL is a request for your Object.

Parameters: from (The path you want the client to use. Don't use a forward slash after the last directory.); **dir** (The directory where the actual files reside. Don't use a forward slash after the last subdirectory.); **name** (An optional parameter that allows you to associate that directory to an Object in addition to redirecting. This function can combine the effect of **redirect** function with an **assign-name** function.

redirect

```
NameTrans fn=redirect from=/ url=http://www.new.com
```
(Under the Server Manager, you can define this function through Content Management|URL Forwarding by defining a URL prefix and a forwarding URL.)

Redirects the client from a URL prefix (virtual path) to another URL. When changing the server path or moving a directory to a new location, this function can be used to replace a request for an older URL with one for a new URL. You can also redirect a subdirectory to a new URL location. Use either `url` or `url-prefix`.

Parameters: from (The directory from which you want the server redirected—that is, the old URL path. In this example, it is the root directory.); **url** (The new URL to send to the client. Use `url` if you intend to use a fixed URL, as in "`http://home.netscape.com/myplace`".); **url-prefix** (The new URL prefix you want to send to the client. Use `url-prefix` when you wish to send just a prefix of a URL, as in `/cities/London`.)

unix-home (UNIX)

```
NameTrans fn=unix-home from=/~ subdir=public-html
  pwfile=/special/passwd
```

This function is for UNIX servers. It translates a URL prefix (for example, `/~`) to the user subdirectory path (for example, `public-html`). A user is also associated to a home directory. You can use the default user password file (`/etc/password`) to identify the user and the user's home directory. This function makes it easy for Internet service providers to make a local user's directories available to the public. A specific URL prefix is translated to a user's home directory. It is recommended that you use this function in conjunction with **Init** function **init-uhome** to have the server read the password file only once at the start of the server. (See also **init-uhome**.)

Parameters: from (URL prefix to be translated.); **subdir** (User subdirectory.); **name** (An optional parameter that allows you to associate that directory to an Object. You can then write your functions to manage these directories and respond to client requests.); **pwfile** (Path and file name of the password file. The default password file is `/etc/passwd`. Lines in the `passwd` file should have the following format:

```
username:<name>:<passwrd>:groupid:<ID>:homedir:<dir>.)
```

user-defined

```
NameTrans fn=explicit-pathinfo separator=","
```

You can write your own **NameTrans** function and pass it any
[name]="[value]" parameter you wish. You can then use these parameters
in your program.

Parameter: Any [name]="[value]" parameter set by you and passed to
that function.

The PathCheck Functions

cert2user (Enterprise Server 2.x)

```
PathCheck fn="cert2user"
 userdb="c:/netscape/server/authdb/default"
```

Maps the client certificate authenticated from the SSL3 session to a user in the
user database (certificate to user). The server gets the user's certificate from the
user and verifies its authenticity. Next, it acquires the user name and password
information and checks it against the user database (HTTP authentication
through access control). If both of these steps are successful (that is, authentication for both the certificate and user name/password), then **cert2user** maps the
certificate to the user in the user database. This process reduces the number of
times that a client must log in with a user name and password to only once—the
first time. The next time a request is made, the server can check the client certificate against the mapped user name and allow or deny access based on the initial
login. (You need to use Netscape Navigator 3.0 or later to take advantage of
client certificate. The certificate file format is different for each major release of
Netscape Server—that is, Netscape Server 1.x, 2.x, or 3.x.) (See also the
PathCheck function **get-client-cert**.)

Parameters: __userdb__ (User database used to verify user name and password
information. You should include full path but **do not include** the file name. The
path is typically the default user database for the server. Netscape Server 2.x uses
the DBM file for access control.); __makefrombasic__ (Uses basic HTTP server
authentication—that is, employs user name and password information. Maps
the certificate to the user if no mapping exists for the user. To choose this option,
set makefrombasic to a value other than 0. This parameter is optional.);
__require__ (Defines whether the client has access even if the certificate cannot be
mapped to a user name. If you set this value to 0, the client will get access, even
when certificate mapping fails. If the value is other than 0, the client will receive
a Forbidden page and the status is set to 403 FORBIDDEN. The default value
is 1. This parameter is optional.); __method__ (Wildcard pattern for the HTTP
method. Typically, this parameter is absent, and **cert2user** applies to all requests.
If you include a method, then pattern matching will occur and only the specified

method will be verified—for example, `method=(GET|HEAD)`. This parameter is optional.)

> **Note ▶**
>
> The preferred method of supporting certificate mapping is to use Netscape's Certificate Mapping API for Enterprise Server 3.x. This API includes functions for performing certificate authentication.

---

check-acl

Server 2.x example:
```
PathCheck fn="check-acl"
 acl="https-foo_formgen-READ-ACL_allow-5883"
```

Server 3.x example:
```
PathCheck fn="check-acl" acl="default"
```
(In Server Manager 2.x, you can set access control rules in the "Restrict Access" form under Access Control|Restrict Access. Turn access control to on. Define where you want access control [which directories or paths]. Set the type of access and define the server response when access is denied. If you are adding more than one user, include each `username` in quotes if it contains any characters other than a character, digit, dash, or underscore. Under Server 3.x, you set the access control rules from Server Preferences|Restrict Access. Choose a resource, existing ACL, or ACL name for which you wish to set or edit the rules. To set the access control for a directory, choose Browse; for a group of files, choose Wildcard. You can then edit the Access Control rules. Server 3.x includes improved and more sophisticated forms for setting up access control rules.)

When you define the "Access Control" information in the Server Manager, a **check-acl** (check Access Control Log) function is added to your **obj.conf** file. ACL files are usually under the `httpacl` directory (for example, `genwork.<server ID>.acl` and `generated.<server ID>.acl`, where `generated` refers to changes that have been made and saved using the Server Manager. `genwork` holds the changes before they have been saved by pressing the final OK button). ACL files provide the necessary authentication instructions. The location of the ACL file is defined with the **magnus.conf** directive **ACLfile**. Under Server 2.x, access control passwords must be no more than eight characters. (See Appendix C for more details.)

Parameters: acl (This parameter points to the specific `acl` [ACL] instructions in the ACL file that define the server's authorization actions for a specific request. For Server 2.x, `acl`'s value is a special ACL function that has a unique name, such as `httpd-foo_formgen-READ-ACL_allow-5883`. This compound name is made up of specific identifiers and instructions. For Server 3.x, `acl`'s value can be a variety of names: a path [`path="c:/netscape/server/docs/special/*"`], a URI [`uri="/special/*"`], a file type [`"*.html"`], or an Object ["default"]. Although this value must be unique, it is not the same type of compound name as for Server 2.x.); **bong-file** (When access is denied, the server responds with the file defined here instead of the default Not Found. This optional parameter is no longer needed for Server 3.x. The ACL file for Server 3.x can include a special instruction that identifies the URL that should be sent when the request is denied [for example, deny with url= "/noway.html";].); **path** (Wildcard pattern—shell expression—determining the path to which the ACL applies. Typically, instead of using this option, an Object is created by associating it to a specific path, and **check-acl** is applied inside the Object. This optional parameter is no longer needed for Server 3.x. With Server 3.x, you can define the path as the value of the acl parameter.)

> ### Note ▶
>
> For Server 2.x, **check-acl** is always the first **PathCheck** directive that the server calls, independent of how **PathCheck** functions are listed in your obj.conf file. For Server 3.x, **check-acl** is invoked after all other **PathCheck** functions, independent of the order of the functions in the obj.conf file.

---

deny-existence

```
PathCheck fn=deny-existence path="*/~*"
 bong-msg="c:/netscape/server/special/forbid.html"
```
Denies the existence of (hides) the resource requested by sending a Not Found (status 404) page. It returns a status 404 not 403 (Forbidden). Instead of letting the client know that it was forbidden access to the resource, it returns not found. The client will not know if the resource is available. It will know only that the resource was not found. (Do not confuse the use of this **PathCheck** directive function with the undocumented use of this function as a **Service** function. For more information on the use of this function as a **Service** function, see **deny-existence** in the **Service** directive functions list.)

    Parameters: **path** (Wildcard pattern of the path for which to deny existence, such as path="*/private/*". If the value of path does not match the requested path, **deny-existence**, instead of sending a Not Found page, returns REQ_NOACTION. If this optional parameter was not used, **deny-existence** assumes that the requested path was a match and returns a Not Found page.); **bong-msg** (Absolute path to a file that the server returns in place of the default Not Found page. This file should be an HTML file. This parameter is optional.)

---

find-index

```
PathCheck fn=find-index
 index-names=index.html,home.html,index.htm
```
(Default value set at installation.)
(In the Server Manager, set your index files in the "Index Filenames" option from the Content Management|Document Preferences menu.)

Defines the index files for the server. When the client requests a URL that specifies a directory but no file, the server looks sequentially in the index file list defined by **find-index** to find an index file for the requested directory. **find-index** locates an index file in the requested directory based on the index files listed in the index-names parameter. If a file was found, it adds the name of the file to the path. If the requested URL includes a query string or if the method of the request is anything other than GET, **find-index** does nothing. If the server does not find an index file, a directory list is sent—that is, if directory indexing is enabled. Often, a client request for your site includes the server name with no index.html file. This function adds an index file to the requested URL path (for example, for the request http://www.foo.com/, the index.html file in the document root directory is dispatched to the client). Do not define the same file name twice, as it will lead to a server error. This function should be included in your **obj.conf** file.

Parameter: **index-names** (Names of the files, separated by a comma, for which the server should look. Do not use spaces unless they are part of the name of the file. These files are chosen in the order they are listed. If you have named more than one index file, the first file in the list that is found is put to use.)

---

find-links (UNIX)

```
PathCheck fn=find-links disable=so dir=/public_html/
```

Searches current path (referenced by the request) for symbolic links to other directories or file systems. This function restricts the file system links (symbolic links).[2] Symbolic links associate a file name to a remote file. They allow access to a file outside of the normal document root as if it was in the current directory. **find-links** limits the use of this type of action on your server. You can use this function to restrict user links to files you do not want others to access from the user's public directory (for example, public_html). The server uses the directory you define to identify any symbolic links and denies use based on how you define the access. The server returns an error for any such request. For example, you can allow a symbolic link from a user's home directory only if the user owns the target of the link.

Although this function is documented for NT and 95, it was intended for UNIX operating systems. It does not work under NT or 95. If you add this function to the **obj.conf** file, the errors log file will report the function **find-links** as not found. Moreover, in the Server Settings|System Settings (in Server Manager 2.x), the function appears highlighted as hypertext, "Symbolic Links," but does not link to any page!

---

2. Under UNIX, you can use the function **ln** to create hard or soft links. (ln -s produces a soft link; ln by itself produces a hard link. You use this function as follows: ln [option] <file to be linked> <new link>. Check under **ln** and **symlink** in your UNIX operating system manual for more information.)

Parameters: <u>**disable**</u> (Choose between h [hard link], s [soft link], and o [permitted user-owned target link made from the user's home directory]. You can combine the options when appropriate.); <u>**dir**</u> (Server looks through this initial directory and all its subdirectories. If defined as a partial path, all requests that include the partial path string are checked. For example, if you define `/private/`, then any request that includes "`/private/`" [such as `home/private/user5`] is checked. If an absolute [full] path is used, only a request to that directory and its subdirectories is checked.)

---

find-pathinfo

`PathCheck fn=find-pathinfo`
(Default value set at installation.)

Extracts the extra path (information that usually comes after the file name) from the path of a CGI request. CGI programs usually use the extended path information to pass a file to the program (`http://` `www.foo.com/cgi/dothis.exe`**`/stuff/info.txt`**). (This desired file, in turn, could hold configuration or other relevant data for the program.) The extra path information, however, does not need to reference another file or directory. It could include any data. **find-pathinfo** resolves the path information for the CGI program by extracting the extra path information from the path. **find-pathinfo** adds `path-info` to the server variables (`Request->vars`). CGI programs access this extra path data through the CGI environment variable `PATH_INFO`. Other server functions can also make use of `path-info`. WAI applications can use extra path information (`PATH_INFO` as well).

Parameter: None.

---

get-client-cert (Enterprise Server)

`PathCheck fn="get-client-cert" dorequest="1"`

Obtains the client's authenticated certificate from an SSL3 session. This function can either check to see if the certificate exists or require the client to select a certificate. The certificate (MIME base-64 encoded, ASN.1 encoded, X.509 formatted certificate) value is placed in `auth-cert` inside `Request->var` (server request variable). By declaring **get-client-cert** in the **obj.conf** file, the server provides the client certificate for your use. This information is also available to your CGI programs through the `CLIENT_CERT` environment variable. Note that security must be set to `on` and the client must be required to send the certificate. You can enable security from the Server Manager's Server Preferences| Encryption On/Off and require certificate through Server Preferences|Encryption Preferences.

A return of `REQ_NOACTION` or `REQ_PROCEED` by this function indicates that the client request can be processed. Otherwise, a `FORBIDDEN` page is returned to the client and the status is set to `403 Forbidden`. (You also need to use Netscape Navigator 3.0 or later to take advantage of client certificates. The certificate file format is different for each major release of Netscape Server [that is, Netscape Server 1.x, 2.x, or 3.x].) (See also the **PathCheck** function **cert2user**.)

Parameters: <u>**dorequest**</u> (The server checks **only** to see that the `auth-cert` parameter is present if this parameter is set to `0`. A setting of `1` demands that the client send the certificate. The client must renegotiate the SSL3 session for the server to obtain the certificate. With Netscape Navigator, the client receives a dialog box from which to select a certificate.); <u>**method**</u> (Specifies a wildcard pattern for the HTTP method. The wildcard patterns are shell expressions. Typically, this parameter is absent and the **cert2user** function is applied to all requests. If you include this method and define it as *shell expression*, then pattern matching will occur—for example, `method=(GET|HEAD)`. This parameter is optional.)

htaccess-find (Enterprise Server 3.x)

`PathCheck fn=htaccess-find`

Provides support for dynamic configuration of the server using `.htaccess` files. The `.htaccess` files are commonly used by a number of HTTP servers to support dynamic configuration (for example, Apache Server). The server uses the instructions in these files to allow limited configuration for the specified directories where these files are placed. An authorized user can use these files instead of the Server Manager or the main server configuration files to set access control rules for the user's designated directories. You need to edit the **obj.conf** file manually, however, to enable this method of dynamic configuration. Note that this method is different from using the Netscape-specific dynamic configuration method supported with `.nsconfig` files. (See the **PathCheck** function **load-config** discussion for more information on using `.nsconfig` files for dynamic configuration.)

The use of `.htaccess` files is provided as an NSAPI add-on application. Unlike **load-config**, this option is not directly built into the server; you must manually load the shared library or DLL that enables this option. You need to first load the shared library or DLL using the **Init** function **load-modules** and then insert the **Init** function **htaccess-init** and the **PathCheck** function **htaccess-find** in the **obj.conf** file. You can find the DLL or shared library for this option under `<server path>/plugins/htaccess`—for example, `htaccess.dll`. (Netscape also provides a Perl script, `htconvert`, for converting existing `.nsconfig` files to `.htaccess` files.) The following code is an example of what you need to add to the **obj.conf** file. (Note that `htacess.dll` has been moved to a new directory under the server path.)

```
Init fn="load-modules"
  funcs="htaccess-init,htaccess-find"
  shlib="c:/netscape/server/htaccess/htaccess.dll"

Init fn="htaccess-init"
. . .
```

```
<Object name="default">

. . .

PathCheck fn="htaccess-find"

. . .

</Object>
```

You should place **htaccess-find** at the end of the list of **PathCheck** functions in the **obj.conf** file, before any **ObjectType** directive function. By adding this directive to a different Object in the **obj.conf** file, you can limit the scope of dynamic configuration to the specific resource specified by the Object. (See also Appendix D.)

Parameter: filename (Configuration file, such as .htaccess. This optional parameter allows you to rename the configuration file—that is, use a different name instead of .htaccess.)

Warning ▶

With .htaccess files, you can use only a user database in NCSA-style text file format (the default user database format of Server 1.x). You cannot use the local database of Server 3.x or an LDAP directory server with this option. There is no support for LDAP and LDAP directories in dynamic configuration files.

load-config
```
PathCheck fn=load-config file=".nsconfig"
```
(In the Server Manager, you can define the dynamic configuration settings through System Setting|Dynamic Configuration Files for Server 2.x and through Server Preferences|Dynamic Configuration Files for Server 3.x.)

Provides for dynamic configuration of the server using specific configuration files that can be used in the document directories. You define the name of the file (for example, .nsconfig) and the base directory where the server should look for these configuration files. The server uses the instructions in the file to allow limited configuration for the specified directories. For instance, the file can include instructions about access control or error messages returned to the client. This function is especially useful for server administrators (such as Internet Service Providers) who allow other site administrators limited configuration options without allowing them access to the Server Manager or the main server configuration files (that is, **magnus.conf** and **obj.conf**). (With Server 3.5.1, you can also use Netshare to set up a workspace in which the users can manage their own server content. From this central location, users can also inspect and change their own user information. Moreover, with Server 3.x, you can limit users' access to the various portions of Administration Server or Server Manager.) (See also Appendix D.)

load-config returns REQ_PROCEED when the configuration files are loaded and REQ_NOACTION when the files are not loaded. It returns REQ_ABORTED if an error occurred.

load-config supports a Netscape-specific dynamic configuration method using `.nsconfig` file directives. If you wish to use a `.htaccess` method of dynamic configuration, which is a more standard method of dynamic configuration supported by other HTTP servers, you need to enable `.httaccess` manually. The `.htaccess` files are supported by Enterprise Server 3.x. (See also the **PathCheck** function **htaccess-find**.)

Parameters: **file** (Name of the configuration file, such as `.nsconfig`. This optional parameter allows you to use a different name for the configuration file. The default name is `.nsconfig`); **disable-types** (Disables the types of files defined here for the specified directories where dynamic configuration is enabled. The server does not process a request for the type of files you defined with this parameter if they are in the directories that support the dynamic configuration. Use wildcards to define the type of files you wish to disable. For example, `*(cgi|parsed-html)` disables CGI files [`magnus-internal/cgi`] and any server-parsed HTML files [`magnus-internal/parsed-html`]. This parameter is optional.); **basedir** (Base directory where the server begins looking for the configuration file. The value should be based on the system's file path. If this parameter is not specified, the server uses the requested URL to identify the base directory. A **NameTrans** directive function will specify the base directory. For example, the document root specified by the **NameTrans** function **document-root** can set the base directory. The client's requested URL is normally verified by **NameTrans** (for example, by the function's **document-root** or **pfx2dir**). The **NameTrans** function then specifies the system's root (base) directory (`ntrans-base`) for the request (for example, `c:/netscape/server/docs`). This directory could also be different from the document root directory. For instance, **pfx2dir** can be used to map a URL path to a specific system path. In this case, this specified system path is identified as the base directory. This parameter is optional.); **descend** (If set to 1, the server continues looking in the sub-directories of the base directory. Typically, for performance reasons, you include all your configuration information in a single file in the base directory, but you are not required to do so. If the server searches subdirectories, **all** appropriate descending subdirectories of the base directory are searched before responding to the client.

> **Warning** ▶
>
> Although you may be able to use dynamic configuration with the FastTrack Server, Netscape does not officially support dynamic configuration under FastTrack. In fact, in the NT and 95 Server Managers of FastTrack Server 2.0, there is no System Settings|Dynamic Configuration Files option.
>
> Furthermore, to use `.nsconfig` files, you need to use a user database in NCSA-style text file format (the default user database format of Server 1.x) or a DBM user database format (the default user database format of Server 2.x). You cannot use the local database of Server 3.x or an LDAP directory server with this option. There is no support for LDAP and LDAP directories in dynamic configuration files.

In other words, for a request of a subdirectory (for example, /docs/public/
image/) of the base directory (for example, c:/netscape/server/
docs/), besides looking in the subdirectory (for example, c:/netscape/
server/docs/public/image/), the server looks in the base directory (for
example, c:/netscape/server/docs/) and any other directory in
between (for example, c:/netscape/server/docs/public/). The
server then responds to the client request. This parameter is optional.)

ntcgicheck (NT)

`PathCheck fn=ntcgicheck extension=.pl`

Adds an extension to a file request that has no extension, or changes a requested
file's .cgi extension to an extension you defined. It adds the extension to path
in *Request->vars* (server variables). For example, if the client requests
/program/hello, **ntcgicheck** adds .pl to the request, which in turn runs
the hello.pl file. This function will hide the type of program from the
casual hacker by removing the file association information from the client's URL
request. It can also facilitate the management of files with different extensions by
defining the association here, rather than in the HTML pages.

Parameter: __extension__ (The file extension to take the place of the requested
file's .cgi extension. Also, the extension to add to a requested file with no
extension.)

Bug Report ▶

(*Tested under FastTrack 2.0a and Enterprise Server 3.5.1 for NT 4.0*) This function is
supposed to add an extension you define to files that have a cgi extension (that is,
*.cgi) or no extension. To add the extension to a file without one, you need to set the
extension parameter to .<*ext*>. You need to add the dot (.) (for example, .pl)
before the extension in the **ntcgicheck** extension parameter. You cannot use the
extension alone (for example, pl), unlike what the Netscape documentation indicates.
Also, an extension with or without a dot does not work properly with the extension cgi.
For example, if the client requests a file such as hello.cgi and the extension in
ntcgicheck was pl, the path will change the file name to help1. Netscape does not
backtrack the right number of characters in the string. To get the extension
parameter .pl to work with **ntcgicheck,** you can use a file without an extension or a
file with two dots and the extension cgi (for example, *..cgi) for the file name
referenced in your HTML page (for example, hello..cgi).

nt-uri-clean (NT)

`PathCheck fn=nt-uri-clean`

(Default value set at installation.)

Denies access to dangerous URL requests, such as ones that include \\, \.\, or ..\
(for example, http://www.foo.com\.\). This function should be included in
your **obj.conf** file. Place this function after any **find-pathinfo** function so that your
programs' extra path information can include the above string.

Parameter: None.

require-auth

```
PathCheck fn=require-auth auth-type=basic
 realm="Private Places"
 auth-group=managers auth-user=(John|Jane)
```

Requires authorization before allowing access to the requested URL. This function can also be used when writing a customized authentication function for the **AuthTrans** directive. It works with the **AuthTrans** function **basic-auth** (or **basic-ncsa**) to limit access to a resource. If you want your **AuthTrans** function to require authorization, you can use this function. On the other hand, if you do not define an **AuthTrans** function, **require-auth** will require client authentication, but cannot verify (authenticate) the client's information. It refuses access to everyone. If you wish to limit access to a specific directory, first define an Object and associate it to the directory. You can then use an **AuthTrans** function and **require-auth** to limit access to those directories. Note that the preferred method of writing authentication and authorization functions for Server 3.x is to use the new Access Control API. (See also the PathCheck and AuthTrans sections in Chapter 2 for more information.)

Parameters: **auth-type** (Authentication type. For now, `basic` is the only option.); **realm** (A string that appears in the authentication dialog box as part of the instructions for the client during the authentication process. It usually identifies which area of the system is being requested—for example, `Enter username for <realm> at <server name>`. You need to include this parameter when using **require-auth**.); **path** (An optional new parameter supported by Server 3.x. With this parameter, you can specify the path for which authorization is required. You can use wildcard to specify the path. For example, if the value of `path` is `"(*private*)"`, the server requires authentication for any request that has the word `private` in its URI.); **auth-user** (An optional parameter that lists the users with access privileges. Use wildcards to list the users. Separate the user names with a pipe symbol [|] and include them in parentheses. Do not include any unnecessary spaces. If it is not used, all users authenticated by the server **AuthTrans** function will have access.); **auth-group** (An optional parameter that lists the groups that can have access. Users can be distinguished individually as `user` or collectively in a `group`.)

> ### Tidbit ▶
>
> If you check in the **obj.conf** of file Server 2.x (for example, Netscape FastTrack for NT), you will find the `path` parameter used with **require-auth** for the LiveWire Object (assuming that LiveWire is installed). Under Server 2.x, however, you may not be able to use this parameter for your **require-auth** function. If you manually add a `path` parameter to a **require-auth** function, no error message is returned. Unfortunately, this function will also not require authorization for the specified path. (You can use this parameter for **require-auth** with Server 3.x.)

set-cache-control (Server 3.x)

`PathCheck fn="set-cache-control" control="public"`
(From Content Management|Cache Control Directives in the Server Manager, you can choose the various control settings under "Cache Control Response Directives." You can also specify to which resources—that is, specific directories—this directive should apply.)

With this function, you can set the cache-control general header. The `cache-control` directive controls the information that is cached by any caching mechanism (for example, a proxy server), along the request-response communication. You can override the default caching algorithm of the proxy server. If the proxy server is HTTP/1.1-compliant, you can specify how the information should be cached. You can use this directive to make sure that the sensitive information that should not be cached is not cached. You can restrict what is cachable, limit what may be stored by a cache, force revalidation of the cache, and set an expiration time for the cache. Netscape Proxy Server 3.5 should support cache control. For more information on cache-control, see the HTTP/1.1 specification (`http://www.ics.uci.edu/pub/ietf/http/`).

Parameter: <u>**control**</u> (Identify how the proxy server should cache the information. You can use a number of values. Values identified through the Server Manager are `public`, `private`, `no-cache`, `no-store`, `must-revalidate`, or `max-age`. `public` means that the response is cachable by any cache. It is the default setting. `private` means that the response is intended for a single user and should not be cached by a shared cache. `no-cache` means that no caching should be used. `no-store` should be used when a response or request must not be stored in a nonvolatile storage—for example, it should not be stored in a back-up tape. No part of the request or response should be stored. This value does not affect the client's ability to store a response outside of the caching system. Use `must-revalidate` if the cached data should be revalidated from the originating server. Use this value when the request can result in an incorrect operation if it is not revalidated. `max-age` specifies that the response sent to the client should not have an age greater than the age you specified. You specify the age in seconds. The `max-age` value should include both the string `max-age` and the seconds. The format for `max-age` is `[max-age]=[seconds]`. For example, for a maximum age of 30 seconds, the control parameter should be `control="max-age=30"`. HTTP/ 1.1 includes additional directives such as `no-transform`, `proxy-revalidate`, and `s-maxage`.)

Warning ▶

If you are using Enterprise Server 3.0, you should update the server with the latest Enterprise Server patch—for example, 3.0i for NT. This patch fixed a number of server problems, including a cache control-related problem.

unix-uri-clean (UNIX)

```
PathCheck fn=unix-uri-clean
```
(Default value set at installation.)

Denies access to dangerous URL requests (such as ones that include `//`, `/./`, or `/../`, as in `http://www.foo.com/./`). This function should be included in your **obj.conf** file. Place this function after any **find-pathinfo** function so that extra path information can include the above string.

Parameter: None.

user-defined

```
PathCheck fn=sdump name=PathCheck
```

You can write your own **PathCheck** function and pass it any `[name]="[value]"` parameters you wish. You then use these parameters in your program.

Parameter: Any `[name]="[value]"` parameter set by you and passed to the function.

The ObjectType Functions

force-type

```
ObjectType fn=force-type type=text/plain lang=en_US
```
(Default value set at installation.)
(In the Server Manager, define the "Default MIME type" option from the Content Management|Document Preferences menu.)

Sets the default MIME type for the requested object. It works as the default **ObjectType** function. If no other types are defined, the server forces the type defined here. For example, the default content type is usually `text/plain`. This function should be included in your **obj.conf** file.

Parameters: **type** (Type [content-type] that is enforced. It is the type you are assigning as a default.); **enc** (If you want to enforce a default HTTP encoding [content-encoding], you can use this parameter. An example of a content-encoding type is `x-compress`. This parameter is optional.); **lang** (Language information defined for the default type, content-language. This parameter is optional.); **charset** (Besides defining the language, you can also define the character set. This option allows you to override the default character set for the language or to define a specific default character set—for example, `charset=iso-8859-1`. This parameter is optional.)

image-switch

```
ObjectType fn=image-switch
```

Tells the server to send a file in another, appropriate, and acceptable format, JPEG. For example, this function directs the server to send an `imagia.jpg` file (a JPEG graphics file) instead of an `imagia.gif` file (a GIF graphics file)—that is, if the file is in the requested directory and has the same name with a different extension. JPEG files use a wider color depth and higher compression ratio. The size of each file is smaller and therefore reaches the client faster. This function must appear after the **ObjectType** function **type-by-extension**. If the client is using a Netscape browser (`MOZILLA` **user-agent**) without a proxy, then the server sends back the JPEG file instead of the GIF file. (When you add this function manually to the `obj.conf` file, the Server Manager may see this function as `Unknown` when you "View Server Setting" from the Server Preferences menu.)

Parameter: None.

---

shtml-hacktype

`ObjectType fn=shtml-hacktype exec-hack=true`

(Under the Server Manager, when you set "Parse which files?" to "All HTML files" in the Content Management|Parse HTML page, the server defines this function, but does not define the **exec-hack** parameter. You must have enabled server-parsed HTML for this function to work.)

Provides additional support for Server-side Includes—that is, server-parsed HTML (see Chapter 3 for more details)—when you want to define parsing for all HTML files. (Here, server-parsed HTML refers to files that contain Server-side Includes [SSI].) Normally, parsing is done for `*.shtml` files. In other words, there is a different MIME type and file extension (for example, `type=magnus-internal/parsed-html exts=shtml`) for parsed HTML type files. This setting limits the number of files that are parsed and improves the server performance. **shtml-hacktype** allows parsing for all HTML files—that is, all files with the extension `.htm` and `.html`. **shtml-hacktype** sets the `content-type` of HTML files, `text/html`, to `magnus-internal/parsed-html`. Under UNIX, you can also specify that only HTML files with the execute bit turned on are parsed. This function works in conjunction with the **Service** function **parse-html**. It is best not to use this function to parse all HTML files, because it is performance-intensive.

Parameter: <u>exec-hack</u> (If this parameter is added, the function checks whether the execute bit is enabled for the file before setting the `content-type` to `magnus-internal/parsed-html`. It checks for the UNIX file permissions of the file to see if the execute bit is turned on. If the execute bit is enabled, the file is parsed. The value of this parameter is arbitrary. You can use any value string you wish. For example, you can use "`true`". This parameter is optional for UNIX versions of the server.)

---

type-by-exp

`ObjectType fn=type-by-exp exp=*.other type=text/html`

Compares the URL path with the expression (`exp`) defined here. If they match, the server employs the MIME type defined here. A wildcard defines the type of file expression. You can also set encoding, language, and character set information. Unlike with the **type-by-extension** function, you actually define your MIME types and file extensions here, instead of using the `mime.types` file. (When you add this function manually to the `obj.conf` file, the Server Manager may see this function as Unknown when you "View Server Setting" from the Server Preferences menu.)

Parameters: **exp** (Wildcard expression that determines the file type you want associated with a MIME type. For example, to associate any file that is in the directory `special` and ends with the string `big`, you can set the `exp` parameter to `*/special/*big.`); **type** (Type [content-type] of association for the wildcard expression you choose. Look in your `mime.types` file for examples of content types.); **enc** (Defines the content-encoding header for the file. You can define the encoding type. If you want to use HTTP encoding [content-encoding] as the type, use this parameter. An example of a content-encoding is `x-compress`. This parameter is optional.); **lang** (Assigns a language [content-language] for the type. This parameter is optional.); **charset** (You can also define the character set, which allows you to override the default character set for the language. This parameter is optional.)

---

type-by-extension

```
ObjectType fn=type-by-extension
```
(Default value set at installation.)

Uses file extensions[3] to determine the content type of the requested file by finding an appropriate MIME type for a given file extension. It uses the MIME types file (`mime.types`) of your server. The **Init** function **load-type** specifies the MIME types file and loads the types into memory, as in the following example:

```
Init fn="load-types" mime-types="mime.types"
```

type-by-extension looks for the requested file's MIME type in the list of types in the `mime.types` file. It then sets the MIME type of the HTTP response-header (for example, content-type). The server also uses this information to invoke the applicable **Service** function. This function should already be in your

---

3. File extensions are the characters after the last period (.) in a file name. Early Windows and DOS users are familiar with this concept, as they probably used the three extension characters to organize their file types. Often, programs will also use extensions to define a file as their own (for example, .doc for Microsoft Word). Extensions, however, can be a source of confusion in Windows95 and Macintosh systems, as you recognize the file not by extension, but by its type. For example, under Windows 95 and NT, you have an option to "Hide file extensions for known file types" (under the View tab in the Options Dialog Box of Explorer's View|Options menu). This option will remove the known extensions from view in Explorer. The file will seem to exist without an extension, even if it has one. In the same dialog box, under the File Types tab, you can see how Microsoft associates a file with a program using the MIME content type often defined through extensions. In fact, you can see the newly added URL file types (for example, URL: File Transfer Protocol is set to Netscape Navigator under the author's NT 4.0 machine).

obj.conf file. Otherwise, files will not be processed correctly by the server. Without this function, for example, `index.html` can appear as a text file instead of a Web page in the client browser, because the correct `content-type` is not sent to the client.

Parameter: None.

---

user-defined

```
ObjectType fn=html2shtml
```

You can write your own **ObjectType** function and pass it any [name]=" [value]" parameter you wish to utilize in your program.

Parameter: Any [name]=" [value]" parameter set by you and passed to the function.

The Service Functions

append-trailer

```
Service fn="append-trailer" method="GET"
  trailer=":LASTMOD:" timefmt="%B %d, %Y" type="text/html"
```

(In the Server Manager, define this function in the "Document Footer" option under the Content Management|Document Footer menu.)

Adds specific text to the end of each HTML document. You can include a variety of general information, such as the date, author, and copyright information. This function adds a trailer to the end of the HTML files. Information is dynamically generated and can include variables (such as LASTMOD, the date the file was last modified). **append-trailer** returns REQ_PROCEED upon success. If the URL path has extra path information (that is, if `path-info` exists), the document is not correctly identified and is not sent. Instead, the client receives a Not Found page. **append-trailer** returns REQ_ABORTED if it failed to open the HTML file. **append-trailer** returns REQ_EXIT if it was unable to write the file to the client. Because this method has performance drawbacks, it is not recommended.

Parameters: **trailer** (Text to be added. The maximum number of characters is approximately 256 for Server 3.x and can include variables, such as :LASTMOD:, and HTML tags. For example, the server replaces :LASTMOD: with the date that the file was last modified. The trailer text should be entity-encoded. Any entities you add in the trailer [such as "] will be decoded after they are accepted by the server and will appear decoded in the Server Manager pages [" will appear as "]. When you submit a trailer, whether in the Server Manager or by editing the **obj.conf** file, you must submit the whole trailer with encoded entities. In other words, re-encode the trailer that appears decoded in the Server Manager.); **timefmt** (Format of the time string that will be used in the trailer. This parameter sets the format of the last-modified date vari-

able in the trailer. You need to specify this parameter if you intend to use the
:LASTMOD: variable. This format follows the **strftime** function convention
defined by the operating system [usually defined in time.h file].)

deny-existence

```
Service fn=deny-existence method="(GET|HEAD)"
 type="magnus-internal/directory"
```

Not to be confused with **deny-existence** as a **PathCheck** directive function. This
function performs a dual purpose. It can be deployed as a **Service** or **PathCheck**
directive function. Its use as a **Service** function, however, is not documented. As
a **Service** function, **deny-existence** can be used to return a Not Found error
page to the client. This function denies the existence of a file based on the MIME
type of the client request. For instance, in the above example, **deny-existence**
responds to the internal MIME type magnus-internal/directory. It
stops the server from responding with a directory listing when a URL request
includes a directory without a file name and that directory includes no index file.
You can use this function instead of **index-common** and **index-simple**.
deny-existence then returns a Not Found page to the client. (See also
send-error in the **Service** and **Error** directive functions list and **deny-existence**
in the **PathCheck** directive functions list.)

   Parameters: **method** (Acceptable method of client request. Wildcards can be
used when multiple methods are acceptable—for example, (HEAD|GET). Uses
GET and HEAD, the standard requests one would make when requesting a directory without a file name.); **type** (MIME type for which you would like to deny
existence.)

> **Note ▶**
>
> You should make sure that this function is supported under your server before using it.
> The author has tested it on NT FastTrack 2.0a without success, but it worked on FastTrack
> for Windows 95 and Enterprise Server 3.x for NT.

IIOPexec (Server 3.x)

```
Service fn="IIOPexec"
```

(When you enable WAI services in the Server Manager from Programs|WAI Manage-
ment, this function along with other IIOP server functions [**IIIOPinit** and
IIOPNameService] are added to the **obj.conf** file.)

   Handles the processing of a client request for your WAI service. If a request from
the client is for your WAI service, **IIOPexec** invokes your WAI service (for example, your Java or C++ Web service's **Run** method). Your program, in turn, returns
the response to **IIOPexec**, which then returns the response to the client. This
method is similar to how **send-cgi** or **livewireService** invokes a CGI or a Server-
side JavaScript (LiveWire) application. The default base URI path for a WAI

application is /iiop. For example, to invoke the WAI application hello available from the server www.foo.com, the client can use the following URL: http://www.foo.com/iiop/hello.

Similar to other specific add-on server applications (for example, Server-side JavaScript), the specific WAI server functions—**IIOPinit**, **IIOPexec**, and **IIOPNameService**—are loaded as server functions through a shared library or DLL at the start of the server using the **Init** function **load-modules**. **IIOPexec** is defined inside an iiopexec Object in the **obj.conf** file.

```
<Object name="iiopexec">
Service fn="IIOPexec"
</Object>
```

The Object is named through a **NameTrans** function, **pfx2dir**, which also identifies the URI path that the client should use to invoke your WAI application (NameTrans fn="pfx2dir" from="/iiop" dir="/iiop" name="iiopexec"). For more information on **IIOPexec** and other WAI-related server functions, see the section Changes to the **obj.conf** File in Chapter 13.) (See also **IIOPinit** and **IIOPNameService**.)

Parameter: Any [name]="[value]" parameter set by you for **IIOPexec** is accessible to your WAI application through a specific WAI method, **getConfigParameter** for C++ and Java or **WAIgetConfigParameter** for C.

IIOPNameService (Server 3.x)

```
Service fn="IIOPNameService"
```
(When you enable WAI services in the Server Manager from Programs|WAI Management, this function along with other IIOP server functions [**IIIOPinit** and **IIOPexec**] are added to the **obj.conf** file.)

Used to register your WAI service or other CORBA services with Netscape's built-in Naming Service. Your Web application service uses the URI path specified for Naming Service to access and register its service with Naming Service. Other CORBA client objects can also get the Object Reference for a registered service (Object Implementation) using the URI path of the Naming Service. The default base URI path is /NameService. To get the Object Reference of a Web Application Service (WAS—a WAI application), the client uses the URI /NameService/WAS/<object name>.

Similar to other specific add-on server applications (for example, Server-side JavaScript), the specific WAI server functions—**IIOPinit**, **IIOPexec**, and **IIOPNameService**—are loaded as server functions through a shared library or DLL at the start of the server using the **Init** function **load-modules**. **IIOPNameService** is defined inside an iiopnameservice Object in the **obj.conf** file.

```
<Object name="iiopnameservice">
Service fn="IIOPNameService"
</Object>
```

The Object is named through a **NameTrans** function, **assign-name**, which also identifies the URI path for accessing the Naming Service (NameTrans fn="assign-name" from="/NameService*" name="iiopnameservice" stop=""). For more information on **IIOPNameService** and other WAI-related server functions, see the section Changes to the obj.conf File in Chapter 13.) (See also **IIOPinit** and **IIOPexec**.)

Parameter: None.

---

imagemap

```
Service fn="imagemap" method="(GET|HEAD)"
 type="magnus-internal/imagemap"
```

(Default value set at installation.)

This function defines the imagemap MIME type. The server processes imagemaps using this function. (See Chapter 3 for the use of imagemaps.)

Parameters: **method** (Acceptable method of client request. Wildcards can be used when multiple methods are acceptable. For example, (HEAD|GET). Methods for imagemap requests are GET and HEAD.); **type** (Defines an imagemap's MIME type, matching the pattern defined in the **mime.types** file. For example, an imagemap can be defined by a .map extension, the common extension for imagemaps. The server then uses this function to process *.map files.)

---

index-common

```
Service fn="index-common" method="(GET|HEAD)"
 type="magnus-internal/directory"
```

(Default value set at installation.)

(In the Server Manager, when you define fancy directory types for "Directory Indexing" under the Content Management|Document Preferences menu, this option is set.)

Netscape allows two types of directory listings when the client requests a directory without specifying an index file. **index-common** is for fancy directory indexing. The server scans the directory and generates an HTML file that lists the content of the requested directory. The HTML file lists the file and directory names, adding reference icons for the directory and file types, and information about the files. Each file or directory appears in alphabetical order as an HTML link. File names beginning with a period (.) are not displayed. (This format is common in NCSA HTTP and CERN—hence the name "index-common.") (See **index-simple** for information on simple directory indexing and **cindex-init** for the format of the fancy directory listing.)

Parameters: **method** (Acceptable method of client request. Wildcards can be used when multiple methods are acceptable. For example, (HEAD|GET).); **type** (MIME type defined for directory listing. It is an internal MIME type [specific to the server], magnus-internal/directory.); **header** (Name of the file added **before** the directory list. It becomes the header [introduction] of the directory listing. This file could be an HTML or a plain-text file. If you have used FTP with Netscape Navigator, you probably have seen introductory text describing downloading rules and general information about the content of the directory before the directory listing. This information can be generated through a file specified in this function. Consider it to be a `readme.txt` file, to be read before the directory is accessed. Use a file name for a file in the same directory or a path relative to the directory with the file name as the value of `header`. You can use a file that begins with a period so that the file will not appear in the directory listing. This parameter is optional.); **readme** (Name of the file that is appended **after** the directory listing. If you use a file name, the file should appear in the same directory that should be indexed. You can also use a path relative to the directory with the file name. This file could be HTML or plain text. You can use this information to customize the bottom of the directory-listing HTML page generated by the server with additional information, such as copyright information. You can use a file that begins with a period so that the file will not appear in the directory listing. This parameter is optional.)

index-simple

```
Service fn="index-simple" method="(GET|HEAD)"
 type="magnus-internal/directory"
```
(In the Server Manager, when simple directory types are defined for "Directory Indexing" under the Content Management|Document Preferences menu, this function is set. See also **index-common**.)

The server generates a simple directory listing when the client requests a directory that does not have an index file. The listing includes no graphics and only a bullet list of the directories and files. Files or directories appear in alphabetical order as HTML links. File names beginning with a period (.) are not displayed. There is no distinction between a directory and a file name, except for the actual name. This index can be generated more quickly than fancy index (see **index-common** for more details).

Parameters: **method** (Acceptable method of client request. Wildcards can be used when multiple methods are acceptable. For example, (HEAD|GET).); **type** (MIME type of the directory listing. It is an internal mime type, `magnus-internal/directory`.)

key-toosmall

```
Service fn=key-toosmall
```
Sends back an error message to the client that the secret key size for SSL communication is too small. When you choose "Require 128 bit secret key size for access" from Encryption|Stronger Ciphers for Server 2.x or from Server Preferences|Stronger Ciphers for Server 3.x, the server adds a Client tag in **obj.conf**. This Client tag specifies the clients with a 40-bit secret key size. The Client tag is added to the Object (template or path) you defined. Inside the Client tag, **key-toosmall** is declared as directive function. Thus any client that uses a 40-bit key size and attempts to access the predefined resource is denied access.

```
<Object ppath="c:/netscape/server/docs/safe/*">
<Client secret-keysize=40>
Service fn=key-toosmall
</Client>
</Object>
```

Do not use this function if you are running an unsecured server. (This function works as both an **Error** function and a **Service** function. It accomplishes the same thing under both directives.) (See also the Error section later in this appendix.)

Parameter: None.

---

parse-html

```
Service fn="parse-html" method=" (GET|HEAD) "
  type="magnus-internal/parsed-html"
```
(In the Server Manager, you define this function by setting the "Parse HTML" option from the Content Management|Document Footer menu.)

Enables server parsing of a predefined HTML type of file. You define the type of file, which is parsed, in **mime.types**. Usually, it is defined as

```
type=magnus-internal/parsed-html exts=shtml
```

In other words, parsing is defined for .shtml extensions. The server reads these files and parses them while looking for specific Server-side Includes that you have defined. It then processes the request and sends the result with the rest of the HTML page back to the client (see the section called Server-Side Include [Server-Parsed HTML] in Chapter 3 for more details). Here, server-parsed HTML refers to files that contain Server-side Includes. This directive can work with **shtml-hacktype** to allow parsing of all HTML files (see the **ObjectType** directive function **shtml-hacktype**).

Parameters: **method** (Acceptable method of client request. Wildcards can be used when multiple methods are acceptable. For example, (HEAD|GET). This method is usually GET or HEAD.); **type** (MIME type for files to be parsed. You define the extension that associates with this MIME type in the **mime.types** file.); **opts** (Options you define for this function. Netscape currently supports only no-exec as an option. If you use this optional parameter, then the server will not accept an executable Server-side Include tag, exec. The exec tag allows a program to run on the server by calling the executable code. You may want to use this option to disable the use of exec tags for security and performance reasons.)

---

query-handler

```
Service fn=query-handler query=*
  path=/cgi-bin/checkinfo.exe
```
(For Server 3.x, you can set the query handler in the Server Manager from Programs|Query Handler.)

Runs a CGI program in response to a request for a specified path. You can also limit the acceptable query string. **query-handler** passes the client's search string to the CGI program as command-line arguments. This function was designed to support `ISINDEX`. You can use it in conjunction with an Object that has been defined for a specific directory. In other words, you create an Object—for example, with `ppath`—and define this function for the Object. Any request for the path defined by `ppath` calls the CGI program defined in the `path` parameter of the **query-handler** function. You can use the `ISINDEX` tag to send the query to the program. The use of this directive or `ISINDEX` is not recommended. `ISINDEX` was intended for sending search strings before HTML 2.0 defined forms. It is now best to use forms to process all client requests, including search strings. As you need to write your own search engine for `ISINDEX`, you might as well use forms and customize your HTML pages instead of using the predefined `ISINDEX` text input field. Also, with Netscape Enterprise Server, you can use built-in, advanced search capabilities. (See ISINDEX in Chapter 3 for more details.)

Parameters: **path** (Points to the CGI file designated to run in response to the request. This program should be a CGI program and not a shell script.); **query** (Defines a wildcard pattern of query that should be present. In the above example, any type of query is accepted.)

---

send-cgi
`Service fn="send-cgi"`
(This function is defined for the CGI Object created by the Server Manager when you set the CGI directory information from the Programs|CGI Directory menu or when you defined CGI as a file type from the Programs|CGI File Type menu.)

Enables and processes your CGI files as programs, and sends the results of the programs back to the client. Netscape allows you to define a CGI Object either by naming it or through file association and directory specification (`ppath`).

The first method for specifying the CGI Object, named `cgi`, is through the Programs|CGI Directory menu. The server has already created the `cgi` Object during installation. You can also define a URL prefix for a CGI directory. The server then specifies the `cgi` Object for the directory. The Server Manager uses the **NameTrans** function **pfx2dir** to define a specific directory as your CGI Object's directory. The server recognizes the directory as the location of the CGI files and expects any files in that directory to be CGI executables. The server also defines the MIME type for the CGI files. Netscape uses the **ObjectType** function **force-type** to enforce the MIME type for your CGI Object, instead of using the `type` parameter of the **send-cgi** function. Hence, any file under this CGI directory should be a CGI program. The MIME type is an internal server type (for example, `magnus-internal/cgi`). The **send-cgi** function, defined for your Object, then processes (runs) your CGI program.

The second method of creating a CGI program is by associating its MIME type to a file type and assigning it to a directory. You specify a directory (or the entire server) where the server recognizes these types of files as CGI programs. You can make this specification through the Program|CGI File Type menu in the Server Manager. This procedure adds **send-cgi**, with the `type` parameter, to the default Object or to an Object that uses the path you defined (an Object by `ppath` association). When you use this method, the **ObjectType** function **force-type** is no longer used. Instead, the server uses the `type` parameter of **send-cgi** to define the MIME type for the CGI files. Finally, the **send-cgi** function processes (runs) your CGI program.

send-cgi also translates the path information from the server variables into a format appropriate for running a program under the operating system (for example, it translates the "/" to "\" for NT).

For organizational and security purposes, it is best to place all of your CGI programs under a specific directory and not allow executables throughout the entire server. Because Windows CGI, Shell CGI, and CGI are processed differently by the server, it is best to give each one its own directory. (See Chapter 3 for more details.)

Parameter: <u>type</u> (MIME type for the CGI type files. `magnus-internal/cgi` is a specific server MIME type defined for CGI programs. The extension that associates with this MIME type is found in your **mime.types** file.)

---

send-error

```
Service fn="send-error" method="(GET|HEAD)"
 type="magnus-internal/directory"
 [path="c:/netscape/server/err/special.html"]
```

(When you choose None for "Directory Indexing" from the Content Management|Document Preferences menu, the server adds the above function to the **obj.conf** file. Unfortunately, the function, as placed by the Server Manager, is missing the necessary `path` parameter. [See the Bug Report box for more detail.])

Not to be confused with the **send-error** function used as an **Error** directive function. This function performs a dual purpose. It can be utilized as a **Service** or **Error** directive function. Although this function returns an error page to the client for both **Error** and **Service** directives, its purpose is different for each directive.

As a **Service** directive function, **send-error** returns an error page based on the MIME type of the client request. This function becomes the default **Service** function for the specified MIME type. **send-error** sends the file specified in the `path` parameter to the client if the client request is of the same MIME type as the one in the `type` parameter. Note that you must add the `path` parameter manually to the **send-error** function to prevent this function from causing a server error. (See also **send-error** in the **Error** directive functions list.)

Parameters: <u>path</u> (File to be sent to the client when the error occurs. Use the full path to the file.); <u>method</u> (Acceptable method of client request. Wildcards can be used when multiple methods are acceptable. For example, `(HEAD|GET)`.

This parameter is optional.); **type** (MIME type for which you would like the server to send the error page. In the example above, `magnus-internal/directory` is the internal MIME type [specific to the server] for the directory listing.)

Bug Report ▶

If you use the Server Manager to add **send-error** for the MIME type `magnus-internal/directory` to the **obj.conf** file, the function will miss the necessary `path` parameter. For example, under NT FastTrack Server 2.x or Enterprise Server 3.x, when you choose **None** for "Directory Indexing" under the Content Management|Document Preferences menu, the server adds the following **send-error** function to the **obj.conf** file.

(If you created this function through Server Manager 2.x, it labels **send-error** as Unknown in the System Settings|View Server Settings menu. The Server Manager does not recognize the function that it placed in **obj.conf**!)

```
Service fn="send-error" method="(GET|HEAD)"
  type="magnus-internal/directory"
```

You choose this option so that the server will **not** send a directory listing of the files if no index file is found in the directory. This function replaces the **Service** function **index-common** or **index-simple**. When the client requests an index page and none exists, instead of providing a defined directory listing, this function should send the client a Not Found or Forbidden page. This function, however, has the unfortunate result of sending a Server Error page. The server reports that the `path` parameter is missing. You must add a `path` parameter manually. The `path` parameter points to the file that the server should return when the client requests a directory that does not include an index file. If you add the path to a specified file, then this function should return that file properly. Note that the server does not send the default Forbidden or Not Found page; instead it expects to return the error page you define in the `path` parameter.

Under Server 2.x, if the file defined in the `path` parameter is not found, the server returns a Not Found page. In other words, if you include the `path` parameter and set its value to a dummy file, the server returns a Not Found page. The server will also not record any error in the error log file. Under Server 3.x, if the file defined in the `path` parameter is not found, the server returns a Forbidden page and reports an error in the error log file. The error states that **send-error** failed to open the specified file.

Alternatively, you can use **deny-existence** as a **Service** function with the same `method` and `type` parameters as the **send-error** above so as to return a Not Found page. With **deny-existence**, the server also records a security error regarding the client request for the directory listing in the error log file.

send-file

```
Service fn="send-file" method="(GET|HEAD)"
  type="*~magnus-internal/*"
```

(Default value set at installation.)

Enables files to be sent back to the client. This directive should already be present in your **obj.conf** file. Otherwise, the server could not respond to the client properly. This default server function (other than internally defined server types such as CGI or your NSAPI programs) returns the requested file to the client.

Parameters: **method** (Method of request, usually GET or HEAD. Wildcards can be used when multiple methods are acceptable. For example, (HEAD|GET).); **type** (Type of file to which this function responds. This MIME type can use wildcards. In the accompanying example, **send-file** is defined for all types except magnus-internal.)

Bug Report ▶

Under NT Server 2.0, the server was unable to send a file larger than 500K. This problem is resolved with Server 2.01 and later.

---

send-range
```
Service fn=send-range
```
Sends back the HTTP byte range requested by the client.

Parameter: None.

---

send-shellcgi (NT)
```
Service fn="send-shellcgi"
 type="magnus-internal/shellcgi"
```
(In the Server Manager, this function is set for the Shell CGI Object defined through the Shell CGI directory from the Programs|ShellCGI Directory menu.)

Enables and processes your Shell CGI programs, and sends the results of running the programs back to the client. **send-shellcgi** uses the operating system's existing file extensions to run a Shell CGI program. You can use this function for any scripting program that needs an interpreter to run. For example, you might have defined all *.pl files to run as Perl programs (that is, the script is passed to the Perl Interpreter perl.exe). Netscape uses this same information to process the *.pl files by running them as a file type you have defined under NT.

When you enable Shell CGI for your server through the Server Manager, Netscape installs Shell CGI two different ways: as a function in the default Object and as a new Object called shellcgi. The line in your default Object, Service fn= "send-shellcgi" type="magnus-internal/shellcgi, enables Shell CGI for all shellcgi type files. As no shellcgi extension is defined in the **mime.types** file, however, no Shell CGI program will run. If you wish to enable Shell CGI for the entire server, keep this line in the **obj.conf** file and add a MIME type for the Shell CGI programs in the **mime.types** file. For example, add type=magnus-internal/shellcgi exts=pl.

The Server Manager also installs Shell CGI as a new Object, shellcgi. The Server Manager uses the **NameTrans** function **pfx2dir** to define a specific directory as your Shell CGI directory. The server recognizes this directory as the location of the Shell CGI files and expects any files in that directory to be Shell CGI executables. The server also defines the MIME type for the Shell CGI files. Netscape uses the **ObjectType** function **force-type** to enforce the MIME type for your

Shell CGI Object, instead of the `type` parameter of the **send-shellcgi** function. Hence, any file under this Shell CGI directory should be a Shell CGI program. The MIME type is the internal server type `magnus-internal/shellcgi`. The **send-shellcgi** function defined for your Object then processes (runs) your Shell CGI program.

This function changes the path variable in *Request*->vars (server variables) to the `perl.exe` path and adds a new variable called `shellcgi-path` that points to the path of your Perl script. For example,

```
path="c:\\PERL\\perl.exe"
shellcgi-path="c:/netscape/server/shellcgi/guest.pl"
```

send-shellcgi also translates the path information from the server variables into a format appropriate for running a program under the operating system (for example, it translates "/" to "\" for NT).

For organizational and security purposes, it is best to place all of your Shell CGI program under a specific directory and not allow executables throughout the entire server. Thus, you may want to remove the **send-shellcgi** line from your default Object. As Windows CGI, Shell CGI, and CGI are processed differently by the server, it is also best to give each one its own directory. (See Chapter 3 for more details.)

Parameter: **type** (MIME type for the Shell CGI files. `magnus-internal/ shellcgi` is a specific server MIME type defined for Shell CGI programs. The extension that associates with this MIME type is found in your **mime.types** file.)

---

send-wincgi (NT)

```
Service fn="send-wincgi" type="magnus-internal/wincgi"
  debug="yes"
```

(This function is set for the WinCGI Object. In the Server Manager, you define the WinCGI directory from the Programs|WinCGI Directory menu.)

Enables and processes your Windows CGI programs, and sends the results of running the programs back to the client. Windows CGI (WinCGI) was designed originally by WebSite (another HTTP server developer company) as a way for servers to work with Windows programs (for example, Visual Basic). These types of programs are not console applications. They do not work with `stdin` (standard input) and `stdout` (standard output), the cornerstones of server information-processing for CGI programs.

When you enable Windows CGI for your server through Server Manager, Netscape installs WinCGI in two different ways: as a function in the default Object and as a new Object called `wincgi`. The line in your default Object, `Service fn="send-wincgi" type="magnus-internal/wincgi`, enables Windows CGI for all `wincgi` type files. As no `wincgi` extension is defined in the **mime.types** file, however, no Windows CGI program will run. If you want to enable WinCGI for the entire server, keep this line in the

obj.conf file, and add a MIME type for the WinCGI program in the **mime.types** file. Unfortunately, this tactic will mean you cannot use the standard `.exe` extension for your WinCGI files. The `.exe` extension is already defined for CGI functions. You can add another type of extension for your WinCGI program—for example, add `type=magnus-internal/wincgi exts=wcgi` to your **mime.types** file. The server then recognizes and runs files with `.wcgi` extensions as your WINCGI programs.

The Server Manager also installs WinCGI as a new Object, `wincgi`. The Server Manager uses the **NameTrans** function **pfx2dir** to define a specific directory as your WinCGI directory. The server recognizes the directory as the location of the WinCGI files, and expects any files in that directory to be WinCGI executables. The server also defines the MIME type for the WinCGI files. Netscape uses the **ObjectType** function **force-type** to enforce the MIME type for your WinCGI Object, instead of the `type` parameter of the **send-wincgi** function. Hence, any file under this WinCGI directory should be a WinCGI program. The MIME type is the internal server type `magnus-internal/wincgi`. The **send-wincgi** function defined for your Object then processes (runs) your WinCGI program.

This function also translates the path information from the server variables into a format that is appropriate for running a program under the operating system (for example, changes the "/" to "\" for NT).

For organizational and security purposes, it is best to place all of your WinCGI programs under a specific directory and not allow executables throughout the entire server. Thus you may want to remove the **send-wincgi** line from your default Object. As Windows CGI, Shell CGI, and CGI are processed differently by the server, it is also best to give each one its own directory. (See Chapter 3 for more details.)

Parameters: <u>type</u> (MIME type for the WinCGI files. `magnus-internal/wincgi` is the predefined server MIME type. The extension that associates with this MIME type is found in your **mime.types** file.); <u>debug</u> (You can "Enable Script Tracing" for debugging purposes by setting this debug parameter to `yes`. This parameter is optional.)

---

user-defined

```
Service fn="formanswer" method="(GET|POST|HEAD)"
  type="magnus-internal/formresponse"
```

You can write your own **Service** function and pass it any `[name]="[value]"` parameters you wish. You can then use these parameters in your program.

Parameters: The standard `method`, `type`, and `query` plus any `[name]="[value]"` parameters set by you and passed to the function.

The AddLog Functions

common-log
`AddLog fn=common-log name="access" iponly="1"`

Logs information into a common log file. This function uses the Common Log Format (CLF) to record the request transaction. This format was originally defined by NCSA and CERN, and is used by most HTTP servers. This function works in conjunction with **init-clf**, an **Init** function. The value of the name parameter defined here must match the *name* parameter in **init-clf**. (See **Init** function **init-clf**.) This method of naming, although a bit confusing at first, allows for multiple **AddLog** functions to work with one log file defined in the **Init** function. You also need to use an **Init** function to open a file once at the start of the server. If you need greater flexibility for your access log file, use Netscape's flexible log file. (See the **AddLog** function **flex-log** and the **Init** function **flex-init**.)

    Parameters: **name** (Points to the log file, as defined in **init-clf**. The name you specify here is a reference to the name you used for the *name* parameter of the **init-clf** and not the actual name of the log file. The value of name must match the *name* parameter of **init-clf**, `[name]=[file path]`.); **iponly** (If you include this parameter, the server will not look up the client `hostname` and will use only the IP address. The actual value of this parameter does not matter, so you can include any value. The Server Manager uses 1 when it enables this feature. This parameter is optional.)

flex-log
`AddLog fn="flex-log" iponly="1" name="access"`
(Default value set at installation.)
(In the Server Manager, most **flex-log** options are set in the "Log Preferences" form from the Server Status|Log Preferences menu.)

This function logs the information into a flexible log file. A flexible log file is an alternative to a common log file, and provides more options and extended data for your log file. It works in conjunction with the **Init** function **flex-init**. You first define the location, name, and format of the log file through **flex-init**. Unlike **init-clf**, **flex-init** includes information about which data will be recorded and how they will be formatted. **flex-log** then logs the information. This method of naming and using the file, although a bit confusing at first, allows for multiple **AddLog** functions to work with one log file defined in the **Init** function. You also need to use an **Init** function to open a file once at the start of the server. Use this function when you want a flexible log format for the access log file. This function should already be part of your **obj.conf** file. (See the **AddLog** directive **common-log** and the **Init** directive **flex-init** for more information.)

    Parameters: **name** (Points to the log file, as defined in **flex-init**. The value of name used here must match the *name* parameter of **flex-init**, [*name*]=[*file path*]. You name the parameter *name* in **flex-init** and point it to the log file. This *name* is then used as the value of the **flex-log** function's name parameter.); **iponly** (If you include this parameter, the server will not look up the hostname of the client and will use only the IP address. The actual value of this parameter does not matter, so you can include any value. The Server Manager uses 1 when it enables this feature. This parameter is optional.)

record-keysize

```
AddLog fn=record-keysize name=keysize
```
Records the key size of each request for a secured server. The client information (its IP or DNS address), plus the date and time of the request, and the size of the key used, are recorded in the file. Use this function with the generic **Init** function **init-clf**. With **init-clf**, you can name and point to the location of the file used to record this information.

Parameter: **name** (Points to the file where information is recorded. You specify the location and name of the file with **init-clf**, an **Init** function. The value of name must match the *name* parameter of **init-clf**, [*name*]=[*file path*].

record-user-agent

```
AddLog fn=record-useragent name=browsersinfo
```
This function records the user-agent's header (from the HTTP protocol header, *Request->*headers) after the IP address of each client in the specified file. Use this function to determine which browser the client is using. The data are recorded for each request, including each request for any embedded multimedia object on the HTML page. The following is an example of the text that is recorded:

```
1.2.3.4 Mozilla/4.04 [en] (WinNT; I)
```

Similar to other **AddLog** functions, you need first to define an **Init** function. Use **init-clf** to specify the name and location of the log file.

As you can log user-agent information using **flex-log** and **flex-init**, you no longer need to use this function to create a separate user-agent file for recording the client user-agent.

Parameter: **name** (Points to the log file where the information is recorded. You specify the location and name of the file with **init-clf**, an **Init** function. The value of name must match the *name* parameter of **init-clf**, [*name*]=[*file path*].

user-defined

```
AddLog fn=Detailed-Log
```
You can write your own **AddLog** function and pass it any [*name*]= " [*value*] " parameter you wish for your programs.

Parameter: Any [*name*]= " [*value*] " parameter set by you and passed to the function.

The Error Functions

key-toosmall

`Error fn=key-toosmall`

Sends back an error message to the client noting that the secret key size for SSL communication is too small for the request. For example, if you set the certification key size to 128, this function checks whether the client is capable of 128-bit encryption. Netscape's exportable browser/server cannot provide this level of security, so this function provides the needed error information for a client who attempts to connect to such a secured area. The server checks on the client's security capabilities. If the client does not have the required capability, the server excludes access to the secured area and returns an appropriate error message written for this function. This function usually works with the client directives (see the Client section in Chapter 2 for more information). Do not use this function if you are running an unsecured server. This function can be used as both an **Error** and a **Service** directive function. It accomplishes the same thing under both directives.

Parameter: None.

query-handler

```
Error fn="query-handler" reason="Unauthorized"
 path="c:/cgi/errorhandler.cgi"
```
(You can set this function in the Server Manager by checking the "CGI" box in the "Custom Error Responses" option under the System Settings|Error Responses menu in Server 2.x and under the Server Preferences|Error Responses menu in Server 3.x.)

Starts a specified CGI program to respond to the client when the type of error code you have defined occurs. You can therefore respond to an error with a CGI program that can include a sophisticated response to the client. You can, for example, recover and log information before sending an error message to the client. If you want to return only an HTML page, then use the **send-error** function instead. (The use of this function as an **Error** directive function is not to be confused with its use as a **Service** directive function. As a **Service** directive function, **query-handler** is used to support ISINDEX.)

Parameters: **reason** (Type of error that calls your CGI program: `Unauthorized`, `Forbidden`, `Not found`, `Server Error`, and so on.); **code** (Type of error code, that calls your CGI program. Instead of using the descriptive text [for example, `Unauthorized`, the `reason` parameter], you can employ the code associated with the error [for example, `401` for `Unauthorized`] to indicate the type of error. You can use both `reason` and `code` as long as they refer to the same error type.); **path** (CGI file activated when the error occurs. Use the full path to the file.)

send-error

```
Error fn="send-error" reason="Unauthorized"
  path="c:/error/error2.txt"
```

(You can set this function in the Server Manager by the "Custom Error Responses" option from the System Settings|Error Responses menu for Server 2.x and from the Server Preferences|Error Responses menu for Server 3.x, and by *not* checking the "CGI" box.)

Sends the HTML error file defined here to the client. You can define the type of error code that causes the file to be sent: Unauthorized, Forbidden, Not found, or Server Error. This option allows for easy modification of the error page that the client will receive. If you want to define a CGI program to be used instead of a file, then use the **query-handler** function. The use of **send-error** as an **Error** directive function is different from its use as a **Service** directive function. As a **Service** directive function, **send-error** sends an error page when a specific MIME type is requested. (See **send-error** in the list of **Service** directive functions for more details.)

Parameters: **reason** (Type of error for which you want the specific file to be sent: Unauthorized, Forbidden, Not found, Server Error, and so on.); **code** (Type of error code for which you want the specific file to be set. Instead of using the descriptive text [for example, Unauthorized, the reason parameter], you can employ the code associated with the error [for example, 401 for Unauthorized] to indicate the type of error. You can use both reason and code as long as they refer to the same error type.); **path** (File sent to the client when the error occurs. Use the full path to the file. The server expects the file content-type to be text/html.)

user-defined

```
Error fn=error_handler code=401
```

You can also write your own **Error** function. Similar to **send-error** used as an **Error** directive function, your **Error** function can be called when a specific error occurs. For the server to run, your error function must specify an error code or a reason string parameter.

Parameters: **reason** (Type of error for which you want the specific file to be sent: Unauthorized, Forbidden, Not found, Server Error, and so on.); **code** (Type of error code for which you want the specific file to be set. Instead of using the descriptive text [for example, Unauthorized, the reason parameter], you can employ the code associated with the error [for example, 401 for Unauthorized] to indicate the type of error. You can use both reason and code as long as they refer to the same error type.) You can also specify any additional [*name*]="[*value*]" parameter to be sent to your function.

ACL Files

The Access Control List (ACL) holds the information about who is allowed access to the different resources of the server. The list includes the rules about users, groups, and clients and their access privileges. ACL also includes information about the method of authentication.

ACLs are normally kept in simple text files with the extension `.acl`. Netscape Server's ACL files are usually kept under the `httpacl` directory. Administration Server 3.x uses separate ACL files found under the `adminacl` directory for the ACLs that apply to Administration Server and the Server Manager. In this appendix, we will briefly discuss the ACL files for Netscape Server 2.x and 3.x. We will discuss the syntax, statements, and functions that can be used in an ACL. The syntax and functionality of ACL are different for Netscape Server 2.x and 3.x. You need to understand the ACL syntax to read and edit the ACL file. In most cases, you can use the Server Manager to make any specific access control modification. Some options, however, require manual editing of the ACL files. For example, for Server 3.x, you need to edit the ACL files manually when you write a customized access control. Using Server 3.x, you can also take advantage of the Access Control API to parse, evaluate, read, edit, create, and modify ACLs dynamically.

The main server ACL files are: `generated.<server ID>.acl` and `genwork.<server ID>.acl` (`httpd-<server name>` is used for FastTrack Server ID, while `https-<server name>` is used for Enterprise Server). `generated` refers to changes made and saved using the Server Manager. The file with `generated` in its file name is the main ACL file. `genwork` refers to temporary changes before they have been saved by choosing the final OK button in the Server Manager; thus the file with `genwork` in its file name is the temporary ACL file. Under Server 2.x, these files are created without any content when the server is installed and are updated when you modify your access control information using the Server Manager (Server Preferences|Restrict Access). Under Server 3.x, there is a default global ACL for the server (`acl "default"`) and a default ACL for agents (`acl "agents"`). The following code is an example of the default ACL file, `generated.https-foo.acl`, generated by Server 3.5.1 during installation:

```
version 3.0;

acl agents;
authenticate (user,group) {
        prompt = "Enterprise Server";
};
deny (all) (user = "anyone");
allow absolute (all) (user = "all");

acl "default";
authenticate (user,group) {
        prompt = "Enterprise Server";
};
allow (read,execute,list,info) user = "anyone";
allow (write,delete) user = "all";
```

The following code is an example of the content of an ACL file for Server 2.x:

```
ACL https-foo_formgen-WRITE-ACL_deny-812(PUT, DELETE,
                                    MKDIR, RMDIR, MOVE) {
    Default deny anyone;
}

ACL https-foo_formgen-READ-ACL_allow-812(GET, HEAD, POST,
                                    INDEX){
    Default deny anyone;
    Default authenticate in {
            Database "c:/netscape/server/authdb/default";
            Method basic;
    };
    Default allow joe;
}
```

The name and location of the ACL file—for example, `generated.https-foo.acl`—is specified in the **magnus.conf** file with the **ACLFile** directive. If you intend to use more than one file, you can include multiple **ACLFile** directives in the **magnus.conf** file. The server then reads and uses all the files at start-up. If you use multiple ACL files for Server 3.x, you should reference the ACLs in the ACL files in the **obj.conf** file.

ACLs usually work in conjunction with the **PathCheck** directive function **check-acl** defined in **obj.conf**. **check-acl** references a specific ACL in your ACL file. It allows the ACL to be applied to a specific Object in the **obj.conf** file. The **check-acl** function is included inside a specific Object's scope in the **obj.conf** file. In other words, it is placed inside the object tags <Object . . . > . . . </Object>, where **PathCheck** directive functions should be placed. The parameter acl for the **PathCheck** function identifies the name of the ACL as its value. You can create the ACL and set access control information through the Server Manager or by manually editing the **obj.conf** file and the appropriate ACL file. You can also limit the access to a specific resource, a server Object, by declaring the **check-acl** function inside the scope of a specific Object, which determines the resource. The following is an example of a **check-acl** function used in the **obj.conf** file for Server 3.x. Inside the ACL file, the specific ACL named by the **PathCheck** function (aclspecial) determines the access control rules. For example, the ACL aclspecial can limit the access to the directory special for users in the group specialists.

```
<Object ppath="c:/netscape/server/docs/special/*">
PathCheck fn="check-acl" acl="aclspecial"
</Object>
```

You can have additional ACLs in your ACL file, which are not referenced by your **obj.conf** file. But, they should not include any erroneous information, such as users that are not part of the user database.

ACLs normally use the server's default user databases for authentication of users. For Server 2.x, the server uses a DBM file for the user database. For Server 3.x, the server uses a local LDAP directory or an LDAP directory server. The user database contains user names and passwords (or group information). You can also specify a specific user database for an ACL. The user database, however, should be one that the server can support. For example, you cannot use an LDAP directory with Server 2.x's built-in access control. Under Server 3.x, you can use a custom database and write an access control program that supports it. If you have an existing user database with access control settings not supported by Netscape Server 3.x, you need to write a program to integrate the database and its user access information with the server.

Under Server 2.x, Netscape does not provide an API for managing ACL files or for writing a customized access control that supports Netscape's built-in access control. With Server 3.x, you can use the Access Control API. We will not discuss this API in this book. If you intend to provide specific access control or authentication features for your server, however, you should definitely check the Access Control API. With this API, you can control access to server resources, write your own attributes for authentication, define a new authentication method or rules, and integrate an existing user database. (See the Netscape document, "Access Control API Programmer's Guide and Reference," at http://developer.netscape.com/library/documentation/enterprise/accessapi/index.htm.)

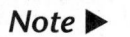

Note ▶

Under Server 2.0, you need to disable LiveWire before modifying the ACL configuration. Also, an access control password should include no more than eight characters.

ACL for Server 2.x

The ACL for Server 2.x looks like a C or C++ function, so we will describe it as a function. The ACL function uses the following syntax:

```
ACL <serverID>_formgen-<action>-ACL_<authorization>-<num>
                       (<request method>){
    <specific instructions>;
}
```

In the ACL file, the name of the function and its parameters are placed on a single line. For the above syntax information, the name of the function is wrapped for printing purposes. The following is an example of an ACL:

```
ACL https-foo_formgen-READ-ACL_allow-812(GET, HEAD, POST){
    Default deny anyone;
}
```

All ACLs begin with the text ACL followed by the name of the function. https-foo (http<d|s>-<server name>) is the server ID. formgen indicates that the function was generated using Netscape's Server Manager. (If you manually add an ACL to the ACL file, you should still use the same syntax.) READ and WRITE (<action>) are actions based on your operating system's file management actions and permission types. They determine whether the ACL function is used for a READ or WRITE action. The client intends to either read a file from your site or write, change, or delete a file in the site. allow and deny (<authorization>) are responses that the server should make. They determine the type of authorization. By combining action, ACL_, and authorization, you create a command (for example, READ, ACL_, and allow together generate the command READ-ACL_allow). READ-ACL_allow (used for a read ACL function) and WRITE-ACL_deny (used for a write ACL function) are the two options available for the ACL. You specify the specific permission settings within the ACL function. For example, for the READ-ACL_allow function, you can include either the Default deny anyone; instruction (denying read access) or the Default allow anyone; instruction (allowing read access). This step is taken in lieu of changing the function from READ-ACL_allow to READ-ACL_deny. While the function name may say READ-ACL_allow, the instruction within the braces ({ }) of the function can either deny or allow access.

The Server Manager automatically generates a unique, random number <num> as an identifier of the ACL function. This number, which is added to the end of the function name, identifies the function uniquely. The Server Manager also generates the **PathCheck** function **check-acl** in the **obj.conf** file. **check-acl** references the ACL function by its name, which includes this unique number identifier. The value of the acl parameter of **check-acl** should match the name of the ACL function. If you decide to write your own ACL function, make sure the ACL function name matches the ACL function identified by the `acl` parameter of **check-acl** in the **obj.conf** file (for example, `PathCheck fn="check-acl" acl="https-foo_formgen-READ-ACL_allow-812"`).

The parameters for the ACL function are the HTTP request methods (for example, `GET`, `POST`, and so on) for which the function is defined—that is, the request methods to which the ACL function should apply. The HTTP request method should match the type of ACL specified by the function name. For example, the `GET`, `HEAD`, `POST`, and `INDEX` HTTP methods are used with an ACL "READ" function—for example, `https-foo_formgen-`**READ**`-ACL_allow-812`. They are intended for the client requests to read data from the server. The `PUT`, `DELETE`, `MKDIR`, `RMDIR`, and `MOVE` HTTP methods are used with an ACL "WRITE" function—for example, `https-foo_formgen-`**WRITE**`-ACL_allow-812`. They are intended for the client requests to write to the server.

The following code is an example of an ACL function for Server 2.x:

```
ACL https-foo_formgen-READ-ACL_allow-812(GET, HEAD, POST,
                                          INDEX) {

    Default deny anyone;

    Default authenticate in {
            Database "c:/netscape/server/authdb/default";
            Method basic;
    };

    Default allow joe;
}
```

Inside the ACL function, you can specify any number of specific access control rules or guidelines. You can define a default response for the ACL function. For example, in the ACL function, you can simply allow everyone access (`Default allow anyone;`) or deny everyone access (`Default deny anyone;`). The access rules are hierarchical, so you should normally first deny access to all (to anyone) and then allow access to specific users or groups. In the previous example, the first rule denies everyone access to the resource. In the last rule, we define an exception to the rule. We allow access to the user joe (`Default allow joe;`).

You can also provide additional guidelines for the ACL inside the ACL function. In the previous example, a default authentication rule is defined that specifies the user database and the method of the authentication. The database is the default user database for Server 2.x. The method of authentication is the basic authentication, in which the client is required to send the user name and password information. All of the rules specified for the ACL are processed before the server can give the client access to the requested resource.

User or group names in an ACL should not include the following characters: &, <, >, \, or ". In Server 2.0, the access control password should be no more than eight characters. If you are adding multiple users to the ACL through Server Settings|Restrict Access, you must put quotes around any `username` that includes any characters except a letter, digit, dash, or underscore. In addition, `username` cannot start or end with white space.

To convert an ACL for Server 2.x to a 3.x-compatible ACL file, you can use the Server Manager of Server 3.x (Server Preferences|Convert 2.0 ACL file).

ACL for Server 3.x

The ACL for Server 3.x does not use the same syntax or rules as that for Server 2.x. The syntax of the ACL does not look like a C or C++ function. Each ACL in Server 3.x begins with the line `acl "<identifier>";`. The various rules and instructions associated with the specific `acl` end where the next `acl` is defined. Thus different ACLs can be sequentially listed in the ACL file.

Following is a brief discussion of the syntax that you need to know to write or modify the Server 3.x ACL file.

General Conventions

All statements in the ACL file end with a semicolon (;) similar to the statements in C. You can add comments to the file by starting the comment line with a pound sign (#), similar to the setup of the server configuration files (for example, **obj.conf**). All ACL files should start with the version information. You need to add the version information before any actual access control entry. You can, however, have comment lines before the version statement. You should use only one version line in an ACL file. The current version of ACL is 3.0. The following code is an example:

```
# ACL file
version 3.0;
```

To make sure the values you specify in the ACL file can accept characters (such as a space) that are otherwise ignored, you should place the value in quotation marks—for

---

Bug Report ▶

Enterprise Server 3.0 and 3.5.1 for Solaris may crash with the following error: `denied by ACL (null) directive 0`. ACL may return the value `null`. The access logs may also log the incorrect time. The hour may jump ahead or decrease by several hours. To resolve this problem, you should upgrade to server patch 3.0J for Server 3.0 and server patch 3.5.1A for Server 3.5.1. For latest server patches, see Netscape's File Library page (`http://help.netscape.com/filelib.html`).

example, `prompt = "Imagination Server"`. You also need to place a list of items in quotation marks—for example, `user = "joe,jane"`.

ACL *identifier*

As mentioned earlier, each ACL begins with `acl "<identifier>";`. Unlike with Server 2.x, for Server 3.x, you use lowercase characters for the word "`acl`" in the ACL file. The *identifier* identifies the type of ACL. It must be unique for each ACL that the server uses. The *identifier* can be a name, a path, or a URI.

For a named ACL, you simply place the name in the quotation marks after `acl`— for example, `acl "default";`. Although by convention, the *identifier* is normally placed in quotation marks, the quotation marks are not required. The name you specify should be referenced by a **check-acl** function in the **obj.conf** file. The name should be the same as the value of the parameter `acl` of **check-acl**. A named ACL allows you to apply the same ACL to different resources in the **obj.conf** file using the **check-acl** function. Netscape adds a default ACL to the ACL file during installation. The default ACL, `acl "default";`, allows read access to anyone and write access to the users in the local database or the LDAP directory server.

Instead of using a name, you can specify a server resource as an *identifier*. To use a path or URI as the *identifier*, you need to include `path="<system path>"` or `uri="<relative URI>"` as the *identifier*. For a path, you need to include an absolute system path to the resource—for example, `acl "path=c:/netscape/server/docs/secrets/";`. You can also specify a file name with the path. For the URI, you should use a relative URI that is recognized by the server, such as `acl "uri=/secrets/special";`. The resources for the URI are relative to the document root. The URI should start with a forward slash. The path you specify does not need to exist directly under the document root directory. If you have associated a system path to a specific URI, you can use that URI for the location of the resource. The use of the path-type ACL allows you to specify a predefined system location independent of the URI that the client uses to access the resource. On the other hand, by using a URI, you can specify a relative path that is independent of the physical location of the resource on your machine. Use a URI if you often change the location of the resources on your machine. Use a path if different URIs are used for a resource that remains in the same system file location on your machine.

Unlike with Server 2.x, for Server 3.x you do not need to use a **check-acl** function for all types of ACLs that you define in the ACL file. Server 2.x supported only named ACLs. In fact, when you convert a Server 2.x ACL file to a Server 3.x ACL file, all ACLs in the Server 2.x ACL file are converted to named ACLs. While you do need to use **check-acl** for named ACLs for Server 3.x, you do not need to use **check-acl** with a URI- or path-type ACL. (You must also use a **check-acl** function to identify any ACL that is not in the first ACL file specified in the **magnus.conf** file.) For URI- or path-type ACLs, the server can use the ACLs without a specific **check-acl** function for the ACLs in the **obj.conf** file. If you do specify **check-acl** for a URI- or path-type ACL, use only the path and URI as the value of the `acl` parameter of **check-acl**. You do not need to include "path=" or "uri=" in the value (for example, `PathCheck fn="check-acl" acl="c:/netscape/server/docs/secrets/"`). When you use the Server Manager to set an ACL for a specific server resource, the server updates the **obj.conf** file with a **check-acl** function for the ACL and adds the ACL to the ACL file.

In choosing an ACL instruction for a specific client request, the server first looks for an ACL referenced in the **obj.conf** file. It then goes through the ACLs in the ACL file that uses a URI or path. In searching for an ACL that is applicable to the requested URL, the server begins with an ACL that matches the file type or a wildcard pattern—for example, `*.html`. Next, it looks at the directory path of the URL for an appropriate ACL. The server traverses the directories in the requested URL, beginning with the first directory in the URL (the left-most directory in the URL). It then steps through the subdirectories and any specified file names looking for a match. If more than one ACL matches the target, the server uses the last ACL that applies. To stop the server from continuing to look for a matching ACL, you can specify the `absolute` attribute with the authorization statement for allowing or denying access. (We will discuss authorization statements shortly.)

Authentication Statement

After the `acl` statement, you can include an authentication statement that determines the method of authentication that should be used by the client and server. By using an authentication statement, you can require authentication for the resource. You must also include a **check-acl** function for the named ACLs or any ACL that is not in the first ACL file defined in the **magnus.conf** file. The format of the authentication statement is similar to a C function, so we will describe it as a function.

```
authenticate (<user and/or group>) {
   /* authentication-related statement
      (method, database, and prompt)
   */
}
```

The following is an example of an authentication function:

```
authenticate(user,group) {
    method = "basic";
    prompt = "special area";
}
```

In the parameters for the **authenticate** function, you specify whether the authentication should apply to the users or groups lists or to both lists in the local database or the LDAP directory server. After the authentication function, you can allow or deny access to the specific user and/or group. (We will discuss this method shortly.)

The default method is `basic`, which means that the client must send the user name and password. If you do not specify a method, the server will assume the method is `basic`. You can also specify a prompt that will appear in the authentication dialog box as part of the instructions for the client during authentication. The prompt usually identifies which area of the system is being requested. The complete string in the authentication dialog box may look like the following: `Enter username for <prompt> at <server name>`. The prompt string is the same as the `realm` parameter used for the **PathCheck** function **require-auth**.

The other built-in method that you can specify is `SSL`, which requires client certificate for authentication. The server must be a secured server (that is, the encryption must be turned on) and the client needs to send an SSL certificate for authentication. If you have written a customized method, you can also specify your method with the method statement.

> **Note ▶**
>
> To change the default method for the ACLs, you add the **Init** function **acl-set-default-method** to the `obj.conf` file and specify the method as its parameter (for example, `Init fn=acl-set-default-method method=SSL`). When you change the default method using **acl-set-default-method,** the server will use the default method you specified when there is no method declared for an ACL.

Another type of statement that you can include with the authentication function is a `database` statement. With `database`, you can specify the database that the server should use for authentication. You can have separate ACLs use different user databases. With this option, you can specify a custom database or an alternative database than the default database used by the server. The server must be able to use the database that you specify. For example, if you have multiple LDAP directory databases, you can use different databases with different ACLs. You can also write a program using Access Control API that supports your special database.

Authorization Statement

You can allow or deny access to a specific resource defined either directly by the ACL's URI or path identifier or indirectly with a combination of a named ACL and **check-acl**. To allow access, an **allow** statement is used; to deny access, a **deny** statement is used. The following format is used for the **allow** or **deny** statement:

```
allow or deny [absolute] (<permissions (access rights)>)
<attributes>
[additional attributes];
```

As with **allow** or **deny** statements in an ACL for Server 2.x, Server 3.x reads the authorization statements for each ACL in the order that they are declared. You normally deny access to anyone (everyone) first, before allowing access to specific users and/or groups. If more than one ACL applies to a resource, the server uses the last authorization statement for the last ACL that applies to the request. If absolute is added to the authorization **allow** or **deny** statement, the server does not look any further for another ACL that matches the request. Instead, the server uses the absolute authorization rule. If there is more than one absolute authorization statement, the server uses the first one that matches.

The specific permissions (access rights) you can use for **allow** or **deny** statements determine the access rights for files or directories. You can limit the type of access that is allowed. The optional permissions include read, write, execute, delete, list, and info. The access rights must also match the type of method used by the client request. read is used for the HTTP request methods GET, HEAD, POST, and INDEX. write is used for the HTTP request methods PUT, DELETE, MKDIR, RMDIR, and MOVE. execute is used for a request to execute an application on the server (for example, a Java applet, agent, CGI application, and so on). delete is used for the permission to delete a file or directory on the server. list is used for getting the directory listing. info is used for getting the HTTP response-headers; it is intended for use by Web Publisher. You can also use all for all permission types. For example, to deny write, delete, and execute access to everyone, you can use the following deny statement:

```
deny(write, delete, execute)
    user = "anyone";
```

The main *attributes* of the authorization statement include the naming of the specific users, groups, or clients that are denied or allowed access. You can define the users and groups that are allowed or denied access using a user or group statement. For example, to deny access to everyone, you can use user = "anyone" with a deny statement. To allow access to the user joe, you can use user = "joe" with an allow statement. anyone is a predefined name used to specify everyone's access, while all is used to specify the access for all users in the server's user database. If you have specified an authentication function for the user list only [authenticate (user)], you cannot deny or allow access to a specific group, or vice versa. To allow or deny access to different users or groups, your authentication statement must include the appropriate user or group parameter. In other words, if you plan to use a user statement, the authentication statement must specify user; if you plan to use both user and group authorization statements, the authentication statement must include both user and group—for example, authenticate(user, group). The following ACL denies access to everyone except joe and suzy:

```
acl "path=c:/netscape/server/docs/special/";

deny (all)
    user = "all";
```

```
allow (read, write)
   user = "joe,suzy";
```

Beside the user and group, you can also use an IP or DNS address (a fully qualified domain name) to allow or deny access to a client from a specific IP or DNS address. Thus you can deny access to any user that uses a specific IP or DNS address to contact your site. You can deny access to any computer using the specified IP or DNS address. With the DNS or IP address, you can also use wildcard patterns to identify a group of IP or DNS addresses. You can also use only a * character for a wildcard pattern. For an IP address, you can only use the * character for the entire set of numbers in the IP address. In other words, you cannot use 204.156.128.2*, but you can use 204.156.128.*. The * character must be the last character in the IP address. You cannot use 204.*.128.200, but you can use 204.*. For a DNS address, you can use a * character for the entire first component of the DNS address. In other words, you can use *.hackers.com, but not *er.hackers.com or master.*.com. You can also list a number of DNS or IP addresses, using a comma to separate each entry. The following deny statement denies access to any client from the domain hackers.com:

```
deny (all)
   dns = "*.hackers.com";
```

You can use the Server Manager to set the specific information discussed so far in the ACL file, but there are also specific statements that you must manually add to the ACL file. For example, you can use the operators and, or, not, = (equal character), and != (not equal character) with the user, group, ip, and dns attributes. This ability allows you to combine a number of different attributes. You can also combine a group of attributes to specify an order of precedence by using parentheses, as in the following example:

```
allow (read, write)
  (user = "joe, suzy" and group="sales") or
  (user="jack,john" and group="secretary");
```

Another option that requires manual editing of the ACL file is the specification of a time of day (timeofday) or day of the week (dayofweek) when the authorization should be performed. You can specify the time in 24 hours based on the local time on the server. Use a four-digit number to specify the time. For example, 2:30 A.M. should be 0230 and 7 P.M. should be 1900. For the day of the week, you can use sun, mon, tue, wed, thu, fri, and sat. You can specify a list of days, using a comma to separate each day of the week. For example, the following statement allows students of the server programming class access to the resource only from 7 P.M. to 10 P.M. on Monday, Wednesday, and Friday.

```
allow(write,delete,execute,list,info)
   (group="serverclass") and (timeofday > 1900
   and timeofday < 2200) and (dayofweek="mon,wed,fri");
```

For timeofday, you can use the following operators: > (greater than), < (less than), >= (greater than or equal to), and <= (less than or equal to).

With a **deny** statement, you can also specify a file that should be returned to the client if the client is denied access by using deny with url="<redirection file>". The file that you specify should be an HTML or text file. For example, to redirect the client to the file /admin/refuse.html when access is denied, you can use the following **deny** statement before you actually specify who is denied access:

```
deny with url="/admin/refuse.html";
```

Appendix D

Dynamic Configuration
of the Server

Often an Internet Service Provider (ISP) or a server administrator may wish to allow users access to some configuration options but not to the main server configuration files (for example, `obj.conf`). With Server 3.x, you can allow authorized users access to a subset of Administration Server or Server Manager options based on the top menu of Administration Server or Server Manager. If you are using Enterprise Server 3.5.1, you can also use Netshare and Web Publishing to allow users to manage and control their server content. To give different users access to a subset of configuration settings for their specific directory, however, you may need to use dynamic configuration. Dynamic configuration allows users to write their own configuration files. For example, with dynamic configuration, users can specify the access rights to their home directories without a need for a specific server program or the Server Manager.

We will discuss dynamic configuration based on the type of configuration file that the user can write. Netscape Server supports `.htaccess` and `.nsconfig` files. Both `.htaccess` and `.nsconfig` are based on the `.htaccess` files used with NCSA HTTPd Web Server. `.htaccess` is a more standard dynamic configuration file supported by a number of other servers (such as Apache Server). These files, when deployed in a specific directory, can determine specific configuration options—for example, access control—for the directory and its subdirectories. Although both `.htaccess` and `.nsconfig` have the same general intended purpose (that is, to provide dynamic configuration support), their support, syntax, and features are different. In fact, `.htaccess` and `.nsconfig` take a different approach to access control.

Netscape Enterprise, Commerce, and Communication Server support `.nsconfig` files. Netscape Server 3.x and Server 2.01 for UNIX and NT with the htaccess patch (`htaccess.zip`) also support `.htaccess` files. You can download the `htaccess.zip` file from `http://help.netscape.com/download/server/enterprise/htaccess.zip`. Although you can manually enable the `.nsconfig` option for FastTrack Server, this feature may not work properly with

FastTrack Server. Dynamic configuration is not intended for FastTrack Server, and Netscape does not officially support this option for FastTrack Server.

For both `.htaccess` and `.nsconfig`, you must enable these features for the server before they can be used. You can enable `.nsconfig` for the server by using the Server Manager or by manually editing the **obj.conf** file. For `.htaccess`, you must manually update the **obj.conf** file. We will discuss how you enable each option shortly.

Warning ▶

You cannot use LDAP, an LDAP directory server, or Enterprise Server 3.x's local database with `.nsconfig` or `.htaccess` files. With `.htaccess` files, you can use only an NCSA-style user database, which is the default user database supported for Server 1.x. With `.nsconfig`, you can use either an NCSA-style user database or a DBM file, which is the default user database for Server 2.x.

.nsconfig

Netscape Server originally developed support for `.nsconfig` files as an alternative to `.htaccess`. Unlike `.htaccess` support, the `.nsconfig` feature is built into the server. The `.nsconfig` files provide features not covered with the `.htaccess` files supported by Netscape Server. With `.nsconfig` files, you can limit access to specific directories, define a MIME type for the files in the directories, and produce a customized error response for the client.

To enable the use of `.nsconfig` files, you need to activate dynamic configuration by adding the **PathCheck** function **load-config** manually or by setting this option using the Server Preferences|Dynamic Configuration Files menu in the Server Manager. With **load-config**, you define the name of the configuration file, its base directory, whether the server should look in all subdirectories for the configuration file, and a specific type of file that you want to disable in those directories. (See also **PathCheck**'s **load-config** function in Appendix B for more detail.)

You can use the parameter `file` of the **load-config** function to specify a different name than the default `.nsconfig` for the dynamic configuration files. The parameter `basedir` can be used to specify a base directory where the server begins looking for the configuration file (for example, `basedir="c:/netscape/server/docs/users"`). The value of `basedir` should be a system file path. If this parameter is not specified, the server uses the requested URL to identify the base directory. The server goes through the **NameTrans** directive functions, which determine the base directory of the requested URI (the value of `ntrans-base`).

With the `descend` parameter, you can specify whether the server should look in subdirectories of the base directory for the `.nsconfig` files. If the value is set to `1`, the server looks in the subdirectories. Multiple configuration files can be created and placed in different subdirectories. In effect, this option creates a distinction along the directory tree so that different configurations can be applied to different directories. If a request is for a subdirectory, any subdirectory that includes a .nsconfig file can extend the configuration setting established by a file in an earlier directory (that is, .nsconfig files found in the base directory or previous subdirectories). This option provides for greater flexibility and control. Different users may provide different configuration files for their directories. On the other hand, you may want to keep all .nsconfig files in the base directory for performance reasons. The server needs to search all subdirectories for .nsconfig files and evaluate the directives in the files, which can have a negative effect on the speed of the response from the server.

The parameter `disable-types` can be used to disable a MIME type for the dynamic configuration directories. You can use a wildcard to specify a MIME type. For example, `disable-types="magnus-internal/*"` disables all internal MIME types used by the server.

It is important that you secure the access to the .nsconfig files. Clients can make HTTP GET requests to read the information in the .nsconfig files. They can also replace or delete the .nsconfig files, if Remote File Manipulation is enabled for Netscape Server 2.x or 3.x, or Web Publishing is enabled for Server 3.x. There are a number of methods for restricting read and write access to these configuration files. For example, you can restrict access by disabling the .nsconfig files using the `disable-types` parameter of **load-config**. First, you need to specify a MIME type for the .nsconfig files in the **mime.types** file—for example, `type=magnusinternal/nsconfig ext=nsconfig`. You can then use this new MIME type with `disable-types`, as in `disable-types="*nsconfig"`. The server returns a server error if the client attempts to access these files. Another method for securing the .nsconfig files is to use the **RestrictAccess** directive in the .nsconfig files to deny access for all files with the extension nsconfig. Here is an example:

```
<Files *.nsconfig>
RestrictAccess type=deny ip=* dns=* returncode=404
</Files>
```

This code denies access to all clients for any file with the extension .nsconfig. It also returns a Not Found error page (status 404) when the client makes a request for these files.

The .nsconfig files look very similar to the **obj.conf** file. The special tag for the .nsconfig file is Files (which is similar to Object tags). Here is the format:

```
<Files [file pattern]>
. . .
</Files>
```

The *file pattern* is a wildcard pattern used to delimit the type of files affected by your directive. For example, the file pattern *.html limits the configuration settings defined within the Files tags scope to only HTML files with the extension .html. If you want the directives to apply to all files for the dynamic configuration directory (directories) specified by **load-config**, use `<Files *>`.

All directives affecting the file type are enclosed within the Files tags. The directives you can include inside the Files tags are **RestrictAccess** for authorization purpose, **RequireAuth** for authentication, **AuthType** for designating a special MIME type, and **ErrorFile** for specifying an error file.

You can have multiple Files tags, each with its own directives in a .nsconfig file. The following is an example:

```
<Files *>
ErrorFile reason="Forbidden" code="403"
 path="/errors/forbidden.html"
</File>

<Files *.html>
RequireAuth dbm="c:/netscape/server/authdb/default/dbm"
 realm="joe's personal site"
RestrictAccess type=allow ip=1.2.3*
</Files>

<Files *.pic>
AddType exp="*.pic" type="image/gif"
</Files>
```

Inside the first Files tags, the **ErrorFile** directive specifies a special error file for status code 403 (Forbidden). The second Files tag applies to HTML files with the extension .html. Inside this Files tag, **RequireAuth** requires authentication for all users. The database is a DBM file found in the dbm directory. **RestrictAccess** allows all users from the 1.2.3 subnet access to the site (for example, 1.2.3.4). The last Files tag applies to any file with the extension .pic. These files are interpreted as GIF files. Their MIME type will be image/gif.

The server processes the **RestrictAccess** directives for a requested resource in the order it encounters them. In other words, if a **RestrictAccess** directive denies access to a client, the server does not allow access to the client even if a later **RestrictAccess** directive permits it. This case is true even if multiple .nsconfig files are used in separate directories. The base directory or a .nsconfig file in a higher-level directive is processed and reinforced first. Once a client is denied access through a **RestrictAccess** directive, the server does not process other access control directives. Therefore, the best way to set access control with **RestrictAccess** is to allow all clients access and then restrict access to those that should be denied access. If you use only **RestrictAccess** directives that allow access, then all clients that are not specifically allowed access are automatically denied access.

RequireAuth directives, on the other hand, are processed after all **RestrictAccess** directives. The server first processes all access control rules set by **RestrictAccess**. If the server still needs to verify whether the client is allowed access, the server goes through the **RequireAuth** directives again based on the order in which they are declared and found by the server.

Any change to the `.nsconfig` file takes effect immediately. The general syntax guidelines for **magnus.conf** and **obj.conf** also apply to this file. For example, a pound sign (#) can be used at the beginning of a line to mark the line as a comment line. As mentioned earlier, the order of directives (as in the **obj.conf** file) is important. The `.nsconfig` file is case-sensitive, so make sure you use the appropriate cases for all directives and parameters. Also, always use a forward slash in a path.

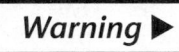

Warning ▶

The lines in the `.nsconfig` files can be only up to 512 characters long.

The following section lists directives that you can use inside the Files tags. As these directives are similar to directives used in the **obj.conf** file, we will use the same format as in Appendix B to describe the directives.

Directives for the Files Tags

AddType

```
AddType exp=*.exe type=magnus-internal/cgi
```

Defines a MIME type for a specified URL request for the prescribed directories. The expression defined in `exp` is a wildcard pattern that the server maps to the MIME type defined in `type` and `enc`. Similar to the **ObjectType** function **type-by-exp**, this function allows the specified subdirectories to have their own MIME type. (See also **mime.types** in Chapter 2 for more details.)

Parameters: **exp** (Wildcard type expression determines the file type to which the MIME type is applied. Use standard wildcards or shell expressions here. The wildcard expression you specify should match the file pattern in the Files tag. You can use the same wildcard expression here [to specify a MIME type for the file] as the one you used in the Files tag. Only define one expression per MIME type.); **type** (MIME type you want to associate with the file type as defined in **exp**.); **enc** (If you want to use HTTP encoding [`content-encoding`], use this parameter. An example of an encoding is `x-compress`.)

ErrorFile

```
ErrorFile reason="Unauthorized" code="401"
 path="/errors/unauthorized.html"
```

Allows a customized HTML page to be sent in place of the default error page (similar to the **Error** function **send-error**). This function sends the HTML file defined in `path` for the error type defined by `reason` or `code`. You define the type of error by the code number or the reason string (Reason Phrase); for example, `401` is the `code` parameter and `Unauthorized` is the `reason` string for the type of error. (For more information on error code and reason string, see the section HTTP Status Codes in Chapter 6.) The server sends the file you specified in `path` when the error type occurs.

Parameters: reason (Type of reason, HTTP Reason Phrase. This error string defines the error type [for example, `Not found`].); **code** (Type of HTTP error code [for example, `401`]. Besides the error string [`reason`], you can also define the error through the code number.); **path** (Determines the URI path for the HTML file the server sends instead of the default error message. The URL path should include the full path to the file without "`http://<server name>[:port]`".)

RestrictAccess

```
RestrictAccess type=allow ip=1.2.3.4 dns=*.foo.com
  return-code=403
```

Defines access restrictions from the specified directories for a client or a group of clients. You can specify whether to allow or deny access. The users are identified by the request's originating IP address or the domain name. (This information is sent by the client browser.) The server processes the **RestrictAccess** directives in the order they are found. Normally, you should first allow access to all clients. Use `RestrictAccess type=allow` to allow access to the clients. You can define the IP address or domain name for everyone with `ip=*` and/or `dns=*`. You can then declare another **RestrictAccess** directive to deny access to specific clients. You can have more than one **RestrictAccess** directive inside the Files scope. If a client is already denied access, no later **RestrictAccess** directive can allow access for the same client. If the **RestrictAccess** directives that apply to a request only allow access, then all other clients that are not specifically allowed access are denied access.

Parameters: type (Type of permission allowed. You can either `allow` access or `deny` access. This action is the same as `deny from` or `allow from` in `.htaccess` files.); **ip** (IP address of the client you want to allow or deny access. You can use wildcards to specify a group of IP addresses.); **dns** (The domain name of the client you want to deny or allow access. You can use wildcards to specify a domain name that identifies a group of host names. You can use **dns**, **ip**, or both.); **method** (Wildcard pattern of HTTP methods for which you want to deny or allow access. For example, to set access restriction for a `GET` or `HEAD` method, you can use `method="(GET|HEAD)"`. This parameter is optional.); **return-code** (Type of code the server returns to the client when access is denied [for example, `404` for file not found].)

RequireAuth

```
RequireAuth dbm="c:/netscape/server/authdb/default/"
  realm="joe's personal site" userpat=al*
```

Requires the client to be authenticated (similar to the **PathCheck** function **require-auth**). The client encounters a dialog box requesting the user name and password for authentication when requesting access to the specified subdirectories. This directive uses the standard basic HTTP authentication. The server first processes all **RestrictAccess** directives that apply to a request before going through the applicable **RequireAuth** directives. You cannot use the default local database of Server 3.x or an LDAP directory server with this directive.

    Parameters: **dbm** (File path to a DBM user database directory. Use either `dbm` or `userfile`, but not both. The default user database file for Netscape Server 2.x is a DBM file. You cannot use this option with Server 1.x for NT. This parameter should be the full physical path to the DBM file. Do not include the actual file name in your path; instead reference the directory.); **userfile** (Path to a user database file that is in NCSA format, an ASCII file with each line consisting of `<username>:<encrypted password>`. Use either `dbm` or `userfile`, but not both. An NCSA-style user database file is the type of default user database for Netscape Server 1.x.); **userlist** (List of the users that are allowed access. List the users with a comma separating each user name. This parameter does not work on a number of Netscape Servers. For example, you cannot use `userlist` with Server 2.x.); **userpat** (Wildcard pattern for the users that are allowed access. For example, `al*` will include users Alex, Alan, Albert, and so on. You can use `userpat` and `userlist` together. Use this parameter instead of listing your users with `userlist`, as `userlist` does not work in a number of Netscape Servers. For instance, `userpat="(john|joe)"` will allow access to the users `john` and `joe`.); **realm** (String appearing in the authentication dialog box as part of the instructions for the client. It usually identifies which area of the system is being requested, as in `Enter username for <realm>` at `<server name>`. `realm` is similar to **AuthName** in the `.htaccess` file.)

.htaccess

If you are familiar with .htaccess, you may want to use this option with Netscape Servers that support it. You can also convert a .nsconfig file to an .htaccess file by using Netscape's conversion utility. htconvert is a Perl script for converting .nsconfig files to .htaccess files. You can find htconvert under *<server path>*/plugin/htaccess. You should specify the path for the **obj.conf** file as an argument in the command line after the script—that is, *<PERL interpreter>* *<htconvert script>* *<**obj.conf** file>*. The script will not delete the existing .nsconfig files.

.htaccess support is provided through an NSAPI extension to the server, though you need to run Netscape Server 2.01 or later to use this extension. To enable .htaccess, you must load the htaccess shared library (htaccess.so) for UNIX or htaccess DLL (htaccess.dll) for NT, similarly to how you register any NSAPI application. For Enterprise Server 3.x, you can find the htaccess shared library or DLL file under *<server path>*/plugins/htaccess.

You must first load the module (shared library or DLL file) using the server's built-in **Init** function **loadmodules**. You specify the path to htaccess.so or htaccess.dll with the shlib parameter. You also identify two specific functions that need to be registered with the server in the **obj.conf** file, **htaccess-init** and **htaccess-find**. **htaccess-init** is an **Init** function that initializes the necessary variables and prepares the server to take advantage of .htaccess files. You should place this **Init** directive function after the **load-modules** function that loads the htaccess module. **htaccess-find**, on the other hand, processes your .htaccess files. It locates the .htaccess files, reads their contents, and fulfills the specific instructions in the files. **htaccess-find** is a **PathCheck** function. With **htaccess-find**, you can also specify a different file name for the .htaccess files by using the parameter filename. The default name is .htaccess. You can change the name of the file so that the server will look for the dynamic configuration information using the name specified in the filename parameter.

The **PathCheck** function **htaccess-find** can be placed within the scope of the default Object in the **obj.conf** file at the end of the **PathCheck** functions list, if you want the server to look for the .htaccess files for all client requests (that is, in all document directories). To limit the scope of the .htaccess files to a specific set of directories, you can create a ppath Object in the **obj.conf** file and place **htaccess-find** inside the scope of this Object. When the server processes a request that matches the path resource you specified for the Object, the server looks for the .htaccess files. Otherwise **htaccess-find** is not used and the server will not look for .htaccess files. The ppath attribute of the Object should specify the directories in which the server should look for the .htaccess files.

The following example gives the lines of code added to an **obj.conf** file for NT to enable .htaccess for the user directory and its subdirectories. You can place the ppath Object at the end of the **obj.conf** file after other Objects. For more information on registering NSAPI applications, see Chapter 7. For information on creating a ppath Object, see Chapter 2. For more information on enabling htaccess, see also **htaccess-find** in Appendix B.

```
Init fn="load-modules"
  funcs="htaccess-init,htaccess-find"
  shlib="c:/netscape/server/plugins/htaccess/htaccess.dll"

Init fn="htaccess-init"
. . .

<Object ppath="c:/netscape/server/docs/users/*">
PathCheck fn=htaccess-find
</Object>
```

As the `.htaccess` files are normally placed in the document directories, other clients can read these files by making an HTTP request for an `.htaccess` file. If you have enabled Remote File Manipulation for Netscape Server 2.01 or 3.x, or Web Publishing for Server 3.x, the clients are also able to delete or replace the `.htaccess` files. For security reasons, you should protect the `.htaccess` files from unauthorized client access. You should take precautions against clients accessing `.htaccess` files by disabling read and write access to these files. You can accomplish this task manually by creating an Object in the **obj.conf** file for the `.htaccess` files—that is, `<Object ppath="*.htaccess">`. Inside the Object, you can specify a server function that denies access to the `*.htaccess` files. For example, you can use the built-in server function **deny-existence** to deny the existence of the `.htaccess` files or you can use **check-acl** in conjunction with an ACL in the ACL file to deny write and read access. You can also set the access rights for the `*.htaccess` files through Server Manager. For Server Manager 3.x, you can specify `*.htaccess` as a resource in the "Pick a resource" option from the Server Preferences|Restrict Access menu. You can then edit the access control rules to deny read and write access to the `*.htaccess` files. (For more information on ACL files, see Appendix C.)

For a requested URI (a request document path), the server looks for the `.htaccess` files beginning with the highest level of the directory in the client-requested path. The server then steps through the subdirectories looking for any additional dynamic configuration files. The server uses the specific configuration information it finds hierarchically. Therefore, the last dynamic configuration file found can determine the ultimate setting. If a subdirectory does not have an `.htaccess` file, the parent directory's `.htaccess` file is used by the server. For example, you can set the server to look for the `.htaccess` file in the `user` directory and its subdirectories. If a client request is for `user/joe/news/news.html`, the server looks in the `user`, `joe`, and `news` directories, in that order, for the `.htaccess` files. Normally, you set the default configuration settings in the base directory and the specific configuration settings in each subdirectory.

The `.htaccess` files that you can use with Netscape Server 2.01 and 3.x allow only access control settings. You can use `.htaccess` with Netscape Server to control access to resources in specific directories. You cannot use other directives, such as **AddType**, or **Redirect**, that are supported by other vendor's servers.

The following is an example of the contents of an `.htaccess` file:

```
AuthUserFile c:/netscape/server/authdb/user.pwd
AuthGroupFile c:/netscape/server/authdb/special.grp
AuthName Joe's Site
AuthType Basic

<Limit GET POST>
order deny,allow
deny from all
allow from .foo.com
</Limit>
```

`.htaccess` Directives

In this section, we will review the different directives that can be used in an `.htaccess` file. **AuthUserFile**, **AuthGroupFile**, **AuthName**, and **AuthType** determine the general authentication setting—for example, the method of authentication and the location of the user database file. The Limit tag is used to set the specific authorization guideline. Inside the Limit tag scope, between `<Limit . . . >` and `</Limit>`, you can specify who is allowed or denied access to the site. You can include the authentication directives before or after the Limit tags, but cannot place them inside the Limit tags. The server goes through the authorization information based on the order you specify with the **order** directive inside the Limit tag and the physical order of the directives inside the Limit tags' scope. You can include multiple Limit tags in a file so as to set different authorization rules for different types of requests.

You do not need to include the authentication directives in an `.htaccess` file, if you do not want the client to be authenticated. Your file could include only the authorization information if you want to deny or allow access to all users or to specific DNS or IP addresses. If you wish to use a user or group name, then you should also include the authentication directives. The clients are then required to send their user names and passwords, which are used to authenticate the users before allowing or denying access to the resource.

AuthType

The **AuthType** directive is used to specify the method of authentication. Currently, you can use only Basic HTTP authentication with `.htaccess` files. The value of **AuthType**, if it is used, should therefore be `Basic`, as in `AuthType Basic`. Basic authentication requires the client to input a user name and password. The server then uses the settings in the `.htaccess` file to verify the user name and password and allow or deny access to the user.

AuthName

AuthName is used to specify the string that appears in the authentication dialog box as part of the instructions for the client during authentication. **AuthName** usually identifies the name of the requested site. The complete string in the authentication dialog box may look like the following: `Enter username for <AuthName> at <server name>`. For example, **AuthName** can let the client know that the authentication is being used to access a user's site, such as `Joe's home page`. The client can use the **AuthName** information to ascertain which user name and password should be sent. **AuthName** is the same as the `realm` parameter used with the **PathCheck** function **require-auth** or the `prompt` statement used with **authenticate** in Server 3.x ACLs.

AuthUserFile

AuthUserFile points to an NCSA-style user database that the server uses to verify the client password information. It points the server to the location of the user database. The path is an absolute path to the user database file. An NCSA user database is a text file that includes the name and password of the user in the following format: `<name>:<base-64 encrypted password>`—for example, `joe:ylia4tjbkhCK1`. (The C function **crypt** is used to encrypt the password.) Each line in the file includes information for a separate user. Netscape Server 1.x uses this type of file for the user database, while Netscape Server 2.x uses a DBM file and Netscape Server 3.x uses an LDAP directory. You cannot use a DBM file or an LDAP directory server with `.htaccess`. You can use only an NCSA-style user database.

AuthGroupFile

AuthGroupFile points to the location of the NCSA-style group definition file. The path is an absolute path to the group definition file, which includes the list of the users for each group. An NCSA group file includes the name of the group followed by the list of the users in the group in the following format: `<group name>: <username1> <username2> <username3>....`

By including both a user and group file, you can take advantage of a group name for authentication. When you deploy a group file, you still need to include a user database file to be able to authenticate the user password. The server uses the group file to identify whether a user belongs to the group. It then uses the user information in the user database to verify whether the user password is correct. Once the client is authenticated, the server can proceed with allowing or denying access based on the authorization rules set inside the Limit tag.

Limit

You set the authorization rules inside the Limit tag. This tag is used to limit access to the resource for specific users, groups, or hosts. With the Limit tag, you also specify the HTTP request methods (for example, `GET`, `POST`, `PUT`, and so on) for which the authorization directives should be deployed. Limit tags are similar to the Object tags in the `obj.conf` file or HTML tags. There is a starting tag `<Limit [methods]>` and an end tag `</Limit>`. What is defined inside these tags is subject to the scope of the Limit tags. Within the starting Limit tag, you specify the request methods. For example, by specifying `GET` and `POST` attributes, such as `<Limit GET POST>`, you confine the use of the authorization directives inside the Limit tags' scope only to requests that use the HTTP method `GET` or `POST`. Inside the Limit tags' scope, you can declare any number of directives that will allow or deny access to certain users, groups, or hosts.

The directives supported inside the Limit tags are **deny**, **allow**, **order**, and **require**.

deny   The **deny** directive can be used to deny access to clients from a specific host or for all hosts. To deny access to all hosts, you can use the `all` attribute, as in `deny from all`. You can use a domain name to deny access to clients from a specified domain. You should use the domain name part of a fully qualified domain name without the specific host name for the value—for example, `.hackers.com`. You can also use a full or partial IP address. For a partial IP address, you can use the first three bytes of the IP address to deny access for a specific group of IP addresses. For example, by specifying `1.2.3` (`deny from 1.2.3`), you can deny access to any client using an IP address from the `1.2.3` subnet. Any client with an IP address from `1.2.3.0` to `1.2.3.255` is denied access. (Do not include the final trailing period for the IP address. `1.2.3` is acceptable, but `1.2.3.` is not.)

allow   The **allow** directive can be used to allow access to clients from specific hosts or for all hosts. As with the **deny** directive, you can use `all` for all hosts, a domain name, or a full or partial IP address. For example, `allow from 1.2.3` will allow access to any client using an IP address from `1.2.3.0` to `1.2.3.255`.

order   Normally, the server reads and applies the directives inside the Limit tags' scope based on the order they are declared in the `.htaccess` file. With the **order** directive, you can predefine the order of the **deny** or **allow** directives used by the server. The **order** directive should appear before other directives in the scope of the Limit tags.

You can use three different options with the **order** directive:

- `deny,allow`
- `allow,deny`
- `mutual-failure`

Use `deny,allow` if you want the server to evaluate the **deny** directives before any **allow** directives. Use `allow,deny` if you want the server to evaluate all **allow** directives before any **deny** directives. In each of these cases, the first group of directives can be seen as the default access rules, while the second group can be seen as the exception to the rule. You normally deny access to all and allow access to specific hosts. If you use mutual-failure, then any host not listed in an **allow** directive is denied access, even if it is not listed in a **deny** directive. You must directly specify the hosts that are allowed access. The order of directives does not matter for mutual-failure. mutual-failure is rarely used as an option.

require   With the **require** directive, you can allow access to authenticated users. The attribute group or user can be used to identify the list of the users or groups that you include. For example, require user joe jack jill allows joe, jack, and jill access to the resource. You can list the users or groups after the identifier group or user. The names of users or groups are separated with a space. If you use a group, then the user must be a member of the group before he or she will be allowed access. Consider the following example:

```
<Limit GET POST>
require group family
</Limit>
```

If the authenticated user is a member of the group family, he or she is allowed access.

You can also use valid-user to allow all users defined in the user database access to the resource. require valid-user allows access for all users in the user database once they have been properly authenticated. In other words, when the requested method matches the method specified in the Limit tags, if the client sends a user name that is in the user database with the correct password, the client can gain access to the resource.

Header Files Included with Server 2.x

> **Note ▶**
>
> This appendix is intended for Netscape Server 2.x users. It also includes references to Server 1.x. Under Server 3.x, with the exception of the general operating system-specific information found in the `systems.h` file, all other server variables, data structures, or function definitions are contained in the `nsapi.h` file.

Under the Netscape Server 2.x root directory (server path), the `/nsapi/include` directory contains a set of header files. You need to include and use some of them in your projects. As with other `#include` declarations, server header files must be chosen and added before you write and compile your code. They help you access and process the information available from the server. You use the data structures and functions in these files to interact with the server and develop your plug-in applications. These header files are a subset of the server's own header files and, as such, give you access to, and great power over, the server's internal workings.

Under the `include` directory, there are two files: `netsite.h` and `version.h`. They determine the type of server (for example, Proxy or Enterprise Server) and a few of the specific definitions of each server. In `netsite.h`, there is a reference to the `base/systems.h` file, which holds other system-specific information (for example, unique definitions for the UNIX and the NT servers). There are also two subdirectories, `base` and `frame`, under the `include` directory. `base` holds low-level, platform-independent functions. `frame` holds server and HTTP-specific functions.

The large set of header files (and the mixture of functions and structures inside) may seem complex and difficult to manage. You do not need to understand all of the functions in these files to program for Netscape Server. Although the files have valuable tools and features, most of them are rarely used and have very specific or limited usage. Mostly, you use a subset of these functions and data structures. Table E-1 lists the files that you will most likely use.

Table E-1   Major NSAPI Header Files

HEADER FILES	USE
crit.h, systhr.h, and sem.h files	Thread and process safety
file.h	File management
buffer.h	File and network buffer management
net.h	Includes network and socket I/O functions
pblock.h	Includes the key parameter block-handling functions
protocol.h	References http.h, used for protocol-specific functions
req.h	Request data structure and functions
log.h	Important **log_error** function used for logging errors
util.h	A variety of utility functions not contained in other files

You should include at least the protocol.h, session.h, and req.h headers in all of your programs. They include the essential data structures of the variables you receive as parameters to your function (that is, pblock, Session, and Request). netsite.h is another file that should be included in your project. As most of the other header files already include a reference to this file (as do pblock.h and session.h, for example), you can safely ignore directly including this file.

Server 2.x Versus Server 1.x

Header files for Netscape Server 2.x are different from those for Server 1.x. Although there has not been a significant overhaul of these files, Server 2.x still includes many changes from NSAPI 1.0. If you are familiar with the first version of NSAPI (NSAPI 1.0), you may want to study these changes. You should also recompile your code with the new headers to guarantee compatibility and to take advantage of the current functionality of the server. NSAPI 1.0 for NT included its own set of NT-specific files (Ntbuffer.h, Ntdaemon.h, and Ntfile.h under include\base\nt, and Eventlog.h, Ntconf.h, and Ntobjset.h under include\frame\nt). Some of the functions in these files have been integrated into the common header files, so that a more platform-independent set of functions is now available. In its simplest form, the #ifdef processor definition declares a set of functions unique to NT and others unique to UNIX in the same file. Other functions (such as **ErrorDialogProc**) are no longer available. Still others are available, but no longer relevant or useful. For example, functions for reading configuration settings from the NT registry are no longer relevant. Server configuration is now accomplished through the text file versions of the **magnus.conf** and **obj.conf** files.

Previously, Netscape provided little in the way of thread or process management. There was only `sem.h`, which included `SEMAPHORE` as a way of managing multiple processes. Specific to NSAPI 2.0, the following files enhance the functionality of programs you may write: `crit.h`, `pool.h`, `regexp.h`, `shmem.h`, and `systhr.h`. The `crit.h` and `systhr.h` files provide a capable series of platform-independent functions for thread safety, management, and synchronization. `regexp.h` adds regular expression functionality to the existing wildcard (shell expression, `shexp.h`) support of NSAPI 1.0. `shmem.h` and `pool.h` provide shared memory and memory pool allocation. To improve performance, Netscape has added caching and shared memory schemes. `MALLOC` and other memory allocation macros now use memory pools and are automatically freed. The `PERM_*` versions of these macros, such as `PERM_MALLOC`, work in the same way as the previous API macros.

There are many other changes in Server 2.0. For example, **net_sendmail**, **net_semaccept_init**, and **directive_num2name** have been removed from the API. There is no longer a `nodelock.h` header file under the base directory. Other functions have been added, such as **conf_vars2daemon**, **http_find_request**, **http_set_keepalive_timeout**, **pblock_dup**, **util_strftime**, **util_mime_separator**, and **util_env_copy**. Under NSAPI 2.0, functions in the header files are defined as `NSAPI_PUBLIC`. In other words, they are identified as special server functions that are available to other programs as public (exportable) functions. Your functions also will be `NSAPI_PUBLIC` functions.

List of Header Files

A review of the following tables will enable you to find out quickly which set of files contains the appropriate functionality for your program. We will list all the header files and briefly describe the frequently used and relevant data structures and functions in each file. The information covered here should point you in the right direction, and supplement any available documentation. You still need to look at Netscape's header files and function API definitions for more options and capabilities. (See also Chapter 5 for a review of the major server data structures and functions.)

Tables E-2 through E-4 include the list of the header files based on the files found in each directory under the <*server path*>/nsapi/include directory. When a file is especially important or new to Server 2.0, it has been labeled accordingly.

Table E-2 NSAPI Header Files in `include` Directory

`include` DIRECTORY	DESCRIPTION
`netsite.h` (important)	Includes definitions and general version information for Netscape Servers—for example, `MCC_PROXY` (Proxy Server) and `NS_CATALOG` (Catalog Server). `MCC_HTTPD` includes the two types of Netscape Server 2.0: `NS_PERSONAL` (FastTrack Server) and the default Enterprise Server. `MCC_ADMSERV` is Administration Server. For servers, the server version (`MAGNUS_VERSION`) and server version string (`MAGNUS_VERSION_STRING`) are defined here. For example, `ENTERPRISE_VERSION_DEF` is defined as the `MAGNUS_VERSION` for Enterprise Server. The actual value of the string is determined by the `version.h` file when the server is installed. For quick checking, the server versions are also defined as numbers—for example, `ENTERPRISE_VERSION` is 1 and `PERSONAL_VERSION` is 2. Functions that deal with server versions are defined here. The functions **system_version** and **system_version_set** are used to identify and set server versions. (See also `version.h`.) `netsite.h` also includes miscellaneous, useful definitions, such as definitions for carriage return (`CR`) and line-feed (`LF`). The file format is different under UNIX and NT, because the UNIX version uses only `LF`, ASCII character 10 (`\n`), whereas NT uses `CRLF`, the ASCII characters 13 and 10 (`\r\n`), for `ENDLINE` (end-of-line characters). `netsite.h` includes macros for memory allocation. `MALLOC`, `REALLOC`, `FREE`, and `STRDUP` are the new macros for allocating and freeing memory. (They use memory pools; see also `pool.h`.) If you use these macros to allocate memory, memory is automatically freed when the request ends. `PERM_MALLOC`, `PERM_REALLOC`, `PERM_FREE`, and `PERM_STRDUP` provide permanent storage for global variables.
`version.h`	Includes the version information string for servers (for example, Proxy, Catalog, and Enterprise Servers). This information is specific to the server installed. For example, the FastTrack Server's strings might be defined as follows: `PERSONAL_VERSION_DEF` is "`2.0a`" and `PERSONAL_VERSION_STRING` is "`Netscape-FastTrack/2.0a`". `version.h` is referenced through `netsite.h`, so it is not necessary to include it in your include declarations. `version.h` is generated through Netscape's server source code and your program's installation compiler. (See also `netsite.h`.)

Table E-3 NSAPI Header Files in `base` Directory

`base` DIRECTORY	DESCRIPTION
`buffer.h` (important)	Includes file and socket I/O abstractions. It provides system-independent functions for both the UNIX and Windows environments. The integer file descriptor (`SYS_FILE`) is used for UNIX, and the file handle (`FILE` structure) for 32-bit Windows. It includes the file buffer (`filebuffer`) and the network buffer (`netbuf`) data structure definitions. `buffer.h` contains functions and macros to read and write using these structures (for example, **filebuf_getc, netbuf_getc, filebuf_open, filebuf_close_buffer,** and so on). Memory mapping (`mmap`) is also supported and can be used with a file buffer but not a network buffer. (See also `file.h` and `net.h`.)
`cinfo.h`	Includes content information (`cinfo`) for files. `cinfo` data structure and functions are used by an **ObjectType** directive function to map a file to a MIME type. The

Table E-3   NSAPI Header Files in `base` Directory *(continued)*

`base` DIRECTORY	DESCRIPTION
	`cinfo` data structure includes `type`, `encoding`, and `language` attributes. Functions include **cinfo_init, cinfo_find, cinfo_terminate,** and so on.

> **Warning ▶**
>
> `description` and `viewer` are defined as members of the `cinfo` data structure in the comment lines above the data structure in the `cinfo.h` file. They are not, however, part of the `cinfo` data structure.

`base` DIRECTORY	DESCRIPTION
`crit.h` (important) (new)	Includes critical-section abstractions. Critical-section functions are used to support thread handling. `crit.h` contains two data structures. The `CRITICAL` data structure and its functions (for example, **crit_init, crit_enter,** and **crit_terminate**) are used to access and lock a thread as well as to protect one thread from another. The `CONDVAR` (conditional variable) data structure and its functions (for example, **condvar_init, condvar_notify,** and **condvar_wait**) are used for conditional thread synchronization. These functions are used for the ownership, synchronization, and isolation of threads. They do not actually start and terminate threads. Unlike semaphore functions, they affect only threads within a single process. (See also `systhr.h`, and `sem.h`, as well as Chapter 11.)
`daemon.h`	Includes daemon-related (server process) data structures (for example, `daemon_s`, `StatHeader`, and `StatSlot`) and functions (for example, **child_status, daemon_run,** and **child_fork**). The functions are used to manage multiple processes and their children. They determine how a connection is made. With the exception of **daemon_atrestart,** you most likely will not use any of these functions. **daemon_atrestart** is a useful function that runs when the server restarts. This function does not work under the NT and IRIX versions of Server 2.x. Under other Netscape 2.x Servers, this function is also invoked when the server is stopped.
`ereport.h`	Includes low-level error-handling functions for recording transactions and reporting errors. `LOG_<degree>` constants define the degree of the error for the **log_error** function (part of the `log.h` file) (for example, `LOG_WARN 0`). Functions include **ereport, ereport_init,** and **ereport_terminate.** To log your errors, you should use **log_error** instead. The special function **ereport_init** allows you to send an error string to a specified e-mail address (for example, the server administrator's e-mail).
`file.h` (important)	Includes system functions for creating, reading, writing, and deleting files and directories. It contains the platform-independent file-handling (or descriptor) data structure `SYS_FILE`. (The actual data structure definition varies based on the specific operating system.) It also references other header files from your system's C header files. For the UNIX platform, it references header files such as `types.h` and `file.h`. Platform-independent file functions include **system_fread, system_fopenRO, system_fclose,** and so on. (Again, how these functions actually get the job done can vary based on the operating system.) The directory data structures are `SYS_DIR` and `SYS_DIRENT`. Platform-independent directory functions include **dir_remove, dir_create, dir_close,** and so on. There are also thread-safe functions that lock a file from other processes (for example, **system_flock**). Thread-safe variants of `localtime` and `gmtime` are also included. Finally, there are functions that convert path strings into appropriate formatting (for example, replacing "/" with "\"). For instance, **file_unix2local** converts a

Table E-3   NSAPI Header Files in `base` Directory (*continued*)

`base` **DIRECTORY**	**DESCRIPTION**
`file.h` (important)	UNIX-style path to a Windows path. These pathrelated functions provide features similar to the built-in **PathCheck** functions. (See also `buffer.h`.)
`net.h` (important)	Includes networking-related functions (such as **net_read**, **net_write**, **net_socket**, and **net_connect**). You normally use **net_write** to write to the client socket. There are also references to other C header files, such as `types.h` and `socket.h` for UNIX and `winsock.h` for Windows. The data structure `SYS_NETFD` is defined as a platform-independent socket descriptor. (See also `buffer.h`.)
`pblock.h` (important)	Includes parameter block structures and handling functions. Parameters (`pb_param`) of parameter block are sets of *name-value* pairs held inside the hash table, `pblock`. You use parameter block functions in a variety of ways (for example, to access values in server headers). The data structures include `pblock`, `pb_entry`, and `pb_param`. Functions to manipulate parameters are **param_create**, **param_free**, and so on. The notable functions manipulate parameter blocks, such as **pblock_create, pblock_findval, pblock_nvinsert,** and **pblock_str2pblock**. These functions are key functions for processing client requests.
`pool.h` (new)	Handles memory pool allocation. It includes functions such as **pool_create, pool_destroy,** and **pool_malloc.** The data structure for the memory pool thread's handle is `pool_handle_t`. Each thread creates its own pool for allocating data. These memory pools are defined to keep each thread safe and independent. You do not usually call the **pool_*** functions directly. Instead, they are used by the platform-independent macros, `MALLOC`, `REALLOC`, `STRDUP`, and `FREE` (defined in `netsite.h`). `MALLOC`, for example, uses the memory pool created for each session, and the memory allocated is automatically freed by the server after the request is processed. (See also `netsite.h`.)
`regexp.h` (new)	Includes regular expression (`regexp`) handling functions. Functions include **regexp_valid, regexp_match, regexp_casecmp,** and so on. Regular expressions are special characters used in a string that provide pattern matching. They are similar to wildcard expressions and shell expressions (`shexp.h`). Shell expressions are the preferred method of handling wildcard expressions for the HTTP server. (See also `shexp.h`.)
`sem.h`	Includes multiprocess "semaphore" support across different platforms. Semaphores under Netscape Server are simply interprocess locks that use files for locking. The `SEMAPHORE` definition type is an integer, except in the Windows and IRIX platforms. Semaphores are used to prevent shared resources (processes) from interfering with one another. Functions include **sem_init, sem_terminate, sem_grab,** and so on. These functions provide mutual exclusion for the entire server. They are different from the thread functions in `systhr.h` and the critical functions in `crit.h`, as they affect all processes and threads. Under NT, however, there are no multiple processes with multiple threads, and they work similarly to the critical-section functions. Use them to exclude access for shared memory or files. Semaphores and shared memory (see also `shmem.h`) can be used to manage and write a multiprocessor NSAPI program. Netscape Server 2.01 added a new semaphore model, counting semaphore. A counting semaphore can be incremented and decreased. It more closely resembles the semaphores with which you might be familiar. For more information on semaphores and counting semaphores, see Chapter 11. (See also `systhr.h` and `crit.h`.)

Table E-3   NSAPI Header Files in `base` Directory (*continued*)

`base` DIRECTORY	DESCRIPTION
`session.h` (important)	Includes session-related data structure and functions. Session consists of the time between when a client connects and when it disconnects from the server. A session persists until the server finishes processing a request. The `Session` data structure holds information relevant for the entire session (such as the IP address, DNS address, and secret key size of the client). It is one of three data structures passed to your function as a parameter. Besides the `Session` data structure, this file also contains functions such as **session_create, session_free,** and **session_dns** that you can use with your function. (See also `req.h`.)
`shexp.h`	Includes shell expression functions for handling wildcards. These shell expressions are loosely based on zsh (the Z shell). (See the Wildcards Options section in Chapter 2 for more details.) The shell expression support functions are **shexp_cmp, shexp_match, shexp_casecmp,** and so on. This file also includes a wrapper for both the **shexp_*** and **regexp_*** functions (two ways of handling wildcards), which start with **WILDPAT_**. The **shexp_*** functions are the preferred method of handling wildcard expressions for the HTTP server. (See also `regexp.h`.)
`shmem.h` (new)	Includes platform-independent abstractions for shared memory. The shared memory data structure is `shmem_s`. Shared memory functions (for example, **shmem_alloc** and **shmem_free**) can be used to allocate and free regions of shared memory. You can use these functions to define a region of memory that is protected from other regions of the program's memory. The designated memory can be shared by the processes and the child processes. Shared memory combined with semaphores can be used to manage and write a multiprocessor NSAPI program. Since Server 3.x does not use multiple processes, you no longer need to use shared memory for Server 3.x. (See also `sem.h`.)
`systems.h` (important)	Includes operating system-specific definitions and functions prototypes. It defines what is particular to each operating system. There is a list of unique preprocessor directives for each system plus some general directives shared between similar systems. This information is used later in other header files to determine the appropriate data structures and their members and/or the appropriate functions for each system. For example, under NT, `wtype.h` and `winbase.h` are included in the project and various definitions such as `MALLOC_POOLS`, `DNS_CACHE`, `FILE_WIN32`, `NET_WINSOCK`, and `DLL_CAPABLE` are defined. This file is included in a few other header files, including the `netsite.h` file, which itself is included in a number of header files. (Unlike other Server 3.x header files, whose contents are now kept under the single header file `nsapi.h`, the `systems.h` header file under Server 3.x still includes the system-specific information.)
`systhr.h` (new)	Includes support for threading mechanisms. The platform-independent data structure for the threads is `SYS_THREAD`. Functions include **systhread_current, systhread_start, systhread_terminate,** and so on. While critical-section functions (in the `crit.h` header file) provide thread isolation and synchronization, these functions provide advanced features for creating and managing threads. If you wish to create threads and control them more closely, you should look to the functions defined in this file. You must always make sure your code is thread-safe. Under UNIX 2.x, these functions affect threads within the current process. (See also `crit.h`, and `sem.h` as well as Chapter 11.)
`util.h` (important)	Includes many useful functions not covered in other files. Many of these functions work independently of the server platform. Functions include **util_getline, util_env_create, util_is_mozilla, util_is_url, util_uri_parse, util_itoa, util_sprintf,** and **util_strftime.** Also included are functions unique to a specific platform. For example, **util_can_exec** is unique to the UNIX platform. Look at this file for useful functions that may be helpful for your program.

Table E-4   NSAPI Header Files in `frame` Directory

`frame` DIRECTORY	DESCRIPTION
`conf.h`	Includes constants, global definitions, and function prototypes for the server configuration. These **magnus.conf**-related functions and definitions deal with ports, spawning children, and other server-related issues. They are related to internal global server information. The file includes an extensive data structure `conf_global_vars_s` that holds the server settings. There are also preprocessor definitions for the variables defined in the `conf_global_vars_s` data structure that provide easy access to the global server information. For example, **server_root** is defined as `conf_getglobals()->Vserver_root` and gives the server's root directory. Function prototypes include **conf_init, conf_terminate, conf_getglobals,** and so on. Usually, you will not use these functions in your program. (See also `object.h` and `objset.h`.)
`func.h`	Handles the server function hash table. The server uses a table of internal functions hashed by a name string. These functions are referenced from the configuration files, specifically the **obj.conf** file. Functions are passed the appropriate data structures: `pblock`, `Session`, and `Request`. FuncPtr points to the function. `FuncStruct` holds a linked list of the name and pointer to the function. The list of built-in server functions and user-defined functions specified in `obj.conf` file is parsed into the hash table at the start of the server. **func_*** functions support finding, adding, and executing server functions (**func_find, func_insert,** and **func_exec**). With these functions, you can manipulate or alter the use of Netscape's built-in server functions. You can remove a server function, replace one with another, put a wrapper (redirection) around an existing function, and so on. (See also `pblock.h`, `session.h`, and `req.h`.)
`http.h` (important)	Deals with HTTP protocol-related concerns. HTTP status codes are defined here (for example, `PROTOCOL_OK 200`). Also included are definitions for the HTTP date format (`HTTP_DATE_FMT`), the default access method for the normal (`http`) and secured (`https`) HTTP server, plus the default ports (for example, `HTTPS_URL` "`https`", `HTTPS_PORT 443`). Most HTTP functions defined here have been redefined as protocol functions. For example, **http_start_response** has been redefined as **protocol_start_response.** Use these redefined functions in your program. They include **protocol_find_request, protocol_parse_request, protocol_set_finfo,** and so on. **protocol_status** and **protocol_start_response** are frequently used. You reference these functions by including the `protocol.h` file (instead of `http.h`), which contains an include declaration (`#include`) for `http.h`. Some **http_*** functions, such as **http_hdrs2evn**, may not include an equivalent **protocol_*** function. **httpd_hdrs2evn** turns headers into environment variables by changing the format of each name to uppercase, adding the prefix `HTTP_`, and turning dashes (–) into underscores (_). This file includes only HTTP-related functions. (See also `protocol.h`.)
`log.h` (important)	Includes the function prototype for **log_error** and an include declaration of `ereport.h`. You reference error log-related functions through this file. Chiefly, you use **log_error** to log an error of a certain degree from a specified function (except when logging an error in **Init** functions). You can also include a descriptive string to be added to the error information. The error is recorded in the error log file you defined in your **magnus.conf** file. (See also `ereport.h`.)
`object.h`	Handles individual HTTP server Objects, which are defined in the **obj.conf** file. This file, in conjunction with `objset.h`, includes the data structures and functions for managing the Objects in the **obj.conf** file. The functions in this file are usually called by the functions defined in `objset.h`. The `object.h` file holds specific data structures and functions for handling individual server Objects (for example, the default Object). The data structures are as follows: `directive`

Table E-4 NSAPI Header Files in `frame` Directory (*continued*)

`frame` DIRECTORY	DESCRIPTION
`object.h`	(each directive function's information); `dtable` (a table of directives, actually a table of functions of a certain directive type); and `httpd_object` (information about the Object, such as its name and its tables of directives [`dtables`]). Functions include **object_create, object_add_directive,** and **object_free.** You can create Objects, add a directive to `dtable`, and so on. Unless you plan to dynamically modify or manipulate the information in the `obj.conf` file, you probably will not use these functions. (See also `objset.h`.)
`objset.h`	Handles the set of HTTP server Objects. This file, in conjunction with `object.h`, includes the data structures and functions for managing the Objects in the `obj.conf` file. This file includes an include declaration for the `object.h` file. You need to include this file only to access the functions. The data structure `httpd_objset` holds the Objects from the `obj.conf` file. It holds the `httpd_object` structures, defined in the `object.h` file, and the list of **Init** functions (`initfns`). Functions include **objset_scan_buffer, objset_create, objset_free, objset_findbyname,** and so on. The Windows NT version of Netscape's Server 1.x used the NT registry for configuration files. This file still includes functions for reading the registry configuration (such as **objset_scan_registry, ProcessObject,** and **GetProductKey**). Unless you plan to dynamically modify or manipulate the information in the `obj.conf` file, you will use neither `objset.h` nor `object.h`. (See also `object.h`.)
`protocol.h` (important)	This file contains the include declaration for the `http.h` file, which, in turn, handles all HTTP protocol-related functions. Include this file in your project to reference **protocol_*** functions defined in `httpd.h` (for example, **protocol_status**). (See also `http.h`.)
`req.h` (important)	Includes request-specific data structure and functions. The `Request` data structure variables apply to only the current request. This structure is normally sent to your function as a parameter and includes parameter blocks (`pblocks`) that hold important data: `vars` (server variables such as `path`); `reqpb` (request-specific headers such as `method`), `srvhdrs` (server response-headers, such as `content-length`); `headers` (HTTP headers, such as `user-agent`); and `aclpb` (ACL **PathCheck** parameter block). Also included are the return codes for server functions: `REQ_PROCEED`, `REQ_ABORTED`, and so on. Finally, there are the function prototypes (for example, **request_create, request_free,** and **request_stat_path**). An important function that you will use to find the HTTP headers is **request_header.** Otherwise, you use the pblock functions (from `pblock.h`) to access the values of the parameters in the `Request` data structure. (See also `session.h` and `pblock.h`.)

osagent and osfind

This appendix describes osagent and osfind, two special utility programs that come with Enterprise Server 3.0. They are part of the Visigenic ORB that Netscape delivers with the server. osagent is especially important for registering and locating CORBA objects for Server 3.0. If you are using Enterprise Server 3.0, you will need to run osagent first before running your CORBA or WAI application. osagent is a proprietary extension to CORBA. It works with Visigenic or a Visigenic-compatible ORB. osfind is used to check on the services (CORBA object implementations) that have registered with osagent.

For Server 3.01 and 3.5.1, Netscape no longer uses osagent. Therefore, you can ignore this appendix if you are running a server other than Server 3.0. In fact, if you are running Server 3.0, we recommend upgrading the server to version 3.5.1 or using the new server patch (P85416) to upgrade the server to the 3.01 version of WAI. With Enterprise Server 3.01 and 3.5.x, you use Netscape Naming Service to take advantage of the functionality for which osagent was intended.

osagent

ORBeline Smart Agent (osagent), also called Smart Agent, is similar to a CORBA Naming Service that provides directory service support. osagent, a Visigenic component, is an integral part of Netscape Enterprise Server 3.0. It supports both client and server objects (object implementations). The server objects register themselves with osagent. osagent, in turn, keeps a list of all persistent server objects. Clients use osagent to find the server object. Under Enterprise Server 3.0, when you want to use WAI or write your own CORBA object using an ISB, you must run osagent first. You can find osagent under the `<server path>/wai/bin` directory. Run osagent before enabling WAI on your server and before running Enterprise Server and your CORBA server object or WAS application. Although Netscape also uses its own Naming Service, osagent is still a necessary part of Enterprise Server 3.0's ISB and WAI package. Enterprise Server's WAI interface, Netscape Naming Service, your CORBA objects, and out-of-process WAS applications register themselves with osagent.

You must run at least one instance of osagent on your local network. osagent can run on any host. For security reasons, however, you should run osagent on the host machine where Enterprise Server and your CORBA object or WAS are located. In fact, you should register osagent to use only localhost: Use the parameter `-a 127.0.0.1` with the osagent. When you run more than one osagent, the client will bind with the first accessible osagent that responds. Just because osagent is on the local network, it does not mean that a client object can register with it. Normally, you must run osagent on each machine that runs a CORBA server object. You must take extra steps to make sure that a server object will find osagent if it is not on the local machine. For example, you can set the IP address and port number of osagent (`OSAGENT_ADDR`, `OSAGENT_PORT`) as environment variables. Each osagent that runs on a separate host machine registers a subset of existing objects on the network. Each osagent then communicates with the others to locate a server object for a client. The osagents find one another through UDP[1] (User Datagram Protocol) broadcast messages. If an osagent is shut down, all server objects registered with it will be automatically reregistered with another osagent, assuming that the osagent can access the remote objects.

The client and the server object broadcast a message to locate osagent. As message broadcasting is used, you must run osagent in a local network. The first osagent that responds will register the object. The point-to-point UDP protocol is used for registration and to find an object implementation. UDP is a simpler protocol that uses fewer network resources than TCP connection. The default UDP port number for osagent is 14000. You can specify a unique UDP port for an osagent by setting the environment variable `OSAGENT_PORT` to the value of the port you wish. The port must be available for this to work. You can also use `OSAGENT_PORT` on different hosts in the same local network to produce separate ORB domains. `OSAGENT_PORT` must be set on all hosts in the same domain that will run a CORBA object or osagent.

The object implementation registers itself with osagent when a call to the method **object_is_ready** (for example, `BOA::object_is_ready`) is made. The object's interface name is then registered with osagent, and the server object is ready to receive requests. If an object implementation is destroyed or shut down, osagent should remove it from the registered list of available objects, although it may still indicate services that were shut down. osagent is also used when your client makes a call to the **bind** method. osagent then checks to see if an object implementation fulfills your

---

1. UDP is a connectionless protocol. It uses the IP address to send a datagram. It also requires less overhead as it does not guarantee that all packets will reach their destinations. UDP is often used for transferring video and audio across the Internet.

client's request. If an object implementation is found, it returns the object reference of the server object.

Although there is a one-to-one relationship between a client and a server object, you can run multiple instances of a server object. If a server object suddenly exits (crashes), or if the connection between the client and server becomes disrupted, the ORB will attempt to connect to another instance of the server object by using osagent. The client does not know about the break in the connection, unless the server object was maintaining specific state information. osagent also updates its list of available object implementations. If a server object has exited, osagent will remove the object from the list.

There are a number of command-line switches (flags) you can use with the osagent program. -v (verbose) displays (or records) additional diagnostic messages. Under the Windows system, this information is saved in a log file under the orb directory (for example, c:\orb20\log\osagent.log). Much of the information may not be directly written into the log file, until osagent is shut down. osagent under Windows system is a Windows application, not a console application.

The -a switch is used to specify the binding IP address of osagent. If this flag is not used, osagent will accept any application (WAS or CORBA object) in your local network. By running osagent as osagent -a 127.0.0.1, you can limit it to accepting connections only from the localhost machine. To reduce security risks, make sure you run osagent with this flag. It will reduce the potential security risks from osagent accepting a connection from an unauthorized object. There is also the switch -p, which specifies a port for osagent.

To allow osagents of different local networks to find one another, you must write the host name or IP address of the remote osagent in a file named agentaddr. As mentioned earlier, these agents use broadcast messages to find one another. They must be on the same local network for broadcast messaging to work. agentaddr simply lists the IP addresses or host names of all osagents. The environment variable VBROKER_ADM (or ORBELINE as specified for the C++ version of ISB) can be used to specify the path of the agentaddr file. You simply make a separate line entry for each IP address or host name of the remote agents.

You may specify an IP address and port for osagent through a runtime parameter for the CORBA application, assuming that the runtime Java interpreter or your program can use the information. You can also specify the IP address of osagent with the environment variable OSAGENT_ADDR. Setting an IP address for osagent allows the ORB and CORBA objects to bypass UDP broadcast so as to locate the osagent. To have the osagent be located through an IP address, set OSAGENT_ADDR (or ORBagentaddr as specified for the C++ version of ISB) to the host name or IP address of the machine where osagent is running. With the environment variable OSAGENT_ADDR set to the IP address or host name of the osagent host machine, the CORBA application will use point-to-point UDP communication to contact osagent. The parameter -DOSAGENT_ADDR or -ORBagentaddr can identify the IP address of the osagent machine for a client or a server object. In the following examples of the switches for a client object named myapp, the first line is based on the C++ specification and the second line is based on the Java specification.

```
myapp -ORBagentaddr 1.2.3.4

<Java Interpreter> -DOSAGENT_ADDR=1.2.3.4 myapp
```

The application you invoke could be a client or a server object. The CORBA object first uses the IP address defined in this parameter to find the osagent. The CORBA object should be written in such a way as to take advantage of the parameters. If the parameter was not found, the object will look for osagent on its local machine. If osagent was not found, it will look for this agent where the environment variable OSAGENT_ADDR is pointing. If this variable is not set, the object will resort to UDP broadcasting to locate osagent. In your program, you will also need to specify the Object Adapter address OAipaddr for the server object.

You can also use the agentaddr file in conjunction with OSAGENT_ADDR to bypass UDP broadcasting and allow access to osagents found outside of the local network. First, write the IP address of each machine running an osagent in the agentaddr file. Next, point the OSAGENT_ADDR environment variable to the location of the agentaddr file. The CORBA objects will then attempt to find an osagent using the IP address or host name in the agentaddr file.

Bug Report ▶

osagent on Solaris Enterprise Server version 3.0 does not always perform as you would expect. It does not accept requests from remote hosts.

osfind

There is an additional useful ORB utility called osfind (ORBeline Smart Finder) in the wai/bin directory. With osfind, you can find the CORBA objects and interfaces running on your network. osfind lists all object implementations of a given interface. It displays objects that are manually started (and registered with osagent) or registered with and activated by OAD (Object Activation Daemon). osfind also lists osagents and OADs running on the network and the names of the machines on which they are running. You must run osagent first before using osfind. The version of osfind under

Warning ▶

osfind is no longer part of Enterprise Server 3.01. osfind is another Visigenic component that is part of Enterprise Server 3.0. It is intended for use with osagent. As osagent is no longer part of Enterprise Server 3.01 and later, you can safely ignore this section if you are using Enterprise Server 3.01 or later.

UNIX is a console application and uses parameters -a, -o, and -i: -a for reporting on the agents; -o for OADs; and -i for object implementations. osfind under NT is a Windows application with menu and dialog boxes for the same options.

Table F-1 lists selected manually started interfaces and objects running on the NT machine. The current agent running is foo, based on the server name foo (https-foo). Enterprise Server is running on the local machine. WAI is enabled, and two sample applications, guest and hello, are running as out-of-process WAI applications. WASip is the WAS example that comes with Enterprise Server running in-process. As you can see, the NamingContext (Naming Service) interface for the server and three WAI interfaces—HTTPServerContext, WebApplicationBasicService, and WebApplicationService—are all manually started. HTTPServerContext provides information about the Web server, such as the server IP address. WebApplicationBasicService and WebApplicatonService are the interfaces that your WAI application uses (for example, guest, hello, and WASip). The right column of the Table F-1 lists object implementations for the interfaces in the left column. Object implementations are identified by the IP address at which they are running (for example, localhost) and the specific name of the object. The IP address is based on the Object Adapters' address. For example, if you initialize IIOP and WAI for Netscape with the parameter OAipaddr=*<new IP address>*, then the Objects will be registered with the new IP address instead of 127.0.0.1. The IP address you use should be based on the location of the server. For more information on IIOP and WAI settings, see the section IIOPinit Parameters in Chapter 13.

Table F-1   Sample of Interfaces and Registered Objects

MANUALLY STARTED INTERFACES	MANUALLY STARTED OBJECTS
CosNaming::NamingContext	\127.0.0.1\ \127.0.0.1\https-foo00000000000https-foo \127.0.0.1\WAS0000000001https-foo
netscape::WAI::HttpServerContext	\127.0.0.1\ \127.0.0.1\https-foo
netscape::WAI:: 　WebApplicationBasicService	\127.0.0.1\ \127.0.0.1\guest \127.0.0.1\hello \127.0.0.1\WASPip
netscape::WAI:: 　WebApplicationService	\127.0.0.1\ \127.0.0.1\guest \127.0.0.1\hello \127.0.0.1\WASPip

Index

Browser
    is Mozilla, 272, 869–870
    name, identifying (user agent), 15, 141, 318, 650
    role of, 5
buffer.h (NSAPI header file), 932
BuildURL (WAI method), 654
    C++ method, 681
    defined (IDL), 657
    Java method, 690
    NSAPI equivalent, 665
ByteArrayOutputStream (Java), 725

C and CGI
    Guest Book example, 155–186
    Hello Client example, 148–149
    server configuration for, 125–126
C and ISINDEX, example, 123–124
C and WAI
    compiling, 790–795
    creating and registering a Web service object,
        747–748, 750–753
    getting information to process client requests,
        709–716
    Guest Book example, 801–831
    header file (ONEiiop.h), 669–675
    Hello Client example, in-process, 787–789
    Hello Client example, out-of-process console,
        769–771
    HttServerContext- and HttpServerRequest-
        related functions, 673–675
    implementation loop, 754
    in-process SAF, 745–746
    logging errors, 733
    main function for console application, 741–742
    redirection, 734–736
    returning responses, 726–732
    run function, 707–709
    starting an out-of-process application, 796
    using NSAPI functions with, 665–667, 828–831
    WAIWebApplicationService-related functions,
        671–672
    WinMain for out-of-process application, 742
CA. See Certificate Authority
Cache(d)
    ACL lifetime, 834
    cookies, 508–509
    debugging SAF and, 361
    directives or requests, 225–226, 266
    DNS entries, 857
    last-modified, if-modified-since, expires and,
        224, 252, 409
    net_write and, 526
    pragma and, 14, 222
    REQ_NOACTION and, 251–252
    stat, request_stat_path, and, 391, 250,
        252
    validation, 226

cache-control (HTTP General-Header), 14, 222,
    508–509
    set-cache-control, 882
cached_* (Request data structure variables)
    date_header, 225
    headers, 225
    headers_len, 225
cache-init (Init function), 361, 855–856
Cache-related directives and directive functions
    ACLCacheLifetime, 834
    cache-init, 855–856
    dns-cache-init, 857
    set-cache-control, 882
    SSLSessionTimeout and SSL3SessionTimeout,
        847–848
Caffeine, 618
Castanet, 521
catastrophe (error type), 86, 309, 732
CERN, 18
Certificate(s)
    Administration Server and, 44
    authentication, 372–373
    Authority, 372–373
    AuthTrans and, 377
    file, server, 835–836
    requiring client certificate, 326, 847, 876–877
    variables (CGI), 142
    variables (NSAPI), 324, 326
    variables (WAI), 651
Certificate mapping, 29, 104, 373
    cert2user and, 872–873
Certificate-related directives and directive functions
    See also Keys; SSL
    Certfile, 835–836
    Cert2user, 872–873
    get-client-cert, 876–877
    Security, 845–846
    SSLClientAuth, 847
Certificate Server, 40, 373
    issuer_dn, 324
Certfile (magnus.conf directive), 835–836
certmap.conf, 373
cert2user (PathCheck function), 78, 389, 872–873
cgi (attribute of SSI exec command), 114
CGI (Common Gateway Interface), 22
    See also Configuring server
    advantages, 124
    C and C++ resources, 148
    C example, 148–149
    data provided by server, 132–134
    enabling, 125–126
    enabling ShellCGI and WinCGI, 127–130
    environment variables, 134–143
    explained, 130–132
    Guest Book example, 155–186
    Hello Client examples, 147–155
    nonparsed headers, 147

CD-ROM License Agreement Notice